THE GREAT LAW
AND THE LONGHOUSE

THE CIVILIZATION OF THE AMERICAN INDIAN SERIES

THE
GREAT LAW
AND THE
LONGHOUSE

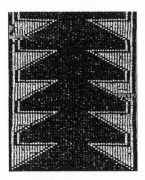

A POLITICAL HISTORY
OF THE IROQUOIS CONFEDERACY

William N. Fenton

UNIVERSITY OF OKLAHOMA PRESS
Norman

ALSO BY WILLIAM N. FENTON

Songs from the Iroquois Longhouse (Washington, D.C., 1942)

(ed.) *Symposium on Local Diversity in Iroquois Culture* (Washington, D.C., 1951)

The Iroquois Eagle Dance: An Offshoot of the Calumet Dance (Washington, D.C., 1953)

American Indian and White Relations to 1830 (Chapel Hill, 1957)

(co-ed.) *Symposium on Cherokee and Iroquois Culture* (Washington, D.C., 1961)

(ed.) *Parker on the Iroquois* (Syracuse, N.Y., 1968)

(ed. and trans., with E. L. Moore) *Customs of the American Indians, Compared with the Customs of Primitive Times, by Father Joseph-François Lafitau,* two vols. (Toronto, 1974–76)

The False Faces of the Iroquois (Norman, 1987)

This book is published with the generous assistance of Edith Gaylord Harper.

Library of Congress Cataloging-in-Publication Data

Fenton, William Nelson, 1908–
    The Great Law and the Longhouse : a political history of the Iroquois Confederacy / William N. Fenton.
        p.   cm. — (The civilization of the American Indian series ; v. 223)
    Includes bibliographical references (p.   ) and index.
    ISBN 0-8061-3003-2 (cloth : alk. paper)
    1. Iroquois Indians—History—Sources.   2. Six Nations—History—Sources   3. Condolence Ceremony (Iroquois rite)—History.   4. Iroquois Indians—Politics and government.   5. Iroquois Indians—Government relations.   I. Title.   II. Series.
    E99.I7F453   1988
973'.049755—dc21   97-19842
                                                                                              CIP

Text design by Cathy Carney Imboden. Text is set in Baskerville.

The Great Law and the Longhouse: A Political History of the Iroquois Confederacy is Volume 223 in The Civilization of the American Indian Series.

The paper in this book meets the guidelines for permanence and durability of the Committee on Production Guidelines for Book Longevity of the Council on Library Resources, Inc. ∞

1 2 3 4 5 6 7 8 9 10

TO THE OLD PEOPLE,
WHO KNOW EVERYTHING

439-4385
mr. FENTIN
SLINGERLANDS, NY

Contents

ILLUSTRATIONS

MAPS

FIGURES

Tables

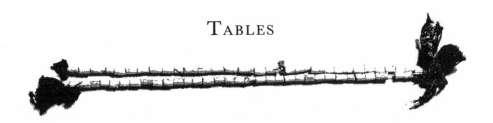

PREFACE

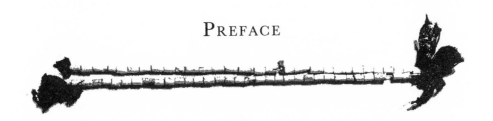

Readers may be interested in how I came to write this book. In the 1930s I had undertaken the assignment to present the social and political organization of the Iroquois to Edward Sapir's seminar at Yale. To prepare, I read the pertinent ethnological sources—Lewis Henry Morgan, Horatio E. Hale, J. N. B. Hewitt, William M. Beauchamp, and Alexander A. Goldenweiser. I really felt on top of it. Sapir called me out after the seminar to tell me I must really go to the field. He suggested I get access to Goldenweiser's field notes on Iroquois work accomplished but never fully reported to the Anthropological Survey of Canada, which he, Sapir, headed from 1910 to 1925. There was a fund for student fieldwork from the Institute of Human Relations, which Sapir controlled.

I wrote to Goldenweiser, and to my amazement a great box of field notebooks and manuscript texts arrived. I soon realized that I must begin more modestly. I had been reviewing F. W. Waugh's notebooks on Iroquois medicines, which Sapir also procured for me from the National Museum of Canada. So I decided to go to the Allegany Reservation of the Seneca Nation of Indians, where my family had some contacts. At Allegany I would be the first anthropologist in training to pursue interests in ethnobotany, social organization, and ceremonialism. No one at Allegany knew much about the traditional League of the Iroquois, but my sources pointed to the life chiefs at Tonawanda, who they said participated in the Seneca tradition of the league.

After two summers and a winter at Coldspring on the Allegheny River, I had stuff for a dissertation on Seneca ceremonialism (Fenton 1936; 1951), and the Longhouse leaders had introduced me at Tonawanda during a Six Nations meeting of the Handsome Lake religion. It was time to learn about the Seneca tradition of the league.

John Collier, then U.S. commissioner of Indian affairs, made that possible. He came to New Haven and addressed the Anthropology Club, of which I was chairman, suggesting that anthropologists might serve the U.S. Indian Service in the manner of their counterparts in the British Colonial Service. I had no interest in becoming superintendent of the New York Agency at Salamanca, which Collier offered me (though his colleagues thought better of it). But several of us had taken the civil service examination for "community worker," which title I accepted because it was vague and entailed no administrative duties, and it avoided a conflict of interest at Coldspring. I set off for Tonawanda in February 1935 to assume the role of community worker.

On two occasions when in Washington I met with J. N. B. Hewitt, native Iroquoianist of Tuscarora descent, at the Smithsonian Institution. In response to my interest in the league tradition, which had occupied him for half a century, Hewitt advised not bothering with Onondaga (Syracuse) but concentrating on Six Nations at Grand River, where the league tradition flourished.

During my two and one-half years at Tonawanda, the one person most seriously interested in the league tradition as a native scholar was Yankee Spring, who became my "friend" in the Iroquois sense. Although Yankee himself did not hold one of the eight Seneca sachemships, or league titles, he had made several visits to the Grand River to learn the league tradition. He took me to meet his sources.

We heard David Thomas, a gifted speaker and ritual holder at Onondaga Longhouse, and Chief Joseph Logan, who then held the title Thadoda:ho? (that of the leading Onondaga chief), expound their theory of Iroquois history. They segmented it into three periods, each marked by the teachings of a prophet: the age of Sapling, the good twin of Creation; the age of the Peacemaker, who brought the Great Law and founded the league; and the age since Handsome Lake, the Seneca prophet. It occurred to me that the three periods, each with its charter myth, might afford a frame of reference for structuring Iroquois political history.

On succeeding Hewitt at the Bureau of American Ethnology in 1939, I faced a formidable body of texts in Iroquoian languages—Onondaga, Cayuga, and Mohawk—that Hewitt had recorded in beautiful phonetic script in the course of his research on the league tradition and its rituals. Hewitt left few English versions. He did leave a manuscript on the Requickening Address, which the Smithsonian editor returned to me for review. Editing and interpreting Hewitt took me three years (Hewitt 1944). In the process, I learned condolence protocol. Hewitt had written the program on scraps of paper.

Hewitt had worked so long in Onondaga that he felt comfortable with the Iroquoian texts. He translated into English but a few pages of John Arthur Gibson's 1899 version of the league tradition. In 1941, Simeon Gibson and I completed the translation. Gibson's 1899 account contained the roll of the founders of the Iroquois League, but it stopped short of the condolence ceremony, which Hewitt had recorded in separate texts. Just how these fitted together posed a problem. Fortunately, Gibson appended the entire condolence ceremony in his 1912 rendering of the league tradition for Goldenweiser (Woodbury 1992). Simeon Gibson had accompanied his blind father during numerous Condolence Councils, but although he was at home in the ceremony, he had never performed it himself. Together in 1943 we translated and annotated that section of his father's 1912 version. We planned further collaboration, but Simeon drowned that fall crossing the Grand River in a leaky rowboat (Fenton 1944).

People who had worked with Hewitt and John A. Gibson and their descendants became my teachers and co-workers. Simeon Gibson and his sister Jemima, children of Chief John A. Gibson; their nephew Howard Skye; Cayuga chief Alexander General (Desgahe?); David Thomas and Onondaga chief Joe Logan; George Buck; and in later years Jim Skye all rallied to my ethnological needs. Several things coincided to make my learning a cooperative endeavor.

The Cranbrook Institute of Science asked me to authenticate a mnemonic cane of pegs and pictographs that had originated at Six Nations Reserve. Hewitt's notes had hinted at its existence. Obviously it was a device for recalling the roll of the league's founders, and at once it was a native organization chart of the league. The digital arrangement of pegs for the titles appeared older than the corresponding pictographs, several of which illustrated items dating from the nineteenth century. To arouse the interest of the chiefs, I distributed blueprints of the two sides of the stick. To my surprise on returning to Six Nations the following year, replicas of the cane appeared, of which some were finer examples than the original. The study had contributed to a restoration and revival. After my monograph appeared (Fenton 1950), condolence canes proliferated. It is even claimed that one reproduction is the original and the Cranbrook specimen a copy.

Hewitt had promised the Gibson family to sponsor a condolence ceremony to elevate Hardy Gibson in the office of Cayuga chief Abram Charles, his mother's brother. Jemima Gibson, as trustee of the title, looked to me as Hewitt's successor to fulfill that pledge. It was an expensive undertaking. I thought of filming the ceremony, an idea that, fortunately, appealed to Paul Fejos, then director of the Wenner-Gren Foundation for Anthropological Research. Robert T. Hatt, then director of the Cranbrook Institute, volunteered as cameraman. A grant from the Wenner-Gren Foundation bought the beef and hung the kettles for the great ceremony.

The council of life chiefs meeting at Onondaga Longhouse had other ideas, however. Making a movie that I probably could not control and that might have showings in Canadian theaters did not appeal to them. But they were going forward with the ceremony, they wanted me to attend, and they urged me to sit in on the rehearsals so that I might learn the ritual as they did and thus prepare myself to understand what I would see and hear. Having translated the ritual texts with Simeon Gibson, and having been coached on the program by Howard Skye, I knew what to expect. The rehearsal proved to be a profound learning experience. I observed spatial relations, recorded the mnemonic for ordering the roll of the founders, which I punched into a lead pencil, heard the chants and songs, and noted the movements of participants—all of which contributed to sharper observations on the great day. Although the chiefs diverted the purpose of my grant, they did me the favor, for which I am ever grateful, of preventing me from viewing the ceremony through a camera lens so that I could see it with my own eyes. I witnessed the ceremony on two occasions—in 1945 (Fenton 1946) and, on their invitation to return, in 1951.

Witnessing the two installation ceremonies ingrained into my consciousness the order of ritual, its symbolic content, and the overall pattern that governed its performance. It occurred to me that surely such an elaborate institution, a veritable cultural showpiece, must have a history. The very league that it celebrated must be quite old. This book is the fulfillment of my quest to discover that history. The search for the roots of the condolence ceremony, for the league itself, and for accounts of its operation, successes, and failures would draw on the methods and techniques of ethnohistory.

Paul Wallace sparked my interest in doing a political history of the Iroquois Confederacy. While writing *The White Roots of Peace* (1946), he came to the Smithsonian to consult the Gibson-Hewitt text concerning the origins of the league, which Simeon Gibson and I had translated at Brantford on the eve of Pearl

Harbor. Within a few months I was deeply involved in the work of the Smithsonian War Committee and the Ethnogeographic Board (a clearinghouse set up by the Smithsonian, the American Council of Learned Societies, and the National Research Council)—activity that suspended further work on the text just then.

After the war, Frank G. Speck inspired me to assemble Iroquoian scholars to identify research problems that might be pursued and to enlist young scholars to enter the field. With the support of Merle Deardorff, banker and avid scholar, and Charles Congdon, attorney and historian of the Allegheny Oxbow, the first Conference on Iroquois Research met in 1945 at Red House in Allegany State Park and was presided over by Commissioner Congdon. The conference has endured for fifty years and gives no signs of demise. It now meets in October at Rensselaerville, New York, which Brooks Atkinson dubbed "the Athens of Albany County." The early strengths of the conference were in prehistory; ethnology flourished until the 1960s. Historians have kept us honest, and work on Iroquoian languages has made remarkable strides in recent years.

What happens when an ethnologist turns to a historical problem? As a fellow of the American Philosophical Society Library, I set out to collect materials for writing a political history of the Iroquois Confederacy (Fenton 1949a). Early on I called on R. W. G. Vail, the noted bibliographer of early Americana, then director of the New-York Historical Society, who charted a course for me in research libraries, including his own, where manuscript collections awaited me. I hoped to carry the perspective of Iroquois society and political organization as going concerns into an examination of sources on Iroquois life in earlier times.

The approach I adopted—that of proceeding from verified present-day observations to earlier, fragmentary accounts by witnesses who barely understood what they were seeing—came to be known as "upstreaming." The method rests on three premises. First, major patterns of culture tend to be stable over long periods of time. Second, one proceeds from what is known to examining sources that may contain familiar elements. Third, the ethnologist favors those sources that ring true ethnologically and resonate at both ends of the time span. Later one can order sequences chronologically.

For the Iroquois Condolence Council, upstreaming enabled me to establish a reasonable chronology, to identify persistent themes and structure, to note changes in content, to mark essential elements, and to suggest that the ceremony had been elaborated over time. In the manner of linguists reconstructing a protolanguage, I reconstructed a paradigm to account for all of the elements. A version of this paradigm became the protocol of treaties.

Upstreaming also enabled me to plot the emergence of the fifty league titles as they appeared in historical documents. Knowing the shapes of the names from living sources helped me identify what earlier scribes had attempted to spell.

Writing a book is a learning experience. The writing takes on a life of its own: wonderful things emerge that one never thought of before; the same sentences recur out of nowhere, months apart. What one professes as style may be only peculiarities.

WILLIAM N. FENTON

Slingerlands, New York

ACKNOWLEDGMENTS

My debt to institutions for access to and use of their collections and for the courtesy of their staffs cannot be satisfied by naming them. Yet it would be remiss not to list them in order of use: Hamilton College Library, Clinton, New York (Kirkland Papers); American Philosophical Society, Philadelphia (Asher Wright, A. C. Parker, Horsmanden, and my own papers); Essex Institute, Salem, Massachusetts (Pickering Papers); Massachusetts Archives, State House, Boston ("Indians," vols. 29–34); Massachusetts Historical Society, Boston (Pickering Papers); Houghton Library, Harvard University (records of the American Board of Commissioners for Foreign Missions); Vassar College Library, Poughkeepsie, New York (Parrish Papers); New-York Historical Society, New York City (O'Reilly Collection); New York State Library, Albany (Beauchamp Papers); New York Public Library (Schuyler Papers); Henry E. Huntington Library, San Marino, California (Loudoun and Abercromby Papers; English Colonial Treaties; E. S. Parker Collection); William L. Clements Library, Ann Arbor, Michigan (Gage correspondence with Guy Johnson); Newberry Library, Chicago ("Documentary History of the Iroquois" photocopies of sources on microfilm); the British Library, London (Haldimand Papers); SPG House, London (Series B letters from Anglican missions, New York and New England).

The following institutions supported my research with grants and fellowships: the American Philosophical Society; the Smithsonian Institution; the Wenner-Gren Foundation for Anthropological Research (fieldwork 1945 and 1981); the Research Foundation of the State University of New York; the Foundation of the University at Albany (Iroquois Research Fund); the Henry E. Huntington Library (1978–79, 1992, 1997); the Newberry Library (NEH Documentary History of the Iroquois Project, 1979–81; NEH Senior Fellowship, 1982–83); and an anonymous private source.

In the manner of Iroquois speakers, "let everyone think that he or she has been thanked." Many individuals come to mind: Merle H. Deardorff and Charles E. Congdon, co-founders with me of the Conference on Iroquois Research since 1945; George S. Snyderman; the late Ernest Stanley Dodge; Frank G. Speck; John R. Swanton and Mathew W. Stirling at the Smithsonian; Paul Wallace; Ray A. Billington and Martin Ridge at the Huntington Library; Francis Jennings, Helen Hornbeck Tanner, John Aubrey, Bob Kerow, and Fred Hoxie at the Newberry Library; George Hammel at the New York State Museum, for photographs and for critiquing the chapter on wampum; Eileen Hardy and Maggie Bartley at Wellesley College Library; and my readers—Hanni Woodbury, Anthony F. C. Wallace, and Elisabeth Tooker. Jack Campisi read and sanctioned the final chapters on the Pickering treaty.

It would be remiss not to name my native Iroquois colleagues and collaborators, whose memories I cherish and to whom this work is dedicated. Most of them have gone the long trail and tasted the berries beside the heavenly road: Simeon Gibson, Jemima Gibson, Dawit Thomas, Joseph Logan (Thadoda:ho?), Alexander General (Desgahe?), Howard Skye, Jim Skye, and Jake Thomas of Six Nations on Grand River. Earlier at Tonawanda in New York, chiefs Henan Scrogg, Edward Black, Solon Skye, and Corbett Sundown contributed to my understanding of the Seneca system. Peter Doctor, Nick Bailey (Billy), and Yankee Spring dissented.

To my editors, who labored to make a book out of the manuscript—John Drayton and Sarah Iselin at the University of Oklahoma Press and especially Jane Kepp in Santa Fe—niawenh (thanks).

NOTE ON PRONUNCIATION

Readers may wonder how to pronounce the Iroquoian words and names of characters in this narrative. Colonial scribes spelled Indian names as best they could, and to guess what they heard is for the most part impossible. Sometimes the shapes of the names in the documents reveal to the Iroquoianist what the scribe was trying to spell. Here are a few rules to afford the reader the sounds of Iroquoian speech. Readers curious about the orthography employed by Iroquoianists may consult Wallace Chafe's *Handbook of the Seneca Language* (1963) or, better yet, his *Seneca Morphology and Dictionary* (1967), and possibly Hanni Woodbury's *Concerning the League* (1992).

Iroquoian speakers voice *k* and *g*, as well as *t* and *d*, somewhere between the two extremes. Some personal names begin with an aspirated *t*, which I write *th*, as in Thadoda:ho?, the Onondaga firekeeper. Speakers tend to stress the next to the last syllable, depending on whether it is odd or even. The vowels are *a*, *e*, *i*, and *o*; to indicate the nasal *e* and *o*, I write a following *n*—that is, *en* and *on*. The colon, as in the foregoing name, Thadoda:ho?, indicates vowel length, not unlike a dotted quarter-note in musical scores. Pronounce *a* as in English "father," *e* as in French "ete," *i* as in French "fini," and *o* as in English "note." The nasalized vowels sound like *en* in French "bien" and *on* in French "bon." The consonants are *h*, *j*, *k(g)*, *n*, *s*, *t(d)*, *w*, and *y*, besides the glottal stop, ?, which sounds the way it does when a Scotsman pronounces "bottle" *ba?l*.

Mohawk preserves an *r*, which becomes *l* in Oneida.

This should get the timid started.

ABBREVIATIONS

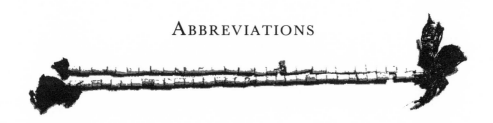

C	Cayuga
M	Mohawk
Oa	Onondaga
Oe	Oneida
S	Seneca
T	Tuscarora
M-1, S-2, etc.	Position on the roster of chiefs: Mohawk 1, Seneca 2, etc.
RC	Roll Call of the Founders

AB	Abercromby Papers
APSL	American Philosophical Society Library, Philadelphia
ASPIA	*American State Papers—Indian Affairs, 1832–34*
BL	British Library, London
BM	British Museum, London
BSP	British State Papers
DCB	*Dictionary of Canadian Biography*
DHNY	*Documentary History of the State of New York* (O'Callaghan 1849–51)
HCL	Hamilton College Library, Clinton, New York
HEH	Henry E. Huntington Library, San Marino, California
HSP	Historical Society of Pennsylvania, Philadelphia
IA	Indian Affairs
IR	Indian Records
JCC	*Journals of the Continental Congress, 1774–1789*
JR	*The Jesuit Relations and Allied Documents, 1610–1791*
LCP	Library Company, Philadelphia
LIR	Livingston Indian Records (Livingston 1956)
LO	Loudoun Papers
MA	Massachusetts Archives
MAI	Museum of the American Indian, Heye Foundation, now the United States National Museum of the American Indian
MHS	Massachusetts Historical Society, Boston
NL	Newberry Library, Chicago
NNN	*Narratives of New Netherland, 1609–1664*

NYCD	*Documents Relative to the Colonial History of the State of New York* (O'Callaghan 1853–87)
NYHS	New York Historical Society
NYPL	New York Public Library
NYSA	New York State Archives
NYSL	New York State Library, Albany
NYSM	New York State Museum, Albany
PAC	Public (National) Archives of Canada, Ottawa
PCR	Pennsylvania Colonial Records
PP	Pickering Papers
PPCM	Pennsylvania Provincial Council Minutes
PPR	Pennsylvania Provincial Records, Harrisburg
PRO	Public Record Office, Kew, England
SPG	Society for the Propagation of the Gospel, London
SWJP	*The Papers of Sir William Johnson* (Johnson 1921–65)
VHS	Virginia Historical Society
VRBM	*Van Rensselaer Bouvier Manuscripts* (Van Laer, ed., 1908)
VSL	Virginia State Library, Richmond
WLCL	William L. Clements Library, Ann Arbor, Michigan

INTRODUCTION

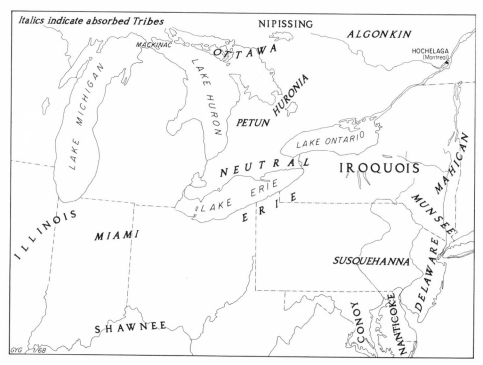

Map 1. Tribal distribution in northeastern North America. Map by Gwynneth Y. Gillette.

THE FIVE NATIONS AND
THEIR TRADITIONAL HISTORY

The aboriginal inhabitants of the lands bordering the lower Great Lakes—Huron, Erie, and Ontario—and the St. Lawrence River, in what are now parts of Ontario and Quebec in Canada, upstate New York, and adjacent Pennsylvania, spoke languages of the Iroquoian family.[1] Among these peoples, the more important ethnic entities were the Hurons of Ontario and the Iroquois of New York (maps 1 and 2). The natives of Huronia, as Jesuit scholars named their country, referred to their homeland as Wendat Ehen, "This Old Island," because they conceived of the world as resting on the back of a turtle swimming in the primal sea. What the French termed Iroquoia, the Iroquois themselves called Wi:s Nihwenjiada:ge:, and the English, the "Five Native Lands" or "Five Nations." The Hurons dominate the literature of discovery, but after their dispersion and incorporation by the Iroquois in the mid-seventeenth century, the colonial records are filled with the doings of the Five Nations—the Mohawks, Onondagas, Senecas, Cayugas, and Oneidas. They became Six Nations early in the eighteenth century when the Tuscaroras migrated from North Carolina to join them. Huronia and Iroquoia may be considered one cultural province.

Iroquois annalists periodize their history by the achievements of three prophets. Native theory speaks first of a time of Sapling, who brought cultural benefits to the people after the formation of the earth. The second period is that of Deganawi:dah, the Peacemaker, who founded the League of the Longhouse, or Iroquois League, and initiated the period of confederacy. The third period comprises the time since Handsome Lake, the Seneca Prophet—the nineteenth and twentieth centuries. Each period is illuminated by a myth about the doings of its prophet, and these myths were, and still are, recited by learned men during public ceremonies. These are occasions for the enhancement of tradition. The three oral narratives rank among the great intellectual display pieces of native North America. Speakers take pride in what they profess is total recall, people honor virtuoso performers, and learned men argue endlessly over variant versions. The myths and accompanying rituals have acquired such inherent power that it

1. This chapter comprises the plan of the book and is adapted from my article "The Iroquois in History" (1971) by permission of the publisher, Random House. An earlier version was prepared for a symposium entitled "Theory and Method in American Ethnological and Ethnohistoric Research," sponsored by the Wenner-Gren Foundation for Anthropological Research and held at Burg-Wartenstein, Austria, in the summer of 1967.

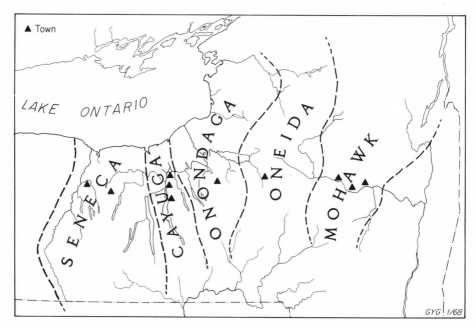

Map 2. Iroquoia in 1600. Map by Gwynneth Y. Gillette.

is thought proper to hold recitals only after the first frost and before the final spring frost, while the earth sleeps.

The cosmological myth of the Earth Grasper, or "The World on the Turtle's Back," tells how the earth, various plants and animals, the celestial beings, and the first humans originated and operated. It is a widespread myth in North America and it occurs in Eurasia, but peculiarly Iroquois touches such as dream guessing and a contest between Sapling and the progenitor of the False Faces render it unique. The Iroquoian cosmology projects into the formative period the paradigm for returning thanks to the spirit forces from the earth to the sky (Chafe 1961; Foster 1974), and it accounts for the origin of clans and moieties. The latter embellishments are ascribed to a fatherless boy who emerges from the bush to lead the community out of a dilemma. The Iroquois say that whenever humankind is up against it, a prophet will appear, and society is attuned to listen.

The Deganawi:dah legend, the tradition of the founding of the League of the Five Nations—the People of the Longhouse—tells how the Iroquois were persuaded to stop feuding, embrace the prophet's message, and join in the Great Peace. It is a legend of epic proportions. The Iroquois in history acted as if it were true, even when they could not make public policy follow its ideal principles.

Although the league as a symbolic system has historical continuity, it remains open to question whether it actually served as a means of organizing and distributing power. Historically, it was the Iroquois Confederacy that was the operating entity: it functioned with available personnel who more often than not were not holders of the fifty famous titles of the founders but who knew the forms and protocol and could speak for the league. By the eighteenth century, the League of the Longhouse was a convenient fiction, and the Iroquois Confederacy had become the effective political institution. This contrast between the league as a symbolic system and the confederacy as the operating instrument of government is new in the literature but not original with me; the distinction was first made by Daniel Richter (1987: 11.) Although the league at its founding was indeed a confederacy, I confine the term "confederacy" to the operating body that emerged in the eighteenth century.

The league legend was first noted by the Moravian missionary Pyrlaeus in 1743 (Heckewelder 1881), a century after European contact, but little of it was known for another hundred years and more (Morgan 1851; Hale 1883; Hewitt 1892; Parker 1916; Norton 1974), even though it underlies an understanding of Iroquois political institutions. Neither Cadwallader Colden, a lieutenant governor of New York, Sir William Johnson, the first English superintendent of Indian affairs north of the Ohio, nor the framers of the United States Constitution give evidence that they knew or understood it or that Iroquois statesmen had communicated it to them. That something so fundamental to Iroquois political philosophy escaped the notice of early writers on Iroquois manners is a problem in intellectual history. It suffices to say that the little we know of the symbolism of the league legend from seventeenth-century writings and the mention of its plot in eighteenth-century sources enable us to speak of its having existed two centuries earlier than it was recorded. Its chroniclers were native scribes who, in the late nineteenth century, had a need to justify traditional Iroquois government to the powers that might abolish it.

Such historical enigmas can never be resolved to the satisfaction of all parties, but they can be examined in the light of new theory and tested with verified historical data. Such data exist for the third period of Iroquois cultural history, from the vision of the Seneca prophet Handsome Lake to the present. During the years since Handsome Lake first revealed the Good Message, or Gaiwi:yo:h, at Cornplanter in 1799, learned preachers have repeatedly recited his words within the hearing of the "guardians of the Good Message" and the "keepers of the faith," who are the Longhouse officers. The Prophet foretold the path that the Seneca people should follow in order to escape the evils of white civilization and reach the heavenly road. His utterances, as a later generation recalled them, now form a code that is preached on public occasions. The code says that the vision occurred during the Berry Moon (June) of the year 1799, an assertion that Quaker missionary journals substantiate (Deardorff 1951; A. Wallace 1952). If such oral tradition can persist for two centuries and maintain its essential historical accuracy through public recitation and constant criticism by its appointed guardians, it stands to reason that other, similarly kept and validated traditions in the same culture merit consideration as oral history.

Temporal problems of another order include new evidence from prehistory that the Iroquois were longer in their homeland than formerly thought. Moreover, the data of ethnography indicate that a number of major Iroquois institutions and customs were distributed widely in the eastern woodlands among both Algonquian-speaking and Iroquoian-speaking neighbors of the Five Nations. Shared culture traits among adjacent peoples afford a different time perspective. Then there is the question of the nature of ethnohistory and how I see and practice it. This much is clear: all that we know about the nature of Iroquois society and the content of Iroquois culture derives from ethnological studies carried out since the late nineteenth century, from the writings of earlier, untrained observers, and from interpretation of the archaeological record. How far such knowledge can be projected into the pre-Columbian past and used to infer the nature of Iroquois society before European contact confronts the paradox of stability and change. Clearly, institutions that survived into modern times and are demonstrably not European either developed during the historic period or are much older; they offer us the opportunity to examine the process of culture change at the same time that they manifest continuity. The best example of this phenomenon is the Condolence Council for mourning dead chiefs and installing their successors, a rite that has ancient historical roots and is widespread in eastern North America.

The Iroquois have expanded their custom of mourning the dead and "lifting up the minds" of bereaved relatives to fashion an institution known as the Condolence Council in which dead chiefs are mourned and successors requickened in the titles of the founders so that the league may endure. This climax form of political ritualism persists today as the validation of chiefship. Its program consists of rites known as the Roll Call of the Founders, the Welcome at the Woods' Edge, the recitation of laws, the Requickening Address, the Six Songs of requiem, and the Charge to the New Chief. One finds this ritual paradigm (or parts of it) in the early historical sources, and a version of it formed the protocol for alliances and treaties in the colonial era. Understanding this protocol is essential for understanding Iroquois views and expectations and for interpreting their relations with Euro-Americans.

With the advent of European colonization, the Iroquois, caught up in the power struggle for control of North America, were manipulated by colonial powers and in turn manipulated colonials to their own advantage. Alliances were indispensable for survival and success, and the old men of Onondaga varied their policy between alliance and neutrality according to the way in which they perceived their self-interest. One thing is certain: whoever came to Iroquoia came on their terms.

□□◇□□

Early in the seventeenth century the Five Nations felt the impact of colonial civilization when the French established Quebec on the St. Lawrence River and the Dutch built Fort Orange on the Hudson. It was soon evident that in the competition between the two centers, first for the trade of the River Indians, or Mahicans, and later for that of nearby Mohawks and Oneidas out of Fort Orange, the free Dutch traders enjoyed the advantages of open ports and cheaper goods over the French royal monopoly. The French would latch onto the established Huron trade and, by extension, trade with the "Far Indians" of the upcountry.

Iroquois encounters with French police—an eighteenth-century concept applied to nations and civilizations in contrast to "savage" tribes—ran from 1609 to 1763. Their trading relations with the Dutch began equally early and terminated officially in 1664, when the English took control of the New York colony during the Second Dutch War of 1665–67. Even after the English succeeded, Dutch traders continued to dominate the Albany scene and served as Indian commissioners well into the eighteenth century. The mid-seventeenth century was the era of the Beaver Wars and marked the climax of Iroquois power, which declined rapidly toward the close of the century following pestilence, wars, defeats, and outmigration to Canada, all of which contributed to a declining population. Wholesale adoptions of peoples whom their wars destroyed as tribal entities failed to make up for Iroquois losses.

The main sources for the French period are Samuel de Champlain, Gabriel Sagard, the Jesuit writers from Isaac Jogues to Joseph-François Lafitau, and the correspondence of governors and intendants of New France. Harmen M. van den Bogaert, Johannes Megapolensis, Jr., and Robert Livingston's "Indian Records" are the principal Dutch sources. Peter Wraxall, Cadwallader Colden, and Sir William Johnson, all English writers, belonged to the next century.

The first authenticated Dutch treaty with the Iroquois was the Mohawk-Dutch nonaggression pact of 1642. The English consummated a similar pact soon after they took over New Netherland in 1664. Livingston's Indian Records (Livingston 1956) commenced two years later; the official New York Indian Records (1678–1751) followed (Wraxall 1915). The perennial problem of border clashes on the southern frontier as settlers encroached on the warpath to the Catawba country brought Virginia, Maryland, and New York together in the so-called first English treaty with the Five Nations (1677). The governors of the three colonies put their hands in the "covenant chain," or "chain of peace and friendship," a symbol of alliance that dominated treaty negotiations for the next century.

From earliest European contact through the seventeenth and eighteenth centuries, wampum served as currency in trade and as the vehicle of international negotiations. Its use emerged from an already vigorous exchange of inland products for coastal shell beads that had begun in prehistoric times. Dutch reporters acclaimed the sources of these shells "the mine of New Netherland," and the new wampum, made with steel drills and whetstones that the Dutch supplied to Long Island wampum makers, became the magnet with which to draw furs out of the forest. Its use in trade expanded rapidly and it became a species of colonial currency. It also became the Europeans' means of approaching the Iroquois and validating agreements.

The eighteenth century, up until 1775 and the American Revolution, witnessed the rise of forest diplomacy and its perfection as a literary art form in the English treaties. If the great issue in the previous century had been who enjoyed the exclusive right to sell brandy or rum to the Far Indians in order to get their furs, land became the dominant issue of Indian and white relations during the eighteenth century. In Indian polity, land titles reposed in the nation or tribe, and the sachems were the trustees but not the owners of the land. Ultimate title rested in the women, who in turn were the trustees of the chiefs.

Typically, Indian delegates who were appointed to represent the nation at treaty negotiations were the front men for the sachem chiefs. Perforce these speakers and negotiators developed reputations as politicians who should be courted and heard. White people in the colonies who became knowledgeable about Indian affairs soon learned to distinguish two kinds of Indian leaders: war chiefs, who raised and led war parties and who in peacetime might be traders, and sachems, or peace chiefs, who confined their attention to civil affairs. What further complicated Indian affairs and confused colonials was that principals typically remained silent and appointed as their speakers artful men who were not of chiefly status. These speakers were often confused with the principals and labeled as sachems in the records. On occasion the principals, who were proper sachems, doubled as speakers, in which cases their names appear in the records.

Interpreters also were to be reckoned with. They had the last say in building an image in the minds of officials who heard them, scribes who wrote the minutes, and officials who read the reports. Individual Frenchmen, notably Louis-Thomas Chabret de Joncaire (1702–66), who was raised among the Senecas, and several of the Jesuits were bilingual. With the exceptions of George Croghan (d. 1782), possibly Sir William Johnson (1715–74), and certainly Samuel Kirkland (1741–1808), no Englishman was bilingual or knew any smattering of an Iroquoian language. At the other extreme, Conrad Weiser (1696–1760), a Palatine German who grew up speaking Mohawk at Schoharie, apparently was more fluent in Mohawk than in English, judging by his journals and letters. Given this state of ignorance in the English colonies, it is no wonder that chiefs were at first confused with "kings" and that deals for land were struck with Indians who had no right to sell. It is amazing, nevertheless, how good the colonial records are, considering that for the most part the interpreters were illiterate or had learned an Indian language during captivity. Few interpreters were scholars such as Kirkland, lifelong missionary among the Oneidas, and even he struggled for words and failed to infuse the fire of Indian oratory into treaty proceedings (Clinton 1812: 36).

Among eighteenth-century writings on forest diplomacy, the works of two French writers stand out. Claude-Charles Le Roy Bacqueville de La Potherie, while serving in New France as royal commissioner, observed the proceedings of the Grand Settlement of 1701 between the Iroquois and the tribes of the upper Great Lakes. His four-volume *Histoire de l'Amérique Septentrionale* (1722) includes a whole volume on the manners of the Iroquois, and the proceedings of the treaty occupy part of another volume. He isolated major themes, and his penchant for detail delights the ethnographer. His work complements nicely Lafitau's systematic treatment of contemporary Iroquois society and politics (Lafitau 1724, vol. 2). Unfortunately, neither writer described the structure and operation of the Iroquois League, although Bacqueville de La Potherie recorded diplomatic procedure and Lafitau sketched a social anthropology of local government at Caughnawaga.

The protocol of forest diplomacy demanded the use of appropriate metaphors. Timing was crucial. The parties manipulated space, and reciprocal action was expected of both sides. The Iroquois expected other parties to observe these forms, which the colonists were obliged to learn to satisfy native demands. Otherwise, to the reader of historical documents, the passing of wampum belts, the distribution of presents, and the enormous expense of providing the expected feast remain unintelligible. Moreover, these activities adhered to a pattern. The ritual paradigm that governed the proceedings guided the behavior of Iroquoian and Algonquian speakers alike throughout the lower Great Lakes; it survives today in the program of the Iroquois Condolence Council (Hale 1883; Fenton 1946, 1950, 1967, 1978a, 1985: 18–19; Tooker 1978).

No English writer of the period quite attained the clarity of the French. Cadwallader Colden (1688–1776), who found so much of interest in North America, discovered in the proceedings of Indian treaties the seeds of a native species of American literature. He was soon seconded by Benjamin Franklin, and there were others in the colonies who read Colden (1727; 1750) and admired the genius of the Five Nations. Indeed, the best minds of the day first experienced diplomatic relations in the conduct of Indian affairs. None of these colonial negotiators, however, described the structure of the Iroquois Confederacy as such. Not Peter Schuyler (1657–1724), first mayor of Albany, who accompanied the "four kings" (three Mohawks and a River Indian) to the court of Queen Anne (Bond 1952); not Conrad Weiser, the Pennsylvania Indian interpreter whom the Iroquois claimed belonged one-half to them (P. Wallace 1945); not Sir William Johnson, who walked in their moccasins and slept in their beds; not Samuel Kirkland, lifetime resident among the Oneidas, Revolutionary War chaplain, and enumerator of the Six Nations by town and clan—not one of them left any systematic account of how the league functioned.

□□◇□□

The eighteenth-century Iroquois were already transformed. They depended economically on the Albany traders; they fully appreciated that dependence; and the fact of it guided policy at Onondaga. Defeated in the west, expelled from conquered lands in Huronia, down in numbers from war and pestilence, they had made peace with the French and to an extent with the Far Indians, and perforce their policy was neutrality. Large numbers of their population had defected to the Laurentian missionary settlements in Canada, where they were manipulated by the governors of New France. Their alliances were accordingly ambivalent in order to prevent further French invasions of their homeland and at the same time maintain the covenant chain with the English governors and secure a credit line with the Dutch traders. The resident Mohawks had grown tired of French Jesuit missionaries and were prepared to welcome Anglicans, as New York governors were urging.

War with the southeastern tribes, egged on by the French, continued to attract young Iroquois men during much of the century. Compensatory English moves to compose these feuds underlay a series of treaty councils held at Albany. Other than Onondaga, Albany was the place of councils where governors and commissioners of the other colonies were obliged to meet and put their hands in the chain of alliances that united much of British America and focused minds on the Six Nations. Although reduced in number, the Six Nations were still a force to be reckoned with. As the nation closest to Albany, the Mohawks would soon deed away their best lands, while the lands of the other members of the Longhouse remained intact. In the process, Iroquois culture was changing rapidly from east to west.

All who described the Iroquois spoke of this change. Colden noted that traditional Iroquois hospitality declined after they learned not to expect it from their white neighbors—they no longer offered their young girls to visiting Christians. Indeed, they had laid aside many ancient customs "and have adopted many of ours; so that it is not easy now to distinguish their original and genuine Manners, from those which they have lately acquired" (Colden 1750: 11). William Johnson was to repeat this observation.

The Five, presently Six, Nations remained a shaky bulwark between the expanding English colony of New York and the French. Although governors of New York sensed the importance of the Six Nations to the security of the colony, they nevertheless failed to get the assembly to raise troops, fulfill promises to the sachems, or mount an attack against Canada. Offsetting just such an attack, Jesuits at Oneida encouraged young men to go out against Indians living at the back of the English colonies in the southeast. Oneida war parties repeatedly headed for the Catawba country, slaughtered livestock, plundered crops, and killed whoever got in the way. Oneida losses were not inconsiderable. Later in the century, Seneca war parties followed the great warrior path to the Cherokee towns. Participation in such raids is difficult to explain in terms other than the traditional drive for honors. For the Iroquois, the economic motive of the fur trade was gone; no one could be expected to pack home deerskins from distant Appalachia to trade at Albany. But the raids embarrassed the English, and the problems they created brought the colonies reluctantly together, first in a series of conferences and ultimately at the Albany Congress at mid-century.

The flow of captives from the southeast altered the already mixed ethnic composition of Iroquois towns. Adoptions failed to replace manpower losses, particularly at Oneida, which lost a good portion of its men in one Catawba campaign. No wonder the power of men declined politically and the power of matrons rose, for they were the continuity of the nation. It was the "she sachems" who decided whether captives were adopted or tortured. They were the trustees of chiefships, the prime producers of cultivated crops, the continuators of family and society, and the ultimate comptrollers of the land. It was the women who stayed home: descent, inheritance, and succession passed in the female line, and women were the conservators of the old culture. Men were the active participants. We do not know as much about women's roles as we know about men's because women seldom enter the literature until the narrative of Mary Jemison's captivity (Seaver 1925).

During the eighteenth century, several refugee populations from the southeast drifted to Iroquoia and joined in the Great Peace. Bands of Tuscaroras and Iroquoian people from the Neuse River in Carolina, defeated in 1712 by colonial forces, moved northward through Maryland and Pennsylvania in stages as displaced people, until a decade later the Oneidas took them under their wing and made them "props" to the Longhouse. Thereafter the Iroquois were known as the Six Nations. Similarly, Siouan-speaking bands called Saponi and Tutelo from Virginia "tramped the bushes down," reaching Cayuga at mid-century, and were adopted. Soon afterward, refugee Nanticokes from Chesapeake Bay arrived and were followed by part of the people called Delaware. Thus, what had been the junior side of the Longhouse—the Oneidas and Cayugas, or "Two Brothers," became known as the "Four Brothers." The senior side, Mohawk-Onondaga-Seneca, stood fast as the "Three Brothers."

These remnant groups presumably introduced some conspicuous southeastern cultural items later identified as Iroquois. The blowgun, which Lewis H. Morgan described (1850: 83; 1851: 379), is mentioned nowhere in historical sources until the last decade of the century, in reference to the Niagara frontier (Weld 1807, 2: 143). Typically, Iroquois splint baskets for washing and sifting corn, frequently in a twill pattern of over-two, under-two weave, which are represented in museum collections from the mid-nineteenth century, resemble cane baskets from the southeast. They are too similar not to be related. Yet they are not the kind of containers mentioned by colonial writers (Speck 1920; Flannery 1939). The diffusion of the calumet and the calumet .dance to the Iroquois is better documented. Both the pipe and the dance came down from the upper Great Lakes after 1680; the ceremony was a feature of the Montreal treaty council of 1701 (Bacqueville de La Potherie 1722, vol. 4).

The Catawbas brought their version of the calumet dance to the Albany treaty council of 1751 (Fenton 1953a: 165ff.). My Seneca informants ascribed the advent of the *tonwi:sas* rite, in which matrons shake Carolina box terrapin rattles while thanking the "three sisters" (corn, beans, and squash) at Green Corn and Midwinter festivals, to the Cherokee wars of the late eighteenth century.

The seventeenth century saw radical changes in weaponry and tactics. The gun displaced the bow and arrow to secondary use. The tomahawk made in Sheffield supplanted the ball-headed warclub, often inlaid with wampum and with a shank fashioned like a human leg. These changes in weaponry prompted corresponding changes in tactics away from massing warriors in slat armor under strict leadership to forming small guerrilla bands. The number of leaders enrolling war parties increased, competition for prestige and war honors was enhanced, and the status of war chief fragmented.

Not until Joseph Brant (1742–1807), a Loyalist Mohawk Christian, was commissioned captain of the Six Nations and put together large raiding parties that ranged out of Niagara during the American Revolution did the war chief's position improve. The multiplying of war chiefs during the eighteenth century also eroded the office of peace chief. When it came to making treaties, the unemployed veterans of the warpath insisted on being heard in council. Moreover, the power of pine tree chiefs—orators appointed for life—evolved from their role as negotiators with Euro-Americans, as is witnessed in the rise of Red Jacket, the Seneca orator, at the close of the century.

These circumstances and the fact that peace chiefs usually spoke through appointed speakers help explain why the names of the fifty founders of the Iroquois League, which descended within matrilineages as ascribed statuses, appear so infrequently in the literature. Occasionally one finds the names of the leading titles of each national delegation. This reflects both the force of incumbents in these titles and the customary usage of referring to each of the Five Nations by these titles.

Thus one may read what Tekarihoken (Mohawk) said or did; that Odatshehdeh (Oneida) supported or dissented; perhaps that Sagochiendagehte, "the name bearer" (a council name for Onondaga but not a title), confirmed it; that Haga?en:yonk (Cayuga) witnessed it; and that Ganyadaiyo? and Sa?dagaenyes (Senecas) were absent. Indeed, the first Seneca title, which the prophet Handsome Lake later held, is less famous in the annals than that of his half-brother Cornplanter, a war chief. Often the Senecas are known by the title "doorkeeper," the fiftieth title on the roll call (Fenton 1950).

Concepts of time are among the most difficult understandings to communicate between cultures. European officials suffered the delays of Indian delegations arriving for meetings on their own time, and they chafed at the deliberateness with which Indians conducted affairs. Indians were never in a hurry. They would arrive "in so many moons," "when the corn is knee high," "when bark is ready to peel for canoes," "when the leaves turn," or "when we get done hunting"—concepts that were important to them but too vague and uncertain for gentlemen attuned to a calendar.

To this day, Indian time is an hour after prevailing time. Meetings are called "when we turn the lamps up" or "when we get done eating." Even now Iroquois tend not to answer a proposition on the same day it is presented. Nor do they press a party for a reply until the party is ready. One listens carefully, repeats the main points of what one hears, and then takes the message home and puts it under one's head for the night. One never interrupts another. Indeed, this bit of forest protocol is sanctioned by ritual. According to Hale (1883: 125), the invocation to the founders of the league says:

> Oh my grandsires!
> Even now that has become old which you established
> —the Great League.
> You have it as a pillow under your heads
> in the ground where you are lying,
> this Great League which you established;
> although you said that far away in the future
> the Great League would endure.

And so the concept endures in the minds of its adherents. Ritual poetry, metaphor, and symbolism, in which the treaty literature abounds, persist in the context of the Condolence Council.

Iroquois delegates expected to devote the first day of a public council to reciting the laws of their ancient government before moving to the conduct of public business. It was the rule that the dead must be condoled and the tears wiped from the eyes of the living. They extended these amenities to Euro-American governors, agents, and their kindred, and they expected the same of others. The English were slow to learn, and we shall discover what they learned. Why Albany continued as the place of council with the English will become apparent, and we shall glimpse how policy was made at Onondaga. The literature that the two parties produced enables us to do this.

It was a natural transition from the Indian custom of exchanging gifts upon making alliances to the trade and payment of presents in European manufactured goods. Diplomacy and Indian gifts went hand in hand. The Iroquois depended on the traders and the treaty negotiations for wampum as well as guns and cloth, the products of European technology. The traders prepared and William Johnson forwarded long lists of the items desired that were manufactured in Britain and the Low Countries. These lists mirror the changing culture of the Six Nations (Jacobs 1950; NYCD; SWJP).

The changes in Iroquois culture reflected conditions of daily contact on the frontier as well as forces far removed on the upper Great Lakes, on the Ohio River, and in Europe. Unable to prevail in the upper lakes and defeated by a coalition of Wyandots, Chippewas, and Ottawas, the Iroquois lost to the infiltrating Mississaugas lands in Ontario from which they had driven the Hurons, Petuns, and Neutrals a half-century earlier (Eid 1979). Likewise, having dispersed former occupants of the Ohio Valley in the previous century, and formerly having controlled access to the valley by the French and the English, the old men of Onondaga now realized that their erstwhile dominion was crumbling at the margins and that the back country was now occupied by displaced former neighbors like the Delawares, Shawnees, and Mingos—the latter defectors from the league. Behind these remnant groups pressed white settlers from Virginia and Pennsylvania during the so-called Westward Movement. Through the eastern door of the Longhouse, Palatine Germans pushed up the Mohawk and Schoharie valleys to occupy recent land cessions. In Albany and Whitehall, the game the English played, unsuccessfully, was to keep the French out of Iroquoia and the Ohio Valley by persuading the Five Nations to grant trusteeship, if not title, to their beaver hunting lands by promising protection that was not forthcoming, by substituting Anglican missionaries for the French Jesuits, and by replacing the Albany commissioners of Indian affairs, who were losing control of the trade, with a single crown-appointed superintendent. In short, military affairs, the missions, the Westward Movement, land cessions, trade, politics, and war were one package called Anglo-French rivalry, and the Iroquois were the string around it.

□□◇□□

Six Nations policy, while adhering to the chain of friendship, shifted in response to British failures to fulfill promises of military aid and segmented Indian affairs up to the American Revolution. From 1701 until 1755 the nations of the Iroquois Confederacy considered themselves not subjects but allies of the crown, each nation party to the alliance with its hand in the chain. A policy of neutrality that the old men at Onondaga adhered to followed the Grand Settlement at Montreal in 1701 and ended in 1755 when William Johnson persuaded eastern warriors of the confederacy to take up the hatchet against the French. From 1755 until his death in 1774, Johnson managed Six Nations affairs in the interest of the crown. In the year of Braddock's dismal defeat at Bushy Run, the victory of Johnson's Indian troops at Lake George earned him a knighthood, although he suffered the loss of his friend Hendrick, a prominent Mohawk chief who had been one of the "four kings." From the viewpoint of the crown, Lake George, the reduction of Niagara three years later, the Royal Proclamation of 1763, and the establishment of the Fort Stanwix boundary line of 1768 ranked as Johnson's major triumphs.

During Johnson's long oversight of their affairs, the Mohawks remained faithful to the English, and nations west of them kept one ear in Johnson Hall, Sir William's mansion in present-day Johnstown, New York. Most of the confederates were willing to leave affairs in his hands because they knew that having acquired a barony of his own, he was interested in keeping other land speculators out. For its sheer volume of documented activity and the importance of the man himself, Johnson's period is unique.

Several characteristics of contact situations were on the rise, including factionalism, witchcraft, and thievery. These symptoms of social disorganization aside, Johnson manifested no doubts about the capacity of Indians for learning. In his opinion, they were put to the English schools too late and then sent back to their own people unprepared to cope with the demands of a hunting, warring society. They did not learn the political mythology or master the expected forms of ritual address.

Johnson's views on education were seconded by Samuel Kirkland, who championed the day school in opposition to his mentor, Eleazer Wheelock (1711–79), and his Indian charity school. Having first visited the Senecas in 1765, Kirkland spent the remainder of his life at Oneida. As a religious "dissenter" and Revolutionary sympathizer, he was politically at odds with the Anglican and Loyalist Johnson, but the two men respected each other's knowledge of Indians. Kirkland learned Oneida, kept journals, and took the first accurate census of the Six Nations. He was keen, systematic, and thorough, and his record is ethnologically superior to Johnson's. To live in the woods, to know the etiquette of campfire and council, and to speak an Iroquoian language, even though imperfectly, were what Indians counted and what distinguished Kirkland from his contemporaries.

The Continental Congress made Kirkland its agent and, in the summer of 1776, on the eve of hostilities, sent commissioners to Albany to secure the neutrality of the Six Nations in the coming war. A British-inspired council followed promptly at Oswego to strengthen the Six Nations' tie to the crown. The sachems advised neutrality, but Joseph Brant, having recently returned from England, roused the warriors. That winter an outbreak of communicable disease carried off three leading Onondaga sachems and ninety others. Torn between these forces, the grand council met in grief at Onondaga in January 1777. There, finding itself unable to maintain a policy of neutrality, its generations at odds and no longer capable of attaining unanimity on policy, the council raked up the fire that had burned continuously since the founders first kindled it. Tradition holds that they covered the fire only for the duration of the war, but for all practical purposes this proved to be the culminating session of the league. The action greatly disturbed Kirkland, who appreciated the tradition of unity that the grand council ideally achieved, and he advised General Schuyler to condole the dead chiefs and rekindle the fire with wampum belts. Failure to act left affairs in the hands of the war chiefs (Stone 1838, 1: 176–77; Graymont 1972: 113; Pilkington 1980: 120).

When the last smoke of hostilities vanished, the embers of the fire that had burned at Onondaga from time immemorial were cold. Families gradually drifted back to old settlement sites but found no shelter in which to lay their heads, and they had little will to build new housing. The refugees at Niagara removed to Buffalo Creek, New York, which became the largest post-Revolution settlement of the Six Nations. Their lands were now in jeopardy and they lived as displaced people, threatened by land speculators and American agitation for their removal westward. There were grievances to be settled with the United States before permanent peace became a reality.

The period of federal treaties that dealt with these grievances had two phases. The first, which I cover in detail in this book, spanned the years 1784 to 1795, when Congress ratified a long-awaited treaty made at Canandaigua the year before. The second ran from the Treaty of Big Tree in 1797, which established reservations in New York state, to the final treaty at Buffalo Creek in 1842. The latter phase overlaps with the reservation period (1784–1924), which in Canada covers the Haldimand grant at Grand River to the Canadian Indian Act and thence to the present, and in New York from Big Tree to the formation of the Seneca Nation of Indians, a republic in 1848, and afterward to the Kinzua Dam cession of 1964 and its aftermath.

The nearly two thousand Loyalist Iroquois and allies who followed Brant to Canada reestablished a replica of the Iroquois League to govern the grant on the Grand River. The original Haldimand grant ran from the river's source to its mouth and six miles on either bank. From a symbolic ember the migrating fire-keepers rekindled a council fire at Onondaga Longhouse near Middleport, which one speaker contrasted with the "glowworm" at Buffalo Creek, and kept it burning until 1924, when the Canada Indian Act imposed an elective council as the legitimate government of the reserve. Then the hereditary chiefs retreated to Onondaga Longhouse, south of the river, where they have continued as an underground government ever since, sustained by their traditional beliefs and by the ritual sanction of the Condolence Council. In recent years confederacy supporters have staged several abortive attempts to regain political control of the reserve. The importance of Six Nations Reserve as a seat of Iroquois studies for more than a century cannot be overstated (Noon 1949; Speck 1949; Shimony 1961; Fenton 1965, 1975, 1978a; Weaver 1978, 1994).

Three "times of trouble" have marked the history of Indian and white relations in western New York since the American Revolution. Each time a major land cession reduced the Iroquois range, displaced settlements, disorganized society, and left the culture to regenerate itself in a new paradigm. In the decade following the American Revolution the Six Nations signed two major treaties with the United States, first a punitive settlement with commissioners of Congress at Fort Stanwix (1784), and then an agreement with Colonel Timothy Pickering, sole commissioner appointed by President Washington, at Canandaigua (1794), to ameliorate the previous terms, secure peace and friendship, and lead the Indians to white civilization. From the Six Nations side, the Canandaigua treaty secured federal recognition and cleaned up the "rusty spots" in the chain of friendship left by the first treaty, and an important agreement ensured that neither party would disturb the other in the peaceful use and enjoyment of its remaining lands or lands already ceded. Colonel Pickering and fifty chiefs and sachems of the Six Nations concluded a just and equitable peace that provided a charter for subsequent Indian and white relations in western New York and was to endure, as the Indian line runs, "as long as the sun shines, water flows, and the grass grows." It lasted until Congress and several administrations, by a process of legislative erosion, appropriated money for planning and building the Kinzua Dam, thereby setting the treaty aside.

Four issues were at work during the decade of the two federal treaties. First was the question of land, manifested in continual disputes over boundaries. Lands were sold fraudulently without consent or supervision of governments, and Indian hunting territories were violated. Joseph Brant and the British were insisting on the Ohio River boundary of 1768. A faction of the Cayugas wanted to sell and emigrate to Canada. Incursions led to murders on both sides, and murders to war. Second, the ever-present danger and horrible consequences of an Indian war might involve a thousand Six Nations veterans, and no one in Congress wanted to let them loose on the border settlements. Nor did they want them to join forces with the coalition of hostile Indians in Ohio. It was in everybody's interest to keep the Six Nations quiet, and that became the purpose of a series of conferences preliminary to Canandaigua. Third, British Loyalists nurtured hopes that with Canada as a base they might recover the Northwest, and they refused to yield the forts at Niagara, Detroit, and Michilimackinac until 1796. The fourth issue was the gradual "civilization" of the Indian, a purpose on the achievement of which Kirkland, the Quakers, and Pickering all advanced strong views.

From the Iroquois viewpoint, Fort Stanwix was bitter medicine. Nothing but trouble emerged from this treaty: the Senecas were injured and angry, and out of it grew a conflict between the state of New York and Congress over the conduct of

Indian affairs and jurisdiction over Indian lands. The new United States government's Articles of Confederation left the question ambiguous; the Constitution reserved control of Indian affairs to the federal government, although Congress has seldom pressed its jurisdiction and New York state has reluctantly acknowledged it.

In the peace settlement of 1783 that formally ended the American Revolution, the British crown forgot the faithful Mohawks and their allies and left them to their own devices. For a while after removal to Grand River, Brant was busy extending the principles of confederation to a coalition of western tribes who were trying to hold lands that they occupied north of the Ohio with the open assistance of the British. These were lands ceded at Fort Stanwix. Not only did the Six Nations once claim Ohio by right of conquest, but the Mississaugas now held lands in Ontario once taken from Huron, Petun, and Neutral peoples. Governors of Canada conveyed the Grand River lands to the Six Nations by proclamation and deed at the expense of the Mississaugas. Brant, assuming title to the grant, sold off tracts of the original grant until the present Six Nations Reserve downstream from Brantford comprised but 44,900 acres (Weaver 1978: 527). In my day, one could still sense the spirit of living history as the old chiefs recounted the removal of their great-grandfathers from New York state, how they looked around and discovered that they numbered a majority of the league chiefships, and how they rekindled the fire and reconstituted the league as local government on the reserve (Fenton 1949a, 1965; Shimony 1961; Johnston 1964; Weaver 1978).

The once proud and numerous Seneca nation, which alone had equaled the rest of the confederacy, segregated into local bands rent by factionalism and mixed in their loyalties. The Buffalo Creek contingent included disparate elements of Onondaga, Cayuga, and other tribal entities. A few Senecas remained at Genesee; there were bands at Tonawanda, Cattaraugus, and Allegheny, each with its own leaders and peculiar interests.

Social disorganization was especially intense in the Allegheny River settlements. Drunken disorder was so bad at Cornplanter's town that the chiefs appointed two men to keep whiskey out of town. These were the circumstances in which Handsome Lake had his vision in June 1799 and began to reveal the Good Message of the Creator. Just then a mission of concerned Friends described the scene and proceeded to revolutionize Seneca subsistence and housing.

Though of a different faith, Asher Wright's mission to the Senecas at Buffalo Creek and Cattaraugus was a natural sequel to that of the Friends. Wright (1803–75) was certainly the best observer of Seneca society immediately preceding L. H. Morgan, and he had unusual gifts in linguistics. Wright's analysis of the causes attending the disorganization of Seneca society is remarkably perceptive for his time (Fenton 1956; Fenton, ed., 1957).

When a pattern of culture is shattered, a people loses its vital spark. The Iroquois had long done things in common, and having reached one mind, they acted. It was abandoning this principle of unanimity, Wright thought, that led directly to the loss of their lands. Scattered on reservations, they were dealt with separately and were forced to act independently of each other. Reduction in the size of their territory increased population density, and formerly autonomous tribes were thrown together on reservations where old lines of tribal distinction and local custom were soon obliterated. Life on the reservation was a new ball game with new rules.

PART ONE

THE CULTURAL FOUNDATIONS
OF THE IROQUOIS LEAGUE

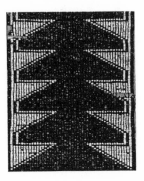

CHAPTER 1

Culture Patterns

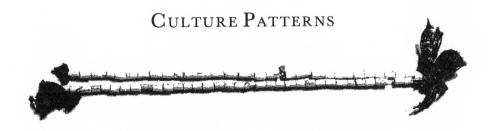

The way of life of the Five Nations as Northern Iroquoians was not unique but was composed of cultural patterns shared by the Hurons and presumably their congenors, the Neutrals, Petuns, and Eries.[1] These last three were destroyed before their cultures became known. We know slightly more about the Andaste, or Susquehannock, people of Pennsylvania. Any attempt to delineate Northern Iroquoian culture patterns is at best a reconstruction. One depends on the early French sources, mainly the Jesuit *Relations*, and calls upon a century and a half of ethnographic research since that of Lewis H. Morgan. The time perspective of this reconstruction extends from twentieth-century observations back to the contact period.

I invoke the legacy of Marc Bloch (1953: 28), the French philosopher of history, that the great problems of historical inquiry derive from the antithesis between continuity and perpetual change. Patterns are the stuff of continuity; the scholar isolates and synthesizes them. Viewed over time, substitutions within their framework afford a diachronic perspective—the stuff of change. Patterns that have persisted for the observation of ethnologists and that are not demonstrably European but can be identified in the early sources represent the Iroquois cultural heritage. Some of these patterns may go back to pre-Columbian times.

For one who arrived at the end of a time span of three hundred years to observe the contemporary Iroquois scene, the logical progression of research is to proceed from what is known best to what is most obscure (Bloch 1953: 45). This approach, now known as "upstreaming," or reading history backward, I find beneficial before restoring time to its historical direction.

□□◇□□

Iroquoia, the territory covered by the metaphorical Longhouse of the Five Nations, south of Lake Ontario, is, with the country just north of the lake, one physiographic and vegetational unit. The south lakeshore is dissected by northward-flowing streams that drain valleys gouged out of sedimentary formations by glaciers. Where impounded, these valleys form the Finger Lakes. High hills rise to the south to the height of land near the Pennsylvania line where the streams flow south into the Allegheny, Susquehanna, and Delaware drainage systems. The uplifted sedimentary formations that form the Niagara Escarpment reach from

1. This chapter was adapted from my contribution "Northern Iroquoian Culture Patterns," which appeared in *Handbook of North American Indians, vol. 15: Northeast* (Fenton 1978a) and is here published by permission of the Smithsonian Institution.

western New York into southwestern Ontario. Southeast of Lake Ontario, between the uplifted plateau and the higher Adirondack Mountains to the north, the Mohawk River with its broad valley cuts through these formations to afford the only water-level route west through the Appalachian chain. The Lake Champlain–Richelieu River corridor between the Adirondacks and the Green Mountains connects the Mohawk and Hudson River waterways with the St. Lawrence River. These were the communication routes of the Iroquois and their neighbors. They were the corridors of trade, war, and peace; for Europeans they became the avenues of exploration, invasion, and westward expansion. The Iroquois were strategically located to exploit the geopolitics of the region.

Before the Europeans arrived, an almost continuous forest of deciduous birch, beech, and maple with admixtures of pine and hemlock covered Iroquoia, giving way in the north to aspen, fir, spruce, and cedar. An Appalachian deciduous forest of oak, chestnut, and yellow poplar reached valleys tributary to the Hudson, and in the hunting range of the Senecas deciduous trees and herbaceous plants typical of the Ohio River drainage intruded. Sycamores, walnuts, and butternuts of prodigious girth are reported from islands and bottoms. Hickories, a source of food, oil, and staves, occurred throughout. Travelers encountered oak openings and savannas on reaching the Genesee country. In all these forests the sugar maple, the American elm, and the white pine were the climax forms that the Iroquois venerated and appealed to in political metaphors. Elm bark was crucial for shelter, containers, and vessels; indeed, the culture could not function without it because birches of sufficient girth for covering canoes, shingling lodges, and making vessels do not grow south of a line encompassing the Adirondacks.

Iroquois travelers could readily find basswood bark or slippery elm bast for making rope, tumplines, and prisoner ties. There was oak or basswood for stanching wounds, and several hundred herbaceous plants were ready to hand for medicines. Such usages were widely shared, with cognate plant names, from the Seneca country to the St. Lawrence Valley, and herbalism is still current in Iroquois communities (Fenton 1942).

Although deer, bear, and small mammals abounded in the forests within a day's travel from settlements—until they were hunted out—it was the beaver that revolutionized the economy and governed politics until the animals were depleted in Iroquoia by the mid-seventeenth century. After that time, demands of the trade drove hunters and raiders farther afield and set off the so-called Beaver Wars.

The spectacular raids of Iroquois war parties, which during the seventeenth and eighteenth centuries reached from Tadoussac to Michilimackinac and from James Bay to the canebrakes of Georgia, misled early historical writers such as Cadwallader Colden into overlooking the fact that for the Iroquois, effective occupancy of territory was confined to their principal towns and to surrounding forests and streams within range of subsistence activities. Territories were defined by heights of land and watercourses. That of the Iroquois League, which was composed of confederated village bands, greeted the sunrise on the Schoharie and saw the sun set west of the Genesee River. The Adirondacks and Lake Ontario were its northern flank, and the headwaters of the Delaware, Susquehanna, and Allegheny invited expansion to the south (Fenton 1940). The so-called Iroquois empire was a myth (Jennings 1984).

□□◇□□

The size of a society has a direct bearing on its political structure. No aspect of New World scholarship has aroused more controversy than estimates of the native population at the time of European contact and earlier. Until recent studies of the epidemiology of introduced European diseases, factored together with rates of decline following dated outbreaks and checked against settlement-pattern archaeology, population estimates for the Five Nations were based on warrior counts made *after* the first serious outbreaks. Such estimates were inevitably far smaller than the sizes of pre-epidemic populations. Naturally, figures for the Mohawk people, who were closer to Albany and more accessible, are more complete than those for the "upper," or westernmost, nations—the Onondagas, Cayugas, and Senecas.

It is now estimated that some 8,100 Mohawks inhabited four main communities in the valley of their name before the great smallpox epidemic of 1633 reached the interior and decimated their towns. Iroquois towns seldom, if ever, exceeded 2,000 persons, being essentially unstable and subject to economic pressures on the land and its resources, which led to groups' budding off to found new towns, if not to division over factional squabbles. Population estimates based on warrior counts probably represent 25 percent of the total population. If the mortality of the Iroquois population in the 1633 epidemic was 75 percent, as the Mohawk figures suggest, and if the same ratio held for the other four nations of the confederacy, previous estimates of the total pre-epidemic population of the league rise spectacularly (after Snow and Lamphear 1988: 23–24; Snow and Starna 1989).

For the seventeenth century, starting in 1660, a generation after the first smallpox pandemic, there are five comparable warrior counts for the Five Nations that average just over 2,000 fighting men but decline toward the close of the century. These figures suggest a total league population of not over 10,000 persons that had diminished by half in 1698. If indeed the original population had lost 75 percent of its numbers, it would have ranged from 32,000 to 40,000 persons, which is too high by half. The towns of Iroquoia had grown larger and fewer in protohistoric times as smaller settlements consolidated, but the largest villages seldom sheltered more than 2,000 people. Iroquoia comprised but twelve towns during the seventeenth century, and of these, only the upper Mohawk "castle," Tionontoguen, and the Seneca capital, Kanagaro (not to be confused with a later Mohawk town of the same name), attained such proportions. An original population of 20,000 for Iroquoia compares favorably with the estimates for Huronia.[2]

The warrior counts serve one other purpose. They demonstrate the relative sizes of Five Nations populations. During much of its history, the Seneca nation was twice the size of the Mohawk, and as time went on it was twice the size of the other four nations combined. But this was after it added two satellite towns of adopted captives to its two main towns. During the seventeenth century Oneida was the smallest nation, boasting 100 to 150 warriors, down to 70 in 1698 but enlarged in the next century by the addition of Tuscarora, Tutelo, and Delaware segments. The three Cayuga towns and Onondaga fielded some 300 warriors each, with

2. Iroquois population estimates are derived from Michelson 1977; from the Jesuit *Relations* and the New York colonial documents as published by Tooker (1978: 421); from Snow and Lamphear 1988; and from Snow and Starna 1989. For Iroquois towns, see Fenton 1940: 203.

populations of comparable size. By 1660 the Iroquois population was a mixed bag of genes comprising various captive and adopted entities including Hurons, Tionontatés (Huron-Wyandots), Neutrals, Eries, and Algonquins of the upper Great Lakes, who replaced losses to war, pestilence, and natural causes (JR, 45: 207). Some of these persons acceded to high office and others became more Iroquois than the natives themselves through a remarkable process of informal education, to which I shall return.

The decline of Iroquois population, including these adoptees, during the seventeenth century affected the transmission of the league tradition in two important ways. There were fewer knowledgeable teachers, and there were fewer eligible candidates for life chiefships. As a consequence, it became impossible to keep the empty seats in the grand council filled with men nominated from the matrilineages in which the fifty titles of the founders descended. The league continued as a symbolic system, but the operating confederacy resorted to other leaders. These effective principals, who conducted the business of the confederacy, often in the name of the league, seldom carried the famous names of the founders.

□□◇□□

Cultures, like armies, move on their stomachs. Diverse subsistence patterns freed Iroquois men part of the year to engage in political activities, funded embassies, supplied war parties, or kept them home at stated seasons. The Iroquois are best known as horticulturists for the slash-and-burn agriculture that women practiced near the villages. But men, in season, cleared the forest, built houses, hunted deer, bear, and small animals, and in spring carried on extensive fisheries. Traditional patterns of Iroquois agriculture and food habits persisted among conservative reservation folk until recent times (Parker 1910; Waugh 1916).

Hunting is less well described (see James Smith's account in Drake 1851), but a recurring theme in Iroquois folklore runs, "They went to the woods to hunt for meat." Next to warfare and attending council, hunting enjoyed great prestige; it was an economic necessity, and no amount of cajoling would bring the old men to a treaty site during the spring or fall hunt.

"Indian tobacco" (*Nicotiana rustica*) was grown for ceremonial and council purposes by all Northern Iroquoian peoples, and still is. It seems to have received little care, but the leaves were plucked and strung to dry. The old men of Iroquoia were never separated from their tobacco pipes. A French observer of a council held in the Seneca main town in 1669 remarked: "It is their custom, on entering, to seat themselves in the most convenient place that they find vacant, without any consideration of rank, and at once get some fire to light their pipes, which do not leave their mouths during the whole time of the council, and they say that '*Good thoughts come while smoking*'" (Margry 1876–86, 1: 129.) This is a persistent theme in Iroquois political life.

Besides tobacco, the triad of maize, beans, and squash—the "three sisters" of Iroquois ceremonial—was cultivated by Northern Iroquoians up to the territorial margins of 120 frost-free days. Complementary to men's hunting, these crops provided the foundation of subsistence and afforded the leisure to develop institutions of sedentary life. In good years they yielded a surplus that was dried and stored for winter use and even held over to lean years. Settlements of up to fifteen hundred persons became possible. Men were free to hunt, repair their gear, and attend council because growing crops was the principal occupation of women in the village (Lafitau 1724, 2: 70ff.). Indeed, the village and surrounding fields constituted women's domain: they planted, cultivated, and harvested in work parties under the direction of a senior matron. They extended sibling terms to the crops they cultivated. Their activities are celebrated in the theme song of "Old-Time Women's Dance": "Women and our life sustainers are as sisters." Work parties of women gathered firewood in a similar manner.

Iroquois life was marked by a diurnal round, a yearly round, possibly a duo-decennial village movement, and a lifetime of activity. Of these entire cycles, one interests us just now. After the harvest, men went hunting in the deep woods for deer. Venison, a paramount item of subsistence, was also the symbol of men's labor, and antlers were the emblem of chiefship. Autumn was also the great season for councils, to the extent that chiefs were not preoccupied with the hunt.

The Iroquois moved easily in their environment and did little to alter it. Population, at least in historic times, was not dense, and the people's effect on the environment was minimal (Ritchie 1955–56). By the late seventeenth century, Seneca fields were extensive, and high yields were reported by the expedition of Jacques René de Brisay, marquis Denonville. John Sullivan's army in 1779 destroyed large plantations that included orchards of introduced peach, pear, and apple trees near Cayuga and Seneca towns. The Iroquois were innovative gardeners, although the British at Fort Niagara stimulated this horticultural activity to make them self-sufficient during the American Revolution.

In general, when soil was exhausted and firewood became scarce—about twice in a generation, although some towns persisted much longer—the town was removed. Removal was a gradual process, one town going up while the other was decaying, a process commemorated in the place-name theme "New Town" and "Old Town." ?Ohgi:we:, an Iroquois variant of the Feast of the Dead (Fenton and Kurath 1951), marked final removal. The Eulogy to the Founders of the Iroquois League, sung on the road during the condolence ceremony, recalls how "the places where they stopped to smoke [hold council] were soon overgrown with brush" and how, indeed, "abandoned fields overlie the places where your bones rest!" (Fenton 1950: 50). Such village removals, recurring approximately every twelve years, constituted a cycle into which each Iroquoian person's life was segmented. Iroquois political life reflected these shifts. The league, originally a confederacy of then-existing local chiefs, underwent changes in town constituencies if not in composition.

The longhouse was the most conspicuous feature of an Iroquois settlement. Typically it had from three to five fires, each of which might be shared by two nuclear families of five to six persons. Houses were, on average, twenty-five feet wide; the length depended on the number of families to be sheltered. Each fire added a two-apartment module of about twenty-five feet to the length of the longhouse. Houses of two hundred feet were not uncommon on Mohawk sites, although the average was about eighty feet (Ritchie and Funk 1973: 299, 318–19). Possibilities expand to a four-hundred-foot house on an Onondaga site (Tuck 1971: 94–96). Comparable data for Cayuga and Seneca sites are not available.

An Iroquois longhouse apartment consisted of a low, wide platform or bench-bed, walled by a section of outer house wall and a partition at either end and open toward the central aisle, where there was a fire shared with the apartment opposite. The platforms, built about a foot off the ground to avoid damp and fleas, were covered with reed mats or pelts and served as seats by day and beds at night. Above, a long shelf or rack held gear and stored food. Between apartments were large bark storage bins for corn and dried food, and firewood was stacked in the vestibules near the end doors (Lafitau 1724: 2: 5–16). In Iroquois thought, the longhouse was synonymous with a residential unit, the household or maternal lineage; it was their own symbol of identity, and together the Iroquois were "the People of the Longhouse," as they called their confederacy.

Important as clothing styles undoubtedly were, the want of museum collections for the seventeenth century, save a pair of black buckskin leggings in the Dauphin Collection (Musée de l'Homme, Paris), leaves us in the dark as to how Iroquois statesmen appeared. When first encountered, as evidenced by the first known portraits, the men were walking galleries of the tattooist's art (see fig. 30). They sported geometric designs, the double-curve motif, and clan crests, which were pricked with bone awls and rubbed with charcoal on face, shoulders, chest, and limbs.

The typical large Iroquois settlement was a cluster of 30 to 150 longhouses surrounded by a palisade and situated on a height of land accessible to drinking water and not too far removed from navigable water. Such a late-seventeenth-century Onondaga settlement, probably drawn by some French military engineer to illustrate the report of Louis de Buade de Frontenac's expedition of 1696, contained sixty bark lodges within a rectangular wall with four bastions, and thirteen lodges outside the fort (Blau, Campisi, and Tooker 1978: 494). Oneida "castle" of 1635 measured 767 steps in circumference and held 66 houses (Gehring and Starna 1988: 13). The upper and largest Mohawk town of the day was somewhat smaller, although of its 55 houses several were 100 steps in length (Gehring and Starna 1988: 9). Two great Seneca towns and two lesser settlements persisted from the mid-seventeenth century until 1687, when Denonville's expedition destroyed them, and Galinée reported populations of 150 each for the former and 30 each for the latter in 1669 (Fenton 1940: 227, 231). The range was from a hamlet of fifty people to a large village of one thousand or more persons. The core of each settlement, regardless of size, was the longhouse: a residential group of kin plus a fringe of spouses married in, all of whom together constituted a microcosm of the larger community.

□□◇□□

The localized character of much of Iroquois culture is as true today as it was when the league was formed out of autonomous village bands. Each village band, or community, is composed of one or more clan segments, or lineages. The lineage is a core of mothers, sisters, and daughters who, in native theory, are a longhouse family, or residential group, together with a fringe of spouses of other lineages. They comprise what the Iroquois call an "ongoing family." Its members identify with an eponymous animal—bird, mammal, or reptile—which becomes their crest, which was anciently displayed on the gable ends of lodges and which might become the name of the community. It was in this sense that the three Mohawk clans were each identified with a particular town, or the town with a clan. Persons whose families identified with the same crest, over the passage of generations, became fictive siblings; they were welcomed at clan lodges, granted hospitality, and accepted as if they were members of the same bloodline. Moreover, each community developed local ways that its members maintained and defended. The importance of local diversity for political history is that something of this character obtained between settlements or village bands and between nations composed of several such settlements or village bands; these differences had to be composed and unified in the formation of the Iroquois League.

The settlement and its chief, who took his name from the place or gave his name to it, are recurrent themes in Iroquois political literature. That the Five Nations comprised a disparate number of such settlements accounts in part for the unequal distribution of federal chiefs. On arriving in a foreign town, an emissary sought the lodge of the chief, who then assembled the community to hear the emissary's message. The chief's lodge was built in proportion to accommodate such gatherings—there were spare apartments for guests—and it became in fact the council house.

Evidence that chiefs were chosen from small residential segments, even a single household, is that multiple chiefships were associated with a single town. There were three principal Mohawk towns, each identified with a clan, and each of these clans owned three chiefships, each of which represented a segment, lineage, or household.

The three main towns of the Mohawks designated by clan names present an enigma. The use of clan names underscores the fact that Iroquois clans have both kinship and local aspects. The lower "castle," Ossernenon, was associated with the Turtle clan; the middle castle, Kanagaro, with the Bear clan; and the upper castle, Tionontoguen, with the Wolf clan (Megapolensis 1909 [1644]: 178–79; Fenton 1940: 203). Dominie Johannes Megapolensis, Jr., who served the Dutch congregation of Albany (Beaverwyck) as pastor, manifested a genuine curiosity about his native Mohawk neighbors. He heard Turtle clan claims to preeminence, boasting descent from the first woman on earth. He wrote that the people of the third town, the Wolf clan of Tionontoguen, were the progeny of the first two.

Although he says that the government "consists of the oldest, the most intelligent, the most eloquent and most warlike men," Megapolensis did not probe further into council composition and structure. The roster of Mohawk titles as eulogized in the Condolence Council and specified in the league epic lists three founders in each of the Mohawk clans and groups them in a tripartite arrangement in which the Wolf and Turtle clan chiefs sit on one side of the fire facing the Bear clan chiefs. Evidently the three clans each comprised three lineages, in which the nine Mohawk titles descended. A nearly identical clan structure and council arrangement existed among the same three clans resident within the palisade at Oneida, a single large town. This tripartite arrangement for counciling became the model for the grand council of the league.

An alternate model that obtained among the upper Iroquois—Onondagas, Cayugas, and Senecas—was the moiety system. This system received its first notice in a French document assigned to 1666 that is preserved and was once displayed in the National Archives in Paris.[3] I once read it to Seneca informants, who equated the terminology with their own. Nine "tribes" (clans) then constituted the Seneca nation. These formed two divisions (moieties), one of four and the other of five clans. The first division was called by a term known to my informants:

3. This document, Colonies C11A2 f.263 = Musée de l'Histoire de France, AE II, no. 1745, is reproduced in Fenton 1978a: 299. O'Callaghan printed it (DHNY, 1: 3–11; NYCD, 9: 47–50). It obviously relates to Seneca social organization at the time.

"four fireplaces," or four clans. The other moiety they called "five fireplaces" or "chimneys," meaning five clans. These are then listed by moiety in the French document. Moiety 1 consisted of the Turtle, Wolf, Bear, and Beaver clans, and moiety 2 encompassed the Deer, Potato (Clear Sand, Snipe), Great Plover, Small Plover, and Eagle (Hawk) clans.

The nine clans had formerly occupied nine villages, but during the protohistoric period they consolidated to sustain warfare. In the seventeenth century, eight Seneca chiefs were divided among the two moieties, each side having one great town and one small one. Onondaga, one main town and a satellite, had fourteen chiefships, undoubtedly representing an accumulation of clan segments at the central fire of the league. The ten Cayuga chiefs were distributed among three towns.

I infer that the nine Seneca clans observed village exogamy, for it is said that the ninth clan, called Canonchahonronon (Kanonhtsahonronon), "partitioned house people"(?), consisted of people from a house remote in the interior that was divided by a partition, separating the household into two intermarrying halves. They had wearied of not finding eligible mates save among themselves. Tonawanda sources had heard the tradition of a people who got around the rule of exogamy by going out one door and marrying in the other end of the house.

The basic patterns of Iroquois social structure have been known since the mid-nineteenth century. Colonial writers remarked on the division of labor between the sexes, which was both functional and spatial. Although Iroquois towns were built and governed by men, and to all appearances the women were drudges, men owed their offices to female succession, and the village and its environs of cleared fields up to the woods' edge were the domain of women. Apart from councils, men's roles were carried out in the forest—hunting, the warpath, embassies of peace and trade. Treaties were consummated at a distant council fire.

Each of the Five Nations was composed of villages and longhouse families and was divided into moieties or phratries. The three upper Iroquois nations adhered to the dual division, whereas the lower Iroquois (Mohawks and Oneidas) operated a tripartite system of phratries that dissolved into moieties in council, as I described earlier, with one clan in "control." Each moiety comprised two or more clans, and the clans were again segmented into one or more maternal families, or lineages. Every maternal family traced its home to some longhouse of which it once formed the household, and so in Iroquois thought the terms for the two entities were synonymous. These lineages, which later formed the segments of clans with which they shared their functions, were the building blocks of the social system (Goldenweiser 1914a: 473).

Viewed by the individual within the system, tribal society rested on certain fundamental organic analogies, the most important of which was a dualism that consisted in the symbolic recognition of the sexes. Starting from the fireside family of husband and wife, it extended to the clans, to the moieties, to the nation, and to the confederacy. In operation it embodied the principle of reciprocity, which governed the function of the moieties, both tribal and confederate.[4]

---

4. Hewitt (1944: 82) attributed this phenomenon to the extension of the rules of incest through the classificatory system of kinship, but a more likely explanation lies in the historical distribution of the same practice among neighboring peoples of the Southeast and the upper Great Lakes.

The simplest unit of Iroquois society is the fireside, or nuclear, family of husband and wife and their children. Stemming from the fireside family, by an arbitrary rule that includes any living siblings of the wife's mother, both male and female, the wife's brothers and sisters, the wife's children and her daughter's children, and the descendants of any of the preceding women in the female line, is the household of fact and legal fiction, or the continuing maternal family. This lineage of persons who trace descent from a common mother forms an exogamic incest group, members of which must take their spouses from other, similar matrilineages. It is what Hewitt termed the "uterine family" and Goldenweiser isolated as the "maternal family" (Hewitt 1944: 82; Goldenweiser 1914a: 467). The senior living woman of the lineage presides over the household and makes ultimate decisions on social and political matters. (Today she is known as the "clan mother.") In time a lineage might occupy several longhouses in several villages, giving rise to segments of a clan.

An Iroquois clan is composed of two or more maternal families who behave as if the members of each generation are indeed siblings, or as if they constitute a single maternal family. Historically, the two maternal families or segments may have originated in a single lineage occupying some distant longhouse, but long since, after some village removal, the connecting links have been forgotten. Possibly a segment derived from an adopted woman and her female descendants. The Iroquois clan, therefore, is a legal fiction. The maternal family is a physical reality that can become extinct if "its ashes get cold," whereas the clan continues. Long after family lines have faded from memory, clan identity is remembered and influences individual behavior.

One or more clans constituted a moiety, acted together, and referred to one another as siblings. The typical Iroquois community and tribe had two such moieties that served one another in crises. The moiety system still obtains in Longhouse congregations of the Handsome Lake religion. Moiety functions are mainly ceremonial: the two sides act reciprocally to condole and bury each other's dead; they may play lacrosse—a game that anciently discharged social tensions— to cheer some depressed person; and they contend at the Great Bowl Game twice a year to commemorate an act in the cosmology. These ritual acts are conceived of and enacted as one side's supporting the other.

Historically, when the Seneca council met, the first moiety ranged itself on one side of the fire and the second moiety occupied the opposite side. When the matter of business that had brought them together was discussed on one side of the fire, the decision was announced with great formality, and if there were two opinions, they were ultimately resolved. This bit of ethnohistory helps explain how, in the formation of the Iroquois League and the conduct of its rituals, the grand council adapted the moiety system of the upper Iroquois when mourning and installing chiefs in the offices of the founders.

At the level of the league, two similar moieties of tribes or nations carry out symbolic functions derived from the lower level of integration. In the Condolence Council, the Mohawk, Onondaga, and Seneca tribes make up the Three Brothers, the so-called *agadoni*, or "sires"—symbolically, the male principle. The opposite moiety, originally Oneida and Cayuga but later expanded to include Tuscarora and Delaware and other adopted peoples, is known as the Four Brothers, who represent the female principle in nature and are termed *kheya?tawenh*, the "offspring" or "nephews" of the Three Brothers. Whether this usage has any historical significance is unknown. (The two halves of the league are sometimes erroneously referred to as Elder Brothers and Younger Brothers.)

These terms derive from the fireside family, which in essence was bilateral and provided the individual with two lines of appeal, first to the mother's line and second to the father's. The two lines defined duties and obligations, particularly to one's mother's brother, who might be the clan chief, but also to one's father's kin. Thus the *agadoni/kheya?tawenh* principle had its operating base in the bilateral family and a symbolic projection in the confederacy.

Although a father's sister held her brother's son under special obligations to replace losses in her family (Lafitau 1724, 1: 552), one's primary loyalty was to the lineage of one's mother. It exercised a moral influence in controlling the nomination and conduct of sachems, or civil chiefs, favoring brothers over first cousins, and first cousins over third. A kind of elite social status adhered to lineages that held title to league chiefships. In sum, descent, inheritance, and succession passed in the female line (Fenton 1985: 10–11).

The Iroquois relationship system, which Lafitau (1724, 1: 552) discovered and Morgan (1877) made famous, groups blood relatives into five generations, the classificatory principle being evident in each. In one's own generation and in the first ascending and first descending generations, parallel relatives (for instance, father's brother and mother's sister) are classed with one's lineal relatives (father and mother, respectively, in this case). Cross-relatives (such as father's sister and mother's brother) are labeled differently. Cross-uncle and -aunt are distinguished, and cross-nephew and -niece show some further differentiation. Cross-cousins (the children of one's father's sister or mother's brother) are called by a single term. One's elder and younger siblings (and classificatory siblings as well) are distinguished with special terms for brother and sister, elder and younger, respectively. An important effect of the classificatory principle is that the lineal bias of Iroquois society is not reflected in the female descendants of the father's sister, as it is in the Crow system of the northern Great Plains and among certain southeastern societies. Indeed, the Iroquois kinship system also occurs among the Ojibwas and Dakotas, where sibs (i.e., clans) are unimportant if existent, a fact which demonstrates that for the Iroquois, kinship does not mirror clanship.

Europeans never appreciated the widespread network of kinship terms that encompassed the Eastern Woodlands peoples, and they misunderstood the values that Indians gave to the terms "brothers," "cousins," "uncles," "nephews," "fathers," and "sons." They assigned to these translations of the native terms meanings conventional in Europe. The English and the Iroquois had little difficulty over the reciprocal term "brethren"; although missing were the nuances of "elder" and "younger" sibling that were important in Iroquois society, the two sides settled on a neutral sibling term equivalent to Iroquois usage. Governors of New France, however, assumed that as "fathers," they enjoyed seniority rights over their "children," a relationship the Iroquois were ill prepared to accept. The symbolic usage of kinship terms among the nations of the Iroquois League was extended to surrounding tribes, and by analogy, similar terms were extended to

Europeans in forming treaty alliances during the colonial period. Just what these terms imply has been a source of confusion.

Neither did characteristic American Indian age grades accord with European usage. The Iroquois revere the dead and include them as the highest grade; they constantly appeal to the wisdom of the founders of the league and the ways that they established, and they deprecate contemporary learning. That the ancestors did something is sufficient sanction for doing that thing today (M. K. Foster to Francis Jennings, cited in Fenton 1985: 11n21). The next grade is the elders, the "old people"—the "old men" and the "old ladies." They next speak of "young people." They invariably include children, "those still on the boards" or "crawling on the ground," and, last, the unborn "whose faces are turned this way from beneath the ground." Indeed, babies are barely separated from the spirit world; as the saying runs, "an infant's life is as the thinness of a maple leaf." There is an element of circular reincarnation in all this, with a tendency for individuals to move up through the grades and statuses that pass in the continuing family, assuming the same names in alternate generations as the cycle repeats itself and society continues.

□□◇□□

The basic patterns of social structure and local organization extend to a wider context. This concept is important for understanding the Iroquois view of alliances and treaties inasmuch as they included governments in the network of symbolic kinship by such devices as the metaphorical "chain." It worked this way: as one moved from the lineage to the clan, to the moiety, to the tribe or nation, and thence to the league, the projected use of kinship terms became more fictional and the expected behavior more symbolic. The principle that operated throughout this extension was duality or reciprocity. Even one's fictional or symbolic relatives were expected to respond in kind with set speeches of condolence, wampum strings or belts or the like, present for present, word for word—and a good host hung a brimming kettle and provided a beverage to wash away the taste of smoking.

The village, its headman, and the council of elders run like a theme throughout Iroquois culture history. Although the clans had separate councils, an ad hoc village council of ranking clan chiefs, elders, and wise men made local policy. In a sense, the same thing happened at national and league levels. The titles and offices of clan chiefs were ascribed in specific maternal families or households, which were segments of clans, and the ranking matron of that lineage presided over the caucus that nominated, censored, or recalled a clan chief. The holders of such titles were also tribal chiefs and represented their villages and nations in the general council of the league. They enjoyed great prestige but had little power.[5]

The Reverend Asher Wright, who spent the great part of a lifetime at the Seneca mission, made the clearest statement of Iroquois political procedures in the mid-nineteenth century. Officers were known by the name of the office, and each clan had its own names and titles that descended matrilineally. These offices were graded. A vacancy, whether created by death, resignation, or deposition, "was

---

5. "Power" in this context means prestige translated into action. In Iroquois polity, no one ordered anyone else around. Issues were argued to consensus, and if agreement was not reached, the matter was dropped. Even when the chiefs attained "one mind," an appeal was made to the people to comply. Those who disagreed simply went their own way.

filled by raising all below a degree higher." The process of review was hierarchical and clear. "Hence at every occasion of filling vacancies, the character and merits of all the officers in the series and of all candidates, were liable to be passed upon first, in the discussion of the families interested; secondly, in the convocation of the clans to which they belong; thirdly, in the meeting of the four clans, which occupied respectively the two ends of the council house; fourthly, by the assembled council of the particular nation; and fifthly, [by the] council at the Longhouse of the Six Nations" (Fenton, ed., 1957: 310).[6]

Further, Wright discovered that there was a regular way to communicate concerns from the least fire to the great council fire of the league, and in turn for the great chiefs to enlist public opinion. In Wright's words: "If any individual desired to bring any proposition before the general council, he must first gain the assent of his family, then his clan, next of the four related clans in his end of the council house, then of his nation, and thus in due course . . . the business would be brought up before the representatives of the confederacy. In the reverse order, the measures of the general council were sent down to the people for their approval. It was a standing rule that all action should be unanimous. Hence the discussions were . . . continued till all opposition was reasoned down, or the proposed measure abandoned."

This process of attaining "one mind," and the ability to speak with "one voice, one mind, one heart," was, Wright thought, what contributed to the power of the confederacy—and it was not "until their councils were divided by bribery and Whiskey of the Whites" and they adopted majority rule that their power declined. This degeneration of power culminated in the negotiations preceding the Buffalo Creek treaty in 1838 (Fenton 1956: 567–81; Fenton, ed., 1957: 310–11).

It was the general pattern in the Northeast, and perhaps a weak echo of the Southeast, to distinguish between civil chiefs—the sachems (an Algonquian term), the *agoianders* of Lafitau, or the *hotiyaneshon?* of the Senecas—whose offices descended in matrilineages or clan segments, and other chiefs, who achieved their rank on the warpath or for council oratory and whose titles died with them and were not hereditary. The first group and their families constituted a class apart. The achieved statuses included the so-called pine tree chiefs, whose honorary titles carried no voting power; the speaker for the women; and the speaker for the warriors. Even the sachems employed a speaker to announce decisions reached in committee, and very few of the sachem titles appear in treaty negotiations. Speakers were chosen for their ability to grasp principle and fact, for rhetorical gifts, and for an enormous memory in a society in which most men and women were walking archives. The speaker's presence exerted a powerful influence on history, since he

6. Although this statement is specific for the Senecas of the early nineteenth century, who had a moiety system with four clans on each side, it probably is not too different from practice among the other nations of the confederacy. Goldenweiser took extensive genealogies at Six Nations Reserve on Grand River about 1912 and discovered similar rules governing descent and succession within matrilineages. I replicated this among the Senecas during the 1930s to get at the nature of clanship and the function of moieties and to collect sets of clan personal names. The "old ladies" who were my sources were often keepers of the names in their respective clans and frequently commented that a certain person, having been given a particular name, was "following" another person and would be expected to succeed to that person's office and duties. This lends credence to Wright's statement (Goldenweiser 1912–14; Fenton 1933–38).

was often identified by colonial recorders while the decision makers for whom he was the voice remained anonymous. Speakers numbered the most famous names in Indian political history. Joseph Brant was a war chief, but Red Jacket came to prominence as speaker for the women and later for the Seneca council.

Civil chiefs were responsible for external affairs, which included trade, alliances, and treaties. An understanding of this responsibility lends credence to a statement by their speaker in 1735: "for the Trade & Peace we take to be one thing" (Wraxall 1915: 195).

One can summarize Iroquois society, in Iroquois terms, as a body of relatives, "my people," who are residents of a place—a village or settlement. The public includes everyone; therefore, any stranger must be adopted. They consider themselves a nation, literally "a native land," a concept that is at once kindred and territorial. And the several bands, tribes, or nations are confederated on the model of the longhouse, which implies both kin and territory.

Vertically, society is ranked into "grandfathers of old," the founders; chiefs (sachems or lords), who are metaphorically called "trees"; warriors, or "mat bearers," sometimes called "big tobacco pouches," otherwise "tree watchers " or "props" to the chiefs; women, "our mothers," who really count in maintaining the ongoing families; and the age grades, already described.

The treaty presented a means of resolving tensions between alternatives that may be expressed in a series of dyads that characterized the life of Iroquois society. The solution to the dyad of relations (kin) versus outlanders was adoption: everyone should have a name and a niche in the kinship system. Therefore, colonial governors were adopted and assigned names. To achieve friendship and overcome feuds (even the trauma of murder), there was a regular way to compound delicts with presents. To achieve peace instead of war, there was the chain, or alliance, reaffirmed by the exchange of wampum belts. To overcome the inevitable conflict between life and death, there was the ritual of requickening, the heart of condolence, which sought to restore light against the darkness of grief by dispelling the clouds and restoring the sun. Persons, clans, and nations unaffected by grief were termed "clearminded"—in possession of their faculties in contrast to the "downminded," whose minds they proceeded to lift out of the depths of depression. Thus the treaty was a way of agreeing to restore normal relations between parties in disparate circumstances. All of this was made explicit to the Iroquois in the charter myth of the foundation of the Great Peace, or the league. Its antithesis was warfare.

□□◇□□

Despite the message of peace inherent in the founding of the league, Iroquois men revered war above all else, and with the fur trade it became a shattering force that threatened the very structure of their society. Enormous amounts of energy were expended on the warpath—in training, preparations, and travel—and heavy losses of manpower were only partly compensated for by adopting captives. As we have seen, the native population of Iroquois towns steadily declined during the seventeenth century, and from the midcentury on there were more outlanders than natives in Iroquoia.

The one perceptive account of the raising and departure of an Iroquois war party was written after the gun had revolutionized strategy and tactics, yet it explicates patterns of social organization that must have been operating for some time (Lafitau 1724, 2: 161ff.; Fenton and Moore 1977: 98ff.).[7] By then guerrilla bands under rising leaders had replaced large expeditions led by distinguished chiefs and shamans. Individual action had supplanted policy and group action. Although Iroquois men loved to hunt and fish, they deemed these activities second to warfare, which summoned the same capabilities in heightened form. Indeed, as Lafitau noted, warfare was a necessary exercise in their culture because it fulfilled a very law of their being. Since manpower was their only asset, the loss of a single person created the demand for his replacement, which entailed an obligation not of his household or lineage but of the *agadoni* (persons related to him as father's kin). The obligation extended to their offspring, who were thus duty bound to their father's lodge, to which otherwise they were strangers. The matron of the lodge of the deceased could force persons so related to her to go to war to make up the loss, or she could keep them at home to prevent further losses. It is evident that the power of matrons increased in relation to such losses at the close of the seventeenth century.[8]

If the matron decided to "raise up the tree" (replace the loss), or if she put on the mat the name of some dead person whom she mourned, she spoke through a wampum belt to a war leader related to her household as *agadoni*, asking him to form a war party. Accepting the belt was his commission (Lafitau 1724, 2: 164; Fenton and Moore 1977: 99.)

The preceding pattern, widely shared in North America, is known as the "mourning war," the continuing and changing implications of which in Iroquois culture history have been thoroughly researched and analyzed by Daniel Richter. He writes in summary: "Nevertheless, despite the weakening of traditional restraints, in the 1670s warfare still performed useful functions. It maintained a tenuous supply of furs to trade for essential European goods; it provided frequent campaigns to allow young men to show their valor; and it secured numerous captives to participate in the continuous mourning rituals that the many Iroquois deaths demanded (though there could never be enough to restock the population absolutely). In the quarter century after 1675, however, the scales would tip: by 1700 the Anglo-French struggle for control of the continent would make warfare as the Five Nations were practicing it dangerously dysfunctional for their societies" (Richter 1983: 544).

□□◇□□

Despite the rigors of change, Iroquois culture afforded the society with models of continuity that kept it in being. First, there was the ongoing human family with its emphasis on matriliny, at the same time acknowledging responsibility to the father's kin. This model of reciprocal obligations and duties, by a process of

---

7. Cadwallader Colden spoke from firsthand knowledge, and he may have had access to Lafitau in writing *The History of the Five Indian Nations* (1727), which appeared three years after Lafitau's work, but Colden missed the nuances of social structure that Lafitau alone perceived (Colden 1750: 5ff.).

8. Lafitau wrote: "The children of these different marriages [by men of other lodges who have marriage links with a particular household] become obligated to their father's lodge, to which they are strangers, and contract the obligation of replacing them [those who are lost] so that the matron, who has the principal authority in this household, can force these children to go to war . . . or keep them home." Lafitau is the only writer for centuries afterward to discuss this bilateral relationship (Fenton and Moore 1977: 99).

projection, afforded the design for both the tribe and the league (see Fenton 1978a: 316). There were metaphors of union, increase, and continuity of life contrasting with death that comprised a series of continuative models. Among these, the ever-growing tree of the long leaves, the metaphor for the commonwealth, contrasted with the metaphor for individual chiefs, who were trees that did topple. Individual chiefs had to be raised up again, just as the Tree of Peace had to be replanted. The deer was man's contribution to the larder, and antlers became marks of identity for chiefs: a rack was installed with his office. But as deer shed their racks, so the antlers were removed from the chief's head in illness, death, or malfeasance in office. During rutting season, deer rub antlers on brush and saplings, and so the great social dance that concluded an installation ceremony was called "rubbing antlers," when the chiefs socialized, diffused their power, and sought dancing partners.

Second, there was constant emphasis on the proper way: life and society were governed by certain procedures and rituals. Third, Iroquois culture redounded with predictions of gloom and set measures for meeting such contingencies (Fenton 1978a: 317).

Finally, the very heritage of the league itself manifested principles of continuity that maintained society. Its cardinal principles of "good word, peace, and power," which constituted the Great Law, had their humbler counterparts in truth (justice, right behavior), health, and physical strength. A note of humility toward the past ran through Iroquois culture: "in later days we have grown destitute," in contrast with the wisdom and knowledge of the "founders who sleep in their graves on the pillow of the law." Hence, respect for the elders, "who know a lot." One hears the constant admonition, "Listen!" And that is how the heritage passes.

CHAPTER 2

"THIS ISLAND, THE WORLD ON THE TURTLE'S BACK"

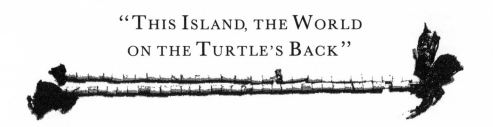

The peoples who spoke languages of the Northern Iroquoian family referred to their country as Wendat Ehen, "This Old Island," which they conceived of as resting on the back of a turtle swimming in the primal sea.[1] Their cosmology tells of the way the earth, plants and animals, celestial bodies, and spirit forces were created and put into operation. The great cosmological myth spells out the duties that each was assigned to perform for the benefit of humankind; it tells how the first human beings on earth learned to adjust to the situation as they found it, and how they responded to crises later on. All of these things constitute the subject matter of the Iroquoian cosmology, which is the first of three such myths by which the Iroquois periodize their history.

Learned men recited these myths at public gatherings or in family lodges where the householders had kindled a fire and cooked a kettle of mush for the myth holder. The telling might fill several days or nights; winter was the season of telling tales. Although each narrator claimed fidelity for his version, each had his own style, and the several versions together composed one genre. For a fact the published versions exhibit a remarkable consistency of plot and incident, although they differ in detail, and probably they differed slightly at each telling.

Our first concern is with the myth of the Earth Grasper; in later chapters I deal with the Deganawi:dah epic of the founding of the Iroquois League and with the revelation of Handsome Lake, the Seneca prophet, that is the ethos of the present Longhouse religion. Locked up in these three epics are the major institutions of Iroquois culture and the themes that have guided Iroquois behavior throughout the people's history and that illuminate certain actions of their descendants today. Just now I shall identify themes found in the cosmology. So let us listen to what "our grandfathers were wont to relate."

□□◇□□

The myth of the Earth Grasper, or, as it is known more commonly, the myth of the Woman Who Fell from the Sky, exists in some twenty-five versions that all adhere to the same general plot and contain most of the essential elements. One continuous mythological tradition confronts us from the first version recorded by Gabriel Sagard in 1623, which was again heard by the Jesuit missionaries Jean de

---

1. This chapter, originally a presidential address to the American Folklore Society, Philadelphia, 28 December 1960, appeared in the *Journal of American Folklore* 75 (298): 283-300. It has been substantially revised.

Brébeuf and Paul Ragueneau ten years later, to the elaborate texts that Hewitt collected from living informants at the close of the nineteenth century. Throughout 250 years, the versions are structurally similar. There is every likelihood that the tradition extends into pre-Columbian times. This is no ethnological freak, nor is the relationship between early Huron versions and later Iroquois versions contrived.[2]

The essential elements in the cosmogonic myth are nine in number. Longer versions contain fifteen or more component motifs that are readily identified in Stith Thompson's *Motif-Index of Folk-Literature* (1932–36). The nine are (1) the sky world, (2) uprooting of the life-giving tree, (3) casting down of Sky Woman, (4) animals diving for earth, (5) establishment of the earth on the turtle's back, (6) Sky Woman's daughter begets twins, Good-minded and Evil-minded, (7) Good-minded as culture hero liberates animals pent up by his brother and procures corn, (8) a cosmic duel with avowed fatal weapons—rushes or maize versus flint or antler, and (9) banishment of Evil-minded while Good-minded and Sky Woman retire to the sky world, promising to return on the last day of the world (Randle 1953: 629). These nine elements form the plot.

Various other episodes embellish longer versions, which include incest, impregnation by the wind, twins quarreling in the womb, Lodge Boy and Thrown-away, constructive and destructive creation, toad holding water until a flood issues from its belly or armpit, father search and son testing, experimental man making, and theft of light. This myth is widely distributed in North America and Eurasia. Peculiarly Iroquoian touches are the dream-guessing contests in the sky world; the struggle for power and control of the earth by a test of demonstrated mountain moving between Sky Holder and Hadu?i?, the hunchbacked mask being, who loses and becomes the Great Defender of Humankind; the rite of returning thanks from the earth to the sky; and the creation of clans and moieties during the formative period of human society. When humans are in trouble, a fatherless boy emerges from the fringe of the bush, defines the situation, proposes a solution, and

2. The cosmogonic myth is reported in an account of Galinée's visit to the Seneca towns in 1670 (see Margry 1876–86, 1: 360–62). Descendants of the Hurons, afterward called Wyandots, were living near Detroit in 1872 when Horatio Hale visited them and collected their ancient traditions (see Hale 1888). Later, Marius Barbeau (1915) confirmed Hale's findings. He collated earlier variants from Sagard and the Jesuit writers with recent sources, and afterward (1960) published the native texts that he recorded phonetically from the last speakers of the language living in 1912 in Oklahoma. David Cusick, a native Tuscarora historian, prefaced his *Ancient History of the Six Nations* (1825) with "A tale of the foundation of the Great Island (now North America), the two infants born, and the creation of the universe" (see also Beauchamp 1892). To the same genre, if not from the same source, belongs Elias Johnson's *Legends, Traditions and Laws of the Iroquois* (1881), Henry R. Schoolcraft's *Notes on the Iroquois* (1846), Erminnie A. Smith's *Myths of the Iroquois* (1883), and Jesse J. Cornplanter's *Legends of the Longhouse* (1938).

New England missionaries at Buffalo Creek also recorded Seneca variants early in the nineteenth century (see Fenton, ed., 1957). Later, folklorists Jeremiah Curtin and J. N. B. Hewitt collected other variants (see Curtin and Hewitt 1918; also Converse 1908: 31–38; Parker 1923: 59–73). Curtin was a pioneer folklorist, Hewitt a native Tuscarora ethnologist at the Bureau of American Ethnology, Converse a poet and journalist, and Parker a native Seneca ethnologist and museologist, the first New York State archaeologist, and the founding director of the Rochester Museum. And to complete the roster of Iroquoianists who collected the cosmogonic myth: early in the century F. W. Waugh recorded Oneida, Cayuga, and Tuscarora variants at Six Nations (see Beauchamp 1922; Randle 1953). Besides, there are four versions—Mohawk, Seneca, and two Onondaga—in Hewitt's "Iroquoian Cosmology" (1903; 1928). Hewitt is my principal source.

leads the community out of its dilemma. One senses that Iroquois tradition has attuned the members of society to listen to prophets (Thompson 1929: 1932–36; Count 1952; A. Wallace 1956, 1958a).

The prophet who would succeed among the Iroquois must use the old words and relate his program to old ways. He is a conservator at the same time that he is a reformer. In the long course of Iroquois cultural history, such prophets have accomplished its several reformations. This is one reason that Iroquois culture has endured so long; it is a tough tradition and a remarkably stable one. None enjoy greater prestige in this society than the men of intellect who perform feats of prodigious memory in relating the myths. These old men "who know everything" single out young men who manifest serious interest and demonstrate a capacity for learning. Soon these young men are marked in the community. Years ago the ethnologist might find himself cast in this role and sit at the feet of the professors of tribal lore. This is how Chief John Arthur Gibson became keeper of the lore of the Longhouse, and it is how J. N. B. Hewitt, a native Tuscarora, came to write it down. After I succeeded Hewitt at the Smithsonian Institution as ethnologist to the Iroquois, I inherited Hewitt's relationship to the Gibson family at Six Nations and came to know something of both men (Goldenweiser 1912b; Swanton 1938; Fenton 1944).

Chief John A. Gibson (d. 1912), a lifelong resident of the Six Nations Reserve on Grand River, was unquestionably the greatest mind of his generation among the Six Nations. While yet a young man he was installed as one of the eight Seneca chiefs who sit in the council of the confederacy, which then governed the reserve. This alert and keen-witted young Seneca chief soon attracted the notice of the senior member of the council, one of the Onondaga firekeepers. Concerned with perpetuating the lore of the Longhouse, the elder councilor decided to tutor his promising Seneca younger brother. Consequently, the customs, traditions, and ceremonies that Gibson mastered were the ancient ways of Onondaga, and when the older man realized that he must lay aside his antlers of office and prepare to take up the long trail, he asked Gibson to stand in his place and lead the ceremonies at Onondaga Longhouse. Although blinded in an early lacrosse accident, Gibson had developed a prodigious memory. After assuming the role of speaker of the Onondaga Longhouse, Gibson spoke Onondaga for the rest of his days, although he occasionally preached in Seneca, his mother tongue, when visiting Seneca communities.

At home the Gibson family spoke the several Iroquoian languages then current at Six Nations, besides excellent English. Small wonder that ethnologists sought after them as informants and interpreters. Indeed, the opportunities for learning Iroquoian languages on the Grand River around 1900 were far better than they had been earlier, when the Six Nations were scattered across New York state. This circumstance, coupled with intellectual curiosity and a keen mind, enabled Gibson to become the greatest living source on Iroquois culture at the turn of the nineteenth century, when field ethnology commenced in earnest. Gibson was never satisfied until he had traced a custom or belief back to its earliest remembered antecedents. No other Iroquois informant approached his work on mythology with Hewitt (1928: 453–54) or on rituals and social organization with Goldenweiser (1912–14). Hewitt thought Gibson's having been blind for some twenty-six years when they worked together had freed his remarkable powers of comprehension and memory for intellectual pursuits.

The Onondaga version of the cosmology that Hewitt recorded in phonetic script in 1900 and published in 1928 runs to more than twenty thousand words and is one of the longest extant Iroquoian texts, constituting some 145 printed pages. It is the best and most complete of the five versions that Hewitt collected and the one that I follow in making my own version. At times Hewitt's pseudoscientific English and biblical style obscure Gibson's Onondaga, which deserves a better fate. Occasionally I dip into the mush pots of Hewitt's other narrators, if only to sample the flavor of their styles.

John Napoleon Brinton Hewitt (1859–1937), when first I called on him before his passing, inhabited a Smithsonian tower office that I was later to occupy. As a graduate student seeking help on my first fieldwork, I approached the then doyen of Iroquoian studies for leads to living sources. Hewitt had married again late in life to a wife who claimed dowager rights in Washington society, and she had gotten him up to resemble her image of a Smithsonian savant: wing collar, Oxford gray coat, striped trousers, and white piping to his vest. He was the last of a notable group of self-taught students of the American Indian whom Major John Wesley Powell had assembled after founding the Bureau of American Ethnology in 1879. Hewitt shared the added distinction with Francis LaFlesche, the Omaha, of being a Native American, by Iroquois reckoning. His mother was part Tuscarora; that made him one, and he had grown up close to her tribal reservation near Niagara.

Although he had planned to follow his Scottish father into medicine, by a series of mishaps he ended up at age twenty-one working as secretary to Erminnie A. Smith, a Jersey socialite and folklorist. He assisted her in collecting myths, and he interpreted among the Iroquoian tribes. Major Powell had commissioned Mrs. Smith as temporary ethnologist at the bureau, and at her death in 1886 Powell called Hewitt to carry on her work. He would serve for fifty-one years. Hewitt soon added Mohawk, Onondaga, and Seneca to his quiver of Iroquoian tongues; these languages plus his native Tuscarora he recorded with painstaking accuracy, employing a phonetic orthography that one can easily read back to native speakers. He became the leading authority on the Iroquois League and its rituals. Being neither a trained linguist nor a schooled scientist, he had the good sense to concentrate on collecting texts, which is just as well, considering the state of theory in his day. His voluminous native-language manuscripts are being mined by Iroquoian scholars continually. The old men of the Seneca nation and of Six Nations on Grand River may be gone, but Hewitt wrote down their words for all time (Swanton 1938).

Hewitt had a philosophical turn of mind and was much interested in comparative religions. His justification for taking texts of myths in the original languages reveals this flair. He prefaced the *Cosmology* with this remark: "Upon the concepts evolved from their impression of things and from their experience with . . . their environment rest the authority of men's doctrines and the reasons for their rites and ceremonies. Hence arises the great importance of recording [texts]" (Hewitt 1903: 134). Essentially he did not differ from Franz Boas on the importance of native texts, although he abhorred Boas and his ilk.

From the four published versions of Hewitt's *Iroquoian Cosmology*, I have isolated the concepts and themes that characterize the culture as I have come to know it from fieldwork and reading.[3] I have also noted literary devices by which the narrator leads his listeners. The versions differ as the personal histories of the narrators differ—in time, in place, and in the narrator's participation in the culture of the day. Close scrutiny tells something about their personalities and provides evidence of culture change. Old John Skanawati Buck in 1889 was closer to sources on the old culture than Gibson, but Gibson was more comprehensive and incorporated all of the system of his teacher, omitting few niceties. One infers from John Armstrong's short Seneca version that the Senecas were mighty hunters and excellent naturalists familiar with the habits of game on which they subsisted. They knew star lore. Armstrong himself was an herbalist. The Seneca version casts the patron, the False Faces, in a friendlier role than does the Onondaga account, which emphasizes the power struggle between the Creator and Hadu?i?. One might expect the Seneca version to differ from Onondaga versions in detail but not in plot. Armstrong's version is foreshortened; it ends in midcourse, leaving one to wonder why informant and folklorist broke off.

Hewitt obtained the Mohawk version in 1897 from Seth Newhouse, the self-appointed chronicler of custom law at Six Nations (Fenton 1949b; Weaver 1984). Mohawks had been in contact with Anglican missionaries since the early eighteenth century, and as might be expected, Newhouse included some Christian elements. His version manifests a passion for legitimacy that is notable in Canada today. It nevertheless cites and explains some Mohawk usages found nowhere else. Newhouse was opinionated, he fancied himself an author, and he regarded Hewitt as a rival. The two native savants had some disagreements (Fenton 1949b: 153–57).

The Onondaga version of Gibson and Hewitt's is the longest and constitutes the second part of *Iroquoian Cosmology*. An analysis of its plot, incidents, and themes shows that it incorporates most of the detail from the three earlier versions.

Hewitt, like other folklorists of his day, sought to derive myths from phenomena in nature, and he spent himself in the futile search for the original and ideal myth. This comment on his career, however, contrasts with his own realization, stated early, that myths are composite cultural pieces and have varied histories in time and space. Considering what he wrote in 1900, it is odd that he did not follow Boas's lead and study myth dissemination: "the great and fundamental fact [is] that all legends are the gradual result of combination from many sources by many minds in many generations" (Hewitt 1903: 139).

Of the factors that enter into myth formation—diffusion, the role of the narrator, and cultural drift between generations—the narrator and drift bear most directly on the cultural history of a single people. We can regard the myth of the Earth Grasper as a mirror of Iroquoian culture without denying that its principal motifs—the celestial tree of light, incest in the sky world, couvade, the woman who fell from the sky, primeval water, earth diver, earth from the turtle's back, twins quarreling before birth, and Lodge Boy and Thrown-away—are at home in the

---

3. I first read these myths as a graduate student. Manifestly what I attempted in 1962 and revise now was impossible then. I shall try to convey some of the thrill of rediscovery. This is an ongoing process largely fostered by the annual Conference on Iroquois Research, where Iroquoianists share field experiences and insights not present earlier. Indeed, the whole field of Iroquoian studies has exploded of late. For the history of the Conference on Iroquois Research since 1945, see Fenton, ed., 1941: 4; Fenton and Gulick 1961; and Tooker, ed., 1967: 1–4.

mythology of neighboring Eastern Woodlands peoples. Two of these motifs, earth diver and rival twins, span the breadth of the continent (Thompson 1929: 279–80). And the notion of a primal sea out of which a diver fetches material for making dry land is among the most widespread concepts held by humankind: its distribution stretches from Finland across Eurasia, including India and southeastern Asia, and covers most of North America, suggesting that the idea diffused eastward to America when people settled that continent (Count 1952: 55–62).

Chief John Arthur Gibson and Seth Newhouse, as guardians of the lore of the Iroquois Longhouse, would probably have been intrigued but surely not amazed to learn that their myth of the creation had such a distinguished global history—although they would probably have claimed priority for it in America. They were certainly its greatest systematists. This drive toward synthesis, which is so evident in the culture of the nineteenth-century Iroquois and which characterizes their two great myths, Earth Grasper and Deganawi:dah, represents a response to the threat of the dominant culture. The narrators of the ancient myths sought to conserve as much of the old culture as possible within an ancient matrix. This motivation underlies the whole history of the Longhouse movement and is exemplified among the Six Nations on Grand River by the career of Chief Gibson.

□□◇□□

The myth of the Earth Grasper has three main parts that correspond to epochs. The first epoch describes the society of the sky world. The creation of the earth upon the turtle's back forms the second epoch, and the third is the world of Sky Holder, or Sapling, the period of primitive human society.

The sky world is the upper surface of the visible sky. Here live humanlike gods whose culture resembles that of pre-Columbian Woodland Indians and who, as persons, manifest the emotional strengths and weaknesses of the Iroquois people of later times. In a clearing stands a village of typical bark-covered lodges that have been extended to accommodate single maternal families. Newhouse said the lodges faced the rising sun and extended toward the sunset, a nice detail reminiscent of the later image of the confederacy, but there was yet no sun. Flowers on the tree of light, a feature standing at the center of the clearing by the chief's lodge and for which he is named, furnish the only illumination. Otherwise the sky-world environment consists of the familiar flora and fauna, specified or not, depending on the interest of the narrator. On entering the end doors of the lodges, one finds along the interior walls beds of rough bark where the occupants sleep on mats and where they sit by day. Each nuclear family has its own fire and compartment. Such units range the length of the hallway to the opposite door.

After the morning meal, the housemates go forth to their appointed tasks. The warriors are in the habit of going out to hunt in the mornings and returning in the evenings. The older versions of the myth imply that this routine affords the opportunity for a girl and boy who are siblings and who, after the old puberty custom, have been secluded, or "downfended," to get together in an incestuous relationship. She goes over and combs his hair, and in this act of symbolic incest somehow gets pregnant. The women of the family question her, but she refuses to tell. The lad, meanwhile, sickens and dies during a couvade over the birth of their daughter. They put him up on a scaffold in a spare room. (Interment came later.)

Gibson cleaned up this incident and elaborated the plot by putting the secluded youngsters under the avuncular authority of the Old Man of the sky people, their mother's brother. The uncle becomes ill over some imagined omen, discloses the nature of death, and asks the Old Woman, his sister, to have him put up in a tree. The Iroquois love their dead, and the daughter or niece spends hours visiting the corpse. In one instance she receives a wampum bracelet in token of paternity, and in two following visits she hears instructions about her marriage to the owner of the tree of light, who is chief of a distant village.

Accounts of the old wedding custom never cease to fascinate Iroquois listeners, who thrill at the most detailed description. Gibson projected to the cosmology the fashion of the nineteenth century: the bride-to-be carries a basket of boiled bread by a forehead strap (the typical burden strap represented in older museum collections) through the woods to the house of the groom, speaking to no one on the way. The bread of sodden corn mixed with berries symbolizes woman's skillful labor in raising corn and grinding it in a wooden mortar. The directions for her journey, the hazards of getting lost and having to cross a stream over a floating maple log, and the taboo on speaking to strangers on the path all contribute to heightening her anxiety at leaving home to qualify as a woman in her husband's village.[4]

The prescribed etiquette states that on arriving at the grassy clearing that surrounds a village, the bride-to-be shall go directly to the groom's house and go right on in through the door to where the fire burns in the center of the lodge. There, before the owner of the celestial tree, she puts down her basket at his feet where he lies on his bunk, saying, "We two marry." Then she sits opposite with the fire between them. He will lay down a string of corn and say, "Soak it and make mush." This was all standard bridal custom as described by Iroquois sources in the 1930s and current until the middle of the nineteenth century.

But in the myth, the mush-making process proves an ordeal. The bride is expected to strip and, without flinching, endure the pain of having her naked body spattered with boiling mush. Then she suffers the added indignity of having ferocious white dogs with abrasive tongues lick her blistered skin. By surviving the test she earns the admiration of torture-loving listeners. She is then persuaded to engage in the most intriguing footsie gambit in aboriginal literature. She makes up her bed at the foot of the groom's and they sleep *pied à pied*. Only the soles of their feet touch, yet in some unexplained way they sit up, their breaths mingle, and she is impregnated. Rather than seeking a sanctimonious interpretation of the act, as Hewitt was inclined, I am confident that Iroquois listeners would deem this funny.

To complete the marriage contract, the groom sends back venison, of which the owner of the tree of light has an inexhaustible supply. He compresses it by shaking it down in the bride's pack basket. Despite its weight and density, she is enjoined not to readjust her forehead strap while going home. She reports his message to the town council and instructs its members to remove the mats from their houses

4. The implication of distant patrilocal residence poses a theoretical problem for the ethnologist as well as for the bride. The later native theory of this society is matrilineal and matrilocal. Daughters should bring home spouses to their mother's longhouse, the residential household and the matrilineage being coterminous.

and spread them out so that it might rain corn and fill them. The people then distribute the magic meat, which expands to fill the council house, whereupon the bride goes back to reside in her husband's village.

If the marriage of Awenha:ih, "Fertile Flower," or Sky Woman, to Hodahe?, "Standing Tree," proprietor of the celestial tree and chief of the sky world, was not an unqualified success, at least it was not dull. As an example of brittle monogamy it is quite familiar to Iroquois listeners, for whom family solidarity depends on the maternal lineage. Confronted by the solid chain that runs from the eldest woman to the umbilical cord of the youngest infant-to-be, Iroquois spouses react sometimes as Sky Chief did. A justifiable suspicion is augmented by jealousy and manifests itself in tests and compulsive behavior. These ordeals are more or less reassuring, but since peace and domestic tranquillity are always threatened and then broken by this strain of paranoia in the culture, individuals end up brooding and depressed. Society then employs several devices for diverting their minds: a game of ball, or "a little dance," perhaps, while people try at random to guess what the person's soul desires, which is usually revealed in a dream. An alternate channel is witchcraft. So when Sky Chief manifests symptoms of jealousy over his wife's pregnancy, the community attempts to relieve his disturbed mind by guessing the "word" (dream) that his soul desires. The dream feast, of which we first read in the Jesuit *Relations* from Huronia, is held beneath the tree of light, and all the supernaturals of the pantheon attend except Wind. Sky Woman is foretold what the verdict will be, so she counsels with her brother Earthquake before returning to her spouse.

In myths of this length the sequence of events is not always clear. Part of the confusion arises from a device that narrators employ to post their listeners in advance of what is going to happen by letting them in on revelations that clairvoyants divulge to actors. This device also builds suspense. Thus, in the Gibson version, Sky Chief has been holding a continuous dream feast dating back before his union with Sky Woman, who, on a visit home, learns from her uncle's corpse the nature of the dream, which ordains and specifies her involvement.

Although people have continually diverted his mind, no one up to now has guessed Sky Chief's particular dream. This dream is a model of paranoid destruction: growing things shall wither, especially the flowers on the tree of light, producing darkness. The tree shall be uprooted, creating a hole in the sky floor into which he shall cast the flowers, and there he and his wife shall sit down on the brink, hanging their feet over the edge, and eat together. She is cautioned not to hesitate. Her name, Awenha:ih, "Ripe Blossom," makes her an acceptable bride because it fits into his plans. In the Onondaga version the key word that signals the dream is "tooth," a reference to the flowers on the tree, and Fire Dragon (Meteor) guesses it. (In one Seneca version the key word is "excrement.") The satisfied dreamer cries "Kuh!" (Onondaga) or "Gwah!" (Seneca), as in the later Midwinter Festival.

It is a cardinal principle of Iroquois culture that the consequences of revealed dreams must be carried out, so the sky people proceed to fulfill them. They uproot the tree, and Sky Woman and Sky Chief sit down as directed to eat the food that she has placed beside them. Suddenly standing, he takes her by the nape of the neck and shoves her into space, where she is peering. Versions differ as to her curiosity or his rage, whether he grabs her by the left leg or shoves her with his foot. Life in the sky world ends with the casting down of Sky Woman and the resetting of the tree.[5]

□□◇□□

The second epoch of the cosmological myth treats of the creation of the world and consists of some eighteen episodes. It opens with the fall of Sky Woman, who becomes Earth Mother, the Old Woman, and ultimately the wicked grandmother. She falls through the sky's crust into darkness. In old John Buck's version (Onondaga), she goes provisioned for her journey into space with three ears of corn, dried meat, and firewood stuffed into her bosom, and carrying her child on her back. Gibson and Armstrong (Seneca) attribute the cultural gifts to Meteor; they comprise a miniature mortar and pestle, a small pot, and a soup bone. In falling, she brings her own earth scraped from the edges of the hole in the sky. The spectacle of Sky Woman falling through space, assisted by waterfowl, to land on the back of the turtle swimming in the primal sea has become a favorite subject with Iroquois artists (fig. 1).[6]

Loon notices her; Bittern, whose eyes are ever on the top of its head, remarks that she is indeed not coming from the depths of the water. Ducks go up to guide her landing while the council of animals sends various divers to fetch up mud from the depths. Muskrat alone succeeds, but surfaces dead, paws and mouth full of mud. Turtle volunteers, and Beaver and assistants plaster the mud on Turtle's carapace. There, Sky Woman is brought to rest. Immediately the earth begins expanding as Sky Woman moves about, and vegetation sprouts in her tracks. The process of the earth's expanding continues throughout creation. This cosmological scheme of superimposed worlds, from the tree of life and the sky dome to the first vegetation springing from the earth on the turtle's back, finds expression in curvilinear symbolism that generations of Iroquois women have worked in moosehair and quill embroidery and afterward in beads in decorating clothing.[7]

A daughter born to Sky Woman grows up rapidly and entertains a procession of animal suitors. On her mother's advice she accepts the fourth, the one with the dirty body who wears a deeply escalloped robe and leggings. Naturally, this is Turtle. He possesses several magic arrows, of which one has no point attached and is blunt, which he continually keeps straightening, a characteristic motor habit of Iroquois arrow makers, unless it be symbolic of an erection. It is this one that he leaves alongside her body as she sleeps. In the Seneca version she is impregnated by West Wind while at play swinging on an uprooted tree; she descends to kneel on the grass, is entered by the wind, and is delighted.

It does not take the Old Woman long to discover that her happy daughter is with child. During a most unusual pregnancy, she hears male voices quarreling within

---

5. This incident is the precedent for uprooting the Tree of Peace in later times, casting weapons of war into the abyss, and then replanting the tree.

6. Notable renderings of Sky Woman's descent to the back of the turtle are those by Jesse Cornplanter and Ernest Smith (Senecas), Tom Dorsey and Oren Lyons (Onondagas), Rick Hill (Tuscarora), and Arnold Jacobs (Cayuga of Six Nations). For a directory of Iroquois painters and sculptors, see Johannsen and Ferguson 1983.

7. Following the lead of Frank G. Speck, the acknowledged discoverer of the double-curve motif in northeastern Woodland art, Arthur C. Parker (1913; 1916b) demonstrated among the Iroquois a rich oral and decorative art involving trees and growing plants.

Figure 1. "Sky Woman." Painting by Ernest Smith (Seneca). Courtesy Rochester Museum and Science Center, Rochester, New York.

her body. Of the twins who converse in the womb, the elder is born normally to become Sky Holder, alias Good-minded, Thrown-away, Sapling, the Creator, whose every act will symbolize and promote growth and fertility.

The younger twin, the ugly one, is covered with warts and has a sharp comb of flint on his forehead, a motif that is memorialized on some Seneca False Face masks. He seeks daylight and erupts through his mother's armpit, killing her. He is Flint (Ice), alias Evil-minded, patron of winter and author of monstrosities, bad luck, and disasters. Flint becomes the favorite of his grandmother when he lies to her about cutting up his own dead mother, whom they bury in the doorway and whose head they put up in a tree for light. The theme of sibling rivalry dominates this period.

That grandmothers can be wicked and reject their grandsons is a hazard of growing up in a society that subscribes to the theory of matrilineal descent, inheritance, and succession. Sky Woman tosses the elder twin into the brush, where he finds shelter in a hollow tree. But she takes the younger twin into her lodge, conspires with him against his elder brother, and refuses to make a bow and arrows for the elder twin. Thrown-away is driven to seek his father.[8] Father imparts certain culture gifts. Sky Holder borrows a bow and, using a second magic arrow that father Turtle had left, shoots at a passing bird. This act parts the waters, revealing his father's lodge at the bottom of a lake. There he visits Turtle Who Holds the Earth in His Two Hands and from him learns the arts of husbandry, the chase, and house building, how to make fire, and how to spit maize for roasting. Turtle gives the son several ears of seed corn.

The Seneca version has father Wind offer a prize to the winner among his four sons of a race around the earth; the trophy is a flute and a bag containing game animals. We read: "So now the youth took up the bundle and packed it home by means of a burden strap." On reaching home he announces that he has changed his name to Maple Sprout—or Sapling, in the Mohawk version.

Sky Holder's acts of creation form the climax of this section. One for one they are opposed and hindered by the evil grandmother, and Flint offsets them with contrary acts. These acts constitute a series of dyads. The growth principle is thwarted by frost, a dualism that symbolizes the alternation of seasons. The contest builds into a cosmic struggle for control of the earth. First come the flora: red osier for medicine, grasses, shrubs, trees, and cultivated plants, including sunflowers for oil. Flint counters with thistle, poison ivy, and other noxious weeds. Next come the birds, starting with Bluebird and the now extinct Passenger Pigeon, which got immersed in bear oil so that afterward its squabs were fat. Handfuls of earth are cast into game animals. Flint makes a cosmic mistake by creating Bat, which, as an old Feather Dance song says, "is the only animal that has teeth and yet flies." Sapling creates rivers having two-way currents for human convenience in travel, but Flint puts in rapids and falls. Overcome by jealousy at the great ears of corn growing in Sky Holder's garden, Flint stunts them because humankind should not have it so good. Sky Holder is meanwhile busy making humans, and out of a

8. The theme of the fatherless boy who becomes the culture hero permeates Iroquois folklore. In Iroquois society, one's father's line is always a second choice, after mother's brother, but is the preferred avenue for certain endeavors such as forming a war party or joining a medicine society.

sense of balance old John Buck and Gibson have Flint making several species of apes, which they must have seen in their travels to zoological gardens—an anachronism that quite enhances the narrative.

When Sky Holder next looks around to view his creations, the game animals have disappeared. Only when Deermouse tells him does he discover where Flint has impounded them in a cave. By moving a rock, Sky Holder frees the game animals pent up by Flint, who tricks him afterward into releasing some monsters that might better have remained beneath the ground. Those that escape in a thundering herd are the familiar game animals, while most of Flint's dangerously large animals remain imprisoned, to be propitiated by the medicine societies of later times. This alternate impoundment and release symbolizes hibernation and spring, as animals annually go to earth and then reappear with young.

The contest reaches a climax in a cosmic struggle between Sky Holder and his enemies, which the uncommitted game animals and humans witness. It has two phases. In the first half, Sky Holder plays the game of peach pits (the Great Bowl Game) against his grandmother. The stake or "great bet" is for control of the earth. Each player summons and exerts his *orenda*, or magic power; each uses personal dice. For Sky Holder the dice are the heads of six chickadees who volunteer and score for him "a clear field"—come up all of a color. Like the peach pit of later times, the chickadee's head is black on top and light-colored beneath. Even today, when the people contend in the bowl game at the Green Corn and Midwinter festivals, they dramatize the duality of nature in the procession of summer and winter. On these occasions the two halves of the Longhouse community alternately symbolize the Master of Life (Sky Holder) and Sky Woman, one moiety taking the eastern position, since east is life, and the other moiety sitting to the west, which represents winter and death.

In the second half, Sky Holder and Flint struggle to the death with avowedly fatal weapons. Flint confesses that the two things that will do him in are antler and flint, and he elicits from Sky Holder that maize and rushes are his weaknesses. (Every native listener knew that antler would chip flint.) So Sky Holder goes around putting these objects up high and handy. Around the world they go, the two brothers heaving rocks and flinging mountains. In some versions the fight goes on until nothing is left but their bones to be gathered up by their grandmother.

At this point in the narrative, two interruptions occur in most versions: a contest of power with Hadu?i?, the mask being, and the theft of light by Sky Holder and animal assistants. These incidents serve to forestall the banishment of Flint and the return of Sky Holder to the sky world.

The dramatic episode involving Hadu?i?, the hunchbacked master of winds, patron of disease, gamekeeper, and tutelary of the False Face Society of later times, is deeply rooted in mythology and evidently quite ancient. It underscores the importance that the Iroquois attach to this grotesque character, who occupies a central place in their world of supernaturals, who is memorialized by hundreds of masks in museums, and whom the traditional Iroquois still honor with ceremonies (Fenton 1987).

The Creator is out inspecting his works, and he and Hadu?i? encounter each other. The two engage in a test of power at moving a mountain while holding their breath. The impetuous Hadu?i? tries first and succeeds in moving the mountain halfway, but in avid curiosity to see Sky Holder's success he turns to look and smashes his nose against the mountain, which has come up behind them, and thereby loses the contest. The forfeit requires a promise not to harm people and to rid the earth of disease in return for the privilege of abiding on the margin of the earth, to come when called, and to coach the False Face Society, whose members shall call him "our beloved grandfather." Hadu?i? agrees to convey the power to cure disease to men who wear masks and impersonate him in return for man's gift of tobacco, which he craves. The contract holds so long as men keep up the ceremonies. Then Hadu?i? leagues with Sky Holder to rid the earth of Flint's monsters. Obviously, narrators have projected into the mythology ritual details that pertain to later ceremonies. As in the white dog sacrifice during the Mid-winter Festival, people send up their words (prayers) to the supernaturals on the smoke of tobacco offerings (Hewitt 1912).

The theft of light by Sky Holder and animal helpers is a separate episode that has no contemporary counterpart. The plot is to secure the head of Earth Mother from the treetop where Sky Woman hung it, or to put it in orbit for the use of humankind. Small mammals work together at canoe building, in voyaging, in guarding the boat, and in the escape of Sky Holder and the animal helpers. In one version Sky Holder makes his debut as Sapling; lacking an instep, he employs antlers as climbing hooks. Gibson has the hero manipulate his feet for shinning. Sapling's sudden descent with the head explains how the sycamore tree got its scabs. Fox escapes with the sun in his mouth, and Black Squirrel takes it over the treetops to the landing, where the magic flight continues. Muskrat or Otter gets clobbered with a paddle for talking back to the pursuing grandmother. Enormous variation in detail, characters, and episodes indicate that this by no means uniquely Iroquoian motif is widespread in North America.

The epoch of creation closes rapidly with the assignment of roles to actors in the mid-pantheon. Some of these characters are destined to serve humankind, and others return to the sky world. Earth Mother becomes Grandmother Moon and regulates women's affairs. Father Turtle, the Earth Grasper, becomes morning star, the Day Bringer. Sky Woman returns home, but her brother becomes Elder Brother, the Day Sun. Monsters get relegated to the mountains or put under-ground, and the Thunders, "our grandfathers whose voices reverberate from toward the sunset," keep an eye on monsters and bring rain to water the crops until the end of time, when they shall come from the east, foretelling the end of the world. The two brothers return to the sky world via the Milky Way, afterward the path of souls; it is forked to accommodate divergent careers and divided minds.

□□◇□□

Sapling's world is the epoch of human society in the first times. The events of those times comprise some sixty pages, the final third of Gibson's text. It is a long period of enormous growth and expansion. Sapling, who appears as the Creator in the older versions, is the first man and the culture hero. Various crises occur for which there are no traditional solutions. These require the Creator to make four returns (four is the magic number) in the guise of the fatherless boy named Sapling, who first proposes the clan system. His several proposals draw heavily on the cultural memory of Gibson's sources, which accounts for the length of the myth and the compulsive character of its contents. Gibson's is therefore a more rigid document than the shorter, freer versions of John Buck and Armstrong, who themselves were closer to the old life, as were their audiences. Gibson felt compelled to add what his hearers needed to know.

I shall confine the discussion to structural, literary, and thematic considerations. Eight episodes are telescoped in the following paragraphs.

Odendonniha, "Sapling," and Awenhaniyonda, "Hanging Flower," are the first couple. They beget offspring and the people multiply. They plant crops, and the Thunders water them when appealed to with tobacco.

The second coming of the Creator is occasioned by the need to teach the people the four ceremonies of thanksgiving. These are sacred to the Creator and constitute the house posts of the later Longhouse festivals. The order of celebration and the content of specified rituals Gibson took naturally from the ceremonies then current at Onondaga Longhouse on Grand River. The ceremonial cycle balances a summer ingathering of crops with a midwinter festival. Coming after the autumn hunt, the great winter ceremonial features stirring cold ashes on the hearths and kindling a new fire, which is followed by guessing dreams and renewing old dreams. It reaches a climax in the white dog sacrifice.

Between festivals it is the matron's duty to return thanks at dawn and at dusk. The myth prescribes the etiquette of hospitality, of greeting and departing. It includes the familiar *kanonhenyonk*, the address of greeting and thanks to the spirit forces of the pantheon that opens all public gatherings and prefaces every day of religious celebration to the present by enumerating the gifts that the Creator left on earth for human use and enjoyment, proceeding from the earth up to the sky world.

The third coming is occasioned by a typically Indian division of kindred into factions. Persons disappear; murder eclipses the sun. Sapling seizes this opportunity to teach the first-fruit ceremonies. "For some time," we read, "the ceremonies were carried on correctly, and then again, there began to be disagreements." Gossip produced intense dysphoria.

The fourth and—since this is the magic number—last appearance of the Creator centers on teaching values that were afterward stressed in the Handsome Lake doctrine. Two aspects of ethnobotany receive attention. The Iroquois manifest a continuing interest in herbal medicine inasmuch as they suffer from real and imagined illnesses. Herbalism depends on botanical accuracy, and it therefore must be imparted systematically, whereas symptomatology can remain vague, as witness the concept of "Disease, the Faceless." In the myth, the introduction of maize horticulture and the cycle of ceremonies attending the growth and maturation of maize is accomplished by sending a pubescent boy and girl to find the "three sisters" (maize, beans, and squash). They discover these cultigens growing in the footprints of the gods leading to the grave of Earth Mother. They return and report to the town council. In this period, inhumation succeeds scaffold burial. Communal agriculture and mutual aid commence. From this episode one can state two themes: first, only the pure may seek and find medicine and discover other cultural gifts; second, there shall be a regular way of organizing group activity. And these two themes become set in ritual.

A human being dies and the elders put the problem to the town council. An unknown young man fulfills the "fatherless hero" theme by proposing that they bury the corpse. It is therefore decided that in such an event the elders shall chose a speaker who will address the relatives and review with thanks the Creator's gifts, especially the herbal medicines that are used in sickness. Moreover, the narrative anticipates that with the formation of clans, the moieties will function in turn to "lift up the minds" of the bereaved relatives. These things shall be the responsibility of elders.

Similarly, woman's priority in matters affecting the continuity of life is affirmed. Control of these affairs shall repose in the hands of the matron of the *ohwachira*, that is, matrilineage. In Iroquois thought, matriliny accords with the forces of nature.

In the legend that explains how clans originated, a young man leads half of the families across a river on a vine, the other half being left on the near shore. This incident also seeks to explain how moieties began. People in camps on both banks are instructed that when women go at dawn to water, always they shall dip with the stream, and they are to observe carefully and remember the behavior of the first bird or animal sighted. These creatures and their actions become the eponyms of the familiar Iroquois clans. Clan sets of personal names are thought to derive from such sightings.

The establishment of a regular place of council poses a further problem that the elders must settle. This concern crops up throughout Iroquois political history, particularly during the treaty period. The seating of the clans and the way they function in governing requires arranging them with respect to the council fire so as to provide communication and movement of issues among themselves and across the fire to their colleagues.

□□◇□□

The cosmology myth, Hewitt tells us (1928), when narrated in council or before a public gathering, "is told partly in the language of tradition and ceremony, which is formal, sometimes quaint, sometimes archaic, frequently mystical, and largely metaphorical." On these occasions the speaker lapses into the high, intoned preaching style of council oratory, which is an art form in itself, and this style markedly affects the impact, if not the form, of the myth.[9] Council style has an important bearing on political history, since speakers at treaty councils regularly employed it. The figures of speech become concrete in the thought patterns of the Iroquois, who regard the metaphors as fact. "Path," for example, has many metaphorical usages: it may refer to a course of action, to one's career, or to the route of souls bound for the hereafter, as when the Creator says, "Where my path will have ended, there you shall find corn, beans, and squash growing from the grave of Earth-mother." As an example of pure aesthetics, the figure "floating foam" must have caught the fancy of some storyteller. River men know the flecks of foam beneath rapids; herbalists see foam well to the surface when boiling roots; and women at streamside observe it when dipping water. I recall as a boy being entranced by Thornton W. Burgess's "bluebird that whistles off the snow"; I wonder now if he realized that indeed it was Bluebird in the Iroquoian cosmology

---

9. A more intimate style of delivery characterizes the telling of fireside tales, when the storyteller impersonates the characters and sings the signature songs of animal actors. He and his audience live out the plot and incidents with appropriate audience feedback.

who gives the death cry—*ko:weh!* (five times)—and frightens off the glacier, thereby breaking up Flint's winter.

One final example. The ever-growing tree stands for life, status, and authority—for society itself. Uprooting the tree and casting weapons of war into a bottomless pit to be carried away by a stream represents a denial of reality so that life may go on. Thus we saw Sky Chief push all living things, including his pregnant wife, Sky Woman, beneath the sky's crust and then replant the tree of heaven. Later Iroquois oratory is replete with this metaphor of the tree uprooted and replanted. Similarly, as we shall see, a pine tree symbolizes chiefship: the tree falls at the death of a chief, but the office continues, so the tree is raised up again with his successor. And finally, a giant elm is conceived of as standing at the center of the earth where the mask spirit rubs his rattle and derives his strength. Tree symbolism takes several art forms (Parker 1912; 1916b: 152–55).

Again, four is the magic number, signaling the hearer to expect four things—imposing four tasks—so that the listener always knows which will be the last. Suspense is created in other ways: Sky Holder directs Sapling, his alter ego, to go around the world picking up antlers and flints where he sees them lying about and to put them up handy. One knows from this that there is going to be a fight. Irony is conveyed when the wicked grandmother addresses Thrown-away, whom she hates, as "my dear grandson."

□□◇□□

I shall now summarize by enumerating the main themes in Iroquois life that emerge from concepts found in the cosmology. They number twenty, which indeed is the price of a human life.

1. The native earth. The earth, our mother, is living and expanding continually, imparting its life-giving force to all growing things on which our lives depend.
2. Renewal. The alternation of seasons and tasks is attuned to ecological time, as are the lives of plants and animals, which rest while the earth sleeps. Ceremonial obligations adhere to the same law.
3. "It is us women that count." A chain of kinship connects all members of society, running from the dead through mothers to the smallest child and reaching even those as yet unborn. Consequently, the Iroquois love their dead and cherish their children. The same concept underlies the chain of peace and friendship.
4. Paternity is secondary: *agadoni* comes after *ohwachira*. The fatherless boy becomes hero; rejected by his matrilineage, he may seek his father to learn. One's father's kin, or *agadoni*, are a second line of appeal in any enterprise.
5. Twins are lucky. They are creative, but sibling rivalry occurs. Only the pure who are "downfended," secluded, may succeed.
6. The law of the kettle. Hospitality is a right and a duty to share. Throwing ashes is the negation of hospitality, sharing, friendship, peace, harmony, and accord; it is typically paranoid behavior that the culture seeks to guard against.
7. Home is where one customarily sits. The bench or bed is the place of rest, reflection, and council.
8. Do not oppose the forces of nature. Going to water, dip with the current when making medicine. When traveling, go around natural objects such as fallen

logs, and part the brush. In ceremonial circuits, adhere to the "living way." Circuits are counterclockwise in life, clockwise in the hereafter.

9. There is a regular way. Life and customary procedures are fairly established. Protocol is vital.

10. *Orenda* (supernatural power). Adheres to inanimate and animate things, to aspects of the environment, and to sequences of behavior.

11. Equanimity. Restraint is important. One must not exert too much power and "spoil it." The equable person succeeds.

12. Impersonation. Acting the role is a means of taking on power.

13. *Kanonhenyonk*, or returning thanks from the earth to the sky. By continual and repeated greetings and thanks one must remember the hierarchy of spirit forces between the earth and the sky that the Creator appointed to assist people in the enjoyment of the earth. All of these must be remembered and balanced in the fulfillment of their appointed tasks.

14. Dreams compel fulfillment. Once the "word" that the soul desires is discovered, it must be fulfilled. Prescribed ceremonies, whether diverting the mind by games, dances, or something else, must be renewed during one's lifetime.

15. Sending up smoke. The column of smoke, which carried the gods back to the sky world, is also a vehicle for sending up words—prayers and incantations. Smoke itself symbolizes thought, desire, community, and government. The metaphorical column of smoke that arises from the central fire of the longhouse at Onondaga symbolizes the league itself. Tobacco is the word: committing it to the fire closes a contract with the spirit forces.

16. Earth shakers. These are friendly spirits such as Turtle, Thunder, Hadu?i?, and "Our Uncles, the Bigheads," the dream heralds of the midwinter ceremonies.

17. A man never refuses when asked, and he never shows fear.

18. Things go by twos and fours. Forked path, divided mind, sex, seasons, moieties, life/death, balance of forces, four tests, four ceremonies. Twenty has a capital value.

19. Reciprocity. This takes place between moieties for requickening life and faculties, for restoring society, and in all associations for renewal.

20. Mind. Culture is an affair of the mind. "Good mind" is prerequisite to welfare, whether personal, interpersonal, or social. It is essential for consensus and indispensable for peace.

Of such was the burden of the Peacemaker's message, to which we now turn.

CHAPTER 3

EARLY VERSIONS
OF THE LEAGUE LEGEND

Next to the cosmology, the second of the great public utterances by which the old men of Iroquoia marked their cultural history was the so-called Deganawi:dah legend, or the message of the Peacemaker, which is the origin legend of the League of the Iroquois. How the People of the Flint (whom we know as Mohawks), the People of the Stone (Oneidas), the People on the Mountain (Onondagas), the People at the Landing (Cayugas), and the Great Hill People (Senecas) were persuaded to stop feuding, grasp the Peacemaker's message, and join in the Great Peace constitutes a tradition of epic proportions. It represents the symbolic justification for the traditional system of life chiefs at Six Nations Reserve in Canada as well as the grand council of the Six Nations Confederacy, the so-called Hodenosaunee, which meets at Onondaga, near Syracuse, New York. By extension, the message of the Peacemaker has supplanted Handsome Lake's code as theology among the traditional Mohawks of Caughnawaga and St. Regis (Akwesasneh) on the St. Lawrence. The epic is still enacted in the Condolence Council for mourning and installing chiefs. It has come down to the present to be regarded by its adherents as a kind of constitution, otherwise known as the Great Law. It has religious overtones.

Although the legend of confederation was yet unpublished in its entirety, Euro-Americans have known about it for at least two and a half centuries: it was first noted in 1743, a good century after contact. But it is doubtful how much of it was known for another hundred years, even though it underlies an understanding of Iroquois political institutions. The Iroquois acted in history as if it were true, often when they could not make public policy follow its principles. A knowledge of the teachings of the Peacemaker goes far to explain Iroquois self-confidence, their professed superiority to their neighbors, and their at times polite arrogance toward representatives of European governments.

How is it that something so basic to Iroquois political philosophy escaped the notice of early writers on Iroquois manners and usages? Are we to infer from the silence of colonial writers that the legend was unknown and the league was not functioning? Why, save for the hint of John Christopher Pyrlaeus, a Moravian missionary, have we to await the emergence of ethnology at the mid-nineteenth century for a description of the league's institutions and ceremonies? By then the Iroquois were living on reservations in New York and in Canada: how did the new circumstances motivate them to preserve and systematize their traditional culture?

Late in the nineteenth century, two parties had motives for preserving Iroquois culture. Politically motivated Iroquois nationalists were actively seeking recognition for ancient law-ways as a basis for conducting local government, and they believed in the efficacy of their own ceremony. It reinforced their image of a glorious past. The then "Lords of the League," as they were styled in Canada, shared with scientifically motivated ethnologists the urge to record for posterity the Deganawi:dah legend in its entirety. The desire to recover aboriginal languages and cultures before they vanished like the smoke of former council fires ran strong in the minds of pioneer ethnologists Morgan and Hale.

But the readers of these pioneer scientists of Darwin's day were literal-minded; they were accustomed to reading scripture and regarded history in the same light. They either read recorded tradition as fact or spurned it as nonsense. To this audience, Deganawi:dah and his alter ego, Hiawatha, either were historical personages or were fictitious. Just as eighteenth-century white men of affairs had practical concerns—staying alive, trading rum for furs, and acquiring Indians' land—that postponed historical or philosophical considerations, so in the next century chroniclers were intellectually unprepared to handle a body of custom or to interpret oral traditions. Folklore as a study was just emerging: it was preoccupied with "survivals" or quaint customs, its practitioners were collectors of tales, and it would only gradually come to share with classical philology the comparative method. It would emerge as a discipline in the twentieth century.

Although versions of the epic are current today, the research for this book is based on two long texts in Onondaga that were collected by J. N. B. Hewitt in 1899 and A. A. Goldenweiser in 1912, both from the same source, Chief John Arthur Gibson. I translated both Gibson versions with the aid of Chief Gibson's descendants. The two versions have been compared and their contents analyzed and then fitted into an expanded revitalization paradigm (A. Wallace 1958a); structurally, the epic comprises three levels of discourse. Kinship usages are projected to the political level, and metaphors are employed symbolically.

With this background, let us examine earlier versions of the legend and explore the circumstances of their composition.

□□◇□□

The first writers on the Iroquois, some perceptive French explorers and missionaries, noted that the Five Nations referred to themselves as one extended cabin (or one family), a recognition that in Iroquois thought the terms for maternal lineage and household were synonymous. Although a Dutch journalist recorded the names of the Five Nations and their term for the league as early as 1635, it was quite late in the seventeenth century before the Albany Dutch began to enumerate the Iroquois nations or mention their meeting in council at Onondaga. Neither the Jesuit ethnologist Lafitau, whose great comparative work appeared in 1724, nor Cadwallader Colden, the first American writer to grasp the nature of the league, in his *History of the Five Indian Nations* (1727), seemingly ever heard of Deganawi:dah, the Peacemaker. Colden simply says: "This Union has continued so long, that the Christians know nothing of the Original of it." To give Colden his due, he did recognize that each of the Five Nations forming the union preserved local autonomy while meeting at Onondaga to iron out differences among themselves (Colden 1727: xiv–xv).

It was an Onondaga boast to the governors of Pennsylvania, Maryland, and Virginia, in closing a treaty council held at Lancaster, Pennsylvania, in 1744, that really shook the colonists and aroused the curiosity of learned men. The gratuitous advice of Canasatego, the Onondaga speaker, has become a famous passage in the treaty literature. The Five Nations were "a powerful Confederacy," he informed the governors: "We heartily recommend union and good Agreement between you our Brethren. . . . Our wise Forefathers established Union and Amity between the *Five Nations*; this has made us formidable; this has given us great Weight and Authority with our neighbouring Nations" (Boyd 1938: 78). These words, documenting the long-established Iroquois Confederacy, were to prove prophetic thirty years later when commissioners of the colonies, meeting in Albany, appealed to the Six Nations for support in the American Revolution (Lincoln 1836: 83, 93).

In the year preceding Canasatego's lecture to the governors on the wisdom of confederating, Conrad Weiser, the Pennsylvania interpreter, went to Onondaga "to take the hatchet out of the heads of the Six Nations." Returning to Philadelphia, he reported on a meeting at the central fire of the longhouse. On such occasions a speaker for the nations lauded the wisdom of their grandfathers in founding the league and deprecated themselves, recited the roll of the founders, performed the ritual of condolence and requickening, and sang the Six Songs of Friendship (P. Wallace 1945: 162–68). These ritual forms, as we shall see, dramatize the content of the league epic.

In the same year, Pyrlaeus, a Moravian and tutee of Weiser's in the Mohawk language, recorded the first sketch of the plot and characters of the league legend. From a Canajoharie Mohawk headman named Sganarady, or David of Schoharie, he learned that Iroquois sources placed the beginning of their confederacy no more than a generation before the coming of the Europeans, when they had united as a nation for mutual defense. Pyrlaeus wrote: "The alliance or confederacy of the Five Nations was established, as near as can be conjectured, one age (or the length of a man's life) before the white people (the Dutch) came into the country. *Thannawage* was the name of the aged Indian, a Mohawk, who first proposed such an alliance."

Pyrlaeus then named the chiefs of the Five Nations who at the time met and formed the alliance: "*Toganawita*, of the Mohawks; *Otatschechta*, of the Oneidas; *Tatotarho* of the Onondagos; *Togahayon* of the Cayugas; *Ganiatario* and *Satagaruyes*, from the two towns of the Senecas, &c. . . . All these names are forever to be kept in remembrance, by naming a person in each nation after them" (Heckewelder 1881: 56n).

These titles are the names of the leading chiefs of each of the Five Nations substantially as they were recalled in the nineteenth century and as they are at present, making this a document of first importance. The first-named founder is, of course, Deganawi:dah, hero of the charter epic. The second title, Odatshehdeh, Quiver Bearer, is the first Oneida lord; the third is Thadoda:ho? (or Atotarho, a Mohawk variant), the Onondaga villain of the piece and later presiding officer of the league. The fourth title is still that of the leading Cayuga chief, Haga?en:yonk. And fifth come the titles of the headmen of two Seneca towns, clearly Handsome Lake (Ganyadaiyo?) and Skies of Equal Height (Sa?dagaenyes), which bespeaks a familiarity with the moiety arrangement still observed in the traditional

Seneca council. The constituent nations were often known by the titles of these leading chiefs. Pyrlaeus found the key to the structure and composition of the league.

In citing Pyrlaeus's manuscript,[1] Heckewelder (1881: 56, 96–97) remarked that the Delawares always considered the Iroquois to be one people, Mengwe, but that the English called them Five Nations, probably to magnify their importance as allies, although other Indian nations considered them merely confederated tribes. In the same manuscript, Pyrlaeus's Mohawk source explained the kinship relations among the nations:

> They then gave themselves the name *Aquanoshioni*, which means *one house, one family*, and consisted of the Mohawks, Oneidas, Onondagoes, Cayugas, and Senecas. This alliance having been first proposed by a Mohawk chief, the Mohawks rank in the *family* as the *eldest brother*, the Oneidas as the *eldest son*; the Senecas who were the last at that time had consented to the alliance, were called the *youngest son*; but the Tuscaroras, who joined the confederacy probably one hundred years afterwards, assumed the name, and the Senecas ranked in precedence before them, as being the *next youngest son*, or as we would say, the youngest son but one.

Inasmuch as we know that the Tuscaroras became the sixth nation in 1722, and if indeed they joined the league a century after the Senecas, Pyrlaeus's speculation would date the league's formation from the first quarter of the seventeenth century, which is relatively recent.

My colleague Hanni Woodbury, on reading an early draft of this chapter, offered the following explanation of the kinship model the Iroquois use to structure the league, to which Pyrlaeus's Mohawk source alluded. Two models emerge from the native language data: first, the model the Iroquois use to describe the moiety structure of the league, and second, the model that describes interactions between chiefs and nonchiefs. The first model can be diagrammed as in figure 2.

In this model, the Mohawks, Onondagas, and Senecas are "fathers" (i.e., father's brothers and therefore fathers under Iroquois rules) to the Oneidas and the Cayugas, who are their "sons" (i.e., a man's brother's son and therefore "son") or "nephews" (i.e., a woman's brother's son and therefore "nephew"). In this system the Mohawks, Onondagas, and Senecas are brothers to one another: the Mohawks are the eldest and the Senecas the youngest. The Oneidas and Cayugas are also brothers to each other: the Oneidas are the elder and the Cayugas the younger. This is the perspective taken when the Two (Four) Brothers (the junior moiety) address the Three Brothers (the senior moiety, Mohawk-Onondaga-Seneca) as *akatu: nih*, "our paternal relatives" (or "our father's kinsmen") and the Three Brothers call the Two (Four) Brothers *kheya?tawenh*, "our offspring."

Woodbury points out further: "There just are no *native language* data to support the idea that the system is one in which the Mohawk, Onondaga, and Seneca make up the set of elder brothers and the Oneida and Cayuga the set of younger brothers," as has been commonly maintained in the ethnological literature.

---

1. Pyrlaeus's manuscript was then in the archives of the United Brethren in Bethlehem, Pennsylvania, but is now at the library of the American Philosophical Society, Philadelphia.

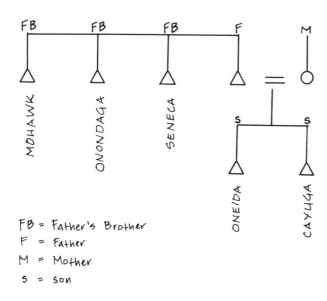

FB = Father's Brother
F = Father
M = Mother
S = Son

Figure 2. Woodbury's model for the kinship relations between league moieties.

The foregoing model accounts for the kinship usage as it is extended to relationships between the moieties at the league or confederate level. At the level of society, the kinship system employs *akatu: nih* and *kheya?tawenh* as affinal terms. Here *akatu: nih* means "my father's kinsman or kinswoman" (affinal because ego belongs to his mother's family), and *kheya?tawenh* refers to the children of a person's male relative and therefore in the Iroquois system means "nephew" when a woman uses it and "offspring" when a male uses it.

The second model, for the terms of address used by a chief and his subjects (constituents) is shown in figure 3. The chief addresses his "subjects" (including the matron and other officials) as *heyenhwa: ten?*, "my nephew," or *kheyenhwa: ten?*, "my niece" (i.e., "my sister's child," hence "my nephew or niece" under Iroquoian rules), and his subjects address him as *kuno?sen*, "my uncle" (i.e., my mother's brother). Interestingly, and in contrast to the moiety terms, these are familial rather than affinal terms and play on the matrilateral relationship rather than on the patrilateral one as do the moiety terms.

Another Moravian missionary, David Zeisberger, knew the Onondagas well enough to compile a dictionary of the language (1887). He also stressed the nature of the extended family compact, saying: "The Iroquois call themselves *Aquanoschioni*, which means *united people*, having united for the purpose of always reminding each other that their safety and power consist of a mutual and strict adherence to their alliance" (Heckewelder 1881: 97).

It is important to recognize that the Moravians of Bethlehem, Pennsylvania, acquired their view of the Iroquois through the eyes of the neighboring Delawares, who, with the Mahicans of the Hudson River, claimed priority for the Longhouse

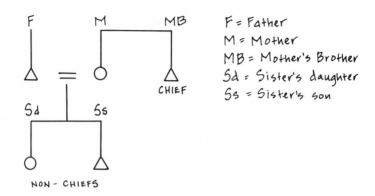

Figure 3. Woodbury's model for the kinship relations between a chief and his subjects.

concept of confederation, and doubtless ethnography supports this view. But understand, too, that the Pennsylvania proprietors and the English merchants of Philadelphia had just acquired lands at the Delaware forks by the infamous Walking Purchase, and to bring the Six Nations into the English interest they had employed as interpreter Weiser, whom the Iroquois claimed as belonging half to them. In this context, the merchants and landowners sought to gain an advantage by elevating the Iroquois Longhouse and denigrating the Delawares.

After Canasatego's boast at Lancaster, Arthur Lee of Virginia wrote to Weiser and later to William Johnson inquiring about the nature of Iroquois government. I find it strange that Weiser, who had experienced and noted the rituals of the league council and who must have known what his student Pyrlaeus discovered, let these things pass unnoticed in replying to inquiries (Heckewelder 1881: 60; Ruttenber 1872: 52, 64; P. Wallace 1945: 160ff.).

William Johnson had recently arrived in America, settled in the Mohawk valley, and established himself in the Indian trade at "Mount Johnson." His Indian experience was only beginning. He was generally too busy to concern himself with political mythology, for he was just learning how to make local Mohawk politics work to his advantage, and it would be late in life before he could write his celebrated letter to Arthur Lee (DHNY, 4: 430–37; SWJP, 12: 950.)

Johnson's letter distinguished near and remote tribes as to their degree of acculturation and noted that those Indians having most contact with traders had altered their system of politics while retaining ancient customs that they were unable to account for. Those tribes farthest removed from contact retained "the greatest part of their primitive usages . . . [but could] give no satisfactory account of their original signification." He also remarked a tendency of the Iroquois to cloak political institutions with mythology. Moreover, he observed that it was more than a century since the Jesuits had first gone among the Iroquois and introduced "some of their own inventions which the present generation confound with their ancient ceremonies" (SWJP, 12: 950).

□□◇□□

Practical considerations and common understandings postponed any urge to write down the old usages and traditions, whatever the state of knowledge. It is a pity that Joseph Brant, in reporting on a grand council he attended at Onondaga during November 1774, merely alluded to ancient usages that he heard rehearsed in opening the council, the substances of which were evidently quite familiar to him. Samuel Kirkland, missionary at Oneida, confirmed this hint a few days later when he heard from visiting Onondaga participants that the month-long council "was opened, their traditionary System [of] politics & counsel of the ancients rehearsed & searched" preliminary to the business at hand. It is our loss that Kirkland, weary from the press of visitors, found neither time nor energy to expand the record (Kirkland 1764–1804; Pilkington 1980: 98; NYCD, 8: 524).

Years later Brant recalled details that he had omitted from his report when answering questions put to him in an interview with the Reverend Elkanah Holmes (Brant 1801). Evidently, Holmes inquired about the date of the league, the tradition of its founding, the names of principals, how its members valued the bond, and how the member nations achieved unanimity with unequal numbers of chiefs representing the several nations. Besides, the interview covered the condolence of chiefs and the installation of successors.

Brant's replies put the legend as we know it squarely in the eighteenth century, when it was already a tradition. He outlined its plot, named characters, and related several crucial incidents. He apparently knew much more (Brant 1801; Boyce 1973: 286–94).

Brant placed the date "a considerable time before the arival [*sic*] of the Europeans." He located its beginning "at the Lower end of the German flatts above the Little Falls, on [the] Mohawk River." The Mohawk village there was on an east-west axis with an "Older brother named *Tekanawitagh* [Deganawi:dah]" stationed at the "East Gate" and of a "peaceable disposition." His

> younger brother named *Adergaghta* was at the West gate and evil inclined . . .—these were the two chiefs of the Village. The Elder brother being grieved at the cruel disposition of the younger, resolved to go westerly and look for a people, and form an alliance with them. He consequently went and met *Odadseghte* of the Onidas. By their conversation the Mohawk was found to be the elder, and therefore the Onida stiled him father.[2]
>
> The Mohawk chief promised to come back the next day, meaning the ensuing year and proceed farther on the business of the Confederacy.[3]
>
> The next year he went to the Onidas according to promise, he explained his intentions naming the divisions forming the Mohawk nation—it consisting of three tribes [clans]: the Wolf, turtle, and bear, and again were each divided into three subdivisions—.[4]
>
> Then the Mohawk got up and sang, mentioning that his son and him were united and that [the] father would be superior. Upon this the Onida stopped him. Then the

---

2. This use of kinship terms is correct, as are the names of the principals.

3. The metaphor of a day for a year also occurs in the Gibson versions.

4. This is the earliest record of the three Mohawk clans being segmented each into three matrilineages.

Mohawk expressed by a song . . . that they both should be equal, and at this the Onidas were satisfied.

Upon this being passed the Onida wished to stop him to rest a little, saying he would throw a tree in his way that he could not get over [the metaphor of the log across the path]. Upon this the other stiled him the *big tree*, so-called.[5]

They went together to Onondaga, they found the chief very obstinate, they with difficulty brought him over to agree, the Mohawk stiling him brother, and equal in the confederacy. When they went to return home, one of the Young men had forgot his maukissons and went back to look for them, as he was by the side of the house he heard the Onondaga singing that what the Father and Son had proposed to him did not suit him and that he could not wear it.—When he overtook them he told what he had heard—in consequence they agreed to return the next year.[6]

[The next year they did return, and] the Mohawk then proposed to the Onondaga (This chief's name was *Thadodarhonagh*) that he should keep the council fire of the confederacy, and he should carry their title. (For that reason he is yet called *roghsena-keghte* [the name bearer].) These condescensions brought him to agree, and they proceeded to Cayuga.

Their [the Cayugas'] chief had a big pipe, for which reason they gave the nation that name—*Shonoenaweadowane*. They stiled him their son, and brother to the Onidas.

From there they went to the Senecas. There was two principal chiefs of these, *Kanyadariyo* [Handsome Lake, lit., "a large or beautiful lake"] and *Shadekaroenyis* [Skies of Equal Height], they also agreed to the Confederacy in consequence of their frontier situation. They called them *roninhohhont*—or the Doorkeeper.[7]

Brant then repeated the titles of the leaders in each nation by which the members of the confederacy were identified. He added no other titles. He supplemented kinship usages among the nations, saying that intertribal bonds were "further cemented by friendships between individuals of the several nations which were held very sacred. In consequence of this they considered themselves as mutually bound to partake in each others good and bad success."

Brant estimated the time lapse of confederation at less than a decade. He was aware of the unequal distribution of sachems in the several national delegations to the grand council. He explained how the founders balanced unequal representation: "The Oneidas and Mohawks each had the same number of sachems, nine each, and that the others had a much greater number. But they all, [it seems, functioned] in the same manner." He also distinguished ascribed from achieved statuses. "Particular families in the nation had the right of choosing a chief or Sachem from among themselves. War chiefs were . . . chosen for their abilities, and it was also sometimes with other chiefs. There never was any other punishment for bad behavior in a chief than the dismissing him, and holding him in contempt. The power of a chief or sachem depends in a great measure on his

5. An alternate synonym for the Oneidas.
6. The incident of the warrior forgetting his moccasins, which he had hung to dry outside the house, is a unique literary device that alerts hearers to what comes next.
7. It is interesting that Brant attributes the doorkeeping function to the two leading Seneca chiefs who first accepted the league in principle, and that he says nothing of the two holdout chiefs, who in later times were called the doorkeepers, being numbers 49 and 50 on the Roll Call of the Chiefs (Fenton 1950: 67). "Extending the rafters" metaphorically brought them into the league.

abilities, in peaceable times they lead, when war takes place they give all power into the hands of the warriors and chief-warriors."

Brant said nothing about the role of matrons in selecting chiefly candidates from within particular lineages, nor of their role in deposing them. Of considerable interest are his remarks on the condoling and raising of chiefs: "If a chief or sachem dies there is a great expense and ceremony, one nation condoling with the other for their loss. In this condolence the commencement of the confederacy, and the chiefs that formed it are mentioned. Another chief is immediately appointed in place of the deceased." Here Brant confirms the Eulogy to the Founders, or Roll Call of the Chiefs, as an integral part of the eighteenth-century ceremony.

Brant is supposed to have left a traditional history of the Five Nations in manuscript, which came into the hands of his political and literary heir, Major John Norton (Teyoninhokarawen), from whom it passed to the Duke of Northumberland. The manuscript survives in Alnwick Castle, the seat of the Northumberlands (Klinck and Talman 1970: 98–105). Norton claimed Cherokee paternity but was most probably a Scot. He lived among the Six Nations of Grand River during the opening decades of the nineteenth century, learned Mohawk, and listened to the learned men of the confederacy. Later, while visiting England, he wrote up his materials, and presumably Brant's. Among the traditions that this fascinating culture broker heard and recalled is an Onondaga version of the founding of the league. Norton's account (ca. 1809–16) connects the Pyrlaeus version with Brant's and bridges the gap to those of Hale, Hewitt, Newhouse, and the chiefs, recorded as the nineteenth century closed and discussed in chapter 4. Its importance lies in demonstrating continuity of tradition before and after the removal of the Six Nations from New York to Ontario. Since it is in print, one need only characterize its plot and incidents.

□□◇□□

Prior to settlement at Onondaga, an extensive village on the Salmon River east of Oswego broke up in a factional dispute. The leaders agreed to remove by canoe and separate. A matron asked her grandchildren to lay her out between canoes of the separating factions and to let her sink into Lake Ontario as they parted. Through the clear water the people saw her transformed into a sturgeon.[8] One division made for Cataraqui (Kingston, Ontario); the other coasted the south shore. While yet in earshot of each other, the two parties began to speak different languages—Dewakanha (Algonquian) and Iroquoian.[9]

A further dispute and fission within the southern party occurred at a creek nine miles east of Oswego. Hiawatha (properly the title of a prominent Mohawk headman, Hayenhwatha, Hayouwaghtenh, Hayenwenthah, or Ayonhwathah) led one band up the creek. They engaged in hunting, salmon fishing, building weirs, and maintaining them. The tradition describes band formation and protocol on

----

8. This incident is symbolic of the trauma caused by abandoning aged persons on village removal.

9. This incident speaks to a sometime Algonquian-Iroquoian community, and it recognizes the two distinct language families. It also suggests that factionalism has always been endemic in Iroquois society.

meeting another band. A visitor is taken to the house of the chief. The two bands occupied opposite banks of a stream.[10]

Eventually the people of both parties descended to sulfurous Onondaga Lake and discovered the Great Salt Spring. Afar they spied lofty Onondaga, its oak forests, and smoke arising to the clouds from the fire of Thadoda:ho?, the Onondaga wizard. Both parties returned to their respective villages before deciding to remove to Onondaga.

Next comes the familiar theme of sorcery, involving the successive deaths of Hiawatha's three granddaughters (daughters in other versions), and his flight into the wilderness. The first and eldest died from the curse of a spurned suitor, whose familiar was an owl, the omen of death. Her father shot the owl with bow and arrow; it fell from the tree and became transformed into the sorcerer, who expired.[11]

The several bands converged on Onondaga and united. The Oswego Falls band became the Bear clan; the Wolf clan arrived by crossing the lake in canoes. Thadoda:ho?, seated on a hillside, saw their approach and conjured a squall, crying, "Do they appear at last?" Although the canoes swamped, some Wolf people survived to meet secretly in a remote wood. It was then, in this version, that Thadoda:ho? conjured a great soaring eagle and caused it to fall at the feet of Hiawatha's pregnant granddaughter, when onrushing warriors, bent on securing the feathers, trampled her to death.

This is the first version to document Hiawatha's depression, his withdrawal from Onondaga society, and his flight into the wilderness. An important decision was announced in a song. "He took up his pouch and bid them farewell," going due south (splitting the sky). At the time Norton wrote, the Onondagas were still familiar with place names in central New York that authenticate the narrative. Four episodes (the magic number) punctuated Hiawatha's wanderings. At every settlement he was greeted by name, as if his advent were foretold to the resident chief. Twice a chief offered to share authority in council, and twice they failed to call him. Overlooked, he took up his pouch, went downstream to another settlement, entered the first house, and sat on a vacant berth until summoned.[12] Each time a returning matron discovered him and ran to the chief, who already expected him.[13]

At the second village Hiawatha encountered friendly and hostile brother chiefs. Again unlike Brant's version, Norton's has the friendly brother have the bowstring of the evil brother cut as a precaution.[14] Once more Hiawatha, ignored, left.

In the third incident Hiawatha reached Oquaga on the Susquehanna and, finding no inhabitants, ascended a branch to its source in a pond. There he encountered geese shedding feathers and transforming themselves into human

10. This is the familiar theme of people living on opposite shores of a lake or stream that is frequently given as the origin of moieties.

11. This is the familiar paradigm of Iroquois witchcraft that lasted into the reservation period.

12. To this day, one is summoned to feasts, ceremonies, and councils by messenger. One does not go uninvited.

13. Protocol calls for taking a visitor by the arm, conducting him to the place of council, and seating him across the fire from his host.

14. Again the difficulty of accommodating a newcomer and sharing authority underscores the problem of unequal representation among the chiefs of the Five Nations when forming the league.

shapes. This is the famous incident in which waterfowl, on hearing him call, fly up, taking water from the pond to reveal wampum, which Hiawatha gathered. It is also the Iroquois explanation of the origin of wampum. Its use in protocol follows.

In the fourth episode Hiawatha reached the Schoharie and followed it downstream to the Mohawk River. As in later times, a Mohawk village stood at the confluence. He entered a house, sat on a berth, and commenced rehearsing a speech over wampum string that he had strung and held in his hand. Once more, a startled matron ran to the chief, Deganawi:dah, who proclaimed, "Hiawatha has come—bring him here."[15]

A host seats his guest across the fire. Hiawatha entered the house of the chief, who pointed to the berth on the opposite side of the fire, saying, "That place is yours." The host offered to share the house and to grant an equal voice in council. When asked why he left kin and country to wander alone in the forest, Hiawatha replied simply, "Thadoda:ho? is angry."

At a council the chief called for volunteers to seek out the habitation of Thadoda:ho?. The first two scouts transformed themselves into cranes, overflew Onondaga, reached the Genesee River (Seneca country), found the openings pleasant, and feasted on abundant ground nuts (*Apios tuberosa*), which cranes were known to favor. Their descendants constitute the Heron clan.

Despairing of their return, a second council commissioned a second pair of volunteers, who assumed the form of ravens. They found a smoke, descended, and became transformed into humans. They were greeted and conducted to the chief's house, where they heard two familiar Iroquois questions, "Where are you from?" and "Where are you bound?" They announced their mission and asked directions. A chief told them that Thadoda:ho? lived on the side of a distant mountain and that occasionally his smoke could be seen rising to the clouds. They had reached Oneida.

Repeating incidents builds suspense and conveys the passage of time. Likewise, throwing a log in the path metaphorically at Oneida delayed formation of the league by at least a year. Other such hitches and hindrances occur in the narrative. Observing protocol took time. Thus, when the Oneida chief told the raven scouts that on returning from Onondaga they should expect a tree in their path, he meant that they should turn off to Oneida village.

On landing at Onondaga and transforming into human shape, the two raven scouts traversed a hillside within sight of a house. The first person encountered cautioned them to speak softly, for that house was indeed the abode of Thadoda:ho?. Persons whispered in his presence. The scouts entered and saw seated a deformed person with hissing serpents for hair. Returning, they stopped at Oneida to report what they had discovered and proceeded safely to the Mohawk settlement.

After hearing their report, Deganawi:dah prepared for his intended embassy. He laid down the wampums appropriate for such a mission. Two Mohawk chiefs

15. Note in this incident that Deganawi:dah is cast in the role of the leading Mohawk chief. Traditionally that status belongs to Tekarihoken, who is first on the roster of Mohawk founders. Moreover, one suspects that Hiawatha and Deganawi:dah are facets of a dual personality. Only the title Hiawatha survives as second on the Mohawk roster. Possibly Norton or Brant confused Deganawi:dah with Tekarihoken.

derived their titles from laying down proportionate shares. For adding an equal amount, one was named "an equal affair," Satekariwategh (Sha?dekariwadeh), and Hiawatha is remembered as saying, "Tekarighhogea wakerighwageron" (I put mine among the whole affair). The second chief became Tekarighhogea (Tekari-hoken), in later times the leading Mohawk sachem (Fenton 1950: 59). Despite the jumbled orthography in the published text (Klinck and Talman 1970: 103), these early interpretations of now-obscure league titles are closer to ancient under-standings than are later renderings of the same names.

In such narratives, repetition serves for emphasis. At the site of modern Utica, the embassy met an Oneida packing a wolfskin quiver whom they dubbed Odatshehdeh, "Quiver Bearer," the leading Oneida chief. Mohawks and Oneidas reached an accommodation on kinship usage as "father and son." Deganawi:dah commented that none of the trees of the forest equaled his age; only the willows along the rivers approached it. He stated that his mission was to re-form the body of the Onondaga wizard and reclothe him. Quiver Bearer underscored the immensity of the task of remaking Thadoda:ho? into an ordinary mortal. He proposed that the embassy lie over at Oneida for a night, metaphorically a year, and next morning (next year) he ventured to throw a log across the path, adding another year to the confederation process. The Mohawk embassy returned home.

In the spring they again mounted the embassy. At Oneida the council assembled and Quiver Bearer opened it by intoning his relationship to Deganawi:dah,[16] who interrupted to insist that their relationship was not one of subordination as father and son. He admonished Quiver Bearer that theirs was a cooperative venture of joint risk—that instead, Quiver Bearer must sing: "My father and I shall risk . . . ." (The Iroquois conception of *thyatatha:wak*, "father and son," joins them as equals.)

The combined Mohawk-Oneida embassy reached Onondaga and entered the house of Thadoda:ho?. The Norton version describes Thadoda:ho? without specifying his deformities. It merely mentions snakes for hair and says that the reformers used wampum to remove his deformities, reclothed him, and put moccasins on his feet (fig. 4). Satisfied that they had done the job, the embassy started home. Again a warrior went back to retrieve moccasins hung outside the house and heard Thadoda:ho? singing that his new garment did not fit. The warrior overtook the chiefs and reported what he had heard. It was agreed to revisit Thadoda:ho? the following year to satisfy him—a further delay in the confederation process.

From this first mission Oneida acquired a new council label, Karontakowa, "Big Tree" or "Big Log," in addition to its national name of "Standing Stone."

The following summer the joint embassy revisited Onondaga. In passing Oneidatown, Deganawi:dah took his son, Quiver Bearer, by the arm. They had decided to make Thadoda:ho? keeper of the council fire of the league, and as further incentive to place the council fire at Onondaga. They found Thadoda:ho? much improved in appearance. One thing remained—"to rectify the concealed parts."[17] They also undertook to change his mind from selfishness to public

---

16. In Iroquois thought, song imparts power to a message, prayer, or public announcement.
17. This is the only allusion in Norton to Thadoda:ho?'s enormous penis.

Figure 4. "The Reformation of Thadoda:ho?." Painting by Ernest Smith
(Seneca). Courtesy Rochester Museum and Science Center, Rochester, New
York.

concern. The reformers, we read, "left their minds with him, meaning that he
should preside over their resolves," and gave him the council title "Rogh-
seanakeghte" (Sagochiendagehte), "Name Bearer."

As further emblems of authority, the embassy presented Thadoda:ho? with a
wing and a staff. The first was to sweep the council fire clean of dust (issues), the
second to prize out threats to public tranquillity, symbolized as "worm, snake, or
venomous creatures." Thadoda:ho? need but shout for assistance from the whole
confederacy.

Norton has Cayuga and Seneca joining the league after Onondaga and not
acting with Mohawk-Oneida in concerted action to persuade Onondaga. Cayuga
came in as a "son" and "younger brother to the Oneida," receiving the council
name "Great Pipe," "Shonnounaweantowa" (Shononawento:wa), an affectation
of their leading chief.

Last the Senecas joined as "younger brother" to the Mohawks and Onondagas and became "Ronninhohonte," "Supporter of the Door" (the post on which it is hinged).

Finally, Norton acknowledged that variant versions of this saga existed among the nations but added that they all concurred in substance. He was left wondering, however, whether the Five Nations had confederated for mutual defense or to promote aggression.

□□◇□□

By 1825, Iroquois affairs of state were no longer pressing, and native writers with time on their hands and the urge to write began to chronicle the past. The most interesting of these native scribes was David Cusick (d. 1840) of Tuscarora. His *Ancient History of the Six Nations* (1825) bears the imprint of his native village. Its later editions (1828, 1848) carry four woodcuts; Thadoda:ho? is delineated seated on a stool smoking a pipe and confronted by two reformers. Snakes surmount his head, and something is wrapped around his waist. Consistent with his deformities, he ate from dishes and spoons made from the skulls of his victims. Cusick has Thadoda:ho? request his own transformation, which was accomplished with a belt of wampum collected among the people. Confederation was of some duration. It took five years before the Tree of Peace was planted at Onondaga to reach the clouds, shade the council, and put out four roots in the cardinal directions. Cusick dates the founding at a millennium before Columbus, which is absurd. The value of Cusick's writing is not in his chronicle but in the establishment from undoubtedly eighteenth-century sources of an important element in the plot.

Among the white captives who were caught up in the whirlwind of the American Revolution and were adopted and raised as Indians, several remained in or near Indian society, served as interpreters, and related tradition to local historians. Ephraim Webster, a farmer at Onondaga Hollow in 1815, had heard the Onondagas relate the tradition of how the league was founded. As he recalled it, the happy thought of a union for defense had come to an inferior Onondaga chief. Perceiving similarities in culture and language and sensing that the Five Nations were threatened from without, this chief made his proposal acceptable by saying that it had come to him in a dream—a culturally sanctioned avenue for innovation. His plan was opposed by a jealous chief, but the hero mustered support by pretending to make long hunting trips when in fact he visited neighboring tribes to consult and co-opt leaders, whom he swore to secrecy. The sequence in which these leaders grasped his message became the order of precedence as we know it from later versions. Webster cited the bundle of arrows as a symbol of union, easily breakable if a single arrow was withdrawn but unbreakable as a bundle (Dunlap 1839, 1: 29–30, quoted in Beauchamp 1892).

During a long career as an Episcopal missionary at Onondaga, the Reverend William M. Beauchamp became a keen student of the Iroquois. In his edition of Cusick's work, Beauchamp (1892: 138) credits Webster with having heard Onondaga sources at the end of the eighteenth century place the age of the league, as Pyrlaeus did, at "about two generations, or one man's life, before the whites came to trade with them . . . about 1586."

Beauchamp is likewise our authority for saying that the most famous name in Iroquois annals—Hiawatha—was almost unknown until the middle of the nineteenth century, when a local historian, J. V. H. Clark, recorded an Onondaga version of the origin myth of the confederacy that featured Hiawatha as co-hero.[18]

---

18. Before his book appeared, Clark published this version in the New York *Commercial Advertiser*. Henry Rowe Schoolcraft used it without credit in his *Notes on the Iroquois* (1846). About this time (1849), Alfred B. Street, then New York state librarian, combined Schoolcraft's account with some original notes from Iroquois sources in composing a metrical romance entitled *Frontenac*. Longfellow took the title from Schoolcraft and the substance from *Algic Researches* (Schoolcraft 1839), which is a collection of Ojibwa tales, and made an Ojibwa out of an Iroquois chief (Beauchamp 1892: 137; Clark 1849: 1: 20, 21; Hallowell 1960: 45).

CHAPTER 4

ETHNOLOGISTS DISCOVER
THE LEAGUE LEGEND

Ethnology as a science in North America began with the publication of Lewis Henry Morgan's *League of the Ho-de-no-sau-nee, or Iroquois* (1851). It is a work on structural lines: it outlines the political organization of the league and refers to the tradition of its origin (1851: 61). Morgan had some reservations about whether to trust native testimony that the system was not of gradual evolution "but was the result of one protracted effort of legislation." He had heard the legend of how hostile bands of generic origin drew together in council to deliberate and formulate a plan of confederation, which a wise Onondaga had promoted. At Onondaga, people showed Morgan the site where Deganawi:dah had called the first council, kindled the perpetual fire, and inducted the village chiefs into offices that have preserved their titles to the present. Evidently, without testing condolence law historically or verifying the traditions, Morgan ascertained the principles and outlined the structure of Iroquois government as it was supposed to have functioned during the previous century. He recorded the titles of the fifty founders (1851: 64–65) and described their powers and duties.

Morgan (1818–81) and Horatio Hale (1817–96) were of an age and contemporaries. It has been the good fortune for Iroquois studies that the field has always attracted gifted minds. During the nineteenth century Hale was a distinguished practitioner in American Indian linguistics.[1] What a tragedy that a mind of his caliber could not be devoted completely to the pursuit of linguistic and ethnological studies! But to gain a livelihood, Hale returned to Harvard to study law; he tried Chicago and in 1856 settled in Clinton, Ontario, to act as a conveyancer of his wife's family properties. Clinton was a strange choice for the law, but it was lucky for ethnology because it brought Hale in contact with the Six Nations of Grand River.

While visiting the Johnson family at Chiefswood, Hale discovered two Indian manuscripts, a Mohawk version and a parallel Onondaga version of the ceremony for condoling and requickening chiefs in the league. He promptly reported his discovery to the American Association for the Advancement of Science (1881), and

---

1. Son of Sarah Josepha Hale, for fifty years editor of the *Lady's Magazine*, and relative of eminent lawyers and jurists, Horatio Hale published a sketch of an Algonquian language while a Harvard undergraduate and on graduation was appointed philologist of the Wilkes Expedition to Oceania. He confirmed the affinity of Malayan and Polynesian languages, and, in the words of Franz Boas (1897), "nowhere was his genius for linguistic research shown more clearly than in his masterly treatment of the difficult languages of northwest America."

his *Iroquois Book of Rites* (1883) soon followed. Chief John "Smoke" Johnson, a famous ritual holder who claimed descent from Sir William Johnson, held the Mohawk manuscript when Hale first saw it in 1879, and John Skanawati Buck, the wampum keeper, quite properly held the Onondaga version. Informants and internal evidence helped Hale trace the Mohawk version to a copy made in 1832 of a still earlier manuscript, written in the eighteenth-century orthography of Mohawk Anglican prayer books, attributed to Chief David of Schoharie. The then living Mohawk chiefs had requested Chief David to write down the rituals and proceedings of the Condolence Council as they were remembered as of old (Hale 1883: 39–42). Smoke Johnson told Hale that he had copied the original during the cholera epidemic of 1832, and that the manuscript also contained, in another hand, an account of the migration of the Six Nations from New York to Canada and their settlement on Grand River. Unfortunately, he neglected to copy this account because the facts were all too familiar to his contemporaries. This bit of history has now passed into tradition, because the original manuscript was destroyed by fire.

The *Book of Rites* set a high standard for ethnological monographs and would serve as a benchmark for measuring the state of the ceremony both for Iroquois ritualists and for Iroquoianists.[2] The chapter on the league and its founders recounts the tradition of its formation. Following the story of the manuscripts comes an analysis of the Condolence Council and the function of the clans in performing the ritual. Hale identified the clans with the classes or committees of chiefs into which the roll call is segmented. He described the all-day performance of the condolence and installation ceremony, which he first observed in July 1883 (Hale 1895), after his book was in print. This accounts for the discrepancy between the published order of ritual and the actual performance. The roll call comes first, not last. A feature of the ceremony is the recitation of the laws of the league, which the Iroquois call "Over the Forest." Hale drew some interesting inferences from the text: how the house was indeed extended and strengthened, and on specific functions of member nations. He found internal evidence that the Mohawk version was composed after the Tuscaroras, Nanticokes, and Tutelos were admitted in 1753. He clearly understood Iroquois character and policy.

□□◇□□

A further inference relates to the era of confederation. Hale found hints that during the period when the nations were separated they made temporary alliances to meet passing emergencies. Then a leader of "peculiar qualities" emerged and, "aided by favorable circumstances," effected "a more permanent union." Hale perceived that confederation was a process and not a single event. He inferred from a projection of linguistic differences the age of separation, cut that in half, and from the evidence fixed the date of confederation at the mid-fifteenth century.

The evidence consisted of field notes recorded "during many visits to the Six Nations on Grand River," which Hale supplemented by two field trips to the Onondaga Reservation near Syracuse. He interviewed "the most experienced councilors, and especially the 'wampum keepers,' the official annalists of their

---

2. James G. Shea, a contemporaneous Catholic historian, declared it "a philosophical and masterly treatise . . . such as we never before had of any nation on this continent" (cited in introduction to 1963 reprint of Hale 1883).

people." By independently corroborating his data in two localities, he tested and compared versions of the Onondaga tradition. The main outlines of the narrative held in both places, but he found that the Onondagas naturally retained a fuller recollection of the events preceding the flight of Hiawatha to the Mohawk country. His Mohawk informants at Grand River knew best the episodes involving their own tribal heroes as founders of the league. Quite correctly he pointed out these facts to later investigators who might undertake to repeat or continue such research, as indeed did Beauchamp, Hewitt, Parker, and I. All writers inevitably make their own version, and so, Hale admitted, when the narratives varied, "I . . . followed that which seemed most in accordance with the tenor of the history and with the evidence furnished by the *Book of Rites*" (1883: 19). Moreover, at their last meeting, just before Morgan's passing, the two friends and colleagues in Iroquois studies reviewed the newly discovered *Book of Rites* together, comparing it with Morgan's field notes: the point at issue was the list of chiefs (Hale 1883: 31; Hale to Morgan, 25 September 1880, Morgan Papers).

Even before their meeting, Hale's letters to Morgan reporting his findings at Six Nations and Onondaga had reawakened Morgan's interest in Iroquois polity. Inasmuch as his old friend and first informant, General Ely S. Parker, was long removed from the Tonawanda scene, Morgan turned to Ely's brother, Nicholson H. Parker, U.S. interpreter at the Cattaraugus Reservation of the Seneca nation. "Nic" Parker replied to Morgan's query on 28 September 1875, remarking the confusion on ancient Iroquois law-ways and complaining that he was not familiar with the matter and that everyone he approached gave him a different account. "The difficulty," he concluded, "seems to be that there is now no one who actually understands the laws of the 'Confederacy' as it was" (Armstrong 1978: 174).

The exact number and order of the founding chiefs and the date of confederation are perennially favorite topics among Iroquoianists (Table 1). Morgan and Hale agreed on the date, which they deduced from the independent testimony of Seneca-Tuscarora informants in New York and Hale's Onondaga sources. Morgan's Seneca sources declared it to have been 150 years before Champlain (or 1459); in 1875 Hale met with the wampum keepers at Onondaga to go over such issues and recorded their answer: "about six generations before the white people came to these parts." If the Onondagas meant Henry Hudson's voyage, and if we allow twenty-five years to a generation, the date is also 1459. Five years later Hale put the same question to Chief John Buck, who thought it a matter of four hundred years since confederation—a reasonable confirmation of the New York Onondaga estimate (Morgan 1871: 151; Hale 1883: 177–78).

All such guess-dates rest on an identification with some European discoverer. (We can dismiss David Cusick's [1825] supposition of a millennium before Columbus as fatuous.) The Mohawks had reason to remember Champlain, although they may not have seen Hudson, but they may also have traded with the Dutch at the mouth of the Norman's Kill before the founding of Fort Orange (1623). And because we now know that the Mohawks were in their valley when Jacques Cartier visited Hochelaga (Montreal) in 1535, and that the Laurentian Iroquois whom he met were a people unto themselves, it remains to find another Jacques, besides Cartier, to satisfy tradition. We now have a likely candidate in Jacob Eelckens, a shadowy figure with various aliases, including "Jacques," who

TABLE 1
SUMMARY OF PROPOSED DATES OF THE FOUNDING OF THE IROQUOIS LEAGUE

AUTHOR	DATE
Pyrlaeus	One generation before contact
Brant	Long before contact; a decade in process
Cusick	A millennium before Columbus
Webster-Beauchamp	One man's life before traders
Morgan	Approximately 1459
Hale	1459
Beauchamp	1559
Hewitt	1570
Fenton	1600 ± 30 years
Fenton	Approximately 1500
Canfield	1451
Fadden-Nash; P. Wallace	1451
Wallace *père* and *fils*	1450
Trigger	Approximately 1440
Tuck; Bradley	1451+
Tooker (1978)	No conclusion

traded in the Hudson area as early as 1613 and who recently surfaced in a manuscript at the American Antiquarian Society (Richter 1982).

With Jacob (Jacques) Eelckens on the upper Hudson River during the second decade of the seventeenth century, we can reconcile Pyrlaeus's phrase—"one age before the white people came into the country"—that troubled both Beauchamp and Hewitt (Beauchamp 1905: 153; Hewitt in Hodge 1912, 1: 618). Three generations, or seventy-five years, is a generous estimate of a man's life in Iroquois society at that period, which would fix the date of confederation somewhere in the middle of the previous century. Both Beauchamp and Hewitt settled on 1570. But there are problems with this date.

No longer saddled with the Laurentian hypothesis that derived the Five Nations from the people who greeted Jacques Cartier, some years ago I suggested that the true date of the confederacy probably lay at 1600, plus or minus thirty years (Fenton 1961: 271). I now regard this date as too recent in the light of ongoing archaeological research. The culture of the Mohawk people is now believed to have evolved from prehistoric sites in and near the Mohawk Valley, and they are no longer thought to have brought their culture from the St. Lawrence. A similar ancestry is being worked out for the other Iroquois in their historical seats (Niemczycki 1984; Bradley 1987). Moreover, the Iroquois tradition in Ontario is much earlier than previously thought (Wright 1966). This all gives credence to the Huron tradition that their confederacy was formed starting at the mid-fifteenth century, and the Iroquois confederacy could not have been far behind (Trigger 1976: 162–63). Elisabeth Tooker (1978: 418–22), in reviewing theories and evidence for the age of the confederacy, came to no conclusion. The true date cannot be known with certainty, but it can be safely said that the process of confederation was going on fairly early in the sixteenth century.

Metaphors that may be quite ancient afford further evidence to bolster tradition. Paul Wallace (1948: 398) identified three metaphorical usages that were
current in league ritual during the mid-seventeenth century and that were then
recognized as being of great antiquity. When Pierre Millet, S.J. (1635–1708), was
adopted into an Oneida family in 1689 (instead of being tortured), he was awarded
the vacant title of the leading Oneida chiefship, Odatshehdeh (Quiver Bearer). We
are told that this title was an "ancient name" of one of the "first founders of the
Iroquois republic," and that his predecessor in the title as such was "a member
of the Council, And . . . was regarded from all antiquity [*de toute ancienneté*, from
the earliest times] as having been one of the mainstays of the Nation" (JR, 64: 91,
101; Hale 1883: 130; Fenton 1950: 60). Traditionally, Quiver Bearer was indeed the
first Oneida to accept the Peacemaker's message, making him a cofounder of the
league. In ceremony his title denotes the Oneida people.

The longhouse itself is writ large in the minds of Iroquois annalists. A Mohawk
protest in 1654 to Father Le Moyne, S.J., that he not go first to Onondaga as
planned but come to the Mohawks employs the image of the longhouse for the
league: the speaker said, "Ought not one to enter the house by the door, and not
by the chimney or roof of the cabin, unless he be a thief, or wish to take the inmates
by surprise? We, the five Iroquois nations, compose but one cabin; we maintain
but one fire; and we have, from time immemorial, dwelt under one and the same
roof." The *Relation* interpolates: "In fact, from the earliest times, these five
Iroquois Nations have been called in their language . . . *Hotinnonchiendi*, that is, 'the
completed Cabin,' as if to express that they constituted but one family." The
speaker went on to list the hazards of entering by the smoke hole and not coming
in at ground level by the door, which the Mohawks held open (JR, 41: 87). One
cannot be sure what seventeenth-century writers meant by the idiom *de tout temps*,
which occurs twice in the *Relation*, but I agree that it pushes the era of the founding
of the league back into or beyond the previous century and earlier than a date
remembered by persons then living.

What on the face of it appears to be precise evidence for dating the entrance of
the Seneca nation into the league is the unsubstantiated tradition that an eclipse
occurred during the travels of the Peacemaker to the westernmost of the Five
Nations.[3] The eclipse incident occurs in none of the major versions of the league
epic recorded on the Six Nations Reserve, which confirm one another. Moreover,
there is a wide range of eclipses that were visible in western New York to choose
from, and only one of these comes conveniently on 28 June 1451 to confirm the
estimated date of Hale and Morgan.

Tradition says: "When the peace messenger of Deganawidah went to the Seneca
Nation he was not at first welcomed . . . by one section . . . who dwelt farther to
the west. As they were thinking it over there occurred a strange event. The sun
went out and for a little while it was complete darkness. This decided those Senecas
who were in doubt. They thought this a sign that they should join the Confederacy.

---

3. Paul Wallace learned of this incident from Ray Fadden (Aren Akweks), of Scots-Irish extraction
married into the Akwesasneh, or St. Regis, band of Mohawks, an extraordinary and imaginative
teacher of Iroquois lore. Fadden had it from George Nash (Torewawaguhn), a Mohawk traditionalist
at Six Nations. Wallace had Fadden write down the tradition before publishing it without claim as
to its infallibility (1948: 399).

This happened when the grass was knee high, . . . or when the corn was getting ripe" (P. Wallace 1948: 399).

Other versions of the epic stress the difficulty of getting the westernmost Seneca chiefs and their towns to adhere to the league. Eclipses did occur, Indians could observe them, and they were deemed ill omens. The darkening of the sky in grief at death occurs as a metaphor throughout the condolence ritual. In council speeches of the eighteenth century, time is reckoned by the height of the corn, the state of its maturation, and similar markers in nature. But note that the grass is knee high in June, some two months before corn ripens. The whole piece then is in character.

What makes this incident difficult to accept is that only one other origin legend of the league mentions an eclipse. Indeed, Ray Fadden, who recorded this tradition, himself produced a pictorial account of the formation of the league in which he referred to the factional struggle between eastern and western Seneca bands over accepting Deganawi:dah's message. He mentions measures taken for composing these differences but makes no reference to an eclipse as the catalyst. There is, nevertheless, a parallel Seneca account that is attributed to Blacksnake, nephew of Cornplanter and war chief of the Seneca settlements on the Allegheny (Canfield 1902: 23–40, 197–200).[4]

The Canfield legend of confederation states that an eclipse occurred just when the Mohawks and Senecas were about to annihilate each other, and this event happened "when the corn was receiving its last tilling," which again fits the date of 28 June 1451.

Inasmuch as Canfield's book had been published for a half-century, and copies of such works inevitably reach Iroquois readers, quite possibly Canfield was the source for George Nash, from whom Fadden obtained the account, or even for Fadden.

□□◇□□

Modern scholarship affords new ways of regarding the time frame. Modern social evolutionists are wrong in saying that little is known of the origin of confederacies. They were the culmination of a series of local alliances specified in tradition and documented historically. Recent work on Onondaga prehistory (Tuck 1971; Bradley 1987) does not date the formation of the Onondaga tribe much earlier than 1451, the eclipse date and that proposed by Hale and Morgan. Hewitt (1894) discounted the value of tradition and, on the principle that leagues were seldom if ever accomplished without the motive of outside pressure, opted for a later date—between 1559 and 1570 in response to European pressure. In Hewitt's favor,

---

4. Little is known of William Walker Canfield (1857–1937) beyond the facts in *Who Was Who*: he was a native of Ellicottville, New York, not far from Allegany Reservation, and later, at the turn of the century, he was a journalist in Utica, New York. He attributed the legends of the Iroquois that he recorded (Canfield 1902) to the great Cornplanter and his nephew Governor Blacksnake, both of the Seneca settlements on the Allegheny and both dead before Canfield's day. The two Seneca war chiefs are supposed to have related the legends in about 1800 to an unnamed surveyor for the Holland Land Company, who recorded them in his field notebooks. Canfield claims to have acquired these notes, to have taken them to Allegany Reservation, and to have reworked them with descendants of the original named informants (1902: 16). These descendants are authentic persons mentioned in genealogies collected in the 1930s (Fenton 1933–34). This is all quite plausible except that Canfield nowhere identified the original recorder, nor have I succeeded in locating the notebooks, if they exist. Canfield reworked the legends for literary effect, which makes the source material even more crucial.

the Creek Confederacy came into being in response to land pressure from Georgia settlers (Green 1982). An alternative hypothesis, demonstrable in the Laurentian case, holds that interior tribes made alliances to break through to the coastal trade.

In concluding his discussion of confederacy formation, Trigger (1976: 163) wrote:

> Yet even if the Iroquois Confederacy was strengthened in response to European intrusion, this appears to have happened with considerable ease. Unlike some later, short-lived confederacies that attempted to bring culturally heterogeneous groups together in opposition to European expansion, the Iroquoian confederacies embraced groups of people who were culturally and linguistically related, and who already shared similar political institutions. In many ways the formation of such confederacies can be viewed as the extension of the same forces that had already created tribal, in place of band, structures. For this reason, it seems doctrinaire and unwarranted to reject the Huron claim that their confederacy began around A.D. 1440.

Anthony Wallace (1958a) favors a mid-fifteenth-century date proposed by his father, but on other grounds. He suggests that a lapse of five hundred years would provide sufficient time "for distortions and variations to have befallen the myth" prior to its recording by later ethnologists. This view does not account for the eclipse incident's dropping out of the major versions, which are far more complete in other details lacking in the two brief snatches containing the eclipse. And there is no way of translating variations into time.

We know from Norton that variation and distortion had already occurred by the end of the eighteenth century (Klinck and Talman 1970: 105). By then the movement to Grand River had separated two Onondaga bands, and a process of drift during the nineteenth century may account for differences between the two localities, leading up to the Newhouse and Gibson versions at Grand River and the Hiawatha emphasis at Onondaga.

Although Norton found no reason for saying the confederacy was formed for defense or aggression, Heckewelder, on the authority of Pyrlaeus, stated that it was formed for mutual defense (1881: 97).

The seventeenth-century struggle between the Algonquian-speaking Mahicans of the Hudson Valley, the so-called River Indians, and the Mohawks culminated in 1675, relieving pressure on the Mohawks and Oneidas from the east and gaining them access to Dutch trading posts. Likewise at mid-century, the Senecas destroyed the Eries, their traditional westward enemy. How long the Five Nations had been compressed from east and west is uncertain, but Hale implies that it lasted for two centuries.

Precise dates for complicated social institutions are at best spurious. Rather than a single event, the formation of the Iroquois League was a process that occupied the lifetimes of its founders. The legend of its founding, to which I return shortly, narrates a long struggle involving internal strife and external threats. The league as such was a confederacy of independent but related tribes or nations; and confederacies, as political institutions, owe their rise usually to the need to compose internal hostilities in order to meet the threat of common enemies. Also, as Ralph Linton wrote (1936: 241): "Most confederacies begin as defensive alliances, gradually developing organization and increasingly strong central control as the necessity for these becomes apparent." They are at best makeshift states and, as we shall see, leave local government largely intact. They permit unequal representation based on preexisting sovereignties; unanimity must therefore be the rule, and they never quite achieve central stability or communication to the margins. But as governments they are peculiarly at home in aboriginal America—among the Hurons and Iroquois and among their neighbors in New England and in the Southeast—and these confederacies had typological relatives in Mexico and Peru. Their success required extremely democratic societies, and, as we are about to learn, the Iroquois made of its forms a ritual and an enduring myth (Linton 1936).

In his cultural history of the Hurons, Bruce Trigger (1976: 162–63), in discussing Iroquoian protohistoric confederacies, makes the following points: (1) The principal feature common to them was agreement among member tribes not to resort to bloodshed to settle grievances. (2) The suppression of vendetta reposed in a confederate council composed of civil chiefs from the member tribes, which met periodically to feast and consult, to judge disputes, and to arrange payment of reparations (these proceedings became highly ritualized: council speeches were laden with metaphor and symbolism, and indeed the conduct of these ceremonies was the principal business). (3) There was no evidence that member tribes were bound to help one another in warfare, although in the Iroquois case the Degana-wi:dah epic states how this was accomplished by putting the warriors of the league under two Seneca chiefs. (4) Foreign policies of member tribes were different. Confederacies did restrain violence and promoted greater security among the members.

□□◇□□

I return now to the epic itself, and the versions of it that preceded Chief John Arthur Gibson's. Before confederation, in the version Hale published (1883), the Cayugas and Senecas were both imperiled by a vindictive Onondaga shaman who was formidable in war and awesome in sorcery. Thadoda:ho?'s foul deeds and loathsome appearance provide the horror episodes in the narrative (Hale 1883: 20–21, 157). Narrators and listeners before Hale's day doted on horror stories, but such incidents were played down by "grave councilors" when reciting the traditional history of the league on public occasions during the Victorian era.

The epic assigns the reformer's role to a middle-aged Onondaga chief of high rank named Hiawatha, a derivative of Hayonwatha or Hayenhwatha. Of significance now is what the original holder of this title represents in the Iroquois value system. Hale makes him out to be the embodiment of the equable man, the ideal chief, who puts public concern above self and family. This legendary kind and generous person was the principal victim of Thadoda:ho?'s machinations: Hiawatha grieved over corruption in government, blood feud, and repeated acts of reprisal by sorcery. Warfare was a constant threat. He conceived a scheme of a vast confederation to ensure universal peace. This was an act of mind, of which the Iroquois are so fond. It was not to be just another confederacy but embodied the idea of permanent government that granted local autonomy and lodged general control in a grand council, or senate, composed of representatives to be elected by each nation who would hold office for life on good behavior. Moreover, built into the system was the capability of indefinite expansion to comprise all peoples who might seek shelter beneath the Tree of Peace. Its avowed purpose was to end war.

But Hiawatha was to suffer the prophet's fate and encounter bitter opposition at home, go into exile, ultimately gain acceptance of his ideas abroad, and then return to Onondaga a hero to reform Thadoda:ho? and make him prime minister of the league. He failed to enlist the support of his own nation in a series of three conferences, all of which the sorcerer frustrated. In Hale's words: "They came together along creeks, from all parts, to the general council-fire" to honor Hiawatha's summons. Thadoda:ho?'s threatening silence shut off debate. Fewer persons attended a second meeting, which ended similarly, and no one came to a third. Depressed, Hiawatha left town to carry his words to more welcome ears.

Hiawatha's plunge into the dark forest, his traverse of lakes and rivers, and his arrival in the Mohawk Valley, to quote Hale, "is to the Five Nations what the flight of Mohammed from Mecca to Medina is to the votaries of Islam." Hale's knowledge of ancient literature is matched only by the rhetoric of the Iroquois.

The meeting of Hiawatha with Deganawi:dah at a Mohawk town, in Hale's account, underplays Deganawi:dah as a character who assumes supernatural attributes in later versions. Whether Deganawi:dah was an Onondaga émigré, a native Mohawk, or, as others would have it, a Huron, is immaterial, for he may well represent the split image of Hiawatha.

In this version Tekarihoken, as leading Mohawk chief, was to have throughout history "the hereditary right and duty of lighting the council-fire, and taking the first place in public meetings" (Hale 1883: 25). He also ranks first on the roll of founders.[5]

Hiawatha anticipated later woods'-edge protocol by waiting at a spring outside the village until Tekarihoken sent a messenger to bring him in. He then met Deganawi:dah, who grasped his message. Their joint progress to Oneida and thence to Cayuga, bypassing Onondaga, and finally to the great hill of the Senecas before returning to Onondaga to reform Thadoda:ho?, constitutes the plot of the epic that will occupy us presently. First, however, there are other versions of the myth that come down to our own day that demonstrate the reverence in which the descendants of the founders hold the Great Peace that was established for them. On emigrating to the Grand River after the American Revolution, according to Hale, "in Canada their first proceeding was to establish, as far as possible, their ancient league, with all its laws and ceremonies." The Onondaga chiefs carried with them a substantial portion of the ancient wampum records, and their Mohawk brethren recalled their leading role in confederation and precedence in council matters. "The history of the League continued to be the topic of orators whenever a new chief was installed in office. Thus the remembrance of the facts has been preserved" for ethnological investigation (Hale 1891: 77; 1883: 34).

□□◇□□

The strength of Iroquois ethnology from the beginning has been the opportunity for one observer to repeat the work of a predecessor with the same informants. Within five years of the publication of Hale's book, Hewitt elicited from John Skanawati Buck "The Legend of the Founding of the Iroquois League" (Hewitt 1892). This was Hewitt's first important contribution, and it represents the beginning of a long research career (Swanton 1938; Fenton 1962: 287–89). Buck's

---

5. Later versions attribute precedence to Thadoda:ho?, the leading Onondaga.

account is concise, for there were then no tape recorders, which is a pity because Buck had much to say and Hewitt complained of the difficulty of transcribing his words phonetically. Later Hewitt took long texts with facility, but his mature writing suffered from prolixity. Nevertheless, the Iroquois idiom comes through in metaphoric and symbolic expressions that state the themes of Iroquois life.

Unique to this version is the incident describing the reformation of Thado-da:ho?, in which for the first time Hiawatha relinquishes first billing to Deganawi: dah and takes his place among the founders of the league whose names descended as titles to living successors. They, unlike Hiawatha, failed to become romantic heroes of nineteenth-century epic poetry. Mythological incidents accumulated around the figures of the Onondaga shaman Thadoda:ho? and the culture hero Hiawatha, who were at first rival Onondaga chiefs and later founders of the league. To their supernatural accomplishments have been added the deeds of historical successors in their titles and roles. As a consequence, a cycle of Hiawatha legends grew up at Onondaga, legends that Erminnie A. Smith regarded "as the histories of a long line of Hiawathas" and that attached to one person who became marvelously endowed (Smith 1883: 47–116, 53–54). Small wonder that Onondaga annalists have confused the attributes and deeds of Hiawatha with those of Sky Holder in clearing rivers, ridding the earth of monsters, and voyaging in a magic white canoe (Hewitt 1892: 131).

The theme of death permeates Iroquois social and religious thought and behavior. Hewitt noted the close similarities between the decennial death feast of Huronia and the Six Songs used in transforming Thadoda:ho? that are preserved in the condolence ceremony. At a modern Condolence Council, the clearminded moiety of chiefs requickens the mourning phratry of chiefs, an act that commemorates the founding of the league and serves to restore society by installing new chiefs in the seats of the dead. The clearminded withdraw on news of the death in the opposite moiety, and they correspondingly converge in a procession to celebrate the ritual that in effect restores social relations. A related theme is putting death out of sight, out of mind, and relegating it beyond the pale of mention by figuratively burying weapons of war, by symbolically covering the grave and never afterward mentioning the deceased person but keeping his name and duties alive by raising another in his place. Death and requickening, then, are reciprocal, reinforcing themes unifying the society, its culture, and its mythology.

"One mind," or "good mind," is the ideal toward which Iroquois polity constantly strives. Sorcery and witchcraft, on the contrary, frustrate all positive action by individuals and groups. As antisocial behavior, sorcery opposes Gaiwi:yo:h and related concepts of civil order and peace. The protocol of public councils suppresses latent hostility, and the devices employed for attaining unanimity overcome factionalism, which is always inherent in the situation. In a complete breakdown of social relations, vengeance respects no blood ties, and such is the situation with which the myth opens.

As in the Hale account, so in the one Hewitt collected from Buck. Thadoda:ho? frustrates a series of meetings called by Hiawatha at secret spots, dominates any meeting that he attends, and conjures a squall to drown persons arriving by canoe. He visits death upon Hiawatha's daughter, out gathering firewood, by conjuring a bird that descends near her; she is trampled by converging sightseers bent on getting feathers. Bereft of kin and striving for release from depression, the hero goes south, exiling himself from Onondaga to wander in the wilderness.

Several literary devices relieve the spectacle of Hiawatha's depression. On reaching and skirting a lake, he is diverted by ducks flying up and taking the water to open a path across, revealing shells, which he proceeds to gather for wampum. Then a series of place names convey his movements: a mountain pass and "tall hickories."

The listener then hears a lesson in etiquette and protocol. A visitor, on reaching a cabin, enters and sits; the owner detains the guest and promises recognition and participation in council. When the promise is not fulfilled in the regular way, the visitor withdraws to a temporary lodge in a cornfield to incant a protest. Aware that someone overhears his protest, he withdraws again, characteristically, to avoid giving offense, and wanders aimlessly. Once more the host inquires why a person of his eminence wanders without purpose.

Journeying, the hero reaches a second cabin and enters. Once more the host inquires why a man of his eminence wanders without purpose, and again it is because Thadoda:ho? is mad and has destroyed the hero's family. The second host, Deganawi:dah, hears the hero's plight and inquires where Thadoda:ho? abides. It is where a pillar of smoke arises to touch the sky. The matter is put properly before the resident chiefs, who decide to wait on Thadoda:ho?.

Evidently it was the custom to make up wampum strings for a particular mission and then entrust the remembrance of specific messages to individual delegates. Twelve themes or matters accordingly were composed under Deganawi:dah's guidance, and the strings were strung up as if this were the first time. Hiawatha added from his pouch a thirteenth to complete the set of requickening strings as we know them today. The "thirteen matters" then strung were hung on a pole, comprising the themes intended for straightening the mind of Thadoda: ho?. We are told that each chief accepted a single theme as his personal responsibility.

It was then, too, that Deganawi:dah devised the customary and later familiar cries of approbation: the *yohen:* and the council reply, *hiya::*, which were to punctuate the proceedings of so many treaty negotiations and attract the notice of eighteenth-century writers. Likewise, it is said that he composed the Six Songs of greeting and farewell, which again were to be heard in other contexts.

Buck has the two scouts who are to seek the smoke of Thadoda:ho?'s fire transform themselves into crows. The first smoke they find is Oneida, where the leading chief obstructs their path with a log so that he is co-opted into the plan.

After much looking they find a second smoke that is indeed massive and touches the sky. Assuming human form, they enter the lodge whence the smoke issues to inquire whether it is the abode of Thadoda:ho?. They are warned by a whisper, "Tci tci," repeated four times by astonished bystanders, as if speaking above a whisper might offend the shaman, whom they point out.

There is no more graphic description of Thadoda:ho? in the literature. "The two spies looked and they were struck speechless and motionless by seeing a thing—a shape that was not human but supernatural and deformed; for the hair of *Thadodaho'* was composed of writhing, hissing serpents, his hands were like the claws of a turtle, and his feet like unto a bear's claws in size and awry like those of a tortoise, and his body was cinctured with many folds of his *membrum virile*— truly a misshapen monster" (Hewitt 1892: 136).

The astonished scouts returned abruptly, resuming their disguise, and reported as requested at the first smoke, where the Oneida leader repeated his friendly obstruction. Thus, after an old principle in Iroquois politics, Oneida became a channel: one reports plans and acts to confederates to secure their allegiance. On returning home, the scouts reported to their chief, Deganawi:dah, whereupon he announced the plan to use the thirteen themes for reconstructing Thadoda:ho?'s mind. They would go to the place of the fallen log and co-opt him. Then they would kindle a woods'-edge fire at Onondaga for Thadoda:ho?, that he in turn might invite them to the "principal place," where they would recite the main themes.

In woods'-edge protocol a visiting delegation pauses where the forest gives way to the clearing, waits until invited into the settlement, and reserves delivery of its message for the principal place, the council fire. In this bit of ritual we witness one variant of a ceremony for greeting strangers that was common to all the woodland and prairie tribes of North America (John R. Swanton, personal communication, ca. 1940).

So the Mohawk delegation took up the path to Onondaga, chanting Atha- hinon?keh, "Going on the Road," the now familiar eulogy or roll call. On reaching the log in the path, they were requested to stay for the afternoon, and they remained overnight, which in the literary language means a year, before resuming the path to Onondaga.

From the sacred stone of Oneida, the trail to Onondaga traversed deep woods, forded several creeks, and threaded swamps until the ground rose abruptly from Chittenango toward the mountain that was Onondaga. The path led to Deep Spring near Manlius, which marked the boundary between Oneida and Onondaga territories, and it was there that delegations approaching from the east rested and sent in messengers to announce their arrival at the woods' edge (Morgan 1851: 520; Fenton, personal observation with A. G. Zellar).

The messenger notified the resident chiefs, saying: "They ordered me their cane to come here," whereupon the resident chiefs went to the woods'-edge fire and extended a greeting.

The terminology of the narrative and the inserted speeches are, of course, the words of the later ceremony that were fed back into the myth. The ceremony at the woods' edge is called "the preliminary part in which mutual greetings are had." Buck said that immediately on kindling the fire the visitors began the Six Songs, a sequence unlike that of the modern ceremony. Although remote, the song had an immediate effect on Thadoda:ho?'s mind. Then, as in the present ceremony, holding a short string for each theme, they spoke three brief words at the fire, promising the full curing ceremony at the principal place in Thado- da:ho?'s lodge. There they would present him with a gull's wing to sweep aside evil from the land. The nature of the cure would compose his mind and transform his hair, hands, and feet, and it promised that his penis, when shortened not to exceed six thumb-widths in length, would make him human. Whereupon they announced: "Let us go to the principal place." And they asked the war chief for an escort.

The report of the scouts had prepared the visiting chiefs (and the listener) for the shock of Thadoda:ho?'s ménage. Entering, Deganawi:dah had the temerity to acknowledge his "pitiable brother Haiyonhwatha," who had come in desperation to his lodge bearing an important message (and this was the first time in a long while that the Onondagas had heard this name spoken). The customary inquiry about the resident chief—"Is this the lodge of Thadoda:ho??"—elicited only the deprecative *tci* (whispered four times). Again Buck repeated the frightful appearance of Thadoda:ho?. Horrified but undaunted, the chiefs responded to Deganawi:dah's command to unwrap the thirteen wampum strings from the carrying pouch and arrange them in order on a horizontal pole.

The incident of transforming Thadoda:ho? into a natural man climaxes Buck's version of the myth. Buck ascribed the transformation to the power of the Six Songs lined out in the text, and they were sung to celebrate the consummation of the affair. This powerful hymn, attributed to Deganawi:dah, is still sung in the condolence ceremony. Whatever its original content, it had a powerful effect on Thadoda:ho?. He raised up his head, an act that he had never been known to do. This act symbolized the elevation of his mind. Buck mentioned a special song of regeneration that Deganawi:dah sang three times to straighten out Thadoda:ho?'s mind, to re-form it like that of a human being. This particular verse remains Thadoda:ho?'s own song, called "a beautiful brushbroom," although its interpretation is moot.

Only one other version of the myth carries the account of re-forming Thadoda:ho?'s body. This was accomplished by the laying on of hands and the use of a string of wampum to designate each body part re-formed. Making his hands and feet human and brushing the snakes from his head and casting them away anticipated the main event. The text says:

> He then delivered another wampum string. "One other thing remains, . . . it is not intended that this should be thus," and then unwinding from the body of *Tha-do-da-ho'* the many fathoms of his *membrum virile*, with which he was girdled many times, and measuring with the eye its natural length, *Deka-na-wi-da* cut away the excessive length, saying, "This shall be so long," and he held in his hand a wampum-string as he spoke and then delivered it, but when he let go the cut member, there was dermal recession. He made three . . . attempts to reduce the recession, delivering every time a string of wampum, but he failed. Then the chiefs said, "Although this will not submit, yet it will not now have the potency to kill persons; hence, leave it; it will make no more trouble." Thus they changed *Thadodaho'* into a natural man. (Hewitt 1892: 140)

□□◇□□

Senecas of the period confirmed what Hewitt heard at Six Nations. At Cattaraugus Reservation, Jeremiah Curtin obtained copies of three native drawings done in about 1840, one of which depicts "*Atotarho* [Thadoda:ho?] confronted by two reformers"; it was published as plate 14 in the Bureau of American Ethnology's annual report for 1880–81.[6] Referring to previous work at Cattaraugus, Curtin wrote:

6. The drawing is described in a recently discovered letter from Curtin to Major John Wesley Powell, director of the Bureau of American Ethnology (Curtin to Powell, Seneca, Newton Co., Missouri, 20 February 1884, National Anthropological Archives). The copies that Curtin sent to Powell are evidently from the same source, if not originals, as published.

The originals were painted, it is said, about forty years ago. The copies were made under difficulties but are of the same size as the originals. The explanations under the pictures are exactly the same. . . .

In the third picture are the three chief characters in the establishment of the league of the "Five Nations," Haiawatha, Ganowida, and Tododaho. . . . Haiawatha is represented [in one story] as the first to use shell wampum. The shells he found on the dry bed of a lake after a tremendous flock of ducks had carried all the water away. Tadodaho the Onondaga chief is represented as a mighty wizard and terrible personage. Whenever he wanted to kill people he shouted and all who heard his voice fell dead. The great snake coiled around his body, which used to thrust its head over his right shoulder, was his *membrum virile*. Haiawatha succeeded in cutting off its head and reducing the trunk to the normal length of the fifth member of a man's body (as the Mohammedans call it). The snakes in his hair were removed altogether, and as an Indian remarked to me the other day are now flourishing in the boots of many American tribes [referring to the cowboy boots that modern Indians fancy].

Two comments on the Hewitt and Curtin findings are in order. It would appear that shamans were suspected of rape in a society where ideally warriors never raped women. All later versions of the myth clean up this reference to the culture hero's sex organs, and some authorities have vehemently denied it, but Hewitt's 1892 paper represents his early and best period of fieldwork.

It is but a step from the metamorphosis of the unnatural Thadoda:ho? to the formation of the confederacy or commonwealth of natural and reasonable men. So the remainder of Buck's account, like other versions, relates to extensions of this idea. Deganawi:dah's message of overcoming blood feud assumes the nature of law. It is a plea for the formation of nations of natural men, which is the true meaning of the term *ongwe hon:we*. In such a polity chiefs must be patient, long-suffering, and courageous; their essential quality is that of men of peace. By extending this principle to other nations, it becomes the law of peace—the Great Law of Equity—which became the leitmotif of the extended house.

Later chapters on the Beaver Wars will enlighten us as to how these ideals were fulfilled—how with a wampum belt in the left hand and a warclub in the right, warriors of the league approached surrounding tribes. The alternatives were to bury the hatchet, come into the protection of the Longhouse, and sit beneath the "tree of the long leaves," or perish. Others might follow the "white roots of peace" that extended to the cardinal directions and reached the warmth of the Onondaga council fire. An eagle atop a tall pine would monitor their approach. It is only natural that the narrators of the myth should feed back into it the stuff of history and telescope two centuries of Indian wars. Nevertheless, the plot remains firm.

The bylaws of the league follow Buck's account as appendixes. Just as the law of composition of murder became by extension the Great Law of Equity, there had to be some hedge against failure. Nations of natural men rest their heads on the "great white roots of peace," but the time may come, tradition warns, "when we may be few and feeble, then we must go to find a great elm tree for support." Meanwhile, let no one strike an ax into the roots of the Tree of Peace, lest blood flow from the root, and from the mouth of the culprit as an enemy of the league.

Completion of the grand plan involved designing emblems of office—antlers for the chiefs. It was decreed that none should succeed the prophet Deganawi:dah, and that the roll of the fifty founders should continually enumerate their titles, which Buck listed and ranked by nation and committee (Hewitt 1892: 143–44). Relationship and assigned duties of nations within the confederacy carry kinship terms and metaphoric descriptions—the Onondagas were designated father's kin to the Oneidas, name bearers, and firekeepers—"where our thoughts are heaped." Provisions for unity and succession were fitted with symbols for remembering them. The constant theme that runs through these passages holds that nothing is certain: not life, kinship, or even death. Symbolism for maintaining the fiction of common hunting grounds suggests a northern hunting people; little is said of agriculture. The prime symbol is the forest, for the Iroquois were indeed a woodland people.

Wampum is the credential of a chief's title, and wampum belts preserve the archival memory of transactions in council. Buck ends his relation with eight memoranda concerning belts that relate to people joining the league in later times. Each memorandum refers to a particular belt that he then held as wampum keeper for the Six Nations council at Grand River. They contain no reference to the founding of the league. (The text speaks of a belt of twelve or thirty-six lines, as the case may be, which refers to belts that many rows deep, just as the New York colonial records read.) The first six records cited refer to Algonquian-speaking peoples of the upper Great Lakes; the seventh relates to the Wyandots, Shawnees of Ohio, and Cherokees. The eighth speaks of taking council brands from the central fire at Onondaga to kindle fires among the Cherokees, Wyandots, and Tionontatés late in the eighteenth century. None of these belts refers to the era of the founding of the league, nor do they reference important transactions with European powers. Evidently the cultural memory of such events had worn thin during a century at Grand River. Before the passing of learned men such as John Skanawati Buck, the chiefs of the Six Nations Reserve would make several attempts to translate the wampum belts into writing.

□□◇□□

Seth Newhouse (1842–1921) was the most prolific and controversial of the native scribes. Although by Iroquois reckoning an Onondaga through his mother, he took the name Dayodekane from the Hawk clan; his father was evidently a Mohawk and he was enrolled that way in the agency records. Fulfilling the propensity at Six Nations for double descent, he passed his political career in the cause of the Mohawk warrior party. An accomplished orator, he served as speaker for the warriors and also for the women before the council of chiefs, of which he was never a full-fledged member. But he was also useful to the old chiefs like John Buck and Smoke Johnson because he had learned to write in both English and Mohawk. This facility enabled him to put down their words, to record the rituals for mourning and installing chiefs, and to codify the laws. The writing activities of Seth Newhouse during the closing decades of the nineteenth century produced some fascinating and at times controversial manuscripts relating the beginnings of the confederacy. He wrote in reservation English, which satisfied neither the chiefs nor the ethnologist Hewitt. At one point Hewitt persuaded him to set his English back into his first language, namely Mohawk, so as to preserve the native style and concepts.

The noted Seneca anthropologist and museum curator Arthur C. Parker afterward acquired, edited, and published a Newhouse manuscript almost verbatim, setting off a considerable literary controversy (Parker 1916b; Goldenweiser 1916; Hewitt 1917; Fenton 1968). Not unlike two rival ritual holders, the two native Iroquoianists remained implacable enemies: it annoyed Hewitt to be scooped, and while he held out for an authentic version that he never produced, Parker somewhat uncritically issued an English version that has become the standard. The manuscript that Parker edited is not known to exist, but its publication and the bitter reviews that it provoked enabled me later to identify the manuscript of still another Newhouse "constitution" (Fenton 1949b). Both Newhouse manuscripts contained variants of the league epic.

Matters of style and unique features not present in other versions concern us just now. Newhouse dated Manuscript I at 1885, but he continued working on it off and on until 1898 (Fenton 1949b). Parker acquired Manuscript II in 1910 and published it six years later. The second is evidently a refined draft of the first.

Manuscript I omits Deganawi:dah's birth and journey but appends it as an afterthought; rather, it opens with the trials at Onondaga of Ayonhwatha, whose name is the Mohawk variant of Hiawatha, and takes him through exile and arrival in the Mohawk country. There he meets Deganawi:dah, and the two collaborate in founding the league.

Two things are immediately apparent about Newhouse. First, old customs obviously interested him, and he loaded the narrative with ethnographic detail. Second, he was a Mohawk patriot. As such he stressed that Mohawk was the first nation to accept the principles of civil authority, peace, and justice. Moreover, he projected into the dim reaches of the past forms of Mohawk ritualism that were current late in the nineteenth century. Likewise, in myth he found justification for the present. Both processes are always at work in mythmaking.

We hear of watch houses in cornfields, a skin pouch for wampum, and wampum headbands identifying chiefs prior to deer antlers at confederation. A screech owl forebodes death. Preoccupation with witchcraft, a perennial Iroquois phobia, manifests itself when an elder Onondaga suitor, on being rejected, assumes the guise of a screech owl, climbs a tree, and regurgitates pellets of clay in true owl manner, only to become the victim of clan vengeance and be shot down with bow and arrow.

Manuscript II improves on these vignettes of early Iroquois life. Etiquette requires a stranger, on entering the lands of another people, to wait smoking his pipe beneath a tree until discovered and brought to town. If he must kill game, he should hang the pelt in clear sight of resident hunters. The narrative describes the making of wampum from unio shells and how it is handled in council.

The earlier version is more specific about the discovery and transformation of Thadoda:hoɁ. He was discovered living south of town in a swale, inhabiting a nest of bulrushes (manuscript II). His discoverers were hushed in the presence of this "preternatural monster," in Hewitt's words; his hair was of snakes, his finger ends snake heads, his forearms crooked, his body crooked in seven places, and his penis passed round his neck to reach the ground. Removing the kinks from Thadoda:hoɁ's body and parts required five strings of wampum, one of which was measured to span from thumb to extended middle finger, the length of a normal male organ.

The first version engages in two bits of projective ritual antiquarianism. At the incident where Deganawi:dah arranged thirteen strings of wampum over a horizontal pole and encoded them with thirteen "words," Newhouse inserted the Requickening Address of a then-respected contemporary ritualist, John Buck, and repeated this bit of business as needed. Likewise, when Deganawi:dah grouped the chiefs and established their rank order in tribal and confederate councils, Newhouse fell back on the familiar Roll Call of the Chiefs and labeled it the "Confederating Hymn." Here he employed the orthography of old Smoke Johnson, Hale's informant, who died at the age of ninety-four in 1887 (Fenton 1950: 40–41, pls. 9–12). Both of Newhouse's sources go back to the settlement of Grand River and undoubtedly reach into the eighteenth century.

Quite early in the narrative Newhouse introduced the concept of a "systematic constitution" comprising thirty numbered articles, and he repeated them, implying that they were composed before confederation; but there is every indication that these bylaws were a recent compilation.

The same version employs a unique literary device for gaining listeners' attention and keeping them informed. As the peace embassy progresses toward Onondaga, a questioning tree knot beside the path asks the passing column, "What's up?" Deganawi:dah replies: "We are on the way to Onondaga to pacify . . . Atotarho." This device serves to connect the thread of the narrative while an hour-long chant is interjected. Allusions to time—a stop overnight, which means a year—more abundant in Manuscript II, indicate that confederation was a process of some duration, not a single event.

It is important to remember that both documents were composed during a period of radical cultural change and political tension when the descendants of the Six Nations were turning their minds to elective government. By this time, changes in the content of the ritual made remembering the old symbolism of union quite difficult, and the alleged details of confederation at this late date seemed, to many, irrelevant.

Dayodekane soon suffered the disillusionment of authorship. Having completed his "constitution," he had it accepted by the council of women, who were the heirs of the titles and trustees of the chiefs in council, meeting in council with the Mohawk warriors, only to have the chiefs themselves defer acceptance and appoint a committee of their peers to prepare an official version. The people were at variance with their chiefs. Like the culture hero Hiawatha, Dayodekane wondered why no one would really listen, and he contemplated exile to Indian Territory (Oklahoma). One is reminded of the theme that an earlier hero muttered over the requickening wampums when he was first discovered lurking in the watch huts of Mohawk cornfields: "Men boast what they would do in extremity, but they do not do what they say!" Newhouse was prepared to offer the thirty articles of his "constitution" as the solution to the procedural ills of his people. There were no takers.

Manuscript II had a long literary career while natives and scholars reworked it to satisfy Parker. It reflects, as Goldenweiser wrote, "Iroquois society . . . distorted by abnormal social conditions . . . during the breakdown of a highly complex and coherent socio-political system, under the stress of modern conditions" (1916: 435–36). Although it has become the standard source for contemporary Iroquois ideology, its importance is for comparative purposes: for constant elements of the plot, incidents, literary devices, symbolism, customs, themes, and rationalization of usage. It enumerates so-called confederate laws, which grew in number from 30 to 117, and these separate into the "Tree of the Long Leaves," the "Emblematic Union Compact," and "Skanawati's Law of Peace and War." This effort to codify custom law in the metaphorical language of ancient usage at times reaches literary peaks, as in the opening statement: "I am Dekanawidah and with the Five Nations' Confederate Lords I plant the Tree of the Great Peace . . . in the territory of *Adodarho,* and the Onondaga Nation" (Parker 1916b: 30).

But despite all this, as Goldenweiser concluded, " 'The Constitution of the Five Nations' is a figment. It does not exist." There is only the legend concerning the formation of the league, and the versions that come as close to the traditional record as we can hope to approach are those of the "chiefs" and Gibson's two attempts.

□□◇□□

One aspect of these several native versions that is little understood is that they all represent an effort to justify the continuance of the hereditary system of chiefs on the Six Nations Reserve, to codify custom law, and to bring system to tradition. The proponents of these efforts were then under attack from reform elements in the native population who were seeking representative government by election. It was to answer these critics, and partly in dissatisfaction with Newhouse, that the old chiefs appointed a Committee on Indian Rites and Customs.

During 1900 the committee labored to prepare a substitute for the Newhouse "constitution," which they had three times heard, found faulty, and rejected. The committee included Chief John A. Gibson because he regularly related portions of the tradition at Condolence Councils and he had dictated the full text to Hewitt the previous year. The committee produced a document that subsequently appeared in two places. Duncan Campbell Scott, for many years secretary of the Department of Indian Affairs and active in Ottawa literary circles, edited the piece and to it added ritual chants from Hale before communicating it to the Royal Society of Canada (Scott 1912). The text of this report was the second of the manuscripts that Parker "discovered" at Six Nations in 1910, which he reprinted without acknowledgment to Scott (Parker 1916b: 65-109). Hewitt, having also acquired a copy of the chiefs' report for the Bureau of American Ethnology (MS 1510), descended on Parker with a fury, as did Goldenweiser (Hewitt 1917; Goldenweiser 1916; Fenton 1968: 38-46).

Although a powerful voice in the committee of chiefs, Gibson seems not to have been satisfied with the English version that the committee produced, for he twice dictated the tradition in the original Onondaga to visiting ethnologists. Hewitt's phonetic transcription, done in 1899, runs to 189 pages of Onondaga text, a language in which Hewitt developed competence and accuracy. In several respects this is the best extant version: it is concise, it embraces the tradition, it contains the major recurring themes, it employs major motifs having supernatural connotations, and it is replete with explanatory elements. Nevertheless, Hewitt kept searching for an "authentic version" that would account for all variants, and he kept correcting and revising the text with other informants, only partially translating the document and never publishing it.

Chief Gibson finished relating the entire tradition to Goldenweiser on 30 June 1912 and died suddenly of a stroke on 1 November of the same year. Goldenweiser transcribed the Onondaga on 525 pages of yellow-lined paper and never translated it. English translations of both Gibson versions were until recently unpublished (Fenton 1975: 134–36). Hanni Woodbury (1992) has since accomplished a linguistic recovery of the Goldenweiser text with parallel English translation.

Having prepared a concordance of all known versions, I shall return to their commonalities later. Meanwhile, my English translation of the Gibson-Hewitt version, in the following chapter, demonstrates the basic structure and affords examples of the literary aspects of the epic (Fenton and Gibson 1941).

CHAPTER 5

CHIEF GIBSON'S ACCOUNT

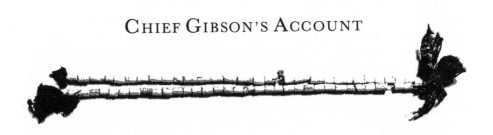

It is said that Deganawi:dah was born in the land that was called *Tkaha:nayenʔ*, where there are bottom lands, but which at the present time is called *Ganyenʔgeh*, "at the flint place" (now Mohawk), situated on the north side of the great lake [Ontario], originally called *Sganyadai:yoʔ*, "the beautiful great lake."

That event happened in this way in ancient time when a mother and her daughter had their house at that place. Moreover when the maiden had grown to womanhood and had not yet been with any man, the old woman, her mother, suddenly noticed that surely her daughter was pregnant. At that time the old woman remarked, "Who is the other person then with whom you are about to have a child?"[1]

The maiden replied saying, "I have said that I do not know, for I have never seen any other person but you."

Then at that time the old woman became depressed in her mind. She said, "Certainly you do not love me, and the reason is that it is impossible for you to tell me the truth about what I have asked you." The maiden replied, "Indeed, I have told you the truth. I do not know the source of the thing that has happened to me."

Then the old woman became very distressed. So then it happened that she had a particular dream in which she thought that she had seen a man who said to her, "Now, you must stop sorrowing because your daughter is about to have a child, for I have come to tell you how this has happened to your daughter's person. It is really true that she does not know the source of her present condition. Therefore I will tell you in truth that it came from the skyworld. It is just this, that the Holder of the Heavens, *Dehaenhyawaʔgih*, chose her as the medium through whom shall be born the one he has sent to work here on earth.

"Moreover, when he shall be born you two shall name him *Deganawi:dah*. And the reason he shall have such a name is that he will travel about on the earth; for he is the principal person both in the skyworld and here on earth.[2] For understand, he brings with him Power, *gaʔshasdenhsaʔ*, and also the Great Law, *gayanehsaʔgo:nah*, so

---

1. The Gibson 1912 version opens by saying that warfare was the normal state of affairs and that the mother and daughter were living in exile north of the lake to escape the scalp raids.

2. The Iroquois concept of *hayaʔdagweni: yoʔ* means the master or ruler of things, the proprietor, or the chief person in rank and importance. They use it for head chief, to designate a place of council, as the site where ambassadors meet, and so forth.

that everything shall become peaceful, *sken:non²*, on earth as well as in the sky-world.[3]

"So that is why I have come to tell you what will happen, so that now indeed you shall continue to feel at ease." After that he said, "Moreover, when it shall happen that he travels about don't either of you interfere with his intentions, for he is about to accomplish a most important work among mankind. This is the sum of my words."

The three versions of the league legend to which Chief John A. Gibson contributed—the chiefs' version of 1900 and his 1899 and 1912 accounts—place the scene in the bottomlands around the Bay of Quinte in the vicinity of present-day Kingston, Ontario. They all reiterate the same recurrent themes and motifs: a time of trouble, virgin pregnancy, revelation by dream, and birth and rapid growth of the hero. There follow the incidents of divination by a bleeding tree and of building, launching, and departing in a white stone canoe for the south shore of Lake Ontario. During the years 1899–1912, Gibson changed the specifications from white birch to white stone, although white remained the magical element.

Deganawi:dah revealed his plans to his grandmother:

I am looking for something with which I may build a canoe. For understand that far on lakes and many rivers I will go seeking the council smoke of some people, holding my course steadily toward the sunrise.

The old woman asked, "How long will it be, perhaps, before you will return?" Then Deganawi:dah replied saying, "I am not able to tell that. But this shall happen when I depart, because then yonder tree standing at the edge of the bluff shall be of assistance to us. And then when I shall have gone away, if it becomes necessary for

---

3. Hewitt left a note (Hewitt Papers) on the three dual concepts comprised in the Great Law:

Morgan, Parkman, Hale and other writers have discussed the structure and laws or ordinances of the League of the Iroquois . . . but they have . . . failed to [grasp] . . . the motives and the working principles which lie at the foundation of the League.

The League of the Iroquois was founded on six basic principles. . . . But these six principles . . . were expressed by (only) three terms, each of which denoted two of these underlying principles. These three terms are: *Ne² Skennon²*, *ne² ga: i²hwiyo*, and *ga²shasdenhsen²*. The first as applied to the body politic denotes *peace*, tranquility, rest; but as applied to the human or living body of flesh and blood, it denotes health or soundness, normal functional condition. War, strife, contention is the antithesis of the first meaning; and disease, illness, obsession or possession by another personality, especially . . . through . . . sorcery [is the antithesis] of the second meaning. Here we have the maximum extension and intention in the connotation of a term.

The second term is *ga: i²hwi yo*, which is not so easy of translation into English. Its first denotation is *gospel*, wholesome doctrine, what is good to be heard, ethical teaching, values, ethics,—righteousness. As its second meaning, it denotes justice, right, as formulated in the customs, manners, religion, and ritualistic summations of the past experience of the people. The first is the teaching of a good doctrine; the second is the establishment of the good doctrine in institutional forms.

The third is *ga²shasdensa²*, whose first denotation is force, as expressed in the war power of the people; and its second meaning is the power, force or authority of the *orenda* or magic potency of the institutions of the people. It was at this point only that religion . . . exerted its influence on the organic units of the social structure.

The institutions arising from these six fundamental principles or conceptions were together called *Kayenensha²go: na*, or the Great Commonwealth of Law.

you to know for certain what my fortune is where I have gone, then you shall go to that standing tree, and when you have arrived there, you shall chop into it: if blood flows from it, immediately you shall infer that already some misfortune has befallen Deganawi:dah; but if blood should not flow from it, you shall then infer that Deganawi:dah's luck has been favorable."

In the 1899 Gibson version, the mother of Deganawi:dah gets transformed into the "Mother of Nations," the later "Peace Queen," to preside over a house that straddles the warriors' path between contending nations. In the 1912 version the two are distinct.

The story continues as Deganawi:dah nears the south shore of Lake Ontario:

Suddenly at a distance he saw human beings moving about . . . so he directed his course there. In a very short time he beached his canoe and disembarked. Then he conversed with those men whom he had seen.[4] Now then Deganawi:dah said, "Where do the people reside?" The men replied saying, "Toward the sunrise." Then Deganawi:dah said, "Indeed then it is a fact that no people lives here?" Then the men replied saying, "No [there are none]." Then Deganawi:dah said, "So then what is the reason that you are stirring about here?" The men replied saying, "Actually we are fugitives." Then Deganawi:dah asked saying, "What is the reason that you are running away, for surely there is nothing amiss now?"

The men said, "Understand that it so happened that where we lived our village was destroyed. So really we do not know the state of affairs there." Then Deganawi:dah inquired, "Who are these people who have destroyed your village?" The men answered, "It is indeed that person who continually harms us named *Dehononhsahenhhwaˀ*, "He whose house obstructs the path."[5]

Now then Deganawi:dah affirmed, "Now as for that, from now on that kind of work shall stop. Indeed understand that such an intention was not in the mind of the Creator of the earth and the skyworld.

Moreover, it is also my aim to put a stop to the killing of one another—that too should cease. This is why I am now traveling. Therefore you must all return home: go back there to the place where you all set out."

At that time the men asked, "So who are you? From what place did you set out?" Then Deganawi:dah said, "What is the reason that you ask this of me?" The men replied saying, "That too is only because there is something amazing about your canoe, and you make it skim so rapidly over the water."[6] Then Deganawi:dah said, "I myself indeed am traveling along for the first time because I wish to inspect the settlements of the people scattered here and there, and I also wish to meet the head ones."

Then the men said, "Perhaps it would not result in good if they should see you, for possibly they would kill you on sight, because they do not know you."

4. Another Hewitt note (BAE ms. 1329, Hewitt Papers) reads: "Then he conversed with a man whom he saw there, named *Thori:hwayeri* [M] (*thai:hwayei* [Oa]) of a refugee family."

5. On a road going from east to west like the old Iroquois trail from the Mohawk River to the Genesee, his house would have stood athwart from north to south, effectively blocking the path, because Iroquois longhouses had doors at the ends. This makes that person an obstructionist or saboteur of government.

6. In other accounts the extraordinary aspect of the canoe was that it was made of white stone and with every stroke of the paddle it seemed to leap through the water (S. Gibson).

Deganawi:dah then said, "Who then is this who does not know me?" Then he inquired further, saying, "So where do they live who have the custom of killing people and eating their flesh?"

The men answered, saying, "Just everywhere."

At this point in the narrative the order of episodes in the Gibson versions is inconsistent. In the 1899 version, on the basis of the recommendation of the men by the lake, Gibson places the visit to the Mother of Nations ahead of the cannibal episode. He meets Djigonhsahsen and establishes a mother-son relationship with her. She cooks for her guest before inquiring about his message, and then he unfolds the plan for the Great Peace. She accepts the concepts of the Great Law, and he explains the concept of the extended house, or league. This clues the listener to the plot that the myth elaborates.

> Then Deganawi:dah said, "I will call it *Ganonhsyo:ni*, the Extended House, and also I will designate it *Gayenenhse²go:nah*, the Great Law or commonwealth.[7] And the reason that it shall have the name the Extended House is that in fact it shall come to resemble only a single household (*sganonhsada²*) when it is completed; and, furthermore, mind or reason will become the source of law (*gayanenhse²*), or human welfare; thinking shall replace killing and welfare eventuate; and thus we shall all be peacefully disposed in the minds of the constituent maternal families. Therefore the united minds will be called *Gayanenhse²go:nah*, the Great Law, or Commonwealth. Moreover, this institution shall endure as long as a single maternal family continues, and until the time when the Holder of the Heavens brings about a transformation of things on the earth."

At that time the Mother of Nations apparently understood the proposition and accepted it. It was then, in this traditional historical precedent, that Deganawi:dah laid down the proposition that women should possess the title to chiefship, inasmuch as the Mother of Nations first accepted the principles of righteousness and peace. Deganawi:dah was then prepared to deal with the cannibal. No other incident in the entire epic merits the full coverage accorded to this one in Gibson's 1899 narration to Hewitt.

□□◇□□

Now then Deganawi:dah departed. It was not long afterward when he arrived at the place where stood the house of the cannibal. Then at that time he looked inside the lodge but no one was at home. Thereupon he climbed upon the house to the place through which the smoke issues, and there he lay flat on his chest.

In a very short time now the owner of the house returned bearing on his back [by means of a tumpline] the dead body of a human being. There indoors he threw down the body, which he proceeded to dismember, cut up, and boil the meat. Deganawi:dah watched the entire process.

And moreover when the meat was cooked, then he [the cook] removed the pot from the fire and rested it there at one side. Just then Deganawi:dah was looking down into

---

7. From this derives the proper title of the epic, *ganonhsyo:ni geha²*, "the extended-house kind," or "concerning the league"; properly, "the legend of the Longhouse," hence *hodinonhsioni*, "the people of the Longhouse." Morgan rendered it *Ho-de-no-sau-nee*, which is the preferred spelling of traditionalists today.

the spot where the kettle stood. And meanwhile the houseowner was walking to and fro everywhere inside the house.

Presently the cook said, "Now, perhaps, I should take out the meat and eat now." At that time he took up a bowl of bark and went over to the place where the pot stood. Now as he thought, "I will take out the meat," he was surprised that a human being was looking up from the depths of the standing pot. Just then he stopped taking up the meat. What's more he withdrew and sat down in the place where he was accustomed to sit.[8] Now for a fact he pondered many things.

In a little while he then pronounced, "Most astonishing what has happened." At that he now stood and again went to where the pot stood. Then again he peered into the depths of the pot. It was just the same: the man was still looking up at him. At that time he said, "Someone, perhaps one of those that wander about, is bewitching me."

Then the owner of the house drew back, and it was then that he looked upward to the place where the smoke is drawn out. Nobody did he see. At that time he said, "So really there is no one attempting to trick me." Now he considered many things. In a little while he then said, "So then it is really I myself that is looking up from the depths of the pot. My personal appearance is most amazing. So, on the contrary, perhaps my manner of doing is not so beautiful, that it should continue thus to be my purpose to keep killing people and eating their flesh. And, moreover, perhaps it is best that I should discontinue my habits. Furthermore, maybe it will happen that I shall see some person, whoever it may be, if, perchance, I shall see someone coming to visit my house, that he will tell me what I should do to compensate for the number of human beings whom I have made to suffer, in order that peace may prevail."

At that time he took up the pot and went outside in the direction of a nearby running stream and there he descended its high bank.

At once Deganawi:dah came down from the housetop, and hurrying, ran toward the place where the houseowner had gone down the bank. Deganawi:dah was approaching quite near when the householder came up the bank carrying the now empty pot, and stopped when Deganawi:dah reached there. Now the one who was standing there said, "It is true that just now I am seeking a congenial friend." Then he added, "Come, let's both go back inside."

At that time they both went back inside the house, and now the houseowner set the pot in its accustomed place. Then the houseowner said, "Be seated over there across the fire; I will sit down here on this side. You as a visitor in my house and I shall sit with the fire between us; and the reason for this taking place is that I have a new experience to relate. So as owner of the house I shall begin and tell it clear to the end. Then you in turn may relate your message to the end. For surely, perhaps, you must bring some message."[9]

At that time Deganawi:dah replied, "You and I agree entirely."

Thereupon the houseowner said, "So this shall be first. I shall relate what happened this very day, a new experience. A very short while ago I went away; I had gone

8. At home a man's place was on his bunk before the fire, out of woman's way. There, when not sleeping, he repaired his hunting gear, played the flute, related his adventures, or received friends with singing and conversation.

9. It is the Iroquois custom for the host to speak first, addressing the guest across the fire. Then the visitor speaks to the very end of the message that he carries. A speaker is always heard to the end, never interrupted. This bit of etiquette becomes expected protocol in treaty negotiations.

hunting for men, moreover I killed one and brought it back. When I returned I cut
up the flesh, and then I boiled the meat. So when the meat was cooked, then I removed
the pot from the fire and set it down over there. At that time I made ready to eat. And
so when ready I then desired to take up the meat; I was surprised that there was a
man looking up from the bottom of the pot. His personal beauty amazed me greatly,
for never before had I seen a person of such form as the one who looked upward.

"Then I began thinking. I thought that perhaps someone was only playing a trick
on me [bewitching me]. And then I looked all around above me where the smoke is
drawn out. I saw nothing. At that time I withdrew and seated myself here where I am
accustomed to sit. And then I considered the appearance of the person who was
looking up from the bottom of the pot.[10] It was quite a long time before I came to the
conclusion that it was perhaps I myself who was looking up from there. At that time
I thought, 'Therefore my body must be beautiful, and indeed my habit [custom] of
killing human beings and eating their flesh is not befitting my form [appearance].' I
decided I would now abandon the habit.

"Then I thought I might see someone, that maybe one would visit my house, and
that he would tell me perhaps what I should do to make restitution to those minds I
had offended by killing people belonging to various bands, so that there might be a
just peace again. Then I arose and took up the pot and went out of the house and
descended the river bank, and there where there is an uprooted tree I poured out the
contents of the pot I was carrying, namely the flesh of a dead human being. I climbed
up the bank. I was surprised now, nearby you were walking along.

"At once my life rejoiced when I saw you. I thought, 'That really fulfills my mind's
desire, to meet a friend.' So now then I have finished. Now then in turn it rests with
you. Moreover, I in turn will listen to whatever message you bring."

Then Deganawi:dah stood and said, "Truly what has happened today is indeed a
wonderful story. Now you have changed the very pattern of your life. Now a new frame
of mind has come to you, namely Righteousness and Peace. Right now you are seeking
someone to come and tell you what you should do in order that peace shall prevail in
the divers places where you have done injury among mankind.

"Now what is more I will tell you [what to do]. This is the very message that I bring.
I too am seeking a certain man [a particular friend] who would work with me; he and
I would collaborate to advance the matter of Righteousness and Peace.

"Now indeed you and I have met, our two minds meet on the level [are quite
agreed]. Therefore this shall come to pass. So then you and I shall work together at
preparing food. Accordingly you shall go for fresh water, and you shall dip it from the
river as it flows along.[11] And as for me, I will go hunt for a game animal. Moreover,
it is enough that when you get back that you shall have the water hot by the time I
myself return. Then at that time you and I will work together at boiling meat. At that
time you and I will merge our two minds."

At that time Deganawi:dah sat down again. Then the houseowner stood and said,
"That is exactly what I have in mind. Therefore it shall come about as you have
outlined it."

10. Water scrying to perceive the identity of a sorcerer is a characteristic Iroquois method of
divination.
11. One should not oppose the forces of nature. In making medicine, water is always taken in the
direction of the current. This is a persistent theme in Iroquois life to this day.

Then Deganawi:dah arose and said, "So now in fact let us two depart. You shall go fetch water, and I will go hunt."

At that time the two set out. And the owner of the house went along rejoicing when he descended the river bank. He hastened to dip up the fresh water. Then he returned home. As soon as he got back immediately he heated the water. Just then Deganawi:dah also returned, having killed a deer with quite large antlers. At that time Deganawi:dah said, "Now indeed the time has come when you and I shall begin to work together; for you and I will put [on the fire] a pot of wild animal flesh [venison]. And it is on this that the Ruler, the Holder of the Heavens, intended that the human beings living on earth should continue to subsist."

At that time in fact the two began to skin the game animal with the large antlers. And the owner of the house moreover now said, "What use shall we two make of these antlers? Indeed will it not be impossible for human beings to live by them?"

Then Deganawi:dah said, "We two shall remove them, and these antlers shall be placed up here [probably pointing to his head] upon humans. At that time it will be possible for all mankind to continue to live by them."[12]

At that time the two men removed the antlers and then cut up the flesh and boiled the meat. Now when it was cooked, working together the two men lifted the pot [from the fire] and set it down to one side. At that time Deganawi:dah said, "In what place were you standing when the thought came to your mind that you had now seen yourself as you actually appear? So stand there."

Then the owner of the house said, "Right here I stood." Now then Deganawi:dah stood in that place and said, "Here in fact is the place where your wisdom [reasoning] lies." At that time Deganawi:dah placed his two hands on the houseowner's head and then passed them down over his face, and said, "One [the Master of Life] has brought you mind [reason]. Now moreover you and I will look into the pot." At that time the two looked into the pot, and for a fact the two men saw that their two bodies appeared identical in the reflections from the depth of the pot.[13]

Then the owner of the house said, "It is wonderful that you and I have similar appearances." Then Deganawi:dah said, "In fact it is true that he [the Master of Life] has endowed both of us with reason." Then he added, "So now you and I shall indeed eat."

And further when the two men had finished eating, the owner of the house asked, "What then shall happen to the part of the human carcass that I have left?" At that time Deganawi:dah said, "You and I will bury it in the earth."

The origin of human burial on a high bluff precedes an explanation of subsistence on venison and antlers as emblems of chiefship. Humans fill their stomachs with venison and rest their minds with confidence on the wearers of antlers. Nature and culture symbolically nurture society. There follows a dialogue defining justice and peace, concepts that will change the minds of men from warfare to coexistence. When asked what he would call the new order, Deganawi:dah replies, "As to that when it is completed people will regularly call it *Ganonhsyo:ni*?, the completed

---

12. Humans subsist on venison, and the antlers of the buck deer, which are to continue as symbols of chiefship, shall sustain the people.

13. Here is the justification for thinking that Deganawi:dah and the house owner are two aspects of a single personality.

house (extended lodge), and also *Gayanensha?go:nah*, the Great Law (or Commonwealth), or the Great Peace." Thus the reformed cannibal accepts the principle, first after the Mother of Nations. He is as yet unnamed.

The identity of the cannibal is in some dispute. Gibson has Deganawi:dah name him Hayenhwatha, "Early Riser," in the 1899 version; the next year the chiefs equate him with the Onondaga sorcerer Thadoda:ho?, as Newhouse did twenty years earlier. But in 1912 Gibson places Hayenhwatha in the Mohawk village council that requires the prophet to undergo an ordeal before accepting his message.

□□◇□□

The main versions feature the test theme in which the prophet is required to climb a tall pine on the brink of the gorge at Little Falls on the Mohawk River, which is then felled into the river. In Gibson's 1899 version, Deganawi:dah is rescued by Hayenhwatha, whom the prophet sent on ahead and so named when the two separated. These separations and alternate appearances become important later. Snatched from the torrent, the prophet sends Hayenhwatha back up the bank in his stead and departs in the canoe for the Cayuga country. But in Gibson's 1912 telling, scouts find the prophet at a smoke rising from a fire at the river's edge by a cornfield. He is escorted to town and names the three leading Mohawk chiefs for their activities and opinions. The formation of the Mohawk council assumes the aspect of a historical event.

All versions feature the episode in which Hiawatha loses his family and "splits the sky" (goes south), but the timing and geography differ in the two Gibson versions, as might be expected, for there is no correct version.[14] Other versions make it an Onondaga event, in which the hero, deeply depressed after losing all of his daughters to the sorcery of an Onondaga shaman, splits the sky into the wilderness, haunts the borders of settlements, is invited to council, but departs again until he communicates the rudiments of woods'-edge protocol, teaches the requickening rite that he devises, and settles down as a Mohawk chief.

In earlier versions of the myth, both Newhouse and Buck place the incident in which ducks magically take up water and reveal wampum during Hiawatha's wandering toward the Mohawk country. Both Gibson versions, however, postpone it well into the confederation process when Deganawi:dah requires wampum beads to make up belts to memorialize the completed league. He instructs Hiawatha where and how he will discover unio shells. Gibson's 1899 text reads:

> Then Deganawi:dah said, "Hiawatha, I detail you to go to yonder lake. And accordingly when you reach there you shall see a large number of species of ducks floating around on the lake, and as you watch them, when they take flight they will take up with them all of the water from the lake. Then at that time go forward and you will see there on the bottom snail shells which you will bring back. And these we shall use in the work we are advancing. And with these we shall lay down symbols that will serve

14. Hanni Woodbury (personal communication, 7 August 1990) notes that because Gibson's 1912 version is much more like the chiefs' version than the 1899 version, she regards this as evidence that participating in the committee of chiefs was a learning experience for Gibson, or at least that it seems to have changed his mind on some issues. She does not agree with me that the episodes exist "more or less at random in the minds of myth makers." This idea of randomness contradicts the point that the versions from Six Nations came out of a politically loaded climate, as I have maintained elsewhere.

as marks of identification for [the concepts of] Power, Righteousness and Peace, and also Mind (Reason): these shall be the foundation of our house."

Then at that time Hiawatha set out and went toward the place to which he was directed. So he arrived there; it was a lake; he saw there a great flock of various wild species of ducks on the water. He approached cautiously, but when he stood, then he saw them all fly up taking with them all of the water in the lake. Then Hiawatha approached, now then he saw it there—several different colors of snail shells scattered about on the bottom. Then right then and there he picked them up and put them in a pouch made of fawn skin. . . . After that he returned to where Deganawi:dah waited.

Twelve years later Gibson ascribed this adventure to Hiawatha alone during a recess in the confederation process. Hiawatha sits there for a long time motionless, but when he stands the ducks take off. This time the shells are white. These would prove better than quills or elderberry shoots when strung or woven into belts to document the Great Law.

These variations in a single narrator's telling simply demonstrate that the incidents and episodes that make up the myth and constitute its genre exist more or less at random in the minds of mythmakers and that no two recitations are ever identical.

One other mythical incident, found in the chiefs' version of 1900 and Gibson's of 1912, deserves notice because it documents the hypothesis that the Peacemaker and Hiawatha represent two aspects of a single personality. Following the ordeal at the gorge, Hiawatha, as emergent survivor and guest, is given a place to sleep in the chief's house. In the night, during an apparent dream, Deganawi:dah comes outside to speak to Hiawatha, who goes out "by the wall" to receive the prophet's report of discoveries during his travels among the upper nations and to outline the prospects for achieving peace among the nations. Both return inside together to sleep, without the chief, who is watching the door, noticing their reentry. The next day Hiawatha is able to produce the prophet, who outlines his plan for confederation.

The account of the process of confederation, although not without its magical episodes—notably the transformation of scouts into birds and the reformation of the shaman Thadoda:ho?—assumes the aspect of a historical narrative. The main events that describe the naming of the principals and explain their relationship as symbolic kinsmen appear in earlier versions. Gibson, however, outlines the structure of the league and relates the investing of leading chiefs with antlers as symbols of identity in considerable detail. The league is now all but complete: the seating in council, the order of debate, and provision for compromise are in place; but there are two head warriors of remote Seneca towns who for years have been unprepared to grasp the Great Peace. By "extending the rafters" metaphorically they are ultimately co-opted and made head warriors of the confederacy and keepers of the western door of the Longhouse. The theme of local village autonomy, which narrators projected into recitals of tradition, runs strong in the confederation process and persisted in later times when the league itself could not be made to work, when new leaders emerged, and when once more government became a confederacy of village chiefs.

Gibson devoted considerable space to symbolism, to which I shall return, while the leading chiefs go home and enlist tribal delegations among constituent clans and villages. These converge on Onondaga to be duly invested with antlers with the titles assigned them by clan mothers.

Bylaws for the operation of the league council take up a substantial portion of text. Provision for deposing wayward chiefs and replacing them follow. When a tree falls (a chief dies) entire moieties go into mourning until a successor is found; his clan and nation prepare to raise up the fallen tree and to requicken and install his successor through an elaborate ceremony of condolence. The rituals of the Condolence Council, which feature the eulogy, or Roll Call of the Fifty Founders of the League, represent a received tradition and project into the past ceremonies current in Gibson's time. They lift up the minds of the mourning moiety and, as here recited by Gibson, constitute the most complete record of these events in the literature.

□□◇□□

Recent scholarship affords two ways of looking at this myth. A myth like the Deganawi:dah epic consists of all its versions, and the various versions may be thought of as belonging together; in that sense the myth has a single identity over time "as long as it is felt to be such" (Lévi-Strauss 1963: 217). Although the Iroquois profess that they control verbatim recall, each narrator has his own version that he never relates precisely in the same way twice, as witness the two Gibson versions. There is bound to be substitution of content over time, and some incidents are lost. Nevertheless, the various versions comprise a single genre, which listeners recognize as belonging to the one myth. One need not seek the one true version, as Hewitt sought in vain.

The myth also may be regarded as a pattern of sequence, which resembles the paradigm of a revitalization movement (A. Wallace 1958a). This approach is essential for understanding the content of the myth and its symbolism. Reconstructing the main outlines of the myth from existing versions, one finds central to the plot the presence of feuding factions who one by one accept the message of peace that is carried by a fatherless boy, the typical Iroquoian culture hero. The hero, or Peacemaker, teams up with a disturbed chief—who is himself the victim of witchcraft—to reform society, create symbols of its identity and unity, and establish rules and procedures for its governance and perpetuation. At the end the hero departs, promising to return on call whenever disaster threatens the system.

The myth has nine constant elements (adapted from Wallace):

1. Villages of male hunters and female horticulturists, widely scattered in the forest, are disrupted and abandoned by the consequences of blood feud—murder, scalping, cannibalism—which amount to warfare among the Iroquois themselves.
2. There exist a few reasonable and concerned individuals who live as refugees at the margins or who are caught in the mesh of existing practices, but who prefer living a settled life with kindred.
3. Deganawi:dah, a fatherless boy, is born to a young woman living with her mother as a displaced person north of Lake Ontario. In the culture-hero mold, he performs miracles, embarks on a mission, preaches, reforms individuals, rebuilds society, and disappears to rejoin the supernaturals.

4. Hiawatha, a recidivist cannibal, has a vision of Deganawi:dah, is reformed, accepts the message that murder should cease because all humans are kindred, and joins the peace mission. But this natural man is soon bereft of his daughters by the acts of a wicked shaman. He quits Onondaga and heads south into the wilderness to wander alone, occasionally camping in field shelters, suffering severe agitated depression until he reaches a Mohawk settlement where he is relieved by the protocol for greeting strangers.

5. A Mother of Nations who has fed passing war parties accepts the message of peace and epitomizes the role of matron in the ongoing human family.

6. Thadoda:ho?, the snake-haired shaman of Onondaga whose acts of sorcery have driven reasonable men into exile and frustrated efforts for peace, is magically cured by song, relieved of hostility, reduced to normal human sexual proportions, cured of his cannibalistic appetite, and otherwise transformed by ritual acts into a natural man who becomes the reasonable and equable presiding officer of the league.

7. Deganawi:dah's code rests on three concepts—the "good word" (righteousness), "power" (civil authority), and "peace" (health of society)—that together comprise the "Great Law" (a synonym for the commonwealth, or league, itself). His message demands that feuds cease, asserts that kinship extends to all men of all nations on earth, and holds that the continuance of the human family depends on it. He devises symbols of identity, invents metaphors, composes songs, and makes ritual speeches to remind people where their confidence reposes.

8. To Hiawatha's concern to find a proper way to console mourners of the dead and to restore individuals, families, and nations to society is ascribed the origin of the condolence ritual that requickens the living in the name of the dead and dissipates the tensions of blood feud.

9. The joint mission of Deganawi:dah and Hiawatha to gain acceptance of the code among the nations employs the strategy of granting local autonomy to gain assent and then follows the tactics of surround and concert. Tribal moieties of Mohawk-Seneca and Oneida-Cayuga combine to bring Onondaga into the league. Confederation was a long process of compromise, reformulating relationships, and providing for the extension of the Longhouse—the symbol of a polity based on kinship—to shelter holdouts and to incorporate other nations who were drawn to accept its principles.

These nine elements, as Professor Wallace demonstrated, may be arranged, with slight modification, to form the portrait of a revitalization movement. In Wallace's view, Hiawatha, an Onondaga who later became a Mohawk chief, was the victim of the social disorganization described in the myth. Hiawatha experiences an episode of agitated depression during which he has visions of two sorts. In one phase he practices cannibalism (which is not historically untrue of the Iroquois), and he has a vision of a supernatural named Deganawi:dah who reforms him and appoints him a special emissary. This view is strengthened by the frequent conversations of the two characters in the myth, as already noted; their clandestine meetings at night and in remote quarters; their alternate roles in the formation of the confederacy; and their infrequent appearances together. Finally, Deganawi:dah declines office, but the title "Hiawatha" remains today second on the Roll Call of the Founders. Wallace suggests further that Thadoda:ho? may represent another facet of the same personality, but I favor his reservation that there may have been a shaman of that name at Onondaga. Today the title Thadoda:ho? stands for the "first Lord of the League," whom contemporary annalists seldom recall as a Freudian monster transformed to a natural man.

Without undertaking a complete structural analysis of the myth, it is apparent that the Deganawi:dah epic is a composite discourse composed of myth and legend that verge on native history. It may be analyzed in stages. Viewed as a historical discourse, it comprises three main parts, or stages: the myth of Deganawi:dah and the conversion of the cannibal; the legend of the conversion of tribes to the cause of peace; and the principles of the league, its internal structure and rituals.

The several versions of the epic represent a learned tradition that native Iroquois like Buck, Newhouse, and Gibson (and even Hewitt) were constantly revising, as if to attain a true ethnohistory. As I have already observed, they were responding to pressures of the day and striving to set standards for their own culture. In part they were reacting to Morgan and Hale by amending and expanding existing knowledge of the structure of their confederacy, its laws, and its ritual procedures. This kind of ethnological feedback has continued to the present. Today when Iroquois patriots claim that their confederacy is six hundred years old, they are manifesting a tendency to assign dates and establish historical priority to phenomena that cannot be dated with certainty. The formation of the league was not an event but a gradual process, and this is quite evident from internal evidence in the myth itself.

Of greater importance than dating its founding is the study of the league's internal structure. This native system, as ascribed to Deganawi:dah, should be considered in relation to the analysis of its structure by ethnologists together with historical observations of actual political practice. The elements of its organization constitute an ideal system that has powerful political overtones and may be considered a symbolic system. It is important to know how it was replicated in practice during three hundred years of known Iroquois history.

Returning to the three stages that comprise the structure of the myth that has become a historical tradition, four genres of mythology relate to the Deganawi:dah myth: the cosmology (already discussed in chapter 2), and outcast children, cannibal, and "naked bear" myths. All of these cycles have in common a polarity between the supernatural and the natural, and between order and disorder. Given the social organization described at the opening of the Deganawi:dah myth, the role of the culture hero is to surmount disorder and establish a new order. As a culture hero, Deganawi:dah on the supernatural side is born of a virgin, enjoys rapid growth, manifests extraordinary power in miracles, and has his career cast in a dream. As a social person, moreover, he is concerned for the social order; but having no father, he is a social cripple for want of father's kin (the *agadoni* principle).[15] And his mother or grandmother tries to drown him.

15. Though not in the Gibson versions, the incident of Deganawi:dah's grandmother's attempt to drown him persists among contemporary narrators. Dr. Woodbury takes exception to the implication that the grandmother's motive was that he lacked father's kin, which Woodbury holds is not in line with Iroquoian social sensibilities and reasoning (personal communication, 7 August 1990).

He never quite identifies with society, he refuses to have his name perpetuated, and he returns to the sky world. As a male hero, and an outsider, he preaches the prophetic gifts of the Good Message, peace, and power—together the Great Law; he names chiefs, establishes rules of succession, devises symbols of identity, decrees council procedures, and provides for mourning the dead and requickening the living in their titles.

In animal myths, the disorder-order polarity assumes the form of monstrosities. Animals first exist in large size, which the hero reduces to a size compatible with human beings. Similarly, the transformation of Thadoda:ho?—the reduction of his monstrous sexual organs, snake hair, turtle-claw hands, and bear-paw feet—follows this process. The polarity might also be expressed as a dichotomy between nature and culture.

The episode of Hiawatha's conversion from cannibalism, when compared with the cannibal cycle, which treats of the problems of different groups in the society, is distinguished by the fact that Hiawatha is converted, whereas other cannibals (not unlike European vampires) become irretrievably lost to society. Hiawatha switches to animal food; venison and antlers become symbols of chiefly office and of manhood.[16]

---

16. For pointing out the direction of this analysis I am indebted to Urzsula Chodowiec, a disciple of Lévi-Strauss's who spent a year with me as a special student.

CHAPTER 6

THEMES AND ELEMENTS
OF THE LEAGUE LEGEND

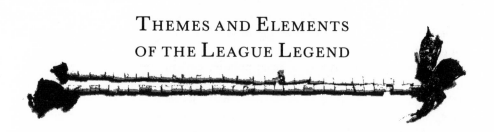

The internal composition of the Deganawi:dah myth becomes evident in a content analysis of the nine major versions when they are arranged chronologically in parallel columns from the most recent (Gibson, 1912) to the earliest (Pyrlaeus, 1743). Several interesting things emerge from this analysis. Modern versions are much more detailed and longer than earlier ones, as if the legend gained content in later times. The longest of the earlier versions (Norton, 1816) yields 86 elements, which contrast with 147 for Newhouse (1880), the 93 of Gibson's first version (1899), 106 for the chiefs' (1900), and 179 for Gibson's second version (1912). The last, however, includes the complete content of the Condolence Council and reduces by 70 elements without it to approximate the dimension of the chiefs' version, to which Gibson was a contributor.

The brevity of earlier versions is undoubtedly a function of communication between informant and recorder. Even the sophisticated Joseph Brant condensed his knowledge in answering the questions of the Reverend Elkanah Holmes, and only John Norton conveys some idea of the richness of content available at the dawn of the nineteenth century.

Certain continuities of actors, incidents, and plot run from the earliest to the later versions. Of these, the traditional elements predominate and bespeak the original historical purpose of the narrative. Recurrent incidents that run like themes to the present commence with Norton. Particular motifs have supernatural connotation. Explanatory elements having temporal, structural, and symbolic significance appear early (Brant, 1801) but drop out or change as traditional knowledge weakens in later times. Finally, the modern versions of Newhouse and Gibson, as previously noted, carry an overburden of modern ritual practice that is projected onto the past, and nineteenth-century political issues are rationalized in symbolic terms.

Today it is taboo to mention the name of the Peacemaker, although he is quoted by name hundreds of times in the narrative. His message has both sacred and political meanings for traditionalists who regard the hero of the epic as a historical personage and the epic as rationale for their national identity and sovereignty, justifying their separatism in the modern world. With this in mind I shall examine the dozen or so constant elements that are present from the beginning. For indeed the historical continuity of the league rests on our ability to trace the early presence of four main features: the myth itself, the Roll Call of the Fifty Founders, the condolence ritual, and the record of regular meetings of the grand council.

□□◇□□

The theme of the troubled nations, of continual blood feud, runs through all of the recent versions after 1880. Neither Norton nor Brant mentions it, but Pyrlaeus states that the confederacy was formed for mutual defense. Conversely, the tradition of rivalry between good and evil Mohawk chiefs (Brant and Norton) drops out of later versions, although Gibson (1899) hints at it. The tension between Mohawk headmen, however, is manifest in the test or ordeal to which the culture hero submits in all versions back to 1816. The cut-bowstring incident (Norton), wherein the hero is saved, gets transformed into making him climb a tall pine tree that is felled into the gorge, ostensibly to drown him.

Heirs to the Mohawk founders insist that the precedence of the Mohawk nation in council stems from a Mohawk leader's first proposing an alliance (Pyrlaeus), and they hold that the ritual chants of the Condolence Council should be rendered in the Mohawk language to constantly validate this priority. The Mohawk priority is further honored by the use of kinship terms among the nations (Pyrlaeus; Brant). The Mohawk nation is the "eldest brother." Mohawk and Oneida are as "father and son," although the culture hero allowed they were equal in status. Lest there be no ambiguity in this structural arrangement, the Mohawk, Onondaga, and, in later usage, Seneca nations were "brothers." The Senecas, being the last to join the league, were first known as "the youngest son," until the Tuscaroras adhered early in the eighteenth century, when the Senecas became the "youngest son but one" (Pyrlaeus). Although they preceded the Onondagas and Senecas into the alliance, becoming "brothers" to the Oneidas, the Cayugas were termed "sons" (or "offspring") to the Mohawk-Onondaga-Seneca phratry (or moiety). The dual divisions of the league are at once "fathers" and "sons," "elder brothers" and "younger brothers," respectively. These structural ambiguities run through history and are probably ancient. Today these kinship or council terms survive in the chant known as Athahinon?keh, "Going on the Road" or "Taking Up the Path," which features the Roll Call of the Founders.

Condolence law states that the dead chiefs must be mourned, the minds of the mourners elevated, and empty seats in the council filled with persons of the name before society may continue and business be transacted. This custom arises from the ancient practice of reinvesting the name or title on a living person of the next or succeeding generation (Pylaeus, 1743, to Gibson, 1912). The approach of the clearminded to the fire of the mourners, the recitation of the names of the founders, and the act of requickening the living in the name of the dead are all mentioned in eighteenth-century versions.

The concept of the completed or extended house as a symbol of the established confederacy runs as a theme throughout all known versions. Narrators employ both the first person plural inclusive form—*agwanonhsioni*, "we of the extended, or completed, house," or the third person plural, "they (the people) of *roti[hodi]nonhsioni*" in Mohawk or Seneca.[1] The colonial records do not reveal an awareness of this concept until well into the seventeenth century. Related to the "one house"

---

1. He-de-no-sau-nee, as L. H. Morgan spelled it, has become the official title of the confederacy in later years and is a poor rendering of *hodinonhsioni*.

concept is the theme of rafters—"extended roof poles, or rafters"—which sheltered other ethnic entities that were taken into the confederacy.

Similarly, the Law of Nomination, which asserts the right and responsibility of a lineage to chose a chief, stands out in nineteenth-century versions (Hale 1883: 31), which stem from eighteenth-century sources.

The Peacemaker's message of "peace, righteousness, and power," which together constitute the Great Law, connotes civil order. The radical nature of this message requires the presence of a counterforce connoting disorder—feud, witchcraft, and murder. The latter role is fulfilled by Thadoda:ho⁷, a character whose person embodies the worst traits of Iroquois personality: fear, suspicion, wrongmindedness. These traits are symbolized by his monstrous physical features. John Skanawati Buck (1892) spared Hewitt none of these details. Norton alluded to them and Newhouse mentioned them, but the committee of chiefs censored them, as did Gibson. Symbolically, the snakes relate to Thunder, the Bear recalls the compact of northern hunters, and Turtle is the father figure in creation.

The theme of Thadoda:ho⁷ re-formed and reclothed by ritual runs throughout the oral literature. That this process of reclothing was not instantaneous is conveyed by an interesting explanatory element wherein a warrior who accompanied the first visit of the reformers returns for his moccasins that he had hung to dry by the side of the house, only to hear Thadoda:ho⁷ complaining that "what was proposed does not fit," by way of indicating that his new garments, symbolizing civil reforms, would take more time to accomplish and require a second fitting.

Other literary devices warn the listener that the league was several years in the making. Newhouse has a whispering tree knot ask passing reformers, "What's up?" An explanation requires the narrator to tell his listeners that the party is en route to Oneida, and thence to Onondaga to re-form Thadoda:ho⁷. The log across the path at Oneida is yet another device to indicate passage of time; it entails a stop overnight, which symbolizes a year. And then there are the concessions made to Thadoda:ho⁷ to bring the Onondaga nation into the league: siting the main fire at Onondaga, making Thadoda:ho⁷ its keeper, referring to him in council as the name bearer, which also stands for his nation, meaning that the chiefs have left their minds there with him (reposed their confidence in him). Moreover, they grant him devices for keeping the agenda clear—a symbolic wing to sweep ashes from the hearth, a rod or pole to dispose of troublesome issues ("to prize out crawling things"). And should trouble arise, he need but shout the length of the house for assistance.

Reform had to await the resolution of the classic Iroquois witchcraft syndrome in which Hiawatha, first an Onondaga reformer and afterward a Mohawk founder, is the principal victim. One by one he loses his kin to the machinations of wicked men, as we have seen. Efforts to relieve his depression fail, and he announces by a song that he will "split the sky," go south to wander in the forest.

Hiawatha's wandering from village to village on the upper Susquehanna watershed, the foreknowledge of his advent, the offers of equal voice in council but failures to summon him to meetings, his repeated departures into the wilderness, the magic revelation of wampum by rising ducks, his gathering shells from the pond slime, his arranging beads in strings, his arrival at the Mohawk town at the mouth of Schoharie Creek, his furtive seclusion in watch shanties by cornfields until a villager discovers him arranging the strings on a horizontal pole while muttering over men's failed promises—all prepare the listener for the "proper way" to lift up the mind of a mourner, to relieve his dark depression, and to return him to the full sunlight of society. All of this is foretold in Norton (Klinck and Talman 1970: 20–30), in both explanatory and thematic form, to be repeated in later versions. The remission of Hiawatha's depression must necessarily precede the reformation of Thadoda:ho?.

Once the protocol is worked out, the words of requickening composed and correlated with particular wampum strings, and the songs learned for driving the message of the Great Peace into Thadoda:ho?'s mind, the remitted Hiawatha can join the prophet Deganawi:dah and take up the path through the nations to where the smoke of Thadoda:ho?'s fire pierces the sky. All versions after Norton's carry this.

Still another literary device places the action in that shadowy time zone beyond tradition when humans and animals conversed readily and assumed the appearance of each other at will. The ducks that Hiawatha encounters converse before turning into birds and flying up, taking the water from the pond. Pairs of scouts sent from the Mohawk country transform themselves into various birds for flight. Norton's cranes (herons) overfly Onondaga to settle in the Seneca country to eat ground nuts and found the Seneca Heron clan.

Modern versions of the epic open with a set of incidents lacking earlier. Among these are virgin pregnancy, anger, depression, and revelation by the grandmother who first attempted to drown the baby, only to learn in a dream that he is a peace prophet. The names of both women symbolize women's roles in horticulture. Modern versions stress the rapid growth of the hero, detail his daily secret departures and returns while building a stone canoe, and relate his prophecy that one may divine his fate by chopping a tree that flows sap or blood as events transpire favorably or badly during his journey. The two women witness from the launching site his magic course over Lake Ontario in the stone canoe, and a refugee camped on the south shore spies his image approaching. The camper then carries the message of the Peacemaker's coming to the Mohawk towns.

□□◇□□

Although not a true state, the Iroquois League was based on kinship, real and fictive. Its formation and successful operation depended on shared kinship usages that reached down to the local level. It accommodated local differences and achieved unity through the principles of unanimity and reciprocity. Each nation had one vote or a veto on the rest. The Peacemaker ended blood feud between villages by co-opting local chiefs, whatever their number, defining their relationships on well-known principles of kinship, and structuring their committees and councils in triads and moieties. He reaffirmed the names of the nations and named the chiefs and assigned them functions, and he granted women the role of chief makers. Further, he ranked society by age and sex: as elders, warriors, women, the public, young people, children, babies on the boards, and "those who face this way beneath the earth" (the unborn). Also available to him was the Iroquois bilateral kinship system, which classifies parallel cousins as siblings, distinguishes cross-cousins but assigns them reciprocal duties, and extends to lineages (by fiction to clans and moieties) demands and obligations of a reciprocal nature. Although the Iroquois ascribe priority of descent, inheritance, and succession to the matrilineage (and by extension to the clan), the system comes into balance by recognizing the father's kindred in the *agadoni* principle of parent (father) and offspring.

Accordingly, chiefs are grouped in triads of siblings, in pairs of parent and offspring, as paired cross-cousins, and in a lone single status that nevertheless is twice *agadoni* to adjacent sets of siblings. Both the dual and tripartite arrangements operated in the grand council. It co-opted two tribal models. On the Mohawk and Oneida tribal council models, each of which was composed of three committees of three chiefs from their respective clans, which shifted to a moiety arrangement with one clan in control, the grand council sat in a tripartite arrangement of Mohawk and Seneca siblings at one side of the fire facing Oneida and Cayuga siblings across the fire, and the Onondaga chiefs sat at the top as firekeepers. But the grand council shifted to moieties of Mohawk-Onondaga-Senecas (*agadoni*, or father's kin) when condoling their "offspring," the Oneida-Cayugas. The moiety system obtained in both Cayuga and Seneca tribal councils.

Although not mentioned as such in the myth, mnemonic devices for recalling these relationships are presumably quite ancient. There is a digital code for laying down kernels of corn, and a similar arrangement of pegs on condolence canes, each unit representing a title of a founder, and there is a circle of wampum for the same purpose (Jenness 1933; Fenton 1950). These digital reminders of the titles and council arrangement of the founders, as memory systems, are obviously older than the present media in which they occur.

Of equally enduring interest are the metaphors for producing unity, as symbols of identity, for cultural maintenance, and as warnings of what may befall should the league fail. Of the first order, metaphors for unity, are the fire and pillar of smoke that touches the sky; the enlarged image of the longhouse sheltering one body of kindred; and the provisions for extension, props to strengthen the house, and measures to secure its doorways. This image of the longhouse as the symbol of a kinship polity proved formidable in history even when the required amenities were not always observed among its housemates. Symbolic antlers of office marked the chiefs, the buck deer being the symbol of manliness, just as venison sustained the people, balancing the "three sisters" (corn, beans, and squash), the produce of women. Chiefs are crowned with antlers; they are dehorned for misconduct. In mortal illness the antlers are removed and set aside pending recovery or death, and then are put on the head of the succeeding chief. To "lock horns" or "rub antlers," like bucks in mating season, is the term for the great social dance that concludes an installation ceremony and reunites society.

Each nation had its own symbol—flint for Mohawk, standing stone for Oneida, great pipe for Cayuga, and so forth—and presumably arrows bore distinctive tribal markings. A bundle of five fragile arrows bound with sinew represented the combined power of the league, which might bend but not break.

Although each of the Five Nations had its own council fire, from their several hearths they looked to the majestic column of smoke that pierced the sky at Onondaga. There was spread the Great White Mat of the Law where they sat in council. Their chairman was provided with an eagle wing and a pole. By keeping the mat dust-free and ridding the discussion of subversive (crawling) things, the head of the grand council and his assistants, the firekeepers, strove to reach unanimity through regularized procedures and set committees. When unable to roll their opinions into one bundle, the council could always, like a university faculty, bury the issue in the ashes. Among other symbols of unity, the chiefs feasted on beaver tail from a common dish.

Two images focused people's minds on the council and helped them to repose confidence in the chiefs. One was the circle of chiefs, and the other was the Great Tree of Peace. The chiefs joined hands in a circle to surround the public; if any chief departed, his antlers of office would catch on the circle and his title would lie within society.[2] Such a circle of wampum with fifty appended strings, one for each chiefly title, arranged by nations, was formerly preserved in the National Museum of Man in Ottawa (Jenness 1933). It has since been returned to Six Nations.

There is also an inverted image of concentric circles within which the chiefs are seated around a fire or in the shade of a tree; they are surrounded at the next ring by the warriors, and, way out, the public is ranged by age grades.

By far the most majestic image of the league is the great white pine with its four white roots extending to the cardinal directions. The tree has long needles ("the tree of the great long leaves"), which grow as the confederacy prospers. The white pine (*Pinus strobus* L.) has clusters of exactly five needles, "one for each nation," it is said. Peoples attracted by the smoke spy the tree and follow its roots to the trunk. If they accept the principles of the Great Law, they may enter the Longhouse as props to strengthen it. People who hack at the roots suffer dire consequences. The main council bench rests at the foot of the tree. An eagle is perched atop the pine to watch out for the safety of the peace.

A tree is also the symbol of chiefship, to be raised up, uprooted at death, and a new one raised or planted in its place. Similarly, a tree is uprooted to bury the hatchet, to cast the weapons of war into the underground stream that carries off pollution of war, and then the tree is replanted.

Maintaining the league through time was accomplished through the rituals of condolence and requickening, which will occupy later chapters. The myth predicts that failure to fulfill condolence law portends dire consequences. The myth closes on a dour note of the calamity that will befall the People of the Longhouse in later times. It foretells that when the chiefs fail to attain unanimity, when they throw ashes in each other's eyes, producing an impasse in council, then the people's heads will roll. The ultimate consequence of such disunity is the dissolution of the league. The text reads: "Then the people shall seek a great rock elm and deposit their heads in the fork of two branching roots." In such an event, Deganawi:dah said, "Call my name in the bushes and I will stand here once again." That day may be upon us.

---

2. In modern times, when a chief from Grand River crosses the Niagara frontier to attend council at Onondaga, where his title may be duplicated, it is said that his antlers catch on the international boundary.

CHAPTER 7

The Good Message
of Handsome Lake

Prophets arise in times of trouble, as in the third period of Iroquois traditional history, when oral history and documentary history combine to substantiate an emergent mythology. This is what happened after the American Revolution when the political power of the old league, and then the confederacy, which had met at Onondaga for centuries, diminished and a new kind of power based on religion emerged. Early in the war the firekeepers raked up the council fire that had burned at Onondaga for centuries and carried an ember to Buffalo Creek, where it burned fitfully in competition with a second fire at Grand River tended by Loyalist Iroquois who had followed Joseph Brant to Canada. Between 1784 and 1796, tribal leaders let their New York lands slip away parcel by parcel in a series of treaty cessions with the United States, New York state, and land companies, until but a half-dozen reservations remained as seats of tribal bands for whom the Six Nations confederacy, and remotely the league, had become symbolic metaphors. The local village autonomy that had preceded the formation of the league and operated throughout the life of the confederacy reasserted itself. Once more local village chiefs and their councilors became political leaders.

The economy, too, had changed. As farming encroached on former tribal hunting territories, hunting practices on the old scale became impossible. The fur trade, so long the hinge of the tribes' economy and the source of European trade goods on which they were now dependent, shifted westward to the Ohio country, and the trade in deerskins, now centered at Pittsburgh, diminished with the decline of the deer population. Only the Allegheny Senecas—Cornplanter's people—still had access to this diminishing asset. Even "our life supporters"—corn, beans, and squash— never recovered from the devastation wrought by the armies of General John Sullivan and Colonel Daniel Brodhead, who burned villages, destroyed crops, and felled orchards bordering the Finger Lakes and leveled the Allegheny settlements.

During this period of radical culture change, social disorganization was prevalent. Persons of both sexes suffered from depression. Warriors, unable to validate their manhood by hunting and fighting, drank to excess. Suspicion of witchcraft reached paranoid proportions, and some individuals resorted to the "fatal root," the traditional method of committing suicide by ingesting water hemlock (Fenton 1986a).

It was to this scene of social disorder, loss of political power, and personal despair that Handsome Lake brought his message of hope, reform, and regeneration

Figure 5. "Handsome Lake Preaching at Tonawanda Longhouse." Painting by Ernest Smith (Seneca). Courtesy Rochester Museum and Science Center, Rochester, New York.

(fig. 5). The tradition, as voiced by preachers of the Good Message (Gaiwi:yo:h) into the twentieth century, relates that it was during the Berry Moon, June, of 1799 that the Prophet, during a prolonged illness, had his first vision of three "angels" who appeared to him bearing signs and portents of what would later constitute his code. Recitations of the code during conventions of his followers, which today are called "Six Nations meetings," have assumed the character of a major tradition. The tradition does not relate where Handsome Lake got his ideas, nor does it say that at the time there were Quaker missionaries present in the Allegheny settlements. These young men, forerunners of the Peace Corps of our day, brought a whole new economy to the Senecas, which the Prophet seconded.

□□◇□□

It was not until the 1930s that the journals and correspondence of these missionaries, who witnessed the revelation of Handsome Lake's visions and left a daily record of his teachings, came to the attention of scholars (Deardorff 1951; Snyderman 1953; A. Wallace 1970). What is most remarkable is that the Quaker records confirm the main outlines of the myth, although later preachers have rearranged certain incidents in the oral code of the Prophet's teachings, which may be out of sequence. What has guaranteed essential accuracy is that the code is always recited publicly, when appointed guardians of the Good Message sit flanking the preacher to ensure accuracy, even counting the number of "words" (paragraphs) recited and later commenting critically. During two hundred years of many preachings, the text has grown with critical embellishments while other detail has been lost.

Since the publication of Edward Cornplanter's Seneca version of the code in English translation by Arthur C. Parker (1913), preachers have used this text as a trot. Still other preachers who themselves learned the code from listening to preachers in the oral tradition profess that they possess the original version. Unfortunately, with one or two exceptions these variant versions of the code have not been recorded, and recent efforts to tape the code from contemporary preachers have failed.

There are several native texts, however. In 1936 Hewitt reported collecting a Mohawk text of some six thousand words from Seth Newhouse, who attributed the version to Chief George Buck in 1884 (Hewitt 1936: 84; Hewitt Papers, ms. 3489). Hewitt also mentioned an Onondaga and a Cayuga version. George Van Every wrote out the text in Onondaga, which Hewitt collected from his son John at Six Nations on Grand River (Hewitt Papers).[1]

It is well known that Chief John A. Gibson preached the code both in Onondaga at Six Nations and in Seneca when on the circuit. There may be a version in Cayuga from Jacob Hess, also of Six Nations. Today one encounters extreme reluctance to allow the Prophet's words to be captured and taken away by ethnologists.[2]

The custodians of the league tradition adhere to the teachings of Handsome Lake, and they are the conservators of the old ways. Jemmy Johnson, Morgan's source at Tonawanda; John Hardy Gibson, who served Hale, Hewitt, and Goldenweiser at Six Nations; and Seth Newhouse, the chronicler of the league tradition, its "constitution," and bylaws, were all preachers of Handsome Lake's code. What was the New Religion early in the nineteenth century—the doctrine of the so-called Pagan Iroquois—became the vehicle of conservatism at the close of the century. Today the followers of the Great Law comprise the Longhouse congregations of Handsome Lake's followers. Exceptions are Newtown and Coldspring longhouses of the Seneca nation, where the league tradition has vanished. Even at Six Nations a substantial portion of the population, largely members of Christian sects, support a government of elected councilors (Weaver 1973).

In August 1935, Chief Edward Black and I carried wampum strings to Grand River inviting the guardians of Handsome Lake's message to attend a Six Nations meeting in September to hear the prophet's words recited (fig. 6). We headed for the home of Onondaga chief Joseph Logan (Thadoda:ho?), who called a council to hear the message and deliver a string to each of the five longhouses in Canada, including Oneida on the Thames. Each string was tied to a stick notched with the number of days until the day appointed to kindle the main fire of the Handsome Lake religion. Delegates cut off a notch each morning and planned to reach Tonawanda the evening before the meeting.

□□◇□□

1. In May 1919, at Onondaga Reservation near Syracuse, Hewitt (1919) reported recording in Onondaga text the complete Handsome Lake doctrine. Whether this is the same as the Van Every manuscript (BAE mss. 449, 2535) remains to be determined. Work is going forward on the Newhouse Mohawk manuscript by a contemporary linguist.

2. In 1958, Wallace Chafe succeeded in taping and transcribing the first day of the code from the late Atkins (Ed) Coury, a Seneca speaker at Coldspring Longhouse, Allegany Reservation, who then succumbed to pressure from his Seneca neighbors and terminated the research.

Figure 6. Seneca chief Edward Black (Hawk clan) displays invitation wampums for a Six Nations meeting at Tonawanda, 14 August 1935. Photo by author.

The documentary sources on the Handsome Lake reformation were generated by Cornplanter's visits to Philadelphia to gain relief from the harsh terms imposed by the 1784 Fort Stanwix treaty. While there he conversed with leaders of the Society of Friends, who manifested a concern for the civilization of the native Indians and who later attended the 1794 Canandaigua treaty conference. The following year the Philadelphia yearly meeting of the Friends established a "committee . . . for the civilization & real welfare of the Indian natives," which implemented the concern by drawing up a plan to introduce plow agriculture and animal husbandry among the Six Nations. They consulted with responsible federal officials, wrote the necessary letters, and selected personnel for the missions. Since persons designated by the society were expected to keep journals and the Friends were habitual letter writers, the Quaker records are a rich source of information on Indian affairs.

Unlike other missionaries, the Friends would not proselytize, and they sought no gain for themselves, nor did they covet Indian lands. After a trial run at Oneida, the committee decided to concentrate on the Seneca nation. In 1798 they selected three young men—Halliday Jackson, Joel Swayne, and Henry Simmons (who had served at Oneida)—as volunteers to staff the mission. In May, John Pierce and Joshua Sharpless of the committee accompanied them to Cornplanter's settlement on the Allegheny River. The embassy of Friends reached Burnt House in mid-May (A. Wallace 1970: 220ff.).

Burnt House, situated in a defile above Kinzua Narrows, was Cornplanter's town and the seat of his kindred, including his half-brother Handsome Lake. Upriver some nine miles on the flats was Genesinghuta (as the Friends spelled it),[3] a settlement most recently abandoned, and a site since known as Old Town. Pierce and Sharpless, before returning home, stationed Simmons at Burnt House to teach Cornplanter's children to read and write. They arranged for Jackson and Swayne to settle at the upper town, away from Cornplanter's personal domain, and charged them to build a house and barn as a demonstration center for the Indians (Deardorff 1951: 86). The young men were told to keep diaries and to correspond with the committee. The Simmons, Sharpless, and Jackson journals constitute the prime sources. Jackson continued to serve the committee and made return visits to inspect advances in technology, matters which he reported at length (Jackson 1830a), and he wrote a brief ethnography (1830b).

William Allinson kept the journal of the 1809 visitation of members of the Indian committee to Allegheny and Cattaraugus settlements, noting various improvements and describing old customs retained. That same year, Major John Norton, en route to the Cherokee nation with a party of Grand River Iroquois, paused at Coldspring, looked up the venerable Skanyadariyo, and congratulated him on reclaiming the Five Nations to sobriety from previously debauched lives. He also commented on Quaker improvements in agriculture and husbandry (Klinck and Talman 1970: 8–12).

Federal sources on the Prophet and his time occur in scattered places.[4] The account of Handsome Lake's calling on the Great Father, his address to the president asking for spiritual endorsement beyond technical assistance, and President Jefferson's reply are items treasured by his followers as evidence of presidential sanction of the Prophet's teachings (A. Wallace 1970: 266–72). Framed copies of Jefferson's endorsement hang in Coldspring and Tonawanda longhouses today when the Good Message is recited.

Soon after the Prophet's death at Onondaga in 1815, Protestant missionaries noted efforts to revive his moral precepts (Timothy Alden in A. Wallace 1970: 332ff.). At the request of L. H. Morgan, Ely S. Parker transcribed in English the first full text of the code as Jemmy Johnson recalled it in 1845 on the day following a Condolence Council at Tonawanda. Morgan attended the preaching session with Parker, who took notes and made a rough translation into English.[5] Three years later, when another session of preaching would occur, Morgan, unable to attend

3. Probably Dyenonhsongohtongeh, "there one passes through the house," as in a ceremonial circuit of the village.

4. These sources include the Knox and Pickering papers, Massachusetts Historical Society; the correspondence of Isaac Chapin, Sr., and Isaac Chapin, Jr., O'Reilly Papers, New York Historical Society; the John Parrish Papers, Vassar College Library; and the Samuel Kirkland Papers, Hamilton College Library (Pilkington 1980).

5. Three copies of this manuscript survive (Tooker 1989): in the Morgan Papers, University of Rochester; in the Newberry Library, Chicago; and in the Parker Papers, Huntington Library, San Marino, California (published in Parker 1919).

the council, wrote to Parker asking him to write down "a fine record of the proceedings." After several exchanges between the two men during the next two years, Morgan published an edited a version of the code in Book II of the *League* (1851: 233–59).[6]

□□◇□□

Returning to Handsome Lake's social and cultural background, Burnt House on the Allegheny River just below the Pennsylvania state line, where the Quakers arrived in 1798, was a unique community of some four hundred persons, a microcosm of Iroquoia at the close of the eighteenth century. Cornplanter, half-brother of the Prophet, having secured a grant from the state of Pennsylvania for his services to the commonwealth, held the land in fee apart from the other Seneca reservations. It was just four years since the Canandaigua treaty had established peace between the Six Nations and the United States and two years after the Big Tree treaty designated the reservations. The Allegany and Cattaraugus reservations were just then being surveyed. Handsome Lake attended both treaties councils and, befitting his rank as a league chief, put his mark third on the list of Seneca signers. At Big Tree he insisted on adding to the list of reserved lands a mile square at Oil Spring (Cuba, New York), a place important to him as a source of medicine. Brother Cornplanter, having made his reputation as a war leader during the Revolution and as the principal negotiator for his people during the treaty period that followed, usually signed ahead of Handsome Lake, and at Big Tree Cornplanter received a cash grant of three hundred dollars (Deardorff 1951: 82; A. Wallace 1970: 182–85).

Handsome Lake's kin at Burnt House were predominantly a segment of the Wolf clan, which included Cornplanter, his nephew Blacksnake (1760–1859) (Abler, ed., 1989), the latter's sister and clan matron, and others. Cornplanter's wife, a native of Burnt House, was a member of the Snipe clan, and likewise her son Henry and his brother and sisters. Both the Prophet and Cornplanter were born at Ganawagens on the Genesee (opposite Avon, New York) during the 1730s. Cornplanter was sired by an Albany trader variously named Abeel, O'Bail, or the like, while the Prophet's father presumably was a native Seneca. When Sullivan's army threatened to invade the Genesee country, the family withdrew to Tona-wanda and the following year removed to the Allegheny, settling at Old Town before concentrating at Burnt House a decade later on Cornplanter's grant. Leadership of the Genesee-Allegheny axis of the Senecas descended to Cornplanter from his mother's brother, old Kiasutha, whose prominence went back to King George's War. This bilateral combination of Wolf and Snipe clan members constituted the elite of Burnt House.

For the Prophet, the title Ganyadaiyo? (Seneca)—Skanyadari:yoh (Onondaga), and so forth—"Handsome Lake," which properly belongs to the Turtle clan, was "a name hung about the neck." Apparently the Turtle matron, lacking a properly qualified candidate of her own, had co-opted a member of the Wolf

6. Parker's rough field notes, which he used in writing the manuscript that he sent to Morgan in 1850, are in the American Philosophical Society Library, Philadelphia (Fenton 1951b: 303, 306–9). Parker's manuscript of the 1848 version of the code that he sent Morgan in 1850 is in the Morgan Papers, University of Rochester Library. The relationship of these several manuscripts is discussed by Elisabeth Tooker (1989: 40–41).

clan, loaning the title for his lifetime. There is no evidence for this, but it is consistent with Iroquois practice. We do not know when he was stood before the people and installed in the title at a Condolence Council, but we do know that the Prophet served as a common warrior in the British campaign against the Americans and that he held the title during the 1790s. His name appears prominently among the fifty-two signers of the Canandaigua treaty on 11 November 1794, when Timothy Pickering, as U.S. commissioner, listed Kon-yoo-tai-yoo, Handsome Lake of the large Turtle clan, "Head Sachem of the Nation by birth." A variant of the name actually appears three times on the treaty: as above, as the name of an Oneida warrior in that dialect, and third on the list of the Seneca delegation.[7]

Handsome Lake escorted surveyors at Presque Isle (modern Erie, Pennsylvania) the following year, when it was acknowledged that he was of the "Nobility," or chiefly rank (Deardorff 1951: 83; A. Wallace 1970: 350n). Jackson, a contemporary, however, stated that he acceded to the sachemship after his visions (Jackson 1830a: 42).

There were at least three white persons living among the twenty or so members of the Burnt House elite, of whom the matrons are seldom named. Peter Crouse, an adopted white captive since boyhood, was to become the forebear of a host of Allegheny Senecas; Elijah Mathews and Nicholas Demuth had taken Seneca wives and served as interpreters (A. Wallace 1970: 185, 188–89). There were as yet no resident missionaries.

Ceremonialism thrived at Burnt House. The old religion was not so much overturned (Parker 1913: 11) as incorporated, systematized, and given new purposes after the advent of the Quakers and following the Prophet's visions. The annual cycle of ceremonies, which I later described at Coldspring (Fenton 1936), had their roots in the previous period. There was the cosmology featuring Sky Woman and the Holder of the Heavens, the good twin known as Sapling, who won out over his evil twin brother, Flint, for control of the earth. Possibly the wooden statue that stood near the riverbank and around which the Burnt House celebrants danced at the Green Corn Festival and where they hung the white dog at the Midwinter Festival represented the good twin, as Wallace suggested (1970: 192). The paradigm for returning thanks from the earth to the sky, without its later embellishments that deified the Prophet, must have been in place. The four sacred ceremonies of later Longhouse religion—Great Feather Dance, Drum (Thanksgiving or Worship) Dance, Personal Chant, and the Great Bowl Game—go back to the roots of Iroquois culture. Intrusion of the thanksgiving paradigm into the first two rites postdates the Prophet's teachings, however; before his day the Drum Dance belonged to the cycle of war dances for recruiting and boasting, and the Personal Chant was a warrior's signature. The Bowl Game stems from the cosmology.

The medicine societies are equally old and underwent metamorphoses of their own after the Prophet suppressed them and their adherents revived them. The

7. Sachem titles in one nation sometimes appear as warrior names in others of the Five Nations. Goldenweiser discovered this in genealogies from Six Nations Reserve, and I encountered the same among the Senecas.

ʔOhgi:we:h ritual, or Chanters for the Dead—the songs of which the Prophet sang out of context—has probably changed the least. But several ritual bundle societies that were once devoted to war and peace, particularly the Eagle Dance Society (Fenton 1953a) and the Little Water Society (Fenton 1979), are now restricted to curing. The False Faces and their patron, Shagodyowehgo:wa:, whom the Creator confined to the margins of the earth, and lesser spirits relegated to the forests who were once concerned with controlling game and granting hunting luck, now concentrate on relieving physical disorders, purging the settlements of disease, and controlling high winds (Fenton 1987). The False Face maskers are only structurally similar to Flint and his progeny. One could go on. The point is that the all-night celebrations of feasts for the medicine societies, particularly those of ʔOhgi:we:h, an unrestricted society, had in the Prophet's day become drunken frolics whenever whiskey was to be had in any quantity. And soon there would be fewer men with war records to boast. Reform was due, and it came.

The traditional economy fared better at Burnt House than in other Seneca communities at the close of the eighteenth century. The women during the summer months were cultivating some sixty acres of corn, beans, and squash in two-acre plots fenced from deer. Although deer were becoming scarce in areas of white intrusion, the mountains of northwest Pennsylvania, where the Senecas then hunted, were still uninhabited and held deer in abundance. In autumn, after the Bread Dance, the men took to the woods, often accompanied by their families, to hunt for meat and, mainly, for skins to trade at Pittsburgh before returning home at midwinter for the great ceremony that marked the longer days. Procuring meat for subsistence was no longer the primary consideration; meat was even left to rot in the woods, for deerskins would fetch both the cash and trade goods on which the Seneca people had long depended. Hunting parties paddled downriver to Tidioute and Tionesta, stashed their canoes before going into the woods, returned to the landing with bundles of skins, and floated to Pittsburgh. Returning laden with goods and whiskey, they lashed their canoes together for safety, put the howling drunks in the center, and struggled upriver against the current. This is the scene that the code describes as preliminary to the riotous drunk that followed for days at Burnt House until the whiskey was consumed (Parker 1913: 20–21).

The huge pinery of the upper Allegheny was another disposable asset. Downriver sawmills, first at Pittsburgh and then later higher up, created an insatiable demand for logs and boards that soon involved Seneca pilots in rafting on the spring and autumn high water. Cornplanter soon had a mill of his own, and the Quakers brought sawmill irons and sent a skilled sawyer. The lumber industry, piloting, and work in the woods for wages quickly supplanted the trade in deerskins and afforded alternatives to farming, which the Quakers, having introduced plow culture, advocated as the way to lead the Seneca people to "civilization."

The amazing success of the Quaker mission to the Senecas on the Allegheny notwithstanding, the Senecas did not become suddenly a nation of farmers. Diane Rothenberg (1976), having reviewed the Quaker sources on the Handsome Lake period, takes issue with Anthony Wallace (1970). Her discussion of sequential economic strategies details the ups and downs of acceptance and rejection of proposed economic reforms. She rejects the idea of cultural persistence that previous anthropologists have advanced (Freilich 1958; Fenton 1963), which the Quakers labeled "habits of mind" for explaining reluctance to taking on new ways. Instead, she resorts to "rational explanations," which she seeks in fundamental economic realities. She finds that the Senecas were open to change and quick to accept innovations. Perhaps anthropologists have overemphasized the sex division of labor in Iroquois cultural history, but Rothenberg herself relies on the pattern of sedentary females and mobile males, a variant of the clearing-and-forest theme, while insisting that "Seneca division of labor . . . arises directly from this circumstance, the women producing those items fixed in the ground and the men exploiting the extensively and randomly distributed resources." Moreover, she notes that both sexes followed "an annual cycle of activities which inhibited their ability to take on new ones" (1976: 149). Women's activities centered in the summer season, and men's work in fall and winter, when furs and pelts were in their prime and women were the least busy.

Women were the least reluctant to take on new activities so long as these tasks did not interfere with their preoccupation with horticulture, particularly if the new activities afforded opportunities for socializing under the leadership of a senior woman and were of the kind from which they derived their prestige. They carried this pattern over into spinning and weaving in the off-season. Their control of subsistence activities in the settlement enabled them to translate prestige into power and elevate their status in politics (Rothenberg 1976: 153). To this day the Iroquois value the life of a woman at twice that of a man, and they deplore as the greatest tragedy the extinction of a family lineage, when, as they say, "the ashes grow cold."

I see no other valid explanation of men's predilection for skilled and dangerous occupations, their love of working in gangs, whether it be in timber felling, piloting rafts, bark skinning for tanneries, or belonging to the regular and extra gangs of railroad track workers, than the structural similarities of these occupations to war parties (Freilich 1958), a species of cultural persistence of equal importance to economic explanations (Rothenberg 1976: 209). Solitary farming never had quite this appeal. Surely the Quaker mission cannot be considered a failure because the majority of Seneca men did not take to farming in Handsome Lake's day or later. Two model dairy farms at Allegany stood out among a dozen subsistence farms in the 1920s, but even these had failed a decade later.

Returning to Handsome Lake's day, white encroachment meant loss of territory, decline of game, and an end of the trade with western trappers (Tooker 1968: 194). More intensive agriculture hardly made up for these losses. More serious was the depopulation during the American Revolution and its aftermath. Kirkland's census of 1788 revealed that the Senecas had lost half their previous numbers (Kirkland Papers; A. Wallace 1970: 194). The vaunted political power of the Six Nations confederacy was no more, the confederacy having broken up over a policy issue during the American Revolution. Its members scattered to the four winds after Washington's armies smashed their villages and scorched the earth, and local leaders like Cornplanter, erstwhile war chiefs, reasserted themselves not unlike the village chiefs who founded the league, according to tradition. Small wonder that people were dispirited.

Depression that assumed several guises resulted in part from public policy. On the eve of the Fort Stanwix treaty (1784), James Duane, member of Congress from

New York and advocate of that state's rights, urged the commissioners of Congress and the governor of New York not to observe the old treaty protocol, not to recognize the Six Nations confederacy as such, to deny sovereignty, to treat the tribal delegates as inferiors, and generally to break down the morale of the once-proud Iroquois. Wallace has noted evidences of social pathology: excessive weeping, alcoholism, violence, witch fear, and disunity. Individuals were frequently depressed when sober and even suicidal (A. Wallace 1970: 196–201; Fenton 1986a). Handsome Lake himself manifested similar symptoms before his first vision.

□□◇□□

The Prophet's visionary experiences produced a catalog of sins, virtues, and expectations that accumulated to constitute the Good Message, or code. His teachings incorporated elements of the old religion—notably four ceremonies and the cycle of thanksgiving festivals—and suppressed the rest. During the first third of the nineteenth century the new religion acted as an integrating force, replacing the confederacy as the leitmotif for the traditionalists. It spread rapidly from Coldspring to Buffalo Creek and Tonawanda; in 1804 it reached Grand River in Canada (D. Smith 1987: 49), where a local prophet had already prepared the way (Kirkland Papers); and at Onondaga the Prophet's travels terminated. The doctrine bypassed Tuscarora, and until quite recently St. Regis (Akwesasneh) and Caughnawaga had no longhouses or adherents to Gaiwi:yo:h (Parker 1913: 7, 14).

Following the sale of the Buffalo Creek Reservation (1838–42), Cattaraugus became a center of the Handsome Lake religion where disaffected traditionalists withdrew and kindled new fires in three longhouses at Plank Road, at Pine Woods on Three Mile Level, and at Newtown.

It was during the Berry Moon of 1799 that Handsome Lake had his first vision, which sparked the fire that became the new religion. As Wallace (1970: 239) points out: "When the misery of poverty and humiliation is combined with a hope of moral and material salvation, the resulting mixture is explosive." Handsome Lake had lost a niece to witchcraft. He was depressed and melancholy; he feared death and felt unworthy of the Creator. He periodically returned thanks for life, but when he got drunk he sang sacred songs supposedly restricted to ceremonies and suffered remorse afterward. These symptoms, as Wallace (1970: 240) wrote, constitute "the classic Iroquois bereavement syndrome compacted of depression, bitterness and suspicion."

The first vision inveighed against four sins: whiskey (one:ga), witchcraft, love charms (onoi?it), and abortion (Parker 1913: 9, 27–28, 41). Whiskey was one of several gifts from the whites—along with playing cards, coins, violin and fiddle dances, and the "decayed leg bone" (syphilis)—that the Prophet condemned (Parker 1913: 17–18). Positive themes were traits derived from the old culture, such as hospitality, generosity, and mutual aid, as opposed to medicine society dances. He praised the work of the honondiont ("keepers of the faith") and participation in the ceremonies and activities of the community.

The vision perceived some virtues to be had from white culture. Improved housing and agriculture were not to be denied. But concepts of land tenure were misunderstood on both sides. The European concept of exclusive title held by individuals directly opposed the Indian concept of land held in common, with the title resting in the tribe or nation, which is the concept governing the reservations of the Seneca nation to this day. The earth and its plants and animals were from the time of Sky Woman and Sapling gifts of the Creator for use and enjoyment by the people whom he released there. On such things the two cultures would never meet.

By sorting out and evaluating old customs, beliefs, and rites, which carried built-in sanctions, the Prophet would arrive at a concept of sin graduated according to the rank of the offender—chiefs, keepers of the faith, and ordinary people (Parker 1913: 44). Such persons who did not confess would not be received by the Creator. Jealousy among chiefs who derided one another and quarreled, behavior that led to the decay of the league (Parker 1913: 45n), should cease. Chiefs who sold land committed the worst offense. To cope with celebrations of the medicine societies that had become drunken frolics, he recommended an experiment: let one party drink whiskey and the other feast on vegetables and fruit, then see who gets murdered. Drinking at planting would blight the corn. He sanctioned the whipping of witches. He gave explicit instructions on the proper way to gather herbal medicines, but held that it was wrong for herbalists to charge a fee for knowledge. He advocated changing mourning customs from an anniversary observance and limiting grief to ten days, for "grief only adds to the sorrows of the dead." One should bury grief in the grave. "The number of our days is known in the skyworld" (Parker 1913: 44–45).

The first vision ended on an apocalyptic note foretelling the signs portending the end of the world. As in the Deganawi:dah epic, when the chiefs, headmen, and *honondiont* disagree, when the earth withholds sustaining foods, when a great plague befalls, when women perform witchcraft in daylight, when others claim communication with the Creator, wonders will be temporary as the work of the evil spirit. When people disbelieve the Good Message, monsters will emerge from the underworld, the faithful may die in their sleep, and then the earth will be destroyed in a holocaust (Parker 1913: 58–59).

The sky journey is a classic motif in Iroquoian mythology. Handsome Lake's second vision related just such an episode. Although cast in the classic mold, the characters whom the Prophet met and the incidents related on his journey pertain to the new world of acculturation. The relation speaks of the "Devil"; it describes drunks canoe-hopping and singing *jihaya?*, the so-called Devil Dance, later forbidden; it introduces a fourth messenger, or "Angel"; and it confuses George Washington with Timothy Pickering, U.S. commissioner at Canandaigua.

Along the heavenly road, the path of souls, the vision recounts eleven incidents in which the visionary stops to witness the treatment of sinners in the house of torment. In one it is noted that a church has but one door and no passage through, an arrangement that would block the celebration of Longhouse ceremonies. Two other incidents relate to Red Jacket's role in the upcoming loss of the Buffalo Creek Reservation. Although the chronology became somewhat confused in later recitations, the fates of sinners here described would become the core of the new religion's theology (A. Wallace 1970: 244–45). One notes the Iroquois preoccupation with fire, as in torture during the previous century, as the symbol of government during peace and war, and now as inflicted by the "Punisher": manifested in the boiling of witches, in burning a wife beater, in serving a female fornicator with hot color-coded penises, in a fiddler's sawing his arm cords with a red-hot iron bow, and in gamblers dealing heated playing cards. To symbolize cardinal social vices, the vision names four persons whom the four angels say cannot be forgiven: the compulsive talker, the glutton, the "hanging kettle," and the "headeater" (Parker 1913: 74).[8]

As in the Orpheus-Eurydice motif of antiquity, the Prophet's otherworld journey walks a narrow road between life and death. Should he meet the Creator, he must stay. Berries grow by the wayside, birds sing, and a spring wells up at one rest stop in magical supply. Farther on he meets his own white dog sacrificed at a previous Midwinter ceremony. At a final halt, a loud voice calls people to assemble for the Great Feather Dance, now one of four sacred ceremonies celebrated at major festivals. At the point of return stands a house of eternal abode where, if one enters, one must remain. So ends Vision II.

At this juncture in the recitation of the code, speakers pause to recount Handsome Lake's periods of residence: ten years at Burnt House, two years at Coldspring, four years at Tonawanda, prior to the hegira to Onondaga, where he died and is buried near the Onondaga longhouse (Parker 1913: 76, 77).

It is known that on recovery the Prophet recited his vision to his brother Cornplanter, who summoned a council to hear it. He also invited the resident Quaker missionary, Henry Simmons, who confirmed the value of visions of heaven, which pleased the Indians. That afternoon the Burnt House folk performed the "Worship Dance," most probably the Great Feather Dance, and feasted on a white dog (A. Wallace 1970: 247). Simmons confirmed the doings in his journal. Cornplanter had mixed emotions regarding Indian and white customs.

The messengers of the sky world appeared to Handsome Lake a third time, on 5 February 1800.[9] They advised him to prepare and take an emetic of witch-hopple (*Viburnum alnifolium*), scraping the bark upward, followed by a sweat bath (Parker 1913: 77n). They reported that the Great Spirit was troubled over the condition of the Indians—whether they had abandoned witchcraft and given up drinking whiskey. The angels deplored land losses and urged Handsome Lake to have his revelations "written in a book" (A. Wallace 1970: 248). They announced the name Hawenose:? ("New Voice"), and for the third time bid the Prophet sing his Personal Chant (*adon:wen?*) for the last time (Parker 1913: 77]).[10] They predicted that the children who were without sin would appoint one to plead that he instruct them.

So Handsome Lake exhorted the people to keep up the old forms of worship, especially the Midwinter Festival. People wept. The Prophet said Cornplanter should visit the towns of the Six Nations and try to unify the chiefs, and New Voice, of coequal rank, urged the Prophet to accept an invitation from the Onondagas at Buffalo Creek. Handsome Lake pined to revisit the scenes of his childhood on the Genesee and soon would start on his hegira.

By the spring of 1800, as Wallace (1970: 249ff.) points out, the preaching of the third vision completed the first gospel of Gaiwi:yo:h, which was essentially

---

8. The latter two are not explained (Parker 1913: 74).

9. The code, section 122, speaks of four messengers (Parker 1913: 77); Wallace (1970: 248) mentions three.

10. The Personal Chant of Handsome Lake is sung to this day on stated occasions during recitations of the code by the speaker.

apocalyptic. It dwelt on three themes: it predicted destruction, it defined sin, and it prescribed ways to salvation. The end-of-the-world theme was rampant. Disagreements among the chiefs (a prediction in the Deganawi:dah myth) foretold cataclysm,

The definition of sin and call for confession would constitute the second gospel. Continued celebration of the four sacred rituals—the Personal Chant, the Great Feather Dance, the Drum Dance with interpolated thanks to the spirit forces from earth to the sky world, and the Great Bowl Game—were the way to salvation. Their celebration should be managed by religious officers drawn equally from men and women of each moiety who would direct the work of the *honondiont*, or keepers of the faith. Handsome Lake's effort to disband the medicine societies, particularly the False Face Society, which met apart, limited its activities to members, and held sacred objects in secret, met with opposition because the maskers dealt with prevalent diseases and members of the society feared the consequences of failure to renew ceremonial obligations (Fenton 1987). The conflict was compromised when the Prophet relented and sanctioned such meetings if strong drink was kept out, if they went public on great days of the ceremonial calendar, and if they were supervised by the *honondiont*. In later times it was said that no one burned tobacco to tell the tutelaries that the specific societies were going out of business and that therefore the Prophet's sanction was invalid (A. Wallace 1970: 252; Fenton 1933–34).

The Prophet's second dictum was to introduce the rite of confession, which to this day precedes the preaching of the code in Iroquois longhouses. A person stands, holds the strands of wampum that symbolize the "light," or fire, of that congregation, and makes a routine or full confession of sins.

A third dictum that urged skipping anniversary mourning rites failed. Today, both the Ten Day Feast and the Anniversary Feast prevail. ʔOhgi:we:h, Chanters of the Dead, annually takes up any slack in fulfilling obligations to the departed.

As Wallace notes (1970: 253), Handsome Lake's role was rapidly shifting from that of preacher to that of dictator. He would presently decree a great witch hunt that had one political consequence: it drove the Delaware Munsee families at Cattaraugus to seek refuge in Canada.

Vision IV (the magic number) occurred fifteen years later during the hegira to Onondaga. The Prophet had set out from Tonawanda with a large following to honor the invitation of relatives, and the party camped at Ganawagens, his birthplace. There he had a dream, which he revealed in the morning, of a path overgrown with grass as if untraveled. The party passed the next overnight at Kanadase:ken ("village site"), modern Geneva, New York. In the morning the Prophet called the people to assemble and, after the familiar thanksgiving address, related hearing an unidentified woman of either Tonawanda or Onondaga—he knew not which—speaking. On reaching the clearing at Onondaga, they stopped. While the Prophet backtrailed to find a lost knife, he was stricken, returned too sick to enjoy a lacrosse game played to cheer the sick hero, as in Hiawatha's depression before him, and, after uttering a few last words, announced that he would soon be going to a new home. He expired on 10 August 1815.

□□◇□□

The political consequences of the Good Message were revolutionary. During his later years (1801-15), Handsome Lake preached the second, or social, gospel and demanded dictatorial powers for carrying it out (A. Wallace 1970: 263ff.), which eroded his conservative political base at Burnt House; made him an outcast at Coldspring, shunned at Cattaraugus, and an exile at Tonanwanda; and annoyed the Quakers and federal authorities. Nevertheless, the faithful carried the "Good Word" to other reserves, where the New Religion flourished and Longhouse congregations became the strongholds of the new traditionalism in upstate New York and Canada. Indeed, five years after the Prophet's death, a Methodist missionary reported no interest whatever among the Cayugas and Onondagas on Grand River, who pointed at their whiskey-drinking Anglican Mohawk neighbors (D. Smith 1987: 61).

Early on, Handsome Lake got embroiled in a bitter dispute with Red Jacket, the dominant force at Buffalo Creek. The two men agreed at a council held at the Genesee River in 1801 on exchanging some parcels of land there and at Buffalo Creek for reforms in the annuity system—warm flannels instead of fine broadcloth—and technical assistance. The truce culminated in the appointment a delegation to go to Washington, the new federal capital, and carry their message to Hanadaganya?s ("Destroy town"), the president.[11] Handsome Lake headed the Seneca party, accompanied by Cornplanter.

In the first of two speeches to the president, Handsome Lake, as if to brief the president on current factionalism, introduced Cornplanter, who was then "being cried down" by the drunken chiefs at Buffalo Creek. The Prophet sought sanctions for his program. The second speech addressed land issues. The party returned armed with letters signed by Secretary of War Henry Dearborn; a guarantee of territory backed by treaty; passports; and a requisition on the commander at Fort Pitt. These documents became Handsome Lake's letters of authority. He interpreted them as meaning that "nothing in the future of any consequence that relates to the Seneca is to be transacted without the knowledge and approbation of *Coniudiu* [Handsome Lake]" (letter of 23 January 1803 dictated by Handsome Lake and written by Jacob Taylor, a Quaker missionary, cited in Rothenberg 1976: 171). This was the height of his power.

His program now, after the second vision, addressed desired social reforms. The new doctrine embraced five principles: temperance, peace and unity, preserving the land base, a pro-acculturation policy that included limited schooling and the new agriculture, and domestic morality (A. Wallace 1970: 277–84). The most important aspect for the future was a radical shift from the matrilineal family and all the implications of the lineage system to an emphasis on the nuclear family and strengthening the marriage tie. In the political world Handsome Lake perceived the destructive force of factionalism in fragmenting the councils of his people. He preached unity, or "one mind," an ideal theme inherited from the Great Law of the league.

Having peaked after his second vision, reaching its zenith in 1803, Handsome Lake's political influence declined rapidly. Current tradition, as preachers now

11. This warrior name was conferred on George Washington during the French and Indian War, although its meaning later was ascribed to General Washington's dispatching the Sullivan and Brodhead expeditions in 1779 to lay waste the settlements and means of subsistence of the hostile nations of the confederacy. In Iroquois fashion, succeeding presidents acceded to the title.

recite the code, forgets what contemporary observers recorded (letters of General Israel Chapin and his son of the same name, U.S. agents at Canandaigua, to the War Department, O'Reilly Collection; Jasper Parrish Papers; Quaker sources cited in A. Wallace 1970: 285ff.; also Stone 1838, 2: 409-29, app. xxix-xxliv). Tradition fails to recall the controversy over the seat of the council fire of the confederacy. It seems that Handsome Lake was acknowledged the leading chief of the confederacy during a council held at Buffalo Creek in 1801, which presumably left it to his discretion where and when to call the next council. Two years later in January, chiefs and warriors of all the villages of the Seneca nation, comprising two-thirds of the male population, met at Burnt House and announced that the fire now extinguished at Buffalo Creek was opened at the new site, where it would continue to burn. From Burnt House the council dispatched delegates to Washington as already described, and it appointed interpreters.

Handsome Lake's attempt to relocate the council fire of the Six Nations, which marked the zenith of his political influence, brought a sharp reaction from Joseph Brant, leader of the Loyalist Mohawks on Grand River; from the council fire of the reconstructed confederacy at Onondaga Longhouse at Middleport, Ontario; and from the leading chiefs at Buffalo Creek, who insisted that their fire still burned. All parties except the Prophet favored Buffalo Creek. General Israel Chapin, the U.S. agent at Canandaigua, reported that Handsome Lake had the support of the warriors and women but that the chiefs opposed him. Chapin regarded the change as an effort to grab the lead of the nation, and he himself insisted that Buffalo Creek was both established and convenient. The controversy over where the fire of both the Seneca nation and the confederacy should continue to burn resolved itself four years later when a grand council met at Buffalo Creek in August to renew the confederacy. Jasper Parrish, U.S. interpreter and later agent at Canandaigua, reported to Secretary of War Dearborn that Seneca chiefs called the meeting, that it adhered to ancient customs, and that they had returned the fire to its former site, where it now burned brighter with Red Jacket as its speaker (Parrish to Dearborn, 3 September 1807, cited in A. Wallace 1970: 286).

Handsome Lake's real base of support centered at Burnt House in his bilateral kin of the Wolf and Snipe clans, whom he proceeded to alienate. He and Cornplanter quarreled over the location of a sawmill. Cornplanter was deposed as chief and reduced to warrior status; the Prophet and his followers withdrew to Coldspring. The Senecas on the Allegheny River now were three factions: Cornplanter's kin at Burnt House, Handsome Lake's numerous adherents at Coldspring, and families favoring Quaker reforms. Cornplanter's nephew Governor Blacksnake supported the Prophet.

Gossip is a powerful sanction in Seneca society. Sachems are supposed to have skin seven thumbs thick, but the Prophet lacked this protection. Social pressure mounted when he succumbed to paranoid delusions of witches and had two women whipped, who later died. His situation reached a climax in 1809 when the Prophet's council tried and axed a visiting Onondaga woman. The subsequent ruckus precipitated his departure for Tonawanda that fall, his political career at an end.

In what must be the most important paragraph in his book, Wallace (1970: 296) analyzes the reasons for Handsome Lake's political failure. They are reasons ordained by Iroquois culture. One is a tendency to bring everyone down to an egalitarian level. Another is pervasive factionalism. A third is "intense ambivalence about dominance [that] was traditionally expressed in the polarity between the politeness of day to day encounters and the violence that erupted in drunken brawls, witchcraft accusations, and in older times, the torture rituals." In short, the Prophet's role as moral censor guaranteed his political defeat.

Judging by contemporaneous accounts, the renaissance of his teachings midway of the nineteenth century, and the vigor of the New Religion as a force for traditionalism in modern times, Handsome Lake as an evangelist produced enduring results (see Tooker 1989). Gaiwi:yo:h, the Good Message, created a third charter in Iroquois culture history, drawing themes from the past and posing new ones for the future.

CHAPTER 8

PROBLEMS IN
IROQUOIS POLITICAL HISTORY

"Prehistory is the discipline concerned with the reconstruction of human history for times and places for which written documentation is not available" (Trigger 1978b: 2). In the light of Bruce Trigger's definition, let us examine the three oral traditions by which the Iroquois periodize their history to see which aspects of them qualify as evidence for ascertaining the nature of Iroquois polity before written records. On the face of it, periodization by the three oral traditions fails to provide a structure that historians might be expected to accept. The code of Handsome Lake is recent, although documents confirm its beginnings and tell us much that the oral tradition has lost, whereas the regeneration of the Handsome Lake religion before the mid-nineteenth century rests mainly on memory ethnology (Chief Henan Scrogg to W. N. Fenton, 7 September 1935, cited in A. Wallace 1970; but see also Tooker 1989). The code has become the charter for the Longhouse religion, and few living informants can exceed its historical dimensions.

Themes afford a sense of historical continuity. A theme is a persistent topic that tends to be repeated throughout the discourse in one form or another. As such it is processual in character. Of the twenty themes identified in the creation myth, almost all reappear in the Deganawi:dah epic, and fewer in Gaiwi:yo:h. Fourteen new themes related to the league, its formation, and its maintenance occur in the second epic, and not all of these carry over to be transformed in the third. These carryovers and transformations become apparent when they are arranged in parallel columns. A few examples will suffice.

The league myth opens on a note of troubled nations, not unlike the "time of trouble" over the sale of the Buffalo Creek Reservation in the 1830s and the Kinzua Dam disaster of the 1960s. The persistent land issues have their origin in the concept of the native earth in the cosmology. Virgin birth, the Mother of Nations concept, the ongoing matrilineal family, and the power of women over chiefs all get supplanted by the nuclear family in the third period. The recognition of paternity in the *agadoni* principle of one's father's kin, which was projected to the league council, fell into disuse, save in the ritual of the Condolence Council among those who adhere to the life chiefs system. Throughout the three periods, emphasis on the "regular," or proper, way continues in woods'-edge protocol, in the concept of "forest and clearing" during the league period, and in the conduct of ceremonies prescribed by the Seneca Prophet. The power of song, which inheres in the concept of *orenda* (supernatural power), underlies the prestige of names of the founders, adheres to council names of nations, and enhances the Great Law; but it has been transformed to ʔotgonʔ, "evil power," in modern times.

Acting in a role increases the prestige or authority of statuses. This was once true of league chiefs. Today, performing as a masker adds a new dimension to the personality of the actor and magnifies the power of the mask itself. Participation at every level, from social dances to sacred ceremonies, is the essence of this theme. Withholding participation is a powerful sanction that few individuals dared risk, whether it was joining a war party or honoring a request. This theme undoubtedly has its roots in prehistory.

The paradigm of returning thanks from the earth to the sky world (*kanonhenyonk*), although Handsome Lake altered its content, and the preoccupation with dreams and dream fulfillment persist through the three periods and must have prehistoric antecedents. The culture hero's paternity is revealed in a dream. Particular dreams foretell obligations to the tutelaries of medicine societies, forecast ceremonial friendships, and the like. Guessing dreams was a perennial rite.

Things go by twos, fours, sevens, and twenties. Magic numbers adhere to moieties and dual statuses such as doorkeeper roles; the fifty founders of the league attained such an aura of eminence; and the Prophet experienced four visions, decreed four sacred ceremonies, and forbade four social dances. Seven strings of wampum signified an urgent message. Twenty strings ransomed a human life. One recalls honorific names like Twenty Kettles, Twenty Canoes, and the like. Some powerful medicines required twenty ingredients.

Closely related is the theme of reciprocity and the patterns for fulfilling it. Reciprocal actions "across the fire" in counseling, in passing wampum, and in cries of approbation and response (the oft-documented *yohen:* with antiphonal *hi:yah* heard at treaty councils) had their antecedents at lower levels of social interaction. Mourning and condoling the bereaved side operated at the village level and structured arrangements of the league in the Condolence Council. Once a theme was adopted at a lower level it was projected to a higher level of integration by a process of perseveration.

The theme of requickening the living in the name of the dead kept alive clan sets of personal names, raised up new civil chiefs in the titles of the founders of the league, restored society, and maintained Iroquois polity. While the league epic claims the origin of the Condolence Council, in which the "clearminded" lift up the minds of the "downminded" moiety from the depths of depression, the roots of the great ceremony go back to the Huron Feast of the Dead.

The oft-repeated line "one heart, one mind, one dish" speaks to the theme of unity or consensus summed up in the concept of "good mind." Its obverse is "divided mind," or factionalism. Its symbolism includes fire, column of smoke, mat of the law, the giant pine tree, and the bundle of five arrows, one for each of the Five Nations. What of this began in prehistoric times and how much was invented in protohistoric times during the formation of the league itself one can only guess; but we do know that much of it dropped out of the Handsome Lake doctrine and that ethnographic details such as cutting bowstrings and the like mentioned in early versions of the league epic were already forgotten by its later narrators.

The theme of path or road, open or obstructed, stands for communication and occurs in several contexts over time. Throwing a log across the path could obstruct and delay an embassy; a house athwart the path at Onondaga meant no passage through to distant nations. In Handsome Lake's sky journey, a church with but one door admits no transit of ceremony. The path of one's life continues on the heavenly road, the path of souls visible in the Milky Way. Ritual circuits on earth follow a counterclockwise route; dance circuits in the sky world are clockwise.

The tree of life theme in the cosmology becomes the Tree of Peace in league symbolism, and a tree that topples and is raised up again is the metaphor of chiefship.

A rack of antlers is the emblem of chiefship, just as venison sustains families of hunters. Rubbing antlers, like the deer in rut, reunites society in the great social dance that concludes the Condolence Council. The antler theme reaches into prehistory, as witness copper-sheathed headdresses in Hopewell burials.

Condolence law requires that empty places in the roster of chiefs be filled by requickening the name of the dead in the body of a person raised up and invested with the title. Requickening gets around the taboo on mentioning the name of the dead. Employing council names as euphemisms for the names of nations serves a similar function. "Name bearers" refers to Onondagas, "great pipe" to Cayugas, and so forth.

When things get unbearable, whether by political division or witchcraft, one withdraws or "splits the sky" (goes south), as witness the wilderness wanderings of Hiawatha or the hegira of Handsome Lake.

Taking one by the arm from the landing or woods'-edge fire to the seat of honored guests in the council house and the concept of linking arms in friendship constitute a single theme of union and continuity that is epitomized in the phrase "we are all tied together by one umbilical cord." This theme underlies the idea of the chain of peace and friendship in the eighteenth-century treaties. The Linking-Arms Dance remains a favorite Iroquois social dance, although Handsome Lake forbade men and women partners to join hands.

Finally, the longhouse, a synonym for a matrilineal household, became the image of the league, *ganonhsyo:ni* or *hodinonhsioni*, "they of the extended house." Capable of infinite expansion by "extending the rafters" to admit adopted nations, the longhouse became the central theme of the Iroquois polity.

Whether these themes show historical continuity is open to question. Gaiwi:yo:h has supplanted the Great Law in modern times, and much of the league imagery has been transformed or has dropped by the wayside. The great variety of themes relating to the league period survive only in the ritual of condolence. Together they comprise a paradigm put together by a reformer, a species of social revolution, to meet a crisis. Similarly, the Seneca Prophet structured a new paradigm to confront the times of trouble following the American Revolution and attending the breakup of the league and the social and personal disorganization of his day. Similar revolutionary changes must have occurred in the past. What is even more amazing is how themes persist over time.

□□◇□□

Some further comments on the three traditions as oral history follow. Their time depth is shallow: even the wampum records annexed to Chief John Skanawati Buck's account of the origin of the league fail to reach back beyond the late eighteenth century (Hewitt 1892). The geography of Iroquoia is faulty in the later Gibson versions of the league legend, particularly on the movement of the heroes, which is natural a century after removal to Canada. But they do reveal a sense of time lapse in the process of confederation—it was not a single event. All of the later versions suffer from presentism, a tendency to project recent phenomena such as familiar ritual practices into the past, and it must be understood that these narratives were composed during periods of tension and social change. They are rationalizations for maintaining the system of life chiefs to confront movements for elected councilors of the Six Nations Reserve. Despite the agreement of Hale and Morgan on a mid-fifteenth-century date for the founding of the league, the oral narratives fail to date events. The chronology of Gaiwi:yo:h is more precise. An early Onondaga tradition speaks of several bands converging and uniting (Norton in Klinck and Talman 1970), a coalescence now confirmed by archaeology (Tuck 1971; Bradley 1987).

Archaeological research, model building, and interpretation, taken together with the French records of the seventeenth century, have only recently supplanted the oral tradition dominant in the nineteenth century for explaining the emergence of the northern Iroquoian peoples before written records (Trigger 1978b; 1985: 55ff.). The general assumption was that the Hurons and related speakers and the Iroquois proper, the Five Nations, and neighboring dialects not too long ago were one people, that they derived from a single family or stock and later diverged and separated, an idea that was first put forth by Father Jérôme Lalemant in 1640 (JR, 21: 193–95). This was essentially what linguists call a dendritic model, and it prevailed until recent times. It undergirded the Laurentian hypothesis—that the Five Nations originated on the St. Lawrence River—which Horatio Hale and L. H. Morgan derived from reading Colden's *History of the Five Indian Nations* (1727) and he in turn had from Nicholas Perrot, a seventeenth-century fur trader. Another assumption was that prehistoric cultures changed very little prior to the ethnographic present, and there was precious little information then for interpreting the archaeological record differently.

The idea of prehistoric cultural succession—namely, that the Iroquoian peoples were intrusive in their historic seats, having displaced previous Algonquian-speaking peoples of less advanced cultures, which were much older—occurred only in the first quarter of the twentieth century to archaeologists like Arthur C. Parker at the New York State Museum and W. J. Wintemberg at the National Museum of Canada. To explain this succession, Parker, following H. M. Lloyd, editor of the 1901 edition of Morgan's *League*, advanced a migrational model that was at once dendritic and has since become known as the southern hypothesis (Parker 1916a; Morgan 1901; Trigger 1985: 63).

Until the southern hypothesis failed for want of archaeological evidence, it found support among Boasians. Franz Boas himself, in assessing "Ethnological Problems in Canada" (1907), and Edward Sapir, in taking up the reins of the Anthropological Survey of Canada (1910), espoused it. John R. Swanton and Roland B. Dixon, in discussing "Primitive American History" (1914), operated on the assumption that the Iroquois were essentially a southeastern people. This is how I found the field in 1940 when I undertook to survey research problems in the Iroquoian field. The resulting study (Fenton 1940) summed up the state of knowledge at the time. I was soon after proved wrong in assuming that much of Iroquois culture was essentially southeastern and came with the people to the Northeast or diffused to them later, but the essay generated a considerable body of new research.[1]

Prehistoric chronology in the Northeast before the advent of radiocarbon dating was a matter of sophisticated guesswork. Unlike the American Southwest, the Northeast held a minimum of stratigraphy and no comparable series of preserved tree rings to indicate precise dates for particular sites. Following the lead of Parker, on the basis of morphological features and content of sites that were obviously pre-Iroquois, William A. Ritchie (1944) distinguished an Archaic phase called Lamoka and a later Owasco culture with pottery and agriculture preceding Iroquois. The early cultures were thought to be those of Algonquian peoples whom the Iroquois supplanted in the region. Later radiocarbon analysis of Late Archaic samples pushed the long-accepted date back from A.D. 300 to a range between 4000 and 1500 B.C. And the Owasco series, had it been anywhere else in the world and not presumed to be the work of Algonquian speakers, might have been interpreted as ancestral to Iroquois. That is how matters stood in the 1940s.

The great pioneering work on the pre-Iroquoian cultures of New York is that of Ritchie (1944), who proposed a chronology of three periods: Late Prehistoric (now Late Woodland), Intermediate (Middle Woodland), and Archaic. He based his scheme on artifact types systematically excavated from sites promptly published (see also Ritchie 1965). He, too, subscribed to the southern hypothesis for the origin of Iroquois incised pottery, small triangular arrowheads, and horticulture, which implied migration and diffusion. The dendritic model would die hard.

It took James B. Griffin and his students in Ann Arbor to stand matters on their head. In 1941 Griffin (1944) assessed the place of the Iroquois in American prehistory, questioned the southern hypothesis, and proposed that Iroquoian cultures had evolved from prehistoric cultures in their historic seats as variants of Hopewell culture from Ohio during the Middle Woodland period. Some years later Griffin presided at the prehistory session of the Conference on Iroquois Research at Red House, New York, and introduced his student Richard S. MacNeish, who reported on a study of Iroquois pottery types and proposed the now accepted in-situ theory, namely, that the historic northern Iroquois peoples had evolved from Middle Woodland antecedents who left the Owasco cultures in New York and Ontario (MacNeish 1952). His monograph sounded the death knell of the migrational model (Trigger 1985: 68). Ongoing research in Canada during the ensuing decade, inspired by MacNeish's theory, enabled James V. Wright (1966) to distinguish a Glen Meyer culture in southwestern Ontario from a Pickering culture north of Lake Ontario and then trace the fate of one at the expense of the other. Both cultures had their roots in Middle Woodland antecedents.

Having abandoned theories of migration, and dissatisfied with the limits of diffusion as an explanatory tool, the archaeologists turned to uncovering entire sites, mapping settlement patterns and interpreting the evolution of house forms for indications of size of society, subsistence patterns, social organization, and polity. Graves and ossuaries were made to yield information on ritual and beliefs. Big-site exploration began in Ontario with the work of William Noble, Norman Emerson, Walter Kenyon, and James Wright; and William A. Ritchie and Robert

---

1. Tooker, ed., 1985 reprints the article in its original format.

E. Funk in New York quickly followed suit (1973). James Tuck, then a graduate student at Syracuse University, with partial support from a New York State Museum and Science Service honorarium, explored and mapped sites in Onondaga County, worked out their sequence and relationships leading to historic Onondaga culture, and defined the horizon for confederation (Tuck 1971). He placed the formation of the Onondaga nation out of two parallel communities at no earlier than the first quarter of the fifteenth century, the pattern prevailing into the late seventeenth century. This process of political consolidation of individual nations initiated the process of confederation, which means the league came after 1450 A.D. (Tuck 1971: 215-16, 225). One longhouse at the Howlett Hill site dating from the late fourteenth century measured 334 feet, the largest house then known in Iroquoia. But at the later Schoff site a single house measured exactly 400 feet. The implications for social organization and ceremonialism boggle the mind (Tuck 1971: 79, 96).

Turning to the Mohawk Valley, in 1965 Donald Lenig, a distinguished amateur archaeologist, outlined the Oak Hill Horizon, which emerged out of Owasco, in turn gave rise to the Chance Horizon, and differentiated into Mohawk-Oneida and Onondaga culture. His dendritic chart demonstrated the relationship of Oak Hill to the development of the other Iroquois nations as well. This pioneering effort preceded the Mohawk Valley research program of Dean R. Snow in the 1970s and 1980s that has enabled him to synthesize Iroquois prehistory down to A.D. 1600 (Snow 1984). The last differentiation occurred around A.D. 1450, and in his view, "the League appears to have been essentially a phenomenon of the historic period" (1984: 257).

Among the more promising efforts to link ethnological and folkloristic data to prehistory now in progress are the provisional studies of George Hamell of the New York State Museum. Hamell explains why native copper, quartz crystals, and marine shells from a wide area of North America appear in graves dating from the late Archaic to historic times. By an analysis of the mythology and religious beliefs of Algonquian, Iroquoian, and Siouan peoples he has demonstrated how materials and objects found in burials relate symbolically to persistent beliefs in underwater spirits and magical properties of bright objects. These studies have aroused the attention of scholars (Ray Fogelson, personal communication; Trigger 1985: 74-75). In part they illuminate the Iroquois veneration for wampum strings and belts and underscore why these were important in treaty negotiations.

□□◇□□

Although Horatio Hale (1883) first attempted to assign relative dates to dialectal differentiation among Iroquoian languages, his estimate of four hundred years for the separation of Mohawk and Onondaga when first recorded in Jesuit dictionaries has proved much too shallow (Fenton 1963: xviii). The separation of these northern Iroquois languages from Tuscarora he regarded as of a much earlier order. His proportions were correct but the time lapse was much greater.

Floyd G. Lounsbury (1961; 1978: 334-36) first applied the lexicostatistical method known as glottochronology to the problem of relative dating of the separation of the southern branch of the Iroquoian family, from which Cherokee is descended, from the northern branch, from which all other Iroquoian languages are descended, and discovered a time depth of between thirty-five hundred and four thousand years for the separation. He also found evidence to support the hypothesis that the second-oldest division within the family occurred in the northern branch and produced Nottaway (of Virginia) and Tuscarora (of North Carolina) as a separate branch, and that this division happened some two thousand years ago. It is uncertain when the next split occurred, that between Huronian and the Five Nations languages plus Susquehanna. Passing over the so-called Laurentian languages of Stadacona (Quebec) and Hochelaga (Montreal), and possibly a third language, which the Cartier vocabularies left to posterity in a mixed bag, the Five Nations languages have survived for study. Of these, Mohawk and Oneida present a close relationship that is also mirrored in their political structure, although they were certainly distinct politically when the league was formed, as we know from the league epic. The separation and differentiation of dialects occurred several centuries before confederation. The division between Mohawk-Oneida and the other three of the Five Nations' dialects—Onondaga, Cayuga, and Seneca—appears earlier, although the relative age of the three remains uncertain. Susquehanna, now extinct, has some affinities to Onondaga. Of the sixteen historically known Iroquoian peoples, linguistic materials of varying quality exist on but eleven of them (Lounsbury 1978: 334).

From these dying speech echoes Lounsbury places the "center of gravity" of Iroquoian speakers in an area encompassing upstate New York and central and northwestern Pennsylvania, perhaps extending into northeastern Ohio. The linguistic evidence, in his opinion, does not support a southern or southwestern origin of the Iroquoian linguistic family within the last four thousand or five thousand years. It favors a long occupation in the north for as much as four millennia. In short, linguistics supports the in-situ hypothesis.

The current sophistication of Iroquoian linguistic studies has enabled Marianne Mithun (1984) to afford us a glimpse of Proto-Iroquoian culture that is available through no other approach. By application of the method of linguistic reconstruction, by comparing sets of words in related languages that are similar in both form and meaning and that derive their similarities from common inheritance, borrowing, onomatopoeia, or chance, she has derived a protolexicon that enables her to infer the protoculture. Inasmuch as the protolanguage and protoculture existed millennia before modern Iroquois languages and cultures, the time depth can be estimated by separations of the Iroquoian family of languages into northern and southern branches some four thousand years ago. Later separations into Proto–Northern Iroquoian, a subsequent split into Proto-Lake to accommodate Huron-Wyandot, and then Proto-Iroquois Proper, into the Five Nations and Susquehanna place the reconstructed semantic complexes in time perspective (see Mithun 1984: 264, fig. 15.2).

The results are fascinating. From the reconstructions we get a picture of the flora and fauna, an emphasis on hunting, a suggestion that maize culture came relatively late to the Northeast after the breakup of the language family. There is a substantial vocabulary relating to water, boats and fishing tackle, and material culture at various time levels. On social relations and polity, the results are meager. The cognates for "clay," "chimney," and "clan" presumably apply to "fireplace." And singing and singing tools have ancient cognates. Proto-Iroquoians were preoccupied with "luck," they practiced medicine, and they danced. Mithun's conclusions distinguish between what Proto-Iroquoians knew and used and what additionally pertains to Proto-Northern culture. The Proto-Northerners hunted with bows and arrows and developed a material culture dependent on forest products such as elm, basswood, and pine. How soon these trees were endowed with symbolism and became themes in Iroquois culture remains uncertain. "Rafters" goes back to Proto–Five Nations.

The Proto–Five Nations knew these things and others. They tapped sugar maples and knew hemp fiber; their women wore skirts and petticoats; they grew corn and beans, pounded corn in mortars with pestles, and made cornbread and mush. This most promising development in Iroquois studies adds a new dimension to culture history.

At a more recent protohistoric level, certain social and political institutions current at the mid-seventeenth century that we know from later ethnographic observations were already of some antiquity. By the method of "upstreaming," Gunther Michelson (1974) used present knowledge to identify phenomena in the past as they occur in Father Jacques Bruyas's *Radical Words in the Mohawk Language, with Their Derivatives* (1862). Father Bruyas, a Jesuit priest, worked among the Mohawks and Oneidas after 1667 and composed his dictionary in Mohawk, Latin, and French around 1675. Michelson points out for us terms relating to the condolence ritual, notably the protocol of passing wampum strings (at the woods' edge) and passages from the requickening ritual. There are references to political organization: the Onondaga responsibility for wampum, the imperishability of the Great Law, raising the Tree of Peace, and the establishment by the ancients of peace as law. Classes of chiefs were already established, particularly chiefships ascribed by maternal lineages, and chiefs were crowned with antlers as symbols of identity. Other offices were achieved or appointed. Mohawk government receives especial attention: the *agoianders* (chiefs) of each town meet as one to hold council; the Turtle clan is said to have nine voices (opinions). Whether this entry refers to the nine Mohawk chiefs in the league council or means that the Turtle clan comprised nine lineages, each with a voice in council, is open to question. The Roll Call of the Founders specifies three titles in each of the three Mohawk clans, implying three lineages per clan. Bruyas may have misunderstood.

Hewitt had marked "L" for matters referring to the league and its rituals in his personal copy of Bruyas's work. Besides items identified by Michelson, I find additionally the following references to house as symbol of the league: "to overset, or destroy it" (25); "when the builders of cabins put something in the way" (obstruct) (51); "rafters" (68); Onontio (governor of New France) "envies our house" (71); "Now the people of the Longhouse have been made infants" (65), a reminder of a line in the condolence ritual—"Sad will be the fate of those who come in later times" (Hale 1883: 123). Other phrases relate to council business: "to allow a space of a day between matters not yet agreed on" (34); "smoking the calumet," "cleaning the pipe" (53); "filling pipe with tobacco" (61); "sending a smoke signal," "to agree in a matter" (78); "the old men consent and cry in approval—yoh hen:h" (85); of "Peace" and "War" (98); "to light the council fire" (to hold council) (106); "to join our voices," "our thoughts" and "feelings"(107); "beneath a tree" (where chiefs meet) (118); "the ancients made it a rule" (118).

Still other terms belong to the ritual of condolence then as now: "One's mind scrambled with affliction" (42); "to throw wampum on a corpse" (67, 83); "to wash the bed" (mat) (67); "the old men mourn" (67); "to regret the earth" (67); "to sorrow for the land" (67); "to place a sack of tobacco (or wampum) on a pole" (69); "curtain" (hung to screen mourners) (75); "to comfort one" (90); "to administer the sweet water of pity" (95); "we are going as in a procession, advancing one before the others" (as in the march of the clearminded to the fire of the mourners) (116). As one might expect, there are numerous references to wampum and its uses in strings and belts: the making of a belt of twenty rows (61, 70); bottom of a strong box (73); to throw a string (80); cylinders (111).

Age grades and rank are clearly distinguished: ancestors, elders, and councilors are synonymous (44); a class of elite persons, both men and women (58); who are "antlered" (66); men of thirty-five to forty years (76); warriors (83); a term for appointed officials (today used for faithkeepers) (91); portions set aside for chiefs (98); men of forty to sixty years. Kinship usages overlap: to have as a child (52, 60); that the governor of New France (Onontio) has adopted us as his children (60); to render as infants the children of the league (60, 65); to have as mother (79); as uncle, as father-in-law (83); as nephew (108); and *atonni* (modern *agadoni*), sire (120).

Some features of the Mohawk people and their geography merit special attention: the "Noses" (Gagonharionni) at the narrows of the Mohawk River, which still mark the road to the Dutch, or Albany (49); and from the "three territories of the Flint (Mohawk) people" (52). In Bruyas's day the Mohawks enjoyed the reputation of being demons in war (36); collectively and singly they were known as the nation of the Flint, or the Bear (75); and their women decorated with wampum beads the long braid at their backs (75–76).

Last, in the evening of burning a prisoner they beat on bark (trays and houses) to drive off the soul of the dead victim. And one ceremony that did not survive was the Dance of the Agoianders (chiefs), in which they cast wampum to the spectators. It is tempting to link this activity to the dance of the chiefs called "rubbing antlers" (*endwana?ganye:*) that today closes the Condolence Council.

Although marginal to the Iroquois proper, Roy Wright's "glottohistory" of the Eries, the "People of the Panther," living west of the Senecas, is a fascinating exercise in linguistic methodology that reviews all extant information and dispels some wrong notions about these people. Unfortunately, we know them only through writers on the Iroquois, mainly the *Relations* of Jesuit missionaries, and cartographers (R. Wright 1974; White 1978b.) Father Claude Dablon at Onondaga reported events that precipitated the Eries' dispersal following 1654 (JR, 42: 31, 57–59, 85–203). Nations of the league mobilized against them an army of twelve hundred Onondagas, seven hundred Mohawks, and an unspecified number of Cayuga and Seneca warriors, an indication that the confederacy could cooperate. The extent to which such cooperation occurred in protohistoric times remains uncertain.

□□◇□□

There is evidence now that the process of confederation could have started in late prehistoric times. Between A.D. 1300 and 1400, during what the prehistorians term the Middle Iroquoian Period, throughout the northern Iroquoian area, villages began to consolidate, grew larger, and were sited in defensive positions and palisaded because warfare was on the increase. The evidence comes from the Oak

Hill horizon for the Mohawks, from Onondaga (Tuck 1971), and from Seneca. The presence of two or more localized clans in the community, each with its offices ascribed in a particular lineage, soon required a town council for the resolution of differences and a mechanism for composing feuds. The next step was to form alliances with neighboring towns, to agree on peace and justice between them, while meeting a common threat of warfare. This is precisely the situation designated by the term "the troubled nations" in the opening of the league epic, and the process of confederating which it describes fits this model of links between localized villages, each with its chief or chiefs (Trigger 1985: 93ff.). As the villages increased in size, some equitable distribution of agricultural resources demanded that women join together under a matron and work in teams to prepare the fields, to plant, hoe, and harvest crops of maize and beans, and to procure firewood. This pattern of mutual aid was to come down to modern times. As the men spent more time away from home hunting or on the warpath, jurisdiction over household, village, and clearing devolved on women and bolstered a system of matrilineal descent, inheritance, and succession. Speculative as it may seem, and devoid of references to a nonexistent literature, as a hypothesis it explains what probably happened.

A new paradigm of Iroquois culture accompanied the consolidation of villages late in the Middle Iroquoian period. Different patterns of reciprocal services between segments of society would emerge locally—a tripartite system in the east and reciprocity between moieties to the west—that would require compromise when merged into a single political system later. After A.D. 1400, ethnic entities ancestral to the historic Five Nations were emerging. In the best case, Tuck (1971: 214–16) demonstrated that the Onondaga nation formed out of two chains of villages that gradually converged to nearby sites about A.D. 1450–75. A similar chain of village removals produced two major towns and the Seneca nation about A.D. 1550 (Niemczycki 1984: 75). The importance of these approximate dates is that formation of the Five Nations preceded the process of confederation.

Clearly, the steps leading to the formation of the league began in protohistoric times during what is termed the Late Iroquoian period. The span of the process described in the Deganawi:dah epic ranged from after A.D. 1450 into the next century. A wide bracket of dates has been advanced (Tooker 1978: 419–22), none of which can be verified but which fall within the range of A.D. 1500 plus or minus fifty years. Hewitt and Beauchamp opted for still later dates, as have some historians, holding that European pressure on northern and eastern tribes produced the response for mutual defense. Process ignores the calendar.

Among the factors tending toward alliances and then confederation was the presence in neighboring villages of kin and clan that bespoke identity of persons sharing the same eponym and demanded reciprocal services to one's father's kin and between cross-cousins. These relationships were soon projected to the fictitious level of clan, to clans of the same phratry, and to opposite moieties. Associations of persons who had been cured by the same medicine society or who shared particular dreams were current among the northern Iroquoians when they were first observed, and such ritual companies undoubtedly go back to pre-Columbian times. One rite of the Medicine Company (*yeiʔdo:s*) today speaks of "cutting through the forest" (*hadihadiyaʔs*), in which one moiety of singers files in as if from another settlement, an act that recalls mutual services between villages at an earlier day. Traditionally, village chiefs encouraged lacrosse matches with neighboring towns, both to keep warriors fit and to discourage intervillage feuds and warfare. Such events still turn out large crowds. And ceremonies for the dead, which began within communities, in the case of fallen leaders drew those affected from afar, setting up the relationship of mourners and clearminded between moieties, towns, and nations that is the heart of the condolence ceremony. Indeed, the Condolence Council, as we know it, has a long history, and its essential features—the Hai Hai chants and the symbolic transportation of the bones of departed leaders—recall the Huron Feast of the Dead.[2] They are of the same genre.

The formation of the Huron confederacy affords a useful analogy. Trigger, in his classic history of the Hurons, reconstructs Huron government and presents intriguing analogues between its confederate council and that of the Five Nations Iroquois (1976: 54ff., 90–104, 156–63). The time frame for these two sets of institutions rests on a comprehensive knowledge of the archaeology of Ontario and New York. Conditions were right for the formation of such confederacies during the century following A.D. 1450. These alliances were at first loose associations for curbing blood feuds and intertribal aggression. Indeed, that is the purpose of the Iroquois Condolence Council, which had its origin in such associations. Although Trigger found no evidence that members of a confederacy were bound to mutual aid in warfare, the Deganawi:dah code specifies just this, and such alliances did restrain intertribal warfare and imparted a sense of corporate identity to all members. The year 1450 must be regarded not as a precise date but only as the start of a long process toward confederation. Trigger's point and mine is that the process began a century before the advent of Europeans in North America. Trigger observes that even if the Iroquois Confederacy were strengthened to cope with European intrusion during the fur trade, this happened easily. Its staying power, moreover, argues for its age. For these and other reasons, he considers it doctrinaire not to heed the Huron claim to the Jesuits that their confederacy began about A.D. 1440 (Trigger 1976: 163).[3]

Warfare between the Hurons and the Five Nations began much later over the fur trade, and there is no evidence for it in prehistoric times (Trigger 1985: 108). It is fashionable now to stress transformations in the native culture in response to European stimuli and to overlook continuities in patterns of culture.

Trading networks covered the eastern woodlands in prehistoric times. Copper from the upper peninsula of Michigan, marine shell from coastal estuaries, obsidian from the Rocky Mountains, and, later, catlinite from Minnesota traveled the trade routes. Partnerships linked individuals near and far, and corporate alliances developed to satisfy urgent needs. The introduction of iron weapons and tools on the St. Lawrence and the Susquehanna developed a demand among tribes nearest the sources, and this hardware at first was not accessible to the Five Nations. The Dutch on the Hudson brought iron tools to the Mahicans and Mohawks before they reached Onondaga or the Seneca towns (Bradley 1980, 1987;

2. Trigger (1985: 102–3) set me to recalling such matters.
3. See my review essay (Fenton 1978b); also Trigger 1985: 104.

Trigger 1985: 161). Bradley found virtually no iron on early protohistoric Onondaga sites and suggests that demand for it contributed to the confederation process.

A difficulty with such protohistoric explanations is that they can be reversed. Factors contributing to confederation are explained by the process of confederation itself. It is made to explain changes in settlement patterns, and these in turn to demonstrate the existence of the confederacy (Bradley 1987: 43). Perhaps that is the best we can do with available evidence. Having discounted upstreaming from seventeenth-century sources to suggest what the confederacy may have been before it was observed, because that approach fails to differentiate continuity from change, Bradley (1987: 104) adopts Wallace's (1970: 42) model of "minimum" and "maximum" purposes. The former relates to the original peace mission of the founders; the latter refers to later extensions to incorporate neighboring peoples and to the chain alliances during the eighteenth century. Bradley is safe in ascribing the former to the protohistoric Onondagas. If not upstreaming, this line of reasoning is certainly a kind of projection of later modeling to explain earlier phenomena. What it lacks is the chain of evidence that true upstreaming demands. I do not regard the model of the "cargo cult" as helpful. Bradley's assertion (1987: 109) that Iroquois militancy in later times was directed at tribes having immediate access to the coast via river corridors rests on firmer ground.

This is as far as protohistory will take us. We now turn to a close consideration of the Condolence Council.

PART TWO

Concerning
the League

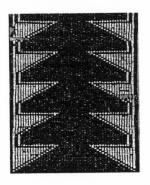

CHAPTER 9

THE HISTORICAL PARADIGM
OF THE CONDOLENCE COUNCIL

In the great ceremony for mourning dead chiefs and raising up their successors in office, traditionalists have perpetuated what is certainly the climax form of Iroquois political culture, the roots of which reach back to the dawn of written history in the Americas. Although recognizable forms of the ceremony appear in the literature of the seventeenth century and occur with greater frequency during the eighteenth, it was late in the nineteenth century before Horatio Hale (1883) first recorded the ceremony from native sources and witnessed a performance (in 1895). On that occasion the principal celebrant was Chief John Arthur Gibson.

Gibson later dictated the complete texts to J.N.B. Hewitt, and again to Alexander Goldenweiser (in 1912). After succeeding Hewitt at the Smithsonian and inheriting his texts, I was privileged to work with Simeon Gibson, a son of John Arthur Gibson, and with Simeon Gibson's nephew Howard Skye, who prepared me to observe the ceremony on two occasions in 1945 and 1951 (Fenton 1946, 1950, and field notes).

Hale's contemporary, William Beauchamp, having attended several condoling ceremonies at Onondaga, New York, before the turn of the century, published an account of one (1895) and noted that although much had changed, it preserved interesting antique features (1907: 351ff.). His monograph (Beauchamp 1907) offers an alternative text to Hale's, features musical scores of the chants, including the Hymn to the Dead Chief, and treats some general features in the old accounts.

After me, Gunther Michelson (1988) was privileged to witness an installation ceremony at Six Nations. I know of no other systematic accounts. In recent years, access to the ceremony has been restricted.

Gibson's text visualized a ceremony in which the Four Brothers (the Oneidas, Cayugas, Tuscaroras, and Tutelos) had suffered a death and were condoled by the Three Brothers moiety of chiefs (the Mohawks, Onondagas, and Senecas). Ideal patterns find confirmation in the reality of observed performances, and Gibson's scenario was indeed the situation I witnessed in 1945. Witnessing live performances also enables the observer to recognize significant behavior, incidentals, failures to adhere to native theory, and omissions. My observations then, at Lower Cayuga (Fenton 1946), and further observations at a turn-about ceremony at Onondaga in 1951 (field notes), coupled with an analysis of Gibson's 1912 text, enabled me to isolate reciprocal and spatial patterns between mourners and clearminded. A detailed sequence of events taking place during the ceremony is given in Appendix A.

After using these sources and observations to establish the program of the ceremony (following Hewitt's lead), I was then able to link the elements of the program to the treaty-making process, to accommodate variants in the earlier literature, and to reconstruct an ideal pattern of treaty protocol. This paradigm illustrates how a symbolic system endures even when the fulfillment of all its forms cannot be accomplished (Fenton 1985: 18–19, 27–30). The structure, content, and symbolism of the amply documented nineteenth-century ceremony facilitate interpreting the often fragmentary earlier accounts, from which one can discern continuities and assess changes during three hundred years.

Throughout the history of the condolence ritual, the learned men of Iroquoia, in acting out this paradigm for maintaining their political system, have believed that it would "strengthen the house." The league epic as given in the Gibson text of 1912 attributes to Deganawi:dah and Hiawatha the protocol for compounding murders, composing feuds, and making peace between nations—a protocol that comprises the rituals of condolence and requickening. This ceremony for maintaining the edifice of government and restoring society, which is known in the literature as the Condolence Council, in turn underlies the protocol of treaties and sets the stage for forest diplomacy.

During the seventeenth and eighteenth centuries, a drama evolved in which the actors were Indian sachems and colonial governors, or their agents. With different casts and slight changes in the script, the play ran for one hundred fifty years, principally at Albany, occasionally at Philadelphia, Lancaster, and Easton, and later at Johnson Hall, Fort Stanwix, and Canandaigua. French actors performed at Three Rivers, Quebec, and Montreal. But in its purest form, with an all-native cast, it opened the great drama festivals held each fall at Onondaga, where it is said that the ceremony originated with the founding of the League of Five Nations before the Dutch or French came to America. Deganawi:dah was the playwright, and Hiawatha, the leading actor.[1]

□□◇□□

To understand the Condolence Council, one must realize that two sides are involved in reciprocal actions. One side, called the clearminded (C), performs the ceremony to condole, or lift up the minds, of the other side, the mourners (M), who have suffered a loss by the death of a chief or relation. Colonial officials and, by extension, royalty came to assume either role. The clearminded are regarded as performing the ceremony so as to put the house in order and restore the faculties of the mourners.

Once the mourning tribal moiety notifies the clearminded moiety that a chief has fallen, the clearminded perform virtually all of the important roles, from approaching the mourning side in a procession to the fire at the edge of the clearing and conducting the several components of the condoling ceremony to charging the new chief with his responsibilities. The aggrieved moiety, however, manages to welcome the condolers at the fire and escort their guests into the longhouse, where the two sides occupy opposite ends.

---

1. After Fenton 1985: 18, 1957: 22–24; and Hale 1883. See also Woodbury 1992: Table 2.

Five fundamental rites compose the framework of the Condolence Council and its program of sixteen essential elements, which I will list shortly (Hewitt 1944: 65). The five are (1) Going on the Road (or Journeying on the Path), the procession of the clearminded to the council place of the mourners, during which the clearminded chant the Eulogy, or Roll Call, of the Founders of the League (Fenton 1950); (2) the Welcome at the Woods' Edge (Hale 1883: 117–19; Fenton field notes, 1945), when the mourners (the hosts) greet the clearminded (the visitors);[2] (3) the Requickening Address (Hewitt 1916; 1944)—part one of which consists of "Three Bare Words" beside the fire ("bare" in the sense of being the minimum essentials), and part two of which consists of four to fifteen "words" in the longhouse, each accompanied by a string of wampum; (4) Six Songs of Farewell to the Dead Chief, or the Great Hymn (see Appendix B); and (5) the reciting of Over the Forest: the Laws of the Founders. Clearly, the performance of these rites, which make up the great ceremony, is an important institution for maintaining the Great Law, or the League of the Iroquois. Condolence law, which mandates that deaths be condoled and empty seats in council filled before proceeding to business, is its supporting sanction.

Within the framework of these five rites, the program of the Condolence Council now comprises some sixteen events arranged in a sequential pattern of a kind that has governed its performance since early times. Its content has changed, and only some of the sixteen events are mentioned in historical accounts. The essential elements that comprise the paradigm, or program, of the ceremony are the following (and see Table 2).

1. Going on the Road: the clearminded go in procession over the path to the house of the mourners, their singer calling out the Roll Call of the Founders.
2. Welcome at the Woods' Edge: the mourners welcome the clearminded at the fire by the woods' edge (clearing).
3. In part one of the Requickening Address, the clearminded and the mourners exchange the Three Bare Words of Requickening—the wiping of tears, the clearing of ears, and the clearing of throats ("tears," "ears," and "throat," for short).
4. The mourners take the clearminded by the arm to the council place.
5. The singer for the clearminded chants the Roll Call (or Eulogy) of the Founders, naming all fifty founders of the League of the Iroquois.
6. A curtain (today a quilt, formerly deerskins) is drawn across the council place to partition it, symbolizing the separation of the two moieties. Behind the partition, the clearminded sing the first five of the Six Songs of Farewell to the Dead Chief (the sixth song is withheld until element 8).[3]

2. "At the Wood's Edge," Deyughnyonkwarakda (Hale 1883: 194) (*deyohnyonkwarakta,* "at the wood's edge; near the thicket"). Note *onniongar,* "thorn bush, bramble" (Bruyas); *akta,* "beside, near to" (Cuoq). The word applies to the line of bushes usually found on the border between forest and clearing. With the cislocative *de-,* it means "on this side of the thicket" (Hale 1883: 194). The rule of the founders about kindling a fire at the edge of the woods is stated in the Address of Welcome in the *Book of Rites* (Hale 1883: 119). "Here they are to condole each other with a few words." The main business, however, is referred to the council house.
3. Frequently, the lead singer is borrowed from the other side. In 1883, the clearminded side borrowed J. A. Gibson from the mourners (Hale 1895: 55 and comments 61, 62–64).

TABLE 2

EPISODE STRUCTURE OF MOURNING AND INSTALLATION RITUALS

THE RITUALS	THE CONDOLENCE PROGRAM BY RITUAL EPISODES
PART 1: THE RITUALS OF MOURNING	
i. On the Journey (Roll Call) (1, 2, 6, 7)*	1 Prologue to On the Journey—at condolers' meeting place (condolers to ancestors)
	2 On the Journey—on way to mourners (condolers to ancestors)
ii. Near the Thorny Bushes (Woods' Edge Welcome) (3)	3 Near the Thorny Bushes—at mourners' fire (mourners to condolers)
iii. Wiping Their Tears (Requickening) (4, 5, 12a, 14a)	4 Wiping Their Tears, part 1—at mourners' fire (mourners to condolers)
	5 Wiping Their Tears, part 1—at mourners' fire (condolers to mourners)
	6 On the Journey, resumed—on way to mourners' longhouse from mourners' fire (condolers to ancestors)
	7 On the Journey, repeated—in mourners' longhouse (condolers to ancestors)
iv. The Six Songs (8, 10, 13)	8 Six Songs, part 1—curtain lowered (condolers—no addressee)
	9 Over the Forest, Prologue—curtain raised (condolers to ancestors)
	10 Six Songs, part 2—curtain lowered (condolers to ancestors)
	11 Over the Forest—curtain raised (condolers to ancestors)
	12a Wiping Their Tears, part 2 (condolers to mourners)
PART II: THE INSTALLATION RITUAL	
vi. The Installation (12b, 14b, 15)	12b Call for the Candidate (condolers to mourners)
	13 Six Songs (songs 1-5: mourners; song 6: mourners to ancestors)
	14a Wiping Their Tears, part 2 (mourners to condolers) [PAUSE]
	14b Presentation of the Candidate and Installation (mourners to condolers)
	15 Charge to the Chief, his Deputies, and his Matron (condolers to officials)**

Source: Woodbury 1992: Table 1. Reproduced by permission.

* The Condolence Terminology I use represents an attempt to correct the record by establishing English language names of Condolence Rituals that reflect the meanings of native language terms as closely as possible. Terms familiar from the English language literature are given in parentheses.

** Fenton (ms. pp. 6, 46, and 49) and Hewitt (SINAA ms. 915) list an episode after the Charge, in which the mourners release the women who will make final preparations for the feast and in which they call on those present to report on 'Dreams'. These consist of announcements of important matters someone in the audience may wish to raise at this time and may include, according to Fenton (p.c. 10/24/88), recitations of sections of the League Tradition.

7. The partition is withdrawn, and the clearminded recite part one of Over the Forest, "the league has grown old."
8. The curtain is again drawn, and the clearminded sing the Sixth Song to the founders.
9. With the curtain once more withdrawn, the clearminded perform part two of Over the Forest, reciting the laws of the league.
10. The remainder of the Requickening Address is recited by the clearminded— "words" 4–15, with accompanying wampum strings. The clearminded threaten to withdraw but are asked to stay until the mourners can compose a reply.
11. The mourners reply: Six Songs.
12. The mourners return the words of condolence and wampum strings 4–15.
13. The clan matron on the mourners' side "shows the face" of the new chief.
14. The speaker for the clearminded gives the Charge to the New Chief and to the public.
15. The mourners host a feast to wash away the tobacco. Cries of approbation on both sides: *yohen:* and *hi:yah!*
16. Rubbing Antlers: the celebration dance. Society is restored.

Native theory holds that the Condolence Council has such potency that it should rightfully be celebrated only between the autumn and final spring frosts, lest it blight growing plants. (Native practice overlooks the rule.) The program sequence reduces its impact by segmenting the episodes and inserting the first part of one episode before proceeding to the second part of an episode already begun. This tempers its inherent power, enabling the mourning recipients to take it in without being overcome.

The ceremony reaches its first climax when the clearminded complete the fifteen words of requickening and feint a withdrawal to the edge of the clearing. In a tension-relieving gesture, the mourners ask them to stay and compose their minds while they return the songs and words of condolence. The mourners, however, do not segment their performance but go through all Six Songs without pause. Iroquois thought regards singing a message as the ultimate form of communication. In treaty negotiations described later, we shall repeatedly encounter the words, "Let me drive it into your minds with a song!"

The ultimate climax in the ceremony occurs when the mourners "hold up the face" of the new chief and the clearminded speaker charges him with the duties and obligations of his office. Then anxiety dissolves and society is restored in the great social dance called Rubbing Antlers, which the chiefs lead and the young people take over.

□□◇□□

Performance of the rites that make up this ritual pattern illustrates two theoretical principles in social anthropology that originated with the functionalists during the first third of the twentieth century. The consequences of one half of the society (the unaffected clearminded's) condoling the other half (whose minds are depressed in grief) to enable the mourners once more to discharge normal social obligations, a ritual process called "lifting up their minds," is an elegant illustration of A. R. Radcliffe-Brown's (1958) concepts of dysphoria and euphoria, the one transformed into the other. The transformation is accomplished by the interaction of the clearminded and the "downminded" in a series of mutual acts, as in Bronislaw Malinowski's concept of reciprocity.[4] Restraint is another principle that operates in the discharge of this paradigm: it is important not to exert too much power. So in lifting up the minds of the grieving party, the two sides employ four additional principles in mutual segments: (1) separation versus approach, (2) alternation and reciprocation of ritual acts by the clearminded and the mourners, (3) interdigitation of rites by the clearminded (introducing a rite by its preface and withholding the balance to follow a second preface), and (4) the clearminded's threat of withdrawal versus the mourners' appeal to them to stay to hear the mourners' rapid return of condolences, wampums, and songs without hitch.

As the climax form of Iroquois political behavior, the ceremony reaches a built-in climax of its own. After traversing the first twelve items of the ritual agenda, which achieve the restoration of society, the ceremony builds to a peak of intensity in raising the new chief in the title of his predecessor (M), charging him with the duties of his office (C), and exchanging "news," referred to as "dreams," which sometimes calls for a recitation of sections of the origin myth. Finally, the terminal feast, always given by the host (M), followed by a great social dance, discharges any tensions and narrows social distance. When the hosts ask the visitors not to be too hard on their women, whom they (M) "release" to the visitors, or "let slip through their fingers," the standard reply by the clearminded invariably is, "We are but old men!"

□□◇□□

Having outlined the spatial and reciprocal actions of the mourning and condoling moieties in performing the condolence ceremony, I now offer accounts of two actual ceremonies that I witnessed in 1945 and 1951. The latter has never before been published, but it is the reciprocal of the published Cayuga installation ceremony of 1945 (Fenton 1946) and of the hypothetical example from the Gibson text of 1912.

---

4. The operation of the concept of reciprocity comes through in Malinowski's writings from *Argonauts of the Western Pacific* (1922) onward, and particularly in *Crime and Customs in Savage Society* (1926).

CHAPTER 10

INSTALLING CAYUGA CHIEFS
IN 1945

Three of us stood shivering in the November afternoon on the common at Lower Cayuga Longhouse.[1] Dr. Robert Hatt and Marcelle Hatt of the Cranbrook Institute and I had parked our cars alongside a row of Indian cars. I had left the Library of Congress sound truck unlocked, knowing that my cameras would be safe, for there were no other outlanders around. From within the longhouse one could hear the chiefs of the Four Brothers' side rehearsing the Six Songs (see fig. 11).

Over at the cookhouse just east of the longhouse, smoke intended for the chimney drifted out the door. One of the two male cooks for the new chiefs ladled chunks of boiled beef out of a great iron cauldron into a wooden trencher. This was part of a quarter of beef that we had procured in Caledonia the day before from William Smith, butcher to the Six Nations. In olden times, eight men were appointed to hunt venison for the feast; they went out all abreast, driving the game until eight deer fell. I remarked to the matron who oversaw preparations for the feast that women are customarily cooks among the Senecas, and men wait on them. But here at Grand River, men regularly do the heavy cooking for longhouse feasts. Indeed, Jemima Gibson, the matron sponsoring the ceremony, quipped, "Here in Canada, Indian and Chinese men are cooks. Therefore, we must have come from Asia. It should interest you as an anthropologist!"

Actually, both men and women fulfill the role of "hanging kettles for the chief" (*honwanajiaha:nink*). Each matron sponsoring a candidate enlists a man and a woman, unless she serves herself.

A car lurched through the gate and chugged up the common. It disgorged a stout Cayuga chief, Hagya?trone? (Alex Nanticoke), and a younger deputy, Shohe:s (Howard Skye). They were returning from Onondaga Longhouse (fig. 7), some two miles west, and they hustled inside to report. About noon, the Three Brothers (Mohawk-Onondaga-Seneca) had dispatched a scout to find out the state of preparations at the fire of the Four Brothers (Oneida-Cayuga-Tuscarora-Tutelo). Going first to Lower Cayuga Longhouse and finding no one there, he returned partway, stopping at the fire of Jemima Gibson, where the cooks were eating. The Onondaga runner, who drove a Ford, was told that the Four Brothers would send

---

1. This chapter has been adapted from my 1946 article, "An Iroquois Condolence Council for Installing Cayuga Chiefs in 1945," *Journal of the Washington Academy of Sciences*, 36 (4): 110–27.

Figure 7. Onondaga Longhouse at Six Nations Reserve, Canada, seat of the traditional League of the Iroquois. Simeon Gibson stands on the stoop. Photo by author, 1940.

a messenger when ready. On returning to the longhouse from dinner, Desgahe? (Chief Alexander General) appointed Howard Skye runner, and Chief Nanticoke drove him. Arriving at Onondaga Longhouse, the Cayuga messenger found the chiefs inside rehearsing the Requickening Address. They stopped on seeing the messenger, who said, "I bear the message of the Four Brothers who sent me to say, 'Now preparations have been completed.' So that is the sum of my message."

With the return of the Cayuga messenger, the hosts knew that the Three Brothers had taken up the path and would arrive momentarily (fig. 8). Warriors were detailed to kindle a small fire near the gate. They cleared away weeds and dry leaves from a spot just east of the path leading from the road to the common, where a cook carried embers from the main fire. Commonly they build the wood's-edge fire just as soon as they hear the singer chanting the Hai Hai, or Eulogy to the Founders, on the path, recounting the roll of the founders of the league, while the procession of condoling chiefs nears the fire of the grieving tribes.

About three o'clock, the prolonged cry of the shouter marching beside the singer floated over the elm and shagbark hickory trees—*kheya?ta:wen:* (my nephews: my male kinsman's children). The cry reached us before we heard the voice of the singer reiterating the Hai Hai. The cry signified that the singer had just completed the roster of a committee of founders. The shout of the "uncles" (father's kinsmen) quavered on the cold wind. I shivered, transported three centuries to the reedy shores of Cayuga Lake, and wondered how the cry must have sounded coming over the forest from Onondaga near modern Syracuse. The clear voice of the Hai Hai next reached us. The singer was Roy Buck, whom the Three Brothers' side was grooming for this role at the rehearsal I had attended (fig. 9).

The procession passed Six Nations Corners and neared the gate. In advance came two warriors at the head of a double column. Next came the singer and crier, followed by chiefs. The chiefs carried canes; the scouts, sticks. Anciently, the two

Figure 8. The Three Brothers, the clearminded moiety in 1945, after stopping for lunch en route to the Condolence Council. Photo by author.

warriors who guard the singer probably ranged far ahead as scouts, for at the founding of the league, enemy warriors lurked in the forest. The order of march did not follow the roll call of nations from Mohawk to Seneca. One wonders that the systematic Iroquois had overlooked the opportunity to regiment the line of march.

□□◇□□

For the Welcome at the Woods' Edge, the mourning Oneida and Cayuga chiefs, their deputies, matrons, warriors, and following public came down the common and ranked themselves in this order facing the fire, the road, and the oncoming procession. The procession of visiting clearminded chiefs, followed by their public—a motley crowd afoot and in automobiles—turned in the gate and took up similar positions across the fire but toward the road. The two guardians of the singer ranged out to flank the front line of chiefs. On reaching the fire the singer stopped.

The principal speaker for the clearminded—the Onondaga David Thomas (Sai?go:na, or Big Knife)—took a front and center position next to Chief Joseph Logan (fig. 10) for the Three Brothers. Deputies formed the second line; matrons and the public ranged behind. Here at the woods'-edge fire was a scene worthy of filming, were it permitted: the two crowds divided by the fire and five yards of common; dead chickory and frosted asters; smoke rising through the bony limbs of shagbark hickories above the Three Brothers; cars, women, babies, men in tailored suits, others in overalls, but none dressed in native costume. One of the scouts glanced apprehensively in our direction, where we stood apart, east of the fire, in order to review equally both moieties. But we held to our pledge not to take pictures, and the scouts relaxed when they saw that we meant it.

A representative of the mourning Four Brothers, Chief Alex General of the Cayuga title Desgahe?, stood to the fore, leaning on his cane, waiting as the

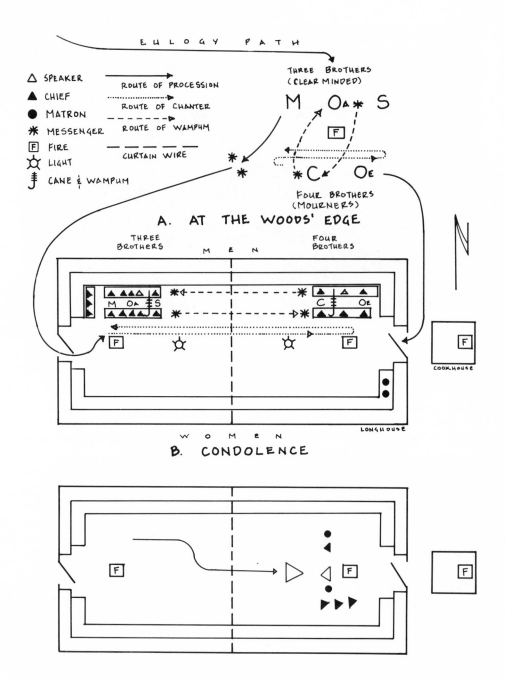

Figure 9. Floor plan for the condolence rite at Cayuga Longhouse, 1945. Drawing by Sylvie Browne.

Figure 10. Chiefs Joseph Logan (right) and Jesse Lewis at Onondaga Longhouse. Photo by author, 1941.

Three Brothers came up and formed ranks across the fire. Presently he took up his cane and paced to and fro, chanting the measured phrases of welcome. This act is called Deyothnyongwa:rakte?, "Beside the Thorny Brush" or "Welcome at the Woods' Edge." The Mohawk words are as printed in The *Iroquois Book of Rites* (Hale 1883: 117ff.), but in performance the phrasing is accommodated to the measured chant—"it takes all of one's breath to express one word."

Onenh wenisera:::de?	Now today
wagadyerengo:::wa	was I greatly startled
deshawennawerade?	by your voice coming
ne? kendeyoho:::don?	to this clearing

The chanting reminds one of high Anglican mass.

Desgahe? had typed out the words from an old penciled script of someone named John Doctor, and there is no telling whether Doctor had it from Hale or both had it from the same source. Desgahe? managed without notes until near the end; there are not quite a hundred "words" to remember.

Thus for centuries grieving tribes had greeted condolers, hosts had received ambassadors, saying, "Great thanks that you have passed safely diverse obstacles and dangers that beset your journey. Journeying you passed places where the founders on whom our faith rests used to meet." The Four Brothers speaking say, "My father's kinsmen, how can your minds be at ease when you kept seeing the traces of our forefathers, and barely perceptible is the smoke still rising at the places where they used to smoke in council, they who sustain our minds, and you saw on the journey the traces of their labors? How then can your minds be at ease, when from your eyes teardrops hang repeatedly, my father's kinsmen? Thanks greatly that you arrived here safely. Now we both have come together with tears in our eyes, and we have sat down [across the fire]." (But they now stand!)

The chanter goes on to conjecture the awful calamity of a death on the trail, or some similar disaster to one of the chiefs. But the founders ordained that a fire should be made at the woods' edge, where they should condole each other briefly, employing but three words. They should reserve the principal matters for inside the house, where the main business should be transacted; there they should rub down each other's bodies, and there they should be taken by the arm and seated on the main bench. A list of town names founded by several maternal lineages concludes the chant. These were sites long ago of Mohawk and Oneida settlements, names for the most part now obscure. The first chant ends abruptly.

□□◇□□

Once more Desgahe? stood front and center before the fire, resting on his cane, for part one of the ritual known as Three Bare Words of Requickening, or the Requickening Address. Hagya?trone?, at his elbow, produced the first three strings of requickening, which are strung of variegated purple and white wampum beads. Traditionally, a horizontal pole resting in the forks of two uprights held the wampum belts and strings at the fire beside the trail. But in 1945 the Cayuga wampum keeper let the three short strings hang from his hand. Nor had the phratry across the fire set up a cross-pole for receiving and racking up the strings. I was surprised to see the mourning chiefs send over the first three strings to the clearminded, because Hewitt (1944: 70) had assigned this act to the latter. But it was to clarify such issues that I had waited ten years and come to Canada to witness the ceremony. Observation serves to correct misunderstood informant testimony.

In the first of the three words, the speaker for the mourners acknowledges the Creator's part in making the day such as it is and causing the number of persons to come on the road with tears in their eyes and to reach the appointed place where the fire rests beside the wood. The Four Brothers deem it remarkable. Now with the white fawnskin of pity the speaker wipes away their tears to enable them to look around with clear eyes and notice passing persons. I observed the speaker's messenger take the first string of wampum and carry it over the fire to the Three Brothers, where it was received by Thadoda:ho?, the first Onondaga chief.

Similarly, the speaker proceeded to remove obstructions from the ears (second string), and then to clear the throats (third string) of the clearminded.

Now enabled to see, to hear, and to breathe freely, the speaker for the Three Brothers replied to the mourners. The clearminded confirmed what their hosts had done and assured them that they approved of the number of matters so far uttered. "Further," they said, "what befell you is not a one-sided affair [it affects both moieties], which is the purpose of the Three Brothers coming. What a calamity has befallen the Four Brothers. Yea, a seat is vacant in the place where you all customarily assemble. Now a man has died, one to whom the people used to look and direct their minds. Now the bench is vacant. And consequently you, the Four Brothers, are in the midst of great tears."

Now the Three Brothers customarily wipe away the tears to enable the Four Brothers to see what transpires on earth. In 1945, a deputy for the condolers carried the first string back over the fire, where it was grasped by the Cayuga wampum keeper. (Since both sides have their own sets of requickening strings, the strings sent over go back in succession to the owners.)

And so the speaker for the Three Brothers, the clearminded, proceeded to open the ears and remove obstructions from the throats of the grieving Four Brothers, sending back the two remaining strings, one at a time, by his deputy as he completed each word.

Now that the mourners were somewhat assuaged—able to see, hear, and breathe freely—by the Three Bare Words, and fortified in their minds by the return of wampum strings, the speaker for the mourning Four Brothers said, "Now we have completed it. The preliminary words are over. We both have rubbed down each other's bodies. Everything on our side is now ready; they shall take you by the arm and lead you to the principal bench (*ganakdagweniyo?geh*), and there one shall seat you in the place where the entire business will be carried to a conclusion, as many matters as remain for us. Thus the appointed warrior chief will take you there by the arm and he will seat you where the benches have been prepared for you."

Just then Howard Skye for the Cayugas and Albert Thomas for the Oneidas stepped across the fire and turned together to face the west entrance to the long-house. As custom dictated, the two ushers preceded the two warriors who had led the procession over the road, the singer and crier for the Three Brothers following.

Meanwhile the hosts, having turned away from the fire, were making for the east door of the longhouse to find seats. Supposedly the chiefs precede the crowd into the building. Actually, many from both sides had crowded in already to preempt the best seats at each end.

Then the two appointed warrior ushers said, as custom demands, "Onenh dwa?dendya?" (Let us proceed).

Once more taking up the Roll Call of the Founders where he had left off on reaching the fire, the singer, Roy Buck, started the procession of the Three Brothers toward the west door. Up to the door he continued to recite names of founders not chanted on the road. It was four o'clock when we followed the procession into the longhouse. We had passed nearly an hour shivering by the fire.

□□◇□□

At the door, another appointed singer takes over and recommences the Roll Call of the Founders from the beginning inside the house, regardless of where the first singer leaves off. Adhering to custom, the visiting chiefs occupied two opposite benches placed lengthwise of the house in the northwest corner, and a third bench placed across the west end of the first two and facing the Four Brothers at the far end of the room. The latter sat on two opposite benches similarly placed in the northeast corner. Men occupied the north half of the longhouse at both ends; women and children sat to the south. Midway of the house a wire stretched across the room, as if to demarcate the zone of the clearminded from that of the mourners, and on it, folded against the north wall, hung a blue quilt fitted with curtain rings (see fig. 9).

Onondaga chief Peter Buck walked slowly the length of the house and returned, cane in hand, on the men's side, chanting the Eulogy to the Founders. It was readily apparent why the eulogy singer must rehearse. He must have the lines fixed in his mind; he must remember the roll of the chiefs in proper order, how they are related as brothers or cousins, their grouping in committees, and how to divide the words to fit the melodic line. From the moment he crosses the door sill, confusion greets him. The mourning side is seated, but his own colleagues are coming in. Escorted to the benches set out for them, the clearminded chiefs seat themselves while the crowd scrambles for seats along the wall. The west door keeps banging and creaks. The air is already fouled: chiefs light up their pipes and cigars; the stoves at each end of the longhouse alternately radiate intense heat or smoke. Babies cry. But the measured phrases of the roll call go on inexorably for an hour (Hewitt and Fenton 1945).

> Haii Haii Now continue to listen
> Haii Haii Our grandfathers of old
> Haii Haii You did establish it
> Haii Haii The Great Law

(Seventeen "words" or lines precede the first name.)

> Haii Haii [four times]
> Haii Haii Continue to hear us
> Haii Haii You who were proprietors [founders]
> Haii Haii Ne Tekarihoken
> Haii Haii They were related as brothers
>
> Haii Haii That was the number of you
> Haii Haii Who worked together
> Haii Haii You did found
> Haii Haii The Great Law
> Haii Raksot [grandsires]

And so the chanter goes on to mention all the names through the rosters of five tribes on both sides of the fire, as they are sires or offspring of each other, going through the chant to the very end as far as it was completed when the league was founded. Moreover, while the chanter walks to and fro performing the ceremony, each time he comes to these lines:

> Haii Haii ne?to hona?de:jon?na
> Haii Haii swa?deihwakhahon?gwa
> ["That was the number of you founders"],

the chief so denominated cries in approbation, "Yohen:::" (in falling tone), and his colleagues of his phratry in unison confirm (in low tone) "Hi:::yen" (stressing the last).

And likewise on their side of the fire, when Four Brothers chiefs hear their names announced, one after another each chief of that nation himself raises the shout of approval, and his own phratry of chiefs supports him.

But when the enumerator, both on the road and inside the house, reaches the vacant title for which the ceremony is going forward to install a candidate, he inserts an address to the deceased chief and his ancestor:

> Haii Haii Know that society is grieving
> Haii Haii They are mourning
> Haii Haii In their minds
> Haii Haii When he did pass away
> Haii Haii He on whom we depended
> Haii Haii He carried away with him
> Haii Haii The minds of those
> Haii Haii Who subsist on the stump[2]
> Haii Haii As the tree puts forth suckers
> Haii Haii Now thou deceased one hear me
> Haii Haii You were a principal [a chief]
> Haii Haii You Daga?en:yonk [second person dual]

Only one principal candidate is named, in this case Haga?enyonk (third person singular), first on the Cayuga list, for whom the Condolence Council was performed. Others who are then installed remain unnamed.

And then the enumerator continues as before until he completes the roll of the Five Nations. The roll call ends abruptly without flourish, leaving the singer midway of the house, whence he returns unceremoniously to his place among the clearminded chiefs and sits down.

It was now five o'clock. It was gathering dusk outside, and the six windows, three on each side of the house, no longer admitted enough light to illumine the interior, even though the logs above the wainscoting were whitewashed. Now the two messengers for the visiting chiefs took down the oil lamps from the chandelier at their end of the house, adjusted the wicks, lit them, and put them up again. Simultaneously, two of the cooks who had hung kettles for the chiefs further fulfilled their duties to the matrons who appointed them by lighting the lamps at the Four Brothers' end.

□□◇□□

Meanwhile, in preparation for the Six Songs, the two servants of the condoling chiefs drew the quilt curtain between the two parties, screening the mourning Four Brothers from the clearminded chiefs who were about to sing. On the women's side, folk could see the whole length of the house.

While this was going on, at the Three Brothers' fire, a cane was put across between opposing benches at the end near the curtain toward the Four Brothers' fire. Tribal delegations were seated together, Seneca chiefs toward the curtain, Onondaga chiefs midway, Mohawk chiefs toward the door. A leading Seneca chief held one end of the cane; the leading Onondaga chief held the other, the speaker next to him. Over the horizontal stick they draped the twelve remaining requickening strings. When all was ready, Chief Logan, having been appointed to this role at the rehearsal, raised the first of the Six Songs. He leaned forward, elbows resting on knees, hands clasped, while his colleagues assumed a similar posture, their heads together as if deliberating some solemn question in council. Indeed, singing

---

2. The chief's maternal family and clansmen.

Clearminded (C): Three Brothers	Mourners (M): Four Brothers

Rehearse
  In charge: Thadada:ho? (J. Logan)
	Rehearse
	  In charge: Desgahe? (A. General)
	Matron (Jemima Gibson)
	  Preparations: pothangers
	Runner (H. Skye)
	Kindle fire (warriors)

Journeying on Road
  Crier
  Chanter (Roy Buck)
  Speaker (David Thomas)	

	Welcome at the Woods' Edge (Desgahe?) Three Rare Words over the fire (Desgahe?)
Three words returned (D. Thomas)	
	Taking by the arm: appointed warriors (H. Skye, A. Thomas)
Roll call to door (R. Buck)	
Second chanter inside from beginning to end (Peter Buck)	
	Pothangers light lamps on mourners' end
Runners light lamps on clearminded end	

————————————————— Curtain —————————————————

1–5 of Six Songs (J. Logan & R. Buck)	
	Curtain Withdrawn
Over the Forest (I) P. John	

————————————————— Curtain —————————————————

Sixth Song (Logan & Buck)	
	Curtain Withdrawn
Over the Forest (pt. 2) (P. John)	
Requickening (pt. 2) (D.Thomas)	

Calling for candidates (Logan)
  Return of short string (invitation)
  Completed number of words
  Feint to leave
	Don't anybody leave

————————————————— Curtain —————————————————

	Return of Condolences
	Six Songs completed (dead chief singing)
	Curtain Withdrawn
	Return Requickening (4–15) (Desgahe?) (Keep one string)

	Showing the Face of the Chief (Desgahe?).
	  Matron (J. Gibson) stands up her candidate
	  (J. H. Gibson), who speaks.

	Announce name (Desgahe?)
	Send string confirming over fire
Title string circulates counterclockwise; touching confirms	
Charge to new chief (Logan): Crosses fire and confronts candidate	
	New chief seated among colleagues.
	Pothangers carry in feast, distribute on both sides.
Ad lib speeches (dreams)	
	Release chiefs of further duties (Desgahe?)

Rubbing Antlers
  Singers (C)
	Rubbing Antlers
	  Release women to guests (M to C)
	Society Restored

Figure 11. Summary of Statuses, roles, and events in the Condolence Council of 1945

the Hymn to the Dead Chief is a solemn occasion for which they had practiced. Now they excelled themselves. No other song is so sacred to the Iroquois. Nothing else quite embodies their feeling for the league.

Chief Logan drew a deep breath and closed his eyes, and his clear baritone voice sang out:

> Hai Hai hi hi i hi [repeat]
> Gayanerenh De skennon—
> —wero neh i
> Hai Hai [etc.]

The leader lined out the song to its very ending: "Yenh!" Then another appointed singer, Roy Buck, picked up the song a second time from the beginning, whereupon all of the Three Brothers chiefs sang in unison, continuing through the entire hymn until the last "hih" fell away, and in unison echoing, "Yenh!" The sustained notes, the breathing in unison, the division of the words to fit the meter so that a verbal suffix commences a new line, and the characteristic ending strike an outsider hearing the choir all the more if he knows the music. I had sat through the rehearsal and previously had recorded the music from a lone singer, but nothing approached the full choir in performance.

All of the songs but the sixth were sung in sequence:

1. Hail, hail. I come to greet the league.
2. Hail, my nephews (offspring), I come to greet you.
3. Hail, the warrior chiefs, I come to greet you.
4. Hail, the matrons, I come to greet you.
5. Hail, our grandsires, what they decreed.

As the response to the fifth song died away, a deputy of the clearminded chiefs drew the curtain aside. It was then quarter past five.

□□◇□□

Because the words of Over the Forest are in Mohawk, it is easier for a native speaker to chant the laws of the league. At the rehearsal, the clearminded chiefs had appointed Peter John in this role. He now arose, cane in hand, adjusted his spectacles, and glanced at the text, which he had written out in a notebook, before starting to pace the length of the house on the men's side between the two fires, chanting the lines that follow. (The chanter prolongs the penultimate of each line, and stresses the last syllable.)

1
Hai Raksotha:hih
Hail, Grandfathers,
now continue to hear us.
Now they do cry mournfully,
your very grandchildren.
Now at this time
it has become ancient [people are no longer interested in],
that which you established,
the Great Law.

Hail. Grandfathers, hail.
Only that it were true
that you might continue to hear us.
2
Hail, Grandfathers.
This is what you said,
that society would become destitute [that sad would be the fate];
that people who come in later times
shall pass this way [in the ceremony].
Even now,
one is uncertain
just how to recite the ritual,
as they were wont to perform it.
3
Hail, Grandfathers.
Now at this time
it has grown old,
what you established,
the Great League.
You have it as a pillow under your heads,
beneath the ground,
where your bodies are lying;
Ye who combined your affairs into
the Great Law.
Would it were really true
that you might still hear us.
4
Hail, Grandfathers.
Isn't this what you decreed:
"In the far future this institution shall be carried on,
that the law shall continue to be observed
by our grandchildren"?
Hail, Grandfathers!

Having intoned four verses, Peter John returned to his place among the condoling chiefs. The curtain was stretched again, and Chief Logan raised up the final, sixth song of the Great Hymn.

tciyatonde:k ne?i: he
tciyatonde:kh [repeat]
Ronkesota tciyatonde:k ne?i [repeat from the beginning]
[Continue to listen, my grandfathers, contine to listen.]

As before, the singer lined out the verse completely before his assistant picked it up; then all the Lords of the League repeated it.

Once more the curtain was "lifted." It was now quarter to six.

□□◇□□

The ceremony continued with part two of Over the Forest. Peter John again stood and resumed chanting and pacing, continuing from where he had left off to recite the laws of the league. This time he consulted his notebook, which interrupted the cadence of the chant. Glossing the text:

The founders provided for succession to office. They decreed that when a chief's life sways like a giant tree between life and death, then shall his antlers of office be lifted off and set on the bed between him and the wall, for it would not do should they be born away into the earth by the passing of a person invested with horns. Should this happen, they said, we should all perish. In such an event, the founders thought, it would be the proper way and would strengthen the league to replace one person with another of equal status. Should the calamity befall that anyone suffered the consequences of being murdered, then should the corpse be placed properly next to the wall, where it should rest in darkness. (Likewise, his kin are in darkness of mourning.)

The founders decided further, lest sunlight disclose the corpse to a child who habitually rummages everywhere, they would save her a possibly awful experience, which would torment her mind until she learned why the corpse was lying there. They would uproot a lofty pine tree, making a great hole, and there into the pit they should cast this thing and the swift current would carry it away. Then they would reset the pine tree, and never should their grandchildren see it again.

And to strengthen the house they provided for a condolence ceremony. "Allowing that we all now wear symbols of identification, that we are invested with antlers, the pity of it being that ere we return to our seats, something may astound our momentary repose. In the event of a loss," they said, "this is what we shall do: we shall place a pole across and on it hang a pouch [of the skin of some burrowing species], and in it we will drop a string, the short string of mourning, to go to either side that is mourning. Whereupon the clearminded shall remove it and follow the path going to the place of mourning. There at the edge of the dust [at the bare spot around a building] one shall speak words of sympathy that at once will lift up the mind of the mourning person and comfort her. Now shall the person take up the path [resume her duties] to the Great Law."

> Finally, the originator of this confederacy
> you yourself, Deganawi:dah;
> and his son, Odatshehdeh [Oneida head chief]
> ye both were joint proprietors [founders];
> and his father's kinsman, Thadoda:ho? [Onondaga]
> ye both were founders;
> and his son, Haga?en:yonk [Cayuga],
> ye both were principals;
> and that one, a father's kinsman,
> Ganyadaiyo? [Handsome Lake, Seneca],
> and you, his cousin,
> Sa?dagaenyes [Skies of Equal Height].
> These were the founders.
> Now this is what they considered:

In later times additions would be made to the framework,
to the great sooty rafters.
Hail, Grandsires.
Now we are failing,
your very grandchildren.
Hail, Grandfathers!"

Ending on this note of humility, the chanter returned to the bench of the clearminded. It was now six o'clock in the evening.

□□◇□□

Presently, the speaker for the clearminded stood and addressed the mourning Four Brothers, resuming the messages of condolence of the Requickening Address, which had begun at the woods' edge with the Three Bare Words. David Thomas, or "Old Dawit," as he was affectionately called, was one of the finest orators among the Six Nations. He waited for his audience before speaking, then commenced slowly, in a well-modulated tone of voice. He was a master of the period, allowing as much time for his words to sink in as passed in utterance. Meanwhile he stood with eyes nearly closed, concentrating on what was to follow. As he warmed to his topic, the pace quickened, and the words flowed in a swift cadence at a high tonal plane that fell away at the end of a clause or sentence. Of such is the "preaching style" employed in the Requickening Address, as in other ritual speeches recited from memory.

What impressed me, even after a decade of association with the Iroquois, was the utter equanimity of public speakers who carry on "in a crowd," as they say, undisturbed by crying babies, banging doors, and the coming and going of children, adolescents, women, and men—even their colleagues, the chiefs for whom they speak. Such poise demands both concentration and knowing the stuff of ritual thoroughly. Besides a wealth of figures of speech, in which the lore of the Longhouse abounds, Dawit employed gestures as graphic and artful as his voice. Irony, even sarcasm, and above all a sense of humor appeal to the Iroquois as Indians. But this was a solemn occasion.

Having cleared the eyes, ears, and throats of the mourning phratry at the woods' edge, the speaker now proceeds to requicken the remaining organs and faculties that were impaired by the awful hand of Death. Picking up after the Three Bare Words, the remaining "words," in summary form, are these:

4. Grief wrenches the internal organs, which the speaker rearranges by pouring in the "water of pity," a sovereign medicine.
5. He wipes clean the bloody husk mat bed.
6. He lets daylight into the deep darkness of grief.
7. The mourners regain sight of the sky, which the Master of Life intended as a source of happiness.
8. This burden restores loss of the sun with all that sunlight implies to a horticultural people.
9. The mourner's mind rolls atop the fresh grave of the dead chief. (This calls for a black string of wampum.)
10. Death, the Great Enigma, has scattered the bones of the founders. The clearminded send over a string (all white in some sets; half black and half white

in other sets) called "Twenty Matters," with which they "bind up the bones of the chiefs and of the nation." Twenty is the penalty for homicide. (This string goes over to the Four Brothers but does not come back until the next Condolence Council.)

11. Moreover, Death has stomped in the council fire and kicked aside the fire logs. This string restores the council fire (civil government) so that neighboring people may see the smoke arising and take heart.

12. This burden acknowledges the preeminence of Iroquois women: birth of men, attending the hearth, preparing food, care of domesticated plants. An early death leaves that much empty space in society for the children she did not bear, and lacking female descendants, the ashes of her ongoing family become cold. The warriors are woman's assistants.

13. The federal chief follows the path of duty. His nephew (warriors) and niece (women) are his immediate care, and the matron warns him when he strays from the path. If he throws her warning over his shoulder, then the head warrior of that family warns him of drifting away from his colleagues and puts him back on the path. The nephew and niece appear a third time, when the chief warrior of the family lifts the antlers of office and hands them to the owner of the title, thereby releasing the man from further duties as a civil chief.

14. Society is warned that following so grievous a calamity as the death of a chief, "anything can happen on earth," even insanity or suicide. People are admonished that certain plants growing on earth are not to be fooled with; indeed, some are medicines but among them are some poisonous plants that will kill a person should she lose her head and trifle with them.[3] (A string is given, half black and half white.)

15. The final burden speaks of the "Torch of Notification" by which the condoling moiety learned of the chief's passing and returns to the pouch on the pole the short, purple string that both sides own equally and use for this purpose. (The string symbolizing the torch is pure white.)

"These are the number of condolence messages."

As he spoke these last twelve condolence messages of the Requickening Address in the longhouse, Dawit lifted the appropriate string of wampum from the cane beside him, where the "words" were ranged in sequence, and held the string in clasped hands until the end of the message, when it says: "Now my offspring, you federal chief, whom I have held to my bosom, the 'word' [attesting wampum string] of thy *adoni* [father's kin] is on its way to thee." Here the appointed deputy took the string from his extended hand and carried it over to the Four Brothers' side, where it was received and hung on a cane. In all, twelve strings crossed the fire during three-quarters of an hour.

But there was one other string. This explains why sources speak of Thirteen Matters inside the house, although Howard Skye told me that but twelve strings crossed the fire during the present ceremony.

□□◇□□

---

3. The reference is to *Cicuta maculata*, commonly water hemlock. See Fenton 1941, 1986.

The speaker now requested that the Four Brothers pay strict attention. It was time to call the candidate.

"Now the Three Brothers have been noticing that the mat [or bench] is vacant where your colleague used to sit. The founders of the league ordained how many trees shall stand erect on both sides of the fire and how to proceed in case a body topples on either side. In that event it shall be urgent that they shall show the candidate's face in front of the chiefs and the public, and moreover that they shall stand him erect and mention his name. That is why the Three Brothers came here, because now the bench is empty where his bench used to be on whom our minds depended. Now that one is gone wherever it took him.

"Now then, point out to us the one who is to be our colleague, so that we may think that the number of words that we have spoken here shall be fulfilled.

"Now, therefore, our means of notification [the short string of wampum that was brought by a runner to the Three Brothers when the Cayuga chief died] now goes back to you. [Deputy carried short string across.]

"Now shall you know that the Three Brothers have completed the ceremony, for this is the number of words."

Three hours had passed since the condoling phratry had entered the longhouse; it was now nearly seven o'clock.

Having ended the formal address, Dawit said, "We are now going to rise as a group and withdraw a little way, as far as the edge of the brush, to kneel and crouch there until further notice."[4]

At once the visiting chiefs made motions as if to leave. Some rattled canes, others reached for hats and coats, and a few stood, canes in hand. Across the room, a speaker for the Four Brothers (the messenger, chief warrior, or a chief) stood and briefly addressed the guests: "My father's kinsmen, we ask you kindly to remain until further notice. That is all."

Somewhat composed, the Three Brothers sat down to await a reply.

□□◇□□

The obligation to return the condolences now rested with the Four Brothers. Accordingly, their deputy drew the curtain. The words of the Three Brothers, attested by thirteen strings of wampum, hung on the cane before them. With them also rested the Six Songs. But the mourning chiefs, too, had rehearsed, and they had appointed a singer and a speaker.

Only four chiefs represented the Four Brothers—three Cayugas and a lone Oneida—supplemented by a singer home from the United States and several knowledgeable deputies. The mourners returned the Six Songs of Farewell to the Dead Chief at one sitting behind the curtain. It took but twenty minutes. It was as if the past chief himself were singing:

1. The law has come to greet and thank me.
2. My father's kinsman comes to greet and thank me.
3. The warrior comes to greet and thank me.
4. The matron [cook] has come to greet and thank me.

---

4. It was the old custom for a visiting delegation to retire and await a summons to hear the reply of the home council.

5. My grandfathers, what they created.

6. Continue to hear us, my grandfathers, continue to hear us.

[The last is the same sixth song sung by the condolers.]

The deputy for the mourners put back the curtain for the last time. Desgahe?
stood and, with great deliberation, returned the burdens of requickening. Confirming each burden, however, was briefer than condoling. Not quite a half-hour
sufficed. Of the strings that had been sent over the fire, all but one were returned.
Howard Skye said he delivered eleven to the Three Brothers' side and that
the Four Brothers kept the one called "Twenty Matters," the tenth burden, which
says:

> Now then does one gather your bones together;[5]
> With Twenty Matters do they bind up your Bones.

This string would be returned at the next condolence held at Onondaga, when the
Four Brothers send it back "by a whisper." Regularly, this string keeps going back
and forth whenever a condolence occurs, although possibly each side possesses
such a string.

In prefacing the return of condolences, the speaker for the mourning phratry
says:

"Now the ruler has made this day just as he prepared the daylight, even the
earth, and he created us people and, therefore, the number of us present. Now
we are two groups met together, my father's kinsmen. And, moreover, already
you made an address, and so now it is the turn of the Four Brothers to reply.
Therefore, you shall all think that we have accepted it, just as you delivered it.
Now you did finish speaking. Furthermore, this is how our grandfathers ordained;
they composed words for carrying on, on whichever side of the fire a chief may
have died. And in that event the clearminded shall come in at the door [of
the mourner]. Accordingly you are following this path, my father's kinsmen. And
what is more, it isn't just one-sided [death may befall either side]: it happens
to both of us alike. Thus from day to day they are toppling over close to thy
person, they are continually dying, thy very nephews and even thy grandchildren.
Consequently right now it is twisting within your mind [you are worried].
Therefore, now they have poured in the decoction of sweet flag [the water of pity],
and when it has settled down it will permeate your body. Then in the future
you shall feel well disposed, and you shall continue to enjoy health for a day
at least."

This is the way the Four Brothers may do, repeating then the number of
condolence burdens and strings exactly as given by the Three Brothers.

□□◇□□

It was eight o'clock when the Four Brothers sent the last of the requickening strings
back to the Three Brothers. Now Desgahe?, their speaker, stood front and center
by the fire, leaning on his cane, and addressed the Three Brothers in the part of
the ceremony called Showing the Face of the New Chief.

---

5. Throughout the ceremony, speakers employ the third person feminine, "she," for society. "It
is as if a woman were doing it." This act covers both living and dead chiefs.

"You now have the completed words of both of us, the [exact] number of my father's kinsmen. And now it becomes possible to show his face right here before the crowd. Now one will raise him to a standing position in front of the chiefs and also one shall announce his name, which is that of the dead chief. Now another thing, one will place him in the vacancy. Now, moreover, my father's kinsmen, you shall think that events have transpired here just as you specified when you did say, 'Now show us the new man who will be our co-worker.' Accordingly, be alert, for this is the real thing! Now you shall take a good look at him. For we are about to show you your new colleague!"

Although others besides myself, including chiefs of the Three Brothers, knew who was going to be the new chief, no one let on, and the tension built while five hours of ceremonial reached a climax. The building overflowed with anxious humanity as people crowded in at both doors and stood up to the stoves to witness the new chief. The crowd probably touched 250 at its peak.

Jemima Gibson, matron of the lineage holding the title Haga?en:yonk, arose as Desgahe? spoke (fig. 12). She crossed calmly from a seat among the Cayuga matrons in the southeast corner to where her brother was sitting in a complementary place among the Cayuga men in the northeast corner. Taking her brother, Hardy Gibson, by the arm, she raised him to his feet and escorted him to a position just flanking the fire on the speaker's right.

During this action the chiefs of the Three Brothers' side and the multitude craned their necks to glimpse the new chief. There they stood, the speaker in the middle of the house, the matron on his right, and the candidate on her right, facing the Three Brothers's side.

The speaker continued: "Now all of you look here, for he is standing here before you, the one who was appointed by the holder of the title, which reposes in that continuing lineage, namely the Bear Clan, whose bench where their great one used to sit was made empty." (Here the speaker validated the new chief's succession from the previous holder of the title, Abram Charles, the candidate's mother's brother, of the Bear Clan. Actually, the candidate had been qualified as a chief when yet a boy.) "And further, this person who came and stood before you then is the one whom they are now crowning with antlers, and henceforth you all shall denominate him Haga?en:yonk." (He repeated the name for emphasis.)

(Actually, the candidate was crowned the moment the matron stood him up.)

"Now, therefore, here is the means by which you may hear the title, Haga?en:yonk." (The speaker held a string of white wampum which, when he had finished speaking, he passed to his deputy to carry across the fire.) "It shall now go across the fire; it is the word of all who have combined their voices with that of the proprietress of the chief's name, comprising both the siblings and the cousins who sanctioned it; and the entire group of relatives have also approved; even the tribes known as the Four Brothers are of one voice. Now, therefore, it shall cross the fire, now their word, which is the means of your being notified, is on its way over [the fire], my father's kinsmen, the Three Brothers." (String.)

The deputy of the Four Brothers carried the string of notification across to the Three Brothers' side. A chief took it, handled it, and passed it to a colleague; and so the string went around the fire in a counterclockwise direction. Each chief

Figure 12. Jemima Gibson, Cayuga matron, and candidate John Hardy Gibson, 1945. Photo by author.

touched the string as it passed among them: taking hold of wampum is tantamount to consent. This act confirmed the appointment.

But the Three Brothers did not reply as yet, because the Four Brothers had yet another candidate. Bill Johnson, a Cayuga warrior in his forties, was raised up in the companion office of Ji?nondawehe?, which stands in a unique relationship to Haga?en:yonk. The two are as "father and son," or, in current native theory, "sons to each other," a relationship that the Iroquois accept with equanimity. In theory, each Cayuga chief, besides the matron, has two assistants: a guardian or deputy who is the chief warrior and an official for ceremonial occasions. Two of the latter were raised to assist the second federal chief.

After questioning the first candidate's pedigree, chiefs among the Three Brothers next asked whether he had ever voted in an election of the elective council, which superseded the council of life chiefs when the Canada Indian Act took effect. Gibson replied that he had always followed the old system, that they might recall that he served as deputy to his late uncle in the old council, and that he intended to keep up the old system for the benefit of future generations. Asked to speak, he acquitted himself well, amazing many persons that he commanded ancient forms relating to the league.

□□◇□□

It was now eight-forty in the evening. The speaker for the Three Brothers then stood to say: "Now it is indeed fulfilled: we have looked over the new one on whom you have placed the antlers of office, and also his guardian, the matron who owns the title; we accept both of them as we are notified by your word.

Therefore the Three Brothers have now sanctioned [accepted] the two new candidates whom you have elevated. Now then get ready to hear something, you two candidates on whom they have placed the antlers of chiefship." Whereupon the first speaker sat down.

It was Chief Logan, Thadoda:ho? himself, the leading chief of the league, who arose to make the Charge to the New Chiefs. This was a great moment because Chief Logan not only held an important office but also was a forthright person of great integrity. The public sensed that the chiefs had entrusted this responsibility to him knowing that he would fulfill it as the occasion demanded. Carrying a heavy bent-wood cane of the type stockmen favor, Chief Logan crossed to the Four Brothers' side to confront the newly installed chiefs. The charge varies with the style of the speaker. Chief Logan said:

"It is an amazing thing that what the founders established many years ago is still going on at the present time. The founders . . . believed that a child was born of virgin birth and that he survived to do away with blood feud and other causes of unhappiness among the people of early times. And that system has worked right up to the present day. Now you two men are the leading Cayuga chiefs: Haga?en:yonk and Ji?nondawehe?ʊ. As such you are as 'sons to each other.' Each shall call the other 'my son.' You two are the firekeepers of the Cayuga nation. It is your duty to preside jointly at councils of your tribe. But although you are the leading Cayuga chiefs, you are no higher than the rest. All chiefs are of equal height."

Having addressed these and other remarks to the two chiefs and to the public, Logan stressed the following virtues of chiefship, at the same time menacing the new chiefs with his cane. He spoke as if everything depended on them:

"You should do all in your power to protect and defend the people and their children as well as the generations to come. Everything depends on you. The welfare of the people depends on how you deport yourselves. Remember always that a chief's skin is of seven spans in thickness (*wa?sagondadensta? djowenhga:da?*, the span of the thumb to middle finger, measured as an inchworm jumps). You will hear a lot of people talking, criticizing. Seven spans of skin will protect you. You will live clean lives so that the people will respect you. You both know the good spirit and the evil spirit.

"I am in a hurry just now [turning away]. There are many more things that I should say, but I am now at the point where I need food. [The speaker always makes a joke of this sort to prompt the cooks. Sometimes he remarks that the young girls want to dance.] But I trust that you will do the right thing."

Chief Logan had already returned to his place when he remembered an addendum. "I almost forgot," he said, "that you should know when the chiefs hold their councils. They meet on the first Tuesday of the month at Onondaga Longhouse. It is your duty to attend."

At the close of the charge, the two officiating Cayuga chiefs took the new chiefs by the arm and ushered them to seats among their colleagues.[6]

---

6. The preceding account of my observations, supplemented by informant explanations, lacks some of the coherence of the text that John A. Gibson dictated to Alexander Goldenweiser in 1912, which I had translated with Simeon Gibson and employed as a control. See Woodbury 1992.

With the seating of the new chiefs, we made a break for the door along with others who had sat through five hours of ceremonial. Outside, the moon had come up and it was crystal cold. Men returning from the brush were gathered in little knots to talk; others walked the circuit around the building worn by the feet of generations of dancers cooling off. We went back inside to recover our seats—a vain hope, because others had taken them.

□□◇□□

We stood in the crowd by the west stove. Pairs of cooks carried in steaming kettles slung from poles over their shoulders. They set a kettle down between the benches occupied by the Three Brothers chiefs, and another for the Four Brothers. Others brought trenchers and basket trays of chunk beef, which they distributed first to the chiefs, before the public. There were great baskets of baker's bread. All distributions went counterclockwise. Hulled white corn soup was the only native food. I was told that it was a small feast by ancient standards, when the women used to cook corn bread.

While the cooks were bringing in the kettles and during the hour from nine until ten that passed in feasting, several of the visiting chiefs were moved to speak. It is customary for the hosts to inquire whether any of the chiefs has dreamed something, or had an inspiration.

Meanwhile, the speaker for the hosts addressed the visiting chiefs, releasing them from further obligation. The clearminded replied: "Now together we have finished the work and all is clear between us. You and I are free."

The Four Brothers, as hosts, replied: "Now then, my father's kinsmen, together you and I have finished everything. Therefore you shall be informed that the Four Brothers have prepared a feast. Accordingly, the time being shall be devoted to this. And so let us eat together for a while. As soon as our meal is finished then the time shall be devoted to rejoicing together that the new one has been elevated; may he strive for the welfare of ongoing generations of our families. Now then we shall rub antlers [name of the social dance of chiefs]. Now, furthermore, it is up to the crowd to have a good time.

"So now, my father's clansmen, I let escape from my hands our womenfolk. Accordingly, you shall use them properly. Don't anyone treat them too roughly!" (This remark always elicits laughter.)

"So now another thing. Time may be devoted to something else. Perhaps one of you may have had a dream [have news to relate]. In that event let us amuse our minds with dreams."

Meanwhile, they feasted. Usually, before anyone among the clearminded has an inspiration, one of them will quip: "No, we have no dreams to relate. We are young people yet and do not sleep much." The implication is that they are out all night and have no time to dream. But someone may reply, "We have only one man here who sleeps much, and he has an inspiration." Then the speaker tells what he has dreamt, which may be a pretense.

On this occasion, chiefs of the Three Brothers' side conducted the final event of the Condolence Council—the social dance called "Rubbing Antlers"—and one of them acted as floor manager. They led off with Trotting, or Standing Quiver, a stomp dance. Garter Dance followed. Soon a throng of dancers followed the leaders. By this time the room was filled with dust and smoke and heat and the noise of dancing. Outside, couples walked around the building. Conversation ran to the importance of the occasion, the complexities of chiefship, and the unwillingness of young people to commit themselves. I returned inside briefly to watch Fish Dance. It was now eleven o'clock. The crowd danced for another hour, I was told, but I was ready to put down my head for the night.

CHAPTER 11

INSTALLING ONONDAGA CHIEFS
IN 1951

At the invitation of the Onondaga chiefs I went up to Six Nations on Grand River in late March 1951. This was my last field trip for the Bureau of American Ethnology, and it followed publication of my monograph on the mnemonic cane for recalling the roll call of the Iroquois chiefs (Fenton 1950). Writing the report had generated questions about the internal composition of tribal councils, for which I sought answers, although some would be resolved later by Annemarie Shimony (1961). I also was curious to observe how the reciprocal of the ceremony was celebrated when the roles of mourners and condolers were reversed. How would the Four Brothers (for all purposes, the Cayugas) perform it?[1]

Protocol requires adhering to the "proper way." A visitor calls at the house of the principal chief. Accordingly, several days before the ceremony I went to the house of the principal Onondaga chief, Thadoda:ho⁷, or Joseph Logan, Sr., whom I had known for some years. The Logan family were most friendly, and the son Josey afterward interpreted for me in the longhouse during the ceremony.

Does the Mohawk nation enjoy supremacy over the rest of the league? This question stemmed from Joseph Brant's role in securing the Grand River lands—the Haldimand grant and the Simcoe Patent. Brant himself exerted such supremacy in council speeches of the period. Seth Newhouse, in his various manuscripts, upheld the priority of Mohawk as the ritual language of the confederacy, as the language of the first nation to adhere to the Great Peace, and I had noticed that ritualists who knew Mohawk took pride in performing the chants in that language.

Another question related to the kinship terms used between nations of the league and between paired chiefships within each nation.[2] The moieties of the league address each other as "father's kin" (*agadoni*) and as "offspring" or "nephews" (*kheya⁷tawenh*), but when the roll call (Fenton 1950: 56) reaches numbers 33 and 34, which designate the two leading chiefs on the Cayuga roster, the terminology shifts to "father and son" or, as the modern annalists maintain, "sons," reciprocally, which contradicts the literal meaning of the term *thyatatahwah*, "you and I."[3]

---

1. There are virtually no Oneida chiefs resident at Six Nations. The Delawares and Tutelos are represented only in the moiety name, the Four Brothers.

2. Hanni Woodbury was to explore this latter question, employing the Gibson text, and present her findings to the Iroquois Conference of 1983.

3. I am grateful to Floyd Lounsbury for putting me right on this, although we do not agree with my informants.

According to Chief Logan: "At the formation of the league, the kinship relation of the several nations was established as *agadonishonʔ*, 'uncles,' in modern parlance, and *kheyaʔtawenh*, 'nephews.' This held until they [the founders] reached Cayuga. It seems there were two village chiefs of separate towns who were brought together in a merging of Cayuga village bands. To assure them equal status, the founders contrived to have them designated as self-reciprocating 'sons' (*thyatatahwah*). The Onondaga refer to them as *hyatatahwah*, "they two are." Decisions were left to a conference and mutual satisfaction of the two. They should agree."

If the Cayugas use "sons" (father and son), I asked, why do the Senecas use "cousins"?

Logan replied: "The first two Cayuga chiefs, *hyatatahwah*, are both on the same side of the council fire: [as such they are] *hondennnon:-denʔ*, 'brothers' [siblings]. But the [paired] Seneca chiefs were of clans across the fire, hence *honaʔsis henʔ*, "cousins.""

Are the Cayuga chiefs all on the same side of the fire?

"No, the last two on the Cayuga roster [numbers 9 and 10, or 41 and 42 on the roll call] are *honaʔsis henʔ* ('cousins'), but the third to eighth Cayuga titles, in sets of three each, have 'brother' and 'cousin' relationships."[4]

As to the relative weights of meanings of "sons" versus "brothers" versus "cousins," sons imply a closer relationship than brothers, and brothers a closer one than cousins.

Chief Logan, then the reigning authority on the composition of the Onondaga council, specified the relationships among the fourteen Onondaga chiefs. The first two Onondaga titles (19 and 20 on the roll call [RC]) are "cousins"; two and three (RC 20 and 21) are "brothers." The next three (RC 22, 23, 24) comprise a phratry of "brothers." These six together form an executive committee of the Onondaga council; they are properly "the firekeepers," although the term is used by the other four nations of the confederacy to refer to the entire Onondaga council. They are sometimes reffered to as "the two fireplaces, or clans."

Thadoda:hoʔ (RC 19, Oa-1) stands as "cousin" to both two and three (RC 20, 21) and to the phratry of three (RC 22, 23, 24), who comprise one phratry across the fire.

The next chief (RC 25) stands alone. Traditionally he is the wampum keeper. His "two uncles" (father's kinsmen) are the next two on the list (RC 26, 27), who are across the fire from each other and presumably "cousins" and are referred to as *degeni dehodoniʔshenʔ* (literally, "the two who are his father's kinsmen").

The next three (RC 28, 29, 30) comprise a phratry. And the last two, thirteen and fourteen on the Onondaga roster (RC 31, 32), the Cayugas say are one chief with two roles.

The preceding relationships are kept in mind by a mnemonic that is laid out with kernels of corn at rehearsals and can be expressed numerically by roll call numbers (fig. 13). The complete chart of the entire roll call is Table 4, page 193.

□□◇□□

Having called on the headman of the Three Brothers, who this time would play the role of mourners, protocol required that I also seek out the ritual leader of the

4. See notes of interview with Alex General (APSL, Fenton Papers, ser. 5, notebook 1945).

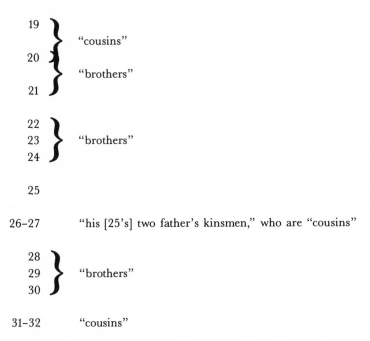

Figure 13. Mnemonic for remembering the relationships among Onondaga chiefs

Four Brothers, who were now in the position of clearminded condolers. Cayuga Chief Alexander General (*Desgahe*?) of the Bear clan was expected to conduct the ceremony for his side and intone specific ritual chants as in 1945. I particularly wanted him to clarify moiety relationships within the Cayuga council. We met that same day.

The Cayuga council has a unique structure, consisting of paired "father and son" (or "co-sons," as native theory insists), RC 33 and 34; then two phratries, RC 35, 36, 37 and RC 38, 39, 40; followed by a pair of cousin chiefs, RC 41 and 42, of which Chief General held the latter title (RC 42).[5] The first two Cayuga chiefs are the firekeepers, the last two doorkeepers.

Chief General, who was later Shimony's informant, told me: "It is a Cayuga tradition that they were the first tribe to organize as a confederacy. They had firekeepers and doorkeepers when first discovered and already had the form of organization later adapted for the league. It is a long story—that Deganawi:dah was having difficulty getting Thadoda:ho? to accept the Great Peace, that he was still dissatisfied [with Deganawi:dah's message], so Deganawi:dah had to find another smoke [people]. Thadoda:ho? knew that another smoke rose to the westward. A messenger was appointed to look for it. That is whom they found, the Cayugas, and this is how they were named.

"The Cayuga headmen insisted that they must smoke first before hearing the two messengers. The two were astonished when they saw these people smoking such a big pipe, hence they came to be called 'The people of the large pipe.' The story goes that every little while Thadoda:ho?, waiting, would lie on the ground

5. The spatial relations are illustrated in figures 18 and 19.

to listen. 'Now I can hear my father's brother's sons (*heyahdawen*?) approaching.' When the Cayuga came to Onondaga they were chanting the roll call."

Having attended the rehearsals at Onondaga Longhouse in 1945, I asked Chief General whether I might attend the Cayuga rehearsals on two nights before the upcoming ceremony. "I don't know what they will say. The older chiefs were very strict. Whenever a stranger entered during a rehearsal they stopped and asked: 'What do you want?'"

Borrowing performers between the moieties is not a new practice. "Roy Buck [Cayuga], son of an Onondaga chief, by rights is on our side. But he is still peeved at the Cayugas, although we have sent word asking him to come back." He is an accomplished ritualist, "and we are short of singers of Hai Hai on the road. Some years ago when the late Chief Robert Davey was running things, Roy came to a rehearsal of the Four Brothers side. They stopped singing when he entered. 'What do you want here?' asked Chief Davey. 'You belong at Onondaga.' Roy left, his feelings hurt. The other chiefs present realized that Chief Davey had made a mistake, but no one went after him. The Cayugas lost a promising performer right then. Ever since he has been with the Onondagas. They have taken in quite a few Cayugas of late."[6]

Not wishing to intrude on the rehearsal at Lower Cayuga Longhouse, I relied on Howard Skye to brief me. He had attended both sessions. Howard knew the program of rehearsals from both sides because the Onondagas formerly rehearsed at his parents' home. According to Skye, the Cayuga procedure was as follows.

First, Desgahe? laid out the fifteen strings of wampum in the usual order on a table.

Second, he uttered the greeting cry *yuhenh::* and heard the response, *hi:yah.* He called it himself twice because there were two nations present—Oneida and Cayuga.

Third, he asked, "Who wants to take up the cane?" (This is the mnemonic cane bearing pegs and pictographs of the roll call.) The Cayugas do not lay out the mnemonic pattern with kernels of corn that I witnessed at Onondaga in 1945 but rely on a reproduction of the cane. Candidates for the singer's role take up the cane and try the eulogy. That year it was Roy Fish who would perform it on the road. The plan was that if George Van Every, who was then in the United States, returned, he would take it into the longhouse. Otherwise they might have to borrow a singer from Onondaga. The Cayuga singers at that time were Van Every, Fish, and Jake Thomas—just in the learning stage. Howard Skye observed that the last time the Cayugas came to Onondaga, Roy Fish had reached number twenty-five (Hononwiyehdi) in the roll of founders on arriving at the fire. Van Every followed in the longhouse.

Fourth, for the woods'-edge ceremony, Desgahe? assumed the address of welcome for rehearsal purposes, as if the Cayugas were both hosts and mourners.

Fifth, Jake Thomas spoke the Three Bare Words. Sixth, Roy Fish led the Six Songs (songs 1–5), and Howard Skye assisted. Seventh, Desgahe? chanted part one of Over the Forest. Eighth came the the Sixth Song. Ninth came Over the Forest,

---

6. At Lower Cayuga Longhouse, the Cayuga nation and the Four Brothers are merged, but there are few Oneidas at Six Nations. Likewise, at Onondaga Longhouse, the nation and the Three Brothers are one.

part two. Tenth on the agenda was lunch. And eleventh, Desgahe? performed the Requickening Address (words 4–15).

The Cayuga rehearsal followed the program of the ceremony, whereas the Onondagas in 1945 followed a different procedure (Fenton 1950: 44ff.), reversing the order of the ceremony.

So much for these preliminaries.[7] For a list of the participants—a kind of cast of characters who perform the roles in the ceremony I am about to describe—the reader is referred to Table 3.

□□◇□□

I made a third call on Mrs. William Thomas, matron of the Onondaga Wolf clan and mother of the candidate, Peter Thomas. She is niece of the late Jesse Lewis (d. 1945), who lived hard by the Onondaga Longhouse and who was the previous holder of the title Awegenhyat (RC 23). Jesse Lewis had succeeded Joe Skye, his mother's brother. Peter Thomas is Jesse Lewis's sister's daughter's son (fig. 14).[8]

Mrs. Thomas traced the steps in selecting her candidate. At first she had no man who would take up the vacant title, her son having once declined to become a chief. (I have known several instances of eligible men who were reluctant.) It went on like that until she decided to refer the matter back to the chiefs of her side in the Onondaga council. Her clan side (phratry) had almost decided to appoint Grant Williams (Wolf clan), her mother's sister's son. Before she went to see Williams to ask him to take the title, her son Peter decided he would now be a candidate.

She returned to her clan's side of the council (the chiefs of her moiety) and informed One?sa:hen (RC 20), another chief of the same clan, of her decision.

After discussion within her phratry, the matter was referred across the fire to Thadoda:ho? (RC 19) (Deer clan) for discussion by the opposite moiety.

When the Onondaga council acts to accept the candidate, they refer it to those of the Four Brothers side (Oneida and Cayuga) who are present. Desgahe? (RC 42, C-10) act next.

The council can veto the matron's nomination. The Onondaga chiefs decide whether the proposed candidate is suitable to take that title. Sometimes the nomination is turned down.

7. Sometimes my queries exceeded Mr. Skye's own knowledge of tradition. He would then put the questions to John Smoke, his native mentor. Regarding the two leading Cayuga chiefs who are mutually "father and son," Howard consulted John Smoke and afterward wrote to me: "When they came to Gadjinondawehe and made him a chief . . . they asked him if there were another man in the vicinity. He said there was another man across the field. The leader of this [inquiring] party suggested Gadjinondawehe get the man to come to their meeting place. When he arrived at the man's place there were a number of families settled there. He related the message to the man, that they wanted the man to come to the council. The man said he would arrive immediately. So Gadjinondawehe returned and reported to the inquiring party. They waited, but the man across the field did not appear. Accordingly, Gadjinondawehe was sent back to fetch the man a second time. The man was no longer there, and the place showed that the people had moved out. Gadjinondawehe went back again and informed his people what he saw there; and he was sent out once more, this time to follow and bring him back.

"When he was bringing the man, Gadjinondawehe asked him why he had run away. He said that when they had played together he was always abused, and now he had seen that Gadjinondawehe had a number in his party and so he feared that [he] might be subjected to ill treatment, which is why he chose to run away. 'I was suspicious (awgagiyonh).' The leader then told him that henceforth he would bear the title Dega?en yonh. So this is how Gajinondawehe and Dega?en yonh became dyatathawak (father and son)."

8. Alexander Goldenweiser first explored the succession of chiefly titles at Six Nations. See his summary reports for 1912 (1914a) and 1913 (1914b).

THREE BROTHERS (MOURNERS)	FOUR BROTHERS (CLEARMINDED)
Joseph Logan, Sr. (Thadoda:ho?)	Alexander General (Desgahe?)
Onondaga speaker	Cayuga speaker
Welcome at the Woods' Edge	Over the Forest
Three Bare Words at fire	Requickening Address (words 4–13)
Presents candidates	Charge to the Chief
Roy Buck (borrowed)	Roy Buck (Cayuga)
Eulogy in house	
Requickening (reply)	
	Howard Skye (Cayuga), messenger
Mrs. William Thomas (Oa)	
Matron, Wolf clan	Roy Fish (Cayuga)
	Eulogy singer on road to fire
Peter Thomas (Oa), candidate	and at longhouse; Six Songs
Elsie Jacobs, second matron	George Van Every (Cayuga) (absent)
	Eulogy singer
Second candidate (name unknown)	
Skanawadi (Oa-14)	Jake Thomas (Cayuga)
	Eulogy singer at rehearsal
	William Thomas (Cayuga), speaker
	Three Bare Words (reply)

I asked whether the matron tells the chief of her clan side (moiety) the proposed title. In the present case she gave both the title and her son's Indian name (personal name from her clan).

As to standards: (1) If he is a soldier, he will not be accepted by the council to become a chief. (This goes back to exclusion of active warriors.) (2) to qualify, he must be a clean-living man. (Married or single was not specified.) (3) He is supposed to be a full-blooded Indian of Iroquois stock. (This last requirement is a virtual impossibility, given the racial admixture at Six Nations and the long history of adoptions among the Iroquois.) I asked about the requirement that a chief have skin seven thumbs thick, which is mentioned in the charge to the new chief. Mrs. Thomas said it was never mentioned when she turned in the title of her candidate.

She also told me about the string of wampum that the matron has to provide by the time of the ceremony. This "title string" has two names: *gayane?da?*, "the title," and *ona?ga?*, "the horn" or "antler." It is kept by the matron and passed along in the family. It is made up for the occasion and consists of a wampum

Figure 14. Mrs. William Thomas, matron of the Onondaga Wolf clan, and her candidate son, Peter, before his installation. Jesse Lewis homestead, March 29, 1951. Photo by author.

string about three inches long. The matron presents it to the Three Brothers side (her own moiety of the confederacy) when she presents the candidate, and this "white string of notification" goes across the fire to the Four Brothers side, which charges the candidate with his duties. The candidate gets no certificate of office, only the name.

The family also procures and cooks the food. Mrs. Thomas made these arrangements for the 1951 ceremony. Her cousin would make the corn soup, and her brother would cook the beef. These persons are known as "pothangers" in two categories: those who hang kettles for the Creator, and those who hang kettles for the chiefs. Pothanger (*owanajaha:nek*) is another name for *honondiont* (usually rendered "faithkeeper"), or "deacon" at Six Nations. Pothangers are of both sexes. A cook at a condolence ceremony is called *owanajaha:nek neh hasennowa:neh*, or *hoya:neh*, "pothanger to the chief" (fig. 15).

A second candidate is frequently installed, and the families share costs and labor. Elsie Jacob proposed filling the office of Skanawadi (RC 32, Oa-14), over which a dispute rages between the Onondagas and Cayugas. The title is linked to that of Ho?sahawih (RC 31), the Onondagas claiming both titles and the Cayugas holding that they are two names for one office. (This relates to a founder who reserved the right to go to war and sit in council as a split personality.) It seems that a family at Syracuse held RC 31, and the Cayugas said no. Onondaga chief Joseph Logan, Sr., went to see the cane of Andrew Sprague (Fenton 1950) and

Figure 15. Pothanger stirs the soup, Onondaga cookhouse, 1951. Photo by author.

found that a peg had been cut off that represented RC 32, indicating that there once had been such a title and office.[9]

Although men conduct the ceremony, women often enough know the content of the chants. Mrs. Thomas manifested a keen interest in the installation ceremony. She knew that there were two kernels of corn together when the roll call is laid out at rehearsals. These relate to the dispute just mentioned. She watched how her late father did it. She also watched them lay out the strings of requickening and learned how to recognize them—all but a few. She can go through and name the strings when they are laid out. She seemed certain that a few more times and she would be able to do it.

□□◇□□

The morning of 31 March 1951, I met Chief General in Ohsweken, the center of Six Nations Reserve, at nine-thirty in the morning. He was carrying a cane and approached from toward the store. We drove north toward the Grand River to turn east down the road that passes the longhouses. We picked up Levi Badeis (Baptiste), a Mohawk, who was walking toward Onondaga Longhouse. At Silversmith's Corners, Howard Skye (Cayuga) came out of his house carrying a reproduction

9. This controversy is the crux of whether there were forty-nine or fifty original founders. Howard Skye consulted the "official" Cayuga cane and reported that "the title peg for Awenhiganhyat was out, indicating that that chieftainship was vacant. But the peg for Skanawadi was not out. It was partly broken so that it could not be removed before the ceremony."

of the original condolence cane of Andrew Sprague, now in the Cranbrook Institute (Fenton 1950). We proceeded on down toward Lower Cayuga Longhouse where the Four Brothers were to rehearse at eleven.[10]

I turned around at Atkins Corners, let out my passengers, and returned to Onondaga Longhouse to await the procession. As I approached the longhouse, I could see smoke rising from fires that the cooks appointed to hang kettles for the chiefs had kindled in cookhouse and longhouse. It was now ten-thirty. Men were going from spring to cookhouse carrying pails of water, others were chopping wood—the usual activities that precede a feast.

At eleven o'clock the chiefs convened at both longhouses to rehearse—the clearminded at Lower Cayuga, the mourners at Onondaga. The clearminded Four Brothers would come over the road to the fire of the mourning Three Brothers.

At noon the Three Brothers chiefs adjourned and gathered at the matron's home for lunch. They filed in, took off their coats, and sat on beds in the adjoining room joking. Onondaga women had made great pans of baking-powder biscuits. Mrs. Thomas and her son Peter, about to assume the title Awegenhyat, are Onondagas; William Thomas, her husband and the father of the candidate, was a Cayuga and speaker for the Four Brothers side. He remarked that he was separated from his wife until after the ceremony, that he could not stay home and eat Onondaga bread. He loaded up his car with bread supplied by his wife for the Four Brothers and went off to join them. The mourners send food to the clearminded side, so food went down from Onondaga to Lower Cayuga.

Between one and two o'clock, the Three Brothers resumed rehearsal at Onondaga Longhouse; presumably the Four Brothers were rehearsing down below. The wampum strings for requickening were spread out on the bench before the chiefs as they had been at the 1945 rehearsal. Roy Buck was pacing to and fro the length of the house reciting the eulogy. On reaching Hononwiyehdi (RC 25) midway of the Onondaga roster, he stopped, saying, "I guess that is enough." (The cane that he carried in the performance belonged to the Onondagas; it bore a few mnemonics, possibly five, but not fifty.)

Meanwhile, the matron gathered her maternal family at her home next door, where I photographed them (fig. 16).

At two o'clock the fires were burning briskly at Onondaga cookhouse. Tension was increasing. Just then Levi Baptiste and Billy Henry kindled the small fire at the corner of the longhouse common for the ceremony of welcome. (I am unsure whether they took fire from the longhouse or cookhouse to ignite it.)

---

10. I counted at this time some three reproductions of the condolence cane of Andrew Sprague (spelled "Spraag" on the cane itself) on the Six Nations Reserve. The cane that Cayuga Chief General carried that morning and used throughout the ceremony that afternoon was a flat, sabre-shaped object that evidently was made after the blueprint I had supplied of the Cranbrook specimen. But Chief General's cane lacked the pegs denominating the chiefs. The cane of Howard Skye was a perfect replica of the Cranbrook piece and was made from specifications that I furnished. It was far superior to the original and had a varnished sheen. A third and fourth cane appeared in the party of T. J. Jamieson, M.D., of Detroit; neither cane, just then, had the pegs or cherry handle of the Skye cane that was used in the ceremony. (Dr. Jamieson afterward made and sent me a walnut replica of the Cranbrook piece, now in the Museum of the Iroquois Indian. Other replicas were later produced by Jake Thomas and may be found in collections.)

Figure 16. Mrs. William Thomas, matron of the Onondaga Wolf clan, and her lineage, 1951. Photo by author.

Sam Silversmith, who had been helping at the cookhouse, along with Baptiste and Henry, kept a sharp lookout from the porch of Onondaga Longhouse for the approaching column. The wind was blowing away from them, so that the scouts could spy the column progressing west on the road from Lower Cayuga before they could hear the voice of the singer. Presently one could hear the cry *agadoni:::::::* of the Four Brothers as offspring addressing their fathers' kinsmen, the Three Brothers, which is shouted every time the singer completes the roster of a committee of chiefs. The chant says: "That was the number of founders, my father's kinsman."

It was two-fifteen in the afternoon when the Three Brothers went out to the fire and drew themselves up flanking the road behind the fire. Chiefs took up the front rank, the Onondagas at the center, the Mohawk chiefs at one end, and the Seneca chiefs at the other. (I failed to notice which was left and right.) Warriors and the public were in the second rank. I stood to the rear listening to the voice of the Cayuga singer, Roy Fish, who marched in the second rank of the approaching column, immediately after the scouts. The wind was blowing sharply from the southwest, and one could hear the drip of maple sap in jars hung on trees around the house of William Thomas. I remarked that it was cold. Josey Logan, who stood beside me, commented that the ceremony must be performed before the buds come on the trees. I noted two exceptions to the rule in the past, which he acknowledged, but he added that for as long as he could remember, and as long as his father could remember, the ceremony had been held either in late winter or in late fall.

The clearminded chiefs reached the fire at two-thirty. They were a double column of perhaps twenty chiefs, fewer than in 1945. The ranks of the Three Brothers waited, lined up parallel to the road, listening to the approaching singer. On reaching the fire, the clearminded Four Brothers halted when their column drew abreast of the Three Brothers across the fire. The singer stopped. As the Welcome at the Woods' Edge opened, the two sides—the Three and Four Brothers—were drawn up on opposite sides of the fire in parallel facing ranks.

Immediately, Peter John commenced the opening chant, "Onenh weniserade::::::" (Today we were surprised to hear your voices coming over the forest . . .). Although a Mohawk chief, Peter John was not nearly as effective in this role as Alex General had been in the 1945 ceremony at Lower Cayuga. He followed a book of written text, marching back and forth by the fire with notes held close to his bespectacled eyes. This lasted perhaps ten minutes.

At two-forty, the speaker for the Three Brothers (Joseph Logan, or Thado-da:ho?) delivered the welcome address, which his son said largely repeated what the chanter had said. The Three Bare Words of Requickening followed at three o'clock. The mourners send three strings of wampum across the fire, one with each word. Billy Henry carried the attesting string across, where it was accepted. A pole was not set horizontally to hang the strings. A chief simply kept them in hand.

William Thomas (Cayuga) replied for the Four Brothers as condolers, sending each of the strings back to the Three Brothers side in the same manner.

It was now three-thirty, the ceremony at the woods' edge having lasted half an hour. Speaking for the Three Brothers as hosts, Chief Logan said, "We will now repair to the principal place where the main part of the ceremony will go forward; there the Three Brothers will await the message of the Four Brothers, our guests."

The hosts escorted the guests to the longhouse. A second singer took over at the longhouse door. Since George Van Every was in the States and had not responded to a letter, the Four Brothers had to borrow a singer from the Three Brothers' side. They came across the fire and borrowed Roy Buck, himself a Cayuga who should by rights have been singing for the Four Brothers. Two members of the Three Brothers' side were appointed to take the Four Brothers by the arm and conduct them to the principal place—usher them into the longhouse. (The Iroquois invariably assign a task to two persons.) We of the public on the Three Brothers' side went back into the longhouse. I still remember Chief Logan marching along in rubber boots, splashing through the wet ditch. He looked at me and grinned as he passed.

The original singer, Roy Fish, continued where he had left off from fire to longhouse door, where he stopped.

□□◇□□

Inside the longhouse the Onondaga chiefs took their customary places in the northwest corner, with the Mohawk and Seneca chiefs flanking them. The public on the Three Brothers' side ranged around the north side of the house, which is to the right of the door. Benches awaited the Four Brothers chiefs in the southwest corner. Dr. T. J. Jamieson, a prominent Detroit physician who was attending the ceremony, carrying a walnut condolence cane of his own making, went to that side saying, "I myself am really a Cayuga by my mother.'' (His father was a Mohawk chief.)

Onondaga warriors escorted the Four Brothers into the longhouse. On reaching the door, Roy Fish left off chanting the eulogy. Then Roy Buck took up Howard Skye's reproduction of the Sprague cane, walked to the north end of the room, turned, and commenced to chant the long Eulogy to the Founders from the beginning, pacing the length of the house and returning. The reason given for this repetition is that it enables the public to hear the chant in its entirety.

Corbett Sundown of Tonawanda—or Shagen?jyo:na (RC 45)—a member of the Seneca Hawk clan who was seated near me, helped keep track of the names. The entire recitation took seventy minutes. We estimated one or two minutes per name. It was four-fifteen when Roy Buck finished and, escorted by Hadya?senhne (RC 37), Alex Nanticoke, returned to the Cayuga side whence the Four Brothers had borrowed him.

That morning, the Onondagas had devised a curtain of two quilts hung by safety pins on a wire stretched across the room in order to partition the space and separate the moieties. A Cayuga aide pulled the curtain, screening the two groups of chiefs.

At four-twenty that afternoon, Roy Fish commenced the solemn requiem to the dead chief.[11] An assistant led the refrain as the condoling chiefs intoned the first five songs addressed to their *agadoni* (father's kinsmen). I noted the following order for the songs:

1. *Agadoni deskennonweroni* (Uncles, I come to greet and thank)
2. *Gayaneren deskennonweroni* (The Law [Peace], I come to greet and thank)[12]
3. *Oyen?gondon deskennonweroni* (Warriors, I come to greet and thank)
4. *Wagonegi deskennonweroni* (Women, I come to greet and thank)
5. *Ronkesota deskennonweroni* (Grandsires, I come to greet and thank)

The singer lines out each song clearly and beautifully, beginning on a high note. The assistant begins on a low note and repeats it, and then the whole chorus of chiefs joins in to greet their father's kinsmen, the league, the great warrior, the women (some say the cooks), and their grandfathers of old who founded the Great Peace. I thought as I listened of Paul Radin's remark that the women are sandwiched between the warriors and the dead grandfathers.

At four-thirty-five, Chief Alex General intoned the first five stanzas of Over the Forest. Peter John (Mohawk), who also performs in this role for the Three Brothers, watched his notebook, checking the progress of his opposite number. Afterward he commented to me, "He left out six words. He thinks that he can

---

11. I had accepted the usage "Farewell Chant to the Dead Chief" from Hewitt, in working with his manuscript notes. It should, perhaps, read ". . . *of* the Dead Chief," for it is as if he is singing. Hanni Woodbury reminds me that there is no mention of the deceased chief in any of the songs. "Rather than saying 'farewell,' these songs greet the mentioned entities. If anything, they seem more like a sort of thanksgiving to all who are presently involved in the great law, as well as it authors" (Woodbury, personal communication, April 13, 1989).

12. This usually comes first.

do it without a book." (I noted later, in the second part of Over the Forest, that Chief General, who depends on his memory, hesitated and then went on.)

At four-forty, the singer raised the sixth song, "Djiyatonde:k:::::: (repeated), "Hear us, hear us!" This plea to the founders is the most solemn of all. It lasted five minutes. The curtain was then put back to the wall.

Chief General completed Over the Forest. Peter John was following him closely with the text, and it was here that I noticed that Desgahe⁷ hesitated. This must have been where he dropped six lines. Evidently, there are among Iroquois ritualists two kinds of minds: virtuosos and literalists. The virtuoso brings to his art considerable accomplishment and quality, and this was possibly the only type of mind that older Indians tolerated. Two performances were never quite identical. Mnemonics are the ancestors of books, and the Iroquois employed several kinds: corn counts, canes with pegs and pictographs, and wampum belts. The compulsive literalist never quite masters the oral text and, fearing that he may forget, relies on a written trot or text, which inhibits him. Roy Buck, of whom Peter John remarked, "He has a good head," managed without mnemonics of any kind. He traversed the roll call without hesitation, having completely internalized the text. On this occasion he never once referred to either the pegs or the pictographs on the cane. Later he delivered the Requickening Address with the same assurance, although Chief Logan and his colleague who kept the wampum strings in order prompted him. The cane, therefore, must be considered a pedagogical device, which is used mainly at rehearsals of the Four Brothers' side. Several Onondaga men then living—notably David Thomas, Peter Buck, and Joseph Logan— depended on their memories, on knowing the ritual chants and speeches, rather than relying on props of any sort.

Desgahe⁷ stood up at four-fifty to complete the articles of condolence. The wampum strings for words four through fifteen hung over a cane that extended between the laps of two chiefs seated on opposite benches. Chief General spoke in his native Cayuga, after the manner of the late Abram Charles. As he spoke he held the particular string in hand. String nine was the one called *dewashen niyoiwaks*, "Twenty Matters," for twenty is the penalty for homicide. That string had been brought down to Lower Cayuga by the Three Brothers in 1945, and it was now returned. This black (purple) string signifying death speaks of "Death the great enigma that has scattered the bones of the founder; and the mourner's mind rolls atop the fresh grave of the dead chief." This string symbolically binds up his bones.

At the end of each message the speaker said, "The word of the Four Brothers is now on its way to thee, my father's kinsman," just as the deputy carried the particular string to the other side of the fire and handed it to one of the Onondaga chiefs, who in turn handed it to Chief Logan, who placed it on a cane stretching between himself and one of the Mohawk chiefs opposite (see Hewitt 1944: 74–75; Fenton 1946:120).

Part two of the Requickening Address took nearly an hour to recite.

It was six o'clock that evening before the mourners were ready to reply. The reply of the Three Brothers to the Four Brothers who had condoled them lasted an hour and a half, just half the time occupied by the condolences of the clear-minded. The shortened time is accounted for by their omitting the eulogy and Over the Forest and proceeding without hitch or alternation.

The mourners drew the curtain and sang the Six Songs straight through. The Three Brothers sang in Onondaga and addressed the Four Brothers as "offspring." They used the past tense. I failed to note any change in the order of verses.

In the return of condolences, Roy Buck spoke for the Onondaga chiefs. He began to speak at six-twenty, returning all but one of the strings.

At seven o'clock, while he was still speaking, the cooks, or pothangers, came in and lit the oil lamps. The tired audience watched one pothanger balance precariously on a bench while putting the lamps back overhead in the chandelier. This afforded a diversion for the children. I wondered what would happen if he dropped a lamp. The speaker went on relentlessly while people came and went, the door banged, a child came to the water bucket and dropped the dipper with a clatter, and everyone whispered discreetly. A chief would get up, go out, and come back. The Iroquois capacity for boredom and the way speakers fail to be distracted always amazes me. Indians learn to live with their ceremonies.

□□◇□□

It was seven-fifteen when Chief Logan stood to address the Four Brothers, saying: "We will presently show the faces of the chiefs." The Four Brothers had asked: "Show us the man who is to take part in the council with us."

The installation is the third part of the ceremony. It commenced about seven-twenty and lasted until eight-thirty that night. It consists of Showing the Chiefs, the Charge to the New Chiefs, a charge to the public, and announcements, called "dreams," as if their recitation were an accepted part of the culture.

Chief Logan stood up and walked out from between the chiefs' benches on the Three Brothers' side and took up a position in front of the men's stove. He summoned the two matrons who were responsible for presenting the two candidates. He said of Mrs. Thomas, whose son Peter stood beside her, "This matron standing here is holder of the title Awegenhyat in the Wolf clan. She has placed the lordship on her son. This is indeed Awegenhyat. He will be your co-worker. Therefore, always speak of him as Awegenhyat. Does he appear to you as one capable of filling the office in which he is to be placed?" (Howard Skye, personal communication). Then he spoke to the faithkeeper, the deputy.

A second matron presented her son as candidate for the title Skanawadi. With the matron and candidate stood a second man, the matron's deputy for watching the chief. Josey Logan commented that the Onondagas, unlike the Cayugas and Senecas, do not have subchiefs. I am uncertain of the standing arrangement, but my notes say the two matrons stood nearest the stove, the candidates flanking them, each with his deputy on his left or right, respectively.

Chief Logan came out, cane in hand, and stood in the center facing the crowd. In presenting the candidates he pointed with his cane at each of the candidates in turn: first at Awegenhyat and then at Skanawadi, taking hold of the top of his head, lifting up his chin, and showing him to the assembly. In doing so, he said: "I now show you his face, this is the kind of person he is; you now see how he looks." His comments amused people.

Of the second candidate he said: "This matron on this side is holder of the title Skanawadi in the Turtle clan. She has placed the lordship on her son. This is Skanawadi. He will be your co-worker. Therefore, always speak of him as Skanawadi.

Does he appear to you as one capable of filling the seat in which he is to be placed?" (Howard Skye, personal communication).

Logan went on about the candidates: "You two new chiefs who have been stood up here, it now remains for you to work for the good. It may be that some family needs advice and counsel, and it is your duty to do them all the good you can." Logan then informed them of the teachings of the Seneca Prophet, Ganya-daiyo?. "It is also up to the chiefs to maintain the word of our maker and to keep it in force always for the good of our people" (Howard Skye, personal communication).

As each chief was presented, Chief Logan took a small string of white wampum from the hand of the matron and sent it over by messenger to the Four Brothers side. "This is the 'drop in the ear,' notification that the candidate has been presented," said Josey Logan. These strings were not returned but were passed among the Four Brothers chiefs and kept.

When Logan had finished speaking about the candidates at length, Chief General for the Four Brothers arose and asked: "Who are the two other fellows?"

Chief Logan returned to say: "They are the guardians of the two chiefs. But they are just ordinary officials, *hodihunda*, in the Longhouse." He announced their names.

Having presented the candidates, Chief Logan once more resumed his place among the Onondaga chiefs and sat down.

There were thus two parts to the installation: showing the faces of the candidates, and the charge by the speaker for the clearminded, the sponsor standing behind the candidate. This latter has two parts: the charge to the chief and the charge to the public.

Chief General for the Four Brothers came out next, cane in hand, and confronted the candidates and their sponsors with the Charge to the New Chiefs. Chief Logan meanwhile got up and walked around to stand behind the candidates, resting his weight on one hip, his cane propped behind him, and one foot to the fore. (The charge is a set speech of which Hewitt took numerous texts, and it occurs in Gibson's of 1912 [Fenton 1946: 125]). The charge lasted from seven-forty-five to eight-ten. There were several questions along the way.

At eight-ten it was announced that the ceremony was over, unless someone had dreamed something. Chief General replied for the other side, "No one here has dreamt anything." Neither side had dreamed, unlike in 1945 (Fenton 1946: 126).

Since no one had dreamed, Chief Logan stood and remarked, "We will now bring in the food. It is time to wash away the tobacco [*oyen?gohaittha?*]," for which the feast is named. The four cooks appointed by the mourners to carry on these duties brought in the food from the cook house—bread and kettles of meat. They presented it first to the clearminded chiefs, who were guests. Second, it went to the mourners. Each group of chiefs in succession intoned three times: "Yo:henh:::::, hii:::::yenh:::." The response recalled the cries that punctuated ancient treaties when the rum and Indian goods were presented.

Sam Silversmith, an assistant cook and scout for the Onondagas, was passing meat from a wooden tray in a clockwise direction, contrary to normal ceremonial circuits. Josey Logan remonstrated to me, "This is a feast, he should go in the opposite way." I commented, "Maybe he thinks it is ʔOhgi:we:h [Feast of the Dead]." Logan acknowledged that that was the only time a clockwise circuit was permitted. There were two kettles of boiled beef, cut up in chunks, one for the clearminded and one for the mourning chiefs. And some women had prepared corn soup, which reminded me that on the day I called on Chief Logan we saw a man going up the road carrying two strings of white corn over his shoulder, followed by a woman. Howard Skye had then remarked, "They are on the way to make corn soup."

By eight-forty-five that night, when I departed the longhouse, six hours of continuous ceremonial had passed. Chief Logan wished me a safe journey home. At nine, when I drove out of the longhouse grounds, I noticed Pete Williams hurrying from a neighboring house carrying a canvas bag over one shoulder by the drawstrings; it contained the drum and horn rattles for the social dance called Rubbing Antlers. Down the road toward Silversmith's Corners, I met a matron and her children coming toward the longhouse. I asked, "Can I carry you down to Lower Cayuga?" She responded, "Oh, is it all over? We were going to the dance." Evidently, for some people the big time comes in the evening when the ceremony and feast are over.

□□◇□□

At the pain of some repetition, let me stress some basic principles at work in the Condolence Council. First, it is essentially a death feast without the corpse. Its purpose is to overcome the dysphoria of death and restore the euphoria of normal social relations. Second, it accomplishes this by several reciprocal acts between moieties of the confederacy. Song is replied by song; speech is answered by speech. The confederate moieties, separated since the death, rejoin at the end of the ceremony. Tension mounts. The clearminded come singing on the road to the clearing, where the mourners greet them with Three Bare Words that are reciprocated. Each ceremonial act is certified by wampum crossing the fire. The main "rubbing down of bodies" is reserved for the main fire (in the longhouse). Mourners withdraw there to await the rest of the ceremony. Clearminded warriors escort guests to the door. An interrupted eulogy, resumed, stops at the door. Thus a preliminary period of welcome at the clearing is followed by five and one-half hours of segmented ceremonial in the longhouse.

Social distance is a third observable principle. It is overcome by gradual alternation of segmented ritual acts, as if to soften the power of the ceremony to relieve grief. Formal distance is accented by drawing and withdrawing a curtain to screen the moieties during the Six Songs.

There is procession and retreat, the pacing to and fro of chanters, and then the rapid return of condolences as the ceremony builds to a climax in the raising up of the new chiefs by the mourners and the charge to them by the clearminded. Society is reunited in an exchange of dreams—the soul of Iroquois tradition—in hosts feeding guests, and in a celebration of the return to normal social relations in a great social dance. Here the women of the hosts are "released" to the guests.

Recall how, in the founding of the league, feuding tribes were brought to confederation. Yet in the process they preserved a sense of tribal identity. They have maintained a facade of tribal differences ever since, even during the past two centuries of living on the Six Nations Reserve in Canada. Hostility prior to confederation gave way to moiety reciprocity. Intertribal moiety reciprocity became a means of making peace and alliances, just as moiety reciprocity within tribes drained off the aggressive behavior of factions.

Tribal diversity in certain cultural items continues. Mohawk is the official language of the Condolence Council; it is spoken by those of the Three Brothers who still know it, but it has been largely supplanted by Onondaga. A few of the Four Brothers speak Mohawk, but Cayuga is predominant. Oneida and Seneca are no longer current at Six Nations. Certain ritual props are used by one side but not by the other. In rehearsing, Onondagas lay down the pattern of the roll call in kernels of corn. Cayugas employ a cane with pegs and pictographs. I am uncertain whether the fifteen wampum strings for the Requickening Address are identical in pattern or differ on the two sides.

The program of the ceremony has changed little within the combined memory of recent generations. I put this and other questions later by correspondence to Howard Skye (Cayuga), who researched them with his mentor, John Smoke. According to them, the Cayugas no longer observe the rule of condoling a death and raising a successor within three days, although I suspect this ideal was seldom fulfilled. Dr. Jamieson, with whom I afterward corresponded on such matters, commented that on the morning of the ceremony they heard the cry of a messenger, presumably Chief General. Mr. Skye assured me that the death cry is given at the time of death of a chief but not on the morning of the ceremony. The cry of death is *gwah:::::heh!*

CHAPTER 12

THE REQUICKENING PARADIGM

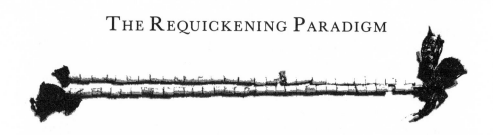

The custom of greeting strangers at a woods'-edge fire or at a landing, usually accompanied by the weeping of real or symbolic tears, has a known history among Iroquoian peoples of at least four and one-half centuries, and it was probably observed throughout the eastern woodlands long before that. In this manner the villagers of Hochelaga (Montreal) greeted Cartier in 1535:

> And after marching about a league and a half, we met on the trail one of the headmen of the village of Hochelaga, accompanied by several Indians, who made signs to us that we should rest at that spot near a fire they had lighted on the path; which we did. Thereupon this headman began to make a speech and to harangue us, which . . . is their way of showing joy and friendliness, welcoming in this way the Captain and his company. (Biggar 1924: 152–53)

An exchange of gifts followed and preceded the escorting of visitors into the village, where the principal business was transacted. Just what was said on these occasions escaped observers unfamiliar with native languages, although one can infer from the tone of the early accounts and the behavior of the Indians what was going on in the light of later, more ample descriptions of similar happenings. Indeed, the nature and content of the ritual paradigm of welcome and requickening became apparent only during the last century, from 1883 to the 1990s, in ethnological field studies by Hale (1883; 1895), Hewitt (1916; 1944), and me (Fenton 1946). The fifteen elements, or "words," composing the ritual paradigm of requickening are quite consistent throughout ten recorded instances and are confirmed by the latest record (Michelson 1988). The elements "tears, ears, and throat" throughout constitute the "bare words" of the Welcome at the Woods' Edge ceremony. The *Book of Rites* texts cover these three plus "wiping away blood" (Hale 1883:21), but Hale, to his amazement, witnessed some eleven to twelve wampums cross the fire during a condolence ceremony conducted after he published (Hale 1895). The celebrant was Chief John Arthur Gibson, from whom Hewitt and Goldenweiser later recovered the texts.

Having plotted the distribution and sequence of the fifteen elements that have constituted the paradigm during the last century, I find Gibson's version for the Three Brothers and Chief Abram Charles's text and strings for the Four Brothers virtually consistent. Following the woods'-edge greeting, which incorporates elements one through three (the Three Bare Words), the second part of the ceremony consists of the following elements: (4) within his breast, (5) wiping bloody mat, (6) darkness of grief, (7) loss of sky, (8) loss of sun (restored), (9) grave covered, (10) twenty, penalty for murder, (11) council fire, (12) woman and warrior (2 strings in Hewitt 1944), (13) chief, (14) insanity (suicide) (item 13 in A. Charles) or, alternatively, torch of notification, and (15) show us the candidate.

Up to element nine, most versions agree. Gibson's 1912 account separates element 9, "mind tosses atop grave," from 10, "Death, the Faceless," which he combines with "twenty matters." Combination of two strings in the twelfth element, and the fact that the "torch of notification" is passed back and forth between the two sides, reduces the requickening burdens to thirteen (Hewitt 1944). Combinations or separations spell the difference between fourteen and fifteen strings (fig. 17). Finally, the so-called torch of notification, a string that is mutually owned and passed back and forth between the two sides (item 14 in Hewitt 1944, 15 in Gibson 1912, and 15 in Charles [Hewitt 1944: 78]), is not essentially a Condolence Council item. Together with the combination of elements 9 and 10, the proper elements of condolence reduce to thirteen, as they are sometimes denominated.

□□◇□□

These are the kinds of elements one should look for in earlier accounts of condolence ceremonies. The order of enumeration and the content of the elements change with circumstances and concerns of the moment; one cannot expect them to be consistent throughout three centuries. Yet some amazing similarities recur. In some seventy-nine condolence events taking place between 1645 and 1805 and recorded in the Jesuit *Relations*, the New York Colonial Documents (NYCD), Wraxall (1915), the papers of Sir William Johnson, records of Indian treaties, and the Pickering Papers, the Three Bare Words recur throughout. The element tears usually comes first, often in combination with ears and throat, but on occasions when blood had been shed, "wiping clean the mat, bed, or seat" comes first. The number and order of the other elements show no consistent pattern. They may number as many as twenty or as few as five.

To gain some control over these data, I plotted the references chronologically and horizontally on spreadsheets in twelve columns: (1) woods' edge, or landing, (2) bare words, (3) internal organs, or water of pity, (4) grave, (5) cast down weapons/riddance of evil, (6) clear path or river, (7) mind, unity, heart, (8) tree planted, (9) dispel clouds/restore sun, (10) fire, (11) song/cries, and (12) custom (a catch-all). The order conforms to earlier historical data.

In 1645 at Three Rivers, Kiotsaeton ("the Hook"), a Mohawk speaker, treated some Frenchmen to the first recorded performance of the Requickening Address to open the proceedings of a treaty (JR, 27: 247–53; Fenton 1985: 128). He stood offshore in the bow of a canoe draped in beads to hail the hosts at the landing as brothers. Welcoming them ashore, he planted two poles and stretched a cord between them on which to hang, in order, the seventeen "words" of his countrymen encoded in wampum strings and belts: (1) a song of peace, (2) take a prisoner by the arm, (3) cast down weapons, (4) clear the river, (5) kindle a perpetual fire, (6) a great belt to bind the parties arm and arm in peace (his tenth), and (7) dispel clouds and restore the sun. The remaining elements treated the business at hand. Early on he affected tears, wiped the bloody mat, and ended the ceremony by

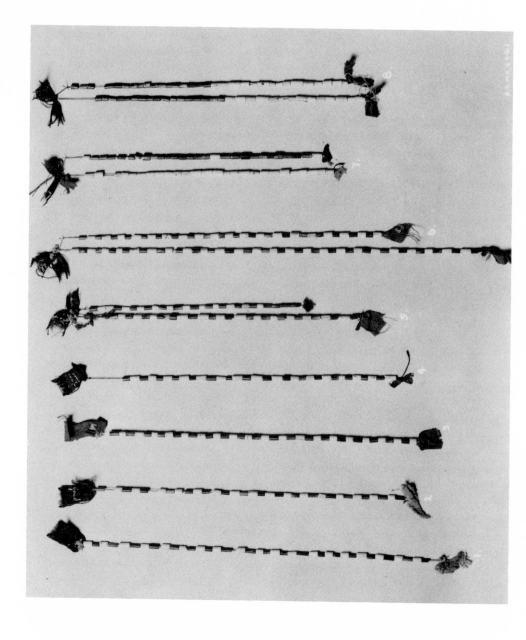

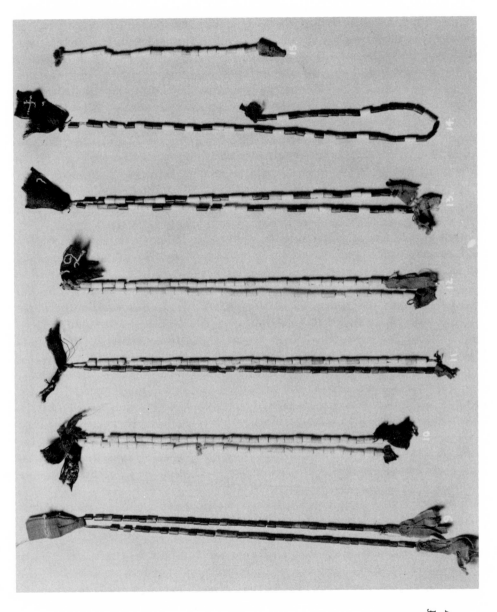

Figure 17 (above and below). The "Fifteen Matters" of requickening; the Cayuga set of condolence strings. Courtesy Royal Ontario Museum of Archaeology, Toronto.

requickening the name of a captive. The affair concluded in a mutual feast and a dance (see also l'Incarnation 1681:393.) I have identified elements found in later performances that make up a pattern constructed to serve a different purpose.

Eight years later at Quebec, an Onondaga speaker performed a less elaborate exposition of the paradigm composed of seven elements: (1) tears, (2) medicine for internal organs, (3–4) cover the grave, (5) cast down weapons, (6) clear path and river, and (7) plead unity and peace (JR, 40: 165–67). These elements were the essentials. The next year, 1654, the same elements occurred in different order (JR, 41: 51ff.). Later in 1654, at Montreal, the speaker enumerated twenty items: (1) the Tree of Peace, (2) unity or peace, (3) administered medicine, (4–7) burned prisoner ties, cut leg cords, etc., and demolished scaffold, (8–10) three nations collaborate, (11) unity, (12) path opened, (13) welcomed Jesuits, (14) cleaned bloody mat, (18) ears opened, (19) link arms (alliance), and (20) invoked sun.

Father Le Moyne took up the invitation, was greeted at the woods' edge outside of Onondaga and ushered into town, heard parts of the eulogy, and addressed the council in "the tone of a Captain" with nineteen words (JR, 41: 99ff.).

Father Chaumonot shared a similar experience the following year: (1) he was welcomed at the woods' edge and led by the arm; (2) he heard two of the Three Bare Words—tears and throat; (3) he was welcomed at the fire and (4) was addressed in kin terms; and (5) he heard "cast down weapons," (6) the path cleared, and (7) a plea for unity (JR, 42: 77ff.).

Garakontie of Onondaga, a master of the forms, journeyed to Montreal in 1658, hung his presents on a pole, and proceeded to condole the French with three words—wiping their tears, clearing their throats, and wiping bloody sites— followed by these elements, among others: (2) giving a medicine to calm the heart, (6) throwing sand on the grave, (8) replanting the "May Tree," (9) reattaching the sun, (10) rekindling the council fire, (11) spreading a mat, (12) clearing the river, and (14) binding the French to four nations—and so on for an agenda of twenty items.

The next year, a delegation of Mohawk, Oneida, and Onondaga ambassadors arrived at Quebec, displayed their presents, and condoled the deaths of three Frenchmen killed at Montreal: they (1) removed the hatchet, (2) covered the grave, (3) cast the dead deep in the ground, (4) planted a "May Tree," (5) kindled a fire in its shade, (6) gave a medicine, (7) prepared minds for peace, (8) restored the sun, (9) again took the French by the arm (alliance), and, after discussing captives, (10) opened their eyes and ears. Such were the elements of condolence in twenty-four items (JR, 45: 81ff.) Later that summer, a Mohawk speaker, thanking the governor of New France for preserving the life of a prisoner, restored two bare words—tears and throat—to the top of the agenda (JR, 45: 99ff.).

A procession of visiting condolers observed woods'-edge protocol while attending a Mohawk Dead Feast in 1667. The nations sat separately, as did the sexes. Myths were recited, but the unsympathetic missionary, excluded for protesting, omitted details (JR, 51: 187).

Speakers for the "whole house" frequently reminded Europeans of the obligation to observe condolence law. A Mohawk, addressing the governor of Virginia in 1685 at Albany, having sung the "Covenant Song" completely, said, "Let me drive it into you with a song" (Livingston 1956: 88–89). This reference to what are now called the Six Songs counted for naught unless something was laid down, namely wampums or presents (Livingston 1956: 49–51).

Following the Schenectady massacre of 1690, a delegation of eight Mohawk sachems from three "castles" came down to Albany "with tears in our eyes" in February to condole the dead. They regarded those who adhered to the covenant chain and sat under the Tree of Peace as their kindred and wept for them. Having (1) wiped the tears, they appealed to the image of the "whole house," which the French had broken at both ends. (2) They gathered the dead for burial, and (3) they appealed to condolence law, having been taught by their forefathers that "when any sad accident befalls any of the Covenant," they should go and bemoan the death, for which (4) they administered "eye water." (5) They wiped away the blood from the defiled house, (6) invoked the "Silver Chain" and pronounced, "Djagon!" (take courage), for "We are of the race of the Bear that does not yield," (7) dispelled clouds and restored the sun, and then proceeded to request military aid (DHNY, 2: 164–70).

Again, two years later, Governor Fletcher of New York learned that a condolence ceremony must be performed before war parties went out (NYCD, 4: 20–22). Fletcher, now named "Great Swift Arrow" (Cayenquiragoe), was at some pains to learn the protocol. And when a later acting governor, Colonel Ingoldsby, failed to condole the Oneidas for their losses, an Oneida speaker warned that no presents were in order if no condolence was performed (NYCD, 3: 842–40).

In 1694, after the Onondaga council had sent nine of its sachems to treat with the governor of New France, Fletcher sent delegates to Onondaga to protest and then convened a great treaty at Albany that summer attended by commissioners from Connecticut, New Jersey, and Massachusetts and delegates of all the Five Nations.[1] The representatives of the league arrived in double-column procession chanting the Hai Hai, or Eulogy to the Founders. A Boston clergyman noted:

> The treaty was held in ye street, yt runs East and West [modern State Street], a little above the meeting house. Ye sachems were attended with many other Indians. . . . [T]hey came two in a rank, Rode, ye Sachim of the Maquase being ye leader, singing all ye way songs of joy and peace. So, likewise, when they were sat down, they sang two or three songs of peace. (Wadsworth 1852: 106)

During the proceedings, speakers employed condolence forms: the Three Bare Words, wiping blood, offering a medicine, planting a Tree of Peace with roots extending to adherents of the chain of peace and friendship. They proclaimed Onondaga the seat of the league, and Albany the site of treaties. Teganissorens of Onondaga reported on the mission to Canada—their efforts to rectify the French governor's mind and clear the river between them—and delivered belts, which Fletcher refused. The next day Sadekanacktie, another Onondaga sachem, sang a long song of peace and used condolence forms and wampum to dispel tension, reporting on conversations with the Ottawas to settle differences. They had dispersed clouds and restored the sun, received a calumet symbolizing the sun, and retrieved the hatchet.

---

1. *Account of . . . a Treaty between Governor Fletcher and the Five Nations, August, 1694* (New York: Wm Bradford, 1694), 39 pp.; Wadsworth 1852; DePuy 1917: treaty no. 3; NYCD, 4: 118.

It is apparent in these proceedings that after 1690 the English equated the "chain" concept with the "whole house" metaphor of the Five Nations, to whom the chain, attached at both ends, was akin to an umbilical cord, important to keep firm and inviolable for all linked in it. According to Sadekanacktie of Onondaga: "The least member cannot be touched, but the whole Body must feel and be sensible; if therefore an Enemy hurt the least part of the Covenant Chain, we will join to destroy that Enemy; for we are one Head, one Flesh, and one Blood."

This was still being said at Tonawanda in the 1930s.[2]

The next winter, so-called praying Indians from Lake of Two Mountains and Caughnawaga came to Onondaga to condole the Longhouse. In the league's reply, Aqueendera demonstrated a unique way of handling the Three Bare Words. He took up "three fathoms of wampum" and touched "one with his finger saying this wipes the tears from our Eyes; touching the other say's [sic] this washes away the blood. Then putting all three together sayd Throw away the bitter Gall out [of] your body Onontio [the governor of New France] and clear up your understanding. Give three fathem wampum" (NYCD, 4: 120). He then proceeded to lecture the French governor, who replied by sacking Onondaga.

Although wampum required for condolences was sometimes in short supply among the Five Nations, at the close of the seventeenth century it was available from Albany traders in fathoms or by the bushel, and it reached Montreal via the Champlain corridor in the contraband trade. Iroquois of Caughnawaga, during frequent visits to Albany, and local Mahicans were the carriers. By this time a cottage industry had grown up that soon evolved into "wampum factories," on Long Island and in New Jersey near the source of marine shells, where domesticated natives perfected the drilling of shell beads.[3]

In the preliminaries to, and during the proceedings of, the Grand Settlement at Montreal in 1701, at least six short forms and three long forms of condolence occurred. "Tears, throat, and wiping blood" comprised the specific bare words. A longer form preceded the negotiations in 1699, when a Seneca led a chanting procession weeping for the dead. The order of elements is somewhat reversed: (1) restoring the sun, (2) planting the Tree of Peace, (3) clearing river and path, (4) casting weapons into oblivion, (5) speaking from the heart, and (6) casting out bile with a medicine. An Onondaga delegation was welcomed at the landing and formed a column to the woods' edge; their speaker, Teganissorens, spoke three words, and they were ushered to council seats. Governor Callière replied in council using three belts; he covered the dead, cast down weapons, and planted a tree. At the height of the treaty proceedings, the death of Kondiaronk, or "the Rat," a Petun Huron chief from the upper Great Lakes who had engineered the settlement, called forth elaborate condolences involving a eulogy procession, wiping tears and clearing the throat, a medicine, restoring the sun, binding the bones, and covering the dead. The funeral next day combined Iroquois and French honors (La Potherie 1722, 4: 136–37, 156–77, 167, 185–86, 193, 200–1, 228ff.; Fenton in DCB, 2: 323).

□□◇□□

2. Chief Edward Black of the Seneca Hawk clan, personal communication to the author about avoiding sides in a trouble case circa 1936.

3. Council with Cayugas, 28 September 1697 (III), PRO England CO5/1040, NL Reel 5; McIlwain 1915: xli ff.; Orchard 1929: 70ff.

By the eighteenth century, the condolence ceremony was no new thing. It was frequently mentioned but seldom described. It mourned the passing of Queen Anne, governors and their wives, Sir Peter Warren, uncle of William Johnson, the French agent Joncaire, and other public personages. Ceremonies for notable Indian leaders reported by knowledgeable interpreters afford greater detail. Seven hands of wampum sent down from Onondaga urged sachems of the other Five Nations to attend a ceremony in Canada to mourn Joncaire, an adopted Seneca (Wraxall 1915: 216).

Conrad Weiser, the Pennsylvania interpreter, botanist John Bartram, and map maker Lewis Evans journeyed to Onondaga in 1743 to "take the Hatchet out of the Head of the Six Nations." Among other wonders, they witnessed a condolence ceremony as passive participants. Greeted at the woods' edge, Weiser arranged for a speaker. Ushered to the council place, they heard the origin of the league rehearsed, the ancestors lauded, and contemporaries deprecated. They watched a pacing chanter recite the Roll Call of the Founders. In the manner of a principal, Weiser fed the belts of condolence to Canasatego, the Onondaga orator, his hired speaker. He greeted the Six Nations by their council names, rubbed down their bodies, and then condoled the mourning families at Onondaga and Oneida: (1) wiping away the blood, (2) covering the graves, (3) restoring the sun (large belt), (4) casting down weapons, (5) dispersing clouds, (6) giving medicine to restore vital signs, and (7) appealing to the chain for unity and peace. Cries of approbation affirmed each message as the wampums were racked up on a pole. Shared kettles of corn soup restored the participants (Bell 1973: 58–61; P. Wallace 1945: 159–63).

The next year, Canasatego, then at the height of his form, led the procession of Iroquois delegates into the treaty site at Lancaster, singing a song inviting the renewal of treaties (Marshe 1800 [1744]: 179). The roll call is not mentioned. In welcoming the Indians, the English custom of a round of drinks superseded usual protocol, while the Indians joked at the size of the glasses. Witham Marshe, a perceptive observer, was at pains to describe the cries of approbation that punctuated the passing of wampum belts:

> By this we were sure the speech was . . . approved by the Indians. This cry . . . is performed thus: The grand chief and speaker amongst them pronounces the word *jo-hah!* with a loud voice, singly; then all the others join in this sound, *woh!* dwelling some little while upon it, and keeping exact time with each other, and immediately, with a sharp noise and force, utter this sound, *wugh!* This is performed with great order, and with the utmost ceremony and decorum; and with the Indians is like our huzza! (Marshe 1800: 185)

With slight phonetic alteration it is what one hears in the Condolence Council today.

During the proceedings, Canasatego, concerned to keep the road open between the two parties, condoled his host for some bad news of Indian depredations. He (1) wiped away tears, (2) cast down weapons, and (3–4) administered a medicine with four strings. One account says that he wiped away the tears with four strings and received three in return (Marshe 1800: 197).

A few days earlier, the Six Nations delegates, recognizing that the governor of Maryland, their host, lacked a council name, unlike the governors of Pennsylvania and Virginia, assigned the honor of naming him to the Cayuga members. They opted for the title of the leading Mohawk chief, Tekarihoken. (Personal names and titles in different contexts were shared among the Five Nations.) The recorded speech conferring the title resembles the modern charge to a new chief.

"And as it has fallen to the Cahugaes' lot in council to consider of a proper name for that chief man, we have agreed to give him the name of Tocary-ho-gon, denoting Precedency, Excellency, or living in the middle, or honorable place betwixt Asserigoa ["Big Knife," governor of Virginia], and our brother Onas [governor of Pennsylvania], by whom our treaties may be the better carried on."

And turning to the assembled commissioners, the speaker said: "We take this opportunity to publish the matter, that it may be known Tocary-ho-gon is our friend, and that we are ready to honour him, and that by such name he may be always called and known among us; and, we hope, he will ever act toward us, according to the excellence of the name we have now given him, and enjoy a long and happy life." Five cries of approbation followed. The commissioners gave three huzzas (Marshe 1800: 194; Boyd 1938: 65).

No Mohawks were present to object to the use of their title.

Six years later, Canasatego died, leaving the grand council in the hands of a hostile faction. Word reached Weiser on the path from his native Schoharie. The league was in disarray, the Mohawk leaders committed to the English interest, Oneida wavering, and the three upper nations inclined toward New France. It was a frustrating time to gain easements for Pennsylvania and Virginia on the Ohio. No business was possible until Canasatego was properly condoled. At Oneida, Weiser enlisted knowledgeable members of the junior moiety of the confederacy— Oneida, Tuscarora, and surrogates for Cayuga—to perform the rites.

Weiser's journal vividly describes the doings at Onondaga. An Oneida member of the council began to sing a "Lamentation Song" just as they set out on the path to Onondaga. This I judge to be the Hai Hai (P. Wallace 1945: 310).

It took several days for the delegates to assemble at the main fire. From the Senecas came word that they could not attend, and the Cayuga council empowered the Oneidas to act for their moiety. As offspring, the Oneida-Cayuga-Tuscarora moiety addressed the Onondaga-Seneca-Mohawk moiety as "father" (agadoni), styling themselves "sons." The Oneida speaker observed the taboo on naming the dead, referring to the deceased Onondaga orator as "that great Man our Word." He (1) wiped the tears, (2) cleared the throats, (3) wiped the mat, and (4) covered the grave. Weiser sought to (5) kindle a fire in Fredericksburg and (6) plant a tree to shelter a treaty council. An Onondaga speaker returned the condolences (P. Wallace 1945: 315–16).

Despite these amenities, Weiser's mission came to naught. The old men were reluctant to go that far, having lost councilors who died on the road going to and returning from treaties in Philadelphia and Lancaster.

William Johnson had begun to observe the proper forms. On 8 September 1753, Onondaga chiefs met him and a Mohawk delegation a mile outside of town. The speaker wiped away their tears and assuaged the grief in their hearts that they might address the council. Johnson addressed the general convention, requick-ening the loss of three named Onondaga councilors with seven words: (1) wiped tears, (2) cleared throats, (3) wiped blood; (4) covered bones; (5) cleared the path;

(6) kindled a fire; and (7) planted a tree. He also gave a wing to sweep dust from the council mat (SWJP, 9: 110–13.)

According to Scaroyady's advice to the treaty commissioners at Carlisle that same summer, only five elements were essential to condolence protocol: (1) wiping blood, (2) kindling fire, (3) covering grave, (4) wiping tears, and (5) restoring sun. The order seems odd: tears should come first, but Scaroyady was an Oneida chief and must have known the ritual (DePuy 1917: 31; Boyd 1938: xii, 127, 128). Four years later, replying to George Croghan at Harris's Ferry, he changed the order somewhat and restored the sun, conforming to the first speaker's sequence (Boyd 1938: 170–1). Evidently the order was not set, although throughout the second half of the eighteenth century the tears-ears-throat cluster predominated, with wiping blood taking precedence as occasion demanded.

Of the many condolence ceremonies that Johnson sponsored at the height of his career during the third quarter of the century, two merit extensive treatment because they are well reported. A third was performed to mourn him and raise up his successor. I treat them together in Appendix C.

The Six Nations Iroquois enjoyed no monopoly on the knowledge and performance of condolence protocol. The neighboring Delawares shared and discharged its obligations with singular éclat, as witness the performances of Teedyuscung at a series of treaty negotiations at Easton, Pennsylvania, between 1756 and 1758 (Boyd 1938: 155ff). Nor was it unknown to the Shawnees, the Nanticokes, and other tidewater Algonquians. The Three Bare Words recur throughout, together with other burdens appropriate to the occasion. Indeed, in both its short and long forms, the performance of the requickening paradigm had become such a common occurrence during the second half of the eighteenth century that chroniclers omit specifics and simply refer to it as "the usual ceremony of condolence." By this time, principals in the colonies and native leaders knew and performed it.

A recent study of the "condolence business" (Foley 1973) confirmed my interpretation of its evolution and its history. The ritual of installation "developed from the condolence at the burial of sachems." To the original burial ceremony were added the customary greetings at the woods' edge, the roll call, and the chant called Over the Forest, the last of which is in part a recitation of bylaws enacted by the founders. In Foley's words, "the condolence at the installation is an elaborated burial ceremony without the body" (Foley 1973: 49). The extension of this fictive burial procedure to members of another nation forms the basis of the alliance mechanism known to history as the chain of peace and friendship.

The essential pattern of the ceremony has remained more or less stable over time (Foley 1973: 50). My own observations in 1945 and 1951 noted a ritual sequence similar to those recorded by Hale (1895) fifty years earlier and Morgan (1851) a century before me. Had one of us witnessed the installation of Guy Johnson as Indian superintendent in 1774, we might know whether certain chants mentioned were those in use today. We note the same sequence, the same separation of confederate moieties, and familiar metaphors of condolence.

In firming and renewing alliances, or at times when two allies or potential allies met in a situation where one had suffered a loss, there was a regular way to act, defined by custom (NYCD, 7: 131). One defined a loss in any of four ways: (1) if any of the principals—translators, sachems, or representatives of an ally—present at a previous conference had died; (2) if condolences were performed but several of the principals were not present, in which case one must repeat the condolences; (3) if any party participating in a public conference had killed any member of another principal party present; or (4) if either participating principal had lost a member of high status, or if a principal had suffered a severe loss. (This last category covered pine tree chiefs, war leaders, and matrons. By extension it included kindred of colonial governors and persons of similar stature.) Circumstances affected the sequence, the omissions, the emphasis, and the kinds of presents exchanged. Woods'-edge protocol might be omitted, and a special occasion might include a procession of singing sachems. A short form might be employed for calling on officials to renew the chain and conduct business. The full classical form might be celebrated before opening a grand council at Onondaga; it resembles the nineteenth-century form that governs the present Condolence Council (after Foley 1973: 51–52; Fenton 1946).

□□◇□□

Now to summarize, as Franz Boas was wont to say.

The requickening paradigm of the Condolence Council has historical roots extending four and one-half centuries into the past. Although the fifteen "burdens," or elements, of the paradigm have remained consistent for a century or more during the reservation period, they clearly evolved from similar elements that were ordered differently in response to deaths by murder and warfare during the eighteenth century and earlier. Then, wiping away bloodstains, real or metaphorical, took precedence. Woods'-edge protocol goes back to the beginnings of written Iroquois history, and the custom of weeping upon greeting strangers gave top priority to the Three Bare Words—tears, ears, and throat—that in some form comprised the essentials of the short form of condolence. Elements of the longer form recur at random, although covering the grave, casting down weapons, clearing the path or river, restoring the sun, planting the tree, and kindling a fire frequently demanded attention.

Each element, or "word," was validated by wampum. Belts came into use during the late seventeenth century as wampum became plentiful, and the use of strings alone during the nineteenth century reflects scarcity. The number of burdens in seventeenth-century performances sometimes ran to twenty, a magic number in Iroquois parlance, but only five were specified at the mid-eighteenth century. Such details partly mirror the record, which varied according to the interpreter and the interests of the audience. Clearly, the modern fifteen have evolved from these earlier fragments, which they have served to interpret.

CHAPTER 13

THE ROLL CALL
OF THE FOUNDERS

The founders of the Iroquois League predicted that it would endure in the far future, and now their descendants lament that they are losing the old ways. The opening stanza to the Eulogy to the Founders, which introduces the roll call, begs forgiveness for any omissions:

> Now to commence at the beginning,
> your grandchildren right
> now take up the path;
> May you excuse them
> if here and there in the ritual
> they shall not perform it in order,
> the way that you used to do it
> when all the words were together
> as you established it.[1]

Four following stanzas speak of abandoned fields overlying forgotten graves of founders lying on the mat of the law; of other sites overgrown with brush where they have taken the league under their heads; of grass covering ancient council places; of erecting a tree (elevating chiefs); and of reinforcing the house. Then follows the roll call of the famous fifty founders.

Although there are ten references to eulogy chant processions between 1667 and 1800, there are only vague hints as to the contents of the roll call before the mid-nineteenth century. Then, commencing with Cayuga physician Peter Wilson's and Abram La Fort's information to L. H. Morgan at Tonawanda in 1845, followed by Morgan's *League* (1851), complete rosters of the founders number eight. The remaining five are those of Hale (1883), Newhouse (1885), Beauchamp (1907), Gibson's 1912 text (Woodbury 1992),[2] and Abram Charles (unpublished text, 1917).

When lined up on a spreadsheet chronologically, these eight versions of the Roll Call of the Founders show remarkable consistency. Allowing for dialectical

---

1. Chief Alexander General, 1943 (Fenton 1950: 50).

2. In 1883, Hale heard Gibson perform the eulogy chant that Gibson later dictated to Goldenweiser, Woodbury's source. For Newhouse and Charles, see Fenton 1950. At Tonawanda in 1845, Morgan obtained independent lists of the chiefs from Peter Wilson and Abraham La Fort. Two years later, Dr. Peter Wilson addressed the New York Historical Society on 28 May on matters affecting the removal of the Seneca nation to Kansas (*Proceedings of the New York Historical Society*, June 1, 1847: 65–74). See also *Literary World*, 15 May 1847: 345–46 (courtesy Professor Elisabeth Tooker).

variations in the sources and for orthographies ranging from the syllabic renderings of Morgan and Beauchamp to the phonetics of Hewitt, Goldenweiser, and Fenton and the phonemics of Woodbury, the lists compose a single genre.[3] The one discrepancy occurs in the Seneca roster, for which I accept Morgan as the standard, since I found it still current at Tonawanda a century later. In lists from Grand River sources—those of Hale, Newhouse, Chadwick (1897), and Charles— the paired titles of the Seneca third and fourth founders, as well as the fourth and fifth titles, are somehow transposed or paired differently. This discrepancy I attribute to the separation after 1784 of the Six Nations on Grand River from the main body of the Senecas, who remained in western New York. Relatively few Senecas emigrated to Canada.

Gibson, whom Hale heard perform in 1883 and who served Hewitt and Goldenweiser, held the third Seneca title, Ga?no:gai? (S-3 in Morgan, S-5 in Hale, S-4 in Newhouse, S-4 in Charles), as in Morgan's listing. His contemporary and brother-in-law, Abram Charles, inverted S-3 and S-4, also S-5 and S-6, as on the cane of Andrew Sprague (Fenton 1950). Evidently, Seneca and Cayuga sources viewed the proper sequence differently.

Even in Hale's day, a good portion of the founding titles defied analysis, their original meanings by then obscure. In the century since, the shapes of names and their meanings have eroded still further as heard by speakers of languages other than the originals. Continual rationalization of tradition by native ritualists has produced false etymologies. Other titles remain transparent.[4] The glosses listed in Table 4 are Simeon Gibson's.

Although Elisabeth   Tooker's article on the league in the *Handbook of North American Indians* carries a table of league chief titles (1978: 424–25) prepared by the editors from a variety of sources, in Table 4 I follow my own rendering of the titles from the Gibson-Goldenweiser manuscript, as modified by Hanni Woodbury's phonemic renderings.[5] Modified forms appear elsewhere throughout this book.

Having completed the Roll Call of the Founders, the chanter disclaims any errors of omission or sequence. He says: "Quite possibly I have performed the ceremony in some way contrary to the way he [the founder] used to recite the words in the ancient day of our grandfathers. For now the people are become wretched; your grandchildren are losing their culture. Grandfathers!"

The metaphorical use of kinship terms in the chant requires some explanation. There are first the moieties of the league—the Three Brothers (M-Oa-S), who sit across the symbolic fire from the Two (now Four) Brothers (Oe-C). The Tuscaroras and a group of adopted peoples—Delawares, Nanticokes, Tutelos—who took refuge

3. It would have been better if Morgan had followed Peter Wilson's orthography, which evidently stemmed from that created by Asher Wright, missionary at Buffalo Creek Reservation (1842), which indicated nasal vowels and provided for the glottal stop, a phoneme in Iroquoian languages. See Elisabeth Tooker (1980: note 2) on the field reports of Isaac Hurd, a companion of Morgan's in the field.

4. In describing the pictographs on the now classic condolence cane, I included much of this lore (Fenton 1950). Editors of the *Handbook of North American Indians*, vol. 15, wisely omitted it (see Tooker 1978: 424–25).

5. Simeon Gibson interpreted his father's text of the Condolence Council for me in 1943. Woodbury, working from the same text, presented her analysis at the Conference on Iroquois Research, October 7–9, 1983.

TABLE 4
THE ROLL CALL OF THE CHIEFS

ROLL CALL NUMBER	ROSTER NUMBER	TITLE	GLOSS
MOHAWK[1]			
1*	M-1	Degai:ho:gen	Of two opinions
2*	M-2	Hayen:hwa:tha?	Early riser
3*	M-3	Sha?degai:hwa:de?	Equal words
4	M-4	Shaenho:na?	Long branches
5	M-5	Deyon:he:hgwi	Double life
6	M-6	Owenhe:?go:na	Big floating flower
7	M-7	Dehanna:?gai:ne	Dragging antlers
8	M-8	Hastawen:?sen:tha?	Enters with rattle
9	M-9	Shosgo:hae:na?	Great branch
ONEIDA			
10*	Oe-1	Ho?datche:hde?	Carries quiver
11*	Oe-2	Ganonhgwen?yo:don?	Erect corn cobs
12*	Oe-3	Deyoha?gwen:de?	Through the clearing
13	Oe-4	Shononhse:s	His house is long
14	Oe-5	(Ha)dwennae:gen?a?	Two voices merged
15	Oe-6	Hadya?do:nen:tha?	His body topples
16	Oe-7	Dehadahonhden:yonk	Droopy ears
17	Oe-8	Honya?dasha:yen	Swallows slowly
18	Oe-9	Honwatshadonhwi	Covered
ONONDAGA[2]			
19*	Oa-1	Dehadoda:ho?	Entangled
20	Oa-2	Hone?sa:hen?	Ties up something
21	Oa-3	Dehatgahdons	Looking about
22	Oa-4	Sga:nya?daji:wak	His dark throat
23	Oa-5	Awe?genhiyat	On the surface
24	Oa-6	Deha:ya?tkwa:i?	Half his body
25	Oa-7	Hononwiyehdi	He conceals something
26	Oa-8	Gowennen?she:ndon	Hanging object
27	Oa-9	Hahi:hon	Spills it
28	Oa-10	Hoyon:nye:ni	He made it for him
29	Oa-11	Shodegwa:tse?	Bruiser
30	Oa-12	Shago:genhe?	He saw the people
31	Oa-13	Ho?saha:hwih?	Carries an ax
32	Oa-14	Skana:wa:di	Over the swamp
CAYUGA			
33*	C-1	Haga?en:yonk	Wonders
34*	C-2	Ji?nondawehe?	
35	C-3	Gada:gwa:ji	Mashed
36	C-4	Shoyon:we:s	His long guts
37	C-5	Hadya?sen:hne	He repeats it
38	C-6	Deyoenhyon:goh	Reaches the sky

continued on next page

TABLE 4 (CONTINUED)
THE ROLL CALL OF THE CHIEFS

ROLL CALL NUMBER	ROSTER NUMBER	TITLE	GLOSS
39	C-7	Deyoto:wehkwi	Doubly cold
40	C-8	Deyawenhe?thon	Two events
41	C-9	Hadonda:he:ha?	He starts
42	C-10	Desgahe?	
SENECA			
43*	S-1	Sganya:daiyo?	Handsome lake
44*	S-2	Tsha?degaenhye:s	Level skies
45	S-3	Shagen?jyo:na	Great forehead
46	S-4	Ga?no:gai	
47	S-5	Nishaye:nen?nha?	Falling day
48	S-6	Sha:dye:nawat	Grasps it
49*	S-7	Ganonhgei?dawi?	Hair singed off
50*	S-8	Deyonihnho:ga:?wen	Doorkeeper

Note: Renderings of the titles are the author's, following the Gibson text of 1912. Spellings elsewhere in this book are simplified.
 * Co-founders of the league.
1. Numbers 1–6 are cousins to 7–9.
2. A dispute rages between Cayuga and Onondaga sources as to whether 31–32 are one or two titles. Onondagas claim them both. Titles 19 to 24 form a single committee. Number 25 stands alone; traditionally he is wampum keeper for the league.

in the Longhouse during the eighteenth century compose the third and fourth entities. The relationship between the two league moieties is that of parent and offspring, "father and son" (*honatathawah*). The Three Brothers stand as "father's kinsmen" (*hodonishen?*) to the Two (Four) Brothers. The Three Brothers refer to the Two Brothers as "my male kinsmen's children" (*kheya?da:wenh*), and so address them throughout the chant. The Two Brothers refer to the Four Brothers as "our father's kinsmen" (*ongwadonishon?*) and hail them as "my father's kinsmen" (*agadoni*).

The considerable generational gap between the ancestral founders and their descendants, the living successors, extends grandparental-grandchildren terms. A founder is a grandfather (*hakhso:t* or *haksothaha*) of a remote kind, referred to collectively as "our grandparents of old," that is, ancestors (*onkhsotahshentahkwa*). Their grandchildren (*etshiya:de:?*), "they, your grandchildren," the living, are, reciprocally, "our descendants" (*onkwa:de:tsen?*). A chief may be addressed in avuncular terms: "my uncle" (*kno?senha*), the reciprocal being "my nephews/nieces" (*akenhwaden?tshae?*).

Within each tribal roster, consulting committees of chiefs are grouped in clusters predominately of three siblings, paired as cross-cousins, and in one case linked as "father and son." In the Onondaga council, the principal founder, Thadoda:ho? (Oa-1), has as "cousin" (*honae?seshen?*) Oa-2, who in turn has as siblings Oa-3 through Oa-6. These, with Thadoda:ho?, are the firekeepers, or executive committee, of the league.

Members of a committee within a nation refer to each other as "siblings" (brothers) (*hontenhnon:ten?*), while colleagues in the league who are on the same side of the fire (moiety) but of other nations are referred to as "younger brothers" (*hontate?ken* or *honatate?kenshon?* [plural]). The opposite moiety, as in the Seneca council, may take an extension of the cross-cousin term.[6]

The preceding considerations should prove helpful later in understanding seating arrangements and models of counseling at the national and confederate levels. They are further made explicit in the diagram for the roll call on the condolence cane (Fenton 1950). But first let us look outside of Iroquois culture to ethnological approaches to leadership in eastern North America for perspective on native polity.

□□◇□□

In recent decades, the subdiscipline known as political anthropology has developed out of theories on factionalism, on the evolution of tribal society and political structures, on the individual in his or her society and culture, and on what Goldenweiser termed "involution." This last phenomenon is the tendency of societies to project to higher levels of integration solutions arrived at on lower levels, as we shall see in the case of the Iroquois Confederacy (Fenton 1986b: passim).

We owe to Ralph Linton (1936) the paired concepts of status and role. He defined status as a collection of rights and duties adhering to a position in the social system, and role as its dynamic aspect. These two concepts translate into what modern job analysts term job description and job performance. But Linton and his followers, working with American Indian and Polynesian societies, identified two entering requirements for statuses. Some statuses were ascribed by birth or by membership in some clearly defined social order and transmitted by a recognized rule of descent. Others, the achieved statuses, were awarded to individuals for life and not transmitted to heirs.

But there is more to status than a set of rights and duties, and that extra derives from expectancies of role fulfillment on the part of persons who enjoy reciprocal relations with persons who occupy leadership positions (Druke 1983). How well do leaders perform? Important as it may be to describe positions in a social system and classify them, even more important are the reciprocal relationships and expectancies that obtain between leaders and followers and that make the system work.

As we shall see, American Indian leaders were expected to advise their constituents, deliberate in council, and then consult the public so as to attain consensus and unanimity of action (if possible). Recall for a moment the role of the crier in a Cheyenne camp who announced that the Council of Forty-Four had met and reached agreement: it was said that the old men had met and gathered their voices into one; "here is their decision, and they hope that you all will agree" (Llewellyn and Hoebel 1941: 96–97ff.)

Evolutionary theorists, disciples of Leslie White and Julian Steward, having reexamined the nature of tribal society and classified types of organization into

---

6. The preceding exposition of chiefship titles, social groupings, and kinship metaphors depends heavily on Woodbury's analysis of the Gibson-Goldenweiser manuscript as presented at the Conference on Iroquois Research in 1983. Many of the terms adhere to my own transcription and translation of the same manuscript with Simeon Gibson, son of the narrator, in 1943.

bands, tribes, and chiefdoms (Fried 1967; Service 1971). Patrilineal and patrilocal bands of hunters peopled the boreal forests in the margins of northeastern North America. They comprised such groups as the Naskapi of interior Labrador and Quebec, the Montagnais, some of the Cree, and interior Athabaskan-speaking groups of the subarctic west of Hudson Bay. By and large, the sedentary horti-culturists of the northeast fell into the category of tribes—the New England Algonquians south of the Merrimac River, coastal Algonquians from eastern Long Island to Cape Hatteras, including the Delawares and the Mahicans of the Hudson Valley, the large block of intrusive Iroquoians around the lower Great Lakes, and west of them the Central Algonquians surrounding the upper Great Lakes south to Ohio and numbering such famous groups as the Chippewas, Menominees, Potawatomis, Sauk and Fox, Miamis, and Shawnees. These were largely egali-tarian societies, some structured on a lineal basis like the Iroquois, others in nonlineal cognatic groups composed of descendants of either or both the father and the mother. The latter practice obtained in well-known tribes on the northern Great Plains among whom sodalities were not based on kinship but were associa-tions based on affiliation of age-grades and of warrior and ceremonial societies (Service 1971: 105). Our concern centers on the nature of leadership in lineal societies, notably the Iroquois and their famous league.

While concentrating on the nature of leadership in Iroquois society, one should not overlook a third category, namely, the so-called chiefdoms of the southeastern Indians with whom the Iroquois have striking affinities. By the eighteenth century the Creeks, Hitchitis, and Choctaws comprised a series of chiefdoms, the native terms for which Europeans translated as "towns." These so-called towns properly fit the technical term "chiefdoms," which anthropologists currently call them (Service 1971: 142ff.). In a general work, *The Southeastern Indians*, Charles Hudson (1976: 202) wrote: "A chiefdom is a type of political organization which stands midway between the egalitarian, highly decentralized tribal organization of the Iroquois, Hopis, and Navahos . . . and the highly centralized state organization of the Incas . . . and the Aztecs." In such polities there is a tendency toward centralization of authority. Chiefs led rather than commanded; they might receive first choice in the distribution of goods and services, but excepting the Natchez, these were not stratified societies. Chiefly names equated with titles, and chiefs occupied privileged seats in the council house. Ritual sanctions reinforced their status. But as Service (1971: 150) reminds us, "chiefdoms may have centralized direction and problems of governance, but no true government to back up decisions by legalized force."

One further point about chiefdoms may illuminate the Iroquois case. When leadership positions become stabilized by rules of succession, sanctioned by mythology, and celebrated in ritual, to the extent that these sanctions are strong and consistent, so also authority becomes strengthened and consistent (Service 1951: 152). Indeed, tendencies of this sort operating in Iroquois polity would reclassify it from a tribe to a chiefdom. The kind of status differentiation that characterized the chiefdoms of the Southeast was at work in Iroquoia. To get at that, I turn to a different kind of analysis.

Three decades ago, Anthony Wallace (1957b: 319) demonstrated that "the Indian tribes of the northeastern agricultural area were characterized by political systems based on the concept of tribe and the tribal territory" and that ethnic confederacies "tended to unify the area socially as well as culturally." Since then I have set forth the nature of Iroquois society and polity (Fenton 1978a; 1985), as has Tooker (1978). It was Alexander Goldenweiser who first analyzed Iroquois society into vertical levels ascending from the fireside family up through the kindred, lineage or maternal household, clan, moiety, tribe or nation, and the league itself (Goldenweiser 1912a; 1914a; 1914b). Similarly, one can view the Iroquois social system from the top down—from the league to the solitary fireside.

What these units of analysis demonstrate is that patterned reciprocal relationships obtained between statuses based on kinship in the same generation (siblings and cross-cousins), between statuses that were age graded (elder and younger siblings), and between generations vertically (father and son; mother's brother and sister's son or daughter; mother and daughter or son; ego's generation and grandparents, and vice versa). Goldenweiser's data further reveal that through a process of perseveration, or involution, as he termed it, relationships established at a lower level were projected to higher levels of integration where symbol superseded kinship. Thus, peace chiefs in the league are grouped within nations into phratries of siblings, or as cross-cousins, and the nations themselves comprise the fires of a symbolic longhouse within which the fires are ranged in two moieties of fathers and sons.

Lest some reader wonder what this has to do with the original founders of the Iroquois League and their successors during the seventeenth and eighteenth centuries, I hasten to demonstrate how this background of anthropological theory affords a way of viewing native leadership in ethnohistorical perspective. By describing the statuses and roles that are observable in tribal society, we learn, first, that certain statuses are (or were) ascribed within particular lineages of clans, that these ascribed statuses carry a particular name that is conferred on the incumbent during his lifetime, and that on his death the name descends to a successor chosen from the same or related lineage and raised up in his place. Indeed, the successor is often known before the demise of the incumbent. These names are tantamount to titles. Second, there are other roles that lead to achieved statuses, and these statuses are not restricted to lineal descendants in the female line of the previous holder; the honor dies with the incumbent. And there are other positions in the system of a more temporary nature, as when someone is appointed for the nonce to fulfill a particular role. War leaders and speakers of distinction occupy achieved statuses; ritual functionaries tend to be temporary.[7]

The principles that govern role fulfillment are in several ways more important than the principles that govern statuses. Followers rate leaders by the way they perform their offices. This reciprocal relationship between leader and follower (between a chief and his constituents) is the essence of leadership. "The head ones to whom we look in confidence" is the way the Iroquois regard the relationship. The equable person is the ideal leader. He is one who consults his colleagues and

---

7. The distinction between hereditary sachems and chiefs of merit was reported to the Royal Society in 1786 by Richard McCausland, surgeon to the King's or Eighth Regiment of Foot, who spent ten years at Fort Niagara, on the authority of Joseph Brant (Thayendanegea) and John Butler, agent of Indian affairs (McCausland 1786: 233–34). He also states that each tribe (clan) had a hereditary war chief with a designated title.

the people and who operates by consent. He never bosses or orders anyone around. His great prestige, occasionally translated into joint action with fellow leaders, constitutes a kind of diffuse power.

In Iroquois social and political action, as well as in the conduct of ceremonies, there is a kind of reinforcing duality of paired performers that violates every principle of Western civil administration as we know it—especially the principle that the same responsibility should not be delegated to two people—but which in Iroquois society works to perfection. The leaders (who are also paired) select two persons, normally from opposite moieties (which the leaders also represent), to perform a certain role. The two consult together, exchange the lead role, and sustain the particular project. This phenomenon, which is most readily observable in the conduct of ceremonies, is also built into the paired relationships of peace chiefs who hold titles of the founders and operate in the league council. There are the triads of Mohawk and Oneida committees that consult to reach one mind, and these contrast with eight Seneca chiefships that are paired as cross-cousins of opposite moieties. The duality is always evident, and tripartite arrangements dissolve to moieties. Both principles—duality, or paired relationships, and tripartite arrangements—are at work in the league.

Quality role performance begets repeated requests of the same person to act in the same capacity, until that person comes to be expected to perform that role and eventually he or she is regarded as virtually occupying a status. This process of role fulfillment is particularly applicable to gifted speakers who often served as ambassadors to outside groups, who came to regard them as "sachems." Representatives of Euro-American powers seldom appreciated the status of these ambassadors at home. This partly explains why the titles of the true league chiefs appear randomly in the Indian Records.

A separation of function by age groups characterizes tribal societies and chiefdoms. The beloved old men, or the ancients full of wisdom, have long since graduated from the warrior class, as have the matrons from the younger women. The roots of such age differentiations are traced in the Six Songs, midway of the Condolence Council, which salute "grandfathers of old," the founders of the league, the Great Law or Great Peace itself. The songs acknowledge the kindred (or offspring), the warriors, and the women, and they deplore the present state of affairs (Hale 1883: 122–23). Inasmuch as the ritual of condolence dates well before the mid-eighteenth century, when it was first recorded by a native scribe, and appears in ethnohistorical sources two centuries earlier, these age distinctions are ancient patterns that have shown remarkable stability over time. This does not mean that the rights and duties of civil chiefs and warriors have not changed. War chiefs lost their principal occupation after the War of 1812. In recent times, elected councilors have replaced hereditary peace chiefs in local governments, and traditional chiefs have become ritualists among the People of the Longhouse.

Nothing has greater force in woodland society than the sanction of ritual and the compulsion of renewal. Leaders are installed in an elaborate ceremony that rehearses and reinforces the code of the ancients. Friendships bonded by ceremony require renewal during the lifetime of either party. Alliances and treaties, then, are regarded as a linking of arms that must be renewed by polishing the chain of friendship, which in the minds of native Iroquois is a symbolical umbilical cord joining the two parties. As the Iroquois saying goes, "if one of us moves, we all feel it."

□□◇□□

Iroquoian languages specify who are leaders and who are followers, and in several contexts the categories are rank ordered. There are three terms for chief, or great one, all in the third person singular masculine: first, *rakowa:neh* (M) or *hagowa:neh* (S), literally "he is a great one"; second, *rahsennowa:neh* (M) or *hahsennowa:neh* (S), "his name is great"; and third, *roya:nehr* (M) or *hoya:neh* (S)—all three sets of which signify "he is a chief." As J. N. B. Hewitt (1920: 535) pointed out, the first two terms are generic and apply to either civil or military chiefs; but the third term specifies civil chiefs of the league and, with a change of prefix, applies equally to matrons who are the trustees of the titles that pass in lineages within clans.

The persons to whom are ascribed the rank of *rotiya:nehr* (M) or *hotiya:nehshonh* (S) constitute an honored group, bordering on an elite, for whom the linguistic precedent and ethnological description go back to the seventeenth century—as witness *gaiander*, "a considerable man or woman" (Bruyas 1863: 58), and Lafitau's account of the elite (1724, 1: 474–75; Fenton and Moore 1974: 293–94). In 1710 the term *agoianders* meant "the ancients, councilors, ancestors." Its root, *-yanehr-*, also means "peace" or "law." The ritual chants of the condolence ceremony address the founders of the Great Peace as "grandfathers of old," but the people address incumbents in the titles of the founders as "uncles" (mother's brothers), who in turn call their constituents "nephews and nieces" (sister's children).

The several terms for warriors have changed over time. The generic term *rotiskenrakehte* (M) or *hotisken'enkehte* (S), third person plural, was current at the end of the eighteenth century. Its analysis remains obscure: the incorporated noun has been variously interpreted as "seed," "mat" (Hewitt), or "weapon" (Druke), although the pronominal prefix and the verbal suffix clearly indicate that "one is carrying something." The term generally applies to men at maturity, and all of the interpretations are plausible. Warriors once carried rolled up rush mats for sleeping; they certainly carried weapons; and they were sires of the nation. The third of the Six Songs, the Great Hymn of the condolence ceremony, greets the warriors as *oyenkondonh*, which Hale derived from the Onondaga *yenkwe*, "men," and labeled obsolete (Hale 1883: 64, 122, 207). In the Gibson Onondaga text of the league epic, the term for warrior is *oyen'gondonh*, "a hanging tobacco pouch," to which the added augmentative suffix *-ko:wa* designates a "warrior chief." This interpretation was the consensus of my interpreters. A warrior installed as subchief or messenger to a particular civil chief is referred to as "guardian of the tree," "the cane," or "prop" to the chief.

Matrons, the senior persons in their respective lineages of clans holding chiefship titles, are greeted in the fourth of the Six Songs as *wakonnnyh*, an obsolete term for "womanhood" (Hale 1883: 64). These women belong to the elite, or *gaiander* (Bruyas 1863: 58)—the *oyander* of the *Relation* of 1671 (Hale 1883: 65; JR, 54: 308, 181–83) and the *agoianders* of Lafitau (1724, 1: 474). They are the "She Sachems" of Kirkland (Kirkland Papers, 1774) and the "Great Women" of McCausland (1786: 234). The root *-yanehr-* applies to either sex. Their role in conferring titles, and their power to censure their appointees and to remove them from office, is well known. Each matron had a warrior who acted as her intermediary with the council, and he might serve as "speaker for the women."[8] Few of these statuses and roles are explicit in the ethnohistorical sources, and there is small evidence in the sources that league titles were confirmed by a Condolence Council, which, as we have seen, is frequently mentioned but seldom described in sufficient detail.

Everyone in Iroquois society, whether born into a clan or adopted, had a personal name. Such names had virtually become titles at the upper levels of Iroquois society, and the Iroquois conferred similar titles on colonial governors and other officials, which passed to their European successors in office. From Arent Van Curler, founder of Schenectady, the Mohawks derived "Corlaer" for governors of New York. Since these officials were appointed by the crown, the great king beyond the water became "Korah," with the augmentative suffix -kowa, "the Great King." Later, among the Senecas, all Indian agents were ko:wek. When Lord Howard appeared in Albany in 1684 to treat with the Five Nations, his name came through the Dutch interpreter as "Hower"—"cutlass," or assaragowa, "big knife," in Mohawk—and Big Knife afterward designated governors of Virginia. The Iroquois are great punsters. Early on they named the Pennsylvania proprietor William Penn onas, "quill," whence "pen." Afterward, Onas became the title of Pennsylvania governors. Governors of New France were Onontio, "great mountain," so-called for Montmagny, first governor of New France (1636–48) (DCB, 1: 372). From the weathervane atop the state house in Boston, some Iroquois wag named the Bay Colony kenzion (kvtsu, M), "fish."

□□◇□□

A rich metaphorical and symbolic language for chiefly roles did not manifest itself in material objects. During the confederation process, the prophet Deganawi:dah proclaimed: "And now we have devised for ourselves marks of identification, and these antlers shall be placed on the heads of the founders, and they shall ensure the lives of generations to come." The antlers of the deer on which people subsist symbolize the contribution expected of hunters to a household. Metaphorically they were placed on the head of a founder by the matron of his lineage; they were to be set aside during mortal illness or on taking up the warpath, and they were removed when the incumbent strayed from the straight path of duty or violated his charge. Iroquois rhetoric is loaded with allusions to "antlers" or "horns of office" crowning Iroquois civil chiefs, but I know of no historical reference to Iroquois officials' wearing antlers. Indeed, at the first quarter of the eighteenth century, Lafitau wrote that "the chiefs have no mark of distinction [and] cannot be distinguished from the crowd." Their deportment in council, however, somewhat made up for this lack, as did their acts of generosity (Lafitau 1724, 1: 293).

Antler symbolism has a respectable antiquity in northeastern North America that may well be pre-Columbian. Antler headdresses are reported for the Illinois Middle Woodland culture and for the Hopewell "chiefdoms" of Ohio, where one notable specimen in a grave was sheathed in copper (Moorehead 1922: 236; Shetrone 1930: 104; Fitting 1978: 46, 49). The Iroquois term gannagaroni, "to

---

8. McCausland (1786: 234) implied that the titles of the "Great Women" (matrons), "to whom they pay great deference," were also hereditary in families. These women did not sit in the council with the sachems but had separate councils of their own.

be invested with antlers," based on *onnagara*, "antler," which meant "to elevate one to high office" (Lafitau 1724, 2: 21), goes back to the third quarter of the seventeenth century (Bruyas 1863: 66; Michelson 1974: 43). And the metaphor was still in use at the mid-eighteenth century among both the Iroquois and the Delawares (SWJP, 11: 324; Druke 1983: 118ff.). In one instance a councilor wished to shift roles and assume another status by laying aside his antlers: he would "lay down the Counsellor, and take up the Warrior" (Indian and Military Affairs of Pennsylvania 1737–75, p. 249, cited in Druke 1983). Evidently, antler symbolism was current throughout the Northeast just then.

A further demonstration of the independence of antlers and incumbents is the circle of chiefs. In this metaphor the chiefs have joined hands to surround the public, and should any one of them seek to escape beneath the circle, his antlers, as symbols of his status, will catch on the joined arms of the chiefs to fall within the circle, thereby stripping him of his office. And if he goes free, he will revert to the status of warrior and never hold office again (Fenton and Gibson 1941: secs. 308–9). A circle of wampum having fifty dependent strings, one for each title on the Roll Call of the Founders, memorializes the circle concept (Jenness 1933).

In later times, after the kindling of separate league council fires at Buffalo Creek, New York (afterward back at Onondaga), and at Grand River, Ontario (Six Nations), duplicate chiefs holding the same title sometimes met on either side of the Niagara frontier, where the international boundary constitutes at least a psychological barrier, although it is frequently denied. At a council held at Onondaga, New York, in 1936, where I was present with a delegation of Tonawanda Seneca chiefs, a Seneca doorkeeper reminded the Grand River delegation, several of whose titles were also held by our New York Onondaga hosts, that an invisible wire stretching along the Niagara frontier had stripped them of their antlers when they crossed into the United States (report of a council at Onondaga Longhouse, 16 March 1936, Fenton Papers, APSL).

A tree is the metaphor of chiefship, and the trees are of equal height. A great tall pine, its roots extending to the cardinal directions, symbolized the confederacy. By extension of the metaphor, the Great Tree of Peace was planted wherever a council fire burned. The chiefs in council sat in the shade of its ever-growing branches. An eagle was said to perch atop the tall pine watching for danger from any quarter. On being named, league chiefs were "raised up" as trees and charged with their duties; whenever the tree toppled (the chief died), they raised up another in his place and invested him with the title and duties of his predecessor. Condolence law in theory required that all empty seats in the league council be filled before business was taken up. This rule accounts for the frequent performance of the condoling ceremony on the first day of treaty negotiations, which colonial officials often found tiresome and failed to record. In practice, the ideal of a full council was seldom attained.

Civil affairs and warfare were separate entities, each with its own leaders. Joseph Brant evidently told McCausland: "When war is declared, the Sachems and great Women generally give up the management of public affairs into the hands of the warriors. It may however so happen, that a Sachem may at the same time be a chief warrior" (McCausland 1786: 234).

Not all league chiefs had deputies who served as messengers and as alternates. Metaphorically, the subchief was the "cane," "prop," or "sucker growing on the stump" of the principal chief. Ordinarily these deputies had no voice in council, but they might represent the principal chief in his absence from a debate. The saying runs that "standing trees inspire confidence toward which the public shall direct their eyes." Deputies are raised up at the same time as principals and charged with their duties.

Although civil chiefs carry no marks of distinction, they receive deference and small honors. At great ceremonies such as the Condolence Council, chiefs are honored first with large chunks of meat. During treaty negotiations, Europeans awarded them lace-trimmed hats and embroidered coats, and during Sir William Johnson's superintendency, medals bearing images of English kings were hung about the necks of important chiefs, a practice continued into the federal period and later, when presidential medals were bestowed.

CHAPTER 14

STRUCTURAL MODELS
OF IROQUOIS LEADERSHIP

I shall now propose some structural models of Iroquois leadership. Mary Druke (1983) has rightly stressed relational aspects of leadership between the polar positions in the leader-follower reciprocal syndrome, that is, the ways in which roles are fulfilled between paired statuses, between leader and constituents. For the nature of this relationship in tribal societies, Robert K. Thomas (1964) coined the term "powerless politics." Conceivably, Thomas was getting at the heart of something characteristic of egalitarian tribal societies.

Until the end of the eighteenth century, there were three types of leadership roles available to the Iroquois: peace and war chiefs (both male) and matrons (female). At the formation of the Iroquois League, certain chiefs who were then war leaders became war leaders of the league council, notably Skanawadi of Onondaga, a split personality having two titles for war and peace, afterward the thirteenth and fourteenth titles on the Onondaga roster. And two hold-out Seneca war leaders came in later by extending the rafters; each was awarded a hereditary deputy for the warpath, while the two originals evolved into civil chiefs and western doorkeepers of the Longhouse.

The system was age graded: war chiefs graduated to councilors or civil chiefs. Individuals oscillated between roles in war and in peace; certain contexts demanded specific abilities: warriors who were good speakers and fit to travel long distances joined or led peace embassies, while older men confined their attention to village affairs and to making policy at Onondaga. Matrons of lineages controlled nominations. The matron of one's father's kin initiated and recalled war parties composed of her brothers' sons, her "offspring." I find no evidence of her decisions being countermanded.

There are two structural models for the Roll Call of the Founders—one horizontal (fig. 18), as Hewitt had it (Fenton 1950: 55), and one vertical, as in the mnemonic for the condolence cane (Fenton 1950: 55–56). There are, likewise, two models for the league, the longhouse writ large, as it functions as a council and as it mourns and requickens its dead. And there is a unique model for the Seneca council. All are based on projections of kinship usage.

The roll call of the Iroquois chiefs preserves the titles of the fifty founders of the Great Peace (see Table 4). They may not all have been there from the beginning, but individual names have a respectable antiquity. In figures 19 and 20, the relationships and groupings of chiefs by tribe are shown in the Iroquois

I Mohawk	II Oneida	III Onondaga	IV Cayuga	V Seneca
1	10	19–20	33–34	43–44
2 T	11 W	21		
3	12	22	35	45–46
		23	36	
4	13	24	37	47–48
5 W	14 T			
6	15	25	38	49–50
			39	
7	16	26–27	40	
8	17 B			
9	18	28	41–42	
		29		
		30		

31–32

Figure 18. Relationships and groupings of Iroquois chiefs by tribe (after Hewitt, in Fenton 1950: 55). Siblings are grouped vertically; tribal cousins are paired on the same row within a column, as are Cayuga "father and son" (33–34). T = Turtle clan, W = Wolf clan, B = Bear clan.

manner as they are preserved in several mnemonic devices and as they are hailed in sequence.

□□◇□□

Identifying these fifty titles in earlier sources poses a perplexing problem. It helps to know the shape of the names and the ethnological content of the chant known as the Eulogy to the Founders, which spells out their relationships in kin and moiety terms. Hale (1883) was certain that the *Book of Rites* had a mid-eighteenth-century source. The title names are evidently ancient, though many are unintelligible today, and they have undergone various interpretations. The spatial mnemonic is probably much older. In searching the literature, I constructed a table of the emergence of the names chronologically, so far as I could identify them (see Table 6, p. 531); nothing like figures 18 and 19, and nothing so elegant as Hanni Woodbury's analysis (1992: fig. 5, Table 2), appears in the historical literature.

Individual titles appear before the mid-seventeenth century, but groupings do not occur for another century. Not until 1802 is there a complete roster for any of the Five Nations. At a treaty held with commissioners of the state of New York, the nine Oneida sachems insisted on signing first and in order before any of the war chiefs (New York Assembly 1899: 258). For brevity's sake, I follow Golden-weiser's nomenclature and abbreviations: M 1–9 (Mohawk); Oe 1–9 (Oneida); Oa 1–14 (Onondaga); C 1–10 (Cayuga); S 1–8 (Seneca), which readily converts to a 1–50 sequence for the complete roll call (RC).

Oddly enough, precedence goes to Oa-13/14, Skanawadi, in his role as war chief in 1647 (JR, 33: 121). Tekarihoken, M-1, first to accept the prophet's message of peace, whom one might expect to find mentioned frequently, in 1653

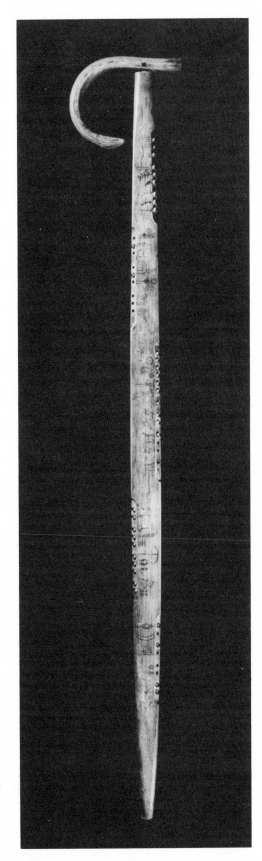

Figure 19. The Cayuga condolence cane
that serves as a mnemonic for the Roll
Call of the Founders. Photograph by
John Brostrop, courtesy Smithsonian
Institution.

Two (Four) Brothers Moiety	Three Brothers Moiety
Younger	Elder
Nephews	Uncles
Offspring	Sires
	I Mohawk
	1
	2
	3
	4
	5
	6
	7
	8
	9
II Oneida	
10	
11	
12	
13	
14	
15	
16	
17	
18	
	III Onondaga
	19–20
	21
	22
	23
	24
	25
	26–27
	28
	29
	30
	31–32
IV Cayuga	
33–34	
35	
36	
37	
38	
39	
40	
41–42	
	V Seneca
	43–44
	45–46
	47–48
	49–50

Figure 20. Relationships and groupings of Iroquois chiefs into moieties of tribal phratries as on the condolence cane. Siblings are grouped vertically; tribal cousins (father and son) are paired on the same row within a column.

was a war captain involved in a peace miracle with the French (JR, 40: 115). Five years later he was still a war chief, and I found one reference to the title in each of the years 1765, 1768, and 1774. The famous Garakontie, not a league title, appears in the role of Sagochiendagehte, "the name bearer," which is a council name for Onondaga, in 1654 heading a delegation of his nation to Montreal. There is no record that he was indeed Thadoda:ho? (Oa-1, RC 19) (JR, 41: 69). In writing about this embassy, Marie de l'Incarnation (1681: 513) stated that the Iroquois had "women of quality" who exercised a deliberative voice in council, made decisions like men, and delegated top ambassadors to treat of peace.

The next bona fide title to emerge is Oa-9, Hahihon, in 1656 (JR, 42: 193); it is cited several times in the next century. Close on his heels comes a keeper of the western door, Ganonhgidawi (S-7), in 1657 (JR, 44: 23), with three mentions a century later. Even more frequently noted after 1666—four times the following century—is Oe-2, Kanongweniyah (NYCD, 3: 126). A possible early candidate (1679) is Oa-7, the traditional wampum keeper Honowiyehdi (Bruyas 1863: 11). But the most consistent performer after 1688 is Oe-1, Odatshehdeh, "Quiver Bearer" (NYCD, 9: 386), the leading Oneida sachem, a title conferred on Father Millet, which occurs eleven times down to 1794.

The most startling break with tradition is that Thadoda:ho?, Oa-1, leading Onondaga chief and prime minister of the league, does not surface until 1745 and then is grouped with the first chiefs of three other nations (Oe-1, C-1, S-1, S-2) by Pyrlaeus in the earliest reference to the formation of the confederacy. His informant was a Mohawk. After 1691, C-1, Haga?en:yonk, the leading Cayuga sachem, performs most consistently in both war and peace roles down to 1794 (NYCD, 3: 774). A holder of this title attended the Albany Congress of 1754, was there again two years later, and was at Philadelphia two years after that.

Colonial governors repeatedly asked for an executive committee of the Six Nations. The leading sachems of the Five Nations plus the Tuscaroras, the sixth nation, would have served admirably, but it never came off. Nor do they appear in clusters of titles that recur from the mid-eighteenth century onward. No more than two of them appear together in the delegations that Sir William Johnson assembled in 1765 and 1768 (SWJP, 11: 984; 12: 621, 628–29). The famous fifty founders made a poor showing at Canandaigua in 1794, when Timothy Pickering, the United States commissioner conducting a peace treaty there, tried to distinguish sachems by birth from sachems of merit and war chiefs. In his list of signers I find S-1 and S-2, Oa-2 and Oa-10, C-1, C-2, and C-6, and Oe-1 and Oe-2. There were no Mohawk signers! And the rest of the great names either stayed home "at the back of the bed" or their seats were empty.

Where, then, were all the sachems who are so punctiliously remembered in the Roll Call of the Founders? The record of Sir William Johnson's march in 1756 leading the clearminded singers to Onondaga (Appendix C) fails to say what and how many names then comprised the list (NYCD, 7: 133). Johnson evidently understood league protocol, but in his celebrated letter to Arthur Lee in 1771 (DHNY, 4: 430–37) he fails to say just how the league was constituted, although he mentions both ascribed and achieved statuses and alludes to changes in Iroquois government without being specific. The missionary Samuel Kirkland, who understood Oneida, strikes me as having better insights; his informants, returning from a grand council at Onondaga in November 1774, reported that the council, which had been in session for a month, opened with a five-hour recitation of "their traditionary system of politics." But to our dismay, Kirkland found neither time nor energy to write it all down (Pilkington 1980: 96–98, 116). At the behest of Guy Johnson, who had succeeded Sir William that summer, Joseph Brant attended and reported on that council, quoting the host speaker for the Onondaga firekeepers as saying:

> "Brothers of the Six Nations Confederacy.
> "We are all assembled this day at our Council Fire, which our forefathers unanimously established as the grand council Fire, and where they made Rules and settled all things in a proper manner." (Here he repeated all the original Rules & Ceremonies and their different Treaties and Alliances and proceeded.) "Brothers we now according to Custom, lay before you all the Business on which we are assembled."
> (Johnson to Gage, Gage Papers, WLCL; NYCD, 8: 524–27)

Brant leaves us in the dark, however, about which rules, ceremonies, treaties, and alliances were reviewed. After the congress, aged chiefs, warriors, speakers, and other persons of distinction came down to Guy Park to report on their deliberations. These sessions yield some information on council procedure: league chiefs preferred to make policy at Onondaga and then inform outside powers; a speaker for the warriors reported on their own councils to the league chiefs, who then persuaded the warriors to adhere to their policy. In a crisis, senior women, the matrons, might intervene in determining issues of war and peace. They addressed the league council through a speaker for the women, usually a man. The Seneca orator Red Jacket came up in that role in later times.

It is all too easy to blame historical sources for not revealing the roots of an ideal system that myth and ritual kept alive to the present century. The sources do suggest that the system failed to renew itself by producing sufficient able persons to make it work, and that others who had achieved distinction as warriors and speakers had taken over positions of local responsibility and became the effective "sachems" or principals during the eighteenth century. Evidently, these emergent leaders worked side by side with the proper league chiefs who appear in the records.

The late seventeenth century witnessed a decline in Iroquois population as warfare and epidemics of European diseases took their toll. Consequently, chiefly lineages lacked qualified personnel to fill empty places in the league council. By the end of the eighteenth century, local leaders of achieved status predominated, and this process, which brought men of achievement into prominence—war chiefs like Cornplanter, Brant, Farmer's Brother, and Fish Carrier, a Cayuga—was really a throwback to conditions that obtained when the confederacy was formed. Then, a series of local chiefs, some of them ascribed in matrilineages and others elevated from the rank of warriors, and even shamans (as in the case of Thadoda:ho?) were persuaded during a process lasting several decades to accept the prophet's message of peace, civil authority, and right-mindedness, which comprises the Great Law.

□□◇□□

Other than tradition, what is the historical evidence for the existence of the Iroquois League at an early date? Early in the seventeenth century, both French and Dutch sources mention such a confederacy. At a council held at Oneida in

1635, a party of Dutch travelers from Fort Orange heard their hosts enumerate and map with seed corn the villages of the Five Nations (NNN: 152; van den Bogaert 1988: 16–17). At a comparable date, French Jesuits reported such a confederacy, and within a decade named its members (JR, 21: 21; 28: 275; 33: 65). By the mid-century, the French knew that the member nations were not always of one mind (JR, 33: 125; 41: 63, 81). They proceeded to found a mission at Onondaga, as if they did not know that the "Hotinnochiendi" were a "completed cabin" (extended longhouse). They were to hear a Mohawk speaker reprimand them for jumping through the smokehole midway of the house and not entering by the door, telling them that indeed the Five Nations were one house, one fire, under one roof, and had been so from time immemorial (JR, 41: 87). Iroquois speakers made a pretense of unity even when the four upper nations met in council without Mohawk representation, claiming that the Five Nations spoke through one mouth (JR, 41: 117). Speakers maintained a facade of unity despite diversity of opinion.

After 1660, French sources designated the Five Nations a "league" (JR, 46: 121–23)that was united and had common enemies (JR, 51: 119). A partial representation might speak for the whole, as when Teganissorens met Frontenac in 1682 without the Senecas, yet invoked the image of the "whole house": for "they had all brought their sticks" to the council fire that Onontio had lighted (MYCD, 3: 324; 9: 184–85). By then, both French and Dutch authorities realized that the league met annually at Onondaga.

Coming late on the scene, English officials learned of the "whole house" concept during the 1680s. References to it abound in the New York colonial documents (DHNY, 2: 20, 165) and in the Livingston Indian Records (LIR: passim). Governor Thomas Dongan recognized its importance and sought to unify the league and exploit it as an instrument of imperial power (LIR: 112). Grasping Iroquois professions of unity—"one head, one body, one heart"—he proclaimed: "The brethren know what trouble and toll I had to unify the Five Nations and also the Northern Indians" (LIR: 141). Dongan had sensed the synonymy of "covenant" and "whole house," which Iroquois speakers were at pains to explain (NYCD, 3: 805, 841; LIR: 168–69). By 1693, the French rendering of *hodinonhsioni*, "whole house," had its English analog, *canossioni*, for *kanonhsioni*, "the league" itself (NYCD, 4: 23, 78, 120, 279–80, 295). The league, then, was a political entity to be reckoned with, and colonial officials kept track of its meetings.

The record of meetings of the league at Onondaga from 1641 until 1774 is virtually continuous. References are scattered at first, and then occur at yearly intervals. That Onondaga was the center of Iroquoia where every year the States General, the Dutch governing body, met to settle differences among its members was explained in the *Relations* of 1667–68 (JR, 51: 237; 52: 153). It was there the Onondaga firekeepers summoned deputies of each nation to assemble (NYCD, 9: 259). In 1686, sachems of all the nations met to discuss policy toward the French (LIR: 133). Some league meetings lasted for a week (LIR: 114ff.), and special meetings were called to deal with crises. Right after Denonville invaded the Seneca country in 1687, all the nations met in council at Onondaga to debate their future (LIR: 133).

Such meetings involved many people and were expensive when held in Albany. Governor Dongan proposed that efficiency demanded paring down representation to an executive committee consisting of two sachems and two warriors of each nation to meet with him in Albany (NYCD, 3: 438–44; Colden 1750: 82). But two years later, he had to be satisfied with sending the interpreter to attend "the general Convention" then in session at Onondaga, where he would find all the sachems (LIR: 148). These general meetings were by then annual events. Reports of the interpreters intrigue the ethnographer, for they speak of antiphonal songs justified as "our old custom," of wampums hung in the "Proposition House," and of other amenities (NYCD, 4: 59ff., 560–62).

Albany in the eighteenth century was the frontier for English governors, and none ventured to Onondaga. Five Nations delegates coming to Albany in 1706 complained that when they held a meeting at Onondaga, "when all the Indian Politicks are Discussed," the governor sent no representative (Wraxall 1915: 47, 49). The big news on 25 September 1714, which was confirmed by a belt, was that the "Tuscaroras are come to shelter themselves among the Five Nations, they were of us and went from us long ago and are now returned. . . . We have received them" (Wraxall 1915: 101). They appeared with a delegation from the Five Nations to meet Governor Spotswood of Virginia in the summer of 1722, and the following spring the interpreter Claessen reported "that the Tuscaroras are received to be a Sixth Nation," to which Wraxall added, "so that from this time the Six Nations take their Date" (Wraxall 1915: 143–44).

The conduct of Indian affairs in the New York colony during the first half of the eighteenth century was concentrated in the hands of Indian commissioners, who were citizens of Albany engaged in the fur trade with the Six Nations and who promoted an illicit trade with Canada. They received at their "fire" runners from Onondaga, official delegations of chiefs, and expatriate Iroquois from Canada. The minutes of their meetings, referred to collectively as the "Indian Records," convey the best picture of the league and its transactions just then (PAC IR RG 10, vol. 20: passim; Wraxall 1915). By 1734 the Albany commissioners were so inured to Iroquois protocol that they dispatched the interpreter to complain to the grand council about not being properly notified of a general meeting "according to Atient Usage," even though seven hands of wampum had been sent to the Mohawks, who informed the commissioners (minutes of the New York Indian commissioners, PAC RG 10, vol. 1820: 54–54v; Wraxall 1915: 190). On this occasion the league adjourned its meeting to the Seneca country.

The next summer, a delegation of fourteen Caughnawaga Mohawks, with their leading sachem, Tekarihoken, at their head, came to Albany in the interest of keeping the "Road to Canada Clean" and concluded a solemn treaty with the commissioners, who failed to notify the New York governor. These visitors introduced the custom of lighting and passing the "Calumet of Peace," from which each of the commissioners took "a Whif," and they requested on behalf of their warriors that the pipe be lodged at Onondaga as a memento to this treaty (PAC RG 10, vol. 1820: 65–66; Wraxall 1915: 193).[1] The pipe was later given to a party of visiting Onondagas.

---

1. The Fox Indians were said to have brought the calumet ceremony to the St. Lawrence a decade earlier. See Fenton 1953: 158.

During King George's War (1744–48), the sachems of the Six Nations "convened in a grand Meeting at Onondaga" and flatly refused to take up the hatchet against the French (Wraxall 1915: 244). The Albany commissioners could no longer sway policy at Onondaga. And at mid-century, the grand council was hedging its bets with French Canada and Pennsylvania. During the third quarter of the eighteenth century, Johnson kept an ear at Onondaga and received reports at his fire in the Mohawk Valley. In transmitting Johnson's journal to the Lords of Trade, Lieutenant Governor deLancey recommended: "Once a year some person with a publick character and some small present should be sent up to Onondago which is the place of the General meeting of the five Nations and where they keep (as they express themselves) their Great Fire & the Tree to which one end of the Covenant Chain is fastened" (NYCD, 6: 808–15; SWJP, 1: 388, 917). In 1755, a Mohawk speaker acknowledged that the fire formerly kindled from Onondaga at Albany was now rekindled at Mount Johnson (SWJP, 9: 155). The main fire would continue as the seat of league policy; the latter two served for reporting (SWJP, 13: 111). So it was at the peace treaty ending the prolonged war with the Cherokees, when, on 4–12 March 1768, "the Three Elder Tribes" (M-Oa-S) took the initiative in approving and renewing the treaty (SWJP, 7: 294–95). Thus a pattern developed and continued down to Johnson's passing in 1774—a pattern of coming down and reporting transactions at the great council fire of the league. To report all of these transactions would be redundant.

□□◇□□

Scholars have generally accepted the date January 1777, when the great council fire that had burned at Onondaga since the formation of the confederacy was raked up, as the effective end of the Iroquois League. Divided loyalties of the Five Nations is the usual reason given. Native Iroquois hold otherwise: that the act of raking up the fire was temporary, not unlike the breakup of the federal union during the Civil War. The immediate cause was not so much political as it was a devastating pestilence that carried off ninety persons, including three sachems. Kirkland at Oneida heard the news and knew that council fires could be extinguished and rekindled. Although the surviving Onondagas insisted that the fire could no longer burn, Kirkland wrote to General Schuyler urging that a condolence ceremony be performed. He specified the design of three large wampum belts to support the "Three Bare Words of Requickening" ("eyes, ears, and throat"), and he proposed the offices of two Oneida speakers "who will model the Speech agreeable to Indian Tradition" (cited in Graymont 1972: 113). Kirkland suspected that the act was a ruse for removing the fire to Niagara (Druke 1983: 284). The proper ceremony went forward the following April, to the apparent satisfaction of the Onondagas. In Iroquois thought the symbolic council fire was continuous so long as condolence law was satisfied.

The fact remains, nevertheless, that the council fire of the Six Nations was rekindled at Buffalo Creek from a symbolic ember carried from Onondaga. It continued to burn there until the Senecas sold Buffalo Creek Reservation in the 1840s. Meanwhile, a large body of Loyalist Iroquois, including the upper Mohawks, upper and lower Cayugas, a band of Onondagas, a few lineages of Senecas, and some Tuscaroras, removed to Canada after 1784 and settled on the Grand River lands granted to Joseph Brant for his followers. Documented tradition holds that almost their first act was to reestablish the league by renewing its laws and ceremonies as the government of the Grand River lands (Hale 1883: 34). The Onondagas had brought a share of the wampum records, many chiefly lineages were present, and the matrons were prepared to assert their ancient privilege of nominating civil chiefs to fill vacancies. Only the Oneidas were missing. Hewitt's and my informants recalled the tradition of these events vividly.

It was not long before the council of chiefs meeting at Onondaga Longhouse near Middleport regarded the fire at "Buffaloe Creek" as "but faintly spark[ling] like the glow worm" (John Norton, Letter Book, NL, Ayer ms. no. 654: 122). In effect, the ancient league had grown old and was disrupted, and the fact that it was rekindled at Grand River, where it persisted as the local government of the Six Nations Reserve until 1924, made Ohsweken a mecca for anthropologists following the footsteps of Hale and Hewitt. Of late, two Iroquois leagues have persisted, one in Canada and the other—the grand council of the Ho-de-no-sau-nee, as Morgan spelled it, which today comprises the New York Onondagas, Tonawanda Senecas, Tuscaroras, and a Mohawk faction—at Akwesasneh (St. Regis).

□□◇□□

My quest for the roots of the league led me to three models of council arrangements that have persisted into modern times. They are sanctioned by ritual, supported by the texts of the league epic, and well may be old, although I have not found them replicated in the historical literature. The first two models pertain to the league itself (figs. 21 and 22); the third is an example of both dual and tripartite seating within a tribal council, which I infer is older than the league (fig. 23).

The first model (fig. 21) shows the moiety arrangement of the Five Nations in condoling one another. They are spaced as the five fires of a symbolic longhouse from east to west, the Three Brothers—Mohawk-Onondaga-Seneca—seated north of their respective fires, and their "offspring," the Two Brothers—Oneida and Cayuga—seated on the south side of their respective fires. In addressing one another, the former, as *agadoni* (father's kinsmen) hail the latter across the fire as *kheya?tawenh* (offspring or nephews), and vice versa.

The second model (fig. 22) illustrates the tripartite seating arrangement of the league council, in which one moiety, Mohawk-Seneca, sits east of the council fire and the junior moiety, Oneida-Cayuga, sits opposite. The presiding Onondaga firekeepers sit north of the fire.

The council of life chiefs of the Six Nations on Grand River, who met at Ohsweken, Ontario, until 1924, had somewhat modified their seating to accommodate Her Majesty's superintendent (fig. 23; Hewitt and Fenton 1945: 306).

In the previous models, the Mohawk-Onondaga-Seneca moiety is *agadoni*, or father's kinsmen, to its *kheya?tawenh*, offspring or nephews, the Oneida-Cayuga moiety. In council, the Onondaga chiefs sit apart as firekeepers while the Mohawk-Senecas of one moiety sit across the fire from the Oneida-Cayuga moiety. Issues originate with the Mohawk chiefs, who, after coming to one mind, consult with the Seneca chiefs, who council among themselves. If the Senecas agree with the Mohawks, a Mohawk speaker refers the matter over the fire to the Cayuga chiefs, who council among themselves and consult the Oneida chiefs, who take up the issue. When the junior moiety is of one mind, its speaker sends

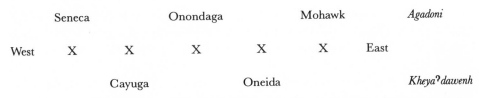

Figure 21. Moiety seating arrangement of the Five Nations in condoling. Each nation's fire is indicated by an *X*.

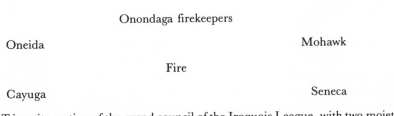

Figure 22. Tripartite seating of the grand council of the Iroquois League, with two moieties across the fire

Oneida   HMS   Mohawk

Fire

Onondaga

Cayuga, Tuscarora,   Seneca
Delaware, and Tutelo

Figure 23. Seating arrangement of the council of life chiefs of the Six Nations. HMS = Her Majesty's superintendent.

its combined opinion back over the fire to the Mohawk chiefs, who, if they agree, pass the combined opinion of the four nations to the Onondaga firekeepers, who review the matter with their colleagues. When unanimity has been attained around the fire, the Onondaga speaker proclaims the decision of the council. In case the council is not of one mind but of two opinions on the matter, the Onondaga speaker refers both questions, with recommendations, to the Mohawks for resolution. The amended resolution then goes back over the fire. Should the council not succeed attaining unanimity, the matter is "buried in the ashes." All of this took time, to the dismay of colonial officials, who learned that Indians could not be hurried.

The first two models (figs. 21 and 22) derive from a third one at the tribal level. Originally, the Mohawks and Oneidas had the same three clans—Bear, Wolf, and Turtle—and there were three lineages holding chiefships within each clan. In both national councils, the triads of chiefs counseled in a tripartite seating arrangement with one triad of chiefs moderating. In the Mohawk council it was the Turtle clan chiefs, and at Oneida, the Wolf clan chiefs. The Mohawk Wolf clan chiefs were "brothers" to the Turtle clan chiefs and sat across the fire from the Bear clan chiefs, who were "cousins" to the Turtles and Wolves. At Oneida, Turtle clan chiefs were "brothers" to the moderating Wolf clan chiefs and sat across the fire from the Bear clan chiefs, their "cousins." At some point the triad dissolved into a moiety system. The Mohawk-Oneida model became that of the league council, the nations acting as a triad of clans when legislating and as moieties in condoling the dead. These seating arrangements are shared in part by the other three nations of the league.

The Cayuga council employs both patterns—dual, two triples, and a dual—the mnemonic for which appears as .. .. on the condolence cane and as : ... ... : when laid down with kernels of corn at rehearsals for a condolence ceremony.

The Seneca council, in contrast, arranges itself in a dual pattern of four committees of two chiefs each, each pair "cousins" and of opposite moieties. Note that the Seneca chiefs in session preserve a paired moiety relationship, but the two doorkeepers, who were the last to accept the Great Peace, sit to one side of the fire. The eight Seneca sachems are paired in four sets of mutual cousins. As representatives of clans of opposite moieties, they sit across the fire from one another.

□□◇□□

The concepts of status and role apply very well to the Iroquois League, which distinguished between ascribed and achieved statuses. As a horticulturally based society it left to women the control of affairs within the clearing and assigned external affairs beyond the woods to men, who provided subsistence to their wives' households by hunting, who engaged in warfare, and who went on embassies. Men held the prestigious offices by the grace of women trustees who kept the names and assured that the ashes of the matrilineage did not grow cold by producing ongoing generations of children. In theory, the league verged on being a chiefdom, although its organization was essentially tribal and it conducted its business on an egalitarian basis, assuring input from all ranks of society. Leaders inspired confidence, and no leader ranked above another, for in Iroquois parlance, "the trees are of equal height, and nobody bosses anyone around."

At the formation of the Iroquois League, certain chiefs who were then war leaders were designated confederate war chiefs. Skanawadi of Onondaga, a split personality, retained both war and peace titles, which are now thirteenth and fourteenth on the Onondaga roster. Two remote Seneca war leaders whose villages were situated to the far west held out and were brought into the league by extending the rafters, after which their roles evolved into civil chiefships as keepers of the western door of the Longhouse. Such imagery lingers today in the minds of traditionalists.

CHAPTER 15

BYLAWS OF THE LEAGUE

The women have a deliberative voice in their councils.—Marie de l'Incarnation, *Lettres à son fils*

In later times the chiefs agreed on bylaws governing the duties of matrons, or "clan mothers," and of the head warriors of constituent clans, and also on bylaws governing the behavior of chiefs. These rules and regulations are laid down in a series of texts that Hewitt collected from Chief John A. Gibson, Chief Abram Charles, and John and Joshua Buck.[1] In the rest of this chapter I quote directly from these texts, adhering to the originals as closely as possible while editing Iroquoian syntax and changing word order for English readers not used to noun incorporation followed by the subject of the sentence. I have left the spellings of Iroquois names and terms as they appear in the originals.

□□◇□□

Goya:nehgo:nah, the Woman Chief, or Matron. Once more the chiefs resolved to add to existing law. They discussed making it a rule as to the place where the titles of federal chiefs repose in the hands of the women owners of the chiefly titles [the wampum strings], among our nations and existing clans. This they decided shall be the rule, that the eldest woman who oversees everyone in the maternal family and upon whom the eyes of the entire family rest shall be the trustee of the chief's activities. She will be the chief's helper in all of his affairs. These, as we know, range from matters of great importance down to small matters, all of which he is obliged to resolve for the peace of mind of people who rest their minds on him in confidence, whenever he is called upon. It may be a public meeting on an issue of some standing, or it might be a chiefs' council. For whatever purpose or how[ever] long they meet, at that time the chief shall turn and speak to our mother who watches over him. He will then hand her the responsibility of putting her hands to preparing that which strengthens our breath [food], that which in fact

1. The texts quoted in this chapter are listed as follows. (1) John A. Gibson, "The Law of the Woman Chief [Goyanehgo: nah]," Onondaga text, 12 pp., Bureau of American Ethnology ms. 894, later revised by Abram Charles, 1923, and John Buck, Jr., up to 1937. English revised from Reg Henry's interpretation. (2) Abram Charles, "Law of the Woman Chief," Onondaga text, 10 pp., Bureau of American Ethnology ms. 1636 (1563), later revised by Abram Charles, 1923, 1928. (Probably notes on 894, above.) (3) John A. Gibson, John Buck, Sr., and Abram Charles, "The Law Governing the Behavior of Chiefs," Onondaga text, 31 pp., Bureau of American Ethnology ms. 484, revised 1917, 1937. English revised from Reg Henry's interpretation.

sustains our lives, which means that she shall cook the food for the people who are meeting, namely the chiefs and also the public. And when she has procured the several varieties of our sustenance, and has everything ready, she shall inform her great one. She shall say, "I have now finished preparing the things that sustain our lives. So now, first of all, you all must eat."

At that time the chief shall proclaim to those assembled there: indeed he shall say, "Now our mother is ready, for now the food is cooked, and consequently business shall come to a halt, whatever we are working on. And that is where matters stand. When everyone is satiated [filled], then we shall resume whatever business we have in progress."

At that moment the meeting will come to a halt. And then the chiefs and the people shall eat. When the people assembled are satiated and their minds are at peace, only then shall they resume business. To the extent that one is strong, so one's mind is vigorous.

This then shall be her life's work to be ever tending her fire, forever sustaining the strength of the council and maintaining clear minds. So now then we shall put her close to the chief, an adjunct to his person, and stand her up [install her] as a chief. And so this shall be the rule in days to come. His dependency on her is quite important. And that is what matrons are appointed for, namely to stand next to chiefs. They are responsible to our nations to see that no man's head is above any one of the chiefs.

Accordingly let us point out the importance of the female chief, or matron. It must be understood that she holds [owns] the title [string of wampum] to chiefship, and that she will undertake hosting functions for the chief [she will cook for him], and that, moreover, the minds of the entire family repose with her, our mother.

Also we shall devise a rule that will unite in one circle the minds of all our nations.

And there is something else that we shall establish. We will appoint a warrior, the eldest male among the holders of the chief's title [the wampum string], who shall assist the great female chief, our mother. And the reason for appointing this senior man is because he is stronger, that he customarily travels as a hunter of wild game, the wanderers of the forests, and also because he provides what the people subsist on. Therefore it is only fitting that he cooperate with the female chief. To enable all the people to feel well disposed shall be their crucial task. And what is more the people will derive sustenance from the Good Word (Gaiwi:yo:h), from civil authority (power of law), and well being (peace)—from the Great Law itself.

Now then the chiefs decreed another thing. That is, "We will establish a rule with respect to families involved in chieftainship among our nations. Accordingly we will determine just where in the families the title reposes. Should it happen that the great female chief [head matron], our mother, or perhaps her warrior helper, whichever one experiences a slackening of duties, failing mind, or perhaps suffers mental confusion verging on a bad mind, to the extent that one of them cannot conduct affairs properly, either the duties of the Great Female Chief, where the minds of her family rest in confidence, as well as those of all of our nations, and where the public have joined their minds with the Great Woman Chief, the overseer, with the result that when her entire family perceives that she has begun to fail in her duties, that she may err by thinking dishonestly, then, at that time, one of her sisters, in that event shall speak out. She will put her back on the path of her responsibilities; and if the matron fails to heed this advice, it shall then devolve on her assistant, the warrior, to counsel her to repent of the errors that she is committing. He shall try to put her back on the right path of her duties. If she again disregards this advice, they shall put the matter before the chiefs. This time it will be up to the chiefs to warn her. If again she fails to heed this advice, they shall refer the matter to the chiefs of the family's moiety and to the public of constituent clans. In the event of this happening it becomes everyone's duty, of women, men, and the public, yea everyone's responsibility who is mentally competent, to meet and decide which woman will replace the Female Chief, what new person shall stand in her place to act as overseer [trustee] and become the Great Female Chief [head matron]."

Accordingly they shall canvas all of the women. They might even decide on a young woman, one whom they perceive is clearheaded and has a good mind, is honest and good natured as well. It shall be everyone's decision, women and warriors equally. At that time they shall put the matter before the principal chief who will consider it. And then if the established system holds true, he will confirm the decision of his nephews/nieces. Then all of the voices will be as one.

And so when this occurs [consensus is reached], then the task of deposing her rests with the warrior, inasmuch as she threw their word (warning) over her shoulder. Now she shall be removed from her charge of affairs [position]. At that time the authority shall pass to the newly appointed overseer. And so now all of their minds shall rest with her, and she shall keep their minds straight, as she becomes the new assistant in the work of the chief. And accordingly the new Female Chief will now be standing here, and the minds of everyone in all nations shall be directed toward her. And so now we have completed the affairs of the matron.

The Warrior. This time we shall establish a rule for the male assistant. He shall collaborate with the Great Female Chief, our mother. We are aware of the kind of road that we established for the head matron, and accordingly her male collaborator's road shall be identical. If his mind weakens, he shall be addressed by three speakers. In case he throws his power over his shoulder [disregards his duties], his first encounter shall follow the rules and procedures applying to the Great Female Chief, our mother. He may then resume his previous duties. Or he may be removed and a new appointee replace him. The Great Female Chief, our mother, would then have a new assistant.

And so now we have finished devising rules and procedures. These will keep our minds clear and keep the souls and minds of our grandchildren straight.

□□◇□□

Succession. And now yet another thing. People held a meeting and recalled what the chiefs said. This time we will establish how it shall be [a rule] respecting families and clans who hold chief's titles among our nations. We people believe that our days are numbered and that life can end suddenly. Our belief holds equally for Chiefs and Great Female Chiefs, and for warriors (equally for women and men). This time we will establish a procedure in case the Great Female Chief, our mother, should fall victim to this great inescapable death (Death the Great Faceless).[2] Should she be so summoned, this would leave her position vacant.

At that point the warrior with whom she collaborated ceases to function since he is grieving for the person on whom his mind depended along with the mothers and children of that maternal family. Now they too will stop functioning. Their collective mourning is directed toward the departed one who no longer exists. And so when this occurs, it also will affect the head chief. He also will now miss her, his former helper.

Accordingly, whenever this happens anywhere, we shall proceed with the mourning ceremony (ritual of condolence). Whenever a mourning ceremony becomes necessary on either side of brother clans [either moiety], it shall be the phratry of the opposite clans [opposite moiety] that shall be responsible for conducting the condolence ceremony. Therefore, [this shall be the rule]: should it become necessary somewhere and sometime to replace a fallen chief [and install a new one], by putting fresh antlers on the chief to be, this shall also be the time to install a newly designated Great Female Chief.

And likewise should the male assistant of the Great Woman die, this is how it shall be done. It shall be the job of the matron trustee to raise up a new one who is to collaborate with the Great Female Chief, our mother.[3]

Consequently, we will mention the several areas of consoling of the minds. All of this shall be forgotten when they see a new face amongst the crowd, and when they stand up the candidate and name him. And he will bring with him fresh ideas, just as suckers sprout around a tree trunk (stump). And a newly designated Great Female Chief shall also stand there. They shall also announce a new name of the male assistant, and stand him up to be recognized and named. And this shall be the rule in the families of our nations. We will complete everything, which will be a continuing process to strengthen the house (the league), as it was intended. It is based on the triad of the Good Word, of power, and of well-being (peace), which together comprise the Great Law (or the league). So this shall occupy the minds and keep it an ongoing thing, involving the host of mothers (women), warriors (men), and even the children and grandchildren.

So now we have finished everything, and it shall be an ongoing process to be carried on through the families of our grandchildren.

So that is what the chiefs established. They proclaimed a rule regarding maternal families in case a chief should die and with respect to surviving assistants, namely the Great Female Chief, our mother, and her collaborator, the warrior. The fact of their survival makes them responsible for the condolence ceremony, and also for presenting a new appointee [lit., "showing his face to the crowd"], for standing him up (raising him up) for chieftainship, for crowning him with fresh antlers, as well as seeing that he gets named after the departed chief. And when he has been declared chief, he then shall be charged. The speaker shall say, "You are all of equal height (at the same level)."

The former assistants to the departed chief shall still remain to help the one newly raised. And the same assistants shall continue to function presently when

2. The Iroquois believed that "Death, the Great Faceless," stalked the forest paths and came up unexpectedly on victims.

3. The matron trustee and the Great Female Chief are the same.

he starts discharging his duties to the laws on behalf of the people, as well as for our grandchildren, and even for those faces approaching from beneath the ground [the unborn]. And he will receive help from the Great Female Chief, our mother, who shall continue to cook for her great one, the chief. And she will work with the warrior.

Therefore everything has been accomplished, and there our minds shall rest [and be preoccupied] with the laws of our nations.

And the one who brought this about was the founder of the Great Law, for he was the principal builder of the Longhouse of the League, namely, Deganawi:dah. And he too was a principal (founder) Hayenhwatha? (M-2); and sharing in the founding as a principal was Ho?datshehde? (Oe-1); and also sharing in the founding was Thadoda:ho? (Oa-1); and likewise sharing in the founding was Haga?enyonh (C-1); and also a co-founder was Sganya:daiyo? (S-1); and sharing with him his cross-cousin Tsa?degaenhye:s (S-2).

This is the sum of the words.

□□◇□□

The Law Governing the Behavior of Chiefs.[4] When the People of the Longhouse established the council fire, they met and recalled what had been said concerning the identical responsibilities for chiefs, warriors, and women in accordance with our bylaws that specify how the Great Law (the league) is structured. The law says: hear and heed the advice of your nephew and niece. Accordingly, their role in affairs has been established, namely that our nephews (both) have two voices in case they desire to address a chief who has strayed from the path set for him. The procedure has been established: should he perhaps throw over his shoulder [shirk] the duties of chiefship to the extent of disregarding their warnings. If need be he shall be removed from office.

At that time the chiefs held council and considered further (the prophet's) decree. "We will devise a procedure that will keep the chiefs aware of their responsibilities. And accordingly we will distribute the procedure among our two nephews (nephew and niece) and ourselves. The rule shall hold for any chief who is observed using his authority for personal gain, committing adultery, or lusting after our precious women, our mothers. Accordingly, when observed indulging in any of these sins, at that time he shall be warned. They shall address his wrongdoing, urging him to mend his ways and repent of his misbehavior. He shall be warned twice. The matron speaks first. But if he just lets it pass over his shoulder, then of the two it shall be up to the head warrior to speak to the chief. If both warnings are cast aside, then the head warrior shall lay down the rules. The two shall demonstrate that he was warned by his trustee, whom he disregarded, and then the head warrior shall take over the proceedings. He will then turn around and address the chief, saying: 'Our mother has made up her mind.

---

4. In the 1899 version of the league legend, Gibson treated the procedure in which the matron warns the chief, the warrior accompanies her at the second warning, and the head warrior takes the case before the council of chiefs, as well as the topic of the council's warning and disposition of the case (Fenton and Gibson 1941: sections 348–43, pp. 173–75). Gibson evidently made a special case of the procedure in the following text to Hewitt at a later date. Seth Newhouse's published version of the "Constitution" spells out bylaws governing "Rights, Duties and Qualifications of Lords" (Parker 1916: 34–36). Article 30 of his manuscript briefs the same material (APSL ms. 1650; Freeman Guide, p. 189; Catlett Guide, no. 821.

She implored you to repent of your sinful activities, and you disobeyed. And the head warrior, who also is of that mind, begged you to repent, and you disregarded both of these warnings by your two nepotic relatives. Accordingly, this will be the last time now that I myself shall beg you to listen and heed the appeal. I will [do this] by reminding you of the rules. And this is what will happen if you still don't obey. Then I will remind you of the rules of authority. You were accorded to discharge your official duties when we crowned you with antlers.' And if a chief still disobeys, then it shall be the responsibility of the head warrior to remove the chief's antlers of office. Then the head warrior shall release the name of the former chief, who, now stripped of his title, shall become like anyone else. The former chief shall no longer enjoy official status.

"So I have now completed the procedure of dehorning. This shall occupy the minds of ongoing generations of our grandchildren."

Malfeasance. Now again the chiefs met for a further purpose. They discussed another rule to keep us upright in our duties as chiefs. This rule pertains to all of the Five Nations. The rule is that if any chief be discovered to be of a double mind [dishonest], if he is unreliable, capable of lying, making false promises to the public, gossiping, cheating, or discovered committing any of the above by his two nepotic relatives, who both have minds of their own, either our mother [his trustee] or the warrior shall reprimand him. She shall say, "What you are doing is wrong. You must cease and repent" [of whatever delict she mentions]. If he refuses, it shall then be up to the warrior.[5]

This time the warrior shall speak out, he shall say: "We both, the matron and I, have joined our voices. She has already warned you. Therefore I too now beg you to quit this bad habit and repent. Thus our joint warnings implore you." And should the chief again refuse, disregarding the combined voices of his nephew and niece, at that time the two shall turn to separate.

The Head Warrior Takes the Case to the Chiefs' Council. Now the warrior visits the Great Warrior, his superior, and reviews for him the transactions to date, that with the combined voices of matron and warrior he warned the chief to repent of his errors. The head warrior will comprehend the problem. He shall then undertake to complete the warning process. He shall now turn to the errant chief and address him: "It is amazing what you have done. It has made you disregard the warnings of both your niece and nephew. And therefore we have said everything. And this time I implore you as chief to repent and do what your niece and nephew have implored you to do."

And so it is now the chief who must speak out. Perhaps he may disobey. It then shall be up to the head warrior to say: "You disregarded three warnings. So now you have discarded it finally. Accordingly I will now remove the symbol of authority, namely, the antlers of office that they placed on you." Now the head warrior shall proceed officially to dehorn him and return the antlers to the matron, our mother, the trustee of the title.

At that point he shall say, "So now then you are released from official duties. You no longer hold an official title."

---

5. Any warrior of the family may act on behalf of the matron.

And now the chiefs proclaimed, "Once more we have established an official procedure that continuing generations of our grandchildren shall bear in mind."

Then the chiefs pronounced, "Now another thing. We chiefs will meet and devise a regulation to keep us honest. And therefore this shall happen, if some chief does not keep to the path, and if he fails to listen and agree with his colleagues, and heed all of the charges bestowed on a chief. Given the sanction of the Good Message, power [civil authority], and peace of the Great Law, and with a clear mind, he shall exercise these powers to reassure the minds and protect his people. But should it ever appear that the chief might seem to be weakening in the performance of his duties, and failing to give his best in discharging his duties, to the end that he is causing dissension among his co-workers, the other chiefs, then there is no road leading to survival for the people in the days ahead. Consequently, when the people comprehend that their great one can no longer discharge the duties of his office, then our mother, the matron, shall speak out and carefully inquire as to his problem. She shall say, "I want you to tell me the reason why you won't try to straighten out people's ways and work for all the people?" Then the chief will reply, asking: "What do I lack to perform correctly? I am doing my best." Having had her say, our mother at that point will turn to go. She will tell her warrior counterpart all that the chief said. Then the warrior shall go to where the Great Warrior resides and lay out the particulars to him, that they have agreed that their great one is no longer competent as a chief, that he himself confirmed his shortcomings, and that he demonstrated how as things were it was the best he could do. He was not helping the chiefs or the people, so that it would not be well for him to hold an official title much longer. It might prove a disaster and people would suffer. Consequently, both voices unanimously, mine and our mother's, have concluded to remove his antlers. And then the head warrior shall pick up the antlers and place them officially where the chiefs of his clan sit. At that time the chiefs of that clan shall consider the fate of that chief, and if they confirm the idea that he should be dehorned, then it shall be the head warrior's task to go forth and lift the antlers of the chief. The head warrior shall say, "You are the one that was unable to perform the duties of your office. Therefore they (the chiefs) remove this title. Now then you are freed of responsibilities. You no longer have an official title. Now then I shall return to the female trustee (clan matron) this wampum title string. And so there their minds shall rest in confidence among our mothers. And they as trustees will carefully chose an appropriate place to install the antlers."

□□◇□□

Installation of a Successor. Again there was something further that the chiefs mentioned. Once more we will establish rules as to what our nephews shall do. And they shall be aware of the rules whenever anyone is stripped of antlers. And this shall be the regular way whenever that occurs. It can occur at any time, not necessarily at a special season, when people voice their sentiments to the chiefs, to the head warriors, and also to the public. And what they shall do is this: they shall hang a kettle and cook. And when the acting officials of the several nations convene, the chiefs, and also the subchiefs, and all the so-called Longhouse people of all the nations are assembled, on that occasion our mothers (the women) and also the warriors (the men) who are the trustees of the titled ones shall take charge. Now the bench where the former chief used to sit has become empty. He has been removed. And another person has been chosen to stand in his place. And then the head warrior shall represent the concerned chiefs in delivering the charge. He shall begin by explaining to the chiefs and also to the subchiefs so that everyone shall understand why the former chief was stripped of his title. And then the head warrior shall pick up the antlers (wampum string symbolic of title) and stand confronting the newly appointed one who then shall be antlered. The head warrior shall say, "There is a sapling that shall replace the old tree. And this one shall now be our standing tree where we shall focus our minds. Therefore, you chiefs, this man shall be your co-worker." As to the wampum: it shall be two strings of mixed white and purple colors that shall be an official emblem of the title of each chief.

Then the head warrior pronounces: "Now indeed you behold him that here he now stands before you officially invested with antlers as a chief. So now then your nephew and niece brought it to a conclusion. Now therefore the matrons and warriors charge him. Therefore, pay attention, you chiefs!"

At that time the head warrior will depart from where the chiefs are circled (seated). Now the remaining acts are up to the council of chiefs (welcoming him, etc.). And now the name bearers (Onondaga chiefs) who are guardians of Deha-doda:ho? (the firekeepers) shall take charge of presenting him to the chiefs. Their speaker shall say, "Now all of the ceremonies have been fulfilled according to the rules so as to perpetuate the Great Law (the league). It will regulate the conduct of all the people. And therefore today we noticed that both our mothers and the warriors followed the path laid out for them and made us observe the proper proceedings for a new co-worker; and moreover we have remarked the meaning of the charge as we heard it delivered to the chiefs."

And now the chiefs shall accept and confirm it with one voice (unanimously). Likewise the war chiefs. And so now he (the new chief) shall be seated in his rightful place among the chiefs, namely . . . [title]. "He shall now serve and cooperate with his colleagues to advance the Good Word. Thus we shall make this a day of reckoning for our people, and also for our grandchildren."

Now that they have cleared away evil things [sins of the previous chief], the new chief is forbidden to engage in any form of sin henceforth. Instead he shall work against sin. All of the ritual acts are performed to put this chief on the path of duty. And his skin shall be seven thumbs [inches] thick; no matter what he is stuck with, it will not penetrate, even if anything sharp is used against him. And for this reason things shall always go well among the council of chiefs, and for the benefit of the people. And so now men shall say: "Hear and heed each other, you chiefs, and pay attention to your two nephews (niece and nephew), for that which will clarify the minds of the upcoming generations of our grandchildren is now completed."

□□◇□□

A brief comment on the preceding bylaws may serve to justify their inclusion in a political history of the League of the Iroquois. Although the Gibson and Charles versions of rules and procedures are prolix and redundant, the texts the two men dictated to Hewitt are characteristic of Iroquois speech, they spell out in detail just what should be done in such crises, they have never before been published, and there is nowhere else in the Iroquois literature anything so complete. Nothing else so vividly illustrates the status and role of the matron in Iroquois society. The Iroquois are known for matriliny and are frequently tagged as a classic matriarchy in popular literature. These texts demonstrate that the matron's status shares its power with that of a male warrior, that she is really a trustee for the title that passes in her lineage, and that responsibility ultimately rests with the council of chiefs to whom a head warrior reports the joint findings of matron and warrior.

The two sets of bylaws represent the philosophy underlying the chapters on the Condolence Council from my own observations.

Up to now, strings of wampum have punctuated the messages of requickening. Still other strings, as indicated in this chapter, symbolize the antlers of office—the emblems of chieftainship—and attest to particular titles. The next order of magnitude is the wampum belts, which were the memoranda of agreements in forest diplomacy and of particular treaties with European powers. Before coming to these matters, I introduce my readers to the nature and history of wampum beads.

CHAPTER 16

WAMPUM, THE MAGNET
THAT DREW FURS FROM THE FOREST

> The Indians prize not English gold,
> Nor English Indians shell:
> Each in his place will passe for ought,
> What ere man buy or sell.
> —Roger Williams, *A Key into the Language of America*

The imagery of the League of the Iroquois was encoded in wampum belts and strings that were hung in the "Proposition House," where the council met, as testimony to agreements reached with neighboring tribes and European powers. After being examined by the public and duly explained, they were taken down and stored in a hemp bag that the chiefs entrusted to a designated wampum keeper. Tradition assigns this trust to Hononwiyehdi (Oa-7), but in practice, so far as the record shows, the chiefs handed their archive to a colleague noted for his memory and upright character who, as occasion demanded, could "read" the belts and teach ongoing generations. In the late nineteenth century, the use of wampum in council lapsed, and surviving belts rapidly disappeared into the hands of collectors. For a century now, most extant wampum belts have been preserved in museums, and their encoded symbolism has dimmed. The Onondaga council in the 1990s sought to recover such surviving wampum, hoping to restore the glory of the league of tradition. What, then, is wampum, and what is its history?

□□◇□□

The term *wampum*, or *wampumpeag*, comes from one of the Algonquian languages of New England and refers to discoidal, and later cylindrical, beads fashioned from marine shells native to coastal waters. Wampum was at first white and later also purple, the latter carrying twice the value of the former. It was graded, strung, and woven into "collars" or belts that increased in size as wampum became plentiful.

Trade in discoidal beads between coastal makers who had access to shells and inland peoples such as the Iroquoians who were removed from the resource began before the first European landfalls in the Americas. The trade intensified and expanded during the years of the fur trade, when wampum became a means of exchange. Explorers and traders soon discovered that wampum was the magnet to draw furs from the forest.

Quite probably the quantities of shell beads that Cartier found among the Laurentian villagers of Stadacona and Hochelaga (modern Quebec and Montreal) came from the south, in Bruce Trigger's view (1976, 1: 198–200). Prehistoric Iroquoian sites in Canada yield only small quantities of shell beads, although the trade in beads resembling wampum may have begun earlier than the data suggest. It was under way in the sixteenth century.

Absentee Huron headmen in 1611, seeking an alliance with the French, sent four strings of shell beads and fifty beaver skins to a council near Montreal that they were unable to attend (Biggar 1922–36, 2: 194–95). Trigger (1976, 1: 268) attributes the fifty beaver skins to Huron clan segments, while the four strings symbolized the four Huron tribes. Evidently, wampum was as yet not plentiful in Huronia. Four years later, however, one band of Hurons offered fifty wampum belts to another band to compound a murder (Biggar 1922–36, 3: 101–3). By the third decade of the century, wampum was sufficiently plentiful in Canada that Father Brébeuf presented the Huron council with a "collar" of twelve hundred wampum beads to "smooth their road to Paradise" (JR, 10: 27–29). Three years later, two Jesuits passed a collar of two thousand beads to the town council of the Neutrals, an Iroquoian tribe inhabiting the Niagara peninsula of Ontario (JR, 21: 207–9). Both Huronia near Georgian Bay and the Neutral country west of Niagara were marginal to Iroquoia, the land of the Five Nations east and south of Lake Ontario. The Iroquois were one step closer to the wampum makers of Long Island. They were intermediaries in the wampum trade, and by 1640 the Senecas, at the "western door" of the Longhouse, had wampum in abundance.

At the eastern door, the Mohawks, having defeated the Mahicans, or River Indians, in 1628, gained firsthand access to the trade at Fort Orange and enforced a policy of not permitting Northern Algonquian Indians to trade directly with the Dutch (Trigger 1976, 2: 464). For a time they monopolized the wampum trade. By the 1640s, they were validating treaties with belts of wampum. At the peace of 1645, the Mohawk emissary Kiotsaeton stood offshore in the bow of a canoe draped in wampum beads and belts and hailed his hosts at the landing with terms of kinship (JR, 27: 251–65; l'Incarnation 1681: 394–96; Fenton 1985: 127–28). The same year a Mohawk war party, surrounded by rival Hurons, laid down wampum belts to disarm them and invite them to confer. They distributed tobacco to the Huron warriors and frightened them into withdrawing, and then, in perfidy, turned on the Huron leaders (JR, 29: 249–51). By the mid-century, belts of large denomination passed from Jesuits to Onondaga, from Onondaga to Huronia, and from the Hurons to the Ursulines after their convent burned (JR, 29: 59; 33: 119; 36: 215–21). This expanding wealth of wampum among the Northern Iroquoians can be traced to a single source—the bead makers of coastal New England and Long Island.

We owe our knowledge of the Long Island wampum industry to the late Professor Lynn Ceci, who extended her research on coastal archaeological sites to systematic study of the collections from Seneca sites in the Rochester Museum (Ceci 1977; 1980; 1987). She then interpreted the ethnohistorical literature in the light of world system theory (1987). Although the generic term *wampum* has been applied to a variety of shell and other beads, the term properly denotes a particular type of white and purple cylindrical shell bead drilled from opposite ends with steel awls and composing Iroquois wampum belts. Ceci (1987: 1–2) points out that this belt wampum, or "true" wampum (Bushnell 1906: 172; Fenton 1971b: 440), is distinguished by three diagnostic traits: species, shape, and size. White wampum beads are "sliced" from the central pillars, or columellas, of two marine species, *Busycon canaliculatum* and *B. carica*, the small northern whelks that formerly were prolific between Cape Cod and Long Island Sound. The lone source of the purple (sometimes called black) wampum is the quahog, or hard clam (*Mercenaria mercenaria*), which is widely distributed on the Atlantic coast from Nova Scotia to Florida and has its greatest concentration at Gardiners and Oyster bays on Long Island and at Narragansett Bay in New England. True wampum is tubular in shape and polished. Ceci's measurements of wampum size average 5.5 mm for length, 4 mm for diameter, and 1 mm for the tiny bores drilled with metal awls (1987: 2).

Shell beads appear as early as the Late Archaic (ca. 2500 B.C.) on western New York sites, but the first "proto-wampum" to meet the three foregoing criteria comes from Middle and Late Woodland sites (ca. A.D. 200–1510). The latter beads are significantly larger, as are the stone-drilled bores. Ceci found comparable materials on coastal sites of similar dates. There was evidently a trade network in shell beads already established before the first European landfalls.

Without access to the shells save through trade, there is no way that the Iroquois could have invented wampum. Indeed, there was no true wampum in Iroquoia (upstate New York) before white contact. Seneca sites south of Rochester occupied after white contact (ca. 1540–1620) produced marine shell beads of increasing numbers and types associated with European trade goods (Wray and Schoff 1953: 56; Ritchie 1965: 270; Wray 1973). White beads appeared first drilled with steel awls. This postcontact white wampum was woven into bracelet-size strips and then, at the end of the sixteenth century, into small belts of increasing width and length. The first purple wampum appeared as figures on white backgrounds early in the next century.

The decades after 1640, the year guns became available, marked a spectacular rise in the number of beads and the appearance of large, broader belts from Seneca sites. One site is estimated to have yielded 250,000 beads and 8 belts, and a second, 100,000 beads and 15 belts. Although data were not available for sites of the easterly members of the confederacy (Cayuga, Onondaga, Oneida, Mohawk) nearer the source, Ceci estimated that millions of wampum beads reached Iroquoia by the mid-seventeenth century. Wampum's rapid spread coincided with the fur trade, and wampum reached the Iroquois country in increasing quantities after the Dutch built Fort Orange (1624) and Albany was settled. This prodigious wealth derived entirely from the work of Algonquian bead makers who gathered the shells, processed them, and finished them on the beaches of southern New England and New York (Ceci 1987: 3).

The numerous episodes involving wampum in Iroquois mythology only under-score its former scarcity. The most famous episode occurs in the league epic when Hiawatha, wandering in the forests, comes upon a pond covered with ducks who fly up suddenly, exposing a species of freshwater shell that he proceeds to gather and devise in strings for the condolence ceremony. He had previously experi-mented with elder shoots, bird quills, and wooden counters. In other tales, wampum exudes magically as the sweat of tortured heroes, as the lice of a bird, and so forth. Both Hiawatha's experiments and the magical incidents substantiate that historically, wampum was something wonderful, the Iroquois could not make it themselves, lacking the shells, and it came by trade from afar. This might seem farfetched if we did not know the facts of its manufacture, its source, the sites where it was made, and how it spread in the trade.

□□◇□□

The Dutch discovered wampum and exploited it. The first navigators quickly learned that the furs native hunters offered in trade were the most profitable North American resource on the world market. Their maps soon illustrated where quality furs were to be had at the heads of navigable rivers. Adrian Block's 1614 map charts locations, including the upper Hudson River, later identified with ethnic entities engaged in wampum manufacture and trade (Ceci 1987: 5-7). The documents do not say just how the Dutch learned that wampum was a negotiable currency with which to procure inland furs, but they soon found European beads negotiable in America as in Africa. Peter Stuyvesant viewed the wampum exchange retrospectively when, in 1660, he responded to a suggestion of the directors of the Dutch West India Company that wampum be reduced to a silver base. Fearing inflation, he declared: "Wampum is the source and mother of the beaver trade. . . . [W]ithout wampum we cannot obtain beavers from the savages." Monkeying with the exchange had produced a scarcity. He preferred to let the market prevail (NYCD, 14: 470-71).

Earlier reports from New Netherland to the States General in Holland stated that wampum was the currency of the Indians, that they manufactured it themselves, principally at Gardiners Bay and Oyster Bay on Long Island, that it was measured by the hand or fathom, and that it was accepted for the payment of duties—formerly at the rate of four for a stiver, but by 1650 at the depreciated rate of six, and ten years later, ten; but it nevertheless constituted such an important resource that the West India Company claimed a monopoly in its trade and worried about sharing it with the English. Secretary van Tienhoven likened it to "the mine of New Netherland," where "at Gardiner's Bay lie the cockles whereof the Wampum is made, from which great profit could be realized" from its trade (NYCD, 1: 269, 281, 343, 344, 360, 365, 459).

The Dutch had reason to worry. In September 1626, De Rasieres, the agent of the West India Company in New Netherland, wrote to the directors in Holland protesting a shipment of copper kettles for the "French Indians," who could get them from the French, saying, "They come to us for no other reason than to get wampum, which the French cannot procure unless they come to barter for it with our natives in the north." The Pilgrims at Plymouth came to the Dutch for the same reason. De Rasieres planned before winter to procure a thousand yards of wampum to stock Fort Orange, where wampum had been in short supply (Van Laer 1924: 223, 227). He also planned to supply duffles in dull colors that would not scare the game. These measures might prevent the Indians from going to competitors (Van Laer 1924: 231).

De Rasieres' letter outlined the elements of a classic economic trade triangle: (1) European investors sent manufactured goods to the wampum producers and exchanged them for wampum; (2) Dutch sloops transported wampum upriver to be exchanged for furs; and (3) furs were baled and shipped to investors in Holland for sale at enormous profit (Ceci 1987: 9). The logs of West India Company sloops plying between Narragansett Bay and Dutch upriver posts document this trade (Jameson 1909: 87; Van Laer 1924: 212). Volume and profits soared yearly.

Not satisfied with a good thing, De Rasieres, on a trading voyage to Plymouth, gave away the advantage by selling the Pilgrims some fifty pounds' worth of wampum and telling them how "vendible" it was at Fort Orange (Jameson 1909: 110). His advice to seek the fur trappers of northern New England helped the Pilgrims pay off their debt on the *Mayflower* voyage. He described wampum making as a winter occupation on Long Island, where the Indians gathered cockleshells on the beach and fashioned them into oblong beads called *sewan* in the local Algonquian dialect. He wrote, "They are as particular about stringing and sorting as we [are] . . . about pearls" (Jameson 1909: 106).

It took two years, according to William Bradford's relation (1952), for the idea to catch on with the Massachuset Indians, who previously had no wampum or very little of it, except "the sachems and some special persons." The Narragansetts and Pequots, Bradford says, were making it and "grew rich and potent by it," but the local Indians, and the English, for that matter, knew nothing of it or its value until advised by the Dutch. Only then did the Massachuset Indians begin to make wampum of shells gathered by the Narragansetts. Wampum had already been in use some twenty years when Bradford predicted, "It may prove a drug in time." Meanwhile, some Indians grew rich in the trade, enabling them to purchase guns, powder, and shot from "sundry unworthy persons, both English, Dutch, and French, which may turn to the ruin of many" (Bradford 1952: 203–4; Jameson 1909: 106, 109–13).

The competition between New Netherland and New England for the wampum trade bid up the costs of wampum and furs (Ceci 1977: Table 10). For a time the Pequots enjoyed a monopolistic position as brokers between the two colonies and the Iroquois. Meanwhile, competing traders introduced steel awls and whetstones, which turned a casual winter occupation into a wigwam industry. Roger Williams, in his charming *Key into the Language of America* (1643), described the situation in New England. He observed that the Indians equated Europe's money with their own, which "is of two sorts; one white, which they make of the stocke of the Periwincle, which they call *Meteauhock* [*Pyrula carica*] . . . and of this sort six of their small beads . . . are currant with the English for a peny. The second is black, inclining to blew, which is made of the shell . . . which some English call Hens, *Poquauhock* ["thick shell," *Mercenaria mercenaria*], and of this sort three make an English peny."

He specifies that wampum was made generally by natives living on the coast. The trade was well established: "The Indians bring downe all their sortes of Furs, which they take in the Countrey, both to the Indians and to the English for this Indian Money [which] . . . the English, French, and Dutch, trade to the Indians, six hundred miles in severall parts (North and South from New England) for their Furres, and whatsoever they . . . need" (Williams 1643: 173).

Inflation attended the rapid increase in the supply of wampum. Improved methods of manufacture contributed. By 1643 a fathom had declined in value from ten to five shillings. This upset the natives, who desired a fixed rate of exchange, and made them impatient with the traders. Black wampum continued to count two of the white (Williams 1643: 175–76).

Before the Indians had awl blades from Europe, Williams tells us, "they made shift to bore this their shell money with stone," but they soon developed new techniques and added words to their vocabulary to describe technical problems encountered. Williams listed terms for "when the awl sticks," "to smooth them," and "whetstone," and a descriptor for the "wooden pincers or vice" that held the bead in drilling. Characteristically, he ended each of his chapters with a quatrain, such as the one I quoted as the epigraph for this chapter.

The function of wampum changed for both cultures. The Indians, accustomed to gift giving and reciprocity, began to participate in a capitalistic market exchange that precipitated competition for resources and conflict—in short, the Beaver Wars. For the colonials, wampum became legal tender "minted" by natives and backed by beaver. A dependency between the two cultures soon led to conflict, fines, and terrorism (Ceci 1987: 11). The Pequot middlemen were soon eliminated, and the remnant native tribes began paying tribute to the Iroquois who succeeded for a time in their role (Ceci 1987: 13).

As the fur trade expanded early in the seventeenth century, inland tribes such as the Iroquois recovered from the shock of being deprived of trade goods, exploited their confederacy for mutual security, and pushed out, subjugating tribes who stood between them and the source of goods at Fort Orange and Montreal. In competition with the French, the Dutch enjoyed several advantages: wampum from Long Island, cloth from the Netherlands, and guns, powder, lead, and rum at lower prices. "French Indians" came down from Canada to Fort Orange just to get wampum. The Indian Records, or records of transactions at Albany, contain the entries of an expanding traffic in which thousands of fathoms of wampum passed from the Dutch to the Iroquois, and they tell how, after 1674, hundreds of wampum belts of varying sizes, designs, and colors were made up and exchanged to attest to political agreements (Wraxall 1915; Livingston 1956; Trelease 1960: 48).

There is no documentary evidence that the Iroquois made wampum of seashells. They evidently had little of it until after the Mohawks defeated the Algonquian-speaking Mahicans in 1628 and drove parts of them to take refuge among relatives in New England. In 1637, they slew the Pequot sachem Sassacus and confiscated his wampum (Winthrop 1929–47, 1: 229). Soon, other New England groups were sending presents of wampum as tribute to the Mohawks (Winthrop 1929–47, 2: 6–7). With access to Fort Orange, the Mohawks began to get wampum in quantity from the Dutch who controlled its distribution (Trelease 1960: 48). A party of traders from Fort Orange visiting the Mohawk and Oneida towns in 1635 doled out *sewant*, the Algonquian term for wampum, by the handful. At Oneida they learned that Frenchmen were giving "six hands of *seawan* for one beaver," but Oneida hunters were willing to bring their furs exclusively to Fort Orange for four hands of it (Jameson 1909: 141ff.; Gehring and Starna 1988: 5, 15–16).

Even the "French Indians" knew that the Mohawks were at one remove from the source of supply. Courcelle's winter expedition in 1665 against the Mohawk towns found most of the Mohawk and Oneida men absent because they had gone "to make war on some other peoples, called 'porcelain-makers,'" leaving only their children and infirm old men in their villages (JR, 50: 135). Years later, some "Far Indians," presumably Ottawas, visiting Onondaga wanted to see New York, where wampum was made (Colden 1750: 107–9).

The quantity and quality of wampum improved steadily after the mid-seventeenth century, despite the importation of European glass imitations, the onset of inflation, and the operation of Gresham's law that poor or cheap money drives good money out of circulation. The Indians insisted on the original marine shell beads in the makeup of treaty belts. The belts themselves increased in breadth and length during the next century and were composed mainly of purple beads with white figures rather than white backgrounds with purple figures as in the earliest belts. In 1687 the Indian Records began to reckon the dimensions of belts in terms of breadth as ten, twelve, or fourteen rows "deep" or "high" (Livingston 1956: 109; NYCD, 3: 483, 485–86). Belts varying from seven to fifteen rows deep and one with five houses on it accompanied a transaction three years later, the depth proportionate to the message's import (NYCD, 3: 712–14).

Beauchamp (1901: 394–95) noted that the supply of wampum and the use of belts flagged for a time but revived wonderfully during Sir William Johnson's term as crown superintendent. During the third quarter of the eighteenth century he dispensed wampum lavishly in the form of strings and belts of "prodigious" proportions, symbolizing union, chain, covenant, road, invitation, war and peace, scalp, and so forth. Speakers for the Six Nations thanked him for reviving their customs. To Arthur Lee of Virginia he wrote in 1771, "Their belts are mostly black Wampum" (DHNY, 4: 437). Following Johnson's death, a speaker for the grand council produced "the great belt of union" and delivered a white belt with "black figure" five feet long and thirty rows deep (Gage Papers, WLCL, 1: 22ff.).

In preparing for a treaty it was not unusual for agents to request fifty thousand to eighty thousand beads of each species for the preparation of belts that might number a hundred (Beauchamp 1901: 438; Pickering Papers, MHS, 59: 56; 60: 140). Timothy Pickering, who had first learned about wampum and its proper handling from the great Seneca speaker Red Jacket, sought the advice of Henry Aupaumut, a Stockbridge Indian, before a treaty in 1793. He would need at least fifty thousand beads of each sort. A few black belts should be made up in advance in case chiefs died. "These may be 8 or 10 rows wide, and two and one half or three feet long." He should have a large belt made up to confirm the treaty, and two or three belts of ten rows each, three feet long, for important speeches. Strings would suffice for minor occasions and could be made up on the spot (PP, 59: 55). The next year a small belt of glass beads was requested from the War Office (O'Reilly Collection, NYHS, 10: 5).

The preparation of belts was usually left to women who were adept at beadwork. There were such artisans among the local Mahican women near Albany and at Stockbridge. But men on occasion produced the belts themselves (Beauchamp 1898: 10–11; 1901: 398). It may be presumed that the technique on a simple bow loom that Morgan described at Tonawanda in 1850 was the time-honored way:

> The most common width was three fingers or the width of seven beads, the length ranging from two to six feet. In belt-making, which is a simple process, eight strands or cords of bark thread are first twisted from filaments of slippery elm, of the requisite length and size; after which they are passed through a strip of deer skin to separate them at equal distances from each other in parallel lines. [These form the warp.] A piece of splint is then sprung in the form of a bow, to which each end of the several

strings is secured, and by which all of them are held in tension, like warp threads in a weaving machine. Seven beads, these being the intended width of the belt, are then run upon a thread by means of a needle, and are passed under the cords at right angles, so as to bring one bead lengthwise between each cord, and the one next in position. The thread is then passed back again along the upper side of the cords and again through each of the beads; so that each bead is held firmly in its place by means of two threads, one passing under and one above the cords. This process is continued until the belt reaches its intended length, when the ends of the cords are tied, the end of the belt covered, and afterwards trimmed with ribbons. In ancient times both the cords and the thread were of sinew. (Morgan 1901, 2: 54-55)

Beauchamp (1901: 380) remarks that most older belts have warps of buckskin, and the edges neatly braided or twisted.

□□◇□□

Wampum was both public and private property. The public treasury, as Lafitau described it (1724, 1: 508; Fenton and Moore 1974: 312), was kept in the chiefs' houses and passed around among them as public sentiment demanded. The years were counted by nights that the wampum had spent in a particular house. Teganissorens, an Onondaga ambassador, made the distinction between public and private wampum in advising the Albany commissioners in 1700 that a belt some Onondaga defectors had carried to the French was not out of the public treasury but was their own (NYCD, 4: 694). The distinction obtained right down to the American Revolution, when warriors frequently owned more wampum than chiefs, judging by their claims of losses (Guldenzopf 1986). Conrad Weiser, the Pennsylvania interpreter, reported that at the death of Canasatego, the Onondaga orator of confederation fame, in 1750, all of the unanswered public belts in his care, received from English governors, were ordered buried with him (Beauchamp 1901: 384; *Pennsylvania Archives*, 1852-1949, 5: 480).

The Onondaga council kept the wampums of the confederacy. It was convenient to have them at the central fire. The firekeepers appointed a keeper among the chiefs, who traditionally was Hononwiyehdi, seventh on the Onondaga roster, but in practice the responsibility fell to someone else. Other nations of the confederacy had belts of their own. Beauchamp (1901: 383, 410) kept a record of the incumbent keepers after the belts were returned from Buffalo Creek in 1847. For over a century they were never in the proper hands.

In the late eighteenth century the British at Fort Niagara kept a supply of wampum for council purposes and employed belts to the exclusion of letters for communicating with Indian council fires (Red Jacket to Pickering, 1791, PP, 60: 97).

Iroquois chiefs never did any serious business without wampum, or a token of the same (PCR, 4: 559ff.; Boyd 1938: 15ff.). They had developed the ritual handling of wampum strings and belts to an art form. Traces of this artistry are still seen during the preaching of Handsome Lake's code and in councils of traditional chiefs. A runner heralded urgent business with seven hands of wampum, that is, a cluster of seven strings tied together. Still more important issues might require a belt. On meeting, the speaker might set up a horizontal pole to rack up the propositions in order, a string or belt for each according to its import. He would then take one down, deliver the proposition, and pass the belt over the fire to the host. To grasp the belt was tantamount to accepting the proposition. The speaker might suspend the belt by one end (see fig. 28), grasp it in the middle,[1] hold it up horizontally by both ends, tie two belts together binding two dependent proposals, tie a knot to choke a path, hang it about his own or someone's neck, or bind it to a captive's arm. The literature from the seventeenth century onward is replete with such references. To throw a belt represented a challenge.

Recipients, to assent, might grasp, pick up, or touch a belt passed in council. To express dissent, they might kick it to one side or flick it out of the council with a stick, or simply leave it lying untouched.

War belts were painted red, and belts might have attachments: a bundle of stick counters, or a notched tally of days to be cut off until a meeting.

All of this behavior had to be learned and understood by persons treating with Indians and advancing proposals with belts. Conrad Weiser, Sir William Johnson, and Samuel Kirkland, missionary to the Oneidas, in the eighteenth century were conversant with the arts of the council fire and wampum handling.

Much has been said about "reading" the wampum. It was an accomplishment possible for persons who, having memorized an oral message or stream at the same time they internalized the spatial design woven into the belt, could later recover its content. So long as the oral and spatial aspects were learned and kept together, one could retrieve the verbal content encoded in the belt. But when belts were separated from their documentation, the one going to a museum and the other to an archive, the message was wiped out, as surely as material nowadays is lost from an erased computer disk. Traditionalists today claim to be able to read belts long out of their possession. Beauchamp doubted that this was possible at the turn of the century. I, too, have questioned the possibility (Fenton 1971b), but my colleague Michael Foster has contradicted my position (1985) and has since undertaken a promising recovery project with Chief Jacob Thomas at Six Nations. The best contemporaneous account of reading the wampum comes from the Reverend John Heckewelder, missionary to the Delawares in the eighteenth century, and is probably applicable to the Iroquois as well:

> For the purpose of refreshing their own memories, and of instructing one or more of their capable and promising young men in these matters, they assemble once or twice a year. On these occasions they always meet at a chosen spot, at a small distance from the town, where a fire is kindled, and at the proper time provisions are brought out to them; there, on a large piece of bark or on a blanket, all the documents are laid out in such order, that they can at once distinguish each particular speech, the same as we know the principal contents of an instrument of writing by the endorsement on it. If any paper or parchment records are connected with the belts, or strings of wampum, they apply to some trusty white man (if such can be had,) to read the contents to them. Their speaker then, who is always chosen from among those who are endowed with superior talents, and has already been trained up to the business, rises, and in an audible voice delivers, with the gravity that the subject requires, the contents, sentence after sentence, until he has finished the whole on one subject. On

1. See the frontispiece in Jacobs 1950.

the manner in which the belts or strings of wampum are handled by the speaker, much depends; the *turning* of the belt which takes place when he has finished one half of his speech, is a material point, though this is not common in *all* speeches with belts; but when it is the case, and is done properly, it may be as well known by it how far the speaker has advanced in his speech, as with us on taking a glance at the pages of a book or pamphlet while reading; and a good speaker will be able to point out the exact place on a belt which is to answer to each particular sentence, the same as we can point out a passage in a book. Belts and strings, when done with by the speaker, are again handed to the chief, who puts them up carefully in the speech-bag or pouch. (Heckewelder 1881: 107–8)

An unusually perceptive observer of Iroquois political behavior, Father Lafitau described the operation of their "Public Treasury":

Their length, width, and the variations of colour are proportionate to the affair's importance. The usual belts are commonly of eleven rows of a hundred and eighty beads each. The bank or public treasury consists . . . of belts of this sort, which take the place of contracts, public acts, of records. . . . For, since the Indians have not the use of writing . . . and are thus given to forgetting things . . . they supply this lack by making . . . a local record by the words which they give these belts, each of which stands for a particular affair. . . .

They are so devotedly attached to this practice that, beside the name of *Gaionni*, meaning belts of this sort, which is the usual name, they also [call] them *Garihoua*, meaning an item of business; that of *Gaouenda*, voice or word [in modern parlance, a treaty]; and . . . *Gaiaderensera* . . . [the word for] grandeur or nobility. These last names are given them because all the matters designated by these belts lie in the domain . . . of the *Agoianders* [chiefs] . . . since it is they who furnish the belts and it is between them [the chiefs] that the belts are divided when presents are made to the village and answer to their ambassadors' belts. . . .

The Agoianders and Elders have, besides, the custom of reviewing them together and dividing among themselves the responsibility of noticing certain ones assigned to them individually so that, in this manner, they forget nothing.

Their wampum would soon be exhausted if it did not circulate but, in almost all affairs, whether internal or external, the laws demand that an answer be made word for word; that is, for a belt, another is given, of almost the same value . . . some difference being observed, nevertheless, of a greater or lesser number of beads since these must be proportionate to the rank of the persons or nations with whom business is being transacted. (Fenton and Moore 1974: 310–11)

Lafitau commented that Europeans had disregarded the need for reciprocity and had retained belts, with the result that the natives cut down on the number of belts, saying that their wampum was exhausted (Lafitau 1724, 1: 505–8; Fenton and Moore 1974: 310–12).

Iroquois envoys were coached on positions to be taken and provided with wampum belts or mnemonic counters so that they would not forget their instructions or exceed their orders (Lafitau 1724, 2: 311; Fenton and Moore 1974: 173).

The meaning of belts was sometimes forgotten in former days, as it is now. A Huron chief named Forty Suns explained that an Iroquois belt had been received so long ago that the old men had forgotten what it said, and he would have to take it to the Senecas to find out its meaning, because the Hurons regarded it a serious matter not to respond to a belt (Margry 1876–86, 5: 290–91).

Condolence Councils in the eighteenth century required belts. The fifteen strings of requickening, described in previous chapters, were in use during preliminaries to the 1794 treaty at Canandaigua (Savery 1837: 355).

In contrast to the belts that documented official business, a message destined only for the ears of an individual could be sent "underground" and was not to be revealed to anyone else. The carrier was told to enter "into the earth" and to surface again at the destination, to avoid being seen, to shun paths, and to traverse the woods (Heckewelder 1881: 109; NYCD, 9: 1086).

No chief paid attention to rumors—the songs of birds—however truthful they might be, until he was informed officially. Otherwise, he had not *heard* it (Heckewelder 1881: 109; NYCD, 9: 1086). What he had heard was encoded in strings and belts, which had symbolic significance as occasion demanded.

□□◇□□

Wampum symbolism operates at two levels. There is, first, a series of more or less arbitrary geometric designs that are limited by the medium in which they appear. They become emblematic, depicting trees, clan eponyms, and stick figures; later they are lettered to convey European concepts such as professions of faith and initials of monarchs. Second, the message that a particular belt might be designed to convey called for an arbitrary selection of appropriate designs to be woven into the belt that would be delivered with the speech; the designs would be recognized and recalled later by the recipients. The spatial design and the verbal stream were learned simultaneously, so that the particular belt would recall the message afterward. This supporting relationship between symbolism and content is essentially ephemeral and lacks the precision of literacy, as history demonstrates. "Reading the wampum" long afterward is a fuzzy business.

With a view to discovering an arbitrary symbolic system, I selected designs from existing belts in museum collections, from Beauchamp's plates (1901), and from belts now in the keeping of the Six Nations. Rarely are belts depicted in the margins of documents, but designs are sometimes mentioned in the records. Brief descriptions of eleven designs follow; where possible I have combined the sources.

1. An open square for a town or nation. Sometimes connected by a straight line or "path." Five squares linked (Force 1837–53, (5)1: 1039). A large covenant belt of thirteen squares (Schuyler Papers, Box 14, 21 July 1779, NYPL).

2. A path, consisting of one, two, three, or four rows. Extends the length of belt and connects squares, rhomboids, diamonds, stick figures. The famous "two-row belt" of tradition, symbolizing separate sovereignties, lifeways, and so forth (MAI no. 17/5205, now at Six Nations).

3. A slant line, sometimes double, rarely composed of staggered squares; single and in multiples. "Props" to the Longhouse. Multiples depicting five or six nations. Late eighteenth-century examples. ·

4. A circle, designating a council fire or meeting place. Usually at center of belt. "A belt of white wampum, made in a circular form, representing their place of meeting . . . in the centre, and crossed by four stripes of black wampum,

presenting all their confederates" (ASPIA, 1: 477, 8 October 1793). A solid disk witnessed the sun.

5. A diamond, single, open, solid, or open with enclosed diamond. Also linked in a chain (the chain of friendship motif), or connected by a path. Numerous examples, early to late.

6. A hexagon, a variant of the square or diamond.

7. A rhomboid, a series of thirteen for the colonies (Force 1837–53, (5)1: 1041–2, 13 August 1776).

8. A cross, single and in series, connected by path, on early Huron belts, Queen Anne's American kings, 1710 (Beauchamp 1901: fig. 184, 236; Bond 1952: 16; MAI no. 20/839).

9. Stick figures, holding hands, or connected by a path. Colonials designated by hats. These are the so-called covenant chain belts of the eighteenth century (Beauchamp 1901: 397; Washington covenant belt, NYSM no. 37310). Linked men–house–linked men. Indian and white men linked by path or chain (purple figures on white background) (MAI no. 3/1899, Gov. Denny [Pa.], 1756[?]).

10. Emblematic, a catch-all for various combinations of the foregoing. Increase in frequency and proportions during the second half of the eighteenth century. Examples: the Penn wampum belt (Beauchamp 1901: 391ff.; Speck and Orchard 1925); the Hiawatha belt, NYSM no. 37309 (Fenton 1960; 1971: 443, 444); the Washington covenant belt (NYSM no. 37310). Tree, men, clan animals (MAI no. 8/4473, Seneca Wolf clan condolence [purple, white figures, at ends]).

11. Lettered. Huron professions of faith, after 1654. Initials of English kings, after 1724. Examples: Chartres Cathedral 1679; treaty at Easton 1757; MAI no. 20/898 "John Tyzacke, 1609[?]" (Wampanoag) (Beauchamp 1901: 391ff.).

I can speak of four belts with some confidence. The Hiawatha belt (fig. 24) is the most interesting on several accounts. The Iroquois date it from the formation of the league, yet it cannot be that old. The wampum belts formerly in the New York State Museum that were returned to the Onondaga council in 1989, including the Hiawatha belt, are nowhere near as old as nineteenth-century scholars thought and the present chiefs believe. Beauchamp first questioned the age of these belts (1880; 1901: 342, 350, 410–11). In 1956, I had the belts X-rayed, in connection with a study of belts in the United States and abroad, to determine their relative age from the manner in which they were drilled. William C. Orchard (1929) had established that earlier beads were shorter, that they exhibited broken channels from being drilled at opposite ends, and that the two channels were offset.

The Hiawatha belt contains beads of several sorts, irregular in size, varying in diameter and length. The drilling, plainly visible in X-ray photographs, shows two extremes of technical skill, some beads having been drilled from opposite ends, the channels not meeting. Other beads closer to the margins of the belt were drilled all the way through in one direction. Since we know that the latter technique was an improvement on the former, it would appear that this belt was done over at some time using beads from two different sources, possibly taken from two dismantled belts of differing ages. It was the practice for the council, when belts

Figure 24. The Hiawatha belt, representing the League of the Iroquois. Courtesy New York State Museum.

were no longer needed, when their contents were forgotten, and when they were deemed unimportant to preserve, to direct that they be unstrung to make new ones. If beads taken from two belts of differing ages were lumped before weaving, we would expect to find them distributed at random in the tapestry. That newer beads occur near the margins of the Hiawatha belt suggest some kind of selection or repair. But what is even more damaging to the authentic age that tradition ascribes to the belt is the presence near its center of a bead that shows up opaque, like a metal object, on the X-ray plate. Presumably it is made of lead glass, and it must have reached Onondaga in colonial times. The offensive bead appears to have been incorporated in the belt when it was first woven, and not inserted afterward. The design is as old as the league; the present belt, which may not be the original, dates from the second half of the eighteenth century, when purple wampum became abundant (Beauchamp 1901: 412; Fenton 1960: 5; Gillette 1970).

The Hiawatha belt, which measured 21.5 by 10.5 inches in 1956, is 38 rows deep and is composed of 6,916 beads, purple with white figures. Its form is that of a mat, the warps of which are buckskin thongs, the outer ones braided, and the beads on which are strung as wefts on hemp thread. A design of white shell beads is worked into the solid purple field, at the center of which is a pine tree (reversed, a heart) flanked by two sets of hollow squares that are connected to each other by a double row of white beads. The design is self-contained. When the mat is oriented east and west like the Longhouse of the Iroquois League, with the Tree of Peace pointing north, the first two squares, on the right, represent the Mohawk and Oneida nations, and the third and fourth squares, on the left, contain the Cayuga and Seneca nations.[2] The path runs from the eastern door of the Longhouse on the Schoharie River to the western door on the Genesee River (Parker 1916a:

2. Beauchamp (1901: 411) noted that there was an additional square at each end of the belt, now frayed, leaving only the foreshortened path.

Figure 25. The Washington covenant belt. Courtesy New York State Museum, Albany.

47–48; Clarke 1931: 88–89; Fenton 1960: 6, 1971b: 443–44). The Oneida and Cayuga squares are connected to the Onondaga pine (heart) by a single row of white beads, possibly indicating their relation as "offspring."

Second, the Washington covenant belt (fig. 25) is the longest of the extant Iroquois wampum belts. It is 15 rows deep and measures 6 feet 3.5 inches by 5.25 inches. It contains 10,000 beads of a consistent sort, mostly white with purple figures. A chain of men wearing hats and clasping hands, seven on the left and eight on the right, hold firm by the interior pair to the Longhouse. (The fourth figure on the left has lost its head, and here the margin of the belt appears to have been repaired with three rows of white beads.) It was commissioned by Congress and conveyed in 1775 or 1789, depending on which of two events it is associated with. The interior figures in each set may represent doorkeepers, and the exterior chains of seven and six symbolize the thirteen colonies (Beauchamp 1901: 413; Fenton 1971: 443).

The third belt (NYSM no. 37420) (fig. 26) bears the motif of the Evergrowing Tree, symbolizing the continuing life of the league, but it has also been known as the "wing" or "dust fan" of the league council (Clarke 1931: 98). It is the widest extant belt, being 50 rows deep; it measures 31.5 by 14.5 inches. This belt and the following one bear symbolism associated with the founding of the league.

The fourth is the so-called Thadoda:ho?, or covenant chain, belt (NYSM, no. 37428) (fig. 27), and it is the second widest belt known. It is 45 rows deep—some 13.5 inches (Beauchamp 1901: 412), or 14 by 27 inches (Fenton 1971: 444). Beauchamp acquired the two wide belts for the New York State Museum in 1898. A single beadworker appears to have made both this belt and the one depicting the Evergrowing Tree, using uniformly matched but irregularly drilled beads. I

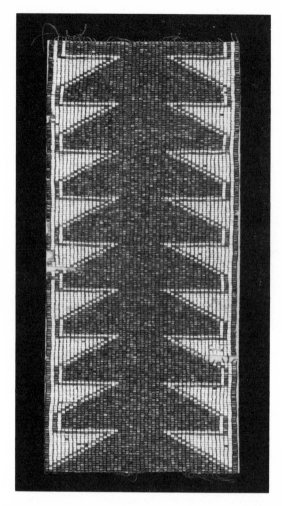

Figure 26. The wampum belt depicting the Evergrowing Tree. Courtesy New York State Museum, Albany.

agree with Beauchamp in placing them in the third quarter of the eighteenth century, in the heyday of Sir William Johnson. The symbolism is obviously older than the belts themselves.

Finally, the structure and composition of the league itself finds expression in a circle of wampum that at once symbolizes the roll of the fifty founders in council, denominates them individually, and separates them into national delegations by pendant strings (Jenness 1933). This important record, until recently preserved in the Canadian Museum of Civilization, was returned to the Six Nations in 1991 (M. K. Foster, personal communication). It contains some eighteen hundred white beads. X-rays show them to be drilled from both ends with steel drills, which places a threshold date of the mid-seventeenth century on their manufacture.

The circle consists of two intertwined strands, symbolizing the Great Peace and the Great Law, and when laid out with the fifty pendants pointing to the center like the spokes of a wheel, one string is noticeably longer than the other forty-nine. This string represents Hononwiyehdi, traditional keeper of the wampums and seventh title on the Onondaga roster, and it serves to orient the Onondaga council

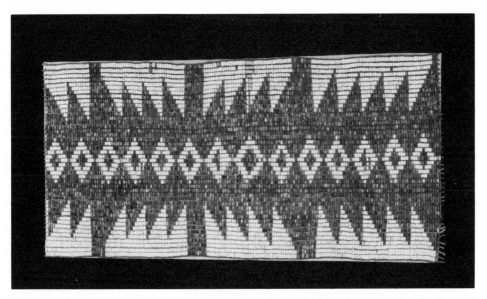

Figure 27. The Thadoda:ho? belt, also known as the chain belt. Courtesy New York State Museum, Albany.

in relation to the other four nations. A join marks the place of beginning. Proceeding clockwise, there are fourteen strings for the Onondaga sachems; then returning to the join and reading counterclockwise there are eight strings for the Seneca chiefs; then nine Mohawk chiefs, nine Oneidas, and ten Cayuga chiefs to the join.[3] The circle preserves the division into national moieties of senior Three Brothers and their two offspring and their seating in council. It also indicates the sequence of deliberating an issue. First the Mohawks introduced an issue and referred it to the Senecas, who sat to their right. When the Senecas returned a judgment, the Mohawk speaker referred it to the Oneidas and Cayugas for deliberation and reply. The Mohawk speaker then laid the matter before the Onondaga sachems, who could confirm or adjudicate a disagreement. Failing unanimity, the matter might go to the council of matrons for resolution. This, at least, is how the league council was supposed to function. History demonstrates that it took on different forms and that individuals without chiefly titles of the founders assumed its offices.

3. The plate in Jenness's article was printed in reverse, and the directions do not conform to his text.

PART THREE

A League for War and Peace
in the Seventeenth Century

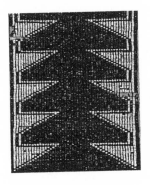

CHAPTER 17

From Champlain to Denonville, 1603–1687

One meets a haughty Savage in a bark hut no less than a proud
Emperor in a gilded Palace.—Jesuit *Relation* of 1661–62

The Iroquois dawned on French consciousness when, in 1603, Samuel de
Champlain attended a feast and scalp dance near Tadoussac to celebrate a
Montagnais-Algonquin victory over the Iroquois, their mortal enemies. The feud
was obviously of some standing, reaching well into the previous century (Biggar
1922–36, 1: 99–103). Champlain's Algonquin hosts described the war routes they
followed to the Iroquois country, and they guided him up the Richelieu, the "river
of the Iroquois," until their longboat grounded (Biggar 1922–36, 1: 141, 160).
Champlain returned to France still curious to see the hilly country of the Iroquois
and meet the dreaded enemies of his Algonquin hosts. Some six years later he
fulfilled this dream spectacularly when he joined an Algonquin-Huron war party
that encountered some two hundred Mohawks near Ticonderoga, against whom
French arquebuses proved decisive (Biggar 1922–36, 2: 90–100).

Nineteenth-century historians to the contrary, this incident did not precipitate
a hundred years of Mohawk vengeance against New France; the Iroquois wars
had economic causes rooted in the fur trade. Champlain was the first Frenchman
to meet the Iroquois in battle; he assisted the next year, 1610, in annihilating
a fortified Mohawk camp on the Richelieu, eliminating the Mohawk threat on
the St. Lawrence until 1630; and he participated in the siege of a palisaded
Iroquois town in 1615—misadventures that he described for his readers. He had
reason to remember Iroquoia; he took an arrow in the knee (Biggar 1922–36, 2:
125–34; 3: 65–78).

The trading of European goods for furs had begun a century earlier, incidental
to maritime fisheries, when Basque and Norman sailors found the natives eager
to obtain iron nails, knives, baubles, and garments. These objects found their way
inland along established trade routes up the St. Lawrence corridor to reach remote
settlements. The demand for such goods soon created a desire to get at the trade
firsthand, eliminate intermediaries, and treat with donors by peaceful or other
means. Frustration and desperation contributed to the Iroquois wars. The
Iroquois had first to end blood feuds among themselves by devising a means of
compounding grievances by confederating as a League of Five Nations. This
enabled them to turn outward against their enemies.

An alternate outlet opened on the Hudson within a year of Hudson's voyage of discovery, in the same summer as the Mohawk rout at Ticonderoga. To gain direct access to Dutch traders and eliminate their trading with northern tribes, the Mohawks made a temporary peace with the French and Montagnais in 1624 and then attacked the Mahicans, or River Indians, whom they finally displaced from the region surrounding Fort Orange at the port of Albany. In effect, they posted Mohawk territory against northern tribes' coming to trade with the Dutch, and when they learned that during the Mahican war the Algonquins and Montagnais had accepted Dutch presents for aiding the Mahicans, the Mohawks resumed warfare with their ancient enemies (Trigger 1971; 1985: 182). Mohawks frequently acted in concert with Oneida war parties independent of the upper Iroquois nations.

During the first half of the seventeenth century, while Dutch trade burgeoned on the upper Hudson, a two-tiered network developed: Hurons, Algonquins, and Montagnais trading with the French, and the lower Iroquois—Mohawks and Oneidas—trading with the Dutch and, after 1664, the English (Rotstein 1972; Trigger 1985: 182). Meanwhile, the upper Iroquois—Onondagas, Cayugas, and Senecas—were at war with the Hurons.

The French policy was to charter monopolies. Champlain held such a concession. Other such exclusive, licensed arrangements followed, with requirements for colonization, regulations limiting competition, and provisions for treating with "savages." Royal marketing policy governing the trade in Canada contrasted with competing Dutch-English mercantilism at Rensselaerswyck and Albany. French traders enjoyed certain advantages: French brandy was superior to rum in quantity, and French powder was less likely to misfire, although French lead and gun flints were inferior. Nearer home, iron tools and implements and, above all, Stroud's cloth abounded and came cheaper at Albany. Northern furs were preferred; the Algonquian natives who trapped them and the Huron trading partners who brought them down to Montreal and Three Rivers should have secured them to the French monopoly, but the Albany Dutch traders controlled the sources, manufacture, and supply of wampum, which, as we have seen, drew the best furs out of the forest.

Soon Iroquois raiders, mainly Mohawk and Oneida, began hijacking Huron fur fleets descending the Ottawa River. These raids, which began around 1640 as beavers became scarce in Iroquoia, evolved later in the century into an illicit but profitable trade between Albany merchants and Montreal sources, a trade in which émigré Iroquois of Caughnawaga were the carriers, plying the Hudson-Champlain-Richelieu water route of ancient war parties.

Such transactions went on between particular individuals who formed interest groups on both sides of the buckskin curtain—between certain Albany merchants and Mohawk trading partners from the Mohawk Valley, between Caughnawaga canoemen and their Montreal sources, and between these voyageurs and Albany outlets.[1] These relationships persisted regardless of the official policies of crowns, colonial assemblies, and tribal councils, and they constituted the real cultural

1. Trigger first applied the concept of the "interest group," derived from Homans (1962), in his history of the Hurons (1976: 23–25) and discussed it further in his revision of Canadian history (1985: 169).

linkages between native Iroquois and Europeans. While exchanging furs for wampum, Stroud's cloth, hardware, guns, powder, lead, and rum, trading partners developed a common jargon, learned each other's ways, and occasionally shared the same blanket. Their offspring became interpreters and brokers between the two cultures (Feister 1973, 1982; Hagedorn 1988).

Trigger (1986: 186) has summarized the nature of Indian trade: "It is clear that in historical times all neighboring tribes either were at war or traded with one another. Archaeological evidence reveals that for millennia trading . . . had been an important mechanism for maintaining peace and friendly contacts among tribes. It is also evident that intertribal trading did not take place in the absence of political alliances." Indeed, years later an Iroquois speaker at an English treaty affirmed: "Trade and Peace we take to be one thing" (Wraxall 1915: 195). The continued immunity of Albany from Indian attack depended on the open market and renewal of alliances.

□□◇□□

Two sets of events radically changed Iroquois life after 1640. First, they had become increasingly dependent on European trade goods, and quality beaver pelts in sufficient quantity were growing scarce within the hunting territories of Iroquoia. Northern pelts were in demand. They could be had by trade or by permission to hunt in Algonquian territories, both of which required peaceful alliances, or by warfare. The Iroquois scarcely measured up to the Hurons as traders, but they were diplomats, and they excelled as warriors. Indeed, the warpath was the way to move upward in Iroquois society. Second, after 1639, English traders on the Connecticut River began selling guns to Mohawks, and the Dutch relaxed prohibitions a year later. Whatever other causes were at work, these two sets of events precipitated the "Beaver Wars" in the ensuing decades (1645–87) (Hunt 1940: 33; Trelease 1960: 118ff.; Trigger 1985: 261.)

The wars of the Iroquois did not mobilize armies of league members but were the work of war parties of tribal villages, sometimes acting in concert with those of a neighboring nation. Mohawk warriors displaced the Mahicans. In raids along the St. Lawrence for European goods, both Mohawk and Oneida parties participated in extinguishing the Algonquins and in hijacking Huron fur fleets on the Ottawa River. The destruction of Huronia was largely the work of Onondaga, Cayuga, and Seneca campaigns, joined by Mohawks and some Oneidas in the final assault. These joint efforts presume a suspension of jealousy between the Mohawks and the upper Iroquois and a policy decision by the grand council at Onondaga to unleash the warriors of the Five Nations to extirpate the Hurons, although the sources are silent. Runners bearing seven strings of wampum and war belts presumably passed the length of the Longhouse summoning assistance.[2]

A second decision the following year to disperse the Petun, or Tobacco, nation, lest they harbor Huron refugees and provide them with a base for recovering Huronia, led to the sacking of the southern of two Petun towns in December 1649, which precipitated a flight westward the next spring of the combined

---

2. On the destruction of Huronia, see JR, 30: 227, 233, passim; Trigger 1976: 725ff.; Trigger 1986: 264–71.

Huron-Petun remnants. Five hundred survivors ultimately reached Chequamegon Bay on Lake Superior.[3]

Iroquois hunters and trappers seeking fine furs to trade with the Dutch brooked no competition from bands of Algonquian hunters, whom they raided and plundered. Those who escaped Iroquois guns and war clubs abandoned hunting territories and followed the Petuns westward. The Nipissing, former trading partners of the Hurons, came under attack in following years but eventually fled westward (Day 1978: 789; Trigger 1986: 271). The Iroquois never colonized or succeeded in controlling the vast areas of Ontario that they depopulated, and the peoples whom they displaced returned with a vengeance later in the century and reoccupied southern Ontario (Rogers 1978: 761; Eid 1979). These southeastern Ojibwas became known as the Mississaugas, who hosted the Loyalist Iroquois after the American Revolution (D. Smith 1987).

The tradition of a vanquished people formerly living west of the Senecas persisted into the twentieth century. The Senecas called them Kahkwaʔgeo:nonʔ, and just who they were remains a mystery. They were possibly the Wenros, a branch of the Neutrals, just east of Niagara, who joined the Hurons in 1638, squeezed out between the Eries to the south and west and the Senecas on the east, who coveted their beaver habitats. The Bernou map of around 1680 places the "Kakouagoga," a dispersed people, on Lake Erie near modern Buffalo, in Neutral territory (White 1978b: 407–8). Iroquoianists now favor the Eries (Pendergast 1994; meeting of the 1995 Conference of Iroquois Research). The Neutrals came next on the Iroquois agenda.

The Neutrals were a confederacy of villagers who occupied the Niagara peninsula in Ontario and Erie County in western New York. Although their villages were concentrated east of the Grand River, their hunting territories extended to Lake St. Clair and modern Detroit. Their vital resources included flint deposits, important to neighboring peoples in prehistoric times, and beavers, besides other sources of fur and hides crucial to the fur trade. Huron traders controlled the Neutral outlets during the first half of the seventeenth century, and after their dispersion, Hurons found asylum in Neutral towns.

This combination stood between the Senecas and the realization of their fur-trade ambitions in the lower Great Lakes (Hunt 1940: 96–100), and the Iroquois perceived the danger of an encircling alliance of Neutral, Erie, and Andaste traders and warriors that would divert the trade to tidewater outlets. Therefore, during 1650, the Mohawks, in exchange for help against the French and to protect the Fort Orange market, formed with the Senecas an army of fifteen hundred that sacked a Neutral town. The Iroquois compensated for a loss of two hundred men by taking Neutral captives for adoption (JR, 36: 141–43; White 1978b: 410; Trigger 1986: 272–73). Although the Neutrals retaliated by attacking the Senecas the next year, the pattern had been set: the destruction of one town sufficed to disperse the rest. One Neutral town was reestablished in Seneca country to become Seneca in time; others fled into the wilderness or to neighboring nations and lost their identity. The ability of the Iroquois to maintain the facade of the Longhouse

3. Trigger 1986: 271; Fenton 1940: 185–86; Garrad and Heidenreich 1978: 394–97; Tanner 1987: maps 6, 7.

stemmed from the institution of the league as a mechanism for composing differences among its members and incorporating outlanders, which is seen in the final case of the Eries.

A people whom the Hurons called the Cat nation inhabited the southern shore of Lake Erie in southwestern New York and the chimney corner of Pennsylvania. We know little about them because no European of record reached their country until after their dispersion. What we know comes from the pens of Jesuit observers at Onondaga who witnessed preparations for the campaign and reported the Eries' destruction at a distance, based on accounts by returning participants (JR, 33: 63; 38: 237; 41: 79, 83; 42: 31, 57–59, 85–203). Again, Huron and Neutral refugees were active in the Erie towns, and where beaver pelts came to market concerned all of the Iroquois. The Senecas suffered losses from Erie raids, and the Eries murdered an Onondaga ambassador. The concern was sufficiently general that the league council must have reached one mind that the Eries had to be extinguished.

In the summer of 1654, the upper Iroquois raised an army of fifteen hundred warriors, including seven hundred Mohawks, that climaxed the campaign by scaling a palisaded town—climbing canoes as ladders—and dispatching the inhabitants. The war lasted two more years, but the Eries, like the Petuns and Neutrals, could not take more than one heavy blow. Some Eries settled among the Senecas, others fled to the Susquehanna, and survivors known as Black Minquas occupied the upper Ohio (Fenton 1940: 197; White 1978b: 416; Trigger 1986: 272–73; Pendergast 1994).

The Erie dispersal opened the Ohio Valley for the western thrusts of Iroquois war parties that decimated the Miamis and Illinois later in the century. Seneca efforts to extend the trade to the upper Great Lakes after the Neutral campaign met with defeats at the hands of the Ojibwa-Ottawa-Nipissing (Tanner 1987: 35). Nearer home and to the south, the Andastes, now called Susquehannocks (Jennings 1978), resisted conquest, raided Iroquois towns, and intercepted Seneca traders bound for Fort Orange.

At mid-century, the Dutch, concerned over competition by Swedes on the Delaware, egged the Mohawks to make war on the Andastes, who were trading furs for arms and other hardware. The results were mixed. After initial success taking captives in outlying settlements, the Mohawks were discovered and routed with heavy losses before they could besiege an Andaste stronghold. The Andastes had Swedish weapons and the support of some one hundred River Indians (JR, 37: 97, 105, 111; NYCD, 12: 431–32; Fenton 1940: 237; Jennings 1978; Trigger 1986: 273). Three years later, when the Dutch took over New Sweden, the Andastes and Mohawks suspended hostilities: each had a Dutch trading outlet. But Andaste raids into upper Iroquoia, combined with smallpox epidemics, severely depleted Iroquois populations. The implication of the Andaste war for Iroquois political history is that the Mohawks were operating on their own, independently of the other four nations. The league as such was inoperative.

The Mohawks were of two minds. As the first nation to accept the Peacemaker's message, they had been the prime movers in advancing the vision of the league to the upper nations. The message of peace and the rituals for reformation and condolence were phrased in the Mohawk language, which, in later times, they insisted should be the official language of the league. Situated as they were at the eastern door of the Longhouse, they insisted that Dutch and French embassies approach the "central fire" through that door. But they acted independently of the upper nations in warfare and in treating for peace and trade. Situated nearest to Fort Orange, they enjoyed a priority in the trade, they were the first nation to get guns, and they dominated relations with the Dutch. They could not control relations with New France, with whom brief peace intervals punctuated continuous raids and open warfare.

During the second half of the seventeenth century, Mohawk and Onondaga relations deteriorated, stopping just short of open warfare. As keepers of the central fire of the confederacy, Onondaga acquired precedence in affairs of state, and an Onondaga chief presided over the grand council. At mid-century this chief was Sagochiendagehte, "the name bearer," which title also became the council name for Onondaga. (Thadoda:ho? would not surface for another century.) The upper nations met most frequently at the central fire, when Mohawk, and sometimes Oneida, delegations stayed home. Moreover, the Senecas, Cayugas, and Onondagas could reach New France by direct water route via Lake Ontario and the St. Lawrence. Trade and peace flowed to Montreal. The path to Fort Orange overland and through the Mohawk Valley was long and beset by dangers. Practically, the league was divided, and that it continued to exist and accommodate these difficulties is amazing. Just what the league was at this period derives from French sources.

□□◇□□

The Jesuit priests who founded the Iroquois missions at mid-century, after the martyrdom of the Jesuit missionary Isaac Jogues among the Mohawks and following the breakup of Huronia, were the products of classical education in the best schools in Europe. They had studied ancient languages and mastered the elements of grammar. French phonetics, with its nasal vowels, adapted more easily to Iroquoian phonemes than did the sounds of English or Dutch. On arrival in New France they immediately turned to the study of native languages—notably Algonquian and Iroquoian. Father Chaumonot sketched Huron grammar, compiled a dictionary, and learned to speak in council. Father Bruyas mastered Mohawk, discovered five conjugations, and isolated radical words (Bruyas 1863; Pilling 1888: 21–22; 37–38).

In the struggle for men's souls, through language the Jesuits found the keys to Iroquois culture. Their journals and reports, now known collectively as *Relations*, written for readers at home in order to enlist support for the missions, carry the only ethnographic reporting on Iroquois manners and political behavior for the period.

That there were five Iroquois nations, as viewed from Huronia—Seneca, Cayuga, Onondaga, Oneida, and, remotely, "Agnie," or Mohawk—and that they were designated "upper" (the first three, and sometimes four) and "lower" (Mohawks and sometimes Oneidas) were first reported in 1635 and with increasing precision thereafter (JR, 8: 117; 17: 77; 21: 21; 33: 65; 40: 161–63). The distinction was essentially topographical—"up above" and "down below" people—but was based partly on the Indians' disposition toward the French and their relations with Huronia. They were all enemies of the Hurons. The Mohawks and Oneidas were especially hostile to the French, but the others might be amenable.

On the eve of the Erie campaign, in 1653, the more numerous and exposed Senecas began to think of peace with the French and induced the Cayugas to join with them. During a truce with hostages, people in Huronia awaited the outcome of a general assembly in Iroquoia, which may not have reached one mind (JR, 40: 117), for the Onondagas and Oneidas pleaded separately and the Mohawks followed later, reluctantly. The nations came down to Montreal in succession. During the proceedings, the French were repeatedly exposed to the ritual of condolence, which they had first experienced at Three Rivers eight years earlier (JR, 17: 247–53; Fenton 1985: 127–30); it was no new thing (JR, 40: 165–69; 185–87). The French were learning, realizing that "one must needs adapt himself to the customs and methods of procedure of those whom he wishes to win" (JR, 40: 167). Before going up to Onondaga the following year, the founders of the Iroquois missions already spoke Huron, a language current in Iroquoia, were fluent in the metaphors of forest diplomacy, and had mastered the expected ritual approaches to the council.

From bitter experience the French knew Iroquois ferocity and cruelty, and they were wary of treachery. Iroquois self-confidence, born of courage and bordering on arrogance, disturbed men reared in a hierarchical society. But the Jesuits came to admire Iroquois civility—their sense of protocol in the conduct of affairs, the style and sheer eloquence of Iroquois speakers in council, council decorum, marked by the rule to hear one out and never interrupt, the ritual sharing of time, and then the withdrawing for rest and reflection before responding. A seemingly unstructured society would suddenly form leagues to meet an emergency and then dissolve into local components. A memory of events and an ability to recall transactions without writing amazed observers (JR, 38: 261).

During these initial transactions, and for convenience, the Tree of Peace was transplanted from Quebec to Montreal, which had become the center of trade and the place of councils (JR, 41: 63, 71).

Le Moyne in 1654, and Chaumonot and Dablon a year later, encountered woods'-edge protocol on approaching Onondaga (JR, 41: 99; 42: 85). Le Moyne performed a eulogy, not to the founders but to local worthies. Sagochiendagehte, the council name for Onondaga, was the most influential name (JR, 41: 69, 89, 109). One of that title had returned a captive with a speech of twenty wampum belts at Montreal, twenty being the price of man's life. The order of symbolic items appears arbitrary, but the speaker saved the "ears" for number 18, the linking of arms in love for 19, and witnessed the sun last (JR, 41: 75). In the condolence paradigm performed at Onondaga in 1656, "tears" came properly first, "ears" sixth (JR, 42: 51ff.). Chaumonot and Dablon adapted the paradigm of condolence and its delivery style to their message of conversion, which was received sympathetically. In reply, they heard an Onondaga version of the Personal Chant and a six-verse antiphonal that suggests the Six Songs of today's condolence rite (JR, 42: 79, 115–17). The text even stressed the key concept *kayendere*, the Huron form of the Mohawk *kayanerenh* (JR, 42: 121–23; Hale 1883: 122). What then meant "excellence, the elite, etc." also referred to the Great Law, or the League of the Iroquois (Lafitau 1724, 1: 474–75; Bruyas 1863: 58).

The lower Iroquois, or Mohawks, though nominally of the league, having reluctantly joined the peace of 1653, were now jealous of the upper nations and resented the French mission station at Onondaga, which abridged the trade. Interior people could now trade with the French and would no longer have to pass through Mohawk villages to carry their furs to the Dutch (JR, 41: 201–3). Tension mounted between Mohawks and Onondagas.

In protesting the Jesuits' having "jumped down the smoke hole to the Onondaga hearth," a Mohawk captain, alias the "Flemish Bastard," appealed to the image of the league as a longhouse with an eastern door: " 'We the five Iroquois Nations compose but one cabin; we maintain but one fire; and we have, from time immemorial, dwelt under one and the same roof.' . . . [F]rom the earliest times, these five Iroquois Nations have been called in their own language, which is Huron, *Hotinonchiendi*, "the completed Cabin" (JR, 41: 87–89). Although the speaker probably used the Mohawk form, *rotinonhsioni*, the Jesuit journalist wrote the more familiar Huron variant. Nothing as close linguistically as these forms appeared for centuries (Morgan 1851; Hale 1883: 75).

Clearly, in 1655 the Iroquois Confederacy was comprised of senior and junior reciprocating moieties, Seneca-Onondaga-Mohawk "fathers" to the "twin brothers," Oneida-Cayuga. The Onondaga speaker assured the missionaries that the twin brothers would embrace the faith, and that the leverage of the four upper nations would bring the Mohawks around (JR, 42: 99, 123). Indeed, the next year the ritual exchange of presents, which was "the common law of the country," exerted a powerful sanction on a Mohawk delegate at Onondaga who expected the Jesuit speaker only to "stammer in their language, like the Europeans who trade with them" (JR, 43: 165).

Just who sat in the grand council at the mid-seventeenth century is unknown, but the titles of four founders surface in the *Relations*: "Aharihon" (Hahihon, Oa-9) (JR, 42: 193), leader of a war party; "Thearihogen" (Tekarihoken, M-1) (JR, 43: 47); "Annonkenritaoui" (Ganonhgidawi, S-7, RC 49) (JR, 44: 23); and Skanawadi (Oa-14, RC 32) (JR, 33: 121). That several of these were war leaders contradicts later native theory that league chiefs may not go to war. Garakontie was then Sagochiendagehte, "the name bearer," or presiding officer (JR, 41: 69; Trigger in DCB, 1: 322). Of such are the fragments of the whole cloth snatched from French sources.

□□◇□□

It is virtually impossible to get a clear picture of the Iroquois polity at the height of its power. If there was an ideal structure, as the league epic stipulates, it was improbable of fulfillment, owing to manpower losses in the wars, the toll of repeated epidemics, and the incorporation of alien populations who outnumbered natives in the fourteen villages of Iroquoia.[4] Onondaga counted seven different nations; Seneca, eleven. Some of these individuals posed security problems, but others became thoroughly acculturated, supplied some of the talent missing among native families, and acceded to leadership roles. Father Millet, later in the century, was adopted by an Oneida matron and requickened in the title of Odatshehde (Oe-1, RC 10), a principal founder of the confederacy (DCB, 2: 473–74). As such, he attended council and discharged the duties of the office, to the advantage of the French and the consternation of English governors.

---

4. See Paul LeJeune, S.J., on the character and customs of the Iroquois (JR, 43: 263).

Whatever the grand council's deficiencies, the Jesuits found much to admire in its conduct as it met annually at Onondaga to settle differences among the member nations. Father Le Mercier wrote: "Their Policy in this is very wise, and has nothing Barbarous in it. For, since their preservation depends upon their union, and since it is hardly possible among peoples where license reigns with all impunity—and, above all, among young people—there should not happen some event capable of causing a rupture, and disuniting their minds,—for these reasons, they hold every year a general assembly at *Onnontae* [Onondaga]. There all the Deputies from the different nations are present, to make their complaints and receive the necessary satisfaction in mutual gifts,—by which they maintain good understanding with one another" (JR, 51: 237).

Writing from Oneida, Father Millet, as incumbent in a chiefly title, described how the Iroquois compounded differences in a series of embassies. Responsibility for rounding up the wampum belts, providing the speakers, and conducting the mission rested with the *agoianders*, the incumbents and trustees of chiefly titles, who usually were senior members of clan segments. There was a public display of wampums, family by family, with appropriate speeches of pride and sympathy. The belts were pooled and entrusted to the delegate. The conduct of the embassy adhered to the paradigm of condolence: woods'-edge, procession of chanters, the speaker coming last, Three Bare Words, a feast with requests for news, a day of rest, and replies. The public danced around the displayed belts; a terminal feast and mutual thanks followed (JR, 58: 185–89).

Factionalism was at home in Iroquois society. The theory of unanimity, or one mind, to the contrary, factionalism operated at every level of the society and between nations of the league. It fed on success and abated only to face a common threat or disaster. The coming of the French missionaries, military victories, and unassimilated captives only exacerbated it (Fenton 1955; Trigger 1985: 274). The Iroquois never resolved the tension between peace chiefs, whose statuses were ascribed within clans, and war leaders, who achieved prestige. It was partly a struggle between kindred and partly the tension obtained between age grades, since the war leaders were allied to the young men, and the peace chiefs often had graduated from their ranks to lay aside the privilege of going on the warpath (Fenton 1955: 335). Following periods of intense warfare, war leaders converted prestige into political power at the expense of peace chiefs. Thus, emergent leaders other than incumbents in the traditional titles of founders came to dominate councils and became, predominately, the "sachems" of historical record.

The Mohawks, as we have seen, were deeply disturbed by the French connection. They warned Father Jogues in 1646 that of the three roads the French might take to visit Iroquoia, the proper route was through the Mohawk Valley, and not via Lake Ontario to Onondaga—as Jogues informed them the French were planning (JR, 29: 57). This was their consistent position after the fact. Internally, of the three clans and named towns composing the Mohawk nation, the Bear clan comprised the war faction, while the Wolf and Turtle moiety would spare captives (JR, 31: 117). Except for brief interludes, for most of the century the war faction prevailed. The other faction felt free to negotiate. However affairs eventuated, the opposing faction could shift or subside (Bacqueville de La Potherie 1722, 2: ch. 17).

Within the league, intense factional strife obtained among the Three Brothers—Mohawk-Onondaga-Seneca—who were the senior moiety. Between Mohawk priority in ritual and Onondaga precedence as firekeepers, tension mounted. Onondagas and Senecas owed a debt for Mohawk firepower in the Huron and Erie campaigns: they could suspend arguments over the trade momentarily. But when in 1656 two Seneca ambassadors returning from Montreal were killed by a Mohawk party, the more numerous Senecas prepared to ravage the Mohawk towns. Composing this affair summoned every ritual device of the league.

A grand council was called to reconcile the Mohawks and Senecas. The Seneca delegation arrived "filling the air with . . . lugubrious chants"; they received a condolence present, and the Cayugas replied in sympathy. But when all the nations assembled, they had first to condole the Onondaga village for a captain who had died the previous night by wiping away the Onondaga tears, restoring speech, and cleansing the council mat of blood. These acts enabled the Onondagas to declare that the council would open after the burial (JR, 43: 101, 167).

The grand council met on 24 July 1656 (JR, 43: 169). Father Chaumonot (Achiendase), having learned their "allegories and metaphors," was asked to mediate and delighted the Iroquois who were present by condoling and requickening the deceased captains. The way was now open for establishing the Onondaga mission (JR, 43: 169–73). Having entered into the kinship system and participated in the annual renewal of reciprocal obligations by exchanging presents, the Jesuits exploited the custom of meeting the night after a funeral to relate stories of ancient times as an occasion to advance the gospel. French activism contrasted with the Dutch claim to have preserved the Iroquois by letting them live in their own fashion (JR, 43: 287, 291).

The Mohawks were a constant source of anxiety to New France. Hoping to get support from home, Jérôme Lalemant in 1660 summarized the condition and character of the Iroquois, particularly the Mohawks. Appealing to the wheel-of-fortune metaphor, he noted that they had been "so many times at the top and bottom of the wheel, within less than sixty years," that history afforded "few examples of similar revolutions. Insolent in disposition, and truly warlike, they have had to fight with all their neighbors." Research on their history was limited to the memory of the old men. "What we learn from these living books is that, toward the end of the last century," the Algonquins had reduced them to the point of extinction. "Nevertheless, this scanty remnant, like the noble germ, so increased in a few years as to reduce the Algonquins in turn to the same condition." Then the Andastes, in a ten years' war, again brought them so low, or humiliated them, "that the mere name Algonkin made them tremble, and his shadow seemed to pursue them to their very firesides" (JR, 45: 203, 207).

It was then thirty years since the Dutch settlers had begun trading for beaver pelts and furnishing the Mohawks with the firearms that enabled them to rout their erstwhile conquerors. "And that is what has rendered them formidable" (JR, 45: 205). Here was the root of Mohawk arrogance: "they think and say that their own destruction cannot occur without bringing in its train the downfall of the whole earth." Lalemant was astonished that with fewer than five hundred men they held dominion for five hundred leagues around. "It is therefore a marvel that so few people work such great havoc and render themselves redoubtable to so large a number of tribes" (JR, 45: 207).

□□◇□□

By 1660, owing to persistent and destructive Iroquois raids, the very existence of New France was threatened. Jesuit writers appealed to France to accomplish the destruction of Iroquoia (JR, 45: 183). Paul Le Jeune, procurator of the mission, addressed Louis XIV: "Sire . . . you are a great King, who while making Europe tremble, ought not to be held in contempt in America" (JR, 46: 199). It took some time for Louis to decide to "plant lillies over the ashes of the Iroquois" (JR, 46: 241), and longer for him to dispatch a famous regiment to accomplish it.

The Iroquois missions varied with the circumstances. Failure in 1658 ended the peace of 1653; but even while Mohawks were attacking Canada, Le Moyne returned to Onondaga to renew the mission to the upper Iroquois. The Mohawks were now at the bottom of their cycle, defeated in the northwest by Great Lakes tribes, decimated by plague, and under Andaste attack (Hunt 1940: 134). But they remained aloof from a peace proposal by the upper nations (NYCD, 3: 121–25).

The Iroquois had finally caught "Le Grand Monarque's" attention. He decreed Canada a crown colony and dispatched the Marquis Prouville de Tracy, a senior but energetic soldier, to be governor of New France. Arriving in 1665 with eleven hundred of the famous Carignan-Salieres regiment, he immediately directed the building of three hundred bateaux, the fabricating of snowshoes and tumplines, and the assembling of stores for an expedition. His first winter foray toward Saratoga failed: the Mohawk warriors eluded him, and food ran out. But in October 1666, de Tracy stove in the Longhouse, burned three well-stocked towns, and retreated in good order while the frightened Mohawks watched from the hills. They sued for peace the following year and laid off attacking Canada for twenty years (JR, 50: 169; NYCD, 3: 125–26; l'Incarnation 1681: 608ff.; Morison 1965: 104–5).

The Mohawks were never the same afterward. Within three years, an emigration of converts to La Prairie (and later Caughnawaga) on the St. Lawrence carried off leading families, including the lineage of the first founder of the confederacy, Tekarihoken. Soon the manpower in the "praying settlements" would outnumber the stay-at-homes. These praying Mohawks became the eyes and ears of French governors, and neither the league nor English governors ever succeeded in repatriating them (JR, 58: 207, 247; NYCD, 9: 79, 84; Winsor 1884–99, 8: 526).

In 1672, Louis de Buade de Frontenac replaced de Tracy as governor of New France. Concerned lest the Ottawas make peace with the Iroquois and carry their furs to Albany, Frontenac, looking to quick profits himself, in June 1673 lined the rapids of the St. Lawrence with his troops, to meet the Iroquois for the first time. The importance they attached to the meeting prompted some four hundred Iroquois to attend, including sixty sachems, warriors, women, and children. They were impressed by the size of the French force, by the military drill, and by the formalities with which Frontenac invested the proceedings. His generosity pleased the women and children. His two bateaux, painted bright blue and red, with mounted cannon, intrigued the native canoemen. Frontenac wined and dined important sachems of the Dutch persuasion. During these preliminaries, workmen cleared a site and erected an enclosure for a trading post that became Fort Frontenac, or simply Cadaraqui (at modern Kingston, Ontario), an entrepôt at which to intercept furs on Lake Ontario.

Knowing no Iroquoian language, Frontenac employed Sieur Le Moyne as interpreter. His imperious address, which advocated Christianity, boasted military superiority, offered merchandise at modest prices, and requested nine children to be educated by the French nuns and taught proper manners and a trade, fell short of his expectations. Assuming the superiority of French kinship usage, he addressed the Iroquois elders as "my children," expecting them to reply, "Father." Father is a relatively weak figure in matrilineal Iroquois society, superseded by mother's brother.

In reply, the Iroquois appeared pleased and remarked that the previous accepted usage between them and French governors was that of "brothers." Next day a speaker for each of the Five Nations answered separately, Garakontie for Onondaga. Frontenac was ill prepared for the "eloquence, shrewdness, and the finesse" with which the several speakers replied. Their demeanor recalled that of members of the Venetian Senate. Nor was he ready to answer sharp questions about the pricing of trade goods. The Iroquois announced that they would discuss the matter of the children after they returned home. They were amenable to a temporary agreement, pending the outcome of war with the Andastes. Frontenac thought he had saved New France by preventing the Iroquois from adhering to the Dutch (NYCD, 9: 95–114; Eccles 1965: 104–6).

For twenty years, until his death in 1677, Garakontie, a Christian convert, led the pro-French faction at Onondaga. When called upon to relate the origin myth of the Iroquois, "he protested that what he was about to say was merely a formula usually followed on such occasions," that the cosmology was only a story (JR, 58: 211). He even refused a dreamer's demand that he give up a decorated bag, his favorite tobacco pouch (JR, 58: 209). The Jesuit priest Jean de Lamberville paid tribute to his passing at Onondaga: "Onne ouagicheia" (Now I am dying) were his last words (JR, 61: 21–29).[5]

While preoccupied with fighting the Andastes to the south and the Mahicans to the east, the Iroquois appeared outwardly docile to the French. Trade expanded to the west from Cadaraqui and Niagara. Illicit smuggling of furs to Albany flourished.

While King Philip's War raged in New England, the Mohawks waited to inflict the coup de grace. As the steam of the war kettles dissipated, in a reversal of form the Senecas grew hostile and the Mohawks quieted. The Andastes were absorbed. With access to either Albany or Fort Frontenac, the Iroquois held the French at a disadvantage (Margry 1876–86, 1: 362; Eccles 1964: 113, 1969: 113).

The Iroquois did not admire French culture. Despite all its glitter, its magnificent architecture, and its awesome military power, some visitors to France, on returning, remarked on the disparity of wealth and the wont of charity. A French observer among the Senecas, however, found Iroquois council protocol remarkable: their restraint in never interrupting a speaker, their praise of a reasoned argument, their coolness in reply, their prodigious memories, and their historical

---

5. Thwaites has this: "See, I am dying" (JR, 61: 27).

sense supported by wampum belts. He noticed their fidelity to friendships and their compulsion to bring home their dead (Margry 1876–86, 1: 343–401, 350, 362). Another observer, the French soldier Baron Lahontan, to the contrary, hated the very sight of them (Lahontan 1905).

The Onondaga council consistently produced diplomats equal and often superior to French and English governors. After Garakontie's passing, Teganissorens and Hotrewati picked up the wampum strings. Two years before Governor La Barre met the Five Nations and faced humiliation at Hungry Bay, Teganissorens called on outgoing Governor Frontenac at Montreal on 11 September 1682 to persuade him that the league had no intention of harming French interests, thereby heading off any countermove. (As he talked, Seneca war parties were raiding the Miamis and Illinois for beaver pelts.) He addressed the governor as "father." As a credential, he stated that he had been requickened in his grandfather's name, Nireguentaron, and as such he spoke on behalf of the "entire house of the Five Nations." Countering the rumor that the Onondagas were sharpening their hatchets, he evidenced a wampum belt as a remedy to relieve suspicion. The French should pay no attention to "evil spirits in diverse cabins" of the league. The "whole house" knew that Onontio (Frontenac) had lighted the council fire, to which all the participants brought sticks. The French should "kick aside" (disregard) wampum belts brought "underground" without league sanction. Teganissorens then referred to the familiar Iroquois concept of the divided personality—a man with two arms and hands, one for peace, the other for war—to explain factionalism within the Longhouse. To counter it, he claimed to have run through the whole house to persuade them not to undertake anything without Onontio's word. The intent was to neutralize the French while the Iroquois destroyed the Illinois, as Teganissorens informed the incoming governor the next year (NYCD, 9: 183–85; Eccles in DCB, 2: 620; French National Archives, AN C 11 A, 6, folio 15c).

Frontenac's reply the next day reveals how thoroughly Longhouse metaphors had permeated French colonial thought. Adhering to his "father" role, Frontenac appealed to the "whole house," alluded to the "invitation belt" as a cable, and honored Indian protocol by returning belts and presents. He spoke of "cleaning the hearth" of confused issues. He noticed that the Senecas, who had not showed at Fort Frontenac, had gone off hunting "at the first running of the sap." Their absence raised an issue of protocol, namely, the rule that once a council fire was kindled at a designated place (Fort Frontenac), it could not be kindled elsewhere without a demonstrable reason that it was extinguished at the first site. Onondaga and Seneca opinion was divided as to where the fire was situated—whether at Oswego or at Cadaraqui. Asserting European supremacy, Frontenac insisted on the prerogative of the "father," not the "children," to designate the place. He was not reassured at the situation in Illinois (AN C 11 A, 6: folio 17c; NYCD, 9: 185–89).

Whatever Frontenac's success in Indian affairs, his conduct of civil affairs displeased the Ministry of Marine at home, to whose minister the governors of New France reported, and he was recalled. Le Febre de La Barre, with Meulles as intendant, succeeded him in 1683, to find affairs in disarray. Fearing that the Iroquois, after polishing off the Illinois, would turn on New France, Meulles addressed the king: "The Iroquois are the only people on earth who do not know the grandeur of your Majesty" (quoted in Parkman 1889: 87).

□□◇□□

The fact of the Iroquois League enabled the old men of Onondaga to play a duplicitous game in the summer of 1684, after Seneca war parties that spring laid siege to Fort St. Louis in the Illinois country. While preparing to outwit the new French governor, they protected their flanks by treating with English governors in Albany. La Barre labored under the misapprehension that the English were promoting Iroquois aggression in the west in order to break the French stranglehold on the fur trade. But the Dutch Albany merchants remained indifferent so long as furs came to them. Consistently the Iroquois tried to divide French allies, treating with one tribe while isolating and attacking another. Urged on by notables in the colony who feared that this process would bring down New France, La Barre resolved to invade Iroquoia and extinguish the western fires of the Longhouse, where manpower was concentrated.[6] His motley army of *troupes de la marine*, militia, and Indians reached "Hungry Bay," La Famine, near Oswego and promptly fell victim to Spanish influenza and extended supply lines.

When Iroquois scouts discovered La Barre's fever-ridden camp, he had no alternative but to accept Iroquois terms as dictated by Hotrewati, the Onondaga orator, in fifteen scornful "words."[7] Satisfied with humiliating the French governor, the Iroquois let the remnants of his army escape downriver to Montreal. La Barre's reports, when they reached Paris, surely did not appeal to the grandeur of His Majesty, who recalled La Barre in disgrace and replaced him with Denonville.[8]

Lahontan, an eyewitness, described the encounter between the Onondaga orator and the proud· governor with candor and no little satire. His "Grangula" (Hotrewati) emerges as a cool cat who sat across the fire concentrating on the end of his pipe as the governor delivered false threats. Once on his feet and in command of the council, he drew fifteen words in reply from the traditional bag of Iroquois treaty speech. The abstracted symbolic metaphors scarcely do justice to Lahontan's oft-quoted account (Lahontan 1905: 79–85; Colden 1750: 71).

First, Hotrewati administered a medicine to alleviate hardship; second, he took the hatchet out of the hands of the "father" lest he strike his "son," the Senecas; third and fourth, he cast animosities into a pit and planted a Tree of Peace; fifth, he asked the father to sustain it; and sixth, he reattached the sun, a symbol of peace affirmed. Subsequent words were the following: (7) the grievance with the Senecas, balanced by mutual losses, did not justify war; (8) the sight of soldiers disquieted the sleep of his children; (9) he would move the fire of peace to Onondaga from Cataraqui, where "grasshoppers prevent his sleeping" and which was too distant for the old men; (10) a belt affirmed that warriors and elders embraced the peace; (11) they agreed not to war against the Miamis; (12) although Iroquois were killed,

6. For the background to, and denouement of, these events, see Eccles 1969: 114ff.

7. Lahontan (1905), an eyewitness to the event, wrote a spritely satire of his countryman, highly favorable to the Iroquois. Cadwallader Colden (1750: 71), who read Lahontan, remarked that this expedition "ended in a Scold between the French General and an old Indian."

8. On receiving the reports, the minister, de Seignelay, endorsed them as "secret" until some decision was reached for the future (AN 11 A, vol. 6, folio 299ff., printed in DHNY, 1: 117–20; NYCD, 9: 236–39.)

their hands were tied; (13) he acknowledged they were at war with the Illinois; and (14) they agreed that the French could restore withdrawn missionaries. Finally, he asked the governor to restrain the Christians of Sault St. Louis from "drawing our people to Montreal and dismembering our nation."[9] In short, the speech, at once satire, ritual sanction, and business, shoved the bateaux of La Barre's sick soldiers off downriver to Montreal.

The minister next turned to the Marquis de Denonville, one of France's ablest military men, who arrived as governor of New France the summer after the disaster at La Famine. Instructed to humiliate the Iroquois and establish a firm policy for their control, Denonville immediately began a year of preparing to smash the western end of the Longhouse by invading the Seneca country, where Iroquois manpower predominated. The English threatened the colony with a giant pincers from Hudson Bay to Albany, with the Iroquois at the hinge. If French diplomacy failed either to purchase the New York colony from James II or to neutralize its governance, the obvious military solution was to hit the Longhouse at both ends. But this would not prove easy.

New York's ablest governor, Thomas Dongan, sought to strengthen the Iroquois League, and he encouraged Albany fur merchants to dispatch experienced voyageurs to the Far Indians and entice them home to trade. Jesuit missionaries in Iroquois towns kept Denonville apprised of Dongan's schemes. They had an ear in the Onondaga council when the league met in general session in June 1687 to discuss the threat (Livingston 1956: 115). Denonville countered by intercepting two Albany trading parties, capturing and jailing participants, and sending them home to warn other adventurers (Eccles 1959: 173–81; 1969: 119).

Having protected his flank on the upper Great Lakes, Denonville risked the hazards of travel and transport to Lake Ontario and kept his campaign to the Seneca country beyond Dongan's reach. Some 400 mission Indians, including native Iroquois, having sung their war songs and feasted on dog flesh, guided his army of 930 Canadian militia and 832 *troupes de la marine*, who were joined at the last minute by 800 regulars, including Chevalier Vaudreuil to command the marines. Had reinforcements arrived earlier, Denonville might have resorted to the original plan of striking the Mohawks and Oneidas as well. But his guides surely would have tipped off their kinsmen.

Advance scouts rounded up scattered Iroquois en route and captured a troublesome Cayuga chief and his followers, settled north of the lake since the Andaste war. Denonville promptly dispatched the men to hard labor on the Mediterranean prison galleys. The Iroquois regarded this as an act of treachery, and the few survivors who later returned had bitter memories of "civilization."

After retrieving Father Lamberville, the erstwhile missionary at Onondaga, returning him to Cataraqui, and reassuring his Onondaga escorts that their nation was not threatened, Denonville's army embarked for Irondequoit to rendezvous

9. The printed version of La Barre's memorandum of 1 October 1684 (NYCD, 9: 239–43) garbles Iroquois personal names from the original manuscript. Eccles regards Lahontan as untrustworthy, but Lahontan conveys the reality of the situation and the spirit of Onondaga oratory. Colden (1727: 72–90) quoted Lahontan but perceived the event from an Albany perspective through the Indian Records. On the participants, see DCB, 1: 442–47, 2: 439–45; Desrosiers 1957; Eccles 1959: 157–72.

with forces from the upper lakes. These were mainly Ottawas and allies under French leadership.

The details of the military engagement with the Senecas are well known and less important than the political consequences. After an ambush failed to rout the French forces, the Seneca warriors withdrew, deserted their towns, and took to the woods, sending women and children to Cayuga. The invading army spent nine days ransacking and burning four villages, destroying every means of subsistence standing and in storage. Besides dogs, they found a few domesticated pigs, later a favorite feast food. A bitter winter of starvation followed.

The Senecas never rebuilt their large towns but fragmented into smaller settlements on Canandaigua and Seneca lakes and along the Genesee River. The eight Seneca founders of the league were by now a ritual memory, and although the offices persisted and incumbents were installed, the new town councils answered to emergent leaders. In less than twenty years, French-led armies had broken the Longhouse at both ends. Both the Iroquois and the English were in shock. They had failed to break the French monopoly of the western fur trade (Fenton 1940; Eccles 1959, 1969: 119). In desperation, the Iroquois responded with all-out war.

CHAPTER 18

FROM TOTAL WAR TO THE
GRAND SETTLEMENT, 1688–1701

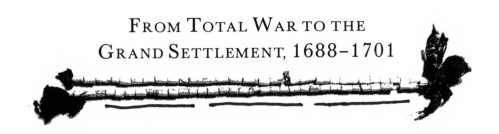

The Iroquois response to Denonville was total war (Eccles 1964: 186ff.). With short intermissions, the war lasted for almost thirteen years and exhausted both sides. It nearly brought down the French colony, it severely depleted Iroquois manpower, and it left the league in disarray. Although the French had smashed the Longhouse at both ends, laid waste to villages, and destroyed crops and food storage, Iroquois warriors took to the woods and survived to retaliate by raiding outlying settlements and rendering it impossible for French inhabitants to farm. To be certain, loss of housing and means of subsistence in Iroquoia sent the homeless and starving victims to the charity of interior neighbors—the Mohawks to Oneida, the Senecas to Cayuga and Onondaga—so that everyone shared the hardships. Similarly, French farmers sought refuge within the walls of Montreal, Three Rivers, and Quebec.

The colony was virtually defenseless against raiding parties that attacked outlying settlements, cut down farmers in the fields, burned buildings, and carried off prisoners to be tortured (Eccles 1964: 187). Few Frenchmen were adopted. Denonville estimated that one hundred Iroquois could lay waste to all the settlements above Three Rivers. Meanwhile, French ships brought measles and smallpox to Quebec, which decimated the mission Indians, including captive Iroquois women and children who had been placed there. Nearly 13 percent of the colony (then eleven thousand) died—some fourteen hundred troops and inhabitants (Eccles 1964: 188). The raiders were not immune. What, then, motivated the Iroquois?

□□◇□□

The roots of Iroquois warfare extend deep into their culture. The persistent theme of requickening the living in the name of the dead flows through these roots as the sap of society and nourishes a concern for ongoing generations. This theme manifests itself in mourning customs which require that clearminded clan segments condole the depressed mourners, lift up their grieving minds, and restore them to ongoing society. It attains its climax form in the fulfillment of condolence law by celebrating the Condolence Council for mourning dead chiefs and raising up their successors in office to ensure continuity of government. It prefaced treaties, and, far more than economics, it motivated the so-called mourning war that prompted matrons to commission the offspring of their father's kin to form war parties and return captives—preferable to scalps—to replace lost kindred (Lafitau 1724, 2: 163; Fenton and Moore 1977: 99; Richter 1983). The mourning-war pattern persisted and underwent changes during the seventeenth and early eighteenth centuries.

"War is a necessary exercise for the Iroquois," wrote Father Joseph-François Lafitau, a perceptive Jesuit scholar, "for . . . it is indispensible to them also because of one of their fundamental laws of being" (Lafitau 1724, 2: 162–63; Fenton and Moore 1977: 98–99.) It was fundamental for two reasons: first, it was the threshold to manhood, the validation of status, and a prerequisite to chiefship, and second, by returning prisoners for adoption and replacement of losses, it sustained or increased the population. Warfare was embedded in mythology, it drew strength from the sun, and it enjoyed the sanction of ritual.

War sometimes resulted from policy that the old men debated and resolved in council (Lafitau 1724, 2: 171), and sometimes from vendettas in which ambitious young men achieved glory, going on the warpath without council sanction. In both cases, the activities of raising a war party, hanging the kettle, setting out, conducting the campaign, taking scalps and prisoners, and returning fulfilled ritual patterns in a sequence that made a ceremony, if not a game, of warfare and locked the participants in a career from which the exits were capture, torture, and death or graduation to the status of old men, the ancients (Fenton 1978a: 315; Richter 1983: 530).

The French learned that Iroquois war parties set out when the leaves were on the trees for concealment, and that they seldom stayed afield in late autumn after the woods were open (Eccles 1964: 162).

Richter (1983: 533) has abstracted from contemporary sources the ritual acts that greeted the return of a war party, which adhered to a sequence from death cry and the gauntlet to torture or adoption. Early observations of ritual cannibalism, which apparently had religious significance, were too shocking to arouse the intellectual curiosity of Europeans !Abler 1980; Richter 1983: 534).

Precombat rituals stressed the importance of human life and the denial of death that the Iroquois regarded as essential to the continuity of society. In practice, the phenomenon assumed two aspects: first, war parties were charged with bringing back prisoners as replacements, and second, leaders must guard against losing the lives of members of the war party. These were strong sanctions (Richter 1983: 535).

The mourning war served as an effective strategy up until 1675, when losses in battle and from periodic epidemics no longer could be replaced by adopting captives (Richter 1983: 537–43). Mohawk population fell by half. Factionalism between traditionalists and converts to Christianity precipitated outmigration to the St. Lawrence mission settlements. Those who went included many adopted Hurons, not completely assimilated to Iroquois ways, but also Iroquois ritualists and office holders. Culture losses were irreparable. Indeed, the mourning war was crumbling.

Iroquois countermeasures to French raids were immediate but less effective toward the end of the century. They reached their peak of success when fifteen hundred warriors sacked Lachine in 1689, two years after Denonville's destruction of four Seneca towns, quite nullifying any French pride. In November of the previous year the Iroquois had laid siege to Cataraqui, the pride of Frontenac, burning its buildings with flaming arrows. Subsequent French expeditions against Schenectady in 1690, against Mohawk towns in 1693, and against Onondaga three years later created a domino effect on neighboring nations. But in each case, pursuing war parties took a toll on returning invaders burdened with captives, short of provisions, and worn down by travel and weather. Returning French armies reached Montreal exhausted and starving (Eccles 1964: passim). By the late 1690s, Iroquois losses had mounted so that warfare was no longer cost effective (Eccles 1964: 267).

During this period, the old men of individual nations, often in the name of the whole house, approached both Montreal and Albany with peace feelers. It was a way of buying time to recoup from a disaster; it was also a means of eliciting support—provisions and munitions—and these missions served to balance and offset the two European powers. Several of these emissaries carried league titles in their respective nations, which indicates the seriousness of such missions and the fact that they represented the facade of the league. Two of three sachems in Albany to report on Denonville's invasion of the Seneca country, though listed as Senecas, bore league titles (NYCD, 3: 444): "Adondaraheera" (Hadonda:he:haʔ, C-9, RC 41), "chief sachem of the Seneca," and "Unedachseno" (Honeʔsa:henʔ, Oa-2, RC 20). The third, "Awitharoa," I cannot identify. He may have been a Seneca, as was a youth of fifteen who fought in the engagement.

During the ensuing spring, Governor Dongan of New York failed to prevent Father Lamberville from persuading the Onondaga, Cayuga, and Oneida councils not to send a delegation with prisoners to Montreal to treat for peace with Denonville. Dongan had insisted that they were subjects of the English crown and could not treat without his permission. Denonville cleverly inquired whether, if this were so, they could negotiate a treaty. This query prompted their speaker, Hotrewati, to declare "that they acknowledged no one as their master; they had received their lands from the Great Spirit and had never been defeated in war by either the English or the French" (AN C11A, 10: folio 48ff.; NYCD, 9: 384–86; Grassman in DCB, 1: 525–26; Eccles 1964: 189–90). Hotrewati, who had appeared in previous negotiations as the Onondaga speaker, was the same "La Grande Gueule" (Big Mouth) who four years earlier had humiliated the previous governor at Hungry Bay. He proceeded to supervise the signatures to the declaration of neutrality. The delegation, he said, would try to get the Senecas and Mohawks to join in the agreement. He insisted that the Cayuga people whom Denonville had sent to the Mediterranean galleys be returned. The agreement did not settle the issue of the western trade. For the Iroquois it was an arrangement of convenience.

The signatures reveal to an Iroquoianist that the delegation included holders of league titles. The orthographies reflect mishearings by the original scribe, further corrupted by printers. From the listing, I recognize the first four names on the Oneida roster of league chiefs: Odatshehdeh (Oe-1, RC 10), "Onakouen[y]oton" (Kanongweniyah, Oe-2, RC 11), "Tiohakwente" (Deyohagwendeh, Oe-3, RC 12), and "Tanonchies," possibly Shononhse:s (Oe-4, RC 13). There is a further Wolf clan chief, "Sagoyenthon," unrecognizable. The Onondaga roster comprises possibly seven names, including that of Garakontie, not a league title and evidently successor to the prominent figure of that name who died in 1677. None of the others is recognizable. The Cayuga roster of five names, however, includes clearly two league titles, "Tiotorekwoui [tiotoreki in ms.]" (Deyoto:wehkwi, C-7, RC 39) and "Tonnoneheiouta" (possibly Teyonhwe:ton) (C-8, RC 40). Could "Tegajami

[Tegaiasni in ms.]" be intended for the leading Cayuga chief, Haga?en:yonk (RC 33)? "Oskonnonton" is clearly a variant for "Deer"; it is not a league title. And "Orehouae" defies recognition. The presence in the delegation of several league chiefs says two things: it was an important meeting to which they sent prestigious leaders, and some semblance of the league was in being.

□□◇□□

Despite these and subsequent negotiations, the position of the Iroquois Confederacy, caught between French and English pressures, steadily deteriorated as the seventeenth century came to a close. The Iroquois were losing more warriors in raids on French settlements than they could replace. They suffered severe losses in the west to an Ojibwa-led offensive that drove them from hunting grounds in ancient Huronia, and raiders reached Seneca settlements (Eid 1979). Starvation stalked Iroquoia following losses of housing and crops. Population declined by half. The Treaty of Ryswick that brought peace to Europe settled nothing in America (Eccles 1964: 268; Richter 1983: 550). Indeed, events in America, though abundantly reported, were seldom understood at either Whitehall or Versailles.

The French in America enjoyed some advantages over the English from the start. Although they were soon greatly outnumbered, one French trait that gained them entrée to Indian society was their willingness to learn and adopt Indian ways. From Champlain's day forward, the birchbark canoe, the tumpline, moccasins in summer, and snowshoes and toboggans in winter proved superior to French bateaux and analogous gear for transport on water and in the woods. The canoe enabled the French to explore the waterways of the continent during the seventeenth century, and voyageurs who learned paddling and poling techniques from Indians followed Indian routes established for trade and warfare. Native-born Canadians equaled Huron and Ottawa canoemen in skill and exceeded the Iroquois, who were essentially landsmen, in running rapids and portaging. The French also learned the native languages both for practical purposes and for religious conversion.

This willingness on the part of the French to adapt to native ways gave them an edge in trade and warfare over the English, who adhered stubbornly to English ways. It is not surprising that the Canadian militia who had learned the arts of woodland warfare from native Indians bore the brunt of the fighting when troops of famous French regiments bogged down or panicked (Wade 1988). The conduct of Indian affairs by courtly governors was not as adept.

Denonville had a plan to take Albany, but before he could bring it off, Frontenac returned as governor in 1689 with instructions to carry it out (Eccles 1964: 199, 201). But the Lachine massacre that August, before Frontenac landed, changed everything. Louis XIV and the Minister of Marine misunderstood the situation, Denonville was unlucky, and the war lasted another ten years (Eccles 1964: 192–5). Frontenac's imperious conduct was unsuited to forest diplomacy, and he misread the military situation. Instead of hitting Albany, the source of Mohawk guns and weaponry, while it was defenseless and in a dither politically over the revolution in England, Frontenac directed a series of border raids on scattered targets in New York and New England. The French raid on Schenectady in January 1690, while a disaster to the inhabitants, fell short of Albany. Mohawk pursuit recovered nineteen captives near Montreal, negating any French triumph (Eccles 1964: 224–25).

Frontenac was clearly wrong. Bochart de Champigny, the intendant, had better strategic sense and urged combining the French forces into a single striking force, avoiding raids on small settlements, and attacking Albany. Such an effort would humble the Iroquois, who depended on Albany for supplies (Eccles 1964: 228).

Meanwhile, in the New York colony, Dongan was recalled in April 1688, and Edmund Andros replaced him in August. Both men were strong governors who strove to harness the Five Nations to the British interest. Albany was the place where the Five Nations did business with the English; Onondaga, the main fire, was where the Five Nations made policy. The device of separating into interior and exterior councils was widespread in American Indian politics. Massachusetts officials particularly resented this, as did Pennsylvania, Maryland, and Virginia—they had to go to Albany if they wished to treat with the Iroquois. Albany merchants, who were primarily Dutchmen, monopolized the fur trade and jealously guarded the right to deal exclusively with native peoples eastward, northward, and westward. These men comprised the commissioners of Indian affairs. What we now recognize as tension between upstate and downstate began early between Albany merchants and crown officials in Manhattan.

Communication between Albany and Onondaga was, then, of crucial importance, and the Onondaga firekeepers made certain that the mayor and principals at Albany were informed. In December 1689, the Onondaga firekeepers and the Oneida sachems sent a messenger with seven hands of wampum from each nation to alert the "Albanians" that the grand council would meet to hear the report of two Cayugas who had been carried off to the galleys. Also, a praying Indian from Caughnawaga would deliver a message from the French governor. There are two accounts of this meeting with different dates, both based on the same source, the Indian Records (Colden 1750:105–13; Wraxall 1915:14–16). The minutes tell how the grand council conducted its business. They also reveal how parties linked in the covenant chain kept each other informed.

The same messenger brought sealed letters addressed to the Jesuit missionary Millet at Oneida, "for the eyes only" (of whom is not clear) and not to be opened until Albanians had seen them.

None of the Albany commissioners saw fit to attend the grand council, but they charged and sent three Indians to convey their views and dissuade the Five Nations from considering a cessation of hostilities.

On the fourth of January 1690, a principal Mohawk sachem came to Albany to inform the magistrates that he had been appointed a delegate to attend the grand council and asked advice. The Albany authorities decided to send the public interpreter, Arnout Viele, and one Saunders, together with two Indians, but no person of consequence carried written instructions conveying their views. This gesture by the Albany stay-at-homes manifested their indifference toward the grand council and was bound to weaken the covenant chain.

En route, the interpreter stopped at Oneida, as protocol demanded, where he discoursed privately with one of the returnees from the Mediterranean and learned that he had no love for the French. He had been impressed by the grandeur of the court and by the French armies, but he resented being badly used. This returnee had been sent to Oneida to enlist the aid of Father Millet, himself an Oneida title holder, in the forthcoming negotiations at Onondaga.

We are indebted to Colden (1750: 106ff.) for the proceedings of this council of the Five Nations, which illustrates "in what Manner a People that we call Savages behave on such occasions."

Eighty sachems had assembled at Onondaga. On 22 January, the Onondaga speaker, Sadekanacktie, stood and opened the council. He addressed the messenger from Albany: he announced that four messengers had come, sent by the governor of Canada, three of whom had been prisoners in France; the fourth sachem was from Caughnawaga. By them Frontenac announced that he had returned as governor and had brought back a Cayuga sachem, Tawerahet, and twelve prisoners. Then, taking up a wampum belt and holding it by the middle, the speaker added that what he had said so far related to only half of the belt. The other half was notice that Frontenac intended to rebuild Cadaraqui and rekindle his fire there the next spring. He invited "his Children," particularly Teganissorens, the Onondaga orator (Eccles in DCB, 2: 619–23), to treat there about the old covenant chain.

Then the sachem of the praying Indians, Adarahta, stood and, with three wampum belts in hand, advised the assembly to meet the governor as specified, if they desired to live. He gave one belt.

Continuing, he gave a second belt sent by Cayuga sachem Tawerahet, which informed of the "Miseries" experienced by their countrymen in captivity and advised them to "hearken to *Yonondio*, if you desire to live."

The third belt conveyed the advice of Father Lamberville and two named Frenchmen to adhere to the governor's invitation.[1]

Next, the Mohawk messenger sent from Albany delivered his message as instructed. It consisted of six articles, omitting nothing. While he spoke, the interpreter followed the written copy of the message, lest the speaker skip anything. Apparently it was preferable to employ a native speaker and leave the interpreter to follow written copy and prompt in the manner of Iroquois principals.

A Seneca sachem, Canehoot (Tekanoet, DCB, 1: 623–24), then presented a detailed report on a treaty concluded the previous summer with a band of Ottawas, on behalf of seven other bands, and requested the other four Iroquois nations to confirm it and include their New York brethren. Three Ottawas were present to confirm details. Ten propositions were attested by belts, a catlinite sun disk, a calumet with catlinite pipe, and so forth. These "Far Indians" wanted to see New York, "the Place where Wampum is made." And they promised to bring prisoners "when the Strawberries blossom."

The Seneca speaker having finished, the Ottawa presents were hung up in the council house. They were later distributed among the Five Nations. Their acceptance ratified the treaty. The Albany delegation received a large belt as its share. The Albany belt was similarly displayed before being divided.

1. Colden (1750: 107) gives the Indian names and their English meanings in a footnote. A report in French that reached London (PRO CO/1038) interprets the three belts shown at this council somewhat differently: the first featured five black squares on a white background, symbolizing accord on the intended embassy; it expressed fear that the Iroquois, or "Rotinonchioni," were about to perish; and it was intended for the use of Teganissorens, their speaker. The second belt was nearly all black and was intended to overset the war kettle of Onontio, "if he doesn't do it himself." The third belt, longest of all, was to be carried across the sea for the eyes of the kings of France and England to reach an accord and report.

New England was represented by a model of a fish, after the cod weathervane on the Boston state house, symbolizing Massachusets' adherence to the covenant. It was handed around, touched by sachems, and then displayed.

With the ritual business concluded, the Onondaga speaker, Sadekanacktie, who had opened the council (uncovered the fire), now concluded that they must govern themselves by the propositions emanating from Albany. Whether he was of the pro-English faction at Onondaga or was stating the sense of the meeting is unclear.

The speaker for the council then addressed himself to the interpreter and asked him to lay before the sachems the instructions he had brought from Albany, which he did. The sachems then consulted together, and the speaker, on behalf of the whole, announced the decision.

The speaker addressed Frontenac's deputies. The Five Nations were determined to preserve their alliance with Albany, they would not go to Cataraqui, there would be no peace, but they would take up the ax (resume the war). He informed them that they had made peace with the Ottawas (Wraxall 1915: 15–16). They encouraged Massachusets to strike at Quebec. The speaker raked up the fire and the council dispersed. Two sachems were sent to Albany to inform the authorities of its resolutions.

Father Millet sat in this council as the leading Oneida sachem, Odatshehdeh. (A second holder of this title led a delegation the previous year, as already noted.) As a double agent, he prevented the junior moiety of nations—Oneida and Cayuga—from endorsing the war belt sent to Albany. It carried only the axes of the three senior nations—Mohawk, Onondaga, and Seneca (Colden 1750: 112). Simultaneously, he maintained relations with Peter Schuyler, an Indian commissioner in Albany, and Godfrey Dellius, pastor of Fort Orange. I find no report of his council activities (JR, 64: 67ff.; DCB, 2: 473–74).

□□◇□□

The American assault on Quebec by Phips and the Massachusetts fleet makes fascinating reading, although it failed; and Frontenac was lucky in mobilizing troops at the right moment (Eccles 1964: 230ff.). Frontenac's efforts to reopen negotiations with the Iroquois were less successful. In 1690 he sent an emissary to Onondaga with an escort. The Onondagas burned the escort and the interpreter, then ran the emissary, the Chevalier Dau, through the gauntlet and sent him to Albany to languish in prison for two years before he escaped.

There were times when Montreal or Quebec might have fallen had the invading Albanians or the Iroquois come at the right moment. Albany, too, might have succumbed to an organized French effort, but supplying the Mohawks and maintaining the contraband trade with Canada granted it a certain immunity. Neither side could win.

In the two years following the diplomatic defeat by the Onondaga council and then Phips's attack, Frontenac, unable to see the larger strategic picture, turned to the "little war." The Iroquois, whom Eccles held were at this time at the crest of their power (1964: 230)—when they were in fact on the brink of a downslide—were, after Lachine, incapable of mounting a major offensive. Both sides engaged in minor successes and suffered local disasters. The Canadian militia was now hardened to guerrilla warfare in the woods, and Iroquois war parties found it less profitable to contest them.

In the autumn of 1691, after Iroquois war parties had retired for the season, Frontenac mustered a force of some five hundred regulars, militia, and mission guides to invade the Mohawk country but then decided it was already too late. No better off a year later, a similar force left Montreal in January on snowshoes, dragging their gear on toboggans. In February they reached two small Mohawk settlements, found most of the men off hunting, encountered no resistance, took villagers captive, and burned houses and stores. This was the second time Mohawk towns had been smashed. Caughnawaga guides flatly refused to kill Mohawk men, their kindred. Three Mohawks escaped, made it to Albany, and warned the authorities. Within four days, 290 Mohawk warriors and 250 Dutch and English militia hit the trail of the retreating invaders, who were slowed by captives and short of provisions. Schuyler's reprovisioned forces harried them to the gates of Montreal, but the Mohawks refused to attack lest they harm their women and children. Most of the Mohawk prisoners escaped or were released (NYCD, 4: 16-19, 9: 550ff.; Eccles 1964: 253, 1969: 122-24).

Even before their villages were destroyed, the Mohawks were impoverished, and the Oneidas were no better off. The previous June, Mohawk sachem Rode had castigated the English for not maintaining alliance obligations, for not mobilizing neighboring colonies against the French, and for "taking their arm out of the Chain" (NYCD, 3: 843). An Oneida speaker complained that Christians failed to condole the Mohawk dead, although the Mohawks had promptly condoled the dead of Christians; that the price of powder was high; and that there was no market for beaver pelts (NYCD, 3: 843). Governor Fletcher's response to these allegations belongs to a later chapter.

There was strong peace sentiment among Oneida families influenced by Father Millet. The upper Iroquois remained hostile. Tareha, an Oneida ambassador, managed to avoid French war parties and make several visits to Quebec in the summer of 1693. The Oneidas alone fulfilled Frontenac's demand that the several nations come treat separately. Tareha, with a belt, proposed that if the French sent authorized persons to negotiate with the Five Nations and the English, then the Five Nations would conduct them safely to Albany for a tripartite peace treaty. Frontenac apparently lost his cool and terminated the talks with a threat (NYCD, 9: 572; Eccles 1964: 257). The English had been working on the Onondaga council. Louis Hector de Callière, the governor of Montreal, perceived that the peace overture was merely a way of frustrating the French and holding up the invasion of Onondaga, which he advocated, while the Onondagas diverted furs to Albany and drew former French allies to trade there.

While buying time, the Iroquois sent ambassadors to the Hurons and Ottawas to treat for peace, to get relief from persistent attacks, and to alienate them from their French alliance while the Iroquois themselves concentrated on the French. The Iroquois ambassadors told the Hurons and Ottawas that they had already made peace with the French, something the French had assured their allies would never happen without native participation. The Iroquois ambassadors had arrived at Michilimackinac just in time to intercept a war party of eight hundred Ottawas ready to set out for Iroquoia. All the French commandant there could do was to send a delegation to Montreal to verify Frontenac's intentions. It found the Iroquois bringing in some French prisoners and interpreted it as proof that Frontenac was double-dealing with the Ottawas and the Iroquois (Eccles 1964: 259–60).

The Iroquois had clearly maneuvered Frontenac into thinking they wanted peace, while Callière and the intendant, Champigny, remained dubious, and at home Louis XIV perceived his royal governor outwitted. He ordered Frontenac to get off the defensive (Eccles 1964: 260–61). Callière had advised the minister that Frontenac's military policy of *petite guerre*, though it achieved minor successes, was costly in men and materiel. Moreover, to totally destroy the Five Nations would be a disaster for New France; their presence in moderate strength assured the economic and political security of the colony. They should be reduced to the point where they could no longer attack New France, but they must remain strong enough so that the Ottawas would continue to fear them and be hindered from going to Albany to trade for cheaper English merchandise (Eccles 1964: 190). Paradoxically, the English wanted the Iroquois kept strong as a barrier between themselves and the French.

Callière was right. In 1695, having overset the Ottawa war kettles, the Iroquois kept their peace emissaries at home and let their warriors slip through their fingers against New France. The renewed attacks, combined with the defection of former allies, moved Frontenac to listen to his subordinates and act on the minister's orders. He began preparations that winter for an assault on Onondaga (Eccles 1964: 263–64).

The Iroquois western alliance, however, soon fell apart. Iroquois hunters had spent the winter hunting with Ottawas. Residual enmity between the two peoples ran strong, and when the Iroquois pushed off their canoes, an Ottawa war party, unable to resist bashing old enemies, passed them in the night and ambushed the returning Iroquois hunters, killing fifty-one and taking twenty-two captive. That ended the alliance, although the Ottawas still held out from joining the French campaign against Onondaga (Eccles 1964: 265).

I shall leave the details of Frontenac's final foray against the Iroquois in 1696 to military historians. Those details are well known. On the approach of his force, the Onondagas set fire to their palisade and flammable bark houses and faded into the forest. The Onondaga citadel was triple palisaded, an oblong flanked by four bastions. "The two rows of stockades that touched each other were of the thickness of an ordinary mast, and outside, at a distance of six feet, stood another row of much smaller dimensions, but between forty and fifty feet in height" (NYCD, 9: 653). In fleeing, the inhabitants deprived the French troops of the glory of a siege, for which they had brought tools and familiar skills. Instead, the troops spent three days cutting standing corn and destroying stores. A detachment under Vaudreuil was dispatched to lay waste the settlement of the "Standing Stone." Oneida deputies met them in a cornfield and pleaded with them, to no avail, to spare crops and habitations.

□□◇□□

As the century closed, French forces had stomped on every fire of the Longhouse save Cayuga. The Iroquois were destitute. The Mohawks had very little corn, Oneida and Onondaga were destroyed, and the writer of the report in the New York colonial documents wondered whether the Senecas would recall that in 1687 the Onondagas had demanded their most valuable wampum belts in return for supplies. It was doubtful that the Cayugas could sustain their neighbors (NYCD, 9: 655–57).

Peace negotiations would consume another three years. France and England came to terms in 1697. Frontenac, who had made the Onondaga campaign in a litter, died. Callière, more adept at forest diplomacy, succeeded him as governor. Eccles, Frontenac's biographer and Canada's foremost colonial historian, on whom this chapter depends so heavily, recapitulates the old count's failures and estimates his true worth (1964: 270–71). His raids of 1690 succeeded only in uniting the British colonies. He never understood Iroquois strategy, which gave the Iroquois the advantage up until 1696. He should have and could have destroyed Albany, which the English feared, but instead scattered his attacks; the destruction of the Iroquois base at Albany would have thrown them on French mercy. Worst of all, he greatly underestimated Iroquois intelligence. They easily deceived him by flattery.

The imperious old count, steeped in the tradition of the French court, failed to perceive the interests of his Indian allies, who often mistook his acts for duplicity. The consequence was that "whenever the Iroquois were in danger of losing their military ascendancy they quickly and effectively waged a diplomatic offensive to split the French from their allies and bring about a cessation of hostilities, during which time they were able to recoup their strength for a fresh onslaught" (Eccles 1964: 271). Frontenac had to be pushed by his subordinates and by royal orders into undertaking the Onondaga campaign that finally brought the Iroquois to plead for peace. Callière, Vaudreuil, and Champigny, who, with the Canadian militia, deserve the credit for the Iroquois defeat, became the principals in carrying out the final settlement.

With Frontenac's passing, imperial *police* ended. The interests of indigenous Canadians were rising. Civilization had barely come to terms with savagism, and the old men of Onondaga had to rethink their own future. For most of the century the Five Nations had maintained an alternate fire on the Hudson, first at Fort Orange and then within the stockade of Albany. The covenant chain was the metaphor of this alliance, and we should examine this accommodation before turning to the "Grand Settlement" that ushered in the eighteenth century.

CHAPTER 19

ACCOMMODATION
BY TRADE AND TREATY

Trade and Peace we take to be one thing.—Peter Wraxall, *An Abridgement of the Indian Affairs*

From early in the seventeenth century, the Dutch and the Mohawks were linked in a chain of mutual dependency. Traders followed in the wake of Henry Hudson's voyage up the North River to the head of tidewater at modern Troy, New York. They found the River Indians, or Mahicans, prepared to offer maize and the kinds of furs Europeans wanted, and the Indians in turn were eager to acquire European beads and metal tools. Evidently, trade was no new thing. One Jacob Eelckens established a post near the mouth of the Normanskill in 1613 (Richter 1982), but whether any Mohawks followed that stream to the Hudson that early is unknown. They surely learned about such traders, but they made no formal treaty with any Dutch parties for another thirty years.[1]

Algonquian-speaking Mahicans occupied the east bank of the Hudson River from its confluence with the Hoosick River southward, and related groups held the west bank from present-day Catskill downriver indefinitely, merging into bands of the Leni-Lenape, or Delaware, people. The Iroquoian-speaking Mohawks did not yet reach eastward of Schenectady and the Schoharie Valley but extended northward toward Saratoga.

The two language families were unrelated and mutually unintelligible. Inasmuch as neighboring peoples, when not at war, trade, individuals on both sides learn the other's language or develop a trade jargon. Evidently, just this process was at work among the three principal groups on or near the Hudson—the Mohawks, Mahicans, and Delawares—when the Dutch arrived. The Dutch first heard the trade jargon from Algonquian speakers, and Algonquian terms persisted even in later times, when English observers described Iroquois customs (Fenton, ed., 1965b). Witness *sachem* (chief), *squaw* (woman), *wigwam* (house), *powwow* (ceremony), and a host of other common terms that entered the American language from Algonquian sources. The literature affords instances of individuals who were bilingual.

The Mohawks had little direct contact, if any, with the early traders until after Fort Orange was established at modern Albany in 1624 (Trelease 1960: 31, 35).

---

1. It seems highly unlikely that the so-called Tawagonshi treaty of 1613 ever took place. The document purporting to support it has been proven a forgery (Gehring, Starna, and Fenton 1987).

This act coincided with the Mohawk-Mahican war, fought over control of the trade with the Dutch, that ended four years later with the Mahicans driven from the Hudson and the Mohawks owning the franchise. No northern or eastern Indians would be permitted to cross Mohawk territory to trade, which meant that furs coming from the north and wampum from downriver must first pass through Mohawk hands. The rule that developed and lasted throughout the century was that no enemy, or potential enemy, should trade with the same European power with which the first party had an alliance. This was the trade and peace syndrome at work (Trigger 1971).

Mohawks and Dutch did not reach an easy accommodation. While still trading with the Mahicans, in 1626 Commissary Van Krieckenbeeck, thinking that firepower would frighten the Mohawks, and in violation of company policy, made the mistake of joining a Mahican war party. The Mohawks had no guns yet, but as "the People of the Place of the Flint," their quivers held arrows with which they ambushed the invaders short of their first town. They killed the commissary and several of his Dutch companions, whom they burnt or roasted, carrying "a leg and arm home to be divided among their families" (NNN: 84–85; VRBM: 306; Trelease 1960: 46–47).

Affairs between the two parties did not improve in the following years. In 1633, Hans Jorissen Hontom, who had long been associated with Eelckens in the trade, became commissary at Fort Orange. The Mohawks hated his guts and refused to trade with him. Instead, they slaughtered the cattle of Patroon van Rensselaer's tenants and burned the Dutch West India Company's yacht. It seems that Hontom had once kidnapped a Mohawk sachem, and after the ransom was paid, emasculated him and "did hang the severed member on the stay," which killed the sachem (VRBM: 302, 304; Trelease 1960: 51).

Years later the patroon was seeking the governor's sanction for an indemnity to be paid to the Mohawks as a means of improving relations between the two peoples (VRBM: 330). As for Hontom, he conveniently perished in a brawl soon after the incident with the sachem and before the matter was settled.

□□◇□□

For a time the Mohawks and the Oneidas traded with both the Dutch and the French. The French connection via Oneida resulted in a trade agreement in 1633, and word of it reached Fort Orange the following year, when the Mohawks closed Fort Orange to the "French Indians," presumably Algonquins. The fur trade declined. The then commissary, Marten Gerritsen, decided to send a party of three company employees into the Iroquois country to find out why business had fallen off and what the French were up to, and to negotiate a new price structure for furs. The three Dutchmen were the first to explore the Iroquois country as far as Oneida and write a report (Gehring and Starna 1988: xix). I shall return in a moment to the cultural and political implications of the journal kept by one of the explorers, Harmen M. van den Bogaert.[2] The three men established the fact of the French

2. Recent scholarship in Iroquois studies has produced an entirely new, annotated translation of the original manuscript journal in the Henry E. Huntington Library (van den Bogaert 1988). Charles T. Gehring of the New York State Library translated the document, William A. Starna of the State University of New York College at Oneonta annotated its historical and ethnological contents, and Gunther Michelson, an independent scholar, rendered the word list into plausible Mohawk.

trade treaty the preceding year and attempted to redirect the fur trade to Fort Orange. They found the lower Iroquois fascinated by firearms, which were still a prohibited item of trade at Fort Orange.

The Mohawks soon found a way of getting around the restriction. English traders on the Connecticut River, under no obligation to honor Dutch West India Company regulations, began selling guns to Mohawks by 1640. Independent Dutch trading partners soon followed suit, and presently the regulation was relaxed. Otherwise, the Indians took their furs elsewhere (see Hunt 1940: 165–72). Mohawk warriors soon became expert marksmen, although dependent on European gunsmiths to keep their arms in repair. Acquisition of guns made the Mohawks formidable in the ensuing Beaver Wars, and it enhanced their political power within the Five Nations: the upper nations owed them favors for mercenary services in the destruction of Huronia and subsequent campaigns.

The time had come for the Mohawks and the Dutch to formalize their friendship. The 1643 pact of nonaggression was the first treaty of "friendship and brotherhood" between the Mohawks and all the Dutch. Sixteen years later it was reaffirmed by boxes of wampum and bound by a symbolic iron chain, the so-called covenant chain that would later extend its links to embrace the English and other allies (NYCD, 13: 112). No treaty of record precedes the pact of 1643.

Dutch pragmatism contrasted with the intellectual interests of the French. To be certain, van den Bogaert recorded names of Mohawk "castles," or villages, paced off houses and noted their relative sizes, and hinted at settlement patterns, noting contrasts between principal villages and satellites. He carried a supply of wampum that he doled out to gain favors, and his party dispensed novelties and hardware. He found the natives fascinated with firearms. At one Mohawk town he witnessed a performance of shamanistic curing, and at Oneida the party attended a rite to assist a sick person—a rite held by one of the medicine societies that may have lineal descendants (Fenton 1942). Of greater significance is the denomination for the first time in any Dutch document of the Five Nations that made up the Longhouse, or League of the Iroquois, and the mapping of their constituent villages (van den Bogaert 1988: 16–17). The map, diagrammed with kernels of corn, has not survived.[3] Van den Bogaert's journal is filled with ethnological niceties such as a description of invited guests bringing bowl and spoon to a feast, and the etiquette of seating and distribution (van den Bogaert 1988: 17).[4] Of more pragmatic concern, the expedition resulted in an improved trade relationship between the lower Iroquois and Fort Orange.

Probing Mohawk grammar and saving souls never ranked top priority among Dutch interests, as they did with the Jesuit missionaries in New France. Dominie Megapolensis, pastor of the Dutch Reformed congregation in what is now East Greenbush, New York, ventured a sketch of Mohawk ethnography in 1644 (NNN: 168–80), which is the lone source on Mohawk culture at this period. Enjoying friendly relations between Dutch and Mohawks following the Mahican war, Megapolensis tried to cope with the Mohawk language, which he recognized was

3. This passage struck me when I first examined the manuscript at the Huntington Library. It was completely misinterpreted by previous editors.

4. Tin pails carried to and from a feast remained the custom during the twentieth century (Fenton 1953a; 1987).

unrelated to that of the Algonquian Mahican. He could get no help from the commissary or other traders in the colony, who made do with a kind of trade jargon but had no grasp of the fundamentals of Iroquoian. He was aware of tenses, a pronominal system, declensions, and conjugations, but did not describe them (Megapolensis 1857: 153; NNN: 172–73.) He glossed some items of material culture, he deplored brittle monogamy, and he commented that his countrymen ran after Mohawk women, who were "much addicted to whoring." (Their progeny in the next generation would serve as interpreters.) Their customs at childbirth intrigued him, as did their capacity for hard work. They regarded the Dutch custom of "lying-in" mere "fiddle-faddle." Torture and cannibalism drew the comment that the "chiefs eat the head and heart" (Megapolensis 1857: 155; NNN: 174). (Bear and hogshead became the prime feast foods in later times [Fenton 1953a].) He mentioned corn ground between two stones but not the wooden mortar and dumbbell pestle.

Of Mohawk arrogance and ingenuity, he wrote with some precision (Megapolensis 1857: 157; NNN: 176). He referred to the Mohawks' elm-bark technology in canoe building, as well as to dugouts. He ascribed the source of shells for manufacturing wampum and fabricating strings and belts, which items the Mohawks valued highly, to coastal beaches. The yearly round of activities attuned to ecological time attracted his notice.

On religion and cosmology, one might expect Megapolensis to have commented. He evidently learned about Aireskuoni, the Mohawk god of war, to whom they made sacrifices, from Isaac Jogues, S.J., whom he befriended during Jogues' captivity among the Mohawks (1857: 158; NNN: 177; see Goddard 1984). The cosmological myth of Sky Woman and the twins did not escape him, nor did the menstrual taboos. He was most candid about Mohawk attitudes toward Christian prayer and sin, and about their query: "Why do so many Christians do these things?" (1857: 159; NNN: 178).

Although quite specific in naming the three Mohawk clans—Bear, Turtle, and Wolf, of which the Turtle clan was greatest and claimed descent from Sky Woman—and their association with named towns, Megapolensis failed to penetrate Mohawk politics. He simply wrote: "The government . . . consists of the oldest, the most intelligent, the most eloquent and the most warlike men. These commonly resolve, and then the young and warlike men execute. But if the common people do not approve of the resolution, it is left entirely to the judgement of the mob" (NNN: 179).

The chiefs were impoverished by generosity in compensating people who had lost kindred in warfare; to them the chiefs awarded prisoners for adoption in place of the deceased. The nine hereditary sachems raised up in the titles of the founders are not mentioned, nor are the matron trustees of the titles. Megapolensis, nevertheless, grasped two essentials: the public independence that enabled Iroquois to ignore council decisions, and the operation of diffuse sanctions in deterring major crimes. "Wherefore," he concluded, "we go wholly unconcerned along with the Indians and meet each other an hour's walk off in the woods, without doing any harm to one another." Nothing else epitomizes the easy relations that seem to have obtained between certain Dutch persons and individual Mohawks just then.

Links of mutual interest took several forms. Indians found shelter in Dutch homes, where they commonly slept on the floor beside the bed (NNN: 175). Such hospitality was common between trading partners. Liaisons inevitably occurred. The interpreters who served the Indian commissioners and interpreted at public treaties during the second half of the seventeenth century were the progeny of such relationships—the children of Mohawk mothers raised as cultural Mohawks—or they were adopted captives who had learned the language in a similar context.

One son of a Mohawk mother and a Dutch father rose to prominence as a Mohawk leader and ambassador to the French. He also served the Dutch and English and, on occasion, the French between 1650 and 1687 (Grassmann in DCB, 1: 307–8; Grassmann 1969: 153). Best known as the "Flemish Bastard," or Smits Jan, he led war parties as "Canaqueese" (Grassmann 1969: 153), and he made the famous pronouncement on the composition and age of the Iroquois Longhouse when protesting because the French mission to Onondaga had not come first to the Mohawks (JR, 41: 87–89). He accompanied Denonville's expedition against the Senecas, and he was claimed by Christian Indians (NYCD, 3: 435). He seems to have gotten around.

An even more prominent contemporary, the native Mohawk orator Kiotsaeton, known as "Le Crochet" (the Hook), proved himself the master of ritual forms during the Mohawk treaty with New France at Three Rivers in 1645, when he treated his hosts to the first recorded performance of the requickening rite of the Condolence Council (JR, 27: 247–53; DCB, 1: 403–4; Fenton 1985: 128). The Dutch and English were yet to witness and record the ceremony. Kiotsaeton left no other mark in the annals.

□□◇□□

The Mohawks at mid-century, having got guns and finding themselves faced with diminishing stocks of beaver to trap and trade, were reaching out in several directions. To the west, Mohawk men answered an appeal to service Oneida women to prevent that tribe from becoming extinct, their menfolk having been wiped out in a Huron engagement. It was afterward said, "That is why the Mohawks called the Oneidas their child" (JR, 27: 295; 28: 279–83). To the east, Mohawks were extracting wampum as tribute and harassing Indians of southern New England, to both the pleasure and, at times, the grave concern of Massachusetts and Rhode Island colonists (Winthrop Papers: passim). To the north they raided the fur fleets when not temporarily at peace with the French. To the northwest, Mohawk warriors leagued with Seneca war parties in destroying the Hurons. This was the height of the Beaver Wars, soon followed by war with the Andastes, or Susquehannocks. To the south, Mohawks mediated a dispute with the Esopus Indians. Meanwhile, at home, Governor Stuyvesant saw fit to regulate the trade at Fort Orange (now Beaverwyck) and Rensselaerswyck and consolidate it into a single jurisdiction under the Dutch West India Company. This move limited Dutch and Mohawk trading partners and afforded less free competition (Trelease 1960: 112–15, 158). Trelease has summarized the situation at mid-century:

There was little more trust and affection between the Dutch and Indians at Fort Orange than . . . at New Amsterdam. Animals were killed, thefts were reported, and mutual suspicion at times ran rampant, yet neither side ever resorted to war. Peace was maintained because both sides had everything to lose and nothing to gain by hostilities. The fur trade was a going concern—not lucrative enough to support the province but sufficient to maintain and enlarge the local community. The two races regarded each other less often as corn thieves, trespassers, or Indian givers than as sources of economic prosperity; what they thought of each other was beside the point. (Trelease 1960: 115)

A manuscript recently discovered in the archives at Arnhem, Netherlands,[5] affords a vivid glimpse at Mohawk-Dutch relations at mid-century, when the house of the colony's director was virtually occupied by native headmen and Beaverwyck was overrun by marauding toughs. The writer, Brant van Slichten-horst, the former director himself, was advancing a claim of fifteen thousand florins for expenses against the patroonship. He asserted:

The Maquaes [Mohawks], not only receive tribute annually from other nations situated 70 [Dutch] miles around them and the colony but also summon them . . . to go fight with them against their enemies the French Christians and Indians who live in Canada.

[Frequently] the field commanders of the Maquaes came into the colony . . . and summoned the other nations to appear there. The patroon's house was their meeting place because those of the fort and the three small houses, which were then in the settlement . . . could or would not offer lodgings, therefore they sent all . . . to the patroon's house; also the sick and wounded. As a result the entire house was full of Indians from front to back; and as one party left another took its place throughout the year. . . .

The field commanders often were so bold as to go sit at the table of their own accord and take food and drink, dividing it among themselves as long as it lasted. I even had to guard against their taking meat and bacon from the garret, although this was done most surreptitiously.

And when the commanders had been well entertained for some days, we then had to provide them with corn, beans, peas, an ax, a breechcloth, or a pair of stockings. And if we were slow about it, then they claimed that they had to fight for us Christians, and that it was necessary to provide them with every weapon: guns, powder, lead, and every other necessity, as the French do for their Indians.

[The Mohawks argued] that the Christians occupied their land that they had conquered from the Mahikanders . . . [and] that they let us . . . live there, so that you had to accommodate them in every way or the Christians might just as well go back over the great water.

And if you did not accede to their foul wishes and demands, then they openly dared to threaten to kill the horses, cattle, and hogs.

Their "campaigns lasted from spring to autumn," van Slichtenhorst wrote, until news came of the French and Indians defeating nearly six hundred Mohawks (on Lake Erie?). There were few warriors left in the first and second Mohawk castles. The writer added that "whenever the Maquaes commanders went out to collect their annual tribute . . . they usually came to the patroon's house, as they went out

5. "De Nederlandse Marcurius" 6 (3): 2–3, September 1990; copy in the New Netherland Project materials in the New York State Library.

and returned, to take up lodging for several days. . . . In addition, many young toughs . . . of every nation ran around daily . . . killing cattle and hogs, and often daring to say openly to me, 'Give us bacon and meat or we will kill those cattle and hogs.'" On one occasion they killed two of Slichtenhorst's hogs and ate them among themselves; he got only one pig's head. Such a present followed the Mohawk feast pattern—the head goes to the chief.

Fort Orange was the Iroquois arsenal, and Oneida was the Dutch horizon (Trelease 1960: 122). The Mohawks held New France under siege and sent war parties against the Abenakis of Maine. When a convenient peace eased expansion, the upper Iroquois surged beyond Georgian Bay into Ottawa territory (l'Incarnation 1681: 128-29, 145; Trelease 1960: 120.)

Politically, the Iroquois League, even at the height of its power, was a loosely knit fabric of alliances. In 1652 a rumor reached New France that the Iroquois intended to combine forces and destroy the colony. But the previous year, when the Mohawks asked for Seneca help on the St. Lawrence, the Senecas replied that they had enemies nearer at home—proposing, however, that the Mohawks help them destroy the Neutrals, which they did. The Senecas were now obliged to return the favor (JR, 38: 61-63; Grassmann 1969: 136-37). When a famous Mohawk captain was killed near Three Rivers, his countrymen resolved to form a general league to revenge the loss, but there is no evidence that this so-called league extended beyond the Mohawks (JR, 38: 61).

The Iroquois political genius was sound, and the Five Nations' strength lay in diplomacy, but their social control was weak (see also Hunt 1940: 155). Individuals acted on their own when they disagreed with official policy. Constituent nations of the league exercised autonomy in war and in peace. The Mohawks held out of the French peace of 1653, harassing embassies of the upper nations en route to Quebec, and they joined the alliance reluctantly at the bitter end. Mohawks and Onondagas ambushed and killed each other over the Jesuit mission to Onondaga. A speaker such as Garakontie might claim that "the Five Nations speak through my mouth" when indeed he represented but part of the league. The ideal was seldom fulfilled, even when the grand council met at Onondaga. Mohawk delegates often failed to attend, or appeared late, and they joined the consensus reluctantly. In the late 1650s, their interests lay elsewhere—in the increased gun and powder trade at Fort Orange, in hijacking fur fleets to pay for these and other goods they were dependent on, and in renewing their alliance with the Dutch (Grassmann 1969: 208, 210).

□□◇□□

In the closing decade of the Dutch regime, things were going badly in Iroquoia. Structurally, the Mohawk castles were deteriorating, and in June 1657 a delegation of sachems from the three castles asked the Dutch, as old friends, to provide them with some horses to haul logs out of the woods to repair their palisades. They anticipated war with the "Sinnekes," which could have meant any of the upper Iroquois (Grassmann 1969: 180-81). Within four years the Mohawks made their first land cession—the flats at Schenectady, then the outpost on the frontier—to Arent van Curler. In 1662 the Iroquois learned defeat on two fronts: a coalition of Chippewas wiped out a Mohawk-Oneida war party in the northwest, and the Andastes repulsed the Onondagas, Cayugas, and Senecas to the south. On top of defeat, after a delay, came the plague, which claimed hundreds of lives. The Andastes then retaliated by attacking western Iroquois towns and intercepting the trade to Fort Orange. And to round out the magic number four, northeastern Algonquians resumed an ancient feud with the Iroquois, raiding and killing.

Finally, native Canadians proved they could retaliate against Iroquois hijackers. The Senecas appealed for a French peace in 1663 (Hunt 1940: 134 and sources). By 1666, fed up with partial peace negotiations, the French under de Tracy, as we saw in chapter 17, visited disaster on the Mohawk towns.

Toward the end of the Dutch regime, following periods of Indian warfare and the hunting out of beavers in Iroquoia, the supply of furs coming to Fort Orange fell off and competition among traders intensified. Governor Stuyvesant took various measures to regulate commerce. To prevent traders from going into Indian castles or intercepting hunters on the Schenectady path, he had a post driven on the hill where the state capitol now stands and forbade traders to go beyond it. But soon, loitering at the post became an offense. The Mohawks complained to the court of physical abuse—being beaten and driven into particular traders' houses (Trelease 1960: 133-35). The court attempted to regulate the rum trade without much success, and it passed some interesting ordinances affecting the baking and sale of white bread, cake, pretzels, and cookies to Indians. Next to rum, the Mohawks had become addicted to such baked goods, and the Dutch inhabitants of Beaverwyck were left to subsist on whole grain, to the serious prejudice of the community. Grain was in short supply. A court minute read: "If this continues the Christians must eat the bran while the savages eat the flour." The situation became acute during the trading season, when, in 1658, the court set the price per coarse loaf of eight pounds at eighteen stivers, "counting eight white and four black wampum beads to one stiver" (Van Laer 1923, 1: 54, 58, 59, 128, 229, 242; 2: 166-67).

Trelease (1960: 137) concludes a survey of commerce at Fort Orange this way: "In almost every context the fur trade reigned supreme at Fort Orange. From the company directors down to the lowliest Beaverwyck trade the primary object of Indian policy was to facilitate the flow of peltry toward the Hudson. Dutch policy toward the Iroquois . . . was cautious, unimaginative, and grossly commercial by comparison with that of New France."

The Dutch had no territorial ambitions to expand beyond the Hudson, and they lacked the military strength to push the Five Nations around, even if they had so desired. They kept their minds on business. The Five Nations, up until the coming of the English in 1664, could hold their own, outmaneuver the French diplomatically, and maintain an alliance for trade and peace with the Dutch traders.

CHAPTER 20

VOICES OF THE FIVE NATIONS

I give you to know, *Onontio*, that my Voice is the voice of the five
Iroquese Cantons. We are born freemen, and have no dependence
either upon the *Onontio* or the *Corlaer.*—Hotrewati to La Barre, in
Lahontan's *New Voyages to North America*

In the final decades of the seventeenth century, the initiative in matters of peace
and war passed to the old men at Onondaga, who were keen to maintain a balance
between Albany and New France and sought an accommodation that verged on
a policy of neutrality. These keepers of the central fire conveyed their views
through appointed speakers who proclaimed themselves the voices of the Five
Nations and spoke for the entire house. The role of speaker was an art form that
the Iroquois polished to a high gloss. A speaker must understand council protocol,
must command the metaphors of council symbolism, must affect the council style
of address, and must be cultivated in handling and passing wampum strings and
belts. Above all, the role required a prodigious memory. Small wonder that
European observers, even though they might not understand an Iroquoian
language, likened these voices to the orators of classical antiquity. Contemporary
observers Baron Lahontan, Bacqueville de La Potherie, and Cadwallader Colden
admired their style. Governor Dewitt Clinton, a century later, confirmed their
remarks. And in recent years, Michael K. Foster has isolated Iroquoian styles of
speech that persist as cultural phenomena. Iroquois speakers over the centuries
voiced the literature of the council fire, which comes down to us in part in the
writings of scribes who were present at councils and treaty negotiations.

The careers of four early Native American voices who played prominent roles
in seventeenth-century forest diplomacy afford insights into the structure and
operation of the confederacy. Three were Onondagas, none of whom held a league
title, and one was a Huron schemer and operator who died dramatically during
the Grand Settlement of 1701. Besides these four, there were two important league
chiefs—the first Mohawk and the first Oneida on the roll of founders—who were
present behind the scenes but who performed minor roles in comparison or
suffered a poorer press.

□□◇□□

The first of these speakers gained notoriety for having humiliated a French
governor. Otreouati (probably Hotrewati), otherwise "La Grande Gueule" (Big

Mouth, Onhwentsiowa:neh), which Lahontan Latinized as "Grangula," was reported by Father Lamberville to have possessed "the strongest head and loudest voice among the Iroquois" (NYCD, 9: 257). He made the scene in 1658 when he and eight countrymen escaped from the Montreal jail by parting the bars to a window (JR, 45: 89). He was by then a warrior and a negotiator who had grown to maturity within earshot of the Onondaga council. Three years later, while Father Le Moyne was treating for peace at Onondaga, Hotrewati raised a war party of thirty Onondagas to assist in revenging the insult of their having been jailed. In a field outside Montreal, they killed and scalped two Frenchmen, took another captive, and beheaded a Sulpician priest and stripped him of his cassock, which Hotrewati put on and paraded in within sight of the habitants. On the way home to Onondaga, Hotrewati, still wearing the black cassock, and his party encountered an embassy of Senecas led by the Onondaga Garakontie, bound for Montreal. The ambassadors, alarmed for their safety, played sick. A council was called, and it went on for hours until pro-French Garakontie, who knew his fellow tribesman well, persuaded the Onondaga warriors to continue on the path (JR, 47: 73, 95).

With apparently no remorse for his previous behavior, four years later Hotrewati served as one of six Onondaga ambassadors to Quebec, where he witnessed the articles of peace along with Seneca, Cayuga, and Oneida delegations, each for their own nation. Somehow, during the festivities he learned of the French governor's design against the Mohawks and advised Garakontie while they were both in the reception room (JR, 49: 179). Whether Garakontie warned the Mohawks on returning to Onondaga is open to question, for relations between the two nations were strained.

Hotrewati escaped notice for the next nineteen years, after which he emerged to prominence during the preliminaries to the confrontation with Governor La Barre at La Famine. Whether he was out of favor with the Onondaga council for nearly two decades is unknown, although there is a hint that his faction gained acceptance when the confederacy needed his unique talents. His name appears frequently in the correspondence between Lamberville and Governor La Barre after 1684 (NYCD, 9: 252-62). By that time, Garakontie had been dead some seven years.

In 1684, La Barre was out to punish the Senecas for depredations in the Illinois country and for interfering with French interests in the upper Great Lakes. In July, at Fort Frontenac, opposite the central fire of Iroquoia, La Barre began to realize the enormity of his task. Intelligence from Onondaga in letters from Father Lamberville revealed that the council was debating both war and peace, that it was prepared for either, and that the Five Nations would unite if La Barre attacked the Senecas. Hotrewati figured in these proceedings.

The grand council of the Iroquois Confederacy was about to convene on 10 July, when the Five Nations planned to unite against the French threat and inform the Senecas that La Barre intended to isolate them from the other four nations. Lamberville wondered why La Barre's staff had not told him that the Iroquois villages were confederated and that the French could not attack one without getting embroiled with the others. The Onondagas were peaceably disposed as neighbors, but the proud and insolent Senecas, who had the most warriors and with whom a war would prove disastrous, might be brought to peaceful terms (NYCD, 9: 252).

Next day a contingent of Senecas was reported on its way to Onondaga to replenish arms and ammunition; it was expected to participate in talks toward an accommodation. Lamberville thought that such an arrangement might benefit Canada. He advised La Barre that there was no advantage in war that year and that the Senecas would not shut themselves in their villages but lie in ambush wherever the French army went. They had already hidden their surplus corn. On learning of La Barre's declaration against the Senecas, they had convoked the grand council, which Lamberville predicted would league against the French if La Barre did not accept the Onondaga peace proposal with Seneca consent. If the French cut Iroquois corn, Iroquois warriors would burn French grain. The Senecas could be neither destroyed nor captured. Indeed, they welcomed war and pitied the French, who, they boasted, "have a great desire to be stript, roasted and eaten," and they wondered whether flesh on a salt diet would be as tasty as the flesh of their other enemies (NYCD, 9: 253). Such arrogance speaks to other documented Iroquois cannibalism. That the Five Nations would feel obliged to unite against a common threat informs the nature of their confederacy.

Two days later, Lamberville reiterated his warning that any hostile act against the Senecas would bring down the whole Five Nations. Seneca warriors in great numbers looked forward to a fight with keen anticipation, but the Onondagas were "men of business" who, having lost some goods but none of their men, saw no point in cutting throats for a few clothes. They would, as moderators in council, endeavor to persuade the Senecas to let them mediate. In effect, they would bring pressure on the Seneca councilors to disavow what their two war leaders were inciting the warriors to do. They would enlist the Oneida and Cayuga councilors in this endeavor. This is evidently how the grand council worked.

The council of four nations met on the sixteenth and seventeenth of July 1684. Lamberville, representing La Barre, addressed the Onondaga chiefs, who replied with three belts. In the same role he also spoke to the Seneca chiefs and warriors with three belts, and they replied with nine, making twelve, which, with Lamberville's letter, were transmitted to La Barre. The Senecas informed Lamberville by a runner that they were prepared to afford La Barre more satisfaction than he demanded and that they would abandon hostilities against the Miamis and other nations if the governor desired, for it was their policy "not to wage war save to secure a good peace." Lamberville thought the Senecas were offering more than might be expected; the Onondagas considered their honor at stake and had "put all sorts of machinery in motion to induce the Seneca to condescend." Apparently the Senecas were obstinate and on the first day of council resisted Onondaga blandishments. Argument was intense and heated, and more wampum had to be produced to attest Onondaga sincerity and persuade the Senecas to confide in them. The Onondagas had recruited Oneida and Cayuga support, and success was attributed to Hotrewati and his "triumvirate," who distinguished themselves in this meeting (NYCD, 9: 254–56.)

Canoes plied back and forth across Lake Ontario and skirted the Thousand Islands for a month carrying messengers and ambassadors between Onondaga and Cataraqui. Hotrewati and someone named Garakontie, possibly a successor to the holder of that name who had died in 1677, made at least one such mission to convey intentions and gather intelligence, returning to brief their countrymen.

On 16 August they reached Onondaga at midnight and passed the night in conferring together. At dawn the chiefs and warriors were assembled to learn the news. Some Senecas in attendance carried home one of La Barre's belts to reassure their kinsmen who were alarmed at armed encroachment. The Onondaga council dispatched runners to Cayuga, Oneida, and the Mohawk towns to notify them to assemble at Oswego to greet La Barre and answer his proposals. Answering La Barre's reassurance not to be alarmed at the sight of his barks and gendarmes, the Onondaga leaders told him "not to be surprised when you will see faces painted red and black at Oswego" (NYCD, 9: 256). The Five Nations were prepared for war or peace.

Hotrewati, as an emissary to La Barre, had gained the governor's confidence and professed his friendship. He and Lamberville met "in the bush," as the Iroquois style private conferences, and Lamberville passed underhand to the orator a belt received similarly from La Barre, whom he complimented for having enlisted Hotrewati's mind and voice. Gifts of *capots* and shirts would also help to influence public opinion (NYCD, 9: 257).

A week later the principals were on the scene and the council was ready to convene. Jacques Le Moyne, a favorite of the Iroquois, represented La Barre, which pleased the Onondaga chiefs, who showed him much attention and promised to end matters in the French interest. In response to the Onondaga summons for the deputies of each nation to assemble, the Cayuga delegates arrived first, bringing two Tionontaté (Huron-Wyandot) prisoners. The Senecas were expected and the Oneidas were hoped for that day, but there was no mention of the Mohawks. Instead, Arnout Viele, the Albany interpreter, came on horseback bearing New York governor Dongan's message that he did not wish the Iroquois to deal with the French without his permission, that he was master of the country and their conduct, "that they belonged to the King of England and the Duke of York, that their council fires were lighted in Albany, and that he absolutely forbad them talking" to the French (NYCD, 9: 257).

Lamberville whispered two words in the ear of Hotrewati, which brought an interesting response in council concerning the illogical stance of Dongan, who had previously urged the Iroquois to satisfy La Barre's demands. When they were two days on the path to Oswego, Hotrewati employed "high words" against Dongan's messenger, "exhorting all the warriors and chiefs not to listen to the proposals of a man who seemed to be drunk, so opposed to all reason" (NYCD, 9: 257–58).

Despite Dongan's attempt to intervene and head it off, and despite a cunning attempt by the Onondagas to postpone the meeting while securing Dongan's permission, in order not to offend him, the confrontation with the French governor took place at La Famine, at the mouth of the Salmon River, on 5 September 1684. In a scathing reply, Hotrewati, as the voice of the four nations present, spoke under fifteen "heads," or topics, first the Seneca positions and then the others listed in chapter 17. Although Lahontan was his witness, Colden later summed up this affair: the great expedition "ended by a Dispute ["Scold" (1750: 71)] between the French General and an Old Indian" (Colden 1727: 90).

The Iroquois gave up little, while the blustering French governor at the head of a sick army escaped with a dubious truce. The Senecas did not attend and were still prepared to fight. Hotrewati pledged a thousand beaver skins as compensation for raids on the French in Illinois, but he refused relief for the Illinois people. The Iroquois promised they would lay off the Miamis. But French voyageurs in those parts were not immune.

In a scathing critique of La Barre's conduct, the intendant, Demeulle, told the Minister of Marine in France how the governor failed to seek the advice of aids who knew Iroquoian and was taken in by the Onondaga speaker. "There came altogether on this embassy only a certain sycophant who seeks merely a good dinner, and a real buffoon, called among the French La Grande Gueule, accompanied by eight or ten miserable fellows, who fooled the General in a most shameful manner, as you will see by the articles of peace I have the honor to send you" (NYCD, 9: 247). The intendant based this indictment of the general on reports of returned officers, and the unfavorable portrait of the Onondaga speaker reflects contemporary French hatred of Iroquois.

On arriving at Cataraqui three years later, Denonville saw fit to send the son and brother of Hotrewati to Onondaga; he characterized Hotrewati as "one of the most distinguished and influential of [that] village, from whom we had derived great assistance in checking the incursions which the Senecas and other Iroquois had made the past year under the instigation of Colonel Dongan . . . and whose influence," combined with that of Lamberville, had frustrated Dongan's designs (NYCD, 9: 362). The previous week a scouting party had picked up a Cayuga of some note who had been watching French movements. They learned that Hotrewati had gone down to Montreal to see what the French were up to, hoping to carry off some French prisoners on the way home (NYCD, 9: 361). Apparently he had been captured and was back in the Montreal jail, charged as a war leader and known persecutor of missionaries (NYCD, 9: 361–62). His incarceration must have been temporary.

The following June, he led the Onondaga delegates who signed a declaration of neutrality with Governor Denonville at Montreal, subscribing their clan eponyms. The Cayuga and Oneida representatives included several recognizable league chiefs (NYCD, 9: 385). By way of explanation, the recorder wrote: "The man called La grande gueule by the French, and Otreouate by the Iroquois, who spoke here at Montreal in public on several occasions in June, and twice repeated what precedes in the speeches, did himself, assisted by two Iroquois, affix the subjoined Totems and delineate with his own hand the figures of these Animals; which he did in quality of Speaker and Deputy of the three Iroquois Nations." The designs include a possible loon superimposed on a man, a raptor similarly posed, a bear, a wolf with erection, and a deer with ten-point rack (NYCD, 9: 385–86).

In early July 1688, Hotrewati appeared at Fort Frontenac with six warriors to request safe conduct to Montreal for the purpose of negotiating a peace with Onontio. Twice their canoe encountered parties of six hundred warriors; they were halted, they parlayed, and they were let pass—a tribute to Hotrewati's status and powers of persuasion. The report of Hotrewati's statement at Cataraqui reads:

After having exaggerated in the presence of Onontio the advantages of those of his Tribe, and the facility with which they could exterminate our people, in consequence of the knowledge he possessed of our weakness, this Savage said, that he has ever loved the French, he had done all in his power to prevent his people executing the project they had formed of burning all our barns and houses, killing all our cattle, setting fire to our grain when . . . ripe, and after we should be [starving] . . . coming the night following and attacking our forts and redoubts; that through his exhortations he had induced them to consent to visit Onontio . . . to make peace on the conditions already set forth; finally, that he was allowed but four days to return to his people; that Onontio should give him a prompt answer and not pretend to delay him any longer, as he would not be responsible for what might occur. (NYCD, 9: 390)

This report, which gives some measure of the man, relates to speeches mentioned in the declaration of neutrality signed at Montreal the previous year. Clearly, Denonville knew the colony was threatened, and he signed—but the Iroquois plan was carried out a year later, despite the treaty, at Lachine. Had Hotrewati gained time, or had the militant faction of the grand council reversed policy? Or was this just another case of the warriors ignoring the policy of the civil chiefs? The Iroquois were not above duplicity.

Contrary to published authority (Grassman in DCB), one of three ranking Onondaga chiefs of the French faction, either this Hotrewati or a successor named Big Mouth, sponsored an "underground belt" that Teganissorens delivered to Frontenac in 1694 (La Potherie 1722, 3: 217). And a year after Frontenac died, the same person came to Montreal in March 1699 to condole the old governor's death; Governor Callière greeted "Big Mouth" (Onhwentsiowa:neh) as an important colleague (La Potherie 1722, 4: 113). But the year 1699 marks the final notices of Hotrewati's career as warrior and diplomat in this title. After that the title disappears from recorded history.

□□◇□□

Five whole Nations address thee through my mouth. I have in my
heart the sentiments of all the Iroquois Nations, and my tongue
is faithful to my heart.—Garakontie, Jesuit *Relations*

From the time of his first appearance at Montreal as leader of a friendly band of Onondagas,[1] Garakontie (1654–77) became known to the French as Sagochiendagehte ("the name bearer"), which was not his personal name but properly the council name of the Onondagas, a status he occupied as its chairman and principal speaker (JR, 41: 69–71, 77, 255).[2] He was said to exercise royal power over the Onondaga nation, "although he does not bear that title" (JR, 43: 277). The Jesuit superior's journal of 1659–60 refers to three presents "given in the name of Sagochiendagehte" at Quebec, where it mentions the escape of Hotrewati and eight others from jail (JR, 45: 89). This was a proper use of the term. Again,

1. See Trigger's sketch in DCB, 1, for the facts about Garakontie's life, and Webb (1984) for extended treatment and interpretation.
2. Stephen Webb (1984: 252) speculates that this title preceded that of Thadoda:ho? as the leading Onondaga league chief. In favor of his view is the failure of the title Thadoda:ho? to surface in the historical documents before 1745. But I must agree with Beauchamp that this "council name" pertains to the nation and not to the man chairing its council.

two years later at a grand council of the league, the journal refers to the nation, not a person (JR, 47: 77). Indeed, this man personified the nation in French eyes. Garakontie was his proper name, and it was not a hereditary title. His status as speaker and chief diplomat of his nation was achieved, not ascribed by membership in the Bear clan.

Garakontie's role as the principal diplomat of the Iroquois Confederacy during the third quarter of the seventeenth century, which made his status synonymous with the council name of the Onondaga nation, questions the primacy of Thado-da:ho? as traditional founder and presiding officer of the league council fire. That the latter title fails to surface in the historical documents until 1745, long after other traditional titles appear, reinforces this doubt. If there was an incumbent in this title at the time, no one mentioned him, whereas the name Garakontie and his diplomatic accomplishments are spread all over the record.

Garakontie had struggled tad struggled to preserve the peace of 1653. As the leading Onondaga chief, he went well out beyond the wood's edge to welcome Father Le Moyne in 1654 and led him by the arm back into town. A master of the condolence paradigm himself, he evidently tutored Le Moyne in its performance, which greatly enhanced the missionary's rapport with the Onondagas and promoted acceptance of the Jesuit mission at Onondaga two years later. Establishment of the Onondaga mission opened a trade channel to Montreal, which threatk monopoly of the trade at Beaverwyck and aroused the keepers of the eastern door to diplomatic protest and military action against Onondaga, until "the ground was stained with blood and murder." Smits Jan, the Flemish Bastard, a Mohawk war chief, made his famous protest over the Jesuits' jumping through the smoke hole instead of properly entering the door of the symbolic longhouse (JR, 41: 87, 89). When in 1658 Mohawks and disaffected Onondagas were plotting annihilation of the Jesuit settlement, Garakontie quietly warned them (JR, 61: 23).

During the military crises that disrupted the confederacy, Garakontie resolved that the French connection was the best policy for Onondaga. Just then the Andastes threatened Onondaga. The disaffected Mohawks were preoccupied with fighting the Mahicans of northern New England. He invited Father Le Moyne to return and reopen the Onondaga mission in 1661. This time Garakontie honored Father Le Moyne with traditional protocol by going still farther out of town to welcome him. He arranged Le Moyne's adoption into his own Bear clan, and the two men exchanged the niceties of council fire ritual and received the approbation of the Onondaga elders. These chiefs, or *rotiyaner*, recognized the wisdom of rescuing Frenchmen from torture in Mohawk fires. While Le Moyne remained at Onondaga, Garakontie secured the release of nine French captives, whom he led to Montreal. Partway, the embassy met Hotrewati's war party returning, as I recounted earlier. Assured that Le Moyne was his security, Garakontie was able to save his prisoners and persuade his rival that the French would welcome the delegation, which inspired the hostages to dub him "the Father of the French." He also bought off an Oneida war party that had hostile intentions toward the French.

During the decade following 1664, only the French alliance kept Onondaga "within two finger-breadths of destruction." In May of that year, Garakontie himself barely escaped an Ottawa and Montagnais ambush at the rapids above

Montreal, when an embassy of thirty Onondagas was decimated. They lost presents and a large quantity of wampum. At home, he was unable to restrain the slain men's kinsmen from seeking to revenge the loss of the Onondaga ambassadors to French Indian allies. And the French regarded pleas for peace as mere rhetorical flourishes, typical of Iroquois deviousness. Indeed, Garakontie's strategy sought to keep the French quiet while Iroquois war parties struck north and south (Webb 1984: 266, citing JR, 49: 137, 139).

In 1665, disease and famine stalked the settlements of Iroquoia. With some Onondaga support, the Mohawks and Mahicans engaged in countersieges, both sides losing men. An Iroquois army failed to breach an Andaste stronghold on the Susquehanna, suffered heavy losses to gunfire, and incurred sickness. A still greater threat loomed in Quebec: Louis XIV sent some twelve hundred veterans of continental wars under the Marquis de Tracy with orders to exterminate the Iroquois. In December, Garakontie led a combined mission of upper Iroquois (Onondaga-Cayuga-Seneca) headmen to Quebec to sue for peace. He brought with him Charles Le Moyne, brother of the late Jesuit, until recently captive at Onondaga, for repatriation and exchange for an Onondaga. Garakontie proclaimed that he was restoring him "in health, without even one of his nails being torn off or any part of his body being burnt" (NYCD, 9: 37–38). He asked for time to persuade the lower Iroquois (Mohawk-Oneida) to join in the peace, but the Mohawks demurred, with disastrous consequences, the following year. Garakontie and Hotrewati had wind of the French intentions, but to no avail. The humbled Mohawks sued for peace in 1667. They were now at the bottom of their cycle—their grain was destroyed, and the prosperous Onondagas were reluctant to heed their appeal for corn.

The French-Iroquois peace of 1667 brought relief to New France and enabled the Jesuits to return to Iroquoia, although the Jesuit historian Charlevoix regarded any Iroquois peace as fragile, and Christianity, to the Iroquois, an optional religion (Charlevoix 1866–72, 3: 111). The league met at Onondaga to smooth out its differences, a policy much admired in the *Relation* of 1667–68 (JR, 51: 237). Garakontie was the key figure in these negotiations. In 1668, having learned from Albany of the French victories in the Netherlands, which would release more French troops to Canada, he visited New France and addressed its governor. He praised Louis XIV for his forbearance in not smashing all the Iroquois, he welcomed Father Garnier to Onondaga, where he built him a cabin, and he requested a *chasseur*, a kind of armed guard or watchman, to assist in repelling Mahican raiders of Iroquois communications (JR, 51: 243). He got what he wanted. Webb (1984: 270) maintains that Garakontie's diplomatic successes and his rapport with the civil, military, and religious officialdom of New France both enhanced his sway at Onondaga and contributed to the preeminence of Onondaga in the league.

Returning home from Quebec, bringing Fathers Etienne Carheil and Pierre Millet for the missions, Garakontie vouched for the former to the leading Cayuga chief with a wampum belt confirming the peace. Before leaving next year for Quebec, Garakontie solicited a letter of recommendation from Father Millet. The Jesuit wrote: "It must be acknowledged that he is an incomparable man . . . worth more esteem and consideration than all the others. . . . [H]e knows how to conduct himself in such a way that he always maintains the fame and authority conferred upon him by his office of Captain General of this Nation, and uses it only to do good to all the people" (JR, 54: 47, 49). With this letter in his pouch, he was prepared to act for all the Iroquois (JR, 53: 41).

While in Quebec to settle a dispute that verged on warfare between the Iroquois and Algonquins, Garakontie proclaimed his faith in Christianity in terms that overcame any Jesuit doubts about his sincerity. Bishop Laval announced publicly that he himself would baptize and confirm Garakontie; Governor Courcelle, as godfather, conferred his name, Daniel, and the intendant's daughter stood as godmother. The ceremony was held in the cathedral, followed by a feast for visiting tribesmen: Hurons, Ottawas, Algonquins, Mahicans, and all but the Cayugas of the Five Nations. Every musket and battery in the citadel proclaimed the event. The governor had hung the kettle in his name for the multitude (JR, 53: 57).

Back home, Garakontie put up a feast and announced his conversion. His speech was a model for the public creed of a *royaner* (civil chief). He would continue to strive in the public interest, to speak when duty demanded, and to risk his life in the national interest. He espoused generosity and charity: the poorest widow would attest his zeal in facing the two main Iroquois disasters—losses of field labor by illness and death, and the loss of possessions and shelter by frequent bark house fires. The honor of the office would continue in his person, although he was a Christian. Other chiefs followed him, and Onondaga was changed forever (Webb 1984, citing JR, 55: 55, 57).

Having avowed his intention to carry on the public duties of his office, Garakontie announced that as a professed Christian he would no longer sponsor dream feasts. He condemned the eat-all feast, and he refused to conduct the Feast of Dreams at midwinter. This celebration of revealed dreams, he maintained, was not, as tradition held, "the mainspring of our country and our lives" but would destroy the nation (JR, 57: 61, 63). And at a public gathering he declared that the Iroquoian cosmology was a fable. Refusal to participate is a powerful negative sanction in Iroquois society (JR, 53: 35).

While Garakontie took on elements of French culture, which he greatly admired, one wonders whether he became literate in French. He celebrated his close ties to Father Le Moyne (Ondessonk) by eulogizing him in the Iroquois manner and building a chapel in his name within his own longhouse. Traditional Onondaga chiefs among his enemies maintained that Garakontie had indeed become French and untrustworthy—that by disclaiming the old culture he was no longer *ongwe hon:we* (genuine Iroquois). But his command of Onondaga affairs was not diminished, he continued to speak for his nation, and no public ceremony took place without his speaking, for "it is He, they say who knows all of the affairs and who is clever as a demon."

Having served his clan, his nation, and the confederacy for twenty-two years as the voice of the Iroquois—until his proper name became a synonym for Sago-chiendagehte, the council name of Onondaga—Garakontie, in the spring of 1676, sensing that he might not witness another renewal of the Creator's blessings, offered three feasts that ratified his prestige and status. The Onondaga elders attended. In the first feast he denounced dream guessing and the belief that compulsive fulfillment of particular dreams prolonged life. In the second, he decried the eat-all orgy. And in the third, knowing that his life span was nearing its end, he sang his death song (JR, 60: 193). His listeners paid close heed. They were convinced that the faith had upset his mind, for he had introduced Christian concepts and phrases into the expected ritual. Despite their misgivings, "the old man," "the elder," had retained their respect by the strength of his mind. He would make one last mission for the nation.

In the last year of his life, Garakontie traveled to Albany and spoke first among the Five Nations in reply to Colonel Henry Coursey, agent for Maryland, there to protest incursions of Iroquois warriors at the back of Maryland and Virginia (Livingston 1956: 43–44).[3] Possibly this was the occasion when, in an act of typical Iroquois arrogance, Garakontie of a Sunday entered the Dutch Reform Church and knelt to pray during the conventicle. "When the minister bade him withdraw, he replied in a loud tone of voice: 'Wait, I have not yet finished my prayer. You make it easily seen that you are not Christians, for you do not love prayer'" (JR, 61: 25).

Returning to Onondaga in August, he made a public confession of his sin of drinking while in Albany. He died that autumn or early winter. Father Lamberville wrote his obituary in the *Relation* of 1677–78 (JR, 57: 139; 61: 21–29). Garakontie's final words in clear Onondaga—"Onne ouagicheria [*o:nenh wagitceria*]," "Now I am dying"—have been badly rendered in the original French as *voilà*, and in English as "see" (JR, 61: 26–27). *O:nenh* ("now") is the commonest Iroquoian adverb!

Garakontie was by all odds the favorite of the Jesuits, and he enjoyed the best press of any Iroquois leader. His skill at diplomacy was unrivaled, and he persistently pursued the interests of his people among both the French and the English. All who heard him marveled at his powers of oratory, even listeners without any comprehension of Iroquoian languages. He saved and restored some twenty-six French prisoners, marking the life of a man with twenty presents, twice that for a woman, in the sequence of the condolence ceremony. Like any Iroquois chief, he had rivals in council, but he maintained his leadership by sheer power of intellect, consistent "good mind," charity, and knowledge of affairs. Only after the "old man's" passing could Hotrewati become the voice of the council. No Indian event in New France rivaled Garakontie's sensational conversion from paganism until the dramatic death of "the Rat" during the Grand Settlement of 1701.

□□◇□□

The devious character known as Kondiaronk, or the Rat (ca. 1649–1701) left a record spanning the last quarter of the seventeenth century.[4] Known also as Gaspar Soiaga, Souias, and Sastaretsi, he led the first generation of Tionontaté refugees at Michilimackinac following the Iroquois conquest of Huronia. There they lived apart among Algonquian bands of Ottawas, maintaining a separate identity but ready to make peace with the Iroquois whenever the latter turned their attention from the Miami north to Michilimackinac.

---

3. We have only a bad translation of his speech, which, nevertheless, preserves some of the elements of expected diplomatic protocol.

4. This sketch is based on my article in DCB, 2 (1969).

A crisis developed presently that brought Kondiaronk to notice in 1682. A Seneca leader strayed while raiding westward and was captured by a Winnebago party, brought to Michilimackinac as a prize, and subsequently murdered. Fearing the Iroquois might annihilate them, the Mackinac tribes appealed to Governor Frontenac. Kondiaronk participated in the negotiations.

After an Ottawa speaker whined that they were like dead men, the Rat acknowledged "that the earth was turned upside down," and he reminded Frontenac that the Hurons, his erstwhile brothers, were "now thy son" and therefore entitled to protection. This shift of kinship neither convinced Frontenac nor satisfied the Kiskakons, a band of Ottawas who knew that without consulting them the Hurons had sent wampum belts to the Iroquois. The Rat excused the Huron action as an attempt to compound the murder of the Seneca warrior, which the Kiskakons blamed on the Hurons. Michilimackinac was a community of uneasy neighbors.

After Denonville's invasion of the Seneca country, Kondiaronk and the allies, in return for loyalty, extracted a pledge from the governor that the war would not be terminated until the Iroquois were destroyed. The old men of Iroquoia might seek a temporary peace, which would relieve pressure on New France but free the Iroquois to concentrate their campaigns westward. Perceiving this, Kondiaronk decided to strike a blow for himself. He raised and led a war party down the lakes to take scalps and prisoners.

Stopping at Fort Frontenac, Kondiaronk was amazed to learn that Denonville was already negotiating peace with the Five Nations. Their ambassadors were expected momentarily for safe conduct to Montreal. The commander advised Kondiaronk to return home at once, to which he assented. Inwardly resenting the French decision, Kondiaronk secretly withdrew across Lake Ontario to Hungry Bay, where La Barre had met humiliation, knowing that the Onondaga embassy must pass there before embarking to the fort. Within a week a party of four councilors headed by Teganissorens, with an escort of forty warriors, approached the landing. The Huron party waited in ambush until the Onondagas began to land before greeting them with a volley. In the confusion, a chief fell dead, others were wounded, and the rest were taken prisoner.

With the captives tied securely, Kondiaronk opened a fateful woods'-edge council. He represented that he had acted on intelligence from Denonville that an Iroquois war party would soon pass that way. The chagrined Iroquois protested through their chief ambassador that they were peace envoys, not a war party, bound for Montreal. Kondiaronk feigned amazement, then rage and fury, cursing Denonville for betraying him into becoming an instrument of treachery. He then addressed the prisoners and Teganissorens: "Go my brothers, I release you and send you back to your people, despite the fact that we are at war with you. It is the governor of the French who has made me commit this act, which is so treacherous that I shall never forgive myself for it if your Five Nations do not take their righteous vengeance." Then he propped up his words with a present of guns, powder, and lead, which convinced the Iroquois, who assured him then and there that if the Hurons wanted a separate peace they could have it. Kondiaronk had lost a man, for whom custom entitled him to request a replacement for adoption: the Onondagas awarded him an adopted Shawnee. They then turned back to their villages, and the Hurons set out for Michilimackinac. Passing Fort Frontenac,

Kondiaronk called on the commandant, to whom he made this chilling boast on leaving: "I have just killed the peace; we shall see how Onontio will get out of this business."

On reaching Michilimackinac in apparent triumph, the returning war party presented the hapless "Iroquois" to the commandant. He, having heard nothing of the intended peace between his government and the Iroquois, promptly condemned the man to be shot. Although the captive protested that this treatment violated diplomatic immunity, Kondiaronk pretended that the man was light-headed and, worse, afraid to die. Kondiaronk sent for an old Seneca slave to witness the execution, told him his countryman's story, and freed him to carry the word back to the Iroquois. Kondiaronk charged him to relate how badly the French abused the custom of adoption, and how they violated their trust while deceiving the Five Nations with feigned peace negotiations.

One member of the Iroquois peace embassy that Kondiaronk had attacked had meanwhile escaped to Fort Frontenac, where the commandant assured him of French innocence in the affair—but the damage done to the peace negotiations was irreparable. The message of alleged French perfidy passed rapidly from fire to fire the length of the Iroquois Longhouse. Wampum belts were buried and war kettles hung. Within a year of Kondiaronk's treachery, war parties of the Five Nations descended on the island of Montreal, sacking Lachine in the summer of 1689. The renewal of French-English hostilities in Europe warranted the New York colony's aiding such Indian attacks, although Baron Lahontan blamed the Rat for provoking the Iroquois to the point where it became impossible to appease them. A decade of warfare followed.

In 1689, Kondiaronk was caught plotting with the Iroquois for the destruction of his Ottawa neighbors. That September, as if to witness his own mischief, he came down to Montreal and returned home unscathed, proving that the French lacked the temerity to hang him. He was worth more alive than dead. The next year he may have motivated the Ottawas to rebuff Frontenac and seek a treaty with the Iroquois to trade at Albany. At mid-decade, Kondiaronk had been reported leading the French faction of the Michilimackinac Hurons against a pro-English Iroquois faction led by one Le Baron, both sides having Ottawa followers. When, in 1687, Le Baron sought to join the Iroquois in destroying the Miamis, the Rat warned the Miamis and overwhelmed an Iroquois fleet in a two-hour canoe engagement on Lake Erie, cutting some fifty-five Iroquois to pieces. This victory reestablished Kondiaronk's eminence, ruined any Huron-Iroquois alliance, and restored the Michilimackinac tribes as Frontenac's "children" (NYCD, 9: 672).

After the Treaty of Ryswick (1697), which ended the War of the Grand Alliance in Europe, and with it King William's War in North America, New York and New France suspended hostilities. The English withdrew support from the Iroquois who, exhausted from a long war, initiated peace overtures to Frontenac that went on for several years preceding the settlement in 1701. Kondiaronk was on hand whenever the Indian allies of the French conferred. At an early meeting between Frontenac and the Ottawas over a truce with the Iroquois, a Cayuga delegate accused the Ottawas of negotiating on their own without the governor's participation. Kondiaronk, "the most civilized and considerable person of the Upper Nations," rebuked the Cayuga, saying: "We are in the presence of our father;

nothing should be concealed from him, so relate the message carried in the wampum belts that you first addressed to us and to the Ottawas." The embarrassed Cayuga declined the challenge.

On the death of Frontenac, Kondiaronk transferred allegiance to the new Onontio, Callière. In 1700 Callière assembled the contending tribes at Montreal and forged an armistice preparatory to the final settlement. As spokesman, the Rat urged the Iroquois delegates to listen to the voice of their father: "Let it not be in a forced or insincere way that you ask him for peace; for my part I return to him the hatchet he had given me, and lay it at his feet. Who will be so bold as to take it up?"

For a while the sparks flew thickly on both sides of the fire. The Iroquois speaker, having listened calmly to Kondiaronk, replied with spirit: "Onontio had hurled the hatchet into the sky [suspended war] and what is up there never comes down again; but there was a little string attached to this hatchet by which he pulled it back, and struck us with it [referring to Frontenac's raid on Onondaga]."

Just then the Rat took charge to remind them that "the Seneca were planning the complete destruction of the French, intending not even to spare his father [Frontenac], whom they intended to put first into the kettle, for an Iroquois [had] threatened to drink his blood from his skull." He said further of the Iroquois that "their hands were covered with the blood of our allies, that the allies' flesh was even still between their teeth, that their lips were all gory with it, [and] it was well known that they were lying to hide what was in their hearts." Further, in Kondiaronk's style, one must dissipate the clouds shrouding the Tree of Peace.

The final Indian congress, or Grand Settlement, began the following year (21 July 1701). Bacqueville de La Potherie, the prime source on the proceedings, met the Iroquois delegates at the village of the mission Indians at Sault Saint Louis (Caughnawaga). The first flotilla to appear consisted of two hundred Iroquois, headed by Onondaga, Oneida, and Cayuga ambassadors, the Senecas having dropped by the way. A Mohawk embassy would follow later. They approached firing their guns, and the mission Indians returned the salute from the shore. The hosts greeted the visitors at a small fire kindled at the water's edge and then led them by the arm to the main council lodge, where they smoked for a quarter of an hour with great composure. The guests were then greeted with the Three Bare Words of requickening—wiping tears, opening ears, and clearing the throat—to prepare them to speak of peace next day with Onontio.

The following day, the Iroquois shot the rapids to the main fire at Montreal, where a crash of artillery saluted them. The smoke of their feasting had scarcely vanished when, in their wake, came two hundred canoes of the French allies— Chippewa, Ottawa, Potawatomi, Huron, Miami, Winnebago, Sauk, Fox, and Mascouten delegates—numbering some seven hundred Indians, to be received ceremoniously at the landing. These Far Indians performed their rite of friendship, the calumet dance.

Negotiations were well under way by 25 July, when Kondiaronk spoke of the difficulty of recovering Iroquois prisoners from the French allies. He wondered whether the Iroquois would comply with sincerity in an exchange or cheat them of their nephews taken during thirteen years of war. He suspected that the allies would be deceived, although they would leave their prisoners as a token of good faith. Next day, the Iroquois admitted to not having the promised prisoners, who as small children had been awarded for adoption among families. They professed that as councilors they were not masters of their young people. This excuse annoyed the Huron and Miami delegates, who had forcibly taken Iroquois prisoners from foster families. Days of wrangling ensued.

The Rat, having persuaded his people and allies to bring the Iroquois prisoners to Montreal, felt duped and humiliated. Shortly afterward, he succumbed to a violent fever. He came to council to discuss the matter on 1 August so ill that he could not stand. Yet everyone was glad when he spoke, according to La Potherie: "He sat down first on a folding stool; [then] a large and comfortable armchair was brought for him so that he could speak with greater ease. He was given some wine to strengthen him, but he asked for an herbal drink and it was realized that he wanted syrup of maidenhair fern," a sovereign Iroquois remedy. Recovering somewhat, he spoke in a languid tone while the assembly listened intently for nearly two hours, occasionally voicing approval of his points. Though obviously chagrined at Iroquois conduct, his political skill summoned a new approach.

He reviewed at length his diplomatic role in averting attacks on the Iroquois, in persuading reluctant tribal delegations to come to Montreal, and in recovering prisoners. "We could not help but be touched," La Potherie wrote, "by the eloquence with which he expressed himself, and [could not fail] to recognize at the same time that he was a man of worth." After speaking, Kondiaronk felt too weak to return to his hut and was carried in the armchair to the hospital, where his illness steadily worsened. He died at two o'clock in the morning.

The Iroquois, who dote on funerals, came to cover the dead. A column of sixty led by Louis-Thomas Chabert de Joncaire, an agent and interpreter among the Iroquois who had been an adopted captive among the Senecas, with the ranking Seneca chief, Tonatakout, walking at the rear weeping, marched in solemn dignity to where the corpse lay and sat in a circle around it while the appointed chanter paced and recited for a quarter of an hour. A second speaker, Aouenano, wiped away the tears, opened the throat, and poured in a sweet medicine to requicken the mourners. Then, producing a belt, he restored the sun and urged the warriors to emerge from darkness to the light of peace. He then temporarily covered the body pending the main rites. Other tribal delegates made similar gestures.

Kondiaronk's funeral the following day rivaled in pomp the cathedral baptism of Garakontie. The French made certain their Huron allies knew how the loss of so considerable a person affected them. A military escort of sixty men preceded sixteen Huron warriors in ranks of four, wearing beaver robes, their faces blackened in mourning and their guns reversed. Then came clergy and six war chiefs bearing a flower-bedecked coffin on which lay a plumed hat, a sword, and a gorget. Behind the train, the brother and sons of the dead chief walked, followed by files of Huron and Ottawa warriors. Madame de Champigny, wife of the intendant, attended by Vaudreuil, governor of Montreal, supported by staff officers, closed the procession. After the Christian burial service—for Kondiaronk was a convert of the Jesuits—the soldiers and warriors fired two volleys of musketry, one for each culture represented in the rites. Finally, each warrior, in passing the bier, fired his musket a third time.

Kondiaronk was interred in the church of Montreal, and his tomb was inscribed, "Cy git le Rat, chef des Hurons" (Here lies the Rat, Huron chief) (Parkman 1889: 470). Today, no trace of Kondiaronk's grave remains. He lies somewhere near or beneath Montreal's Place d'Armes.

□□◇□□

Teganissorens (ca. 1682–1718), a contemporary of the previous three voices and a principal in the negotiations that produced the Grand Settlement of 1701—although he did not participate in its ratification—apparently succeeded Garakontie and Hotrewati as the voice of the Onondaga council during the final decades of the seventeenth century and the opening decades of the eighteenth (Eccles in DCB, 2: 619–23). He was equally at home in the councils of the French and the Albany English and was a considerable favorite of Cadwallader Colden, who witnessed him in action in his later years: "Decannesora had for many Years the greatest reputation among the Five Nations for speaking. . . . He had a great fluency . . . and a graceful Elocution, that would have pleased in any Part of the World. His person was well made, and his Features . . . resembled much the Busts of Cicero." He had a knack for making affairs seem less disagreeable to English ears when his people sought accommodation with the French, which was contrary to the English interest (Colden 1750: 156–57).

Following his previously described encounter with Kondiaronk, Teganissorens embarked on a brilliant diplomatic career. By 1693 the Five Nations were tired of war and began treating separately for peace with the French and their allies. During these negotiations, Teganissorens came to prominence in both Quebec and Albany. Frontenac, having returned as governor in 1689, listened to Iroquois proposals and agreed in 1694 to suspend hostilities, providing the Iroquois send two representatives from each nation and that Teganissorens be one of them.

To hedge its bets that winter, the Onondaga council sent Teganissorens to Albany as speaker to inform Governor Fletcher, through Major Peter Schuyler, that the Iroquois intended to make peace with the French unless the English increased aid (Colden 1750: 157ff.). At a council held at Onondaga, the upper four nations chose their delegates, including Teganissorens, whom they charged to inform the Mohawk chiefs and Albany. All of this was to have been done in November, but, as Teganissorens told Schuyler, the chief sachem of Onondaga, whom the "general council" at Onondaga designated speaker for the Five Nations, "had a sore Leg, and could not travel." Colden (1750: 158) notes this idiom as "signifying a trifling Excuse of an unwilling Person."

The speaker went on to specify the three propositions, supported by belts, that the council resolved to send to the governor of Canada, and how Father Millet, now the leading Oneida sachem, Odatshehdeh, and a French captive empowered as an Onondaga sachem, had added two propositions. The first belt, while the speaker withheld two others, referred to the kettle of war; the second overturned it; and the third upheld the four nations' alliance with the English so long as the two powers were at war. The two added belts were documented by letters, which were read in Albany. Aware that the English mistrusted the Jesuits, the speaker softened the impact: "We know that the Priest favours his own Nation, and deceives us in many Things; but it is not in his Power to alter our Affection to our Brethren, we wish you would bury all Misunderstandings that you have conceived on his Account; and we likewise wish you gave less Credit to the Rum-Carriers than you do." On this reference to the contemptible character of traders, Colden (1750: 160–61) remarked that the management of Indian affairs was entrusted to these same people.

Teganissorens closed in typical Iroquois style: "'The Governor of Canada's Words, and the Resolutions of the Four Nations are now before you, consult therefore what is to be done, and if it be necessary for the Brethren to go to our Castles to advise us farther, be not unwilling'; and then he laid down a large Belt eleven Rows deep, and seven Fathom of Wampum" (Colden 1750: 161).

In response, Schuyler denied consent for any treaty with the French and set a date seventy days hence for another conference with Governor Fletcher. But to his several specific requests, Teganissorens stated that as "now Minister of the General Council," he could act only at the council's direction. He could only lay the belt down in each of the castles; he could not promise compliance (Colden 1750: 162).

In the spring of 1695 the Onondaga council sent delegations both to Albany and to Canada. Leading the delegation to Quebec, Teganissorens arrived wearing a scarlet coat trimmed with gold braid and a laced beaver hat, gifts of the New York governor. While in Quebec, members of the delegation dined at the governor's table or were entertained by persons of rank. After three days of dignified delay, Teganissorens addressed Frontenac, his staff, and the clergy "with great solemnity" and stated the Iroquois terms for peace with ten belts (La Potherie 1722, 3: 219; NYCD, 9: 579ff; Colden 1750: 169; Eccles in DCB, 2: 621).

First, a general peace settlement with the French would include the English colonies allied to the Five Nations in the covenant chain at a treaty conference to be held at Albany. Second, after reviewing the history of warfare under previous governors and French perfidy in retrieving the hatchet thrown in the sky and fishing it from Hungry Bay, the Iroquois proposed casting it into the bowels of the earth. Belts three to five related to adoptions and mission Indians. The sixth mourned losses of chiefs and pledged not to avenge them; it desired that the French notify Indians of the upper country of the peaceful intentions of the Iroquois. The seventh ministered a "medicine" to expel "bad stuff" from French hearts. The eighth would wipe the blood from ground underlying Cadaraqui and restore the site for a peace conference (NYCD, 9: 579–81). (In his Albany account of the Quebec proceedings, Colden [1750: 173] has Teganissorens say bluntly: "Onondio, we will not permit any Settlement at Cadarackui; you have had your Fire there thrice extinguished; we will not consent to your rebuilding that Fort; but [ninth belt] the Passage through the River shall be free and clear.") Moreover, the mat was prepared for council at Onondaga, the place for transacting important affairs. The tenth belt dispelled darkness and restored the sun.

Frontenac and his staff were of two minds. Although the governor refused to concede it, the staff were convinced that the Iroquois were stalling for time while they enticed tribes allied to the French into their own alliance system. Proof came the following year, 1696, when the Iroquois renewed raids on the habitants near Montreal. Having received reinforcements from France, however, Frontenac retrieved his position by restoring Cataraqui and, in 1696, smashing Onondaga and Oneida.

Unfortunately for the Iroquois, during negotiations leading to a peace settlement, Teganissorens lost his Christian Mohawk wife, who was from Caughnawaga.[5] He withdrew from public affairs and secluded himself. Only on the earnest entreaties of the Albany commissioners, who appreciated his skills as negotiator and feared what might transpire at Montreal without him as speaker, did he return to the council (Eccles in DCB, 2: 621).

The return of captives proved the sticking point that delayed ratification of the treaty. When Kondiaronk accused the Iroquois of bad faith, Teganissorens gave the standard explanation—that having been adopted into families, they were beyond retrieval by the council; and if they were forcibly returned, the French should load the mission Iroquois into canoes and repatriate them. The Iroquois needed every available person.

In the spring of 1701, Governor Callière greeted Teganissorens with two kisses, persons of quality discoursed with him—one suggested he sit for his portrait— and the governor presented him with a double-barreled gun, a laced coat and hat, and tobacco. At week's end, when Teganissorens declared his intention to return to Onondaga to arrange the return of captives, Callière, knowing that the account of his visit would spread the length of the Longhouse to Albany, wisely shoved him off in a canoe manned by three voyageurs and instructed them that his guest was not to lay hand to paddle (NYCD, 4: 890; Eccles in DCB, 2: 621–22).

When a French delegation consisting of Joncaire, Father Bruyas, and Le Moyne de Maricourt, an interpreter and negotiator, approached Onondaga to retrieve prisoners, Onondaga hosts at the landing "threw themselves into the water up to their waists" in order to carry their guests to dry land, carried their packs, and offered them food. An aged war chief harangued them, offered hospitality, and told them to rest that day to recover from the fatigue of the journey. Next day, they were stopped a quarter of a league from town so as to form a column. Teganissorens came outside the palisade to welcome them with the Three Bare Words of requickening—he wiped away their tears over losses, he opened their throats so they could speak, and he cleaned the mat of blood where they were to sit in council. They were then escorted into a guest cabin and fed (La Potherie 1722, 4: 149–50; Colden 1750: 200; Charlevoix 1866–72, 5: 103–5).

Teganissorens was cowed by the blandishments of neither governor. Replying to Father Bruyas at a grand council held on 10 August 1699, he stated that the council would not welcome a return of the Jesuit missionaries: that they now preferred Protestants. When Maricourt violated a principle of Iroquois protocol by threatening war in a council called for peaceful purposes, Teganissorens reportedly said: "You come and speak of peace and scarce are set down to smoke a pipe, but

---

5. Teganissorens's wife was murdered for alleged witchcraft. She was said to have learned "poisoning" from the Jesuits, but the description of her act of poisoning fits the classic pattern of Iroquois witchcraft. Her victim was the son of Aqueendero, the chief sachem of Onondaga who alternated speaking roles with Teganissorens. Witchcraft is symptomatic of the intense factionalism between pro-French and pro-English parties that beset Onondaga just then. A relative of her victim spied her in Albany and beat out her brains (NYCD, 4: 689).

talk of coming and knocking us on the head, and therefore I say nobody knows your heart."[6]

When the newly arrived English governor, Bellomont, sought to establish and garrison a fort at Onondaga, Teganissorens, whom he thought an English servant, devised delaying tactics that frustrated the project. He had a positive knack for making the Onondaga interest palatable to English ears. Eccles credits Teganissorens with proposing to the French in 1703 a treaty of neutrality between New York and Canada, which both sides accepted (Eccles in DCB, 2: 622). He later made a secret mission to warn Governor Vaudreuil of English plans to attack Canada in reprisal for French attacks on northern New England.

Teganissorens visited Albany several times in his later years. Land issues were now to the fore. In 1715 he proposed sending delegates from each of the Five Nations and the Mahicans to England to voice their grievances to the crown, drawing on the precedent of a voyage that had been accomplished five years earlier and had brought results (Bond 1952). He blamed the English for letting the French establish a post at Irondequoit that would be stocked with English goods supplied in the illicit trade with Montreal. His memory faded in his final years, when he contradicted his previous position on the rum trade. The Onondaga council finally chose another speaker when Teganissorens could no longer fulfill the role. The Albany authorities had come to regard him as a double agent in the French interest. Colden (1727), who heard him speak as an old man, wrote of him as having already gone the long trail.

□□◇□□

Had the League of the Iroquois been functioning as tradition prescribes, we should have heard more from the life chiefs whose titles descended from the founders. The title Tekarihoken, that of the leading Mohawk who, by tradition, was first to accept the message of the Great Peace, occurs in the French sources in 1653 as leader of a war party near Three Rivers. He negotiated the release of some Huron refugees from Quebec four years later. The next year he headed a war party of twelve hundred against the Ottawas and then appeared in Quebec with Father Le Moyne to exchange prisoners. I recall no notable records of his voice.

A successor in that title went with the Mohawk hegira to the St. Lawrence missions. Either he or his successor resided at Caughnawaga during the first quarter of the eighteenth century. One of that title came to Albany and met with Governor Burnet, who failed to persuade the Iroquois in Canada to pull down the French post at Niagara, which was on Seneca land. A favorite of Governor Chauvignerie, he joined the governor on a trip to Oswego and Onondaga in 1728, when he visited the British fort with local Iroquois and reported the discussions (Trigger in DCB, 2: 624–25; NYCD, 6: 796).

More consistent performers were holders of the first Oneida title, Odatshehde (Quiver Bearer). This was already an ancient title of a founder of the confederacy when in 1689 Father Pierre Millet was awarded to the lineage in which it descended

---

6. Eccles in DCB, 2: 622. I have failed to locate this in the sources. Charlevoix (1870, 5: 105) attributes this reprimand as having been directed toward the emissary of the English governor Bellomont: "I do not understand . . . what my brother means, in desiring us not to hearken to our Father's voice, and to sing the war-song at a time when everything invites us to peace." La Potherie does the same (1722, 4: 154).

to replace one of that name. During the 1690s Millet functioned in that role and assumed his seat in the grand council of the league. One of that title appeared with Hotrewati in Montreal in 1688 (NYCD, 9: 385). Successors figure prominently in the next century (JR, 64: 91; NYCD, 4: 85–88, 279, 561; L. Campeau in DCB, 2: 473–74).

Holders of the first Cayuga and second Seneca titles appear at about the same time. None left notable records until the next century.

None of these holders of distinguished titles attained the eminence of the men who were the "voices of the Five Nations." Speakers of the council inevitably attracted the notice of European governors, commissioners of Indian affairs, and colonial secretaries. Their names figure prominently in treaty proceedings and in negotiations that preceded permanent agreements. As in all governments, they were the effectives who were charged with missions and got things done. In effect they were the "sachems" of record, while the holders of titles descended from the founders of the league remained largely unsung.

CHAPTER 21

THE ENGLISH TAKEOVER, 1664–1700

> In 1664, New York being taken by the English, they likewise immediately entered into a Friendship with the Five Nations, which has continued without the least Breach to this Day; and History, I believe, cannot give an Instance of the most Christian or most Catholick Kings observing a Treaty so strictly, and for so long a Time as these Barbarians, as they are called, have done.— Cadwallader Colden, *History of the Five Indian Nations of Canada*

In the first meeting between the Five Nations and the English after Britain took possession of New York in 1664, four local chiefs represented the Mohawks, and four nominal "Senecas," of whom two were Onondagas and two Cayugas, covered for the other four nations (NYCD, 3: 67–68; Beauchamp 1905: 216). (The Dutch at that time lumped any Iroquois west of the Mohawks as "Senecas" and only later applied the term to the westernmost nation of the five.) It was agreed during this meeting that previous trade relations with the Dutch were to continue; that personal injuries, upon complaint to the authorities, would be redressed by both parties; that the English were not to aid the New England Indians, who had murdered a Mohawk leader; and that the English would assist in making peace with the River Indians. The sachems' witness marks to the agreement extend linearly east to west, but the signatures (made by a scribe) do not agree with the orthography of the printed text. The geography of Iroquoia west of Schenectady was terra incognita to Albanians just then, and there was no one yet who could cope with Iroquois personal names.

The agreement alludes to Mohawk involvement with the Indians of northern New England, which for some years had concerned both the Dutch and the English of Massachusetts. The former wanted a peaceful settlement; the latter applauded raids on the hostile Sokoki, Penacook, and Pocumtuck settlements but feared any Mohawk-Abenaki rapprochement that would free northeastern war parties to raid the English frontier. Governor Stuyvesant gave some thought to arranging peace among the Mohawk, Mahican, and the Abenaki tribes, in order to free them to go beaver hunting for the trade, but he got diverted by other duties in New Amsterdam (NYCD, 13: 240, 296–99, 302–4, 355–56; Trelease 1960: 129). The war that began in 1663 between the Mohawks and the southern New England tribes lasted some ten years, until the end of King Philip's War in 1675. The

Sokokis and their confederates mounted an unsuccessful attack on the Mohawks in 1669, perhaps in response to a Mohawk raid on Penacook. Losses were considerable on both sides. Each side murdered the other's ambassador. New England groups displaced by these hostilities, and various refugees, came to rest at Schaghticoke at the falls of the Hoosick River near the Hudson (Day 1978: 150).

The Mohawks enjoyed a bad reputation in southern New England, among both the Indians and the Puritans (Gookin 1792: 186–88; Winthrop 1929–47: passim; Vaughan 1965: 291). Daniel Gookin, a contemporary Massachusetts Indian agent, devoted a chapter of his book (1792: 16–28) to Mohawk raiding tactics and the terror they caused the Indians within his jurisdiction. In it, he relates an amusing incident that illustrates the Mohawks' curiosity about English domestic culture and their sangfroid in custody.

Although they were very cruel, they ordinarily did not molest the English and left the praying Indians alone. Gookin tells of five armed "Maquas" who entered a house in Cambridge, "that they [might] better see and observe the English manner of living," did no harm to the inhabitants, offered no resistance on being apprehended by the sheriff, and were held in the local jail pending trial. "At their being imprisoned and loaden with irons, they did not appear daunted or dejected; but as their manner . . . is, they sang night and day, when . . . awake." They were tried, remonstrated, and sent home with a letter to their sachems, despite the protests of local Indians who wanted them killed (Gookin 1792: 24; MA, 30: 127).

There is no more vivid description of the fear Mohawks engendered in southern New England Indians than that in Colden's writings, set down some fifty years after the events from the memories of old men of New England. Colden himself claimed to have witnessed the anxiety manifested by local Indians so long as two senior Mohawks were present to collect wampum tribute. "An old *Mohawk Sachem*, in a poor Blanket and a dirty Shirt, may be seen issuing his Orders with as arbitrary an Authority, as a *Roman* Dictator" (Colden 1750: 3–4).

Affairs at home in the Mohawk Valley did not warrant such arrogance. A recent outbreak of smallpox had taken its toll. Manpower losses in continual warfare left women without spouses. At least a few entered lifetime liaisons with Dutch men who, in the absence of Dutch women, disregarded a Rensselaerswyck ordinance forbidding such arrangements. Their genes descend in old Albany families (Trelease 1960: 172).

□□◇□□

The management of Indian affairs in Albany between 1664 and the end of the century gradually shifted to accommodate English imperial policy. Colonial governors, who were nominally in charge, were instructed to purchase large tracts of land adjacent to settled areas and to promote trade. The English were inclined to recognize Indian title, which the Dutch had ignored. Among a procession of English governors—Nicolls (whose term began in 1666), Andros (1674), Dongan (1683), Andros again (1688), Fletcher (1692), and Bellomont (1698)—Andros and Dongan sought seriously to stabilize affairs with the Five Nations. The former stressed the policy of land acquisition; the latter proposed appointing an executive committee of the league to expedite business. Fletcher sanctioned some huge land deals. None of this was easy, for the Dutch and the Iroquois resisted intrusions into their accustomed ways of relating to one another as trading partners. The governors, as infrequent visitors to Albany, were essentially outlanders who had as yet to learn Iroquois protocol. What New Yorkers recognize today as the "upstate-downstate" cleavage in politics began early (Trelease 1960: 193, 204).

Although the governor was responsible to the English crown for the management of Indian affairs, he was entirely dependent on the Albany magistrates, who were essentially traders, for the day-to-day conduct of Indian business and the direction that policy took. Only after 1690 were the magistrates officially "commissioners for Indian affairs." They conducted their business in Dutch, and the town clerk kept the minutes. After 1675 the office of town clerk was combined with that of secretary for Indian affairs in the person of Robert Livingston (1654–1728), a Scot who had learned Dutch in exile. The links in the chain of communication between Iroquois speakers and literate governors ran the gamut: from Mohawk to a Dutch interpreter, to a secretary writing a gloss in Dutch, to an English translation entered in the Indian Records that began in 1666, to a letter to the governor, and finally his report to Whitehall. It is amazing how much comes through, and it is all that we have.

Under English rule, Albany, inhabited by Dutch traders, evolved from being the magnet of the beaver trade to become "for three-quarters of a century the diplomatic center of British North America" (Buffington 1922: 327). Albany was the place of treaties where the Five Nations kindled a fire for the conduct of affairs outside the Longhouse. Dutch relations that began with the Mohawks seldom reached beyond Oneida, but the metaphor of the chain, which was forged jointly by the Iroquois and the English, linked the nations of the Iroquois League with neighboring tribes and with the emerging commonwealth of British colonies (Jennings 1984). The symbol that native speakers at first invoked as a rope hawser fastened from ship to a tree atop what is now State Street hill metamorphosed into that of an iron chain that adherents to alliances grasped and that was stretched westward to be secured at Onondaga. Frequent renewal of alliances polished the chain of friendship and kept it free of rust from neglect. In time, a silver chain was substituted in the metaphor for one of iron. Of such was the axis of communication.

Albany, at the head of tidewater on the Hudson, with its port ice-free during much of the year, was accessible from New York and overseas. Northward stretched the Champlain corridor to Canada. Onondaga, on the high ground near modern Syracuse, seat of the league council fire where the Iroquois made policy, was more remote yet central to a network of trails that anticipated modern highways and connected villages of the Five Nations. Accessible waterways flowed northeast to Canada, southeast to Chesapeake Bay, and southwest to the Ohio country. The Great Lakes gave access to the northwest.

The overland road to Albany, though downstream and a portage for the Mohawks, was not the easiest route for the upper Iroquois nations. Had it not been for the Andastes before 1675, they might well have floated the Susquehanna. Nevertheless, the Five Nations' long-standing alliance with the Dutch, enhanced later by the English and celebrated by the symbolic chain, was backed up by mutual economic advantages that determined the policies of both the Iroquois and Albany. These interests outweighed geographical hazards. Iroquois military success rested ultimately on guns, powder, and lead purchased at Albany. Political imagery encoded in mnemonic strings and belts of wampum greatly magnified the prestige of the Iroquois in the sight of their Indian neighbors. And European powers gradually learned the rituals of forest diplomacy. The Dutch merchants of Albany were prepared to offer wampum beads by the string (fathom) or *scheppel* (bushel). Dutch interests revolved around furs; they had virtually no interest in politics. Land was the English interest; imperial politics was an obsession. In the Iroquois, the English met their match. To do business with them, the English would have to learn the protocol of forest diplomacy. That they did is a tribute to Iroquois insistence and a relaxation of British pride. The English encountered a native people who "proudly asserted themselves to be, the subjects of no master, but an independent power." Other than the trade, the Dutch burghers paid little heed to the activities of the French, who soon were at odds with their old rivals and British imperial policy (Buffington 1922: 328).

Dutch trading methods continued under British rule into the next century. Merchants sought to confine trading to the town and established rules for the conduct of business with the Indians. Hailing passing Indians from the stoop was forbidden; Indians were no longer to sleep in Dutch houses; posts and shelters were set up on the hill. Above all, policy opposed intercepting inbound Indians bearing furs on the Schenectady road; trading was prohibited in Schenectady; and no settlement was to be established west of there (Buffington 1922: 329; Trelease 1960: 131–37).

Before 1664, a restrictive trading policy obtained in the absence of free competition. Massachusetts Bay was too far for Iroquois to travel there; trade with the French was interrupted by frequent wars; competition from Pennsylvania for deer hides awaited the next century. Albany offered a price advantage. Albany was all business (Buffington 1922: 330; Norton 1974).

The English takeover ended Albany's isolation. Competition increased. Louis XIV responded by assuming more control over Canada. The Dutch merchants of Albany soon found themselves caught up in a diplomatic struggle for control of the continent that involved their erstwhile trading partners among the Five Nations, the French, and the English. The struggle ultimately found a military solution. Meanwhile, Albany became the vortex of the storm. For the Five Nations, it was the place for trading and treating. For the English, it was the outpost of empire. And to the French, it was an anathema—a place of bargain prices where the Iroquois obtained firearms to destroy French-allied Indians and divert the best furs to Albany. The historian Arthur Buffington questioned whether the Albanians ever grasped the importance of their position. Only the trade mattered to them (Buffington 1922: 331).

A few British imperialists perceived that control of the west was of crucial importance. The country around the Great Lakes was by then the source of the fur trade. To supply Albany, the Iroquois must kill beavers in the hunting territories of resident tribes, a privilege either granted in alliances or secured by warfare. With Albany's backing, they succeeded at either course only temporarily. An Iroquois–Far Indian alliance that would divert furs to Albany jeopardized French alliances with the same tribes and threatened the Montreal market. French leaders clearly understood where their interests lay. They must protect their alliances, secure the west, and undertake, as we have seen, to punish if not destroy the Iroquois. That the Albany traders failed to exploit their opportunities ɪsgusted British imperialists, notably Cadwallader Colden, New York governor George Clinton, and Peter Wraxall, secretary to the Albany Congress and later to Sir William Johnson (NYCD, 9: 65, 80; Buffington 1922: 332–33; Trelease 1960: 205–7).

Albany policy hinged on relations with the Five Nations. The local economy grew up and prospered on the Indian trade, and from the Five Nations' viewpoint, trade and good relations were one. Friendship demanded reciprocity; each party needed the other. Albany policy mirrored that of Onondaga. Therefore, Albany merchants were not about to dispatch trading parties to the west so long as the Iroquois preferred to carry rum and blankets to the Far Indians of Green Bay and return their furs to Albany (Buffington 1922).

This arrangement lasted some twenty years after the English takeover, as trade policy evolved in three stages. First, Albanians began to assume a broader political perspective and to view the continent with a wider lens. Second, they reached out for the western trade and encountered bitter rivalry from the French. They joined with New England in an abortive effort to conquer Canada. Third, they relapsed into neutrality, traded with Canada, contrary to imperial policy, and earned the criticism of Colden and Wraxall (Buffington 1922: 334; Colden 1724; Wraxall 1915: 48n1).

The magistrates, later the board of Indian commissioners, were a self-perpetuating body on whom the old men of the Iroquois Confederacy depended. Governors came and went and, with notable exceptions, stood at one remove from the management of Indian affairs for which they were responsible. The pivotal figure was the town clerk of Albany, who served also as secretary of the board. What the governor learned was colored by Albany interests, which determined policy whether or not the governor had any. He depended on the magistrates, and later the board, to carry out his policy, but any policy with which they disagreed stood small chance of reaching the Indians. The so-called commissioners, through their interpreter, continued as the sole means of communicating with the councilors of the Five Nations. In the words of Buffington (1922: 335), "the one constant factor in British Indian policy was the policy of Albany."

Iroquois leaders encountered the same obstacles in reaching the governor. The governor had some control over the commissioners. He appointed them from a double list of magistrates submitted by the remaining magistrates. After 1668, the commandant of the Albany militia was ordered to sit and preside over the commissioners in "matters Capitall or treatys with the Indians," and he was to cast the deciding vote in case of a tie (Palstits 1910, 2: 307–90).

The Five Nations began to sense the long reach of British imperial policy between 1674 and 1687, during the terms of Sir Edmund Andros and Thomas Dongan, both strong governors. Andros set the tone of British administration of Indian affairs, organized the Indian commissioners, pacified some long-standing Indian wars, and conducted the first English treaty. Dongan perceived the French threat, exploited the chain as a metaphor of imperialism, regularized the treaty process, established Albany as the seat of colonial negotiations with the Five Nations, and proposed ways of strengthening the Iroquois League itself. Jennings (1984: 141–85) has covered this period admirably.

□□◇□□

Andros set foot on Manhattan on Halloween of 1674. He immediately got busy. In the spring he went upriver to Albany, renewed British protection of the Mahicans and Mohawks separately, and settled their differences. He apparently journeyed some fifty miles up the Mohawk Valley to Tionontoguen, the third and largest Mohawk "castle," to treat with the Five Nations. Who beyond the Mohawks were represented is unknown, for no minutes of the proceedings have surfaced. The Mohawks named Andros "Corlaer" after Arent van Curler (ca. 1600–67), a title which thereafter descended to governors of New York (NYCD, 3: 254; HEH, HM 3028, after PRO 1682; Jennings et al. 1985a: 160). Andros reported that the Mohawks "submitted in an extraordinary manner," for they evidently took on the task of knocking on the head King Philip's warriors, who included some Mahican kinsmen, a task they accomplished with brutal efficiency. Andros resettled the survivors at Schaghticoke, within his jurisdiction. He then arranged peace without vengeance between Massachusetts, Connecticut, and his newly adopted "children" (Jennings 1975: 323; 1984: 148).

Dutch and English sources reveal little awareness of the operation of the Iroquois League at this time. It is all "Maquas" and "Mahikanders." Nevertheless, during earlier peace negotiations between Mohawks and Mahicans in 1666, the Albany justices had the Mohawks give wampum also to the Oneidas and Onondagas "to seal the peace with the Mahikanders" (LIR, 35). Clearly, the confederated Iroquois and the River Indians shared some customs. The three Mahican bands condoled the death of the patroon Jeremias van Rensselaer in 1674–75, and they understood wampum taxonomy (LIR, 37).

The first of the "silver" covenant chain treaties, made in the spring of 1677, linked New York, Massachusetts, and Connecticut at one end to the Five Nations and the River Indians at the other end. Again, the minutes are missing, although snatches appear in other sources (LIR, 39; Jennings 1984: 148). The New Englanders, having a strong tradition of covenants, refused to acknowledge that the Indian parties were entirely within Andros's jurisdiction and insisted on a formal meeting and a full understanding of mutual obligations. In their view, the Indians were "free" agents. This was not Andros's idea of how things should be. He later found the Indians "insolent." They refused to acknowledge being British subjects. He nevertheless came around to accepting the treaty-making process, which was largely the Iroquois way (Jennings 1984: 149). The Mahicans reassured the Massachusetts commissioners of open communication: "There shall be no shrubs or rubbish grow along ye Rivers." The Hudson would remain clear "quite downe to N. Yorke" (LIR, 40).

Meanwhile, Andros, in promoting the treaty of 1677, had used his good offices to end the bitter war with the Andastes, or Susquehannocks, that had immobilized the Iroquois Confederacy up to 1675 (NYSA, Colonial mss. 201/25: 124). Jesuits among the Iroquois had reported that the Iroquois at long last had defeated the Andastes (JR, 60: 173), a myth that Jennings has exploded (1984: passim). The lower Iroquois had been more amenable to the peace than the upper nations, particularly the Senecas, who were reported "most arrogant and insolent" (JR, 60: 173). Andaste survivors removed from the Susquehanna Valley to settle in Seneca towns, and as adoptees they replaced Senecas lost in the wars and in pandemics. The same source reported that some two hundred captives were brought a distance of two hundred leagues to work in the fields (JR, 60: 185). Ending wars with the Mahicans and Andastes that had kept the Iroquois docile for so long now freed them to threaten New France. In Eccles's words, "in 1676, the whole basis of peaceful relations between the French and the Iroquois was shattered" (1964: 113; 1969: 113).

Frequently, peace terms required the return of captives, something the sachems found difficult to satisfy. Mohawk sachems felt the pressure acutely, being close by; the remote Seneca sachems felt it less. In 1677 the Mohawk sachems asserted that "they would not be made the laughing stock of the other nations." Prisoners belonged to the warriors until distributed among families, but once adopted, they were beyond the jurisdiction of the sachems. The sachems protested that "while we are indeed sachems, we cannot simply turn our backs on soldiers, for they are our protectors and have to fight for us since we are old people" (LIR, 41). This complaint runs like a theme through the treaty literature and is frequently offered as an excuse for failure to comply with treaty provisions. That the sachems could not control the warriors was a weakness in Iroquois polity.

Iroquois warriors, abetted by French agents, were at this time raiding to the south, creating all manner of havoc at the back of Maryland and Virginia. Frontier settlers were losing cattle, hogs, crops, housing, and their lives. Reprisals for encroachments on the warriors' path elicited complaints and prompted efforts to resolve the problem during the next half-century. Disposition of the Susquehannocks at the spring 1677 treaty had been accomplished without Maryland's participation, and the Maryland authorities soon learned that to make peace with the Iroquois they had to deal through Governor Andros (Jennings 1984: 154–57). They instructed Colonel Henry Coursey to go see Andros in New York and commissioned Coursey to make a treaty with the Susquehannock and "Cinnigo" Indians—the "Senecas," or all of the four upper nations (PRO CO1/40: 74–5).[1]

This affair, the second "silver" covenant chain treaty, held in July–August 1677, turned out to be an expensive learning experience for Maryland and a triumph for Andros and the Iroquois. In Manhattan, Andros proceeded to edit Coursey's instructions to his liking before they both went up to Albany. Coursey was to tell the Iroquois that Susquehannocks had committed the murders that the English blamed on the "Cinnigos" (PRO CO1/40: 74–5). The parties to the treaty, in Iroquois terms, were Maryland and, across the fire, the Iroquois and Delawares. I shall examine the ethnological implications of this affair, which Jennings has interpreted with insight in considerable detail (1984: 156–65).

Each of the Five Nations replied separately to the Maryland propositions. There was no league reply as such, but the Onondaga speaker spoke first, followed by Oneida, Mohawk, Cayuga, and Seneca.

Garakontie headed the Onondaga delegation of four sachems.[2] None of them carried names of the founders (PRO CO1/40; LIR: 43).[3] He affirmed unity of

---

1. The term "Cinnigoes" (Senecas) still referred to the four upper nations beyond the Mohawks, although the Five Nations were by then known individually to Yorkers by their proper names.

2. See Trigger in DCB, 1: 322–23. This may have been the brother of the famous Christian convert of the same name, or the same person, who died in the following winter of 1677–78.

3. The spellings of sachem names by delegation varies between PRO and LIR: 43–48, and they are not all present in the latter source.

heart and head, buried the past in oblivion, and sang a song to proclaim a new covenant. His second song was to forget any enmity (LIR, 45–47).

The Oneida sachems, who were present during the Onondaga speech, replied the same day. Swerisse, speaker for the four, none of whose names suggest titles of founders, approved the speech of their Onondaga "fathers," a term they extended to "Christians of this Government" (LIR, 44). They were prepared to obey King Charles, although their warriors were already on the warpath, having left before the treaty and therefore deserving to be excused (PRO CO3/40: 82). They acknowledged depredations but denied killing any Christians. They were prepared to join the Onondagas in the covenant, although some twenty Oneida warriors were still out fighting southern Indians and would remain uninformed.

A copy of the original treaty attested by Robert Livingston (HEH, HM 787), dated 6 August 1677, carries the Mohawk answers, names the delegations by castle, and designates their speaker, Canondondawe, as head of the largest delegation of four sachems from the third castle. He complimented the governor for fixing upon Albany, convenient to the Mohawks, as the site of the meeting. He declared that he and the governor were of one heart and one head (mind). He avowed that the bond between them was so strong that "if thunder were to strike it, it would not break." He reported that six hundred Senecas had been on the way but had turned back in fear. (Smallpox had been prevalent.) Things in the past should be buried: "We consider ourselves innocent of having injured any people from Maryland and Virginia." Then, to drive his words into the mind of his host, he sang a peace song, then repeated it for emphasis, as if Coursey should appreciate the power of song in ritual. He reported that the Senecas preferred another place to confer. Finally, he thanked His Excellency for releasing his two sons, who were alleged to have beheaded a Susquehannock sachem.

It was late August before the Seneca and Cayuga replies came in. Of six Seneca sachems, Adondarechaa was the speaker. One sachem name suggests Donin-hogawen (S-8, RC 50), keeper of the western door.

The Cayuga delegation of seven employed Attarachrett as speaker. Listed are two uncertain candidates for founder titles: "Degaweyoo" (possibly Haga?en:yonk, C-1, RC 33) and "Sonnondaendowannne" (possibly "the great pipe"), the council name of the Cayugas in the league epic.

The Seneca speaker promised that all of the Seneca sachems would come to Albany next year to treat with Colonel Coursey. The Cayuga speaker confirmed the Seneca speech. They had reached a consensus. This was the first time they had seen a representative of the Maryland government. They promised to publish the news at home and make reparations for future damages.

In May, preceding the treaty, Andros had sent Wentworth Greenhalgh and an unnamed companion on horseback the length of the Longhouse to the farthest Seneca town on a fact-finding mission. They were to urge the Five Nations to send delegations to meet with Colonel Coursey (NYCD, 3: 256). Greenhalgh's observations enumerated and sited tribal villages, counted houses, estimated numbers of warriors, remarked on the condition of crops, and guessed distances between tribal settlements. His figures are generous.

He found the populous Senecas least acculturated. They were most curious "to see us ride our horses, which we did: they made great feasts and dancing, and invited us yt when the maides were together, both wee and our Indyans might choose such as lyked us to ly with" (DHNY, 1: 13). The Oneidas had recently resettled in a new town and were forced to buy corn at Onondaga. The Seneca cornfields were most extensive. The party witnessed the torture of incoming captives from the west and reported cannibalism (see Fenton 1940: passim). These observations comprised the first English intelligence on all the Five Nations, who could then muster some 2,150 warriors (NYCD, 3: 250–52).

After this intelligence and the Maryland treaty, an Oneida delegation reminded the Albany commandant and magistrates that from the Seneca towns to New York, the Five Nations were under one government (Wraxall 1915: 9). The existence of the league was beginning to dawn on English consciousness.

Within two years, agents of Virginia came to Albany on the same mission, demanding that Indians passing near Christians should stand still and lay down their arms in friendship. Again, Mohawk, Onondaga, and Oneida sachems appeared seriatim and replied separately (LIR, 48–61). A Virginia commissioner died before the meeting convened. The Mohawk speaker ritually cleansed the council house before welcoming Colonel William Kendall and complimenting him on such a long journey for a senior person. He then renewed the covenant. To commit recent mischief to oblivion, he presented a belt "14 high," and he approved the new rule of approach. Finally, he acknowledged and lamented the sudden death of Colonel Littleton but observed that it was their custom not to lay anything down as a present on being notified of a death. But he did give a belt thirteen rows deep to wipe away Kendall's tears (LIR, 50–51).

Affairs dragged on. Ten days later, a lone Onondaga sachem showed. The Onondagas had received the invitation belt through official channels, but they had expected the southerners at Onondaga, the place of business of the Five Nations. He had come, nevertheless, although smallpox prevailed and hindered the chiefs from traveling.

Governor Andros sent a message to Oneida that Kendall was bringing an "oneyda squa," evidently taken from a war party. Kendall expected an exchange of captives. Late in October, two Oneida sachems, neither with league titles, appeared. They said that smallpox had kept them. They acknowledged that their warriors had taken prisoners but protested that they had snitched only a few ears of corn and tobacco. They asked that the rest be forgiven. Although the "Pale or Stake of unity" had fallen, it was now raised up again, so let the past be forgiven and cast into a pit of oblivion, beneath which a strong river current runs. The covenant was renewed and the chain brightened. The Oneidas had indeed been the principal offenders in pursuing the Susquehannocks, who were now destroyed. They advised, however, that it was beyond the power of the sachems to return a Christian girl, but they would speak to the matron who had adopted her, and then the sachems would sit on the issue. They would be pleased when she was freed. A belt twenty rows deep underscored the seriousness of the issue. (Twenty was the price of a woman's life in later times [LIR, 55–57].)

It was November before Kendall met with the Onondaga sachems. The grievances were similar. Garakontie spoke for the delegation of four sachems, none with league titles. He likened their young men to a child with an ax in hand, unable to discern good from evil. He thanked Kendall for the complaint, he too presented a belt twenty rows deep, and he praised Kendall for charity to the Oneidas, "our children" (LIR, 60–61).

Although the Mohawks were less culpable for the southern raids, they had not kept their covenant with Massachusetts. Mohawk warriors continued to harass the Naticks, to march in a warlike manner through English settlements, and to enter houses, as we have seen. Governor Bradstreet wrote to Andros requesting a peace settlement, and Andros resolved to go up to Albany (MA 30: 251ff.). Major John Pynchon addressed the Mohawks in November 1680. Their speaker thanked him for coming, acknowledged his propositions, and pleaded that there were not many Indians at home at this season—they were off hunting—to make wampum belts for the proceedings. But they would retire, consider the issues, and answer next day.

Canondondawe spoke for the delegation of six sachems, none of whose names suggests a league title. First, they grieved over the guilt of their young men with a belt fourteen rows high. Second, they said that they wished to preserve the covenant. Third, they were not ashamed of their children and urged the same with a belt twelve rows high. Fourth, Christian Indians, once adopted, could not be reclaimed. "They are our children." Canondondawe made no promise to return them, for "it is hard for any man to part from flesh and blood." A belt fourteen rows high underlined this verity. Fifth, the war with the Naticks was of long standing, and it was difficult now to lay down the ax, but they would nevertheless do it in gladness, "for we never had any delight in this warr." Canondondawe produced and laid down a belt seventeen rows high. Sixth, the present speeches should be published throughout New England, but since Pynchon could not understand Mohawk, the speaker proclaimed the *yo he::::!* (MA 30: 252–54).

Pynchon went home reassured that there would be no further incursions or captives taken. He paused at Springfield to summarize the negotiations: the Mohawks had buried the hatchet; there was great cause for Mohawk shame; they would make the peace known to other Indians and avoid occasions for further trouble; but captives could not be returned. Pynchon had received more wampum belts than his listed presents—duffels, blankets, a dozen shears, wampum, rum, and tobacco (MA 30: 255).

The previous Maryland treaty did not end the incursions. Within three years Colonel Coursey was back in Albany trying to restrain Iroquois war parties. During the proceedings, four wampum belts were left lying on the ground and were not taken up by the agents of Maryland and New York, which inaction indicated that the issues were not resolved. The Indians retired from the meeting to consult alone (NYCD, 3: 325; LIR, 64–67).

□□◇□□

In my view, the ablest of the colonial governors was Thomas Dongan (1634–1715), who landed in New York in October 1683 to succeed Andros at the behest of the Duke of York. A native of Ireland, Dongan was a Catholic, he had served in France, and he understood the Gallic mentality. He soon teamed up with Robert Livingston, the secretary of Indian affairs, who coached him on the politics of the Five Nations and who shared with him a distrust of French expansion in the west to dominate the fur trade. Both men perceived that enlisting the goodwill of the Iroquois was the key to British success in North America. Dongan inherited the silver chain from Andros, and it was up to him to keep it polished. Dongan was "the first Englishman to see the vital connection of trade and policy, and to understand the immensity of the issues involved in Indian relations on the North American continent" (McIlwain 1915: lxi). He was the last man to let this trade go to the French. He soon had plans to build forts at strategic points, and during his five-year term, traders out of Albany voyaged beyond the Seneca country seeking furs among tribes in the upper Great Lakes. Before Dongan's coming, no Englishman had traveled west of the Genesee River (NYCD, 3: 395, 477; Wraxall 1915: lxi).

Dongan reported home that the Five Nations, the most warlike people in America, were "a bulwark between us and the French and other Indians" (NYCD, 3: 393). In 1684, Lord Howard of Effingham, governor of Virginia, journeyed four hundred miles to Albany with Dongan's blessing seeking relief from incursions by the war parties of the Five Nations on the expanding frontier of his colony. The recent Iroquois raids down the Ohio into the Miami and Illinois country alarmed the Virginia gentry, who perceived those areas as fruitful resources for land speculation. On hearing the complaint, Dongan sent Arnout Viele, the interpreter, up to Onondaga to acquaint the Five Nations, collectively and individually, that although he did not consider the alleged acts a breach of the previous peace, he did demand that they recall their young men. His words evidently offended the chiefs. Viele was also to post the king's arms on all the Iroquois castles (Beauchamp 1905: 229; LIR, 70).

Meanwhile, an agent of Massachusetts, Stephanus van Cortlandt, improved the opportunity to renew a previous covenant with the Mohawks. The parties met on the eve of the main treaty. The Massachusetts present to the Mohawks—some ninety guilders of wampum, thirty ells of duffels, twelve shirts and stockings, three vats of rum, and four rolls of tobacco—elicited an instructive reply. Odianne, the speaker, prompted by Canondondawe, himself an orator, delivered the message of five other named sachems, none with league titles. The speech of eight "heads" thanked the Bostonians for the previous agreement—that they would mutually keep the covenant firm—now renewed by the present. It declared that the cleared path was to be kept open, the present covenant house was to be kept clean, the covenant chain was to be brightened, and the branches of the Tree of Peace would reach to Massachusetts, as well as to Virginia and Maryland. Canondondawe reminded his listeners that any covenant must be renewed "in this court house"; and in renewing the covenant, both parties must "keep the chain bright and clear, and suffer no rust to come upon it" (MA 30: 281–84).

The main treaty convened on the last day of July 1684. Across the fire from the two governors, Dongan and Lord Howard, sat sachems of four of the Five Nations: eight Mohawks, three Oneidas, three Onondagas, three Cayugas. The Senecas were off campaigning. The principal purpose of this meeting, according to the Indian Records, was to bury the ax and make a firm and lasting peace between the Virginia and Maryland Indians and the four nations just named. The record reads that the four nations requested the Duke of York's arms to post on their respective castles. In presenting the arms, Dongan urged a good understanding among them, and if there were differences he would compose them. They were not to make any covenant with the French without his sanction. They were to say the same to the Senecas (Wraxall 1915: 10).

Colden used the Indian Records, misconstrued dates, and published an elaborate series of replies that pertain to a conference held a year later, on 15 September 1685 (Colden 1750: 48–55; Leder in LIR: 71, 84–91). His account is nevertheless rich in symbolism and deserves attention. Wraxall preserved the address of the Onondaga and Cayuga sachems to Dongan (1915: 11–12; NYCD, 3: 417–18). There is also an abstract of preliminary proposals (NYCD, 3: 347).

The two nations wanted English protection from the French; otherwise they would face the loss of beaver hunting territories north and west of Lake Ontario, in parts of modern Michigan, and in the Ohio Valley. They would put themselves under the protection of the English king. They had already conveyed to New York the Susquehanna lands, which, they told Effingham, William Penn's people might have bought and settled (see map in Leder, LIR: 70). Further, they were a free people and, in uniting themselves to the English, exercised the right to give their land to whichever sachem they pleased. They gave a great belt of wampum for the king, a smaller belt for the Duke of York, and a beaver pelt to Dongan for transmitting their proposal.

Everyone in Iroquois society must have a personal name. The Onondagas and Cayugas, in addressing Lord Howard, called him "Brother Assarigoe" (Aʔsareʔko:wa), Big Knife, a pun on the Dutch *hower*, a cutlass or sword, which title pertained to later governors of Virginia (NYCD, 5: 670).

The formal speech in council, at the Albany courthouse, elaborated items agreed on "in the bush." Addressing Dongan as "Brother Corlaer," the speaker said: "Your Sachim is a great Sachim and we are but a small people." He reminded them that when the English first came to New York, Virginia, and Maryland, they were but a small people, and "we a large Nation," and that finding them a good people, they gave them land and treated them civilly. He likened the recent grant to a "branch of the great tree that grows here, whose top reaches the sun, under whose branches we shelter ourselves. . . . Our fire burns in your houses, and your fire burns with us, and we desire it ever so may continue (Wraxall 1915: 11–12; NYCD, 3: 417). He acknowledged that the young Iroquois warriors were like wolves of the forest. He manifested concern for lands to leave their children.

Several days later the Senecas answered an unrecorded speech by Dongan. They complained that the French governor styled himself "father" and called them "children," that he supplied their enemies with ammunition, and that they had intercepted French gun runners. They welcomed the Duke of York's arms and put themselves under English protection (Wraxall 1915: 12–13). That evening the Senecas told Effingham they were prepared to bury the hatchet with Maryland and Virginia.

It was then that Dongan offered the Five Nations some excellent advice. They should not maintain correspondence with the French without informing him and gaining consent as British subjects. To strengthen the league, he suggested they form an executive committee of two wise sachems from each nation and one or two war chiefs, to manage their affairs in concert without expensive public meetings. Third, they should make alliances with the Ottawas and Miamis of Ohio and open a path for them to trade at Albany. Fourth, likewise they should bring back Mahican refugees among the Ottawas. Fifth, they should send runners in the name of the Five Nations to invite Christian converts home from Canada. Sixth, he advised them to bury corn outside their castles for security. Seventh, they should not allow French priests among them, for the one at Onondaga (Father Lamberville) reported everything to the French. Eighth, he urged that the chiefs keep their people sober (Wraxall 1915: 13–14). For Dongan, a Catholic, to move against the Jesuits was quite a concession.

In concluding his address to the four nations present, and later to the Senecas, Lord Howard proposed that two hatchets be buried in the courtyard; that the following summer he would send a deputy with some Indian sachems to make a lasting peace; and that meanwhile, parties bound southward should keep to the foot of the mountains, away from the heads of rivers, there being no beaver there, and lay down their arms as friends on any approach to residents (LIR, 71–72; Colden 1750: 47–48).

□□◇□□

Despite the confusion among the sources—Colden, the Indian Records, and the official minutes of the treaty proceedings—certain Iroquois political metaphors and other symbolic acts become clear.[4] They are as follows.

1. The covenant chain. To the Iroquois it was both a "linkage of arms" and an agreement between two parties (VSL: sheets 9, 12). Even thunder and lightning may strike but not break the chain. Let no one pull arms from the chain (Colden 1750: 51).

2. The power of song. "Let me stamp understanding into you" (Colden 1750: 49). "Let me drive it into your mind with a song" (LIR: 89, 91). The covenant song (LIR: 88) descends in the Six Songs of the modern condolence ceremony.

3. Bury the ax. Uproot a tree and cast weapons in the pit of oblivion. An underground stream carries away evil (Colden 1750: 49, 51, 52; LIR: 74, 94).[5]

4. The Tree of Peace. Planted in the hole created by burying the ax, it reaches to the sun. It shades the parties to the covenant, and its branches extend to shelter additional participants. Warfare may shake or fell it; renewal of the covenant replants it.

5. Fire, the symbol of civil government. Exchange of fires: "Our fire burns in your houses; yours in ours (Colden 1750: 54).

6. Names and kinship. Granting a name embraces one in society. Kinship terms indicate rights and duties, relative status. "Brothers" in an alliance were equals; "father" and "children" usage created ambiguities.

7. The continuing family superseded the tribe or nation. Captives, once released to a matron, were hers to dispose of. Once captives were adopted, the sachems repeatedly protested that they were powerless, save for moral suasion, to retrieve and return them. They were "family" and occupied whatever status had been held by the person replaced.

4. The official minutes of the treaty proceedings are in the Virginia State Library, Richmond: Colonial Papers, Folder 4, Item 2a. Photocopy in the Newberry Library, Chicago, cited in Jennings 1984: note 23.

5. With all the excavation and rebuilding of downtown Albany in recent years, no hatchets have surfaced from "the southeast courtyard," near State and Pearl.

8. Wampum belts confirmed any of the foregoing, and, indeed, transformed them into symbolic acts. The relative size and depth of the belt conveyed the importance of the gesture.
9. The path: the symbol of communication. It was the road of embassies; keeping the path clear and free of obstructions was the way to preserving and renewing alliances. Throughout the treaty literature it is a continuing theme.

An enigma rises over a metaphor that first appears in conferences dating from the final decade of the seventeenth century. The metaphor of the bundle of arrows may not have originated with the Five Nations, as apologists for Indian influence on the U.S. Constitution maintain. The fasces bundle was known in Europe from Roman times, although the Iroquois may have invented the bundle of arrows metaphor independently to illuminate the strength of their confederacy. It was employed by a spokesman for the Indian commissioners at a May 1690 conference in Albany. It was immediately taken up by Tahaiadoris, the Mohawk speaker, as if he knew all about it. He proposed a union of the colonies to resist the French and rejoiced that the commissioners now understood the Iroquois concept of the whole house and were so well informed. The Mohawks simply wanted a bow to shoot the arrows, which meant larger powder bags. The speaker ended by presenting a belt thirteen rows deep depicting the five houses of their confederacy (NYCD, 3: 712–14; PRO CO5/1881; Grassmann 1969: 517–19).

From the same welter of sources there also emerges the order of precedence among the Five Nations. Who speaks first? The party that kindled the council fire opened and set the agenda. The host symbolically "rubbed and greased the legs" of the travelers with "three bare words." The invited embassy acknowledged the host and retired to prepare. Next day the host made the principal address, and the guests listened and requested time to prepare their replies. In these early treaties the Five Nations replied separately—partly because they arrived singly, the Mohawks often first, being nearest to Albany—although a Seneca speaker might invoke a consensus of linked arms reached in passing through intervening villages (LIR, 80).

When William Byrd followed Lord Howard of Effingham in 1685 to implement the arrangements Effingham had made the previous year, Garakontie of Onondaga replied first on the difficulty of retrieving a prisoner (LIR, 87). A Seneca speaker next protested that their warriors had "passed around the mountains," and he chided the sitting sachems of the other four nations. A spokesman for the Oneidas alone explained how difficult it was to free a prisoner from the families to whom they had been given (LIR, 88). A Mohawk speaker, Canondondawe, absolved his people of blame and sang the complete covenant song to admonish his own people and then the Indians of Virginia.

Colden (1750: 48–49) has the Mohawks replying first to Lord Howard. Their speaker, Cadianne, after excoriating the other nations as "stupid and brutish" for threatening the covenant, addressed the Oneidas as "children," called the Onondagas "brothers" deaf from filth, and urged the Cayugas to mend their ways. They must keep the covenant with the respective parties. He gave a belt to stamp understanding and to remember. (Mohawk and Onondaga rivalry for some time was intense.) He had planted the Tree of Peace and taken the hatchet out of their hands. There was no reason to bury a Mohawk ax, for they had done nothing. Second, an Onondaga named Thanojanihta spoke for the other three nations. Then axes were buried.[6] So much for native protocol.

History is unkind to native theory. Despite professions of unity within the league and insistence on precedence, evidence of disunity abounds in the historical record. Discrepancies between policy and action were not much different in New France and New York. Officially, a treaty of neutrality between France and England, concluded in 1686, governed policy on North America, but Louis XIV had already charged Denonville, who replaced La Barre, with recovering France's honor lost at Hungry Bay. Dongan, who knew French, corresponded with Denonville, but policy did not prevent Denonville from preparing to invade the Seneca country the next year. Rode, a Mohawk speaker, was reassuring Dongan with symbols of unity that the league was intact and explaining how the confederates were quick as foxes and could communicate news of any disaster by relays of runners from the Seneca towns to the Mohawk Valley, where a horse would cover the last lap to Albany. An Oneida injected a note of humor—that there were young Indians who did not sleep at night and would discover and inform them.

On the contrary, evidence of disunity within the league is considerable. The grand council met in May 1686 for seven days trying to reach a common policy to meet a common threat. We have no minutes. The Mohawks and Senecas (despite a heritage of feuding) were aligned against the Onondaga, Oneida, and Cayuga delegations, who favored meeting the French at Cadaraqui "when the bark peels" (June), which proposition the former two rejected.

Mohawk sachems protested to the magistrates that Arnout Viele, the interpreter, on a mission to the upper nations, by-passed the first two Mohawk castles. Protocol required that an embassy should pass through, not by, the door (LIR 101, 102, 103, 109, 114–15). Later, a Seneca delegation committed the same error by going silently past the Mohawk castles en route to Albany when the sachems were abroad (LIR 115), instead of waiting to go down together.

□□◇□□

In the spring of 1687, the threat of a French invasion hung like a dark cloud over the Seneca hills. Governor Dongan saw clearly the importance of the Five Nations to the British position in America, and this is why he again sought to strengthen the league and unify Iroquois policy before the scheduled June meeting of the league outside of Onondaga. He urged the Mohawk and Seneca doorkeepers to bring the interior nations into line and prevent them from attending the Cataraqui meeting. He complimented them on joint action against the Miamis, which would benefit the trade, and "wished the Brethren were alike in other things."

The Oneidas feigned absence when the Mohawk messenger arrived, and said they had gone to listen and decide what was fit (LIR: 112, 114). The Onondagas could give no answer before the general meeting. They claimed the Seneca messengers went silently by their castle. The Cayugas would attend the meeting to accept the return of some Oneida prisoners from the Ottawas. The Cayugas had given their votes to the Senecas; the Oneidas entrusted theirs to the Mohawks. This use of proxies at

---

6. These proceedings, which Colden had from the Indian records, are missing from Wraxall's *Abridgement* (1915: 14).

a grand council may be unique in the literature (LIR: 116). Dongan reiterated his suggestion of an executive committee composed of a sachem and a warrior from each nation to meet with him (LIR: 135). He wrote home to Lord Sunderland, the British secretary of state: "The great dispute between the French and us is which shall have the Five Nations" (BSP 371: 1262, in Grassmann 1969: 428).

Denonville was out to humiliate the Iroquois, and he succeeded. In the campaign in 1687, he smashed the Seneca towns and shattered the league. He recruited Mohawk guides from Caughnawaga and Oka (Eccles 1964: 151), which compounded the divisions within the league, particularly among people of the lower Iroquois towns whose relatives had emigrated to the St. Lawrence. Neither the émigré guides nor their relatives at home wished to engage each other. The Senecas were somewhat remote and made an easier target.

A runner brought news of the disaster to Albany, where, in late June, a Cayuga speaker admitted to the magistrates that disunity prevailed among the nations of the league. Rumors coursed the woodland paths: for example, there was a roomfull of Indian shoes and a store of powder and lead at Cataraqui, which should have warned the English of a French attack. There was little Dongan could do but talk.

Close on the heels of Denonville's sacking the Seneca towns, Dongan advised the Five Nations that he had sent someone to the king, that a raid on the king's subjects might bring war with France, that the raid was not without provocation, and that the Five Nations should not offer peace to the French without his consent, or hearken to any treaty, but should depend on the treaty of peace between the two kings. They should hold any French prisoners without harm for exchange. He proposed a meeting of the executive committee and urged them to keep their designs private. They should offer to bury the hatchet with the Ottawa, Miami, and other "farr" Indians allied to the French, by returning prisoners, urge them to come into the chain, invite them to trade at Albany, and charge them a yearly toll for use of the path through the Longhouse.

News of the Seneca disaster reached Albany the same day as the battle (LIR: 126, 129). Relays of messengers had run from village to village the length of Iroquoia. Dongan went up to Schenectady promptly, and the grand council met on 18 July. In early August, the executive committee met with Dongan, who was relieved that the losses were not greater. He urged that the Iroquois open a path enabling the "North Indians" and the River Indians to come home from their refuge among the Ottawas, allowing them to pass freely through the Five Nations without injury. He urged that the Iroquois make one further attempt to persuade the Christian Indians in Canada to return to their native country and that they get rid of the French priest, Father Lamberville, at Onondaga. Dongan threatened the Oneidas, who had not kept the covenant, with digging up the arms they had buried and returning them to Lord Howard. The Senecas alone, Dongan said, were brave, honest men who kept their word (NYCD, 3: 439–41).

Dongan had learned to listen only to sachems. A Mohawk sachem, addressing the other sachems of the Five Nations, reminded them of Dongan's speech the previous day. He recalled that they had made a bad peace with the French at Onondaga three years previously. Turning to the governor, he explored possible reasons why Denonville had invaded. He mentioned various incidents in the fur trade when the Iroquois had hijacked furs, seized a bark, stolen brandy, and cut a cable. He then commented on those of Dongan's proposals that the sachems approved and would perform. They would let him know when they would accept English Jesuits, and they would open a path to the Far Indians. And yes, their young men were unruly (NYCD, 3: 441–44).

The leading sachem of the Seneca delegation that briefed Dongan on the invasion is reported to have been Adondaraheera, which is a Cayuga league title (Hadonda:he:ha?, C-9, RC 41). Possibly the delegation comprised both Seneca and Cayuga members, but its spokesman clearly held a Cayuga league title, an indication of its stature.

Soon after these events, Dongan interviewed a Christian Mohawk. He wondered whether the French knew that the Five Nations were united. The answer was no. (The real question was not whether the French knew the league existed, which they knew very well, but whether they knew it was functioning.) He learned that Kryn, the Christian Mohawk leader, was about to make overtures through the first Mohawk castle to the Oneida and Onondaga councils. Clearly, the Christian Mohawks were of two minds concerning the French invasion. The real reason they would not come home was that they wanted freedom to practice Christianity apart from pagan drunks (NYCD, 3: 433).

Denonville, for certain, smashed the western door of the Longhouse and frightened the daylights out of the Albanians, but his campaign was not an unqualified success. Although his invasion brought the Iroquois to terms, he lacked sufficient troops to really defeat them. War threatened in Europe, and reinforcements were not forthcoming. His effort left Canada in a bad way. Unless peace could be arranged, the colony faced a long war of attrition. French manpower losses were aggravated by epidemics of smallpox and measles that carried off 9 percent of the population (Eccles 1969: 119).

The English and French governors continued to correspond, but relations between them deteriorated after the Seneca campaign. Both men advanced counterclaims to jurisdiction over the Five Nations. Denonville addressed them as "children"; they were reciprocally "brethren" to Dongan. The sources fail to distinguish "elder" and "younger" brothers, or whether they were just siblings. The three parties construed kinship in their own ways. Attitudes of rectitude did not compensate for misdeeds and neglect. The crisis drove Dongan to seek defensive assistance from Massachusetts and Connecticut as well from the Five Nations. Here began the effort to unite the colonies over the Indian problem that would occupy them during the next century (Grassmann 1969: 454; NYCD, 3: passim; 9: 369–71).

Meanwhile, Dongan was recalled. Before he embarked, he met with the Six Nations and Mahicans in Albany at midwinter 1688. His tenure, they told him, had shed a "great light" upon them. They regarded his claims to extensions of their territory with mild tolerance, but pooh-poohed the conquest theory of sovereignty implied by both powers. Particularly, they held, the French had no proper title to Cataraqui, Mount Royal, or the lands toward the Ottawa, Tionontaté, and Miami territories, which they themselves had invaded. Nor could the French pretend to title for having invaded the Mohawk country, burned some bark houses, and cut down corn, or, more recently, for having devastated the Seneca country. If that were good title, they themselves could claim all of Canada for having subdued whole nations, demolished their castles until "now great oak trees grow where they were built," and afterward confined the French to their houses so that "they were not able to go over a door to urinate" (NYCD, 3: 534).

Peace between the Iroquois and Canada was a left-handed affair, whereas the Five Nations kept their right hands fast and firm in the covenant chain with the English (NYCD, 3: 534). When Sir Edmund Andros returned to replace Dongan in August 1688 and reiterated the claim that the Five Nations were British subjects, they insisted that though poor, they merited equal status reciprocally as "brothers" (NYCD, 3: 557–61). That kinship terms carry different meanings in different cultures is manifest in Andros's reply. He was bound by the class system to put them down.

Louis XIV had sanctioned Denonville to negotiate a peace with the Iroquois. He met a delegation of three nations at Montreal in June 1688. In a bad way themselves, the delegates pretty much accepted his terms and agreed to return the next year to sign the treaty (Eccles 1969: 119; AN C 11A, 10: fol. 48ff.; NYCD, 9: 384–86). That the Iroquois deemed the negotiations a serious affair is manifested by the composition of the delegation. The Oneida council sent four sachems with league titles (Oe-1 through Oe-4, RC 10–13). Garakontie and Hotrewati represented Onondaga, and of three Cayuga sachems, clearly two held league titles (C-7 and C-8, RC 39–40), and possibly another did as well (C-1, RC 33). The representatives of the interior nations (Oneida, Onondaga, and Cayuga) signed the document with appropriate clan eponyms. The treaty marked the advent of the policy of neutrality that was on the mat when the league met the following winter.

The Albany magistrates and merchants were less mindful of the revolution in England than of what went on at Onondaga. They sent Viele, the interpreter, and a man named Saunders, together with two Indians, to represent their interests at the "Grand Meeting" of the Five Nations at midwinter of 1689–90. Two Cayugas who had been carried off to the galleys in 1687 and had now returned were present. A praying Onondaga came to persuade the league in the French interest, inviting them to meet at Cataraqui in the spring to forge an alliance with the French governor. After hearing Indians present the Albany proposals, the English faction of the council prevailed. As subjects of the English king, they had no power to ally themselves with the French, with whom England was at war. A Seneca speaker reported on a treaty with the Ottawas, three of whom were there to confirm it. An Onondaga speaker stood and plunked for the Albany position.

"The Speaker for the whole Assembly then addressed himself to Arnout [Viele] . . . and desired him to lay before the Assembly the Instructions he brought from Albany," which he did. "They then all consulted together." The speaker, on behalf of the whole, then announced the decision. The Iroquois were determined to preserve the English alliance. The speaker next turned to the deputies of the governor of New France and said that the Five Nations would not go to meet at Cataraqui. There would be no peace. They would continue to take up the ax. The French were still in for it.

The ax had already fallen, literally, on 5 August 1689. At dawn that day, fifteen hundred Iroquois emerged from the mists around Lachine. The French settlers were roused from their slumbers by war whoops. Many were axed before stepping outside, others as they fled. Still more were led off to be tortured or held in captivity. Of seventy-seven habitations, fifty-six were burned to the ground. The habitants and the militia were unprepared, and as a surprise attack, for the Iroquois it was a complete success. In late afternoon the warriors withdrew to the south shore of Lake St. Louis, where survivors in the garrisoned forts could see faint fires around which the Iroquois, celebrating their first victory in a war that would last for a decade, burned a few prisoners (JR, 64: 23–25, 87, 91, 272; NYCD, 9: 431, 434, 435; Colden 1750: 88, 90; Eccles 1969: 120). Had the Iroquois understood siege tactics, New France would have fallen.

□□◇□□

Frontenac returned to Quebec in October 1689 as governor and immediately began plans to retaliate against the Iroquois. Uncertainty reigned in the English colonies that year in the aftermath of the "Glorious Revolution" in England. New York underwent a political rebellion, the so-called the Jacob Leisler affair, and there was apprehension over Indian attacks from Canada. Should the French alienate the Five Nations from the chain alliance, it would be the ruin of all the English settlements, as Francis Nicholson wrote to the Lords of Trade in London, to whom colonial governors reported (NYCD, 3: 574–76). Frontenac had designs on Albany, but it escaped because he went at it piecemeal.

Meanwhile, the Penobscots, who were at war with New England, made overtures through the Mahicans to get the Mohawks to strike at the English. But the Mohawks wanted to fight only the French (DHNY, 2: 189; NYCD, 3: 611). In late August "the general Convention" met at Onondaga to resolve this and other issues. Agents of the New England colonies spoke to the River Indians, employing the covenant with the Mohawks to remind them that as His Majesty's subjects, it was their duty to destroy the king's enemies, namely the Penobscots and other troublesome New England Algonquians (LIR: 148–49).

In late September 1689, Viele, the interpreter, delivered a delegation of the Five Nations to hear the New Englanders appeal to the ancient chain alliance and suggest signs that the Iroquois could use to identify their presence—holding up the butt of a gun during the first six months, both hands the next six moons (LIR: 150–53). Of the sachems present, only one carried a league title, which belonged to the Cayugas (C-9, RC 41), and he is listed as a Seneca. They selected Tahaiadoris, the chief Mohawk sachem, as their speaker; he repeated the propositions made to them the previous day and delivered the answer of his confederates. He affirmed that the two parties were met in the "Prefixed Place" appointed by the Christians for the conduct of treaties with the Five Nations. He thanked the New Englanders for renovating the iron covenant chain, now replaced by a silver chain, which linked all of His Majesty's subjects from the Seneca country as far east as any Christian subjects resided, and southward to Virginia. The covenant chain was old and of long standing. Under its terms the confederates had pursued English enemies and saved Christian blood. But Iroquois manpower was now low, which cut down on campaigns. Nevertheless, having taken up the ax against the French, "we will never give the French a smile . . . so long as there is a Frenchman alive" (LIR: 154).

The speech of Tahaiadoris illustrates a separation of powers within the league. His seventh item spoke for the Mohawks alone: they would guarantee to convoy the New England agents home, lest some Penobscots ambush them. Five Mohawk men would escort them. They knew not what the other four nations would do (LIR: 156).

His ninth item reverted to the business of the Five Nations, namely the covenant chain, which they promised to keep inviolate. Here the speaker appealed to the sun as witness, with two belts, one for sun itself and one for its beams.

In the final metaphor, the nations planted the Tree of Peace and Tranquility, its roots fast in the ground and extending to the utmost bounds of the colonies. If the French came to shake it, the roots would move and the Iroquois would sense it.

That event would soon come to pass.

The speaker had managed to avoid answering two main points. The New England agents complained that the Five Nations were still entertaining four eastern messengers and that they had not declared them enemies. The speaker answered that they had no orders from the sachems to deliver the messengers. Moreover, the eastern Indians had committed no hostile acts against the Iroquois, who could not, therefore, declare war on them. Later on, however, the confederates sent the two interpreters to request a private meeting with the New England agents. What they would not say in public was that they had a design to attack first the Penacooks and then the Penobscots (LIR: 157-58). Colden held that the Five Nations were divided on the matter, some favoring the eastern Indians. Secrecy was paramount for the hostile faction (Colden 1750: 103-4).

Adondaraheera, Seneca spokesman (with a Cayuga title), rejoiced at the private arrangement and at their renewing the league and strengthening the chain.[7] He thanked the Mohawks for detailing five men to escort the New England brethren home. He would do the same but for living so far removed. He would nevertheless send an able man for that service (LIR: 158).

One final note on this affair. William Smith, the historian of the New York colony, commented on the extraordinary memory of Tahaiadoris, the Mohawk speaker, and his ability to repeat transactions of the previous day. The way the speakers propped up their memories was for the presiding sachem to prepare sticks in advance and distribute them to individuals, charging them with recalling stated parts of the address. Thus the orator was briefed beforehand to repeat every part of the message and could be prompted if he faulted. This was the custom pursued at public treaties (Smith 1757: 63-64, after Colden 1747: 2, 100).

The Mohawks themselves that summer took the precaution of repairing the palisade of the third castle, Tionontoguen, and asked the magistrates for three teams and six men to help remove it a mile higher upriver, for which service they promised to pay in due time (DHNY, 2: 87-88).

As the year 1689 wound down, the Albany magistrates, it is clear, preferred to stay at home and to use Mohawk sachems and interpreters as legs and ears in council to influence policy at Onondaga. Their mission was to forbid Onondaga from naming ambassadors to treat with Frontenac. The Onondagas had demanded that the Mohawks bring belts to support the English position. Two of thirteen returned Iroquois who had been carried to France would attend a grand council. But none of the news from Canada would be communicated before all the sachems were assembled, it being Iroquois policy not to discuss a matter until the principals were present. Unlike the New York magistrates, the Iroquois were "not

7. It is unclear which league he refers to—the League of the Five Nations or the alliance with New England.

going to lie on their backs in consequence of . . . tidings of peace, and learn to fight only by looking sideways at it." Numbers of their war chiefs were still captive in France, or had died in captivity (DHNY, 2: 137–39).

The magistrates met two days after Christmas. Five Onondaga and Oneida sachems came to hear the news. The sachems confirmed previous news of the threatened Miami attack on the Senecas, that Cadaraqui was abandoned, and that the "farr Indians" had returned two Seneca prisoners as a peace gesture. They wanted Schuyler and some others of such stature to attend the upcoming grand council to advise on matters of such consequence as a French peace proposal, "for they were resolved to do nothing without the knowledge and content of all those included in the Chain" (Colden 1750: 106–7; DHNY, 2: 139–41).

The magistrates were unanimous in not sending any Christians to the grand council, but limited representation to two interpreters and three Mohawks. (For an account of the January council at Onondaga, see chapter 20.) An English agent at Oneida reported that the assembled Iroquois sent an express runner to the Oneidas inviting them to join the other nations at Onondaga to assist in composing their reply to Onontio. The Oneidas showed him three belts: one of five squares on a dark background marking the Five Nations—the *rotinonhsioni*, or "whole house";[8] a second black belt threatening to overset Onontio's war kettle; and a third belt, the longest, destined for the king of France to compose his differences with the king of England. These were to be carried by an Iroquois embassy. The "whole house" concept was beginning to dawn on the English conscience (PRO CO5/1038, ca. 1690).

□□◇□□

Although the Canadians were confident they could raze Albany to the ground and destroy the Iroquois base of supplies, Frontenac moved with caution. Having failed to alienate the Five Nations away from the English at Onondaga the previous summer, a French force employing Caughnawaga guides sacked Schenectady in the winter of 1690 but failed to strike Albany. The Caughnawaga guides were unwilling to strike their kinsmen. The Mohawks learned of the Schenectady disaster two days later. They took two measures: warriors took up the trail of the raiders, killing some and recovering captives, and eight Mohawk sachems (none of whose names suggests a league title) came down to condole the panic-stricken Albanians, stating that such was their custom and urging them not to flee (NYHS Colls. 1869: 164ff.; DHNY, 2: 164–67; DePuy 1917).

Both the Mohawks and the Albanians were discouraged. The Albany palisades were so low that "the Indians jump over them like a dog." But the two partners could find refuge in symbolism. The ritual of condolence had cleansed the blood from the defiled house of public treaties. The chain held the covenant fast. The image of the "whole house" of the Iroquois Confederacy was now understood in Albany. Thereafter, officials there would appeal to it and would receive the congratulations of their hardy Mohawk brethren of the race of the Bear, who urged them to take courage (*jagonya*). The Mohawks asked for help from the River

---

8. The Reverend Mr. Dellius communicated to Governor Fletcher a slightly different interpretation of this belt by Millet at Oneida: that it contained "five black squares on a white ground" (NYCD, 4: 79–80).

Indians and for smiths to repair their guns. The Albanians reiterated Dongan's idea of an executive committee of the Five Nations and awarded the Mohawks six belts, duffels, tobacco, and provisions. The Mohawks expected the upper nations to consult with them and were confident that they would condole the English (DHNY, 2: 167–70; NYCD, 3: 712). The French had attacked both ends of the chain. The Mohawks sensed the anti-English bias of the Albany Dutch, which encouraged the southeastern wars, and asked why they allowed English soldiers in the fort when a Dutch prince reigned (Colden 1750: 94ff.).

It was confusion that reigned in the aftermath of the destruction of Schenectady. In May 1691, Governor Sloughter, who served less than a year, met with a group of local praying Indians, the erstwhile flock of Dominie Godfrey Dellius, who had succeeded Megapolensis. They professed to represent the three Mohawk clans and proceeded to condole the governor for the deaths of ship companions lost in the winter voyage. They disclaimed being sanctioned by the Mohawk sachems to treat of public affairs, being only praying Indians and the governor's children. They planned to settle at the mouth of Schoharie Creek, where they desired Protestant teaching. They presented the governor with a warrior's pouch decorated with porcupine quills (NYCD, 3: 771–72).

A month later, Sloughter addressed the upper four nations, the Mohawks having gone off to make peace with the French in the confusion of the Leislerian affair. Thirty-two sachems attended, of whom I can identify but two as having league titles—one Seneca (S-2, RC 44), and the other Cayuga (C-9, RC 41), who is listed as Seneca. The Onondaga "Rottsaganna" suggests Oe-9, RC 18. Several days later they were joined by Mohawks who then invoked the whole house of the confederacy. Having welcomed the new governor, the speaker for the upper nations recalled the history of the covenant, bound by the chain that tied them together in one genetic unity. He invoked the Tree of Peace, its roots extending to the Seneca country. Following Iroquois political usage, he urged the magistrates to fill up the empty benches to completion, naming three men who were adopted Mohawks. Last, he recommended interpreter Hilletie van Olinda, whom they accepted as a daughter (NYCD, 3: 774, 777).

Frontenac had sent a belt to advance peace with the praying Indians in Canada, which Sloughter "spewed" (rejected). It was left lying on the ground. It requested the release of some Caughnawaga prisoners among the Senecas (NYCD, 3: 778–80).

Men at war could not hunt and were compelled, the Mohawks said, to kill domestic animals of the colonists, lest they starve.

When the governor asked for two hundred men to go out and fight, he learned that the upper nations had to go home and consult, and they were prevented from prompt action by an upcoming grand council at Onondaga, to which they invited the governor to send delegates.

Within a fortnight, death struck down Tahaiadoris, leading chief and speaker of the third Mohawk castle. Although the warriors of the first two castles were armed and ready to depart, condolence law prevented his mourning relatives from undertaking any action until after the ceremony, a delay of weeks. This occasioned the remark that Tahaiadoris "never did good in his lifetime" (BSP in Grassmann 1969: 545–46). Thus, the death of a sachem delayed a war party. Major Peter Schuyler departed for Canada without it (NYCD, 3: 800–5).

Meanwhile, some Mohawks who had visited their kin at Caughnawaga brought intelligence that the French across the river were making some two hundred canoes for a design against Onondaga. While the praying Mohawks had no compunction about fighting the Onondagas, they warned their kinsmen to stay away and did not want them involved.

In the Iroquois view, the covenant chain carried mutual obligations. Governor Sloughter, on a visit to Albany, "found the place in great disorder" but got the message. The Iroquois were goading the colonies to unite and form an alliance against the French. He wrote to the governors of Virginia, Maryland, Pennsylvania, West Jersey, Connecticut, Rhode Island, and Massachusetts conveying the sentiments of native statesmen about "how far they think you are obliged (being in the same covenant with them) to aid and assist us against the French." Should Albany fall, the colonies on both sides would suffer. It was only the place itself that kept the Indians "steady to us, and a loss of that must be a loss of them, and the loss of them must be the loss of all the king's interest of this Continent" (NYCD, 3: 784).

In September 1691, a delegation of Seneca, Oneida, and Mohawk sachems (none with league titles) administered a "draft of understanding" to the governor. A Seneca speaker from "Basswood castle" offered propositions loaded with symbolism. Although the Senecas were a nation dispersed and scattered by the French invasion as far as Onondaga, they urged that the house be kept clean by condoling the Mohawks for their recent losses. He appealed to the "Tree of Prosperity" as the sign of peaceful relations, with its roots firm and stable, extending throughout the whole house to the margins of government. Beneath the shade of its leaves, all who maintained the covenant sought shelter.

A Mohawk speaker chided the English for failing to condole them and the Oneidas for their losses. Albany authorities replied using the tree motif with great effect, demonstrating an understanding of Iroquois metaphors. They contrasted "the rest of the house" with the Mohawks, who were stalling and not committing themselves to the proposed joint effort. The Mohawk excuse, they said, was that "you can't peel bark after the season is advanced"—not the death of their sachem. The Mohawks are quoted as saying, "It is not our custom to stop a general resolution for the loss of some dead" (NYCD, 3: 808).

At year's end, the Mohawks and Oneidas had lost their principal captains in an engagement near Lake Champlain, which had a severe impact on all the Five Nations (NYCD, 3: 814–16). Where were the reinforcements from neighboring colonies? The conflict of cultures had not abated.

When Sloughter died suddenly after a few months in office, Colonel Ingoldsby, as ad interim governor in Manhattan, advised the assembly that the treasury was exhausted and he could not buy presents for the Iroquois. The assembly managed to appropriate funds to sustain two hundred fusiliers for the defense of Albany, but it referred to a committee the matter of raising six hundred pounds for the Indian presents (Leder 1961: 9, 22, 25).

In late May 1691, Ingoldsby hastened upriver to meet the principals of the four upper nations. They asserted that although of one body and blood with him, they could not sustain the war without ammunition. Next day he urged them to carry the fight to the enemy and gave them one hundred pounds of powder and two hundred pounds of lead. He had to admit that Christians were not as good in the woods as Indians, and he hinted at support from other colonies (NYCD, 3: 840–42). A week later Oheda, chief sachem of the Oneidas, and Rode, likewise of the Mohawks, joined the other headmen.[9] The former complained that the Mohawk dead were not condoled, that the governor spoke only of the loss of Christians, and that the nations would have come down to condole the deaths of his men but were engaged in the war at home (NYCD, 3: 842–44). He reaffirmed the covenant, planted the evergrowing Tree of Peace, cleaned the house, and commended the interpreter, Hilletie van Olinda, for "she is our mouth." Rode asked whether neighboring colonies had drawn their arms out of the covenant chain: "How can they be brethren and not of one family?" At their end of the alliance, the Iroquois demanded performance of certain expectations. "Unite and we will show you the way to overcome" (NYCD, 3: 843).

As mayor of Albany, Peter Schuyler knew too well what it meant to have 350 Indians encamped nearby. Best to present them a dog, a pistol, and a sword, provision them, and hasten them out of town. Otherwise, they were killing cattle, destroying fences, and stealing corn. He did lecture them on public versus private property—how the colonists' cattle were no more common property than beavers were to the Iroquois, notwithstanding their memory of the understanding with Governor Andros to the contrary.

The military details of the campaign against Canada are of less interest than Iroquois confidence in strong ties of kinship between themselves and their relatives at Caughnawaga—ties that Schuyler mistrusted, deeming the Caughnawaga Iroquois enemies in the European sense. A Mohawk was confident that he could go inside and parlay with his *agadoni*, his father's kinsmen, but Schuyler insisted they meet outside (LIR: 162–68). A further misunderstanding arose over the Albanians' usurping of relations with the Shawnees, traditional enemies of the Iroquois, without first informing the Five Nations and gaining their consent. Normal protocol demanded that the whole house meet first and discuss the matter. Common consent was of the essence (LIR: 168–69).

□□◇□□

In the summer of 1692, the home government began to recognize the needs of the Iroquois and undertook to lift some of the burden from the New York colony. Governor Fletcher landed in August, bearing royal instructions and funds for presents to the Iroquois. A soldier of the king, he was not inclined to sit idly and wonder, but, ignoring the council's advice, he would survey the situation himself. Almost immediately he went upriver to Albany and Schenectady to meet the magistrates and make arrangements to renew the covenant chain. The visit pleased the Indians. Fletcher maintained that if the Shawnees made peace with the Five Nations, they should remain in the chain. These efforts to the contrary, he was unable to stave off disaster the next winter when the French struck the Mohawk castles for the second time since 1666 (Trelease 1960: 308–9; Eccles 1964: 192).

When word of the attack reached Fletcher a fortnight later, he immediately called up the militia, arranged for transport by land if the North River froze, and, with a favorable wind, reached Albany in a record three days. This swift response

---

9. Could Oheda be Hodatchehde (Oe-1, RC 10)?

so amazed the Mohawks that they named Fletcher Cayenquiragoe (Kayv:kwira-kowane, "Big Arrow" [Michelson 1973: 125, 72]), usually rendered "Great Swift Arrow," which actually may be a typical Iroquois pun on the name Fletcher. The Mohawk pursuit of the French, under Schuyler, ended when captive spouses and children were threatened (NYCD, 4: 16–19). In his dialogue with the Mohawks, Fletcher berated them for unpreparedness and for not keeping scouts out, which they admitted the same day. Schuyler reported to Fletcher that "the enemy have now twice been at the Gates to their Castle undiscovered and tied a bunch of small reeds or straws at the very door" (NYCD, 4: 65). The Mohawks' loss should be revenged, Schuyler told him, but grief and anxiety delayed them, and it was their custom, Fletcher should know, that the deaths first be condoled. Want of ammunition diminished their capabilities, and it would be easy to reduce Canada if only the colonies would unite (NYCD, 4: 21–25).

The devastation of the Mohawk castles did not completely shatter the Mohawk tribe. They relocated their three main settlements to more secure sites south of the river. Though they were diminished in numbers, that year marked the end of the diaspora to the Laurentian missions. The Mohawks were tired of the Jesuits and were disposed to entertain Protestants. At Oneida, Father Millet was still active as leading chief, siphoning intelligence to Frontenac and worrying Fletcher. A report that the Onondagas had also been defeated spread alarm in Albany and prompted a proclamation forbidding residents to depart (Grassmann 1969: 588). The league was to meet at Onondaga to hear a French peace overture, and Fletcher would try to frustrate it. Meanwhile, he got the brush-off from the other colonial governors. Affairs had reached the low water mark.

The old men meeting at Onondaga, discerning that military aid was not forthcoming from the other colonies, determined to keep the path open to both European powers. They would assert their independence as free men—they were not subjects of either king, nor were they the king's children, except in a polite sense. Fletcher, perhaps more sensible to Iroquois kinship usage than Frontenac was, styled himself "elder brother"—still a status ranking "younger brothers." The grand council was already leaning toward the policy of neutrality that would prevail in the next century.

The Iroquois peace movement centered on Oneida, where Millet served the interests of Frontenac, who sought to neutralize the confederacy—realizing that he could not destroy it, even if that were desirable (Trelease 1960: 313). He sent belts and instructions to Millet, information that the Iroquois promptly shared with the English, just to balance things.

Having learned of Frontenac's designs, Fletcher did what he could to preserve the illusion of the covenant chain. He prepared and conducted two major conferences with sachems of the Five Nations during the next two years. William Bradford, having removed to New York in 1693 to become the father of printing in the middle colonies (Winsor 1884–99, 5: 248; 8: 529), printed a journal of the first meeting and an account of the treaty of 1694.[10] The proceedings of these

---

10. "Journal of Stephen Courtland and Nicholas Beyard . . ." (Wm. Bradford: New York, 1693), and *An Account of the Treaty between His Excellency Benjamin Fletcher . . . and the Indians of the Five Nations . . . 1694* (Wm. Bradford: New York, 1694). I saw copies of these works in the Henry E. Huntington Library, San Marino, California.

conferences convey substantial material on the symbolism and ritual of treaty procedures as they illustrate Iroquois political protocol, which colonial officials were beginning to share.

The war had gone badly for the Iroquois and they were not jumping to Fletcher's tune. He could not prevent their listening to French emissaries at Onondaga, nor could he head off Iroquois delegations exploring peace with Frontenac. Fletcher's best efforts failed to convince the Iroquois that they were British subjects; they consistently maintained their independence. The Oneidas were the least cooperative and were inclined toward the French. They gave the English authorities but three weeks' notice of the grand council meeting to hear Frontenac's message. Fletcher was not amused and promptly fired off a message repeating former demands and promising support, which he signed "yor freind and *elder brother . . . Caijenqiragoe*" (NYCD, 4: 32ff.). (Whether his use of a ranking kinship status had any effect remains speculative.) Dirck Wessels, who carried this message to Onondaga, reported the breakdown of the negotiations and the posture of the league as summarized by Aquadarondo, then the chief Onondaga sachem: "The Mohaques [who declined attending] are as if conquered, the Oneijdes wavering, the Senekes [the greatest force] more inclined to bever hunting than warr so that the Onondages ly in the greatest danger. You hear in your ears the cry of the women & children for the losses of their husbands & relations."

Aquadarondo went on to protest that the Englishmen's great promises to take Quebec five years earlier had not materialized. He carefully avoided referring to "Our Brother Caijenquiragoe" who, he said, "behaves like a soldier but recently here." But other long-time members of the covenant chain—New England, Maryland, and Virginia—do nothing. Fletcher's renewing the covenant for them "doth not knock the enemy in the head" (NYCD, 4: 59–63; Trelease 1960: 314–15).

In short, the Iroquois were confused. If anything, they favored peace. Aquadarondo further explained to Wessels that it was Iroquois policy to hold public meetings on all occasions, and Wessels observed that when the whole house met it was customary for the presiding Onondaga sachem to lead the sachems of the other nations in an antiphonal song, which presumably affirmed that they were of one mind.

To strengthen the British position vis-à-vis the Five Nations and to relieve the mounting anxiety in Albany, Fletcher took several measures. He put Peter Schuyler in charge of Iroquois affairs, relieving Robert Livingston, the long-time secretary of the magistrates. In 1696 he created a three-man board of commissioners. He procured the issuance of a royal letter asking help from neighboring colonies, but he failed to gain either political control or military command of any other militia (Trelease 1960: 309, 315–16).

Without this kind of support, the Iroquois realized that alone they could not drive the French from Canada, and so they temporized by sending a diplomatic mission to Frontenac, suggesting ways in which he might make peace with the English, which he rejected. Meanwhile, to cover their bets, Teganissorens, their most able diplomat, who was also a favorite of Frontenac's, appeared before the Albany magistrates in February 1694 to report on the mission of Tareha, an Oneida, to Canada, describe the belts passed, and relate the preliminary proceedings at Onondaga. The grand council then included two voting sachems—

Millet of Oneida and an Onondaga—who were adopted native Frenchmen, and they had introduced writing to document wampum belts, which were read. There was intelligence on war preparations in Canada: Frontenac had commissioned the weaving of some two hundred to four hundred burden straps (tumplines) for carrying packs (NYCD, 4: 85–92, 87; Colden 1750: 159–60). To Schuyler's request that the Iroquois stop all correspondence with the French for seventy days, Teganissorens replied that he had no authority to answer Schuyler. He would lay down a belt in each of the castles informing the nations of the request, but he could not promise compliance (Colden 1750: 161).

In May 1694, Teganissorens led nine Onondaga sachems, more than half their number in the league council, to Canada (Colden 1750: 165–66). Other sachems met with Fletcher in Albany. The speaker for the latter group admitted that fear motivated the mission to Canada. He protested Fletcher's agent's interfering at a general council at Onondaga and ordering the fire removed to Albany. "The Privilege of meeting in General Council, when we please, is a Privilege we have always enjoyed." No former governor had obstructed this privilege. At Albany, he said, the Iroquois had planted a Tree of Peace with extending roots for business of the chain—that is, colonial affairs.

The Iroquois, he went on, intended to keep that tree and sit in its shade. Such prohibitions of their assemblies would have evil consequences (Colden 1750: 165). Onondaga had been the place of council before the arrival of the Christians. "There . . . from the beginning, a continual Fire [has] been kept burning; it is made of two great Logs, whose fire never extinguishes. As soon as the Hatchet-makers [Europeans] arrived, this General Council at Onondaga planted this Tree at Albany, whose Roots and Branches have since spread as far as New-England, Connecticut, Pennsylvania, Maryland, Virginia; and under the shade of this Tree all these English Colonies have frequently been sheltered" (Colden 1750: 167).

At this May meeting, Fletcher gave the Iroquois one hundred days to return and declare who was for him and who against, which suggested that the latter would be treated as enemies.

In August, having cut the notches from memory sticks, twenty-five sachems of the Five Nations paused at the edge of the pine bush that then reached well into modern Albany. The delegation comprised five Mohawks, with Rode as their speaker, three Oneidas, seven Onondagas, with Sadekanacktie and Teganissorens as speakers, four Cayugas, including Dekaeijow (Haga?en:yonk, C-1, RC 33), the lone league title, and five Senecas, plus a "queen," or clan mother. Fletcher had assembled the governor of the Jerseys and agents from Massachusetts Bay and Connecticut. Aside from its avowed purpose to renew the covenant chain, sort out loyalties, and hear Teganissorens relate his negotiations with Frontenac, this was a most important treaty that asserted Albany's supremacy in Indian affairs. It is well documented and it is loaded with ritual symbolism and metaphor.[11]

The treaty was held in the middle of present-day State Street, just above the meeting house. The sachems sent a messenger to inform the governor, their host, that they were ready. An honor guard awaited them. The sachems, led by Rode

11. Bradford 1694; Colden 1750: 170; NYCD, 4: 38–47; LIR: 170–72; Wadsworth 1852; Duane 1869; DePuy 1917, treaty no. 3; Trelease 1960: 317–18; Sewall 1973, 2: pp. 319–21; Jennings 1984: 203–4.

singing peace songs, came down the hill in ranks of two, not unlike the procession in the modern Condolence Council, to confront their hosts across the symbolic fire. Rode continued to pace and sing two or three songs while the sachems were seated on planks laid on the ground. (This recalls the resumption of the eulogy by the clearminded on arrival at the mourner's fire.)

Teganissorens stood and asked permission to sing a song of peace before the speakers began their discourse. During the first three days (15–17 August) of the eight-day treaty, nothing was said "but what was said by the Indians," according to Sewall and Wadsworth, which means that the Iroquois, as respondents, had the advantage of speaking first (Foster 1984). Fletcher made no welcoming speech.

Rode, as Mohawk speaker for the eastern door, addressed the sachems of the Five Nations, congratulating them on seeing Brother Great Arrow and participants in the covenant chain, with whom they were about to consult on matters affecting the public good. The chiefs responded with two more songs of peace.

The confederacy entrusted its main address to Sadekanacktie of Onondaga. He first reminded his colleagues how long they had enjoyed friendship with inhabitants of the New York colony and other crown subjects in America. He cited acts of mutual friendship and related the origin of the covenant chain (Wraxall 1915: 25).

He then turned to the governor, addressing him as "brother" and by his council name. "You expected to see us here, and we are come." The sachems had met the deadline of one hundred days. "Who will be for you, and who against you?" They were of one voice. Last May they had given an account of messengers sent to Canada, were rebuked and then received back in favor with a wampum belt confirming the covenant chain.

Their numbers were greatly diminished, Sadekanacktie continued, and the hunting was poor. (This is a recurrent theme, but just then they had suffered losses in war and from disease.) He repeated the evolution of the covenant chain from twisted bark to iron and finally to silver, and he reiterated the obligations of participants to avenge violations. Others have been attracted to put their hands in the chain, he said. Iroquois hands were tired and stiff from holding the chain while neighbors sat and smoked. In a metaphor of decrease, Sadekanacktie remarked: "The Greese is melted from our Flesh, and drops upon our Neighbours, who are grown fat, and live at ease, while we become lean: They flourish and we decrease."

Then, naming the English plantations, he said, "We are envied by our Enemies round about, and particularly by the French, who are very unconstant." Should the French attack, he urged combining forces. He implied that the chain alliance was already ancient and that it required full participation, so that "Thunder itself shall not break it."

He next appealed to the metaphorical Tree of Peace, with its roots extending to neighboring colonies, "which we now make green and sapid. Whoever touches that tree or its roots, must not only be made aware of it, but its adherents must rise up and fall upon and destroy them." And as if to acquaint the governor with a historical precedent, he declared that the Five Nations were resolved to continue an ancient custom of keeping their meeting place at Onondaga. They would send word of general meetings and would welcome attendance. For certain, the league had met at Onondaga before Fort Orange was established.

The Iroquois acknowledged disobedience in going to Canada to treat with the French. It was a matter of gaining intelligence for survival, Sadekanacktie claimed. There was the usual plea for cheaper goods and ammunition.

Having renewed the covenant with all parties, and with special regard for New England, from whom the Iroquois hoped to receive continued military support, the speaker presented to their agents, as a token to remind them, a salmon painted on a blank paper that the Bostonians had previously sent to the Iroquois. They presented Fletcher, as head of the covenant, with a wampum belt and asked him to notify the other governments that the chain was renewed. Having said what they planned for that night, they would relate next day the transactions in Canada and describe tokens received from the Far Indians.

On 16 August, Teganissorens reported on the mission to Canada. He had addressed the governor of Canada as "father," telling him that if peace were not concluded now, it would lie at his door, not theirs—that they had taken the hatchet from the hands of the allied River Indians while he had put one in the hands of the Ottawas, and that he was untrustworthy. Teganissorens blamed Frontenac for starting the war. "But we have never hated the House of Ockquese [ʔAkwi:se], our [adopted] son" of Montreal, and he would be welcome at Onondaga.

Teganissorens said he had appealed to the praying Indians of Caughnawaga, who knew Iroquois customs better than the governor, to advance the peace. As for those at Kanehsatageh (Oka), the second castle, he held them to be worse than the French for deserting and siding with the enemy.

"Father, you have almost eat us," Teganissorens had told Frontenac, meaning that the war had consumed the best of Iroquois manpower. While the Iroquois had thrown the hatchet into a rapids, Frontenac had retrieved it and hurled it into the sky with a string attached to the helve, and then pulled it down. In retaliation, the Iroquois had fallen on Lachine. Notwithstanding, they wiped away and covered the blood shed on both sides. To drive away evil thoughts and purge Onontio's heart, Teganissorens administered a "Cordial or Drink" as an emetic. (This item remains as the fourth word of the Requickening Address.)

The Iroquois had twice quenched the fires at Cadaraqui, Teganissorens said, and would admit of no further rebuilding there. Nevertheless, they "cleared the river" that the French might have free passage to Onondaga. They cleared the sun and dispelled the clouds and darkness. As for prisoners, Teganissorens explained the Iroquois custom of distributing them to families to replace losses. (They were beyond council jurisdiction.)

In reply, Frontenac had maintained that any peace with the English was up to the king of France, and he insisted on keeping two hostages, which displeased Teganissorens; but an Onondaga and a Seneca volunteered. Frontenac would erect a Tree of Peace at Cadaraqui. He laid down a belt for Governor Fletcher to send people of his own. There was a second belt from the Tionontatés (ex Hurons) requesting relief from the war with the Five Nations. (Both belts were later rejected by Fletcher.)

On the following day (the seventeenth), the delivery of a second report was entrusted to the leading Onondaga sachem, Sadekanacktie. (Thadada:hoʔ was not present.) He sang a lengthy "Song of Peace" before relating negotiations with the Ottawas and Tionontatés. The Iroquois had sent home two prisoners with belts. The captors were prepared to reciprocate. The captors observed condolence forms and used wampum strings, notably "a cordial and potion" to settle the heart. The metaphor of an open door extending as far as Albany, which Sadekanacktie employed, is a variation on the path theme. The Onondaga custom of preparing a room for invited guests anticipates Bartram and Weiser sixty years later (Bell 1973). An understanding of how to compose future differences called for black wampum. The two parties dispersed clouds, dispelled the darkness of war, and restored the sun of peace. A catlinite stone pipe disk brought to Onondaga represented the sun. The Ottawas and Tionontatés had placed a hatchet in the hands of named Central Algonquians to war against the Five Nations. They would now retrieve it. They regarded the Senecas as stupid creatures whom they warned not to go hunting far from their villages in the territories of the Central Algonquians and then blame us. The speaker gave a stone hatchet pipe. (This last reflects mounting pressure from midwestern Algonquians, as well as the Ottawas and Mississaugas, to reclaim Iroquois conquests [Eid 1979; 1985]).

Fearing that the Far Indians passing through Iroquoia to trade at Albany would observe their weakness and report it to Canada, the Five Nations suggested that the Far Indians be admitted no farther than the Seneca country. (This would give the Senecas a trade advantage.)

The Onondaga speaker deferred other replies until another day. Fletcher also wanted time to consider.

Three days later (20 August) the conference resumed. Sadekanacktie, speaker for the Five Nations, deferred to the governor, who approved of their renewing the covenant on the first day. He wanted to know whether they had really made peace with Canada. Sadekanacktie replied that Five Nations losses were such that they could not sustain a war with the French, that they could no longer serve as a barrier between the English and the French, and that they had brought their enemy's answer, which they laid at Great Arrow's feet, referring the whole matter to him to work it out.

Governor Fletcher wanted to know what they meant by making peace with Canada providing he approve it. In effect, the Iroquois had negotiated despite their promises not to, had made a de facto peace without his approval, which he regarded as a violation of the covenant, and had left him the alternatives of approving the peace or declaring war upon them. He would, to use their metaphor, tie up his hatchet, but he could make no peace with the governor of Canada. Iroquois diplomacy had failed to stabilize the situation, but an English governor began to speak the language of forest diplomacy.

While protesting Fletcher's doubts about Iroquois integrity and fidelity in keeping the covenant chain, Sadekanacktie elaborated the chain concept (as the umbilical cord of the Five Nations). "The least Member cannot be touched, but the whole Body must feel and be sensible." Should an enemy hurt the least part of it, they would all join to destroy that enemy, "for we are one Head, one Flesh, and one Blood."

Fletcher having rejected the wampum belt of Frontenac, Sadekanacktie suggested sending someone to a neutral place where the two governments could confer.

Two things that worried Fletcher were the rebuilding of the fort at Cadaraqui and the presence of Jesuits among the Iroquois. He twitted the Iroquois, "the antient and most War-like Nations of Indians upon this Continent," for creeping so low as to beg peace of the governor of Canada. The Iroquois speaker manifested some understanding of the levels of power in the two governments and suggested ways of communicating between the parties. Fletcher demurred. Frontenac's writing, then available to Fletcher, put the Iroquois in a subservient position. Frontenac consistently assumed the position that he stood in the relationship of father to his Iroquois children. Fletcher understood this European view of kinship, which was not the Iroquois view, and held that this made the Iroquois subject to Frontenac's correction. Sadekanacktie responded that "father" was only a name that they had given Frontenac "because he calls us 'Children,' not that we own him as our Father."

□□◇□□

Teganissorens was maneuvering the Onondagas toward neutrality, which the grand council would adopt as policy presently. The praying Indians had assured him that they would hold fast to the peace that their "father," Frontenac, had made with the Five Nations. He had persuaded warriors prepared to attack the English not to.

As the treaty proceedings continued that August 1694, Fletcher made an ill-advised attempt to bluff the Five Nations, saying that he would not attack them for their misdeeds and would let pass their peace efforts in Canada, when they must have known how impotent he really was.

In a private afternoon session with the governor regarding a proposal that the Five Nations send a mission to the eastern Indians, Sadekanacktie admitted that Onondaga was as short of diplomats as it was of warriors. The manpower shortage extended to sachems. Here is further reason why incumbents in league titles seldom were represented at treaties (Bradford 1694: 24). Fletcher acknowledged that the Iroquois had their own methods of making peace (with the Far Indians), but cautioned them not to be rocked to sleep by their ritual.

Indians desired that goods be sold cheap. Attributed to Sadekanacktie is the remark that such would make Albany desirable when the Far Indians came, "like a fair Maid that has many Lovers, so all people will flock thither." (Is this an Onondaga metaphor?)

New York governors preferred Albany meetings for the business of the covenant chain. Fletcher professed no objection to the Five Nations' meeting at Onondaga for the conduct of their own affairs, but he could not promise to send representatives to Onondaga on chain affairs. Later, in a public meeting, he reiterated his stand. Only when peace or war was treated need he be present. Treaties should be held in Albany, where the covenant chain was born (Bradford 1694: 29–30).

The Onondagas were aware of factions in their council and of leaks to the French. "We have but one Eye and one Ear, whatever we see or hear, your Excellency shall see and hear forthwith." Aware that there were persons present in his delegation who would report to the French, Sadekanacktie advised the governor to omit sensitive matters from his public speech. He disclaimed knowledge of a belt rumored to have been sent by the Senecas to Indians on the Delaware River, attributing it to Indians who had fled the league, then living on the Susquehanna.

By 22 August, after a week of meetings, the Indians were eager to receive their presents and go home. Fletcher desired the Iroquois to work on the praying Indians to come down and ask him to bury the hatchet. He reiterated a denial of any pretense to hinder their ancient custom of meeting at Onondaga on their own affairs, but he insisted that treaties involving war and peace be held at Albany, birthplace of the chain. Realizing that the Five Nations would be sending embassies to Canada, he advised them to limit the delegation to a few sachems. They should keep their young men at home and not listen to the Jesuit Millet. He laid down a wampum belt to seal the renewal of the chain.

On the eighteenth, Fletcher treated independently with the River Indians. They professed to have been once strong but now to be weak. Fletcher admonished them for slipping aside in New England and getting drunk after hunting, thereby depriving their families of sustenance. On the twenty-eighth, he met with the "Mahikanders," the "Lower River Indians, and the Shawnee." The Mahican speaker condoled the loss of some Christians killed on a recent joint venture. Their relationship with the English, they said, was that of "parent and child." Obviously, the Mahicans shared Iroquois ritual forms.

Colden commented on this treaty that neither governor could make peace without its first being made in Europe. He recognized that the Onondaga council was divided into factions. He remarked how conscientious these "Barbarians" were in keeping the terms of their treaties, even at a time when their own exigencies would demand independent action. When the grand council met at Onondaga to consult on terms offered by the French, Colden wrote, they were divided in their opinions: the Cayugas and part of the Senecas favored the French proposals, but a majority of the sachems absolutely opposed allowing the French to rebuild the fort at Cataraqui. Nor would they admit tribes allied to the French into the treaty. The peace faction formed a delegation and went to Canada returning thirteen captives, notably Father Millet, who had been taken in 1689, and Joncaire, long among the Senecas. Both men had advanced to sachemships (Colden 1750: 179).

Ten Mohawk sachems met with Fletcher at Albany on 28 August 1695 to report on affairs among the upper nations. Beyond their unsuccessful appeal for military support, they reported that the letter and belt of wampum that Sadekanacktie and Teganissorens had brought to Onondaga that spring had been shown to all the Five Nations and had been well accepted (Penn Letters 2: folio 300, APSL).

The management of Indian affairs at Albany took a turn in 1696. From 1675 onward, the magistrates had been de facto commissioners, with Robert Livingston, town clerk, as recorder. Fletcher took Indian relations out of the hands of the magistrates by formally creating a board of three commissioners, soon to be four. Livingston, temporarily out of it, went to England to settle accounts of funds spent in Indian matters but not reimbursed during two decades. He also got even with Fletcher, who would soon be replaced by Bellomont, by convincing the authorities that he had indeed served twenty years as secretary for Indian affairs and getting the office established with a salary (Trelease 1960: 207, 309–10; Leder 1961).

Following Fletcher's big conference renewing the covenant chain, the Iroquois peace effort came to naught. League policy shifted as the militant faction evidently gained the ascendancy. War parties went out, with or without the sanction of the old men, and Frontenac terminated negotiations and resumed his military buildup. He moved troops to Cadaraqui and rebuilt the fort. This act unified the league in opposition. Within a year, Frontenac would lead an attack on Onondaga and Oneida (see chapter 18).

The news frightened the Albanians, and as tension mounted, many of them fled downriver. Persistent rumors of a French fleet headed for New York harbor kept Fletcher in Manhattan contending with a miserly colonial assembly unwilling to fund additional troops. No help came from neighboring colonies. Fletcher blamed the Indians for their own bad luck—a result of their drunken, negligent, and careless ways, he believed—and sent them home to rely on themselves. Small war parties harassed New France, and Indians allied to the French retaliated, infiltrating Iroquois towns and raiding farms near Albany and Schenectady.

As the Iroquois perceived, the rebuilt Cadaraqui became a staging area for Frontenac's attack on Onondaga. The news reached Albany and sped downriver to New York. Fletcher proposed taking several hundred men to defend Onondaga, but the council stalled for want of funds. Too late, Fletcher went up to Albany in August 1696 to hear Mohawk and Oneida sachems describe the magnitude of the disaster. He could only call another conference and order corn supplied to the victims at public expense. Had the council approved, Fletcher's plan would have failed. It was too far to Onondaga, and the French outnumbered him four to one. Clearly, New York could not fulfill its promises to the Iroquois, and they knew it (Trelease 1960: 318–21).

After Frontenac's raid, stores of corn were nearly exhausted in Iroquoia. The Mohawks had very little, the Oneidas were ruined, and no one could predict whether the Senecas would recall the Onondagas' having charged them their most valuable wampum belts for supplies after Denonville's invasion. The Cayugas' harvest was intact but of uncertain quantity to provision their confederates (NYCD, 9: 657).

Despite the Five Nations' losses and diminished numbers, securing their friendship remained a vital British concern. They must not go over to the French, and the Senecas were crucial. To continue them in His Majesty's service, Lavinas van Schaick wrote the Lords of Trade, the most proper method was to renew the covenant chain, and this was always done at Albany with presents. The cost would approach one thousand pounds sterling (NYCD, 4: 168–70). Goods were expensive, but personnel were vital, for no Englishman in the colonies then spoke an Iroquoian language, which differed one from another (NYCD, 4: 181). A plan called for raising some English youths among the Indians to learn their language, customs, and manners perfectly (NYCD, 4: 183–84), but this was never done.

Fletcher made one final effort to retain the loyalty of the Five Nations by renewing the covenant chain. No French fleet having arrived off Manhattan, he went up to Albany in September. With him went a substantial present from the king, nearly matched by the New York colony, which—what with conference expenses, scouts, and repair of guns—amounted to 660 pounds (NYCD, 4: 236). The civility of the Iroquois, despite their plight, was remarkable in the light of the recent disaster and their long-standing grievance over the failure of the colonies to mount an attack by land and sea against Canada. This time they made their plan explicit by mapping French settlements along the St. Lawrence on a bundle of beaver skins to demonstrate to the English "the smallness of the enemy" and how such an attack might be accomplished. They asked that the map be sent to the king (NYCD, 4: 198, 236-37).[12] To be certain that the map and their proposals reached the king, they gave five additional beaver skins to pay for pen, paper, and ink. They remained adamant in the face of Fletcher's protest that to transmit their message to the king and expect an answer and action by spring was impossible. Only when Fletcher agreed to write to the king did they renew the covenant. Indeed, so insistent were the sachems in their desire that their words reach the king's ears that two of them went as far as New York with the thought of shipping to England, but turned back.

This conference was of such surpassing interest in the colony that William Bradford published the journal of the proceedings.[13] On 2 October, Dackashata, a Seneca sachem, addressed the governor under twelve heads. He condoled losses with a belt. He had come with the whole house to consider matters affecting its welfare. They were there to renew the chain with all parties that they might partake of the fire, which he recommended they keep up. He would drink and deliver the cup. They had come to remove the dark cloud, as morning sun dispels darkness. They confirmed the tree of safety and welfare planted at Albany. They made fast all the roots and branches for participants of the covenant, that all in the chain might sit quietly in its shadow. He renewed the chain on behalf of the whole house. They had lately lost two castles by enemy action, and both parties should assist them. Finally, they appealed to the king (NYCD, 4: 238).

The sachems greeted the feast and drinks with the litany of approbation that was to punctuate treaty negotiations for a century and that still occurs in the modern Condolence Council. The principal Mohawk sachem raised the cry—*ohee* (*yohenh:*). The whole assembly replied, *heeeeee hogh* (*hi:::* *yenh*). This antiphonal was repeated for each of the Five Nations. In each case the principal sachem gave the cry (NYCD, 4: 239; Bradford 1696 in DePuy 1917: treaties no. 8, 10-11).

The Iroquois were now beset and diminished. During nine years of what in Europe was called King William's War, with almost no English colonial support, they had harassed the French. These campaigns, as one scholar has written, "combined with disease, had taken a terrible toll of their ranks. At the beginning of the struggle for the west their warriors had numbered some 2,800; by 1698 they were reduced to 1,320," of whom 1,000 were Senecas (Eccles 1964: 201). Meanwhile, the population of New France rose from 10,523 in 1688 to 12,786 ten years later. Peace was the only alternative for the Iroquois, and that would come at the turn of the century.

---

12. Compare "Draft of this Country 1696/1697" in LIR: 172-73.
13. "A Journal of what passed, etc. between Gov. Fletcher and the Five Nations at Albany . . . " (New York: Wm. Bradford, 1696), 11 pp.

CHAPTER 22

THE GRAND SETTLEMENT
AT MONTREAL, 1701

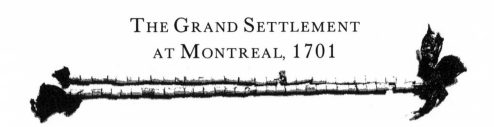

> The Iroquois are the fiercest and most redoubtable nation in
> North America; at the same time the most political nation and the
> most judicious that can be known.—Bacqueville de La Potherie,
> *Histoire de l'Amérique septentrionale*

After twenty years of almost continual warfare between the Iroquois and the colony
of New France, with its allied tribes of the upper Great Lakes and the Ohio
watershed, neither the French nor the Iroquois could knock the other out. All
parties were exhausted, entire settlements had been destroyed, and the toll of
human life was incalculable.

The Longhouse was no longer safe. Previously invincible Iroquois war parties
that had terrorized neighboring peoples during the Beaver Wars met defeat late
in the seventeenth century. The Miamis checked them in the southwest, and the
combined Ottawa-Mississauga tribes drove Iroquois hunters out of Huronia. Far
Indian scalpers skulked the trails and lay in ambush. Iroquois women feared to go
into the fields or gather firewood. The grand council of the league was a shambles,
rent by pro-French and pro-English factions, its seats usurped by parvenues,
unable to reach one mind. But new leaders emerged, men who could talk like
Teganissorens, and who knew compromise.

Though Stroud's cloth and rum were cheaper in Albany than French brandy
was in Montreal, the English were all bluster, big promises, and little help.
Iroquois policy veered toward a French settlement while keeping the path open to
Albany. Their strategy aimed at keeping both the French and the English alive:
although they were dependent on the English, they worried lest the English wholly
destroy the French or, conversely, the French the English. Both European powers
needed the Iroquois as a buffer between them. Three times the French had bashed
the Iroquois Longhouse at both ends and the middle but stopped short of
exterminating the inhabitants, who took to the woods and regrouped. The English
resorted to the alliance known as the covenant chain, which they repeatedly kept
bright with presents.

At last, in the Grand Settlement of 1701, the French stabilized a de facto
situation that had evolved from these circumstances—a situation in which the
power of the Iroquois had become eclipsed and they found it advantageous to
adopt a policy of neutrality.

The proceedings of this treaty appear in two primary sources—Bacqueville de La Potherie's *History of North America* (1722) and Governor Callière's reports to the Minister of Marine in Versailles (NYCD)—written by, respectively, an eyewitness and the presiding official. Pierre F. X. de Charlevoix, S.J., came a decade later (1744), read the official reports, and interviewed participants. Francis Parkman (1899), Anthony Wallace (1957a), and Richard Aquila (1983) rely on these sources. (See also Brandão and Starna 1996.)

La Potherie (1663-1736) submitted his manuscript to the royal censor in the year after the treaty, but for various reasons his book did not appear until twenty years later, just two years before Lafitau's *Moeurs* (1724) and twenty years before Charlevoix's *History and General Description of New France*. He devoted the last two of his four volumes to the Iroquois. In the genre of the day, La Potherie couched his work in the form of letters. He was at his best when describing events that he witnessed. Although a royal commissioner, fortunately he was free of responsibility during the treaty so that he could observe the preliminaries, summarize the speeches of governor and chiefs, praise the role of Kondiaronk, the Huron speaker, and recount his demise and spectacular funeral. Unlike his contemporaries, La Potherie considered the Iroquois anything but barbarians. Like Lafitau, he was at heart an ethnographer; his failure to assign specific dates to events gave one historian fits (Pouliot in DCB, 2). He was more interested in recording customs, cataloguing metaphors, noting the structure of Iroquois society and politics, describing the sequence of treaty protocol, marking wampum usage, and commenting on the personalities of participants (La Potherie 1722, 3: passim). These topics of political ethnography can await consideration of the treaty negotiations.

Two virtually simultaneous Iroquois treaties during July 1701 at Albany and at Montreal ended twenty years of warfare and ushered in a policy of peace with the Far Indians and of armed neutrality between the Five Nations and the rival European powers that lasted well into the eighteenth century. This policy promoted trade and enabled the old men of Onondaga to manipulate affairs with neighboring tribes. By adhering to it, they succeeded in balancing French and English interests. As a result, neither power knew which way the Iroquois would turn and neither gained ascendancy. The French provided the initial motivation for this shift in policy (Wallace 1957a).

□□◇□□

A decade of uncertain events preceded the Grand Settlement at Montreal. For thirty years, French policy had opposed any rapprochement between the Five Nations and the Huron-Ottawa peoples that would send the preferred northern furs to Albany. The Hurons had favored the Senecas in 1687, and the Ottawas withheld from Denonville's campaign all but a few warriors, who were reluctant participants (Blair 1911-12, 2: 42-43; Wallace 1957a: 226). The Iroquois retaliation at Lachine scared the daylights out of the Ottawas, who summoned neighboring tribes to Michilimakinac to consult on measures to confront the new situation. The council resolved to send a mission to the Senecas, consisting of two old Iroquois men whom they freed, with the message that the Ottawas were severing relations with the French and desired an Iroquois alliance (Blair 1911-12, 2: 44-45; Wallace 1957a: 227). The French faced a conspiracy of erstwhile allies whom they could not control, although they could at times rally small war parties. A delegation of three Ottawa chiefs paddled down the lakes to Iroquoia and presented calumets to formalize a peace planned before the Lachine disaster, hoping to satisfy two interests—trade and support against their Siouan neighbors (Blair 1911-12, 2: 41, 95, 105; Wallace 1957a: 227). Reciprocally, Iroquois wampum belts traveled up the lakes, openly and "underground," to condole the dead of previous encounters and to confirm alliances that the French opposed and the English favored.

In effect, the Iroquois were in no position to field large war parties. They were all talk. By 1694, the Five Nations were down to fifteen hundred warriors and had lost so many chiefs and warriors that they were enfeebled (La Potherie 1722, 3: 43, 195). That year, Tareha, an Oneida emissary, came to Canada to advance peace, which the English attempted to block. La Potherie thought the French should have attacked Onondaga at that time but for the difficulties and military requirements of such a campaign (La Potherie 1722, 3: 195-96; NYCD, 9: 578). In March, on Tareha's return, the grand council met at Onondaga to hear his report and resolved on two things: they would send Teganissorens, their best hope of averting disaster, to meet with Frontenac, but first they would dispatch Hotrewati's nephew with a belt to notify the governor of New France of their resolve. After being fished out of Lachine rapids, and not finding Frontenac at Montreal, the nephew presented the belt to Callière with the message.

The English, meanwhile, responded to this perceived defection by sending Peter Schuyler to meet with the grand council. He was caught in a May snowstorm at Oneida and failed to reach Onondaga, but the Iroquois councilors got the message and delayed further execution of their plan. They hedged by sending three Mohawks to Albany with belts (La Potherie 1722, 3: 198-200). From Albany, the *agoianders*, "the head ones of the Five Nations," sent three belts to their relatives in the Canada missions by way of informing the French that they were unable to come to Canada in the spring, since Governor Fletcher had called them to meet in Albany in April 1694, which they had decided to do. (In effect, they had canceled the Canadian mission and opted for Albany.) The second belt opened the road for the mission Iroquois to come and go in safety. The third belt "tied up their hatchets" (suspended hostilities). Callière was present when these belts were delivered. It was feared that Frontenac, who had refused Tareha's belt, would refuse these as well. The real purpose of these belts was to sound the minds of the Five Nation's mission kin and the French (La Potherie 1722, 3: 200ff.).

Frontenac was not impressed. He sensed that the Iroquois preferred dealing with "Big Arrow," Governor Fletcher, "who was only their brother," and not their father (in the European sense). He, Frontenac, would deal only with principals; but unless Teganissorens showed up on St. John's Day with the headmen of other nations, prepared to regret past misdeeds, the door no longer stood open for them. Second, Onontio replied, the French would guarantee secure passage both ways to the old men, who feared being held hostages. The Iroquois should stop sending people "to carry their words on the wind." Third, as French "subjects," the Iroquois did not need security, nor did the French going to Onondaga. Traffic depended on securing his, Frontenac's, good graces. He would not tie up the hatchet until assured that the Iroquois reciprocated. They might sharpen it when they observed him grinding his own (NYCD, 9: 578; La Potherie 1722, 3: 203-4). (Indeed, Frontenac was preparing for war.) As La Potherie concluded, "This response seemed haughty to a people who believed that they themselves had intimidated us."

Means were found to amuse the messengers until Teganissorens and two deputies reached the Lachine rapids in May 1694. There they were joined by "the Plate," a principal Caughnawaga Mohawk chief, and three old Mohawks who were yet in Canada. Although Onnagoga, then ranking chief of the grand council, headed the embassy, the council had charged Teganissorens with carrying the word to Frontenac, who esteemed him. The word consisted of ten belts, which the speaker and his assistant proceeded to arrange on a tabletop before addressing the host (see chapter 20).[1]

Although the ten messages conformed to expected protocol, the sanction of ritual was not binding. Frontenac remained unconvinced. He sensed that the grand council was not of one mind. He must have known that while Teganissorens pleaded for peace, a pro-English faction of chiefs was renewing the covenant chain with Governor Fletcher in Albany. Onnagoga and Teganissorens reinforced French doubts when they supped with Vaudreuil and, during a private meeting, presented him with an "underground" belt, or a "ferret," which La Potherie explains (1722, 3: 217): "When the Indians desire to speak of some agreement in particular, they give a belt in secret to the person with whom they are treating."

This particular belt conveyed the views of the three most important Onondaga chiefs of the time—Garakontie, Hotrewati, and Thoronthisati—who demanded continued French esteem and sought to persuade Vaudreuil that they were doing their best to engage both their relatives and the entire Onondaga settlement to hear his voice. Frontenac acknowledged the pleasant memory of these three chiefs with a belt of his own.

The reciprocal action required in speeches, which impressed the minds of participants, the passing of wampum belts, and return of presents—the very essence of Iroquois gift giving—had the sanction of custom law. Although Teganissorens had accepted a coat from Governor Fletcher, who hoped to divert him from going to Quebec, he returned the accompanying belt, breaking the bond, thanked the New York governor for the coat, and went to Canada anyway, sporting the coat. Not to be outdone, Governor Frontenac sent Teganissorens home with a double-barreled gun, which he in turn gave to Onondaga warriors and which was interpreted as a sun symbol. Similarly, Frontenac felt obliged to reply to the underground belt sent by the three "families" (clans) with one of his own (La Potherie 1722, 3: 217–19). Evidently, the three named Onondaga chiefs headed clan segments.

The Five Nations were not yet prepared to present a solid front for peace. Instead, they temporized: emissaries of single nations appeared sequentially in Canada while others went to Albany. Following Teganissorens, a Cayuga delegation arrived in council and condoled the governor with the usual three strings, which, La Potherie said, "served to dispose the audience to accept the belts that followed relating to the return of prisoners." One belt conveyed a "medicine to straighten the mind like a row of white wampum." Another announced that the Cayugas might return in thirty sleeps, but meanwhile they were going to sound

1. The speech of ten belts (La Potherie 1722, 3: 205–11) is printed in NYCD, 9: 579–81, together with Onontio's reply (La Potherie 1722, 3: 211–18; NYCD, 9: 581–83). The latter document is the better of the two.

out Great Arrow—Governor Fletcher—on Frontenac's terms. Several days later, Frontenac answered the three strings of condolence, accused the Cayugas of bad faith, and kept the belt on prisoners, returning the others as unacceptable. The Iroquois must come down together prepared to make a general peace (La Potherie 1722, 3: 236, 237–38).

Oneida embassies made two appearances at Montreal. First came Father Millet, who had been taken captive in 1689 and requickened in the title of the leading Oneida chiefship, joined by Tareha as chief of delegation. They presented three strings of condolence—tears, throat, and ears—on behalf of themselves and the Onondagas (La Potherie 1722, 3: 248–49).

Subsequently, "Otaxeste" (Odatshehdeh), clearly holder of the same title as Millet, appeared on behalf of those of his nation who were prepared to settle among the French and reported on his reception at Onondaga. The council resolved to send two of its headmen to carry belts to Canada on behalf of all the nations, but a dispute detrained the project when some rash young men, bent on revenging the death of a prominent Onondaga killed by a French-sponsored party, went on the warpath. La Potherie commented: "The Iroquois is so burdened with vengeance that nothing in the world can smother his resentment, until he has apparently washed his hands in the blood of someone" (1722, 3: 295–96).

Meanwhile, the bag of wampum containing the belts for Canada was still on the mat at Onondaga, pending resolution of the dormant issue of whether or not to send a mission to New France (La Potherie 1722, 3: 296). The council finally decided to send the Oneida leader, who had visited them, back to Montreal with three belts notifying the French of the delay, saying that they were in mourning, and asking if they still would be well received. Frontenac, whose patience was wearing thin, replied with a single belt.

In the midst of the Oneida negotiations, a Seneca delegation headed by the "naturalized" Joncaire, whom they had named and commissioned to do business, came down the rapids to Montreal. Joncaire addressed Frontenac on behalf of three chiefs of the two Seneca towns—namely, Gayaraougon, Gariotario (clearly Ganyadaiyo?, S-1, RC 43), and Sagotiarakon—concerning trouble the Senecas were having with tribes of the upper lakes allied to the French.

These diplomatic overtures by single tribes of the Iroquois Confederacy tell us several things about Iroquois polity. The Iroquois were running scared, and perceiving French military preparations, they were bidding for time. The council of the confederacy was not of one mind, the civil chiefs could not control the warriors, and, judging by the composition of the delegations, the league was not a functioning entity. The tradition of its having been founded as a league for peace, however, lived on in the persons of an Oneida and a Seneca delegate who bore titles of the founders.

Iroquois diplomacy failed to deter Frontenac from sacking Onondaga and Oneida in 1696, as we have seen in earlier chapters, and the raid brought the Iroquois to heel. Frontenac died in November 1698, soon after the Treaty of Ryswick in 1697 ended King William's War in Europe, producing a radical shift in Iroquois posture vis-à-vis the French and English in America. If the two European powers ever attained a united policy on Indian affairs, the Iroquois were finished. They had to get busy.

□□◇□□

Some two years after Frontenac's passing in 1698, word of the event having reached the Iroquois, a delegation proceeded to Montreal to properly condole his death and to recognize Callière, whom the French had "raised up" in Frontenac's place as governor of New France. Callière was equally interested in forging an Iroquois alliance to forestall an English invasion of Canada should hostilities resume between the European powers. The Iroquois knew Callière from previous negotiations as a no-nonsense realist.

Onhwentsiowa:neh (Big Mouth) of Onondaga addressed Callière. By his first belt, he said, "We are aware of the death of Frontenac, our father. All our households have wept for him. We have learned that you have taken his place, which is why we have been obliged to come to you on behalf of all the Iroquois" (La Potherie 1722, 4: 113ff.).

Onhwentsiowa:neh went on to say that the people at the rapids (Caughnawaga, or Kahnawakeh) and "at the mountain" (Kanehsatageh, or Oka), their kindred, had assured the Onondagas that if important members of the Onondaga council came to address Callière, he would listen—if the powerful Senecas showed. The Onondagas had made an effort to attain consensus among the nations of the confederacy by strongly urging the Cayugas and Oneidas to consider peace, and they had solicited the Senecas and Mohawks. They brought three French captives, for whom they requested release of four "nephews" detained by the French.

The Onondaga speaker proposed that Callière send Maricourt, a captain of the marines, and Father Bruyas to Albany to recover prisoners whom they would assemble there, an act which they deemed feasible because of the peace between France and England, which had given them some ideas. La Potherie commented that this deputation was "a trait of their politics, to try to penetrate our feelings," and that "the hearing ended without deciding anything" (1722, 4: 118–19).

Callière responded to this exploratory mission by insisting that the fire for such transactions burned at Montreal, not Albany. Moreover, his kettle would hang until the Iroquois included the French allies in the peace. These were the two conditions essential to peace: the council fire for doing business must be kindled at Montreal, and it must be done conjointly with all of the allies (La Potherie 1722, 4: 120).

When Callière asked whether the Iroquois would comply with the two provisions, the emissary, typically, told him that he must wait for a reply. The emissary would have to go home and consult the council. It would make known its latest thoughts in sixty days (two moons), when Callière could expect two or three deputies who would tell which of the provisions the council would accept. They would then return home and the council would send deputies to represent each nation. In short, the Iroquois would not be rushed; they would adhere to the "proper way."

Meanwhile, the hatchet would be hung up by both sides during the sixty days. The Iroquois would continue to hold their captives, who, La Potherie recognized, had been successfully enculturated into native society. He was equally impressed by the strategy the Iroquois adopted when beset by conflicting pressures (La Potherie 1722, 4: 120–22).

The English were doing their best to frustrate an Iroquois-French settlement. From the French viewpoint, the close union that the English had contracted with the Iroquois was a great obstacle to concluding peace. La Potherie commented that the English authorities in America were yet unaware that changes in government from a far country had transformed the entire face of affairs in America, turning upside down all the measures the Iroquois wished to take for the confirmation of this new alliance (La Potherie 1722, 4: 123–24). Indeed, Louis XIV did not inform Governor Callière of the terms of the Treaty of Ryswick until two years after the fact, and the Iroquois learned of it late in that year (1699) from Callière (NYCD, 9: 698), much to their consternation (La Potherie 1722, 4: 123–24, 130).

If the English authorities at Albany were aware of the peace in Europe, they kept the Five Nations in the dark. Keeping the chain bright with presents was the English insurance policy.

At Onondaga, there was a want of unanimity about just how to treat with the French and get prisoners back from the Montreal jails without alienating Albany. Teganissorens, who represented the pro-English faction and who played both ends against the middle, came down to Albany in the dead of winter that year with the unpleasant news that Onhwentsiowa:neh had gone to see "his father in Canada" without a belt. The council had decided that sending belts would violate its agreement with Lord Bellomont, the English governor. Teganissorens told the Albany commissioners that on reaching Lachine, Big Mouth had observed a woman making moccasins at the rate of thirty pairs per day, which clearly indicated preparation for a war party. The commissioners decided to send their interpreter, along with an Indian, to Onondaga to alert the councilors that Colonel Schuyler and others would follow to head off any Five Nations embassy to Canada (NYCD, 4: 492–95).

In late March 1699, word came from Onondaga that Onhwentsiowa:neh and Odatshehdeh had returned from Canada with Maricourt, bringing five belts in the interest of recovering French prisoners, of keeping the general meetings at Onondaga, and of reestablishing the Jesuit missions in Iroquoia. The Onondaga council underscored the message with seven hands of wampum, telling the Mohawk sachems that the four upper nations would meet in twenty-five days and urging them to attend. Such calls to council were accompanied by a tally stick attached to the wampum, a notch to be removed each day (Beauchamp 1905: 251). The upper nations also desired Peter Schuyler and Major Dirk Wessels to attend the general meeting (NYCD, 4: 497–98). The Albany negotiators reaffirmed these facts and reported uncertainty that negotiations with Canada could be interdicted. Aqueendera, with Teganissorens—the two head sachems at Onondaga—refused to meddle, although the latter leaned toward Albany (NYCD, 4: 558–60). The issue was uncertain.

The matter was of such consequence that the New York council and assembly in April ordered Captains John Schuyler and John Bleeker to go up to Onondaga and seek to head off the Five Nations' treaty with the French in Canada. They were to leave the interpreter at Onondaga to watch and report on the movements of the Indians (NYCD, 4: 498–500).

The New York delegation—Captains Schuyler and Bleeker, John Baptist van Epps, and Arnout Viele—having sent a runner ahead, left Albany the evening of 22 April. They were a week on the road. No Mohawks were at home. At the third Mohawk castle they found two elderly sachems too enfeebled to make the journey, who sent their proxy supporting the New York position by seven hands of wampum.

They disapproved of any of the league's people treating with the French governor. The messenger preceded them at Oneida, where the sachems were alerted to attend the meeting and would follow next day. Likewise, the Cayuga and Seneca sachems were summoned with seven hands of wampum. The Cayuga sachems, having gone to the woods to catch passenger pigeon squabs, would be a week late. Such were the difficulties of assembling a grand council (NYCD, 4: 560–63).

Meanwhile, Odatshehdeh, the leading Oneida, himself a Papist and a frequent ambassador to Canada, went home in a huff over the prospect of English interference with the peace settlement.

The Onondagas evidently had erected a new council house that the journalists referred to as the "Proposition House." There, the Mohawk proxy of seven strings was racked up for all to see (NYCD, 4: 563). Discussion revolved around bringing French prisoners to Albany for their repatriation to Canada. No time was set for an Albany meeting. When one of the sachems asked for the five belts brought from Canada, a young Indian got them and threw them toward the first sachem, but not quite to where he sat. "Another Indian disdainfully kicked them toward him," and they then related the accompanying messages. This bit of behavior relates to sanctioning a position implied by picking up and handling belts. Evidently, both men wished to dissociate themselves from the French connection.

The Iroquois council tradition favors moderation and calm demeanor on the part of speakers. Conflicting arguments may be advanced without apparent emotional overtones. One does not speak of warfare or threaten sanctions in a council called to discuss terms of peace. So when Schuyler overstated the English position and forbade the Five Nations to hold any correspondence with the French, the council listened, asked the advocates to withdraw, and proceeded to consider the English governor's propositions. Teganissorens notified the English delegates an hour later that the council would reply when done.

Two days later (9 May 1699), Teganissorens delivered with fine rhetoric the council's answer to Bellomont's propositions for Schuyler and Bleeker's ears. He spoke under eight heads, which in substance were as follows. (1) If the Iroquois could not go to Canada, there was no way they could get their prisoners back. Albany offices were ineffective, "without love." (2) Albany had frustrated previous efforts at recovery of prisoners, Bellomont's military efforts to dislodge the French were ineffective, and the Iroquois were meanwhile beset by Far Indians. The council disbelieved that its sending a delegation to Canada would break the chain that had subsisted for years. (3) There was no need for English forts in peacetime. (4) A fort at Onondaga might be necessary if war with France resumed. (5) As for the Iroquois being the king's subjects, at least the English should act like brothers and render real assistance in warfare. (6) They looked forward to a previously announced meeting at Albany. (7) A belt confirmed that all of the sachems of the Five Nations would attend that conference, and they expected the governor to be present. Meanwhile, they would not go to Canada. (8) Let goods be cheap; get our prisoners there. We are sorely vexed. Forty-eight hands of wampum notified their coming to Albany in fourteen days (NYCD, 4: 564–65).

Meanwhile, the Iroquois took advantage of the lull in affairs to raid the Miamis and Illinois, allies of the French. La Potherie commented: "They never stop to recollect not having kept their word" (La Potherie 1722, 4: 124).

□□◇□□

The Albany meeting of the Five Nations and the commissioners convened on 12 June and got down to business next day (NYCD, 4: 567–73). Not much was accomplished. The commissioners read Lieutenant Governor Nanfan's instructions, Bellomont having gone off to Boston as governor of New England. According to those instructions, if the Indians insisted on going to Canada, they were to be reminded that they were crown subjects and that the government would undertake release of their countrymen by sending two agents to negotiate.

Next day, Teganissorens allowed that the English had stopped the path to Canada and that the Five Nations would adhere to it. Aqueendera of Onondaga denied that they had other motives in going to Canada and claimed that although the path there was shut, there was an open road from Albany to Montreal via the Champlain corridor—"yea, a beaten path knee-deep"—worn bare by recent travel. Why, he asked, was there no response to their request of Bleeker and Schuyler last fall to effect an exchange of prisoners? The Iroquois had forsaken a plan to send one from each nation for that purpose the previous summer in favor of Schuyler's offices, which had succeeded only in securing their people even faster in their imprisonment. After an Oneida had carried five small belts to Canada on behalf of the three interior nations, the French had spread the rumor that the four upper nations had made a separate treaty with them, excluding the Mohawks and New York, "only to raise jealousy among us" (NYCD, 4: 569–70).

Further, having brought their French prisoners to Albany as requested, they had lost them one by one without having any of their own people returned. They were fed up with English incompetence. They proposed a joint effort to get the job done. They succeeded in getting a joint planning committee of five from each side—one from each of the Five Nations, and five "gentlemen."

The plan for retrieving the Onondaga prisoners from Canada hinged on some imponderables. There were still two Onondagas in Canada who were no longer prisoners but who lingered hoping that the Five Nations would come and retrieve them by a separate treaty. The plan called for sending two trusted Indians to inform them that the road to Canada was shut, and they were not to depend on the Five Nations coming. Instead, they were to come along with the two messengers. The sachems, after considering the plan and approving, appointed two Senecas—one a sober sachem whose son had been taken by the Tionontatés the previous summer along with a Frenchman, now back in Canada, whom the sachem could ask how his son fared. The messengers were not to discourse with French officialdom but were to bring the two Onondagas back to Albany. As a cover, they were outfitted with goods to trade. Meanwhile, they would hold the French prisoners left at Albany last fall pending the outcome of negotiations. The report of this plan was not for publication.

Such conferences were always a mixed bag. The son of the principal Onondaga sachem, Aqueendera, had died, apparently by poisoning, and his passing was condoled by the hosts' giving white wampum to the sachems, which was kindly accepted. A Seneca couple brought news that the Tionontatés had been summoned by the governor of Canada to treat, and if the Five Nations failed to show and treat, Callière was resolved to make war on them. Other information had it that a new trader had settled on Cayuga land without permission and threatened to draw off the furs of seventy Cayuga beaver hunters.

The Iroquois sachems begged off, saying, "We have spoke a great deal in this house—if it were all heaped up together it would make a great Piramide" (NYCD, 4: 571).

The Champlain corridor was indeed open to Canada. During the meeting, three Frenchmen arrived bringing two Onondagas who reported that the two former prisoners being sent for were free and hunting north of Lake Ontario. Accordingly, the sachems consented to releasing the French prisoners to return to Canada (NYCD, 4: 572). Intelligence from Canada depicted hourly expectation that the Five Nations would appear to treat, while military preparations went forward to invade Iroquoia (NYCD, 4: 574). Such Albany conferences clearly frustrated Governor Callière.

The departing Five Nations sachems proposed five things. (1) The English should expect private individuals to visit relations in Canada. (2) If any Iroquois took wampum belts and treated without council sanction, let that not be considered a breach of the covenant chain. (3) The English should forget about a fort at Onondaga. (4) Likewise, they should forget about sending Protestant ministers. (5) The commissioners should give the Indians provisions for the journey home. The commissioners agreed that they would condone private visits by oversight and would mention forts and ministers to the governor, and they granted the provisions. The Seneca sachem who had been "pitched upon to goe to Canada" could now go home (NYCD, 4: 573).

That summer, Far Indians continued to harass Seneca villagers, Nanfan and Callière exchanged letters regarding the release of Iroquois prisoners, rumors of French and English conspiracies to extirpate the Longhouse traveled from fire to fire, a bitter factional struggle divided the grand council, and pro-French and pro-English parties sent emissaries to Canada and Albany (NYCD, 4: passim). Indians of the lower Hudson, erstwhile enemies of the Mohawks, questioned paying further tribute for fishing rights (Palstits 1910, 1: 35–36). And the New York commissioners for Indian affairs worried that an Iroquois trade mission that went to Pennsylvania would divert the exclusive trade from Albany, "in breach of the Covenant Chain" (Jennings et al. 1985a: 164; NYCD, 4: 596–97).

The commissioners in Albany learned from an Onondaga messenger that a Seneca sachem named Old Smoke had appealed to the Onondaga council to send a mission to Canada seeking relief from French-instigated incursions by Far Indians for the fourth time since the peace in Europe. But the Onondaga sachems, of another opinion, had decided to appeal through Albany to Bellomont (who was now serving as governor of both New England and New York) to intercede with Callière. The messenger also reported that all the sachems of the Five Nations were now met at Onondaga, that they had called hunters home to watch the motions of the French, and that a French embassy was en route to Onondaga to make proposals (NYCD, 4: 597–98). The commissioners commended the council's decision and urged the Five Nations not to treat with the French.

Bellomont next winter addressed the Lords of Trade, opposing any rumor of a plan to disarm the Indians, who depended on their guns for hunting. He doubted they would submit, and commented that they would go any distance to hunt beavers. He urged that if "speedy and effectual course is not taken" to beef up garrisons at Albany and Schenectady, the British would lose the Five Nations, "a discerning people," to the French interest—and they were the only barrier just then between the French and the exposed Virginia and Maryland colonists, as well as New York. Bellomont clearly foresaw the background of the raids into the southeast by Iroquois war parties during the eighteenth century (NYCD, 4: 608-9).

□□◇□□

Although the Five Nations repeatedly asserted their independence, they were beholden to the English for presents and wary of provoking further French reprisals. Down in manpower, deprived of former hunting territories, beset by Far Indian scalpers, and divided in council, they fell back on keeping the paths of diplomacy open both ways. They could still talk. One ruse was to use the good offices of mission Indians to represent their views and probe French intentions. Securing their own hostages and retaining or returning French captives adopted into Iroquois families were the sticking points in a troubled case that dragged on for two more years. Early in 1699, sensing that Callière was fed up with their devious ways, the council dispatched a chief to beg Callière not to be impatient if they could not send deputies of the several nations for some time (La Potherie 1722, 4: 123-27, 133-34). It seems that when their emissary returned from Quebec the previous autumn, he found only two old men in residence, the rest having gone on the fall hunt.

"The Iroquois commenced to have serious thoughts," La Potherie wrote (1722, 4: 135). They held a series of councils that summer of 1699, "where their most judicious persons reviewed everything" done during a decade of relations with Frontenac, their own irruptions into Canada, his reprisals, and their resolve to end with the new governor what they had left off with his predecessor. They resolved to send a formal embassy of six to Canada, charged them with belts, and instructed them in proper protocol. Seneca opinion prevailed, and the Great Hill people dominated the delegation.

The French were delighted to see the six Iroquois ambassadors land at Montreal—two Onondaga and four Seneca chiefs.[2] After resting several days, the delegates made their formal approach from the landing to the governor's residence—some three hundred paces. With their adopted son Maricourt escorting them, Teharstakout, a Seneca, led the column of chiefs chanting a lamentation for all the French dead, the chant we now know as the "Going on the Road" of the modern condolence ceremony. In La Potherie's words, he sang: "Oh you dead . . . thrust your heads above the ground so as to hear what I say, and do not demand any more vengeance. Peace is achieved." He finished with these words: "*Hai, hai,* which is the saddest lament of which this ruthless nation can let themselves feel" (La Potherie 1722, 4: 135-37).

The same Seneca chief addressed the governor as "father" and deferred to the Onondagas as his "elder brother," saying, "he is brighter than I . . . and has come to address you on behalf of four nations." (Frontenac had assured them they could do business without the Mohawks.) They first wanted to know whether the two

2. The delegates are variously named in La Potherie 1722, 4: 137, and the French document printed in NYCD, 9: 708. The latter dates the event 18 July 1700. The discrepancy in dates is typical of the former.

European powers, having made peace, would combine and punish them. The Senecas had gone hunting, assured of peace, and had suffered fifty-five men killed by Ottawas near Detroit. Would the governor or his allies remove the hatchet from their heads? They wanted the war kettle overturned. The speaker appealed to the usual metaphors—witness the sun, planting the Tree of Peace, clearing rivers and paths. The ambassadors commissioned Joncaire plenipotentiary for the Senecas, and Maricourt for the Onondagas. By three strings they condoled the death of Joncaire's father and installed Tonatakout, the closest relative of his family, in his place. The sachems said they represented but two nations of the confederacy because Peter Schuyler had come from Albany to dissuade them from coming. They had sent a mission to their offspring, the Oneida and Cayuga nations, to learn why they opposed missions to Canada (La Potherie 1722, 4: 137–41). (Clearly, the senior and junior moieties of the confederacy had become factions. Thus three strings, in this instance, served as a kind of footnote to impart relevant information.)

The speaker then reminded the Algonkins present of their joint hunt the previous winter, how as true brothers they drank broth from a common kettle, and how he brought them "the most precious thing among us other than manpower, which is a belt of wampum." When some Abenakis present laid into the Iroquois with fury, accusing them of speaking with the tips of their tongues, not with their hearts, the Iroquois hardly seemed embarrassed. La Potherie wrote: "It is strange that three or four thousand souls can make a whole world tremble. . . . [T]hey are feared over an extent of territory of more than 1500 leagues by our allies" (La Potherie 1722, 4: 147).

After several days of feasting, Callière replied (La Potherie 1722, 4: 142–43; NYCD, 9: 708–11). He had requested deputies from each of the Five Nations—where were the Oneida and Cayuga delegates? He would like to believe that the speaker addressed him in the name of the absentees. He would comply with their requests on condition that they leave hostages, and he would release prisoners when and if the requested delegates showed up. The Iroquois listened carefully and left four hostages.

The date was set for September to light the fire of peace. This would afford time to appoint Iroquois delegates and round up the tribes allied to the French.

An embassy of Bruyas, Maricourt, and Joncaire accompanied the returning Iroquois to Onondaga to retrieve French captives. They were received at the landing with the niceties of woods'-edge protocol, refreshed on the path with sweet corn stalks, and then halted outside Onondaga while Teganissorens requickened the party with three strings: wiping their tears, clearing their throats, and cleansing the mat, followed by a fusillade. The hosts then took the visitors by the arm and led them to a clean cabin, where they were fed. Empowered Seneca, Cayuga, and Oneida delegates awaited them. Preliminary inquiry found that the French captives lacked enthusiasm to return, and their foster parents were unwilling to yield to presents. Particular prisoners so used to Indian life flat out refused.

The deputies of the Five Nations assembled on 10 August in the council house, where the French ambassadors were called and seated.[3] Both sides exchanged

3. La Potherie's dates, where he gives them at all, are notoriously unreliable, or perhaps his printer erred in dating a council held two days after this one on 10 August as being held on 7 July (La Potherie 1722, 4: 151, 158).

greetings. The Mohawks, although not parties to previous transactions of the upper nations, had made sure that they had deputies present "as ears in the council."

Father Bruyas spoke first, invoking the Holy Spirit and appealing to the expected Iroquois metaphors—Tree of Peace, hatchet buried, war kettle overset, and sun as witness to the proceedings. He then presented three belts: (1) that Onontio was their father, (2) regretting the deaths of some Seneca chiefs (that was well received), and (3) on behalf of Asendase, a name the Iroquois had conferred on the Jesuit General in Canada, an appeal to accept missionaries. "Do you want them returned?" (La Potherie 1722, 4: 151).

The proceedings were interrupted by a young Englishman who came on horseback from Schenectady with a message from the English authorities.[4] He held a string warning the Iroquois that they must not listen to rumors. Invoking English precedence, the message forbade the council to treat with the French and ordered it to remove to Albany within six to twelve days, when Governor Bellomont would meet with it. These were written orders.

The tone was so imperious and the manner of speaking so fierce and haughty that the message very much surprised the Iroquois, who regarded it as undignified and inappropriate. The presiding councilor did not want to tell the Englishman that he had not previously explained to the French ambassadors the motive for Colonel Schuyler's coming to Onondaga. But Teganissorens, unable to dissemble his feelings, cried out that he would tell "Our Brother Corlaer" (the New York governor) "how had he agreed to that? If there was in fact peace in Europe, how come he still sings of war? Why does he prevent our listening to the voice of Onontio [the French governor]?"

The council was about to visit the sanction of ridicule upon the English emissary. Its members voiced their approval of the previous questions. They would carry on. The proud emissary did not let it show how disconcerted he was, although he surely knew from what he heard during two hours that the Iroquois had turned him into a subject of ridicule. He suffered the chagrin of listening to the reproaches of the French, the Iroquois councilors, and especially the Iroquois speaker, who on this occasion favored the French interest over the English. This deputation engendered dissension in the council for several days (La Potherie 1722, 4: 155).

Meanwhile, Joncaire embarked for the Seneca country to recover captives. Warriors saluted his landing with a fusillade, and Chief Tegancot shook his hand, saying, "Yonder is a kettle of soup and a platter of meat." People covered his canoe and stowed his gear. They feasted him before escorting him up the great hill, where he was received with three words—tears, throat, and bloody mat cleansed. He reported on the Onondaga council and next day rounded up reluctant captives (La Potherie 1722, 4: 155–56). He appealed especially to the warriors to abandon attacks, and to pledge them he gave belts of three thousand beads to each of four named chiefs.

---

4. This was probably Peter Schuyler or his agent of that name, who made several appearances at Onondaga that spring and summer (La Potherie 1722, 4: 151; NYCD, 4: 654–61).

Back at Onondaga, the council met two days later and gave Joncaire a "Sun of Wampum" to light his travels, and especially their business. They hung about his neck a collar of wampum to symbolize to people that he was indeed their plenipotentiary. Three other named chiefs gave him yet another belt, which they divided in half to be shared with Maricourt to sanction the two men's activities. They named a captive among the Miamis whom they wanted returned. Joncaire forced one reluctant captive to embark (La Potherie 1722, 4: 157–58).

The grand council reassembled several days later to authorize Bruyas and Maricourt to repatriate French captives. The Onondagas wanted the English deputy to witness the firm peace that they were about to make, independent of English participation. Addressing the full council, Teganissorens said that they had heard the voice of their father, Onontio, and that one or two delegates from each nation were leaving for Montreal. Then, addressing the Englishman, he said: "I do nothing secretly. I am quite relieved that you are present at this council that all of the Iroquois have held on the mat of Sagochiendagehte [Onondaga]. You may tell my brother Corlaer that I am going down to Montreal where my father Onontio has lit a fire of peace. I shall also go to Orange, where my brother calls me. And so that you are ignorant of nothing, here is the belt that I shall carry to my father Onontio" (La Potherie 1722, 4: 158–59). Having spoken, the orator took out five wampum belts in the name of the Five Nations, demonstrating their unity and autonomy.

The council resolved a conflict of interest between French Jesuit missionaries and Dutch Protestants by rejecting both appeals. They showed no embarrassment in answering the belt of Bruyas in the name of Asendase (the Jesuit General); they were more interested in a smith to repair their weapons (La Potherie 1722, 4: 161).

□□◇□□

Iroquois policy was to keep the path open to Albany and maintain the chain alliance, yet to hold the English at arm's length. New York Governor Bellomont perceived the urgency of securing the friendship of the Five Nations with presents lest they trade with the French. He feared the Jesuits and foresaw the need of Protestant missionaries. He dispatched Schuyler and Livingston to Onondaga to advance the English interest and head off a French alliance. He would commission Colonel Romer to survey a site for a fort at Onondaga and map the approaches through Iroquoia to the Ohio country before the French got there first (Bellomont to Board of Trade, Calendar of State Papers, 1700, no. 167: 90–97; Winsor 1895: 13–14).

In March 1700, Schuyler reported that the Mohawks were out hunting, save three families who, disturbed at recent alarms, sent a small belt to Albany to learn the news. Reassured, they went hunting too. Schuyler expressed hope that Bellomont could get a policy approved that would head off French designs. As Montreal fortified, the Albany garrison was nearly naked (NYCD, 4: 663). The governor authorized the two men most acceptable to the Iroquois—Robert Livingston and Peter Schuyler, with Hendrick Hanse and the interpreter—to go up to Onondaga in April and invite the sachems to come down to Albany in four and a half moons to treat. Both Livingston and Schuyler kept journals, and together they filed a report (NYCD, 4: 648–52, 654–61; Leder in LIR: 175).

Matter-of-fact Livingston kept a table of distances, named Mohawk towns, and drew a map. The Mohawks were weakened by the last war, and two-thirds of them were now in Canada, where they were clothed and fed. The remainder complained of English impotence to protect them, and of English neglect in not sending ministers to replace priests. Livingston recommended moving the Mohawks, Oneidas, and Onondagas closer to Albany on lands purchased for them. He observed that factionalism at Onondaga had reached a crisis in which pro-French Iroquois were poisoning pro-English members. For strategic reasons, Livingston thought a fort at Onondaga essential.

The Mohawk sachems were not at home but on their fishing stations during the April salmon runs. Finding them, diverting their attention to business, and assembling a grand council at Onondaga was a time-consuming and frustrating task for Livingston and Schuyler. Two sachems appeared ignorant of French designs to alienate them from the English, complaining that the French never informed them, assuming they were pro-English, but confined their attention to the upper four nations. They learned of the design indirectly from others. A praying Seneca told the English agents of the French plan to build five forts at strategic sites. The Mohawks were confident that the great king would not let them be penned in (NYCD, 4: 654–55). Further, there was a rumor from Onondaga that the English were scheming to destroy the Five Nations by depriving them of guns, powder, lead, and weapons. Supposedly, the French quoted Bellomont as saying that bows and arrows were sufficient.

The commissioners replied to the complainants with a belt that said the governor would meet them on 10 August in Albany.

The Onondaga sachems were similarly dispersed. Only three were at home. The chief sachem, Aqueendera, was on his way home from his fishing camp beyond Oneida Lake. Meeting with Schuyler and Livingston in the bush, he proclaimed adherence to the chain and related for Corlaer's ears the intricacies of Onondaga factionalism. Word from Canada, intended exclusively for Teganissorens and not for himself, but which he had learned from a mutual friend, related to an English plot to kill members of the pro-French faction by poisoning, to destroy the Five Nations by withholding supplies, and similar schemes.

Further, Aqueendera reported, two Seneca sachems had independently sent two belts to the governor of Canada through an Onondaga intermediary, hoping to recover two prisoners detained by the governor. These were the same two sachems "pitched upon by the Five Nations last year at Albany." Callière had held out for two sachems from each of the Five Nations. He would not countenance independent action. A message concerning these gestures destined for Albany via the Mohawks had stopped at Oneida and not been forwarded because of deep snow.

Finally, according to Aqueendera, five belts sent by Callière to the Senecas had come to Onondaga and lain there a long time, and when carried up to Seneca, that council had disowned forwarding belts to Canada. The two Seneca sachems named had done so without council sanction (NYCD, 4: 657–58).

Livingston and Schuyler at last managed to assemble a grand council in late April 1700. When the two commissioners approached Onondaga on the twenty-sixth, two sachems greeted them with the usual woods'-edge formalities, conducted them to their lodgings, where the other sachems awaited them, bid them welcome with wampum, and sent in the customary kettle of mush to be hung for them (NYCD, 4: 658–60).

Iroquois speakers have a way of repeating in open council words spoken in the bush. The Onondaga leader, Aqueendera, again mentioned the English plot to destroy the pro-French Onondagas. With Millet at Oneida, Bruyas at Onondaga, and other priests destined for Cayuga and Seneca, resistance to the Jesuits in Iroquoia was mounting. Moreover, Bruyas had called upon Lord Bellomont to learn his objections to their return, and queried why Bellomont should send for the Five Nations to come to Albany to treat when Onondaga was the place of council sanctioned by ancient custom.

The commissioners examined the source of Teganissorens's confidence regarding the French rumor of English poisoning and disabused the council of any such intention. They delivered Bellomont's invitation to meet at Albany on 10 August, 104 days hence, four and one-half moons from that day. They confirmed the English intent to build a fort at Onondaga, promised Protestant missionaries, and delivered three additional belts for the absentee Oneida, Cayuga, and Seneca sachems, to be sent by trustworthy runners. Their instructions: keep Corlaer informed; concentrate settlements; don't trade at Cadaraqui.

The Onondaga speaker thanked the commissioners for Bellomont's invitation, which eased their minds, and requested that they send up the interpreter to remind them as the day approached. When the sachems returned home they would advise and consult (NYCD, 4: 660–61).

When the grand council met that spring, the sachems were not of one mind. To satisfy both the pro-French and pro-English factions, they sent deputies to both Montreal and Albany. Six emissaries representing each of the upper four nations reached Montreal in July 1700. (The Mohawks would show later.) Some principal chiefs absent from the delegation had gone trading pelts to the English. Initiative came from the Senecas, who were suffering from French-instigated raids by allied Indians. The Seneca speaker complained that their hunters had been attacked by Ottawas at Detroit, by Illinois on the Ohio, and by Miamis on the Chouegen. Onontio should make them drop the hatchet and exchange prisoners (La Potherie 1722, 4: 164, 166–67; Wallace 1957a: 229).

The preliminaries leading to the armistice of 1700 have been sketched in the vignette of Kondiaronk, "the Rat," in chapter 20. The principals agreed to hold a general council the following year, and the instrument was ratified by Callière and staff, while the deputies of the nations each affixed his sign—distinctly, the Cayuga pipe, the Oneida stone, the bear for the absentee Mohawks, and, for the allies, the Huron beaver, the Abenaki deer, and the Ottawa hare. The nearly starving French got respite; the Iroquois went hunting and were caught in the act of breaking beaver lodges in Ottawa territory. There were casualties (La Potherie 1722, 4: 174). Moreover, Ottawas and Mississaugas and Nipissings seized the opportunity to recover territories in Huronia that the Iroquois had gained in the Beaver Wars (La Potherie 1722, 4: 179–80; Eid 1979). The Onondagas lodged a protest.

The key man that year at Onondaga was Teganissorens, who, though courted by both governors, was his own man. He went up to visit Governor Callière that spring to listen to French views, discuss the return of captives, and learn what he could in the interest of his nation. The French knew he was a valuable property and were concerned to save him for an important issue. They believed he could influence the warriors of his nation, they sensed that he leaned toward the English, and they worried that the English might get established at Detroit. La Potherie wrote of him: "He came here, listened quietly to all that was said to him, and then went home to Onondaga and spoke against the establishment" (La Potherie 1722, 4: 184). He gave the warriors his presents and assisted in prisoner exchange, but, in mourning over his wife's death, he did not participate in the treaty.

□□◇□□

By mid-June 1701, the season being far advanced, it was time to complete the treaty negotiations. I have already described Teganissorens's role and the amenities observed in greeting the French expedition to retrieve prisoners at Onondaga (chapter 20; see also La Potherie 1722, 4: 185–86). At the same council, representatives of New York and New England invited the sachems to meet at Albany and reaffirm the chain alliance. The ruckus in Europe over the Spanish succession must have meant little to the Five Nations, except for the threat of possible war between France and England. They were urged to remain quiet on their mats and to go treat at Albany, a request to which they listened attentively (La Potherie 1722, 4: 189).

A fatal accident added to uncertainty, and mandatory mourning delayed the Seneca and Cayuga delegates, when one Seneca sachem paused to rest beneath a leaning tree that hung by the roots, and the tree crashed (La Potherie 1722, 4: 191–92).

The treaty preliminaries began in Montreal on 21 July 1701, and the proceedings started on the twenty-fifth. Again, La Potherie is our best source. Although not officially involved, he was free to observe (La Potherie 1722, 4: 193ff.).[5] From their arrival and throughout days of wrangling, the Iroquois maintained "un grand sang-froid." The French-allied Indians had brought prisoners; the Iroquois had withheld theirs. This was the main sticking point. "For several days the Iroquois had been considering their position. It was feared that they might go home and burn the captives, rather than give them up." At last, their speaker, Tekaneot, rejected the idea of the French holding returned allied prisoners "on the mat" (in escrow) until the Iroquois delivered theirs. He asserted, "This proposition has never been made since the world began. Keep them if you wish. We will go home and think no more about them." But if Callière would loan them their adopted son Joncaire and deliver "our nephews" (the captive Iroquois), they would be delighted to return the allied captives now in Iroquoia. This was a tough proposition, to which the allies reluctantly consented and which Callière granted. If the Iroquois failed to fulfill their pledge, sanctions would follow (La Potherie 1722, 4: 238).

It was agreed that in case of war between the French and the British, the Iroquois would remain neutral. Iroquois hunters might hunt now in Michigan and trade at Detroit.

Having accomplished the business of the treaty in two days, the parties commissioned several Indian women to make up the necessary wampum belts (La Potherie 1722, 4: 239). Anxiety over spreading sickness hastened the end of the treaty.

---

5. I described the preliminaries in chapter 20 in the sketch of Kondiaronk, whose dramatic role, tragic death, and obsequies preceded the treaty proper.

The fourth of August was the day set for concluding the peace. Elaborate preparations went forward for the ceremony that was to be held on the lawn outside Montreal. The French hosts erected a double brush fence enclosing an area some 128 feet long and 72 feet wide, with an alley of 6 feet all around. An arbor 29 feet long and 25 feet wide faced outward on the enclosed space. Notables and ladies of Montreal occupied the arbor, facing more than one thousand Indians with their deputies seated on the lawn in groups wearing distinctive tribal dress and headgear. Soldiers of the garrison, drawn from famous French regiments, surrounded the camp (La Potherie 1722, 4: 239; Charlevoix 1866–72, 5: 149).

Callière, as host, spoke first. He removed the hatchet and buried it deep in a symbolic pit so that no one could raise it. Interpreters translated in the several languages: Anjelran in Ottawa, Bruyas in Iroquoian, Bigot in Abenaki, Perrot in Miami-Illinois, and Garnier in Huron. With the exception of the trader Perrot, who had learned a Central Algonquian language on his own, Jesuit linguistic accomplishments in Algonquian and Iroquoian languages predominated (La Potherie 1722, 4: 240–41; Charlevoix 1866–72, 5: 150). Cries of approbation greeted the speech.

To sanction the agreement according to native law and make it inviolable, some thirty-one wampum belts passed to the chiefs of the nations present. Speakers of each nation replied in that nation's own distinctive way during the return of Iroquois captives by the allies. Hassaki, chief of the "Cut-tails" (Parkman 1899: 472), gave a string, then added a calumet that was carried to the Seneca Takaneot, who received it. The Iroquois replied with four cries as four nations, each by a chief. Forty-Pence, surrounded by eight "slaves," recounted the difficulties in rounding the prisoners up among the Miamis, and, seeing no prisoners of his own nation among the Iroquois, threw his wampum belts on the ground (La Potherie 1722, 4: 243–44).

A string and a calumet served as signature for Central Algonquian speakers. A Mississauga chief wore a headdress of prairie bison, replete with horns and ears, which he doffed upon speaking. He presented a calumet on behalf of himself and then one for the Potawatomis. Again came the four cries (La Potherie 1722, 4: 245–46).

The Fox orator afforded the comedy relief. Three prisoners followed him into the enclosure. His face painted red, he wore an old powdered wig that he doffed like a hat, to the amusement of the assembled gentry (La Potherie 1722, 4: 246–47).

A poignant moment for the Iroquois that epitomized their decline as warriors occurred when the Alonquin chief, an extremely well-built young man dressed like a Canadian but sustaining the tribal roach with drooping feather, approached deliberately. He had led the Algonquin war party, all youths under twenty, that had recently cut an Iroquois party to ribbons and ended the war. One Black Kettle, a redoubted Iroquois war chief, fell that day, saying, "Must I who made the whole earth tremble now die at the hands of a child?" (La Potherie 1722, 4: 248–49).

Following remarks by the Iroquois who lived "at the rapids and at the mountain," Caughnawaga and Kanehsatageh, the Iroquois proper spoke last. In typical Iroquois style, having listened quietly, they replied with four belts, one for each nation present. Auenano, a Seneca chief (DCB, 2: 20), said, "Onontio, we are delighted with what you have done, we have listened to what you have said, and these four belts are our words to reassure you that we shall be firm in keeping your orders. As for the captives that we have not brought to you, we have made you master of them, and you shall send to fetch them" (La Potherie 1722, 4: 252–53).

The governor and council deemed it fitting to confirm this grand alliance with a spectacle. Nothing was more appropriate than the calumet dance of the upper Great Lakes, of which the allied tribes were masters. Callière, Champigny, and Vaudreuil smoked the pipe, which was carried next to the Iroquois and to the deputies of the allies. Three Frenchmen performed the dance alternately, back and forth before the native assembly seated on the grass. La Potherie wrote: "They stepped in cadence, their faces animated, and the movement of the body responded to the emphasis of the words. The soldiers also marked the cadence" (1722, 4: 253–54).

A feast ended the event. The cooks carried in ten great kettles in which three beefs cut in small pieces were boiled. Our observer thought the feast sparse for so many people. The habitants then kindled a bonfire behind the enclosure, to the din of beasts, muskets, and cannon. Finally, the deputies ratified the treaty document by each making his mark or drawing his totem or clan animal.

A distribution of presents from the king's stores followed the treaty signing. It all ended on 7 August 1701 (La Potherie 1722, 4: 255–64). That day the four Iroquois nations asked for an audience with the governor. They had entrusted their own people as prisoners to him to be redeemed when they delivered ones they held. The governor, in the generosity of the moment, handed over all but five.

The Mohawk delegates who had failed to show up arrived late, several days after the settlement was reached, but they approved. The governor loaded them with presents; they left theirs and went home satisfied.

The Grand Settlement of 1701 marked the official beginning of Iroquois neutrality. Even before it was signed, however, an even larger contingent of sachems, warriors, women, and children from all of the Five Nations had taken up the path to Albany the previous summer to honor Lord Bellomont's invitation, as we shall see in the next chapter.

CHAPTER 23

THE ENGLISH
RENEW THE CHAIN, 1701

The "chain" was a metaphor for the alliance made between the People of the Longhouse and traders on the Hudson soon after the first Dutch vessel was tied to the shore. It was essentially an Indian idea that manifested itself in several forms, evolving from the image of a hawser made fast to a tree to that of an iron chain kept free of rust by renewals. Finally it became a silver chain, permanently bright. From a tree on the shore, its mooring moved up the hill toward the Mohawks and then to the great hill where the fire of the confederacy burned at Onondaga. The chain's strength was such that not even thunder and lightning could strike down those who put their hands in it. As symbol of an alliance capable of infinite expansion to admit both native and European parties, the chain had metamorphosed from the Iroquois concept of linking arms in friendship—of persons tied by a single umbilical cord so that if one moved or was struck, everyone felt it. To take guests by the arm and escort them to lodging and hospitality was the way to greet strangers. Such was the custom in eastern America.

After 1664, the English renewed the previous alliance and, having joined in the chain, extended it to include other colonies. What had been a native concept became, in history, an English acquisition. Lord Bellomont, governor of the New York colony, faced an ongoing institution.

In midsummer of 1700, having cut the last notch from the wampum tally, some fifty sachems of all of the Five Nations, escorted by warriors and accompanied by women and children, reached Albany to honor Bellomont's invitation to renew the chain. Then governor of both New England and New York, Bellomont sailed from Boston to New York and a week later ascended the North River by sloop to welcome his Iroquois guests. They comprised the largest company ever assembled there for a treaty. From the Longhouse came eleven Mohawk, six Oneida, eleven Onondaga, eleven Cayuga, and eleven Seneca sachems. The numbers in no way conform to a pattern laid down in the Great Law, which reads 9-9-14-10-8, and the temptation to equate the magic number fifty to the number of Iroquois League founders is unwarranted, since but one of their listed names identifies with a name on the Roll Call of the Founders.[1] There were some fifty young Indians besides. Bellomont approached with a heavy heart, unable to gratify the Iroquois on two

---

1. I compared the list of Indian names (NYCD, 4: 728–29) with the manuscript at the Public Record Office (PRO), Kew, England (CO5/1045: 20–41), on which they appear in the margin, which is frayed. The seventh Cayuga name is Sanagie, not Sauagie, not recognizable; but the tenth Seneca

points—to build them a fort or supply Protestant ministers. He also knew that they were a very observing people who, on seeing the poor condition of the fort and shabby garrison, would ask how the king could protect them from the French (NYCD, 4: 687, 728ff.). Some things were going on before either party reached Albany that deserve attention.

□□◇□□

Two visitations preceded the main event. In June, some praying Indians of Caughnawaga, having come to town to trade, appeared before the commissioners for Indian affairs to protest the sharp trading practices of the Albanians: loaves of bread were small, and certain traders let Indians sleep in their houses and plied them with food and drink in order to gain a price advantage. Some sachems of the Five Nations who were in town had given them tips on the trade. When chided for having left their fires in the Mohawk Valley to seek Christian teaching in Canada and for refusing to return, they replied that had there been English missionaries they might not have deserted. Clearly, the case for Anglican missionaries was building. Bellomont had the minutes of the meeting copied and sent them to London (NYCD, 4: 692).

It was customary for an advance party to clear the way for a treaty. The five sachems who were in town were empowered by the grand council to seek a remedy for the French's instigating the Ottawas to kill Iroquois hunters. With Teganissorens as its speaker, the delegation included another Onondaga, a Cayuga, and two Senecas (the main victims)—all of the pro-English party. They addressed the commissioners in the presence of Aqueendera,[2] the designated treaty speaker, and one Henry, a Mohawk.

Five Ottawas had come to Onondaga, they reported, and warned them to be on guard, saying that the French would not take the hatchet out of the Ottawas' hands until the Five Nations submitted to the governor of Canada and made peace, which "our great Brother Corlaer forbids us to do." Further, the Five Nations were distracted by conflicting loyalties and severely divided by factions, and, although the English had shut the path to Canada, two sachems had gone to Canada on their own carrying private belts not out of the public treasury. The sachems asked Corlaer (Bellomont) to intercede. They also reported that five Ottawas presently at Onondaga desired to be brought into the covenant chain but feared to come down to Albany to trade lest they be killed by drunks on the way (NYCD, 4: 694–95). The commissioners agreed to send the interpreter up to Onondaga to interview them (Livingston 1956: 177). The commissioners were also concerned to learn what the Jesuits Bruyas and Maricourt were up to.

Early in July, speaker Aqueendera dutifully reported to the commissioners the names of three Onondagas and one Oneida who had met recently with the

name, Ganogarie, not Garogarie, could be Ga?nogai (S-4, RC 46), of which the modern Mohawk form is Kanokareh (Fenton 1950: 67).

2. Bellomont, in a postscript to his letter of 26 July 1700 to the Lords of Trade (NYCD, 4: 689), identified Aqueendero as the chief sachem of Onondaga, who had spoken for all the Five Nations at a conference two years previously and was now a refugee living on Colonel Schuyler's land, forced out by intense factionalism. His son, in a classic case of Iroquois witchcraft, languished with handfuls of hair coming out a sore on his side. The Christian Mohawk wife of Teganissorens was the suspected agent (see note 5, chapter 20). Beauchamp (!1905: 255) questioned whether Aqueendero might be Thadoda:ho?.

governor of Canada—names he had learned from visiting Caughnawagas. They had told him that the praying Indians of Caughnawaga and the Rondax Indians (*atirun:taks*, "bark eaters"), Algonquins, intended to adhere to the terms of a previous peace treaty. They related the governor's growing impatience with Iroquois complaints of Ottawa raids; he would speak to them no further by belts until they were prepared to come and treat with him on his terms. They were to inform the Iroquois but not the "Christians." But the refugee Iroquois of Caughnawaga still considered themselves bound by the covenant chain to inform the commissioners. They gave but one belt, since they were now short of wampum. The commissioners commended their fidelity, made no reply, and decided not to forward the belt to the Five Nations, pending the arrival of Bellomont at Albany (NYCD, 4: 695–96).

Bellomont was still in New York at the end of July when an express from Colonel Schuyler reported that the English faction at Onondaga had announced by runner the arrival of Bruyas and Maricourt. Bellomont explained to the Lords of Trade that these were both important men in Canada and Iroquoian speakers, that the French had as many friends at Onondaga as the English, that the Onondagas were the most warlike of the Five Nations, and that the Mohawks had dwindled to almost nothing (NYCD, 4: 689). He was clearly worried that the confederacy might defect to the French and drive the English out of the continent.

The treaty conference finally opened on 26 August and lasted a week (NYCD, 4: 727–46). To Bellomont, the meeting "was the greatest fatigue I ever underwent in my whole life." (He died soon afterward.) "I was shut up in a close chamber with 50 Sachems, who besides the stink of bear's grease with which they plentifully dawb'd themselves, were continually either smoking tobacco or drinking drams of rum. They seem'd sullen and out of humour at first, but by degrees I brought them to perfect good temper" (NYCD, 4: 714).

With a crowd of some two hundred Indians, which attests the importance they attached to the treaty, the hosts were at some pains to round up victuals to feed them.

It was the obligation of the host to speak first. The topic of the first day was religion—one topic per day so as not to burden the Indians' memories. In the name of the king, Bellomont pledged support; he sought to dispel Jesuit rumors of a royal plot to destroy the Iroquois, saying he hoped English hospitality would prove the Jesuits liars; and he touted Protestantism, having already sent to England for ministers. It would take a year for one to learn Mohawk. (It would, in fact, take even longer to deliver them.) He urged the Iroquois to use all means to bring the praying Indians home, which would strengthen the Five Nations.

The second day belonged to the sachems. Their speaker was Aqueendera, alias Sadekanacktie, who headed the Onondaga delegation and embodied the Onondaga council name of Sagochiendagehte, "the name bearer." (His successor later assumed both names and the title [Beauchamp 1905: 255].) They had come at Bellomont's invitation, Aqueendera said, and were now convened. They had heard that Bellomont would disarm or poison them, but they did not believe the French rumor. If the king would protect them from the Ottawas, the Miamis would break off relations with the French. The promise of Protestant ministers was joyful news—something they were promised at Onondaga a year ago, when the French

Jesuits sent belts asking to renew their missions. The French had often deceived them. Both requests—for protection from the Ottawas and for the return of the Jesuit missionaries—had been refused. They feared the return of their delegates to Canada fed and clothed—a standard French practice they doubted the English king was prepared to assume. They desired that Protestant ministers be sent as soon as possible to Onondaga, the center of the Five Nations, to counter fraud in Jesuit teaching.

The sachems then withdrew to let some Protestant Mohawks address the governor. Their speaker, Henry, claimed they had prevailed on five of their people not to be seduced and go to Canada, for which the governor commended them.

On the third day the parties exchanged views. That morning the governor commented on the reply to his opening address. The Iroquois zeal for Protestantism would please the king. But he would station ministers at Onondaga only when they consented to let the English build a fort in their country, which the assembly had resolved to fund, and for which the engineer, Colonel Romer, was seeking a suitable site. (This matter of the fort at Onondaga clearly forecast and underlay the royal grant of silver communion plate by Queen Anne a decade later.) The king would most probably fortify Albany and Schenectady, and he would resent injuries to the Five Nations, his subjects. He would maintain the beaver trade at Albany and regulate it, of which regulation he discerned a lack among Dutch traders. (This last proposal, to abandon a free market, must surely have annoyed the commissioners present.)

That afternoon the sachems replied to the governor's morning proposals. Sadekanacktie, their speaker, addressed the governor under five heads. First, the Ottawas planned to settle north of Lake Ontario, for which the speaker promised to "lay down a few hands of wampum as a cord to draw [invite] them by"; this is the first mention of wampum at this conference. In addition, the Iroquois accepted the idea of stationing two ministers at Onondaga, although they feared the English would not clothe converts in the French manner; they desired ministers to instruct them at Albany and Schenectady; they agreed to confining the trade to Albany and wanted it regulated with reference to the chain; and indeed, trade was the basis of the chain, which should not be broken for the faults of a few. There was no mention of the fort.

Bellomont questioned the credentials of the speaker: did he really represent the Five Nations? The speaker cleverly acknowledged the governor's remarks by saying the Five Nations would welcome the engineer Romer. Bellomont told them plainly: no fort, no ministers. Unlike the Jesuits, an Anglican could not survive in the Indian style, and all the beavers the Five Nations could take in a year would not induce an Anglican minister to go live alone in their country and hazard his life.

The perennial problem of the inability of sachems to control warriors arose in connection with a Virginian held captive five years in Iroquoia. "Some of our young men are like doggs that snatch at a peece of meat when one's back is turn'd." The Iroquois promised they would deliver him.

The following day Bellomont and ten sachems, two from each of the Five Nations, met in private. He warned that the combined Central Algonquians and Huron allies vastly outnumbered the Iroquois, and rather than be destroyed they should bring them into the covenant chain, which would open their hunting territories and entice them to trade. Indians working on the fort would receive the same pay as the English. He offered one hundred pieces of eight for every Jesuit brought captive to Albany.

At a second private conference held on 30 August, eleven sachems attended—the same representation plus a Christian Mohawk. But each of the Five Nations brought one more from each nation, alleging that all business of moment should be transacted by the three "ensigns" (clans) comprising the Five Nations, namely Bear, Wolf, and Turtle; therefore, they asserted that each of these clans in each nation should be represented.[3] The request for expanded representation reflects the distribution of authority in Iroquois society and the importance the sachems attached to the business at hand.

Their speaker, Sadekanacktie, said that they had come to answer the heads proposed by his lordship yesterday—to draw their kin from Canada, make peace with the Far Indians, and deliver Jesuits. The three issues merged. The council thought it advisable first to make peace with the Ottawas and then to draw people back from Canada before meddling with the Jesuits. Second, Jesuits among all the bands of Far Indians would interfere with a peace, and they would prevent Iroquois converts from returning from the St. Lawrence. Therefore, make peace before acting. Third, the rest of the sachems presently were met up on the hill deliberating on the remaining proposals, which Sadekanacktie enumerated. It was evidently the practice to refer questions to parts of the council for consideration and reporting. They would recommend which sachems were to select the site of the fort at Onondaga, and also the matter of guides for Colonel Romer.

The Iroquois controlled the agenda. When Bellomont asked the leaders who were meeting with him whether they would now relate the message that Maricourt and Bruyas had brought to Onondaga, or whether they would wait until all the sachems were convened, they told him the latter. Again, on the design of the fort, he would hear from all the sachems. The garrisoning of the fort was a matter for the warriors, Sadekanacktie said: they would have to consult the young men before giving a positive answer. When Bellomont, accustomed to British command structure, replied that he thought the sachems had sole command and controlled the young men, the speaker reminded him: "Wee have often proposed something to you and you have told us that you would write to the King . . . about it, which gave us satisfaction and we never importuned you any more about it; and therefore pray be satisfyed with what we now have answered." The diffuse nature of Iroquois social control indeed was a mystery to his lordship.

A message came from the sachems meeting on the hill that they had concluded to send twelve men from each of the Five Nations to help build the fort in Onondaga country. On another matter—that of sending their children to be educated in New York—the sachems replied, "We are not masters or disposers of them; that is a matter that relates to our wives . . . while the children are under age." Children were beyond the jurisdiction of the headmen in a matrilineal society.

On the morning of the sixth day, the conference met in plenary session to hear his lordship's valedictory. He would admit the French traders among Far Indians

3. These were the three clans of the Mohawks and Oneidas down to historic times. The upper three nations acquired additional clan segments during the Beaver Wars by incorporating captive populations. A process of clan fission segmented older clans.

to Albany, but not the Jesuits. He wanted all the details of the Maricourt-Bruyas mission to Onondaga. He preached of Iroquois duty to king and Protestantism. He assured them of fortifying the country and concentrating the beaver trade at Albany. He commanded them, as king's subjects, to reject all French offers. All this in awarding the king's present, a considerable inventory of goods, not to mention rum (NYCD, 4: 740).

On the afternoon of the sixth day, in his reply to Bellomont, Sadekanacktie gave a lesson in alliance. The Five Nations pledged to remain steadfast. In their view, being instructed in Protestantism, remaining firm in the covenant chain, and remaining subjects of the king were a package. They likewise recommended that the English remain steadfast in religion and keep up friendship. (Friendship meant an obligation to continual renewals.) The speaker appealed to creation: "The Sunn has shined long upon us, and we have lived many years in peace. . . . [L]et us go hand in hand and support one another. Wee were here before you and were a strong and numerous people when you were small and young like striplings, yet wee were kind and cherished you, and therefore when wee propose anything to you, if you cannot agree to it, let us take council together that matters may be carry'd on smooth, and what we say may not be taken amiss." He expressed hope that such severities as whipping that the Jesuits used in proselytizing would not be employed by the Anglicans (NYCD, 4: 740).

On the matter of regulating the trade, the main accomplishment of the conference, Sadekanacktie replied to Bellomont that the French might come to Albany, but the Iroquois wanted the king to set the boundary with the French; they wanted cheap goods; and they would fix the trade at Albany and forbid English traders from coming into Five Nations country demanding a beaver skin for spoonfuls of rum. They were grateful for powder, but there were no duffels in which to wrap it and keep it dry.[4]

The Iroquois agreed that they would try to make peace with the Ottawas. But the peace in Europe should apply in America: "Write to your King."

Then came a full report on the visit of Maricourt and Bruyas to Onondaga that summer, substantially as related in the previous chapter. Two things bear notice. The French emissaries had brought a belt of wampum. Bruyas had hinted that allowing Jesuits to reestablish the missions and instruct the Iroquois would banish plagues and distempers. Smallpox and flu were evidently taking a toll. But this belt was not accepted because the Iroquois had already accepted a previous belt for a similar purpose brought by English emissaries, "which belt being given first, had the preference."

When asked what four sachems were doing in Canada, the speaker replied that they had waited two years for the English authorities to retrieve their captive kinsmen and then decided to do it themselves.

At Onondaga, Bruyas had raised the question of the New York governor's not informing the Five Nations of his correspondence with the French governor—of keeping them in the dark. He claimed that the French governor kept nothing from his Indian children. Furthermore, unlike Corlaer, Onontio made no claims

---

4. Duffel was a coarse woolen cloth named after a town of the same name near Antwerp. The other desired cloth was Stroud's, a blanket cloth still woven at Stroud in Gloucestershire, England.

on their land, and he left them free, while Corlaer pretended they were subjects (NYCD, 4: 742–43).

Henry, a Mohawk Protestant, thanked Bellomont for vacating some land grants that the Reverend Mr. Dellius and others had connived to get. It seems that in making grants to Mohawk lands, Governor Fletcher, despite protests from Albany citizens, had mistakenly awarded a grant to the Dutch Reformed minister Godfrey Dellius, who was also an Indian commissioner. Dellius, with four associates, had suborned their offices to finagle certain Mohawks separately into a faudulent sale of lands in the Mohawk Valley. It had devolved on Lord Bellomont, on orders from England in 1698, to rescind the grant (Nammack 1969: 14–15, 30, 52).

While Lord and Lady Bellomont were yet in Albany, the River Indians, settled on Rensselaer's land at Scaghticoke on the Hoosick River, made the usual gestures to renew the covenant chain. Having removed from New England after King Philip's War, they had planted a tree and since sat in its shade. They begged protection so as not to remove again. Indians east of them desired admission to the chain. That same day the governor renewed the alliance, urged its Indian members to invite the Penacooks to join them and strengthen the chain, wished they would become Protestants, promised to do the reasonable thing to recover prisoners, and distributed presents (NYCD, 4: 743–45).

□□◇□□

Save as a delaying action, this conference did not accomplish much, and it scarcely may be termed a treaty. It was held with one faction of the Iroquois Confederacy while another was in Montreal. For Lord Bellomont, it was a not-so-pleasant learning experience in Iroquois diplomacy. The lessons were conducted by a leading Onondaga sachem then living on the lands of the Schuylers more or less as a refugee but serving as the local resource on Indian matters for the Albany commissioners. Unfortunately, Bellomont did not live to put the experience to work, although in October 1700 reports of the conference got the attention of the Lords of Trade (NYCD, 4: 701).

Early in March 1701, Bellomont died, and negotiations with the Five Nations fell to his deputy, Lieutenant Governor John Nanfan. In July, Nanfan conducted a so-called treaty at Albany at which the Five Nations conveyed to the crown their beaver hunting territories north and west of Lakes Ontario and Erie (Winsor 1884–99, 8: 529). (That same year saw the founding of Yale College, where later Anglican missionaries to the Mohawks were educated and where, in the twentieth century, Iroquoianists were trained.) Just then, and for the next half-century, rival French and English interests focused on the Ohio country, the territory between the Ohio River and the Great Lakes, which had remained open only to hunters ever since the destruction of the Eries midway in the previous century. As pressure from settlement on the East Coast mounted, both Iroquoian and Algonquian remnants took up residence in the area, often in joint settlements. Pennsylvania traders followed the Indian hunters, while Virginians encroached on the Appalachian summits south of the river. French canoemen traversed the waterways and portaged the hogbacks from the St. Lawrence to the Ohio, while rivals ascended the Mississippi from its delta to the Ohio rapids and contended at Versailles for jurisdiction over its resources.

The English in New York, plainly worried, concocted a counterclaim based on their alliance with the Five Nations, an alliance which they translated into subjugation. They were alarmed that the Five Nations could not prevent the French from establishing a fortified post at Detroit, and Bellomont, like Dongan before him, feared the insidious teaching of the Jesuits and communicated the native desire for Protestant ministers (NYCD, 4: 717; Lydekker 1938: 8–11; Wallace 1957a: 231).

Moreover, the Grand Settlement at Montreal that summer meant that the English could no longer depend on the Five Nations to shield their northern frontier. The Iroquois had to be persuaded to let the Far Indians come to trade at Albany; otherwise, the French would continue to rule the upper lakes. Trade and alliances ran together (Eccles 1969: 128–30). All this lay behind the so-called treaty at Albany with the Five Nations (Winsor 1895: 66).

When the twenty sachems of the Five Nations met the new governor of New York, John Nanfan, in July, there had been deaths on both sides.[5] In June, the Onondaga council had notified the assembly that Sagochiendagehte had died over the winter and they had raised up his brother in the same name (Bleeker journal, NYCD, 4: 891). The Indians spoke first on the opening day, hoping the new governor would continue the "love and affection" of his predecessors. Nanfan then announced the death of the Earl of Bellomont and his own appointment.

The Indians expressed sorrow next day but deferred formal condolence. They welcomed a vigorous successor who could travel. They acknowledged Albany as the place for treaty negotiations and expressed hope that the covenant chain would be maintained. They confessed: "Wee have been brought very low" by "the death of many of our men" and the "great breach in our contry by seducing our people to Canada" (NYCD, 4: 897–98). As for treaties that they had made with the Ottawas and other Far Indians, the speaker cited a map with castles painted on a large skin that they had given to Captain Bleeker, and added that they had made peace with seven enumerated nations, including the Adirondacks. They had failed to entice their kin to return from Canada because the Jesuits controlled them and the governor of Canada had them in his service (NYCD, 4: 899).

Four days later Nanfan expressed gratitude for their confidence but showed little sympathy for their troubles with the Far Indians. They should defend themselves like men, and not complain to the French governor. They should reassert their previous conquest of Detroit. He appealed to the chain and promised to fortify Schenectady (NYCD, 4: 900).

The sachems confessed their inability to prevent the French from fortifying Detroit, and on 19 July 1701, the twenty sachems signed a deed to the English king quitting "for ever" title to a tract some eight hundred miles long and four hundred miles wide, including Detroit, which they alleged to have acquired by right of conquest. They thought they were putting the land under protection of the English crown (Jennings et al. 1985a: 165; NYCD, 4: 908–10).

The sachems trusted Robert Livingston more than the new governor. As secretary for Indian affairs, Livingston had recorded their Albany meetings for many years. They asked that he be sent to talk in person with the king, and they

---

5. Livingston, as secretary, listed the names of the tribal delegations, among which only two Oneida names faintly resemble titles of the founders (NYCD, 4: 897–98). They appear again on the deed with different spellings. The original at PRO might be helpful.

feared that if he did not go and explain how the French were encroaching on their domain, their letters would be read, laid aside, and forgotten. Nanfan paid little heed at first, until the sachems reiterated their request. Somewhat taken aback, Nanfan then promised to consider it. Apart from this official business, Livingston had a backlog of expense accounts that the New York assembly had not satisfied. He had made two trips to London in 1695 and finally made another in 1703, on both official and personal business. He was genuinely interested in the welfare of the New York colony, and he appreciated the plight of the Five Nations (Leder 1961: 101, 164, 168ff.). While in London he spoke with members of the Society for the Propagation of the Gospel concerning the desire of the Five Nations for Protestant missionaries and the wisdom of having them as tenants of the deeded territories (Lydekker 1938: 11, 13–14).

□□◇□□

Before turning in the next chapter to Anglican efforts to propagate the Gospel among the Mohawks, two other matters demand attention. The first is the geopolitical situation in North America following the 1701 treaties. The second is the sociopolitical ethnography of the residual Five Nations and their expatriates in Canada.

The two sets of treaties were diplomatic compromises all around. During a half-century of wars with their neighbors and with New France, the Iroquois had lost more people than they could replace by adoption. Recurrent epidemics took an even greater toll. Defections to the Catholic missions on the St. Lawrence outnumbered residual populations in eastern towns. Warfare was no longer a productive choice. The Iroquois had raided but failed to reduce New France, the campaigns against the Miamis and Illinois had fallen short of success, and the Far Indians of Michilimackinac had expelled them from lands previously conquered in Huronia and were lifting scalps in Iroquoia. The vaunted Iroquois League was an unworkable memory, and the Five Nations needed time to rebuild the confederacy.

Similarly, the French needed breathing room. They had failed to reduce Iroquoia, they could no longer control their Far Indian allies, who were seeking trade agreements with the Iroquois and Albany, and they were willing to let the market work so long as the Iroquois remained neutral.

Albany was the source of guns during the Beaver Wars, of wampum, of Sheffield cutlery, of Stroud's woolens, and of New England rum—at prices generally cheaper than the French monopoly could offer. English military support, however, was fitful or wanting. While the Iroquois fought alone, the English alliance known as the chain was useful; but having settled differences with the French and their Indian allies, the Iroquois veered toward a policy of neutrality, of playing the French off against the English, of selling their furs on a free market, and of rebuilding their polity (Wallace 1957a: 233–35).

Until Cadwallader Colden (1727), English sources show a singular lack of insight into the nature of Iroquois government. Captain William Hyde's "Observations on the Five Nations of Indians at New Yorke, 1698" (Fenton, ed., 1965b) manifests great interest in warfare and torture and says nothing of civil government. He was intrigued by Iroquois drinking habits and left a notable vignette of their law of sharing. "I have seen Seaven or Eight of these fellowes sitt Round uppon the Grounds all drunke, and to maintain faire Justice among them in drinking a young handsom Squa sate in the middle with a Cagg of Rum, & measur'd Each mans due proportion with her mouth into a dish and soe it went Round" (ms. p. 13). Apart from Iroquois behavior in negotiations, the composition of delegations to treaties, and the Five Nations' insistence on protocol, on proper reference, and on attesting with wampum belts agreements reached in council, the New York Indian Records leave us in the dark about the structure of Iroquois government.

For subjects such as village form and composition, village autonomy, clan representation, the various ranks, offices, and age grades and their functions at the local, tribal, and confederate levels, the role of orators, affairs of state, and civil versus military affairs, the best account of Iroquois polity comes from the pen of Father Lafitau, a scholar who resided among the expatriate Iroquois at Kahnawakeh for five years in the early eighteenth century, read the *Relations*, quizzed senior colleagues, and wrote a pioneer comparative ethnology (Lafitau 1724; Fenton and Moore 1974). It was La Potherie and the trader Perrot, and possibly Lafitau, who inspired Colden.

Lafitau sensed that legitimacy in Iroquois polity passed matrilineally, and it was by women that care of civil affairs was entrusted to men; that all villages governed themselves in the same way, as if autonomous; and that "we see in each, the same distribution of families [clans], the same civil laws, the same order, so that anyone who sees one, sees them all" (Fenton and Moore 1974: 287). Affairs of common interest united the nation in a general council of deputies from the several villages, who strove for consensus.

There were in each village three clans—Wolf, Bear, and Turtle. Each clan had its chiefs, *agoianders* (persons of rank), elders, and warriors, who together formed the body politic. The names of chiefs descended in matriclan segments. The clans segmented during village removals that were necessitated by requirements of agriculture and fuel (Fenton and Moore 1974: 289, 290).

The will of the clan reposed in the clan chief, and from that will flowed his dignity and jurisdiction. Each status was marked by linguistic usage, which Lafitau discovered (Fenton and Moore 1974: 290–91). The clan chief was at once the "distinguished one" and spokesman of the clan, referred to by clan eponym in the form "he the Wolf [Bear, Turtle] said or did it." Or he was referred to by age grade: "the Old Man." By extension, the spokesman for a nation assumed its council name—for Onondaga, Sagochiendagehte, "the name bearer." The Senecas (Tsonnontouans, "Big Hill People") might be referred to by the titles of the two doorkeepers of the confederacy—in Lafitau's Mohawk usage, Tsonnonkeritaoui and Te-Ionninnokaraouen ("Hair Singed" and "He Holds the Door Open"), respectively (Fenton 1950: 67).

Lafitau said the chiefs were of equal rank and authority, but he sensed that one in each village who represented its founding lineage enjoyed greater prestige, although he could not decide whether ability was more important. He traced descent and succession in the matrilineage, he witnessed the showing of the new chief to the village by "holding up his face" to the public, and he remarked the publication of the news in other villages of the nation, and at allied nations, with public solemnities (Fenton and Moore 1974: 292). Clearly, the chiefs embodied the metaphor of the tree that fell, was reerected, and required added roots as props in event of a regency, so that civil authority over the chief's "children" or "nephews" was maintained in the clan. Iroquois chiefs enjoyed greater prestige than power and exercised no coercion. Order was kept by consent. Iroquois chiefs, with rare exceptions, bore no mark of distinction (Lafitau makes no mention of antlers of office, real or metaphorical). They presided at meetings and feasts, and they generally impoverished themselves by generosity (Fenton and Moore 1974: 292–93).

The chiefs were assigned deputies, with whom they shared sovereignty over the territory and together comprised the class *agoianders*. This class looked to its leader, called *roiander goa* (*royandergo:wa*), "the great one." Within each clan, each matrilineage had one person appointed by the matrons of this class to represent it. Lafitau states that a woman might occupy this position and that she was recognized in council, but her office was not revealed publicly to allied nations, as were the chiefs. These women trustees watched out for local interest, kept an eye on the public treasury, and audited its use.

The senate was composed of an indeterminate number of old people—persons who had attained maturity and respect.

The young men able to bear arms comprised a fourth category, warriors, or *agoskenrhagete* (*rohskv?rakehte* [Michelson 1973: 68]). Warriors were led both by clan chiefs graduated from the warrior class and by war chiefs (Fenton and Moore 1974: 294).

Lafitau is at his best in describing councils (Fenton and Moore 1974: 295ff.). The women deliberated first and apart, advised their clan leaders, who assembled the clan elders, and carried the issue to the national council. The warriors, too, counseled apart on issues in their purview and sent a speaker to the council of elders, who held open and closed sessions and announced their decisions publicly. They received ambassadors, hung the war kettle, and mourned the dead with proper ceremony. Secret councils were by invitation. The council fire was lighted in the lodge of a chief or in a public council house. In an oft-cited passage, Lafitau wrote:

> They are a troupe of dirty men seated on their backsides, hunched up like monkeys, with their knees up to their ears, or lying in different positions, either flat on their backs with their stomachs in the air, who, all of them, pipes in their mouths, treat affairs of state with as much coolness and gravity as the Junta of Spain or the Council of Sages at Venice. (Fenton and Moore 1974: 296)

Whether Lafitau experienced a "Council of the Ancients" such as the one he quotes almost verbatim from Brébeuf's description of a Huron council in the *Relation* of 1636 is uncertain, although several of its features apply to council behavior among Iroquois descendants today (Fenton and Moore 1974: 296–97). The behavior is generically Iroquoian, although the observations are specifically of Hurons.

The same might be said of Lafitau's passage on orators (Fenton and Moore 1974: 297–98), whom he most certainly heard at Kahnawakeh. It is a pity that Lafitau never visited Onondaga, which he knew but remotely, and he nowhere described the composition of the league or representation in councils of the confederacy. He mentions the symbolic Longhouse of the "Builders of Lodges," specifies its five member nations, their five dialects, and their division into upper and lower segments, and shows awareness of their union, all of which one reads in the *Jesuit Relations* (Fenton and Moore 1974: 86–87). And he knew titles of some leading chiefs, as we have seen (Fenton and Moore 1974: 291–92). The rest, Father Bruyas could have told him, had he not died just as Lafitau entered on his mission. His mentor was Father Garnier, who, like Bruyas, had toiled sixty years in Iroquoia (DCB, 2: 237).

The Jesuits' tradition of enlightened inquiry and their interest in learning native languages—albeit for the purpose of saving souls by converting natives to Catholicism—stand in marked contrast to Dutch and English concerns with trade and land acquisition, their ignorance of Iroquoian languages, and their belated realization that Protestant missionaries might offset Jesuit success. Indeed, at home the Lords of Trade in Whitehall were only dimly aware of the limits of Canada and ignorant of the geography of Iroquoia. It would take a spectacle in public relations launched from Albany to get their attention.

PART FOUR

Balancing Onontio and the English Crown, 1702–1759

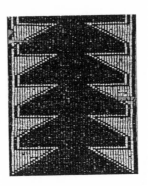

CHAPTER 24

Kings in the
Court of Queen Anne

When Queen Anne acceded to the throne in 1702, her subjects at home and in America had acquired, in Albany Indian parlance, a "squaw sachem," or, in Iroquois usage, a *goyanehrgow:wa*, "grand matron," or clan mother.[1] For the next decade her regime focused on wars on the continent that left little time for thought of America. The Lords of Trade were dimly aware of where Canada began and left off. In Paris, concerns might be more sharply focused, but as Voltaire remarked: "Canada was so many acres of snow!"[2] A few men in the colonies, including some Indians, three British officials, and one or two Albanians, knew that something had to be done. Together they pulled off the greatest publicity stunt of the century.

Three forces in America—Iroquois, French, and English—sought recognition of their interests in Europe. Following the Grand Settlement at Montreal in 1701, the Iroquois Confederacy embarked on a policy of neutrality in wars between the two dominant European powers, a policy which the French and British honored at their convenience and which was threatened by both sides. Factions still rent the confederacy: the Senecas, beset by Ottawa war parties, favored the French; the Onondaga council played it both ways; and the Mohawk leaders were pro-English. The need for protection from French forces supported sentiment for an English fort at Onondaga and the appeal for Protestant ministers. Dependency on the trade at Albany sustained the chain alliance, which the New York governors renewed with presents and with promises of military aid that was seldom forthcoming. Acting as a bulwark against the French had wasted the confederacy. As if honoring the 1701 agreement, French-supported war parties raided New England, destroying Deerfield, Massachusetts, and carrying off captive women and children to Caughnawaga. Pressure to relieve such attacks came from Bostonians who complained about the neutrality of the Five Nations and urged countermeasures from New York and the confederacy (NYCD, 5: 42; Winthrop and Leverett to Lovelace, HEH, HM 3030).

1. Properly, *squaw* was the Algonquian term for "woman," and it was in common usage in Albany at the time, both by the River Indians, who spoke a dialect of Algonquian, and by the Dutch and English. Only later did the term become confused in Mohawk as a reference to female genitalia, so that now the word is offensive to modern Iroquois. See "Squaw" in Hodge 1912: 629–30, and "Squaw Sachem" in SPG ms. A1, no. LVI.

2. See the discussion of Voltaire in Fenton and Moore 1974: front matter.

But the confederacy had lost half its population to Jesuit success in enticing converts to emigrate to the St. Lawrence missions and practice Christianity undisturbed by pagan kin. Fed up with a half-century of Jesuit devices, the stay-at-homes were sympathetic toward accepting Protestant missionaries. Holders of some traditional titles had defected to Canada, leaving empty places in the grand council at Onondaga, which meant restructuring the representation of the Five Nations as a confederacy. In this process, coupled with the policy of neutrality, the confederacy supplanted the Iroquois League as the operating entity, and the league as an institution became a memory.

The restoration of the Iroquois Confederacy during the first half of the eighteenth century hinged on an ad hoc policy aimed at restoring Iroquois economic, political, and military strength. In a recent study, Richard Aquila contends that this was a unified policy that comprised four major strategies: neutrality; an accommodation with the tribes of the upper Great Lakes; cooperation with Pennsylvania in taking over the remnant Indians; and redirecting warfare toward the tribes of the Southeast, abetted by the French (Aquila 1983: 16–17). The southeastern wars unified the attention of a generation of young men, but their raids on the backs of the English colonies embarrassed their elders, who confessed they could not control the warriors, and it weakened the linkages in the chain. English governors protested in a whole series of treaties. The sachems who represented the confederacy were now predominately former war leaders. Few, if any, were league chiefs, although they acted the part in representing their interests to the English and French governors.

Vaudreuil succeeded Callière as governor of Canada in 1703 and served until his death in 1725 (Winsor 1884–99, 8: 530; Zoltvany 1974: 33; DCB, 2: 565–74). He sought to maintain the benefits of the Grand Settlement and to avoid another costly Iroquois war, despite the outbreak of hostilities in Europe over the Spanish succession, a conflict known in North America as Queen Anne's War, which lasted until the Peace of Utrecht in 1713. Although hotheads in Canada urged launching an all-out campaign against New York and New England, Vaudreuil heeded other advice. Recalled to France, former intendant Champigny advised the Minister of Marine against such attacks, telling him that the New Yorkers wanted to be left alone in peace and that the risk of the Iroquois taking up the hatchet was too great. Instead, the Iroquois treaty of neutrality was a better model for negotiating with the English colonies. Let the Jesuits insinuate to the Iroquois that if the English would suspend hostilities, the French would follow. The onus would be on the English (Eccles 1969:133). The minister went along.

The economy of New France faced a crisis. The inventory of beaver pelts and other furs from years of overbuying jammed the warehouses, prices fell, and erstwhile allies from the upper Great Lakes threatened to turn to Albany, where inventories were down and prices higher. When the Iroquois were at war, French-allied hunters could not go great distances to where beavers prevailed. Loss of the trade threatened alliances with the Far Indians on whom New France depended, and it left the Iroquois unchecked (Zoltvany 1974: 33–34).

The Iroquois, too, sensed the need for peace. Dependent as they were on Albany, trading also at Montreal gave them access to the best grades of gunpowder; and French brandy, when they could get it, was smoother than New England rum. For strategic reasons, the upper Iroquois were less enthusiastic about Protestant ministers and petitioned for the return of Jesuit priests. Father Lamberville went back to Onondaga, and Garnier and Vaillant to the Senecas. Their presence might deter raids of tribes from the upper lakes, traditional allies of the French among whom other Jesuits resided. Onondaga warriors welcomed a French smith to repair their weapons (Zoltvany 1974: 35).

Policy among the Five Nations was localized and hinged on strategic and pragmatic considerations. The upper nations would follow a policy of independent action so long as English support was not forthcoming. The Mohawks inclined toward Albany. They would tolerate the Jesuit missionaries while it served their purposes of gaining concessions from the French and frightening the English. The basic Iroquois policy was to remain independent while keeping communication open both ways, balancing the English off against the French, whom the Iroquois distrusted. Neutrality was at the core of this policy, and carrying it out required considerable finesse (Zoltvany 1974: 35–37).

In 1703, the Iroquois opened the way for the Far Indians to trade at Albany—at first the Hurons and later the Ottawas and Miamis, with whom they patched up a peace. To the French, this was a disaster because it represented the first breach in the Iroquois barrier that the French had relied on during the previous century (Eccles 1969: 135, citing Zoltvany 1964). Until then the Albany traders had stayed at home and procured western furs via Montreal, which Caughnawaga and French canoemen delivered to Albany. This gray market trade continued into the eighteenth century, to the dismay of British imperialists (Colden 1724). Before opening the path to trade at Albany, the Iroquois had not allowed either power to establish posts in Iroquoia. In Eccles's words, "Whereas before, Iroquois strength had been the main threat to New France, Iroquois weakness now proved to be an equal, if not greater menace" (Eccles 1969: 135).

Ultimately, the French responded by fortifying western posts and consolidating the links in a chain of strong points stretching from Niagara to Detroit, down the Ohio Valley, and along the Mississippi to New Orleans.

Vaudreuil's policy was to accommodate the Iroquois, spare the New York frontiers, and strike New England. This policy suited mission Iroquois because it enabled them to avoid fighting their kin. The Abenakis were troublesome and were flirting with Massachusetts governor Dudley. The attacks on Deerfield in 1703 and Haverill five years later prompted New England to pressure New York and the Iroquois to invade Canada. The English enlisted all but the Senecas to rise with them against the French and ultimately expel the Jesuits from Iroquoia (Winsor 1895: 71).

□□◇□□

British imperialism encountered colonial self-interest, which was further segmented by local interests. The governors of Massachusetts, Virginia, Maryland, and Pennsylvania reluctantly looked to New York on matters affecting the Five Nations; there was not yet any unified policy on Indian affairs. At Albany, the commissioners of Indian affairs, who were traders, met frequently with delegations of the Five Nations, viewed the Indian business in their own lights, heard the Indians' demands, and communicated their needs to the governor of New York and his council, who remotely perceived the situation on the frontier and had other

interests. Securing and maintaining the New York frontier that began at Schenectady was an enormous expense to the crown, running to thousands of pounds per
year for presents to Indians alone, besides expenses of the commissioners, fees to
interpreters and payment for their travels to Onondaga, and outlays by the
secretary of Indian affairs. And there was an Albany garrison to clothe, feed, and
pay. For formal treaties, the governor chartered a sloop, voyaged the 150 miles up
the North River, endured the lengthy councils, returned downriver promptly, and
ultimately reported to the Lords of Trade in Whitehall.

Colonel Robert Quarry, as surveyor general of customs in North America, in
1702 wrote the lord high treasurer of England that Massachusetts and New
Hampshire alone were spending some thirty thousand pounds yearly for defense,
that the Iroquois alliance demanded constant bribes to the chiefs to secure a shaky
trust, and that continual repairs to the fort at Albany drained funds, while the
outposts were in ruins. The remedy was to drive the French from Canada (Quary
to Godolphin BL 28, HEH; Winsor 1895: 69).

To accomplish this, several things became gradually apparent: maintaining the
covenant chain between the Five Nations and the colonies required a unified
English policy on Indian affairs; the Jesuits had to be replaced with Protestant
missionaries; and the command of the militias and garrisons had to be
coordinated, with military aid from the Royal Navy. The Five Nations recognized
Albany as the "fire" for doing business with the English colonies, although the
main fire of Iroquois policy burned at Onondaga. Colonial governors and their
commissioners avoided traversing the wilderness to Onondaga but came by water
and overland to treat with the Five Nations at Albany. With the exception of
Pennsylvania, they gradually yielded priority in Indian affairs to the governor of
New York. It would take another fifty years before the colonies attained a unified
policy and the crown placed responsibility for Indian affairs under a single head.

Although British authorities considered placing Protestant missionaries in
Iroquoia as tenants on the lands deeded in 1701, the Iroquois, aside from their
more pious motives, understood this as putting their lands under the protection
of the crown. Eastern members of the confederacy got their first glimpse of an
Anglican minister in 1704, when the Society for the Propagation of the Gospel in
Foreign Parts (SPG) sent out the Reverend Thorgood Moore, who took up residence in Albany but manifested little appetite for living with the Indians. The
Dutch minister Lydius introduced him to some Mohawks, and in late November
he ventured to the first Mohawk castle, where one Indian took him by the arm,
addressed him as "father," and escorted him into town to a small guest house
where the sachems left him to rest. The Mohawk council hesitated to accept an
Anglican mission without the sanction of the other four nations, who still perceived
"a Light arising in Canada" (the Jesuit missions).[3] The Jesuit fathers had brought
a bell to summon them to worship, and the concept of a church mystified them.
The Mohawks told Moore that he must first acquaint them with the program of
the SPG. Then they would inform the other four nations, "for we are all but one
house." Then they would give him a definite answer: "sudden Answers were

3. "Light" (*gaji:sta?*) is still the name of the wampum belt held at Tonawanda for the Handsome
Lake religion.

not their custom" (Lydekker 1938: 17–20). The following year, Moore threw in the towel.

The Iroquois realized they could not expect too much of Anglican missionaries, who were poorly prepared to reside in their villages. More mundane considerations dominated Indian thought. Three cultural demands were uppermost. Wraxall (1915: 49) summarized his reading of volume one of the Indian Records to 1706 under three heads that the Indians constantly stressed: (1) that someone who understood their language be empowered by the government to reside among them, attend their councils, and make an occasional progress through their settlements; (2) that a smith be stationed at Onondaga; and (3) that they desired powder and lead for hunting and war at reasonable prices. These three demands surfaced at every public conference—they were very important to the Indians, and "neglect of them [was] very impolitic."

The sachems perceived their own interests clearly. Whenever they had matters of consequence to communicate to the governor, now Lord Cornbury, they did not wait for him to come up from New York but instead went to Albany and spoke directly to the commissioners. Their three mutual concerns in the summer of 1707 were failure to get the praying Indians, who were by then entirely under the influence of Governor Vaudreuil, to return home; peace with the Far Indians; and the fact that the French were inciting their young men to go out against the Flatheads, or Catawbas (Wraxall 1915: 50; Colden 1937: 361).

In the hands of rival European powers competing for Iroquois allegiance, the condolence ceremony metamorphosed into an alliance weapon. Vaudreuil tried to persuade the Five Nations of Cornbury's insincerity by pointing out how Cornbury had failed to send a present to condole his Mohawk neighbors when a prominent Mohawk sachem died that year (Colden 1937: 363–64). Indeed, Cornbury's administration was a mess all around. Among other things, he abolished Robert Livingston's job as secretary of Indian affairs as an unnecessary expense and disallowed Livingston's back salary and expenses (Leder 1961: 203–4).

Robert Livingston was one of the few men in the colonies who saw the big picture. He had wisely gone to London in 1703 to petition the Privy Council directly for reimbursement of accounts that the New York assembly had not paid. On returning in 1706, he wrote an indictment of Cornbury's conduct in office, which brought the governor's removal. While in London, he succeeded in getting two Anglican missionaries sent to the Iroquois. He combined public service with personal profit in the Indian trade, he saw the strategic advantage of gaining Detroit as the focus of the western trade, and he recognized that bringing Palatine Germans to produce naval stores and settling them on the Mohawk and Schoharie rivers would exert a stabilizing influence greater than that of the treaty of 1701 (Leder 1961: passim; Winsor 1895: 72–73).

The one commissioner in Albany whom the Iroquois respected was Peter Schuyler (1657–1724), familiarly known to them as "Quider," there being no labials in Iroquoian languages. It would fall to Schuyler—trader, leader of Mohawk war parties, militia officer, emissary to Onondaga and Quebec, and first and long-term mayor of Albany—to organize and conduct a group of Iroquois ambassadors to the court of Queen Anne in 1709–10 (DCB, 2: 602–3; Lydekker 1938; Bond 1952).

Lord John Lovelace, Baron of Hurley, landed in Manhattan in December 1708 to take over from the deposed Cornbury. Lovelace had two programs in mind. One of them—the transplanting of Palatine refugees to produce naval stores—did not come off for several years, and as for the other—the so-called Glorious Enterprise to reduce Canada—Lovelace would not live to see it end in disaster. He died in May of the following year. Four nations of the Iroquois Confederacy, excepting the Senecas, condoled his passing and wiped away Queen Anne's tears (Colden 1937: 377-78; Leder 1961: 203-5).

Samuel Vetch (1688-1732) in Boston had conceived the plan for the Glorious Enterprise, which involved a naval thrust against Acadia and an army assault from Albany. Colonel Francis Nicholson (1655-1728), former governor of Virginia, experienced in colonial warfare, volunteered to assist by commanding militias of Connecticut, New York, and New Jersey, which were to advance from bases in Albany and Stillwater via the Champlain corridor to the heart of Canada. Queen Anne in March 1709 approved Vetch's plan, commissioned him to get the expedition moving, and instructed him to take a ship to New York and deliver letters of authority to the governors, stipulating quotas of manpower and supplies. He was to enlist the Five Nations and the River Indians (Bond 1952: 24). The latter would take some doing.

To advance recruiting, Schuyler convinced Nicholson to send five Indians to Boston to view the fleet expected momentarily (Colden 1937: 379, 380). Within a month, five Mohawks reviewed Colonel Hobbey's regiment, and the governor hosted them at the castle and at Nantasket to show them the strength of the fort. To demonstrate further Her Majesty's intentions, the five men-of-war in the harbor "spread all their Finery to set out the Ships" (Sewall 1973: 623, 624). Presumably, the Indians went home duly impressed.

Through Lovelace, Vetch enlisted Schuyler and Livingston, Vetch's uncle and father-in-law, respectively, to round up Indians as spies, emissaries, and ultimately guerrillas for the militia (Waller 1960: 161-65; Leder 1961: 205; DCB, 2: 496-99, 650-52). The Iroquois, however, were not about to set aside proper protocol. They made a clear distinction between status and role. When the commissioners proposed to a delegation of sachems meeting in Albany that they scout out the French and Indians, the sachems answered that as a matter of protocal it was not their custom, when they came to treat of public affairs, to be asked to undertake the office of scout or spy. But if the Christians were to come to treat in their country, and if there were an apparent danger, they would send out some of their own people to scout and observe the motions of the enemy. They would not expect protection from those who came to treat with them or ask them to undertake such an office (Wraxall 1915: 60; Colden 1937: 368). The Senecas remained neutral in these negotiations (Wraxall 1915: 68-69; Colden 1937: 372-74; Livingston 1956: 206ff.).

Despite pressure from Massachusetts on Governor Lovelace early in 1709 to prevent further defections of Mohawks to the French and to allow the Five Nations to act offensively in the present war, it was no easy task to persuade the confederacy to abandon its policy of neutrality (Winthrop, Wait, and Lamont to Lovelace, NYPL). At the council fire at Onondaga, the sachems failed to reach agreement. The Seneca representatives held that it was rash to take up the hatchet against

Canada and later complained that when the council resolved to make war against the French, "the Five Nations did not make a Compleat or full house," inasmuch as only one Seneca sachem was present and the nation had not empowered him to act on the matter (Colden 1937: 376). This failure to attain unanimity was not new in the confederacy, nor did it prevent the other four nations from going off on their own.

For a decade, neither the promised Protestant ministers nor the campaign to reduce Canada materialized. Four nations, despite their avowed policy of neutrality, nonetheless sent several hundred warriors to scout for and guide a combined force of militia and regular troops that sat on the upper Hudson too late in the season in 1709, awaiting word to advance once a Royal Navy squadron had anchored off Massachusetts Bay. Word never came. The army dispersed and the Indians went home disgusted. Something drastic had to be done to get Queen Anne's attention and preserve the chain with the confederacy.

□□◇□□

Just who fathered the first great American public relations stunt remains uncertain. It was an obvious idea with established precedents: the French had taken Indians abroad to exhibit them at trade fairs and at court. The idea unified the interests of the Iroquois, the Albanians, and the imperialists in the colonies. It was a combined effort between Peter Schuyler and fellow officers encamped at Wood Creek, who petitioned Vetch in Boston. The officers' proposal to send representatives of the Five Nations overseas was a logical extension of Vetch's earlier invitation that New York send some Indians to Boston to impress them with preparations for the naval campaign against the maritimes. Peter Schuyler, who enjoyed the confidence of the Iroquois, acted as principal in selecting the delegation and conducting it abroad (Bond 1952: 32–33).

An ideal delegation would comprise five sachems and deputies selected equally from the Five Nations. But the remote Senecas were neutral, which limited selection to four nations, and even this proved impracticable. Instead, Schuyler enlisted three trusty Mohawks with Christian names—Hendrick, Brant, and John—none of whom was yet a sachem, and a lone River Indian, a Mahican named Nicholas.[4] Hendrick, who was descended from a Mahican mother but had grown up a Mohawk, served as their leader. The four undoubtedly had Indian names, although their titles as spelled in the English sources, to the extent that one can resolve them to Iroquoian personal names, suggest that they acquired more prestigious titles for the occasion.

Hendrick (c. 1680–1755), a Christian convert who had rounded up Mohawk warriors for the abortive campaign of 1709, headed the party and spoke for it (fig. 28). The Mohawk Wolf clan named him Theyanoguin (the accepted spelling; DCB, 3: 622), but for the trip abroad he acceded to the illustrious title Tee-Yee-Neen-Ho-Ga-Row, as the English heard it, a variant of the Mohawk Teyohninhohakara:wenh, or Deyonihnho:ga:ʔwen, the fiftieth title on the roll call of league chiefs—that of the Seneca doorkeeper (Fenton 1950: 67).[5] Nobody in

---

4. Whether there were four or five sachems in the delegation has confused later writers. One version holds that there were five, but one died at sea, leaving a delegation of four. I follow Bond (1952) in opting for four. Likewise, there were several trips to Boston.

5. League titles in one nation sometimes occur as personal names in other nations.

Figure 28. Hendrick. Portrait by Jan Verelst, 1710. Public Archives of Canada, neg. no. C-92415.

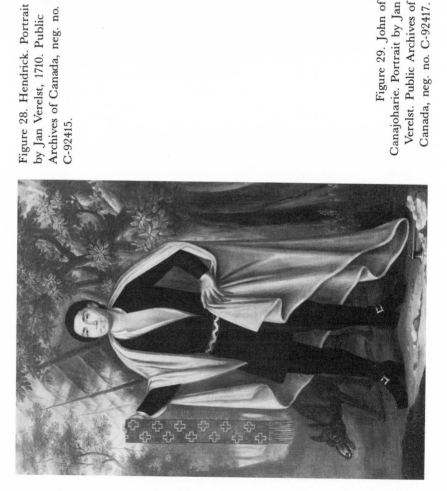

Figure 29. John of Canajoharie. Portrait by Jan Verelst. Public Archives of Canada, neg. no. C-92417.

Figure 30. Brant. Portrait by Jan Verelst, 1710. Public Archives of Canada, neg. no. C-92419.

Figure 31. The Mahican Nicholas. Portrait by Jan Verelst. Public Archives of Canada, neg. no. C-92421.

London knew the difference, and the title did not hinder a distinguished career. Hendrick later participated in the Albany Congress of 1754 and died a year later in the battle of Lake George.

John of Ganajohore (now Canajoharie), the third, or upper, Mohawk castle, where "the kettle washes itself" (the earlier upper castle, Tionontoguen, was by now abandoned), belonged also to the Wolf clan (fig. 29). In London, printers spelled his title "Oh-Nee-Yea-Ton-No-Prow," although there is no *p* in Mohawk. His proper Mohawk name eludes us, and no record of him survived the visit.

Brant, of the Bear clan, his proper name unknown, in London became "King of the Maquas," with the title Sa-Ga-Yean-Qua-Prah-Ton—again the errant *p* crept in. The title probably was Sagayen?kwara:ton, "Vanishing Smoke," which name later in the century belonged to a prominent Seneca war chief, Old Smoke (Sayenqueraghta in Hodge 1912: 482). Brant died soon after returning home. He probably was not the grandfather of Joseph Brant; instead, his fame now rests on the elaborate tattooing preserved in the portrait of him by the artist Jan Verelst (fig. 30).

Albanians regularly dealt with River Indians, the remnants of Hudson River and New England Algonquians. Nicholas, who attained no later distinction, in London became Elow-Oh-Kaom, a name that no Algonquianist has resolved, to my knowledge. He posed for Verelst brandishing a ball-headed warclub of the period, with a cutlass, or *hower*, at his belt (fig. 31). Either he spoke Mohawk, or his three companions, as close neighbors, had acquired some Mahican, for Algonquian and Iroquoian languages comprise distinct families (Bond 1952: 40, et seq.).

Schuyler appointed his brother John as his deputy, informed the Mohawk sachems with seven hands of wampum, and departed with the four chosen Indians for Boston in the early winter of 1709 (Colden 1937: 381). There, the party met the governor and local worthies, they were wined and dined, and, lest they get bored waiting for their ship, Josiah Parker of Cambridge took the "Four Sagamores" hunting—and then had to go to court to collect his overdue expense account (MA 31: 87–89; Bond 1952: 41).

HMS *Reserve* weighed anchor on 28 February 1710 and arrived off Portsmouth on 2 April, a remarkably short voyage for the time. Aboard were the four Indians, Colonel Peter Schuyler, a surprise passenger, Major David Pigeon (Sewall 1973: 62), and Captain Abraham Schuyler. Colonel Francis Nicholson had preceded them and smoothed the path. They reached London by Easter Monday (10 April that year) to end Lent.

Two central concerns—Protestant missionaries and establishing a fort— occupied the minds of the Indian delegates; but securing a guarantee of military support for the Glorious Enterprise dominated the thinking of their escorts. The distractions of London, however, immediately transformed the mission into the sensation of the London season, with both sides experiencing culture shock. In all the excitement, it is clear that the native New Yorkers faced the situation with aplomb.

London was already astir with the impeachment trial of Dr. Sacheverell, a High Church divine, on 19 April, the day the queen received the Indian sachems (Churchill 1957, 3: 84ff.). As Londoners watched two royal coaches progress toward St. James Palace carrying the Indian sachems—now "Indian Kings of Canada"—to their audience with the queen, excitement mounted. The Duke of Shrewsbury, the new lord chamberlain, presented them, Captain Abraham Schuyler interpreted from Mohawk, and Major Pigeon read an English version to Her Majesty (Bond 1952: 1). Presumably Hendrick was the Mohawk speaker.

The speech to the queen represented Iroquois concerns of the day over their fate in the struggle between England and France for North America and requested English missionaries to minister to the Iroquois people. Broadsides carried the text for Londoners to read (Lydekker 1938: 26-28; Bond 1952: 93-95).

In their speech, the sachems said they had undertaken a long and difficult journey to relate to the queen in person what they thought essential for her good and for the good of their people, her allies on the other side of the Great Water. They had lost their best men in defending the security of her subjects. On hearing of the great plan to reduce Canada, they had rejoiced, hung the war kettle, and taken up the hatchet. They had sent a delegation to Boston to view Vetch's preparations to go against Quebec by sea while they, Nicholson, and Schuyler went overland to Montreal. Hendrick used the adopted names of the principals: Anadaissa (Vetch), Anadagariaux ("village destroyer") (Nicholson), and Quider (Peter Schuyler). They had waited long for the expected fleet, Hendrick told the queen; they felt frustrated, and they feared that the French would think them no longer able to make war against them. They considered the reduction of Canada vital to their hunting and their free trade with the English. They presented the queen with wampum belts "as a Token of the Sincerity of the *Six Nations*, and in the Name of [those] present."[6]

As for themselves, they said, in the interest of their families, they must decide whether to forsake their country and seek other habitations or stand neutral, neither of which appealed to them.

The petition closed by reminding the queen of the Five Nations' long-standing alliance with the English, her children; it claimed some knowledge of Christianity on the part of the Indians; it referred to the insinuations of French priests and to presents from liars hoping to persuade the Iroquois to come over to the French interest; and it appealed for the queen to send over some persons to instruct them, whom they would welcome. The sachems now left these matters with the queen for consideration.

Queen Anne was impressed. She ordered gifts and commanded her lord chamberlain to entertain the sachems at her expense and to show them the city. The audience concluded, protocol reversed itself. The kings rode back to their lodgings at the Two Crowns and Cushions, an upholster's shop in King Street near St. Paul's Church. They were now on the town.

One pamphleteer, quoted by Bond (1952: 2-3), described the Indian "kings" in part as follows:

They are well form'd . . . of a Stature . . . within an Inch or two of six Foot . . . their Limbs muscular and well shap'd . . . their Hair black and long, their Visages are very awful and majestick, and their Features regular enough . . . and the Marks with which

6. The Tuscaroras had come north that year, and this is the first mention of their adoption by the Oneidas as the sixth nation.

they disfigure their Faces, do not seem to carry so much Terror as Regard with them. . . . [T]hey wear . . . black Waistcoats, Breeches, and Stockings, with yellow Slippers [moccasins], and a loose scarlet mantle [blanket] cast over them . . . their hair ty'd short up, and a Cap . . . [like] a Turbant upon their heads. They are generally affable . . . and will not refuse a Glass of Brandy or strong Liquors from any hands that offer it. They never sit on Chairs or Benches, but on their Heels, which makes their Knees, when they stand upright, bag out before. They feed heartily, and love our *English* Beef . . . with the best of Wines; but they seem to relish our fine pale Ales before the best *French* Wines.

They were soon caught up in a round of social activities: "The Duke of Ormande had them out to dinner at his country place on 20 April. Next day a royal barge carried them to Greenwich to view the instruments of the Astronomer Royal, the hospital, and the Woolwich docks and yards of the Admiralty. A day later they banqueted at Whitehall. By then one of the Kings was done in and had to rest a day at the 'Two Crowns and Cushions'" (Bond 1952: 3).

The Iroquois love ceremony, and the four kings, by now a sensation, were about to witness the London theater. The manager of the Queen's Theatre in Haymarket, where Congreve's *Old Bachelor* was on the boards, saw a way to fill the house. He announced in the *Daily Courant* a performance "For the Entertainment of the Four Indian Kings" on Monday, 24 April. At the last minute the play was changed to *Macbeth*. But three of the sachems attended. The mob went wild and demanded their money's worth: the kings before the bill. A special epilogue honored them (Bond 1952: 3–4).

Not to be outdone, Powell's Puppets at Punch's Theatre published a playbill for 1 May at seven, picturing "the Four Kings A–D" and naming them. The competition heightened when the Theatre Royal in Drury Lane announced two plays for the kings and additional attractions—cockfights, a "Battle Royal," and the presence of "Ladies of Quality." And so it went. Accustomed as the American visitors were to traditions and even episodes of ritual torture, I imagine that fighting cocks, pit bulls, and swordplay might have appealed to them.

But there was business to be done. On 25 April they called on the Duke of Ormonde and appeared before the Board of Trade and Plantations (the Lords of Trade), who promised assistance. Next day they reviewed four troops of the Life Guards in Hyde Park and made a fine speech of thanks to the duke, which was printed and aroused some controversy. Not to be outdone, the New England and New York merchants entertained the sachems on Friday the twenty-eighth; that day they saw a hospital and a workhouse and witnessed the poor of London. One of the sachems allowed a woman to kiss his hand and gave her a half guinea to buy blankets (Bond 1952: 6–7). They must have found the inequalities of eighteenth-century London appalling.

Queen Anne had meanwhile directed the Earl of Sunderland to transmit the sachems' request for missionaries to the archbishop of Canterbury, to the president of the Society for the Propagation of the Gospel, of which Colonel Nicholson himself was a member (Lydekker 1938: 30; Bond 1952: 7), and to the knowledgeable member of the select committee charged with examining the request. The committee's report addressed realities and became the basis for the SPG's resolution to send missionaries to the Mohawks. The committee interviewed Schuyler and the sachems, who "profest great satisfaction and promised to take care of the Ministers . . . and that they would admit no Jesuits or other French priests among them" (Lydekker 1938: 30). Besides sending two missionaries and an interpreter, the society's program called for erecting a chapel and a house for the missionaries and constructing a fort to protect them. It provided stipends of 150 pounds each for the missionaries, and 60 pounds for the interpreter. They would be stationed next to the main Mohawk settlement, where they would promote English for Mohawk children and Iroquoian for colonial youths. They would also undertake to translate Anglican texts into Mohawk for printing and distribution. The society would urge colonial governments to enact laws prohibiting sale of liquor to Indians, which the sachems requested. Finally, the SPG board ordered four copies of the Bible in quarto, together with the Book of Common Prayer, bound handsomely in red Turkish leather, for presentation to the sachems. They signed their written acknowledgement by drawing their clan eponyms—Wolf, Bear, and Turtle.[7]

Of the sachems' further activities, the enduring mementos are their portraits by three artists (Bond 1952: 9ff., 66ff.). On 2 May they sat for Bernard Lens the Younger, who painted miniature portrait busts, which Bernard Lens the Elder engraved as a quartet from which prints were struck on a single sheet (NYPL; Bond 1952: frontispiece, 68). Lens captured facial tattooing on two of the Mohawks, elaborate chest tatoos on one of them, and down tufts at the ears of all four.

Queen Anne meanwhile commissioned Jan Verelst, a Dutch painter resident in London, to do full-length portraits of the four kings in full regalia. These are the most famous portraits of the kings, showing them draped in gold-trimmed red blankets, bearing customary weaponry, bare chested to reveal tattooing, and girdled by decorated tumplines. Three of them are in moccasins; Hendrick wears shoes and is dressed in black, displaying a wampum belt of crosses. All of them are sustained by their clan animals. The backgrounds are woodland scenes, in two canvases showing distant hunters running down deer, and in one, a scalping scene. For years these paintings were lost to view, until they were discovered in the gatehouse of Ingatestone, Essex, and subsequently sold to the government of Canada.[8]

Verelst was persnickety about seeing his work reproduced faithfully, but he allowed John Simon, a Huguenot engraver, to make drafts of the four portraits. Numerous black-and-white prints were struck from the blocks, and they were widely distributed at the time. Until recently, the Simon mezzotints were the prevailing images, but they have since become scarce (Bond 1952: 66–67, 132–33; I have seen copies at the New York Public Library, among other places).

John Faber the Elder did a third set of portraits from life, but they were confined to busts. He also executed and sold his own mezzotints. His portrait of Hendrick, "The Emperor of the Six Nations," illustrates face-painting (Bond 1952: 80, 134; copies in NYSL, Newberry Library). The subject has a pensive look.

The four kings created no less a stir in London literary circles. Verses and ballads were composed in their honor, commenting on their dress and footwear.

---

7. Similar signatures appear on their letter to the Archbishop of Canterbury (Bond 1952: 8).

8. Several years ago, the Verelst portraits were on loan to the Albany Institute of History and Art, when full-color prints 24 inches by 18 inches (image size 18 inches by 13 inches) became available for sale.

One ballad related "How a beautiful Lady conquered one of the Indian Kings" in St. James's Park, her reply to his request, and his lament:

> But I fear she cannot love me,
>   I must hope for no such thing:
> That sweet saint is far above me
>   Altho' I am an Indian King.

The visit did not escape the newsprints of the day. Besides pamphlets, both the *Tatler* and the *Spectator* carried comments by Steele and Addison.

Apart from the stir that the four kings created in the London theater, the competition among painters and limners for their images, and all the versifying, the mission accomplished its purposes. The sachems succeeded in gaining official attention to the importance of America's native people, they strengthened England's military policy toward Canada, and they convinced the SPG to send out missionaries to the Iroquois. The aftermath of these efforts was mixed.

Before departing for their ship, the kings had a final audience with the queen. They thanked her before "shoving off their canoe," paused at Windsor, and sailed from Southampton next day.

Gift giving is always reciprocal among the Iroquois. I shall skip the inventory of some two hundred pounds' worth of English goods that the visitors took away, none of which survives today, to mention the gifts they made in return (Bond 1952: 12–13). To Sir Hans Sloane, inveterate collector and founder of the British Museum's ethnographic collections, they donated a swordlike purification or emetic stick and tumplines, both plain and decorated, which their hosts thought to be prisoner ties. Such survive today in the collections of the Museum of Mankind (Bushnell 1906; Braunholtz 1953; Fenton, personal observation 1991). They apparently also left their moccasins and several wampum belts to attest to their words.

Having boarded HMS *Dragon* the first week in May, the four sachems landed in Boston on Saturday, 10 July 1710. Voyages of ten weeks in the westward crossing were not remarkable then. Nicholson, the Schuylers, and Pigeon accompanied them. An escort of English fighting ships carrying marines and regular troops for the assault on Quebec anchored off shore. By Monday the sachems, eager to get home, announced to Schuyler that they were leaving on Thursday, and Schuyler informed Governor Dudley. They would need nine horses and gear to transport them and ten armed horsemen to guard them as far as Springfield. Before departing, they did not neglect to write Queen Anne, thanking her for English hospitality and for transporting them home, and they reminded her to send the promised missionaries and of their hopes for a chapel and manse. They wrote to the archbishop of Canterbury, too, signing both missives with their clan symbols (Bond 1952: 44). They also requested a fort commanded by officers who could speak their language, a post for which they recommended Abraham Schuyler and for which Peter Schuyler also applied (HEH, HM 348, 22270).

Queen Anne later responded to the appeal of the four kings by commissioning Francis Garthorne, silversmith, to make up communion plate—salver, bason, chalice, paten, and flagon—for each of two royal chapels to the Mohawks and Onondagas. Each set was inscribed with the royal cipher and coat of arms and labeled "The Gift of Her Majesty Anne, by the Grace of God, of Great Britain, France and Ireland and of her Plantations in North America, Queen, to her Indian Chappel of the Mohawks (Onondagoes)." The title to these objects, now treasures, clearly remained in the Church of England. The royal gift included more perishable furniture—altar cloth, "large Cushion with Torsels [tassels] for the Pulpit, 2 Common Prayer Books (one for the Clerk), and 4 Imperial Coats of Arms painted on Canvas, to be placed in the Mohawk Chappel and three Castles." Archbishop Tenison sent "twelve large Octavo Bibles" and "a Table of the Society's Seal [SPG] painted in proper Colours to be fix'd likewise in the Chappel" (Lydekker 1938: 31; Bond 1952: 59). Of these objects, only the communion silver survives today, as we shall see momentarily.

The four kings rode west toward the Hudson, laden with gifts and mindful of the sights, sounds, massive buildings, Yorkshire beef, and lager beer of eighteenth-century England—a life-style that they could not possibly convey to their kindred. No wonder all but Hendrick vanished into the forest. Within two months Brant was dead; no word is known of the others. Only Hendrick, to my knowledge, weathered the transition to native life and lived to negotiate between the two cultures.

□□◇□□

The Glorious Enterprise was not dead yet. Before committing themselves, the Mohawks demanded reassurance that the English meant business and that military support would be forthcoming. Raising a fighting force of several hundred Iroquois warriors, equipping them, feeding them, and holding them together while an army of regulars and provincial militia sat waiting for word to advance up the Champlain corridor toward Montreal would tax English diplomacy. Schuyler knew that idle Iroquois warriors grew restless and were apt to go off on their own. Without English action they might listen to their relatives from Caughnawaga and go over to the French. Something had to be done to hold them intact.

The Mohawk council sent a deputation of three sachems to Boston to see for themselves what British ships and troops were actually in port for the naval assault on Canada. The sachems reached town on 22 July 1710, and next day Nicholson presented them to Admiral Walker, who wowed them with a tour of his immense ship and entertained them with wine, music, and dancing sailors. Not to be outdone, the sachems replied with the rite of Adon:wa (Adon:wen?), each man singing his Personal Chant while pacing to and fro on the deck, leading the admiral by the arm, the others sitting and keeping the cadence and giving the appropriate cries "at distinct Periods of his Dance; . . . their Way of Dancing . . . was in a very different Manner to anything ever seen in Europe" (Bond 1952: 51; see also Colden 1937: 379–80; Sewall 1973: 623–24). Clearly, the two cultures were an ocean apart.

On the sudden death in 1709 of Lord Lovelace, governor of New York, Queen Anne had sent over Robert Hunter, a veteran of the battle of Blenheim in the War of the Spanish Succession, who went up to Albany the following summer, met with the returned kings—who pleaded for restrictions on the rum trade—and then renewed the covenant with sachems representing the Five Nations. The interpreter, Lawrence Claessen, recently returned from a tour of the Five Nations, reported to Hunter that French agents at Onondaga were agitating to prevent

Iroquois warriors from joining the English invasion of Canada. The sachems complained that their men, while waiting for action, had not gone hunting, that they had no beavers to trade, and that their families were hungry. Hunter observed that with French instigation, Iroquois war parties were yet raiding the Catawbas, and their young men were killing the cattle of settlers beyond Schenectady. Hunter told the sachems that the queen had heeded the petition of the kings for missionaries: were they prepared to accept the building of chapels and to saction the garrisoning of forts in their castles? The four kings, having no doubt informed the other leaders of their visit to England, confirmed the might of the queen's armaments and denied the vain boasts of the French. Hunter presented medals bearing the queen's image—twenty to each nation—for the chief warriors to wear about their necks. He made a similar appeal to the Schaghticokes, who were important to Albany.

On 19 August, Kaquendero (Aqueendera) replied for the Five Nations sachems. They were pleased by the queen's choice of governor and reassured that he had arrived safely. They condoled the death of Lovelace. They acknowledged that some of their brethren had visited England and were returned safe—"and altho' they were native Mohogs . . . we are as well satisfied as if there had been one from each of the Five Nations being all united." They had seen the queen and were well treated, "for which we are very thankfull" (NYCD, 5: 217–25).

Just then sentiment at Onondaga favored accepting missionaries, erecting a chapel, and garrisoning a fort in each of the Iroquois castles. This view held so long as French-inspired Ottawa war parties threatened the security of Iroquois towns. But as an accommodation was reached with the Ottawa allies, this sentiment would change. So would the position of the Senecas shift between French and English.

From the viewpoint of the Iroquois, both the first and second Canada expeditions aborted. For the 1709 campaign, they had pledged 443 men, mostly Mohawks and Cayugas, including 60 River Indians, but no Senecas; Teganissorens counted them with sticks. Two years later, after Peter Schuyler made a tour of the Five Nations and the interpreter Claessen attended a grand council, they sent to Albany 682 warriors, including 182 Senecas and 26 Shawnee tributaries of the Senecas, who marched with 132 local Indians north to Wood Creek (Fort Anne). When the army learned that the English fleet had foundered in the St. Lawrence, it returned home. The Indians must have taken a dim view of English military prowess (Wraxall 1915: 69, 91, 92).

Hunter waited until Nicholson was free of the campaign to seek his advice on the design and construction of the fort and chapel at the mouth of Schoharie creek. He let the contract to five Dutch carpenters of Schenectady on 11 October 1711 (NYCD, 5: 279–81; Lydekker 1938: 32–33). He intended to go ahead with similar construction at Onondaga as soon as the Mohawk facility was finished. But there was no road to Onondaga, no contractor would undertake the job, and by then Onondaga sentiment had shifted as danger from western enemies abated: the Ottawas carried their calumets to Onondaga and sang the ritual of peace. The Five Nations were now about to be six. The Tuscaroras had come north as refugees from a bitter defeat by white Carolinians, and they were filled with rage against whites. A fort at Onondaga was out of the question.

The situation having changed, Governor Hunter sought sanction from the SPG for placing the "Onondaga" plate, books, and altar furnishings at the service of Her Majesty's chapel in the Albany fort for the use of the garrison. Apparently the bishop of London approved. The communion plate passed to St. Peter's Church at Albany a few years later when that church received a royal charter, and it has remained there to this day, where it is displayed in the foyer and used on the altar at Christmas and Easter (NYCD, 5: 315, 317; Demille 1946: 4, 5, 8, 10–17). The original church of St. Peter (1715–1803), above the junction of modern State and Pearl streets, sheltered public meetings and Indian treaty councils throughout the century (Lydekker 1938: plate 6). The "Mohawk" silver, which graced Her Majesty's chapel to the Mohawks at Fort Hunter, remained intact until the onset of the American Revolution, when it was buried for safety and then dug up and carried off to Canada by Loyalist Mohawks. They then divided it between the band at Tiyendanega Reserve and Her Majesty's chapel to the Mohawks erected by Joseph Brant at Brantford in 1784 (Lydekker 1938: plate 4).[9]

Hendrick attended a conference at Albany between Hunter, Nicholson, the commissioners, and the sachems of the Five Nations, led by Teganissorens, when the contract respecting the forts was discussed. Hendrick presented a letter to Canterbury, thanking the queen for the care she had taken to convert them and asking Nicholson to lay their wants before the archbishop, to whom they sent a belt of wampum confirming their request (NYCD, 5: 279; Lydekker 1938: 33). One wonders which of the belts now in the British Museum might be the one.

The Society for the Propagation of the Gospel found the Reverend William Andrews, who had been in America, where he had acquired "some knowledge of the Indian language" (SPG Journal 2: 173, 178). He reached New York on 12 April 1712, after the "Queen's Fort" was completed. The Reverend Thomas Barclay of St. Peter's went up to Schoharie in October, met the sachems, and dedicated the chapel. In mid-November, just before winter set in, Andrews made it to Albany, where Hendrick, his kinsmen, and Albany notables greeted him at the landing. Hendrick conveyed the thanks of the Mohawks to the queen for answering his belt. Five days later, Andrews, who really had no Mohawk, set off for the fort with a Dutch interpreter, the mayor of Albany, a church warden, a Schenectady justice, and the Reverend Mr. Barclay, who recommended his clerk to interpret from Dutch to English.

Andrews, having endured a hard winter at the fort, at "iceout" in March 1713 related his first impressions of Mohawk culture in a long letter to the society. A misunderstanding arose over the tithe, which ran counter to Mohawk expectations. Hendrick, who had been in England, possessed them of the idea that the minister, by taking a tenth of their possessions, would become a burden to them. The rest of the sachems, on being reassured, proceeded to depose Hendrick. Barclay held the Dutch traders responsible for spreading the notion because they feared interference in the trade (Lydekker 1938: 35–37; NYCD, 5: 358).

9. In 1956, all of the silver except that at Tiyendanega was brought together once more for an exhibition featuring the artifacts and literary memorabilia of the four kings at the New York State Museum and New York State Library, Albany. The Brantford silver joined that of St. Peter's when councilors of the Six Nations Reserve and the chaplain of the Mohawk chapel brought their silver to Albany and attended the opening by Governor Harriman.

Andrews found the slightly acculturated Mohawks least reliable, they having picked up the worst traits of the Dutch and being "much given to lying, cheating, profanity, and drinking." Those who knew a little English were the worst, and to his credit, Andrews resolved to learn Mohawk and teach in the native language.

Andrews included a vignette of Mohawk culture. The adjacent settlement contained an estimated 260 adults resident in some forty or fifty bark houses within a palisade. Some twenty miles west stood another chief town of twenty to thirty houses, and there were scattered clusters of seven to eight houses in between. The sachems later advised Andrews that the town by the fort, called Teyawenda-rokough, held 360 inhabitants, that the second town twenty miles beyond was Canojoharie, and that a third town, Anandagie, four miles further held 180 persons. In a fourth settlement twenty-four miles (southwest) of the fort, called Eskahare (Schoharie), there were 40 persons, making an estimated total of 580 Mohawks.

The natives wore blankets or bearskin mantles, slept on mats or skins, painted and greased themselves with bear's fat, and cut their hair from one side of the head. Some wore a scalp lock with feathers, favored tufts of fur at the ears, and fancied nose pendants and strings of wampum or beads at the neck and hocks. Andrews noted the sex division of labor with the usual aspersion that the men were lazy and the women overworked, packing in venison and firewood and tending the fields of maize while carrying infants at their backs. They waited on their husbands, ate after them—and for all that, the Mohawks said, "Women court the men when they design Marriage." He found the Mohawk language virtually unattainable, having been assured by Lawrence Claessen, the interpreter, that it had taken him five years of intensive immersion as a child to learn the language. Despite apparent brittle monogamy, most couples remained faithful till death. In general, the Mohawks were "a civil peaceable quiet people." Andrews continued his mission until 1719, when he resigned and went to reside in Virginia (Lydekker 1938: 51).

□□◇□□

For thirty years the Anglican mission made little progress. It faced an unstable political situation because the upper nations of the confederacy wavered in fidelity to the British. Its great fault lay in its institutionalized nature, linked as it was to the established church and the crown. It would enjoy two bright moments at mid-century when Henry Barclay (1712–64) and John Ogilvie (1724–74), both educated at Yale, started schools and translated scriptures into Mohawk. They found young Indians who wanted to learn English and to write in their own language. The mission found staunch supporters in William Johnson, rising trader and later superintendent of Indian affairs for the Northern Department, and in Hendrick, veteran of the London journey. Johnson's protege, Joseph Brant, or Thayenda-negea (1743–1807), having attended Wheelock's boarding school, assisted in translating Gospels into Mohawk and soon moved easily in both cultures (Kelsay 1984). For the traditionalists, one David of Schoharie wrote out the ritual texts of the Condolence Council (Hale 1883).

None of this speaks to politics. The grand council continued to meet at Onondaga, but we learn little about its composition. The sachems, of indeterminate number during the first half of the eighteenth century, kept coming to

Albany to meet with the commissioners and, on stated occasions, with the governor of New York. But aside from Hendrick's being put out of his honor, we occasionally learn only that one chief succeeds in the title of another, and the rules for succession are never stated. The ability of the Iroquois to improvise in order to maintain an ideal pattern continues to amaze us. Three Mohawks and a River Indian could assume prestigious names and perform the roles of sachems of the Five Nations, gain the status of foreign kings in London, make representations on behalf of the confederacy, and still find confirmation of their roles by their own people, although the Reverend Barclay held they were persons of no stature.

The coming of the Tuscaroras and their acceptance as the sixth nation enhanced the diminished numbers of the original Five Nations. But they arrived full of rage, which made the path from the Mohawk Valley to Onondaga dangerous, and a conspiracy to recruit others of the Five Nations threatened the Carolina colonists. It would require considerable skill on the part of the original Five Nations and the commissioners, along with the interpreter's intervention, to calm the Tuscaroras, avert a campaign, and clear the path between Albany and Onondaga. We shall see presently how this was accomplished.

CHAPTER 25

TUSCARORA,
THE SIXTH NATION

While yet in London in 1710, the visiting "four kings" on occasion referred to themselves as representing Six Nations. By then but a few Tuscaroras had come north from the Carolinas to seek refuge among the Oneidas (map 3), and years passed before officials recognized the confederacy as the Six Nations in 1723. Even before that, a sentiment of kinship prevailed between the northern Iroquois and their southern linguistic congeners—that they were once one people who had separated (Wraxall 1915: 101). The Tuscarora War (1711–13), which ended in the Tuscaroras' final defeat, precipitated a northward migration that had already begun when local encroachment by white settlers, which went on without plan or sanction, made life intolerable (Landy 1978: 518). The flight northward continued for some ninety years.

The Tuscarora War resonated in the north. Governor Robert Hunter, as a former governor of Virginia, knew how southern settlers regarded Indians, he worried about Iroquois raids down the Appalachian chain against the Catawbas, which disrupted settlers and their livestock, and yet he appreciated that the New York colony depended on the trade and goodwill of the Iroquois. When he learned that the Tuscaroras had sent belts of wampum to Onondaga requesting the confederacy to intervene in a war with the English, he wrote to the Lords of Trade: "The war betwixt the people of North Carolina and the tuscarora Indians is like to embroil us all" (NYCD, 5: 343, 347, 371). He blamed the Five Nations' sympathy toward the Tuscaroras upon the French, whose agents visited Onondaga frequently, and he promptly sent agents of his own "to dissuade them from this fatal design." This would take some doing and require presents.

The grand council of the confederacy met without adjournment in 1711–12, during the Tuscarora crisis. When French agents appeared, the sachems sent messengers to Albany with seven hands of wampum, the sign of urgency, desiring Peter Schuyler's presence at Onondaga (Wraxall 1915: 81, 93; Colden 1937: 399; Livingston 1956: 219). Wraxall (1915: 93n) commented: "Seven Strings [hands] of Wampum is a Solemn Sanction among the Indians to any News or Message that they bring" (see also Colden 1937: 410–11). The Five Nations were not to be dissuaded from sheltering the Tuscaroras, but they hedged their bets and stood neutral, maintaining their alliance with Albany, where trade and peace were synonymous. They even offered to mediate between the Tuscaroras and the

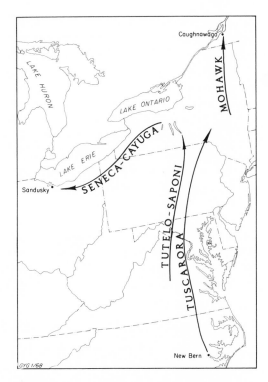

Map 3. Iroquois migration, 1700–1784.
Map by Gwynneth Y. Gillette.

English and thought it strange that the English took no notice of their proposal (Wraxall 1915: 4–5, 96; Colden 1937: 409).

The coming of some five hundred Tuscarora families to Iroquoia over the years considerably swelled Iroquois manpower, which in 1712 totaled an estimated eighteen hundred men (Lydekker 1938: 49; Livingston 1956: 220). The refugees numbered six hundred fighting men and four hundred old men and boys, according to Colden (1937: 414). The accession of a whole nation enhanced the Iroquois's sense of well-being, as governor of Montreal Ramezay wrote to the Minister of Marine: the Iroquois "have never appeared so haughty as they are at present; for they have been strengthened by the accession of a nation . . . who were settled near Carolina and took refuge among them, so that they now number 3,000 men capable of bearing arms" (Wisconsin Historical Collections 16 [1902]: 315, 321; Boyce 1987: 155).

The Peace of Utrecht on 31 March 1713 made the Five Nations subject to England, but the old men at Onondaga were in no way subservient. Governor Hunter proclaimed the peace in New York but admitted to Secretary Popple that the Five Nations were not to be persuaded from sheltering the Tuscarora refugees, nor was he able to furnish out of his own pocket the presents they expected on such occasions (NYCD, 5: 371). In September, he sent two commissioners and the interpreter up to Onondaga to confer with the sachems. Teganissorens, chief sachem of Onondaga, met the delegation at Schenectady, the eastern end of the Longhouse, having intercepted the messenger bearing seven hands of wampum sent to each nation to notify them of the visit. The message had been stopped at

Canajoharie for want of funds to forward it, but Teganissorens had sent it on by one of his own men and was confident it would be delivered. Had he met the commissioners in the Mohawk country, he would have turned back, but he asked the commissioners to wait while he went on into Albany, slept overnight, and returned next day as promised. Just then the Onondagas were apprehensive at what might emanate from Albany.

The embassy proceeded up the Mohawk Valley toward Oneida, picking up delegates on the way. Teganissorens and the Mohawk delegates grew anxious about the exact nature of the mission and asked for some hint before reaching Onondaga. In return, Teganissorens imparted bad news: namely, the Indians had heard that the English were resolved to cut off the Five Nations, and they took the rumor seriously. It had been confirmed from two quarters, with wampum belts. (This was a persistent rumor, sometimes involving a conspiracy between the French and the English.) Commissioner Hansen resolved to go on and manifested no fear on approaching Onondaga, which reassured his escort. At Oneida they were treated in a friendly manner. Two Oneida delegates joined them.

The journal of Governor Hunter's deputies describes the manner of receiving public delegates at the woods' edge:

> 19 September. Toward evening we reached Onondaga. . . . [W]hen within an English mile of the Castle we were met by about one hundred and fifty Indians old and young, who afterwards surrounded us and set up a wild shrieking and uproar; after having been ordered by our people to remain still, they desisted from further noise, and the Sachems there present made us a very friendly address. . . .
>
> "Brother Corlaer, we are rejoiced to see you here in health; that you have not met with any accident on the road, nor broken any legs or arms, nor encountered any robbers by the way, nor been drowned in any kill or river, and escaped all other troubles and misfortunes that by accident might overtake you." We very heartily thanked them, and they, and the entire assemblage which had come out to meet us, then brought us to the Castle, to a house that they had expressly cleaned for us, which we found a very comfortable lodging, where we were entirely free of any drunken Indians.

This was the familiar protocol for greeting visitors beyond the settlement, welcoming them, and escorting them to a place prepared in advance of their coming.

The sachems having met on 20 September, by order of the Five Nations the speaker addressed the visitors "with three strings of Wampum in their loftiest style," welcoming them to Onondaga, hoping to hear them speak with pure heart the governor's message, and saying that should the message contain any objection that exceeded their comprehension, they would endeavor to refute it.

The commissioners replied with three strings of wampum, thanking the Iroquois for the reception, stating that the Indians must consider what they said as the words of His Excellency, to whom the commissioners would report, and assuring them that the commissioners would not exceed their orders (NYCD, 5: 373–74).

The hosts returned thanks and withdrew. (Both parties had fulfilled the required protocol of the Three Bare Words, which are not spelled out in the document.)

At two o'clock that afternoon, the sachems being assembled, they sent messengers to inform the visitors that they were ready to hear the governor's message. "We then demanded if the entire body of the Five Nations were assembled; they said, Yes." The visitors then resolved to accompany the messengers to the council house, where the Five Nations were met.

The visitors, as petitioners, spoke first, under six heads. (1) The governor was concerned to keep the covenant chain unbroken and inviolable, for which the commissioners' speaker laid down five belts of wampum, one for each of the Five Nations. (2) Queen Anne had proclaimed the Peace of Utrecht, of which the governor had dispatched word to Canada. The speaker laid down another belt. (3) The governor excused himself for not meeting the Five Nations at this harvest because news of the peace had arrived too late; it was their hunting season, and he faced two meetings of the New York assembly, but he planned at the next meeting to take the hatchet from their hands, for which the speaker laid down three strings. (4) A belt warned them not to render assistance to enemies of the crown. (5) Intelligence held that the governor of Canada was at war with his own Indians, and when he sought help from the Five Nations, they should not accept the hatchet. Another belt. (6) The Five Nations were not to hinder the passage of strange Indians bound to trade with the English. Three strings of wampum validated this request.

The following day, 21 September, Teganissorens replied for the Five Nations. "Brother Corlaer," he said, meaning Governor Hunter, "it affords us great pleasure and satisfaction to hear you say that you have come here to renew the ancient Covenant chain, and we right cordially thank our brother Corlaer . . . but we hope it is not the expression merely of the lips, but that it is the intention of the heart, and we promise on our parts that it shall be preserved inviolable." He "laid down 2 beavers, 2 Wampum belts and three strings of Wampum"—a sign of the chain's importance to them.

Under five additional heads, Teganissorens assured the Albany delegates that the Five Nations were glad of the news of peace and hoped it would last (three strings of wampum pledged their allegiance); with three further strings, they accepted the governor's excuses; they promised not to aid Her Majesty's enemies (a belt was laid down); they would not accept French belts to fight for the French (this rated only an elk hide); and they would not hinder free passage of strange Indians but let them pass freely to trade with the English (this merited three more strings of wampum). This ended the first meeting.

Having answered the governor's propositions, the speaker invited the commissioners to stay and hear four Indians from Maryland state the object of their mission. "We shall immediately order them to speak, which they did."

This tidewater delegation addressed its hosts as brothers. The speaker for the delegates reported that they had come to fulfill a request of two years' standing, namely, that whenever the Five Nations needed them, they should always be ready at their service. Further, the path between them and the Five Nations would remain clear for the passage of both parties. They condoled the deaths of those deceased and professed to be under the command of the Five Nations: they "dwelt on their land, . . . were their subjects, and . . . wherever they . . . tell them to go and reside, there would they make their dwelling" (NYCD, 5: 375). These petitioners presented a written statement supported by twenty large belts "and twice 3 strings of Wampum." They inhabited the "Siaerdsies" (Chesapeake Bay) in far-off Maryland; were they perhaps Conoys or Nanticokes?

On the following day, 22 September, when the commissioners were about to return to Albany, the sachems showed them a belt that had been sent to them from "the South of Carolina" which they said brought news that their brother Corlaer designed to destroy all Indians, which they found hard to believe. The senders had laid down a skin to confirm this.

The Dutch Reformed commissioners ascribed this news to the devil's trying to intercede between brothers through one who dared not show his face to them; such stories should be buried deep underground, where no one would think further about them. The commissioners laid down a belt, which gave the sachems great satisfaction.

Then Teganissorens, "in a full meeting not only of the Sachems but of all the Inhabitants of Onondaga," spoke of the Tuscarora War on the Neuse River in Carolina, attributing the information to Corlaer (he may have picked it up in Albany). "These Indians went out heretofore from us, and have settled themselves there; now they have gotten themselves into a war, and are dispersed and have abandoned their Castles. . . . The English have got the upper hand of them . . . and they are scattered hither and thither." The sachems asked the governor of New York to intervene and act as a mediator between the English of Carolina and the Tuscaroras, "that they may no longer be hunted down." The sachems would oblige the Tuscaroras not to do the English further harm, "for they are no longer a Nation with a name, being once dispersed" (NYCD, 5: 372-76).

□□◇□□

In May 1714, Commissioner Hansen came down from the Mohawk country to report, having heard privately from a trusted Indian that there was soon to be a general meeting at Onondaga, not only of the Five Nations but including all the Indians living at the back of New Jersey, Pennsylvania, Maryland, Virginia, and Carolina. There was a death penalty out for anyone informing the English. The Mohawks expected daily a summons to attend the meeting. The commissioners, fearing "that this lies on no good bottom" and that it implied a threat to crown subjects, resolved to enlist "a good and trusty Indian to go to Onondaga," pay heed to the motions and resolutions, "dive into their design," and report as soon as the meeting broke up.

The commissioners secured the services of Hendrick, "a Christian Sachem of the Mohawk Nation," who went up to Onondaga and reported on 22 June. The meeting had resolved that some of the sachems should carry ten belts of wampum to the governor of Canada, Vaudreuil, telling him that since he had made repeated attempts to destroy them and had failed, he should in the future let them live in peace. Whenever he had something to say to them, he should either come himself or send messengers, and they would do likewise. They would refuse to take up the hatchet for the English against the French, but would remain neutral. They would not tolerate his Indians attacking Her Majesty's subjects. Former agreements held Indians on both sides to neutrality. The Indians promised to divert the trade for cheap powder. They proposed a firm and lasting treaty of peace and friendship, to be published broadly. They requested openness and sincerity in negotiations, and once the French were persuaded of their friendship, free passage between their two countries (Wraxall 1915: 96-97). The deputed sachems carried two discretionary belts that empowered them to ask the French governor anything else they thought appropriate to the interests of the Five Nations.

Knowing the inclinations of the Senecas and Onondagas, the commissioners wrote Governor Hunter that they feared French interests might prevail. French emissaries and Jesuits were continually active among them (Wraxall 1915: 98).

Within a month, sachems of the Five Nations were in Albany to report on and inquire about a belt sent to them from Maryland Indians informing them that the English of that colony aimed to cut the Maryland Indians off from the Five Nations and to express their desire that the path between them be kept open. Was there any truth to this intelligence? Private individuals had informed the sachems that the New York government had a similar design. What about this one?

Along the length of the Appalachian range from Carolina to New York, from the Tuscaroras to the Iroquois, rumors traveled the Indian paths reporting white aggression along an expanding frontier. Indian refugees fled campaigns bent on destroying them, and the Longhouse of the Iroquois afforded possible shelter. What worried the old men at Onondaga and the Albany commissioners of Indian affairs was whether official policy, the lack of it, or benign neglect on the part of the English supported these rumors.

The Albany commissioners did their utmost to dispel these rumors. They wrote to Governor Hunter, who agreed to meet with the Five Nations in September 1714; but ultimately the governors of the several colonies would convene to reach an accommodation with the Five Nations. Meanwhile, the commissioners got the visiting sachems to agree to send a belt to stop the delegation bound for Canada until after their meeting with Governor Hunter.

Sachems of all the Five Nations came to Albany on 20 September in response to Governor Hunter's invitation to renew the covenant. The sachems intended to receive a large present; they would refute rumors, request a smith for the Seneca country, discuss missionaries, forts, and chapels, and announce the adoption of Tuscarora refugees as their children. The governor immediately issued a proclamation forbidding the selling of rum to any of the Indians during his five-day stay in Albany (Wraxall 1915: 99; NYCD, 5: 382–89).

As respondents to a summons, the Indians spoke first. Teganissorens, the eminent Onondaga, opened: he invoked the Creator for the day and said that none of the sachems of the Five Nations was missing, that they had come in response to the governor's command, that they were glad to see him in good health, and that they welcomed him with eight beavers, one fisher, and a raccoon.

Second, they were there to renew the covenant chain with a belt that the governor had sent up to Onondaga by Hansen, but they were concerned about rumors that clouded the alliance. There was a rumor of a conspiracy of colonies, supported by two belts, a short and a long one, to extirpate the Five Nations, which disturbed them. Were powder cheaper, they would not worry.

Third, notwithstanding these reports, they had come at the risk of their lives. And fourth, they acknowledged that forty Senecas and one hundred Onondagas had gone out fighting, but they had recalled them.

Hunter answered that the rumors were groundless. He came up with considerable powder and lead, and he promised a future price drop. (His generosity no doubt reflected the French threat.) He was glad the Iroquois had stopped the war parties directed at Her Majesty's subjects, and he intended to take the hatchet away from them permanently. The speaker, Teganissorens, replied that the Five Nations were pleased, and they intended to inform all of their people of their reception and treatment.

Three days later, on 23 September, their host, Governor Hunter, spoke first. (During the recess, small groups met in the bushes.) Hunter asked, Who brought the two belts? Where were they now? He had come in Her Majesty's name, he said, to renew the covenant, a mutual obligation. She had brought peace to the world, particularly peace with France, the previous year. He proceeded to take the hatchet out of Iroquois hands, and he enjoined them to control their young men, lest they, in their southern raids, involve everyone in war.

Second, the governor reserved the trade to British subjects. No French should be permitted to settle in Iroquoia, he said. (He was anticipating the building of trading posts at Irondequoit and Niagara by the French.) The Iroquois were to give free passage to the Far Indians to trade at Albany. He had ordered a handsome present; it included 100 bags of powder, 45 gallons of rum, 37 red coats, 2,000 flints, 20 guns, and more. In private, to the sachems went 14 blankets, 18 bags of powder, a dozen shirts, and 2 gallons of rum (NYCD, 5: 385). The distribution came at the end.

Third, Hunter referred to the mission of the four kings to England and the response of the Society for the Propagation of the Gospel. He urged the Five Nations to give an ear to the missionary William Andrews, a good and pious man. The fort and chapel were being built and maintained, he said, at considerable expense to the crown.

Fourth, white frontier inhabitants had complained of Iroquois war parties killing their cattle, destroying gardens, and stripping fruit trees in their marches. Such parties should be provisioned by their own people, the governor said. "Let no further suspicion rust the covenant chain."

The sachems deliberated on the governor's propositions for two days and answered on the twenty-fifth under eight heads. First, they were now convinced the rumors were false. Second, they renewed and strengthened the covenant chain with a belt. Third, they repeated and spoke to the governor's several proposals, with particular reference to campaigns against the Flatheads, or Catawbas, to Hunter's efforts to disarm those people, and to the uncertainty over when the campaigns would end. There had been no reply to their offer to mediate the dispute in the Carolinas.

Fourth, with reference to the "kings" who had gone to London, and to missionaries, forts, and chapels, the speaker, having no wampum left, gave a stick promising to send a belt when they returned to their country, where they would repeat the propositions. "We have no belts now to lay down, according to our custom, but must make use of a stick but shall send down belts for them" (NYCD, 5: 386). Fifth, the English should not worry about the French who had come to lodge for a night or two in the Seneca country (a night being a metaphor for a year in Iroquois symbolism). Sixth, as to complaints of war parties killing cattle and destroying orchards, the sachems would try to forewarn the young men, if they would but listen. They would grant free passage to the Far Nations to trade. As for not supporting the missionaries of SPG, they could not attend church dressed in "an old Bear skin" or a deerskin, nor could they afford the clothes until goods were cheaper. Seventh, they desired to send some people to Maryland with belts in reply to the ten they had received. That would confirm the peace. They had spared a belt to confirm that desire.

Finally, the speaker announced, "The Tuscarore Indians are come to shelter themselves among the five nations. They were of us and went from us long ago and are now returned and promise to live peaceably among us, and since there is peace now every where we have received them." They had spared a belt for this last item. "We desire you to look upon the Tuscaroras that are come to live among us as our Children who shall obey your Commands & live Peaceably and orderly." Some beaver and other skins confirmed this news (Wraxall 1915: 101).[1]

The governor failed to acknowledge this statement, and Livingston omitted it from his final minutes that were forwarded to the crown (Jennings et al. 1985a: 170).

This treaty conference fulfilled a previous lapse in ceremony where a simple message with a belt had been thought to suffice. It further served notice that the Five Nations hereafter would be six, strengthening the confederacy with augmented numbers.

That same day, "Blew Bek," chief sachem of the Senecas, appealed for a smith to be stationed midway between the Seneca and Cayuga territories to reside in the village of an old sachem named Oraqui, who would protect him. (Neither name appears on the Seneca roster of league chiefs.) The governor demurred. There was already a smith in the Mohawk Valley to whom tools and weapons could be brought for repair until such time as a second smith could be found (NYCD, 5: 387).

"Blewbeck," as the English knew him—properly Kayen?kwarahte (Old Smoke), a war chief attached to the English interest—questioned the Albany practice of daily trading for French goods via the Champlain corridor while official policy prohibited the Five Nations from trading with Canada (Colden 1937: 430). His pro-English activities so aroused the French that in 1719 the agent Joncaire, who was continually among the Senecas and spoke the language, got him deposed and removed from the Seneca council (Colden 1937: 432). Joncaire further prevailed in getting the Senecas to raise up in his place someone of Joncaire's nomination. The Albany commissioners responded by sending one Myndert Schuyler and Robert Livingston the next year to the Seneca country to get Old Smoke restored and his replacement degraded (Wraxall 1915: 127; NYCD, 5: 542–45).

□□◇□□

French activity in building and garrisoning posts at Irondequoit, Niagara, and Detroit, which would divert the trade, genuinely concerned the commissioners. The English felt that they had a deed to these places. They sought to prevent the French from instigating Iroquois warriors to go out against the Catawbas, and they wanted no hostilities with the Far Indians, but free passage to Albany. The French traders claimed permission of the Seneca warriors, but neither the Seneca council nor the English interpreter succeeded in removing the intruders (NYCD, 5: 550).

---

1. Elsewhere it is said the Tuscaroras were received into the league as the sixth nation "on the cradle board" (Jennings et al. 1985a: 117).

Second only to hostility toward the French, rivalry among the English colonies embittered colonial life. Residents of Carolina, as well as Massachusetts, complained that "Yorkers"—the people of upstate New York—could do more to prevent Iroquois war parties from ravaging border settlements, raiding down the Appalachians, harassing tribes friendly to Carolina interests, and indiscriminately destroying what came in their path. Having taken Tuscarora refugees under their wing, warriors of the confederacy did not hesitate to lift the scalps of southeastern Indians who had assisted the Carolinians in dispersing the Tuscaroras. Iroquois messengers had gone south "with their lives in their hands" to urge the Choctaws to keep the peace. They remained fairly solid in the English interest. Governor Hunter worried: "If the war does not end soon, the confederates will go south in greater force" (Winsor 1895: 133). So far, no effectual method had been devised for uniting the divided strength of the colonies for defense of the whole (Hunter to the Lords of Trade, NYCD, 5: 417).

Whatever the disposition of colonial governors, the Five Nations held firm to their resolution to treat with the English nowhere but at Albany. They made policy at Onondaga; they made treaties at Albany. The reason they could make this arrangement stick, according to Colden (1937: 428), was that "these Indians are of much more Consequence & much more haughty as well as politick than any oother Nation." They could not be treated as the English southerners treated their native neighbors. Consequently, the neighboring colonies "ought to consent" to come to Albany "where the treaties can be carried on with the greatest safety and with the best advice."

An internal schism, not unlike a structural fault, rent the body politic of the Iroquois Confederacy during the first quarter of the eighteenth century. The sachems, who came regularly to Albany to renew the covenant chain, admitted that they could not control the warriors. French agents easily appealed to the warlike genius of the young men, for whom the warpath was the route to glory and the way to achieve status. The southeastern wars that continued through much of the century extended the mourning wars of the previous century as a means of replacing dead relatives (Colden 1937: 428; Richter 1983).

Just how the immigrant Tuscaroras contributed to this situation between 1713 and 1722 is known from missionary reports to the SPG. In 1716, Claessen, the interpreter, warned Andrews not to venture to Onondaga because the path traversed the country of the Tuscaroras, people who had every reason to hate whites. They took a dim view of Christianity, and they were blamed for stirring up their Oneida hosts and the Mohawks to oppose Andrews's mission. In passing the fort containing Queen Anne's chapel to the Mohawks en route to trade in Albany, they mocked "Mr. Andrews when he would offer to talk to them about Religion; and when he proffered to go to their Abode, they absolutely forbad him" (Humphreys 1730: 305-6, quoted in Boyce 1987: 156, 200).

Just then the Anglican missions ranked below the western trade in the minds of Albany merchants who sat as Indian commissioners. When Governor Vaudreuil got wind of the English plan to erect a post at Niagara that would cut off the trade from the upper Great Lakes, his man Joncaire got there first, and the English in 1720 faced a fait accompli (Eccles 1969: 142-43). Governor William Burnet, having succeeded Hunter, might protest vigorously, but to no avail. The Five

Nations were deeply concerned, and to maintain the balance between the two powers, they were prepared to grant permission for the English to fortify a trading post at Oswego in 1724 (Eccles 1969: 142–43). The confederacy faced two intruding sovereignties in Iroquoia.

Sentiment mounted in Massachusetts for some joint action with respect to Indians, even though the Lords of Trade regarded the idea as mutinous (Winsor 1895: 162). Treaty conferences with individual governors outside of New York were ineffective. In July 1721 the governor of Pennsylvania, Sir William Keith, and Secretary James Logan intercepted at Conestoga an embassy of Senecas, Cayugas, and Onondagas headed by the Seneca Ghesanont, on its way to treat with the governor of Virginia concerning peace with the southern Indians. When Keith claimed to have come a long way from home to meet them, Ghesanont replied that they, too, had come a long way to speak to him (DePuy 1917: 7).

Keith, having called the conference, spoke first. He granted safe conduct through Pennsylvania but forbade their traveling the Susquehanna Valley as a warrior's path. He warned them that the governor of Virginia expected them not to hunt east of the great mountains south of the Potomac River, an area reserved to his Indians, and promised that his Indians would not hunt north of the Potomac or west of the mountains. Although unlettered, Ghesanont maintained that the Iroquois kept previous treaties fresh in their memories. He complained that traders treated them like dogs—and so they behaved accordingly. He appealed to the chain metaphor and held that as speaker he embodied plenipotentiary authority of the confederacy. In Iroquois thought, the speaker and his object identically represented the original parties to a contract, the parties should adhere to council protocol, and they expected mutual respect and treatment as equals. Everything in a treaty should be firm and good on both sides. Although this treaty did not satisfy competing claims, it held lessons for future negotiations (DePuy 1917: 7; Andrew Bradford, Philadelphia, 1721, APSL 970.5, no. P26 50074).

In September 1721 Governor Burnet met the sachems of the Five Nations at Albany to renew the covenant chain. The attendance of commissioners and notables reflects the issues at hand. Burnet, as host, spoke first. He lauded the Five Nations' great name, their wisdom, and their freedom as his children. To brighten the old covenant chain he gave a belt (WLCL, Sherburne Papers, vol. 45; NYCD, 5: 635–40). He cautioned against French intrigues, particularly those of the Jesuits, and warned that the French intrusion on Iroquois lands at Niagara posed a threat to the English. He gave a belt to keep the path open for traders and for the Far Indians to come through. Burnet cited a letter received from the governor of Virginia, pursuant to Conestoga, restating restrictions on hunting territories: any Iroquois Indian caught east of the mountains or south of the Potomac would be brought to justice; and runaway slaves should be returned. Burnet asked for reassurance.

Two days later, the speaker for the Five Nations replied. "We have understood . . . you call us Brethren, and so we ought to love one another as well as those that have suckled one Breast, for we are Brethren indeed." They were glad to renew the chain, relieved that Burnet was safe over the great water, and pleased to see him there in health. They promised "to keep the Chain invincible as long as the Sun and Moon endure." The speaker laid down a belt of wampum.

The speaker declared with a second belt that the Iroquois would not trust the French, and with a third that they were resolved to tell the French to pull down the house at Niagara. A fourth belt proposed to keep the path open and encourage the Far Indians to come trade at Albany, "although they are unruly and may kill your cattle."

Belt five confirmed boundary and warpath restrictions in Virginia. And with a sixth belt, the Iroquois owned up to raids by their young people, who killed cattle; they confessed to their want of command over them but said they would try persuasion. With a final belt they promised to comply. But they requested that powder be sold "not so dear." Beaver prices were depressed.

Having learned that Burnet had recently married, as a token of their rejoicing they gave the bride a few beaver pelts for pin money and added that "it is Customary for a Brother upon his Marryage to invite his Brethren to be Merry and Dance . . . which they did according to their custom" (NYCD, 5: 640).

□□◇□□

There was trouble all along the frontier in 1722 that only a conference of principals meeting at Albany could settle. In March, after a murder occurred near Conestoga, the Five Nations sent down a large belt of wampum bearing the figure of a "Ryndlet [cask] and a Hatchet" to the Indians settled on the upper Susquehanna, with orders to stave all the kegs of rum encountered. Tokaachroon (possibly Haga?en:yonk, C-1, RC 33) was the Cayuga deputy (PPCM, 3: 154). The governor of Pennsylvania, on the death of a Seneca hunter, sent a belt to the Senecas to wipe away their tears (PPCM, 3: 154). In May, the Seneca leader Ghesanont, having died, was condoled (PPCM, 3: 167). Governor Keith of Pennsylvania was preparing a speech to deliver at the upcoming treaty at Albany, "that our words . . . pass and be recorded . . . to be sent down to" succeeding generations and "last as long as the Mountains and Rivers and the Sun and Moon shall endure." He was learning Indian metaphors of time (PPCM, 3: 195).

With provisions now scarce in Iroquoia, people of all ages looked forward to the treaty and a good feed at crown expense. A large delegation showed up in segments. Burnet met the chiefs on 27 August to prepare them for the governors of Pennsylvania and Virginia. In the presence of members of Her Majesty's council, which included Colden, and commissioners of Indian affairs, Burnet spoke first. He stressed Iroquois promises not to deal with the French, thanked the Five Nations for not joining French Indians on the warpath south—each with belts—and asked, How clean had they kept the chain?

Four days later (1 September), the Five Nations answered. The leading Oneida sachem, Odatshehdeh, spoke for the confederacy (VHS, Westover ms., 369-80, mss. 1B9966A). Several sachems had not yet arrived, but they would answer later. As to the chain, the sun had scarcely gone down since its last renovation, which was fresh in their memory. It was now a year since they were forbidden intercourse with the French. They had granted the Far Indians free passage, and agents sent to them had not yet returned. They had observed boundaries restricting fighting in Virginia with reference to the Potomac River and the Blue Ridge. But some parties went against the Catawbas, who were old enemies. They stood ready to discuss matters of moment and seek mutual advice. One belt sufficed (NYCD, 5:

657–59). Rather than joining French Indian war parties bound for the Southeast, they would try to stop them.

The coming of the Tuscaroras had brought structural changes to the Iroquois Confederacy. Intelligence at Albany noted warlike preparations among the Five Nations. The speaker explained: "Two years ago (1720) two Tuscarores brought a belt of wampum from the governor of Virginia (as they said) and thereby in (his name) desired the Five Nations to make War and destroy the Tadirighrones (Catawbas), but being informed that the governor of Virginia was to be at Albany we deferred any resolution about that affair, till we had spoke with him ourselves" (NYCD, 5: 660).

Old Smoke, the chief sachem of the Senecas, and other sachems were expected daily. Nearly two weeks passed before the whole conclave met on 13 September. While waiting for all the delegations to arrive, a large gathering of Indian men, women, and children were exhausting provisions in Albany. The town fathers must have complained to the commissioners and they to Governor Burnet, who opened the treaty conference. The three governors of New York, Pennsylvania, and Virginia appeared together in the name of the British colonies. They were, in the Iroquois idiom, of one heart and one mind as they prepared to wipe any stains from the covenant chain with a belt.

Burnet announced that the eastern Indians had declared war and destroyed frontier New England settlements. The governor of Massachusetts had sought to get the Five Nations to interpose and send deputies to the eastern Indians expressing indignation at their actions, demanding they cease fighting, and obliging them to make peace with the Bostonians. The Iroquois ambassadors were expected in Boston to pick up passports, meet an escort, and collect a reward. A second belt was offered (NYCD, 5: 665).

Burnet further announced a severe law to stop the trade to Canada for Indian goods. Cadwallader Colden, in his "Account of the Trade of New-York" (NYCD, 5: 685–90), had sought to discourage the trade to Canada and encourage trade directly with the Far Indians.[2] To that end Burnet had dispatched Abraham Schuyler to Irondequoit in Seneca country to push the trade toward Albany. Several of the Indian commissioners present who were deeply involved in the Canada trade and stood to lose must have resented Colden's attendance.

Burnet asked whoever went to Canada to report. He then complained about the large numbers of young people who tagged along to treaty conferences and then got into mischief in town and country, injuring the inhabitants or being injured by them. He asked the Indians not to bring more than sixty or seventy persons, limited to sachems, warriors, women, and children, so that he could provide ample provisions at future treaty conferences. He failed to appreciate that Indians equated the size of a delegation with the importance of a meeting. A belt signified that in Burnet's estimate, "this has been a great and solemn meeting" never to be forgot, and his hope that the covenant chain would endure as long as the rocks to which it was fastened (NYCD, 5: 666; DePuy 1917: 10).

2. Colden developed this thesis much further in his 1724 "Memorial concerning the Furr Trade" (NYCD, 5: 726–33).

The following day, the Five Nations delivered a second reply by Odatshehdeh. Claessen interpreted into Dutch for Livingston, who wrote the English minutes (NYCD, 5: 667-69). The speaker held the agreements binding the four parties to be inviolable and promised they would imprint them upon their posterity for ever. They would answer the principal heads to propositions agreed upon among the parties renewing the chain.

For the benefit of the visiting governors, Odatshehdeh recited the origin legend of the covenant chain: "When the Christians came to this Country our Ancestors fastened the ship . . . behind a Great Mountain with a Chain in order to secure the same which Mountain lyes behind the Sinnekees Country, so that the one end of the Chain, being fastened there and the other end at ye Ship, if any body would steal away & molest this ship the chain will jingle & make a noise & so alarm all the 5 Nations who are bound to defend this ship & this is the foundation & original of the covenant chain." He laid down a belt of wampum (NYCD, 5: 667).

Odatshehdeh told the governors that the Iroquois Confederacy had selected one from each nation (five men) to go to Boston and command the eastern Indians to make peace. Since they lacked a belt to confirm this item, they would substitute the one given them requesting this service. The confederacy, however, questioned the logic of their not going to Canada when peace and amity supposedly prevailed among all people, especially when they went there to promote understanding. They hoped that it would not be ill taken if some of their people went there. They did not consider the prohibition of the trade with Canada as their business and wished to be excused.

As to the size of treaty delegations, they agreed to limit future embassies to sixty or seventy persons, being fully aware of damages done by their ungovernable young people. A belt confirmed this. Finally, the speaker observed that formerly goods were cheaper at Albany, while powder was now dear. Moreover, the Albany traders abused them. They sought some remedy (NYCD, 5: 669).

During these proceedings, representatives of the Five Nations met separately with the governors of Virginia and Pennsylvania. Each of these worthies made special requests of the sachems, and each had a traditional Iroquois name that the speaker explained. Governor Spotswood of Virginia stressed boundaries restricting Iroquois war parties north of the Potomac and west of the Blue Ridge (NYCD, 5: 670).

Addressing Spotswood as "Brother Assarigoe"—Big Knife—the Oneida speaker for the Five Nations plus the Tuscaroras, who had come to the conference at the New York governor's message, acknowledged that the sachems of the Six Nations had paid great attention to the Virginia governor's message. He further elaborated on the chain metaphor. Accidents or mischief committed by either side should be forgot and forgiven and not allowed to breach the chain. There were two places where parties with hands in the chain might settle differences—Albany and Onondaga. Without going further into traditions, they would proceed to address Spotswood's propositions with proper respect and hope that he would excuse any omissions.

They promised not to pass over the Potomac or east of the Blue Ridge, but wished Spotswood had brought some leaders of the Toderechrones (Tutelos), their inveterate enemies, so that they might put their hands in the chain and make peace. The speaker gave two belts of wampum—one for the Virginia government and one for its tributaries (NYCD, 5: 671).

Thus, according to Wraxall (1915), the sachems and warriors of the Five Nations, together with three Tuscarora chiefs recently settled between Oneida and Onondaga (Wraxall 1915: 143), through their speaker Odatshehdeh, the leading league sachem of Oneida, fully agreed to the English governors' propositions regarding peace and boundaries and signed a treaty document with appropriate symbols. (Wraxall gives the date as 6 September 1722.) John Randolph, secretary to the treaty, carried their signatures back to Virginia (VHS, Westover ms., p. 373, ms. 1B9966a). Among the six Mohawk sachems' names there appears Thonnen-hokarawe, alias Hendrick of the four kings. Also, one Ighuedaats:arya signed by drawing a buck deer. The second of four Onondaga sachem names, Ayeghwaghta, is clearly a Mohawk title (Hiawatha, M-2, RC 2). The fourth signature is "Decanisore" (Teganissorens), "Great Sachim of Onnondague." Of the three Seneca sachem signatures, I recognize only "Sagayengwarachton" (Old Smoke), alias "Blackbick," among other spellings.

Several days later Spotswood specified the ethnic entities dependent on Virginia whom he represented in a peace settlement: Nottoway, Meherin, Nansemond, Pamunkey, Chickahominy, and Christiana Indians (the Iroquois called this last group Todirichroones, but Virginians comprehended them under their individual ethnic names), along with Saponi, Ochineechee, Stenkenock, Meipontsky, and Totero (Tutelo) people—all of whom resided east of the Blue Ridge between the Potomac and Roanoke rivers (Feest 1978: 268–69; Mooney 1894). Remnants of these entities—notably the Tutelos and Saponis—would seek refuge among the Cayugas at mid-century, after which one moiety of the league, comprising Oneidas, Cayugas, Tuscaroras, and Delawares (Saponi and Tutelo descendants having merged with the upper Cayugas at Grand River), came to be called the "Four Brothers."

In a further reply to Spotswood next day, the Five Nations (not yet six in public usage) agreed to observe restrictions on their travel and promised to use his Indians peaceably wherever encountered. The speaker then informed the governor that just as he represented ten nations, so the Iroquois were Five Nations who spoke also for the Tuscaroras, Conestogas, Shawnees, Mohawks settled at Onoh-quageh, and the Ostanghaes settled on the west branch of the Susquehanna in Pennsylvania, all of whom were leagued with the Iroquois.

On 10 September, the Oneida speaker addressed Pennsylvania governor Keith as "Brother Onas"—"quill" or "pen," a pun on the name of the original proprietor, William Penn. He removed rust that had collected on the chain since the last meeting at Conestoga. The Iroquois thought it hard, the speaker said, that one of Keith's people who had killed one of theirs in a drunken brawl should suffer in jail, and they thought he ought to be released. They acknowledged the governor's wiping away and covering the blood of their dead friend and desired that the matter be forgotten and never mentioned again.

□□◇□□

Governor Burnet, after his long stay at Albany with the governors of Virginia and Pennsylvania, felt satisfied with the results. He reminded the Board of Trade and Plantations of an agreement reached in 1701 when the Five Nations deeded lands to the crown, not just to Niagara but also to Detroit (PRO CO5/972, p. 71; cf. NYCD, 4: 904–6). Concern was mounting over French expansion, just as the French were concerned at English efforts to offset their posts at Niagara and Detroit (Vaudreuil to Ramezay, 27 December 1722; see Jennings et al. 1985b: 78).

That autumn, an Oneida messenger in the delegation bound to remonstrate with the eastern Indians died in Boston and was buried in the south cemetery (Sewall 1973: 997). As late as May the next year his death had not yet been condoled, but Claessen reported that the Tuscaroras, who were settled near Oneida, were now accepted as a sixth nation, and from the year 1723 the Six Nations take their date (PAC RG 10, vol. 1819: 16–17; Burnet to the Lords of Trade, 25 June 1723, PRO CO5/1085; NYCD, 5: 684; Wraxall 1915, 144).

Preparations were under way for a full-scale conference between the Six Nations, the commissioners, and the Bostonians. When three Massachusetts commissioners met with the New York commissioners at Albany on 28 May that year, the speaker for the confederacy mentioned all Six Nations, although the Onondagas and Senecas were absent. He said, "We Sachems of the Five Nations and the Tuscaroras—80 in number—are empowered by the Six Nations to treat with you." The Onondaga and Seneca sachems declined to attend this meeting, they said, because they were still mourning the deaths of three sachems the previous autumn, and their deaths were not yet condoled. As if to remove that pretense, the interpreter borrowed three Stroud's blankets and a shirt and proceeded to condole their deaths. When he told the sachems of the two nations that he had done so (some of them being present), they replied that they had concluded not to attend unless the meeting were held the following spring. They gave seven hands of wampum to say a general meeting at Onondaga would discuss such Five Nations affairs (PAC RG 10, vol. 1819: 16–17). The real reason for their not attending was that Joncaire had persuaded them to the contrary.

Just what role the Tuscaroras played as the Sixth Nation in the affairs of the confederacy is open to interpretation. They came into the confederacy under the arm of the Oneidas. They were never part of the league as such, although in later times their chiefs were installed at Condolence Councils by the Three Brothers moiety as if they were indeed holders of league titles. Nor did they vote in league councils, where the Oneida sachems represented them. But the league itself had evolved from local village councils, and in its formation local chiefs were co-opted and their titles were ascribed to clan segments or lineages. By 1722 the league was a tradition, largely symbolic and seldom complete, whereas the confederacy co-opted local leaders once more and became the operating political body. Inasmuch as the Tuscaroras lived apart in two settlements at Oneida Lake and on the upper Susquehanna drainage, they enjoyed the same sort of local autonomy as the original settlements of the Five Nations. Yet the Tuscaroras, not being part of the symbolic league, occupied a subordinate position in the political scale. Their descendants, in my experience, lacked the self-confidence of Seneca leaders whom I knew in the 1930s when I dealt with both councils. In contrast with the traditional council of the Tonawanda Senecas, the Tuscarora chiefs were a high-strung lot. I once mentioned the contrast to a holder of a Seneca league title, who commented: "Years ago we took the Tuscaroras under our wing, but they lived to itch us like the fleas" (Chief Henan Scrogg, personal communication 1936).

Boyce, in a recent study (1987: 157ff.) using a range of sources, comes to a more balanced view. Intense localism operated against concerted action by the confederacy. The Tuscaroras afforded added strength but soon lapsed into the traditional pattern of village autonomy tempered by multiethnic alliances that they had enjoyed in the south and that was mirrored in the scattered villages comprising the Iroquois Longhouse (Fenton 1951a). The two early Tuscarora settlements at Oneida Lake and Oquaga lay off the east-west path that traversed Iroquoia. Messengers bypassed them, they seldom attended general meetings of the confederacy, and on occasion they refused to go to Onondaga. The two communities developed opposing views of Europeans: most people at Oneida Lake were pro-French; the mixed Mohawk-Tuscarora village at Oquaga was pro-English. A third Onondaga-Tuscarora settlement at Ganaseraga, toward Onondaga, became consistently pro-English. Acceptance of a particular sect of Christianity was a matter of local option.

Tuscarora interest in Protestantism developed slowly, except at Oquaga. As might be expected, the three Tuscarora settlements took different courses during the American Revolution. The Oquaga people were Loyalists. Those near Oneida followed Kirkland in the American cause. The Ganaseraga group found neutrality impossible and joined the British (Fenton 1951a: 158; Graymont 1972).

Perhaps ethnologists, when interpreting sources, rely too heavily on structural considerations such as local diversity and the original conditions of Tuscarora adoption. To be certain, people who "came in on the cradleboard" as "children," people no longer with status as a nation, will always bear the marks of inferior status. Seth Newhouse thought as much in drafting bylaws for his so-called Constitution of the Five Nations (Parker 1916b: 50–51). In looking back from my own fieldwork to the historical roots of what I observed, I favored stability over change. Boyce, as a historian, sees the Tuscaroras from a different perspective and makes a case for gradual evolution of Tuscarora political institutions, stressing change. He takes his lead from Hewitt, a native Tuscarora, who held that the Tuscaroras, after their adoption, passed through successive probationary periods until they mastered the ways of the confederacy (Boyce 1987: 159). This view overlooks the fact that during the nineteenth century, when the Seneca nation withdrew from the confederacy and the league titles clustered at Tonawanda and Onondaga while a re-creation of the old league assumed the tasks of governing the Six Nations Reserve on Grand River in Canada, hereditary chiefs still governed the Tuscarora Reservation on the American side at Niagara Falls. By then the confederacy, having less to do than formerly, assumed new functions and began to condole and install Tuscarora chiefs in office, as if they enjoyed league status.

CHAPTER 26

THE COUNCIL BRAND
PASSES TO PENNSYLVANIA

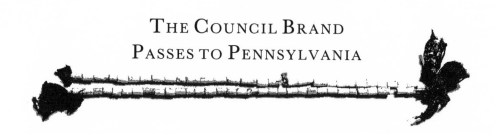

Nothing more revives & enlivens affection than frequent Conferences.—Oneida speaker to the commissioners, 1740

Just as trade and peace had dominated the previous century, land was the big issue of the eighteenth century. As the frontier of white settlement expanded westward and Iroquois war parties followed the warrior path to the southeastern tribes, the two forces inevitably clashed, and the center of gravity of forest diplomacy shifted from New York to Pennsylvania. The sachems of the Six Nations, who habitually said they represented Five Nations, carried the council brand from Onondaga to Philadelphia, kindled a third council fire there in 1732, and cleared the path between the two fires of "every grub, stone, and stump."

Conrad Weiser (1696–1760), who had learned Mohawk as a boy at Schoharie, wore out his shoes in traveling that path as emissary for the Pennsylvania colony's proprietors, to bring the sachems down and interpret their words. In the north, Mohawks complained that grants of land filled their valley with white settlers who fenced them in from all sides. The Mohawks' big grievance was the Kayaderosseros Patent to their hunting grounds, a vast tract north of the Mohawk Valley adjoining the stream of that name in what is now Saratoga County (Nammack 1969: 53–69).[1] They had abandoned interest in the Susquehanna Valley. Pennsylvania farmers encroached on Delaware holdings, and the infamous "Walking Purchase" of 1737 took a great swatch of Delaware lands,[2] which the proprietors got the Six Nations

1. In what became a landmark swindle, Governor Lord Cornbury, who was so corrupt that he was refused communion, in 1704 granted to Sampson Shelton Broughton, attorney general and member of the New York council, license to purchase within the year a tract of land. Having selected the area, Broughton and associates in October agreed to purchase the lands (of indefinite extent) for Indian goods worth sixty pounds in New York currency from Indians named Joseph, Hendrick, and Cornelius, who were designated in the deed as Mohawk sachems and "Owners and Proprietors." Supposedly, the three men represented the three Mohawk clans—Bear, Wolf, and Turtle. But a deed dated October 6, 1704 (NYHS Misc. mss.) carries the marks of four—Joseph, Hendrick, Amos, and Gidion—whom the Mohawks later claimed represented but two of the clans. Sir William Johnson held that this invalidated the deed and rendered the transaction fraudulent. Mohawk opinion stated that they would never sell such a large tract for a mere sixty pounds' worth of trade goods. The grant had a tangled history down to the 1768 Stanwix treaty. By then, land jobbers had subdivided the tract, it was largely settled, and it was too late to accord the aboriginal proprietors even moral satisfaction.

2. In September 1737, Thomas Penn and James Logan organized the swindle known as the Walking Purchase of Delaware lands above Tohickon Creek in Buck's County, Pennsylvania. Delaware sachems reluctantly agreed to relinquish all the land that a man could walk in a day and

to sanction by claiming that they had subjugated the Delawares and "put skirts on them," which made of them women who had no right to sell lands.

For a decade previously, the Six Nations had held sway over the upper Susquehanna Valley, and the Onondaga council appointed an Oneida chief known by his Delaware name, Shikellamy, whom they stationed at Shamokin at the forks of the Susquehanna River (now Sunbury, Pennsylvania) as "regent" to preside over local residents, who were Delawares. Iroquois war parties regularly floated the Susquehanna and then cut overland to the back of Maryland to cross into Virginia east of the Blue Ridge and on to the Catawba country. Settlers complained that Indian raiders killed cattle and ravaged their crops, and when the militia sought to impede them, lives were lost on both sides. In a series of treaties between 1732 and 1744, the governors of Pennsylvania, Maryland, and Virginia sought to restrict Iroquois hunting to north of the Potomac, to move the warrior path west of the Blue Ridge, and to extinguish Iroquois title to lands that they claimed by right of having conquered the resident tribes east of the mountains.

By the first quarter of the eighteenth century, French and English readers could gain some understanding of Iroquois politics. Hard on the heels of La Potherie's *Histoire* (1722) came Lafitau's great comparative work, *Moeurs des sauvages amériquains* (1724), although another 250 years passed before it became available in English (Fenton and Moore 1974; 1977). It afforded the best description of local government in action, although not of the confederacy. People read Colden's *History of the Five Indian Nations* (1727), and its expanded London editions (1747, 1750) reprinted proceedings of several treaties. Colden cited La Potherie and possibly read Lafitau, but he himself knew Iroquois diplomacy at first hand, having participated in Albany treaty negotiations. He described the external features of the Iroquois Confederacy, admired the style of its orators, and even inquired into its origins and antiquity, but he seems unaware of the "Great Law," or the league as a system, its composition, and its operation. He quoted the Indian Records—the proceedings of the Albany commissioners of Indian affairs, which Peter Wraxall abridged—but even these registers of conference proceedings leave us outside the door of the Iroquois Longhouse as a political system.

The external features of the system were more obvious. When someone of importance to their external relations died, the Iroquois promptly condoled his death, and they expected the same from others within the chain of their alliances. They memorialized the death of Queen Anne. The passing of the governor of Montreal, M. de Ramezay, demanded an Iroquois gesture to restore relations. It was their custom, they announced, and that of their ancestors, to weep for the dead and to cover their bodies—acts that "we never fail to do when we lose a friend, a relative," or some considerable person. Such a death affected all the Five Nations. They wiped the tears, wiped the mat, rekindled the fire, restored the sun, and went through the rest of the paradigm (Archives Nationales, Paris, C11A, vol. 47, fol. 442–48).

The custom of condolence as preliminary to establishing or maintaining good relations was not just an Iroquois institution. Neighboring peoples of the woodlands

a half. Provincial agents hired runners who raced along a road cut straight into the Lehigh Valley, leaving Delaware observers far behind. By noon the next day, the relays had covered fifty-five miles (Jennings et al. 1985a: 178; Grumet 1995: 239–40).

and Great Lakes understood and acknowledged the gesture and themselves practiced some form of it. It was so widespread in practice and persistent in the records
that it must have been ancient. When word reached Detroit in 1727 that Peter
Schuyler had died three years earlier, the news prompted the local sachems to send
two Potawatomi sachems to Albany to appear before the Indian commissioners
and verify the fact. Their speaker presented a "Calumet pipe painted blew" and
asserted: "We come to condole his death and cover his grave with a beaver coat
that it may not be exposed to the rain." They filled the pipe, lighted it, and passed
it among the commissioners, who each took a whiff. The minutes noted that this
unique act of peace and friendship was what these Far Indians used in their treaties
with neighboring nations, for indeed the calumet was to the Great Lakes
Algonquians what wampum was to the Iroquois (PAC IR RG 10, 1819: 188–89a;
Fenton 1953a).

Such gestures were fundamental protocol preliminary to peace and trade,
passports, and shared hunting. The trading house at Oswego was up and open for
business, the path clear, and the Albany warehouses stocked with goods at cheap
prices in expectation of great numbers of Indians from the upper lakes coming to
trade. Rum and Stroud's cloth were not the least incentives.

As we shall see presently, the neighboring Delawares shared the Iroquois forms
of condolence, which are manifested in the Pennsylvania treaties throughout the
century.

A second feature of forest diplomacy, the protocol of greeting visitors at the
woods' edge outside the settlement, caught the attention of French and English
participants alike. Not just the Iroquois but also peoples throughout the eastern
woodlands observed the custom. It must have derived from an ancient era
(Archives Nationales, Paris, 19 March 1728, C11A, 50: 405–18).

Third, some hint of the perpetual succession of sachems appears in the Indian
Records. In October 1728, Oneida sachems reported to the commissioners that
they had raised up a fit person in the title of Odatshehdeh (Oe-1, RC 10),
"deceased, who was one of their chiefs and a Tree of Peace." They presented the
new sachem, who now held the same title and whom they recommended as firm
to the English interest. They had charged him with taking care of public affairs,
which he promised to do, and they asked that he be accepted by the board of
commissioners as a sachem of their nation. His was indeed the title of a league
founder, which they validated with a string of wampum. The commissioners
acknowledged his acceptance with a shirt (PAC IR RG 10, 1819: 277–78).

Two years later, in the dead of winter, fifteen newly appointed commissioners
heard some Cayuga sachems report their recent loss by death of eight sachems, but
the Cayugas presented no replacements. The commissioners properly condoled the
deaths by wiping off the tears and covering their graves with three blankets of
Stroud's cloth, while expressing hope that their replacements would be experienced men who would have proper regard for their country and be faithful to the
province. The commissioners were concerned about French intrusions into
western New York (PAC IR RG 10, 1819: 311–12).

Fourth, the grand council of the confederacy continued to meet regularly at
Onondaga. The sachems maintained repeatedly that they were not subjects of the
English crown but allies in the chain. With this sense of independence went the

policy of neutrality that they sustained down to 1746, in the wake of the outbreak of King George's War (1744-48), the American manifestation of the War of the Austrian Succession in Europe. Typically, the firekeepers dispatched two runners with seven hands of wampum in relays to Oneida and then Canajoharie, from where two Mohawk messengers carried the word to the commissioners, who notified the governor in Manhattan that the council would convene in so many days. In May 1729, for example, after three hundred Mahican and Shawnee families sent word that they desired to settle among the Six Nations, the sachems announced that a general meeting of the confederacy to discuss the matter would open within seven to eight days at Onondaga castle. They asked the governor to send one or two persons to attend; the commissioners sent the interpreter and an assistant (PAC IR RG 10, 1819: 284).

The sachems, however, did not always include observers at grand councils. On a later occasion, when the Mohawks acquainted the commissioners with seven hands of wampum that the Onondagas had scheduled a general meeting with all of the Six Nations without notifying the commissioners, they sent the interpreter to find out why. The council did not meet at Onondaga during his stay but moved the site to the Seneca country on the pretext that some visiting Pennsylvania Indians intended to condole the deaths of some confederate sachems. The Onondaga council wanted Seneca sachems to accompany them to Canada to condole the death of a great man, but the Senecas refused. Just then the Senecas were busy forging an alliance with the Ottawas. The confederacy was not always of one mind (PAC IR RG 10, 1820: 54, 62-63).

The Onondaga council on occasion held impromptu sessions, with or without the sachems of the other nations. In a sense, the Onondaga firekeepers met in continuous session and could assemble in a hurry an ad hoc council to hear any proposition affecting the confederacy. The commissioners, worried about a French threat to Oswego, in the winter of 1740-41 sent the interpreter Claessen up to Onondaga to investigate what business two Onondaga sachems had transacted with the governor of Canada. On arrival, he had the sachems called together. The council declared unanimously that the two went on no public business other than condoling the death of French agent Joncaire and a priest lately deceased. Claessen told the council that the commissioners were credibly informed that the sachems had schemed with the French to cut off Oswego in the spring. He pleaded with them to be truthful, to affirm or deny it, passing a belt of wampum in the name of the English government.

The ambassadors replied that on the way to Montreal they had met three Oneidas who had heard that the commandant at Niagara would be relieved and a second officer would replace him, bringing reinforcements for the command of the first officer, who would cut off Oswego. (This intelligence had most likely reached the commissioners from Mohawk sources.) But as for themselves, they pleaded ignorance. Their mission was to condole the dead. That being the case, they returned the belt, "not thinking it worthwhile to give any other answer" (PAC, IA, RG 10, 1820: 202-202v).

□□◇□□

The interests of both Albany and the lower Iroquois focused on the French threat, while the upper Iroquois, or western members of the confederacy, looked to the south. This division of interests helps explain the want of Mohawk participation in Pennsylvania treaties. Just when the first Pennsylvania treaty negotiations commenced in the summer of 1732, eight Mohawk sachems were more interested in getting their friend David Schuyler released from jail for a debt to the Livingstons (PAC IR RG 10, 1819: 355).

It was mainly Senecas, some Cayugas, and a few Oneida sachems who came down to Philadelphia that summer to light the council fire in the name of the Six Nations. This first of the so-called Pennsylvania treaties resulted in no formal document attested by both parties with signatures and pictographs. It was, rather, a conference to explore land issues, hear grievances, and renew the chain of friendship between the Pennsylvania proprietor and ambassadors of the confederacy (Boyd 1938: xxiv–xxv; P. Wallace 1945: 47; Jennings 1984: 314).

Three years earlier, some forty Iroquois, a majority of them Cayugas, had visited Philadelphia to polish the chain, complain about traders, swear off rum, and discuss land sales. It took Secretary James Logan another five years to bring Thomas Penn, the second proprietor, to visit the colony and meet its original owners. Meanwhile, trouble mounted with the Delawares and the Six Nations. Logan was convinced that securing the goodwill of the Iroquois held the key to Pennsylvania's interests. The governor and council resolved: "As the Five Nations have an absolute Authority over all our Indians and may command them as they please, it is of great importance to Remove any impressions . . . to the prejudice of the English" (HSP, Penn mss., Indian Affairs, 1: 34; PCR, 3: 271–76, 295–98, 307–26; Boyd 1938: xxii–xxiii).

Holding a treaty conference might accomplish this. Beyond the local issues lay the threat of French control of the trans-Allegheny country and the Shawnees, whom, Logan foresaw, the Iroquois alone could influence. He dispatched Shikellamy, the Oneida chief stationed as "regent" at Shamokin, to Onondaga bearing invitation strings. This time, predominately Senecas responded, with a few Cayugas and Oneidas. The Onondaga sachems later begged sickness at home. Smallpox was abroad. No Mohawks attended.

The conference ran from 23 August to 2 September. Thomas Penn, having landed on 12 August, had barely a week before the sachems reached town in which to prepare for his first encounter with forest diplomacy. Conrad Weiser—Tarachiawagon to the Mohawks and "Honest Conrad" to Pennsylvania governor George Thomas—arrived on the eighteenth with the Indians. He became the best informed and most reliable interpreter in the colonies, and in the next decade implemented Logan's policy of giving official support to the authority of the Six Nations. Tyoninhogara (Doninhogawen, S-8, RC 50), traditional western doorkeeper of the league, with Hetaquantagechty ("Earth Carrier"[?]) as his speaker, headed the delegation. With them came some eight other Seneca chiefs. Tiohogwanda (Deyohagwendeh, Oe-4, RC 12), "Through the Opening," an Oneida league title, is listed as leader of the Cayuga party of four other chiefs, while Shikellamy, alias Swatanaey, the brother of "Big Tree," and two others represented the Oneidas (HSP, Logan papers, vol. 11; Boyd 1938: xxv; P. Wallace 1945: 471–48).

Forest protocol awarded the courtesy of speaking first to the host. Pennsylvania had kindled the fire. Penn reiterated his father's policy of friendship and justice to the native Indians. This meant purchasing any lands occupied. He also urged the Six Nations to extend and consolidate their influence over other Indian nations, thereby enhancing their power, particularly over the Shawnees, who had removed to the Allegheny and should be brought back. They were to avoid wars with the Catawbas and Cherokees. Further, they were to inform other nations that an alliance with the Six Nations leagued them also with the English (PCR, 3: 433–52; Boyd 1938: xxv). Throughout, the natives listened attentively without remark or hint of their inner thoughts, as was their wont.

Hetaquantagechty introduced his Pennsylvania hosts to the art of council-style speech replete with metaphors and laced with humor. Paul Wallace (1945: 48) thought the Indians, throughout the proceedings, outperformed their hosts. They complimented Penn, overlooked his patronizing ways, and answered questions about their relations with the French. They had told a French governor who had proposed that they "sitt still and look on" while he fought the English that he was not wise to make war on Corlaer, for they would join the New York governor. "If we fight with you, we may have our Father Onontejo [Onontio] to bury . . . be wise and live in Peace." And the way to bring the Shawnees home was to recall the traders from the Allegheny. The Six Nations let Pennsylvania know that in no way would they become dependent "sons" in the English sense; their status was that of siblings or equals, as it was in New York. They would go home, the speaker said, and report to the general council (Jennings et al. 1985a: 177).

The conference set the tone for future relations between the parties in a series of treaties that followed during the next thirty years. Benjamin Franklin, who would print the subsequent treaties and who first recognized them as a native American literary genre, attended the meetings and wrote a favorable account (Franklin 1962, 1: 277). Here began Franklin's sustained fascination with the Iroquois Confederacy.

The conference enabled Pennsylvania to gradually dispose of four trouble spots in Indian relations: the lower Susquehanna, the forks of the Delaware, the Ohio River valley, and the Lebanon Valley in Pennsylvania. The last was accomplished that year. The other three would entail bloodshed and treaty negotiations for the next thirty years (P. Wallace 1945: 49).

Although smallpox prevented the Six Nations sachems from revisiting Philadelphia the next year, they did meet Governor Cosby in Albany. After exchanging condolences, they renewed the deed to their hunting lands toward Detroit. Cosby, worried about competing French activities, asked the sachems to stop Iroquois war parties from raiding south. But the sachems confessed that seldom could they control their young men, who pretended to go out hunting and then met to form war parties (Wraxall 1915: 188). Lack of social control vertically and horizontally marred the structure of Iroquois polity.

Another reason the Mohawks stayed home to attend to local business was that they had few good men to spare. Pestilence and emigration had greatly reduced their numbers. More than half of their population, including some titled lineages, had removed since the 1680s to the St. Lawrence missions. When fourteen Caughnawaga chiefs in August 1735 concluded a treaty at Albany with the commissioners of Indian affairs over trade matters, none other than Tekarihoken (M-1, RC 1) headed the delegation and prompted the speakers. In earnest of peace they presented a calumet and introduced the ceremony of passing and smoking the pipe, a ritual that the Fox Indians of Wisconsin had brought to Montreal a decade earlier, which the commissioners thought remarkable. On behalf of their warriors, they asked that the pipe be lodged at Onondaga as a means of reconciling differences between the exiles and the confederacy, to which the commissioners agreed (PAC IR RG 10, 1820: 65-66; Wraxall 1915: 193; Fenton 1953a).

The following month, Governor Cosby himself met with the Six Nations chiefs, condoled recent losses, and renewed the covenant. Among more serious matters— Oswego, French agents resident in Iroquoia, an argument over the Caughnawaga trade proposals, and the southeastern wars—the governor delivered the calumet for Onondaga. The sachems accepted it, thanked him for the condolences, confirmed the covenant, expressed concern over prices, decried crooked traders at Oswego who watered rum, welcomed smiths, and declared that "Flatt Heads are a people who have no reason." As for French traders among them, the Indians reminded the governor of an essential truth: "The Trade and Peace we take to be one thing." Wraxall, in a footnote, agreed (PAC IR RG 10, 1820: 71-72v; Wraxall 1915: 194-95).

□□◇□□

Four years passed before representatives of the Six Nations came down to Philadelphia to renew agreements reached in 1732 and conclude a formal treaty with Thomas Penn and the Pennsylvania council. This "Treaty of Friendship" proved a landmark event: it extended the covenant chain to Pennsylvania, and it established a mode for future land cessions. It was the first of the treaties printed by Benjamin Franklin (DePuy 1917: no. 16; Boyd 1938: 1-14), and it is now the rarest of treaty documents (Boyd 1938: 303). The Iroquois intended to continue and strengthen the chain "between all the English and all our Nations," including the Delawares, Conoys, and Indians living on the Susquehanna. It ceded the lower Susquehanna Valley to Penn.

A preliminary council at Secretary Logan's Stenton home set the agenda. Afterward, Weiser met with returning chiefs "in the bushes" at Shamokin, where Pennsylvania recognized the Iroquois as having sole right to sell Indian lands in the province and accorded them exclusive right to speak in treaties for other Indians. The Iroquois asked Pennsylvania to intercede with Maryland toward settling Iroquois claims to "conquered" lands north of the Potomac. The sachems signed a quit-claim deed to lands that other Indian tribes occupied in Pennsylvania, which in effect ceded the lands to Pennsylvania (Jennings et al. 1985a: 177-78). These issues would linger beyond mid-century.

The treaty felled a log across the traditional warpath. For years the Susquehanna Valley had been the route north for the Catawbas and Cherokees in raiding the Iroquois, as well as the way south for northern Iroquoian war parties. George Washington, as a young man surveying at the back of the settlements, frequently encountered such war parties (Freeman 1948). It was in the interest of the English governors, both north and south, to put an end to the wars between the northern Iroquoians and the Catawbas, as well as the Cherokees (Winsor 1895: 180-82, 185).

When Weiser learned that the Six Nations delegation was on its way to the preliminary council, he high-tailed it for Shamokin, where the east branch joins the main Susquehanna River. Protocol required that he greet the ambassadors, take them by the arm, and usher them to the main fire. To his amazement, eighteen canoes carried some one hundred people of all ages, including twenty sachems and Hetaquantegechty, the Seneca speaker of the previous conference. Weiser, overwhelmed at the size and distinction of the delegation's makeup, greeted the ambassadors by shaking hands, which pleased them.[3]

The sachems held their own council, reached their own agenda, sent for Weiser, placed him between the two senior Onondagas, and proceeded to instruct him, as well as their speaker and Shikellamy. The troupe then repaired to Logan's country house at Stenton, where they were entertained for three days and nights before entering Philadelphia. The proprietor and members of the council rode out to meet them (PCR, 4: 79ff.; P. Wallace 1945: 68). They brought the required wampum so that Weiser, for Thomas Penn, could condole the Six Nations with the Three Bare Words of Requickening. Each nation responded with the cry of approbation before their speaker replied in kind.

Smallpox in Philadelphia occasioned concern on both sides. Despite the danger to the Indians, the treaty convened in the Great Meeting House on 2 October and went on for two weeks. Logan greeted the Iroquois delegates and explained the purpose to the general audience. Then, through Weiser, he turned the meeting over to the Indians, who, having called the council, spoke first. Hanickhungo, the designated Seneca speaker, made three points, attesting to each with a present. A white belt of eleven rows carrying four black crosses, one for each of the original Five Nations present, read, "We are now come down from the Towns of several Nations to give an answer to the great Treaty . . . [of] four Years ago." Their grand council had carefully considered the matters then agreed upon, when "you undertook to . . . keep a Fire for us. . . . We are now come to warm ourselves [at that fire], and we desire and hope it will ever continue bright and burning to the End of the World" (see Speck and Orchard 1925: pl. 2).

Having assured his hosts that matters of the fire, the road, and the chain had been satisfied, the speaker invoked the symbols of unity—one heart, one mind, one body—to be preserved by oncoming generations of both peoples. Although not equal to his hosts in writing, he assured his listeners that the Indians had a unique way of preserving and transmitting the memory of transactions. He said:

> We who are now here, are old Men, who have the Direction of Affairs in our own Nations; and as we are old, it may be thought that the Memory of these things may be lost with us, who have not, like you, the Art of . . . Writing: We nevertheless have Methods of transmitting from Father to Son, an Account of these Things. . . . [T]he Remembrance of them is faithfully preserved, and our succeeding Generations are made acquainted with what has passed, that it may not be forgot as long as the Earth remains. (Boyd 1938, Treaty 1736: 6)

3. Several of the listed names of the sachems, who were then the most considerable Six Nations leaders, resemble the shapes of league titles, particularly C-7, RC 39, but none of the Onondagas or Oneidas listed, whom Weiser wrote Logan were "the wisest of their nation," equate with the famous founders (HSP, Logan Papers, 10: 59; P. Wallace 1945: 65–67; Boyd 1938: 3–4). The delegation comprised five Senecas, five Onondagas, four Cayugas, two Oneidas, and two Tuscaroras, but no Mohawk chiefs.

It is a tribute to Weiser that so much of ethnographic interest got printed in the treaty. Both the Iroquois sachems and the Pennsylvania councilors found satisfaction in Weiser's performance. He established himself as liaison between Pennsylvania and the Six Nations. Shikellamy, until his death, and Weiser would play complementary roles. Each had a foot in the other's moccasins.

Later, Charles Thomson (1759) complained that the published minutes of the treaty omitted much that was done "in the bushes" to alienate Delaware and Shawnee claims and affections. He should have known that these private caucuses were how the Iroquois reached consensus before publishing decisions in open council (Lafitau 1724, 1: 478ff; Fenton and Moore 1974: 295ff.) The 1736 treaty did little to abate the Iroquois-Catawba war.

Governor Gooch of Virginia asked the Pennsylvania authorities by regular embassy to entreat the Six Nations to come to Williamsburg, where he had arranged for the Catawbas and Cherokees to send deputies to settle the troublesome war. Meanwhile, a truce should obtain for one year. James Logan sent Weiser to Onondaga to bring the Six Nations down. Weiser left home in late February 1737, before iceout, picked up Shikellamy and a guide above Shamokin, and, after fording swollen streams and traversing snow-covered mountainsides, reached Onondaga barely alive in early April. His 1737 journal reads like the horror story of the eighteenth century (P. Wallace 1945: 76–94).

Weiser, by sending a string from five miles off, notified the chiefs that he carried a serious message. Word came back that their fire was kindled and burning, and chiefs of all the Six Nations were there. They greeted him with amazement, affection, and concern, lodged him in the best house in town, and brought him food. By a string they invited him to speak, but suggested that he rest until recovered, "for you look like Dead Men." After consulting with Shikellamy, conscientious Conrad said he would speak next day. The chiefs appointed the house where he was lodged as the place of council next morning. Takanunty, an Onondaga participant in the 1736 treaty, opened the council and signified that they were ready to hear the message, which Weiser divided under two heads: first, by a string, the invitation of Governor Gooch to a treaty at Williamsburg with the Catawbas and Cherokees, and second, by a belt, the request of Pennsylvania for the Six Nations to lay down the hatchet pending the peace treaty.

Not to be rushed, the chiefs, after eating, deliberated apart in council and, sensing the urgency of the issue, announced that they were ready that evening to reply. They returned to Weiser's lodging, attached his invitation string to a stick, and hung it for the public to see. They repeated the message, and then Takanunty "spoke as a Man of great Authority and Prudence loud and slow and great Silence and order was kept during the whole." He referred to the message of Assarigoe (the governor of Virginia) and spoke affectionately of Onas (Penn), Logan, and the Pennsylvania council. Then he delivered the clincher: the Six Nations could not go to Williamsburg to a treaty of peace because "there is no Road to that place. We never travel through Bushes to Treaties of Peace. It is too dangerous and we have no fire at Williamsburg. . . . Such a thing cannot be done in a corner, it must be done by a public fire." Assarigoe could come to Albany, together with the Catawba and Cherokee chiefs. A string confirmed this message, and Weiser's string was taken off the stick and put by (P. Wallace 1945: 91).

Having disposed of the matter, the council observed for Logan's ears that they doubted the sincerity of the Catawbas. Had they been sincere, they might have come safely to Onondaga. They knew less of the Cherokees, but thought them reasonable. The next day the council dispatched runners east and west to the other five nations to inform them of the news and proclaim putting aside the hatchet. There followed the usual terminal feast, to which each chief brought his own dish and spoon (P. Wallace 1945: 92).

Several days later the council reassembled all the males at home to hear Weiser's message repeated and verified. Subsequently, Weiser became quite ill and a local practitioner administered an emetic and physic, the effects of which the journal describes. The Onondagas held Weiser in such esteem that they urged him to stay on for a month's rest, but to no avail. He did visit the salt spring. He measured longhouses of one hundred feet, five fires, and as many families. He was amazed at the incredible crops of corn. The journey home by canoe was less arduous than the outbound trip (P. Wallace 1945: 93).

That spring, the interpreter Claessen reported that the Six Nations desired a treaty in Albany with the governors of Virginia and New York. Lieutenant Governor George Clarke of the New York colony met the chiefs there in June. The sachems welcomed him with assurance of their pleasure that he had escaped accident, illness, or other mishap en route. But they also reminded him that first they must condole the deaths of two sachems according to the custom of their ancestors before they could conduct any public business. He scolded them for letting Joncaire persuade the Seneca council to let the French build a trading post at Irondequoit. Clarke refused to renew the covenant chain until reassured that the deal was cancelled. On behalf of His Majesty, Clarke wanted to purchase from the three western nations "all the lands on the south side of Lake Cadarague [Ontario] from Oswego to the falls of Iagara [Niagara]." He intended to fortify Irondequoit, asserting that it would improve the trade and prevent the French from intercepting it.

When the interpreter summoned the chiefs to caucus on the matter at the home of Nicholas Bleeker, Clarke became upset and reprimanded the agent and the host. The chiefs held that the owners of the lands desired were just then in the Seneca country, and that those present had no power to sell the lands in question. The chiefs finally reassured Clarke that they would permit no Frenchman to settle there but reminded him of English inactivity near Niagara and at Crown Point, which was Mohawk territory. As for the removal of the Shawnees from the Susquehanna into the French orbit, it was up to Pennsylvania to bring them back. They had not sold the ground from beneath them. Penn had bought it.

At one point in the negotiations, the native speaker reminded Clarke of how the Iroquois remembered everything of previous transactions and transmitted the knowledge to their youths in a way more effective than records written in a book and not read by successors. He also invoked the metaphor of the British government as a ship of state moored behind a great elm where people took refuge, later lifted and stretched as a chain and secured behind the great hill at Onondaga (NYCD, 6: 106; Wraxall 1915: 201). He said that the Iroquois took no notice of the French governor's invitation to join his campaign against the Fox Indians because he had failed to send a wampum belt with his message (Wraxall 1915: 204).

□□◇□□

The years 1737–42 were a time of trouble among the Six Nations. A smallpox epidemic swept through the Longhouse in 1738, carrying off nine sachems, including several bearing league titles. When duly condoled, the sachems presented their nominees for successors to the New York governor and asked him to accept and install them. The grand council continued to meet at Onondaga, the sachems were seldom of one mind, and on one occasion they deferred answering a crucial issue saying it would have to come before the women. The council was powerless to control independent action by its autonomous nations, as when three Seneca sachems granted an easement to a Frenchman to establish a trading post at Irondequoit, nor could they prevent the Oneidas from levying tolls on the Wood Creek portage. Both of these actions were later reversed after pressure from Albany.

A principle was at stake, as Onondaga spokesmen had stated in 1726 to Governor Burnet, and that principle was the law of unanimity. "They say that it is customary among their Tribes for One to Negotiate Business with any other People, which if afterwards approved by the other Tribes stands good; but if not, the Transaction is null & void, And that in this Affair [the Seneca easement to the French at Niagara] their Proceedings were disapproved by the rest of their Confederate Tribes & therefore of no Force" (Wraxall 1915: 165).

Niagara had passed to the French while Oswego, as a British outpost constantly threatened by the French, survived at the whim of the ambivalent Onondagas, who complained about the cheating traders watering their rum and deplored the violence in drunken routs. Famine stalked the Longhouse as crops were not planted or brought to harvest. Men were too weak to hunt. People no longer lived in nucleated, palisaded villages, as settlements spread out in a defenseless pattern. The Senecas and Cayugas were most scattered. English authorities urged them to concentrate once more in their "castle," but the sachems replied that they would consult with their people when they returned from hunting, especially with their women, "who have so much to say in that affair," and then answer (PAC IR RG 10, 1820: 218v–219; Wraxall 1915: 223).

The French made various claims to strategic spots in Iroquoia, but the Mohawks asserted that Wood Creek and its portage to Lake Champlain lay within their hunting territory. French agents kept inciting Iroquois youths to go out against the southeastern tribes. The New York authorities in 1740 countered by sending Claessen to Onondaga to bring down the sachems in June, while they could still peel bark for canoes, to meet with Lieutenant Governor Clarke and renew the covenant. The sachems were pleased at the prospect of making peace with the southern Indians, but they preferred that the latter show in person. Clarke dallied until August, and the sachems had to walk. Clarke renewed the covenant chain and extended it to include southern and western Indians who were formerly French allies. Some Caughnawaga observers attended to keep their options open (PAC IR RG 10, 1820: 186–87; NYCD, 6: 172–78). In what amounted to an installation ceremony (without the condolence), the speaker presented the governor with nine young sachems recently appointed in the "rooms" (places) of deceased officers, including two league titles, S-1, RC 43 and Oe-2, RC 11, and a possible third, Oa-3, RC 21. The governor duly charged them with the English interest (PAC IR RG 10, 1820: 196–197v).

Whenever the Onondaga council sent a delegation to call on the governor of New France, the English authorities worried. The old men of Iroquoia sensed this and used it to serve their own interests, favoring the English and treating the French with caution except when the interests of the other two served their purposes. Peter Wraxall commented: "To preserve the Ballance between us & the French is the great ruling Principle of the Modern Indian Politics" (Wraxall 1915: 219n).

In Philadelphia, James Logan, who shaped Pennsylvania's Indian policy during the first half of the century, reduced it to a nutshell: "If we lose the Iroquois, we are gone" (Boyd 1938: xix). This policy became that of the proprietor, Thomas Penn, who had seen his first Iroquois at age seven when the "four kings" visited London, and who met the Iroquois embassy at Stenton in 1736.

While the Pennsylvania authorities enlisted Weiser to help clean up after the Walking Purchase of Delaware lands in 1737 (P. Wallace 1945: 95–101), the Six Nations pursued more pressing matters at home. The grand council held general meetings in January 1741 to reassure Claessen that the Onondagas who had called on Governor Beaucours at Montreal "went on no publick business," and in March it sent a delegation to explain to the commissioners that extending the chain to include some former French allies merited diplomacy. The council resolved in August to protect Oswego, but urged peace between France and England (PAC IA RG 10, 1820: 202–202v, 205). Three Seneca sachems, headed by the doorkeeper, Tyoninhogara, reversed a former cession and deeded Irondequoit to His Majesty in consideration of one hundred pounds (NYCD, 6: 204–5). Uncertain which way the wind blew, Caughnawaga sachems called on the commissioners but remained evasive. Of greater significance, negotiations began that spring to settle the long-standing feud between the Six Nations and the Cherokee and Catawba nations. The Cherokee "Beloved Old Men" manifested good faith by pledging a pipe and eagle fan, while the Catawbas appeared tentative and the Six Nations skeptical (NYCD, 6: 208, 210–11). The Senecas desperately needed provisions, lacked powder and lead to hunt, and were in no shape to travel. A diplomatic settlement of the southern wars would await further conferences in Albany and two Pennsylvania treaties (PAC IA RG 10 1820: 214).

At a June conference in Albany, Lieutenant Governor Clarke, in renewing the covenant, spoke first, urging the Six Nations sachems to include the southeastern Indians in extending the chain, specifically the Catawba, Cherokee, Chickasaw, and Choctaw nations. The sachems had told a visiting Cherokee deputy that they were ready to exchange prisoners, but they would make no positive answer to the Catawbas, "a designing people," until they saw the faces of the negotiators (PAC RG 10, 1820: 227v–228v; NYCD, 6: 16–19).

□□◇□□

The big Philadelphia treaty was a year late. At mid-October 1741, two Cayuga chiefs and followers arrived unannounced. The governor, wondering why they had come, sent for Weiser to learn what news they brought, or what matter of consequence. It seems that the previous spring, the Six Nations chiefs had agreed to come down that summer to visit Brother Onas and receive payment for lands sold. But the winter had been severe, and some of them had perished. They had gone to Albany instead, where there were victuals. They had agreed that they should all set out at the end of the next full moon and meet at Wyoming (modern Wilkes-Barre, Pennsylvania) to float the Susquehanna. When the others failed to show, the Cayuga contingent decided to come down alone. Some Onondaga and Seneca chiefs had gone to Canada to confer with the French governor and "repair the road." Although expected to have returned by then, the visitors had no news of what might have detained the others. The governor told them that Penn had returned to England but hoped to meet them next summer and had left goods and provisions for their return upriver (PCR, 4: 501).

As the time for the Philadelphia meeting approached, the scattered pattern of Iroquois autonomy prevailed. No longer interested in the Susquehanna lands, Mohawk attention focused on Albany. Six Cayugas and some Oneidas and Tuscaroras requested a meeting with the commissioners in January to regret the death of Lawrence Claessen, whom they were not yet prepared to condole. Some Mohawk sachems attended. Without Claessen, they said, it was difficult to convey their words (PAC IR RG 10, 1820: 223–24v; Wraxall 1915: 224). They would suspend campaigns southward for two years and try to concentrate their settlements. The Reverend Henry Barclay reported to the Society for the Propagation of the Gospel his having appointed two Mohawk schoolmasters in the upper and lower castles, but the scarcity of food that spring impeded their efforts (SPG mss., London, B10: 111–12). In early summer, Tyoninhogara and two other named Seneca sachems acknowledged selling Irondequoit to Arent Stevens, agent of the commissioners (PAC RG 10, 1820: 234; NYCD, 6: 204; Wraxall 1915: 228).

The Philadelphia treaty of July 1742 formalized the alliance made six years previously. In theory, the Six Nations were to receive further compensation for Susquehanna lands released earlier, but the treaty's actual purpose was to squelch the Delawares at the forks of that river. The proprietor and governor of Pennsylvania hoped to hold down the number of Indians attending the treaty conference, especially the local Delaware residents. The meeting promised to be expensive, but the Indians were hungry, and their numbers matched the importance that they attached to its outcome. In June, Richard Peters, an Anglican clergyman and the Pennsylvania provincial secretary after Logan, authorized Weiser to go up and meet the Indians, leaving to his judgment what provisions to take and how far to go. But Weiser was scarcely prepared for nearly two hundred Iroquois men, women, and children, "most of them in a starving condition," who were joined by some forty others from Conestoga upriver (Boyd 1938: xxxi).[4] Principal Delaware and Nanticoke leaders showed up anyway. Richard Peters counted 220 Indians present on opening day (P. Wallace 1945: 126).

The roster of the Six Nations delegation numbered 69 chiefs and Indians, including 13 Onondagas headed by Canasatego, the speaker, 19 Cayugas, 14 Oneidas, 3 Senecas, and 20 Tuscaroras, but no Mohawks. The sparse size of the Seneca contingent was due to the famine in their country. Besides, 5 Shawnees, 4 Conestogas (Oneida speakers), 4 Nanticokes, and 6 Delawares from Shamokin attended—a total of 88 Indians listed. Conspicuously few names suggest titles of league founders; they are ascribed to the wrong nations, and none had prominent roles.

4. Paul Wallace (1945: 125) says 160 Indians showed up at Weiser's plantation in June.

The Cayuga "Tohatgaghthus" suggests Dehatkahdos (Oa-3, RC 21). The Oneida "Onughkallydawwy, a noted young chief," may be an Oneida rendering of Ganonhgidawi (S-7, RC 49). Evidently, famous titles were shared by other nations, or else the recorder misplaced them (Boyd 1938: 22–23; Horsfield Papers, APSL, 1: 9; PPCM, PPR, vol. K: 257–59).

This was an Onondaga show with Canasatego in charge. The Onondaga council had sent him south while another deputation went to Albany. An experienced diplomat and a powerful speaker, of compact build and extroverted personality, he liked to drink and give advice, as we shall see at this treaty and two years later at Lancaster. Though not the holder of a league title, he dominated politics just then at Onondaga. The proceedings began on the second of July with a preliminary council at James Logan's house. As host, the governor opened with a statement of background and purpose. Six years ago, he said, half of the compensation for lands the proprietor had purchased was delivered to the Six Nations, and half withheld at their request, which the proprietor was now prepared to deliver. By accepting it, the Six Nations would agree to release claim to both sides of the Susquehanna River, including the Walking Purchase of lands in the upper Delaware Valley.

As was the Iroquois way, Canasatego announced that the Indians proposed to rest for four days to recover from the fatigue of the journey. Before the formal treaty opened on 6 July, at informal dinners the governor and Canasatego took up several minor matters. Why were so few Senecas present? It seems that "the Senecas were in great Distress, on Account of a Famine that raged in their Country, which had reduced them to such Want, that a Father had been obliged to kill two of his Children to preserve . . . the rest of his Family's Lives" (Boyd 1938, Treaty 1742: 7). Canasatego assured the governor that he need not be concerned at Iroquois overtures to the French—they had no intention of taking up the hatchet against the English. Their policy was neutrality, but if the French attacked, they would come to the aid of the English. Delegates of each nation present affirmed this by raising the "Mark of Approbation" (*yohee:*).

The speaker observed some other bits of tribal law and protocol. Some naive warriors had sold land, he said, but such transactions were properly confined to sachems, who had rebuked them. Because no wampum had passed hands, there was no deal. The governor inquired formally with a string of wampum as to who had brought scalps to a Shawnee settlement—a trader had written that eastern Shawnees had discovered scalps in the baggage of Miami visitors and let the visitors escape before discovering the identity of the victims, where the scalps had been taken, and who had lifted them. The speaker acknowledged the seriousness of the matter by replying that the delegates would retire to consider it and reply (Boyd 1938, Treaty 1742: 6).

The conference met in plenary session at the Meeting House on 6 July. As host, the governor spoke first. Contrary to Iroquois protocol, in which distributions of food and goods come last, he read over the list of goods held in escrow for six years in final payment for the Susquehanna lands. He also spoke of impending war between England and France, its implications for the alliance, the Iroquois position near Canada, and the importance of the treaty. His mention of the fire and the chain evoked further cries of assent, repeated as many times as there were nations present. Again, Canasatego asked for delay to retire, consider, and reply next day (Boyd 1938: Treaty 1742, 11).

Listeners on 7 July heard a sample of Canasatego's wit and rhetoric. Weiser interpreted and a secretary wrote:

> Brethren: We received from the Proprietors, yesterday, some Goods in Consideration of our Release of the Lands on the West-Side of *Susquehannah*. It is true we have the full Quantity according to Agreement; but if the Proprietor had been here himself, we think, in Regard of our Numbers and Poverty, he would have made an Addition to them.—If the Goods were only to be divided among the *Indians* present, a single Person would have but a small Portion; but if you consider what Numbers are left behind, equally entitled with us to a Share, there will be extremely little. We therefore desire, if you have the Keys of the Proprietor's Chest, you will open it, and take out a little more for us.
>
> We know our Lands are now become more valuable. The white People think we do not know their Value; but we are sensible that the Land is everlasting, and the Goods we receive for it are soon worn out and gone. . . . [W]e are not well used with respect to the Lands still unsold by us. Your People daily settle on these Lands, and spoil our Hunting. We must insist on your Removing them, as you know they have no Right to settle to the Northward of *Kittochtinny-Hills*.—In particular, we renew our Complaints against some People who are settled at *Juniata*, a Branch of the *Susquehannah*, and all along the Banks of that River . . . and desire they may be forthwith made to go off the Land; for they do great Damage to our Cousins the *Delawares*. (Boyd 1938, Treaty 1742: 12–13)

This was clever speech that put the governor on the defensive. He could be more generous, since he wanted help in a quarrel with the Delawares over title to their lands. The upshot was that the Iroquois got an additional present valued at three hundred pounds.

In further elaboration of his point with respect to squatters, Canasatego said: "It is customary with us to make a Present whenever we renew our Treaties. We are ashamed to offer our Brethren so few [skins]; but your Horses and Cows have eat the Grass our Deer used to feed on. This has made them scarce, and will, we hope, plead in Excuse for our not bringing a larger Quantity" (Boyd 1938, Treaty 1742: 13).

At this point, Governor Thomas played Indian: he would have to refer the matter of an increased present to the board for consideration and reply later (Boyd 1938, Treaty 1742: 15).

The Indians at dinner that night settled two matters of consequence. In a matter of protocol concerning an assault on a settler at the forks, the Six Nations council had found the culprit and reproved him, and the victim had recovered; therefore they considered the matter settled, and the speaker returned the string, having complied with the request. Had the victim died, they would have put the Indian to death. "Indians know no Punishment but Death. . . . [I]f a man be guilty of a Crime he is either put to Death or the Fault is overlook'd" (Boyd 1938, Treaty 1742: 16).

In the matter of the trader's letter about scalps discovered in visitors' baggage, the issue was one of procedure. The council had considered just how the matter referred to them should be handled. They knew that the visitors in whose baggage the Shawnees had discovered the scalps were Miamis. The Shawnees had sent the governor a message to which he should have replied with a present and a sharp message, reproving the Shawnees for letting the visitors get away before giving a true account of when and where they got the scalps and the identity of the victims !Boyd 1938, Treaty 1742: 15).

The conference reached its climax on 9 July. The governor presented his case against the Delawares at the forks and documented it with deeds and letters. Weiser interpreted and explained the evidence to the Six Nations chiefs at some length, and then the Delaware chiefs presented their side of the case. Canasatego had three days to listen and muster his thoughts before he rose to indict his cousins, the Delawares, on the twelfth. Addressing the governor and council, he was made to say:

> Brethren . . . The other Day you informed us of the Misbehaviour of our Cousins the *Delawares*, with respect to their continuing to claim, and refusing to remove from some Land on the River *Delaware*, notwithstanding their Ancestors had sold it by a Deed under their Hands and Seals to the Proprietaries, for a valuable Consideration, upwards of *Fifty* Years ago; and notwithstanding that they themselves had about [blank] Years ago, after a long and full Examination, ratified the Deed of their Ancestors, and given a fresh one under their Hands and Seals; and then you requested us to remove them, inforcing your Request with a String of Wampum.—Afterwards you laid on the Table our own Letters by *Conrad Weiser*, some of our Cousins Letters, and the several Writings, to prove the Charge against our Cousins, with a Draught of the Land in Dispute.—We now tell you we have perused all these several Papers: We see with our own Eyes, that they have been a very unruly People, and are altogether in the Wrong in their Dealings with you.—We have concluded to remove them, and oblige them to go over the River *Delaware*, and quit all Claim to any Lands on this Side for the Future, since they have received Pay for them, and it is gone thro' their Guts long ago.—To confirm to you that we will see your Request executed, we lay down this String of Wampum in return for yours. (Boyd 1938, Treaty 1742: 21)

Then, holding a belt of wampum in hand, Canasatego turned to the Delaware chiefs and delivered his famous scold:

> Let this Belt of Wampum serve to chastise you. You ought to be taken by the Hair of the Head and shaked severely, till you recover your Senses and become sober. You don't know what Ground you stand on, nor what you are doing. . . . [Here he commented on the merit of Brother Onas's cause.] We have seen with our own Eyes a Deed signed by nine of your Ancestors above *Fifty* Years ago for this very Land, and a Release signed not many Years since, by some of yourselves and Chiefs now living, to the Number of fifteen or upwards.—But how came you to sell Land at all: We conquered you; we made Women of you; you know you are Women, and can no more sell Land than Women; nor is it fit you should have the Power of selling Lands, since you would abuse it. This Land that you claim is gone through your Guts; you have been furnished with Cloaths, Meat and Drink, by the Goods paid you for it, and now you want it again, like Children as you are.—[Here he contrasted the Delawares selling in the dark with the public land sales of the Six Nations at formal treaties.] . . . You

act a dishonest Part, not only in this but in other Matters: Your Ears are ever open
to slanderous Reports about our Brethren; you receive them with as much Greediness
as lewd Women receive the Embraces of bad Men. And for all these Reasons we charge
you to remove instantly; we don't give you the Liberty to think about it. You are
Women. Take the Advice of a wise Man, and remove immediately. You may return
to the other Side of *Delaware* where you came from: but we don't know whether,
considering how you have demeaned yourselves, you will be permitted to live there;
or whether you have not swallowed that Land down your Throats as well as the Land
on this Side. We therefore assign you two Places to go, either to *Wyomen* or *Shamokin*.
You may go either of these Places, and then we shall have you more under our Eye,
and shall see how you behave. Don't deliberate; but remove away, and take this Belt
of Wampum. (Boyd 1938, Treaty 1742: 21-22)

Clearly, Canasatego's rhetoric on this occasion exceeded logic or precedent.
There is no historical record that the Iroquois Confederacy ever conquered the
Delawares, unless it occurred in prehistory. And on several known occasions,
Iroquois sachems protested that they could not sell lands without the sanction of
the women. Canasatego extrapolated from the fact of a few Delawares at the forks
selling a particular piece of land to Penn to an indictment of the Delaware nation,
which, he claimed, had no right whatever to sell land (P. Wallace 1945: 130).

Although there is no record, Canasatego was not the only Iroquois to boast that
his people had defeated the Delawares in warfare, and the Delawares never publicly
denied this charge. C. A. Weslager (1972: 181) has steadfastly advanced the view,
which he first expressed in 1944, that indeed the Iroquois had subjugated the
Delawares and reduced them to a subservient position. He cites instances during
the first half of the eighteenth century when Iroquois asserted superiority, when
the Delawares after 1709 were paying tribute in wampum, and when Iroquois were
asserting overlordship in Pennsylvania. Relegated to the status of women, the
Delawares were prohibited from going to war or negotiating treaties. Jennings
(1984: 342ff.) maintains that Canasatego fabricated a convenient myth, that he got
carried away by his own rhetoric (a tendency that perseveres among his descendants today), that he considerably exceeded his terms of reference (much to the joy
of his patrons), that in removing the Delawares from the forks he opened the gates
to colonial settlement beyond the Appalachians, that the Shawnee and Delaware
bands who slipped away to the Ohio country returned to visit vengeance on white
settlers, and that the drift of Senecas and Mingos into the Ohio country, beyond
the reach of the old men of Onondaga, weakened the Iroquois Confederacy
(Jennings 1984: 344-46).

As usual, the Indians wanted better prices for their deerskins. Deer were
growing scarce, and the market economy was as much a mystery to the Indians
as it was to some Russians in 1990. In other treaty business, it remained but to
thank their hosts and compensate for messing up their accommodations. And they
were especially indebted to Weiser for translating Onondaga into his acquired
Mohawk and then into broken English for their hosts. Despite these deficiencies,
the secretary managed to produce a document with literary merit that attracted
readers at home and abroad. Again, Canasatego acknowledged the debt with
some grace:

Brethren: The Business the *Five* Nations transact with you is of great Consequence, and requires a skilful and honest Person to go between us; one in whom both you and we can place a Confidence.—We esteem our present Interpreter to be such a Person, equally faithful in the Interpretation of whatever is said to him by either of us, equally allied to both; he is of our Nation, and a Member of our Council, as well as yours. When we adopted him, we divided him in two equal Parts: One we kept for ourselves, and one we left for you. He has had a great deal of Trouble with us, wore out his Shoes in our Messages, and dirty'd his Cloaths by being amongst us, so that he has become as nasty as an *Indian*.

The public business was now over and the treaty had been a dry event. The hosts had fed the Indians well, but they would now welcome, they said, some rum to wash away the taste of their smoking, and they desired provisions on the road and wagons to transport them to the water route home. The Pennsylvania council appropriated one hundred pounds for Weiser's expenses and ordered "Twenty Gallons of Rum for the aforesaid Use" (Boyd 1938, Treaty 1742: 23-25). Five pounds and two Stroud's each were ordered for Kakshayon, an Onondaga headman, and Shikellamy for their services.

At the close of the treaty, Canasatego reminded the Pennsylvania governor of a promise made six years earlier to write to the governor of Maryland about Indian claims to lands in that province. The council, alarmed, met immediately and concluded that "should those Threats . . . be put into Execution," the inhabitants of both provinces would be threatened and all of His Majesty's subjects in America might be in big trouble. Canasatego's remarks amounted to an ultimatum: "Let him [the Maryland governor] say *Yes* or *No*: If he says *Yes*, we will treat with him; if No, we are able to do ourselves Justice" (Boyd 1938: xxxii–xxxiii). Richard Peters, in writing to the proprietors, suggested "what a resolute and powerful people the Six Nations were and how prejudicial it might be to the British Colonies to disoblige them at this time" (Boyd 1938: xxxiii). The governors decided to treat two years later at Lancaster.

CHAPTER 27

THE TREATY
AT LANCASTER, 1744

> While their advantage lasted, a league of ragged villages held off two great empires, inflexibly and proudly forcing the empires to treat with them in the village language.—Carl Van Doren, Introduction to *Indian Treaties Printed by Benjamin Franklin*

While the sachems returning from the Philadelphia treaty of 1742 were sobering up at the Delaware settlement of Tulpehocken, Conrad Weiser obtained a list of eight peoples with whom the Six Nations had made alliances, their situation, and their number of fighting men. They inhabited the borders of the Great Lakes and the Ohio country, and they were former allies of the French (PCR, 4: 586; APSL, Horsfield Papers, 974.8, no. H78, fol. 11). Pennsylvanians wanted to know what support the Six Nations could muster, but they were mainly interested in trade possibilities. Meanwhile, trouble was brewing both at home and abroad.

While the sachems were treating in Philadelphia, a war party of Onondagas and Oneidas took up the path south against the Catawbas. Neither the Iroquois nor the Catawbas had buried their enmity. Settlers had encroached on the path against the mountains, and the party ran into the Virginia militia. There were casualties on both sides. Word of "the late unhappy Skirmish in Virginia" reached Madame Montour's settlement on the Susquehanna in January 1743 when the prolonged "Dead Cry," "Que, Que, Que" (*ko:weh*), sounded over the river, as trader Thomas McKee explained to the Pennsylvania governor and council (PCR, 4: 630–33, in P. Wallace 1945: 145).

Governor Thomas sent Weiser to Shikellamy, the Oneida chief living at Shamokin, to notify the Six Nations, the Shawnees, and others in the alliance to hold steady until he could mediate with Governor Gooch of Virginia. Weiser found Shikellamy mourning a nephew lost in the engagement, condoled him properly, and reminded his Tuscarora and Delaware listeners of the treaty. Weiser took things in hand. He sent Shikellamy, another nephew, and the Tuscarora chief Saghsidowa to Onondaga to prepare the grand council for his own mission to smooth the way for a settlement of the issues with Maryland and Virginia at Lancaster.

When the advance party returned to Shamokin, Weiser was there to meet them. As the voice of the Six Nations, Saghsidowa delivered the stern message of the grand council. Shawnee and other warriors were to stay home. He thanked Onas (the governor of Pennsylvania) for mediating. The Six Nations would adhere to an ancient policy: not to avenge a first injury. They would first treat. If the offense was repeated, the Six Nations would rise and knock their enemies down (P. Wallace 1945: 153). The Virginians had struck the hatchet into the head of the Six Nations; they must first wash away the blood and bury the grievance.

Governor Gooch was ill-prepared to go to Albany to fulfill what Governor Thomas informed him was expected of him. He countered by requesting that Weiser go up to Onondaga as Virginia's ambassador to perform the necessary offices and arrange a time and place to settle the major land issues. Weiser was the only choice. As an adopted son, he had more influence on the grand council than any colonial governor. Weiser's third journey to Onondaga proved a diplomatic triumph, and the reports of negotiations yield rich ethnographic information.

□□◇□□

This time Weiser did not go alone. John Bartram, a Quaker farmer and botanist, and Lewis Evans, a surveyor and map maker, came up from Philadelphia on 5 July 1743 to make the journey, each with his own agenda of exploration. The three men represented the dawn of the Enlightenment in Philadelphia in the year the American Philosophical Society was founded. All three kept journals, of which Bartram's is the fullest, Weiser's excels on council procedure, and Evans's stresses geography (Bell 1973: 105–12; Weiser in PCR, 4: 660–69).[1]

They rode down into Shamokin on the eighth of July, and Bartram learned there not to despise good Indian food. They picked up Shikellamy and his son and set off again on the tenth, following Weiser's trail of 1737. It pains me to skip Evans's description of the mountains, his speculation on their probable origin, and their relation to the prevailing theory of the biblical deluge (P. Wallace 1945: 138). They passed two cultural landmarks in Iroquoian worldview—a mountain where a good hunter discovered corn, beans, squash, pumpkins, and tobacco, brought by Sky Woman, and the shallow lake near Tully where ducks flew up taking water to reveal shells that Deganawi:dah gathered and strung for condoling. Signs of maple tapping and fruit trees marked the margins of Onondaga cultivation as the travelers approached the central fire of the Longhouse on 21 August 1743.

Five miles out they paused, and Weiser sent a messenger to alert the firekeepers that he carried a message from Onas (Pennsylvania) on behalf of "Assaryquoa" (Virginia). The firekeepers that day dispatched runners to summon the council of the Six Nations. Weiser's messenger returned to tell him that they would lodge at the house of a named chief. This bit of protocol omitted only their hosts coming out to greet them at a fire kindled at the margin of the clearing. They simply rode into town. Children climbed to the rooftops to glimpse the famous bearded interpreter. Friends greeted them warmly, ushered them into the longhouse, which Bartram described, showed them where to stow their gear and where to sleep on fresh mats spread for them, and assigned their guides space across the fire. They feasted on eels boiled in hominy.

Several chiefs, including Canasatego, called on them and inquired about their kindred in Philadelphia, the governor and the proprietor. They smoked a pipe of Philadelphia tobacco and chatted.

---

1. Paul Wallace (1945: 154–70) combined all three accounts, and Whitfield Bell (1973) reprinted the three journals with an introduction.

Next morning early, Tocanontie (Tekanontie:), also known as "the Black Prince," a noted war leader, brought Caxhayion (Kakshayon) to express joy that the visitors had traveled so far over many obstacles just to bring the Six Nations a disagreeable message, a kind of Indian joke. Next came Canasatego bringing Caheshcarowno (Kaheskarowaneh[?]), the head chief at the time, and several others to spend the day hearing of their journey.

Small talk over, on the following day, the twenty-third, petitioners Weiser and Shikellamy called on Canasatego to request a "Meeting in the Bushes" to plan strategy, review Weiser's instructions, assign wampums to topics, and enlist Canasatego to speak for Virginia.

Following this private session, Canasatego went directly to Kaheskarowaneh's house, and a messenger soon summoned Weiser to meet the Onondaga chiefs in council there. Tekanontie: was speaker. The chiefs desired to hear the matter, which affected them directly, the speaker said, before it was put to the "Council of the United Nations," who would answer the message Weiser had brought from the Virginia governor. Apparently the Onondaga chiefs, as firekeepers, constituted a kind of screening committee for matters coming before the grand council of the confederacy. Weiser thanked them for their goodwill and withdrew.

Aware of the Virginia message, the Onondaga council sat a second day (the twenty-fourth) to summon and hear the leader, with two of his companions, of the unfortunate war party that had encountered the Virginia militia the previous winter. The war captain, Jonnhaty, told the story from beginning to end; Weiser afterward wrote it down for him to verify in the presence of some chiefs. Bartram thought it wise to gain warrior assent before the issue came before the council (Bell 1973: 62).

This same Jonnhaty put up a feast the following day, honoring Virginia (by Weiser) and Pennsylvania (by Shikellamy) over a cask of rum. Eighteen attended. Songs thanked the honorees, dispelled clouds, and restored the sun. Hearty Canasatego toasted Virginia, and Kaheskarowaneh toasted the Pennsylvania governor. A kettle circulated with a wooden spoon for each man to drink from between smokes. The customary cry of *yo-hee!* for each nation and delegate saluted the empty kettle. Guests dispersed.

Tribal delegations drifted in from the twenty-fourth to the thirtieth of August. First Cayugas, then a party of Nanticokes (Algonquian speakers), of whom none could speak a word of Iroquoian, although one knew some English. They got Weiser to interpret for them in council. Oneida and Tuscarora delegates came in on the twenty-seventh and twenty-eighth; the Onondaga headmen held a last private council on the twenty-ninth to agree on speakers, apportion wampums to items on the agenda, and designate goods for the mourning families. The Mohawks were last to arrive, on the thirtieth, the day the grand council met at noon. From the time the runners went out, it had taken about ten days to assemble a full council. The Senecas did not show.

Weiser and Bartram provide us with eyewitness accounts of the ritual marking the opening day of a league-confederacy council that regularly preceded consideration of national business (PPCM, 4: 663–64; Bell 1973: 73–75). We can now interpret these observations in the light of ethnological studies made during the last century and a half by Morgan, Hale, Hewitt, and succeeding Iroquoianists. Recall that Hale traced the *Book of Rites* to David of Schoharie at this very period. Moreover, 1743 is the year that the Moravian Pyrlaeus first noted the plot of the league epic, also from David of Schoharie (Heckewelder 1881: 56).

Although the following celebration embodied league ritual, I shall refer to it as a confederate council because none of the participants, so far as I can judge, held titles of the league founders. It would appear that the reigning Onondaga sachems invoked the league, although they were not of it; instead, they constituted the operating effectives of the confederacy.

The council met in the council house at noon and declared themselves complete. Ceremonies took up the first day. "First, the Onondagas rehearsed the beginning of the Union of the Five Nations ['Concerning the League']." They praised the wisdom of their grandfathers for forming the union, which made them formidable, and deprecated themselves ['Over the Forest'].

Second, as hosts, the Onondagas, by their speaker, Tekanontie:, with a string of wampum "rubbed down the bodies" of the visiting deputies, who had suffered hazards on the road and escaped "evil spirits in the woods." Chanting, the speaker paced the length of the house. The visiting delegates conferred and appointed one of their own to return thanks for their reception with a string.

Third, walking the length of the house, this same speaker praised the union and recited the names of its founders (the Eulogy to the Founders, or Roll Call of the Founders, performed by visiting moiety of chiefs).

The council was proclaimed open. It was announced that "Asarykowa" (Virginia) would speak next morning in the same house. Each nation cried *yoh-hee:* (Weiser in PCR, 4: 663). The chiefs emptied four great kettles of corn soup and then dispersed, each to his home (Bell 1973: 74).

On the second day, the thirty-first, the grand council met at late morning. A host speaker told Weiser that the delegates were ready to hear Onas and Asarykowa. (The host opens and lets the visitor speak first.) Weiser asked Canasatego to address the open council for Virginia, while he prompted him, article by article, as agreed. Canasatego, who knew the expected ritual, elicited approval. He greeted the united nations (the confederacy) by their council names: Tekarihoken, Mohawk, "our brother"; Nitarontakowa ("they of the great log"), Oneida, "our son"; Sononnawentona ("great pipe people"), Cayuga; and the Tuscaroras, "our younger sons." "And our absent Brother Ounghcarrydawy [Ganonhgidawi, S-7, RC 49] and Honinhohonta [Doninhogawen, S-8, RC 50]," the Seneca doorkeepers.[2]

Weiser held three broad belts and five strings of wampum to document his requests. He fed them to Canasatego, who passed them across the fire, where they were racked up on a pole laid across from one apartment to another over the passageway (Bell 1973: 75; PPCM, 4: 664–65).

Canasatego outlined the background of Weiser's mission bearing the message of Virginia to "Sagogssaanagechtheyky" (the place of the name bearers), or Onondaga. "Now you will hear our Brother Asarikowa himself who has been brought to our fire by Brother Onas." Thus the speaker assumed the voice of Virginia, as prompted by Pennsylvania. Weiser took up a belt of wampum and

2. I have reconstructed several of these names from Hale 1883: 78–79.

handed it to Canasatego, the speaker for Virginia. The proceedings then unfolded in the following steps:

1. Canasatego addressed the confederacy convened at the place of the name bearers. He referred to the skirmish in Virginia and awarded the belt to the mourning families at Onondaga to moderate their grief. The whole house responded.
2. Weiser handed another belt to the speaker and prompted him. This belt went to the mourning families at Oneida. The whole assembly responded.
3. A large belt dispelled the dark cloud attending the skirmish and restored the sun. Virginia did not dispute blame. He (as speaker for Virginia) had come here to fetch home the hatchet and bury it. "The solemn Cry . . . was repeated as many Times as there were Nations present."
4. Continuing with a string, Canasatego buried the incident underground and laid a heavy stone to hold it down forever.
5. Strings of wampum specifically dispelled the dark cloud and restored the sun. The usual response ensued.
6. Further strings served to remove "Bitterness of Spirit" and purge the confederacy of an overflow of gall, a serious distemper. Canasatego laid down four rows of wampum. There came the usual cry.
7. "This String serves to mend the Chain of Friendship." He again laid down four strings and got the usual response.
8. He issued the invitation to meet and treat. His old men had met and appropriated a present, he said, which they lodged in the hands of Onas. They would send commissioners next spring to discuss lands now in Virginia's possession that the Six Nations claimed. "Let the place and time be appointed for certain that we may not miss one another." He laid down the invitation string and requested a speedy answer.

For the terminal feast, women brought in kettles of hominy, of which the "divider" (head woman) placed the largest before the guest speaker for Virginia. Some sixty people partook. Bartram noted that the conference lasted until three o'clock in the afternoon, after which three great kettles of corn soup laced with dried eels and fish and garnished with young squashes fed the crowd. Then came a great bowl of Indian dumplings made of soft corn scraped from the cob, mixed with beans, and wrapped in corn leaves (Bell 1973: 75).

Having eaten, the sachems of each national delegation walked out as units, presumably to caucus. They soon returned and sat as a legislative body for some two hours, when, in an unusual move on the same day, their speaker announced that Virginia was to have an immediate answer. Now the house was packed with every man in town, many standing outside.

The speaker then asked Asarykowa to "give Ear" to the appointed speaker, Tekanontie:. In the great tradition of Iroquois orators, often from the warrior class, he delivered the grand council's reply in the following steps:

1. Referring to the "unhappy Skirmish" in Virginia, he said: "[A] Smoke arose from the bottomless Pitt, and a dark Cloud overshadowed us; the Chain of friendship was indangered & disappeared, and all was Confusion. We, the

Chiefs of the united Nations, took hold of the Chain with all our Strength. We were resolved not to let it slip before we received a deadly Blow. But to our great Satisfaction, in the Darkest Time, our Brother Onas entered our Door and offered his Mediation." Both sides were drunk with the overflow of gall, he said, and the blood that was shed corrupted their hearts. He praised the visitors' coming to condole the mourning families, thanked them, and laid down a belt to comfort the mourning families in Virginia. Weiser thanked him.

2. The speaker again thanked the visitors for healing the hearts of mourning families at Onondaga and Oneida and laid down a second belt for the same purpose in Virginia. The usual thanks.

3. Although the Virginians had initiated hostilities, Tekanontie: said, that was now of no consequence as compared with the enmity among the Catawbas. The old men of Onondaga disapproved of the action and thanked Virginia for removing the hatchet and burying it under a heavy stone. "Let this Belt . . . remove our Hatchet from You, and not only bury it, but we will fling it into the bottomless Pitt, into the Ocean, that there shall be no more Use of it." The usual approbation.

4. Addressing Virginia: "Let this String of Wampum heal the very mark of the Wounds" to remove from sight and sound any mention from this day, either in public or private. He laid down four strings, which elicited the usual cry.

5. A string to dispel the dark cloud and restore the sun. "Let us look upon one another with Pleasure and Joy." Again the cry.

6. Tekanontie: thanked Virginia for purging them of gall, but remarked that the Europeans labored under the same distemper, "in particular your back Inhabitants. . . . Let this string purge your People. . . . We thank you for good advice." Four rows of wampum elicited the usual cry.

7. Four more rows of wampum thanking Virginia for mending the chain brought the usual response.

8. Finally, a string acknowledged the invitation to treat at a place called Canada-gueany (Lancaster) in Pennsylvania next spring. The Indians looked forward to the meeting with pleasure. "We will set out from our Towns after eight Moons are past by, when the ninth just is to be seen, this present Moon, which is almost expired, [is] not to be reckoned." They would leave on the ninth new moon counting from the next lunar cycle.

After the customary cry of approbation, Tekanontie: announced that they had no more to say. But they would not permit Weiser to depart, desiring his presence until the Senecas, still on the road, brought in some Cherokee peace emissaries. They also needed him to interpret for the Nanticokes the following day. A second meal of boiled bread, six or seven inches in diameter and two inches thick, terminated the second session.

The grand council met in its third session on 1 September to hear the Nanti-cokes go through the condolence paradigm in English with three belts and five strings; Weiser interpreted it into Mohawk. They entreated the Six Nations to protect their women from insults while afield hunting. Bartram says this went on for four hours (Bell 1973: 76–77). Evidently some friction had developed as the Nanticokes moved up through Pennsylvania.

The council of the united nations held a final meeting on the second. They asked Weiser to write down for Onas's eyes their view of the Catawba war. They predicted it would go on to the end of the world. There was no trust on either side. With a string they asked the governor to notify the back inhabitants to behave in a friendly manner to Iroquois war parties. They had moved the road presumably beyond former settlements, but the mountains prevented moving it further. Settlers had sat down on the new road.

In a final act, the Onondaga speaker gave two strings to put out the council fire on both sides. In Weiser's words: "After all was over, according to the Ancient Custom of that Fire, a Song of Friendship and Joy was sung by the Chiefs, after this the council fire on their side was put out. I with the same Ceremony put out the Fire on behalf of Assaryqoa & Onas" (PPCM, 4: 668; Bell 1973: 131). Was this song a predecessor of the Six Songs of the Condolence Council?

The hosts provided provisions for the road, and the three ambassadors rode out.

□□◇□□

The year 1743 saw the end of a long era of peace and the struggle of the Six Nations to maintain their policy of neutrality in European squabbles. King George's War in America (1744–48) adhered to the same pattern as Queen Anne's War (1701–13). New York merchants wanted no active role. The contraband trade with Montreal that involved the Albany Indian commissioners was too profitable. Their Iroquois friends manifested no interest in carrying the hatchet to Canada. The Pennsylvania merchants, good Quakers, opposed any war and looked to their profits. Only New Englanders saw the opportunity to seize Louisbourg from the French (Eccles 1969: 150).

Weiser's visit to Onondaga set New York's commissioners of Indian affairs' teeth on edge, and the governor was equally concerned lest the initiative in Indian affairs pass to Pennsylvania. Word had reached the commissioners of the skirmish in Virginia and of Pennsylvania's intervention with Virginia and Maryland. They sent their interpreter up to Onondaga, once to reprimand the Iroquois for the "murders" in Virginia (only to hear that the Virginians had been the aggressors), and a second time to learn what Weiser was up to. The Mohawks shared their concern and told the interpreter that properly the commissioners should condole the Six Nations for their losses in Virginia as their mutual treaty required (PAC IR RG 10, 1820: 242).

New York governor George Clinton got around to renewing the covenant chain with the Six Nations at Albany in June of the following year, just before their delegation reached Lancaster. I find no list of delegates who met the governor but surmise that distinct personnel were involved. Governor Clinton told the delegates about the war in Europe. He asked the Six Nations to intervene both "offensively and defensively" vis-à-vis the French, but they chose only the latter option and absolutely refused to expel French residents from Iroquoia. Once more it became obvious that the sachems could not control their warriors (Jennings et al. 1985a: 180–81; PAC IR RG 10, 10: 251 and passim; NYCD, 6: 262–66).

Although Weiser had cleared the road to Lancaster, the Maryland commissioners distrusted him because he was Pennsylvania's interpreter, and they worked on the Virginia commissioners to prejudice them against him. A running boundary dispute between Maryland and Pennsylvania complicated the issue. The Marylanders suggested Annapolis as the meeting place, but Weiser advised that the council site depended on where and when the Indians could peel bark for wigwams (HSP, Peters Papers, 2: 5). The time and place of the meeting bothered the Virginians, too. In late May 1744, Weiser became ill, and Richard Peters, the Pennsylvania secretary, worried that the interpreter might not be able to attend the treaty. Neither the two Virginia commissioners nor "the seven flaming fine gentlemen" in their entourage knew the Indian business at first hand. The shared ignorance of the two southern delegations to the treaty probably accounts for Maryland's appointing Witham Marshe, a Maryland legislative secretary, to record the proceedings in detail. His journal, one of the finest records of an Indian treaty, contains pen pictures of the participants and sketches of the doings (Boyd 1938: xxxvi–vii; Marshe 1800: 171–201). William Black served in a similar capacity for the Virginia delegation, but his journal (Black 1877), although covering the preliminaries, leaves off just where Marshe's begins.

The Lancaster treaty with the Six Nations proved to be a pivotal event in the history of the colonies. It opened on 22 June 1744 on a note of mutual suspicion and closed 4 July in friendship and mutual respect. The Iroquois controlled the agenda, and native protocol prevailed. Canasatego gave a virtuoso performance of council rhetoric, replete with metaphorical flourishes, but unwittingly he and his colleagues signed a deed to lands beyond the mountains that their ancestors had acquired by conquest. This cession opened the way for Virginia's expansion into the Ohio country, which became a bone of contention between Indians and whites for the remainder of the century. The treaty proceedings proved a learning experience for the commissioners of Virginia and Maryland. They came disposed to treat the Iroquois as savages but soon learned that racial superiority would not work. They went home fascinated by native diplomacy, and at least one Virginian sought to learn more of native customs and usages.

The Lancaster treaty conformed to a pattern of sequence that governed other such negotiations. Traditional council-fire protocol governed the proceedings: the formal invitation, the time appointed, the delegates selected, their travel and approach, their reception at the landing, their conduct to the treaty site, and the procession into town. Ritual hedged the entire event. After the preliminary welcome, the visitors withdrew and camped apart by nation, establishing a temporary village, a replica of Onondaga, where they could council apart. Preliminaries settled who would speak first, and the Iroquois requested two days to rest. Parties to a treaty had to have Indian names and be properly condoled and charged. A treaty involved a formal agreement. The hosts hung the kettle for a concluding feast. Valedictory speeches sealed mutual amity. A climactic dance united the participants.[3]

Canasatego, then the dominant figure at Onondaga, set out for Lancaster in mid-May, intending to hear the response to the ultimatum he had issued at Philadelphia two years earlier. Would the colonies treat with the Six Nations over Indian land claims in what had become Maryland, or would they fight? The Iroquois invariably sought first to treat.

---

3. For the complete paradigm, see chapter 12 and Fenton 1957: 23; 1985: 28–30.

The Onondaga council had sent messengers to the several towns of the Six Nations instructing the delegates to set out on 18 May. They and their families each assembled at the nearest headwater branch of the Susquehanna to make bark canoes. (Mid-May to mid-June is when elm bark peels readily.) As Weiser wrote to Peters, the Oneidas finished their canoes first and floated down to Otzininky (Chenango), near the Tioughnioga, a branch that comes down from Onondaga through modern Cortland, presuming that the Onondagas were making their canoes at its head. Not finding them, the Oneida party kept on to the mouth of Pine Creek, a great branch of the Susquehanna that comes down from the Cayuga and Seneca country. Not hearing of those parties either, the Tuscarora deputies, who had accompanied the Oneidas, waited while six Oneida men went ahead to Shikellamy's at Shamokin, reaching there on 30 May. The Oneida regent assured Weiser that the several delegations had set out at the appointed time. He was confident they would all arrive shortly; the Onondaga council had promised to send him an account by special messengers, whom he was awaiting. Shikellamy was happy that the commissioners had arrived in Philadelphia, but until he heard from the second messenger, "nobody needs to stirr." Of such were the uncertainties of assembling a body of Six Nations delegates (Boyd 1938: xxxvii; Weiser to Peters, 2 June 1744, in Black 1877: 414–15).

Miserable conditions in the colonies that spring contributed to the anxiety of the commissioners waiting in Philadelphia. Besides boundary disputes, the displaced Shawnees and Delawares threatened to defect to the French. Securing the Six Nations became crucial. Richard Peters advised Weiser to importune the speaker of the Pennsylvania legislature and to convince Governor Thomas to attend the treaty and guide the southern commissioners in the proper conduct of an Indian treaty, because they were ignorant of Indian ways, were condescending, and were demanding that Weiser be replaced as interpreter. Without him, Thomas wrote to Governor Gooch of Virginia, "neither your Government nor that of Maryland will be able to carry on the Treaty" (P. Wallace 1945: 184).

It was mid-June before word reached Weiser that the Onondaga, Cayuga, and Seneca delegations were at last approaching Shamokin, the hub of the Pennsylvania Indian universe. Weiser at once went up to take them by the arm and bring them down to Lancaster. A horseman rode out to notify the commissioners to hasten to the treaty site without delay. They reached Lancaster in time to see the Iroquois enter town. Witham Marshe (1800: 178–79) witnessed the procession:

> During our dinner, the deputies of the Six Nations, with their followers and attendants, to the number of 252, arrived in town.[4] Several of their . . . wives, with some small children, rode on horseback, which is very unusual for them. They brought their fire-arms and bows and arrows, as well as tomahawks. A great concourse of people followed them. They marched in very good order, with *Cannasateego* . . . at their head; . . . when he came near to the court-house . . . [he sang], in the Indian language, a song inviting us to the renewal of all treaties heretofore made and that [are] now to be made.

4. Paul Wallace (1945: 186) gives the number as 245, whom Weiser met.

The composition of the procession and the mode of singing conforms to the pattern of chanting the eulogy on the path to the Condolence Council.

Weiser "conducted them to some vacant lots in the back part of town, where sundry poles and boards were placed. Of these, and some boughs of trees from the nearby woods, the Indians made *wigwams* . . . wherein they resided during the treaty. They will not, on any occasion whatsoever, dwell, or even stay, in houses built by white people" (Marshe 1800: 179).

The visiting party, in staying apart during the treaty, maintained its separate identity. Separation into moieties, approach, and withdrawal are principles operating in treaty proceedings as well as in the Condolence Council. The Indian camp replicated the seating arrangement of the grand council. Marshe (1800: 179) understood this: "They placed their cabins according to the rank each nation . . . holds in their grand council. The *Onondaga* nation was placed on the right hand and upper end; then the others according to their several dignities." They lacked only the Mohawks.

A list of named Indians present at the treaty enumerates 20 Onondagas, 26 Cayugas, 12 Oneidas, 4 Senecas, and 16 Tuscaroras, making 78 of the Six Nations. Besides, 13 Conestogas were Oneida speakers. There were also 9 Shawnees, 10 Nanticokes, 8 Conoys, and 9 Saponi residents of Shamokin, who made a grand total of 127 men. The Six Nations chiefs forbade the Delawares from attending the treaty. I fail to identify a single name in the peculiar orthography as that of a league title (Pennsylvania Historical and Museum Commission, Harrisburg, Exec. Corres., RG 21).

Canasatego and Tekanontie: carried the burden of speaking for the Six Nations. Later on, the council by lot assigned to the Cayugas the right of conferring an Iroquois name on the governor of Maryland. They appointed Gachradodon (Ka?hrado:don, "Standing Sun," or "Standing Moon"[?]) to charge him with his duties (Boyd 1938: 65–66).

Marshe described Canasatego. He was "a tall, well-made man; had a very full chest, and brawny limbs . . . a manly countenance, mixed with a good natured smile." Marshe supposed him to be sixty years old, "very active, strong, and had a surprising liveliness in his speech." The second speaker, Tekanontie:, a renowned war chief, was a tall, thin man, of part African ancestry, his chest tattooed with gunpowder designs. He, too, had represented his nation at conferences. He was a particular favorite of the then governor of Canada, who favored his presence in Onondaga delegations.

Weiser cautioned southerners visiting the Indian encampment not to discuss the Indians, not to laugh at their dress or appearance, and not to remark on their behavior, for some of them understood English, although they would not speak it while engaged in a treaty. Such conduct would provoke resentment.

Among the English principals, the Pennsylvania governor, George Thomas, presided. Thomas Lee and William Beverly were the Virginia commissioners, and Edmund Jennings and three others served Maryland.

On 22 June 1744, Governor Thomas, acting as host, performed the official welcome that Indian protocol prescribed. Following a round of handshaking, the Iroquois delegates seated themselves in council order on the steps flanking the bench where the hosts arranged themselves. Through the interpreter, the governor said he was glad to see them, that they would do no business that day, and that they might rest from their journey for two days, as was customary, before he opened the treaty council on Monday. Canasatego thanked him. After smoking, they washed away the taste of tobacco with a round of punch and wine, and the Indians withdrew to their shelters.

The right to speak first belonged properly to Maryland, which had called the conference, but it was left to Pennsylvania to open, and the host commissioners would follow (Marshe 1800: 181; Boyd 1938: 43–44; P. Wallace 1945: 188–89). The Virginians insisted that because theirs was the oldest colony, precedence belonged to them. But, as Wallace (1945: 190) indicated, it was an Iroquois conference, and Iroquois protocol demanded that "the party who had called a conference should lead off with a statement of its purpose." When Colonel Lee sought to assert English notions of propriety and tried to bribe Weiser to influence the Indians to grant Virginia preference, he learned that "it was nothing to them who was the oldest Colony." It was Maryland's invitation string that had brought them to Lancaster, and therefore Maryland should speak first. If Brother Onas wished to reorder the ceremony, that was up to him. They would never so insult their host as to object to his wishes (Peters to Penn in Wallace 1945: 190).

The Iroquois did not stir from their camp for two days. Marshe, who visited the encampment on Saturday night, noted that it was usual for them to rest two days after traveling and before treating with the English. But the young men grew restless, and he found them engaged in a stomp dance, which I readily recognize from his description as *ga?da:syo:t*, "Standing Quiver" (Marshe 1800: 181–82).

Governor Thomas had some work of his own to do. The southern commissioners had come prepared to take a high tone with the "savages." The Virginians thought they could frighten the Indians out of their claims. Thomas thought it necessary to warn Jennings, Lee, and the others that provoking a war with the Six Nations would prove a serious blunder, and even if the English defeated them it would be a disaster to the English interest in America, for it would remove the only effective barrier against the French (P. Wallace 1945: 189).

The treaty got down to business on Monday, 25 June, after noon. The hosts resumed their seats and the Indians entered and sat as before. In his opening speech, Governor Thomas referred to the request that the Six Nations had made at the 1742 treaty that he write to the governor of Maryland regarding lands at the back of that province, which the Six Nations claimed by conquest but which had since been trespassed upon by settlers. The request also involved lands in Virginia. Determining title to these lands constituted the main issue of the treaty. The unfortunate skirmish at the back of Virginia compounded the crisis. Virginia had paid one hundred pounds in reparations to bury the matter, and additional goods lay by, ready for distribution. The English regarded peace and friendship with the Six Nations as essential for both parties. But they were bothered that the confederacy's policy of neutrality allowed free passage of French agents through Iroquoia. They wanted the confederacy tied to the British interest exclusively. Clearly, an accommodation would prove cheaper than a war.

It appears that Pennsylvania and Virginia had worked out this opening statement in advance, although Virginia was not about to yield its claims (Boyd 1938: 44–45).

Then, continuing for Virginia and Maryland, Thomas appealed to appropriate symbols: they were here to enlarge the fire, which was almost out, and brighten the chain, which had become rusty, that their friendship might endure like the sun, moon, and stars. He advised the Indians to receive the two southern colonies into the chain as one body and soul with them. Then he warned them of the intrigues of Canada. He paused and laid down a belt, which elicited the response, *yo-hah!*

The cry of approbation intrigued Marshe (1800: 185), who wrote: "This cry is usually made on presenting wampum . . . in a treaty, and it is performed thus: The grand chief and speaker . . . pronounces the word *jo-hah!* with a loud voice, singly; then all the others join in this sound, *wugh!* This is performed in great order, and with the utmost ceremony and decorum; and with the Indians is like our English huzza!" The literature contains no better description of cries heard in the modern condolence ceremony: *yoh-henh*, and the antiphonal *wa? wa:?*, or *hi:yenh*.

Canasatego, replying for the Six Nations, recapitulated the governor's speech in the usual Iroquois way, returned thanks for the advice, and promised to heed it where possible. But it was the custom, he said, that a belt given called for one in return, which would take until afternoon to provide, when he would answer them (Boyd 1938: 46). (This was women's work.)

That afternoon, Canasatego, with belt in hand, replied to the governor's speech on behalf of Asarykowa (Virginia) and the nameless governor of Maryland, whom the Iroquois had always regarded as brothers. But they deferred brightening the chain until pending disputes over lands formerly belonging to the Iroquois and now possessed by the colonies were adjusted. Again he cited the Iroquois custom of first removing any obstacle and then proceeding to friendship. (This passage was partly underlined in the copy printed [Boyd 1938: 47].)

This time the interpreter gave the *yo-hah!* for the governor.

Governor Thomas acknowledged the belt. He mentioned that the one hundred pounds sterling which the governor of Virginia had paid as reparation, fulfilling Weiser's statement at Onondaga, awaited the Indians. He then awarded the chair to the two host governments and volunteered to withdraw.

It was now Maryland's right to speak first and welcome the Six Nations with a string of wampum, which elicited the usual response. The Marylanders, too, had decided that it was wiser to treat than fight. Their speaker presented a belt to brighten the chain. He then appealed to precedent: an earlier treaty made with the Susquehannocks (1654?), a treaty between the Five Nations and Maryland in 1674, and a Five Nations' deed to the crown in 1684. He appealed to the symbols of continuity with a second belt and received a response.

Presently, Canasatego acknowledged having heard what was said of the "olden times" but replied that the Six Nations could not answer now; they would consider Maryland's speech and answer tomorrow. Meanwhile, they would like to have their guns and hatchets mended, as was customary at treaties. It was so ordered (Boyd 1938: 48–49).

The following day (26 June), Canasatego returned string for string and belt for belt and delivered an elaborate lecture on the metamorphosis of the chain. "What is one Hundred Years in Comparison of the Length of Time since our Chain began?" He traced the cultural history of his people from their emergence as stone-age hunters in precontact times to the Dutch introduction of metal tools. He described the chain as the Dutch ship's hawser fastened to bushes, then to a tree, then extended to the rock at Oneida, and finally made fast to the mountain at Onondaga. "We . . . rolled Wampum about it; and, to make it still more secure, we stood upon the Wampum, and sat down upon it, to defend it, and to prevent any Hurt coming to it."

He traced the English succession and the renewal of old treaties. A silver chain replaced the rope. The English supplied Stroud's, knives, hatchets, and guns, which replaced buckskin, stone tools, and bows and arrows. They were now in straitened circumstances, deer were scarce, and they were done in "particularly from that Pen-and-Ink Work that is going on at the Table." He told how the Six Nations gave their Susquehanna lands to the governor of New York to hold in trust, but how he went to England and sold them to Penn. Fortunately, they had been repaid for them.[5]

He came to the point. "We now come nearer home. We have had your Deeds interpreted to us, and we acknowledge them to be good and valid . . . that the *Conestogoe* or *Sasquahannah Indians* had a right to sell those Lands . . . for they were theirs." He then claimed that the Five Nations had conquered the Conestogas after they had deeded lands to Maryland. But the lands they were now claiming were the Potomac lands in dispute, which Maryland had not possessed for a hundred years, let alone ten, but had since settled and divided between the two colonies (Maryland and Virginia), and for which the Six Nations expected compensation (Boyd 1938: 51-53; P. Wallace 1945: 191-92).

It was Virginia's turn to speak on the morning of 27 June. After the welcome, a string, and approbation, the commissioner advanced Virginia's claim to title, asserting that the Six Nations had relinquished their lands to the crown, which had possessed Virginia for 160 years. The governor of Virginia had asked the governor of New York to lay this matter before the council at Onondaga. Two years earlier, the Six Nations in Philadelphia had claimed lands only in Maryland. What nations of Indians had conquered lands in Virginia? A string. Approbation.

He then adverted to a chest of goods, an incentive for brightening the chain.

"Tachanoontia" (presumably Tekanontie:) answered "Brother Assaragoa" that the Indians would reply that afternoon. The treaty reconvened at five o'clock to hear the Black Prince reply to Colonel Lee (Marshe 1800: 187). He presented one string and two belts. After recapitulating the Virginia speech, he asserted the right of conquest, "which cost us too much Blood" to relinquish out of hand. The chiefs wanted to see the letter and signatures relinquishing land last year, and wanted to know who was the interpreter. "Some of our Council would easily remember it." They denied giving up any such right.

He went on to name the ethnic entities conquered or displaced: Conoy, Kanawa, Tutelo, and "House-corner people," while noting that Virginia had never conquered any groups beyond the mountains. A string. Approbation. He acknowledged the chest of presents with a belt.

He next specified the mountains that were validated by a Virginia belt given in Albany in 1722, which symbolized a fence on the Blue Ridge that marked limits

_____

5. Canasatego's traditional history is printed in Jennings 1984: 357-59, as well as in the treaty minutes, as cited.

to settlement and removed the warrior path west of it. A belt elicited the usual ceremony.

Governor Thomas resumed the chair next morning (the twenty-eighth) to bring up the sad matter of trader John Armstrong's murder by three Delaware Indians, which had nearly wrecked the treaty. So as not to impede the business of the treaty, the Six Nations might take their time to answer, which they promised to do.

That afternoon, Maryland offered goods in the amount of three hundred pounds for lands in that province that the Six Nations could define. The chiefs were not entirely satisfied, but after counseling apart, agreed to give up lands already settled.

And Virginia acknowledged the road that warriors should follow as it was defined in Governor Alexander Spotswood's 1722 treaty at Albany, a treaty that made the Five Nations responsible for preventing four other nations besides themselves from crossing that line into Virginia. They had thought to avoid this issue by settling the Catawba war, which would erase the need to cross the line. That night the young people staged a mock war dance (Marshe 1800: 189; Boyd 1938: 58–62).

Canasatego, having traced the lines of some rivers on a deal board, replied to the Maryland commissioners. The chiefs were willing to renounce the right to lands two miles above the upper fork of the Potomac, near Cresap's post, with a proposed alternate, so as to comprise all settlers. A belt. Marshe describes the debate, which was eased by "bumbo punch" (Marshe 1800: 191; Boyd 1938: 62–63).

□□◇□□

In a shift of speakers, Gachradodon opened the morning session on the thirtieth with a strong voice and suitable action. He spoke first of cultural and racial differences between the parties, in the manner of later cultural relativists. He asserted that his people remembered great things, but they had no cultural memory of ever being conquered by the king. They did remember being employed by Maryland to conquer the Conestogas and, in a second campaign, taking them captives. As for peace with the Catawbas, it could be accomplished only in a face-to-face meeting. But the Catawbas never came. They refused an invitation by letter. The Iroquois had confirmed a peace with the Cherokee nation. As to the way south, a wagon road, it was reasonable between friends to expect victuals when hungry. Finally, they wanted the chest of goods opened for inspection. But the commissioners were holding out until Monday (Boyd 1938: 63–64).

In Iroquois polity, every participant must have a proper name. Weiser advised the commissioners after dinner on the thirtieth that up until then, the governor of Maryland was a nonperson, which the chiefs proposed to remedy. Marshe caught the moment:

> That as the Lord Proprietary . . . was not known to the Indians by any particular name, they had agreed in council, to take the first opportunity of a large company to present him with one: And, as this with them was a matter of great consequence, and attended with abundance of form, the several nations had drawn lots for the performance of the ceremony; and the lot falling on the Cayuga nation, they had chosen Gachradodon, one of their chiefs, to be their speaker, and he desired leave to begin.

Permission granted, he spoke from "an elevated part of the court house, with all the dignity of a warrior, the gesture of an orator, and in a very graceful posture"

(Marshe 1800: 194). "This Gachradodon is a very celebrated warrior, and one of the Cayuga chiefs, about forty years of age, tall, straight-limbed, and a graceful person, but not so fat as Cannasatego. His action, when he spoke, was certainly the most graceful, as well as bold, that any person ever saw. . . . [It was later said of him] 'that he would have made a good figure in the forum of old Rome' " (Marshe 1800: 200).

Gachradodon proceeded to deliver a typical charge to a new chief:

As the Governor of Maryland has invited us here, to treat about our lands, the united Six Nations think themselves so much obliged to him, that we have come to a resolution, in council, to give the great man . . . a particular name, by which we may hereafter correspond with him. And it has fallen to the Cayuga's lot in council to consider of a proper name for that chief man. We have agreed to give him the name of *Tocaryhogon* [Tekarihoken, M-1], denoting Precedency, Excellency, or "living in the middle," or honorable place, betwixt *Assaragoa*, and our Brother *Onas*, by whom our treaties may be the better carried on.

And then, turning to these gentlemen, he added:

As there is a company of great men now assembled, we take this opportunity to publish the matter, that it may be known that *Tocarryhogon* is our friend, and that we are ready to honour him, and that by such name he may be always called and known among us; and, we hope, he will ever act toward us, according to the excellence of the name we have now given him, and enjoy a long and happy life. (Marshe 1800: 194; Boyd 1938: 65)

The chiefs responded with five individual cries of approval; the English gave three huzzahs. It is ironic that no Mohawks were present, yet the name selected was the title of the leading Mohawk and first founder of the league.

After a round of toasts, the commissioners had Weiser announce that the deed releasing Six Nations' claim to lands in Maryland was ready for signatures. Canasatego promptly made his mark, followed by thirteen others. The rest marked the deed two days later, as printed in Marshe (1800: 196–97). The Maryland copy of the deed bears their marks, often as graphic representations of clan eponyms— Bear, Deer, Turtle, Beaver—or the bow and arrow of warriors following their personal names. The interpreter signed both as Conrad Weiser and as "Tarrugh-hiawaggon" (Sky Holder) in bold script (Maryland Historical Society, Calvert Papers, mss. 174, no. 400). The chiefs present relinquished western Maryland, including all settlements, for three hundred pounds' worth of goods. Virginia laid out two hundred pounds in Pennsylvania currency, added two hundred pounds in gold, and defined the road, by which, as Jennings points out (1984: 360ff.), they got a bigger bargain—access to lands in the Ohio country. The Indians just then were more concerned with getting rum to drink and going home. This pretty much wound up the treaty, except for some details (Boyd 1938: 69–70; VSL, Colonial Papers, Folder 41, Item 10).

That same morning (2 July), Canasatego condoled Governor Thomas for the murders of Indian trader John Armstrong and his two men. The alleged murderers were Delawares under Six Nations' jurisdiction. He gave a string to clear the path once more. He referred to three Indians killed on the Ohio at different times, of which they had not complained. Don't be too concerned, he told the commissioners. "To take the Grief from your Heart, we give" a second string. On the way down, they had learned of the Armstrong murders, conferred with the Delawares, "Our Cousins," and charged them to make satisfaction. On their return, they would demand that the Delawares send down some chiefs with two men for examination by Onas. A third string. Finally, some Conoys, having removed to Shamokin, wanted payment for their land. A fourth string (Boyd 1938: 66–67). The governor promised a fair trial (Boyd 1938: 68).

On the morning of 3 July, Governor Thomas recapitulated the proceedings. He referred to the 1742 treaty, which had widened the road, enlarged the fire, and strengthened friendship by an exchange of presents. They had now joined with them two southern colonies. In a mutual exchange of information, he reported British victories on land and sea. Now it seemed appropriate to renew the covenant with William Penn, whom he embodied. A belt; *yo-hah*.

This prefaced a plea for the Six Nations to keep the French at bay. Emphasis required a second belt; *yo-hah*.

Having satisfied Pennsylvania's concerns, after a pause Thomas turned to Virginia's desire to adjust the Iroquois-Catawba war. The Virginia commissioners seconded this proposal by delivering the goods and gold and proposing that the Iroquois send three or four children to Virginia to learn the language, customs, and religion of the white people. They promised to accord them the same care as their own children. A string. Response.

Maryland, not to be outdone, offered one hundred pounds in gold to adjust any misunderstanding and build links in the chain. A belt. Response.

Canasatego, addressing the three entities by their Iroquois names, acknowledged these matters of moment, which the chiefs would give due consideration, and notify them when ready. They would meet in council next morning. He added, "You tell us you beat the French; if so, you must have taken a great deal of Rum from them, and can better spare us some . . . to rejoice in your Victory." The governor ordered a dram of rum to be served in "French Glasses" (Boyd 1938: 70–73).

The final day of the treaty, appropriately 4 July, belonged to Canasatego, who tied up the bundle of remaining matters with wit and delivered his famous valedictory on civil government to the colonies. Throughout the proceedings the Six Nations had controlled the agenda set by their hosts, intriguing the curiosity of one Virginian who would later correspond with Weiser. We shall hear more of this in a later chapter.

Canasatego's first string thanked the Six Nations' hosts for holding the meeting and clearing the road between the parties. With a belt, he acknowledged to Onas news of the war in Europe, which enhanced the importance of renewing the covenant between them.

A second belt addressed the need for mutual assistance in facing the French threat in America. He appealed to the metaphors of unity—one heart, head, eye, ear, and hand. They would forbid the French to pass through Iroquoia to hurt their brethren, the English. Presently, he "mended" his speech to add that they would use their authority over nations formerly allied to the French, particularly the émigré Iroquois at the gates of Montreal, to keep them neutral. Governor Thomas thanked him for mending his speech.

Turning to Virginia, Canasatego agreed that the Six Nations were glad the dispute over lands was ended, although the deed took away more than he had realized. His belt confirming the chain between them appealed to metaphors of continuity. As for the Catawbas, "your brethren," they were a contemptuous lot. He gave a string to bring them northward for a settlement on reasonable terms.

In responding to the Virginia offer to educate some Indian youths, Canasatego demonstrated remarkable insight into the enculturation process. "We must let you know we love our Children too well to send them so great a Way, and the Indians are not inclined to give their Children Learning. We allow it to be good, and we thank you for your Invitation; but our Customs differing from yours, you will be so good as to excuse us."

He went on to praise Weiser and express hope that he would be "preserved by the good Spirit" to a ripe old age. When he was gone, it would be time to look for another interpreter. "While he lives there is no Room to complain." This subtle reminder recalled Virginia's earlier insistence that Weiser be replaced. A string returned the invitation.

By brightening the chain of friendship, Canasatego said, the Iroquois, too, were inclined to renew previous treaties. He reminded the Virginians that the chain required continuous attention to prevent rust. A belt in confirmation. The usual response.

And now to some lesser concerns. He gave a string to reopen the road to the Tuscaroras that mischievous warriors had caused the Virginians to stop. He asked that messengers might go the old road. Response.

Several families of Conoys living among the Tuscaroras wanted leave to pass through Virginia to join the rest of their nation among the Six Nations. A string.

Reciprocity is a cardinal principle in Iroquois society. They had received handsome presents; they must make a return. "We should return you something suitable to your Generosity; but, alas, we are Poor." The traders' and settlers' "Cattle have eaten up all the Grass, and made Deer scarce." As a token present, Canasatego gave three bundles of skins to be divided equally among the hosts (Boyd 1938: 76-77).

His now famous valedictory on confederation would compensate for the want of material wealth:

> We have one Thing further to say, and that is, We heartily recommend Union and a good Agreement between you our Brethren. Never disagree, but preserve a strict Friendship for one another, and thereby you, as well as we, will become the stronger.
>
> Our wise Forefathers established Union and Amity between the *Five Nations*; this has made us formidable; this has given us great Weight and Authority with our neighbouring Nations.
>
> We are a powerfull Confederacy; and, by observing the same Methods our wise Forefathers have taken, you will acquire fresh Strength and Power; therefore whatever befals you, never fall out one with another. (Boyd 1938: 78)

This advice, given at a time when the Iroquois Confederacy was eroding at the margins, awakened some inquiring minds in the colonies and provoked some amusement among the English intelligentsia. It suggested the germ of confederation without the structure for accomplishing it.

Ending the treaty on this euphoric note, Canasatego, caught up in his own rhetoric, proposed a toast of rum, this time from English glasses rather than the previous, smaller, French glasses. He thought that the hosts could afford this switch, considering the booty reported taken from the French. The request granted, the Iroquois, in order of precedence in the confederacy, gave five *yo-hehs*.[6] They drank the health of the English king, and three loud huzzahs by the whole company put an end to the treaty.

One final bit of protocol that evening marked the tenor of forest diplomacy throughout the treaty. Governor Thomas, in taking leave of the Indians, returned a string of wampum for one he had received from them; it had requested the governor of Virginia to suffer their warriors to pass through Virginia unmolested, which the present treaty had rendered unnecessary.

---

6. The absentee Mohawks should have been first; the fifth cry must have been that of the Tuscaroras.

CHAPTER 28

New Treaties,
Precarious Balance

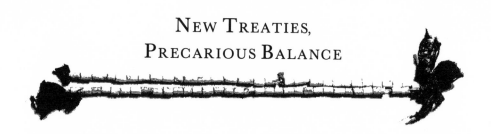

Richard Peters worked over the rough manuscript minutes of the Lancaster treaty before Benjamin Franklin edited and printed it in Philadelphia in 1744 (fig. 32; DePuy 1917: 22; Boyd 1938: 41–79).[1] Peters came away from his reading thinking that Canasatego had outshone the commissioners, and he wrote to Thomas Penn: "I make no doubt that the Indian treaty will give everyone pleasure that reads it and the Indians really appear superior to the Commissioners in point of sense and argument, it will raise people's opinions of the wisdom of the Six Nations and give the government at home higher notions of their consequence than they could have before" (Boyd 1938: xl). Franklin evidently agreed.

Of the fifty small books containing the transactions of some forty-five treaty conferences that appeared in the century prior to the American Revolution (Wroth 1928: 749–66), Franklin printed thirteen in stately folios. Printers in the colonies undertook these publications at private risk to satisfy a general concern with Indian affairs, and several were reprinted in London. Franklin, with his keen eye for excellence, sensed in the ritual and rhetoric of the Six Nations participants a certain literary appeal that prompted him to run off three hundred separates of the Lancaster treaty of 1744, which he shipped to William Strahan in London, hoping that "the method of doing business with those barbarians" might amuse him (Van Doren 1938b: vii). Here was a new form of literature that was native American, as straightforward as a play, replete with homegrown metaphors, and possessed of a certain style that found immediate appeal.

William Parks, a discriminating printer of Williamsburg, Virginia, reprinted the Lancaster treaty, prefacing it with an explanatory account of the Six Nations confederacy and the protocol of their conferences, which he had from Colonel Thomas Lee, a Virginia commissioner at the treaty (DePuy 1917: 23). Colonel Lee's source was Conrad Weiser, for whom he developed an admiration and with whom he corresponded after the event. Parks's second source was Cadwallader Colden, who had written an account of the conference that Franklin also printed in Philadelphia in 1744 (Winsor 1884–99, 5: 566). The Williamsburg preface reappeared in the *American Magazine* of London (December 1744: 665–69). The

---

1. Boyd (1938) says the Franklin editions are generally more satisfactory than those printed in the *Pennsylvania Colonial Records*, which were taken likewise from the official fair copy (PCR, 4: 698–737).

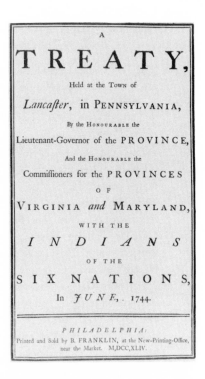

Figure 32. Title page of the Lancaster treaty of 1744, printed by Benjamin Franklin. Reproduced from Boyd 1938, courtesy Historical Society of Pennsylvania.

treaty next surfaced in the London edition of Colden's *History of the Five Indian Nations* (1750: 87–152), without the Williamsburg preface.

The friendship between Conrad Weiser and Thomas Lee that grew out of the Lancaster treaty produced a series of questions and answers relating to Iroquois custom, law, and government (P. Wallace 1945: 197–98). From his boyhood in Schoharie, Weiser had participated in and observed Iroquois life at first hand, and he spoke Mohawk, the principal language of the Great Law and the Iroquois League. No one at mid-eighteenth century was better qualified to answer Colonel Lee's queries. Not unlike the later anthropologists, Weiser also understood the ways of the whites and could mediate between the two cultures.

Weiser had little to say about the structure and function of the Six Nations confederacy beyond "what pertains to their transactions and demeanour with other nations, for in that respect they take great pains: Each nation of the six tribes sends Deputies to the great Council at Onondago once or twice a year to confer with each other; they are slow in coming to a decision in the Council, and have good rules which are looked to and kept inviolably" (P. Wallace 1945: 198). After discussing the handling of some cases of trouble, he went on to estimate numbers of warriors by tribes, listing some eleven allied nations and their manpower.

From long personal experience among a nation imbued with a great warrior tradition, Weiser had learned one proverbial truth: "A European who wishes to stand well with them, must practice well the three following virtues: (1) Speak the truth; (2) Give the best that he has; (3) Show himself not a coward, but courageous in all cases" (P. Wallace 1945: 201).

The Williamsburg preface summarizes Lee's understanding of Weiser on government:

This Confederacy [has] been generally stiled the Five Nations of Indians . . . but since the Junction of the Tuscaroras of Carolina, they are called the Six Nations. [They are:]

1. The . . . Mohawks; [who were] the first Promotor of the confederacy. He (they always stile a whole Nation in the singular Number) is stiled in the Council of all the Nations, *Docaryhoogoo* [Tekarihoken, M-1] . . . President, or Eldest.[2]

2. The Onayiuts, or Oneidas, were the first who join'd in the confederacy with the Mohawks, by putting themselves under their Protection. He calls the Mohawk his Father, and in return he is called a Son: The Mohawk used him for his Ambassador to the other Nations: In Council he is stiled Niharontaquoa [Niharontako:wa] or the great Tree.

3. The Onontagos were the next that joined, and of their own Accord became Confederates; they are therefore called by the Mohawks, Brothers; and by the Oneidas, Fathers, because they had not been forced into the Alliance as the Oneidas were: He is called in Council Sagochsaanagechteront, the Arms, or Names-bearer.

4. The Jenontowano's [*tionontowa:neh ononh*, "great hill people"] or Sinikes [Senecas], next joined in the Alliance of their own Consent; they are stiled by the Mohawks and Onondagas, Brothers, and by the Oneidas, Fathers: His Title in Council is Onughkarydaawy [Ganonhgidawi (S-7, RC 49)], whose signification is not known, and Dyionenhookaraw [Doninhogawen (S-8, RC 50)], Open Doors for Friends and Enemies.[3]

5. The Caiukquo's [Cayugas], the last of the Five Nation Alliance, being compelled thereto by the rest, is Brother to the Oneyders, and Son to the others; is stiled in Council Ganunawantoowano [Sononnawentona in Hale 1883: 79], "the Great Pipe."

6. Tuscarora's joined in the Alliance about thirty two years ago [1712], being compelled thereto by the English of Carolina: He is Brother to the Oneyders and Cayukquo's, and Son to the others; has no Title in Council, but is frequently called a Fool.

Dependents and tributaries of the Six Nations follow (pp. v–viii):

The Mahicans of the Hudson River, as do the Delawares, refer to themselves as "Women" when addressing the Five Nations. At other times the Five Nations call them Cousins [nephews?], and in return are called Uncles.

The Shawnee are Brethren.

The Nanticokes are allied, but not tributary to the confederacy.

A few Tutelo wards, from Virginia, are at Shamokin.

For some eight listed tribes, no kinship terms appear. Number eight, "Kerhawgue Roanu" (*karhagwe ro:non*), "the people of the wilderness" (literally, forest), hunters, fishers, and gatherers then living on the north side of Lake Huron, suggests the mysterious *kahkwage onon* of the Senecas.

---

2. Here is justification for treating the names of the several nations in the singular form as collective nouns.

3. The Senecas were hardly volunteers, and the Onondagas came in last under pressure, according to the league epic. Weiser was not infallible.

Before taking up Colonel Lee's contribution, it strikes me that Weiser must have had access to the tradition of the Iroquois League. He possibly misunderstood his informants on the sequence in which the Five Nations accepted the Great Peace and the conditions of acceptance. All later versions of the tradition grant primacy to the Mohawks. But the Oneidas, after a delay, joined next, of their own volition. The Onondagas were last, preceded by the Cayugas and eastern Senecas. The two specified Seneca war leaders held out and came in later when awarded special duties at the western door.

Weiser clearly understood the kinship terms employed by the Mohawks, Onondagas, and Senecas—the fathers—for their offspring or sons, the Oneidas and Cayugas, and the reciprocal terms, which implies that he understood the moiety arrangement of the league and the confederacy. The adoption of the Tuscaroras and, later, the Tutelo and Delaware remnants gave rise to current usage: the Three Brothers and Four Brothers.

The author of the preface continues (p. viii):

Their Form of Government is a Council of their oldest and wisest Men, who have been great Warriours. Every one of the Six Nations [has] such a Council, in which Matters relating to that Nature [sic; nation] are determined. And if it is of great Moment, they consult their young Warriours, and the Business is debated with great Deliberation. In Foreign Affairs, which relate to the Union in general, every one of the Six Nations send Deputies out of their Council, to a General Council. . . . [T]his General Council, as well as the Particular Ones, consult the young Warriours, and have their Concurrence, before any Matter of great Consequence is determined. All their Debates in Council are managed with great Decency and Deliberation; and the Resolution is imprinted in the Memory of One chosen from among them, of great Reputation and Elocution, who is appointed to speak in Publick. He is assisted by a Prompter, who puts him in Mind of any Thing he forgets. They have no coercive Power over their young Warriours; they can only persuade and admonish; nor have they any Punishment but Death; Crimes that by their Laws do not deserve that are forgiven, after proper Reproofs.

The preceding sketch of the form of government most probably derives from Colden (1727), although the exact passage does not occur in Colden's first edition.

The Williamsburg preface (p. ix) next describes the "shout of approbation," substantially as it appears in Marshe's journal. It adds this comment: "If it [the matter] is of great Consequence, the Speaker gives the U—huy thrice, and they make the Shout as often. It is usual, when the white People speak to them, as they give a Belt or String of Wampum, for the Interpreter to begin the U—huy, and the Indians make the Shout. . . . The Wisdom of the Chiefs in this Confederacy hath gained them no less Reputation than their Courage."

The preface closes with a plea for equitable treatment of these men as human beings who are by no means barbarians or savages (p. xii): "One sees, in the following short Sketch of the Behavior of the Indians, strong Traces of good Sense, a nice Address in the Conduct of their Affairs, a noble Simplicity, and that manly Fortitude which is the constant Companion of Integrity. The Friendship of a Nation like this, tho' under the Appelation of Savages or Barbarians, is an Honour to the most civiliz'd People: I say nothing of the Advantage which is derived from them by Commerce: And the French well know, by dear Experience, how terrible they are to their Enemies in War."

The author reinforces his view with a quote from Bacqueville de La Potherie's *Histoire* (1722), as cited in Colden (1727), which establishes that Colden was indeed his source. So much was available to readers in the eighteenth century beyond the experience of individuals who participated in treaty negotiations.

□□◇□□

The Lancaster treaty of 1744 not only awakened colonists to the importance of the Six Nations confederacy in the struggle with the French but was also effective in other ways. The Six Nations promised neutrality in King George's War, and there was general agreement that a peaceful settlement between northern and southern Indians was desirable. Residents of South Carolina breathed easier. The Catawbas wanted Thomas and Weiser to persuade the Six Nations to recall their warriors. Although neither the governor nor the interpreter trusted the sincerity of the Catawbas, Weiser, nevertheless, soon braved another difficult journey to Onondaga to try to convince the Six Nations to come down to Virginia to treat on the matter (Boyd 1938: xl–xli).

Factional politics beset the confederacy just then, and Onondaga was at the eye of the storm. Canasatego led his followers home laden with goods and gold—more lavish presents than had been received at previous treaties. The Six Nations had pledged to remain neutral, but an invitation to treat with the governor of Canada at Montreal awaited them, and they accepted. At stake was their long-standing policy of neutrality that enabled them to balance the two European powers and extract presents from both, to threaten defection, and to force compensation for land claims.

Having distinguished himself in treating with representatives of three colonies as equals at Lancaster, Canasatego's prestige at Onondaga reached its zenith. Translated into action, this meant power. But he faced a difficult role. Individual distinction in Iroquois society inevitably aroused jealousy in others who felt threatened and who countered with covert if not open reprisals. Individual Onondaga leaders aligned themselves in pro-French and pro-English factions. Dominance of one over the other upset the balance and threatened the Six Nations' neutrality. Similarly, the confederacy manifested disunity at its extremities: the Mohawks would eventually take up the English ax from Sir William Johnson; the Senecas, abetted by the Joncaires (father and son), favored fighting on the side of the French; and the Cayuga and Oneida moiety supported Onondaga neutrality. Recent losses to the south lessened interest in war. By this time Mohawk and Seneca families had drifted into Ohio to hunt, where they reached an accommodation with the Shawnees, who leaned toward the French. While displaying a bold front of neutrality, indeed the confederacy as a fabric was fraying at the margins. Although Canasatego succeeded in sustaining a policy of neutrality despite the defections of two senior moiety members, the power of the confederacy was diminished. After the Treaty of Aix-la-Chapelle ended the War of the Austrian Succession in 1748, and with it King George's War, the fulcrum of the balance shifted to the Ohio. Canasatego himself would disappear from the scene six years later in an apparent political assassination (Boyd 1938: xli; P. Wallace 1945: 131n19, 309ff.). This was some ways off.

The "Great White Roots of Peace" that extended in the cardinal directions from Onondaga enabled the Six Nations to sense threats to the policy of neutrality from all quarters. From the north, French intrigue menaced unity within the confederacy. Toward the sunrise, Abenaki peoples sacked New England villages. Toward the sunset, Central Algonquians, formerly allies of the French, still leaned that way despite Iroquois attempts to bring them into the chain. And to the south, the Catawbas remained intractable. They drained off Iroquois manpower, and neither side trusted the other. Early in 1745, Governor Gooch of Virginia urged Governor Thomas of Pennsylvania to send Honest Conrad up to Onondaga to promote a peaceful settlement of the long-standing feud. Although Weiser had no love for the Catawbas, he willingly undertook a third journey to the main fire of the Six Nations and scoffed at any personal danger. As an ambassador he had nothing to fear among adopted kin.

The French worked in subtler ways. Indeed, they were provoking disunity within the Six Nations, preventing the nations from coming to one mind on issues. Their trade emissaries from the Catholic missions infiltrated Albany and Schenectady, spreading rumors that the English were about to "cut off" the Six Nations, and they influenced the Indian commissioners, who were traders, to oppose the English interest. Joncaire the younger kept the Senecas on the French side. Only the three interior fires of the Longhouse—Oneida, Onondaga, and Cayuga—stood neutral. The Mohawks favored the English, although land scams, mistreatment in Albany, and persistent rumors eroded that loyalty.

Weiser looked forward to revisiting the Mohawk Valley of his boyhood. Before he left home, New York governor George Clinton requested Pennsylvania governor Thomas to have Weiser inquire into the "Strange Alarm" among the Mohawks that the English intended to destroy them. A half dozen Mohawks, returning from some Schenectady grog shop at mid-winter, alarmed the lower Mohawk town in the dead of night, warning that the white people were coming in force to "cut them All in Pieces," which news precipitated a flight in panic to the woods (Barclay to SPG, in Lydekker 1938: 56–57). The alarm spread to the upper town, where hotheads prepared to make reprisals. The Reverend Henry Barclay suspected the French were behind the rumor, and chief Hendrick fingered Joncaire.

Some other French amenities had reached Onondaga. Instead of the customary protocol at the clearing, a parade accompanied by violins, flutes, and drums ushered Weiser into Onondaga.[4] He immediately confided his mission to Canasatego and Kaheskarowaneh and the following day addressed the Onondaga council, inviting its members to Williamsburg to treat with the Catawbas and reporting that the Shawnees had defected to the French (PPR, 4: 780). The council deliberated and answered next day. It deferred the proposal to treat with the Catawbas until its embassy returned from Canada, and it warned that the warriors must be consulted on such a matter. Moreover, a peace treaty proposal must come before the general council of the confederacy, when the war captains would meet jointly with the sachems. Meanwhile, they would keep their warriors at home. Under no circumstances would the sachems go as far as Williamsburg to meet

---

4. At least one Oneida Iroquois learned to play the violin while interned in France, and the Seneca prophet Handsome Lake later preached against "fiddle-playing."

Catawbas until preliminary ceremonies rendered it suitable. Without first kindling a council fire there and opening the road, there would be no show. Philadelphia would be a proper site for the treaty (PPR, 4: 781; P. Wallace 1945: 221).

On the Shawnee matter, Tekanontie: replied that they would take Weiser's belt to Canada and seek restitution. A feast followed by a dance capped the proceedings. If Weiser had failed in his mission, he had at least followed the proper way, and he reported fully on the protocol observed.

His business discharged, Weiser went up to Oswego, visited the fort, met once more with the Onondaga delegates bound for Canada, and heard their complaints that the commissioners of Indian affairs at Albany, who opposed their mission, told them only of English successes, whereas the French acknowledged losses. They would, they said, nevertheless report on their mission to the New York authorities. Having shoved off their canoes on Lake Frontenac, Weiser returned to Onondaga before going on to the Mohawk Valley and passed a day with Canasatego and Kaheskarowaneh, who were tending the fire pending the meeting with the New York governor.

That day Weiser heard his hosts outline Six Nations policy on maintaining the balance of power in America by remaining neutral in the current struggle between France and England. Now they were courted by both, but should either party prevail and drive the other out of the country, the Six Nations would no longer merit presents and would ultimately come under the laws of the conquerors.

Quite possibly this was the occasion when Canasatego contrasted Iroquois hospitality with his treatment in Albany, an account that Weiser related to Benjamin Franklin, who (from memory late in life) quoted it in his famous *Remarks Concerning the Savages of North America* (Franklin 1987: 973–74; P. Wallace 1945: 225–26). The piece represents Franklin's continued interest in the Iroquois, it demonstrates his esteem for the native culture, and it exemplifies his use of that knowledge for social criticism.

There were just then two main Mohawk towns. At the upper town, Canajoharie, Hendrick, of London fame, Abraham, and Arughiadekka (Aronhiade:ka), "Burning Sky," served clan segments. They greeted Weiser warmly, inquired about his transactions at Onondaga, manifested concern over how New York would treat the late alarm, and wondered how matters then stood. Hendrick was particularly exercised over recent scams involving Mohawk lands in the valley. Although they favored the English interest, they had backed the mission to Canada just to assert their independence of the Albany commissioners, who, they alleged, backed the land scams, had prevented the Bostonians from coming to them directly, and had forbidden them to speak to the Mohawks save in their presence. The same men, they charged, engaged in the contraband trade, supplying gunpowder to the French through Kahnawakeh (Caughnawaga) canoemen (NYHS, Hormanden papers, no. 20: 82–89).

Downstream beyond the promontories called the "Noses," the lower Mohawk town, Dyiontorogon, stood near Fort Hunter at the mouth of Schoharie Creek. There, Aaron, or Asaragehty (Ax Carrier [NYCD, 6: 293]), Joseph Brant, and Thomas received Weiser and set a date for the council to meet two days later to hear him. Resentment against the Albanians ran strong, although wiser heads denied the rumored threat by the whites, and for the moment the matter was reconciled. But they said that at the time, "the dead Cry was heard everywhere, Que, Que, Que" (*ko:weh*).

Both as Pennsylvania's interpreter and as one who had heard the Onondaga and Mohawk sachems express their views, Honest Conrad aroused the enmity of the Albany traders and Governor Clinton. When he went back to Albany in October, he found that they had it in for him. They envied his inside information and sought to discredit him. The rumor that the Six Nations had taken up the French hatchet scared them to death.

The 1745 Albany treaty was conceived in haste and born into confusion. The commissioners, having inquired of a "Trusty Mohawk" what happened in Montreal, learned that the French governor had thrown down a black belt with the figure of a hatchet interwoven, and that the Onondaga emissaries had picked it up but answered that they would take the belt back to Onondaga for consideration by a full council of the Six Nations. The commissioners, fearing the Six Nations were wavering in their attachment to the British interest, wrote to Governor Clinton saying, "There is now an End of the Neutrality" and they might expect an attack presently. They urged him to summon a conference including commissioners of the neighboring provinces to consider the emergency (APSL, mss. class B, no. 182, vol. 4, fol. 115–18; Wraxall 1915: 240). There was no cause yet to panic.

Clinton, at odds with the assembly and as yet unversed in Indian affairs, heeded the advice of Colden and wrote to the neighboring colonial governors inviting them to meet on 4 October with representatives of the Six Nations. He hoped to induce them to declare war against the French, and he wanted to get to the source of the alarms that the English were about to do in the Six Nations. He resolved to identify the instigator, or a convenient scapegoat. The Pennsylvania interpreter would be a likely target, inasmuch as Pennsylvania recently had gained the lead in Indian affairs.

The Albany commissioners were not happy at the prospect. They were dismayed that the New York assembly proved niggardly in funding presents for the Indians (PAC IR RG 10, 1821: 93). (Only Colden and one other supported the governor.) They sent their own interpreter, Arent Stevens, up to Onondaga to invite the Six Nations to come down and to find out whether they had accepted any belts from the governor of Canada; if so, they should bring them (PAC IR RG 10, 1821: 92). In mid-September they sent Stevens back to Onondaga to inform the council that Massachusetts and Canada were at war (PAC IR RG 10, 1821: 96). Meanwhile, two Caughnawaga Indians came to Albany with a pass from the governor of Canada regarding an exchange of prisoners. It upset them that they could no longer trade there as usual, since they had kept the treaty of neutrality. It was not their fault, they said, that other Indians had broken it (PAC IR RG 10, 1821: 97–98).

Commissioners of Pennsylvania, Connecticut, and Massachusetts arrived in Albany with different expectations and distinct interests. Each colony jealously held to its own position. Pennsylvania instructed its commissioners to charge the Six Nations with violations of the neutrality pledged at Lancaster. Iroquois war parties still went out against the southern Indians, despite their promise to Weiser in June. Pennsylvania traders were being robbed on the Ohio. And what of the report that the Six Nations had accepted the French hatchet at Montreal (Boyd 1938: xlii)? The New England commissioners sought relief from northern Indian war parties' burning frontier villages and carrying off or scalping Christians. They wanted the Six Nations to declare war against the northeastern Indians and join the British effort to reduce Canada.

On accepting the governor's invitation string, the Six Nations raked out their fire and covered in the ashes some important issues: the Catawba peace, trouble with the Shawnees, and the report of their recently returned delegates from Montreal. In deferring these matters in favor of renewing the chain, they looked forward to the usual treaty hospitality at Albany, and they expected the business to go forward in the customary way (P. Wallace 1945: 229).

In contrast with Montreal, the Six Nations found Albany a poor show. New York failed to hang a full kettle and provide ample shelter for them. Disregarding treaty protocol, Clinton instituted an inquest with a view to pinning blame on someone for instigating the rumors. This was no way to impress the sachems with the power of the English colonies. He impelled Weiser to interpret, although he was there to serve the Pennsylvania commissioners. When Clinton privately examined an individual Mohawk suspected of spreading the alarm, the Mohawk sachems became outraged at his not raising the matter in open council. At a meeting for the same purpose including two Onondaga leaders and some Mohawk chiefs, Hendrick, while demanding redress of recent land scams, became so enraged that Weiser took a belt out of his hands and Canasatego rebuked him for bad council manners.

Next day Hendrick identified one Andrew Van Patten as the alarmist, but Brant whispered that Hendrick himself and Aaron were the authors. Seeing that the inquest was getting nowhere, Weiser persuaded Clinton to drop the matter. Anyway, Van Patten could not speak Mohawk. Hendrick's grievances, however, were genuine, and the governor promised to adjust them before leaving town. As for Weiser, who had stepped into the breach and who was, as a Pennsylvania employee, "working out of title (as we moderns say), he got no thanks. Instead, the governor cursed him (Weiser in Boyd 1938: 309–10). The uproar subsided.

The treaty finally opened on 10 October. For days a committee of commissioners had worked over a joint statement for delivery by Clinton, who hoped to impress the French with a united front of the English colonies. But the issue of Iroquois neutrality brought small agreement, and Pennsylvania withdrew when two Quaker commissioners refused to countenance a declaration of war against the French; they decided to treat separately and not to attend the opening-day ceremonies.

Having convened the treaty, Clinton spoke first. His address invoked the covenant chain, condoled the absence of Senecas, and, in declaring war on the French, asked the Five Nations and their allies to join. Upon this, the interpreter threw down a black war belt with a hatchet interwoven at the feet of the Indians, who responded with a loud shout. Their young men were about to start the war dance when their elders restrained them. Big promises filled out the speech, which elicited the customary *yo-heh!* (PPCM, 5: 7–15; Boyd 1938: 310).

The old men of the Six Nations took two days to debate the question and come to one mind. They were lukewarm to any war with France; they would need more time to council, enlist Seneca participation, and line up their allies. Let the French and English fight it out on the saltwater. Moreover, the English were already dominant and increasing faster than the Indians, who were declining in numbers. Canasatego, who favored neutrality, reminded Weiser that previous French and

English wars had "et up their People." He asked Weiser in private why the Pennsylvania commissioners did not attend opening day. During these discussions, the Albany interpreter asked Weiser to help persuade the Indians to war so as to please the New Englanders. The governor and the Albany Indian commissioners stood behind the gesture, willing to use the offices of a mere interpreter to suit their patrician purposes; but the Pennsylvania commissioners advised caution, and Weiser was no fool. Moreover, the Six Nations knew the views of their exiles in the Catholic missions, who regarded the hostility of the New England tribes as no new thing: they deemed the New Englanders worse than their enemies. The Six Nations agreed to send peace emissaries to the New England tribes the next spring, but in no way would they engage them in war. This view suited the New York and Pennsylvania commissioners, who wanted merely to secure the friendship of the Six Nations, should matters reach a crisis (Weiser in Boyd 1938: 310, col. 2).

The Six Nations delivered their formal reply with belt and string to the governor of New York on 12 October. While not rejecting the hatchet, they condoled the deaths of New Englanders by northern Indians and asserted that they would take up the hatchet against their enemy, but before using it would "hide it in our Bosom" pending the mission to the New England Indians. The prudent approach was to try for peace first before striking them.

It is a rule in Iroquois council never to interrupt a speaker. Nevertheless, the impatient Boston commissioners stopped Canasatego's delivery with a large belt. Governor Clinton tried to smooth over the difficulties created by the New Englanders, who had declared war without notifying him. It was a bad show.

At last Canasatego finished his reply with a sermon on unity. "Let this belt tie you together as of one mind, one heart, and one body. . . . [I]f one is touched or hurt, all feel it." He ended with the usual complaint that the price of goods was dear. The failure of the colonies to reach any sort of agreement on policy and to act together was all too apparent to the old men of the confederacy.

Clinton replied out of hand, without consulting his colleagues. His conduct affronted the Indians, and he hurried away without fulfilling his promise to take up and relieve their grievances over land. The New Englanders went home disappointed, and the Indians were mad as hornets: "Now you see yourself how we are treated" (Weiser in Boyd 1938: 311).

□□◇□□

While the English colonies failed to reach a unified policy on Indian affairs, French agents advanced the policy of neutrality and achieved disunity among the Six Nations. The Senecas and Cayugas refused to join any campaign against Canada; pro-French and pro-English factions divided the Onondaga council; the Oneidas wavered; and one segment of the Mohawks withheld participation in the English cause. When French and Indians, including some Caughnawaga Christian Mohawks, burned Saratoga, within Mohawk territory, they ended any English hope of unity. The Albany commissioners sent Arent Stevens, the interpreter, up to Onondaga to inform the Six Nations that the English had taken up the hatchet against the French and expected them to join in the war. But the sachems of the confederacy "convened in a Grand Meeting at Onondaga" and flatly refused to take up the hatchet against the French. They were of one family with the people of Kahnawakeh, intermarried and of one nation, and they would not make war on one another. If they did, making peace with the other group afterward would prove difficult. They did not consider the covenant chain broken by this refusal. They remained adamant (Wraxall 1915: 144).

The New Englanders did not give up; they were back in Albany the following summer, 1746, as was Clinton, although the Pennsylvania commissioners "stayed home in the back of the bed," as the Iroquois say. Several hundred of the Six Nations braved the dangers of smallpox and returned, despite the meager hospitality the previous autumn.

Between smallpox and a malignant fever, Albany was a pesthole that summer. With the exception of Phillip Livingston and Colden, the members of the provincial council declined to go upriver with the governor, who conscripted the local commandant, John Rutherford, to eke out a quorum. Lacking immunities, Clinton lodged aboard the sloop to avoid infection. Much of the business fell to Colden, and he evidently wrote up the proceedings.[5] William Johnson, a trader and landowner in the Mohawk Valley, painted and in Indian dress, made his debut as head of the Mohawk delegation. Even the Mohawks were not of one mind until Colden succeeded in persuading the Turtle clan leader of Canajoharie, where Colden had previously been adopted by the Mohawks. Some Mississaugas appeared as a seventh nation in the confederacy.

The real business of the treaty sought to stir the Indians to action on the English side of the war with France by inducing them to take up the hatchet that they had kept in their bosom since the previous treaty. Colden advised not bothering the Indians with military affairs in Europe, not to overload their memories, but to concentrate on what was properly their business. A further difficulty arose when the public interpreter became dangerously ill. Several substitutes knew enough Mohawk to make themselves understood and could comprehend spoken Iroquoian, but none could speak "with Propriety and Distinctness" the language of forest diplomacy expected and customary at treaties.

As usual in intercultural impasses, both sides improvised. They would get a selected sachem to understand the commissioners' speech as rendered by a common interpreter, and he in turn would deliver it paragraph by paragraph in proper Iroquoian. At first the commissioners pitched upon a Mohawk, but the sachems advised selecting one of the opposite confederate moiety—a speaker from the Oneida-Tuscarora-Cayuga half—because a Mohawk might be suspected of partiality toward the English. They proposed an Oneida sachem. This device apparently worked. The man readily comprehended the content of the speech, rehearsed it several times in private, and learned where to make the stops. Afterward, an Albany commissioner who understood both languages allowed that the Oneida speaker had delivered the sense of the speech clearly and distinctly.

With Governor Clinton ill on 19 August, it fell to Colden to deliver the speech. It renewed the covenant chain, related French attacks and the fall of Louisbourg to the English, and dwelt on frontier depredations, notably Saratoga. In response to these murders His Majesty had ordered the mid-Atlantic colonies to join with New York in attacking Canada by land. The New England colonies would go by

5. Treaty between Governor Clinton of New York and the Six Nations, held at Albany in August and September, 1746, printed by James Parker, New York, 1746, 23 pp. (DePuy 1917: 25). It was reprinted in Colden 1750, pt. 3: 153–96. Copy seen HEH H16393.

sea. He invited the Six Nations to join, appealing to past glories, reminding them of French invasions of Iroquoia, and recalling their reprisals. Belts and shouted responses punctuated the stops. Where six cries were expected, eight were heard, two additional nations having joined in the chain. The official proceedings spell out the names of the Six Nations plus the Mississaugas, a "Far Nation" (NYCD, 6: 317–26), but I am uncertain that they were all present. Some Susquehanna and Oquaga tributaries followed.

The several nations caucused separately until they came to one mind, when one informed the governor that they were ready to reply at a time when he was prepared to hear their answer. He named the next day, but three days passed before the commissioners convened to hear them. An Onondaga sachem who had formerly spoken on such public occasions (most likely Canasatego) stood and delivered the joint reply. This much came through the public interpreter as screened by several who understood Iroquoian:

1. The Six Nations assembled as their speaker announced taking in the Mississaugas as a seventh nation. The governor's adherence to the custom of their forefathers in employing the Three Bare Words of condolence—wiping the tears, clearing the throats, and washing the bloody bed—pleased them. He returned three strings.
2. A belt reaffirmed the chain, to which they mutually held fast.
3. The French having destroyed Saratoga, the Six Nations now had use for the hatchet given them last year, meaning all Governor Clinton's children. (Here the speaker threw down a war belt, the Indian custom in declaring war.)
4. A belt of mutual union.
5. A belt confirming the conquest of Cape Breton, with hopes of a land victory.
6. A promise not to admit further French priests and a pledge of warriors, of whom the Mississaugas comprised eight hundred men in five villages. The speaker gave a belt of union incorporating figures of several persons joined hand in hand.

This time the interpreter sounded the *yohe:* at the end of every item, instead of the war cry, which prompted laughter among the Indians. On realizing his mistake, he raised the war cry, which the Indians joined.

Anxiety over the spreading sickness hastened the distribution of presents, the most elaborate ever given. The Boston commissioners, in a hurry to get home, awarded theirs separately. The sachems had little to offer in return, since hunting was poor. They could promise few fighting men immediately because many men were afield hunting, trading, or fighting their enemies. They would endeavor to recall them.

A day passed dividing the presents into eight equal parts—two shares to the Mississauga deputies. Next day the hosts hung the war kettle and the Indians performed the war dance singly, which the recorder was at a loss to describe.

Smallpox took its toll of the Far Indians, who lacked immunity. Several died in Albany, and others fell victim on the way home. Women and children who accompanied the Six Nations delegates carried the infection to their villages, where it spread rapidly. The governor hastened to get the Indians out of town, both for the expense of feeding some seven hundred people and to remove them from contact with local carriers. Some twenty had already come down with the sickness.

The epidemic rendered it impossible to fulfill promised quotas of fighting men. Many of the Six Nations took sick before reaching the Mohawk castles, and the Mohawks lost "a considerable number of the briskest young men." It was too much to expect war parties to go out while the Indians were mourning their dead.

Any expedition against Canada would conflict with loyalties to émigré Mohawk kin in the St. Lawrence mission settlements. On arriving at the lower Mohawk castle, the Six Nations sachems met six returning men bearing a message from the governor of Canada, who had called in the Kahnawakeh headmen and complained that some Six Nations warriors had killed some of his people. He asked them to go among the Six Nations, find out the reasons, and warn them that if it happened again he would make reprisals. The Kahnawakeh warriors should return a prisoner taken at Crown Point "without eating his Flesh!" He urged the Kahnawakeh men to go out against New England.

The Kahnawakeh spokesman answered the governor that he was wrong to expect them to gather intelligence among the Six Nations, or to threaten them, which would only incite them to mobilize their numerous allies to destroy Canada. He could do his own dirty work.

The Kahnawakeh council sent an escort with the returned prisoner, but when they neared the Mohawk towns, the escort sent the prisoner on alone to relate the message. It was that word of the recent treaty had reached the Christian Mohawks and that their Mohawk kin should pay no heed to Clinton's effort to set them against each other, lest both parties all die. By all ties of friendship they invoked the Six Nations to inform them of any plot against them. They looked forward to a joint council next spring at Kahnawakeh. Meanwhile, the Six Nations should not be angry at their destroying Saratoga; "Colonel Schuyler dared us. . . . [W]e gratified his wish."

Runners promptly carried the Kahnawakeh message among the Six Nations, an act the authorities mistakenly interpreted as proof of Iroquois sincerity in complying with the treaty. William Johnson reported that the Mohawks to a man were under arms, but his influence ended with them, and the rest of the Six Nations sat on their hatchets. Weiser, who showed up alone in Albany to scout out the situation in September 1746, just before Clinton left town, learned why. In an hour's conversation with an Iroquois friend, his source confessed that it was only their lips that spoke, not their hearts. His people regarded it as a bad omen that so many accidents had happened. When first they came to town they were hit by smallpox, and then by the "long fever," which spread from the Albany people to the Indians, most of whom fell sick and many of whom died before reaching home (P. Wallace 1945: 238-39). The epidemic proved far more effective than French military action in aborting the Canada expedition.

□□◇□□

The governor of Canada had neutralized the Six Nations. English prestige declined. The long-serving Albany commissioners of Indian affairs were of two minds; some absented themselves from meetings, Clinton distrusted them, and they resigned, ending a tenure of fifty years. Management of Indian affairs involving the Six Nations passed to William Johnson, who would gradually take control for the northern colonies and serve until his death in 1774. The Indian problem would bring the colonies together, and in Whitehall the idea of unified management was dawning. The Six Nations confederacy, able to represent unanimity when in fact its members were divided, occupied the fulcrum in a balance between the English and the French.

CHAPTER 29

THE CHAIN IS BROKEN

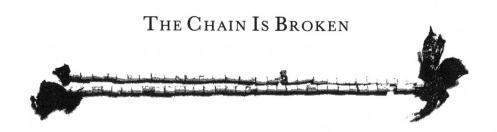

The Six Nations confederacy had commenced to unravel just when the English colonies began to see the need to unite. William Johnson, who had come to the Mohawk Valley in 1738 and bought land for himself north of the river the following year, soon monopolized the Indian trade, began to learn Mohawk, readily picked up the fundamentals of Mohawk culture, and observed the rules of Iroquois society by going on the hunt, eating Indian food, sleeping on the ground, taking up the hatchet with the warriors, and "trying on the moccasin" with the village beauties.

The chief Hendrick, although an Anglican and a Mahican raised among the Mohawks, dominated politics in the upper Mohawk town at Canajoharie. He became Johnson's mentor. Each had something to gain. Having succeeded as a trader and estate builder, Johnson's leverage in colonial politics hinged on his ability to deliver manpower for the defense of the colony. Hendrick, outraged at the rapid alienation of native lands, looked to Johnson to influence governors and councils. The English horizon, which for years had stood at Schenectady, crept up the valley past Fort Hunter and the lower Mohawk town to bypass Canajoharie. While the Albany Dutch were content to sit in Albany and let the trade come to them, land hunger replaced the fur trade as the dominant theme of the eighteenth century as the English sought fertile valleys in which to farm, locate mill sites, and establish towns. Palatine German farmers brought over by Robert Livingston took up the flats and spilled over into Schoharie.

Mohawk society was greatly reduced by warfare, disease, and defections to the Catholic missions on the St. Lawrence. Manpower in the two Mohawk castles declined further during the three decades after Johnson came to the valley in the 1730s.[1] Yet the thirst for blood revenge prevailed, and the mourning sanctions to replace deceased kin roused young men to go on the warpath. Hendrick had led such war parties, and Johnson soon learned to throw wampum belts, hang the war kettle, and take up the hatchet. Hendrick hated the Albany traders and Indian commissioners and preferred Johnson to intercept furs once destined for Albany. The city of Albany, including members of the Livingston family, had secured a patent to Mohawk flats south of the river, and Hendrick himself had signed the Kayaderosseros Patent to 800,000 acres bordering that stream in Saratoga County,

---

1. Warren Johnson's journal of 1760–61 estimated the decline at from fourteen hundred to three hundred men, which greatly exaggerates the male population when compared with other, contemporaneous figures (SWJP, 13: 194; DHNY, 1: 17, 22, 26).

which became a bone of contention down to the Albany Congress. Johnson later claimed that representatives of only two of the three Mohawk clans had signed the deed (Nammack 1969: 54).

Mohawk society was indeed incomplete. Whole lineages, including holders of chiefly titles, were living as émigrés in Canada, where the Mohawk population equaled, if it did not exceed, that of the valtey. The sachems of the remaining two villages, who comprised the council of the nation, had names other than those of the nine traditional founders of the league. The lone league title that appears in the documents, that of Tekarihoken (M-1), belonged to a lineage at Kahnawakeh. The Six Nations confederacy nevertheless functioned, invoking the symbolism of the league as necessary.

Johnson attended council at the lower and upper Mohawk castles, he met with the sachems at Mount Johnson, and he appeared with Mohawk delegations in Albany. But until 1748, when he went up to Onondaga to participate in a grand council and enlisted the help of Mohawk speakers to ensure proper protocol, his knowledge of the confederacy did not extend much beyond its eastern door. Cayugas and Senecas he knew of by hearsay. From his council fire, kindled first at Mount Johnson, next at Fort Johnson, and later at Johnson Hall, he saw the confederacy and its ancient league through Mohawk eyes.

Having dismissed the remaining Albany commissioners of Indian affairs, in August 1746 Governor Clinton commissioned Johnson as "Colonel of the Six Nations" (SWJP, 1: 60–61), which concentrated Iroquois affairs in his hands and put him in considerable debt. In the eighteenth century, collecting an expense account from the crown was no easy task. The Mohawks gave Johnson a name based on his activities—Warraghiyageh, "in the midst of affairs." Within a year he tried to persuade the Iroquois to repatriate their kinspeople at Kahnawakeh and the people beyond at Kanehsatageh (Lake of Two Mountains) and enlist them in the English cause. The delegates present deferred the question to the grand council at Onondaga, knowing too well that the policy of neutrality would prevail (NYCD, 6: 359–60). Johnson would have to meet the grand council in person.

The confederates marked Johnson's progress through their villages in April 1748 by hoisting the English colors and beating drums, exceeding his expectations. As he entered Onondaga, the warriors and sachems lined up in rank order and fired a volley to announce his coming, to which his escort responded. Gone was the exchange of condolences at the woods' edge. Principal sachems then led him by the arm to a large house cleaned out for his use, with fresh mats spread for him to lie on. They had cleared out a second large house for his Mohawk entourage and two additional houses for others of his party.[2]

Within an hour of his arrival, a caller assembled the sachems of the several nations to meet in council and sent for Johnson to attend the meeting, "a very full one."

Canasatego, then the presiding Onondaga, spoke first to welcome Johnson to the fire of the confederacy with three hands of wampum. (Recitation of the Three Bare Words had moved from the woods' edge to the council fire.) The speaker went on

2. William Johnson's journal from the New York State Archives, *Council Minutes*, 21: 300, describes the grand council in action. It is fairly detailed, and I have mined it for ethnographic information.

to relate the hardships of complying with the request to stay home and not go to Canada, the deprivations of not going afield hunting, and the high prices at Oswego. The Six Nations had honored Johnson's request to meet with them, Canasatego said, although food was short. A wampum belt stressed urgency, and strings underscored it. While waiting for him, out of patience and hungry, they had been about to break up when a runner brought news that Johnson had reached Ganaseraga, a day's travel distant, whereupon they had decided not to break up but had procured hogs and corn to feed their guests while hearing Johnson's news. They meanwhile returned thanks for his supplying their wants. That was sufficient for the day. Another belt verified the speaker's words.

Johnson answered his "Brethren of the five Nations" by thanking them for his reception. He expressed his pleasure at seeing them at the traditional meeting place of "our Forefathers whose Steps I have now traced" so as to keep the road open between the two parties, an agreement that he hoped they remembered. He had come at the governor's orders, was fatigued from the journey, and would rest before delivering his message tomorrow. Meanwhile they could ease their minds while that night he would put up a feast for the sachems, and a second for the warriors and village dancers. He gave wampum to conclude for the day.

Johnson spoke first on the following day, 25 April 1748. He assured his brethren that he had hurried to meet them, but the roads were so dangerous that he dared not come without a guard, which, together with the logistics of bateaux laden with presents and stores, had delayed him.

He began with a treatise on "Brothership," the relationship between the Five Nations and New York as siblings, an affair of long standing, which some of them had forgotten but which he, a foreigner, had discovered in the writings of their forefathers, namely, the legend of the covenant chain, which the French were trying to get them to let go of. This relationship called for a large belt of wampum (SWJP, 1: 158).

Governor Clinton had ordered Johnson to Onondaga to stop the Six Nations from going to Canada, but he had no intention of stopping their other roads. He and the governor as one mind urged them to exert their interest everywhere but Canada. A belt estopped the path to Canada.

The Six Nations were not only to stay home from Canada, Johnson said, but they were also to leave it to the New York authorities to retrieve their blood relations from the Laurentian missions, an endeavor in which the Iroquois had previously tried and failed. (Johnson's confidence that the New Yorkers could bring this off would prove misplaced.) A belt.

A delegation of the confederacy had come to Johnson the previous spring and presented several belts requesting permission to go to Canada to fetch their kindred. They were to return within a month. But they had stayed all summer and brought home no relatives, which made Johnson think that they had other business with the French governor. Meanwhile, they had asked Johnson to keep all their warriors at home, although the warriors were ready to go out against Canada. The old men had duped Johnson in order to protect their ambassadors from reprisals. This had not prevented Kahnawakeh warriors from lifting English scalps. A belt urged them not to listen further to the deceitful French (SWJP, 1: 160).

Johnson next reminded the sachems of the metaphors of unity—one flesh, one blood, one heart, one head—symbolizing their old agreement, which meant that what happened to one affected the other. The French ax was stuck in the English head. Their Kahnawakeh kinsmen had done it. Heaps of bones were scattered all over the country. A very large belt asked them to emulate their ancestors. They should drop France and stand by the English. The king had ordered Governor Clinton to protect Iroquois castles and gather Indian families within forts built for the purpose, and to clothe and feed them. Two more belts.

As was customary, the Six Nations answered belt with belt. (1) It delighted them that Johnson had discovered the chain legend, and they hoped he would not let it be lost again. The French would never get them to drop their friendship with their brethren. (2) It was cruel to be hindered from fetching their blood kindred who lay rotting in irons in French jails. But they agreed not to go to Canada providing the English could arrange an exchange of prisoners. (3) They confirmed having asked Johnson for permission to make one last attempt to bring their émigré kin home from Canada. While the delegation was at Montreal, news came of the Five Nations' killing some Frenchmen, whereupon the ambassadors were ordered to Quebec, threatened with jail, kept prisoners for ninety-two days, and finally released to bring home but two of their people held in irons. The others were still being held pending cessation of hostilities. Otherwise they would be put to death. Consequently, the sachems had begged the warriors to confine their activities to scouting the woods near home, hoping they could persuade the Kahnawakeh council to withhold theirs, in which they now confessed they had failed. (4) They would adhere to the rules of their forefathers and would continue to keep the English ax in hand. (5) They had held the ax for appropriate use while the English raised an army, and they had enlisted foreign Indians in their interest who were ready to act, but they had seen no sign of an army, and they could not predict what these outlanders might do. (6) They acknowledged the offer to fortify their castles, providing they agreed to it and gathered their people, whereupon they would notify the English. They were grateful for having the presents delivered and avoiding the hardship of going down after them. They awaited the governor's call.

Johnson covered the fire with satisfaction at their compliance. He would reassure the governor (SWJP, 1: 165).

This instance of grand council procedure speaks to two things: it exemplifies Six Nations political behavior at the mid-eighteenth century, and it demonstrates Johnson's command of expected protocol, his discovery of the chain legend, and his use of appropriate symbolism. He obviously employed a Mohawk speaker, and his command of the Mohawk language at this time remains uncertain. One suspects that he never attained the competence of Conrad Weiser. Johnson undoubtedly developed oral comprehension, although the orthography of Mohawk terms in his later writings shows little grasp of the phonetics and structure of the language, even though he could make himself understood. Johnson found in the Indian Records no tradition of the founding of the Iroquois League as we know it from nineteenth-century sources, and the league as such had long been supplanted by the confederacy. Johnson would soon make it over to suit his own purposes. Canasatego still presided at Onondaga, but a rising pro-French faction threatened to take over.

□□◇□□

At mid-century, Onondaga, still the axis of the Indian world, wobbled between Montreal, Albany, and Philadelphia. For two decades it was Shikellamy's world— the Oneida leader whom the grand council stationed at Shamokin to serve its interests during his lifetime—and the world of Conrad Weiser. With the advent and rise of Johnson, the orb of Indian politics would shift toward the Mohawk Valley while the Joncaires, *père et fils*, pulled it in the other direction. By their activities among the Senecas, the French in effect split the confederacy. The upper Iroquois—Senecas, Cayugas, Onondagas, and at times Oneidas—became pro-French. The settlements of émigré Iroquois on the St. Lawrence—Kahnawakeh (Caughnawaga), Akwesasneh (St. Regis), Kanehsatageh, and Oswegatchie (Ogdensburg)—exerted a powerful attraction. Émigré Iroquois refused to come home, operated mainly for the French, and neutralized the grand council.

Famine, disease, and rum weakened and diminished the population. Treaty delegates visiting Albany and Philadelphia encountered ship-borne diseases. Eminent sachems died and were buried on the spot, others succumbed returning, and survivors reaching home brought the viruses to their families. Small wonder the sachems expressed reluctance to revisit Philadelphia.

People of all ages became addicted to rum carried by Albany traders to Oswego. When the chiefs kept traders from the villages, both men and women took their pelts to Oswego and packed kegs home to the settlements. Witnesses describe the horrendous brawls that went on for days until the kegs were empty. The Moravians Cammerhoff and Zeisberger, visiting the Seneca villages, found little to eat but escaped with their lives thanks to a matron who hid them overhead in a loft until a brawl subsided. The council never managed to meet to hear their message. Men did poorly hunting, and the "three sisters" yielded little to the women that summer. Conditions were little better at Cayuga and barely tolerable at Onondaga. Intolerance to alcohol and drinking to excess had plagued the Iroquois for a century, but by 1750 it had virtually destroyed Deganawi:dah's message of peace and equity (Cammerhoff in Beauchamp 1916).

Such was the situation at Onondaga at the close of Canasatego's regime. A notable drinker himself, when sober he advocated the image of the confederacy, lauded its conquests, and cited its diplomatic feats to the English, while the faction of his rivals espoused the French connection and younger members drifted to Ohio, where game was abundant, traded deerskins with Pennsylvanians, forged new alliances, and asserted their independence.

The Delawares and Shawnees had preceded them, moving westward from the Susquehanna, leaving Shikellamy to preside over a few families at Shamokin. Traders out of Philadelphia and Lancaster followed, carrying rum in their pack trains over the Allegheny Trail that led to settlements of mixed populations near the forks of the Ohio. Back over the trail came pack trains laden with deerskin bundles destined for eastern tanneries. Conflicts of interest arose on all sides. The old men of Onondaga perceived a loss of control, a weakening of the confederacy.

Darkness descended on Shamokin in December 1748 when the enfeebled Shikellamy went the long trail (P. Wallace 1945: 274–76). He for Onondaga and Weiser for Pennsylvania had fashioned Pennsylvania Indian policy. The Three Brothers raised up another Oneida, Scaroyady ("Beyond the Sky"), and instead of dispelling the gloom at Shamokin, stationed him in Ohio, where he would collaborate with Johnson's agent, George Croghan. Weiser saw an opportunity and proposed buying the depopulated Juniata Valley (P. Wallace 1945: 264–78). Abuses in the trade cried out for a remedy.

The treaty was the time-honored way in Indian affairs. Between 1747 and 1753, a series of attempts sought to regulate the trade, to mitigate grievances between colonists and the Indian hunters in Ohio, and to settle the Six Nations' stance vis-à-vis the French. Just then the Six Nations confederacy claimed title to the headwaters of the Ohio and lands in its watershed and maintained the right to sanction any easements or cessions to Indians or Europeans. English land speculators ignored this claim, which the French recognized, although they were prepared to prevent the English from encroaching. They foresaw that the English were less interested in the deerskin trade than in acquiring land: they warned that trading posts would give rise to farms, that domestic animals and clear-cutting of forests would drive out the game, and that the native occupants would be displaced. French forts would not wipe out hunting territories: in short, two contrasting patterns of land use were at stake.[3]

Early in 1747, the Six Nations council met to discuss and compose such issues, on which they were divided. Mississauga ambassadors, having crossed Lake Ontario, laid down several "fine tobacco pipes adorned with wampum and feathers," pledging a shift of alliance from the French. The council was of two minds, but its members agreed to send a message to Canada and a second message to Albany requesting that the English tie their canoes and bateaux to the bushes for a few days and hold up their expedition against Canada until the Six Nations' messengers had returned from there. Meanwhile, Mohawk warriors had gone off on their own and joined the English without the sanction of the Six Nations council. The Onondagas, followed by the Oneida and Tuscarora sachems, declared in open council never to abandon "their eldest brother and founder of the Union" (Weiser to Provincial Council, 9 July 1747, PPCM, 5: 83–86).

This kind of fancy maneuvering did not appeal to the young men in Ohio. A party of Iroquois warriors appeared one November night in Philadelphia to visit the Pennsylvania government regarding their concerns over French and English hostilities in the west (Weiser in *Pennsylvania Gazette*, 12 November 1747, no. 987). They had come representing others without formal invitation. The president and council met them next day in a formal setting or "treaty," with Weiser interpreting. They were annoyed at the old men at Onondaga, who had refused to honor the English request that they take up the hatchet after Indians allied to the French had attacked English settlements. Originally they were asked to remain neutral. Their young men and war captains, after consulting together, had resolved to take up the English hatchet, to disregard the will of the old men, and to lay them aside "as of no use but in time of Peace." They would build their own council fire on the Ohio in the spring. Having done this, they had come to ask for better weapons. "We put a great deal of fire under our kettle and the kettle boiled high," meaning that they were carrying on the war briskly. "The Frenchmen's heads might soon be boiled." But the fire under the English kettle was nearly out, and

3. See sources cited in Eccles 1969: 158–59. See also Gipson 1939, 4: 217; NYCD, 10: 235.

"no Frenchmen's heads were like to be in it." Scaroyady, their leader, asked why the English, having brought them into the war, would not fight. With seven strings he urged the English to put more fire under their kettle.

They received a plausible answer and a present worth 150 pounds, which included four barrels of gunpowder; they were promised another present the following year. They said they were satisfied (DePuy 1917: treaty no. 26; PCR, 5: 145–52; Boyd 1938: 101–8; *Pennsylvania Gazette*, nos. 988, 996).

The meeting paid off. Weiser learned that the Miamis had told two western groups who intended to attack the Pennsylvania settlements that attacking the English, who were allies of the Six Nations, would be the same thing as attacking the confederates—all of which underscored the importance of the friendship of the Six Nations to Pennsylvania that he, Weiser, had cultivated (*Pennsylvania Gazette*, no. 990: 556–57). The president of the council concurred (*Pennsylvania Gazette*, no. 992).

This meeting with the insurgent Iroquois of Ohio represented a pivotal point in Pennsylvania Indian policy. Previously, the Pennsylvania council had treated solely with the Iroquois confederacy on all important Indian matters, recognizing Six Nations jurisdiction over other native tribal entities within the colony. Weiser was their emissary, as we have seen; but even he began to shift his view of Indian affairs in the light of the western drift of the Delawares and Shawnees and of family segments of the Iroquois to the Ohio country. Although the grand council appointed viceroys to watch this shifting population and report, the old men of Onondaga were losing control. Power would reside elsewhere in the future (P. Wallace 1945: 258ff.; Wainwright 1959: 17).

Conrad Weiser first perceived the shift and set his sights on the Ohio. Single-handedly he changed Pennsylvania's Indian policy and resolved to go there. With the demise of Shikellamy, that chief's role passed to the Oneida Scaroyady, through whom the people on the Ohio heard from Onondaga. Presently, the Miamis sent strings of wampum indicating their desire to enter the chain alliance and requesting that a road be cleared and that those already in the chain act as intermediaries to admit them. They petitioned Scaroyady to act on their behalf and lead their mission, but he suffered a fall on the road to Lancaster the next summer and could not speak for the mixed band of Miami, Shawnee, Delaware, Nanticoke, and Six Nations Indians, some fifty-five emigrants who appeared seeking English friendship. Instead, he deputed Andrew Montour to deliver his speech and interpret for the Algonquian-speaking Delawares, Shawnees, and Miamis. Weiser interpreted for the Six Nations.

As the first order of business, the interpreter was ordered to condole with the delegates for the accident before delivering the speech of Scaroyady, who lay encamped in Weiser's orchard and coached the proceedings at a distance. The Miamis described themselves as living in some twenty towns on the Wabash and having a thousand warriors. They presented thirty beaver skins and a calumet pipe "with long Stem, curiously wrought & wrapp'd round with Wampum of several Colours" (PCR, 5: 309; Boyd 1938: 116), which both parties to the treaty smoked.[4] They sought admission to the chain alliance with the English. They announced

4. The calumet was to the central Algonquins what wampum was to the Iroquois and writing to Europeans (see Fenton 1953). Throughout the eastern woodlands the same symbols or their synonyms prevailed.

that some twelve other nations awaited their success before approaching the English. The Shawnees, having broken a previous treaty by traveling through the bushes to Canada, were put on probation. There were then some 730(?) Six Nations warriors settled on the Ohio (PCR, 5: 307–19; P. Wallace 1945: 261; Wainwright 1959: 19). The treaty pleased the Pennsylvania proprietor, who feared the fragmentation of the Six Nations and deemed a strong confederacy essential to the English interest (Penn to Peters, in Boyd 1938: xlix, n98, 109–22).

The summer of 1748, when Weiser set out over the Allegheny Trail to treat with the Delawares, Iroquois, Shawnees, Mahicans, Wyandots, and various Central Algonquians at Logstown, marked the zenith of English predominance in the Ohio drainage before the peace of 1763 (Boyd 1938: li; P. Wallace 1945: 261ff.). Weiser faced a mixed bag of ethnic entities jointly occupying settlements but lacking a common language and a firm tradition of political unity, unlike the Six Nations confederacy. He asked them to enumerate their fighting men; they counted 307 Iroquois, 165 Delaware, 162 Shawnee, 100 Wyandot, 40 Chippewa, and 15 Mahican warriors (PCR, 5: 351). These nearly eight hundred men had two things in common: an interest in the trade and a desire for guns and powder. If held together, this coalition represented a gain to the English; if alienated, it posed a considerable threat to the Pennsylvania frontier. The liquor traffic was ruining any Indian advantage in the equation. Weiser's previous diplomatic experience paid off. The treaty increased the furs and deerskins coming to Philadelphia for export, and his journal awakened Pennsylvania investors to the rich soils of the region. George Croghan, a trader, emerged to prominence just then as an effective Indian manipulator, and he presently would serve as Johnson's deputy in the region (Wainwright 1959).

Besides the Logstown negotiations, satisfying Onondaga preoccupied the Pennsylvania authorities. Settlers were encroaching on the Juniata Valley in advance of its purchase from the Six Nations, and colonists from New York to Carolina desired an end to the Catawba war. Pennsylvania took the initiative. The old men of Onondaga, mindful of their own interests on the Ohio and of their claim to former Delaware lands, sent a delegation down to Philadelphia under Canasatego. This occasion proved the old orator's final appearance and witnessed his windiest utterance.

Meanwhile, the mounting western trade after Logstown worried the merchants at Montreal. The treaty with the Miamis at Lancaster the previous year posed a real threat to them and brought French efforts to regulate the Indian trade. Gallissionaire, then governor of New France, dispatched the Celoron expedition to take possession of strategic points, plant plaques claiming title, discover the temper of the Indians, and drive off the English traders. The Pennsylvania traders were about to lose their monopoly. The French brought off this coup with less than half the manpower of the Pennsylvania population alone (Boyd 1938: liii; Winsor 1895: 252ff.; Margry 1876–86, 6: 666–726). Celoron was amazed at the dramatic increase of the mixed Indian population in the region in the ten years since his previous visit. Johnson soon learned of the foray when a Cayuga chief brought one of the lead plaques to him (Parkman 1884, 1: 66). The English trade dropped by half.

□□◇□□

How much of this Canasatego knew when he set out from Onondaga for Philadelphia is uncertain. Catawba was on his mind. The others of the Six Nations had agreed to send deputies; they planned to rendezvous at Wyoming and then go down together. But when the others failed to show at the appointed landing, three Senecas, two Onondagas, and several Tutelos, Nanticokes, and Conoys came on without them. Weiser, having recently condoled the relatives of Shikellamy and finding affairs in a muddle without him, awaited the delegates at the landing with instructions to charge them with a message so that the proposed sale of the Juniata Valley lands would appear to come from the Indians (Boyd 1938: lvii).

This running council, not a formal treaty, introduced the new Pennsylvania governor, James Hamilton, to forest diplomacy. The agenda covered land problems and peace with the Catawbas. Two Senecas spoke first. While waiting at Wyoming, one speaker said, they had confirmed that white people were encroaching east of the Blue Ridge. The second speaker stated that the Conoys had entrusted their case to them: the Conoys had sold land between the Delaware and Susquehanna rivers, including their town site, for which they had not been paid. The governor issued a proclamation that termed the meeting with the Senecas a treaty and acknowledged that although the Conoys had lived on the land they had sold for a while before removing to the Juniata Valley, the government had honored the Six Nations' desire not to give money to tributaries for land. The government would remove those settlers who had not paid. The Indians received a considerable present.

Weiser had warned the government to keep quiet about the western settlers until after the Six Nations chiefs came downriver, when they could not but notice the western drift across the Susquehanna and would themselves complain. After that, everyone would see the need of a new land purchase (P. Wallace 1945: 278). He was authorized to send a message by the returning Senecas to the council at Onondaga inquiring whether they would sell any additional lands to the proprietors (P. Wallace 1945: 279). He charged the Senecas with heading off any straggling deputies of other nations.

But early in August 1749, Canasatego showed up at Weiser's uninvited, leading a host of 279 hungry Indians who looked forward to a good feed and a drink in Philadelphia. No matter that the business had already been transacted and the presents awarded—Canasatego insisted on pressing on. At Shamokin he had recruited sundry Delajare, Tutelo, and Nanticoke Indians. When Weiser questioned the size of the delegation and the presence of the Shamokin volunteers, he learned: "Everyone is at liberty to come along or stay at home on such occasions." Canasatego had come so far with the deputies of the other Six Nations that he could not turn back without visiting Philadelphia. Size was a measure of the importance attached to the business at hand. Weiser was fed up with Indians. He let them know that they were not wanted (P. Wallace 1945: 280–81).

The interpreter's blast shook numbers of the Indians. The Oneida delegation prepared to turn back, but Canasatego maintained a facade of affability. He reminded Weiser that regularly Indians invited Europeans to accompany them on missions and share amenities. Such a reprimand was unprecedented. They would not trouble the Pennsylvanians again; they would return home without sustenance and presents. Perhaps now that Pennsylvanians had got their lands, they no longer felt obliged to honor obligations. He demanded that Weiser produce the orders that they turn back (Boyd 1938: lix; P. Wallace 1945: 283).

There was no alternative to leading the throng to Philadelphia. Some 260 (one account said 290) Indians of eleven different nations straggled into town of a Sunday evening in mid-August (*Pennsylvania Gazette*, 17 August 1749, no. 1079). They got a cool reception. The council met on Wednesday, when Canasatego, in the manner of later attorneys, requested an adjournment until afternoon, which was granted. He then managed to find business enough to discuss in his longest speech on record (PCR, 5: 399–403; Boyd 1938: lix–lx). He reminded the governor and council of the road established by previous treaties (a string of wampum). A belt of eight rows invoked the custom, after long absence, of brightening the chain of friendship. A second belt affirmed that despite interim accidents, the Indians' attitude toward the Pennsylvanians had not changed. A third belt reminded them that the Six Nations, still the barrier between them and their enemy, so far had kept the war from them. Having brightened the chain, belt four meant that they could as siblings now proceed to other business. Canasatego found the governor's proclamation insufficient to restrain the European squatters in the Juniata Valley, who, like his own younger generation, were out of control. He complained of the mistreatment of some minorities present in their previous locations. A belt of twelve rows and a string.

A further belt documented inflation of land values. A string called for an inquest into the murder of his own nephew. A belt of seven rows spoke to the grievances of the Nanticokes enslaved by Marylanders. There was the usual request to mend hatchets and guns. Finally he returned two belts and strings sent by Governor Thomas to procure peace with the Catawbas at a proposed treaty in Virginia: the Six Nations preferred Philadelphia. Fearing they would get no present, he proposed selling some lands east of the Susquehanna.

The government responded to this unwanted visit and contrived speech by giving a sneaky deed that failed to show the headwaters of the Susquehanna, so as to conceal from the Iroquois that the purchase included the reserved lands around Wyoming. Indeed, since Pennsylvania's interest now focused on the Ohio, this act demonstrated the end of mutual respect between Pennsylvania and the Iroquois. Pennsylvania had grabbed the land that the Six Nations had wrested from the Delawares when they took them by the hair in 1742. Richard Peters blamed Governor Clinton of New York for the decline of Iroquois honesty in council: "The Old Six Nations lose their Influence every day & grow contemptible." The real reason was that Canasatego, in his usual diplomatic style, "had impaled the proprietorial officials on the horns of a dilemma" (Boyd 1938: lx; P. Wallace 1945: 285).

□□◇□□

Pennsylvania Indian policy could no longer cope with the "Indian problem." The proprietor, now John Penn, favored working through the Onondaga council. Thomas Lee of Virginia, who, since Lancaster in 1744, had maintained a steady correspondence with Conrad Weiser on Iroquois customs and politics, came up with a grand design of uniting the British colonies from Nova Scotia to Georgia in an alliance with the Iroquois Confederacy. He proposed that Weiser invite the grand council to send deputies to Fredericksburg to meet with representatives of the colonies, settle the Catawba problem, and forge a national Indian policy. As it turned out, the Six Nations declined to honor Virginia's invitation, and William Johnson preempted the Catawba negotiations. With the passing of Canasatego, the whole scene at Onondaga shifted in favor of the French. Nevertheless, Weiser's journal of his mission for Virginia gives a vivid picture of Iroquois politics at the mid-century (P. Wallace 1945: 298–320; PCR, 5: 470–80).

This time Weiser followed the Delaware Watergap path to Minisink, went thence to Esopus, or Kingston, on the Hudson, called at Livingston Manor on the east bank, and recrossed to Albany. There, at some predecessor of today's Keeler's or Jack's restaurants, he treated Henry Peters and Nickas, two Mohawk chiefs, to several bottles of wine. They had recently visited Canada, they said, where the French had given them a hard time for having served the English in the late war. Still in good spirits a day or so later, they advised Weiser that most of the Onondagas had gone over to the French interest and converted to Catholicism. They informed him that Colonel Johnson had been commissioned to seek peace with the Catawbas, but Peters doubted that he could bring it off. Peters volunteered privately, however, that if the governor of Carolina made him a handsome present, he personally could do it.

Revisiting Schoharie, where he had passed fifteen formative years speaking Mohawk, Weiser learned that the upper three nations had made the French connection and that some Oneidas leaned that way and chided the Mohawks for remaining loyal to the English while the New York governor, since the peace, had neglected to address and thank them for their services. When the chiefs at Fort Hunter asked whether his mission related to the Catawbas, Weiser assured them it followed from the Lancaster Treaty six years earlier.

No traveler of the day could escape the hospitality of Colonel William Johnson or fail to communicate his business before leaving the Mohawk Valley. Johnson informed Weiser that peace with the Catawbas was his responsibility, that Governor Clinton had entrusted the matter to him, and that he had already begun negotiations. Johnson and Clinton had agreed that it was best for Weiser to say nothing about the Catawbas at Onondaga, thus removing the matter from Weiser's hands. Governor Glen of South Carolina, at the Catawba end of the matter and in accord with Virginia, had entrusted the matter to two different people.

Iroquois protocol demanded that an embassy pause to build consensus at each fire of the Longhouse. Weiser next stopped at Oneida, enlisted a delegation to conduct him to Onondaga, and requested that the Oneidas send a messenger ahead to foretell his coming. He gave an extra string to the runner to be relayed by a second runner to Cayuga and to the Senecas. The Oneida chiefs asked him to stop for a day or two, inasmuch as it would take at least a week to assemble the grand council, which would afford leisure to discuss state affairs. The Oneida council knew in advance of Weiser's coming, and they understood that his mission was to invite them to Fredericksburg to treat for peace with the Catawbas under the aegis of A?sare?ko:wa, the governor of Virginia. Weiser asserted that the British king had ordered the conference to renew the chain with the Six Nations, and they would see no Catawbas there. The Oneida chiefs insisted that the English had been taken in by the Catawbas, who had boasted to the Tutelos that they would never sue for peace with the Six Nations—that even "after their Death, their very Bones shall fight." The Catawbas held the Six Nations in contempt, unlike the Cherokees, who had come to the frontier towns of Iroquoia to sue for peace. Now the Catawbas should undertake the same. "The Six Nations were too great a People and had too much Honour to kill the Deputies of their Enemies in their Towns."

The then leading Oneida sachem, who no longer carried the title Odatshehdeh but the name Disononto, whom Weiser described as a man of seventy yet strong and nimble, sat up until midnight quizzing Weiser about factions in the New York colonial government—Why were the governor and assembly at odds?—and other questions that Weiser could not answer.

Next day on the path to the Tuscarora town some eighteen miles distant, a messenger from Onondaga intercepted Weiser to announce that owing to the death of Canasatego two nights before, there would be no general council while they were mourning. Weiser noted that performance of the condolence ritual marked the status of the deceased: "It is to be known that the Six Nations don't meet in Council when they are mourning till some of their Friends or Neighbours wipe off their Tears and comfort their Heart; it is a certain ceremony, and if they appear in Council without that Ceremony being performed, the dead Person was of no Credit or Esteem, and it is a certain affront to the deceased's Friends, if he has any."

After Weiser's arrival at the Tuscarora settlement, a second messenger came from Onondaga to inform him that the Onondaga council, on second thought, had decided to hear him, contrary to custom and "notwithstanding the melancholy Event," since Weiser had come so far. A grand council of the Six Nations was summoned.

Weiser's party in this situation became the clearminded, representing the Oneida-Tuscarora-Cayuga moiety. As the offspring of their father's kinsmen, the Three Brothers (Mohawk-Onondaga-Seneca), it was their obligation to condole the moiety in mourning. Accordingly, a senior member of the council, an Oneida, began to sing the "Lamentation Song" (Athahinonʔkeh, Going on the Road), as they took up the path to Onondaga.

At Onondaga, Weiser lodged as usual with Tohashwachdiony (Kakhswenthioni, "Hanging Wampum Belt," also known as Red Head),[5] successor to Canasatego but a convert and French partisan. It is a tribute to Iroquois hospitality that politics did not abridge a friendship, particularly with an ambassador. Various members of the council not in mourning called on Weiser, particularly Saristaquoah (Saristako:wa, "Big Sword, Steel, etc."), who came twice. Onondaga had lost several headmen of late, specifically three men who had died traveling to and from Philadelphia.

While waiting for the council to assemble, Weiser learned that half of the Onondaga population had defected to the new French mission at Oswegatchie (Ogdensburg) on the St. Lawrence. Those who returned hocked their French finery for liquor. French authorities had told converts that there was no need for Indian government—only traditionalists supported it.

5. See "Kakenthiony" in DCB, 3: 321–22. Another of this name was on the Ohio after the mid-century (DCB, 3: 319–20).

It took just seven days for a quorum of the council to assemble. On 13 September, five Oneida and Tuscarora deputies arrived; the Cayugas could not come but deputized the Oneidas, of their moiety, to represent them. None came from the Senecas. Members of the clearminded moiety met with Weiser apart "in the Bushes." They agreed to condole the mourning Onondagas over the death of Canasatego, and an Oneida chief named Ganachquayieson (Kanakwayie:son) would act as their speaker. At noon the Onondaga chiefs and company received them and consented to hear Kanakwayie:son.

With the Three Bare Words of the Requickening Address, he addressed the senior moiety:

> *"Father"* [*agadoni*] (So the Oneiders, Cayugers, and Tuscaroras stile . . . the Onondagers, Sinickers, and Mohawks), We, your Sons, the Oneiders, Cayugers, and Tuscaroros, jointly with your Brother Assaryquoah [Weiser, representing the governor of Virginia], entered your door in a very melancholy time, when your Eyes were almost blind with the Tears you shed, and when your Heart is sorrowful to the highest degree for the Death of that great Man our Word, who died but the other day (a dead man's name must not be mentioned among those People); we, your Sons and your Brother before named, make bold to come near you in order to comfort you in your trouble and to Wipe off the Tears from your Eyes, and to clean your Throat, to enable you to see about you and to speak out again; we also clean the Place where you sit from any deadly Distemper that may remain on it, and might perhaps have been the occasion of the great Man's Death.

On behalf of his moiety, the speaker gave a string of three rows symbolizing the three words—eyes, throat, and mat. Weiser gave another of similar size. He then covered the grave of the deceased with a belt of wampum. This act concluded the required condolence.

The council was now prepared to hear his message. After a polite interval, Weiser asked to be heard; the hosts assented to hear him. Addressing "the United Six Nations" as "Brethren," he enumerated their council names—first, the senior moiety of the Three Brothers, then their offspring.[6] He then issued the Virginia governor's invitation for them to treat at Fredericksburg and receive the king's present in consequence of the Lancaster treaty of 1744. A large belt of wampum.

At sunset, the Onondaga speaker Kakhswenthioni returned the condolences, giving three-row strings to the junior moiety and to Weiser. He desired that they might be comforted over the death of the great man.

On the evening of the fifteenth, the council having met all day, three of its members brought word to Weiser that his answer would follow at Oneida, which they hoped would be satisfactory.

On the sixteenth, Weiser, as custom required, extinguished the council fire that he had kindled and took leave of Onondaga. The Oneida and Tuscarora deputies accompanied him to Canasaraga.

On the party's reaching Oneida next day, the Oneida chiefs met in council for two hours before summoning Weiser to hear the answer of the Six Nations to the

6. These were Tekarihoken (M-1), Sagochiendagehte (the name bearers), Dyionenhogaron (doorkeepers); Neharontoquoah (great log—Oneida), Sanonowantowano (big pipe—Cayuga), and Tuscarora.

governor of Virginia. Although they took kindly to the invitation, they had lost so many great men traveling to Philadelphia of late that they desired moving the council fire to Albany and kindling it there. They would return Virginia's wampum belt when they met, but they gave a large belt to Weiser to convey their answer.

Weiser indicated that he believed the governor of Virginia, instead of coming to Albany, might give the king's present to the Indians on the Ohio who were kindred of the Six Nations. The sachems present responded that the Ohio Indians were mere hunters and neither councilors nor chief men; they had no right to receive presents due the Six Nations, "although they might expect . . . a share . . . from the Six Nations Chief under whom they belong."

On his way home, Weiser paused at the upper Mohawk castle to relate the proceedings at Onondaga. He had found "the Six Nations quite of another disposition than formerly . . . that their Heart was turned from their Brethren the English." His Mohawk sources confirmed this view: the French now dominated the upper Iroquois, which they ascribed to English mismanagement of Indian affairs.

While Weiser was at Onondaga, the chiefs had inquired about the disposition of lands bordering Juniata Creek. They insisted repeatedly that the Indians on the Ohio had no right to sell any land in Pennsylvania. He had also found Onondaga thick with French praying Indians who had come there to visit friends and who behaved civilly toward him.

Canasatego had taken the public trust into his grave. His successor, Hanging Wampum Belt, now the presiding chief, told Weiser "that all the Belts of Wampum belonging to the Publick from the several English governors that remained unanswered at the Death of Canasatego, and found in his Possession, were by his orders *buried* with him."[7] This made Canasatego a thief after his death, although some people believed his widow and family had stolen the belts.

While at Onondaga, Weiser learned why his Moravian co-religionists had failed to establish an Onondaga mission. They had dealt "in the Bushes" with Canasatego's faction, bypassing the general council. They were therefore answered "in the Bushes" and got no council sanction.

□□◇□□

The news that Weiser brought back to Philadelphia shook the Pennsylvania authorities: Canasatego was dead, his successor was a Roman Catholic and pro-French, most of the Six Nations inclined that way, and Weiser had found the whole atmosphere at Onondaga, though still civil, less friendly than formerly. Interest now centered on the western tribes, who outnumbered the Six Nations. Losing the Six Nations meant that the French threat was now general and affected the other colonies, and efforts began to enlist other colonial governors in a united approach to Indian affairs. Governor Clinton of New York would have to act.

The concept of union in the management of Indian affairs was emerging. As early as 1745, Pennsylvania governor Thomas had suggested the need for effective management. Thoughtful men saw beyond colonial rivalries, jealousies, and dissensions between governors and legislatures to the general good. The proprietor

---

7. The printed journal reads "burned," which is inconsistent with Iroquois inhumation, for they did not cremate the dead (PPCM, 5: 480).

Thomas Penn had perceived the advantage and suggested a form of representation and shared funding. Archibald Kennedy of New York and Benjamin Franklin at mid-century promoted the idea, which would culminate in Franklin's famous statement to his fellow printer Parker four years later. Governor Glen of South Carolina urged a Williamsburg conference to settle the Catawba question, noting that the French were always united in their councils (Boyd 1938: lxi-lxii).

Iroquois leaders at Logstown in May 1751 struck a positive note for the English colonies when they spoke for the western tribes in the manner of the great men of Onondaga. In a confrontation between Joncaire and George Croghan, when the Frenchman threatened Croghan and warned the tribes to cease trading with the English, an Iroquois chief intervened, questioned Joncaire's manhood, and told him: "Go and tell your Governor to ask the Onondaga Council if I don't speak the Minds of all the Six Nations." He then returned Joncaire's belt by way of rejection. The deference to Onondaga on a matter of policy was reinforced by a response to a Virginia request for a land grant on an Ohio tributary: the power to dispose of lands still rested with the Onondaga council (PCR, 5: 530-32). In presenting the governor's message regarding the land grant, Croghan employed the condolence paradigm, which the Delawares and Shawnees clearly shared. Johnson had invoked this practice among the Mohawks. Croghan also put the myth of the chain metaphor to service in forging his own alliance (PCR, 5: 535).

That summer, Clinton called a conference to meet the threat to Oswego posed by the French at Niagara. Its stated purpose was fourfold: to renew the covenant chain with the Six Nations; to exhort them to forge strict military and free trade alliances with neighboring nations; to get them to send sufficient men to Niagara to stop the French from building any new works and to demolish any existing ones; and to make peace with the Catawbas (Clinton to the Lords of Trade, NYCD, 6: 714).

Only Massachusetts, Connecticut, and South Carolina sent commissioners to the conference. The other colonies were not yet ready to commit themselves to an alliance. Pennsylvania, suspicious of Clinton's motives, sent Weiser with instructions limited to condoling the death of Canasatego. Clinton, anxious that Weiser not speak first, before Clinton himself did, demanded that Weiser submit his remarks in writing for approval. Weiser was told that he might speak as soon as the Catawbas who were in town had received their answer. But various Indians, including Dyoninhokaro (S-8), approached Weiser on a personal basis (PCR, 5: 541-43).

The Catawba delegation, much awed by the Six Nations, approached singing, their gourd rattles decorated with feathers, and offered a calumet to their hosts. Catawba, a Siouan language, proved a hazard to the interpreters. Weiser finally rendered the English substance into Mohawk, which satisfied the chiefs. All had grown weary of the war and gladly welcomed the sight of a wampum belt and feathered stems tied to a post (P. Wallace 1945: 327). The Six Nations gave the Catawbas a wampum belt to wear about their necks symbolizing friendship, but they cautioned that until a second or third visit returning prisoners, their custom of suspending peace would prevail (P. Wallace 1945: 328),

The formalities concluded but the presents not yet distributed, the Indians waited by the door while Clinton granted Weiser permission to speak and then left town without saying good-bye or taking the Indians by the hand, which greatly affronted them. Weiser, more sensitive to ceremonial requirements, hired Ganach-quayieson, an Oneida chief who had served him previously, to fulfill the necessary ritual. While Weiser ordered a round of drinks for the seated Indians, the Oneida ritualist paced the room and sang "lamentation Songs over the death of Cana-satego and others, naming all the Chiefs that died of late." Having finished the eulogy, he sat down, paused, and then stood to announce to the Six Nations that the governor of Pennsylvania had sent Tarachiawagon (Weiser) with a message. He gave a string and proceeded. Not only had Canasatego died but others of the chiefs had also succumbed returning from Philadelphia. Pennsylvania condoled their loss and wiped the tears from the eyes of their relations. The son of Seneca chief Old Smoke, killed by the French, was properly condoled, and a piece of Stroud's was given to cover the graves of those who had fallen in the service of the king. Times were tough. Abram, a Mohawk, apologized that the Mohawks lacked presents to give to the governor of Pennsylvania (P. Wallace 1945: 330; APSL ms. 134; APSL, Papers on the Indian and Military Affairs of the Province of Pennsylvania [1737–75]: 123–28).

For the second time since 1745, Clinton had bungled a conference. This one failed to achieve unanimity: few colonies attended, and Weiser and Johnson were at odds. Clinton did renew the covenant, and peace negotiations with the Catawbas began, but the Six Nations were unhappy that Johnson had resigned and wanted him reinstated. There was a chance that the crown might honor his expense accounts and recognize the need to entrust the management of Indian affairs to one person.

Even before the conference opened, the Six Nations had requested a private audience with the governor to convey what they had agreed in council. Hendrick spoke for them. When Colonel Johnson had sent a belt through the Six Nations informing them that he would no longer act on their behalf, they had been shocked because he understood their public affairs. They thought of him as an Indian and likened him to a tree that had stood during wartime and now had fallen. They would not welcome some stranger ignorant of their affairs, and they gave the governor a belt of wampum "to raise up the fallen Tree." They wanted an answer, and they wanted Johnson, "for he has large Ears . . . and what he hears he tells us; he also has large Eyes and sees a great way, and conceals nothing from us." Moreover, their fire was kindled at Colonel Johnson's, but it was going out, so they gave a string to have it renewed (SWJP, 1: 340).

Clinton tried to dissociate the person from the position and offered to find someone else and kindle a fire elsewhere, to which the Six Nations responded that only half of Colonel Johnson belonged to his excellency; the other half belonged to them. And since his excellency had not persuaded Johnson to come down, they asked leave to send a runner with a string, to which Clinton consented. Johnson had already started out, and the runner met him east of Schenectady, so that he was present within two days. He would not resume the management of Indian affairs, short of reassurance that his previous expenses would be paid. He agreed to serve during the present conference, and Clinton promised to press his claim in London (SWJP, 1: 342–44; NYCD, 6: 726; Colden's memoir on Indian affairs, NYCD, 6: 739). The Six Nations had prevailed.

Outbreaks of smallpox prevented further treaty conferences from being held at Albany during the next two years. In June 1753, Johnson and a contingent of Mohawks met the governor in New York City, where Hendrick, their speaker, demonstrated contempt for his excellency's neglect of the Six Nations by declaring the chain broken. He asserted that the Mohawks were the acknowledged head of the Six Nations. A belt would notify the others. The chain would not be mended before the Albany Congress the following year (NYCD, 6: 781ff., 788).

CHAPTER 30

THE ALBANY CONGRESS
MENDS THE CHAIN

Preservation of the whole continent depends upon the proper regulation of the Six Nations.—Archibald Kennedy, *The Importance of Gaining and Preserving the Friendship of the Indians*

From diverse quarters abroad and at home, parties added sticks to kindle a fire where all might assemble to mend the chain. The Lords of Trade, by the Duke of Halifax, wrote to the governor of Pennsylvania recommending that "a junction of commissioners" representing the several colonial governments meet with the Six Nations, renew the covenant chain, and make the presents customary on such occasions. The lords urged care in choosing the commissioners: they should be men of character, ability, and integrity, and familiar with Indian affairs. The time and place of the meeting was up to the governor of New York (APSL ms. 124, Papers on the Military and Indian Affairs of the Province of Pennsylvania, 1737–75).

Andrew Montour, interpreter and go-between for the Ohio Indians, Pennsylvania, and Virginia, whom the Six Nations would presently "antler" to represent the Ohio Indians, visited Onondaga in the spring but found few at home. He encountered universal opposition to the building of forts by either the British or the French, and he heard disapproval of either Virginia's or Pennsylvania's treating with the Ohio Indians. There was little the grand council could do, however, but grumble about it. Neither would they go to Winchester to treat with Virginia.

While at Onondaga, Montour witnessed seven French Indians arrive and present a black belt (a war symbol) some six feet long and "twelve grains wide," informing the Six Nations that a French army accompanied by Indians was descending on Ohio to build forts and drive out the English traders (P. Wallace 1945: 340). The report said that Kakhswenthioni, "Hanging Wampum Belt," or Red Head (Weiser's host and now headman at Onondaga) had sent word back to Onontio that the Ohio lands belonged to the Six Nations, that they would keep them, and that the Six Nations meant what they said; they declined to accept the black belt and returned it to the sender.

Concerned, Governor Hamilton of Pennsylvania wrote to Governor Clinton of New York and dispatched Conrad Weiser on a fourth mission to Onondaga that terminated in the Mohawk Valley. Weiser waited several days in Manhattan for an audience with Clinton before going upriver, while Clinton's haughty letter forbidding his going alone to Onondaga—that is, without William Johnson—lodged in the pocket of a wagoneer, to be delivered on Weiser's return.

At Albany, the mayor summoned the commissioners of Indian affairs to concert measures for returning some Pennsylvania prisoners from Canada. It seems that some Caughnawaga warriors, having set off against the Cherokees, had encountered a mixed force of Indians and English and captured some of each. One was given to a Caughnawaga warrior; the others went to jail. A Mohawk matron from the Laurentian settlements held one whom she had accepted to replace her deceased son, who had held the leading Mohawk league title, Tekarihoken. The title evidently had gone to Kahnawakeh in the emigration from the Mohawk Valley. The last incumbent, this matron's son, had died in 1751. (Weiser's fluency in Mohawk astounded the woman.) During the next week, Weiser met with and delivered his message to the Mohawk chiefs. His journal enumerates "Seth *Degarihogan*," followed by Kanadakayon ("Old Town") and others. The stay-at-homes had resuscitated the title Tekarihoken, and Kanadakayon was their speaker.

Johnson attended and invited Weiser home. From the Mohawk speeches and conversations with Johnson, Weiser could infer the views of the Six Nations on the French threat, affairs in Ohio, and English neglect. Some Senecas told Johnson that with French forts built on Six Nations land, "it would be over with the Six Nations and their Union would signify nothing more." Abraham, brother of Hendrick and himself a Mohawk chief, told Weiser that the Six Nations feared the French because the Six Nations were so divided and the French alliance so strong among them that they were powerless to resist French operations, despite their wish to oppose French possession of Ohio. Kanadakayon confirmed this view.

After Weiser and Johnson compared instructions from their respective governors, and Johnson did not invite Weiser to accompany him to Onondaga, Weiser judiciously withdrew, deciding that his mission was unnecessary, although Johnson did not openly oppose him. Weiser headed back to New York, where again Clinton used him badly. When news of Johnson's coolness and Clinton's mistreatment of the Pennsylvania interpreter reached Thomas Penn in London, and when some ministers in England read Weiser's journal, they found another job for Clinton and recalled him. Although Weiser's journal is no literary gem, it signaled "a clean-up of American colonial affairs" (PCR, 5: 642–47; P. Wallace 1945: 339–44).

□□◇□□

Treaty conferences at Winchester, with Virginia, and at Carlisle, with Pennsylvania, in the summer of 1753 accomplished little beyond distributing presents to Ohio warriors. Frightened by the French incursion into their homeland, Scaroyady led a mixed band of a hundred Five Nations, Delaware, Shawnee, and Miami Indians to meet and redefine relations with the Virginians. Mainly they wanted arms, which the Virginians withheld. Scaroyady reversed a previous request for a fort. In a hurry to get home, the Indians refused to go to Philadelphia or even to Lancaster but met the Pennsylvania commissioners at Carlisle in September (PCR, 5: 685; Gipson 1939: 286–87; Wainwright 1959: 54). The significance of Carlisle to Iroquois politics derives from Scaroyady's imposing Iroquois ceremonial requirements on the conduct of the treaty, which illustrates Iroquois prestige in Ohio. And for later history, the Carlisle treaty launched Benjamin Franklin's diplomatic career (Van Doren 1938a: 209).

Scaroyady instructed the commissioners on treaty protocol. A proper condolence ceremony required that presents be "spread on the ground" before a word was said. The form and content of the condolences were prepared in advance. The essential elements consisted of wiping the bloody seat, digging a symbolic grave to bury the bones of warriors, covering the grave, and wiping the tears that the bereaved might see the sun. "The proper strings and belts were made ready."

During advance meetings in the bushes, a messenger brought word from Tanacharison, the Oneida chief also known as the "Half King" who represented the grand council on the Ohio, that the French had rejected with contempt the three warnings the Six Nations customarily gave before making war. The French commandant threatened to throw Brothers Onas (Pennsylvania) and Assaryquoah (Virginia) over the hill. Scaroyady warned Pennsylvania traders not to cross the Ohio River, lest the French harm them. He advised his Delaware and Shawnee companions to wait on this gloomy message and confirm it at home (Boyd 1938: 125–27).

On the opening day of the treaty, the commissioners, as hosts, spoke first, invoking the name of the Six Nations in delivering the condolences. Then Scaroyady proceeded to condole the tribes present seriatim. For the Wyandots he introduced a theme of deprivation present in later Condolence Councils—"We are informed that your good old wise Men are all dead, and you have no more left." Then for all he rekindled the fire, recommended union, and urged keeping the covenant chain free of rust and damage. The allotted goods were then distributed.

The following day, the commissioners, having laid down the presents, sealed the affair with a union belt of six figures representing the five nations present and Pennsylvania, cautioning that if the union were broken in any part, the belt would fray and beads run off (Boyd 1938: 129).

On the third day, Scaroyady, on behalf of the Miami, Shawnee, Delaware, and Wyandot persons present, acknowledged wiping the blood, wrapping the bones of warriors, covering the graves of wise men, wiping tears, and restoring the sun. They would take the union belt home, where their wise men sat in council, and return an answer.

The ethnologist, ever keen to kinship usage, finds the Delawares in one context "grandfathers" to the Shawnees (Boyd 1938: 130) and in another, "uncles." Whether grandchildren or nephews, the Shawnees, out of deference for the Six Nations, earnestly requested the conference to lay all its transactions before the Onondaga council, to assure the council that "we do nothing in the Dark." Likewise with proceedings at Winchester.

That afternoon, the Miamis delivered a calumet decorated with feathers; a sacred shell painted green on the concave side, with wampum string attached, the symbol of the heart; and a large belt of fourteen rows that the Six Nations had sent to the Piankashaws, a Miami subtribe. They also attested to a Miami-Shawnee alliance and proclaimed the "Chain of Friendship" subsisting between the Shawnees, Six Nations, Delawares, and English.

Scaroyady acknowledged the several speeches and assured the authors that the substance would be communicated to the Six Nations. This observance of the forms and this concern that the right ways be followed mirror the image of the Onondaga council among the Iroquoian and Algonquian residents in Ohio (Boyd 1938: 130–32). Iroquois prestige was still a force to be reckoned with.

The final act of the commissioners assured the participants that they themselves would send the proceedings to Onondaga (Boyd 1938: 132-33). Scaroyady favored entrusting the matter to Andrew Montour, of whom he remarked to the commissioners, "We have set a Horn on Andrew Montour's Head," meaning that the Six Nations had antlered him—made him a counselor—and he was now a great man among them (Boyd 1938: 134).

The commissioners, having learned something about treaty protocol, came away not overly sanguine about the future. Whichever way the Ohio Indians leaned made little difference, they reported to the Pennsylvania governor. The liquor traffic had greatly increased, was already ruining these Indians, and would soon destroy them as an effective barrier to the French (Boyd 1938: 134). Matters were now out of Pennsylvania's hands.

□□◇□□

New York awakened from its apathy. The previous year, Hendrick had come down to Manhattan, taunted the English for sitting in peace at Albany, declared the chain severed, and walked out of the meeting in contempt. Clinton, thoroughly shaken and fearing an Indian war, asked Johnson to go up to Onondaga and mend the chain. Johnson had not made the mission when Weiser visited the Mohawk Valley, as we have seen. When Johnson received orders from Lieutenant Governor DeLancey, he got busy.[1] With Mohawk help, he set out for Onondaga just as Weiser and the Pennsylvania commissioners met the western Indians at Carlisle (NYCD, 6: 808-9).

Although Weiser afterward thought that Johnson had merely "dreshed the old Straw over again" by condoling the death of Canasatego three years after his demise and extolling the annexing of "two nations" to the confederacy—the Tutelos among the Cayugas, and the Nanticokes—who in fact were but a few families and "a miserable lot," Johnson nevertheless managed to please his hosts by resorting to the ancient symbolism of the league and mending the chain (P. Wallace 1945: 350).

In July, Hendrick responded to Johnson's invitation by remarking that "it is not usual for us to speak first when sent for." But the issue was of such urgency and Mohawk hearts were so full that they would break the rule. Following Johnson's speech, they agreed to assist him at the general council.

On 8 September, the host sachems met Johnson and the Mohawks a mile east of Onondaga and assured him they were ready to receive him. Woods'-edge protocol is implied.

Johnson's journal says that upon his party's entering Onondaga and being seated, Red Head, "one of the Chief Sachems," addressed the visitors: "As you enter our Meeting Place with wet Eyes, and sorrowful Hearts . . . we do by this String of Wampum wipe away your Tears and asswage your Grief, that you may

1. Clinton's replacement, Sir Danvers Osborn, served the shortest term as governor on record. He landed at Manhattan on 7 October 1753 and hanged himself five days later. James DeLancey acted ad interim (MHS Collections, 5, 1836: 37; NYCD, 6: 803-4.) The commissioners of Indian affairs whom Clinton had appointed during Johnson's temporary withdrawal inspired small confidence in the New York assembly and even less at Onondaga, and DeLancey pitched upon Johnson as a person of stature among the Six Nations.

speak freely to this Assembly." The remainder of the Three Bare Words is omitted (SWJP, 9: 110; DCB, 3: 320–21).

Johnson's speech to the general council, whether made by himself or by Hendrick, followed directly. With three belts of wampum he condoled the deaths of three named men who had made the council complete. The belts symbolized three words—tears, throats, and blood. Stroud's blankets covered their bones. A further belt deferred a summer meeting with the new governor, pending his arrival. Resuming the familiar symbolism, a fourth belt cleared the road and made up the fire.

Having renewed the fire, Johnson proceeded to sweep clean the council space with a new "white wing," which he hung near the fire, handy to brush aside dust and dirt brought in by strangers. This symbolic act out of the league epic rated a string.

He next proceeded to set upright the shady tree planted by the Five Nations' ancestors to shade the council—which tree he had on arrival found leaning—that it might flourish and that the roots might extend as formerly. Persons sitting or standing on the roots, feeling them shake, should set about securing the tree. A belt.

A larger belt celebrated the fire now burning and the tree growing in the old place, which called for quenching the "Fire made of Brambles" at Oswegatchie and bringing home the deserters. He could not prevent their going to Canada, but he warned that the French, a "delusive People," were infiltrating the Ohio and alienating allies of the Six Nations.

To improve communication, something of mutual interest, Johnson urged the Six Nations to return to the old custom of sending their own people directly as far as they intended a message to go, and to abandon the practice of relaying the word from castle to castle until it arrived distorted. A belt.

He reminded the Seneca delegates of their traditional role as the western doorkeepers of the Six Nations. They should hang a new door and communicate directly with Onondaga. They should attract near western tribes and bring them into the Six Nations' orbit. A belt.

With another belt, Johnson reset the Oneida stone, the great boulder that lent the name "people of the standing stone," and rubbed off accumulated moss and dirt. He advised concentrating the settlements of the Five Nations near those of their children, the Tuscaroras, and those of the recently allied Nanticokes. He fixed "a New String to the Cradle . . . hung up by your Forefathers when they received the Tuscaroras" to feed and protect them.

(Weiser deprecated the significance of the Nanticoke and Tutelo adoptions, which Johnson likened to two additional links strengthening the chain of friendship. According to Weiser, they were a few lineages at best, "a good for nothing people as any among the Indians," who had recently left Shamokin [P. Wallace 1945: 359].)

Turning to the Cayugas present, Johnson expressed the wish that they would not live so scattered and that they would stop listening to the French, a people with whom they never had an alliance. He welcomed the news that they were incorporating the Tutelos, an eastern Siouan remnant, for whom he gave a belt and a pass.

Johnson expressed concern that scalping parties recently had gone out against the Catawbas, despite the peace concluded the previous year, which he had attended. (This was the grievance that Weiser had sought to adjust and which he felt Johnson slighted.) A belt might not do it.

The council deliberated for two days and delegated Red Head to reply. Addressing Johnson reciprocally as "Brother Warraghiyagey," the council acknowledged his speech and thanked him for condoling the loss of the three named councilors, especially because it conformed to the traditional way. No further mention should be made of the loss. The reply continued, item by item and belt for belt, or string for string, in the sequence of the petition. Indeed, they knew very well the use of the white wing to sweep away what might keep the fire from burning with a pure flame. As for the tree of shelter, they were so hemmed in by both French and English that their hunting territories were preempted. "If we find a Bear in a Tree, there will immediately appear an Owner . . . to challenge the Property, and hinder us from killing it." The Senecas acknowledged themselves "the Door of the Six Nations," and the council thanked Johnson for refurbishing the Oneida stone, for adding a string to the cradle for the Nanticokes, and for recognizing the Tutelos at Cayuga. Although the chain was "almost Eat through with rust" from neglect, they wanted the two new nations added as links.

Johnson had returned their three belts requesting prohibition of the rum trade. They were grateful it was stopped, but wished it included Oswego.

Finally, Johnson's speech had employed familiar symbolic metaphors, which pleased them. "We . . . return you a great many Thanks for speaking in Our own way, which is more Intelligible to us, because [it conforms] to the Custom and manner of our forefathers." They hoped he would come on call, for they had often stretched out their necks in expectation but had been disappointed. Style was more important than substance (SWJP, 9: 110–20). The speech might not concentrate the Six Nations in their castles, but it would bring delegates to Albany the next summer.

□□◇□□

Well before the Lords of Trade instructed the colonial governors to develop a plan to face the crisis posed by the French incursion on Six Nations lands under crown protection in Ohio, a few thoughtful men in the colonies were exchanging ideas on their own. Franklin, ever a realist, regarded the Indians "with a humane curiosity and natural respect" for a people with a way of life different from his own. Out of his experience in sitting through an early Philadelphia treaty as a member of the assembly, in printing the treaties, and in serving as a Pennsylvania commissioner at Carlisle, he had come to admire the Iroquois Confederacy. He found in it a model for inspiring his contemporaries to support a plan of union that he was drafting for the upcoming Albany Congress.

In advance of the meeting, on 20 March 1750 he wrote what amounted to a referee's report to his fellow printer James Parker in New York, who appended it to a pamphlet by Archibald Kennedy (1751: 41), in which Kennedy suggested a confederacy of the colonies. Franklin's words:

> It would be a strange thing if Six Nations of ignorant savages should be capable of forming a scheme for such an union, and be able to execute it in such a manner as that it has subsisted ages and appears indissoluble; and yet that a like union should

be impracticable for ten or a dozen English colonies, to whom it is more necessary, and must be more advantageous, and who cannot be supposed to want an equal understanding of their interests." (Van Doren 1938a: 207, 209; Franklin 1962, 5: 335, 1987: 444)

Franklin's famous words were not uttered at the Albany Congress, as sometimes has been alleged. This bit of satire on Franklin's contemporaries has of late inspired proponents of the idea that the writers of the United States Constitution derived its structure and separation of powers from the Iroquois Confederacy, a doctrine for which supporting historical evidence has escaped responsible scholars. None of Franklin's contemporaries—not even Colden, Weiser, or Johnson—left an account of the internal workings of the confederacy for James Madison to follow. Not until the middle of the nineteenth century did such appear in Lewis Henry Morgan's classic *League of the Ho-de-no-sau-nee, or Iroquois* (1851). Like much of what else is advanced today as politically correct, this spurious doctrine represents invented tradition (Tooker 1988; Johansen 1990).

I need not add to the already abundant literature on the Albany Congress. Instead, I shall examine Iroquois participation in the light of current "politically correct" rhetoric that it was an occasion when native participants held up the Iroquois League/Confederacy as a model for the colonies. In reality, native participants were far more interested in promoting their own grievances.

The commissioners of the several colonies came to Albany by request of the Lords of Trade to deal with two issues: mending the chain alliance with the Six Nations and devising some plan for uniting to cope with French aggression (Gipson 1939: 9). Among the commissioners sent by the several colonies, the New York delegates, led by acting Governor DeLancey, particularly Johnson, in addition to Franklin from Pennsylvania, aided by Weiser, were acquainted with expected native protocol. The Iroquois representation, predominantly Mohawk, included few headmen of the upper nations. Mohawk leaders spoke for their nation and in the name of the Six Nations. Arent Stevens interpreted. Weiser acted as a resource person, although his Mohawk was thought rusty and not deemed up to treaty standards. English was his third language. Nevertheless, although Franklin made the conference famous, Weiser enabled it to achieve its original purpose (P. Wallace 1945: 358).

During the two weeks preceding the adoption of Franklin's plan, accepted Iroquois treaty protocol prevailed while the commissioners reforged the chain with the Indians. The speech of the colonies employed the usual metaphors of welcome: the path, the fire, wiping tears with three strings, brightening the chain and forging new links, and clouds hanging over the council, which implied a need to restore the sun. Someone had coached DeLancey.

Kanadakayon, "Old Town," speaker for the lower Mohawk castle, told the governor that the Six Nations were present that day by the Creator's will, "to which place you have led us by the hand," to the "old meeting place," where they would lay their complaints. They would open their minds. They hoped that the governor would take time to consider and not be too hasty or answer in two or three words, and then turn his back on them in the manner of Clinton. Land was their major issue, specifically the Kayaderosseros Patent to lands north of them,

Figure 33. The Mohawk
chief Hendrick, drawn
around the time of the
Albany Congress, 1754.
Courtesy Williams College
Archives and Special
Collections.

which Kanadakayon described. With this long-standing grievance, the lower
Mohawk town drove an entering wedge into the proceedings, speaking first and
resetting the agenda, before the Canajoharie Mohawks could present their
grievance.

The next day, Hendrick (fig. 33) and other headmen of the upper Mohawk
castle appeared together with sachems representing the other Five Nations and
waited on the governor. Hendrick explained the delay. The upper Mohawks had
been at Johnson's when the message to meet "where the fire burns" had reached
them, and they "came down running" as soon as they received it. "The Six
Nations are now here complete." It had taken some time to assemble them.

The governor welcomed them and condoled their losses with a string to wipe
their tears, take sorrow from their hearts, and open their minds to speak freely.

Hendrick reciprocated. Then, turning to the Six Nations, he briefed them on
how he served Johnson at Onondaga and how Johnson had told the chiefs there
about the death of the new governor, Osborn (Clinton's replacement), soon after
Osborn's arrival—before they could meet him. Hendrick said he was glad to see
the acting governor, to whom he would declare his grievances.

As to why the Canajoharie delegation had arrived late, he gave a somewhat
convoluted explanation: after they had gone down to New York the previous
summer and had their complaints ignored (and after having walked out of the
meeting), they thought the covenant chain was broken. "It seemed to us that the
Governor had turned his back upon the Five Nations, as if they were no more."
In contrast, the French were courting them and drawing their people off to
Oswegatchie. The Mohawks had been strong in former times, when Colonel

Schuyler had frequently visited them, which had kept the Anglo-Mohawk alliance intact. Now the Mohawks were in a bind. Their own people blamed them behind their backs for things they did not deserve. The Onondagas had liked Johnson's speech last summer but had attributed its authorship to the Mohawks. The other nations regarded them as Johnson's counselors, supposedly hearing all the news from him. This was not the case. Johnson neither received much news from them nor imparted much news to them. This was why they had stayed behind, letting the other nations go down first to hear the governor's speech. Had they come first, the other nations would have said the Mohawks had made the governor's speech. The Mohawks could hear it afterward.

All of this speaks to the tension between Mohawk arrogance and jealousy of the remoter nations. Hendrick admitted that some Mohawks "who have large open ears" had learned to speak broken English and Dutch. From overhearing settlers, "we came to understand that we are looked upon as a proud nation." For that reason they had stayed behind. "Tis true and known we are so, and that we, the Mohawks, are the head of the other nations. Here they are, and they must own it." For a fact, native tradition assigns the Mohawks priority in forming the Iroquois League, and as we have seen, Mohawk is the official language of league ritual. To a degree, their insistence on this precedent to this day irks the other nations.

This brief glimpse into the internal structure of Iroquois polity is about all the commissioners would get. Several days later, Hendrick made a second speech replying for the Six Nations to the general address of the commissioners by Governor DeLancey. First, Abraham, brother of Hendrick and also a sachem of the upper Mohawk town, asked the assembly: "Are you ready to hear us?" Following the governor's assent to this bit of council protocol, Hendrick stood and proceeded to renew the chain of friendship between the colonies and the Six Nations. The Six Nations, he said, rejoiced to meet the commissioners face to face, thanked them for condoling their dead, and reciprocated with three strings of their own, the bare essentials. Then, holding the chain belt given them by the governor and commissioners, he returned grateful acknowledgments for their renewing and brightening the chain. Inasmuch as this belt representing the alliance was of great importance to the "United Nations," they would take it to Onondaga, where their council fire burned, keep it, and consult over it. He mentioned two added links; they expected more as they filled up vacancies in the chain. This was a mutual obligation of both parties. Theirs was the view of those present and of absent brethren (in Ohio).

As for their living dispersed, with half the Onondaga population then at Oswegatchie, Hendrick explained that Canada prevented their several attempts to retrieve their kin and concentrate them in British territory. They would keep trying. But the real reason was that New York had neglected them for three years. (He meant that no treaty conferences had met.) Then, in a gesture of contempt, he took a stick and tossed it behind his back: "You have thrown us behind your backs and disregarded us." The French were subtler, forever trying to alienate his people. This item warranted a belt.

Without the Six Nations' consent, Hendrick continued, the French had encroached on their lands and built forts. Meanwhile, Virginia and Pennsylvania were disputing rights to lands of the Six Nations in Ohio, which surely would precipitate destruction of the Six Nations. He gave a belt to clear the clouds of confusion and restore the sun.

Indeed, the speaker avowed, Albany was the ancient place of treaty, where the fire of friendship had formerly burned, but the Six Nations had not been called to a treaty in three years. Clinton's appointed commissioners had never invited them to smoke (confer) with them. Instead, they dealt with Canadian Indians engaged in the trade. He boasted that Mohawk warriors could have taken Crown Point, the French fort on Lake Champlain, but were deterred, while the English had burned their own fort at Saratoga, leaving unfortified Albany open to attack. Beaver pelts filled trading houses, but the money went to Canada along with powder, lead, and guns destined for Ohio. "The French are men . . . but you are all like women, bare and open." On this shameful note Hendrick ended.

His brother Abraham continued. The Six Nations' chain of memory was long. Three years earlier, when Johnson laid down the management of Indian affairs, they had expressed their anxiety to Clinton. He had promised to convey their concern to the king, on returning home, so that his successor might reappoint Johnson. The Six Nations now embraced this new opportunity to remind the acting governor, DeLancey, of their request by laying down a belt. The Mohawks wanted Johnson reinstated. Their previous request must have "drowned in the sea."

Turning to the New York commissioners of Indian affairs, Abraham declared: "The Fire here is burnt out." With this gesture of no confidence, the session adjourned.

In their joint reply to the Six Nations, to which several delegations proposed additions during the debate, the commissioners tried to reassure the natives that the chain was brightened, the fire burned clear, and they hoped both sides would find things pleasant thereafter. They acknowledged neglect, affirmed that the Six Nations did not consent to the French encroachments, and denied allegations that either Virginia or Pennsylvania had sent soldiers to the west or built forts there. In clarifying these matters, Conrad Weiser emerged from relative obscurity to set the record straight in a published memorandum on the background of the Ohio situation (MHS 5: 46-47; DHNY, 2: 585-86).

Governor DeLancey recovered the agenda to defend the Albany traders. As for Johnson, he would not reappoint him yet but would keep the Indian commissioners for another year on trial and charge them to be more responsive to Indian interests. A Massachusetts commissioner then reported on depredations in northern New England.

Two days later, the Six Nations confirmed the actions of the commissioners with several belts. They accepted the Indian commissioners for another year but renewed their plea for Johnson. They thanked the commissioners from the several governments for meeting to discuss Indian affairs. They thanked the New York governor for acknowledging "that [the right to sell land] is in us." They had been unable to go down to Virginia to accept the king's present. They affirmed what Weiser had said. They reiterated concern for the safety of defenseless Albany, for themselves, and for the personal safety of Johnson from French agents, he "being also one of the Five Nations" and one of their sachems (MHS 5: 52).

The grievance over Canojaharie lands threatened to impede the Albany Congress. Delancey held two meetings "in the bushes" to settle the matter. He persuaded two heirs to the patents to release their rights. But DeLancey had left the pertinent papers in Manhattan and would have to examine them on his return. The Indians left these matters in the hands of their "elder brother," as they distinguished the governor from the other commissioners, "their brothers." It was agreed not to appear to differ on policy matters while there were French Indians in town (MHS 5: 59).

The following day, the secretary read the report of a public conference of commissioners and sachems the previous evening. It covered four topics: the enforcement of laws respecting the rum trade; approval of the Mohawk request to build a church at Canajoharie; the satisfaction of land grievances; and a decision not to ration gunpowder "on the hill" but to send it in bulk to Schenectady.

The host then covered the fire, which Hendrick acknowledged. The Six Nations were pleased. Both sides must not fail to keep fast the covenant chain. Hendrick implored his host to tend the "fire of friendship." "We wish this tree of friendship may grow . . . to a great height, and then we shall be a powerful people." The "United Nations," looking to the increase of a stronger confederacy, might "retrieve the ancient glory of the Five Nations" (MHS 5: 61).

As some thirty wagons carried the Indians through the pine bush toward Schenectady, the colonial commissioners summarized the results of their negotiations with some melancholy conclusions. They worried over the defection of half the Onondaga population to the Oswegatchie mission, and they contemplated the rumor that the Seneca nation, the most numerous, was wavering, inclined to the French. Confederacy representation had been poor: only 150 men of all the nations attended the conference. Mohawk participation dominated. The commissioners attributed this to their very great neglect of Six Nations affairs. They acknowledged the evils of the rum trade, private land deals, and patents to insiders. Some regulation was in order. They contemplated building forts for each nation. And they agreed that Indian complaints in these matters merited serious attention.

Having discharged its first obligation, the congress turned to consideration of a plan of union. This now famous document contained provisions for holding treaties, regulating the Indian trade, and purchasing Indian lands—matters that would ultimately come under federal jurisdiction.

Nowhere in the document, or in the negotiations leading up to it, does one find evidence that the Iroquois projected a model of their league or confederacy or that the commissioners understood its structure and operation. Other than Hendrick's asserting the primacy of the Mohawks and the other nations present not objecting to his stating traditional precedent, there is nothing to support current dogma about the Six Nations' having held up their confederacy as a model for the colonies. Indeed, the Mohawk leaders were far more intent on clearing title to their lands than on instructing the commissioners in their manner of governing themselves. Title to western lands was another serious consideration.

The British claim to the Ohio lands rested on an interpretation of the Treaty of Utrecht (1713), at the end of Queen Anne's War, in which the English held that the Five Nations had given them jurisdiction over their lands. These lands comprised the Ohio country by right of Iroquois conquest. The French held a different view of the treaty. Endless disputes and a half-century of warfare ensued (Gipson 1942: 79–80). The British claim underlay the assumptions of the Albany Congress, but the commissioners of the several colonies held individual views that resulted in conflicting interests. Connecticut had its eyes focused on the Wyoming Valley, and on the side during the Albany Congress the commissioner Lydius got for the Connecticut Company a deed to these lands—a deed which the Onondaga council later repudiated. And Weiser, not unfamiliar with doing business "in the bushes," found some "greedy fellows for money" who signed a deed to Pennsylvania covering a vast tract of western lands that overlapped the grant the Six Nations had made to Virginia at the Lancaster treaty ten years earlier (Jennings et al. 1985a: 187). Weiser went home with a questionable document; Lydius went about soliciting additional signatures.

□□◇□□

William Johnson emerged from the Albany Congress the big winner. The Mohawk speakers had demanded his reinstatement to manage their affairs. DeLancey had temporized by supporting the hated Albany commissioners for another year, but in London the ministers were perceiving the wisdom of concentrating Indian affairs in a sole superintendent, namely, Johnson. In April 1755, Johnson was appointed major-general of the Provincial Army (DHNY, 2: 651). Within a year of his commission, he expanded his horizon to include all of the Six Nations. He removed the treaty fire from Albany and rekindled it at Fort Johnson, his home upriver from modern Amsterdam, where he hosted a series of conferences that adhered to traditional council protocol. He addressed his guests with familiar metaphors and validated his words with strings and belts of wampum. Nothing pleased Indians more than observing their customs, unless it was hanging a big kettle. Johnson proved a generous host.

In these matters, Hendrick and his brother Abraham served Johnson as mentors. He employed Arent Stevens and others to interpret: Johnson's fluency in Mohawk is difficult to demonstrate. He co-opted Daniel Claus, who had recently learned Mohawk, to translate speeches that he read in English and to brief native speakers between formal sessions. Peter Wraxall, an experienced chronicler of Indian affairs, drafted the English versions of council proceedings that come down to us, which reveal a command of expected ritual forms and symbolism. Johnson would remodel the confederacy in the name of the league as he understood it to accommodate his needs for doing business. Johnson's league was a reinvented tradition.

Johnson first tried out his scenario at the neighboring lower Mohawk castle. He wiped the Mohawks' tears and cleared their throats with a string that they might speak freely. He raised up the metaphorical tree and strengthened its roots that its branches might shade the council. With a belt, he announced his appointment as sole manager of their affairs and proclaimed the embers of the fire removed from Albany to Fort Johnson, where they might light their pipes. A string served to clean the council room that no snake might crawl in to obstruct the harmony. He wanted the Six Nations summoned to the new fire to hear the speech of General Edward Braddock, with whom he had met in Alexandria, Virginia, upon his commission into the Provincial Army.

After the chiefs retired to consult, Abraham, sachem of the upper castle, replied for both towns. Typically, the chiefs deferred responding to details of the request until after the Six Nations met. Meanwhile, the speaker returned the condolence string with thanks, welcomed Johnson with another, evoked the replanted tree, and recognized the embers removed. He expressed the hope that the fire might continue to burn clear with lasting wood. He reminded his listeners that their forefathers had kindled the original fire at Onondaga, whence they carried embers to Albany. where the fire had never burned clear and was about to expire. They rejoiced to hear that Johnson had rekindled it here. Having thanked Johnson for cleaning the council room, Abraham concluded by saying that he would withhold specifics until the general council that Johnson had requested (SWJP, 1: 626–31).

Johnson also met with the Mohawk warriors and their leaders, who had a voice independent of their uncles, the sachems. Canadagaia, chief sachem of the Bear clan, vouched for the three Mohawk clans present (Wolf and Turtle are not mentioned). The war song should not begin without sufficient cause, he said. The chief warriors were present, and the sachems would leave it to their nephews to do what they deemed proper (SWJP, 1: 638–39).

The conference with the nine so-called "nations" opened on 21 June 1755. Johnson, immediately on returning from his meeting with General Braddock, had dispatched messengers carrying belts throughout the nations announcing his appointment and summoning them to his new fire. With a view to the kettle, on 22 June Johnson ordered the interpreters to enumerate the men, women, and children of each nation gathered for the council. They counted 1,071 persons as follows: Mohawk, 408; Oneida, 200; Onondaga, 100; Cayuga, 103; Seneca, 67; Tuscarora, 64; Tutelo, 9; Nanticoke, 19; Delaware, 101. It was proclaimed the largest attendance of men at any meeting so far (SWJP, 9: 189).

Johnson's welcoming speech in English was translated into Iroquoian by the method already described. With a string he offered two words of condolence— tears and throat—and reported on his meeting with Braddock. Then with belts and strings, he invoked familiar council metaphors: the planted tree, its roots and shade; the fire, removed and rekindled, extinguishing all others; cleaning the council room; and the bundle of sticks, unbreakable when bound, symbolizing unity. Braddock had sent presents (NYCD, 6: 964–66).

The chiefs having withdrawn and deliberated, two days later Hendrick announced that the confederated nations were ready to reply. Johnson heard a lesson in league council protocol. Hendrick explained to Johnson and for posterity the method of their forefathers. They had arranged the league council into moieties, of which the Mohawks, Onondagas, and Senecas were the elder brothers, and at such public conferences the speaker was invariably drawn from that side without preference. Hendrick urged the warriors and youths to take notice and remember the custom. The Oneidas, Cayugas, and dependents comprised the younger brothers (NYCD, 6: 966, 988).

Wraxall recapitulated this separation for the benefit of officialdom: "The eight confederate Nations are subdivided into two grand Divisions vizt The Mohawks, the Onondagas, and the Senecas, who are called Elder Brothers of the Confederacy; the Onejdas, the Cayougas, the Tuscaroras, the Schaniadaradighroonas ["beyond the bay people," Nanticokes] and the Tiederighroonas [Tutelos], which five are called the younger Brothers, the Delawares are looked on as the children of all these Nations" (NYCD, 6: 988).

The joint council of sachems and warriors had first chosen Hendrick as speaker, but, he explained, he had declined, proposing Red Head of Onondaga instead, who had agreed to serve. This was a stroke for unity because Red Head had previously espoused the French. The speaker returned the condolences with a string. With a second, he proffered a caveat should he forget anything. Then, one by one with belts and strings, he repeated the metaphors of Johnson's speech, applauding his role. The Six Nations would kick away other fires. This brought a shout. On union, he commended the bundle of sticks (NYCD, 6: 968).

Addressing the senior moiety, the chief sachem of Oneida announced the death of a sachem and the raising up of a boy in his "room."

Again on the following day, speakers divided the role, with Mohawk and Onondaga speakers for one side and Oneida sachems for the other.

In his second speech, Johnson, having opened their ears, called upon the Six Nations to witness the four volumes of Indian Records on the table. From this source he had extracted the legend of the covenant chain, a metaphor for the alliance with the crown. The chain called for a union belt of considerable proportions standing for solidarity of the alliance and requesting a pledge. Johnson had hung the war kettle over the fire, his canoe was ready to be launched, his gun was loaded, and his ax was sharpened. The Six Nations should take up the hatchet and join the English. He wanted scouts for Braddock. A large war belt went to Abraham, the Mohawk (NYCD, 6: 974).

On the twenty-fifth, Red Head opened, prompted by Hendrick. Johnson read Braddock's speech and threw down a war belt in Braddock's name. An Oneida sachem took it up, and immediately the interpreter began the war dance while Johnson set down a large tub of punch. Cayuga and Seneca participation was minimal.

The following day, a Cayuga sachem arrived with nineteen warriors accompanied by a Mississauga party from north of Lake Ontario, complaining that the French were hindering trade at Oswego. Although the linkage between the two parties appears to have been weaker than an alliance, the north shore people brought belts seeking to join the Six Nations (NYCD, 6: 975-76).

The elder moiety of nations met and without hitch approved Braddock's speech. The younger nations, owing to a lack of unanimity among themselves, did not attend council. Some sachems having died, the chiefs presented Johnson with candidates for installation whom they hoped he would accept. Thus began a practice of letting Johnson vet the grand council.

On 29 June, Kakhswenthioni delivered the reply of the elder moiety under nine heads, among which he recapitulated Johnson's second speech. The governor had strengthened the union of the Five Nations by putting Johnson in charge. A belt recognized the king as their master. The covenant chain was renewed. A belt thanked Johnson "for putting us in mind of our ancestors . . . we are but weak children in comparison." They combined the war belts of Johnson and Braddock in a single declaration. They favored the bundle of sticks as a symbol of a strong union, and they would return their people from Oswegatchie.

The Oneida speaker for the junior moiety concurred, although the Cayugas, worried about their relatives at Kahnawakeh, remained hesitant to take up the hatchet. Bringing home the émigrés remained a perennial problem.

Johnson urged the confederates, as "children of the Crown," to acquaint their allies with the agreements reached. Let the young men go home to prepare for war: some should go to aid Braddock, others should assist Governor Shirley of Massachusetts, who was en route to the English fort at Oswego on Lake Ontario. Crown Point on Lake Champlain was Johnson's own target. He would send a message to Kahnawakeh. Meanwhile, here were the king's presents (NYCD, 6: 980–82).

Scaroyady had reported the loss of six Mohawk warriors at the hands of Creeks. Condolence law required the junior moiety, under Oneida leadership, to carry the ceremony to the upper Mohawk castle. The Onondaga speaker for the elder moiety then confirmed the rite in both Mohawk castles, both for his moiety and for Johnson, who covered the warriors' graves with a black Stroud's.

It was announced that the Nanticokes had been taken into the confederacy as children (NYCD, 6: 983–84).

The Oneida speaker, taking up a large belt with a smaller one attached, requested that their host bung the rum kegs; they wanted corn instead. Their main concern, however, was the deed that Lydius had procured the previous year at Albany to the Wyoming and upper Susquehanna lands. He castigated Lydius, who was present, describing his method of persuasion and bribery, and protested his methods of recruiting for Shirley.

Dissatisfaction prevailed among the junior nations. The Cayuga delegates said they would report home, hold council, and decide about sending men. Shirley's men were already felling trees along Oneida waterways. The French cast a long shadow over upper Iroquoia. Red Head wanted a fort at Onondaga. But the Six Nations were happy that they now had a person appointed over them whom they had requested their father, the king, to appoint. They hoped this expedition would not turn out like previous fiascos. As usual, despite what the sachems said, the young men were zealous for war. Although Seneca participation was slight, the senior moiety solidly supported Johnson, and the reluctant Cayuga delegates, when pressed, declared that they would follow their elder brothers (NYCD, 6: 985–88).

The Lydius deed to Wyoming Valley lands had alarmed the Pennsylvania authorities. Early in 1755 they had sent Scaroyady, who the year before had succeeded Tanacharison as Half King, leader of the Ohio Iroquois, to Onondaga to put the matter of the Connecticut Company's purchase of the Wyoming Valley to the grand council and urge it to invalidate the deed in a letter to the Connecticut governor. On Weiser's advice, Daniel Claus brought Hendrick and a party to Philadelphia via Schoharie and an interior path, avoiding Albany so as not to alert the New York government. An indication of the seriousness of the mission is the presence in the delegation of the holder of the leading Mohawk league title, Tekarihoken. Hendrick, having signed at least one of the deeds, and with the land under his own upper castle in jeopardy, gladly obliged. In his last visit to a Euro-American city, he condemned the Wyoming deed and complained bitterly against the New York authorities, who tacitly sanctioned the Connecticut deed and would not move to reverse it. The Pennsylvania government, rather than offend New York, had Weiser write to Johnson to quietly quash the whole affair (PPCM, 6: 274–91; P. Wallace 1945: 376–77). The incident enabled the Mohawk leaders to exert leverage on New York while supporting Johnson's management of their affairs.

Scaroyady, having returned from Iroquoia in late March, qualified his report to the Pennsylvania authorities and his fellow Ohio Iroquois by asserting that he had not just looked into houses where he visited but entered and stayed some time to observe what was going on. Having passed the Mohawk castle, where some chiefs were absent, he went on to Oneida, which he found pro-English. Learning that he had messages for the Onondaga council, the Oneida council advised him not to go on to Onondaga, which they said was not well disposed toward the English, but to stop and deliver the messages at Oneida. "No body cared to do [English] business at Onondaga." His audience included some Mohawks, Tuscaroras, and Nanticokes who urged him, in the name of the Six Nations, to deliver his messages to them, as if they were at Onondaga. Inasmuch as the issue of Frenchmen being in Ohio was an issue of territory, and inasmuch as warriors have charge of territory, Scaroyady had to address them first as a warrior, "as one that lived among the bushes in the Wilderness" (PCR, 6: 340–41), and not as a counselor. Clearly, outlanders were representing the grand council, which was being bypassed.

□□◇□□

Few Six Nations warriors, if any, answered Johnson's call to support Braddock's army. Hendrick told Governor Morris in Philadelphia that the Six Nations no longer controlled their tributaries in Ohio. Not even Scaroyady could keep them in line. One could not expect a declaration of war to involve everyone. It was the Indian custom that when anyone offered a hatchet, some took it up and others did not. The three clans of the Mohawks might support the English effort, but it was too much to expect other nations to conform (PCR, 6: 283). George Croghan was supposed to manage the Indians for Braddock, but the southern Indians that Governor Dinwiddie promised, fearing reprisals, failed to show. The Six Nations, on hearing of his recruiting, held back lest they get embroiled with old enemies. And Braddock, having spurned available Indian advice and scouts, lost his army and his life.

Braddock's defeat in his attempt to take Fort Duquesne from the French in 1755 has been called "the Pearl Harbor of the Seven Years War" (Morison 1965: 163). It would turn the Indian world on its head and send wavering allies into the French camp. A fortnight after the rout, "the incoherent, unexpected, unintelligible, not to be credited damned bad news" reached Johnson in the midst of his preparing for the Crown Point expedition (SWJP, 1: 759, 767). He hustled home to Mount Johnson to confront the principal leaders of the three upper nations, to whom he had the guts to communicate the now confirmed disaster pretty much in its true light. They in turn, having heard the bad news, agreed to stand by their engagements (SWJP, 1: 794–97). Johnson had the solid support of the two Mohawk towns, but the émigrés at Kahnawakeh posed an uncertainty. Neither side favored fighting its kin.

While Shirley failed to take Niagara, General Johnson managed to defeat the French at Lake George, although he fell short of taking Crown Point. Hendrick, Johnson's friend, too enfeebled to run the woods, fell victim to some women and children while escaping an ambush set by French-allied Indians. When the reports of Johnson's victory reached London, the king raised Johnson up as a baronet in absentia. From his manor at Johnstown he would manage the external affairs of the Six Nations confederacy for two decades.

CHAPTER 31

JOHNSON REMAKES
THE CONFEDERACY

Sir William Johnson emerged from the battle at Lake George a certified hero (Jennings 1988: 164). Some forty Mohawk warriors and Hendrick fell during the engagement and took up the long trail to the hereafter. A few Senecas were also involved. As was their constant custom, the survivors of the battle went home to mourn their losses. It would be weeks and months before they were all condoled and free to take up the hatchet again or do any business. Johnson, with the help of Peter Wraxall, promptly sent the colonial governors a report of the battle, which was printed in the *London Magazine* (Winsor 1884–99, 5: 581, 584). Coming two months after the Braddock disaster, news of even a partial victory raised hopes at home and abroad (NYDH, 2: 691–95, 696).

Johnson did not sit long contemplating the scalp pole. He held a series of conferences that fall and winter with various segments of the confederacy, the proceedings of which were collected in "An Account of Conferences Held" (London, 1756). This now scarce book honored Johnson's knighthood. In the words of the publisher, "He who knows the valour and military qualifications of Sir William Johnson, together with the importance of the Indians in North America, especially the Six Nations, to us as well as to the French, will here be agreeably entertained with specimens of the political talents of that victorious general, and the sagacity of the Indians" (Account: ii). It is the latter that claims our attention.

Johnson set out to consolidate his gains with the Six Nations and urge them to neutralize their émigré kindred in Ohio, their Delaware nephews, now chafing at being "women," and the troublesome Shawnees. Bringing them into the British orbit might not be possible. Besides the loss of Hendrick, the death by alcoholism of the Half King, Tanacharison of Oneida—the grand council's man on the Ohio—the year before had bereft the English cause of two influential Iroquois advocates. The council had raised up Tanacharison's deputy, Scaroyady, in the office. A seasoned warrior, he was active and eloquent.

When Pennsylvania authorities wavered on whether to support the Delawares, Mingos, and other Indians over whom Scaroyady watched on the Ohio, lest they go over to the French, Scaroyady remarked, "You can't live in the woods and stay neutral" (PCR, 6: 553; P. Wallace 1945: 389). Pennsylvania and the Six Nations needed each other. Tohashwughtonionty (Belt), who shared a name with the Onondaga sachem Tohashwachdiony (Kakhswenthioni, "Hanging Wampum Belt," or Red Head) but was himself a Seneca who had fought with Braddock and was "reckoned amongst the greatest Warriors among the Six Nations," told Weiser that the Six Nations had sent a large belt of wampum to the Indians on the Ohio telling them "they must now Sharpen their Arrows and prepare with all speed to engage in the War with the Six United Nations against the French" (PCR, 6: 614; P. Wallace 1945: 395). From Shamokin, Scaroyady informed the Pennsylvania governor that the Six Nations had sent a fathom-long black belt ordering their Delaware cousins to shed their petticoats and clap on a breechclout (PCR, 6: 615).

The Delawares remained ambivalent. The Shawnees and related tribes inclined toward the French. Scaroyady, having returned from Shamokin, where he warned the Nanticokes, in October challenged the Pennsylvania assembly to give them the hatchet so that they themselves could fight. "If they would, he had something further to say. If not they would soon know what to do." Then, in the so-called Delaware Declaration of Independence—what Boyd (1938) called "the most dramatic spectacle that the State House saw prior to the Revolution"—Scaroyady took up a double belt of wampum, one black, with a string tied to it representing Braddock's defeat, and the other white, to make the hatchet sharper. Addressing the assembly for the tribes he represented, he proclaimed: "We do, therefore, once more invite and request you to act like men, and be no longer women, pursuing weak measures that render your names despicable." His people wanted to know what course Pennsylvania would follow before they decided themselves. Scaroyady threw the belts on the table, declaring, "One word of yours will bring the Delaware to join you." The assembly failed to reach one mind. Carnage visited the frontier. The Six Nations no longer held a war club (*casse-tête*) above the Delawares, for neither Iroquois prestige nor diplomacy fazed the western tribes (PCR, 6: 685–87; Boyd 1938: lxix).

Pennsylvania's failure to act decisively left Johnson in the lurch. He would urge the Six Nations to put pressure on the Delaware and River Indians, their supposed dependents, and put a stop to the barbarities they were committing on the Pennsylvania frontier.

Representatives of four nations—Mohawk, Oneida, Tuscarora, and Seneca— met with Johnson in December 1755. The Onondaga council failed to send anybody. Some Senecas had gone to Montreal in October to greet the new governor of Canada, the Marquis de Vaudreuil (the second governor of that name). Johnson underscored the seriousness of his request with two wampum belts, one quite large to gather intelligence, for which the Iroquois reciprocated, promising to inform the Delawares and keep the path open (SWJP, 9: 328–29). He warned the Six Nations that if they did not exercise the authority that they boasted over the Delawares, they would soon have them as enemies.

Three nations returned the day after Christmas, with Tuscarora and Oneida spokesmen, to thank Johnson for ammunition, large guns, and paint. The Oneida chief Canaghquayeson (Kanaʔkwaye:son, possibly Kanongweniyah, Oe-2, RC 11)) assured Johnson that they were "on guard against the malicious designs of the French." He confessed that they had been drunk for several years but asserted that they were now looking after the River Indians and Shawnees. They requested a fort to protect their consolidated settlement. They would not go to Oswegatchie to meet the French. Four large belts sent to persuade their allies to the south not to make other alliances were communicated to the French. A follow-up message requested that the River Indians and Shawnees come speak with them in the interest of stopping further bloodshed. If the River Indians and Shawnees failed to show, Oneida and Tuscarora sachems would go after them (SWJP, 9: 332–34).

It was mid-February before Johnson replied (SWJP, 2: 434). The Oneidas were "elder brothers" of the Tuscaroras, some Nanticokes having joined them. Johnson had come to depend on these ethnic fragments. He wished they had come to their senses earlier when the French invaded their hunting grounds. But he complimented them on not going to Oswegatchie. Pleased at their upcoming conference with the Delawares and Shawnees, he awaited results.

Meanwhile, the sachems who had carried Johnson's message to the Delawares returned from Tioga (modern Athens, Pennsylvania) to Onehughquagey ("place of wild grapes," according to Hewitt) bearing the Delaware version of the quarrel (reported in a letter from Gideon Hawley to Johnson, 27 December 1755, SWJP, 9: 334). According to their version, the trouble had begun on the upper Susquehanna near the "Big Meadow" (*skahendowaneh*), or Wyoming, in a misunderstanding with an English trader who failed to stay east of the river. He blamed the cause on the Delawares and their "uncles," the Six Nations. Some Pennsylvanians, on hearing that Delaware warriors were mobilizing at Wyoming, made prisoners of some 232 domesticated Delawares. The account of what followed is unclear; what is clear is that when three gentlemen showed up bearing a commission to build a fort to protect the Indians, but having no wampum to validate it, the Indians objected, became suspicious, and in the ensuing fracas knocked them on the head. Only the Indian trader escaped.

The Delawares' answer to Johnson professed that they did not know the cause of the quarrel. They acknowledged being subjects of the Six Nations and "women." "Our uncle must say what we must do; he has the hatchet." They were obliged to Johnson for telling them to stop. They heard, and they would stop and repent. But then followed the usual excuse that their young men had gone off on their own, although they would try to recall them. The reply ended by asking leave to use paper, instead of wampum. (Perhaps they had none.) Delaware professions of peace seemed doubtful (Account: 10–14; SWJP, 9: 334 ff.).

For political support and intelligence, Johnson had come to rely on minor ethnic entities dependent on the Oneidas and living on the upper reaches of the Susquehanna River. They were in council during February 1756—Ohkwages, Tuscaroras, Nanticokes, Chugnuts, Mahicans, and Shawnees. Their speaker, presumably an Oneida, opened by condoling Johnson's loss of his sister and her husband, an officer killed at Lake George. There are no details (Account: 15; SWJP, 9: 393–94).

Johnson, at his home in the Mohawk Valley, employed the Mohawk sachem Kanadakayon (Old Town) in replying to the Delawares' speech transmitted in Gideon Hawley's letter. Communication required three interpreters. Besides the Iroquoian language Tuscarora, at least two Algonquian languages were represented. To satisfy the Delawares' grievances, Johnson promised a fort to protect them from French Indians. His listeners, despite the difficulties of translation, assured Johnson that they should "never forget it [the promise of the fort] as long as the waters of the Susquehanna run" (Account: 18).

□□◇□□

In the days leading up to the big conference at Fort Johnson at mid-month, three Onondaga runners brought three strings of wampum from the sachems notifying Johnson that the headmen of the Onondaga, Cayuga, and Seneca nations were on the path. The first two arrived that day, and fifty Senecas would follow the next.

Mohawk sachems brought word that Oneida and Tuscarora representatives were expected at Canajoharie to condole the great Hendrick and other chiefs of that castle who had fallen at Lake George. They expected Johnson to attend. Johnson supplied the requisite wampum belts and asked the Mohawks to act for him. As host to many Indians just then, he could not get away. They understood. When still more Senecas arrived, Johnson performed the necessary ceremony of welcome.

Having condoled Hendrick and the others, the Oneida and Tuscarora sachems reached Johnson's clearing several days later, when Johnson formally welcomed them. The Oneida sachem Canaghquayeson explained the delay: "We have been clearing up the road of our forefathers" (condoling a loss). Canajoharie had lost two great men, and they had raised up two others in their rooms. They deplored other nations' having passed by and neglected the ceremony. That they were now complete should ease Johnson's mind. A belt.

Being present in the council room where the affairs of the Six Nations were transacted, the speaker invoked the white wing, which he proceeded to take down to sweep the council chamber free of dust and dirt that nothing might impede their deliberations. Three strings of wampum confirmed this symbolic act (Account: 20-21; SWJP, 9: 349-51).

Hendrick's surviving brother, Abraham, sachem of the upper Mohawk castle, privately thanked Johnson for fortifying and garrisoning Canajoharie, thereby securing the old people and children during the delegates' absence. Johnson was convinced of their loyalty.

The grounds at Fort Johnson seated 586 members of the Six Nations and their allies on 18 February 1756. Before the meeting could open, Johnson condoled the united nations. A party of remote Senecas had lost three men in an engagement with English settlers. The paradigm called for cleansing the beds of those who had fallen (wiping blood), covering the dead (burying the affair forever), and dispelling clouds (restoring the sun), that they might proceed with business. The balance of the ceremony addressed first the Cayugas and Tutelos, covering their dead, followed by the remaining nations present who had lost men at Lake George. Six French prisoners taken in that engagement were formally delivered to replace named individuals (Account: 23-25; SWJP, 9: 355-57).

Next day a Seneca named Red Head returned the condolences on behalf of his nation and the assembled nations. They thanked Johnson for drying their tears, driving sorrow from their hearts, taking the ax out of their heads, wiping the blood from sight, and covering the graves, "agreeable to the antient custom of our forefathers," which he confirmed with appropriate strings and belts. Johnson had settled their distraught minds and reminded them of the harmony that had long subsisted between their forefathers and the English, which tradition had handed down from father to son. Each nation present confirmed Red Head's statement with a belt.

The Six Nations as a body next acknowledged Johnson's affection in cleansing their habitations of the blood and defilement caused by the death of so many of their principal men. (The speaker did not specify the number.)

Johnson had given them a large belt emblematic of the Six Nations joined hand in hand. Taking up this belt and holding it aloft, the speaker focused his listeners' attention and reminded Johnson and themselves of mutual obligations contracted when Johnson began to manage their affairs. "We look upon them as sacred, and shall, on our parts, punctually perform them as long as we are a people."

Taking up a second large belt given the Six Nations by the governor of New York some years previously, the speaker reiterated promises made to them on that occasion. They hoped the English would remember and fulfill them. They promised to do the same, depending on their memories, not records.

With three strings, the speaker next referred to the Pennsylvania governor's puzzlement at the barbarous behavior of their Delaware nephews, which he attributed to the French having deluded them. The Six Nations would do what they could. They hoped the English would do likewise. Meanwhile, Johnson should inform the governors that the Six Nations had not neglected this important affair but had sent an emissary to take the hatchet out of the hands of their nephews. Withdrawing troops from the frontiers would facilitate recovery of captives. A belt (Account: 25–28; SWJP, 9: 357–60).

A party of warriors from remote parts of the Seneca country, from the very "door of the Six Nations"—probably Geneseo, New York—who had never come down for a previous council, met with Johnson the same day. Kayandagaron, also known as Kenderondy, their speaker, said they had made the journey with several of their sachems to take Johnson by the hand and hear him speak. This gesture pleased Johnson because it extended his acquaintance to the far end of the Longhouse (Account: 29; SWJP, 9: 361).

In greeting the assembly next day, Johnson demonstrated further control of council metaphors. Belt by belt he invoked the fire, sun, and tree. He thanked those who had fought at Lake George, although he said he could have used more warriors. He brightened the covenant chain "that has so long linked us," so that it might endure "as long as the sun shines, or the rivers continue to water the earth"—a theme to run in later treaty negotiations. He had sent a black belt by a Seneca to stop the raids of the Delawares, their nephews. In replacing Braddock with Shirley, the king had commanded Shirley to protect their lands. Confronting French designs on Oswego, Johnson proposed a general meeting there in the spring.

In replying for the Six Nations next day, Red Head—the Onondaga speaker, not the Seneca of the same name—expanded these metaphors of continuity felicitously. The allies would mutually collect fuel for their common fire, he said, that it might burn bright as the sun and moon. The roots of the tree they had planted reached remote settlements, its branches sheltered their allies, and friendly streams watered it. A belt brightened the chain, the symbol of their alliance and unity. The Six Nations had regarded the Delawares as being the first responsibility of Onas, the Pennsylvania governor, who had neglected them. They hoped Shirley might help recover their lands. They found the notion of taking embers from Onondaga to start a council fire at Oswego acceptable and planned to warm themselves at that fire next spring (Account: 35–39; SWJP, 9: 362–66).

A few days later, in response to another Johnson speech, Red Head reviewed the history of Delaware subjugation, saying that the Six Nations had twice warned them. That proving abortive, an Oneida emissary had reminded them of their subordination, demanded an explanation of behavior contrary to the covenant with the English, and urged them to cease hostilities.

Cleverly, the Onondaga Red Head recognized Johnson as one of their own body and dumped the problem of the insubordinate Delaware and Shawnee nephews in the laps of Johnson and the eldest brother, the Mohawks. "As the Mohawks are the head of our confederacy, we leave the management of that affair entirely to them." This he confirmed with a large belt (Account: 43-45; SWJP, 9: 373-74).

With what may have been the largest belt presented at the mid-century, said to contain figures representing the Six Nations and wrought with a sun symbol, the confederacy expressed its intention with respect to the far nations, vouched for the union, and invited them to join in the covenant chain. The speaker said they would send the belt to the Senecas, who would convey it to the remotest nation (Account: 45-46; SWJP, 9: 375).

To crown the thousand pounds' worth of presents, Johnson had commissioned for the occasion "the largest pipe in America," which he instructed the delegates to take home and hang up in the council chamber at Onondaga and to smoke at important councils. Red Head assured him that they would make proper use of it when they reflected on their engagements. One is reminded of the Seneca aphorism to Father Hennepin in the previous century: "From smoking comes good thoughts" (Account: 47; SWJP, 9: 377).

At the close of the conference, the speaker announced that the Six Nations had agreed that the Mohawks should accept responsibility for settling the Delaware problem, and they were further of one mind that several delegates of the Six Nations should join in the effort. They were sending a message by Nanticoke and Oneida runners inviting the Delawares to meet with them at Otseningo (near modern Binghampton) (Account: 48-49; SWJP, 9: 382).

During these conferences on the Mohawk River, the crown commissioned Johnson sole superintendent of the Six Nations (fig. 34), knighted him in absentia, recalled Shirley, and summoned John Campbell, the forty-one-year-old fourth earl of Loudoun (Flexner 1959: 172), as British general in America. Franklin would compare Loudoun, who left a splendid paper trail, to a tavern sign of a mounted horseman who is ready to ride but never takes off (Pargellis 1933). A self-proclaimed king of the Delawares named Teedyuscung just then emerged at the forks of the Delaware to proclaim his own confederacy and question the dominance of the Six Nations (A. Wallace 1949; Jennings 1988: 254ff.).

□□◇□□

Delawares and Shawnees on the Ohio operated independently of their eastern members. Johnson's agent George Croghan learned that the Onondaga council was unhappy with the English for pushing settlements so far back that the natives felt squeezed between them and the French forts. The council, sensing a loss of control over erstwhile satellites, communicated a scheme for incorporating the Delawares, Shawnees, Munsees, and Nanticokes into the Six Nations confederacy (HEH, Loudoun papers 757). Croghan wondered whether the Six Nations had

Figure 34. Sir William Johnson, Her Majesty's Superintendent of Indian Affairs. Portrait by John Wollaston. Courtesy Albany Institute of History and Art, 1922.2.

reached agreement on the scheme. His informant doubted Mohawk and Oneida participation.

Iroquois politics were indeed fragmented, though no more so than politics among the colonies. For more than a half-century, three factions—pro-English, pro-French, and neutralist—had dominated or cohabited in the town councils of Iroquoia and rendered the grand council at Onondaga at times virtually inoperable (Richter 1992). At mid-eighteenth century, the pro-English faction dominated the Mohawk castles. At Oneida, sentiment alternated between the first two poles. Pro-French or neutralist views prevailed at Onondaga, and Cayuga and Seneca towns favored the French or identified with émigré kin in Ohio. Warriors acted independently and in accord with geography. Cayuga and Seneca warriors raided in the west. Onondaga and Oneida warriors joined French raids on settlements in former Mohawk territory, and only the Mohawks remained steadfastly pro-English. Iroquois warriors did observe one treaty covenant: they "did not attack colonials in lands that acknowledgedly had been ceded by treaty to Pennsylvania" (Jennings 1988: 261–62).

Pennsylvania, having long regarded the Six Nations as the key to securing trade and settlement to the west, continued to treat with its northern neighbors even though the crown had vested the exclusive right of management in Sir William Johnson. Conrad Weiser continued to advise Governor Denny; the Quakers, having opposed military action in the assembly, sought friendly means to pacify the aroused Delaware-Shawnee-Mingo hostiles; and all parties looked to Scaroyady and Croghan to mediate. Random delegations of individual Iroquois nations, composed of warriors and the odd member of the grand council, showed up to listen, deliberate, and reply. Frequently they carried the matter home for referral to village or national councils for decision. It took time to assemble a general council, and communication was slow.

Conrad Weiser left a list of Indians who showed up at Carlisle, Pennsylvania, in January 1756 for a conference whose goal was to rally the Indians on the upper Susquehanna and gain their confidence. With so few present, not much was accomplished toward mitigating raids on the frontier. Led by the Seneca sachem Belt, they represented but one faction of the Ohio Iroquois. Scaroyady, Belt's rival as successor to Tanacharison, failed to show. The list included Silverheels, Seneca George (Atsinonto), New Castle (Cashawayion), the Half King's son Gahickdodon (Khikdo:don, "Standing Thorn"), Zigerea, and, among others, John King, a Nanticoke (HEH, HM 305). Belt said they were all warriors, though few in number. They blamed hostilities on the French, on whom they would eventually seek revenge. They thought it prudent to wait for the return of messages sent to the grand council of the Six Nations. Travel was impossible just then. They advised building a fort at Shamokin immediately (P. Wallace 1945: 421–24).

When Pennsylvania, having long sat (like a captive) with its head bent to its knees, declared war, the Friends began negotiations for peace. In April, they rounded up Scaroyady, then Half King of the Mingos, who was conveniently in Philadelphia and away from his minions in Ohio, and six of his followers to meet with them at the house of Israel Pemberton. The Friends reminded their Indian guests of the peaceful conduct of their forefathers, assured them of their good feeling, and urged the Indians to find some way to reach the Delawares and turn their minds to peace.

Scaroyady, somewhat amazed at the turn of events, nevertheless rose to the occasion and delivered some splendid examples of Iroquois council oratory. Answering in the name of the Six Nations, he urged observing proper protocol with the Six Nations council, who were glad to hear that there were some people left with peaceful principles. Would that they had been told sooner, and that "you had always spoke and acted agreeable to this principle." Although the Delawares had struck the first blow, if the Pennsylvanians had taken proper precautions in time, "you might have kept them under your eye as children." But now, as the interpreter explained, the Delawares "had grown stiff like a strong tree, and not easily bowed." In a graphic gesture, Scaroyady proclaimed, "We will hold it fast (clasping his hands, and keeping it close) till we come to the Six Nations, where we are now going, and then we will lay it open to them in a strait line (opening his hands wide, with the back of it on the table, and setting his fingers and pipe strait before him) . . . and when I relate it to them [Pemberton's peace proposal], it will make their hearts melt."

In reply to a large white belt ratifying the Friends' peace proposal, Scaroyady expanded his previous statement. "Your fathers declared that they had nothing but love and good-will in their hearts to all men. We thought that the people of that profession, had been all dead and buried in the bushes or ashes; but we are very glad that there are some of the same men living" who would mediate between "our cousins the Delawares" and this government. The evil spirit must have risen from beneath the ground and spread all over the country. "We are very glad at your rising up and holding the white belt in your hands, as an emblem of peace" (Account: 65–77; DePuy 1917: treaty no. 37).

Conrad Weiser, one of three interpreters, listed the Indians attending and the presents received (HEH, HM 3036). Two notable names stand out: Newcastle[1] and Ochzigerea, or Satagaroyies (Sa?dagaenyes, "Skies of Equal Height," S-2, RC 44), the title of a Seneca league founder. Why he was in Philadelphia remains a mystery; if he represented Mingos, the title must have passed westward to Ohio. He and "Captain Newcastle" were clearly of the Six Nations; they, William Laquis, and Augustus of Bethlehem (two Delawares) comprised the mission appointed to carry the governor's message to the hostile Indians at Tioga on the upper Susquehanna River, a journey too dangerous for Quakers. They reported in June (APSL, Horsfield Papers 1: 115-19). Johnson regarded the mission as meddling; it resulted in a long series of conferences with Teedyuscung, the rising Delaware spokesman.

With Mohawk help, Johnson consolidated his position during June and July 1756 by carrying the requickening ritual over the path to Onondaga (see Appendix C). He also held up his new title, by which he would henceforth be called "Sir William," for the grand council to witness. (The Iroquois regard name and rank as vital to social placement. "What is your name?" and "What is your clan?" are perennial questions.) The name Warraghiyageh took on new significance.

While Johnson was at Onondaga taking the petticoats off Nitimus, the aging sachem of the eastern Delawares, Teedyuscung, an emerging leader of warriors, had gone to Niagara to assess the quality of French preparedness and found the garrison on short rations. He decided to hedge his bets in Pennsylvania (A. Wallace 1949: 99-102; Jennings 1988: 271-72). He would assert his power at Easton that year and face Iroquois scorn two years later. In a moment of drunken bragging, he announced that he was the king of ten nations: the Six Nations and the Munsee, Unami, Mahican, and Lenape branches of his own people. Pennsylvanians, eager to make peace with someone, did not question his qualifications (A. Wallace 1949: 107).

He should have known better. At Tioga he had heard Captain Newcastle, the Iroquois speaker, outline the protocol for transacting important affairs, which should be done at a public place, namely Tioga. He insisted that the chiefs of the various related Delaware settlements should come there. When the chiefs met, Newcastle, in proper Iroquois style, announced that he carried a message from the king of England, but before he delivered it, he condoled them with the Three Bare Words of requickening (A. Wallace 1949: 94), a gesture that the Delawares and Shawnees appreciated.

Captain Newcastle reminded his listeners that the Six Nations had sent deputies to a conference at Otseningo, where they had met some three hundred hostiles, blamed them for taking up the hatchet against the English, and told them to lay it down and deliver their prisoners.

The delegation to Tioga, consisting of two Iroquois, a Delaware, and a Moravian, returned to Philadelphia and reported on the last day of May. They had heard Shawnee chief Paxinosa invoke familiar metaphors—dark clouds, eyes running tears (both parties), clearing the mind, and opening the passage from heart to mouth so as to speak freely. He noted that his listeners had come a great

---

1. Newcastle could be literally *kanondase:?*, "new town," as opposed to *kanondakayonshen?*, "old town," familiar usage today.

way through dangerous passages where evil spirits reigned and threatened the traveler with all manner of obstacles—all essential elements of the condolence paradigm that the Shawnees evidently shared (Boyd 1938: 138).

Not to be outdone, Teedyuscung dwelt on dark clouds, professed to spit out unhappy times, acknowledged the Six Nations as "uncles," and confirmed the Otseningo agreements (Boyd 1938: 139; A. Wallace 1949: 94–95).

In summoning a treaty conference, one must designate a place and time to kindle a fire. Provisionally, Lieutenant Governor Morris of Pennsylvania proposed kindling the fire at the home of Conrad Weiser, a member of the Six Nations council and public interpreter for Pennsylvania. Weiser had so advised him, but observed that the Indians were free to name another place. They preferred the forks of the Delaware, modern Easton (Boyd 1938: 140).

This first Easton Treaty was provisional and preliminary to the official treaties of 1757, 1758, and 1762, held under the auspices of Sir William Johnson. But it witnessed Teedyuscung's boast that the Six Nations had become ten nations, that the Delawares were now men, and that he represented the lot. Governor Denny, having professed not to interfere with Johnson's new status, nevertheless ignored a letter from Lord Loudoun, recently arrived in America, advising that His Majesty had taken out of the hands of governors all rights to treat with Indians and lodged that responsibility with Johnson as sole agent. This was bitter medicine for the Pennsylvania authorities, who asserted an influence on the Six Nations of some standing beyond anything of Sir William Johnson's. When Morris failed to get either council or assembly approval to conduct the treaty, but instead backed Johnson, and when Teedyuscung refused to come to Philadelphia to treat, Morris went up to Easton with a military escort. Quakers who claimed injustice as the cause of the alienation of the Indians showed up in force, attended all sessions, advised the Indians, and delivered a wagonload of presents. Thereafter, Quakers became a third force, a quiet conscience in Indian affairs.

Previous scholars have navigated these crosscurrents of colonial politics (Boyd 1938: lxxvii–lxxxi, 141–47; P. Wallace 1945: 439–51; A. Wallace 1949: 111–15). My concern is with examples of political behavior shared by Iroquois and Delawares that are more explicit here than in previous literature on the Iroquois. In an opening speech on 28 July, Teedyuscung stated his credentials in less pretentious terms than he had declaimed earlier. "I am here by the Appointment of ten Nations, among which are my Uncles the Six Nations, authorizing me to treat with you, and what I do they will all confirm" (Boyd 1938: 142; A. Wallace 1949: 111). And it was also true, he said, that he was one of two "kings" appointed by the ten nations to transact public business.[2] But he felt impelled to acknowledge, "I am but a Messenger from the United Nations, though I act as a Chief Man for the Delawares" (Boyd 1938: 142). He then illuminated two other concepts: business done in public versus business done "in the bushes," and courageous, or effective, conduct—termed in Delaware *whish-shicksy* and familiar in Iroquoian as *jagoyon*,

---

2. The Iroquois invariably designate two persons, often of opposite moieties, to carry out a specific task. The grand council thus selected two Mohawks and two Cayugas, of opposite sides of the confederacy, to monitor the activities of the eastern Delawares. When Oswego fell in August, they sent two messengers from Onondaga to relate the taking of Oswego and subsequent massacre (LO 1601, 1603). The same arrangement obtains in the conduct of Iroquois ceremonials today.

which he explained meant "be strong," or "do it effectually" and with dispatch (Boyd 1938: 142). This was how he expected the negotiations to proceed.

Nowhere in the treaty literature is there a more vivid explanation of wampum symbolism than in this address by the Delaware speaker. Teedyuscung took up a large wampum belt and held it up before the governor. The belt featured purple (black) stick figures of two men with arms outstretched from each end toward a hollow square between them, against a white background. This belt, Teedyuscung said, carried several interpretations. First, it was the "Independence Belt" wherein the Iroquois had made men of the Delawares. Speaking for Nitimus, who had made peace with the Six Nations at Onondaga, he now renewed the covenant between the Six Nations and the Delawares. "They have made Men of us, and [granted us] Authority . . . to make peace." Second, the belt meant "that whoever will not comply with the Terms of Peace, the ten Nations will join against him and strike him; . . . strong Men on both Sides; Hatchets on both Sides; whoever does incline to Peace, him will I join."

The third meaning on the belt was symbolized by "a Square in the Middle, meaning the Lands of the Indians, and at one end the figure of a Man . . . the English; and at the other End another . . . the French," both of whom "coveted our Lands," so "our Uncles [the Six Nations] told us." Teedyuscung said he expected the Pennsylvanians to join with them to protect their lands. Peace was evidently contingent on Pennsylvania's guaranteeing the territorial integrity of the Delawares and Six Nations (A. Wallace 1949: 112; Boyd 1938: 144–45).

This example demonstrates that wampum belts could carry several meanings and brings into question the reliability of subsequent "readings." Certainly when the verbal stream associated with each belt was lost, belts became unreliable documents.

Confronting this ambiguity, the governor and Conrad Weiser turned to Captain Newcastle for advice on how to treat the belt and what it meant. Newcastle insisted that the belt was of consequence because the Six Nations had sent it to the Delawares. They should keep it among the council wampum. His interpretation of the belt next day, from the Iroquois point of view, put the Delaware "women" in a shameful position:

> Cousins the Delaware Indians: You will remember that you are our Women, our Fore-fathers made you so, and put a Petty Coat on you, and charged you to be true to us, and lye with no other Man; but of late you suffer'd the String yt ty'd your Petticoat to be cut loose by the French and you lay with them and so became a common Bawd, in which you did very wrong and deserved Chastisement, but not withstanding this we have an Esteem for you and as you have thrown off your Piece, and become stark naked which is a shame for a Woman we now give you a little Prick & put it in your private Parts and so let it grow there, till you shall be a compleat man. We advise you not to act as a Man yet but be first instructed by us and do as we bid you and you will become a noted man.
>
> Cousins: The English & French fight for our Land, Let us be strong and lay our hand to it, and defend it. In the meantime turn your Eyes and Ears to us and the English our Brethren & you will live as well as we do. (A. Wallace 1949: 113; P. Wallace 1945: 450)

Newcastle said he hoped the council bag was filled with wampum, which he recommended dumping in Teedyuscung's lap because he would need it in subsequent negotiations with his Ohio kin. Clearly, wampum was not plentiful among the Indians but could be had in local trade centers. At his further suggestion, Indian women were employed to make a belt for reply, to measure one fathom (six feet) by sixteen beads wide. Its center would feature a figure of a man (the governor), and each side would depict five other figures, together representing Teedyuscung's ten nations. It was done in a day (Boyd 1938: 147).

□□◇□□

While Pennsylvanians debated their role in Indian affairs, desperately sought an end to Indian hostilities, and wondered just whom Teedyuscung represented, events transpired elsewhere. After two years of undeclared warfare, England and France made it official in May and June of 1756, beginning the Seven Years War that devastated Europe and ended in America with the fall of Quebec. In July, Lord Loudoun, loaded with advice on how to handle the Six Nations and under orders from George II, arrived belatedly in New York to assume command. Johnson hastened to Albany to meet and size up the new general. Johnson had much to report.

He had just made peace, he told Loudoun, with the eastern Delawares, Shawnees, and Mahicans, who had arrived after the fire was covered at Onondaga and followed him to Fort Johnson. The Six Nations addressed the Shawnees as "brethren," signifying equality, but the Delawares were "nephews," implying dependence (HEH, Loudoun Papers [hereafter LO] 4079; SWJP, 9: 476). The Tioga Delawares had no control over those in Ohio. He had left Daniel Claus at home, and Claus had reported the woods full of skulking Indians. A Six Nations delegation of Onondaga and Oneida councilors heard Governor Vaudreuil urge them not to take up the English hatchet and to abandon their villages. They rejected his proposals. The French general Montcalm was reportedly moving on the English fort at Oswego (it would fall a month later). Loudoun, apparently pleased, recommended publication of Johnson's proceedings, as we have seen ("An Account of Conferences Held"; DePuy 1917: 38; NYCD, 7: 152–61).

The Six Nations were of three minds—Johnson's pro-English Mohawks, Onondaga neutralists, and the pro-French Cayugas and Senecas—and they were hungry. They would come down where power centered. For the moment, the neutralists predominated. Loudoun wrote home that "those we call friends, are no more than Neutrals" and went on to describe the independent actions of individual colonies, notably Pennsylvania (LO 1522). Inflation affected Indian affairs and made their affections expensive and subject to alienation (LO 1525). Wampum was in short supply. Indian business in Pennsylvania had used up available wampum, none was to be had in Philadelphia, and newly appointed Governor Denny expected Johnson to supply belts and strings for upcoming conferences (LO 1537, 1580; SWJP, 9: 505).

Doubts lingered in Philadelphia that Johnson was up to his task. An officer wrote Loudoun wondering whether Albany's principal families could be reconciled to act in concert with Johnson. These alumni of the former Indian commissioners still had considerable interest with the upper nations, whereas Johnson's interest centered among the Mohawks. In the officer's opinion, this made it impossible for Johnson to gain the confidence of the others, who remained jealous of his partiality for the Mohawks, Indians being naturally jealous. The French employed different agents for each nation (Major John Rutherford to Loudoun [LO 1549]).

Johnson had his work cut out for him. Faced with a deteriorating military situation that threatened the Mohawk Valley and frustrated Loudoun's plans, Johnson set out to remake the fragmented confederacy into an instrument for confronting the French and "doing business."

From time out of mind the hereditary village chiefs had met annually at Onondaga to sort out and settle differences among the autonomous "nations." This was the League of the Iroquois that the Jesuits had found operating a century previously (Le Mercier's *Relation* of 1667: 237). But this league had ceased to govern and had seconded its functions to headmen who had achieved status as war leaders and orators. The league had metamorphosed into the confederacy of the five (later six) nations that operated in the name of the original league, now a symbolic entity. The village council, composed of both hereditary chiefs, or sachems, and headmen of achieved status, continued to function as local government and sent delegates to a tribal or national council and to the grand council at Onondaga. Thus Lafitau could write his famous treatise "Political Government," in which he described how an Iroquois village council operated, and make only passing reference to the council names of the constituent nations of the league (Fenton and Moore 1974: 287ff., 291). Indeed, the village council was the core element of Iroquois polity.

Onondaga's preeminence in the original league emerged from its position at the geographical center, midway between the Mohawks and Oneidas to the east and the Cayugas and Senecas to the west. There, the annual sessions of the grand council met, its "States General" in the eyes of Europeans. There also reposed the hereditary titles of the league's legendary founders. An Onondaga was keeper of the wampum, the so-called national treasury, which he held in a hemp bag containing belts and strings symbolic of the league and commemorating various transactions—for no agreement was valid unless wampum passed across the fire, and no credit was given to any statement unless it was properly attested by string or belt. Only Mohawks disputed the preeminence of Onondaga, claiming to be head of the league and confederacy for having first accepted the Great Peace. Mohawk speakers frequently advanced this claim and made it stick. By virtue of location and frequency of meetings there, Onondaga engrossed privileges and authority that it did not possess at the founding of the league, for Onondaga was the last nation to accept the Great Peace.

There is a principle that students of the Iroquois must inevitably learn: the way a thing is done is often more important than the issue at stake. As Merle H. Deardorff observed in the late 1960s, "The body of etiquette and protocol developed by these people is truly formidable, and much of it [is] beyond our comprehension."[3] Persons who master this protocol and observe the forms achieve status in Iroquois eyes. Inasmuch as league business was transacted at Onondaga, the central fire, resident speakers became the acknowledged masters of the art. Over time it became the rule that league business could be transacted only at Onondaga. Later, observing the rule became impracticable, so a symbolic compromise became expedient: the presence of a single Onondaga headman could make

3. Merle H. Deardorff, "Memorandum on the League of the Iroquois," 20 October 1968, Fenton Papers, APSL. Copy from NL collections, courtesy Francis Jennings.

a meeting official wherever the meeting convened. This compromise validated meetings at Johnson's fire and at various treaty sites. Agreements reached elsewhere could be validated at Onondaga later.

At the founding of the league, according to the Deganawi:dah epic, Onondaga was established as the central fire partly to placate the reformed Thadoda:ho?. The historical record does not support the idea that the Onondagas were any more than first among equals. This record begins in 1655 in the Jesuit *Relations*. What the Jesuit writers described was a voluntary association of five nations sharing a more or less homogeneous culture who met for a limited purpose every autumn to settle any differences that had arisen between them in the previous year. This they accomplished with an agreed-upon mechanism for composing feuds, namely, the condolence ceremony. We do not know what changes had occurred in the composition of these meetings, its delegations, or in its structure during the century prior to contact with Europeans. We assume it took the shape and operated as the league described in the epic. Originally, men bearing the titles of its fifty founders composed its grand council. How long they controlled its operation and transformed their prestige into power by action remains a mystery.

We do know that by the turn of the eighteenth century, headmen of achieved status had succeeded to the roles of the founders. These were the men who presided over the grand council, made embassies to Europeans, and signed treaties. Only rarely do the titles of the founders appear in documents, although a distinction remained between honorific hereditary chiefs and headmen who did business. The league of tradition had become the confederacy, although the confederacy continued to appeal to the former institution. Like what happened among the Pueblos in later times, the league became the interior polity while the confederacy became the mechanism for external affairs. Deardorff labeled this second phenomenon "League #2"; Richter (1992) distinguishes it as "the Confederacy."

The confederacy emerged as a response to the need for doing business with European powers. Just as the league co-opted then-existing village chiefs, so the confederacy was managed by headmen of achieved status in village councils. Occasionally, holders of hereditary titles filled both roles. This was the government that Johnson took over, manipulated, and reformed. He perceived it as an instrument for resisting the French. As superintendent of Indian affairs in the Northern Department, Johnson became the channel for dispensing crown favors in the form of presents, passports, and medals to Indians (fig. 35). By mid-century, Iroquois culture depended on European manufactures: guns, powder, lead, Stroud's blankets, knives, axes, needles, and rum. Controlling these goods and other favors, Johnson could name the recipients. In doing so he adhered to the rules of Indian etiquette and observed proper protocol. He never used excessive force. He never pushed people beyond their limits or ordered them around. His power remained unobtrusive but understood, and therefore effective. Early on, as we have seen, principals informed him of successions to chiefly office and requested his approval. His sanction became vital.

Johnson soon recognized that he must operate within the context of two political systems: hereditary chiefs of the league and those he named "chiefs to do business." He gradually came to install both. The Iroquois themselves remained ambivalent about the two classes. The hereditary chiefs bearing titles of the founders of the league enjoyed prestige but lacked power to put it in action. Those

By the Honorable Sir William Johnson Bart His Majestys sole Agent and Super-Intendant of Indian Affairs for the Northern Department of North America. Colonel of the Six United Nations their Allies and Dependants &c. &c.

To

Whereas I have received repeated proofs of your Attachment to his Britanic Majestys Interests. and Zeal for his Service upon Sundry occasions. more particularly

I do therefore give you this public Testimonial thereof as a Proof of his Majestys Esteem & Approbation. Declaring you the said to be a of Your and recommending it to all his Majestys Subjects and faithfull Indian Allies to Treat and Confider you upon all occasions agreable to your Character. Station. and Services

Given under my Hand and Seal at Arms at Johnson hall the day of . 17

By Command of Sir W: Johnson

Figure 35. Sir William Johnson's passport for Loyalist Indians. Its illustration shows an Indian being presented with a medal as the two parties sit across the fire from each other, sheltered by the Tree of Peace. Also depicted are the chain, the heart, and the calumet of peace. Courtesy New-York Historical Society, New York City.

of achieved status were in control, and it is their names that appear on agreements and treaties, with the rare exceptions that I have noted. Deardorff maintained that Johnson held the machinery of both polities in his hands, for all practical purposes.[4]

As we shall see presently, the dual system persisted into the federal treaty period, 1784–97. Meanwhile, let us examine contemporary French comprehension of treaty protocol and Iroquois polity.

4. A modern analog of this dual system has existed at Six Nations Reserve in Canada since 1924, when the Indian Act abolished the hereditary chiefs, who retreated to Onondaga Longhouse. Since then the hereditary chiefs who bear league titles have enjoyed the prestige of a traditional elite, while Ottawa recognizes elected councilors who discharge the business of the reserve. In that sense the latter resemble Johnson's "chiefs to do business" (after Merle H. Deardorff).

CHAPTER 32

IROQUOIS POLICY
VACILLATES AS POWER SHIFTS

Throughout the Seven Years War a fundamental policy issue divided the Iroquois Longhouse. Where did its loyalty lie? At the eastern door, Mohawk leaders favored the English; the Seneca keepers of the western door, facing attacks from nations allied to Canada, remained pro-French. Seneca sentiments prevailed among the upper Iroquois nations, although the old men of Oneida were of two minds. Disagreements did not prevent the grand council from meeting at Onondaga, as it always had met annually to settle similar differences, and pro-Anglo sentiments did not deter Mohawk headmen from attending. But the Six Nations confederacy had no consistent foreign policy as such. The one thing its members agreed on was to maintain their territorial integrity from further incursions by British or French.

Both the French fort at Niagara, in Seneca territory, and the British outpost at Oswego, where the "Onondaga River" emptied into Lake Ontario, represented such incursions. Onondaga elders stood by and watched Montcalm sack Oswego, and no Iroquois war party went to its relief. A few Iroquois warriors may have joined the Far Indians in the massacre that Montcalm sanctioned. They were relieved to be rid of an eyesore. The confederacy was in no mood to assist the British. Instead, the upper nations saw the pendulum swinging toward the French.

Late in 1756 an embassy of the upper nations approached Montreal to parlay with Governor Vaudreuil. They came on their own initiative, and no one greeted them properly at woods' edge or landing. Besides the four upper nations, the delegation included Tuscarora, Tutelo, Nanticoke, and "Canaoneuska" (Conestoga?) dependents; several Cherokees had come along. Some Iroquois of Two Mountains attended, along with Algonkin, Nipissing, Ottawa, and Potawatomi units identified with the French—in all, some 180 men, women, and children.

French observers had a good eye for ritual and a good ear for language. Of the two accounts recording these meetings, the official report is strong on detail, but a later letter by Montcalm conveys the symbolism (NYCD, 10: 499–518, 553, 561; Jennings 1988: 325). Although the negotiations did not achieve a major goal, they nevertheless reveal some aspects of Iroquois polity just then. A divided confederacy, to achieve unity of policy, confined itself to the upper nations and excluded the Mohawks until such time as they cut loose from Sir William Johnson. Metaphorically, they had chopped off a segment of the Longhouse. But their apparent gratitude at the sack of Oswego did not signify willingness to submit as children to a French patriarch; rather, it conveyed joy over recovery of lost territory. No contemporary treaty document clarifies so well a fundamental principle in Iroquois polity, which applies equally to the league and the later confederacy, namely, ritual (the repeated performance of set forms), which is always paramount to structure. How a thing is done (the proper way) is more important than content or who does it. Thus a virtuoso performance of the condolence paradigm with appropriate strings and belts does not require the services of a league titleholder. The orators on this occasion, unknown to us previously, fulfilled the canons of Iroquois oratory.

One Chinoniata, an Onondaga chief, spoke first in the name of the Five Nations, the original members of the league, as if to invest his message with the greatest authority. He remarked that no one had come to meet them, a lapse in protocol, which immediately put the French on the defensive. Then, by some fourteen belts and several sets of strings, he made the confederacy's case.

Addressing the governor as "father," he began with the most serious affair: two belts attested how eight nations had come out of the darkness of grief to properly condole the deaths of a French father and son who had watched the Tree of Peace. The Onondagas in particular covered their graves with a first belt in the presence of the bereaved relatives. A second belt represented the Tuscaroras.

Then he got into the paradigm. A belt from Onondaga spoke for the Five Nations, who collected and covered the bones of warriors and other dead. A half-belt kindled a new council fire; the other half promoted "work at good business." Another half-belt requickened those lost among their successors to do business; the other half organized their assistance. Dispelling dark clouds and restoring the sun divided a sixth belt, including a disclaimer of current wisdom compared with that of the ancients.

A seventh belt conveyed medicine for the heart to enable the French to speak plainly—a custom always observed by the Five Nations. An eighth belt symbolized a tobacco pouch, which their forebears had used "when they perceived anything bad; they placed it on the shoulder and labored at good business." The belt renewed the pouch; some added strings (being short of wampum) kept it always filled with tobacco. (Theme: smoking promotes good thoughts.) A ninth belt cleaned the council chamber of filth accumulated since the last council. Strings affirmed the governor's desire to renew ancient councils; speaking from the heart required uprooting a pine so as to bury bad business.

By a tenth belt bearing the eleventh message, eight nations erected the Tree of Peace, already old, and renewed its *three* sustaining roots that extended north, south and west. The council would retire beneath it to do business. The belt included the Delawares.

The leaves of the Tree of Peace that had withered between councils were restored by an eleventh belt to afford shade for the council. Three strings put a beaver's tail and a plug of tobacco in a dish for all parties to partake in mutual friendship.

A twelfth belt had originated with the governor's predecessor and sanctioned the Iroquois war against the Catawbas and Chickasaws. Half of the belt added roots to the Tree of Peace; whosoever touched these roots would rouse all nations to unite. Permission was requested to strike them.

Belt thirteen remarked English posture and threats. It urged the French to hold fast to the peace and remain quiet on their mat while the Iroquois, equally balanced, stayed neutral. Belt fourteen addressed "good business," commended the governor's son, who kept them informed, and acknowledged their obligation to the French for clearing the barrier at Oswego and reopening the path to Montreal. By two sets of double strings they petitioned for the renewal of trade at Cadaraqui (Fort Frontenac) and for cheap prices. The second set asked for similar fare at Niagara and begged restoring the portage business to native bearers.

The following day, an Oneida speaker announced the death of a chief named Tharia, their pro-French mentor not yet replaced, who had evidently accompanied an Onondaga-Oneida embassy to Montreal earlier that year (NYCD, 10: 445ff., 503, 508).

Several days later, the interpreter delivered the governor's reply, belt for belt and string for string, addressing the natives as "children." While adhering to the expected forms, the speech took a decidedly pro-French twist and anti-British bias. It admonished the Five Nations to work at "good business," which meant to promote the French alliance or stay quiet on their mats.

Within two days, Koue?e, an Oneida chief, delivered the confederacy's assent to the governor's final belt. Yes, they agreed not to permit the English to infringe on their territory, or to assist them, but they would defend themselves, which would not prove difficult because "he [the English] does not know how to travel in the woods." They would lose no time in showing the governor's belt to the Mohawks, indicating the governor's willingness to pardon them, and would add a belt of their own, "inviting him [the Mohawks] to withdraw from the English" and urging him to "work at good business" (NYCD, 10: 513).

An account of this embassy that accompanied Montcalm's letter the following April (NYCD, 10: 555) dilated considerably on the official proceedings, revealing in footnotes an understanding of the confederacy and its policy of granting citizenship by adoption so that, though the confederacy by now comprised ten nations, its members continued to refer to themselves as Five Nations. The notes further explain the nature and uses of wampum strings and belts: chiefs kept them and designed their length, width, and color proportionate to the affair being negotiated. Ordinary belts comprised twelve rows of 180 beads. The notes demonstrate even greater verbal sophistication, defining the terminology for belt, affair, speech or message, and the concept of greatness or nobility, which in Iroquoian stem from the same root (NYCD, 10: 556).[1]

Speakers for the Five Nations at the end of each item carefully acknowledged the source of each belt presented, the share, if the belt represented a joint subscription, and the proportion of wampum donated, crying out by name the canton or nation that furnished it (NYCD, 10: 563).

The notes further comment on the French lapse of protocol. The initial speaker had insinuated that no one had come out to meet them—that they had not been received with the usual ceremonies. "The Five Nations are the only ones for whose reception there is an established etiquette." They expected to hear the Three Bare Words and receive as many strings outside of town, and to be saluted with five cannon shots on entering. It was also the custom for visitors to return an invitation belt and for the host to acknowledge it. After this initial speech, Governor

---

1. The terms are *gaionne* (*gayone*), usage for belts; *garihoua* (*garihwa*) "affair," lit., "word"; *gaouenda* (*gahwenda*) "speech, message" (*gaswenhda?*, "wampum belt," Seneca [Chafe 1967: 81]); and *gaianderensera* (*gayendarensera*) "greatness or nobility."

Vaudreuil had then thanked the delegation for coming and made amends for the lapse with six strings—two for each of the three words: tears, ears, and throat (NYCD, 10: 557).

The Iroquois speaker, after announcing that the Five Nations were first to inform the English of the demise of Oswego, reported how the English army had destroyed its own outposts and retreated. The speaker ended the session by presenting six strings of similar dimensions by way of thanking the governor for wiping their tears, cleansing their throats, and opening their ears, and he concluded by condoling the governor's losses, which would enable the governor to speak and hear his children.

When the delegation was fully assembled, its main speaker, an Onondaga who would deliver the fourteen belts and two sets of strings already described, made his entrance dancing and weeping (NYCD, 10: 558). (Weeping upon greeting strangers was a widespread custom in the eastern woodlands from the seventeenth century onward.)

The Five Nations pitched upon a Cayuga orator to address the second session. After relating some post-Oswego events and requesting a resident French agent in Cayuga country, he presented two strings announcing the death of their principal chief and presented his replacement, a lad of sixteen, who saluted the governor. This practice of showing the faces of newly raised chiefs to colonial officials, both at Fort Johnson and at Montreal, would lead to confirmation and appointment of chiefs by governors and agents.

Similarly, an Oneida speaker recalled the Six Nations' ancient attachment to the French, invoked the memory of Tareha and the senior Vaudreuil, and with four strings presented the new chief to fill the empty seat. He mentioned a recent alliance with the Cherokees, who were present.

The Cayuga orator then closed the council by eliciting the cry of approbation serially from each nation, according to rank (NYCD, 10: 560).

The several Algonquian-speaking nations present sustained the governor's reply several days later, admonishing the Five Nations to distance themselves from the English and adhere to the French. This roused the Cayuga speaker in the name of the Five Nations to assure Vaudreuil of their good intentions. They had "cut off from their cabin the Mohawks, whose heart was wholly English; yet he hoped, by dint of shaking their heads, to make them recover their lost senses and to bring them back to their Father. He then called the roll of the Nations, and the Assembly adjourned" (NYCD, 10: 560–61).

Following the conference, Vaudreuil and Montcalm reported to the ministry a diplomatic triumph. The Iroquois speakers, in the name of the Five Nations, could go home and proclaim that upper Iroquois sentiments had prevailed. Neither party gained much. Although the Mohawks for the moment were immobilized, if not cut off, the facade of the Longhouse was maintained.

□□◇□□

With support confined to the Mohawks, and unable to entice the Senecas to take up the English hatchet against the French so long as the Mississaugas and Ottawas threatened the western door, Johnson, as crown superintendent, turned his attention south to settling the troubles between the Delawares and Pennsylvania. Under his direction, George Croghan conducted three treaties at Easton in the years 1757, 1758, and 1762. An Iroquois presence put the kibosh on the rantings of Teedyuscung (Boyd 1938: lxxxi).

Intelligence of affairs in upper Iroquoia reached Johnson even when the English withheld military support. A mounted warrior, six days out of Cayuga, said his chief was lame and would follow, that he rode horseback for dispatch. The Cayuga chief, Dyaderowane, reported that while the Six Nations delegates were in Canada, "they saw a great Number of Western Indians there who had joined the French Army." The delegates called them to a meeting and spoke to them with a belt, saying the Iroquois thought their joining the French in the war was precipitate. No one could foresee how affairs would turn out. The English had never harmed them. They should return home and stay neutral. The French, on seeing their Indians leave and on learning that the Six Nations deputies were to blame, reprimanded them. Further, the French planned to attack the British at Lake George within the month and destroy Johnson's house; the deputies had seen the forces gather.

What was more, affairs on the Ohio deeply concerned the Cayugas. Two months previously, another Cayuga sachem, Hayendisere, had visited Fort Duquesne. A French officer had produced a large black war belt, which represented a large ax capable of destroying all it touched, urging Hayendisere to deliver it to the Six Nations and use it against the English. When the officer threw the belt toward him, Hayendisere kicked it away, saying that to charge him with such a message was improper, and he would never carry it to the Six Nations.

Finally, not unlike the Six Nations, the western Delawares were divided in their minds. The Six Nations recently had sent them a message urging them to cease hostilities against the English. Half of their people had accepted the message; the other half refused. The first half begged the Six Nations to intervene, lest faction-alism lead to bloodshed. The upper Iroquois, wanting the matter settled, would carry that view to Easton (HEH LO 1887; SWJP, 9: 539–41).

Under Johnson's orders, Croghan went to Philadelphia to investigate the Indian situation and convince the natives to maintain friendly relations with the Six Nations and to cooperate with the British army in its 1757 campaigns. He was also to inquire into the causes of the alienation of the Delawares and Shawnees and to seek justice. His arrival in town put both colonial factions in a dither. The Quaker party, led by Israel Pemberton, having raised substantial funds to promote peace with the Indians, was backing Teedyuscung. The proprietors, although responsible, were at a disadvantage. That Johnson had fully empowered Croghan to act and investigate the Indian situation stunned both factions. Both sides tried to influence him. Croghan, to the dismay of the proprietor's party, insisted that all the lands west of the Allegheny Mountains that the Penns had purchased in Albany during the congress of 1754 and which they had not yet paid for must be given back to the Indians, since that purchase had provoked great dissatisfaction among both the Iroquois and the Ohio Delawares (SWJP, 2: 657–58; Wainwright 1959: 118–19).

The Ohio Delawares were in no mood to be pushed around. Having regained their status as men, a Delaware delegation that had been held six months at the Seneca town on the Genesee defied the Seneca leaders to prevent their going to Niagara, saying, "We have been once Women, and ashamed to look down at our Petticoats, but as you have taken off our Petticoats, and encouraged us to quarrel with the English, we are determined to never submit to that ignominious State while there is one of us alive" (HEH LO 2976).

George Croghan, representing Johnson, held two preliminary meetings in the spring of 1757 at Harris's Ferry and Lancaster. Little was accomplished, but the proceedings attract our interest for two reasons: they outline the basic elements of the condolence paradigm, which Croghan had learned from Scaroyady, and although all of the Six Nations and the Delawares sent deputies, Teedyuscung and his followers failed to appear to settle the claims he had advanced the previous year at Easton.

Ancient custom required that Croghan, as host, speak first, mixing the tears of the two parties, wiping blood from the seats, wiping tears, dispersing clouds, and restoring the sun, so as to heal the hearts and free the minds of his guests, rub down their weary bodies, and brighten the chain. In reply, the Oneida Scaroyady congratulated Croghan for observing an ancient custom, sharing their grief, wiping blood from council seats, wrapping bones, wiping tears, and restoring the sun. These, then, were the essential elements of the paradigm—much fewer than in later times (DePuy 1917: 40; Boyd 1938: 170–72).

The visiting chiefs, fearing smallpox, refused to go to Philadelphia to meet the governor but compromised on Lancaster. Removing the council fire required an additional belt. The Lancaster council proved to be Scaroyady's final appearance on the treaty scene; the dreaded disease overtook him regardless and led the steadfast old Oneida on the long trail.

The Indians had waited for weeks while the oak leaves reached the size of a squirrel's ear: it was time to get home and plant. The Mohawk Little Abraham, son of Hendrick's brother, declared that a treaty must be concluded. He further insisted that the proper way to contact the Delawares was through the western door of the Senecas, the only people the Delawares still acknowledged as uncles (Boyd 1938: 176–78; P. Wallace 1945: 469; Wainwright 1959: 122, 124).

Why did Teedyuscung fail to appear and state his claims in the presence of the Six Nations? His biographer offers an explanation (A. Wallace 1949: 153). Teedyuscung was unfamiliar with Iroquois polity. He had grown up in the white settlements of New Jersey, beyond the sound of council oratory, and had witnessed only peripheral Iroquois operations. He failed to realize that Iroquois unity rested on occasional shared sentiments. Had he known how the old men of Onondaga achieved consensus, his position would have been stronger. As it was, he was not prepared to face the Six Nations at Lancaster. The image of the Iroquois still loomed large over the forests.

That year witnessed simultaneous Indian negotiations north and south. While Croghan was meeting with the Six Nations and others at Harris's Ferry and Lancaster, a delegation of Mahicans, Shawnees, and Nanticokes from Otseningo on the Susquehanna came to Fort Johnson by mistake. Sometimes invitation belts conveyed the wrong message. A folded wampum belt could carry two different messages (HEH LP 3253). The Shawnees had been asked to stand ready to aid the British when called upon, which they interpreted as an invitation to treat with Sir William. He had asked the Cayugas to bring them in, but the Cayugas would not budge from home, standing ready to defend their Oneida siblings in the junior moiety, who expected the French to attack (HEH 15091; DePuy 1917: 41).

As the summer conference at Easton approached, Pennsylvania governor Denny worried about the expense of presents necessary for condoling the Six Nations, who were expected to attend in large numbers at Johnson's invitation. There was also Teedyuscung's following. Would the crown defray the expense? Loudon ruled no; Pennsylvania should bear the cost (HEH LO 3485, 3562).

The treaty sessions ran from 21 July through 7 August 1757.[2] A host of hungry and nigh naked Indians arrived early: 150 adherents of Teedyuscung, 119 of the Six Nations, mostly Senecas, as expected, including women and children. The treaty's principal accomplishment brought peace between the eastern Delawares and Pennsylvania. Teedyuscung behaved irrationally, ranting for days about land issues, the inferior position of the Delawares as women, their status as subordinates to the Six Nations, and so on. When told that the crown had handed the resolution of land questions to Sir William Johnson, he demurred. He apparently feared a confrontation with the seasoned diplomats of the Six Nations, who would displace him from the council circle. After days of scolding, an old Delaware declared that they had come to make peace and had heard talk only of land. They should settle the peace and defer land disputes until afterward. Croghan realized that the treaty had merely produced a truce (Wainwright 1959: 132).

Great quantities of wampum, including belts of eight to seventeen rows, besides strings, passed between the parties at this treaty. The most remarkable belt was to confirm peace. Governor Denny "gave a very large white Belt, with the Figures of three Men . . . representing . . . King George, taking hold of the Five Nation King, with one Hand, and Teedyuscung, the Delaware King, with the other, and marked . . . G.R. 5N D.K., for King GEORGE, Five Nations, Delaware King" (Boyd 1938: 204). Such lettered belts came into use at this period.

The treaty concluded with the usual bonfire and Indian dances.

□□◇□□

Back in the Mohawk Valley, Sir William Johnson sought to extend his tenuous grip on the Six Nations. The council had met at Onondaga that spring, when the three upper nations declared themselves neutral while the Oneidas and Tuscaroras, who were in shock over the destruction of nearby forts, withheld opinion. Half of Oneida was pro-French (Beauchamp 1905: 310-11).

In June, Seneca and Onondaga delegates appeared at Fort Johnson, preceding a Cayuga party. Mohawk leaders soon joined them. Oneida principals came belatedly. None of the Seneca sachem names equates with a league title. One of the old castle was named Tawistawis ("Sandpiper," "Snipe"). Likewise, the Onondaga sachem names defy recognition, but one "Head Warrior," Tyohaqueande, shared the name of the third Oneida founder (Deyohagwendeh, 0e-3), which demonstrates that Iroquois personal names were not the exclusive property of one nation. Nor does Skahyonwio, "Big Canoe," the Cayuga spokesman, appear on the roster of Cayuga league titles. Apparently the participants were acting out a tradition with proxies.

As usual, the sachems failed to control the warriors of the upper nations. Big Canoe, speaking for the Cayugas, acknowledged the truth of the allegation that

2. In a bibliographic note, Jennings (1988: 342n) discusses the three versions of this treaty critically. I shall follow the version by Croghan, who knew Indians, for its ethnological content as printed by Franklin (Boyd 1938; DePuy 1917: 42).

warriors of the upper nations had gone out against the English, but he said that they had thrown a belt to keep the Cayuga warriors from participating in the future (NYCD, 7: 256). As if to attain consensus, the Onondaga speaker, addressing the Mohawk and Seneca nations, convoked a caucus of the Three Brothers, the senior moiety of the confederacy, saying it was proper for them to withdraw and take the matter under consideration. His answer next day implied that they had included the Cayugas in their deliberations, invoking the image of the grand council, without the Oneidas of the junior moiety.

Fear of the Mississaugas had immobilized the upper nations and prevented them from taking up the English hatchet. In this situation the grand council had opted for neutrality, which did not prevent renewing the old covenant chain with the English. No doubt trade considerations weighed heavily. The presence of the nearby Mohawk leaders elicited the encomium that they were the head of the confederacy.

Holding fast to the chain invoked related symbols: dressing up the council fire, now at Fort Johnson, the sheltering tree, weeding its perimeter to promote its growth, and so forth. This was not just the resolve of three nations but included Oneida and Tuscarora—the whole confederacy (NYCD, 7: 258).

Johnson's answer stressed the essence of the chain: "The English and the Six Nations shall consider themselves as one flesh and one blood, and . . . whenever any enemy shall hurt the one the other is to feel it and avenge it, as if done to himself" (NYCD, 7: 261). (Theme: linked arms or common umbilicus.)

In private conversations, Johnson remarked on actions inconsistent with the old covenant chain. The Onondaga speaker declared that they had come away from the grand council resolved to settle any such matters. On leaving their respective castles they had laid hands on all fighters to keep them home until they returned. This pledge to restrain war parties lacked certainty. Moreover, the Senecas had interposed and prevailed on the Ohio Delawares to lay down the hatchet. They awaited an answer. Senecas present did not know why Teedyuscung had stayed away from Lancaster. To validate their adherence to the covenant chain alliance, which they declared reached to the farthest Seneca town on the Genesee, the speaker delivered the covenant chain belt that Sir William had presented to the remote Seneca castle (NYCD, 7: 264).

That evening the Senecas spread out a prodigious belt of thirty rows, twice the usual width, figuring the sun in the middle and the Six Nations at one end. They had sent it to retrieve all the scattered remnants of their own people and to invite other nations to remove nearer and join the confederacy. Messages had gone out to allies to send deputies to a grand council at Onondaga next moon to consider the general welfare (NYCD, 7: 254–66).

Three Cherokee warriors showed up at Fort Johnson at the end of July. In the presence of Seneca, Cayuga, and Oneida delegates, Johnson performed the rite of condolence, wiping their tears with a string and performing other acts that custom demanded. In returning the string, the Cherokee speaker confessed, "We are warriors and do not understand these matters and hope you will excuse us." Days later a Seneca sachem named Belt spoke for them, returning Johnson's welcome. The Cherokees would attack the French fort on the Ohio (NYCD, 7: 324–25).

In September, four of the Six Nations (without Onondaga) met Sir William in the name of the confederacy. They declared themselves sufficient to act for the whole. In addition there came some River Indians and several Cherokees, who, merely warriors, were instructed to return with delegates prepared to make peace at Johnson's fire and nowhere else. Johnson supplied a long, broad white belt to cover the peace message and a black belt for the Cherokee warriors. The speaker proclaimed the nearby Mohawks and Oneidas "the heads of the confederacy," at whose fires the chiefs of the Six Nations would meet with the Cherokee ambassadors. Indeed, traditionally the two were the first nations to adhere to the league (NYCD, 7: 324-28; SWJP, 9: 831-53).

In reading eighteenth-century sources today it is hard to appreciate the time lapses and hazards of communicating just then. The natives had not yet acquired writing. Runners charged with strings and belts took several days or even weeks on the path, "where every stone and tree [that] lay in the way was avoided" (HEH LO 4733). Letters wrapped up in birchbark might be hung on a bush to be picked up by a passing scout, which was the common way of sending letters between enemies (HEH LO 1986). Sometimes letters got partly or entirely burned in trailside camp fires. "Beloved men"—chiefs and priests—of the Cherokees instructed their emissaries to the Mohawks to leave a stone with a painted cross turned upside down wherever they camped. Mohawk warriors were to do the same (HEH, Abercromby Papers [hereafter AB] 26). It seems a wonder that word ever got through.

Invitations to council were sometimes ambiguous. An illustration of this, and an example of how Johnson dealt with Indians, occurred in March 1758, when Johnson met some Oneidas, Tuscaroras, Cayugas, Delawares, and Schoharie Mohawks at Fort Johnson. Save for the last, these comprised the junior moiety of the confederacy. The firekeepers had summoned a general council at Onondaga, but in the absence of an invitation with a string, those present urged Johnson not to attend. A belt came from the Cayugas to their elder brothers, the Oneidas, asking: Why had they, as senior members of the moiety, not called a moiety meeting? The Oneida speaker replied: "The Onondagas have given a Shout to Acquaint the Nations that the Fire is kindled." This removed any doubt. It was up to the Mohawks to decide whether to bring Johnson. Snow lay yet deep on the road, and scalping parties were out. Johnson left it to the Mohawks to judge whether it was safe and prudent for him to attend the meeting, but he thought his presence unnecessary. He would await the results. Privately, Johnson urged a strong union and concerted action among the Six Nations on behalf of the English. French influence at Onondaga worried him. Before they departed, in the presence of all the Oneida sachems Johnson reinstated one of their number "with the usual Ceremony and marks of Distinction" (SWJP, 9: 879-86).

□□◇□□

Skipping over military affairs of moment, such as Abercromby's defeat at Ticonderoga, the building of Fort Stanwix (modern Rome, New York) at the Oneida "carrying place" into Oneida Lake, and Bradstreet's success at Fort Frontenac, which severed the French supply line to the west, let us follow the diplomatic scene, which shifts to negotiations in Pennsylvania leading up to the grand treaty at Easton in the autumn of 1758. This treaty has generated considerable discussion among historians, most recently by Francis Jennings (1988: 396ff.). My interest centers on Indian participation and the light it shines on native polity.

During the preceding summer, Teedyuscung honored the invitation of Governor Denny that brought to the Pennsylvania state house some Delaware and Mahican leaders. Teedyuscung spoke first. His performance demonstrates that the Delawares shared the same metaphors and ceremonial forms in use by Iroquois orators, which he had learned of late. He swept the council chamber clean with a wing, and with three bare words and four strings wiped the dust from the eyes of his hosts, cleaned their ears with a feather, and removed dust from their throats. The governor's invitation had cleared bushes and grass that had overgrown the path to the Delaware settlements. The path, formerly kept open, should be kept free of obstacles. This warranted a belt of four rows. Speaking from the heart, not just the mouth, manifested sincerity in council and guaranteed continuity to both sides. To press the grass down and part the bushes on but one side of the road symbolized a failed mission. To smoke good tobacco from the same pipe used by their grandfathers reassured participants. To press on together with both hands exerted power. To bring a medicine—a plaster to heal wounds—would relieve injuries inflicted by the French. In returning a captive, one Sarah Decker taken by the Minisinks, Teedyuscung explained that no captive was his or her own master. Likewise, he had nothing to do with another white man married some ten years to an Indian squaw and now his own master (HEH AB 422).

Denny's reply several days later clearly reflects his efforts to learn Indian protocol. Conrad Weiser was his tutor. He proceeded to return the same forms and metaphors. He could afford generosity with strings and belts, for it seems that in such negotiations the English always had access to wampum, which was relatively scant among Indians.

News of the previous Easton treaty had not reached the Ohio. Two old men living there, unaware of the peace made a year earlier, returned to visit their birthplace in eastern Pennsylvania. They had to be briefed on the peace terms, in hopes they would publish them on returning home. It seems the Six Nations had informed Pennsylvania that at a great council held at Onondaga the Delawares had acknowledged their fault in striking the English. On hearing this, Pennsylvania sent messengers to Tioga to ascertain the truth, hoping to bring a confirmation from the mouths of Delaware headmen. Fortunately, Teedyuscung was then at Tioga, a council was called, he brought confirmation, and peace was concluded. Teedyuscung's boast of ten nations apparently did not include the Delaware émigrés.

The road from Ohio was now opened. The governor asked Teedyuscung to join another belt to his. Teedyuscung then stated that he sat in the middle of that road, where the Six Nations had stationed him to control traffic. He would no longer sit still with his pipe in his mouth but would be active in the English cause. He bemoaned the bodies, lying in the brush, of persons killed by the French (HEH AB 433).

Late in August, Croghan reported that twenty Indian messengers had left Wyoming carrying invitations to the forthcoming treaty. Already the upper nations were assembling, and from the number of Indians of importance gathering with their deputies, he foresaw a fair prospect of uniting Indian sentiment favorable to the English and establishing a lasting peace (Denny to DeLancey, HEH AB 587). Adding to French disfavor, some French emissaries spread the word in

Detroit that the Iroquois were doomed to be annihilated, which boast reached the Senecas through the Delawares. It was the kind of rumor that Johnson could exploit to great advantage (Winsor 1895: 389).

Johnson was fairly confident that, with the possible exception of the remote Seneca villages, very few of the Six Nations would join the French against the English. He was convinced that their chiefs predominately tried to maintain a policy of neutrality. He understood that the Onondaga chief who had accepted a French hatchet at Montreal the previous year was severely reprimanded by chiefs of the other nations. This man and his followers might still defect. Similarly, the Oneida village at the lake was largely pro-French. What is more, Johnson detected readiness among the confederacy to delegate chief men to the meeting at Easton. Visiting Senecas informed him that some six weeks earlier they had sent emissaries up the lakes to incite former French allies to fall upon French settlements (HEH AB 668; SWJP, 10: 4–7). At the same time, negotiations were going forward for peace with the Cherokees.

The Easton treaty fell toward the end of the deer hunting season. Chiefs of all the Six Nations attended, with strong representation from the upper nations. "Tocaaoyon" (Teka?en:yon, or Haga?en:yonk), the title heading the Cayuga roster of league chiefs (C-1, RC 33), was among the five hundred Indians gathered at Easton. Besides Iroquois, eastern and western Delaware, and Shawnee principals, there were Tutelo, Nanticoke, Conoy, Chugnut, Unami, Mahican, Mohegan, Minisink, and Wappinger entities. The presence of Mohawk leaders would serve to chasten Teedyuscung and reduce him to pleading for a place to live, in a speech "which for beauty, imagery and pathos deserves to live" (HEH 3037; Boyd 1938: lxxxvi, 230).

The Easton treaty marked the end of Pennsylvania's ascendancy in treaty negotiations. Conrad Weiser and Richard Peters deserve most of the credit for what was accomplished. The conference was held to settle much of what the previous Easton treaty had left in limbo. The previous year, Teedyuscung had assumed the role of the great one and did all the talking for his people. But now Six Nations sachems were present, and one of the first questions they asked was, "Who made Teedyuscung a great man and wherefore is he called a King?" (DePuy 1917: 44; Treaty Minutes 1758 in Boyd 1938). Careful as Teedyuscung was in their presence to address them as "Uncles," the delegates of the Six Nations treated him with scant courtesy. Teedyuscung had promised the previous year to return all the captives he held, but he had not done so. An Oneida chief rebuked him: "Remember, Cousin, you have made this promise in our presence. You did indeed before and you ought to have performed it. It is a shame for one who calls himself a great man to tell Lies" (Boyd 1938: 243).

An examination of Iroquois participation in the treaty illuminates the way they controlled its course. Their avuncular relationship to the Delawares lay at the root of it. What the governors planned as a formal affair soon metamorphosed into forest diplomacy as Iroquois speakers took charge and reasserted customary kinship rights and usages. Croghan expected this.

Early in October he sent the interpreter Montour and the Mohawk Nichas to conduct the big Seneca and Cayuga delegation from Fort Allen to Easton. Croghan knew that Seneca warriors had gone to support the Delaware raiders and that Seneca headmen protected them. Tagashata, a war chief who headed the Seneca delegation, was Teedyuscung's alleged advisor. Toka?en:yon, the leading Cayuga sachem, graced the Cayuga party. Peace with the upper Iroquois nations took precedence over considerations of national ranking and status. Croghan set Mrs. Montour, the interpreter's mother, to fabricating the wampum belts and strings needed to validate his welcoming address. The success of the treaty depended on bringing the two principals—the Senecas and Cayugas—to a right mind. Nichas and the Oneida Thomas King might support them (Wainwright 1959: 146–47; Jennings 1988: 198).

It soon developed that the Iroquois delegates had not reached one mind on the Delaware connection. The Seneca and Cayuga headmen insisted that they were the sole directors of the Munsees and Delawares, excluding the other Six Nations. The game plan that Croghan and the proprietor's men followed sought to get the Iroquois to reassert their dominance over the Delawares. In private sessions, the strategy that developed called for Tagashata to force the Delawares to profess friendship and acknowledge that they were wrong in taking up the hatchet against the English. Then the Six Nations would intercede for them. Reducing Teedyuscung to size, a game the Iroquois were very good at, would nullify Teedyuscung's previous negotiations and undermine his claim for restoration of the Walking Purchase (Wainwright 1959: 148; Jennings 1988).

Tagashata prepared to speak first at the plenary session on October 11 by laying out on a table the belts and strings in order of his argument. Teedyuscung, now visibly anxious, preempted the agenda, ignoring Croghan's question about the propriety of his interrupting the council, and proclaimed that he would have nothing to do with the treaty since he had already made peace. Tagashata, at this breach of protocol, adjourned the council to next day. He then proceeded to declare peace on behalf of both Teedyuscung and the Ohio Delawares. Teedyuscung, having got himself thoroughly drunk, entered council and heckled the Iroquois speakers, boasting that he was king of all the nations and all the world. The Six Nations were fools. Only he could make peace or war. The only way to make peace with the English was to make war on them and cut their throats. That he had done and would continue to do as long as he lived (Wainwright 1959: 149–50).

Without entering into the controversy between the Quakers, who supported Teedyuscung, and the proprietor's men, who worked through Croghan to reassert the dominance of the Iroquois Confederacy, the Iroquois speakers fulfilled their roles in a manner that brought the desired results. The two moieties of the confederacy met privately with the two governors on 15 October: the senior Mohawk-Onondaga-Seneca half sat across the fire from the Oneida-Cayuga junior half, with its Tuscarora, Nanticoke, and Tutelo dependents—the familiar Three Brothers and Four Brothers of later times. The order of speakers preserved this arrangement. The issue on the mat was the status of Teedyuscung.

Properly, the Mohawk chief Nichas spoke first. The chiefs had spent the previous day considering the matter, he said. "[Teedyuscung] gives out, he is the great Man, and Chief of Ten Nations. . . . Now I, on Behalf of the *Mohawks*, say, we do not know he is such a great Man. If he is such . . . we desire to know who made him so. . . . We want to enquire and know whence his Greatness arose."

Tagashata spoke next for the Senecas, seconding Nichas. And Assarandonguas of Onondaga remarked that he had never heard that Teedyuscung was such a great man, nor was it ever said in any Onondaga town.

The question now devolved on the junior moiety. The Oneida chief Thomas King spoke on behalf its constituents. "We Five are all connected . . . and if any Thing is said to one of us, it is communicated to all the rest." The junior side proceeded to disown Teedyuscung.

Toka?en:yon, the Cayuga sachem, addressed the question of captives not returned. "If there be any of them that have gone down our Throats, we will throw them up again."

Nichas followed on behalf of the Three Brothers, the senior moiety, saying that on their return they would search every town for captives, bring the matter before their respective councils, and produce them. He reiterated the promise with a string of seven rows to heave up any captives that had gone down their throats (Boyd 1938: 224–25). Indeed, the Iroquois were known to have burned and eaten captives.

The Indians needed wampum for their speeches and they depended on the commissioners to supply it. It is not generally understood today that the bulk of available wampum during the treaty period was concentrated in the hands of European merchants. It was not being produced in Iroquois towns but had become a cottage industry in Albany, in New Jersey, and on Long Island, where it had originated in the previous century.

After several days of talks in the bushes, during which Governor Denny tried to explain his role in the rise of Teedyuscung, matters came to a head on 18 October. The councilors having importuned the Delaware and Minisink chiefs to release their captives, Nichas announced that the councilors were turning the matter over to the warriors, who would speak next. Thomas King was appointed to deliver their words, which both moieties of councilors had approved. He proceeded to relate a series of incidents in which the Six Nations had been involved that had led to the recent frontier war.

The Six Nations, having eased their minds of any burdens, were ready to go home. Teedyuscung, shorn of his exalted status, stood to air his grievances and explain what had happened to the peace belt of fifteen rows and a fathom in length given the previous year. It had gone upriver to Tioga and two other named towns, whence the council decided to send it to their uncles via the Senecas, whence it presumably passed through the Six Nations. This took a year before it came back to the Delawares. He would do whatever the uncles decided: he too would search the settlements and return any captives. While trying to mollify his uncles, he mistakenly claimed the headwaters of the Delaware as belonging to his people; he then disclaimed any lands belonging to his uncles that included all the lands bordering streams flowing into the Susquehanna. While he spoke, and as he took up another belt, the Six Nations chiefs walked out. The matter was sorted out later (Boyd 1938: 230–31; Jennings 1988: 399).

Several days later, Toka?en:yon summed up the Six Nations' position on the treaty, not at all what the proprietaries expected. Addressing Teedyuscung, he said:

Cousin, I thank you for your Openness and Honesty on this Occasion, freely to declare the Truth. We wish our Brethren, the English . . . were so honest and precise.

They have called us down to this Council Fire, which was kindled for Council Affairs, to renew Treaties of Friendship. But here we must hear a Dispute about Land, and our Time is taken up, but they don't come to the chief Point.

The English first began to do Mischief; we told them so. They only thanked us for our Openness and Advice, and said they would take Care for the future, but healed no Wounds. In short, when they speak to us, they do it with a shorter Belt or String than that which we spoke to them with; tho they can make Wampum, and we cannot.

They ought not thus to treat with *Indians* on Council Affairs. Several of our strong Belts are lost in their Hands entirely. I fear they speak from their Mouth, and not from their Heart. (Boyd 1938: 237)

□□◇□□

The main accomplishments of the Easton treaty of 1758 were, first, that the Pennsylvania proprietors ceded back to the Indians the northwestern lands purchased at the Albany Congress. Second, the Pennsylvania governor promised to restrain settlements in Indian territory, which led to a royal proclamation in 1763 that delineated crown lands reserved for Indians. Third, the western Delawares took home the agreements for ratification by their own council. They withdrew from defending Fort Duquesne, which soon fell to General Forbes. And fourth, the Iroquois managed to reassert their dominance in Indian affairs by reintroducing the concept of the covenant chain. As Croghan's biographer wrote, "The main problem at Easton was not the coddling of Teedyuscung, so typical of previous treaties, but the proper handling of the Iroquois chiefs" (Wainwright 1959: 151).

The latter was an art in which Sir William Johnson excelled. He encouraged pro-English sentiment among the Six Nations wherever he found it. In October, he sent Silverheels and another Seneca among the Cayugas and Senecas. He had discovered a pro-Anglo faction led by Ottrowana, a principal Cayuga sachem, and seconded by another Cayuga chief, the so-called "Englishman . . . the most leading Indian amongst them." On a visit, the Englishman had promised, with a belt of wampum, to keep the English informed on the movements of the French. He had now sent a large one via Captain Fonda at the Oneida carrying place. The Englishman had constantly favored a policy of neutrality. This being the situation, Johnson remained confident that the Six Nations would make no military alliance with the French (HEH AB 721–22, 723, 726; SWJP, 10: 21–26).

This incident illustrates a principle in Iroquois politics discovered by Mary Druke. Unanimity does not mean that the minority subsides; it simply withdraws for the moment until opportunity arises to reassert its views, short of removal from the scene. Thus factionalism is a corollary of unanimity (Druke 1983; 1985: 92–96; 1987).

Events would conspire in 1759 for pro-Anglo sentiment to surface among the Six Nations. In April, Johnson met the Six Nations and their subsidiaries at Canajoharie and heard the desire of both moieties of the confederacy to support the British interest. Then Johnson, with the help of Seneca and Shawnee warriors and Onondaga diplomacy, captured Fort Niagara in July. Previous intelligence had reported that the palisade was rotting. General Jeffrey Amherst retrieved Abercromby's disgrace by taking Fort Ticonderoga, and Quebec fell to General James Wolfe's army in September, although both he and Montcalm died of battle wounds. Indeed, all of North America would soon be British. The role of the Iroquois in the latter two engagements was minimal. How would they manage diplomatically without the French to counter British aggression and land hunger? The policy of neutrality was now dead. What would replace it? The answer might lie in Johnson's negotiations.

The April conference at the upper Mohawk town of Canajoharie brought the confederacy into the British camp. Both moieties of the confederacy were represented, and the reciprocal action between the two sides, mentioned in the Easton treaty, becomes explicit in the proceedings. The day before the conference opened, sachems of the senior moiety called on Sir William, as was their duty, to inform him of deaths among the Cayugas. The junior moiety, including Tuscarora, Tutelo, Saponi, Nanticoke, and Conoy tributaries, must be condoled before doing business. When the assembly convened next day, it fell to Johnson, an adopted Mohawk, on behalf of the senior moiety, to condole the Cayugas specifically and the junior moiety by courtesy. Then followed "the usual Ceremonies of Welcome and the customary condolences to all the Nations." The custom was now so well established that it was not described.

A particularly "black affair" further inhibited proceedings. It seems that a Cayuga warrior who had been generously hosted among the English had murdered and scalped a trader near the Oneida portage. Outraged British authorities demanded that the murderer be brought to justice. This "trouble case" brought out the best of Iroquois ritual diplomacy. The junior moiety met and appointed Conochquieson (Kanongweniyah, "standing ears of corn," Oe-2, RC 11), a chief sachem of Oneida, to speak on behalf of the murderer's kin. He proceeded to deliver five named captives in fulfillment of the recent Easton treaty. He then spoke to the renewal of the covenant chain. But as to the other parts of Johnson's speech, the trouble case, he referred that to the senior moiety, saying: "As we are only the Younger branch of the confederacy & and in a manner but children we shall not take upon us to answer thereupon but refer you upon those Matters to the Onondagos & Senecas, who are our Fathers" (NYCD, 7: 378–82). Thus, in a figurative sense the senior and junior moieties related as fathers and sons. Until the senior moiety of the Three Brothers chose to respond, Johnson must decide what he really wanted out of the meeting.

The Oneida sachem was again the speaker selected to reply to Johnson several days later. He explained the delay as owing to weather and bad roads, which had kept their senior people, responsible for conducting such meetings, from getting there. But they had taken up the trouble case and Johnson's demand for a remedy. "You desired a Medicine from our Warriors to heal the . . . wounds you have received. . . . We have asked our Warriors present . . . what sort of medicine or Plaster they chose to apply" (NYCD, 7: 386). Although their numbers were depleted, the warriors stood ready to revenge English and Iroquois blood shed by the French. (Note that Iroquois polity separated civil from military affairs. The murder was committed by a warrior; therefore, it was up to the warriors to provide a remedy.) They had resolved on unanimity before leaving home. This followed from an ancient and fundamental agreement in the confederacy, "that if any one of either of the Nations was killed by an enemy, the whole were to join in revenging it." The French had killed an Oneida sachem at Fort Stanwix. The resolve to join the English cause against the French ought to satisfy Johnson's need of a remedy for grievances against the Oneida-Cayugas. The speaker ended by throwing a large belt on the ground toward Sir William, which, according to custom, vouched for his sincerity (NYCD, 7: 386–87).

The confederacy anticipated the success of English arms. The younger branch had already delivered its white captives; those still among the Onondagas and Senecas of the senior branch, including their Delaware nephews, would be delivered to the governor of Pennsylvania.

That evening the Onondaga nation gave an ox roast, the beef supplied by Johnson, to which the chief sachems and warriors were invited, where one or more of every nation performed the war dance.

Next day Johnson acknowledged the speech of the junior moiety, which called for a display of the covenant chain belt, a very large black belt with figures representing ten nations and the English. This act symbolized renewal of an ancient alliance replete with associated metaphors.

In fulfillment of the Easton treaty, Johnson surrendered with his own hands to the Onondaga speaker the deed to lands on the Ohio that Pennsylvanians had acquired during the Albany Congress (NYCD, 7: 388). It remained only to offer General Amherst's hatchet by throwing a war belt, which a Mohawk immediately took up and danced with, followed by warriors of other nations. The Onondaga speaker expressed pleasure that Johnson had not loaded their memories with too many things.

Next morning the Oneida sachem Conochquieson spoke to Johnson's belts. They would take them home and publish the resolutions (NYCD, 7: 389).

It was now up to Johnson to hang the kettle for a war feast. By now Johnson had learned how to do a feast up in style, and this one had the desired results. The account is among the best in the literature. Of an evening the carcasses of two oxen were cut up and boiled in five kettles. The chunks of meat were laid out in the Indian manner. The sachems and warriors sat in two opposing lines across the several fires kindled in the center. Old Belt, "a Great Seneca Sachem and Warrior," stood with belt in hand and addressed Sir William and the nations present. He said that the Chenussio Indians, from one of the most considerable Seneca towns near Niagara, had authorized him to declare publicly at this war feast that they heartily concurred in the resolutions reached at this meeting to join the English against the French. Further, twenty-six of their warriors present had determined before leaving their country not to return until they had faced the enemy. They were prepared to march wherever Johnson sent them. Up to now the Genesee Senecas had withheld from the rest of the confederacy what they had resolved the previous winter: to commence hostilities against the French. They were prepared to assist the English in destroying Niagara, which had been built in their country. They had kept this resolution secret not only from the rest of the confederacy but also from "the Drunkard himself the Head of the whole Seneca Nation." They thought the reduction of Niagara sufficient "Plaster" for Sir William's wounds. Belt then led off the war dance (NYCD, 7: 391).

Three sachems of each of the nations called on Sir William next day. They urged him to move speedily on Niagara, the sooner the better. Others, strangers, might not be as familiar with their customs as he was. They implied that Johnson should lead. Their belt featured Niagara at one end and Sir William's name at the far end.

To the Niagara belt they added a white belt with purple figures to dispatch two emissaries to retrieve their kindred from the St. Lawrence missions. Otherwise, the latter should stay out of the way of British armies. News of the Oswegatchie pledge came in and was proclaimed by crier throughout the camp.

□□◇□□

Johnson had succeeded in getting the whole confederacy to pledge to join the British in the war. He was set to march on Niagara. What had caused the confederacy to abandon its policy of neutrality and shift its loyalty to the British?

Indian policy was determined not by religion or by the national traits of either the British or the French but by who held the balance of power, something the Six Nations thoroughly understood. Recall that when renewing the covenant chain, Indians regularly asked for cheaper goods, other concessions, and removal of whites. As Peter Wraxall discovered, they took trade and peace to be one thing. They knew how important it was to maintain their confederacy, and they invoked the image of the Iroquois League of tradition to enhance its image. Consistently they opted for peace first and war second. Historians have stressed the importance of gifts in determining policy (Jacobs 1950), but the important thing in cementing relations was exchange, or reciprocity. The Iroquois expected and succeeded in getting both sides to observe the ritual of treaty protocol, which assuaged grievances and promoted friendship in any important conference. They continually evaluated the relative strength of both the French and the British. The latter were poor performers at first—big on talk and poor on fulfillment—and the Indian orators let them know it.

Traditional ties or enmities of long standing shaped native alliance structure. Algonquin-Iroquois wars reached from precontact times to the mid-eighteenth century. Iroquois contempt for the Delawares occupied the first half of that century. The Delawares and Shawnees were natural allies and hostile to the British.

The covenant chain appears to historians as an alliance between the British and the Iroquois (Jennings 1984), but the Iroquois viewed the alliance from the concept of linking arms, or the concept of a common umbilical cord. The realities of the situation often overshadowed tradition. Throughout the history of treaties, the Iroquois managed to adapt tradition and symbol to the particular situation. Although the chain became rusty at times, it was declared broken but once—by Hendrick in 1753. Whenever French arms succeeded, the Iroquois let the chain sag.

There were principals, or key men, who acted as go-betweens among both Europeans and Iroquois. Weiser, Johnson, and Croghan served the British; the Joncaires and various Jesuits upheld New France. But the Iroquois produced their own statesmen as occasion demanded, notably Hendrick, Canasatego, and an Oneida called Good Peter, of whom we shall hear more later. The key to success was active participation.

The real name of the game was survival and ending up on the winning side. This explains some of the shifts in Iroquois policy. The grand council strove to keep its policies flexible enough to allow it to approach one side without severing ties to the other. It kept sending embassies to Montreal in order to keep French forces from attacking the Six Nations' vulnerable towns, and it maintained constant touch with Mount Johnson and Albany in order to keep the trade open.

The Iroquois adhered to the policy of neutrality until one side demonstrated superiority. It was detente with the French and polishing the chain with the British. When a British victory became apparent in 1759, they dropped the policy of neutrality and joined Johnson's campaign against Niagara.

Their participation in Amherst's campaign against Montreal would lessen their enthusiasm for the partnership in the future. Amherst was not a man who liked Indians, and they soon knew it.

PART FIVE

BALANCING CROWN AND COLONIES, 1760–1777

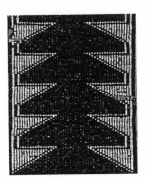

CHAPTER 33

THE SIX NATIONS
FENCED IN

We . . . are penned up like Hogs.—Joseph Pepy, speaking for the
Six Nations at Easton, 1761

Sir William Johnson tried without success to convince General Amherst that
Indians were human beings. To Lord Jeffrey, Indians were not to be trusted; their
main business was to give intelligence to both sides; their demands for presents far
exceeded his budget; spies deserved court-martial and death, "the best way of
treating Indians"; and as allies they were more trouble than they were worth. He
would soon dispense with them (Amherst 1931: 97, 109, 173; Long 1933: 90, 93–94,
97, 117). Just then, however, he needed them. He decided to visit Johnson and
view the Six Nations for himself, and he issued a proclamation assuring Indians
protection of their lives, lands, and property so long as they remained loyal to the
English crown.

En route to Oswego after visiting Johnson in July 1760, while waiting for
bateaux to arrive at Oneida Lake, Amherst, out of curiosity to learn Iroquois
customs, visited Oneida castle, "a pretty situation on a Hill" east of Oneida Lake.
There he estimated a population of sixty warriors, besides women and children.
Some were at prayer. One house was filled with dried eels, salmon, and other
species of fish.

Next day he crossed the lake to the west shore and found an Onondaga family
encamped at a fishing site where three rivers joined. He counted a man, a
"squaw," two children, a dog, a small canoe, a gun, and a fishing rod. His host
pointed out the extent of his domain around the compass. Amherst gave them
some salt pork, which they ate—even the little child, who devoured it abundantly
and then suckled. He remarked that the parents were vastly fond of the child and
indulged it (Amherst 1931: 216–17).

Johnson endeavored to show Amherst Indians at their best—Indians gardening,
at prayer, weaving, engaging in village life. But there were less pretty scenes,
unscheduled. One evening the Indians got drunk on some forbidden rum and in
their frolic cut a horse to pieces. Amherst wrote, "They are devils when drunk,—
when sober, quiet enough" (Long 1933: 129).

Some 11,000 men, including 1,300 Indians under Johnson, rendezvoused at
Oswego that summer in preparation for the campaign against Montreal. The
Indians whom Johnson had mobilized included women and children, leaving

possibly 600 warriors. They represented all the Six Nations but predominantly the upper Iroquois. Mohawk manpower had declined from some 1,400 when Johnson arrived in America to 300 (Warren Johnson's journal, 1760-61, in SWJP, 13: 180-214, 194). Smaller numbers of dependents, including émigrés to Oswegatchie, were enrolled. Johnson got rid of the women and children as soon as possible (Amherst 1931: 224-25). Some 155 warriors reached Montreal (SWJP, 13: 173-78). "Tekarihogo" (Tekarihoken, M-1) of Canajoharie and "Kanahokeayat" (Awekenyat, Oa-5, RC 23) of Onondaga bore names of the founders (SWJP, 10: 180-85).[1]

The plan was to advance through the Thousand Islands and shoot the rapids to Montreal. The voyage required a vessel more stable than canoes. Amherst laid down a battleship called a "snow," rigged like a brig, armed with nine guns, and capable of carrying his command. He had a large flag made with an Onondaga Indian painted on it, which ran up the mast just as he broke a bottle on its head, christening the ship HMS *Onondaga*, which pleased the Indians no end. Thomas Gage's regiment fired a volley, the fort fired a gun, the Royal Highlanders fired a volley, and the ship's nine guns replied. Amherst made a speech, and Sir William stood a round of punch. The delighted Indians promised to be fast friends and declared they were ready to start (SWJP, 10: 223).

General James Abercromby wrote to Lord Loudoun that if the Iroquois were as hearty in the British cause as they appeared to be, they would strike terror among the Canadians. Further, an Oswegatchie chief had promised not to interfere (HEH LO 6259).

The *Onondaga* embarked on Lake Ontario on 10 August, setting her course to Cape Vincent and the head of the St. Lawrence and down the hazardous rapids. She flew the union jack and the Onondaga flag, and her nine black-muzzled cannon promised a formidable defense to any attacking party. Bateaux followed. In canoes the Iroquois, painted and feathered and whooping it up, coasted the shores, flanking the army. One wonders how the several hundred Senecas and the comparable number of Cayugas, who were essentially landsmen, fared in the white water (Long 1933: 130, citing Amherst journal, 15 August).

The fun was soon over. In taking possession of La Gallette Island, Amherst forbade the Indians to go ashore, lest they commit atrocities in reprisal for those committed by French Indians. To his horror he discovered that, deprived of live victims, the Indians raided graves and scalped corpses. They were proving slippery allies, and to pacify their dissatisfaction with Amherst's orders, Johnson was kept busy in day-long conferences without much success. Under cover of night, more than two hundred slipped away, stole boats, and returned to Oswego (Long 1933: 131). Amherst praised Johnson for keeping the Indians within human bounds so that "not a Peasant, Woman, or child has been hurt by them, or a house burnt," in the enemy's country (Amherst to Pitt, in Long 1933: 136). He wrote too soon. On two abandoned islands the Indians found scalps taken on the Mohawk River, plus miscellaneous hardware. Amherst ordered the tools saved, but the incensed Indians burned the chapel, French houses, and Indian huts. Johnson, having gone

1. The list that reached the Public Record Office in England counts 185 who reached Montreal, exclusive of 506 who left after the surrender of Fort Levi (SWJP, 10: 185). The more modest list in the hand of Daniel Claus segregates the Mohawks into their clan designations—Turtle, Bear, and Wolf (SWJP, 13: 173-75).

ahead to Akwesasneh (St. Regis), found a priest and ten men there and assured them they would not be harmed; they promised to stay quiet. From the military stores taken in the fall of Montreal, Johnson commandeered Indian goods intended for France's Indian allies, including some 64 necklaces, 242 pounds of silver trinkets, 119 pounds of wampum belts, 6,000 cords of birchbark for canoes, and 44 anchors of brandy.

Not to crowd his luck further, on reaching Akwesasneh on 22 September, Amherst ordered the Indians home. For the fewer than two hundred Indians who had stuck it out to Montreal, Amherst ordered silver medals struck and engraved with the personal names of individual recipients. Sir William got a gold medal. The Indians, however, valued substantial presents for the group over honors to a few. Johnson knew that subsidizing whole tribes was the way to keep them peaceable. Amherst disagreed. Nor would he grant permission to Johnson to publish on his career in Indian affairs. That was up to the ministry (List of Indians, SWJP, 10: 180–85; Warren Johnson's journal, SWJP, 13: 189, 190; Long 1933: 138, 158; Gipson 1946–54, 7: 449–54).

□□◇□□

That summer of 1760 witnessed a high watermark in Indian affairs. Canada passed into English hands; the ancien régime ceased to rule New France. Conrad Weiser had just died, ending a long and useful career as Pennsylvania's man with the Six Nations that climaxed in the 1758 treaty at Easton. Johnson and Croghan had taken charge. English traders no longer had French rivals, and Amherst was about to stop payment on presents to the Indians. The Six Nations and their tributaries had fallen from the position of balancing power between rival nations. From now on the British would call the shots. George II died that autumn, although the news did not reach Boston until Christmastide. How would the Six Nations respond to the new situation under George III? What role would they play in the rising tide of nativism in the old northwest?

In September, Johnson held a conference at Montreal, assembling the Six Nations and Laurentian mission Indians. The Six Nations recognized the mission Indians as "Eight Nations of Canada" (previously known as the "Seven," which they became again when the Iroquois of Oswegatchie joined their kin at Akwesasneh) (Jennings et al. 1985a: 192; SWJP, 13: 163–66). The speaker for the Seven, having thanked Sir William for bringing them together, opening the road, and strengthening the old covenant chain, assured him that they would satisfy any requests he made of them. They would bury the French hatchet in a bottomless pit never to be seen again by their posterity. The speaker then assured the Five Nations that the Seven were prepared to reunite with their Six Nations kin as formerly. They requested deputies be left behind to transact the necessary business.

A war chief of Kahnawakeh then addressed Sir William, confirming what the sachems had agreed upon. He recommended dismissing the former interpreter of Governor Vaudreuil. In return for standing neutral during the war between England and France, the Kahnawakeh people requested continued possession of their country. Proper strings and belts attested to respective items in the chiefs' speech. Several black belts were made of the more valuable purple wampum (SWJP, 13: 163–66).

The following March, the Kahnawakeh and Kanehsatageh (Lake of Two Mountains) folk "in public Council unanimously resolved that, Times and Events being what they were, they would never again take up the hatchet for the French against the English." They would simply tend to their hunting (Claus to Johnson, HEH AB 174; SWJP, 3: 361).

But resentment of the British boiled up in Iroquois kettles. Grievances rankled, particularly among the Senecas, who were traditionally pro-French and had remained aloof from Johnson's reach but who had sent several hundred warriors to the Montreal campaign. They had assisted in the reduction of Niagara but found the British garrison an even less welcome tenant. The trade was down, prices were up, guns and ammunition became scarce. Within a year, sentiment favored driving the British from the continent, and schemes to accomplish it by extending the rafters of the Longhouse beyond its western door dominated talk around Seneca fires.

Two Seneca war chiefs, Kayahsota? ("it erects a cross") (c. 1725–94) and Tahaiadoris, focused hostility in a red wampum belt that they carried to Detroit and circulated among Wyandot and Central Algonquian tribes residing in the vicinity of the fort, hoping they would rise against the English. The scheme failed when Croghan's interpreter tipped off the commandant. When the two war chiefs later arrived somewhat dejected at Fort Pitt, Croghan bought their secret: they had foreseen a concerted uprising against every English settlement from Detroit to the German Flats at Johnson's doorstep, some two years before Pontiac's Rebellion (Abler in DCB 4: 408; Wainwright 1959: 179–80).

To offset this plot and extend his aegis to cover the western tribes, Johnson made the arduous journey to Detroit in September 1761. He had in mind a league embracing Delawares, Shawnees, Wyandots, and various Central Algonquians, on the familiar model of the Iroquois Confederacy. At the Detroit conference, Kayahsota? denied his alleged involvement in the plot, but an Ottawa chief identified him as the "bad Bird lately amongst us." Johnson tried to mollify the detractors and met Kayahsota? privately to persuade him to follow the path of peace. Although Johnson intended this western league to be similar to but separate from the Six Nations, he later made no bones about exerting his utmost to create a misunderstanding between the Six Nations and the new confederation so as to head off a coalition. For the moment, Johnson had stomped on the spark brought by the two Senecas (Wainwright 1959: 182–83).

Johnson heard a second bit of bad news just as he embarked for Detroit. Pennsylvania's acting governor, Lieutenant Governor James Hamilton, was back in the treaty business in a final effort to get the western Indians to ratify the Easton treaty. Johnson was furious. During the first two weeks of August 1761, Hamilton and others met at Easton with representatives of nine tribes: all of the original Five Nations except the Mohawks sent representatives, as did the Nanticoke, Mahican, Delaware, Tutelo, and Conoy tributaries—some five hundred Indians. Land and return of captives were at issue. The Delaware Teedyuscung tried and failed to reopen questions that he himself had settled at previous treaties. Some Connecticut claimants had settled at Wyoming on lands purchased from the Six Nations, who now wanted the sale of any lands previously sold to Connecticut annulled. The Cayugas asserted that they had returned all white captives previously held, although the Delawares and others had not fulfilled promises to return captives made three years ago at Easton (DePuy 1917: 46; Boyd 1938: 245ff.). The meeting afforded the Indians an opportunity to complain about Johnson's trade practices, particularly his prices, and his administration of Indian affairs. Would Pennsylvania open a trading post at Tioga?

Both parties to the treaty conference, whatever else it accomplished, observed the required ceremonial amenities. The governor welcomed the native deputies with a string, and with others wiped the sweat from their bodies, removed the thorns and briars from their limbs, cleared their throats, and opened their hearts to speak.

Seneca George spoke for the visiting nations, invoking with a string a clear sky and an open road. With a second string he recited the Three Bare Words, washed blood, swept the council chamber, and threw the dirt outdoors (Boyd 1938: 247–49).

By a black belt of eight rows, streaked with white, the visiting nations condoled the deaths of settlers. A white belt of seven rows, with four black streaks, condoled the death of Conrad Weiser. A white belt of five rows, with three black bars, dispelled clouds and restored the sun.

Holding a belt by the middle, Seneca George raised up another interpreter, Sammy Weiser, Conrad's son, whom the half-Iroquois-half-German father had placed with a Mohawk family to learn the language. The son should succeed his father. A black-and-white belt of eight rows.

An Onondaga chief had sent a string by a deputy to request that the governor place at Onondaga a resident interpreter who would translate letters to the chiefs. The speaker presented one James Sherlock, a captive, for this role.

This ended the visitors' message. They were sufficiently rested to hear the governor. The host would set the time and place and notify them. The Indians had seized the initiative.

Two days later, however, the visitors still held the floor. This time, Teka?en:yon (Haga?en:yonk), the leading Cayuga sachem, who had participated in the Easton treaty three years previously, stood and spoke. He proceeded to return a large white peace belt of eighteen rows that the governor had given the Six Nations when he told them he had removed the small Easton fire to Philadelphia, site of the great fire that their ancestors had kindled to make alliances and treaties. A second belt joined to the first confirmed that the road had been opened there. By a white belt of seven rows, striped, the governor had opened the ears of the seven nations; by six white strings he had cleared their eyes; and by three strings he had relieved their shyness.

The seven nations living over the Great Lakes, formerly in the French interest but recently allied to the Six Nations, had sent a string requesting membership in the chain. Of the seven named entities, I recognize but three: Warontas, "Bark-eaters" (Abenaki); Kahnawakeh, "At the Rapids" (Iroquois); and Kanehsatageh, "At the Mountain" (Oka) (Boyd 1938: 249). Ten white strings followed.

With multiple strings, the sachem returned the invitation string to acknowledge their welcome and the joy of seeing each other. The rubbing down of their bodies and the Three Bare Words merited four checkered strings.

Clearly, belts sometimes lost their meaning. The Cayuga chief Teka?en:yon returned three such belts brought to Onondaga by an Oneida messenger without accompanying speeches but alleged to pertain to the governor's business. Perhaps Hamilton might know their meaning. The governor later disclaimed them.

Teedyuscung spoke that afternoon. Although a Delaware, he shared the Iroquois style, demonstrated facility in passing wampum belts, and employed metaphors not unlike those of his uncles of the Six Nations. In explaining his position as monitor of traffic over the mountains, he said: "My Uncles have now put some Tobacco in my Pouch" so that Englishmen coming over the mountains might light a pipe and approach the Mingos (émigré Iroquois in Ohio) (Boyd 1938: 251).

Whoever wrote the governor's reply, which he gave on the fourth day, demonstrated an understanding of expected native protocol. The writer repeated the condolence paradigm, touched on the death of Weiser, and then invoked the ancient Iroquois custom of taking from among the relations of any great man a person fit to serve in his place. Since Conrad Weiser was by adoption a Mohawk of the Six Nations (although by birth a Palatine), the governor recommended casting eyes on one of his children, namely Sammy, who alone "has any Knowledge of the *Indian* Language" and life. He joined the petitioner's belt to another. It was now up to the Indians to raise Sammy up. The governor was less than enthusiastic about the Onondaga request for James Sherlock.

The great peace belt went back to the Six Nations and their tributaries with a reminder from the governor of its purpose: to brighten the chain and to put fresh earth on the roots of the Tree of Peace, that it might withstand storms and endure "whilst the Sun should shine, and the Rivers run." This was all written down in the previous treaty, of which the belt should continually remind them (Boyd 1938: 252–53). It was destined for safekeeping at Onondaga, site of the grand council fire (Boyd 1938: 254).

Teka?en:yon resumed speaking several days later in the name of the Six Nations. Here was one treaty conference in which the principal speaker for the Six Nations held a league title—the first on the Cayuga roster, and thirty-third on the roll of the founders. The burden of his complaints over land issues and Johnson's trading practices are less important just now than how the league functioned vis-à-vis the confederacy at the mid-eighteenth century (Boyd 1938: 255).

In a third remark to the governor, Teka?en:yon spoke on behalf of the Nanticoke and Conoy refugees from Maryland whom his own nation had adopted. And on the closing day he requested wagons to transport sick Tutelos, who were also Cayuga wards (Boyd 1938: 260, 261).

The English often did not understand wampum belts, and they still had a few things to learn about running a treaty conference. As if to prompt the governor, their host, to cover the council fire, the sachem added, "We heard what good Words you spoke to us. We have no more to say at present, and we see likewise that you have nothing more to say to us. . . . We will acquaint our People with what we have heard. We heartily thank you for good Usage."

It was now up to the host to distribute presents, bring in the kettles, shake hands, and disperse (Boyd 1938: 261–62).

□□◇□□

The failed Seneca coup that confronted Johnson in Detroit and the complaints emanating from Easton concerning his conduct of Indian affairs prompted his summoning the Six Nations to meet him at Johnson Hall in April 1762. The several nations were acting independently and the confederacy had lost its sense of unity. Seneca head warriors intrigued with western Indians and were slow to return captives. Tension mounted between Onondaga and Mohawk sachems over Mohawks boycotting meetings of the grand council, while Mohawk sachems, facing a loss of hunting territory, declared the Connecticut purchase of Wyoming lands a fraud. Johnson would try to reunite the confederacy and extend his management of Indian affairs.

On receiving Johnson's belt inviting them to meet in thirty days, the Onondaga council dispatched young men who wore themselves out in trips to the Cayugas and Senecas, relaying the invitation. The roads were deep in mud. The Seneca sachems decided to stay home and collect captives still among them for delivery to the governor of Pennsylvania; to Johnson's meeting they sent a delegation of warriors fit to travel. Johnson's belt fetched 47 Onondagas and 33 Senecas. Some 109 Cayugas, 26 Tutelos, and 31 Tuscaroras followed (SWJP, 10: 436-37).

As host, Johnson opened with the customary ceremony of condolence, deferring his speech until the following day. Above four hundred Iroquois, including women and children, turned out to hear him. But first the Onondaga speaker performed the reciprocal condolence rites on the Six Nations' behalf, returning Johnson's string with thanks for condoling them and for covering the grave of Onondaga chief Bunt's son.

Johnson expressed his displeasure that the Seneca delegates had taken so long in coming down and had sent so few sachems and chiefs capable of discussing the issues on his agenda. He scolded them for conspiring in the upper Great Lakes against the English who had brought them peace (SWJP, 3: 690-715.) Returning home from Detroit after learning that their scheme had misfired, he had asked Seneca leaders to meet him at Niagara. Instead, after making Johnson wait, they had sent word that he could talk with Sonajoana (Shagenjowa, S-4, RC 46), who was then at Niagara with a few followers. If indeed this was the sachem of the Hawk clan and holder of a league title, it was not unreasonable that he could relay Johnson's demand to the Seneca council that they send a proper deputation to Detroit to clear themselves. Possibly Johnson did not know the man's identity, but in any case he felt slighted and remained convinced that the Senecas could not justify their behavior. He wanted an explanation returned for his belt, which he held up with the belt sent by those Senecas to Detroit (SWJP, 3: 692).

The Mohawk Abraham, son of Hendrick and namesake of Hendrick's brother, addressing the confederacy, appealed to the metaphor of the chain and reminded the assembled sachems and chiefs of their duty to preserve it. The bad news from Geneseo about the Seneca scheme threatened the ancient alliance. Should they break ancient treaties? He joined Johnson in castigating those Senecas.

The unnamed Onondaga speaker requested that the belt which the Senecas had sent to Detroit be turned over to them to hold until the Senecas repeated the message sent on it and answered the charge. This being done, the chief of the Genesee Senecas stood. He explained that after the reduction of Niagara, the Wyandots had sent several messages warning that proliferating English posts and settlements would shortly surround and hem in the Six Nations. Wyandots repeated this theme whenever they met any Iroquois. The next fall they had spoken with a string to Awetharungwaghs, a Cayuga chief (a name not on the league roster) settled at Presque Isle (Erie, Pennsylvania). Early the following spring, the Potawatomis and Wyandots had jointly sent eight strings encoded with messages via the Senecas for a joint meeting at Sandusky. The Senecas were expected to transmit the message the length of the Longhouse, but the last runner reached Oneida and the Oneidas failed to relay it to the Mohawks. When none of the other members of the Six Nations responded, the Senecas sent a second notice, which was also disregarded. Given this breakdown in communication, the Senecas decided to act on their own to consult with their western neighbors, the Shawnees and Wyandots, and find out whether they intended peace or war. That was how Kayahsota? and Tahaiadoris had gotten involved in a mission of discovery; they were expected to report back to the council. The belt they carried had originated with Joncaire, the French agent. It was an ambivalent belt—one half of it meant war, the other half, peace.

It seems that when the two Seneca emissaries reached Detroit, Tahaiadoris, who spoke French, made some pretext for crossing the river and, without consulting his partner, told the interpreter that the Five Nations planned to attack the English within ten days. The Wyandots heard the message and, fearful that the commandant knew of the plot, surrendered the belt to clear themselves. Kayahsota? and other deputies, according to this version, though strangers to Tahaiadoris's behavior, took the blame and were accused in Johnson's presence (SWJP, 3: 695–97). On the contrary, the Seneca speaker maintained, the Seneca nation intended to hold fast to the covenant chain.

The Seneca speaker segmented his speech, deferring answers to Johnson's charges until the next day. He attributed the presence of so few Seneca sachems to the weather and bad roads. The sachems had decided to stay home and send agile young men able to travel and transact business. "Consider that we, are in fact the People of Consequence for Managing Affairs, Our Sachems being generally a parcell of Old People who say Much, but who Mean or Act very little." The delegation was empowered and able to act. Indeed, this quotation goes far to explain why so few recognizable sachem names appear in treaty documents.

Having justified a war party of fifty Senecas going out against the Cherokees as provisioned and sanctioned by Fort Pitt, the speaker delivered a belt of eight rows and sat down.

The chief sachem of Oneida, Conoghquieson (Kanongweniyah, Oe-2, RC 11), interposed to say that the Seneca speaker, being slightly ill, had deputed the Onondaga speaker to continue. The sparse intelligence he gave on the Shawnees is of less interest just now than the procedure in council. In reporting on captives still held at Geneseo, the speaker delivered a bundle of nine sticks and a belt of six rows. Following separate pleas to stop traders from carrying rum to Onondaga and Oneida, the Onondaga speaker addressed the Mohawks, repeating their advice to the confederacy and thanking them, especially not having heard them speak for some time. "And as you are the head of the Confederacy, your Silence turned our heads, and occasioned great Uneasiness Amongst Us." The speaker alleged that the Mohawks had failed to attend councils at Onondaga and Fort Johnson. The Onondaga firekeepers hoped in the future the Mohawks would adhere closely to ancient custom and that they would not fail to attend the upcoming council at Geneseo (SWJP, 3: 701).

The following day Johnson renewed the covenant chain and urged the Six Nations to hold fast to it. He stressed the sanctity of treaties and assured the sachems that His Majesty's government would honor them. He conveyed the belt of the covenant chain. (The broad belts held now by the Six Nations' descendants and until recently preserved in museums are of this period [Fenton 1971b; 1989].) He reopened the road to his fire, addressed the issues of captives yet undelivered, cited deserters living among them, favored regulating the rum trade, and deplored irregular acts of violence. He would reward the faithful tomorrow (SWJP, 3: 702–4).

The Mohawk sachems waited a day or two to answer the charges of long silence and failure to attend meetings of the grand council. Abraham addressed the confederacy: true, they had not attended as formerly; they were not invited. "*We are the head of the Confederacy*; Whenever our presence is Required, we shall meet you." They would attend the council at Geneseo. They had supported Johnson's mission to Detroit. No wandering people, they were determined to leave their bones where the bones of their ancestors were deposited (SWJP, 3: 704).

After a final council, Kanadiohora,[2] chief of Geneseo, attempted to bury the Detroit grievance by casting the trouble into a deep pit, offering a medicine to wash away its memory, dispelling dark clouds, and restoring the sun. The Seneca warriors agreed to return captives, and being the most active and ruling people in Seneca society, they pledged to deliver them. They would expect an additional present (SWJP, 3: 706–7).

The confederacy had directed the Oneida sachem Conoghquieson to complain of the ill treatment Oneidas had encountered at fishing sites between German Flats and Oswego from members of British garrisons who shot at them and ran at them with bayonets. He also advised Johnson, who had excluded women from the conference, that it was customary for women, whom they greatly esteemed, to attend treaty councils, "in that we proceed from them, and they provide our Warriors with Provisions when they go abroad." The women, evidently, had resolved to come and hear the good words (SWJP, 3: 707–8). They, too, would expect presents. Such a serious matter rated a belt of ten rows.

The Onondaga speaker then thanked Johnson for renewing the covenant chain. It was not their custom to forget good works. It was good to have the road opened so that Johnson and the Mohawks might attend the grand council. He next appealed for cheaper goods by returning to Johnson a belt he had given the Six Nations while on his way to Niagara three years earlier, which was to remind Johnson of his pledge regarding the trade, a matter of consequence to them (SWJP, 3: 708–9).

But Indians did forget. The speaker next displayed and gave back a covenant belt that some previous governor had given in Albany. All those who were then present had since died. The living chiefs would like to know the particulars of what it said. The Onondaga wampum keepers having no records, the greater part had been forgotten. He commended the wants of the Seneca warriors and women and begged indulgence (SWJP, 3: 709).

---

2. Was this Kanadayohora, a variant of Ganyadaiyo? (S-1, RC 43), the leading Seneca sachem, a title held later by the Seneca Prophet?

In satisfying their demands, Johnson replied that he could not recover the meaning of the covenant belt, since the Indian Records were at his other house (Fort Johnson) (SWJP, 3: 712).

As usual, the Indians asked to have their guns repaired, and Sir William complied. To the heads of delegations he made some private presents.

On the final day, Abraham addressed a Mohawk grievance over the sale of Susquehanna lands to Connecticut people, for which, he alleged, Lydius had obtained a deed after getting some chiefs drunk during the 1754 Albany Congress. Timothy Woodbridge of Stockbridge pleaded: "Your great men had Two Thousand Dollars of my money. . . . And I have many witnesses that you was Sober when you signed my Deed." Of such was the unbridgeable gulf between the two cultures (SWJP, 3: 714–16).

After this conference, Cadwallader Colden wrote to Johnson congratulating him upon his success with the Indians and warning that Lydius was a dangerous man deserving prosecution for his land deals (HEH, HM 8321; SWJP, 10: 467).

The problem of Teedyuscung and the Walking Purchase of 1737 still hung fire. The crown finally instructed Johnson to hear the complaint and settle the matter. At Easton that June, Johnson acted the role of an Iroquois sachem toward Delaware nephews, a role Teedyuscung acknowledged by symbolically putting "the largest Buck Horns" on his head; the Delawares evidently shared the antlers-of-office concept (SWJP, 3: 763). Johnson managed to persuade Teedyuscung to drop the charges of fraud, and Pennsylvania gave his people a large present on behalf of the proprietor, Thomas Penn, which outraged the Quakers but earned Johnson support in London (SWJP, 3: 760ff.).

□□◇□□

In August that same year, Pennsylvania governor Hamilton met representatives of the northern and western tribes at Lancaster. This was the final treaty printed by Franklin, in 1763 (DePuy 1917: treaty no. 47; Boyd 1938: 263–98). On the fifth day, there arrived representatives of four of the original Five Nations (no Mohawks) and tributaries of the now Six Nations. They were led by holders of league titles, notably the first Cayuga and the third Oneida, representing Onondaga. The meeting featured the delivery of colonial captives, their release in the name of their captors, and the announcing of the localities where they had been taken. The big issue was the Connecticut claim to lands at Wyoming on the Susquehanna, for which some Indians had received Woodbridge's two thousand dollars at Albany in 1754. The Iroquois asserted that the deal had never been discussed in the councils of the Six Nations and was therefore void.

Several participants had private agendas. Augus, chief of the lower Tuscarora village at Onohquageh ("hulled corn soup place"), on arrival—following the usual condolences—asked the governor for information on his people's kin still resident in the Tuscarora Valley, whom they intended to visit.

On the fifth day, the Oneida Thomas King began his lectures on Iroquois council protocol by declaring: "We are of different Nations, speak different Languages, we shall take time to consider and explain . . . and Tomorrow . . . I shall give you Notice when we shall be ready to speak to you" (Boyd 1938: 272–73).

Three days later, King spoke in the style of his forefathers, addressing the governor as "brother." String by string, he returned thanks for their hosts' health and for the day, he thanked the governor for removing briars from their legs and stones from their feet, he opened the governor's ears and cleansed his throat and passages to his heart, he wiped tears from his eyes, and so forth. He then directed the discourse to the business at hand. The main items required belts (Boyd 1938: 277–78).

King attributed the Indians' slowness in returning captives to differing tribal customs, linguistic diversity, and different concepts of time, and their fewness to mixed colonial and crown jurisdictions. He then turned to the great tradition of the chain of friendship, invoking the metaphor of the hatchet: gathering bones from diverse places, uprooting the great pine, burying the hatchet, and replacing the tree. "I own you are my eldest Brother," he told the Pennsylvania governor (Iroquois kinship implies a tutorial relationship between elder and younger siblings.) This lesson rated "A Belt of Seven Rows."

Late differences had caused dark clouds to obscure the sun, which the speaker restored by clearing the sky with a belt of six rows.

The old people believed that trouble caused bile to rise in the throat from the heart. The grandfathers had instructed that for times when the Iroquois "found our Brother's Heart and Throat to be foul," they had left a medicine to be drunk as a physic that would cleanse the throat and heart "and pass through their Body down to the Ground. . . . By this String I bury it in the Ground," he said on behalf of fourteen nations.

He then named the nations who "first brought about the good Work of Peace." He added that "the Mohocks and Oneidas were the eldest of the Six Nations, and both of a Height." As first to grasp the message of peace, they were of equal status. It was important for Onas, the Pennsylvania governor, to understand the channels for communicating with the league (or confederacy). (Pennsylvania had been dealing directly with Onondaga during Weiser's term as interpreter.) The proper way, he implied, was to pass through either the eastern or the western door of the Longhouse. In King's words: "The *Mohocks* are the eldest, yet are the furthest off to the Eastward: When they hear any Thing, they pass through the *Oneidas* to the *Onondagoes*, where the Council Fire burns: Likewise, when the *Senecas* hear any Thing, they come to the *Cayugas*, because they are next to the *Onondagoe* Council; so whenever they hear any Thing to the East or West, it is carried to the *Onondagoe* Council." The meaning was clear: diplomatic messages to the Onondaga council must be sent either to the Senecas or to the Mohawks (Boyd 1938: 280).

The treaty literature abounds in mention of wampum belts, but seldom are they described in detail. In brightening the chain of friendship, Thomas King cited symbols of unity inherited from the Five Nations' grandfathers and delivered a belt of nine rows carrying the figures of two men at the center, a heart between them, flanked by six diamonds on each side. One male figure represented the Indians, the other the English. The diamonds stood for native participants.

King went on to explain the relationship of counselors and warriors in achieving a lasting peace. "Counsellors can do nothing, unless the Warriors . . . consent." Here a belt of seven rows, with two diamonds, represented the two parties united in council (Boyd 1938: 281).

The warriors, however, went home from this council unsettled in their minds on keeping the peace.

□□◇□□

The next year, 1763, the storm swept from the west in what became known as Pontiac's Rebellion. War parties of Central Algonquians, Wyandots, émigré Iroquois, so-called Mingos, and western Senecas wrought havoc in a wide area. It was their reply to Amherst's Indian policy. The Peace of Paris ceding Canada to Great Britain meant little at first on the frontier. A Mohawk, Onondaga, and Cayuga delegation journeyed to Hartford in the interest of settling the dispute over the deed to the Wyoming lands. The Senecas boycotted Johnson's rally against the western tribes at German Flats in July, and in September they were reprimanded as "covenant breakers" when the Caughnawaga chiefs met with the confederacy at Johnson Hall (NYCD, 7: 553–59).

Some three hundred Indians of the confederacy attended this council. Six Senecas of the eastern towns came under confederate protection, and some 250 dependents joined them from as far away as Owego on the Susquehanna. A Kahnawakeh delegation wanted title to a grant from Louis XIV to the Jesuits, which Johnson thought possible since the order had been suppressed in France. In return Johnson wanted the Kahanwakeh warriors to bury the French hatchet.

According to the Onondaga speaker, confederate emissaries had spoken to the errant Senecas three times to get them to return to the covenant chain and work for the public good. No word yet from the remote Seneca towns. Johnson strove to maintain a facade of equanimity so as not to alienate the Senecas present. The Oneida sachem Conoghquieson reaffirmed that all the nations were friendly as far as the eastern Seneca town of Kanadase:ken (modern Geneva, New York), but he warned Johnson that he had a wide foot, and when traveling the road of peace upcountry, he should not step on friends.

Toward the end the Onondaga speaker held up the covenant belt received at Albany in 1754 by way of renewing the alliance on behalf of eighteen nations.

Land claims remained a burning issue. Johnson and the Mohawks still sought restoration of nearly a million acres taken in the Kayaderosseros Patent some fifty years earlier (NYCD, 7: 561–62). But the first definition of Indian rights— a definition that became central to subsequent policy—came in the British North America Act of October 1763, which prohibited the advance of colonial settlement west of a line defined as the boundary of crown lands reserved for Indians. This royal proclamation would undergo some negotiation in subsequent treaties.

Counting Indians remained an uncertain business, and no two enumerators agreed. Taking attendance at treaties was more accurate than making estimates of warriors sight unseen, which usually favored the cause being advanced. Johnson, at the height of Pontiac's Rebellion, computed that the Senecas in some twenty villages could field 1,000 men, and the rest of the confederacy 1,200, for a total of 2,200 (SWJP, 10: 878). But a month later, in a tabular enumeration of Indians within his department, he increased the Seneca count by 50 and reached a total of 1,950 for the Six Nations proper, with an additional 280 adopted dependents, giving a smaller total of 2,230. To this figure he added 630 allies in Canada and 1,100 Indians of Ohio—Shawnees, Delawares, and Wyandots—for a grand total of 3,960 (NYCD, 7: 582–83). The western tribes that follow amount to twice as many. That the united Iroquois could mobilize nearly 4,000 warriors seems unlikely.[3]

When the Genesee Senecas signed a peace treaty with Johnson at Niagara in the summer of 1764, the entire Six Nations confederacy came under British jurisdiction. The seven named Seneca signers were apparently war chiefs; none of the names resolves into a league title. The warriors evidently also made peace. The seven Senecas delineated their clan eponyms: Heron (a bird); Wolf, to the left; and Snipe, Deer (possibly Hawk), and Beaver on the right (NYCD, 7: 651–53).

Johnson had mastered the ritual forms and was prepared to instruct other Englishmen in how to conduct themselves so as to gain favor with the Six Nations. He understood the moiety system of the confederacy. He was about to ratify candidates for chiefship advanced in the "rooms" of deceased members of national councils. Having experienced the contention between his Mohawk neighbors and the Onondaga council, he would seek to unify the confederacy and strengthen it in order to advance British dominion in North America.

The Genesee Senecas and incorporated Delawares had proved tough nuts to crack. Their eyes were focused on, and their ears were attuned to, movements among the western Indians rather than on Onondaga. After two years of diplomacy backed by some force, the Genesee Seneca–Delaware contingent, which had perpetrated most of the damage between Niagara and Fort Pitt and east to the Susquehanna during Pontiac's Rebellion, hailed into Johnson Hall bringing Squash Cutter and Long Coat, the two chief warriors in the Susquehanna raid. Johnson had insisted on their delivery (SWJP, 11: 706).

An Onondaga delegation followed on their heels. Having met their host, but before retiring to consider the losses they had suffered during the recent campaign, the Onondaga speaker, Teyawarunte, presented to Sir William "those young men whom we appointed to assist us in our councils as our sachems are now too few to manage matters properly." The empty seats in the Onondaga council concerned the sachems because Onondaga was the "proper Council fire for all the surrounding nations, our allies and dependents." The speaker proceeded to show the faces of seven young men, whom he named. Although the written list of names includes twelve sachems (Table 5), only seven of them have named sponsors. This list of Onondaga sachems and their guardians is an important document because it enables us to identify the predecessors of later Onondaga chiefs of the same name, as a group, and their clan affiliations in 1765.[4]

Diaquande, the chief of the Onondaga warriors, whose name suggests that of the third title on the Oneida roster (Deyohagwendeh), took responsibility for one new sachem, unspecified. There follow the names of six others, generally older men, who agreed to watch over the younger sachems.

---

3. A similar enumeration of fighting men of the Six Nations the following year gives a smaller figure for the Senecas (800), and lists for the Cayugas 150, for the Onondagas 200, for the Oneidas 150, for the Tuscaroras 70, and for Canasaraga 30, yielding a total of 1,400 (the Mohawk figure is missing). Another 100 Delawares among the Senecas brought the overall total to 1,500 (NYPL, Schuyler Papers-Indian Papers, 1764–74, folio 13). A second list from the same source gives a Six Nations total of 1,635, which may include the Mohawks.

4. The later Merle Deardorff alerted me to this list in 1954, but I was not then in a position to cope with it.

TABLE 5

NEW ONONDAGA SACHEMS PRESENTED TO SIR WILLIAM JOHNSON IN 1765

NAME	CLAN	PROBABLE LEAGUE TITLE
Wathatodarho	Bear	Oa-1, Thadoda:ho?
Onessarakung	Beaver	Oa-2, One?sa:hen
Owigaiat	Turtle	Oa-5, Awekenyat
Tayiatquari	Turtle	Oa-6, Dehayatgwa:e
Ononwisaghti	Wolf	Oa-8, Gawennensen:donh
Wahagheirong	Deer	Oa-9, Hahihon
Oyuwanis	Eel	Oa-10, Hoyonyenni
Tughhaghsi	Turtle	Oa-11, Shodegwa:tsi?
Sagagare	Eel	Oa-12, Shagohenhe?
Amadagia, Bunt's son	Snipe	
Tawanasaroonda	Turtle	
Tawaskughta	Turtle	

Source: SWJP, 11: 706ff.

The Onondaga speaker, having concluded the presentation of candidates, expressed the hope that these newly appointed sachems would adhere to the rules laid down by the ancestors and work for the interest of the English. He asked Johnson to sanction these appointments, to which he agreed.

When the Onondaga warriors assembled on the Sunday following, Johnson charged the young sachems at length and promised them the usual marks of distinction, namely, a laced coat, a ruffled shirt, and a medal. He then shook each man's hand, wishing him long life to serve his country and the English (SWJP, 11: 708–11).

The importance of this list to history is threefold. First, the Onondagas were reasserting the tradition of league government in confederacy affairs. Second, these eight or nine league titles, a substantial part of the Onondaga roster, comprise the largest assemblage for a single nation and the earliest record of titles that were still extant on the Grand River during the nineteenth century, when they were recorded by Hale and Chadwick, and by Morgan in New York state, and which survive today. And third, with this list, single names that occur randomly throughout the historical documents take on a new significance (Table 6).

Such was the relative strength and position of the confederacy on the eve of the first treaty at Fort Stanwix (1768), which met to establish the boundary of Indian lands prescribed in the royal proclamation.

TABLE 6

THE EMERGENCE OF LEAGUE TITLES, 1647–1803

TITLE	1647-60	1661-72	1673-86	1687-99	1700-12	1713-25	1726-38	1739-51	1752-64	1765-77	1778-90	1791-1803
M-1	x x						x	x x		x x xx		
M-2				x								
M-3									x			
M-4												
M-5												
M-6												
M-7												
M-8												
M-9										x		
Oe-1				x xx	x	x		x			x	x x
Oe-2		x			x	x			x xx	x	x	x x
Oe-3				x				x			x	x
Oe-4							x		x	x		x
Oe-5												x
Oe-6											xx	x
Oe-7											xx	x
Oe-8												x
Oe-9					x							x
Oa-1	x?							x?	x x xx	x		
Oa-2										x		x
Oa-3								refC-3				
Oa-4										x		
Oa-5										x		
Oa-6										x		
Oa-7										x		
Oa-8												

continued

TABLE 6 (*continued*)

THE EMERGENCE OF LEAGUE TITLES, 1647–1803

TITLE	1647–60	1661–72	1673–86	1687–99	1700–12	1713–25	1726–38	1739–51	1752–64	1765–77	1778–90	1791–1803
Oa-9	xx											
Oa-10										x		x
Oa-11												x
Oa-12										x		
Oa-13										x		
Oa-14	x							?				
C-1				x								x
C-2								x		xx x		x
C-3								refOa-3				x
C-4												
C-5												
C-6										x		x
C-7												
C-8												
C-9												
C-10												
S-1								x x				x
S-2				x				x				x
S-3									x			
S-4												
S-5									x	x		
S-6												
S-7	x	x								x x		
S-8							x	x				

CHAPTER 34

THE BIG GIVEAWAY AT
FORT STANWIX, 1768

Two related issues—peace with the Cherokees and the boundary line of colonial settlement—that had beset William Johnson and the Six Nations for a decade now approached resolution. In May 1767 the Six Nations met Johnson at German Flats to discuss boundary issues, particularly that of running the Mason-Dixon line over the Allegheny Mountains, and to prepare for peace with the Cherokees when delegates of that nation arrived. Sporadic raids continued. Small war parties enjoyed an advantage in the southern wars, although no major conflicts had occurred in recent years (NYCD, 7: 947; SWJP, 12: 309–15). Although tribes bordering settlements had diminished, several of the Six Nations were increasing. Johnson urged strengthening the confederacy and rejoiced that 160 Tuscaroras had migrated from North Carolina to augment the sixth nation (NYCD, 7: 883; SWJP, 12: 312). The chiefs on whom he had relied for twenty years expressed concern at Johnson's health, and they themselves were aging.

Some "bad belts" circulated among the upper nations. A drunken brawl erupted between some Senecas and Mississaugas at the Niagara portage, sending one of the latter badly wounded to the fort and leaving the commandant to mitigate the dispute (DHNY, 2: 868ff.). French agents kept Onondaga in turmoil. Settling a factional dispute between Onondaga sachems and warriors kept Johnson at Oneida Lake for three weeks in October 1767. Admitting traders and rum to Oswego and the Onondaga settlements were at issue. Johnson employed an Oneida speaker to compound the loss of the principal Onondaga sachem, and he met apart to placate the leader of the warrior faction (SWJP, 12: 368–72; DHNY, 2: 831ff.). It took six days to assemble the confederacy to condole the principal chief of Onondaga, who did not bear the title of a league founder. Seneca matrons intervened in the confusion of bad belts circulating to stop their young men from taking up the warpath (Beauchamp 1905: 331).

Back in the Mohawk Valley, the grant of the lower flats and the Kayaderosseros Patent at Saratoga to Albany speculators hung fire and aggrieved the Mohawks. Two main issues topped Johnson's agenda: settling the boundary line with the Six Nations and making a lasting peace with the Cherokees. These concerns took precedence over other distractions.

Cherokee deputies coming by water reached the Mohawk Valley at years's end to convene with some 760 Iroquois at Johnson Hall in March 1768. Johnson immediately sent runners with invitation belts to the entire confederacy, but the

Six Nations came late and reluctantly because of weather and some nasty murders of six of their people in Pennsylvania. They were joined by representatives of Caughnawaga and the Seven Nations of Canada. As usual, private meetings to discuss boundary issues with various delegations preceded formal councils. Johnson, having kindled the fire, welcomed the delegates and condoled their losses with the customary three words of condolence before going through the rest of the paradigm. He hoped that a boundary line protecting their hunting grounds might be speedily settled. Business would start next day.

The assembled chiefs designated the second Oneida sachem to acknowledge the condolences, explain their circumstances, and thank Johnson for adhering to customary ways. Although he had removed the hatchet from their heads and buried it, the speaker pointed out that he had neglected to perform the same act for the English.

When the congress convened the next afternoon, the Cherokee delegation refused to open its embassy because one did not start a meeting after noon, a taboo that the Iroquois observe to this day: they suspend preaching the Good Word of Handsome Lake when the sun reaches the zenith.

Accordingly, on 6 March, Johnson, always a stickler for protocol, cleared the way for the Cherokee chiefs. Their speaker, Ouconastota of Echota, who had visited England during the reign of George II, stood and arranged his belts, calumets, and other props in order before addressing the assembly. Clearly, the Cherokees and Iroquois employed common council forms and metaphors. A Cherokee sachem of Chotte had sent a particular belt to Onondaga, hoping the Six Nations would take hold of it. Another belt and calumet with attached eagle tail went to Johnson. A third belt applauded the good talk of the neighboring Mohawks for speaking "in their Fathers' tongue." Cherokee matrons sent their own belt to Iroquois mothers. Two belts would clear the path between their respective towns. Although Mohawk and Cherokee were the closest of remote Iroquoian tongues, several interpreters were required.

On 7 March, Iroquois warriors asked the sachems to move the council to the open court that they might hear and witness the peace negotiations. The second Oneida sachem held forth. Peace with the Cherokees was essential to the boundary settlement, first put to them at German Flats. Johnson should request the several colonial governors, especially the governor of Virginia, to restrain their people from crossing the path, lest the transgressors close it to travel.

The two Iroquois confederacies—Six Nations and Caughnawaga—next addressed the Cherokees as "Younger Brothers," as if assuming seniority in political matters. They had come down to the meeting in the manner of their ancestors, "whose Kettle was always ready with their Packs and Seven Men allotted to each Cannoe [sic] and with a good Stick in their hands ready to chastise evil doers." A large white belt attested that both confederacies were ready to make peace.

Business halted next day because a Kahnawakeh Mohawk chief named Onaharrissa had recently died, and his people wanted him condoled. The Oneida sachem, on behalf of the younger moiety of the confederacy, performed the entire ceremony of condoling the elder Three Brothers, the Mohawk-Onondaga-Seneca moiety. The Onondaga speaker formally thanked the junior moiety for adhering to the custom of their forefathers (NYCD, 8: 38-45).

Having assembled the Six Nations chiefs in council, Johnson displayed a letter he had received from Lord Shelburne instructing him specifically how to settle the boundary line within the year. Johnson stressed its benefits to their interests.

Having met privately, the chiefs appointed a speaker who delivered their reply that afternoon. He thanked the Great Spirit for the present meeting, promised to address honestly the subject of Johnson's speech, and declared the causes of their anxiety, which had reached a feverish pitch on their arrival. It was Johnson's turn to open his ears and listen, and then seek a remedy, which was the only way to secure the peace.[1]

English promises made at the beginning of the Seven Years War had not been fulfilled and lingered as postwar complaints. Traders continued to abuse the Indians, the speaker said, and rum bottles hung at every door. Would-be English protectors stole their land. The Mohawks were about to lose land at their very doors. "If you wont do justice to our Fathers the Mohawks . . . if you wont keep the people away from the Rivers near Ohio, and keep the Road open making Pennsylvania and Virginia quiet we must get tired of looking to you, and turn our faces another way."

The English king might have good intentions in drawing the boundary, the speaker continued, but the Cherokee chiefs had told the Six Nations that they were surrounded by the line drawn in their country the previous year. The Iroquois would have more to say when the time came.

Johnson, in commenting on the Cherokee-Iroquois peace treaty now ready for signature, dwelt further on Iroquois losses and efforts to give satisfaction. He had by then clearly mastered the ritual forms of condolence. The Cherokees had at last grasped the covenant chain.

On the final day, Oneida warriors remedied a lapse on the part of the sachems by metaphorically collecting the bones of deceased warriors strewn along the path south to the Cherokee country and, in the manner of their ancestors, burying them deep in a pit where an underground stream would carry them forever from sight. They stood ready to take the Cherokee delegates by the hand and escort them safely home through the towns and along the warpaths until the good news of the treaty spread (NYCD, 8: 38–53).

□□◇□□

The Cherokee peace was the last of a series of negotiations to implement the Proclamation Line of 1763. Colonel John Stuart in the south and Sir William Johnson in the north had commenced negotiations in their respective regions in 1764, and for Johnson the effort climaxed in the autumn of 1768 when 3,100 Indians assembled at Fort Stanwix (the site of modern Rome, New York). Authorization to conclude a final treaty had not not come until January of that year, when the Earl of Sherburne authorized Stuart to proceed. Stuart concluded the Treaty of Hard Labor on 14 October. It reaffirmed his earlier negotiations and projected the demarcation line to the mouth of the Kanawha River. Completing the boundary north to the Great Lakes remained for Johnson to accomplish that same fall.

---

1. The text reads "place" instead of "peace," an obvious misprint (NYCD, 8: 46).

Early in the year, the Lords of Trade instructed Johnson just where to draw the boundary line and sent him a map.[2] The line was to start at Owego, New York ("Owegy" on the map), run down the Susquehanna to Shamokin and then up the west branch, cross over the mountains to the Allegheny at Kittanning, and then follow the Ohio River to the mouth of the Great Kanawha (see map 4). The Six Nations had agreed substantially to this line when Johnson met with them in 1765 (Billington 1944: 184). What prompted Johnson to alter these instructions is another story that relates to the growing speculation in western lands among colonial enterprisers from Virginia to New York. Everyone of any consequence was involved.

Johnson set the date for the treaty at 20 September. His Mohawk runners went out earlier to alert the tribes, presumably carrying notched sticks with attached wampum strings, a notch to be cut off for each day until the date they were expected at the clearing. He himself went up to Fort Stanwix on the nineteenth in order to welcome the arrivals the next day. Dr. Thomas Walker, representing the interests of Thomas Jefferson and his Virginia neighbors, arrived early to talk with Johnson, although he later stated that he merely witnessed the treaty. Indians straggled in, late as usual.

The Shawnee, Delaware, and Seneca delegates improved the opportunity to transact business in the several towns they passed through. Some 805 Indians arrived by the first of October to begin devouring prodigious quantities of provisions. The greater number and those of consequence being delayed, Johnson dispatched messengers to hurry them along, only to learn that the sudden death of a Seneca chief and the invariable condolences on such occasions would further detain them in the Seneca country.

Crown expenses were mounting (NYCD, 8: 104–6). By 22 October, Indian attendance had swelled to 2,200, with several large parties expected the following day. When all were assembled, including the chiefs of the upper nations, attendance totaled 3,100. Johnson prepared to kindle the council fire on the twenty-fourth.

Of the listed participants, interest focuses on the roster of twenty-seven Indian chiefs and which of them held league titles. The Mohawk delegation of seven boasted the first name on the roll call—"Tobarihoga," which is clearly meant for Tekarihoken. (Labials are strangers to Iroquoian languages.) None of the four Onondaga and two Seneca names listed resembles a league title. But among five Oneida chiefs listed, I recognize Oe-2 and Oe-4. And the leader of the three listed Cayugas, "Tagaaia," was indeed Haga?en:yonk (C-1). The remaining twenty-three names do not appear to be titles of league founders.[3] The order in which the nations were listed conforms to the moiety system of the league and confederacy; it begins with Mohawk-Onondaga-Seneca, the "Three Brothers" of the senior moiety, and the Oneida-Cayuga-Tuscarora-Delaware moiety, the "Four Brothers," follows.

Sir William employed Abraham, a Mohawk whose name heads the list, to welcome the native and colonial delegates. He prepared them for the business at hand by resorting "to the ancient custom established by our Forefathers" of

2. Hillsborough to Johnson, 12 March 1768 (NYCD, 8: 35–36). The map appears in SWJP, 5: op. 286.
3. Footnotes to the edited text (NYCD, 8: 112–13) and Billington (1944) dwell on the colonial personages, especially Dr. Thomas Walker of Virginia.

performing the condolence ceremony proper to such occasions. He gave three strings of wampum for the three indispensable words: tears, opening passages to the heart for clear speech, and wiping blood from their berths (seats). He then rekindled their several council fires (with a belt).

With another belt he dispelled the darkness that overshadowed their several countries by reason of losses, and restored the sun. Their ancestors had left a set of rules and directed that they be followed; Sir William had Abraham enumerate the rules. Sachems and councilors should on occasion consult the war chiefs, who are generally men of experience and judgment. In turn, the young men must pay heed to the sachems and councilors, whose sage advice seldom is amiss.

The confederacy recognized but two fires—one at Johnson Hall, the other at Onondaga—where one must stand ready to attend and, it was hoped, conduct business properly for mutual benefit. Councils adhered to the rule of unanimity; councilors should reside in their respective countries and not scatter or settle among other nations, a practice that weakened the confederacy.

Johnson gave a pouch containing three strings of wampum to use whenever the confederacy suffered a loss, to promptly condole the affected moiety. Finally, he presented "a Torch or candle" for traveling by night in an emergency and communicating the news. His hearers punctuated the discourse at the proper places by giving the *yo-hah*, the shout of approbation.[4] Clearly, Johnson was concerned that the confederacy was fraying at the margins, he sought to strengthen it, and he had mastered the ritual forms for appealing to its constituents.

Next day, the ranking Oneida sachem, Conoghquieson, addressed the assembly, remarking that although several American governors had Indian names, the governor of New Jersey was anonymous, a deficiency that he wished to make up by bestowing upon the governor his own title—that of Kanongweniyah (Oe-2). Governor Franklin perhaps never realized what this honor entailed.

The speaker then replicated Johnson's condolences and conveyed the thanks of the confederacy to Johnson for observing the ancient ceremonies. They would follow the recommended rules for good government.

Overnight the Six Nations, evidently dissatisfied with the Oneida sachem's having given his own name, that of a league founder, to Governor Franklin, met in council to find a suitable substitute. They decided to honor Franklin's people's justice for imposing the death penalty on some murderers of Indians by renaming him Sagarihwioghsta, "Doer of Justice" (NYCD, 8: 117n1, after Bruyas 1862: 91–92).

This was Johnson's day to renew and strengthen the covenant chain that it might endure "as long as Grass shall grow and waters run" by presenting a belt of fifteen rows with human figures at each end. He also stressed the benefits of mutual union and invoked the metaphors of path and rivers cleared of obstructions.

Much of these preliminary formalities went on while the delegates waited for ninety-six Onondagas led by Diaquande to arrive. Meanwhile, Johnson conducted business in private conferences, or "talks in the bushes," which Billington (1944) construed as opportunities for private deals—as well they may have been. But as Lafitau stated a half-century earlier, the Iroquois brought nothing to open council

---

4. The torch of notification is the fourteenth article of the Requickening Address (Hewitt 1944: 77); the fawnskin pouch is featured prominently.

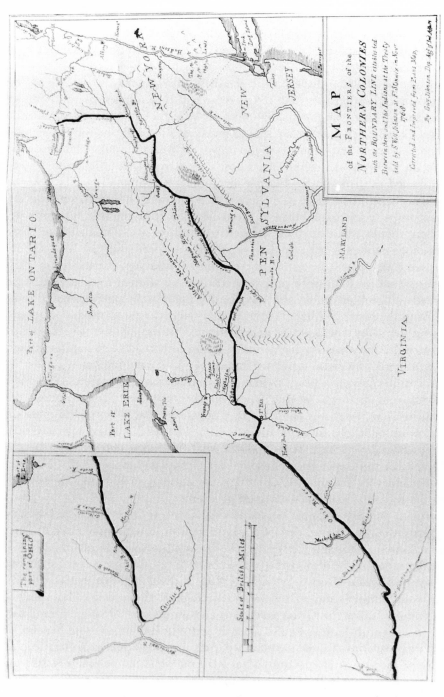

Map 4. The 1768 boundary line limiting colonial settlement established at the treaty of Fort Stanwix (*Johnson Papers*, 7: 450–51).

that had not been discussed and decided beforehand in such sessions (Fenton and Moore 1974: 295ff.). This Iroquois device, which Johnson exploited, enabled Thomas Walker to advance the interests of his fellow Virginia speculators in lands west of the Blue Ridge Mountains without making a public record. This may partly explain how Johnson came to exceed his instructions.

The Indians, moreover, after meeting privately, asked for an audience with Johnson. They were concerned that if the boundary line between them and the English did not extend northward from Owego, their villages would lie open to invasion, and they believed such a line would be mutually advantageous. Johnson had already mapped such a line and invited the chiefs to inspect it, which they did. Johnson's proposed northern extension stopped short of Lake Ontario at Wood Creek, east of Oneida Lake just west of Fort Stanwix, which secured the portage route from the Mohawk Valley to Oswego (NYCD, 8: 120, and map, 136). Starting at Wood Creek, the line ran due south following Tionaderha Creek, crossed the east branch of the Susquehanna overland to the Mohawk (east) branch of the Delaware, and followed it downstream to below Popackton Brook. Thence the line continued due west to the Susquehanna's east branch and downstream past Owego to Awandoe Creek, up that stream and over Barnett's Hills to Tiadaghton Creek, up its west branch, then across country to Kittanning on the Allegheny and downstream to Fort Pitt (map 4). This extension of the line represented a departure from the Board of Trade's instructions in three respects: (1) it settled the western New York boundary, save for the open segment north of Wood Creek to Lake Ontario; (2) it opened to Pennsylvania settlement lands at the forks of the Susquehanna; and (3) its western limit bypassed the Great Kanawha, where it was supposed to link up with Stuart's Cherokee boundary, and instead the line followed the Ohio to the mouth of the Tennessee, or Cherokee, River, a considerable distance downstream.

Pressure from all sides motivated Johnson to exceed his instructions. On 28 October, the speaker for the Six Nations reminded him that the Iroquois title by right of conquest in the previous century reached well south of the Great Kanawha, as far as the Cherokee River, and not to acknowledge it was unworthy of the warriors who fought there. And they wanted the northern extension moved east to end at Lake George to exclude lands already patented. Having issued this reminder, the Indians withdrew to reconsider. The sachems would have to consult the warriors. Over the weekend, the warriors consulted apart and directed four sachems to present their reservations to Sir William on Monday. They would part with no lands west of Oriskany, the Wyoming Valley, or the Great Island, south of modern Utica, New York, which they reserved for their dependents.

The presence of an agent of Eleazer Wheelock's seeking a site for removing Wheelock's Indian school from New England to Oneida territory further distracted the Indians, outraged Johnson, and threatened to displace the Reverend Samuel Kirkland's mission at Oneida. Had the matter proceeded with quiet diplomacy, Dartmouth College today might be situated near Utica.

The failure of the long siege to restore the Kayaderosseros Patent to its native proprietors, along with similar intrusions by white settlers on Mohawk and Oneida territories, convinced Johnson that further restraints on colonists were impracticable. But stubborn resistance by the Indians prevented his running the boundary to Lake Ontario. The concessions to Pennsylvania were beyond his control. Ray Billington (1944) has ascribed the extension of the treaty line to the mouth of the Tennessee, which opened Kentucky lands to Virginia speculation and settlement, to the clandestine persuasion of Dr. Thomas Walker, the Virginia commissioner who really represented Colonel Andrew Lewis, Thomas Jefferson, and associated speculators. Although Walker later protested that he signed the treaty only as a witness, his role behind the scenes was unmistakable. Surrender to the land speculators created, in Billington's words, "one of the worst treaties in the history of Anglo-Indian relationships."

Although Johnson was later admonished by the crown for taking too much territory and was directed to re-cede some of it, from the Iroquois point of view the Fort Stanwix treaty was the greatest giveaway in history. They were in no position to defend what they claimed, but they tried to reserve rights to hunt. The confederacy was no longer a great power; its resources had wasted. Reciting the chain myth with its constituent metaphors of path and fire might boost Iroquois morale, but it no longer stood for a balanced alliance: as English strength rose, Iroquois strength fell. Of the six principal chiefs who signed the deed on behalf of their respective nations and the confederacy, only two held titles of the founders: the second Oneida and the first Cayuga. The league of hereditary chiefs ascribed by matrilineages had become a symbolic memory; headmen of achieved status had taken over the confederacy.

The Iroquois confederacy, nevertheless, still projected a powerful image. In imperial circles the Iroquois were the accepted native negotiators for the entire region of northeastern North America between 1765 and 1768. "It was with the Six Nations that the line was to be settled" on behalf of their dependents and the Delawares, Shawnees, Mingos, and other ethnic entities in the Ohio Valley. The Fort Stanwix treaty climaxed these negotiations. Dorothy Jones (1982) claims it was a moment of power for the Six Nations. Indeed, it was they who signed both deed and treaty. She takes issue with previous scholars who held that ending the line at the Tennessee River and granting the Kentucky region to Virginia was the price of giving up lands at the forks of the Ohio to satisfy Philadelphia merchants, and she holds that the Iroquois were the active participants in the Stanwix negotiations. The final boundary was pretty much what the Six Nations had agreed to in 1765. The Iroquois asserted their right to the entire area and proclaimed their continued dominance over dependents between the mountains and the Mississippi; they made their claims stick regardless of the fact that they never controlled this vast area (Jones 1982: 88–89; Fenton 1940: 239ff.).

□□◇□□

After the treaty, and for the next six years, the Shawnees differed with Iroquois policy and alienated the youths of the confederacy. In April and May of 1768, George Croghan met at Fort Pitt with warriors of the Six Nations and with Delaware, Shawnee, Munsi, and Mahican residents of the Ohio watershed to deliver Pennsylvania's condolences for murders committed by whites on the frontier and to hear complaints that settlers were encroaching on Indian lands. The Indians accepted three thousand pounds in compensation, and a commission was charged with ordering squatters off Indian lands (Jones 1982, citing PCR 9: 481, 483; Jennings et al. 1985a: 196–97). The Shawnees asserted their own rights, protesting the Iroquois policy of supporting British interest and asserting that the British seizure of Fort Pitt from the French did not make them masters of territory that was Indian property. The Iroquois present did not let this divergence from Iroquois policy go unchallenged. The right to dispose of the lands remained with the Six Nations, they claimed (Jones 1982, citing PCR 9: 528).

A year after the Stanwix treaty, they could scarcely back up their words with deeds. Johnson toured the upper nations to find the Onondagas short of provisions after a crop failure, and the arguments intensified as he moved westward. Returning to Onondaga from private meetings with various chiefs in their hunting camps, Johnson's canoe capsized, and in climbing the bank he fell and cut his previously wounded leg, nearly disabling himself. In meetings of the grand council, worries mounted over a European war, and doubts increased that the Six Nations could keep the Cherokee peace. They feared that intrusion of New Englanders into Pennsylvania would draw them into war. Some five hundred people met Johnson at Cayuga, where tension was palpable. Four times that number answered his summons to meet in the Seneca country. Western nations were militant. Before the grand council, two formerly faithful Seneca chiefs told Johnson that their labors to prevent bad belts from circulating had largely failed to offset general discontent. The Seneca speaker opened by reciting a long list of grievances: relations on the frontier had deteriorated, white inhabitants had murdered their people, and withdrawal of inspectors had increased fraud in trade. Word came that Cherokee chiefs were en route to Onondaga for a general congress, to which the Canadian confederacy was invited. A western confederacy supported by French agents posed a threat. Johnson concluded that control lay in keeping the several confederacies from uniting (NYCD, 8: 183–86).

The Cherokee delegates got their wish and met with the Six Nations at Onondaga during the winter of 1769–70. Their speaker passed twenty belts to the Six Nations in renewing and strengthening their recent peace treaty. In return, they expected the Six Nations to join them in attacking several western and southern nations who were common enemies. The Six Nations, having withdrawn to council, cagily demurred that they would first have to seek Warraghiyageh's (Johnson's) advice. Meanwhile, they would take care of the belts and calumets while their deputies asked Sir William to call a congress. Johnson wrote to Lord Hillsborough, one of the Lords of Trade: "We must either agree to permit these people to cut each others throats, or risque their discharging their fury on our Traders and defenceless frontiers" (NYCD, 8: 203–4).

Johnson kindled the fire at German Flats in July 1770. Of a Sunday at midmonth, he came down from Johnson Hall accompanied by his two deputies, Daniel Claus and nephew Guy Johnson, and the then secretary for Indian affairs, Dr. Richard Schuckburgh.[5] Weary from his Onondaga travels, Johnson needed all the help he could get. Some 1,600 Indians awaited him, and more were expected. Their numbers soon swelled to 2,320: 1,446 Six Nations, among whom 354 Senecas predominated; 510 dependents, of whom 193 were Nanticokes and

---

5. Schuckburgh supposedly was the composer of *Yankee Doodle*. Johnson had appointed him in 1759, on the death of Peter Wraxall, but he was not confirmed until later. Witham Marshe, the Lancaster treaty diarist, served ad interim until 1768, when Schuckburgh filled the office (NYCD, 8: 244n). He lacked Wraxall's knowledge of Iroquois custom and treaty protocol.

Conoys; 126 from Canada, largely from Kahnawakeh and St. Regis; 2 River Indians; and 7 Cherokee ambassadors (NYCD, 8: 227–44).

With that many Indians attending, things were bound to happen. Delegates were delayed. Diaquande, Onondaga's head warrior and Johnson's friend—he appears on the roll call as the third Oneida sachem (Deyohagwendeh, Oe-3, RC 12)—at first withdrew from participation, the ultimate sanction, and joined another camp. He had to be coaxed. Thomas King, a chief of Onohquageh, killed a young Tuscarora but next day returned to submit to the will of the deceased's kin. King was valuable and would be needed later. Johnson interceded.

The Seven Nations of Canada, who apparently were not represented at the winter council at Onondaga, were first to return the invitation string, by Level Sky (compare S-2, RC 44) of Akwesasneh. The second Oneida sachem followed for the Six Nations, who had heard the Cherokee request at Onondaga to join them against troublesome enemies westward. The grand council had at that time deftly referred the matter to Johnson, requesting that he assemble the entire confederacy, including that of Canada.

Before they got down to business, mutual losses called for multiple observances of the ancient custom of condolence, with variations of the Three Bare Words according to the status of the deceased and the speaker, but invariably with three strings.

The speaker for the Oneida warriors, the same Thomas King, complained that the sachems had failed to brief the warriors, who were primarily affected by the Cherokee request and considered it their business. An Oneida chief, Tagawara(?), responded for Johnson, addressing first the Seven Nations of Canada, then the warriors and Cherokee delegation, and finally the general assembly, welcoming them and urging decorum.

That afternoon Johnson held a series of private meetings with the chiefs and resorted to an executive session to which the principal nations each sent a sachem and their head warrior. They met far into the night. Johnson learned that warriors were bent on war with the southern Indians, but he managed to convince the sachems that peace was in the interest of the Iroquois Confederacy. Despite insults received from the Indians on the Wabash, they should ratify the treaty and send the Cherokee embassy home. These talks "in the bushes" proved valuable to both parties because they flushed out issues before they surfaced in public sessions.

The plenary sessions or councils occurred outdoors, where a bower shaded the participants. (Presumably the Indians found shelter in lean-tos such as those they readily erected when traveling or hunting.) A speaker for the host announced the agenda for the day, followed by speakers for constituent items. The Mohawk Abraham performed the first task and introduced the Onondaga Teyawarunte, speaker of the Six Nations, who, as Sir William's surrogate, performed the entire condolence ritual for several Iroquois: a Mohawk chief recently deceased, a Cayuga killed by a tribesman, and a Seneca chief who had drowned. He passed the requisite belts for each and covered their graves with a black belt, eliciting the customary *yo-hah*s from the audience.

After consultation, the council chose from the junior moiety the second Oneida sachem, Conoghquieson, to return the condolences, which host Johnson acknowledged. A Cayuga chief concluded by covering the grave of the Tuscarora murdered by Thomas King.

In abstracting the treaty proceedings, which are themselves summaries of much longer ritual acts, one cannot but admire the patience of Sir William Johnson, who had learned that adhering to Iroquois customary ways was the sure way to get what he wanted out of a council. Others of his contemporaries who found Indian ceremony tedious and who bridled at the waste of time accomplished far less.

Johnson made his big pitch the following day in public council. The Cherokee ambassadors had come via Onondaga charged with belts and a pipe to solicit aid from the Six Nations against the Piankashaws, Weas, and allied tribes. The Six Nations handed the matter to Johnson for advice. Johnson listened to Thomas King, who had escorted the Cherokee ambassadors north, and he consulted General Gage, who sought the king's sanction for the meeting and authorization to implement the Stanwix treaty. Johnson cautioned the confederacies against any action that would strengthen a Wabash confederacy, which he suspected the French of abetting. Any attack on behalf of the Cherokees would divide Iroquois manpower and weaken the Six Nations. Rather, they should attempt friendship. A belt of nine rows.

Johnson cautioned the Cherokee deputies to adhere strictly to their original terms of reference and not embellish them. They agreed.

The following morning the sachems and chief warriors of both confederacies, "or Leagues of the Six Nations," met apart in their camps to consider Johnson's proposal. They counseled all day without reaching one mind. Toward evening they delegated a chief to apologize to Sir William for not replying within the day, as promised. The militant warriors gave the sachems a hard time. The senior moiety of the confederacy had agreed on an answer, but the others had not. This lack of unanimity called for more private sessions. Time and scarce provisions after native crop failures motivated an early resolution. By the next afternoon they had achieved consensus (NYCD, 8: 235).

The Onondaga speaker introduced the Mohawk Abraham to deliver the decision of the Six Nations and their dependents. They would make use of their Shawnee younger brothers, Abraham said, to work on their troublesome southern allies and bring them to peace. Sir William urged them to recall war parties already gone south. In showing the map of the Fort Stanwix cession (map 4), he indicated that the king did not require quite all that land, if it were inconvenient. He did not say that he had exceeded his instructions but put a good face on it, asking them to ratify the treaty and the deed of cession.

Johnson invariably made certain that he got what he wanted. That night he resorted to the device of meeting apart with a sachem and warrior of each nation. This was a good way to head off growing suspicions of future British intentions— that the Iroquois would be wholly disregarded and neglected. The Mohawks had long been Christianized, but of late the Church of England had failed to send out a missionary. Although a private matter and not confederacy business, the example foreboded a dark future to the upper nations. Moreover, British interest in Kahnawakeh had declined markedly since 1763 (NYCD, 8: 238).

On Monday, 22 July, the Indians and Johnson met in full council. The Six Nations having come to one mind, the second Oneida sachem asked Sir William: was he ready to hear their reply? On assent, Abraham delivered the answer of the Six Nations and others to Johnson's speech on the king's reaction to the Stanwix proceedings and deed. (The alternation of speakers between the junior and senior moieties of the confederacy, the former deferring to the latter, adheres to Iroquois council protocol.)

Abraham expressed amazement that anyone could question Iroquois title to the lands ceded. "Our Title has always been indisputable." The title was clearly held by the Indians, and they had ceded their own property. They confirmed the transaction.

The issue of their relation with the southern Indians was more troublesome. Their people were frequently robbed or murdered on the southern frontiers. Their young men thirsted for revenge and were difficult to control. A black belt of ten rows confirmed their anxiety.

Promises of security, freedom to travel, and abundance of trade at cheap prices had not materialized. A belt of ten rows sought redress.

Again, speakers alternated between moieties. The pattern of alternation probably was not accidental, but the Oneidas were deeply concerned because their parties were committed to the southern wars. The second Oneida sachem announced the agreed-upon solution. They had fixed upon four chiefs, headed by Thomas King, who could be depended upon to faithfully "deliver our words to the Shawanese." They would seek to get the Shawnees to influence the Wabash tribes to a more peaceful disposition. The full message was communicated to Johnson a day later.

Just then, the speaker informed the Six Nations and Johnson that the death of the Tuscarora sachem Gawehe had created an empty seat at the council fire, which they filled by raising up one Tarriwahge with the usual ceremony (NYCD, 8: 240). (I do not recall an earlier instance of condoling and installing a Tuscarora chief.)

The Mohawk Level Sky spoke for the Seven Nations of Canada, who were resolved for peace, saying that the people of Kahnawakeh would keep their eyes on the Six Nations council at Onondaga while the people of Kanehsatageh would keep their eyes on groups westward up the Ottawa River. They were men of their word, the speaker asserted; they seconded the message of the Six Nations to the Shawnees, and they were prepared to send a delegation of their own with the same message on a belt, which they displayed.

It was apparently the custom to return a belt as assurance of having complied with a request. The previous fall Johnson had sent a belt to the Onondaga council requesting that it withhold its warriors until further notice. The council complied: Abraham returned it. He returned a second belt that Johnson had sent the previous spring to the Seneca country, requiring that the Senecas round up and deliver horses taken from white people. They promised to comply.

The main purposes of the conference were accomplished: peace with the Cherokees was confirmed, and the Fort Stanwix treaty and deed were ratified. Appointment of a delegation to lean on the Shawnees bypassed the Cherokee demand that the northern Indians join them in fighting their western enemies (Jennings et al. 1985a: 197). Unanimity having been attained among the parties,

Johnson renewed and brightened the covenant chain. Each nation responded with the *yo-hah*.

He then addressed each participating nation. Abraham answered in the name of the Six Nations and the Canada confederacy, confirming the covenant.

The Onondaga speaker informed Sir William that the Indians had appointed Taganaghquaghsee (compare Oa-11, RC 29) to replace the deceased Kanajiakaia, and another man, from Karaghiadirra, to replace the war chief Odongota.[6] Johnson, as was now expected, approved and charged them. The replacements were not of the same names as their predecessors, nor were the names considered titles.

The final business was to approve the message that Thomas King's party was to carry to the Weas, Piankashaws, Kickapoos, and related Central Algonqians. Sir William met with the chiefs of the nations present. The embassy should inform these people that the Cherokees had made peace with the Six Nations and northern Indians. The delegation should take the western folk by the hand and take the hatchet from their hands. If they proved obstinate and persevered, the combined confederacies would come down upon them. The embassy would carry a large belt already made up to back up their words.

Johnson ordered up the provisions for the journey home and covered the council fire (NYCD, 8: 244).

□□◇□□

It was against the background of these negotiations that Johnson, on 28 February 1771, replied to the queries of Dr. Arthur Lee of Virginia on the customs, manners, and languages of the Indians (DHNY, 1: 430–37; Lee 1772). He wrote as a weary man to satisfy two sets of queries from Dr. Lee. In neither his first letter nor in a second one written between 6 November 1771 and 28 March 1772 did he explain the moiety system of the confederacy, which guided the protocol in treaty proceedings and which he understood (compare Wraxall 1915). He had participated in the operation of the grand council, but unlike Lafitau before him and Morgan a century later, Johnson did not inquire into or explain the function of moieties at the tribal and local level, the nature and function of clans, or the Iroquois kinship system. These fundamentals of the social system, which were projected symbolically to the confederate level, are essential to understanding the Iroquois League and the confederacy, but no one in the eighteenth century other than Lafitau really understood them and made them explicit, although the image of the confederacy loomed large on the colonial horizon.

One wonders why Johnson never left a systematic description of the Iroquois Confederacy. To Lee he pleaded that previous concerns had kept him too busy for philosophical reflection or for recording his considerable knowledge of Iroquois political structure and its workings. He recognized defects in contemporaneous general works on American Indians, which failed to take into account changes in their manners and customs, so that a "description of them at a particular period must be insufficient" (Johnson to Lee in DHNY, 4: 430–37; SWJP, 12: 950). He distinguished a degree of acculturation between near and remote tribes and noted that the Indians having most contact with traders had altered their system of

---

6. Karaghiadirra (*karaghiyadirha*) appears on Guy Johnson's map, "The Country of the Six Nations" (map 5) on the site of modern Belvidere, Allegany County, New York (NYCD, 7: 723n). Its modern cognate in Seneca is Caneadea (*kaneyadi:a*).

politics while retaining ancient customs that they were unable to account for. While those peoples farthest removed from contact with Europeans retained "the greatest part of their primitive usages," they could "give no satisfactory account of their original signification" (DHNY, 4: 431). Johnson's Iroquois sources tended to cloak political tradition with mythology, and it was more than a century since the Jesuits had been among them and introduced "some of their own inventions," which Johnson's generation confounded with the natives' own ancient ceremonies.

He most certainly must have heard some account of the origin myth of the league, and he must have sought some explanation of its structure as we know it from nineteenth-century sources. But he left no written account of it. Nonetheless, Johnson's account of the duties of chiefs and of how they were elected and installed fails to jibe with Morgan's and Hale's findings as they were spelled out in nineteenth-century texts of the condolence ceremony, which we know date from Johnson's period.

In his letters to Lee, Johnson merely characterized each of the Five Nations by its collective symbol: flint (Mohawk), stone (Oneida), great mountain (Onondaga), pipe (Cayuga), and several unexplained symbols for the Senecas, who were remote and whom he knew least.

Johnson was certain that the power of the chiefs was waning. He noted that formerly, one person in each nation appeared to have more authority than the rest, and this was still the case among the remoter nations, but that in general, and especially near white settlements, humility was the best policy for Indian survival. It was his view that chiefs were chosen by public assembly, presumably by men, and were recruited from the ranks of the warriors. He said nothing about the role of women in the naming of chiefs, although "she-sachems" operated at the time (Pilkington 1980: 98). Ascribed statuses did exist, however, as Johnson acknowledged: "Some families have a kind of inheritance in the office and are called to this station in their infancy."

Clearly, late in the century superior ability and tacit consent counted more than inheritance of office in determining which Iroquois officer mediated between the two cultures. In cases where the office descended unilaterally, Johnson continued, "should the successor appear unequal to the task, some other sachem is sure to possess himself of the power and duties of the office" (Johnson to Lee, 28 February 1771, DHNY, 4: 433; SWJP, 12: 1952).

The duties of chief sachems, in Johnson's day, comprised custody of the wampum belts, keeping the records of public transactions, prompting speakers at all public treaties, and attending the grand council when not otherwise involved in the affairs of a particular nation. National councils included a variety of officers, but regularity, decorum, and avoidance of interrupting the speaker marked all of their proceedings (Johnson to Lee, 28 February 1771, DHNY, 4: 433).

A further accommodation to change affected the power structure. Johnson noted that Indians formerly had lived under "more Order & Government" than at present; their recent intercourse had been with the lower classes of colonial society, from whom they learned only vices, and their long wars and immoderate use of liquor had so reduced them that they could no longer maintain policy and order. The relatively recent reduction of Canada wrought a further change in their system of politics: "Their eyes are upon us . . . and much of their Time is spent in intrigues of State" (DHNY, 4: 436).

Arthur Lee's communication to the Royal Society of London of some extracts from Johnson's letters (Lee 1772) caught the attention of William Robertson of Edinburgh, who was preparing his *History of America* (1777). Robertson fired off questionnaires to correspondents in America, seeking information on American Indian customs, which elicited the opinions of George Croghan and Guy Johnson, Sir William's nephew (Wainwright 1947; Hamilton 1953). Robertson seems not to have used much of the information, but several of the answers in the original replies bear on the present inquiry into eighteenth-century knowledge of Iroquois political organization and behavior. Croghan's reply to a query regarding the authority of sachems in war and peace pretty much confirms Sir William's opinion. Good behavior, prudence, and persuasion invariably converted to power in council. He hinted at an ascribed elite but regarded achievement as paramount. Croghan knew the condolence ceremony but professed it impossible to translate the texts (Wainwright 1947: 157–58).

Guy Johnson completed a schedule of questions received by Sir William just before his death (PAC, Claus Papers; Hamilton 1953). In comparing Croghan's and Guy Johnson's returns, Milton Hamilton concluded that Guy Johnson's views suffered from oversophistication and a zeal to interpret rather than report. Otherwise, on most points the two agreed. Rather than depending on authority, sachems or chiefs depended on diffuse sanctions: they could convene people and propose questions; success depended on influence derived from previous achievements (Hamilton 1953: 321). While Guy stressed achievement over ascription, he reiterated Sir William's reference to "particular Families, who, (by ancient Prescription) furnish a Sachim to their Tribe." We have seen that when a minor was named, the Iroquois appointed a regent to act in his behalf, and these candidates were presented for approval to the superintendent, who responded by conferring a medal. Offices such as that of wampum keeper were often hereditary and were charged with keeping and transmitting the *kayenarongsersa* (public concerns) of the nation to the young people (Hamilton 1953: 321, 323). Guy seems to have been ignorant of the teaching power of the league epic and the didactic nature of condolence chants and texts. He was aware of the speaking style employed in public transactions, in contrast with ordinary conversations (Hamilton 1953: 325).

Guy Johnson shared the duties of deputy with Daniel Claus during the final years of Sir William's life and took over at the great man's death, as we shall see presently. But beyond imperial circles, the career of the Reverend Samuel Kirkland, missionary at Oneida after a bad start among the Senecas, would carry through the American Revolution into the reservation period among all the Six Nations. Kirkland's views on the destiny of the people came to differ markedly from those of the royalist Johnsons.

CHAPTER 35

ONE WHO WALKED WHERE THE EARTH IS NARROW

THE REVEREND SAMUAL KIRKLAND

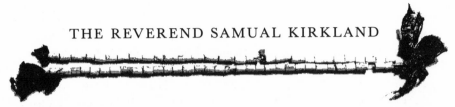

Of the "dissenting" missionaries to the Iroquois, Samuel Kirkland (1764–1808) appeals most to the anthropologist (fig. 36). Although the Honorable Society in Scotland for the Propagation of Christian Knowledge sent him out to enlighten the Indians, what made him unusual was that he strove to learn native Iroquoian languages, he carefully observed customary ways, he kept a journal, and he regarded the native people as human beings. Kirkland grew up in the atmosphere of the "Great Awakening," a religious reform movement that shattered the long-established religious formalism of Puritan New England. He imbibed a concern for the revitalization of personal religion in which, for these so-called dissenters, the congregation constituted the church. Such theology embraced the need to missionize the Indians. The dissenters were anathema to the Johnsons, who adhered to the Anglican faith and promoted the established church and the Anglican missions among the Mohawks.

Kirkland reported at first to his old Connecticut schoolmaster, Eleazer Wheelock, a Congregationalist, although he himself became a Presbyterian while attending Princeton. Master and pupil came to differ in ways that extended beyond matters of doctrine to education of Indians—whether in boarding schools removed from their "pagan" kin, as Wheelock preferred, or in day schools within sight of their parents, as Kirkland advocated—a controversy that persists to this day in Indian education.

The call that Kirkland heeded is difficult to appreciate or evaluate now. But judging from his journals of life among the Iroquois between 1765 and 1774, from his role as negotiator with the Indians when he applied his knowledge to Revolutionary politics, and from his authorship of a remarkable plan for the education of Indians that bore fruit in the founding of Hamilton College after his death, the man stacks up as one of the more considerable personalities among the founders of our nation.

While at Wheelock's school at Lebanon, Connecticut, Kirkland came in contact with Indian youths with whom in 1761 he began to study the Mohawk language with a view to missionary work. That fall, Sir William Johnson received and encouraged him. For the next three years Kirkland was enrolled at Princeton, but eight months before commencement he went on his mission to the Iroquois without waiting for the formalities. By the time his classmates graduated, Kirkland had contacted the Oneidas, made the hazardous journey to the Senecas, and left

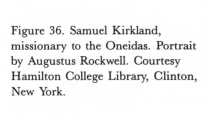

Figure 36. Samuel Kirkland, missionary to the Oneidas. Portrait by Augustus Rockwell. Courtesy Hamilton College Library, Clinton, New York.

an account of travel and transportation in Iroquoia that rivals John Bartram's and Conrad Weiser's. Even though Kirkland wrote his journal of 1764–65 late in life from scattered memoranda, his observation of Indian customs was almost continuous and enabled him to select the most striking aspects of aboriginal life as his subject matter (Lothrop 1848; Fenton 1953b: 586; Pilkington 1980: 3–39).

In assessing Kirkland as an ethnologist, his qualifications for success as a missionary—faith, courage, patience, veracity, and hardihood—are subordinate to two questions: what did he have to know to survive, and how well did he see? To live in the woods, to know the etiquette of campfire and council, and to speak an Iroquoian language were what counted and what distinguished Kirkland from his contemporaries. Until 1766 he worked on a grammar and dictionary of Seneca (now lost), and by 1789 he had completed a census of the Six Nations—by towns, families, clans, households, and personal names, with sex and age of inhabitants, which he transmitted on the occasion of his election in 1791 to the American Academy of Arts and Sciences in Boston. That copy has never surfaced, although the original notes survive in the Hamilton College Library (HCL) in Clinton, New York.

It is a maxim of ethnology that one's first observations in a new culture are sharpest. The longer one stays in the field, the more one's increased knowledge tends to cluster, and only what appear to be new items are noted. Prolonged residence has a leveling effect on the observer. Repeated visits enable one to replicate observations. Soon one must begin to systematize the data, whether on language or social organization, into patterns. The rigors of missionary life—mere survival—afforded Kirkland little leisure for such pursuits. He did attempt a grammar, and his census is a mature summation. Historically, his early journals are the best, but his later unpublished letters of negotiations between 1774 and 1794 are richer, more meaningful documents. One incentive to notation was the requirement that he send journals regularly to the missionary societies that supported his work. Whenever pen and paper were at hand and strength permitted, Kirkland wrote down what he did, what he saw, who came to see him, and how the Indians behaved.

□□◇□□

When Kirkland first went into the Indian country, Johnson received and hosted him, took his measure, and decided that this young dissenter deserved support. While Johnson waited for a trustworthy Seneca to guide Kirkland to the eastern capital of that nation, which was the limit of Johnson's influence just then, Kirkland visited Onohquageh near modern Binghampton, residence of Good Peter, a later supporter of the Oneida mission, who thought the Senecas were too "disturbed in their minds" to receive a missionary yet.

At length, when two Senecas arrived to whom Johnson felt he could entrust Kirkland, they set off in the dead of winter on the long journey to the Seneca country. Winter travel entailed carrying forty-pound packs while walking on snowshoes, which caused the neophyte muscular strain and swollen ankles. His guides insisted on breaking trail, and they bathed his ankles in cold water. As hosts, they assumed responsibility for making camp beside the path, which left Kirkland free to describe the process of making a wooden trammel and frame for hanging an iron trade kettle, fashioning wooden spits and bark serving platters, and providing wooden spoons.

Travelers on the east-west path through Iroquoia made courtesy calls at the constituent towns of the confederacy. At the main Oneida town, the party received the usual hospitality. Echoing an episode in the league epic, the Oneidas asked the travelers to stop for a night, which meant tarry for a year, and then visit the Senecas. This was an old story of keeping new culture from distant neighbors.

It took two days of travel over hilly terrain to cover the fifty miles to Onondaga. It being midwinter, the chiefs did not come out to meet them at the woods' edge but received them at the council house, which was some forty feet long and contained four fires. With customary hospitality, the Onondaga hosts put their weary guests to bed, saying that they did not hear messages of peace in the dark of night but in the light of the next day. Kirkland's journal describes the council assembling next morning at ten, the seating, and the protocol of lighting pipes, after which the chief sachem declared that they were ready to hear the visitors' message.

Johnson had charged one of the party with his message on a belt, which the guide displayed as he stood to speak. Kirkland described the style of delivery and the replies made by the seated sachems, who responded in unison at the end of a speaker's paragraph with "Ne?tho dogenske!" ("Indeed that is true"). The old Onondaga speaker confirmed what was said. The Indians' practice of shaking hands and kissing both cheeks, however, recalls French presence at Onondaga during the previous century.

The party evidently by-passed Cayuga. The journal describes the travelers' reception at Kanadasegea, the principal Seneca town east of the Genesee River:

According to Indian Custom we halted, at the skirt of the town, sat down upon a log to rest and lighted our pipes. Presently a runner was dispatched from the town and came at full speed to us, and asked whence we came and where we were going & what was our desire. One of the convoy answered we are only bound for this place & wish to be conducted to the house of the chief Sachem. He then told us to follow him & we soon entered the chief Sachem's house & were cordially received. The Speaker one of my convoy just informed the chief that we had a message from Sir William to communicate to their Chiefs so soon as they could conveniently assemble. (Pilkington 1980: 7–8)

The leading chief took notice of the message and told the visitors to rest until the morrow, when he would gather the sachems and head warriors in council to hear what they had to say. No business would be done until then. "Possess your minds in peace for this night." The evening passed in pleasant conversation concerning news of the colonies and abroad. The sachem's wife spread Kirkland's blankets on a bunk, directed him to sleep there, and added one of her own for warmth.

The council of welcome met at noon next day; one may infer that an opening address was offered before the chiefs heard Sir William's message. A silent minority did not join in approbation.

The head sachem, Sakayengwalaghton, or Old Smoke,[1] made the formal reply, thanking Sir William for introducing this young man among them, thanking the ministers to the east for sending their young brother to teach them good things, and saluting the convoy for bringing him safely on an arduous journey in winter. He then passed the belt to the sachem next to him and so around the circle. Kirkland observed: "Some would stroke it up and down with the hands & perhaps make some remarks; others would only look upon it, apparently with intenseness of thought & not open their lips and . . . passed it to the next. This ceremony took up more than twenty minutes by my watch."

A guest resides in the chief's house until the town council decides where to assign him, and that assignment to a household is tantamount to adoption by an extended family, for a household is a kinship unit. A smaller family council then assigns the guest to a particular fireside family. From Kirkland's assignment we learn something of the concept of the "good man" to whom he was entrusted. "He is what we call a good man, a sober & temperate man, & honest; he tells no lies. He is likewise very industrious, always at work doing something & and a man of *few words*." After the assignment was made, the village chief publicly directed Kirkland's removal from the council house to the dwelling of his fireside family.

Had this arrangement lasted, Kirkland would have been in a happy situation for learning the Seneca language. His orthography suggests to me that he lacked a phonetic sense, and I wonder whether he ever mastered an Iroquoian language, although he understood much of what was said and, like later ethnographers, grasped the basic patterns of the culture. A younger contemporary, James Dean,

1. "Disappearing Smoke," commonly "Old Smoke," was a prominent war chief title and principal of the eastern Senecas. Kirkland gives the Oneida version of the name. See "Sayengueraghta" in Hodge 1912: 482.

who learned Oneida as a boy before being educated at Dartmouth and becoming an interpreter, held that Kirkland never spoke Oneida well.

In Kirkland's observations on Seneca reaction to a sudden death—when his foster father died on the fourth night of Kirkland's residence with the family—and in his account of his trial by the town council he achieved his greatest triumph in ethnology. Here his powers of observation, sharpened by anxiety for his life and fed by the solicitude of his loyal Seneca family, produced the finest account of such a trial in the Iroquois literature. The resolution of this "trouble case," though in Kirkland's favor, nevertheless resulted in the failure of his Seneca mission.

This crisis at Kanadasegea brought out two sequential patterns in Seneca life: one of death, grief, and funeral, and the other of inquest, trial, and justice. Sudden death shocked the community and raised questions about the stranger. Runners notified neighboring towns. Meanwhile, Kirkland remained loyal to his grieving family and visited the corpse at intervals, a gesture that the kin, in the darkness of death, noticed. The funeral itself was sparsely attended, mainly by some 150 wailing women and girls; the men were all in council. Kirkland described how the corpse was dressed. The council meanwhile held an inquest to examine probable causes, whether witchcraft or natural. The anti-Anglo faction of a war chief named Burnt Milk held the former view and tried to indict Kirkland for witchcraft, which would sanction anyone to tomahawk him.

On hearing that the malcontents had sent to Oswego for rum, Kirkland's family hid him from uncontrollable members of society so that justice might prevail. Reports of the daily council proceedings, which went on in secrecy, emerged slowly. The national stake in Kirkland and his sponsor, Sir William Johnson, overshadowed other issues. He was a guest of the nation. They had received him and adopted him. Fear of his writings motivated the opposition. Writing threatened the traditional culture.

Old Smoke, as principal village chief, though not a holder of a Seneca league title, manifested great skill in conducting the proceedings. He opened the council for discussion. He let Burnt Milk blow off in a kind of masculine protest typical of a warrior chief. The council then summoned witnesses, members of the immediate family and neighbors. He listened to these persons carefully and asked questions, but did not comment. He reserved a discussion of death by natural causes until last. He cited the Iroquois concept of allotted life—a man's days are numbered. He contrasted with natural death the occasional suicides by persons taking the "fatal root" (*Cicuta maculata* L.) (Fenton 1941). Finally, he appealed to precedent and the honor of the Seneca nation. Although the council fell short of consensus, rationalism had momentarily quieted those of a different mind. Kirkland was spared.

As is usual in Iroquois affairs, the dissidents withdrew unrequited. Even when apparent unanimity is obtained, the opposition seldom feels bound to the decision but goes off and waits for an opportunity to do its own thing. Although Kirkland's family watched over him in the village, he had developed a cordial relationship with the headman of another settlement. He describes vividly how, as he was returning on ponyback from a visit to this man, a warrior of Burnt Milk's faction, painted for war, tried to waylay him near Seneca Lake outlet and failed only because of a damp gunlock (Pilkington 1980: 38).

A more serious threat to Kirkland's Seneca mission than physical harm was possible starvation. By mid-March 1765, the Senecas had run out of provisions. Game was scarce. They had eaten the meat from the winter hunt, and what was left had spoiled. With little corn left in the town, they were eating white-oak acorns, which brought on a violent colic relieved only by drinking bear's grease. Corn commanded a high price at Cayuga. Seneca agriculture had declined during the Seven Years War, when most of the nation was encamped at Niagara. With famine threatening the ensuing season, Kirkland and his immediate family considered going east.

The journey east to the Mohawk Valley after iceout in an elm-bark canoe would prove even more hazardous than winter travel on snowshoes. Kirkland held out until mid-April before proposing to his "elder brother" that he accompany his kinsman's family to visit Sir William. At issue were the health of the elder brother's wife and looming starvation, it being the wrong season for hunting. It took three men three days to find a suitable tree, peel a sheet of bark by rolling the log on hot coals, and fashion a canoe that would hold a family of nine persons and their gear. After six days of paddling, the travelers reached the west end of Oneida Lake, where they rigged a sail of blanket, paddles, and tumpline for the crossing. But they were soon overtaken by a gale; the canoe sprang a leak and took water so rapidly that it required two hands to bail constantly with kettles and dishes. Kirkland nearly went overboard unstepping the mast. The elder brother, quite pale at the thought of his family, untied a squirrel-skin pouch and cast two pinches of sacred powder on the waves, defying the wind to overpower them.[2] On shore they dried their gear, boiled water for tea, and repaired the canoe (Kirkland journal 1765, transcripts, p. 21, HCL; Fenton and Dodge 1949: 19–20).

Exposure, possible hypothermia, and short rations reduced the entire crew. The elder brother's wife, who was ill from the start, suffered most and died soon after reaching the Mohawk Valley. Johnson declared Kirkland a ghost and offered hospitality, but he failed to persuade the young man to abandon his adopted family encamped by the river. Kirkland's act of reciprocal loyalty earned him great credit with the Indians, brought the respect of Sir William, and eased his reception at Oneida the following year. Moreover, Kirkland kept the confidence of the Senecas and, as his brother Tekanade advised him, did not disclose to Sir William "that profound secrecy had been enjoined respecting what took place . . . in the condoling council at *Kanandasegue*" lest one of Johnson's confidants report the breach.

Not only had Kirkland stayed with his brother during the sickness of the brother's wife, but he also returned to the Seneca country, this time by bateau, with his mourning kinsman. Such loyalty during the mourning period earned him the accolade of a "good man." Presently the women and young girls of Kanada-segea fulfilled the custom of packing home great loads of firewood which they deposited at the door of the bereaved family, as if to rekindle the fire extinguished during mourning. Some forty to fifty relatives and friends, the old women in front, stood by the hearth singing funeral songs and weeping in memory of the departed. Kirkland had withdrawn to sit silent on a log beside the path where the women returned from the woods. He was soon told that because he observed their most

2. This incident suggests the Little Water Medicine bundle known to later ethnology.

ancient and sacred customs they considered him a deep and heartfelt mourner, which earned him both respect and kindness from the body of kindred.

During Kirkland's return east, his old enemy Burnt Milk sought to enlist a war party of young men to go out against the Cherokees and bring back prisoners or scalps as testimony of valor. Although taking the warrior path to the Cherokees was a tradition, they declined. Burnt Milk, who was prepared to violate the move of Johnson and the confederacy toward a Cherokee peace, suspected Kirkland of poisoning their minds with white people's notions. His people, he declared, would soon be reduced to performing the tasks of Negro slaves, domesticated Indians, and women. He was out to get Kirkland, come what may. The pro-Anglo faction in the friendliest Seneca town could not protect a dissenting minister.

□□◇□□

Kanonwalohale, "Head on a Pole," was the principal Oneida town just then. Situated about twenty miles west of the Mohawk River and fifteen miles south of the eastern end of Oneida Lake, it became the site of Kirkland's mission to the "people of the standing stone" in the summer of 1766, and his residence for the rest of his life. From the start, drunkenness and social disorganization vexed him. Public discussion and staving rum kegs made some difference. Kirkland wisely got the town to appoint eight headmen and empowered them to seize and destroy any liquor found brought to town. By December only two holdouts opposed the policy, and one, a veteran warrior, vowed to get its perpetrator. Kirkland described this incident in a letter to Eleazor Wheelock (MHS 101.90).

In a classic trouble case, Kirkland destroyed the liquor belonging to a habitually drunk woman whose husband promptly called on the dominie to learn his reasons. After two hours, as the husband prepared to depart, he insisted that Kirkland pay half the cost of the liquor. Kirkland refused, saying that to grant his request would be worse than breaking the keg of rum. The dissatisfied plaintiff went off, bent on revenge. He soon purchased liquor from some passing Onondagas, got drunk, and toward evening proclaimed his intentions. Next morning he reappeared at Kirkland's house, entered in a haughty manner, and threatened the missionary. Asked to leave and invited to return when better composed for conversation, the man made no move to go. Kirkland suspected he concealed a knife under his blanket, a suspicion that proved groundless. As Kirkland gently eased him to the door, the man tried to grab Kirkland by the throat, upon which Kirkland closed with him and put him down, calling upon an aide to help bind him. Kirkland seemed amazed at his own success, for the warrior had "twice too much strength," although in falling his adversary disabled an arm. The man's wife promptly arrived in a terrible passion and demanded his release. Frustrated, she turned on Kirkland, striking and attempting to bite him. Fortunately for the minister, another Oneida matron intervened and diverted the attack on herself. She had her hair pulled and her life threatened afterward.

The humility of being bound was more than an Iroquois warrior could stand. The man felt compelled to threaten Kirkland's life and recited the record of his murders to frighten him. One is reminded of the appeals of warriors in torture, begging to be killed, and ten minutes later wishing their captors "to ye lowest Hell." Kirkland released the man, sober, to return to Oneida castle, where he repeated his threats in public.

The Oneida headmen, now concerned for peace, felt impelled to counsel together and came as a body to Kirkland. They admitted that as civil chiefs they were powerless to curb a warrior who had threatened and sworn bloody vengeance, thereby reiterating a theme that pervades the treaty literature. Kirkland was convinced that the Oneidas had no government.

Just then the frustrated recidivist hung around the skirts of town in an attempt to take one of the missionary's cattle and slit its throat, not unlike a Cheyenne visiting vengeance on a rival's horse. Finally, the community expressed its anxiety in confused rumor, those who would put the matter to rest saying the bad lot had gone to Canada, and others fearing he would momentarily return from hunting and fulfill his threat.

News of the incident surely reached Johnson, who already had the measure of the man, before Kirkland's letter informed Wheelock what his pupil was up against. They both knew that the missionary was dead serious. Johnson promptly wrote to the Society for the Propagation of the Gospel in London that the time was ripe for the appointment of an Anglican missionary, offering, if necessary, to pay the salary of a middle-aged man who would be zealous in the discharge of his duty and not extreme in temperament—a little less gloom and not too much levity (SPG ms. B 2 87; Lydekker 1938: 116). Johnson, who had had his fill of dissenters during the 1768 Stanwix treaty negotiations, when Wheelock sent agents seeking land for removing his college to New York, became convinced that an Anglican clergy demanded an episcopate. That dissenters from New England were spreading the Revolutionary spirit greatly concerned Johnson (SPG ms. B 2 89; Lydekker 1938: 118–20).

Information on the Oneida mission during the next several years is fragmentary. Kirkland was busy learning the Oneida language so that he could preach in it. His sermons, given progressively in the native language, affected individuals differently and soon divided the community politically. The Oneidas found his doctrine more demanding than that of previous Christian missionaries, notably the Jesuits. He developed lifelong friendships with Skenandoa, who survived Kirkland and asked to be buried beside him, and Good Peter of Onohquageh, warrior, orator, and peacemaker, whose name derived from his piety. An Indian friendship was a special relationship between two individuals, bound by ceremony and carrying mutual obligations during the life of either participant. It reached beyond the kinship system to bond persons outside the kindred of blood and marriage, and it is a persistent theme in Iroquois culture. Both of these men embraced Christianity and brought considerable support to Kirkland's mission.

A "pagan" faction soon developed that included numbers of the life chiefs, or sachems. Factions are essentially unstable and may not develop into organized political parties, which was the case at Oneida, although the divisions became known as the "Christian" and "Pagan" parties.[3] To balance these forces required considerable skill and self-reliance. The Oneida mission began to develop an integrity of its own and attracted notice in New England. For example, Benjamin

---

3. Kirkland challenged traditional beliefs. As Campisi points out (1978: 482–83), it was no coincidence that his followers were warriors, who were beyond the control of the chiefs. He provided religious validation to political reality, further weakening the hereditary chiefs, who therefore opposed Kirkland's doctrine and his politics.

Gale, a physician of Killingworth, Connecticut, manifested an interest in Iroquois medicines then popular among white colonists by asking Wheelock to have his messenger find out from Kirkland what medicines "the Indian Parturient Women take antecedent to Delivery which occasions so easy a Travail—they have given some of our Captives" (Dartmouth College ms., 21 July 1769).[4] We do not know that Kirkland answered this query.

The following year, 1770, Kirkland came under the direct control of the Boston Board of Correspondents for the society in Scotland, which auspices gave a new thrust to the Oneida mission. A series of works projects during the next several years mobilized Indian interest to build a public meetinghouse, erect a sawmill, and site a gristmill. Board funds purchased oxen and farming implements. Despite the customary contempt of Iroquois warriors for engaging in women's hoe culture, some Oneida men began to farm. A blacksmith shop where young men could learn to work iron answered the perennial plea at treaties to have guns repaired and tools mended. Later came the climax project of raising a steeple for the Indian church.

Kirkland visited Boston and got married. Within a year his bride, Jerusha, who had stayed behind near Stockbridge, bore him twin sons, whom the Oneidas greeted with the Iroquois reverence for twins of the Creation and promptly named John Ahganowiska, "the Fair Faced," who was destined to become the only Oneida-speaking president of Harvard, and George Lagoneost, who later caused his father endless anxiety (Lothrop 1848: 229).

The Anglicans meanwhile were busy getting their mission started at the upper Mohawk castle, where Johnson had built a chapel. But Kirkland's Oneida mission stood at the crossroads of the Longhouse. He was besieged by guests from all of the Six Nations traveling the east-west path between Albany and Niagara. Appealing to the society in Boston on 12 November 1770 for support in building a meetinghouse, he wrote: "We are on the public rode [sic] (Tho' a foot path) thro' the Five Nations; we have from time to time crowds of travellers; we are exposed to so much company; 500 or a thousand have passed this way at a congress or general meeting; most of the Five Nations have their eyes fixed upon this place."

The mission was indeed expanding to include Tuscaroras "much concerned for the state of their souls" (Pilkington 1980: 60). Two or three hundred Indians from five villages attended the dominie's sermons. Demands on his time left Kirkland short of sleep that winter. But while the Anglican missionary John Stuart, sent by the SPG to the Mohawks in 1770, encountered difficulties learning his charges' language (SPG B 2 197), Kirkland was exploring such political subtleties as the relation of warriors to councilors. He observed that in all their public addresses, the warriors styled the councilors "uncle," and "for the most part the Warriors are uncontrolled by the Sachems or *Lords*, as this title signifies in their own language" (Pilkington 1980: 66). He noted that his appeal to the public to proceed with one heart and one mind brought support from the sachems, who nevertheless feared a separation might follow between them and the warriors (Pilkington 1980: 68). Luckily for Kirkland, several of the head warriors converted to Christianity, which weakened the warrior faction and underscored its separate political existence from the sachems.

4. On Iroquois herbalism and colonial medicine, see Fenton 1942.

□□◇□□

The Six Nations were feeling the centrifugal forces of cultural change, religious schisms, and political rivalries. As Kirkland's message gained followers at Oneida, the "Faithful Mohawks" adhered to the Church of England and to Sir William Johnson, who planned to put the Mohawk mission on a permanent footing sustained by quitrents (SPG B 2 66–67). Johnson sensed the change and expressed it in his letter to Arthur Lee of Virginia cited in chapter 34. The nearer tribes were losing their customs fastest and were most confused by differing interpretations of western culture. Their political systems were changing rapidly. Johnson, in his final years, was already training his nephew, Guy, to succeed him, and his Mohawk protégé, Joseph Brant, was coaching the Reverend John Stuart in the Mohawk language. The next four years would witness the climax and decline of British rule of Indian affairs as it took the path westward through the Longhouse beyond Niagara.

The Fort Stanwix treaty did not make British control of the Six Nations any more secure. The western Senecas had acted independently, they were in constant communication with tribes in the Ohio region, and it was greatly feared that they would league with them against the British. Indeed, in the spring of 1771 George Croghan learned that ever since the treaty, Seneca agents had been "telling the western tribes that the English had not bought their western land but had stolen it," and that they had instigated the union of western and southern tribes, who were waiting for Iroquois war parties to join them in attacking British posts (Wainwright 1959: 274). Such news did not dispose Johnson to look favorably on independent action at Oneida near home; he reacted strongly on reading Kirkland's 1771 journal report to the Board of Correspondents (DHNY, 4: 460). An Anglican memorial to the prime minister on converting the Iroquois, to which Guy Johnson contributed his now famous map of the Six Nations (map 5), deplored the sinister Boston influence (Charles Inglis in DHNY, 4: 1089–1117).

Word had reached Johnson in February 1771 that a great council recently held at the plains of Scioto had ended apparently without achieving its purpose of promoting a union with western and southern tribes, which the Ohio Indians favored and which Johnson had tried with all possible caution to obstruct. The deputies from the northern confederacy, led by Thomas King and carrying a hundred belts from the Six Nations and from Johnson in accord with the treaty at German Flats the previous summer, had met Indians from Scioto at Fort Pitt in December and ordered them to reassemble at Scioto promptly, when (and not before) they would communicate the resolutions of the northern Indians (NYCD, 8: 262). Johnson had every confidence in the ability of these deputies.

The very real danger of the alliance was for the moment averted. But Johnson, knowing Indians, gave Lord Hillsborough in England his own assessment of their views. Indians had begun to have more respect for the English and their resources, Johnson wrote, although because of the unwise behavior of some English people and the natural suspicions of the Indians, they had gradually become increasingly alarmed for themselves. They still believed that they could deliver such a check as to prevent the English "from attempting what they apprehend we have in view. Many will talk, some will think, and a lesser number will act otherwise; but this is nevertheless the true political state of their sentiments" (NYCD, 8: 263).

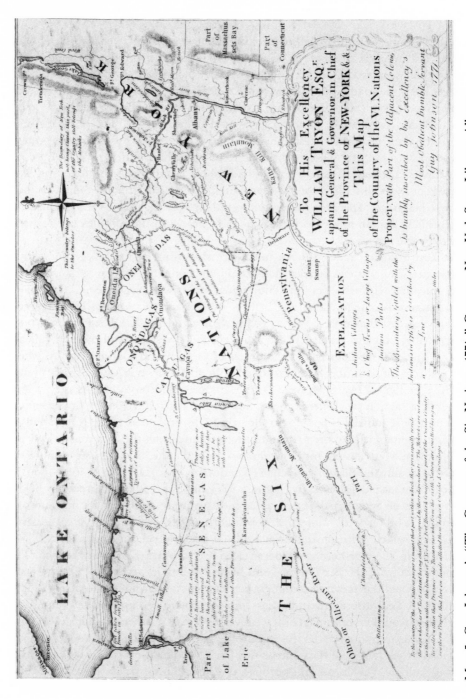

Map 5. Guy Johnson's "The Country of the Six Nations, 1771." Courtesy New York State Library, Albany.

That an Indian war was probable was plain to all sides. Various delegations of the Six Nations explored with Johnson its possible implications on the frontier and in Europe (NYCD, 8: 263). Kirkland's Oneidas expected war in the west by the next spring or autumn (Kirkland to Wheelock, 20 January 1772). That summer of 1772 it appeared that the commotion might subside, but the westward movement of colonists from Virginia across the Ohio River would break into open hostility two years later in Cresap's, or Lord Dunmore's, War. The Shawnees and Delawares, sometime tributaries of Onondaga, having been joined by renegade bands of Iroquois, were now less inclined to listen to the old men of the confederacy.

Meanwhile, Johnson would exert diplomacy to avert it. In July 1771, he summoned the Six Nations to Johnson Hall and demanded an explanation of intelligence concerning allegations of their participation in exciting the Shawnees, Delawares, and related nations to make war on the English. Some 350 attended. In response to Johnson's charge, the speaker for the Six Nations, Tyorhansera, gave a long explanation to which Johnson replied that he could not deem their answer satisfactory until they delivered up the belts mentioned in their speech. This they promised to perform. Clearly, wampum constituted legal documentation of an act or intent. For some time Johnson had doubted the friendship of the Genesee Senecas and the émigré Senecas in Ohio.

Tyorhansera's explanation illustrates how the confederacy conducted an inquiry. In response to Johnson's charge, he said, the Iroquois had made the strictest inquiry among their several nations concerning Johnson's intelligence. The persons questioned first came from the eastern division of the nation, the so-called upper Seneca villages, and not a single one admitted to knowing anything about the alleged incitement. Then Old Smoke, chief of those towns and Kirkland's savior, examined persons from the farthest Seneca castle who declared that any residual trouble proceeded from previous activities of Gaustarax, erstwhile chief of Chenussio, who was now conveniently under the ground. He had busily engaged in clandestine activities done in the name but without the sanction of the Six Nations. He had sent a hatchet belt with speeches to the Shawnees and their allies but kept it secret from Old Smoke, knowing he was pro-English. The belt proposed moving the western door of the Longhouse from Chenussio to Scioto and said that Gaustarax counted on the western Indians' assistance to fight his way there. All of this came out much later. Gaustarax had met some Ohio Indians at the Fort Stanwix treaty and afterward sent them belts with various instructions. He recommended that they concentrate on the Scioto plains and apply themselves to hunting for three years in order to purchase supplies for war. When they were ready, he would assist them.

The Six Nations proper had no part in these negotiations, Tyorhansera added. Old Smoke's source had known all this for some time but thought the scheme had been abandoned. Now that Thomas King and the deputies of the Six Nations had gone to the Ohio country, the matter should be settled.

Johnson remarked to Hillsborough that the English might count on the advantages of jealousies between Indian nations (NYCD, 8: 280–83).

The return of Thomas King and the Six Nations delegation appointed at the German Flats treaty to the congress at Scioto was anxiously awaited. They had been gone the better part of two years. The sad news reached the Mohawk Valley that the leader and his deputy had died on the way home, King in Charleston and Anawaacka, his deputy, aboard ship to Philadelphia, where the survivors landed in February. Instead of getting a full report, Johnson had to piece together what happened from some young men who brought him a considerable number of belts and calumets (the currency of alliances among Central Algonquians) with which they reconstructed the proceedings.

King had first met at Fort Pitt with Shawnees who assured him that the Weas would shortly send deputies to the Six Nations seeking continuance of friendship. Upon arrival at Scioto, King had summoned all the nations in the region. He first addressed the Shawnees, reprimanding them for withdrawing so far down the Ohio and confederating with people who neglected their obligations. He repeated his charge to each nation.

The Shawnee excuse held that the Six Nations had neglected to fulfill a promised grant of land between the Ohio and the Great Lakes. In distress, the Shawnees had boarded their canoes and floated downstream, but the Six Nations had stopped them some years ago at Scioto and shook them by their heads, charging them to settle there and live in peace with the English. They had observed the military posture of the Six Nations during Pontiac's Rebellion, and when the Iroquois intensified their abuse, they had sent belts to strengthen their union with the Six Nations through the Senecas. They surmised that Gaustarax, then the keeper of the western door who received the belts, did not publish them to the confederacy. No belts came back to them.

The Shawnees displayed emblematic belts linking them to the Illinois Indians with a chain of ten intervening nations. There was even a Choctaw belt promising to be guided by the Six Nations.

After accusing the Shawnees of misrepresentation and detailing their acts contrary to the behavior expected of allies, King offered to restore them to their senses by opening a road to the council fire at Onondaga and thence to Johnson Hall, in a solid alliance with the English.

Returning through the Southeast to gain adherents as offsets to the Scioto coalition, King's party found the Cherokees grateful for the peace of 1768. At Gohi they met the Creek headman, who was cordial and promised to open a road to Onondaga. Catawba guides, former enemies, led them over the mountains to Charlestown. The principal survivor of this expedition, Nicaroondase (Nikaron-dase:ʔ), Johnson's source, carried a name resonant of Sapling, the culture hero of the cosmology.

A second embassy to a congress at Scioto followed the one-hundred-belt embassy of Thomas King. This time the Six Nations appointed chiefs and head warriors from every nation of the confederacy, and Johnson sent his own deputy, whom he instructed how to behave in various contingencies. The confederacy still acted as if it could translate its prestige into power. The second embassy returned in October 1772 and promptly related the transactions to Johnson. The Six Nations had waited for days, but the Wabash, Kickapoo, and Piankashaw delegations failed to show, their excuse being that during the previous year an Iroquois-Cherokee war party had killed some of their people. The Six Nations deputies nevertheless laid out their belts and delivered a reprimand to those present. They also demanded the surrender of belts exchanged between the Seneca

Gaustarax and the Scioto confederation without the sanction of the Six Nations confederacy. Persons present did not have the belts in question because the Cherokees had stopped them, but they thought they could be collected and brought to a general congress at Onondaga. Among the belts finally delivered to Johnson was one of the largest he had seen, which he attributed to the French on the Mississippi. The same Indians failed to appear at the "Grand Fire Place" at Onondaga within the allotted time. Johnson urged the Six Nations to assert their rights growing out of the land sale at Fort Stanwix and advised them to withdraw their people from the Ohio. The leader of the Ohio émigrés, Kayashota, a Seneca of considerable stature with whom Johnson had later dealings, was present and agreeable (NYCD, 8: 300–1, 314–17).

The confederacy persisted and called a third congress at Scioto. The Six Nations' third appearance in Shawnee country did not evoke more than promises, later unkept, while the Shawnees continued to promote their own confederacy. When Johnson later questioned Iroquois tolerance of broken promises and failure to take decisive action, they reminded him that it was their custom to call three times on erring nations before they struck (Jones 1982: 106, citing *Documents of the American Revolution* 5: 212). Indeed, four is a magic number in Iroquois culture.

During these comings and goings, Johnson, Governor Tryon, two members of the New York council, and staff met in July 1772 at Johnson Hall with upper Mohawks of Canajoharie to hear their grievances over questionable land surveys. The proceedings reveal the inner workings of Mohawk polity. Decarihoga (Tekarihoken, M-1), who held the title of the ranking Mohawk sachem, now back in the valley, spoke first, saying that the sachems, tired of delay and still without satisfaction, had resolved to put the business in the hands of their young men, the warriors. Whereupon Joseph (Brant?) stood and spoke for the warriors, outlining the problem. He recalled that the Mohawks had joined with the confederacy in ceding lands to the king at the Stanwix treaty, but they had excepted land neighboring their villages, to which the Livingstons and others had staked claims. A speaker named Hendrik reiterated the same. Governor Tryon, in replying to the Canajoharie speaker, said he could not approve of the sachems' giving over responsibility for their grievances to the warriors. He deemed it highly inappropriate for them to quit the conduct of public affairs when negotiating with the king. He had come to deal with sachems as officers of peace and men of wisdom and experience. In a state of war, he would deal with warriors. Evidently Johnson had coached him.

In this case, to enlist the support of the new governor, the sachems reversed themselves, agreeing to let the business go on via the old channel.

Local autonomy prevailed. The upper and lower Mohawk towns dealt separately, each with its own speaker.

Oneida sachems and warriors took advantage of the governor's presence to share their own concerns over land. The familiar Conoghquieson (Oe-2, RC 11) headed the delegation and spoke for them (NYCD, 8: 304–10). This conference summoned the participation of at least two holders of league titles in significant roles.

□□◇□□

During the negotiations in the west just related, which Johnson sought to control, Kirkland continued to labor at his Oneida mission while awaiting the outcome.

Oneida remained a key stop on the east-west path between Albany and Niagara. Since the founding of the Iroquois League, a log had lain across the path at Oneida. Runners and embassies bound for the Mohawk Valley or headed west to the upper nations stopped, put down their heads for the night, and related the nature of their mission. The rare traveler who ignored this custom earned the sanction of the sachems. News of expected war in the west in early 1772 created such a "commotion among the Indians," particularly the warriors, that the mission halted and Kirkland removed his family to the safety of Stockbridge, where he wrote to Wheelock on 20 January: "The present state of affairs among the Indians affords a gloomy prospect in regard to spreading the Gospel. There is no small commotion among the distant Tribes—which begins to affect the confederate Nations—who are generally of the opinion that an Indian War is unavoidable and expect its commencement by this spring and next autumn."

By June it began to look as if the commotion might subside. Perhaps the missions to Scioto were taking hold. But that hope would prove overoptimistic some two years later, when white expansion across the Ohio River would incite the Shawnee-Delaware coalition into the open hostility of Cresap's War.

Oneida was showing signs of social disorganization in the spring of 1772, when Kirkland returned there alone. A student missionary sent out by Wheelock to assist him gave up in disgust and delivered a thirty-count indictment of Indian failures ("David Avery's Farewell to the Oneidas," 20 June, in Kirkland Papers). The failure was perhaps the student's own, owing to his being ill suited to the fatigues of Indian life, for he sought a softer life in Virginia. But it was a bad year for a neophyte at Oneida; Kirkland commented the same day on the low state of religion among the Oneidas:

> I have discovered more of Indian deceit, art & hypocricy this last year than ever before, during the whole of my residence among them. . . . After seven years service & scholarship I begin to understand a little of Indians. . . . By searching into Indian traditions—National temper, past conduct under Providence [contrasted] with the present state of the different Nations and tribes. . . . By stubborn facts & long experience I am now obliged or constrained to give up my hope of the Indians ever being called in as a people or Nation—which hope I have held & hugged as my life for many years. (Kirkland to Rodgers, 20 June 1772)

Politically, the best information that Kirkland could get detected a general uneasiness prevailing in the confederacy and among more remote tribes that war in the west could be prevented. Nor was he reassured when young warriors appeared thirsty for blood and could scarcely be constrained. He transmitted this intelligence with some anxiety that if it were published and got back to the Indians he would be severely handled (Kirkland to Rodgers, 20 June 1772; also Kirkland to Thornton, 29 July 1772). Messing in Iroquois politics was a dangerous game for missionaries, as later it became for anthropologists.

Early in March 1773, the grand council of the confederacy met at Onondaga, where some two hundred sachems and warriors gathered to hear the grounds of uneasiness among the Senecas and more distant tribes with which they were affiliated. The council sat for nearly three weeks "and to all appearance matters were settled to the Joy of many, though to the disappointment of some who were thirsting after blood, and in high expectation of a war" (Pilkington 1980: 82). Kirkland rejoiced: "The long threatened & expected storm seems to withdraw— the clouds disperse, which gives universal joy to all my people—we begin to hope for a day of peace" (Kirkland to Jerusha Kirkland, 24 March 1773).

For eight years Kirkland had walked where the earth was narrow—a reference to the Iroquois path to the hereafter, which follows a ridge and crosses over an abyss on a precarious log. He had learned that to preach the gospel he must stay out of Indian politics. He had endured and survived the physical dangers of life in the wilderness. He manifested great moral as well as physical courage, traits that Iroquois admired, and he had participated in Indian life to the extent of learning the language, acquiring a working knowledge of social structure, and making two solid friendships. Although he deplored native ceremonialism, he brought innovations and taught skills of European culture. But as Conrad Weiser had learned, one cannot live in the woods and stay neutral. Kirkland now differed with his old mentor, Wheelock, and he would soon break with the Johnsons, who by now regarded him as both a dissenter from established religion and a subversive in politics. Kirkland's Boston connection brought him news of Revolutionary thought and actions in New England—doctrines that the Johnsons accused him of relaying to the Oneidas. But although a pagan faction opposed him, Kirkland had acquired a rival following of headmen who would defend him.

The fire that burned at Johnson Hall, however, was about to flicker and go out. It would be rekindled briefly before being quenched as storm clouds again approached Onondaga.

CHAPTER 36

DARK CLOUDS
OVER ONONDAGA

British relations with the Six Nations reached a climax in 1774. Sir William Johnson died in council trying to stave off a coalition of tribes in Ohio from forming a hostile confederacy involving the Six Nations. His passing ended two decades as superintendent of the Northern Department of Indian Affairs, a landmark in the colonial administration of native peoples. With the support of sachems and warriors of the confederacy, Guy Johnson (fig. 37), Sir William's nephew and son-in-law, was raised up in his place and given a new Indian name. Together with Thayendanegea, or Joseph Brant, Sir William's Mohawk protégé, Guy prevailed on the council at Onondaga to deny a Shawnee request to take up their quarrel with Virginia. Guy wrote extended reports of these doings to impress General Gage in Boston and the ministers and king in London. The Iroquois sachems, in visiting sanctions on Cayuga warriors who had gone on the warpath to join the Shawnees, listened to the matrons who held the strings of office in their hands. This was one of the last times the grand council of the Iroquois Confederacy was to act as a government: three years later the Six Nations raked up the embers and covered their fire, unable to agree on the path to follow during the American Revolution. An independent view of these happenings flowed from Samuel Kirkland's pen at Oneida while his followers raised a steeple on the mission church.

□□◇□□

Johnson spent his final year in distant diplomacy, employing Seneca intermediaries with the emigrants of the confederacy then living in Ohio, whom the old men at Onondaga could no longer control. Bringing them home would strengthen the confederacy and get them away from efforts to seduce them into a hostile union. The real problem was to unite the two divisions of the Seneca nation, who numbered as many people as the other nations combined; a solid Iroquois Confederacy was in the British interest. For years Johnson had been able to rely on chiefs from the eastern Seneca towns while those west of the Genesee River remained aloof and dealt secretly with elements in Ohio (NYCD, 8: 361–62).

To these ends the chiefs of the Six Nations came to Johnson Hall in April 1773. The grand council had met a month before coming down, as Kirkland has told us, and "brought the Senecas to a sense of their misconduct" while persuading them in the future to adhere to the true interests of the confederacy (NYCD, 8: 361). Because of the usual delay while the chiefs straggled in, the Onondaga

Figure 37. Guy Johnson and an unidentified Mohawk who accompanied him to London. Oil portrait by Benjamin West. Courtesy National Gallery, Washington, D.C.

speaker opened with the short form of the condolence ceremony: just three bare words and three strings. Johnson hastened to business.

The Onondaga speaker immediately reviewed recent transactions with the Miamis, Piankashaws and others. He deplored the impropriety of private transactions to the neglect of conducting affairs at the proper fireplace. He thanked Johnson for advising "the Mohawks and Onondagas, as elder Branches of the Confederacy," and for bringing the Senecas who were present to a sense of their true interests as the third member of the senior moiety of the confederacy. He could blame their defection, the speaker said, on Gaustarax (now conveniently deceased), "the old chief who turned his face the wrong way" and failed to perform properly as the western door of the Longhouse. Hereafter, the Senecas would "keep their face toward the great Council fire at Onondaga." The ethnologist wonders who the proper doorkeepers were just then. And what of Ganonhgidawi (S-7, RC 49) and Doninhogawen (S-8, RC 50), who figure prominently in the Eulogy to the Founders (Hale 1883; Fenton 1950)? Those functionaries, the speaker asserted, were supposed to keep the door continually open to receive bad news and transmit it to Onondaga. They had sent word to Kayashota, the Seneca leader of the Ohio émigrés, to advance their requests; as soon as their messengers returned, the grand council would meet at Onondaga and summon the Miamis, Piankashaws, and other troublesome nations to appear and answer for their behavior. Belts of appropriate dimensions and design attested to the points made.

Renewing the covenant chain to include both divisions of the Senecas prompted a recitation of the chain myth, symbolized by a belt of twelve squares, eleven rows deep.

Two days later, Johnson applauded the restoration of the senior moiety of the confederacy to include the Senecas. Whatever misdeeds Gaustarax had performed, Johnson wanted the "bad belts" retrieved and turned over to him. He relied on Kayashota's cooperation and the support of the warriors. With reference to the upcoming grand council at Onondaga where the Miamis and their adherents, agreeable to ancient custom, would be summoned for the last time, Johnson reminded the chiefs present how well he knew their ancient customs. Long ago, so as to make no mistake in observing them, he had committed them all to writing at a time when such matters were better understood than they were at present. (One wonders what happened to this memorandum. The four volumes of the Indian Records that Wraxall abridged contained the first treaties with the English.)

Brightening the chain of friendship to include the Senecas invoked the sanction of ritual. Regulating the western door in order to exclude issues offensive to nations at the middle and eastern end of the chain reaffirmed its original purpose as defined in the league epic.

The large chain belt of thirteen rows, "Black with White Squares," with which Johnson confirmed the covenant recalls the "Hiawatha" belt recently repatriated from the New York State Museum (see fig. 24).

As for the "bad belts," Seriohana (Serihowaneh[?]), now chief of the Senecas on the Genesee, held that they were no longer in force. They were somewhere far south, one in Cherokee hands, both sender and recipients now dead, and unrecoverable unless Kayashota could pick up one (NYCD, 8: 362–68).

Kayashota (*kayahsotha*?, "it stands up a cross" [Chafe 1963: 57]) showed up at Johnson Hall at the new year to report on his transactions at Fort Pitt with the western nations. He and Johnson evidently shared a good rapport. After reiterating Johnson's messages, he related the answers of the Hurons and Ottawas at Detroit and of the Miamis who headed the confederacy on the Wabash. George Croghan had conducted the meeting. Though virtually illiterate, Croghan had a way with Indians that compensated for other shortcomings. He had mastered forest diplomacy, communicated in native tongues, and had acquired considerable prestige, if not power, to achieve his own ends. As agent, he nominated, charged, and installed chiefs.

According to custom, the Hurons had taken the war ax out of Miami hands, Kayashota said, and buried it to oblivion in the Miami village, thereby opening the road to Fort Chartres. In response, the Miamis had complained that the Shawnees distorted messages received from the Six Nations, adding speeches of their own urging a union against the English. The necessity of relaying messages from tribe to tribe contributed to distortion, if it did not create an opportunity for deceit. The Shawnees in turn had complained to Kayashota that the Scioto Senecas continually manifested hostility to the white people; the Shawnees wanted them removed close to Fort Pitt, where Kayashota could watch them. Huron, Seneca, and Delaware persons present wondered why the Shawnees entrusted the message to a white man (Croghan) and did not deliver it themselves, inasmuch as they were responsible for prevailing on the Senecas to remove sixty miles downriver in the first place. Kayashota faulted traders for stirring up trouble on the frontier.

Kayashota next addressed the Delaware Captain Pipe, who was being raised up to replace his mother's brother, charging him to concentrate his straggling people from Venango, where the Six Nations had assigned them, to a site on Beaver Creek nearer Fort Pitt. He would similarly concentrate the Senecas scattered in Ohio upriver of the fort.

Croghan accused the thirteen Shawnees present of having spoken with a double tongue after receiving the advice of the Six Nations. Their leader had responded by lighting and passing a pipe of peace and then presenting it to Johnson's surrogates, promising to heed their advice in the future. The Shawnee speaker also reported that a branch of the Illinois called Kaskaskeys could not come to the Iroquois country, being engaged in a war at home. He concluded with an elaborate excuse about why the Shawnees had not brought a combined delegation of western tribes to Onondaga two years earlier. It seems that of the two Iroquois messengers who had brought the invitation, one, instead of returning home immediately, had stayed behind in order to give advance notice when the embassy set out. Tired of waiting, he had run off and was overtaken by two Shawnee runners one hundred miles from Scioto, where they ordered him to stop until the grass was a foot high (mid-June), when he could depend on the embassy's setting out for the proposed congress. It was all the traders' fault for keeping them drunk at home. Of such were the hazards of forest diplomacy. Shawnee duplicity, Kayashota reported, appeared to be a hopeless case.

At their closing meeting, in the presence of Seneca, Onondaga, and Oneida chiefs, after mutual condolences, Johnson complimented Kayashota on his previous mission and sent him back charged with messages for the Hurons, whom he considered heads of the western confederacy, the Shawnees, and the Miami confederacy, who were victims of some "Bad Birds." From now on they were to "stop their Ears" to such and keep their eyes focused on Johnson. Kayashota thanked Johnson for his speeches and promised to deliver them faithfully with the particular belts (SWJP, 12: 1055–60). That was the last they were to see of each other.

Johnson, in his final year, began to impose British criminal law on the Six Nations. At his insistence the Senecas in April delivered at Johnson Hall two of their young men who had murdered some Canadians on Lake Ontario and hijacked their goods. Johnson prevailed on them to turn the men over to British justice, and he confiscated the goods. Colonel Guy Johnson (1740–88), whom Sir William had chosen as his successor from among his deputies with Six Nations' approval, wrote: "This is the first instance of their complying with our Laws at the Expense of their Antient Customs" (BM 24, 323, folio 15). Guy hoped this set a precedent. One of the men died in custody and was condoled; the other was finally released (BM 29, 237).

□□◇□□

Guy Johnson and Samuel Kirkland had little use for each other. Several issues separated them: tension on the frontier over the boundary line that Sir William had set and was responsible for maintaining, and danger of an Indian war should the Six Nations cast their lot with the Shawnees versus Virginia. Kirkland, a dissenter, identified with New England and with rising discontent against the Stamp Act. The Oneidas and the Mohawks, traditional leaders of the two complementary halves of the confederacy, confronted a religious struggle between dissenting patriotism and adherence to the Church of England and the crown, a schism that would eventually break up the Longhouse.

Sir William balanced the two sets of loyalties. So long as he lived, he and Kirkland maintained a semblance of good relations. But Colonel Guy's sympathies were entirely with the crown, and as a zealous Anglican he worked among the Six Nations for church and king. He set out to destroy Kirkland and discredit him at Oneida. Yet when the wampum belts were down, Kirkland had the support of the Oneida council, who sent Guy a belt and a speech: "We love and esteem our father, the minister; he lives in great peace among us; he does no one any harm; he meddles not with state affairs. . . . We do not desire his removal, nor are we willing to part with him. . . . We therefore beg you will desist from any further attempts to drive him off" (Lothrop 1848: 235).

Kirkland and Guy Johnson had one thing in common: they both wanted to keep the Six Nations quiet and out of the Shawnee's war with the Virginians—what historians know as Lord Dunmore's, or Cresap's, War. The Six Nations never believed that white people would respect the 1768 boundary line that followed the Ohio River, separating settlers and Indians. Land speculators among the Virginia gentry had set their eyes on the whole valley, and common folk disregarded the treaty line. Violations became known as the Westward Movement. Policy made in Whitehall reached colonial governors, but folk on the frontier turned deaf ears to it.

As we have seen, the problem for the Iroquois Confederacy focused on their satellites: émigrés from the Six Nations settled in Ohio who identified with the Delawares and Shawnees, former dependents who had thrown off their skirts to regain the breechclout and warclub. A confederacy of Miamis and Central Algonquians loomed on the western horizon. New council fires with new sovereignties threatened Iroquois supremacy. By enlisting Kayashota, leader of the displaced Senecas, or Mingos, as "Ear to Onondaga" and ambassador for Sir William Johnson, the Longhouse and Johnson maintained communication and some control. At home, the perennial struggle between generations—the sachems and warriors—and between official statuses and informal roles would inspire the matrons to intervene. Moreover, the governors of Virginia and New England interpreted policy differently.

This was the situation that confronted Sir William at his final council with the Six Nations at Johnson Hall. His old friends among the sachems had remarked on his declining health and expressed to Sir William their concern both for him and for their own future unless he named a successor familiar with their affairs and not some stranger to their politics and customs. Guy Johnson felt he was the choice of both parties (Guy Johnson to Gage, 21 October 1774, Gage Papers, WLCL).

Oneidas returning in June from the spring hunt heard rumors of an Indian war to the south. White people near Fort Pitt had killed, among others, nine Senecas. If the report was true, and if the Senecas' kin sought revenge, dire consequences were forecast. The Oneidas expected two hundred Tuscaroras to remove from North Carolina within a year and settle nearby (Kirkland to Eliot, 13 June 1774; Kirkland journal 1774–75). They would considerably augment the sixth nation.

Meanwhile, at Johnson Hall the congress preliminaries began on 19 June when a large advance party of Onondagas came in to announce to Sir William that chiefs of all the confederated nations were traveling the path to his house to confer on the current state of Indian affairs. For nearly three weeks delegations kept coming in, until their numbers approached six hundred. The day before the congress opened on 9 July, one of the two prisoners jailed for the murder of Frenchmen on Lake Ontario died, and the chiefs asked for the release of the other prisoner to their custody. They had brought all the pelts taken in the robbery, and in view of their misfortune to the south, begged relief. Sir William, knowing it was good politics, acceded to their request.

Next day Conoghquieson, the second Oneida sachem, opened the congress by condoling the Senecas on the death of their kinsman the previous day. His choice as speaker preserved the moiety arrangement of the confederacy.

A Seneca chief named Serihowane, "Great Log" or "Lofty Tree" (also a Mohawk hereditary name, M-4, usually rendered "Big Tree"), then spoke first, addressing Sir William as Warraghiyageh (NYCD, 8: 474–84). He returned the invitation string and then, to demonstrate that his people kept their old engagements, displayed a chain belt that Johnson had given the Senecas at Niagara in 1764.

The onus was on the Seneca nation, because it was mainly its people who had defected to the Ohio and its branches whom Johnson had asked to have repatriated, and because its young men had committed the murders. The speaker blamed the Senecas' inability to accomplish the repatriation on traders who intercepted hunters with rum and goods in their hunting grounds instead of trading at established posts. Moreover, white people, disregarding the line established at the Stanwix treaty, encroached on Indian lands. Nevertheless, he promised on behalf of the chiefs and head women to keep the young men quiet until Kayashota returned from his mission.

The Six Nations, having considered the distressed situation of the Montauk Indians, bereft of their lands on Long Island, had agreed to place them at Cana-waroghere, an Oneida village, annexing another entity to that nation.

Having listened to a Cayuga war chief complain about traders bringing liquor into the Indians' villages, Johnson made his formal reply two days later, on 11 July. Addressing the Six Nations as siblings, he followed the sequence of the previous speaker, as was customary, speaking to each head. He remarked on the tenderness of the English government in restoring the surviving prisoner. It pleased him to see the great belt he had presented at Niagara preserved, and he hoped the Senecas would fulfill its symbolism. Regulation of the trade, he said, had been turned over to the colonies, who needed time to work it out. The deplorable encroachments on the frontier mainly affected the Six Nations' southern dependents, although lack of a unified colonial policy was the root cause. Nevertheless, chiefs of the tribes in Ohio should be held responsible for mischief done by Indians. Johnson approved of his deputy Croghan's role in mediating these conflicts, as well as Kayashota's efforts. He would use his good offices to relieve the Cayugas of trader abuses. A single belt sufficed.

The people of Canajoharie lodged a complaint against "that old Disturber of our Village *George Klock*," delivery of which they entrusted to Tekarihoken, their resident headman and leading Mohawk sachem. In presenting the Mohawk case, the eminent sachem invoked the sanction of the entire confederacy, confident it would back him in convincing the English authorities of native rights. Johnson, in his final act, asserted that the Mohawks need not have involved the confederacy, it not being the other members' business, but he urged patience, for "Klock's conduct was disagreeable to the King" (NYCD, 8: 478–79).

Having ordered pipes and tobacco and liquor for the Indians, Sir William, visibly worn out by chronic illness and public affairs, retired and within two hours died. The falling of the great man threw the Indians into confusion. They assembled immediately to inquire of Colonel Guy Johnson whether the king had granted their earlier request to empower him to take up their affairs. They hoped he would take over until the matter was settled. When they proposed sending runners with alarm belts throughout the confederacy, announcing that the great tree had fallen, Guy persuaded them to retire to their encampments until he could respond next day.

Guy Johnson's efforts to convince General Gage and the ministers in Whitehall of Sir William's intentions and the Indians' expectations that he accede to Sir William's post comprise an abundant record for the ethnohistorian of how Iroquois condolence protocol shaped a colonial appointment.[1]

On 12 July, Guy Johnson assembled the chiefs. Although a mourner, he spoke first, explaining that according to their custom he properly should have declined to address them until after the condolence ceremony, had they not stated their intent to send messengers throughout the nations proclaiming the sad news. (The

---

1. Gage Papers, American Series, William L. Clements Library, University of Michigan; Haldimand Papers, British Museum; Kirkland Papers, Hamilton College Library; NYCD, 8: 518–24; PAC, Indian Records, Ottawa.

approaching runner shouts the death cry—*ko::weh!*—repetitively. It is an alarming sound.) They should be reassured that Sir William had endorsed their desire to the consideration of the king. Meanwhile, they could send word through the nations that the fire still burned and the road was open to Johnson Hall. He asked for their support until the matter was decided. The chiefs returned thanks and agreed to send such a belt. They would plan a proper condolence after Sir William's burial. They asked permission to attend the funeral.

Unless one has experienced an Iroquois funeral, one cannot imagine their reverence for the dead and the importance they attach to proper ceremonies. In short, they cherish the dead and attain their best in ritual. Out of both affection for Sir William and their desire to witness an Anglican service, they wanted to be part of it. The procession following the bearers extended from Johnson Hall into Johnstown to the church that Sir William had erected, where his remains were deposited in the family vault. Some two thousand people from the countryside attended, including the Indians, "who all behaved with the greatest decorum and exhibited the most lively marks of real sorrow." The funeral must have been the spectacle of the decade. Back at Johnson Hall, the Indians informed Guy Johnson that they would perform the condolence ceremony next morning, 14 July.

The chiefs were ready early. Now was the opportunity for colonial officials to witness the climax form of Iroquois ritual. (Edmund B. O'Callaghan, editor of *Documents Relative to the Colonial History of the State of New York*, was at pains to identify these dignitaries, but not the native participants.) Because Warraghiyageh was an adopted Mohawk, of the senior moiety of the confederacy, conducting the ceremony rested with the junior moiety, from which the chiefs chose Conoghquieson as speaker. One can infer from Guy Johnson's abstract only the ritual content: three words (with three strings); covering the body (double belt); covering the grave (belt of six rows); and remarks to the mourner: relief that the fires would continue to burn at Johnson Hall and at Onondaga (belt of seven rows). With a second belt of similar dimensions, the speaker swept the fireplace clean. A bunch of strings requested that Guy attend when their ceremonies were performed and advise the young men in the manner of Sir William.

Knowing that the mourner was loaded with grief, they metaphorically cleansed his body and washed his insides with clear water, that he might again tend to business. Both sides were obscured by clouds, which the speaker dispelled, after which he restored the sun to its proper course (two strings).

Finally, toward reaffirmation, he added that since it pleased the "Great Spirit to take from us our Great Brother *Warraghijagey*, who long desired at our Request to put you in his place, we . . . rejoice to find you ready to take this charge . . . without which we should be in Darkness, and great confusion." A belt of six rows urged Guy to assume responsibility and follow in his master's footsteps. Clearly, Guy Johnson was the choice of the chiefs (NYCD, 8: 481).

Then Tyerhansera, a Mohawk chief, spoke of the troubles to the south that had consumed Sir William at his death. He blamed the white rum traders for preventing the repatriation of his people. He urged Guy to stand firm.

Conoghquieson now stood, holding a large black-and-white belt. He spoke this time on behalf of the whole confederacy and its dependents. They exhorted Guy to assume charge of their affairs in the manner of the great man who preceded him. (One does not mention the dead by name.) They commended their words to the king, hoping he would grant their wishes. (This was by way of a charge to the one newly raised up in the place of the dead.) Thereupon, they withdrew to await Guy's reply.

In a measure of urgency, Guy Johnson that same afternoon acknowledged the condolence ceremonies occasioned by the death of the late superintendent. He could now raise his head and go about official business. He would tend the fire that they had rekindled. In reply to Tyerhansera, he would address their grievances but urged greater effort toward repatriation and cooperation with Kayashota. This would beef up the confederacy. The dependents merited a special word concerning their grievances and encouragement to assure their integration in the chain. "And I desire that these my words, may go to the *setting Sun*" (a belt).

He treated the chiefs with the usual pipes and tobacco, a custom that General Gage would deplore.

By way of "shoving off the canoes," Colonel Johnson gathered his guests on 15 July to convey his pleasure at their unanimity and their promise to check their dependents, "who run about like drunken men." In turn, he would seek some relief from their grievances, communicate their good intentions toward the Montauks, and speak to the governor about George Klock. The Indians returned thanks for his speech and shook hands.

Before they departed next day, Colonel Johnson had a special word with Old Smoke about the dangers facing the Senecas in Ohio. The chiefs had agreed to send delegates from each nation with belts and messages designed to support Kayashota's mission, and they sent him some private instructions on how to frustrate the Shawnees by diverting other tribes from joining the Shawnee plot (Johnson to Gage, 26 July 1774, Gage Papers, WLCL). Thus the sanction of the confederacy was to be visited on the Shawnees. Johnson made a handsome present to the chiefs, particularly to those who had apprehended murderers.

One should note that Guy Johnson signed this report, which became the first step in his campaign for confirmation (NYCD, 8: 474-84). From the Iroquois viewpoint, he had been properly condoled and raised up in office. They had yet to decide on a new name for him.

□□◇□□

Although opponents politically, Guy Johnson and Kirkland in common wanted to keep the Six Nations quiet and out of the Shawnee war with the Virginians. The word of Sir William's death threw Kirkland's Oneidas into confusion, just when they were erecting the steeple on the mission church. Kirkland did his best to reassure his congregation. And Guy Johnson did prevail on the assembled chiefs not to send out belts spreading the disturbing news that "the great tree had fallen" until he could get himself confirmed and installed. Both men attributed the success in keeping the young men quiet in their beds to "the Head Women of the Confederacy." These combined maneuvers produced a nearly complete record of the Condolence Council for mourning and installing new chiefs. And they afford a glimpse at the proceedings of the grand council at Onondaga.

Joseph Brant, having sat in the grand council at Onondaga as Guy Johnson's ear, later reported that the program for opening the council featured a recitation of the ancient laws of the league, but he did not favor us with any details. Afterward,

Kirkland listened for more than five hours to the report of Oneida delegates returning from Onondaga but protested that he was too tired to write it all down. Here was the plot of a great historical drama without most of the lines. Given the outline of events, Indians and a few colonials of the eighteenth century could supply the missing parts.

Guy Johnson was still without a warrant to act officially, which might trouble the some two hundred Indians expected daily for the formal Condolence Council (Johnson to Gage, 8 September 1774, Gage Papers, WLCL). Word that His Majesty had commanded that he "do for the present" had not yet reached him (Dartmouth to Johnson, 8 September 1774, NYCD, 8: 489).

In September the chiefs returned to Johnson Hall to formally condole Sir William's passing and to invest Colonel Guy Johnson as superintendent with a new name. Bunt, as headman at Onondaga, with Tagawarunte as his speaker and with head warrior Diaquande, in company with Old Smoke, headman of the eastern Senecas, and others not specified, met privately with Guy Johnson to convey their sympathy and concern that they were not present when Sir William died. Bunt recalled the many times that Sir William had befriended and trusted him, and he assured Guy of his confidence. The head warrior, a long-time friend, reiterated Sir William's confidence that of his two deputies he expected Guy to succeed him, and he recalled the instruction to go among his people and keep them from turning their heads elsewhere. Colonel Johnson regarded this renewal of friendship and confidence a "mark of a good mind."

The Onondaga speaker addressed Colonel Johnson as "Brother Gorah" ("Great One").[2] He returned thanks to the Creator for enabling the chiefs and warriors to be present there to see him, hoping that the dark cloud occasioned by their great loss would soon be dispelled. Those who did not attend the previous congress would continue grieving until the condolence ceremony passed. Then with three strings he performed the ceremony, covering the grave, wiping away the tears, relieving the heart of grief, clearing the sky, and restoring the sun, in the manner of the clearminded.

As mourner, Colonel Johnson was obliged to thank the speaker, return the words of condolence, and send the three strings back over the fire.

It was the custom on the death of a friend to recapitulate favors received and return gifts of the deceased to his heir. Accordingly, Bunt's eldest son recited such acts and returned the presents—sword, laced hat, medals, and so forth—that Sir William had given him. Others followed. Conforming to past usage, Colonel Johnson in turn thanked them, hung the medals about their necks, and restored the gifts to each of them, requesting that they preserve them as mementos of past friendship. In doing so he confirmed his status in the relationship and assumed a reciprocal obligation.

The chiefs asked to defer the main business until chiefs of unrepresented nations arrived. It amounted to a rule of the confederacy that important issues required the token presence of all the Five Nations. On Monday morning, Serihowanenh

---

2. From *gorah* derives modern Seneca *gowek*, the term for Indian agent. Compare Chafe 1967: 66, no. 1032.

(Big Tree) of Seneca and Atrawana of Cayuga joined the Onondagas and others already present, for a total of some 235 persons.

Further sentiments of condolence, memories of Sir William's acts of generosity, and congratulations dominated the proceedings of the two-day congress held at Johnstown on 11–12 September. Perhaps celebration of ritual acts counted more than substance in assuring loyalty. Some of the chiefs in attendance had not been present at Sir William's demise. They now made up for that concern in tributes to the great man, recitations, and the return of medals and gifts once bestowed. They expressed great satisfaction in Guy's capacity to serve them. One speaker summed it up: "He trusted and expected that you would succeed him."

In a more formal setting the following morning, the Onondaga speaker invoked a codicil of condolence law: mourners may not conduct public business. This meant that some chiefs present could not participate in council until a ceremony of condolence was performed. Repetition of the proceedings was inevitable.

After thanking the Great Spirit for permitting the chiefs and warriors present to see their host that day, and after expressing hope that the dark cloud had been lifted from him, Tagawarunte said, "As some of the Principal men now present did not attend the Last Congress they must continue in Grief until the ceremony of Condolence is Performed when they will be enabled to attend to Publick Affairs." Whereupon the speaker, with three strings, went through the ceremony of condolence, covering the grave, wiping away the tears, removing grief from the heart, and so forth. It was then up to Johnson to respond and return the presents of the deceased. Now the public business might begin (NYCD, 8: 496–506; Gage Papers, WLCL).

A second rule of council protocol required that participants have names consistent with their status. Indeed, "the first people of the Confederacy"—league chiefs, speaker, chief warrior, and sundry other headmen—had come to see that Guy Johnson was raised up and given a proper name.

While these dignitaries were condoling Guy Johnson on the lawn of Johnson Hall, Lieutenant Colonel John Caldwell, the British commandant at Niagara, reported that other Seneca chiefs had gone to meet the Shawnee deputies (and presumably escort them to Onondaga, if not to Johnson Hall). But, Caldwell added, the Shawnees were reported meanwhile to be in council, and the outcome was doubtful to those of his sources who should know (Caldwell to Gage, 11 September 1774, Gage Papers, WLCL).

According to intelligence that reached Johnson in the days of his inauguration, some tribes around the Great Lakes, on the advice of Kayashota, had rejected Shawnee belts inviting them to take up the hatchet. Evidently Croghan's maneuvers lay behind Kayashota's success (Wainwright 1959: 292). The same Shawnee council that Caldwell mentioned next decided to send three deputies to Onondaga to appeal to the Six Nations warriors, claiming the right of protection from their enemies. Johnson's emissaries reached the Shawnees first, however, and succeeded in checking those elements who were most inflamed by recent losses. The Shawnee deputies were told they could expect no aid from the Six Nations, who were about to hold a congress of the confederacy at Onondaga to advance pacific measures (Johnson to Dartmouth, 10 September 1774, NYCD, 8: 490).

Back at Johnson Hall, on Thursday, 15 September, all the councilors being seated, Tagawarunte of Onondaga, speaker for the Six Nations, stood and addressed his host as "Brother Aghscare." He held a belt given to the Six Nations by Sir William to bring the Shawnees, their "Younger Brothers," to council. Messengers carrying Colonel Johnson's belt announcing the death of Sir William had met the oncoming Shawnee delegates and returned with them to Onondaga. Tagawarunte quoted their speech. The Shawnees had addressed the Six Nations as "Elder Brothers." The Shawnee case rested on the premise that Virginia had struck both themselves and the Six Nations. The Six Nations did not agree, but announced a general congress to which the Shawnees could send deputies. The Shawnees wanted the matter kept from the superintendent, but a Seneca and a Cayuga chief were joined by others to the contrary.

The Onondaga speaker then held up the same belt of twenty-one rows symbolizing the covenant chain that Sir William had presented to the Six Nations in the presence of nine governments. The Six Nations had kept it free of rust, he said, and held fast to it. They remembered the words spoken when it was given, and they looked to it when anyone threatened to disturb the peace and harmony between the two parties to the agreement. The bad words of the Shawnees would have no effect on either party.

The speaker then held up a second belt of fourteen rows, also given by Sir William to keep in their minds their obligation to the covenant chain. They now delivered the belt to Colonel Johnson as evidence that they had followed Sir William's advice. A third belt of six rows expressed their satisfaction at the continued custody of their affairs by two men familiar with their customs, namely Colonel Johnson and Colonel Claus.

They were now prepared to raise up Colonel Guy Johnson in Sir William's place and hang a new name about his neck, in the manner of an Iroquois chief. This was a New World version of civil service. The Iroquois were assured that Colonel Guy was long familiar with their affairs and customs, and they expected him to walk in the footsteps of Sir William. The speaker concluded his charge by saying: "At this time Brother we speak to you Empty Handed, but we shall take a time to Raise you according to our antient Custom" (NYCD, 8: 490). A belt of six rows.

Having concluded the remarks of the Onondaga sachems and warriors with another belt of eight rows, and having assured Johnson with a belt of six rows that the Six Nations would adhere to the covenant chain, the speaker for the firekeepers sat down.

It was now up to the first nation of the senior moiety of the league to raise up Colonel Guy in the office of Sir William.

"Then *[Te]Carahoga* as Titular head of the Mohawks" arose and announced briefly that the Six Nations had met privately the night before and, according to ancient custom, had fixed on a new name for Colonel Johnson consistent with the office he was performing. "The Onondaga speaker then stood and repeated the same on behalf of the Confederacy." He proclaimed the name Uraghquadirha, "Rays of Sun Enlightening the Earth." Johnson stood while a chief of each nation repeated the name, after which each constituency shouted "Yo-hah!" in approval. The speaker directed "that the same might be proclaimed in Every nation of the Confederacy" (NYCD, 8: 496–506).

Efforts were under way on both sides to strengthen and regularize the confederacy. Guy Johnson and Joseph Brant were in the thick of it. Johnson wanted to make the best use of the upcoming congress at Onondaga. Before that, he had to return the belts presented to him and document them. Certain belts relating to old business, having lost their importance, could be dismembered. A prime consideration on both sides was to fill up seats in the grand council, inasmuch as several chiefs had died and others were too old to serve. The Oneida and Onondaga speakers announced new chiefs they had appointed and asked Johnson to charge them. In the words of the orator, "To shew our sincerity we of the Great Council and Fireplace at Onondaga Considering the great age of our Chief the Bunt, a true friend of the English, and that all our Late appointed chiefs may be known to you, [we] do now introduce them that you may be well acquainted with those to whom our Affairs are committed." None of those mentioned in the text has a recognizable league title, save Diaquande, whose name resembles the Oneida title Deyohagwendeh (Oe-3, RC 12) (Gage Papers, WLCL; NYCD, 8: 506).

To preserve the council fire, it was agreed that if an issue disturbed any member of the Iroquois Confederacy, its members would meet and toss it out. Unanimity fueled the fire.

Addressing their agent by his new name, the speaker introduced messengers sent by Kayashota to report that the Virginians had obstructed his mission but that the Delawares had sent four strings saying they would keep their young men home. Kayashota, however, added that but two Iroquois families among the Shawnees agreed to come home, and he despaired of persuading others. (Four strings.) The speaker presented a bunch of strings sent by Colonel McKee and Croghan at Fort Pitt in token of their efforts to assure peace on the Ohio.

The head warrior of Onondaga informed Johnson of a conversation with a Seneca chief who, returning from a previous meeting with the new agent, expressed pleasure at their private talk. He was prepared to cooperate for peace and sent a belt as proof.

The following day Johnson acknowledged the previous speeches and returned the great covenant chain belt, as well as a "Belt of 14 Rowes" given by Sir William on a memorable occasion to reinforce the covenant, not to mention other matters.

On the final day of the congress, 18 September, the chiefs put some further problems to Colonel Johnson. They posed one of little interest to historians but fascinating to an ethnologist because it documents how belts were unstrung and rewoven for new uses. The Oneida chiefs of Conawaroghere, having discovered among them a large black belt with two axes which they had received from the French at the close of the last war, worried that keeping it might threaten the tranquility of the confederacy. Their speaker, Thomas, a Christian, alias Adionghkonras, related that a former keeper appointed to watch the movements of the French maintained that when the French raised themselves, the belt would shake and notify him that he too was to rise. Evidently the belt bothered the keeper to the extent that on his deathbed he divulged the story to his brother, whose wife had the belt just then and wondered whether she might unstring it for the sake of the wampum. Otherwise he would have brought it to the congress. Johnson wanted to see it, and offered to compensate the woman. The Oneidas had some other wampum problems on which they requested assurance. They also had replaced a chief killed in the late war with an incumbent they hoped Johnson would accept, which he did.

The Onondaga chiefs, too, had replaced their head and several leaders whose names they submitted to Johnson for approval. Bunt, a true Anglophile and head of the grand council and fireplace at Onondaga, was now superannuated. And they had appointed others whom the speaker now introduced by name and put forward that Johnson might know to whom their affairs were committed. Onagogare would succeed Bunt and follow in his footsteps. I do not recognize any of those named in the minutes as holding a league title.

Joseph Chew, the newly appointed secretary of Indian affairs who wrote the minutes, lacking an Indian name, was awarded that of Decariaderoga, a variant of "Between the Lakes" (NYCD, 8: 501, 506.)

□□◇□□

The congress at Onondaga to consider the Shawnee request for aid was planned for the last week in September 1774. Invitations went to Canada, and Johnson expected the more influential chiefs to consult him en route. The Shawnees, who were affiliated with part of the Senecas, had reported that the Six Nations would aid them. Seneca influence might prove troublesome, but Johnson held that the majority of the Six Nations could be relied on not to take the part of the Shawnees. French traders south of the Great Lakes still had an ax to grind.

The satellite communities of Mingos (émigré Iroquois) in Ohio had been subject to alienation for some time. Guy Johnson, like his predecessor, urged bringing them home. Most recently, on hearing that their people had been killed, some eighty Ohio Senecas and warriors of a village southwest of Geneseo had joined the Shawnees, according to Onondaga intelligence, and the Shawnees were taking great pains to seduce more to follow their example. According to a Seneca chief, when a Shawnee messenger demanded of the Six Nations that they take up the hatchet against the Virginians, Bunt, "the King of the Six Nations," threw the belt back indignantly to the Shawnees (Caldwell to Gage, 29 September 1774, Gage Papers, WLCL; NYCD, 8: 507–9). Lieutenant Colonel Caldwell at Niagara was reasonably confident that the Shawnee position would be rejected at Onondaga. The Shawnee petitioners were playing the local autonomy of individual tribes off against the rather diffuse powers of the confederacy.

The purpose of the coming congress at Onondaga was to make the sanction against the Shawnees general. The sachems knew full well what they faced at Onondaga. They were in concert on the proper channels for reporting. Warriors should consult the sachems and follow their advice. Individual warriors should report to a war chief and he to a sachem, and act on his advice or orders. It was thought that this arrangement would prevent individuals from independently carrying out blood feuds. One wonders whether this was an Iroquois or a British plan. That it represented a recent improvement suggests the latter.

Guy Johnson was fairly confident as he and Joseph Brant planned the agenda. Johnson designed to consult all members of the confederacy so that their determination might be general. He wrote to Gage that he was seeing the "first people of the whole Confederacy," of whom many were Sir William's firm friends. Indeed, the British, who loved procedure as much as the Iroquois did, intended the make the confederacy work.

Late in September, while Guy Johnson was preparing for the congress at Onondaga, Kayashota arrived from Fort Pitt to report on affairs in that sector, condole the death of Sir William, and advise his host. After a long stay, he set out to return to the Ohio on 5 October, charged with a large belt addressed to the Mingos, Delawares, Miamis, and other well-disposed groups, urging them to work for tranquility and to keep their eyes fixed on the "Councils of the Confederacy" (Johnson to Gage, 6 October 1774, Gage Papers, WLCL; Johnson to Dartmouth, NYCD, 8: 494–95.) Old Kayashota, having barely avoided a Shawnee ambush, would find safety in the hills of the Allegheny country.

During the third week in October, the headmen of the confederacy were assembling at Onondaga for a congress that would last several weeks, after which Johnson expected the chiefs to come down to Johnson Hall in a body. (He preferred to feed just a few.) The Mohawk delegation, well instructed, set out on the twenty-third, and Johnson had his own men there to watch and influence the others.

Samuel Kirkland got home to Kanonwarohale from Boston just in time to hear reports of the grand council. He returned later than expected, but his people thought that he timed it well. He wrote in his journal on 24 October 1774:

> Their grand Congress at Onondage is now sitting, and the upper Nations are very jealous of the Onoides in such deliberations when I am upon the spot, lest I be too soon acquainted with the consultations.
>
> This is one of the most important meetings that the Six Nations have had for many years—and the consequences more extensive. I am informed that if the Six Nations agree to join and aid the Shawanese in their quarrel with the Virginians, six or eight of the western tribes stand ready to unite their strength. I have no apprehension that any of the Onoides will join the Shawanese. They appear more and more averse to meddling in the affair, notwithstanding repeated solicitations. (Pilkington 1980: 96–97)

Fortunately, we have two independent reports on what happened at Onondaga during the congress that opened on 21 October and lasted until 11 November. On one point they happily agree. The traditional system of politics and counsel of the founders was rehearsed and searched before the delegates took up the principal business. On this point Kirkland and Brant support each other; but they leave much to be desired as to just what the original rules and ceremonies were that the Onondaga firekeepers thought their forefathers had established when they first kindled the council fire. There is just enough to give historical depth to ceremonies that I witnessed at Six Nations on Grand River 175 years afterward (Fenton 1946; 1950).

It took some time for a grand council of the confederacy to assemble, and even longer for it to reach consensus. The Cayuga and Seneca delegations attended reluctantly and only after several urgent messages. Having waited for them to arrive, the congress got down to business on 5 November. A party of Seneca junior chiefs whose fathers were at Onondaga engaged in affairs of state came down to visit Guy Johnson. Johnson manifested concern that the Indians, who were at home with factions, should not hear of factions within "our government," implying that some weak persons had been spreading tales (Gage Papers, WLCL). Kirkland at Oneida, however, was closer to the source, and on the twelfth had some real intelligence from a Cayuga chief who had come over from Onondaga out of curiosity to see the new Oneida church. He told Kirkland "that things were like to have a favorable issue. . . . The Six Nations and their Confederates utterly decline granting any assistance to the Shawanese in their quarrel with the Virginians."

People started drifting back from the Onondaga council on the fifteenth. Presumably they were on the way down to see Johnson, but Kirkland had the news two weeks beforehand. We can be grateful for his journal, but we might wish he had written more:

> Next day Two of their Sachems came in to acquaint me with the result of their Grand Council at Onondage, which has sat for a month past. Delegates from each tribe of the six united Nations and from the northern confederates upon the St. Lawrence, which consist of seven small tribes. They inform [me] that after several messages to the Senekas and Cayugweas they gave their attendance. The council was opened, their traditionary system of politics and counsel rehearsed. The petition and demands of the Shawanese brought upon the Carpet. Finally concluded that they were under no obligation to join the Shawanese in their quarrel with Virginia, and determined it was bad policy to meddle in this affair, otherwise than advise the Shawanese to an immediate reconciliation with Virginia. They very severely censured the Cayugue nation, as regards of the general good, in allowing a small party of their tribe to set out for the southward for aiding the Shawanese before the minds of the body confederate were known in general council.

Kirkland added:

> The rehearsal of their deliberations and transactions were nigh five hours in length. I am only sorry I had not leisure at the time to commit their relation to paper. They exhibited . . . strength of will, penetration, good policy, and some degree of benevolence in their deliberations, particularly the governesses or she-Sachems in their address to the Sachems and warriors. (Pilkington 1980: 97–98)

We, too, are sorry that Kirkland ran out of time and energy; but the Six Nations' act of censuring the Cayugas for sending out a war party before the general council could meet and deliberate, and the decisive role of the matrons in this sanction, occupy a unique niche in Iroquois political history.

The outcome so pleased Kirkland that he wrote to his wife, Jerusha, describing how he preached to nine Seneca and Onondaga sachems who called to hear about Christianity. Other concerns occupied Guy Johnson, who had the news two days later. Public ignorance of the power of the Six Nations, who could still muster 2,100 warriors and who numbered some 10,500 people, lay behind the present troubles on the frontier. Up to now they had been managed for the most part as friends. "The Frontier People never consider this" (Johnson to Gage, 24 November 1774, Gage Papers, WLCL).

Although Guy Johnson already knew the results, nothing short of required protocol would satisfy the aged chiefs, who came down in the dead of winter to report and deplete the larder at Guy Park before going on the winter hunt. They numbered sixteen principal men and ninety others. Johnson already had Brant's written report, and he knew pretty much what the chiefs were going to say. His agents had overcome the jealousies of the Cayuga and Seneca delegates, the Shawnees were rebuffed, and once more the Iroquois Confederacy had translated its prestige into action to dispel the tension on the southern frontier.

Following three words of condolence by Abraham, the resident Mohawk speaker, which the Onondaga speaker, Tagawarunte, returned so as to open the way for business, the Onondaga orator promised to reiterate his opening address to the grand council. He could do this with some assurance, he said, inasmuch as Joseph Thayendanegea (Brant), by Johnson's authority, "took down in Writing what passed." Confident that Brant did this exactly, the report could be brief.

But Iroquois speakers and their audiences are never satisfied with less than the full text. The proceedings say that five days later, while waiting for the upper Seneca delegates to arrive, Tagawarunte addressed the Six Nations confederacy just as he had at Onondaga.

> We are all assembled this day at this our Council Fire, which our Fore Fathers unanimously Established as the Grand council Fire, and where they have made Rules and settled all things in a proper manner. (Here he Repeated all the original Rules & Ceremonies and their different Treaties and Alliances. . . .) We the Onondagas who keep the great Fire, Remember almost Every thing that our Fathers did, and agreed upon, and we resolve to follow their advice.

He ended with an allegory: "Our Fathers meant when they said, if anything should happen after we have made Every thing good, or if a *Bad Creature* or Snake should *Come near the fire*, we are to join all hands to take a stick and throw the snake away."

Tagawarunte having laid down the Shawnee belt and five scalps, which the confederacy tossed aside in the manner prescribed, Tekarihoken of Canajoharie arose on behalf of the Mohawk, Oneida, and Tuscarora sachems to declare their unanimous decision to uphold the peace. A Cayuga chief affirmed with a large belt.

When the Seneca sachems proved reluctant, the firekeepers had sent them a great belt of union, one that Sir William had given them before 1755 and that had always lain at the central fire, to prop up the western door of the Longhouse. It was a belt of thirty rows, five feet long, containing a figure in black wampum. Its original purpose had been to repatriate the Ohio Senecas. A Genesee Seneca speaker acknowledged that the door was now repaired. Putting hand to belt affirmed a deed. The Senecas gave a large black belt in return for that of the confederates.

Having reached unanimity on the matter before them, according to order in council, the Mohawk speaker recommended their agreement to the Onondaga firekeepers, "who in a manner are head of it all," keep the council fire, and attend to the welfare of the whole confederacy. He reminded the Cayuga and Seneca delegates that it was a long-established custom for the warriors to seek the advice of the sachems and never to be the aggressors, a rule much honored in the breach. The speaker assured Johnson that belts he returned would be carefully put up overhead at Onondaga with other important belts.

□□◇□□

The dark clouds that hovered over Onondaga that fall were dispelled by the deliberative procedures of the grand council as sanctioned by the Great Law. Both Guy Johnson and the sachems made sure that the procedures went into operation by laying the groundwork in a series of tactical maneuvers that involved the principal segments of Iroquois society. Seneca war chief Kayashota, leader of the émigré Mingos in Ohio, abetted by George Croghan, Johnson's deputy at Pittsburgh, embodied the prestige of the grand council and the power of Iroquois war parties in carrying out diplomatic missions to the Shawnees and their confederates. He managed to lure Shawnee delegates to the council fire at Onondaga and submit them to the rigors of Iroquois council protocol. We know how this worked thanks to Joseph Brant, who, as eyes and ears for Guy Johnson, kept the minutes, and to Samuel Kirkland's journals. In an act rarely reported in the literature, the clan matrons exercised their right to raise and recall war parties by censoring those Cayuga and Seneca zealots who had taken up the Shawnee hatchet before the grand council met to hear the Shawnees plead for aid and come to one mind on the issue of war or peace. Kirkland, by then the accepted source at Oneida on Revolutionary thought in Boston, manifested a deep concern for the outcome of the grand council deliberations, listened to returning participants, and recorded just enough detail for the ethnohistorian to appreciate the historical depth of Iroquois traditional polity as we know it from nineteenth- and twentieth-century studies.

CHAPTER 37

THE STRUGGLE
FOR NEUTRALITY

The dark clouds over Onondaga were no sooner dispelled than another storm loomed on the southwest horizon. Intelligence brought to Onondaga so alarmed the Six Nations that they sent a delegation of sachems back to Guy Park in the depths of winter. Some of the sachems were old men who traveled slowly, for snow covered the roads, so they sent a messenger ahead to alert Colonel Johnson to expect them in a day or so. White people were stirring up trouble among the satellites and alienating their affection from the crown. The want of a unified Indian policy among the colonies intensified Johnson's problem of communicating through channels to London. Lord Dunmore's War, in the interest of Virginia land speculators, was a prime example.

Protocol took precedence over urgency. The deaths of some Oneida and Cayuga chiefs had to be condoled before the council could open. Teyoharisera, the Mohawk head chief, spoke the Three Bare Words of Requickening, and an Oneida speaker passed the three strings back over the fire, clearing the way for the confederacy's speaker to relate their mission.

Their erstwhile satellites had lost the battle of Kanawha to the Virginians. The Shawnee messenger who brought the news was the sole survivor of his village; three Senecas of Ohio were among the thirty casualties. Lord Dunmore, governor of Virginia, had put some Mingo petitioners in irons and packed them off to Williamsburg. The Shawnees requested that the Six Nations remove their ancient fire from Onondaga to Fort Pitt, nearer the crisis zone, but the sachems of the confederacy held that Onondaga was the proper place. So did Guy Johnson, who advised them to have no part in the quarrel and avoid the snare. Teyoharisera, appointed by the whole to reply to Johnson, affirmed that there never had been an occasion to change the fireplace or meet a satellite anywhere other than at Onondaga or at their superintendent's residence. They had rejected the Shawnee request and instructed two Shawnee chiefs to bring their people to Onondaga. But the Shawnees twice had refused to heed a summons to the great council fire. The Six Nations asked Johnson to write to the governor of Virginia and ask him to send representatives to a meeting where the Six Nations would state their policy of neutrality in such disputes.

The problem of the satellites, both for the old men at Onondaga and for Johnson, arose from the fact that since 1768 the center of political gravity had shifted from Onondaga to the forks of the Ohio, where the eyes of the Senecas and

Cayugas focused. The western door of the confederacy had sprung its hinges; the Longhouse was being pulled apart. At its eastern end, Mohawk primacy in the league faded into memory as the Mohawks' lands slipped away and their village sites were preempted, forcing them to consider taking refuge among the Oneidas. Oneida and Cayuga, the junior moiety of the confederacy, were at odds. Both Sir William and Guy Johnson, as we have seen, sought to strengthen the confederacy by repatriating émigrés from Ohio and consolidating settlements. Both efforts failed. Managing Indian affairs remote from the Mohawk Valley became increasingly difficult.

But Johnson perceived a more immediate problem at home. He regarded the missionary Kirkland as a subversive. Kirkland had been on the ground longer, he was in daily contact with Oneida villagers, he spoke the local language, and his congregation numbered a substantial following. Situated halfway to Onondaga, he received news of the grand council several days to a week before runners went on to Guy Park. Councilors frequently asked him to interpret written documents, including letters and abstracts of proceedings of the Continental Congress. Johnson viewed these services with alarm.

When, in mid-January 1775, Johnson began hearing country reports of Kirkland's activities of the sort that he ordinarily discounted, he informed Gage that he would try to authenticate them (Gage Papers 125, WLCL). He listened carefully a few days later as Conoghquieson, speaking on behalf of the Oneida delegation to a congress of the Six Nations, recited a litany of complaints against the missionary. The Oneida sachem alleged that Kirkland (unlike previous Jesuit missionaries) had refused to baptize children of parents who were not his communicants; he gathered news and related activities of the white people; he operated a store; and he meddled in public affairs. He said the Oneidas wanted Kirkland removed. Evidently this sachem did not reside at Kanonwalohale, where Kirkland was stationed, but in a distant village, so that much of his testimony was hearsay. An Onondaga speaker next alleged that Kirkland intercepted messages and advised his constituents not to forward any news that might prove disagreeable but to burn it. Johnson, although he deferred to clergy, manifested respect for the testimony and cautioned his Oneida source in the future not to encourage unauthorized persons to meddle in public affairs. He added that he had ordered a literate native in His Majesty's service to keep him informed and had supplied him with writing materials for that purpose.

Conoghquieson further alleged that Kirkland was the source of Boston stories about how the New England people had surveyed all of the Indian country and taken a census of each nation, with a view to possessing arable flats. On a recent return from Boston, Kirkland had brought bad news: the king wanted to recover colonial expenditures with the Stamp Act, which had precipitated the Boston Tea Party. From now on, powder and Indian goods would become scarce and expensive.

With a belt of six rows, Guy Johnson conveyed hope of dispelling the fears of the Six Nations over the consequences of the Boston Tea Party by assuring them that General Gage's grasp of the affair and His Majesty's friendship gave them nothing to fear and much to hope. Both Johnson and the sachems surely knew that hope without gunpowder would not put meat in their corn soup (Gage Papers, 126: 1–23, WLCL).

Discontent ran like an infection through the confederacy. The Seneca warriors, still half the manpower of the confederacy, were idle but well armed and concentrated at Niagara in numbers exceeding those of any other time. They had reason to be unhappy, for seven of them were taken hostage and put in irons at Fort Pitt. It was feared that the long peace would be the ruin of their nation, for the warriors, without exercise, were losing their manhood—their youths would become women (Caldwell to Gage, Johnson to Gage, Gage Papers 126, WLCL).

Although Mohegan survivors from New England were on their way to Oneida, where the Six Nations had offered them asylum and in return would gain some manpower, the Oneida sachems were about to split with their Cayuga kindred of the junior moiety, weakening the confederacy further.

Matters between Johnson and Kirkland came to a head in mid-February, when Johnson wrote Kirkland an arrogant letter asking him, administratively, what the hell was going on? It seems that Kirkland, in going down country and in returning from Boston and Stockbridge (where his wife and children had taken refuge when the Shawnee crisis threatened), had passed Guy Park without calling, not yet knowing that Johnson had been confirmed as superintendent, but had stopped to visit with Daniel Claus, an old friend who had learned Mohawk and also served as Sir William's deputy. Guy felt slighted. He repeated the allegations, implying that Kirkland was obstructing His Majesty's service. The Oneida council, however, took it upon themselves to clear Kirkland and then called him into public council to hear the message they had sent, apparently independently, to Johnson.

> We esteem the office of Superintendent and love our minister of the Gospel. Such reports that our Minister has wrote things abroad to our disadvantage, and that he meddles with political affairs, and is charged with many thing of this nature . . . we Indians think to be . . . utterly false. The labors of our Minister are wholly confined to religious instructions. . . . We do not know that he ever meddles with or opposes civil Government, but labors faithfully to discharge his ministerial function.[1]

In a letter to Johnson dictated by seven Oneida chiefs, translated and written down by Kirkland, the chiefs went on to ask for clarification and rectification of differences in a face-to-face meeting conducted in a civil fashion without any "hard speeches" from either side (Pilkington 1980: 110–11). The whole affair was very disturbing to the Indians, who thought the fault lay with the white people. In the same letter, Kirkland noted that no Indians except a man called Kanahgwaes had ever charged their minister with such crimes, and Kanahgwaes, in a belated visit to the Oneida fireplace, had appeared before the council and admitted that Joseph Brant, with whom he had talked in the bushes, had coached him in how to appeal to Johnson's prejudices. (None of the seven chiefs of the town council bore a name resembling a title of the original nine Oneida founders of the league. Since these titles later emerged, one wonders who held them.)

To the Indians, this controversy was a dispute between siblings, and they wanted no part of it. And they regarded the growing quarrel between colonists and king as an argument between parent and offspring, not their affair. Although neither

---

1. Johnson's and Kirkland's letters appear in Pilkington 1980: 105–10. See also Graymont 1972: 56–58.

party would leave them alone, they intended to remain neutral. The Oneidas stated their policy to Governor Trumbull of Connecticut: "We are unwilling to join on either side of such a contest, for we love you both—old England and new. Should the great King of England apply to us for our aid—we shall deny him—and should the Colonies apply—we shall refuse" (Kirkland Papers, in Graymont 1972: 58).

As we shall see presently, neutrality was fine policy but a vain hope. Oneida relations with the New Englanders were too close to avoid getting involved. Even Eleazer Wheelock, the pious founder of Dartmouth College who had educated Indians of the Six Nations both at his charity school in Connecticut and at Hanover, New Hampshire, sought to attach them to the patriot cause. Sons of the Caughnawaga and Akwesasneh Mohawks on the St. Lawrence had often been represented among the students at Hanover. To renew the friendship of the Laurentian Mohawks, Wheelock sent James Dean, a young white man who had grown up from age nine speaking Oneida as a native, without trace of accent, as a recruiter to Caughnawaga near Montreal, where alumni of the missionary school resided. Dean, who was undoubtedly bilingual in Iroquoian, would encounter little trouble converting the Oneida *l* to the Mohawk *r*; he had some previous experience, having interpreted for the missionaries at Onohquageh.

Dean, who was apparently very bright, set out with boyish enthusiasm to recruit students for the college and for the New England cause. Wheelock thought that should occasion arise, Dean "should be properly authorized for . . . he could influence all those *Six Nations* to join these Colonies against any invasion . . . attempted against them." Dean found the Caughnawaga council strong for neutrality and ready to banish any young warriors who took up the hatchet against the Americans. Only when the Canadian governor, Guy Carleton, threatened to confiscate their lands if they did not support the British did they tell the governor that they would defend him if Montreal were besieged, but they would not send warriors to defend the frontier posts. Dean, knowing how Indians did change their minds, warned his American friends to provide for the worst. His influence at Oneida became crucial in later years (after Graymont 1972: 59–60; Schuyler Papers, box 13, NYPL; APSL film 1101; DCB, 5: 141–55).

From the center of rebellion in Boston, General Gage warned Guy Johnson against the influence of New England men on affairs to the south and west. The missionaries were their agents. Gage instructed Johnson to encourage the Indians to turn these troublesome people out, and he suggested seeking a temporary missionary from among the Anglican clergy of Albany who were good royalists (Gage Papers, WLCL).

Johnson was not particularly encouraged. It was not going to be easy to get rid of Kirkland without splitting the Oneida community down the middle. Clearcut evidence that Kirkland was engaged in Revolutionary activities was not forthcoming. The last party of Oneidas who had spoken in Kirkland's favor were his own "Deacons," and they were just as impartial as the chiefs who were against him. Kirkland himself went to see Johnson to clear up the charges. He told Johnson that his Oneida friends reported Johnson's speaking of him "in a manner as devoid of Truth as probability." Kirkland admitted having "at their request explained passages out of the Prints" to the Oneidas, which act related to his own interpretation of events flowing from the Stamp Act (Gage Papers 126, WLCL).

In this controversy Gage and Johnson had one thing going for them. As Gage perceptively reminded Johnson, the crown had always stood behind the Indians in land disputes, while the colonists had consistently violated royal proclamations, transgressed dividing lines, and sought by every means to displace Indians and possess their lands. The Mohawks were particularly vulnerable to this argument because they had been victimized by their white neighbors and were virtually landless. Gage thought that in a choice between land-hungry Yorkers and their friend, they would chose the king (Gage Papers 125, WLCL; Nammack 1969; Graymont 1972: 61).

□□◇□□

By the spring of 1775, missionary work at Oneida had become untenable. The community segmented into factions. Johnson, now of a mind with Gage, prepared to oust Kirkland. He invited John Stuart, the Anglican missionary to the Mohawks, to extend his ministry to Oneida. Stuart had acquired a working knowledge of Mohawk and could probably cope with Oneida. Indians respected him, so did white settlers, and he was loyal to the king. Kirkland admired Stuart, but he protested to Johnson, refusing "to accept the meddling of the missionary from Fort Hunter," and Stuart had no stomach for a church quarrel. Kirkland alleged to Johnson that his life was threatened by a speech of Johnson's and departed with his grievances for Boston. He would not return without Johnson's protection (Johnson to Gage, Gage Papers 127, WLCL).

Other than with Gage, Kirkland's Boston connections were solid. In late March, when tension was mounting, Kirkland wrote to Andrew Eliot of the Boston missionary committee, to whom he reported that it was urgent to secure the friendship of the Indians in the upcoming crisis. The proper way to do it was to get the Continental Congress to send a formal speech to the Six Nations. But Kirkland wanted his name kept silent, lest word get back to Oneida and put his life in danger. Eliot agreed to communicate this proposal to Congress without revealing its author, while urging Kirkland to stress to the Indians that engaging against the colonies would bring utter ruin upon themselves (Kirkland Papers; Graymont 1972: 60).

It would be late summer before Congress took up Eliot's proposal. Meanwhile, news reached the Indians of a battle between British regulars and some Bostonians (Ayer ms. 7, NL). Details were scant, for the informants were young men. Guy Johnson, in mortal fear of being captured by "Bostonians," was being watched over by Mohawks, and three Mohawk principals, with Joseph Brant as interpreter, went to Oneida seeking help (Force 1837-53, ser. 4, 2: 665). Johnson had already moved against the missionaries. In May, as Kirkland returned from Boston, Johnson ordered him held under house arrest, preventing his return to Oneida. Kirkland, though treated politely, got no rest during the "noise and confusion" over an alarm that the Yankees were coming to take Colonel Johnson captive.

The magistrates and committees of Albany and Schenectady were equally apprehensive. Little Abraham of Fort Hunter, son of the Mohawk sachem Abraham, addressed them on 20 May on behalf of the loyal Mohawk council, saying that the Mohawks would support their superintendent and not see their council fire extinguished. The whole confederacy would resent it if that happened. The Mohawks were deeply disturbed by troop movements, Little Abraham said.

They feared the innocent might fall with the guilty. They were so desirous of maintaining the peace that they were unwilling that the Six Nations should know the bad reports already spread among them. Let the white people settle their own quarrels. Kirkland interpreted (Ayer ms. 6, NL).

Within a fortnight, twelve Oneida sachems signed a declaration of neutrality, a first on the American continent, written by Jacob Reed, a pupil of Kirkland's, and dated at Kanonwalohale, (2) June 1775. It was addressed to the people of New England, and a delegation of the nation carried copies to Hartford, Providence, and other eastern towns. This and other documents in the Kirkland Papers show how, for a time, the Oneidas carried the rest of the confederacy on a policy of neutrality. It read: "Not only we of the Onoida nation, But other nations with whom we are connected . . . desire . . . to be nutrail." They would exert their utmost efforts to keep their brethren of the Six Nations, and other nations further back, from disturbing the New Englanders in these difficult times.

Just when is not certain, but the Oneida sachems, hearing that Kirkland had abstracts of the proceedings of the Continental Congress, insisted on knowing the contents. Kirkland later told the Albany committee of the New York Provincial Congress that he could not deny reading the abstracts to them, notwithstanding his cloth, although otherwise he had been extremely cautious not to meddle in political affairs. Word soon reached Johnson. Nevertheless, Kirkland thought in retrospect that his reading of the doings of Congress to a group of sachems was worth more than five hundred pounds in presents (Force 1837–53, ser. 4, 2: 1310).

The Continental Congress had not been idle. Sensing the importance of the Indians in the upcoming struggle, in June it created an Indian Committee, which within a month recommended creating three Indian departments, including one for the northern district, for which it appointed four commissioners: General Philip Schuyler, Major Joseph Hawley, Colonel Turbot Francis, and Oliver Wolcott (JCC, 2: 174, 176–83). The committee followed the advice of Samuel Kirkland, who came down to Philadelphia and spent a week testifying before Congress and instructing the Indian Committee how to draft a proper speech to the Six Nations that adhered to expected protocol and employed the customary symbolism of forest diplomacy. It would enable the commissioners to invoke the tree and the chain and refer to Onondaga as the central fire and seat of the council house of the confederacy—the time-honored metaphors that got results in treaty negotiations. All of this would be ratified with wampum belts in dimension and design commensurate with the topic, on which Kirkland left instructions (Schuyler Papers, box 13, NYPL; NYCD, 8). The Congress resolved that Kirkland be allowed three hundred dollars to cover his traveling expenses and further to secure the friendship of the Six Nations and sustain their policy of neutrality. For the next five years Kirkland would serve the Continental Congress as agent and interpreter and as chaplain to the Continental Army.

Before Kirkland went to Philadelphia, Johnson, who had been planning a congress of the Six Nations above German Flats, suddenly, on the last day of May, left Guy Park for good with a retinue of 90 Mohawks, 120 whites, and his staff, including Daniel Claus and John Butler, bound for Fort Ontario via Fort Stanwix. Johnson feared capture by the Tryon County patriots. A party of Oneidas, Tuscaroras, and Senecas greeted him at Fort Stanwix. He offered them presents to come along to the meeting at Fort Ontario, but the Oneidas refused the presents and departed. Johnson could not expect unanimous support from the confederacy.

At Fort Ontario, across the river from Oswego, some 1,458 men, women, and children of several nations of the confederacy, together with some Huron Wyandots from Detroit, assembled to parlay with Johnson concerning their role in the upcoming struggle. Johnson thought they had "agreed to defend communications, and assist his Majesty's Troops in their operations." They should avoid white settlements. He excoriated the busybody missionary at Oneida for spreading Indian intelligence abroad before he himself got wind of it. The Indians assured a visitor from Albany that they had no intention of fighting against the settlers, but they would keep communications open along the Mohawk River (Graymont 1972: 64–65, and sources cited).

Among those present, Joseph Brant, yet to lead a war party, stood in the shadow of Little Abraham as speaker for the Flint People. Years later, Governor Black-snake, nephew of Cornplanter, recalled that few or no Senecas of importance attended the congress (Abler, ed., 1989: 36). That Johnson held a quorum of the confederacy remains uncertain.

The grand council of the confederacy that summer pondered its own destiny. In July 1775 the leaders of the constituent nations struggled to reach one mind on a policy about which way to turn in the gathering storm. Among the rumors that flew, one prevailed among the inhabitants of German Flats that the Five Nations were coming down to cut them off. The council dispatched two Oneida runners "to undeceive the People." The Oneida council sent the two Oneida messengers on down the valley to Albany to inform the Albany committee that the headmen of the confederacy were then gathered in council at Onondaga and that the confederacy was favorably disposed toward the settlers. The Five Nations were friendly: reports to the contrary were not to be believed (Duane Papers, NYHS; Schuyler Papers, box 13, NYPL). It remained uncertain how long the grand council could maintain a policy of neutrality and withstand the tendency of its autonomous members to fragment under pressure from the British and the Americans. Besides counting on a tradition of loyalty, mercantile Britain could afford presents to Indians made in its own factories. The impoverished Continental Congress, nevertheless, had seized the diplomatic initiative and armed its commissioners with a speech to the Six Nations that Kirkland had written for them and Philip Schuyler was expected to deliver (HEH, HM 14186).

The initiative for the Albany treaty came from Kirkland's Oneidas to the Committee of Safety in Albany, and General Schuyler passed it on to the Indian Committee in Congress. When the nearby Mohawks got wind of the upcoming meeting, they sent a delegation of three headmen to Oneida, where they summoned Seneca, Onondaga, Cayuga, and Tuscarora principals to press the Oneida council not to send emissaries to a conference called by Americans. The Mohawk speakers reminded the assembly of Guy Johnson's admonition at the Fort Ontario conference to stay away from white settlements. Albanians would only deceive them, murder them, or turn them over to New Englanders.

The junior moiety of the confederacy was of one mind in opposition. As custom demanded, they waited a time after the Mohawk speaker sat down before rising to respond in order—first the Oneida and then the Cayuga speakers—to reprimand the Mohawks for "taking up arms in a peaceable country." The Mohawks had insulted white people, they said. The Mohawks acknowledged their aggressions. Kirkland's Oneida parishioners then mounted a defense of their missionary, whom Johnson had threatened to deal with on his return from Canada, saying that any tribe that harbored him would gain the king's displeasure and be cut off. This alarmed the upper nations, Onondaga and Seneca. They and the Cayugas feared that any harm to Kirkland would incur the wrath of New England against the confederacy. "We therefore propose whether it be not wise, that your Father the Minister should retire for the present, or that we all agree to support and defend him at all hazzards" (Kirkland Papers, cited in Graymont 1972: 70).

The treaty at Albany in August 1775 between the commissioners of Congress and representatives of the Six Nations followed the classic mode. The preliminaries at the woods' edge took place at German Flats in the Mohawk Valley, near modern Herkimer, because some chiefs objected to coming down to Albany for fear of smallpox and dangers on the road. Nevertheless, those willing to go were "taken by the arm" to Albany a week later. On each occasion the host spoke first, and various Iroquois speakers replied. Strings and belts of wampum, prepared for the occasion to match the speeches, passed over the fire and were returned in kind. The sources describe some of these in detail. The hosts cited precedents in previous treaties and employed customary metaphors. Sessions ended with a round of drinks; final agreement warranted a feast, distribution of presents, and help getting home.

To accommodate the Indians, two of the commissioners, Volkert P. Douw of Albany and Turbot Francis of Massachusetts, made the eighty-mile journey up the Mohawk Valley from Albany to German Flats, where sachems and warriors of the Six Nations greeted them on 15 August. Commissioner Francis kept a journal (Francis 1836; see also NYCD, 8: 605–31). He spoke first on behalf of the commissioners, the hosts, inviting the Indians to come down to Albany where they would meet the remaining commissioners, rekindle the council fire, and ascertain the intentions of the united colonies. Kirkland interpreted.

The commissioners noticed the poor representation of the Six Nations—the upper nations were not present. The commissioners' message, composed of three words, matched in number the conventional Three Bare Words. The first, a token of their affection, urged the Six Nations to send a representative delegation prepared to discuss the present situation with the colonies at a general council. The second, a belt, invited the Seven Nations of Canada to attend the Albany conference and asked the Six Nations to appoint four or six principals, commensurate with the business to be transacted. The third word was a belt to shut Indian ears against hearing reports hostile to the united colonies on their way down.

The Oneida sachem Conoghquieson, erstwhile opponent of Kirkland's mission, replied with typical Iroquois irony: "You have now opened your minds. We have heard your voices. Your speeches are far from contemptible. But as the day is far spent, we defer a reply till to-morrow, as we are weary from having long sat in council. We think it time for a little drink; and you must remember that the Twelve [*sic*] United Colonies are a great body" (Francis 1836: 76–77).

An Oneida sachem, Tiahogwando (Deyohagwendeh, Oe-3, RC 12) delivered the promised reply the following day. "Brother *Solihoany*" (Colonel Francis?) and "our Albany Brother" (Douw), "Listen!" It would take a year to assemble the extremities of the confederacy, he said, "as we extend very far." But when the present council fire was raked up, the Six Nations would inform the people at the margins and their allies. It was not going to be easy to deliver an invitation belt to Caughnawaga and the Seven Nations because a certain unnamed man there would frustrate efforts to bring those people to an American conference. Anyway, the minds of the peoples on the St. Lawrence reposed at the Onondaga council house. Accordingly, the speaker returned the invitation belt.

Clearly, this Oneida sachem with a league title appealed to a rule that one or more nations could act for the confederacy, a part for the whole, and then inform the rest—an act which, unless the other nations objected, was binding.

The Oneida reply disturbed the commissioners. Colonel Francis asked what Englishman in Canada they meant. The Mohawk sachem Abraham, in an effort to relieve tension, answered that they saw no reason to be explicit, for they took it for granted that the commissioners knew whom was meant.

The Indians regarded the road to Albany as unsafe. Tiahogwando, in a second speech, asked the commissioners to admonish their own people not to molest the delegation on its way down to the council fire at Albany. Their free passage should be published. In contrast, by a belt the speaker declared that the road was open for passing and repassing throughout the Six Nations, as it had been for a long time. They expected reciprocity.

Colonel Francis promised white guides who spoke the native language. Presumably he covered the council fire for removal to Albany, where it was rekindled nine days later.

Five hundred Indians were in town on 23 August when the commissioners, joined by General Schuyler, rallied the principal gentlemen of the place to call on and welcome them. A Colonel Barlow observed that they were "very likely, spry, lusty fellows, dressed very nice for Indians. The larger part of them had on ruffled shirts, Indian stockings and shoes, and blankets richly trimmed with silver and wampum." He noted that on the day the council opened the Indians made "a very beautiful show, being the likeliest brightest Indians I ever saw" (Beauchamp 1905: 351).

In response to the commissioners' greeting, Conoghquieson deftly cadged another drink. He allowed that they would cheerfully share a glass and a pipe with the gentlemen. The commissioners' reception gathered town and Indians at five o'clock at Cartwright's Tavern. Well humored, the Indians put up a social dance that evening to honor the town.

On the eve of the congress, a deputation of sachems called on the commissioners at their lodging to explain that the Albany committee had invited them to come down before Congress and had appointed them as treaty commissioners, and they felt it only proper to meet first with the committee and answer its questions, which would take little time. The commissioners asked the sachems to appoint one of their number to act as interlocutor to explain to the Six Nations the propositions that the commissioners would put to them. The sachems picked Abraham, a chief of the lower Mohawk castle. They had no objection to the suggestion of encircling the treaty site with a guard. And the commissioners complied with a request to mend kettles, axes, and hoes—items that Indians now depended on but could not themselves repair.

The commissioners graciously delayed their own treaty for a day so that the Albany committee and the Indians could exercise their priority. The committee opted for Yonkers Street, behind the Dutch church, and invited the commissioners. They sent a bellman around the city calling people to attend. Senghnagenrat, an Oneida chief, spoke first on behalf of the Six Nations. He asked the assembly to inform him when its body was complete. He then said that the day had come and they had arrived in accord with their invitation. The committee had promised to "open the ashes and rekindle the old council fire at Albany." This symbolic gesture pleased the Indians. At German Flats the Oneidas were solid for peace, Senghnagenrat reported. Guy Johnson's threat to remove their minister, Kirkland, disturbed them greatly. They had promised to relate what was done at the Oswego council fire, but the Oneida delegates had told the committee that it would be better to send two men to German Flats to hear the report of the Oswego conference at first hand. Continuing his review of events, Senghnagenrat said that the committee representatives at German Flats had told the Oneidas they would not expect assistance in their struggle with their adversaries overseas. Instead, the committee had produced testimony to the ancient covenant—a belt of twenty rows between the Oneida nation and Quider (Peter Schuyler) of Albany, and another given by Sakayengwalaghton (Old Smoke) of the Seneca nation—which they held up for inspection by all the Six Nations at the rekindled council fire at Albany.

The speaker then asked the commissioners as well to listen. It was the policy of the Six Nations and their allies, who extended from Detroit and Ohio to Kahnawakeh, to maintain peace. "We rejoice that nothing more has been asked of us. . . . We shall remain at peace and smoke our pipes" (NYCD, 8: 612). They would keep the path open. In case of hostilities, he asked that others show compassion for old women and, especially, the younger ones, who represented the future of the nation. Finally, as for their father, the minister Kirkland, who stood by him interpreting, it would be wise for him to take a sabbatical and reside with his family until the quarrel subsided. He had now unburdened his mind, the collective will of the Six Nations, and these were the sum of his words.

The committee would answer after the appointed commissioners of the united colonies had transacted their business.

□□◇□□

What proved to be the last Indian treaty held with the Six Nations at Albany opened on 25 August in the Dutch church. Commissioners Schuyler, Francis, Wolcott, and Douw presided. They were joined by Abraham Yates, chairman of the Albany committee, and the town's principal inhabitants. Kirkland and Dean interpreted. Not a great deal was accomplished, although both parties observed proper protocol and employed some fine rhetoric.

Having been invited at the woods' edge with three strings, it devolved on the speaker for the Six Nations to speak first and return the strings intact. Again they chose the Oneida Senghnagenrat. (Indeed, this treaty was predominantly an Oneida affair.) He spoke in the name of the Six Nations, who desired that the great council fire be kindled up. He urged the commissioners to heed only that voice and pay no attention to individual Indians.

The commissioners, as hosts, were punctilious in observing proper protocol. The great pipe of peace was lighted and passed around. As the smoke permeated the corners of the church, the sachems opened their minds to listen as their host spoke. By now the commissioners knew what to say and how to say it. Kirkland had taught them. They rekindled the ancient council fire at Albany that William Johnson had removed upriver to his residence, and they heaped it with enough fuel to keep it burning bright and clear so that it might not be extinguished again. They renewed the covenant chain, promised to keep it bright and clean and free of rust, and gave a belt to strengthen it. (Kirkland had commissioned Stockbridge Indian women to make up the belts for the treaty and furnished them with thirty-nine thousand wampum beads. He later billed the Indian Committee of Congress nearly thirty pounds for this and related expenses [Kirkland Papers, HCL].)

In what is the first solid evidence of the impact of the Iroquois Confederacy as a model on the united colonies (although Franklin had cited it in 1754), the commissioners' speech next adverted to the advice given a generation earlier by Canasatego at the Lancaster treaty of 1774. Those famous words had sunk deep into the consciousness of the commissioners' forebears, and they had followed the chief's advice. "The Six Nations are a wise people," they said. This appeal to the ancestors was bound to please the Iroquois listeners. The commissioners then referred to the bundle-of-arrows motif as a symbol of strength in union (a single arrow would break), a symbol they evidently shared with the Iroquois (although both sides now claim it). The colonies had formed a confederacy, lighted a council fire at Philadelphia, and sent sixty-five councilors to speak and act for the whole. The commissioners would deliver the speech entrusted to them by Congress next day.

The speech of Congress on the twenty-sixth appealed to the two groups' similar confederate political structures and then proceeded to recite their common history on "this island," their joint participation in the French and Indian War, and colonial grievances against the crown. The commissioners would have more to say on Monday the twenty-eighth. A broken belt.

Appealing to familiar kinship usage, the commissioners' speech on the twenty-eighth argued that affairs between Old England and America were not unlike relations between father and son. (Reciprocal duties and benefits in matrilineal Iroquois society between mother's brother and sister's son are more like ties between father and son in Euro-American society. Iroquois listeners could find an equivalent.) This justification for taking up the hatchet against the crown called for a black belt. Here was a family quarrel that did not concern the Indians, who should stay out of it. They should stay home and keep the hatchet buried deep, but keep the path open. They and the Americans shared the same ground and had a common birthplace. The speech invoked other symbols of unity: one heart, one hand, the chain, the desire to sit together in the shade beneath the tree of peace. "Let us water its roots, and cherish its growth, till the large leaves and . . . branches extend to the setting sun, and reach the skies" (NYCD, 8: 619; Francis 1836: 90). This passage is right out of the league epic.

Other, more ominous metaphors invoked this island shaking on its eastern shore, a dark cloud looming east over the great water, restoring the sun, and the covenant chain slipping from their hands. Having returned to metaphors of unity, the speaker delivered the "union" belt, which Kirkland had procured. It probably resembled the Washington covenant belt lately in the New York State Museum (see fig. 25)

To keep the great road that ran through the middle of the country open and to remove from it every thorn, briar, and stone that might impede a traveler, the speaker gave a second belt of Kirkland's provision—the "path" belt—to promote communication between the Six Nations, their allies, and the Congress.

Further to promote peace and assure neutrality, to shut Indian ears against false rumors, and to afford a remedy for any future breach, the speaker presented a pipe of peace with six small strings attached, symbolic of the Six Nations. He urged the sachems to hold fast to the covenant chain, to acquaint their allies that the chain had been renewed, and to deposit the words of the Congress in the central council house at Onondaga to be handed down to posterity.

Conoghquieson acknowledged the speech, saying, "We have sat around and smoked our pipes at this our ancient place of kindling up our council fire." They had heard all of it and found nothing unpleasant, and since it treated matters of great importance, they would sit down next day and deliberate coolly, and answer the day after that.

It took the Indians two days to come to one mind and charge the Mohawk Little Abraham with their reply. He promised to touch lightly on each head but went on at some length. The Six Nations rejoiced, he said, to have the council fire replenished on orders of the great council at Philadelphia. They would keep the wampum belts as instructed but use them as mnemonics. He said: "Brothers, As you desired your belts might not be returned, but be deposited at our central council-house, we shall only make use of them to refresh our memories and speak upon them as we go on with our answer."

Continuing, Little Abraham noted that a brother of Canasatego's, now himself an old sachem, seated nearby remembered the words of his brother at Lancaster. The commissioner's metaphor of bound arrows to illustrate the necessity of a union to oncoming generations impressed the Indians. And they applauded the concept of replanting the tree of peace at Albany so that they could come sit in its shade and water its roots, so that the branches flourished and reached the sky. "This the Six Nations say shall be done" (NYCD, 8: 621).

The commissioners had told them to take no part in their family quarrel with the king, the speaker said, but to sit still and mind nothing but peace. Indeed, Colonel Johnson had told them the same thing at Oswego. The commissioners should listen closely. The Six Nations had fully considered this matter and resolved it. "The resolutions of the Six Nations are not to be broken or altered. When they resolve, the matter is fixed." They were determined not to take part in this family affair. They would sit still and let the parties fight it out. They had told Colonel Johnson the same thing. (Just how infallible this decision would be remained for the future.)

They were deeply grateful to have the covenant renewed, Abraham declared. Future generations would see the covenant belt at Onondaga and be reminded of the pact. And they would inform their allies. Keeping the path open was contingent on keeping the covenant.

Abraham asked protection for Sir William Johnson's son, born among the Mohawks of a Dutch mother, as well as for the Anglican missionary to the Mohawks, who did not meddle in civil affairs. The Six Nations desired to be kept informed of anything affecting them. As for the presentation pipe, probably made by an Albany silversmith, Abraham described it as "on one side the tree of peace, on the other a council-fire; we Indians sitting on one side of the fire, and the representatives of the Twelve United Colonies upon the other." They would keep it at the central council house for further use in official business.

To the Mohawks, land was the grievous issue. Two main parcels had been taken without compensation, and no less than restoration would satisfy them.

Grateful as they were for the commissioners' honoring the ancient customs of rekindling the fire and planting a tree of peace at Albany, the committee and commissioners had neglected one thing. Ancient custom required that whenever a fire was kindled and a tree of peace planted, some one person should be appointed to watch it. The Six Nations took it upon themselves to remedy the oversight. They proposed appointing the descendant of their ancient friend Quider (Peter Schuyler)—presumably General Philip Schuyler, a commissioner. They expected him to say whether or not he would do it. They would supply him with a wing to brush away insects that might come near the tree, which was the custom at Onondaga for the firekeeper. A belt of ten rows of wampum underscored the importance of this proposal.

The Oneida nation, too, had a grievance. Tiahogwando, third title on the Oneida league roster, raised the controversy over the Wyoming Valley lands in northern Pennsylvania, then being infiltrated by Connecticut people. The commissioners opted out of this affair, saying land problems lay beyond their jurisdiction. (The Oneida nation was going to have to get used to big government.)

The customary shout, *yo-heh*, from each of the Six Nations affirmed the end of the treaty on 1 September.

There remained some other matters to be cleaned up between the Indians, the commissioners, and the Albany committee. Neither the Oneida nor the Mohawk people were to be deprived of their ministers, and the Six Nations reaffirmed their intention to remain neutral, but the land issues had already come before the courts and the Indians were not then or ever to get satisfaction.

The Indians requested that James Dean be sent to Onondaga to explain the terms of the treaty to the grand council. This was a tribute to Dean's command of council speech. Dean would find the grand council fractionated and unable to come to one mind on the policy of neutrality. He reported in November that the Mohawk, Cayuga, and Seneca segments who had followed Guy Johnson from Oswego to Canada had returned saying that they had taken up the hatchet against the Americans (Graymont 1972: 74). So much for the solidarity of the confederacy. Disunited, the Six Nations could not maintain a policy of neutrality, and the several nations opted for different sides in the struggle that followed.

□□◇□□

Neutrality proved a fragile policy. By the spring of 1776 the western tribes of the confederacy favored the British, and Dean reported to Schuyler that the Oneidas had hosted a ceremony for condoling the death of a headman called "the Cagg." A large party of clearminded Onondagas and mourning Cayugas (fellow members of the junior moiety of the confederacy) had come to town to perform the rites. The amenities over, the two parties of the junior moiety engaged for three days in the fiercest debate since the founding of their union before the Oneidas prevailed in their firm attachment to the colonies. Fish Carrier, a Cayuga chief, accused the

Oneidas of paying more attention to Albany than to the ancient council fire at Onondaga. The Cayugas wanted the Oneidas to join them in retrieving the hatchet that the Oneidas had surrendered at the Albany treaty instead of observing proper protocol, which demanded that a hatchet be returned to the party who gave it, namely Colonel Johnson. Such partial acts violated the confederate policy of neutrality. The Oneidas replied that they had suspended the matter pending the approval of the whole confederacy, which would guide their conduct. Meanwhile, they rejected any thought of joining a Cayuga party to Albany. Reluctantly the Cayugas agreed to turn back, although disaffected and disgusted (Dean to Schuyler, 10 March 1776, Schuyler Papers, box 13, NYPL; Kirkland to Schuyler, 11 March 1776, Kirkland Papers, HCL).

Oneida headmen perceived that for the Americans to capture Fort Niagara would unite the confederacy in support of the colonies, but the Continental Congress was ill prepared to act. Meanwhile, Mohawk messengers passed and repassed daily on the pretense of having gone only to the Seneca country, although they carried letters from the British commandant at Niagara, Caldwell. The colonists were beginning to discover, as the Indians asked for trade, smiths, and weapons, that the covenant carried obligations as well as benefits.

Already, early in March, a delegation of some one hundred Senecas, fresh from a meeting at Niagara, awaited the return of the Onondaga and Cayuga headmen at the central council house of the confederacy to hold a general meeting to review the results of the Albany treaty and, they hoped, maintain a policy of neutrality. The individual nations of the confederacy, torn in two directions by outside forces, would find it difficult to attain one mind. The Oneida and Tuscarora delegations, stricken by the death of the principal Tuscarora sachem, could not leave home to attend the grand council until after the funeral. They intended that their delegation include Dean, who regularly sat with them. Mohawk threats to kill Dean if he showed up did not sway the Oneida headmen, who left it up to Dean to decide for himself. They would protect him. They needed him to balance John Butler (Guy Johnson's man), who had come from Niagara with the Senecas.

"The face of things among the western tribes," Kirkland wrote, began to change that spring, and he feared that the expectations of neutrality aroused at the Albany treaty had already faded. The Oneida headmen knew they faced opposition at the general council. Mohawks coming from Niagara threatened Dean's life if he dared appear. The Onondaga firekeepers, sensing the Mohawks' determination, sent a runner to intercept the Oneida delegation and warn Dean not to proceed further. A runner went back to inquire how the firekeepers planned to recapitulate the commissioners' speeches without Dean's assistance. The Oneida sachems would stay put and not proceed to Onondaga until the firekeepers returned a satisfactory answer.

As they waited, Little Abraham, accompanied by a Mohawk fresh from Niagara and himself party to the plot, overtook the Oneida delegation. Their arrival in the Oneida camp immediately called for a meeting, at which Little Abraham publicly questioned the Mohawk about his involvement in the plot against Dean and assured him it would be vain to equivocate because the truth was bound to come out. Embarrassed, the lad confessed that some Senecas had agreed to take Dean prisoner, should he appear at Onondaga, or to kill him if his protectors interposed.

Onondagas favored the plot; otherwise they would banish such miscreants from their council fire and advise the Oneidas to proceed. No news came from Onondaga.

On the twenty-fifth, a messenger arrived from Onondaga instructing the Oneida-Tuscarora-Caughnawaga delegations to proceed and assuring Dean that the miscreants had laid aside their plot. An immediate council decided that Dean should accompany them, and the "female Governesses" of Kanaghserageh, jointly with the Oneida matrons present, in a speech to the council opened their minds: they worried over the threat to them should harm come to Dean and urged him to turn back. Dean thanked them for their advice, told them to possess their minds in peace, and replied that he was sent with the great men on important business and must go on as directed. Next morning the chiefs sent their own messenger to Onondaga requesting lodging on arrival.

At the woods' edge three miles from Onondaga, the visitors heard that they could not be accommodated as a group but would be distributed in twos and threes throughout the town. The visitors, in council, rejected this solution as unsatisfactory and decided to camp together outside of town. They marched in Indian file as usual, but with Dean flanked by a guard of warriors, to a hemlock grove a half-mile from the council house, where they bedded down for the night.

Next day no summons to council came from the Onondaga sachems, who had located some liquor and were busy getting drunk.

On the twenty-ninth they were called to council, but the day passed with "their usual introductory speeches" composed of the Three Bare Words of Requickening to mutually open their minds. Dean then briefly stated his business and who sent him. The speaker thanked him for coming and reassured him.

As a rule, those who kindle the council fire provide the wherewithal (berry juice or liquor) to wash the mouths of those whom they call to sit around it. (To wash away the taste of smoking tobacco is a recurrent theme at Iroquois feasts to this day.) It therefore came as a shock to the visitors when the Onondaga speaker concluded by asking Dean, would he send for something to wash the taste of tobacco from their mouths?

The council returned that day to condole losses of the Kahnawakeh and Tuscarora visitors. And the Onondaga speaker answered the condolence speeches of Butler and the Senecas for an Onondaga headman and others killed defending Canada from an American invasion. Several "new trees" were raised to replace those who had fallen. Sakayengwalaghton, or Old Smoke, the Seneca sachem, then told the Oneidas that he was aware of their scheme with General Schuyler to deliver Butler or his scalp at Albany and advised them that if the rumor were true, they should consider carefully what they were about. The Oneida sachems reviewed the whole affair and demonstrated that the report was false and malicious.

Next day, the Seneca speaker recapitulated Colonel Butler's five speeches. In the first, he reminded them of commitments made at Oswego the previous summer. The second asked them to weigh his speeches against those of the Bostonians to see who spoke most of peace. The third manifested grief over the divisions within the confederacy. They should heal the breach. The fourth promised that the king in two months would voyage to Boston to talk of peace and, if the Bostonians refused, punish them. The Six Nations should observe neutrality as a policy. Fifth, he would kindle a council fire at Niagara for both the Six Nations and the western tribes in six weeks to discuss peace. The Seneca speaker had thus unburdened his mind. The Mohawks present had threatened to divulge these speeches if the Senecas did not. This threat promoted a further speech in the name of the senior moiety, Seneca-Onondaga-Mohawk, to the junior moiety, Oneida-Cayuga-Tuscarora, promoting unity.

The process of uniting the minds of the confederacy and composing answers to Butler's five speeches occupied another day.

The want of clothing, powder, and other necessities on which they now depended deeply distressed the Six Nations. Although the upper nations toward Niagara favored British rhetoric, inventories of trade goods at the fort were down. The senior moiety addressed a speech in its own name to the other nations of the confederacy proposing consideration of addressing the American commissioners directly concerning their plight. For goods to reach them, they desired opening the bottleneck at Quebec and keeping the passage free at Fort Stanwix. The matter was left on the mat until they reviewed the speeches delivered by the commissioners at Albany. Dean noted general approbation. They would not return the supporting belts but would keep them as instructed, since the commissioners desired that their talk might remain at Onondaga. In camp that night the delegation of Oneidas, Tuscaroras, and seven tribes of Canada discussed and unanimously disapproved the address proposed by the upper nations.

As charter members of the junior moiety, the Cayugas felt left out of the loop. Next morning they came to the Oneida camp to learn the Oneidas' sentiments on the proposed address. To their dismay they heard that the Oneidas were prepared to reject it and would urge patience until the matter could be brought to an Albany meeting that summer. This reply greatly dissatisfied the Cayugas, who insisted that the matter come before the council immediately and be presented as soon as possible.

Dean describes how the grand council worked. The Oneida speaker, in a civil manner, presented his nation's sentiments on the subject for the sachems' determination, together with supporting arguments that led the Oneidas to desire deferring the matter to some future meeting in Albany. The senior moiety immediately withdrew to caucus on the matter. While they were out, Dean received General Schuyler's letter relating the reduction of Boston. The senior moiety, on coming back in and being told that Dean had just received a letter from General Schuyler, wanted to hear its contents directly. Schuyler couched his report of the British evacuation of Boston in a speech to the Six Nations, which Dean read and interpreted to the assembled councilors. "A variety of passions appeared in the faces of the assembly on the recital. Some seemed elated with joy, and others as much depressed with vexation and disappointment."

Tegawanonde ("Between the Hills"?) of Onondaga brought in the reply of the Three Brothers to the Oneida proposal. Any speech to the commissioners should be made in the name of the whole confederacy, and if their requests were not complied with, an alteration in their minds would follow. Senghnagenrat responded for the Oneida sachems, who rejoiced and were thankful that trade in British goods via Quebec would be restored (now that Boston was closed to the British), and that the Stanwix passage over which those goods traveled to the Oneidas and Mohawks would not be shut by the Americans. The senior moiety would in effect "blow away the mind" of General Schuyler (and render him unnecessary), and they would of course get their entire request. This bit of irony silenced the opposite moiety but did not foreclose their design to keep Schuyler in the loop.

The Oneida speaker then turned to the whole assembly to proclaim that the Oneida and Tuscarora position on neutrality was "unalterably fixed"—they were determined not to interfere in the present quarrel or to impede the military operations of either party, so long as they themselves remained uninjured. A head warrior confirmed the position of the Oneida sachems.

Dean wrote that the Oneida sachems could not fathom Seneca perseverance in their insistence on addressing the commissioners, unless they had a speech in hand written by Colonel Butler that they concealed from the open council because he, Dean, was present.

The firekeepers on 2 April extinguished the council fire, after which Cayugas that evening visited the Oneida camp and restored amicable relations with their Oneida siblings of the junior moiety (Dean's journal in Force 1837-53, ser. 4, 5: 1100-4.)

Such detailed accounts of council procedures are rare, and the preceding relation constitutes our final view of the grand council as it struggled to reach one mind before its breakup two years later. Neutrality as policy and practice survived until the end of May 1776, when the Oneidas and Tuscaroras deemed such policy no longer feasible or possible. After that, individual nations fragmented and polarized to one side or the other, succumbing to outside pressure. Barbara Graymont (1972) has told the story of the Iroquois in the American Revolution with such clarity and detail that we may turn confidently to its aftermath in the treaties at Fort Stanwix in 1784 and, finally, peace and friendship at Canandaigua ten years later.

PART SIX

THE FEDERAL TREATY PERIOD, 1777 – 1794

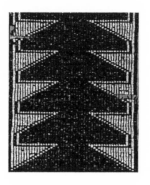

CHAPTER 38

BITTER MEDICINE AT
FORT STANWIX, 1784

Early in the new year 1777, word reached Fort Stanwix that pestilence had struck Onondaga and toppled a number of principal chiefs. The grieving and disheartened survivors, divided in their minds, raked up and covered the council fire that had burned since the founding of the Iroquois League. Patriot Samuel Kirkland saw the opportunity to win the Iroquois over to the American cause and urged General Schuyler to condole the grieving nations, but no strings or belts passed over the fire. The league had long since ceased to function, and the confederacy stayed divided during the remaining hostilities of the American Revolution. The greater part of Kirkland's Oneidas joined in the American cause, but the upper nations held fast to the covenant chain with the crown. After an expedition led by Major General John Sullivan in 1779 sacked Onondaga, destroyed Cayuga and Seneca cornfields, cut down orchards, and reduced housing and storage to ashes, the survivors fled to eke out a living on rations from Fort Niagara. In revenge, war parties out of Niagara pillaged and burned Oneida while the Oneida and Tuscarora inhabitants fled to Schenectady until the end of hostilities.

The council fire of the upper Iroquois now burned at Buffalo Creek, or Toshiowen, "Basswood Place," where the Onondaga firekeepers had carried the council brand. The wampum keeper shouldered the wampum bag and followed. Farmer's Brother and Young King were the resident war chiefs. Red Jacket, somewhat younger, rose to power as speaker for the women. His rivals for control of the Seneca nation, Cornplanter and his nephew, Governor Blackchief, veteran war chiefs, counted substantial adherents at Ohi:yo?, the Allegheny settlements.

During the Revolution the Loyalist Mohawks abandoned their valley and followed their war leader, Thayendanegea, or Joseph Brant (fig. 38), to Canada to sustain the British cause. When the Treaty of Paris that ended hostilities in 1783 made no provision for the Mohawks' future, Brant, in a friendly gesture, visited Philadelphia but failed to establish rapport with the Indian Committee of Congress or officials of the Department of War. Back in Canada he appealed to Governor Haldimand, who awarded him a grant of land for his followers on both banks of the Grand River from Lake Erie to the river's source in upper Canada. There the Loyalist Iroquois—save Deseronto's band, which stayed behind at the Bay of Quinte near modern Kingston, Ontario—began to congregate during 1783–84: the Mohawks at Brantford, the Bearfoot band of Onondagas at

Figure 38. Joseph Brant.
Portrait by Charles Willson
Peale, 1797. Courtesy
Independence National Park,
Philadelphia.

Middleport, and the upper and lower Cayugas, Delawares, Tutelos, and a few
Tuscarora dependents at "up above" and "down below" along the Grand River.
A few Senecas came later.

It was inevitable that these segments of the confederacy would again confederate
on the model of the ancient league. Among them were holders of hereditary titles
who recalled the legend of the league's founding and could teach others the rituals
for condoling the dead and installing new chiefs to fill out the rosters of the Five
Nations. Indeed, they reinvented the league along traditional lines to govern what
later became the Six Nations Reserve. The Grand River league kindled its fire at
Middleport in the custody of Thadoda:hoʔ and the Onondaga firekeepers. For a
time, Grand River chiefs attended council on both sides of the Niagara frontier,
but in time local pride came to regard the fire at Buffalo Creek with disdain.

In Albany, the crisis revived the commissioners of Indian affairs for the
Northern Department with the familiar names Douw, Duane, and Schuyler. They
met with Oneida sachems and warriors in February 1780 to hear the outcome of
an embassy sent to Niagara with flags and letters from the commissioners, inviting
the hostiles to peace. Grasshopper explained that arthritis and public duties had
kept him home during the mission to Niagara; Good Peter and Skenandoa had
taken his place. They carried the consensus of the sachems, warriors, and women,
the three principal ranks of Iroquois society, who had individually charged them.
They were to talk to their former confederates but have nothing to say to the king's
emissaries.

Not all Cayugas were hostile, the Oneida chiefs reported. Two had arrived at
Oneida to inform their brothers of the junior moiety that Senecas and other enemy
Indians had kindled a fire at Kahnawagens (Avon, New York, on the Genesee), the

one Seneca village left undestroyed between the Genesee and Niagara. Grass-hopper said he had proposed that the messengers meet there and interview their adversaries apart from British agents. No further word had come.

Meanwhile, Oneidas did not dare to plant in their own country, where they had buried their possessions and fled. They begged land nearby, and as usual they needed wampum—to make belts for an alliance with the Penobscots of Maine (NYPL, Schuyler Papers, box 14).

A delegation of Oneida headmen visited Philadelphia a year and a half later. A committee of Congress expressed sorrow that enemy Indians had destroyed their villages and looked forward to restoring their lands. Congress further promised preferential treatment soon to relieve the suffering of their faithful allies. The Indian Committee would write to the commissioners of the Northern Department instructing them to assist the Oneidas on their return (NYPL, Schuyler Papers, box 14).

□□◇□□

General Philip Schuyler conveyed his views on the management of Indian affairs in a letter to Congress on 29 July 1782. These views essentially guided the policy of the Indian Committee prior to the second Fort Stanwix treaty two years later. George Washington wrote to James Duane, a committee member, that his own views on the conduct of Indian affairs and land matters agreed substantially with Schuyler's (Washington to Duane, 7 September 1783, in Washington 1891: 303–12). Washington abhorred the thought of land jobbers overrunning former Indian holdings to the prejudice of individuals and the government. He outlined his ideas on the proper line of conduct toward the Indians under three heads: (1) all prisoners held by the Indians should be delivered; (2) the Indians should be informed that after eight years of struggle for the sovereignty of the country, Britain had ceded all lands to the United States within limits set by a provisional treaty; and (3) the Indians, despite advice to the contrary, had sided with Britain, shared their fortune, and would have suffered banishment by a less generous people than the Americans. A boundary line separating Indians from whites should be established and reasonable effort made to restrain persons not engaged in trading, treating, or other business from crossing that line. Americans should neither yield nor grasp too much.

The legislature of New York, Washington continued, should be restrained from insisting on expelling the Six Nations from their prewar holdings—something Schuyler seemed to worry the legisture might do—lest it end in another Indian war. The Six Nations would not give up their country without a struggle, but Washington thought they might compromise for part of it. It was cheaper to purchase than to fight. A proclamation prohibiting trespass on Indian land might help keep away surveyors and other intruders.

One way of preventing land jobbers from skimming the cream of the country at the expense of suffering officers and soldiers of the Continental Army lay in Congress's establishing land grants in lieu of back pay. Washington wrote that he believed administration of land grants should not be put in the hands of agents like the Johnsons. Rather, Congress should define the agents' duties, circumscribe their powers, and pay them a fixed salary. They should not trade.

The entire Indian question and the policy for Indian administration inevitably involved the formation of new states. Again, purchase was cheaper than fighting

Indian wars (Washington 1891: 303–12). Washington had heard the grievances of the Oneida Indians when he was recently on the Mohawk River, and he had ordered a pound of powder and three pounds of lead per man issued from the military magazine that they might go hunting. Schuyler's letter carried a similar recommendation. Yorker Duane, the recipient of Washington's recommendations, viewed the Six Nations as New York's historic concern. He took a hard line.

The Indian Committee of Congress received Schuyler's and Washington's recommendations and proceeded, nevertheless, to visit conquest theory on the hostile Indians. Both New York and Pennsylvania had inquired of Congress concerning peace with the Indians. The matter was referred to a special committee that included, among others, Alexander Hamilton and James Madison; the committee indicated that the Ninth Article of Confederation vested in Congress "the sole and exclusive right and power of regulating the trade and managing affairs with the Indians [who were] *not members of any of the States*" (emphasis added). The committee assigned Indian affairs under Congress to the Department of War, resolved to suspend offensive hostilities, and urged immediate measures to communicate with the several tribes toward a final peace. It further recommended appointment of four commissioners by districts, including one for the northern district that comprised the Six Nations and their dependents (JCC, 24: 264).

Colonial governors had long asserted that the Iroquois were dependents of New York and that Albany was the place of treaties. The old Board of Indian Commissioners had consisted of Albanians and traders who had managed the conduct of Indian affairs until the crown vested the superintendency of the Northern Department in Sir William Johnson. That act had removed Indian affairs from meddling by provincial officials and recognized the de facto sovereignty of the Six Nations (SWJP, 4: 817, 838, 850, 863; Manley 1932: 23–24).

The Articles of Confederation left the question of jurisdiction up in the air. The Indian Committee of Congress prepared to exercise its jurisdiction in managing Indian trade and affairs while the legislature of New York insisted on its rights to treat and obtain land cessions from the Six Nations as members of that state. The whole issue of mixed jurisdiction would plague relations with the New York Indians for two hundred years. Today the Iroquois insist they are sovereign nations. New York would have them dependents, and Congress has never conceded its ultimate right to the state of New York.

Leaders of the new nation came down on opposite sides of the question. Governor George Clinton, General Philip Schuyler, and James Duane favored state jurisdiction. Other members of the Indian Committee favored Congress or were ambivalent. For James Monroe and James Madison, it was a constitutional matter, and they discussed it in subsequent correspondence.

The Indian Committee reported to Congress in the autumn of 1783. It proposed as terms of peace that "the savages shall without compensation abandon part of their country to the United States who claim it by conquest" (Manley 1932: 26). After some assertion of states' rights by Pennsylvania, on 15 October Congress adopted resolutions for holding a treaty of peace. To avoid a separate negotiation, the Pennsylvania authorities would be notified of the time and place of the general treaty with the United States. A Pennsylvanian would be named one of the commissioners. Strong sentiment favored naming a New Yorker to the panel as well, but the final panel, originally of five members, after withdrawals consisted of three commissioners: Arthur Lee of Virginia, General Richard Butler of Pennsylvania, and Oliver Wolcott of Connecticut (JCC, 25: 680–91). The superintendent of finance would purchase a quantity of goods for the Indians and entrust them to a storekeeper (JCC, 25: 747). To that role he appointed Griffith Evans, a Philadelphian, who will presently afford us an eyewitness account of the treaty proceedings.

While Congress deliberated, New Yorkers were not idle. The New York assembly numbered heads of Mohawk Valley families who had lost lives, buildings, and crops to hostile war parties. They threatened to expel the Iroquois from New York. They were only slightly more sympathetic toward the Oneidas and Tuscaroras who had suffered similarly for espousing the patriot cause. The assembly proposed removing them to a district carved out of "vacant" Seneca lands in western New York. The hostile Senecas, Cayugas, and Onondagas should be driven out or made to follow the Mohawks to Canada. To accomplish this, the assembly appointed three commissioners—Abraham Cuyler, Peter Schuyler (of whom more later), and Henry Glen—and committed them to this exchange (Manley 1932: 28–29).

Word of these doings reached the Iroquois council at Buffalo Creek and the British commandant at Niagara. Officers of the garrison regularly attended council meetings. Intelligence was frequently distorted. The Seneca chief Abeel (Cornplanter) informed a council held on 2 July 1783 that two young men, Oneidas, without asking the chiefs, had recently visited relatives at Canawaroghere, the Oneida capital, at the moment when forty Americans passed through en route to Onondaga, ostensibly to build a house for General Schuyler. Be that as it may, the (Oneida?) chiefs next morning expressed regret that the chiefs of the Six Nations had not seen fit to attend a council called by General Schuyler the previous spring to hear his speech, which they repeated.

In substance, Congress had directed Schuyler to inform the Six Nations that peace had been agreed upon between the king and the Americans, who were now "masters of this island" and could dispose of the land as they saw fit. Those Iroquois, Schuyler is reported to have said, who had gone to join the British troops at Niagara and elsewhere had "forfeited their lands to us. . . . [W]e are the conquerors." At the time the hostilities began, Schuyler had asked the Six Nations to stand neutral, but they paid no attention. Their lands were now forfeited. The king had relinquished the lands to the United States, which now held them on the theory of conquest. Yes, the Indians could move across the Great Lakes to British lands. Schuyler would regard the Oneidas and a few Cayugas who had served him during the war more favorably than the hostiles. Not surprisingly, Brigadier MacLean, then commandant at Niagara, flatly contradicted this speech, declaring it a fabrication. The Six Nations should listen to him (NYPL, Schuyler Papers, box 14).

The Buffalo Creek council thought it best to keep the channels open. They got Jacob Reed, an Oneida, to write a letter and sent it home by Skenandoa and Peter to hand to General Schuyler. They wanted "to be straight." Joseph Brant, to be safe, sent along assurances of friendship to the Americans and to Schuyler personally (HEH A 803). The letter reached Schuyler on 29 July 1783.

That day Schuyler wrote two letters: one in reply to the belt brought by Skenandoa and Peter, the other to Congress containing his thoughts on peace terms with the Six Nations. In the first, he denied having sent any such message to those Indians as they reported, not since the letter Peter and Skenandoa had been charged to deliver to Niagara. That earlier message had been calculated to restore peace and friendship, Schuyler said, but it was ignored. Those same Indians had disregarded the advice of the commissioners of Indian affairs early in the war. It must have stung the Buffalo Creek council to be addressed as "those Indians of the Six Nations who sent a belt." Schuyler concluded his message to "those Indians" who wanted a quick answer by sending the following advice in the spirit of reconciliation: "They should send a deputation composed of four or five Sachems and as many principal warriors of each Nation to the Commissioners of Indian Affairs, instructed to request that peace may be established between the Americans and the Indians." As evidence of sincere desire for peace, the deputies should bring every prisoner in their possession. Before the deputies began their journey, they should send a runner saying they were coming and when they would likely reach Oneida. Then the commissioners would appoint a place to meet them. Immediately Schuyler would write to Congress requesting instructions to the commissioners (NYPL, Schuyler Papers, box 14).

Schuyler's letter to Congress, conveying his thoughts on peace with the Six Nations, reveals his respect for the dignity of Congress and his hope not to drive the Indians to despair. He saw no sense, he wrote, in continuing a war with a people who might abandon their country anyway and whose land could be had for less expense than that of a further Indian war. He trusted that Congress would take this into consideration in preparing terms for a treaty. Second, there would be no obstacle to timbering and farming at the margins of land the Indians currently retained, because the approach of settlement inevitably brought a scarcity of game that would induce the Indians to withdraw further and make them more willing to dispose of their lands, until their holdings dwindled to nothing. This had been the history of Indians living near civilized people. Third, if expelled, they must retire to and reside in British territory, which would strengthen that nation and might prove troublesome later. Fourth, should the Indians continue to harass United States frontiers, it would take an enormous expense to defend them. Schuyler knew full well how difficult it was to contend with Indian warfare. Fifth, warfare would totally disrupt the fur trade. Schuyler added that Congress must consider the size of garrisons needed in peacetime and in war, and that Congress should not forget bounty lands promised to the army. The New York legislature had already assigned Onondaga and a greater part of Cayuga country to veterans of the Continental Army (NYPL, Schuyler Papers, box 14). Schuyler's letter to Congress silenced New York proposals to expel the Iroquois (Manley 1932: 32).

Schuyler wrote a third letter that same day to Joseph Brant, in response to Brant's message delivered by Skenandoa and Peter. Schuyler had released all Indian prisoners taken by his army, he said, giving them friendly advice that he wished they had followed. He was still for peace and would promote it if the Indians would follow the advice given in his speech, which he hoped would be clearly interpreted. They should cease to be amused by idle stories that would lead only to their ruin as a people, a possibility he deplored (NYPL, Schuyler Papers, box 14).

Schuyler's peaceful sentiments were soon dashed by British-inspired responses to his speech and letters. The council at Buffalo Creek stood willing to treat, it replied, but on condition that the Indians there not be disturbed in possession of their lands. They preferred to treat not with Schuyler but with Congress. Little did they know that Schuyler's view had inspired both Washington and Congress. The Indian Committee of Congress advanced Schuyler's name as a treaty commissioner, but he declined to serve (Manley 1932: 36; JCC, 26: 73, 198).

Brant sent a letter accompanying the reply of the Six Nations to Schuyler that appears to be his own speech in council. It makes some interesting points. The council had awaited the return of some principal warriors from a council at Sandusky, Brant reported, which suggests an effort to extend the confederacy to include entities living north of the Ohio River. Congress had sent several messages to Buffalo Creek signifying willingness to make peace. The Indians were willing on condition that Congress act on some agreed-upon fixed principle in settling terms honorable to both sides. "Do not think that we were drunk when we gave our assistance to the King." The Six Nations knew how to make treaties. It was serious business carried forward in a regular manner established by the ancestors. Brant questioned whether Schuyler enjoyed the confidence of Congress. Congress should appoint a place somewhere between the parties to meet and kindle a council fire. His people stood ready to return captives. They decried surveys and settlement beyond the boundary line fixed in the 1768 Stanwix treaty. Finally, Brant wrote that Schuyler had not understood the Six Nations' speech as delivered by Skenandoa and Peter. "It was sent in the name of the Whole Six Nations & not in the name of any particular party," as Schuyler had implied (NYPL, Schuyler Papers, box 14).

Not much came of Schuyler's negotiations. He met with the Six Nations the following winter, but the Indians were not prepared to face the reality of their situation, nor was Schuyler ready to forgive their breaking promises of neutrality in 1776. He told them he had never invited them to make peace; he had merely *advised* them to (Manley 1932: 35).

□□◇□□

Various adventurers set out to see the frontier for themselves, or to gather intelligence. Major Ephraim Douglas got as far as Detroit and Niagara. Brigadier MacLean assured him that the Indians would never surrender their lands without a fight (Manley 1932: 39). Ebenezer "Indian" Allen of Pennsylvania, late in the Revolution, lived among the Senecas on the Genesee trading and "trying on the mocassin" with several native women. An early double agent, he communicated with both the governor of Canada and Congress. On a visit to Philadelphia he informed Congress that the Senecas held about one hundred American prisoners who were rapidly degenerating into savages. They were inclined to peace but ready for war. He returned with a wampum belt and a letter to the Indians. Brant, however, repudiated Allen's mission, informing Schuyler that the Iroquois would never send a white man on Indian business. He returned the wampum belt.

Washington would not be satisfied until he saw upstate New York for himself. His long-standing interest in land, his early contact with Indians, and the need to inspect military outposts sent him to the field. On 18 July 1783 he set out from headquarters at Newburgh, proceeded north by Albany to Lake George and Lake Champlain, inspected Crown Point, traveled southwest by land to Schenectady, and journeyed upriver to Fort Stanwix. (He undoubtedly talked with General

Schuyler on the way.) Crossing the Wood Creek portage to Lake Oneida, he visited and addressed the Oneida nation, directed Colonel Willett to issue powder and lead from the arsenal for their hunting, and listened to the Indians' troubles. From Oneida he rode south over the hills to Lake Otsego, viewed the headwaters of the east branch of the Susquehanna, and made the Canajoharie portage from the lake to the Mohawk River. Inland navigation preoccupied him. He contemplated an extended tour of the eastern states and Canada west to Lake Michigan the following year (Washington 1891: 228, 290, 312, 324–25).

These travels afforded Washington opportunity to consider Indian policy and formulate thoughts that he expressed in correspondence with James Duane, chairman of the Indian Committee of Congress, General Schuyler, and later Monroe and Madison. Governor Clinton had escorted Washington from Newburgh to Albany, and Duane had the governor's ear as well as Schuyler's and the Livingstons' (see Washington to Duane, 7 September 1783, in Washington 1891: 303–12). Washington's views on Indian policy, and to an extent Schuyler's, transcended the local prejudices of state legislatures, but later Duane took a hard line toward the Six Nations. He made a clear distinction between the authority of Congress to make peace with Indians and the territorial rights of states over Indians who were members of a state. He advocated abandoning long-established protocol for making treaties with Indians as nations, dropping native metaphors, abolishing the style of addressing them in kinship terms, and no longer recognizing the Six Nations as a confederacy (Manley 1932: 57–58).

On the matter of land purchases—something of considerable significance in view of later controversy between New York and the general government—even after passage of the 1790 "Non-Intercourse Act" Washington wrote: "No purchase under any pretence whatever should be made by any other authority than that of the sovereign power, or the legislature of the State in which such lands may happen to be."

The question of where such jurisdiction rested would afterward occupy the minds of two younger Virginians, both future presidents, who visited Fort Stanwix before the treaty (in the case of James Monroe) or during it (in the case of James Madison). British garrisons yet occupied the western posts when Monroe, during the summer break from Congress, set out to test by personal observation a plan he had advanced for taking possession of the posts. He wrote to Thomas Jefferson, his mentor, on 20 July 1784:

> I . . . shall commence for the westward upon the No[rth] river, by Albany. . . . I shall pass through the lakes, visit the posts, and come down to the Ohio and thence home. . . . In this trip . . . I may perhaps acquire a better knowledge of the posts wh[ich] we sho[ul]dd occupy, the cause of the delay of the Brit.h troops, the temper of the Indians towd. us, as well as the soil, waters, and in general the natural view of the country. (Monroe 1898–1903, 1: 35–38)

Monroe reached New York in August, when he again wrote to Jefferson, describing his revised itinerary: from Albany he would follow the water-level route to the lakes and go as far as Detroit and thence to the Ohio, where he planned to buy horses for the journey home. He had about given up on seeing Montreal and Boston. "It is possible that I may lose my scalp from the temper of the

Indians, but if either a little fighting or a great deal of running will save it I shall escape safe" (Monroe 1898–1903, 1: 39).

Plans changed along the way. Governor Clinton advised that getting by the British posts might prove difficult. At Schenectady Monroe learned that it was impossible to get past Oswego without a pass from the commandant. That did not deter him from going on to Fort Stanwix ahead of Governor Clinton's New York state treaty delegation.

Monroe evidently reached Niagara in September. His gentle manners charmed the garrison and Joseph Brant, who escorted him west. An incident on Lake Erie in which members of a landing party were killed turned them back. Colonel Depeister at Niagara sent Monroe home via the St. Lawrence to Montreal and south through the Champlain and Hudson valleys to New York (Monroe 1898–1903, 1: 40).

These travels afforded the background for Monroe's later correspondence with Brant, Jefferson, and Madison concerning the Stanwix treaty and jurisdiction over Indians. He also learned that the British commandants had received orders to retain possession of the posts at Niagara, Detroit, and Michilimackinac, which fell within the American cession line, and that they had since recommissioned vessels on the lakes that had been decommissioned by the preliminary treaty. The British ascribed this action to the behavior of New York and Virginia, the latter with respect to pre-Revolutionary debts owed to British merchants (Monroe to Benjamin Harrison, 30 October 1784, in Monroe 1898–1903, 1: 39.)

The New York commissioners reached the treaty grounds at Fort Stanwix ahead of the commissioners of Congress and tried to exact concessions from the Indians. They accomplished little; the Indians favored treating with Congress. But a collision was unavoidable. Governor Clinton had no intention of waiting around for the general government to usurp the prerogative of New York state to deal with the Six Nations, whom he regarded as members of that state. He instructed his own Indian commissioners to draft terms of a treaty. The hostile nations were expected to compensate the citizenry for injuries sustained, but they would not be driven from the country. They were to deliver all captives and relinquish all land east and west of a certain tract bounded by two lines drawn from Lake Ontario south to the Pennsylvania border, location yet unspecified (NYPL, Schuyler Papers). The governor had sent a messenger to the four hostile nations inviting them to meet in May at German Flats, hoping the Indians would sense the propriety of dealing with New York. Peter Ryckman, as his courier, ran into the confusion caused by the exodus of Loyalist Iroquois from the Niagara frontier to the Grand River. Brant and other leaders preferred making peace with the several states. The Indians chose to hold the treaty at Fort Stanwix. They were expected to arrive in July (Manley 1932: 50–53).

By that time, Governor Clinton's plans were well advanced. Abraham Cuyler, Major Peter Schuyler (nephew of Philip), and Henry Glen had been named as the New York commissioners, and they had their instructions. (General Philip Schuyler had declined to serve either New York or Congress.) All this while, Congress solicited the several states for troops to protect its own commissioners. New York would not fulfill its quota. The federal commissioner Arthur Lee reported to Congress in August that the New York legislature had authorized holding its own treaty independently of the general government's, which act outraged members of Congress. In response to a letter from Commissioners Lee and Butler, Clinton said he would hold a treaty anyhow. He did not object to the commissioners of Congress taking advantage of their presence at his treaty to do the United States some good, but they should make no agreement with Indians residing within the jurisdiction of New York state, with whom he intended to treat. For Congress to do so would prejudice that state's rights.

Commissioners Lee and Butler, still in New York on 19 August, reminded the governor that the season was already advanced, the Indians were expected at Fort Stanwix, and the commissioners must meet them to conclude a peace in the name of the United States. Moreover, without knowing what business the governor planned to transact with the Indians, it was impossible to judge whether his intentions were compatible with their commission as defined by Congress. They left it to Clinton to decide whether his business might "be more properly transacted at the same time and in subordination to the General Treaty." Pennsylvania had made such an arrangement. Clinton and his advisors decided not to answer the letter, lest they provoke an "altercation" (Hough 1861: 18–33; Manley 1932: 554–56).

That summer, messages traveled back and forth along the east-west trail. Brant and his followers delayed coming east to Fort Stanwix in June as he had proposed to do in his message to Governor Clinton. The provisions and rum reached the fort a month before any Indians showed. The traders got there first. Brant awaited confirmation that the United States would be represented at the treaty and wrote that the western nations were coming with the Six Nations. He asked Clinton to inform Congress that the Indians desired representatives of the whole United States to attend, in order to settle matters finally (Hough 1861: 18; Manley 1932: 59).

Clinton sent Peter Ryckman with a letter to Brant on 14 August assuring Brant that he had forwarded the message to the United States commissioners, but he stressed the fact that he and his commissioners represented the state of New York, which enjoyed historic priority in treating with the Six Nations. Clinton said he intended to exercise that right first, even if United States commissioners were not present.

The Six Nations council at Niagara, perhaps with British advice, matched its delegation with its estimate of Clinton's proposal. It sent with Brant not a single sachem but ten principal war chiefs, whom the council authorized to explore but not conclude a treaty of peace. The delegation included representatives of allied western nations. They were to settle some points prior to a general treaty of lasting peace between all the nations and the United States. Ryckman and Brant's runners met and exchanged letters at Canasaraga, a Tuscarora town under Oneida jurisdiction. Clinton's urged the Six Nations to come at once to Fort Stanwix; Brant's stated that with the chiefs at hand he could make peace with the state of New York but not with the United States (Hough 1861: 30; Manley 1932: 60). The council saw no need for all the chiefs to attend a treaty with a single state.

James Dean, the Oneida-speaking interpreter, and Samuel Kirkland were meanwhile communicating between the friendly Oneida-Tuscaroras and the commissioners of Congress, who had warned the Indians not to cede any of their lands. The Oneida-Tuscaroras had a distinct federal bias. Dean managed to avoid

Clinton's request that he interpret at the state treaty by claiming urgent business elsewhere. Instead, he carried a message from the commissioners of Congress urging the Six Nations to get on down to Fort Stanwix for a federal treaty.

The New York treaty proved a fiasco. It challenged federal authority to treat with Indians and failed. Preliminary messages passed through Oneida, but the Oneida and Tuscarora councils sent no delegates. Unanimity being the cardinal rule of Iroquois grand councils, the Six Nations could later claim its decisions not binding. Worried, the New York commissioners sent a committee to Oneida to assure the chiefs of goodwill and persuade them to attend. Nothing would be said about land cessions.

On 4 September, Governor Clinton addressed the chiefs assembled at Fort Stanwix for the New York state treaty, employing the classical mode of treaty speech, completely ignoring Duane's advice. He stated that the business of the treaty was to establish boundaries, and he cautioned the Indians against sales to unauthorized parties.

The speaker for the Oneida-Tuscaroras reciprocated in kind (Hough 1861: 40–47). They had not put any stock, he said, in rumors that the state had designs on their lands. The speaker repeated in several forms the point that siblings did not displace siblings. They were pleased to be reassured of protection of their lands. As for the eastern boundary, it was set in 1768, as the state well knew.

Next day the governor addressed the Mohawk, Onondaga, Cayuga, and Seneca spectators to the previous day's performance. Reminded of recent hostility, the state of New York sought reconciliation and solicited their views. He explained that the right and power to regulate the affairs of Indians who were not members of any state was vested in Congress and its commissioners appointed for that purpose; but he and his commissioners were appointed by the New York legislature to superintend affairs of Indians residing within the state. Brant's letter of 11 August had informed him that the Six Nations, in alliance with others, had sent a delegation to settle some points prior to a general meeting. What were those points? New York was prepared to follow the ancient custom governing conduct of treaties established by their respective ancestors. Why depart from the old way? What were their credentials?

It rained next day, affording the Indians time to compose their reply. Cornplanter, a Seneca war chief (fig. 39), opened the council, introduced the matter, and cleared the way for Captain Brant to speak. Essentially, Cornplanter explained, dual jurisdiction under two separate bodies caused some "Difficulty in our Minds" and disagreed "with our ancient Customs." The chiefs preferred to meet first with commissioners of the whole thirteen states. Any residual matters could be discussed with any particular state.

Brant's further explanation cleared up one matter. His delegation, he said, had been authorized by and represented the Six Nations; it did not represent the western confederates, who had refused to treat at any site east of Niagara (Manley 1932: 68–71; cf. Hough 1861).

The state treaty concluded on 10 September. The governor was not prepared to request the cession of a particular tract, but he reminded the Indians that they were subject to the ancient rule that no lands within the state could be ceded without state consent.

Figure 39. Cornplanter. Portrait by F. G. Bartoli, 1796. Courtesy New York Historical Society, New York City.

Brant, Cornplanter, and the other delegates returned to council declaring that they recognized the authority of the state commissioners within their jurisdiction, that some land cession might be reasonable, and that they were not empowered to act but could recommend such to their respective national councils. They would first treat with the commissioners of Congress. They would abide by the ancient rule and would not cede lands within the state without its approval (Manley 1932: 71–72).

Having accomplished little, the governor covered the fire. He and the New York commissioners returned to Albany in the morning, leaving Peter Schuyler and Peter Ryckman in charge of surplus provisions, mostly rum. They were to stay and observe the treaty with the U.S. commissioners. They would prove a nuisance to the delegates of Congress.

□□◇□□

Colonel James Monroe, the other young Virginian and a member of Congress, attended three days of the state treaty sessions. During his travels near Niagara he and Joseph Brant had discussed treaty matters and apparently agreed, as Brant later wrote to Clinton (Manley 1932: 66). How much these conversations influenced Brant is uncertain, although they prepared Monroe to observe and correspond afterward with Madison and Jefferson.

Griffith Evans, storekeeper for the commissioners of Congress and clerk to the Pennsylvania commissioners, reached the treaty site several days after Madison arrived with the Marquis de Lafayette (Gottschalk 1950: 58). Evans left an eyewitness account of the proceedings and a fascinating description of the environs. (His manuscript journal, preserved in the Huntington Library, was edited and published by Hallock F. Raup in 1941, nine years after Henry S. Manley's monograph *The Treaty of Fort Stanwix, 1784* appeared.)

Evans landed at Albany on the afternoon of 22 September and there met and dined with Arthur Lee and Richard Butler, commissioners of Congress. Within a few days he mustered the stores and embarked by bateau to row some 109 miles from Schenectady to Fort Stanwix. His description of the Mohawk Valley, its natural resources, and its inhabitants ranks among the best accounts of the region at the period. He found the low Dutch around Herkimer unsociable, in contrast with the more enterprising Germans who occupied the flats of their name below the fort. They had suffered greatly in both life and property from Tory and Indian raiders, for whom they held an abiding hatred.

Fort Stanwix (or what had survived a fire several years earlier) stood on the south bank of the Mohawk River. On 2 October there remained but three small blockhouses situated a half-mile south of the previous works. Evans inspected the outworks, trenches, and abatises with an experienced military eye, estimating the number of men required to defend the place. Having looked to the safe arrival and security of the stores, he turned to meet resident traders and the Reverend Samuel Kirkland, whom the Oneidas had petitioned the Board of Correspondents in Boston to restore to them, and who was there in the role of interpreter.

General Oliver Wolcott of Connecticut, who had been taken sick on the road, arrived late the same day. Wolcott was the senior commissioner. Evans, having lodged with him in Albany, characterized him as studious, of sound judgment and judicious, but not possessed of a lively imagination.

The following morning, 3 October, Evans met the entourage of the Marquis de Lafayette, including a young French nobleman named Marbois, and James Madison of Virginia, who had arrived several days previously. (The New York commissioners were already on the ground, as were numbers of Indians awaiting the commissioners of Congress. I shall stick to Evans and come back to the others.)

The United States treaty began on 3 October 1784. Evans wrote: "This day, the Indians for the first time were called together and the council fire kindled. The continental commissioners opened the business." In a short speech, General Wolcott introduced the French gentlemen and his fellow commissioners. He said it was their plan to treat for peace and friendship, deferring the particulars. They would go fully into the business when the several nations were represented.

Cornplanter made the customary brief acknowledgment. Evans developed a high regard for the Seneca chief's intellect, great confidence, and natural abilities. "His speech was short and to the subject. He congratulated them on their arrival, expressed the willingness of the natives to treat, and the spirit of pacification that prevailed with them." (Cornplanter's words are reported in Craig 1876, 2: 497.)

Evans found more to say about native speakers than about the substance of the treaty. Lafayette spoke that morning "with much . . . elegance calculated to serve the interest of his king and to promote the continental business," upbraiding the tribes who had honored their covenant with the English crown and committed depredations in the late war, and praising those who had espoused the patriot cause (an incident described later). Evans commented on the responses of old Grasshopper and Onegenta of Kahnawakeh, as interpreted by Kirkland: "I now for the first time hear men savage in almost every respect harangue on important subjects with eloquence, force and coherence, which I found by explanation to be . . . respectable in every sense, and was told 'twas far inferior to the original" (Evans 1941: 208).[1]

Evans spent 6 October fishing in the company of a Mr. Crain and caught some fine trout. Keeping up his journal occupied the next two days. Again, three days later (9 October), in company with a Mr. Fisher, Evans went to "Canada creek" (West Canada) for trout and caught a "fine parcel." He wrote: "This creek abounds with this kind of fish in greatest plenty. A person of skill can take as many almost as he chooses" (Evans 1941: 209).

Evans much admired the work of beavers that felled birches five or six inches in diameter, hauled them over paths to the water, and worked them into dams, turning sizable streams into ponds. Evans enjoyed these moments of quiet on the stream, removed from mounting tension at the treaty grounds.

Let us now leave Griffith Evans temporarily to his fishing and return to the Marquis de Lafayette and his entourage. James Madison, by prearrangement, had met Lafayette in New York, and the party had ridden up from Albany ahead of the U.S. commissioners. They reached Fort Stanwix on the afternoon of 29 September (Gottschalk 1950: 98). There they found only a small band of Iroquois and other Indians encamped in bark lean-tos while waiting between treaties for the commissioners of Congress to arrive. Typical of Indian hospitality, the Indians afforded a lean-to for Lafayette's party to crowd into. The French soon learned that factions still divided the Indians vis-à-vis the United States. Noise of brawls kept them awake, and a fight broke out between two brothers. Kindred interceded to settle the quarrel with a pipe.

The French tradition loomed large in Oneida eyes. Men lived who had served under Lafayette's command during the American Revolution. In 1778 the Oneidas had given him the name Kayewla, after a famous Oneida warrior. They had treated with Onontio, the French governors of Canada, from the seventeenth century to the Seven Years War. Some Oneidas had visited France, one or two spoke French, a French Jesuit had once held the leading league title, and Father Bruyas had written a grammar. No one else in America but Lafayette was French, American, and Oneida at the same time (Gottschalk 1950: 97). Neither French, British, Americans, nor Oneidas could overlook Lafayette's presence at the treaty.

Kirkland, still at Oneida in late September, in advance of the treaty, sensed that Lafayette's presence might turn the negotiations in a favorable direction. He tried to get Lafayette to address the Indians there even before the commissioners appeared. Lafayette diplomatically wrote to the commissioners seeking their instructions and suggesting that perhaps he should fulfill Kirkland's request. The letter reached Lee and Butler on the road; Wolcott, indisposed, would follow. Lee was opposed; Wolcott apparently agreed. In any case, the treaty could not begin

---

1. The Indian speeches as printed nearly a century later put Algonquian terms for the Great Spirit into the mouths of Iroquoian speakers. "Manitou" and "Kitchy Manitou" seem hardly credible coming from a Mohawk orator, although Lafayette may have used them, inasmuch as many Algonquian terms first heard in New England and the Hudson Valley had by 1784 entered American speech. But Lafayette undoubtedly spoke his first language—French (see Craig 1876, 2: 470–71).

until Wolcott arrived. But the commissioners agreed that they would afford Lafayette a chance to speak as he felt proper.

A visit to Oneida temporarily resolved the dilemma. On the afternoon of 30 September, Lafayette, Marbois, and the young Chevalier de Caraman traveled the eighteen miles from Fort Stanwix to Oneida, where the Oneidas hung a kettle for them, Grasshopper, who had visited Philadelphia in 1781, still wore the Bavarian hunting costume that the French minister had presented to him. Another host had served under Lafayette. The party drank from wooden bowls, except for the guest of honor, who had a broken glass mended with gum. Afterward, by request, the hosts put up a social dance. The tom-tom (water drum) accompaniment to what the French observer described as "one word and two notes" (nonsense vocables) suggests the old-time "Moccasin Dance" !Kayo:wa) or the modern Fish Dance. It went on for two hours until Lafayette's former servant requested they stop and let their tired guests retire. They were back at the fort next day (Gottschalk 1950: 100–101).

Louis Gottschalk credits Marbois with some anthropological observations, which I find minimal. The Oneida people were quite honest: stray horses were quickly rounded up. Frequent brawls were mediated. "Easy marriages" obtained between hosts and guests. Divorce was common. Enlightened readers in France might find the "children of nature" unlike descriptions by writers who had never seen them (Gottschalk 1950: 101). Of Lafayette, Marbois wrote: "Those who have seen him before have a great urge to see him again" (Gottschalk 1950: 102).

Back at Fort Stanwix, the Oneidas and Senecas composed their differences and buried their hostility in order to present a united front to the commissioners when they arrived. In what resembles a variant of woods'-edge protocol, Grasshopper, representing the Oneidas, who had supported the Americans, escorted by five warriors, approached the Seneca encampment. The chief of the Seneca delegation, probably Cornplanter, came out to meet him. "They sat down together on the grass, exchanged compliments [undoubtedly the Three Bare Words of Requickening], smoked a pipe of peace, and then separated." Next day the Senecas carried the same ceremony to the Oneida encampment (and returned the words of condolence). Marbois, who witnessed the exchange, says nothing about passing wampum strings, but wrote: "I thought myself at the Diet of Ratisbon" (Gottschalk 1950: 102, after Chase 1929: 205).

Whether Lafayette's presence acted as a catalyst to bring about peace remains open to question. He certainly radiated the kind of charisma that the Indians admired. But he posed a problem to the commissioners of Congress, whom he upstaged. The Indians expected him to speak; the commissioners wished he wouldn't, but they reluctantly accorded him a spot on the first day, after chairman Wolcott finally arrived.

It was a cold morning on 3 October (according to Evans) when the commissioners called the Indians together in council for the first time and kindled the council fire. The composition of the Indian side is not specified. Cornplanter led the Seneca delegation; neither Red Jacket nor Brant was present, although Aaron Hill later spoke for the émigré Mohawks and others, and for western allies. Grasshopper fronted for the neighboring Oneidas and Tuscaroras. Some Kahnawakeh chiefs attended, and some Shawnee observers looked on. Precisely who the Six

Nations were just then and who might represent them at the treaty would become a bone of contention later. There were some forty warriors present, some with arms, others in "masquerade" (Montbas 1929: 96).[2]

As host, Commissioner Wolcott spoke first, welcoming the delegates and introducing Lafayette and his party. The main business of the treaty would await full representation of the nations involved.

I shall not dwell on Lafayette's celebrated speech. He made two important points: he urged the Indians to accept the terms offered by the U.S. commissioners, and he upbraided those who espoused the Loyalist cause. Grasshopper, for the Oneidas, and Onegenta of Kahnawakeh responded to Lafayette with considerable fluency. Despite the limitations of Kirkland's interpreting, Evans was amazed at their logic and eloquence. In further reference to these preliminary exchanges, Evans confided to a friend: "I am very much surprised at the force and comprehension of their Ideas and [how] generally [they are] coherent." He had been compelled at first to lodge with the Indians in a "wigwam," which he found disagreeable, but after several days of living with them and seeing them constantly he preferred their company to sleeping outside without fire or blanket (Evans to John Nicholson, NYSL, 13515).

On 4 October, following Lafayette's address, Grasshopper, on behalf of the friendly nations, opened the council, thanking Lafayette for his advice. They recalled how Kayewla seven years earlier had warned them against the British. His words then had proved true, and they would follow his present advice. To confirm his words, the old Oneida chief presented Lafayette with a wampum belt that he had received long before from the hands of Montcalm, that great French soldier. It pleased Lafayette that the Oneidas had kept the belt intact, but he returned it, saying he would hold one end of it while the Americans held the other (Gottschalk 1950: 104).

Hearing these exchanges, Marbois found the Iroquoian sentence structure and syntax baffling, Iroquoian being given to polysynthesis and noun incorporation. "They heap up all sorts of incoherent ideas and facts." When Lafayette proposed to one of the more eloquent orators that he learn English, the man replied that he feared corrupting his native tongue (Chase 1929: 26; Gottschalk 1950: 105).

□□◇□□

The treaty proper did not commence for several days after Lafayette and Madison departed. Madison would comment later on interference by New York state, the first problem; the second was that clearing the treaty grounds of rum traders raised the specter of local option and the jurisdiction of the county sheriff. Governor Clinton had stationed Major Peter Schuyler at the fort to watch the movements of the commissioners of Congress, to oppose whatever struck him as detrimental to the government of New York, and to do what he could to frustrate it (Hough 1861, 1: 63; Evans 1941: 210). The commissioners took umbrage and after several incidents ordered the guard to escort Schuyler and the traders from the grounds, post sentinels, and seize and store the liquor until after the treaty concluded. Evans, having found these parties amiable, regretted their departure.

---

2. Available sources do not specify masks as such, or face painting.

Following the departure of Lafayette's entourage, Evans took his meals in the mess of the U.S. commissioners, which until then had been crowded with guests. The new situation kept him au courant with inside conversations. On one of his days in camp (8 October), Evans heard Cornplanter reply to the commissioners' general terms of the treaty. Cornplanter, Kirkland informed Evans, could be likened to "Cicero for force, eloquence and accuracy,"

After the preliminary skirmishes, the treaty got under way in earnest on 12 October. The commissioners faced fewer Indians and persons of lesser rank than they had expected. None of the named participants carried a league title. Additional Iroquois, Shawnees, and Delawares had arrived several days earlier with the Mohawk Aaron Hill, Brant's surrogate. Captain Hill felt obliged to explain why so few of the Six Nations were present (he viewed the treaty as preliminary to a major congress), that the Wyandots had returned home from Niagara, and that although the delegates had brought no prisoners, Brant would have them collected and sent down promptly. The commissioners chose not to reply. Instead they turned to Cornplanter, with whom the "headmen of the Six Towns" (of the Seneca nation) had sent a "writing" naming him their representative. It would please the commissioners to do business with a person of his wisdom and good name (Manley 1932: 87).

The commissioners then read their commissions and, in a set speech delivered by Arthur Lee in a tone "by no means accommodating or flattering" (Evans wrote), and "quite unlike what they used to receive," the commissioners "made the Indians stare." They declared that the hostile nations of the Iroquois Confederacy were now a conquered people who must submit to terms imposed by Congress, which included expected land cessions. Lee urged the Indians to give the matter deep consideration and reply when ready. It was up to them to propose a boundary line. He then raked up the council fire.

Five days passed before the Indians replied. Several incidents delayed them. A wounded traveler to Niagara limped in on the thirteenth, having been shot by some Mahican irregulars. The Indians counseled the commissioners not to let the incident interrupt the proceedings. Similar occurrences during the next three days were relieved by exceedingly fine weather. Evans reported that they were "living in the highest style . . . too sumptuous for my constitution."

The council reconvened on the seventeenth. Nine Senecas had come in, bringing word that a son of Cornplanter's had died. On hearing the sad news, Cornplanter remarked (according to Evans) that while the Good Spirit had brought them together and cleared their lungs to speak clearly and dispose their minds to peace, "Evil Spirits without face [Death the Faceless] had come amongst them and struck a hard blow from behind to send one of their young men under the earth."

Ancient custom required performing the ritual of condolence to lift up Cornplanter's mind before proceeding to business, which was done in the presence of the commissioners. Belts passed both ways between clearminded and mourners.

The Mohawk Aaron Hill, being unaffected, seized the moment to challenge the commissioners in a not-atypical display of Iroquois arrogance. Evans characterized Hill as "an enterprizing warrior but impolitic statesman." His speech, of which I offer only an abstract, is an excellent example of Iroquois oratory (Craig 1876: 418–20).

The Great Spirit had convened the council to make a lasting peace, Hill declared. A treaty was a mutual affair. He spoke in the name of the warriors, "for there are no Sachems amongst us." Warriors were men of the world, hardened by war; their words were strong, and they were empowered to make a lasting peace. The proof of their character lay in their strict adherence to the crown covenant. He spoke in the name of the Six Nations but also in the name of their allies, which strengthened his words. They were a free and independent people, the king having broken the chain. (A string.)

He took up the belt given to validate the Congressional commission, which meant more to the Indians than the writing. The Six Nations agreed that no particular state enjoyed priority over Congress. (A string.) They preferred to deal with the general government.

As to the boundary, they adhered to the 1768 line. It now defined the United States. Common justice would have required the king to mention his faithful Indian allies. (A string.)

Corresponding to the commissioners' powers, the Six Nations were the only people empowered to treat for a list of Central Algonquian, Wyandot, and Muskogean tribes. (A string.)

A black-and-white string marked a cession of all French lands to the United States.

Then, taking up one belt, laying it down, and taking up another, Hill said that the latter belt referred to captives not returned. He proposed that the Americans come and get them, a daunting task. (A belt.)

It being late in the day, the commissioners raked up the fire and retired.

Next morning (18 October), Cornplanter resumed where Captain Hill had left off. In a "long and artful speech," Evans noted, he drew the boundary within which the Six Nations hoped to live and which they wanted ratified. It was essentially the 1768 line. Cornplanter said that the day was too short to solve such a vital question, "for we Indians love our lands." He blamed much of the tension between his own Senecas and the Mohawks on Colonel Guy Johnson, who kept moving the council fire from place to place. After conferring with the Onondaga council, the Senecas had delivered to General Schuyler the hatchet that Johnson had given them at Oswego. It had originated with their blood kindred at Kahnawakeh, whom they loved. Kinship obligations prevailed over the request of the United States that they remain neutral, and that was how they had entered the war.

"I who stand before you am a warrior," Cornplanter said. As such he would be distressed if the commissioners did not tell him if his words failed to meet their approval. The lands in question belonged essentially to the Seneca nation, he asserted. Warriors need a large area to range and hunt. They must provide for the future generations. "By this belt you can see my mind."

He then introduced a colleague who would attend the surveys to assure that the proper boundaries were drawn between the Senecas and American settlers. The commissioners promised a reply and raked up the fire (Craig 1876, 2: 420–23).

A treaty was no occasion to be bored. On the afternoon of 18 October, teams from Oneida and Kahnawakeh (twelve on a side) entertained the crowd with a game of lacrosse. The prize was twenty dollars. The players stripped and partook generously of rum. Evans observed that this game, skittles, and dancing were the Indians' main diversions.

Evans described a social dance that began after dark, as such performances still do. It led off with Ga?da:trot, "Standing Quiver Dance," a variant of the widespread stomp dances of the Eastern Woodlands peoples. (I infer this from Evans's attempt to reproduce the nonsense antiphonals between leader and followers, and his description of the motion of the dancers.) It pleased the Indians when Evans and others joined in (Evans 1941: 213).

The Indians heard the bad news two days later, on 20 October. Arthur Lee replied for the commissioners (Craig 1876, 2: 423ff.; Manley 1932: 89, who ascribed it to Butler; Evans 1941: 214). Lee's tone alarmed his hearers. These were the main points: that the native orators pretended they spoke for all nations, north and south, surprised the commissioners: "We summoned the Six Nations only to this treaty." The delegates of the Six Nations had offered neither writings nor belts to substantiate their claim. (The commissioners themselves had not distributed written copies of their speeches lest they be misinterpreted by partially literate persons having private interests.) As for the Indians' pretenses of keeping covenants, where were their pledges of neutrality made at treaties in 1775 and 1776? They were neither free nor independent nations but a subdued people. They had been conquered. They could expect no repetition of the present offers. Peace rested on two concessions: they must deliver up all captives, and they must propose a boundary that the United States could accept. The Indians had given no satisfaction on either point. It was fatuous to expect Americans to retrieve the captives. Much of the land within their proposed boundary had already been sold to Pennsylvania, and the lands southeast toward the Cherokee River had been ceded in the 1768 treaty and were already partially settled.

The commissioners then outlined their conditions for peace and the protection of the United States. These four conditions, which composed the text of the treaty as later published without the proceedings, were all that were available for some ninety years (*American State Papers—Indian Affairs*, 1: 10; Craig 1876, 2: 425-27; Manley 1932: 92). The commissioners restricted the conditions to the four hostile nations—Mohawk, Onondaga, Cayuga, and Seneca.

In summary: (1) The Indians should deliver immediately six hostages to be held until all captives (white and black) were delivered. (2) The Oneida and Tuscarora settled lands were secured for those tribes. (3) The western boundary of the Six Nations would be demarcated by a line drawn from "the mouth of Oyonwagea Creek on Lake Ontario, four miles east of Niagara south to the mouth of Buffalo Creek, and east of the Niagara portage, thence due south to the northern boundary of Pennsylvania, thence west to the end of that boundary, thence south along the west boundary of that state to the Ohio River." The Six Nations would cede all lands west of that line. (4) The commissioners would order goods delivered to the Six Nations upon their signing the treaty.

The commissioners felt constrained to add a few remarks on the four articles, which they deemed moderate and equitable. (To the Indians they were bitter medicine.) First, the Six Nations' failure to deliver captives, requested by General Schuyler in the name of Congress six months ago, demanded hostages. Second, the United States secured those nations faithful to them in the free use and enjoyment of their lands. Third, the king had ceded to the United States, by right of conquest, the whole of his possessions (except Canada). So far the United States had claimed but a small part; now the veterans of the Continental Army must be provided for. And fourth, although the present distress of the Six Nations was their own fault, the United States intended to minister relief.

Cornplanter, knowing he faced criticism at home, replied with dignity: "You have this day declared your minds to us fully, and without disguise. We thank you for it; this is acting like men, for thus men speak. We will take what you have said into our most serious consideration, and when we shall have prepared ourselves to answer to what you have proposed, you shall hear our voice" (Craig 1876, 2: 427).

After the usual ceremonies, the commissioners ordered the council fire raked up and retired from the council house.

The Indians replied promptly next day (21 October). The Mohawk Aaron Hill, who was destined to be one of the six hostages, protested that the Indians had been misunderstood, that they actually loved peace, and that they were now relieved of their covenant with the king. They were again free and independent people. They would remain neutral should war break out again. No, they had not brought any words with them but had left them with the council fire that burned among the Shawnees on the Miami River.

The commissioners were not impressed.

That same day Good Peter, a great Oneida speaker, made an elegant speech on behalf of the Six Nations, they having agreed to the commissioners' proposals (Evans 1941: 214). Two more mornings of conferences passed before the Indians signed the treaty. Of the listed signatures, two from each of the Six Nations save a lone Cayuga, none bears the title of a league founder. Cornplanter, himself a warrior, signed apart from the others at the foot of the list (Hough 1861, 1: 65).

The Pennsylvania commissioners, having stood by and observed the sessions of the U.S. treaty, on the following day (23 October) seized a favorable opportunity to purchase previously unavailable Indian lands contiguous with their state. These lands comprised Seneca hunting territory. As a token to Cornplanter, they excepted some eight hundred acres on the Allegheny River, just south of the New York state line, afterward known as the Cornplanter Grant, for the exclusive use of his descendants. He would also receive an annuity. Red Jacket later would cite these emoluments to destroy Cornplanter's reputation among the Seneca people (Manley 1932: 95).

On the twenty-sixth, Grasshopper signed the receipt for the federal treaty goods in Evans's charge. Evans walked up on the green to observe the distribution. He noted that the Indians accomplished it with "the greatest decorum and apparent impartiality," apportioning "the goods to each tribe with much exactness [and] not a word of dispute or dissatisfaction" (Evans 1941: 214–15).

□□◇□□

The harsh terms imposed by the 1784 Stanwix treaty sparked the breakup of the Six Nations confederacy. Factionalism divided the Seneca nation between Cornplanter's adherents on the Allegheny and the followers of Farmer's Brother and Red Jacket at Buffalo Creek. Traditionalists at Grand River sought unity by reviving the Iroquois League. Joseph Brant's followers sought to extend the idea of confederation to include western tribes. A decade of Indian warfare in Ohio followed American military expansion. During that decade, the United States would lose two armies in the wilderness before General Anthony Wayne defeated the coalition of hostile Indians at Fallen Timbers and Timothy Pickering negotiated peace and tranquility with the Six Nations at Canandaigua in November 1794.

CHAPTER 39

PRELUDE
TO CANANDAIGUA

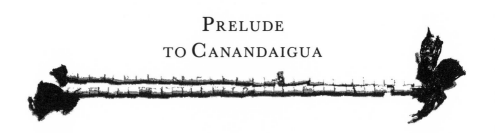

> And the United States will never claim the same, nor disturb the Seneka Nation . . . in the free use and enjoyment thereof. —Article III, Pickering treaty, 1794

This pledge from the pen of Timothy Pickering, whom President Washington commissioned as sole agent to treat with the Six Nations at Canandaigua in the autumn of 1794—a pledge signed by him and fifty sachems and war chiefs—became familiar to thousands of newspaper readers at the time of the Kinzua Dam controversy in 1959. It was repeatedly cited by lawyers for the Seneca nation and by friends of the Indians, and it echoed in the halls of Congress. Yet no one bothered to look beyond these words to see how and why they were written.

The Kinzua Dam controversy has come and gone. The Seneca nation lost a substantial portion of the Allegheny Valley below Salamanca to the rising waters, and the 130 Indian families who had called the valley home, having first learned to live like muskrats, fled to higher ground and relocated in two suburban housing settlements built by their own enterprise. Other Americans, having assuaged their guilt, soon forgot it, but a generation afterward trauma lingers among Seneca families for whom the Canandaigua treaty was the charter that guaranteed free use and enjoyment of their remaining lands.

No one up to now has examined the original sources with a view to finding out what the state of affairs was when the original agreement was signed. The record is not readily available, but it exists. Timothy Pickering, who conducted the treaty, on his return to Philadelphia in December 1794 wrote only the briefest of reports to Henry Knox, the outgoing secretary of war, just before Knox retired and Pickering succeeded him. Knox had been an able and conscientious administrator at a time when Indian affairs were lodged in the War Department, and he had laid a firm basis for an Indian policy that, once the hostile Indians were subdued, would accord fairer treatment to peaceful tribes than they could expect from the several states. But Pickering succeeded Knox before he could file a full report, with the result that the treaty alone, without the supporting documents, went from Pickering to President Washington, who transmitted it to the Senate for prompt ratification. The documentation never became part of the public record. The Senate ratified the treaty without delay, the president proclaimed it on 21 January

1795, and the original bearing the Indian signatures was deposited in the office of the secretary of state, then Edmund Randolph. It is now in the National Archives.

Henry Knox must have been among the first public servants to depart the government for business reasons—to conduct his personal affairs in Maine. Both he and Pickering were in the van of public officials who carried home the records of their offices. Indeed, their foresight proved fortunate, for New England was spared during the War of 1812, while the War Department records were burned when the British sacked Washington. Perhaps it was a sense of history that yet characterizes eminent New Englanders that prompted these two Federalists to retain their papers. Afterward, Pickering's son Octavius put the papers in order and wrote a biography of his father. Later, the Pickering family deposited the Pickering papers, which included three volumes of Indian negotiations, with the Massachusetts Historical Society in Boston (Pickering 1896), which also holds the Knox papers. There I was privileged to examine them. Descendants of that name who still occupied the Pickering house on Chestnut Street in Salem, Massachusetts, in 1948 gave me access to letters that Timothy wrote to his wife, Becky, from Canandaigua.

I was the first person trained in anthropology with some knowledge of Iroquois culture to examine these sources. I had then some fifteen years of intensive and intermittent field experience among the living descendants of sachems and chiefs who signed the treaty. It was their sense of oral history and their tradition of politics that turned me to testing their views of their own past in the materials of history. Coming from living sources in the field to reading literary sources in the library, I brought the critical apparatus of ethnology and some understanding of Seneca culture. This approach has become familiarly known as ethnohistory.

The old men of Iroquoia were a legalistic lot who quoted the treaties at will. I used to wonder just how reliable were the memories of these old men of the Seneca nation—men like Walter "Boots" Kennedy and Johnny Button of Cattaraugus, Jonas Crouse, Oscar Nephew, and Howard Logan of Allegany, and Peter Doctor and Nicodemus Billy (Bailey) of Tonawanda—who spoke with such authority about "Indian law" and the Pickering treaty? I met these men in the 1930s; for two and one-half years I sat with them in council as representative of the U.S. Indian Service; and as an adopted Seneca by the Hawk clan I listened to discourses when I sought their opinions. To these old men of prodigious memories I owe my postdoctoral training in Indian politics. Of all the palefaces, from whom they suffered so much indignity and of whom I was so often a minority of one, they revered the names of Washington, Pickering, and the Quakers of Philadelphia.

The essence of civilization is literacy. The Indians say we palefaces are forever writing things in books, yet we forget more rapidly than they do, and our records have a way of getting lost, misplaced, or burned up. Could I, as an ethnologist, determine what depth there might be for the Indian tradition of their negotiations with Euro-Americans? Would the extant records of the political history of the Six Nations reflect sufficiently the native point of view? What light would the records throw on the processes of culture change? Ethnologists and culture historians constantly seek the principles that explain culture change and conservatism, which are facets of the same phenomenon. Conceivably, Iroquois traditionalists who speak

confidently of agreements that their forebears entered into may be better custodians of the spirit of history than we later Americans who remain preoccupied with
the written record.

The Pickering treaty provided the Seneca nation and the rest of the Six Nations
with a charter for their corporate existence. It vouchsafed their reservations, land
being their essential identity. Nothing before Kinzua really set aside the principle
that the lands were theirs until they chose to sell, and then they could sell only to
the people of the United States. This has always meant that ultimate jurisdiction
resided in the federal government, as set forth in the Constitution of the United
States. Section eight of Article 1 defines the general powers of the Congress,
namely, "to regulate Commerce with foreign Nations . . . and with Indian tribes."
As we saw in Governor Clinton's demeanor during the 1784 Stanwix treaty, New
York state has always maintained its priority in dealing directly with the Six
Nations, particularly in the purchase of lands; it sees this right as descending from
its status as a crown colony of the king of Great Britain, which preceded formation
of the "general" (federal) government by the Articles of Confederation and the
Constitution of 1788. From the beginning of the nation, jurisdiction over Indian
affairs has been mixed, and not surprisingly, public officials have perforce been
ambivalent in defining the situation. The Indians, too, have played it both ways,
taking from the state while falling back on the federal government when pushed.

When the courts ruled that Congress, in appropriating funds for preliminary
explorations for the Kinzua Dam, had in effect abrogated the 1794 treaty, which
Congress had the right to do, the Seneca nation was bereft of its charter and had
just cause to feel "disturbed." I shall not discuss further the history of the Kinzua
Dam crisis, which warrants a separate book, but will concentrate in the next four
chapters on the background, proceedings, and substance of the Canandaigua
treaty itself, to which the Senecas appealed. It may be helpful first to examine the
terms of the treaty and the issues it addressed.

□□◇□□

The seven articles comprising "A Treaty between the United States of America,
and the Tribes of Indians Called the Six Nations," dated 11 November 1794,
constitute an agenda of the issues of the day. Each article became the subject of
considerable negotiation, and several engendered anxiety on both sides of the fire.
The seven provisions represent the best agreement the Indians and Pickering could
reach. They resolved some issues that had hung fire for a decade, issues that were
vital at that juncture in our national history.

The preamble to the treaty defines its conditions, states its purposes, names the
parties, and expresses hope for its permanence. President Washington stood
squarely behind it. I agree with George Heron, then president of the Seneca
Nation of Indians, testifying before the U.S. House of Representatives during the
Kinzua crisis, that the Seneca people believe "Washington read the 1794 treaty
before he signed it, and that he meant exactly what he wrote" in proclaiming it.
Its purpose was to remove "from their minds all causes of complaint" arising from
previous treaties and to establish "a firm and permanent friendship with them"
(House of Representatives 1794: 276).

In appointing Timothy Pickering "sole agent" of the United States to treat with
the Six Nations, the president clearly excluded other commissioners, particularly

those of Pennsylvania and New York state. The other party to the treaty consisted of "the Sachems, Chiefs, and Warriors of the Six Nations"—the three ranks of Iroquois polity. The treaty text is one of the truly great pieces of American documentation. It is a pity that more people have not read and studied it.

A third party, the Society of Friends of Philadelphia, whose presence Seneca leaders requested and whom the president invited to attend as observers, chose not sign the document but stood as a moral force to the equity of both parties. The Friends committed their views to their journals.

Of the seven articles to the treaty, article 1 established "peace and friendship" perpetually "between the United States and the Six Nations." This is no empty phrase, considering that the Six Nations in New York and Canada then numbered some forty-five hundred, including more than a thousand seasoned warriors, according to a systematic census that the missionary Kirkland had just completed. The president and Secretary Knox charged Pickering with keeping the Iroquois quiet in their seats lest they be loosed on the frontier of New York and Pennsylvania. The last thing President Washington and his secretary of war wanted was another Indian war while General Anthony Wayne's army was somewhere in Ohio. An Indian war cost manpower, goods, and money; treating for peace cost far less and might prove permanent. The Quakers manifested a concern that the treaty settle differences arising from previous treaties. At Buffalo Creek, at Grand River, and at Cornplanter's village on the Allegheny, the great debate raged: should the Six Nations accede to Joseph Brant and join the western coalition of Indians to defeat Wayne with British military aid, or should they turn their backs on the "red coats" of Niagara and Detroit and treat with Washington's government in Philadelphia?

Article 2 of the Pickering treaty acknowledged that the parcels of land that the Oneidas, Onondagas, and Cayugas had reserved in their respective treaties with the state of New York were indeed their several properties. The United States pledged never to claim those lands or disturb their Indian owners "in the free use and enjoyment thereof." It pledged that these lands were theirs "until they chose to sell," and that the "people of the United States had the right to purchase."

In the decade following the Fort Stanwix treaty, Indian transactions with the state of New York went on apace, and these land cessions were now an accomplished fact, although some of them violated the Non-Intercourse Act of 1790. Pickering sought to reassure the several nations involved that what few lands they still held were not in jeopardy, nor were previous transactions invalid. As we shall see, Pickering devoted considerable time to reassuring the several nations at Canandaigua and afterward at Oneida. In the 1960s, the Seneca Nation of Indians would rest its right to retain the lands jeopardized by the Kinzua Dam on article 2.

Article 3 defined the territory of the Seneca nation, then the most extensive tract in western New York. In 1788, six years previously, Oliver Phelps and Nathaniel Gorham had purchased the Massachusetts preemption right to two and one-half million acres of land lying east of the Genesee River and a small tract lying west of it, between that river and a line drawn on the meridian just west of modern Geneva on Seneca Lake, and comprising what are now Ontario, Steuben, Yates, and parts of adjacent counties. The Stanwix treaty defined the western border of

Seneca lands, subject to the Erie Triangle, which was patented to Pennsylvania in 1792 so as to afford access to Lake Erie at Presque Isle.

This last transaction had greatly disturbed Cornplanter and his warriors, who, up until the last minute, awaited word to take up the hatchet. Defining these bounds involved protracted negotiations before the treaty could be signed. The article concludes by making the same assurances that the lands are the property of the Seneca nation and that the United States will never claim them or "disturb the Seneca nation . . . in the free use and enjoyment thereof."

After the treaty document described and acknowledged which lands were the property of the Six Nations individually, article 4 affirmed and quit claim to those lands and promised never to disturb the owners, who in turn promised the same with reference to lands that they relinquished to the people of the United States. The very essence of the treaty centers on this mutual agreement to quit claim and never disturb each other in the free use and enjoyment of their respective property. On it rests the idea of sovereignty in either case.

Article 5 provided for a wagon road to afford travelers free passage around the Niagara portage. This provision emerged from a compromise: Pickering wanted a corridor at Cayuga Creek, but the Senecas worried about encroachments on the strip from buildings, saloons, and other enterprises that would ruin their lives, deface the landscape, and spoil the fisheries. They settled by terminating the road at Buffalo Creek.

Article 6 provided that in consideration of the foregoing, the Six Nations would receive ten thousand dollars and an increased welfare fund, at the time amounting to $4,500, to be paid as an annuity forever—for purchase of clothing, domestic animals, farm implements, and the like, and to compensate "resident artificers." The presents were what Indians came for, but the definition of benefits to be paid as an annuity, which came to be known as "unity goods," fulfilled a plan for the gradual "civilization" of the Indian natives that had multiple authors. Kirkland had first advanced it, the president and his cabinet officers promoted it, Pickering drafted a plan for agriculture and industry, and the Quakers had already experimented with technical assistance. Indian leaders saw the need to return to an economy not dependent solely on hunting but also relying on women's maize-bean-squash horticulture, which had languished during the war years. They would supplement those crops with other cereal grasses and farm with domesticated animals. Spinning, weaving, and blacksmithing represented important skills not yet acquired. A United States superintendent would guide this revolution.

Article 6 also attempted to bring the custom of blood feud and compensation for injury by means of the condolence ritual into harmony with Anglo-Saxon law. Pickering and the chiefs understood only too well that injuries done or sustained produced a chain reaction leading to Indian wars. Pickering knew how reluctantly Indians gave up offenders to trial in courts of law, and that it was virtually impossible to get a jury to convict a white man of murdering an Indian. From now on the Indians were supposed to complain to the president through their agent, but not to seek revenge. Local peace officers were to leave Indian crimes to federal officials, as in later times murder, rape, and arson became major crimes subject to the federal courts. This was how it was going to be until "the great council" (the Congress) should make other provisions. Article six built in protection that Indians of later times would covet and relinquish reluctantly.

Finally, article 7 excluded Indians residing in Canada from receiving annuities. This exclusion addressed some amusing situations in later times when Iroquois families living on the Grand River and having relatives at Buffalo Creek, or intermarried with Iroquois families in other Niagara frontier settlements on the New York side, became adept at boundary hopping and collected annuities in both countries.

The United States and the Six Nations comprised the two nominal parties to the treaty. Pickering signed as sole agent for the government, and fifty-nine sachems, chiefs, and warriors of the Six Nations and their dependents each marked an *X* next to his title. Eight important citizens witnessed the document, as did four interpreters, of whom one was a Seneca. For reasons of conscience, the names of four Quaker observers are absent.

Two signed copies of the treaty survive. The National Archives preserves the government's copy; the Indians' copy, somewhat worn from frequent consultation, is on view at the Ontario County Historical Society in Canandaigua, where it was executed.

Although the tribes named are the Six Nations, the Canandaigua treaty was primarily a Seneca affair. Seneca signers predominate; there was virtually no Mohawk representation. Pickering secured but one Mohawk signature, which scarcely warrants the claim of Mohawk descendants today that their forebears were party to the treaty.

□□◇□□

Timothy Pickering (1745–1829) of Salem was nearing the peak of his career at age forty-nine when he came to Canandaigua that autumn (fig. 40). An imposing figure of a man, above six feet in stature, he had evoked the name Kanehsadeh, "on the side of a hill," when the Senecas adopted him four years earlier at Painted Post. Red Jacket, no mean intellect himself, sized up Pickering for what he was. Pickering had graduated in 1763, the year of Pontiac's uprising, from Harvard, where he had studied law. He married Rebecca White, and they bore ten children. His letters from Canandaigua to Becky and to his son John, afterward the noted linguist, contain human insights on the treaty. His business interests ran to the improvement of agriculture and land investments. Having raised a regiment at the outbreak of the Revolution, Colonel Pickering became adjutant general of the American army within two years and served as quartermaster general after 1780. With the cessation of hostilities, the claims of New Englanders to the settlement of the Wyoming lands in northeastern Pennsylvania engaged his attention.

In 1791 President Washington appointed Pickering postmaster general, and meeting Pickering one day on a Philadelphia street, the president asked him to double as commissioner of Indian affairs under Henry Knox, secretary of war. As such, Pickering conducted a series of meetings preparatory to Canandaigua. One of three commissioners to the Indians at the Maumee Rapids in 1793, a mission that failed to pacify the western coalition of hostiles while General Wayne kept his eager army quiet, he learned that council-fire protocol did not always succeed. He was determined to leave no stone unturned at Canandaigua. Surely there is no better training for diplomacy than learning how to meet the expectations of

Figure 40. Timothy
Pickering. Engraving by
T. B. Welch, after a portrait
by Gilbert Stuart. Courtesy
Massachusetts Historical
Society.

participants of another society and different cultural heritage. At that Pickering
succeeded better at Indian affairs than afterward as secretary of state. President
Adams dismissed him.

Affairs were being put in train for Pickering's arrival at Canandaigua. Strings
of invitation wampum went out to the principal fires of the Six Nations—eastward
to Onondaga and Oneida, and westward toward the sunset. The chiefs at Buffalo
Creek would relay runners to Cornplanter's settlement on the Allegheny and to
the Grand River in Canada. The Indians would all come hungry. Stores were
assembled, beefs purchased and driven in, and warehouses emptied for receipt of
Indian goods that Pickering had ordered sent by water from Philadelphia to
Albany and thence inland. Traders laid in rum and cheap whiskey.

Pickering could delay his departure overland until he thought the Indians would
come in, knowing that arrangements at the treaty site were in competent hands.
The Israel Chapins—father and son, *yatathawak* in Iroquois usage—were fellow
Revolutionary officers who inspired confidence on both sides. General Chapin had
explored the Genesee country for Phelps and Gorham, had helped found
Canandaigua in 1788, and resided there. As deputy superintendent of the Six
Nations, he adhered to Knox's Indian policy—"that a fair and kind spirit should
mark the national intercourse"—winning the Indians' respect for patiently
hearing their views. He had restrained land grabbers, maintained calm, and
played down armed force when the Senecas appeared moody and might defect to
the western coalition. Above all, the elder Chapin had earned respect for wearing
out his moccasins going to Presque Isle to avert an armed clash the previous
summer, a journey that quite ruined his health. General Chapin was now a sick
man.

The Senecas regarded Captain Chapin as one of their boys and treated him with affection. He probably knew the language passably. Two years previously he had conducted Joseph Brant, the Mohawk war captain, safely from Canandaigua past the scenes of recent massacres to Albany and Philadelphia on a mission to meet President Washington and Secretary Knox, a journey that the British opposed and might have cost Brant his life. Hostility toward the Six Nations still ran high in upper "York state."

Among the interpreters for the treaty, several had learned Iroquois as captives. Farmer's Brother, leader of the Buffalo Creek Senecas, characterized two of them, Jasper Parrish and Horatio Jones, as "the little boys who were caught up in the whirlwind and cast into our arms to be adopted into our families." Both were carried off by war parties, ran the gauntlet, survived, and grew up in Seneca families. They became bilingual and bicultural. Parrish acquired both Iroquois and Delaware; Jones was entirely Seneca. Each stayed on the frontier after the Revolution as trader and Indian agent, roles that favored ambivalence. Jones became party to the most secret Indian negotiations; Parrish belonged more to the whites. They both died in 1836.[1]

Four Quakers from the Yearly Meeting for Sufferings of Philadelphia attended the treaty. Their journals, along with the Pickering papers, compose the primary sources on the proceedings. John Parrish and William Savery (1750-1804) had earlier attended the abortive treaty at the Maumee Rapids; David Bacon and James Emlen (1760-97) were neophytes at Canandaigua. William Savery spoke for the four and was the most literate: his journal, printed afterward in Philadelphia and London (1837), has been the sole resource for previous writers. Bacon's diary (Haverford College Library, ms.) describes Indian customs; Emlen's journal (New York State Library) ranks next to Savery's in quality and coverage (Fenton, ed., 1965a). Emlen was a better observer of natural phenomena than Savery, but his account skips the last ten days of the treaty proceedings. Savery evidently wrote from his own notes and the combined journals of the other three.[2]

Some sixteen hundred Indians, a good third of the population of the Six Nations, converged on the Canandaigua council fire. Attendance measured how important they regarded the treaty. Jones and Parrish helped Pickering and Savery estimate the combined population of the Six Nations just then at 4,500, including 1,900 Senecas, 400 Cayugas, 500 Onondagas, 600 Oneidas, 300 Tuscaroras, and 800 absentee Mohawks in Canada. (An actual census by village that Kirkland made four years earlier totaled five hundred fewer.) People came by foot over the well-worn trail that connected the main fires of the Longhouse, which today the New York Thruway traverses. A Seneca matron matched her one hundred summers in miles walked from Buffalo to witness her grandchildren part with their heritage. Skenandoa doubled his age in miles of trail from Oneida and seemed none the worse for the journey. Matrons and leaders in the next century would

1. Jones, who was barely literate, merited a biography by George H. Harris of Rochester (1903: 383-526), and the same volume carries a sketch of Captain Jasper Parrish, pp. 527-46. The Parrish Papers at Vassar College Library are silent on matters about which he was most knowledgeable.

2. The late Merle Deardorff, in reading a 1965 draft of this manuscript, commented that all versions of the Quaker journals published under Quaker auspices were heavily edited to eliminate items unfavorable to the Society of Friends. This is particularly true of the Savery journal.

recall being packed on cradle boards at their mother's backs. Only the very aged and crippled stayed at home "in the back of the bed."

It was important to make certain that the right Indians were present and signed the agreement. This avoided argument later. Pickering insisted that all ranks of Indian polity—sachems, councilors, warriors—sign the articles of the treaty, a wise move, as affairs developed. But it remains unclear how many of the fifty-nine signers qualified, and whom they represented. Numerically the signers represented individual nations unevenly: 27 Senecas, 9 Cayugas, 8 Onondagas, 6 Oneidas, 1 Mohawk, 4 Tuscaroras, and 2 each of Munsees and Mahicans.

The Iroquois League tradition made a poor showing. Of the fifty known titles of league founders, but two of eight Seneca titles appear: Ganiodaiyo? (Ganya-daiyo?), or Handsome Lake, afterward famous as the Prophet, and Tca?takeonye:s (Sa?dagaenyes), Skies of Equal Height. Pickering learned that the head Onondaga sachem, "a sensible old man," lame and "not to be tempted over the fire by the British," remained behind at Buffalo Creek. Could this have been Thadoda:ho?? Of the fourteen Onondaga titles I find only Onesahen (One?sa:hen), Oa-2, RC 20). None of the nine Mohawk titles appears to complete the senior moiety.

Four possible titles of founders signed for the junior moiety. Of the nine titles on the Oneida roster, the first two—Odatshehdeh, Quiver Bearer (Oe-1, RC 10), and Kanongweniyah (Oe-2, RC 11)—head the list in proper order. Only two of ten titles on the Cayuga roster—Teyoenhyongo (Deyoenhyon:goh, C-6, RC 38) and Odegwa:shon (Gadagwa:ji, C-3, RC 35[?])—are suggested by the listed signers. Fish Carrier, however, a sachem by merit and not the holder of a league title, led the Cayuga delegation and signed first.

The Six Nations put forward the best men available to represent them. They were the so-called councilors, or "headmen to do business." Accordingly, Farmer's Brother (Honeyewas, or Honanyawus) and Red Jacket (Shakoye:wa:tha?) of Buffalo Creek managed the Seneca delegation and signed ahead of Handsome Lake and Skies of Equal Height.

Cornplanter (Kayenthwahkeh), the most considerable of the Seneca warriors present, led the Allegheny faction, although two war chiefs whose titles descend from the league's founding outranked him: Sonehso:wa (Snipe clan) and Then:wonya?s (Wolf clan), of the opposite moiety, who in later times served the sachems as runners.[3] Others had achieved the status of sachem in recent years, including Big Kettle (Sononjowa:neh); Little Billy; Little Beard, or "Hanging Spear" (Segwidon?gwi), of Geneseo; Kanehshongo, or simply Shongo; Half Town; Stinking Fish; and others, not to overlook "Heap of Dogs" (Kajiageonh), still a favorite name.

Two Oneida war chiefs came under comment: John Skenandoa, who signed, and Peter, who departed angry after the sachems reprimanded him for usurping their authority.

---

3. Jemmy Johnson, L. H. Morgan's informant on the Handsome Lake code, held the title Shosheowa:?, or "Big Burden Strap" and may have been the same person referred to in the Canandaigua treaty sources as Sonehso:wa. Governor Blacksnake of Allegheny, Cornplanter's nephew of the Wolf clan, who held the title Then:won:nya?s, "Chain Breaker," most probably attended the treaty (Abler 1989).

Two representatives of the sixth nation, Sword Carrier and Green, his mixed-race interpreter, impressed the Quakers by pleading for technical assistance, missionaries, and schoolmasters. (Tuscarora has no league titles.)

Women occupied a unique niche in Iroquois political structure. Their presence with children at Canandaigua spoke to the continuity of matrilineal society. The women possessed the land and made the chiefs. Land was a big issue, and they were there to see how the chiefs performed. Nor did they intend to play a passive role. They asserted their importance by demanding equal time to hear their voice in council, particularly after the frontier prophet Jemima Wilkinson managed to address the opening council, exhorting the Indians to repent of their sins. Pickering, in characteristic deference to women, had allowed her to speak. The women also had an interest in the goods to be distributed following the signing. Stay-at-homes did not share in these goods.

Absentees exerted a negative effect. Brant's Mohawk faction, under British influence, remained at home on the Grand River, eighty miles west of Niagara. For part of a day they had an ear in council, but notable Mohawk titles are missing from the signatures. In the strictest sense, the want of Mohawk representation somewhat impaired the validity of the articles; in another sense, it made the Canandaigua treaty typical of other Indian treaties that in the main are somewhat imperfect.

Yet overall, the Canandaigua treaty fulfilled the Iroquois idiom of "a column of smoke that touches the sky"—something that both parties might view with awe. The United States and the Six Nations concluded an equitable peace that was to endure "as long as the sun shines, the waters flow and the grass grows." In the haze of contemporaneous events, it was an amazing accomplishment.

□□◇□□

Four issues had marked the drift of events in recent years. First, land, the perennial issue of the century, manifested itself in boundary disputes, fraudulent sales by the wrong persons, cessions without consent or supervision by governments, and trespass on hunting territories. Indian insistence on agreed-upon boundary lines, just then the Ohio River, got little respect from land-hungry settlers. Incursions led to murders, and murders to war.

Second, the ever-present danger of an Indian war threatened the existence of the young republic. Keeping the Six Nations quiet in their seats and from joining a coalition for war that threatened the frontier like a gathering storm governed the tenor of Indian policy in Washington's government and guided the major purpose of the treaty.

Third, Loyalists in Canada dreamed of recovering the Northwest Territory, or at least rendering it neutral by creating an Indian buffer state. Anglo Loyalists and Anglo-Mohawk Loyalists resettled at the Bay of Quinte (Kingston, Ontario) and at Brantford, having both lost their Mohawk Valley homes, rallied to support militant governors Lord Dorchester (Guy Carleton) of Quebec and John Graves Simcoe of Upper Canada. These men directed imperial army commandants to hold a string of forts stretching from Oswego to Michilemackinac for ten years after the peace. Concern over British intervention in an Indian war influenced Indian policy.

Fourth, the gradual "civilization" of the Indians occupied the minds of public officials, Friends, and concerned citizens. The several parties agreed on acculturation of the native Indians as the desirable course but proposed as many different plans for accomplishing it. Washington thought the Friends held the key to technical assistance and asked them to attend the treaty. They also manifested a concern to inquire into the title to Hopewell lands in Virginia.

Although it was not an issue at the treaty, some white Americans hoped that the Indians would take to reform. Periodically Indians had raided the border settlements, stealing livestock, burning, scalping, and carrying off survivors into captivity. Would they agree formally not to disturb white people or ever claim lands previously ceded? This hope would prove the hinge on which the negotiations swung. To work, it must be reciprocal.

To the Six Nations, the memory of being coerced to sign the treaty at Fort Stanwix ten years earlier tasted like bitter medicine. Two states and Congress had sent commissioners that time, each charged with obtaining a treaty. They had tried to get the tribes to sign individually, according preference to the Oneida-Tuscarora patriots. As a Mohawk war chief, Brant had come briefly to Fort Stanwix before the New York state treaty began, to seek grounds for a general treaty later at Niagara. Cornplanter, in parallel capacity, had signed the Fort Stanwix treaty in hope of saving some Seneca lands in western New York, to regret it for the rest of his days. Red Jacket and the Buffalo Creek faction never let him forget that making peace belonged to the sachems.

Cornplanter, Half Town, and Big Tree had addressed their grievances directly to President Washington in December 1790. The written text of their famous plea to their "Father," usually attributed to Cornplanter, also bears the signatures of Half Town and "Great-Tree," marking it a joint effort. Big Tree, one of the great Seneca orators of the day, may have delivered the oral address; powerful figures of speech come through even in Joseph Nicholson's interpretation (ASPIA 1: 1, 143–44).

Father:
   The voice of the Seneca nation speaks to you, the great councillor, in whose heart the wise men of the Thirteen Fires [the original states] have placed their wisdom.

   It may be very small in your ears, and we therefore entreat you to hearken with attention; for we are about to speak of things which are to us very great. When your army entered the country of the Six Nations, we called you the town destroyer; and to this day, when that name is heard, our women look behind them and turn pale, and our children cling close to the necks of their mothers. . . .

   When you gave us peace we called you father, because you promised to secure us in the possession of our lands. Do this, and, so long as the lands shall remain, that beloved name shall live in the heart of every Seneca.

   Father: . . . When our chiefs returned from the treaty at Fort Stanwix, and laid before our council what had been done there, our nation was surprised to hear how great a country you had compelled them to give up. . . . [A list of grievances follows.]

   Father: You have said that we are in your hand, and that by closing it, you could crush us to nothing. Are you determined to crush us? If you are, tell us so that those of our nation who have become your children, and have determined to die so, may know what to do.

In this case, one chief has said he would ask you to put him out of pain. Another, who will not think of dying by the hand of his father or of his brother, has said that he will retire to Chateaugay, eat of the fatal root, and sleep with his fathers in peace.[4] . . .

We have already said how we came to join against you; we saw that we were wrong; we wished for peace; and you demanded that a great country to be given up to you; it was surrendered to you, as the price of peace, and we ought to have peace and possession of the little land which you have left to us.

Father: When that great country was given up, there were but few chiefs present, and they were compelled to surrender it, and it is not the Six Nations only that reproach those chiefs with having given up that country. [The nations of the westward lands] ask us, *Brothers of our fathers* [sires, so to speak], where is the place you have reserved for us to lie down? . . .

Father: You have compelled us to do that which has made us ashamed. We have nothing to answer to the children of the brothers of our fathers [parallel cousins, or siblings]. When last spring, they called upon us to go to war, to secure them a bed to lie upon, the Senecas entreated them to be quiet. . . .

Father: We will not conceal from you, that the great God, and not men, has preserved the Cornplanter from the hands of his own nation.[5] For they ask, continually, where is the land which our children, and their children after them, are to lie down upon? [Here he refers to the east line and the west line of Seneca lands specified in the Stanwix treaty, since intruded upon by the persons designated to protect them, and points to Cornplanter's dilemma.] He is silent, for he has nothing to answer.

J hen the sun goes down, he opens his heart before God, and earlier than that sun appears again upon the hills, he gives thanks for his protection during the night: for he feels that, among men become desperated by their danger, it is God only that can preserve him. He loves peace, and all he had in store, he has given to those who have been robbed by your people, lest they should plunder the innocent to repay themselves. The whole season which others have employed in providing for their families, he has spent in his endeavors for peace; and, at this moment, his wife and children are lying on the ground, and in want of food; his heart is in pain for them. . . .

Father: The game which the Great Spirit sent into our country for us to eat, is going from among us. We thought that he intended that we should till the ground with the plough, as the white people do, and we talked to one another about it. But before we speak to you concerning this, we must know from you whether you mean to leave us and our children with any land to till. Speak plainly to us concerning this great business. . . . All the lands we have been speaking of belong to the Six Nations; no part of it ever belonged to the King of England, and he could not give it to you. The land we live on our fathers received from God, and they transmitted it to us for our children, and we cannot part with it.

---

4. The fatal root was water hemlock (*Cicuta maculata* L. Moensch.) (Fenton 1941; 1986b), which grows in the marshy coves of Chautauqua Lake. Big Tree fulfilled his own prophecy two years later on learning of the death of a friend, his companion-in-arms, General Butler.

5. This passage suggests that Cornplanter was not the speaker.

The speaker here distinguishes between the western lands in Ohio, as the property of the Six Nations, and the residual lands of Iroquoia that came down to the Senecas, which they had continually occupied. From the Iroquois standpoint, neither the conquest theory of the state nor the right of discovery from English common law had any bearing on Indian land titles.

Washington, in a letter that has been widely printed, replied to the three Seneca chiefs at the end of the month, summarizing actions in train to relieve their grievances. He and Knox had just charged Pickering with "taking the hatchet out of the heads of the Six Nations." Pickering's report of negotiations at Tioga lay on the president's desk as he wrote (Pickering Papers 61: 61–93, MHS). First, in true Indian fashion he sought to bury past miseries. Second, he asserted that the general government now had sole power to treat with Indian nations respecting land sales. Any treaty "held without its authority will not be binding"; all future land sales must be "held under the authority of the United States." Third, the courts were now open to Indian nations for redress of wrongs. Fourth, he reassured them that they alone had the right to sell and the right to refuse to sell their remaining lands. These concepts formed the foundation of language in the Canandaigua treaty, and they are basic to understanding it today.

The Congress had just enacted the "law on trade and intercourse with the Indian tribes"—now famous as the Non-Intercourse Act of 1790—that reserved supervision of land cessions to the general government and deprived the states of a right descending from colonial times. Pickering had interpreted the law to the Six Nations at Tioga Point; it enabled him to exclude New York governor Clinton from interfering in the Canandaigua treaty but did not stop Clinton from ignoring the law in subsequent state treaties.

Having answered the principal points of the Seneca plea, the president encouraged the Senecas to practice agriculture, promised technical assistance, and addressed the frustrating problem of bringing white murderers of Indians to justice. He pleaded for their loyalty as the closest of the Six Nations to the scene of Indian depredations on the Ohio, a concern that ran through his communications for the next four years. To secure their loyalty, he authorized paying Cornplanter a substantial present of money or goods. He promised to appoint an agent to reside close to them. He selected General Israel Chapin as the first federal agent to the Six Nations.

As the president's emissary to Tioga Point in the autumn of 1790 "to take the hatchet out of the head of the Six Nations and bury it," Pickering learned the protocol of forest diplomacy that he put to use at Canandaigua four years later. That summer, irresponsible frontiersmen had murdered two Senecas of the Turtle clan found hunting on Pine Creek in northern Pennsylvania. This incident halted surveying operations on lands acquired at Fort Stanwix and threatened to loose war parties on the frontier. Efforts of Pennsylvania and the federal government to bring the perpetrators to justice did not satisfy the aggrieved relatives, for whom Iroquois custom demanded blood revenge or compensation. Pickering approached Tioga with an open mind, determined to find out what the circumstances required and to satisfy the aggrieved with the means at hand. He soon learned that an Indian mission demanded enormous patience, time, and the procurement of quantities of food, drink, and wampum. Above all, one must fulfill the ritual of condolence.

At Tioga, Pickering met the principals with whom he would deal during the next four years. He gained an estimate of particular Indians and interpreters. He found Horatio Jones a creature of the Senecas and devious, but felt he could trust Jasper Parrish and Joseph Smith. Farmer's Brother and Red Jacket took pains to instruct him and gave him the Indian name Kanehsadeh, "Side of a hill, on which an old town formerly stood of ye same name [while] we enjoyed peace," as Red Jacket explained. The two told Pickering that although they were young, they would instruct him in the ancient ways of their fathers: he must not just pull the hatchet out of their hands and merely cast it behind him, but bury it and plant a stake or tree to mark the place. Otherwise their eyes were not yet washed that they might see, their throats cleared that they might speak, the bloody places washed from their beds, or the rust removed from the chain of friendship. These acts comprised the political requisites, but society demanded more.

Farmer's Brother reminded Pickering that in matters closely affecting the family, Indian women merited attention. "Our women expect you will show them equal attention." His audience responded to what must have been an old Indian joke, which one still hears: "Perhaps in taking them by the hand, you may see one who may please you."

The ritual uses of wampum pertain to "those rules which were in the minds of our forefathers," continued Red Jacket. "These were the rules and they told their sons to observe them as long as the world might last." A belt should be given to the closest relations of the deceased to comfort their minds. Further rules pertained to distributing goods among the several ranks of society: sachems, war chiefs, warriors detained from hunting to run messages, women, and children.

Transfers of cultural information seldom go one way. Pickering in turn explained the implications of Article 1, Section 8, of the U.S. Constitution, ratified the previous year, which reserved to Congress "the regulation of commerce . . . with Indian tribes." The general government had, in effect, assumed jurisdiction for Indian affairs previously in the hands of the several states. Pickering went on to explain the implications for the Six Nations of the 1790 "Act to regulate Trade and Intercourse with the Indian tribes" and gave them a copy of it.

In accepting the document, Red Jacket rehearsed the heads of Pickering's speech to make certain that the interpretation was correct, and then resumed his discourse on Indian custom law for Pickering's benefit. This would brighten the chain of friendship, he said. He reminded Pickering that in Sir William Johnson's day certain ways of doing things had been established, which the Indians seemed to remember if white men had misplaced their writings. There was a regular place of council, mutually agreed upon. Relations between the two peoples should be stabilized—this was what was meant by the chain of friendship—to enable women and children to live in quiet. Rubbing the chain was good exercise, and no one was ever killed doing good. His people were continually troubled in their minds about their lands. Purchasers initiated negotiations at unauthorized places for their own convenience and without security, representation, or consent. Frauds if not misunderstandings ensued (Pickering Papers 60: 92; 61: 191, MHS).

Pickering, a reformer at heart, met in Red Jacket an equally conservative adversary. As to the Indians' attachment to the ways of their ancestors, Pickering countered by advising that they might improve treaty procedures considerably and expedite matters by appointing a deputation of chiefs to go conduct the business and then report back to the tribe, attesting their words with written transactions. For the Indians this took all the fun out of it: it was a hopeless cause, a change the Indians were loathe to accept. It deprived them of the most colorful event in their lackluster existence, Red Jacket explained. The whole tribe preferred to witness the event in the making, and wampum belts, not writing, composed the vouchers of their word. This was an old issue, which the two men would argue again.

Pickering's report to the president, which coincided with Cornplanter's visit, anticipated several plans for the education of Indians in practical arts that would revolutionize their culture. Pickering, Kirkland, and the Friends advanced similar schemes for introducing farming, blacksmithing, sawmills, weaving, and domestic arts. Kirkland, who knew what the Indians faced, became so caught up in Cornplanter's plea and so impressed with the man himself that he stayed on in Philadelphia through the Christmas season. He turned down the superintendency of the Six Nations; he hoped it would be offered to James Dean instead, but thought the president would offer it to Pickering. He was right, but Pickering declined. It went to General Chapin. Washington sympathized with these plans but faced more immediate concerns.

Cornplanter, Half Town, and Big Tree likened the president's reply to their speech to "the first light in the morning to a sick man. . . . He rejoices, but he is not cured." They would return home and call a council to establish a policy on future land transactions. "The blood that was spilled near Pine Creek is covered, and we shall never look where it lies." They would welcome the promised instruments of acculturation. Change was in the air.

Other steps must go forward first. The president turned to Pickering, but Pickering said he could not accept a formal appointment, although he indicated that he would serve on demand. Improvement of agriculture occupied the back of his mind, and neither the president nor the Indians would let him off. Although the Senecas might be ready to accept new technology, the hostile Indians on the Wabash must be dealt with first.

The president and Secretary Knox resolved to exhaust every possible means before resorting to warfare against the Wabash tribes. To give General St. Clair time to build up his army in the Ohio posts, they sent Colonel Thomas Proctor on a peaceful mission to the Wabash. He was to go by way of Cornplanter's town and use his good offices to secure an escort of chiefs and warriors, which might prevent their going over to the enemy and might bring the hostiles to peaceful terms. If Proctor's mission proved a diplomatic failure, it was at least an ethnohistorical success. The search for Cornplanter led Proctor from the Allegheny settlements to Buffalo Creek, where, in a long series of councils, he persuaded the chiefs and matrons to let their warriors guide him to the Wabash. The mission failed because the commandant of Niagara denied them transportation on Lake Erie. Proctor observed and recorded the disposition of settlements, food habits, dress, transportation, council protocol, and social dances. His sketches of the character and personalities of persons he dealt with afforded intelligence to Knox and Pickering. Proctor's journal must have been exciting reading in Philadelphia (ASPIA, 1: 149–62); today, ethnohistorians may find it a delight.

□□◇□□

In May 1792, when it appeared that Proctor might not succeed, cabinet officers urged Knox to instruct Pickering to secure the Six Nations to the American cause. Armed with the Cornplanter speeches, Pickering set out for Painted Post near modern Corning, New York, to "impress on the minds of the Indians that their interest and happiness" depended "upon the protection and friendship of the United States." His real purpose was to keep them quiet and prevent them from joining the confederacy of hostile Indians, whose warriors were as troublesome as at any time since Braddock's defeat. The president warned that the Six Nations should abstain from joining the enemy and, in a gesture of friendship, send their warriors to join the United States Army, on the payroll. Further, if Brant showed up in council, Pickering was to invite him to visit Philadelphia at public expense. Pickering should resume talks on gradual civilization and keep a journal.

The transactions at the Painted Post councils document Pickering's further preparation for ultimate success. His mentors included the Senecas Farmer's Brother and Kayashota, who had served Sir William Johnson; Good Peter of Oneida, who supported Kirkland; the Mahican Captain Aupaumut, or Hendrick; Clear Sky of Onondaga; and Fish Carrier of Cayuga, all of whom would reappear at Canandaigua.

This time—June 1792—Pickering came prepared to validate his written speech with a wampum belt as Red Jacket had instructed him. As voice of the Six Nations, Red Jacket responded: "We are not willing to throw away all our old rules, but are willing that both should live. Tis the opinion of the Six Nations here that we cannot take all the ways of the white people at once, but by degrees. . . . Now to this day we have the rules of our forefathers in ancient times. We cannot transact business but in that way" (Pickering Papers 61: 191, MHS).

As he spoke, Red Jacket held a wampum belt as if to document the fact that while the Indians grasped certain innovations, change would come in a traditional manner.[6] He observed that although the Six Nations' loyalty to the British had been continuous since Sir William Johnson's day, "we do not give ourselves entirely to them." Moreover, Indians were deliberate and would not be rushed. Above all, they desired peace.

Just then Brant was gone on a peace mission to the Shawnees and Delawares, Red Jacket reported. They were hopeful. Captain Hendrick would soon set out on a similar mission. Referring to the oft-repeated assertion that "savages" continually move about without settling down, Red Jacket observed that white people as well as Indians moved about, as witness the western movement, of which the Indians were victims. He closed by delivering a white belt of ten rows, two and one-half feet long, two and one-half inches wide, marked by purple diagonals: three sets of two, one, and three.

Several days later, Red Jacket responded to criticism that Indians took American speeches to Niagara to have them read. He explained that the British, who better understood the wampum art, invariably accompanied their messages to the Indians with wampum. Pickering must learn not to listen to birds that told ugly

---

6. This may be the beginning of the idea expressed in the now famous "two-row wampum belt"—that the two sets of cultural premises should be put down side by side but never intersect.

stories. "If you had told us to fetch the British speeches to you, we would have packed up our wampum, and thrown the pack down before you; then you could have read the whole." Red Jacket undoubtedly knew that Pickering could not "read" the belts. Pickering reported to Knox that the Iroquois treated documents marked with attached ribbons as if they were belts and at times confused them.

A year of tentative peace overtures and diplomatic intrigue immobilized most of the Six Nations, but the year ended with the worst Anglo military disaster since Braddock's defeat at Bushy Run. Hendrick failed to gain the ear of the western confederates. Only a few Senecas from the Allegheny went on the warpath to Ohio, as an adventure; they were present to see St. Clair overwhelmed and lose his artillery. The fault lay partly with army contractors but mainly with a partially trained militia. Washington, though deeply angered, kept his counsel and gave a candid report to the people. He turned to "Mad Anthony" Wayne and charged him to prepare an army while negotiations continued.

Having defeated two American armies, the Indians living north and west of the Ohio River turned a deaf ear to peace overtures that would compromise any territory north of that boundary. Instead, they revived the western confederacy in the late summer of 1792. Although he spoke an Algonquian language that some of them must have understood, Captain Hendrick Aupaumut accomplished little more than four previous agents. The Ohio council sent Seneca messengers with its reply to Buffalo Creek, where the elder Israel Chapin heard the news on November 6. Compensation did not appeal to the western Indians; they wanted their lands restored. Ohio was to be Indian.

Washington did not give up. His autumn message to Congress gave first priority to Indian affairs, and he voiced hope of achieving a peaceful settlement of the issues. People on the frontier committed outrages against the Indians; they must be constrained from violating treaties. Early in 1793, Washington co-opted three prominent men willing to serve as commissioners to negotiate at Detroit with the hostile Indians in Ohio. Timothy Pickering, Benjamin Lincoln, and Beverly Randolph—two New Englanders and a Virginian—accepted the commission. The Society of Friends of Philadelphia named John Parrish and William Savery, who would reappear at Canandaigua, and the Moravians sent John Heckewelder, veteran of the Delaware mission on the Muskingum, to accompany them.

Never was a mission better planned that failed. The commissioners had authority to give up lands previously ceded by the Indians at a treaty at Fort Harmar in 1789, to promise evacuation of two forts, and to offer fifty thousand dollars, plus a ten-thousand-dollar annuity, if the Indians would let the Fort Harmar treaty stand. The Indians refused to treat on these terms, insisting on complete evacuation of all lands north of the Ohio River. Without meeting the Indians in council, the commissioners returned the way they had come.[7]

The mission was not entirely barren. Pickering and the Friends gained a detailed knowledge of the Iroquois country—its natural resources, flora and fauna, and Indian settlements. They participated in Indian councils at Buffalo Creek,

7. *American State Papers—Indian Affairs*, 1: 352ff., carries the official reports, but General Lincoln's journal (Lincoln 1836) is the best firsthand account. Other details appear in the Pickering Papers, vol. 59, and in Parrish's journal (HSP, AM 565, cat. no. 468).

witnessed the goings and comings of Indian embassies, and learned council protocol, all of which made Pickering a sharper negotiator and Savery a closer observer at Canandaigua. They gained some insight into British management of Indian affairs at Niagara and Detroit.

In June, Pickering confided his frustrations to his wife. He was "satisfied that it will be much more tedious than I expected," and returning in late August he added that he had had enough of the "*man* or *men* [British officers] who direct their measures." This may explain his intemperate outburst directed at a British agent who appeared uninvited during the treaty the following autumn.

The one prominent Mohawk who did not participate in the Canandaigua treaty, Captain Joseph Brant, nevertheless in his ambivalent behavior preceding it profoundly affected its conduct and outcome. Brant, or Thayendanegea (1742–1807), protégé of Sir William Johnson, product of Wheelock's Indian school, and a Loyalist, led war parties out of Niagara against erstwhile white neighbors in the Mohawk Valley during the Revolution. The name Brant was anathema to New York frontiersmen who had seen their their barns burned and their relatives killed, scalped, or carried off into captivity. In their eyes, the abandoned Mohawk settlements and hunting territories were now forfeit, and Brant merited neither military courtesy nor Christian charity. But as Kirkland wrote to Secretary Knox, "few gentlemen in Canada . . . could set more plate on the table than Captain Brant" (Kirkland Papers, HCL). Aware of the hostility back in the original Mohawk territory in New York state, Brant responded in characteristically Indian fashion: he withdrew. He built a church—St. Paul's Chapel of the Mohawks at Brantford—where half of the Queen Anne communion plate resides today; the other half is at Deseronto. He busied himself with Loyalist Mohawk affairs and with Grand River leases. He advanced the model of the Iroquois Confederacy to the tribes in Ohio and supported the Ohio River boundary as drawn in 1768. Just how prominently he figured in the formation of the western confederacy remains uncertain.[8]

Brant sensed that the Indian interest must present a united front. They must unite, independently of white people, as he told his old friend Samuel Kirkland in 1788; a committee of chiefs had sent embassies as far as the Creeks preaching this message. Brant shared the Indian conviction that Indian land titles were valid: the doctrine of right of discovery and the conquest theory of the state had not displaced Indian title the moment some European stood offshore in a vessel. The British encouraged him to support the western tribes in maintaining the Ohio River boundary to a buffer state. This issue went back to the earlier Fort Stanwix treaty in Brant's young manhood.

Kirkland was the one man in the United States who appreciated Brant's genius. Having known Brant from his youth and kept in touch with him, Kirkland could count on their friendship and stood a chance of securing him to the American interest. Kirkland had lived in the woods, had learned the etiquette of campfire and council, and spoke an Iroquoian language—matters that counted among Indians and distinguished him from his contemporaries.

8. See Isabel T. Kelsay's full biography (1984).

In the winter following the St. Clair disaster, Secretary Knox turned to Kirkland to bring to Philadelphia the Six Nations chiefs whom Pickering had invited the previous summer at Painted Post, and especially to get Brant. Kirkland knew full well that this was no time to alter the Indian custom of representation by limiting the delegation: the more the better; the wider the representation, the broader the involvement. Attendance by ranking councilors meant immediate commitment. Friendly Oneidas enabled Kirkland to effect the first rapport with the Genesee Senecas since the split in the confederacy that quenched the traditional council fire in 1777. By kindling a council fire on the Genesee, one hundred miles east of Niagara, Kirkland enrolled the headmen of Buffalo Creek without submitting to British scrutiny. The Oneida Good Peter secured the Buffalo contingent, including Red Jacket and Farmer's Brother—some forty chiefs and warriors representative of the Five Nations, excepting the Cayuga Fish Carrier, who feared to come, and one village on the Allegheny (Kirkland to Knox, Kirkland Papers, HCL). The "female governesses" and the chiefs had failed to restrain Cayuga warriors from joining the Indian army and taking scalps.

Reports of the Indian victory over St. Clair's forces in November 1791, near present-day Fort Recovery, Ohio, produced a sensation in the Iroquois settlements, arousing the spirit of veterans and posing opportunities for young status seekers. Would the western tribes attack the Six Nations if they refused to join? Would the British support them? Would the British take reprisals if a delegation went to Philadelphia? What if the Americans finally prevailed? These questions the Buffalo Creek council debated in secret. Meanwhile, it appeared that the British meant to supply the western posts. The Indians could tell from the sharp rise in barrels containing military supplies passing over the Niagara portage.

What further diplomatic maneuvers would it take to keep the Six Nations quiet in their seats? Bringing the principal chiefs to the council fire of the United States and awarding them presidential medals might just do it.

CHAPTER 40

THE TORTUOUS ROAD
TO CANANDAIGUA

In early 1792, the two main fires of Indian diplomacy burned at Buffalo Creek and Philadelphia. Having failed militarily, and until Wayne could recoup the disaster in Ohio, Washington's cabinet opted for diplomacy. Much as it does today, confusion reigned in the capital. Some believed that bringing the principals of the Six Nations to town, according them the dignity of their own protocol, acknowledging their sovereignty, and treating them to Philadelphia hospitality might ensure their loyalty. The word went out from Knox to Pickering to Kirkland to bring Brant in. Brant, the biggest fish in the pool, yet ambivalent, would prove amenable to a Philadelphia visit, but on his own terms.

Kirkland signed his Oneida name to a personal appeal to Brant, urging him to accept Pickering's invitation and join the other Six Nations chiefs bound for Philadelphia. But like a lunker salmon holding at the bottom of a ding, Brant refused to rise to Kirkland's fly. His situation in the Indian world was complex and undergoing change, and he faced a loss of status. He was depressed. Illness had kept him at Grand River while the western coalition defeated St. Clair, and the victorious leaders had sent word by his own returning warriors, whom he had failed to restrain. Still, the coalition complained that his warriors were too few and chided Brant for not being with them. Kirkland heard that Brant, in apparent frustration over his declining power in the west and continuing criticism from his own people, had sought solace in the bottle.

Regardless, Kirkland reminded Brant that he had once expressed "curiosity at getting a look at the great American chief." Brant told Samuel Ogden, the land speculator who delivered the message, that he would go to see the president, provided the president personally sent him a written invitation. The Iroquois are great sticklers for protocol, particularly when reluctant to honor a request. A proper messenger should come and take him by the arm to the seat of government, Brant said. Pickering still appeared naive about council procedure, and the British would oppose any Philadelphia visit. Brant delayed answering Kirkland and then politely declined, citing dates that would have prevented a rendezvous at the Genesee. He hoped to go later. Before making any commitment he wanted to know what to expect in the way of a treaty.

Brant held himself above "common" Indians who so frequently and habitually visited the seat of the republic for notoriety and a handout. Instead of accepting, within a few days Brant sent a belt by runner to Kahnawagens (Avon, New York), where Kirkland awaited the arrival of the headmen still at Buffalo Creek: the belt invited Kirkland to a council at Buffalo Creek instead. But Kirkland heeded Red Jacket's advice: one may not extinguish a council fire by lighting another. Kirkland held the priority. His report to Knox on these negotiations indicates how these issues were resolved and how they could be used to advantage in the game of forest diplomacy.

A proper invitation from Secretary Knox to Brant would take some time. Meanwhile, Kirkland assured the Mohawk chief that no one intended "you should be rounded into the company of all the old chiefs and dragged along with them promiscuously thro the proposed tour." Knox assured Brant of the president's interest, and Kirkland transmitted the sealed invitation in care of the commandant of Fort Niagara, all parties presumably aware of its apparent content. Given the circumstances, acceptance would embarrass relations with the fort; British influence had already failed to keep the Buffalo, Genesee, or Allegheny chiefs at home. Postponement, however, would afford Brant an exclusive state visit under altered circumstances. The president would have to wait. (See also Kelsay 1984: 459–64.)

Meanwhile, a delegation of forty-eight chiefs escorted by Kirkland approached Philadelphia. Their hosts dispatched escorts to greet them on the road with the ceremony of the woods' edge. The ritual of the council fire would be enacted in Philadelphia, clothing the chiefs in new garb and hanging medals around their necks. Red Jacket, who did most of the speaking, received a splendid medallion bearing the president's name, image, and the year 1792, which he wore during his lifetime on state occasions and when sitting for portraits (figs. 41, 42) (Stone 1841: 66–108; Hubbard 1886: 128; Snyder 1978). The desperate Americans sought to stabilize the Six Nations; the chiefs knew they were in a bind between pressure from the western nations and the British and Americans to the east. They accepted annuities and friendship and promised to do what they could to quiet the tribes at Miami in the fall.

With the departure of Kirkland and the chiefs to Philadelphia, responsibility for affairs on the Genesee devolved on General Israel Chapin, who that summer metamorphosed from land agent into the first United States Indian agent to the Six Nations. The annual salary was then $500. Enticing Brant to visit Philadelphia, which Brant's English friends opposed, became Chapin's first task. At this point, Brant's estimate of settling peacefully the border disputes of the Indians motivated him to accept Chapin's hospitality and guarantee of safe conduct, to honor Knox's invitation, and to risk the displeasure of crown officials in Canada.

Traveling the water route where possible, via Albany and New York, Brant and Captain Israel Chapin, Jr., arrived in Philadelphia on 20 June for a ten-day visit. Their reception was correct but cool. Brant saw the president next day, but most of his conversations were with Knox. Afterward Brant claimed that they offered him substantial "allurements of gain" and twice his half-pay British pension to use his good offices for peace. "But this I rejected." Knox did not confirm any such offer. Knox did induce him to go to Miami with instructions as one of several peace emissaries. Once more Brant would find his prestige diluted by a large Six Nations delegation appointed for the same purpose.

While Brant was in the city, a delegation of three Quakers waited on him, and John Parrish, who would lead the Quaker observers at the Canandaigua treaty,

Figure 41. The Red Jacket
medal. Courtesy Buffalo and
Erie County Historical Society.

Figure 42. Red Jacket. Portrait by R. W.
Weir. Collection of the New York Historical
Society, New York City.

communicated to Pickering a favorable impression of the man. Brant convinced the Friends that his concern for peace was sincere and he would "do all in his power toward bring[ing] about a reconciliation," although he appeared pessimistic of success short of restoring part of the lands that Indians complained had been taken from them unjustly.

Knox seemed satisfied with the visit. He found Brant judicious and sensible, and he flattered himself that the visit would give Brant great satisfaction for having been made acquainted with the humane views of the president. He communicated his optimism to Chapin, Wayne, and Governor Clinton of New York. Knox asked Clinton to satisfy Fish Carrier and the Cayugas about their reservation, a strictly New York matter but one of particular concern to Brant and therefore a bit ticklish—it might affect the polarity of Iroquois factions.

Knox handed the departing Captain Chapin what may be the classic federal travel order. The letter covered an advance of $600 to be delivered to his father, which would defray the expenses of Brant and his party to Niagara. It authorized Brant to take two horses from Philadelphia, but it limited Captain Chapin to purchasing a low-priced horse in Albany, which he must turn over to General Chapin, his father, who must exercise every economy in the conduct of his office, unlike the "helter skelter conduct which was observed under the later management." The new agent must get along with part-time clerical assistance (NYHS, O'Reilly Collection, 8: 28).

The one person dissatisfied with Brant's visit to the president was Kirkland, who had done the most to facilitate it. He complained that Brant had not so much as called upon him when he bypassed Oneida going and returning. "He must act the Indian sometimes with all the civility he is master of."

En route to Niagara, Brant paused at Canandaigua on 24 July, where General Chapin found him highly grateful for attention paid him. From Fort Erie Brant wrote to Knox and Chapin that delegations of Senecas and "Seven Nations of Canada" awaiting passage to Detroit and Miami cluttered the facilities. Brant hoped to go up by the return of the next vessel. The lake was the only safe route to Miami for peace embassies because hostile hunters ranged the intervening woods to the south. All sources agreed that the essential requirement for peace was a new boundary line. The word from Detroit held that the Indians were elated over recent victories and doubted American motives—they suspected the Americans of fortifying while negotiating. Brant worried about his status among the western Indians since his Philadelphia visit.

Although the British still held the forts at Detroit and Niagara, they had chosen a contingency site opposite Buffalo against the day they must surrender Fort Niagara to the United States. There, a Boston correspondent found Colonel Butler of Cherry Valley fame holding council with chiefs who were informing him on their Philadelphia visit. The journalist opined that presents from Congress could not be expected to hold the savages, who had daily access to handouts of clothing, cooking utensils, ammunition, and so forth at the British forts. Americans deceived themselves over cultivating good relations with the Six Nations. Indeed, the old people stayed quietly at home while the young men joined hostile forces. The observer predicted that the good offices of the Buffalo Creek chiefs to influence the western tribes to peace would have little effect: power alone would bring peace (MHS Collection, 1: 284–88).

This species of American realism thought even less of the idea of applying to Lord Dorchester, governor of Quebec, and having him appoint garrison commanders as commissioners to draw a boundary line between Indians and Americans, thereby creating a buffer state. Nor did this view regard the Indian as perfectible for life in civil society.

Brant's return to the Niagara frontier brings us full circle to the grand council of western tribes in the late summer of 1792 at the Miami rapids, and to the ill-fated mission to Detroit the following year.

□□◇□□

Iroquois participation in the affairs of the western confederacy recalls "Turtle's War Party," a classic Woodland fable involving Skunk, Rattlesnake, and Porcupine, who shoot their special weapons and fall by the trail. Hendrick Aupaumut failed to convince the western tribes to consider peace; Brant, ill, arrived after the council broke up; and Cornplanter, with forty-eight Six Nations chiefs including Red Jacket as speaker, was rebuffed as peacemaker. A Shawnee speaker taunted the Six Nations for having urged them to form a confederacy and now coming "with the voice of the United States folded under their arms." This was like withholding a wampum belt for later presentation. The grand council suspended activities for the winter hunt, pending a meeting with United States commissioners at the Maumee rapids in the spring of 1793. They would insist that the Ohio be the boundary.

During the quasi truce, officials expected General Anthony Wayne to hold up military operations while the president's commissioners journeyed to negotiate with the hostile Indians. But the evident rigor with which Wayne drilled his troops and prepared for combat worried wiser heads like Brant and Colonel McKee at Detroit and brought protests of truce violation that alarmed General Benjamin Lincoln, who was yet at Fort Erie awaiting passage to Miami in the summer of 1793 (Lincoln 1836: 130ff.).

Whatever royal policy may have been, military preparations went forward in Canada, where official opinion held that with Indian allies they could win. This view convinced the Indians. The expectation that the king's men and military supplies would be forthcoming would prove a mistake. Logically, since England had declared war on Revolutionary France, the ally of the United States since 1778, war between the United States and England, and therefore Canada, would follow. Least of all did leaders in Canada expect John Jay, then in London as United States commissioner, to negotiate successfully a peaceful settlement of the border dispute.

Anti-American sentiment hardened in Canada with the appointment of two royal governors—Lord Dorchester (Guy Carleton) at Quebec and John Graves Simcoe at Niagara for Upper Canada. Little Turtle visited the Seven Nations of Canada, who waited on Dorchester concerning the boundary issue. Dorchester's reply on 10 February 1794, that he should "not be surprised if we are at war with them in the course of the present year," caused a sensation on both sides of the lakes. This remark represented his interpretation of reported movements of Wayne's army, certain hostile appearances on the Lake Champlain frontier, mounting pro-French sentiment in the United States, and American resentment over Britain's impressing seamen and interfering with commerce on the high seas.

It encouraged Brant to think that British aid would be forthcoming (Kelsay 1984: 507). The word spread through the Indian world that their father in Quebec had spoken; some two thousand warriors responded to strike the war post. It emboldened Cornplanter's warriors to identify with the western Indians.

In these circumstances, neutrality seemed the logical position to wiser heads among the Six Nations. They should encourage tribes of the upper lakes to support the Ohio tribes, but they should withhold their own warriors. Open hostility would expose the Allegheny and Buffalo settlements to American attack. Cornplanter's and New Arrow's towns astride the New York–Pennsylvania border lay at the cutting edge of the frontier.[1]

Iroquois culture prescribed several solutions: withdrawal, war, or peace. Would Cornplanter take the path of Big Tree, who, depressed at losing his friend General Butler, threatened to eat hemlock, fulfilling the classic Iroquois suicide syndrome, and then stabbed himself? Delaware settlers removed their women, children, and elders from Allegheny to Cattaraugus. A few Seneca warriors just then were with Wayne's army in Ohio. Others stayed home to defend their towns. Brant dispatched some Cayuga warriors, veterans of St. Clair's defeat, from Grand River to support Cornplanter's warriors in keeping the Allegheny corridor in Iroquois hands and to prevent other Cayuga warriors from joining the western confederacy. Nevertheless, warriors of the Six Nations did join the forces against Wayne. War was one way out; peace might not retrieve Cornplanter's prestige. A precarious balance of forces that summer preceding the Canandaigua treaty stabilized events in the Genesee-Allegheny corridor—the land lying between Lake Erie and an arrow pointing southwestward from Canandaigua to Venango (Fort Franklin).

Congress had patented the Erie Triangle to Pennsylvania in 1792. This act intended to afford American traders an outlet on Lake Erie at Presque Isle. For two years the woods would be full of surveyors, whom the Indians regarded as a threat. In the autumn of 1793, after the unsuccessful peace mission to Detroit led by Pickering, Lincoln, and Randolph, a council at Buffalo Creek proposed Venango as the site of a general peace treaty to convene on 15 May 1794. Peace seemed possible, but between the fall hunt and spring planting, affairs took a turn, largely because of Dorchester's speech and Simcoe's strengthening of the forts. President Washington presented the matter to Congress with supporting documents, and he made representations to the British ambassador. Brant could not be counted on, and Cornplanter wavered from friendliness to near hostility.

But let us return to the council at Buffalo Creek in the autumn of 1793. Farmer's Brother delivered the word of the western confederates, speaking as if their words were his own. Both the British Indian superintendent, Colonel John Butler, and the United States Indian agent, General Israel Chapin, heard him. On inquiry they learned that the league between the Six Nations and the Shawnees had stood for "three lives," with the understanding that if either party were in distress, the other would come to its aid. The Shawnees now offered the Iroquois a place to come, bring their beds, and sit down. A Wyandot spoke through a large wampum belt, which pictured the Americans, the Six Nations in the middle, and themselves

---

1. New Arrow's town, situated on the flat opposite Wolf Run, later known as Old Town, was completely abandoned in the nineteenth century.

at the far end, to express the Wyandots' sorrow that the American commissioners were gone before they could speak to them. Brant arrived a day late to advance the Mohawk (British) position that claims to Indian lands were the persistent cause of wars with Indians; he insisted on some assurance on the boundary line issue.

These communications in Chapin's reports prompted Knox to issue invitations to the Indians in the president's name to treat at Venango, beyond British ears. Knox advised the western tribes to come by water to Presque Isle. Chapin delivered the invitation at a council held at Buffalo Creek in February 1794, and he attended again in April to hear the reply of the Six Nations. The president included the reports of these meetings among sundry papers that he laid before Congress. Several factors caused the delay between invitation and reply: the Six Nations' desire to retire and consider the matter privately in council at the Seneca village, their submitting the invitation to the British for scrutiny, and the hardening of the British attitude as reflected in Dorchester's speech. The boundary issue hung like a curtain between the parties. The Six Nations stalled for time on the pretext that some of the chiefs were afield.

By April, dark clouds hovered over the frontier from Canandaigua to Pittsburgh, and people quaked like the aspen before the gathering storm. A few strong individuals, both white and Indian, stand out like giant pines in the intervening forest. Chapin at Canandaigua and John Adlum, the Pennsylvania surveyor, heard the alarm but refused to believe that war would occur. Cornplanter and Red Jacket, leaders of opposite factions, prepared to withstand the storm. But it was the Onondaga Clear Sky whom the council chose to turn down the president's summons to Venango. Because of its importance, the council had considered the president's speech at length, but the sachems replied, "It is not now in our power to accept." After rehearsing their relations with the Americans during the decade since Fort Stanwix, Clear Sky stated: "In the absence of any pre-agreement on a boundary line, we cannot, at present, rise from our seats and attend your council at Venango." He concluded by asserting the independence of both the Six Nations and the United States. They would put themselves under the protection of the Great Spirit. Although their patience might be worn, yet they wished for peace. Accordingly, they returned the invitation belt and the speech to Secretary Knox.

Unshaken, Chapin asserted that he did not believe that war would take place. He asked, Why do the Indians need be called out to forward the pretensions of Great Britain? They could rest assured that the president would not take up the tomahawk without warning them.

Canandaigua was an open town. Utica lay 112 miles east through unbroken forest, Buffalo some 100 miles west through oak openings. Chapin returned home to find the place in a flap. Townspeople urged erecting a blockhouse to shelter women and children should the Indians rise. Chapin opposed such evidence of fear lest it provoke a raid, but he did ask Knox to forward twelve hundred to fifteen hundred stand of arms and ammunition. Indians came and went daily without apparent unfriendly intention, although one story held that an Indian approached a white woman, circled the top of her head with his finger, and with a threatening look said, "Bime by [by-and-by] you." It was not in Chapin's official reports, but it was alleged that friendly sachems informed him that a council was set for September to determine whether settlements on the Genesee should be cut off.

Cornplanter assured Chapin that he would communicate the result by one of his swiftest runners. Should the runner bring bad news, Chapin thought there would be lead time for the women to reach Utica before war parties struck.

The council met, and when it reached a decision, Cornplanter, it was said, started a runner at daybreak with news for Chapin. Indian runners traveled in breechcloths and moccasins, carrying only parched corn and dried venison, and the frontier whites knew their gait as the "Indian lope"—a long, swinging stride. Tension mounted while Chapin waited at home. As the sun sank behind Arsenal Hill, the runner came down Main Street. Chapin met him. "*The runner had made ninety miles upon the trail between the rising and setting sun of that day.*" Canandaigua was safe.

This record run was the talk of the town. What lends credence to the story is that the athlete was pointed out to Friends Emlen and Parrish when they came to Canandaigua that fall. Emlen identified him as "Sharp Shins" (Fenton, ed., 1965a: 296). Other runners took two and one-half days.

□□◇□□

Chiefs visiting Canandaigua that spring en route to Albany and returning insisted that the principal chiefs were the proper owners of the land, that Buffalo was the proper place of council, and that all officials who desired to do business with them must come there. They meant this for the governor of New York, and they remained adamant to the bitter end that Pickering observe the same protocol. Chapin honored their request three times during 1794. His willingness to observe the amenities of Indian protocol contributed to keeping them neutral. He assured them that the governor acknowledged them proper owners of the land and that they alone had the right to sell, and he then held that the governor had the right to purchase. Indeed, he quite wore out his moccasins on the path to Buffalo Creek; that summer he would exhaust himself traveling to Presque Isle to relieve the crisis over the Erie Triangle. By November he was a sick man who would die soon after the treaty.

In the eyes of the Buffalo Creek council, a few Indians, not the nation, had sold Presque Isle. Even Cornplanter, whom they accused of selling it, very much regretted having done so and now wanted relief from the terms of sale. He prepared to prevent its occupation. Pennsylvania, having acquired the northwestern lands in 1784 and the Erie Triangle by United States patent in 1792, was proceeding to survey and sell tracts for settlement. In the year preceding the treaty, the Pennsylvania assembly authorized laying out a town on Lake Erie. The following spring the governor sent an expedition under Captain Ebenezer Denny to fortify the port. He charged Denny to use extreme caution not to offend the Indians or alarm the British garrison. News of the move soon reached the Niagara garrison, which stirred up the Indians. It soon became apparent that both the Six Nations and the western Indians claimed this corridor. In their view it must stay open. The Six Nations foresaw that closing the corridor between them and the western confederacy spoiled their argument for recovering part of their lands. On this, Brant, the Buffalo chiefs, and Cornplanter were of one mind.

The tempers of the Six Nations were growing short. Learning that Denny had fortified Le Boeuf (Waterford), only sixteen miles from Presque Isle, the Buffalo Creek council summoned Cornplanter and the Allegheny chiefs to hear their position. At Fort Franklin, General Wilkinson observed that "the English have soured their minds." The claims of the Six Nations rose with the military success of the western Indians and with British assistance. There would be no treaty at Venango that spring. The council sent a runner to Chapin, calling him to Buffalo to hear them refuse Knox's invitation.

A nasty murder brought the Presque Isle issue to a head. One May day a young frontier hothead, somewhat drunk, killed a Delaware Indian friendly to the garrison at the scene of the proposed treaty. Although the commandant at Fort Franklin arrested the offender, now the Indians had a real issue, and presents to the contrary, nothing short of Pennsylvanians' evacuating the area would satisfy them.

Communication was slow and confusing. Dispatch riders took a week between Canandaigua and Philadelphia, and equal time for the return; likewise from Fort Franklin via Pittsburgh. Runners covered Buffalo Creek to Canandaigua in two days, summoning Chapin to council, while he waited for instructions. Secretary Knox yearned for reports, if only negative, by each post. Couriers passed between the War Office and the Pennsylvania governor. Small wonder that reports crossed orders and that the president counteracted the Pennsylvania governor and legislature. Cooperative federalism has never been simple.

By the end of May the president had decided it would be expedient to humor the Six Nations and suspend the Presque Isle establishment. Knox so informed Pennsylvania governor Mifflin. Chapin, sensing the policy drift but still lacking instructions, responded to the Indians' demands and reported the situation on 7 June. Through an agent he sought a personal interview with Brant, hoping to win him over to the United States. But he began to doubt the steadiness and reliability of Cornplanter, whom the British had lately loaded with presents. On returning home, Cornplanter had sent out runners calling a council at Allegheny, intending to descend on Venango and inquire into the circumstances of the murder. Responding to a runner from Buffalo, Chapin went as far as the Genesee and learned the purport of the message, but he deferred going on to Venango until his son returned from Philadelphia with instructions. The Indians agreed to wait. Chapin suspected that the reason Cornplanter had called the council was not the murder, but Cornplanter saw in it an opportunity to extricate himself from difficulties that had plagued him for ten years. Cornplanter and a few Senecas had sold the Presque Isle lands to Pennsylvania without the consent of the nation. No division of the money was ever made. He repeatedly denied having made the sale, which the nation held invalid. In the eyes of the Six Nations, Pennsylvania had sent troops to occupy lands owned by Indians. Cornplanter was indeed in a spot. Chapin sensed that the Venango meeting might be crucial for war or peace, and that it was his duty to attend. There he could confer with Indians without British interference. Knox advised that the British were strengthening the garrison at the Miami rapids to nine companies, the obvious intention being to encourage the hostile Indians, to whom they were supplying arms and ammunition.

The president wanted the Indian war ended that year. Knox wrote Wayne that he did not think the British would seek a war with the United States just then, that he rather hoped Jay would succeed in adjusting any differences, and that the president had no intention that Presque Isle should upset negotiations in London or bring the Six Nations down on the frontier. It was far cheaper to fund a treaty. To Chapin he sent a list of goods wanted by the Indians with instructions for distribution and accounting (Knox to Wayne in Knopf 1960: 327, 332; Knox to Chapin, O'Reilly Collection, 10: 16, NYHS).

By mid-June the Venango conference shifted to Buffalo Creek. Three successive runners brought Chapin summonses requesting his immediate attendance. He stalled, hoping his son, Captain Chapin, would return with instructions, but left on the thirteenth without them, full of apprehensions over Presque Isle. It was one thing for Knox to sit in the War Office and enunciate policy; it was another matter to meet the chiefs on their own ground. The state of Pennsylvania may have purchased lands within the Erie Triangle from the Six Nations, but the Indians were in no mood to permit a settlement, regardless of what Knox ordered.

After three days on the road without hearing from Knox or being overtaken by his son, Chapin reached Buffalo Creek to find the Indians disturbed and impatient over Pennsylvania aggression. They had debated the matter for three days and come to one mind. The Canadian Indian Department interpreter, a man named Johnson, had participated in their decision. Since the issue constituted an infringement of territory, the council had turned the matter over to the warriors. As head warrior, Cornplanter addressed the American agent as if speaking to the president himself, calling him "Brother" (equal in status)—though sometimes "Father," but on second thought, "Friend." (The Iroquois equated the president's status with that of civil chief.) He asked the president, as head of the nation, to disregard previous actions of Congress and, in justice, hear the plea of the Six Nations for a parcel of land. They had fixed a boundary and marked it on a map. The matter was now in the hands of the warriors to find room for their children. Eight strings of white wampum attested to the seriousness of the matter.

A second item for which they had kindled the fire dealt with missing persons. Cornplanter interpreted Big Tree's disappearance, a known suicide, as murder. Alluding to the death of the Delaware Indian at Venango, he cited custom law on compounding a peacetime murder, which demanded that "those who have done the injury, go to the injured party and make satisfaction." The mention of death required delivering ten strings of black wampum.

Addressing General Chapin, in whom the Six Nations reposed their confidence, the council requested Chapin to go with Johnson, the British interpreter, to Presque Isle and remove the trespassers back over the line marked on the map. Ten warriors would escort them. The two would report back to the council. (Six strings of black and white wampum symbolized friendly compliance, or the consequence.)

Chapin complied with the request but disclaimed any power to drive the white settlers off; he could only advise them. Since he shared responsibility equally to the United States and to the Indians, however, he felt accountable to both. They could rely on the president's friendship and his attending to their business as soon as he received their speeches. But to maintain the pacific intent of their mission, he asked that sachems accompany him in addition to the ten warriors. Four agreed to go, besides Johnson and a servant (NYHS, O'Reilly Collection, 10: 43; ASPIA, 1: 520).

General Chapin kept a journal covering the Presque Isle mission, from 13 June to 7 July, in which he described the voyage along the lakeshore, the negotiations, and the return (NYHS, O'Reilly Collection, 10: 43). The second day out, Cornplanter met them at the mouth of Cattaraugus Creek, bringing fresh intelligence that Chapin promptly dispatched by runners to the commandant at Venango. "Ten great men" had sent for Cornplanter; he wished not to appear in person but would send his voice by the deputation to Presque Isle, where those men would meet the embassy. He had bad news that another of his warriors was missing.

Considering the lag in communications, it is amazing that things went as well as they did. While strong headwinds grounded Chapin's party for twelve hours, Knox, in Philadelphia, was dictating orders to him and to Wayne, which fortunately covered actions already taken. Meanwhile, the missing Captain Chapin had left Philadelphia on the tenth, burdened with goods for a treaty, and consequently did not overtake his father. On reading of reprisals near Fort Franklin, Knox realized that an understanding with the Six Nations, particularly those on the Allegheny, was essential for peace, and he considered settlement of the Presque Isle matter the great task for Chapin to accomplish. The British role worried Knox, but diplomacy might change it. Was it true, he wondered in a letter to Chapin, that the British were strengthening the garrison at the Miami rapids?

No one greeted Chapin's landing party at Presque Isle on the twenty-fourth, so he proceeded inland to Le Boeuf, where Captain Denny of the Pennsylvania militia and surveyor Andrew Ellicott greeted the group. On a cold and rainy Thursday, two days later, the council met to hear Chapin read the eviction notice prepared at Buffalo Creek. The United States and Pennsylvania should withdraw their forces and remove any settlers south of a line drawn from Cornplanter's town near the state line on the Allegheny to French Creek, just below present-day Meadville, and thence to the head of the Cuyahoga River and westward. The alternative to the federal government's establishing and enforcing the new boundary line was the threat of war. Although disturbed over injuries received, the Six Nations still were opposed to war and desired to live in peace with the United States. But establishing a garrison at Le Boeuf might involve them in a war with the western nations. They opposed the surveying of their lands for legal reasons (Kent and Deardorff 1960: 268).

To resolve this impasse, Chapin recommended appointing commissioners to settle differences among the Indians, the United States, and Pennsylvania. The Six Nations wanted this treaty held at Buffalo Creek, the regular place of their council fire.

Two days after hearing Chapin's report, the Onondaga chief Clear Sky opened the council and turned to Cornplanter, the speaker appointed for the occasion, who addressed General Washington as "Friend." Cornplanter found satisfaction in only one thing that the people at Le Boeuf had said, namely, Ellicott's reference to the Pennsylvania grant of land to himself; the rest was deception. He made repeated assertions about the boundary line and the status of the Six Nations as free people. Eight strings of black and white wampum attested to these assertions.

In properly acknowledging this speech, Chapin expressed hope that the Six Nations would remain easy in their seats until he could communicate their words to President Washington. He would recommend an early settlement of their grievances (Chapin to Pickering, 9 July 1794, Pickering Papers, 59: 267, MHS). Knox informed Pennsylvania governor Mifflin and forwarded Chapin's recommendation to the president (17 July 1794, ASPIA, 1: 522). Washington was ready to name a commissioner to hold a treaty with the Six Nations at the Genesee, removed from British influence. He hoped that such a person might also act for Pennsylvania. States' rights to the contrary, the Constitution reserved to the general government regulation of trade and intercourse with the Indians. This time New York state would not interfere. By the third week of July, cabinet policy had crystallized on holding a federal treaty with the Six Nations at Canandaigua on 15 September. If Pennsylvania declined to name a commissioner, the federal commissioner would become sole agent empowered to act for all interests. Thus Timothy Pickering's role as U.S. commissioner would become crucial (ASPIA 1: 522–23).

□□◇□□

Moving the council fire to a spot east of the Genesee River would have to await the outcome of Wayne's campaign. Meanwhile, Cornplanter kept his own fire at the long eddy above Kinzua while his warriors ranged the dark forests of the Genesee-Allegheny corridor and the women planted and harvested the "three sisters" on the big flat at Old Town, as did their kindred on Cattaraugus and Buffalo creeks. Any person who ventured into this borderland must be courageous, resourceful, wary, and fleet of foot if he hoped to escape with his hair.

The situation produced such a man in John Adlum, a Pennsylvanian who arrived to survey the lands on the upper Allegheny in 1794. His memoir is a remarkable ethnohistorical source on the Senecas (Kent and Deardorff 1960). Through Adlum we meet Cornplanter just after Chapin's mission and just before Wayne's victory, when the old chief was abandoning loyalty to the whites and reverting to his own people. By shear guts and resourcefulness Adlum managed to obtain clearance for surveys and an escort to protect his crews, whom he kept interested by rationing diluted drinks. He managed permissions in council by gaining the support of the matrons and old people, who in turn worked on the chiefs. He left us a record of council procedures and war customs, including the best extant account of an Eagle Dance—one held in his honor. Adlum's undated map of part of Pennsylvania and southwestern New York encompasses the Allegheny corridor and locates precisely the Indian towns of the period.

Adlum had been among the Senecas during the Pennsylvania boundary survey, when someone had schooled him in Iroquois customs and beliefs, especially in the power of dreams. At Fort Franklin he encountered a party of Seneca hunters who were being recalled for a council. He befriended them and by judicious hospitality persuaded Chief Half Town to lead him to their towns and pledge his safe return to the fort. The two men engaged in a contest of dreams, by which Adlum managed to save "a ten gallon keg of whiskey and one of five gallons filled with wine" until they reached the Indian towns. Adlum ingeniously concocted a vision of Kayashota and his first wife, the old war chief having recently died, which was interpreted as portending some event to the nation. Adlum exploited this belief to his own advantage by asserting that unless they offended the Great Spirit, they had nothing to fear. He held that the vision was meant to help him observe Seneca ethical behavior and enlist their help in knowing what conduct on his part would be appropriate. It was a wonderful device for establishing rapport.

As the flotilla reached the long sheet of quiet water below the town of Burnt House (Tyononhsate:kenh), Cornplanter, their host, had gathered his warriors and stationed them in a single file some six feet apart along the west bank. Adlum counted some eighty, dressed and painted for war, with swan's down on their heads. At Cornplanter's signal of three loud whoops, the warriors fired in succession over their heads, aiming as close as possible without hitting their guests. Adlum, unruffled by this dangerous tribute, went ashore with all his papers. He carried a letter from Knox informing the Senecas that the president had appointed Pickering to treat with them at Canandaigua, besides a commission from Governor Mifflin, who was displeased at the delay in settling the Erie lands. This made Adlum an ambassador from the state of Pennsylvania.

Whether he knew from prior experience or from instinct for the situation, Adlum quickly sensed from the number of older women and men at the landing, who reappeared at the council house to ask questions, that if he could enlist their aid, "there would be no war." His memoir affords the best evidence of how the matrons and elders influenced council opinion for war or peace. Adlum was taken by the hand at the water's edge, conducted to the council house, and seated between two principal chiefs. From the central fire Cornplanter lit a large feather-stemmed pipe, which he had loaded with tobacco mixed with viburnum (or possibly dogwood bark), and started it counterclockwise around the council. Each man as he passed it lit his own pipe to fulfill the theme, "from smoking comes good thoughts." The house by then was crowded.

The dignity of council ceremony contrasted markedly with the want of social control as young men and boys mounted the tie beams of the building. In lieu of the customary cries of assent marking articles of a speech, "the young Indians on the beams above saluted me with an universal roar, *vulgarly called farting*. I heard several of the elderly women exclaim *Yaugh-ti-Yaughti* . . . shame, scandalous" (Kent and Deardorff 1960: 304). Cornplanter reprimanded them, as did another chief, followed by the sister of Kayashota named Hummingbird (Jithonwentonh), "one of the great women." The ethnologist could not want a better illustration of a perennial schism in Iroquois society—the incivility of young men of the warrior class—and the power of shame as a social sanction when administered by matron and headman.

After the usual day's recess, the council met to answer Adlum's request to survey. He had given them a map of Pennsylvania, which they spread on a deerskin. (Iroquois ability to conceptualize their country from maps amazed the earliest observers.) Cornplanter complained that they had not received value for lands ceded to Pennsylvania at Fort Stanwix. They deemed trespassers enemies. Cornplanter reasoned that the British, having fortified the Miami rapids, would provision the Indians, issue arms, and probably join them if they went to war. They had heard Dorchester's declaration. War was their last chance of recovering part of their country. This baleful influence, irresistibly at work in bringing on an Indian war irrespective of what the king might do in Europe, assumed the symbolic proportions of the Naked Bear, an Iroquois horror tale: "As he had caused a great beast to run over our country, who would cause us to be at war with each other before the end of the Summer." Cornplanter laid an arrow on the map, marking a corridor from Burnt House to French Creek (modern Meadville) and on to the head of the Cuyahoga. War was the consequence of this strip's not being returned to them. Cornplanter played a desperate game at which Adlum was equally adept.

That General Wayne would not defeat the western Indians never entered Adlum's mind. In his reply, he reviewed Indian participation during the Revolutionary War; he condoled their losses and noted that their ranks had diminished while they were allies of Britain. He mentioned Jay's mission to England to demand surrender of the frontier posts, which they could depend on being in American hands within another year. Wayne would move his army against the western Indians in a matter of days. It would therefor be prudent to await the outcome of the expected battle. Their participation would not divert Wayne from the operation planned, nor could Cornplanter's warriors get there in time. Wayne's trained troops would surely prevail. He offered these comments, he said, as friendly advice.

In contrast with their previous dependence on hunting and fish drives, Adlum continued, Cornplanter's towns had enjoyed better harvests in the last three years. The women had planted the flats, and Adlum saw corn hanging in their houses two years old and in abundance. Hogs had replaced bear meat as feast food, but game was scarce. People were better clothed. It was not worth losing all this for a bad alliance.

An appeal to the prejudices of a matrilineal society proved Adlum's most compelling argument. He told the council that he would like to speak to the women— "all the principal ones, of both towns"—whom he hoped could be persuaded to prevent the ruin of the society, inasmuch as they were the ones who cultivated the corn, packed in firewood for winter, tended to domestic animals, and hung the kettles. Besides, "they also were the mothers of the nation, which ought to command the[ir] respect." Putting the women between himself and the headmen and warriors revealed a keen insight into Iroquois society; it was sound but dangerous strategy. Men would both respect and resent him.

A petitioner withdraws while the council deliberates. Seated in Cornplanter's house, where he bunked, Adlum inferred from the reaction of his interpreters to the loud talk issuing from the council house that the debate was heated, but he refused to let his interpreters eavesdrop. He banked on the matrons. He knew they would call him to the council house to hear the decision. The matter was put over and debated again until noon. At three, a horn sounded to reassemble the council, and two principal chiefs took Adlum by the arm inside.

After the preliminary smoking, Cornplanter spoke their mind. Concentrating on events of the past decade, he stressed the duress under which he had acceded to demands of the United States commissioners at Fort Stanwix. He alleged that white men were crueler than Indians both in war and in peace; he raised the old issue of differing concepts of land tenure: Indian rights to hunt and fish versus exclusive ownership. They could not comprehend how the king gave away land that he did not own. If they had forfeited all right to title, it was for want of power. They now asked for a small part of what they had given up. In sum, they would grant an easement to land south of an arrow laid on the map before him, and no more, although this area represented but half of the lands in question.

By engaging the favor of the women, Adlum had made matters more difficult for the council. The women liked his advice and opposed military measures, although the chiefs and warriors felt confident that what had been done twice could be repeated. They refused to concede that Wayne exceeded or differed from Generals Harmar or St. Clair. White armies held no magic.

It is characteristic of Iroquois councils that if they do not completely reject a proposal, they may accede to part of the request. They agreed to provide Adlum's surveyors with an escort to protect them from western Indians who ranged eastward to French Creek. Adlum would need to clothe and provision the nine warriors and three chiefs and their womenfolk. The council allotted but forty of the eighty days requested to complete the survey. They argued that running the line would in no way prejudice any future treaty. All this for a consideration of two more kegs of powder, lead equivalent, a barrel of flour to each town for the women and children, and some linen, calico, and blankets.

□□◇□□

While Adlum's surveyors and guides went off into the wilderness for forty days to drink diluted whiskey and run concession lines, Chapin made arrangements for the treaty at Canandaigua. Once the decision to hold the treaty was made, the initiative passed to the Americans. Before leaving Buffalo Creek, Chapin settled his account with C. Winney, a local trader, for fifteen quarts of whiskey, besides corn and cash advanced to individual Indians. Brant and Red Jacket were two-quart men, ten others received a quart apiece, and five half-pints went to warriors (NYHS, O'Reilly Collection, 10: 47). It would take more than a case of whiskey to move the council fire east of the Genesee River, and so on reaching home, Chapin planned accordingly. He sent long lists of goods desired by the Indians to Pickering, who placed orders with Philadelphia merchants for shipment to Albany by water. He wrote to Pickering, Brant, and Governor Clinton informing them about the truce reached at Presque Isle, Indian land claims, and the plan to hold the treaty at Canandaigua.

The original dates of 8, then 15, September that Knox set for the treaty in late July would prove unrealistic. It would take Colonel Pickering, the named commissioner, longer to procure the goods and clear up the business of the Post Office. Chapin would notify the Six Nations and persuade them to come to Canandaigua, but they would come on their own time. Knox sent Jasper Parrish to Chapin with an advance of $1,500 for provisions and with five thousand wampum beads to make up the invitation and treaty belts (NYHS, O'Reilly Collection, 10: 56).

While Parrish rode the wilderness trail to Canandaigua bearing instructions, Chapin received intelligence from the west. A white man from Detroit informed him that a party of Indians had come in with prisoners, scalps, and horses from the southward. They had evidently tangled with one of Wayne's patrols, and the trophies taken scarcely compensated for the losses sustained. Chapin later learned that the Indians had lost seventy men in this engagement. The survivors were sore at the Six Nations for not supporting them (NYHS, O'Reilly Collection, 10: 63).

In response to a report that western Indians had beset Fort Le Boeuf, the Six Nations were said to be withdrawing women, children, and old people from Allegheny to Cattaraugus and might accept a British invitation to remove north of Lake Erie, where American troops could not cut them off. Amid these rumors, Chapin reassured the Six Nations that if they remained quiet, they would not be disturbed. The reports of these events had a basis of fact, as Adlum revealed, although the British gesture smacks of psychological warfare. Chapin predicted that if any of this occurred, the Senecas would make their stand at Cattaraugus Creek. He regarded Cornplanter's friendship to the United States as unreliable, the chief being burdened with guilt over personally selling the Presque Isle land, which the Six Nations deplored inasmuch as they were not party to the proceedings. Indian enmity and the sanction of constant criticism had displaced Cornplanter toward the British, who benefited by such schisms (NYHS, O'Reilly Collection, 10: 57).

Chapin thought that the British would remain at the Miami rapids, although they had not sent more troops. Wayne was on the march, but how many opposed him? The Six Nations sat quietly, awaiting an answer to their speech to the president. Chapin waited for Parrish to bring orders and deliver goods, when Chapin would send word to the chiefs that they might come view them: "An Indian's hopes of receiving something by & by is more gratifying than Present possession." One may judge from the liquor bills that Chapin later submitted that councilors came by Chapin's, glimpsed the goods, stopped at Berry's tavern for a drink, and went home to report.

Chapin's intelligence was substantially correct. On 30 June an escort of Wayne's riflemen and fifty dragoons met an attack by numerous Indians under the walls of Fort Recovery and beat off two waves of assault with considerable Indian losses. Wayne estimated that between fifteen hundred and two thousand warriors were engaged. They were led by British officers in red coats and supported by Detroit militia with blackened faces. Wayne's men had already discovered St. Clair's artillery hidden beneath fallen logs where the Indians had hidden it (Knopf 1960: 346; O'Reilly Collection, 10: 57, NYHS).

An Indian informant told Chapin on 12 August that the Indians had lost seventy men in this battle and that he himself had seen a wounded Caughnawaga warrior returning home. Surely the Six Nations had the word first. Clearly, Wayne's progress would affect the disposition of the Six Nations toward the treaty. Appearances were good. Chapin predicted compliance with reasonable terms. Appearances and his sources indicated that the Six Nations had not gone off as a body and joined the hostile Indians but remained at home, satisfied with the withdrawal from Presque Isle (NYHS, O'Reilly Collection, 10: 63).

The president disposed of the Presque Isle matter by inviting the Six Nations to a treaty at Canandaigua on 10 September 1794. The Chapins, father and son, on 15 August drafted the invitations "to the Head Chiefs, Sachems, and Warriors of the Six Nations" (NYHS, O'Reilly Collection, 10: 64). General Chapin being ill, Captain Chapin next day carried the wampum strings to the Buffalo Creek council, asking its members to notify the other villages, "particularly Captain Obeel [Cornplanter] and his people." The draft of the speech delivered at Buffalo on 20 August is wordy, but in the Iroquois idiom it meant, "He invites you all to assemble in a treaty to be held at Canandaigua in ____ days from this day," a form that enabled the council to prepare invitation sticks notched with the appropriate number of intervening days. Colonel Pickering would attend and take charge. In effect, the speech continued, the president has spared no pain to ease your minds and to assure that on your return you may remain easy on your seats.

Runners covered the seventy miles from Buffalo Creek to Cornplanter's towns on the Allegheny, whence Captain Crow, or "Big Hemlock," in the space of two days found Adlum deep in the Allegheny forest at Kuskuskee Narrows. The message, somewhat premature, said Colonel Pickering had arrived at Canandaigua and Adlum was wanted at the Cornplanter towns. On reaching the upper, or New Arrow's, town on 23 August, Adlum was immediately conducted to the council house. The speaker told him that they had received that day an invitation to go to Canandaigua to meet with Colonel Pickering. But they had decided that if the colonel wished to speak to them, he must meet them at Buffalo Town. They wanted Adlum to go with them. They did not wish to treat until they had an unequivocal answer to the question, Had Pickering come to restore the land they had asked for—"yes or no?" The alternative was war. They expected next day a party of reinforcements representing various of the Six Nations living beyond Lake Erie, who would join them against the United States if their request was denied (Kent and Deardorff 1960: 440).

In late August the Allegheny Senecas appeared determined to take up the hatchet to keep open the corridor to the west. Any treaty to which they were a party must restore some lands and guarantee title to lands retained. Adlum explained that logistics prevented Pickering's coming to Buffalo Creek; there were no roads west of the Genesee by which to transport heavy presents, and it was easy for the Senecas to go cross-country on a path known since La Salle's day. Pickering might possibly entertain a request to meet at the Genesee River, but Buffalo was out of the question. He deserved a civil answer (Kent and Deardorff 1960: 443).

The Indians nevertheless remained adamant: they had not requested a treaty, they didn't want presents, they simply wanted a part of their country restored. Adlum cautioned that they should not exceed the possibility of getting an answer to their question. They should at least send delegates to meet the representative of "the *greatest man known* and a very powerful people" (Kent and Deardorff 1960: 443). Whatever they did must be by the authority of the chiefs. An insolent answer from warriors would lead only to Pickering's covering the fire and turning his back on them until they recovered their senses.

The arrival next day of nineteen warriors led by Duquania, "a very muscular man" of French and Cayuga parentage, coming from Grand River to help guard the frontier only reinforced the warlike spirit. Adlum described their martial reception (Kent and Deardorff 1960: 444). As was customary, they were escorted to the council house and fed, and after they had rested, "the chiefs and warriors called upon them to hear the news." Adlum wisely did not attend.

No one on the Niagara frontier had yet heard any news of Wayne's decisive victory during the week preceding Duquania's coming to New Arrow's town to peddle the Dorchester-Simcoe line to the Senecas. The Iroquois in Canada were still acting on the presumption that war between Britain and America was imminent. Having heard that the Six Nations of Buffalo Creek had requested the return of part of their country, Duquania offered the support of seven different tribes in Canada ready to join when needed.

While Duquania lectured the men, Adlum talked with the women. Somehow he sensed that they were key to the situation. He wrote, "I found the women invariably for peace and most of the old men." He could speak to these two ranks of Iroquois society without giving offense. "But it would have been thought highly indecorous and impertinent, to attempt the young men called warriors" (Kent and Deardorff 1960: 445). There was another way.

There is no more effective way to shorten social distance among the Iroquois than giving a feast sanctioned by a dream. Adlum hung the kettle for the warriors of two towns by presenting them with a fat hog, as his dream prescribed, that they might make a feast after their own customs. Since this variant of the Eagle Dance or Brag Dance has been fully described and published (Kent and Deardorff 1960: 446–52; Fenton 1953a), I skip the ethnographic detail to remark that Adlum's sheer guts in sitting out the ceremony at the striking post, as blows came increasingly closer to his head, while a first interpreter fled to the "shelter of women's petticoats," earned him the respect and compliments of the participating warriors.

As the smoke of the cooking vanished, Cornplanter, as host, struck the war post three times and, after recapitulating the day's proceedings, presented Adlum with a pair of embroidered moccasins that symbolized his travel orders. Cornplanter did not believe that Wayne could defeat the western Indians. Little did the participants realize, as they carried home the feast food, that instead of celebrating a Brag Dance to honor Adlum's departure, they were indeed holding a Ten Days Feast for their kinsmen killed at Fallen Timbers. Cornplanter cited Adlum's influence over the women, the old men, and the young warriors. They were at peace momentarily, they guaranteed his safe conduct, he must depart on the morrow; but if their land was not returned, they would break up the frontier from the Genesee to Pittsburgh. Later, Adlum learned that he should have made a speech, as good manners required.

To dispel any misapprehension about their intentions, Cornplanter invited Adlum to witness at sunrise the instruction and departure of three scouting parties from the council house. Fifty-six men painted for war ranged themselves behind their leaders: Duquania, Little Crow, and Nephew. They were instructed specifically where to hunt, pending further orders. Meanwhile, the local chiefs and the "great women" would be attending an intertribal council at Buffalo Creek, where the council would decide the plan of operations and communicate it to the hunters in the woods. The matrons would meet with the matrons of other towns and tribes. "We would give you orders at once, but our great women are opposed to going to war: "*and we may . . . thank our friend for that*." Adlum's strategy had paid off. But Cornplanter hoped that the women might change their minds when the three ranks of society—chiefs, warriors, women—met in council.

A messenger had just come from Buffalo bringing an inquiry from their brother chiefs about going to Canandaigua to meet with Colonel Pickering. Cornplanter spoke for the Allegheny chiefs: this would be unnecessary, since they neither desired nor requested a treaty; if the colonel had anything to say to them, he could come to Buffalo prepared to say yes or no about returning their lands. Cornplanter seemed unimpressed by Adlum's advice on the protocol due the president's sole commissioner. He hoped the Buffalo chiefs would agree. Cornplanter would risk war to retrieve his reputation.

□□◇□□

News of the battle of Fallen Timbers on 20 August took three weeks to reach Buffalo. Chapin knew on 16 September and wrote to Knox next day (NYHS, O'Reilly Collection, 10: 72). Cornplanter's faction acted as if they disbelieved it; the British at Detroit and Niagara tried to suppress the news; and Chapin briefed Pickering upon his arrival at Canandaigua on the nineteenth. Philadelphia was in the dark. Wayne, busy consolidating his victory, had waited eight days to file a report (Wayne to Knox, 28 August 1794, in Knopf 1960: 351–55).

"The shout of war & news," three whoops, interrupted an ongoing debate in the Buffalo Creek council between Cornplanter, for the warriors, and a Mrs. Chittiawdunk, for the matrons, just when she was invoking the supernatural sanction that traditionally enabled women to exercise a right that they would not relinquish, namely, "to prevent madmen and fools from doing mischief." Adlum, who was present, learned from an interpreter whose mother was a matron "that if the Indians go to war without the consent of the great women, the mothers of the *Sachems and Nation*, the Great Spirit will not prosper them in War, but will cause them and their efforts to end in disgrace" (Kent and Deardorff 1960: 465). Cornplanter complained that he had long submitted to this ancient custom, but it was now time for the men to decide for themselves. While the matron was speaking, the news of Wayne's victory came in. The council suspended business until the news was related. Dead silence fell on the assembly for a time, until one old man rose and observed that friends and kin to the westward had participated in that battle. He proposed adjourning until survivors brought more news. One hundred warriors of the Six Nations saw action that day, according to Wayne's report (Knopf 1960: 357).

The council opened next morning with the usual ceremonies. Several recent arrivals from the battle scene related that indeed the British had shut the gates while Indians were trying to gain access to the protection of the fort. This news came as a great shock to councilors who had been led to expect British support. Just then an old man who had listened to Adlum and remembered his prediction spoke. He reminded the council of what they had been told at Burnt House, which "so far came out to be true." Therefore, in his opinion, "the best thing they could do was to go to *Canandagua* . . . meet Col. Pickering, and make the best terms they could." Several approved; none dissented. No one spoke against it.

Having sat through many Iroquois councils in this century, I find Adlum's memoir to have the ring of veracity. All too seldom is there information on how decisions were taken in Iroquois councils. The present case bears on the disposition of the Six Nations to come forward and treat at Canandaigua more than two hundred years ago.

Cornplanter, having been worsted by the women and old men, went home unhappy at the Buffalo Creek council's decision. The debate had gone on for several days before the dire news of Fallen Timbers came in. Tired of the women's obstinacy, he had argued for abolishing the supernatural sanction that gave women the right to veto warfare. He held that men had submitted too long to this ancient custom handed down from their ancestors—that it was time to change the rule and let the men decide for themselves. His real concern was that Colonel Pickering would argue them into accepting peace terms, much as they had suffered Adlum to amuse them for sixty days. Otherwise they might have attained unanimity for war. He favored sending out runners then and there to order the hunting parties to make a stroke. This was the only way they could take this power from the women. He knew the women would never give in. Indeed, the matrons had taken the measure of the most famous war chief of the Senecas. He never recovered from this humiliation. He would prove difficult at Canandaigua.

CHAPTER 41

PICKERING KINDLES A FIRE
AT "KANANDAIGUA"

Great events have a way of running on Indian time. While Cornplanter hung the war kettle, while Adlum surveyed the woods, while Wayne prepared to advance, and while the Chapins drafted invitations, official business kept Colonel Pickering chained to his desk with little hope of departing Philadelphia before 10 September, the date originally set for the treaty. Knowing how deliberately Indians approach an event—that they cannot be hurried—Pickering estimated that arriving in Canandaigua on the eighteenth would be in plenty of time to greet the Indians. As a gesture of good will, he was bringing Cornplanter's son, Henry Abeel, who had gone to Philadelphia to be educated, to see his father (fig. 43). Anticipating that the local tavern would be crowded with people attending the treaty, Pickering asked Chapin to put him (Pickering) up and to find a convenient place where he could entertain. Canandaigua, in the backwoods, would lack certain amenities, so he shopped for "liquors, coffee, tea, chocolate," and he brought a servant, but no cook. The "Indian Goods" had already reached New York for transshipment to Albany and should be in Canandaigua in time for the treaty (MHS, PP, 62: 176–84; NYHS, O'Reilly Collection, 16 August 1794).

Meanwhile, the Meeting for Sufferings of the Society of Friends in Philadelphia, being duly informed of the treaty and encouraged to attend, seriously deliberated on this important movement. Four Friends—Bacon, Emlen, Parrish, and Savery— saw it as their religious duty to go. The society furnished them with an address to the Six Nations, signed by forty-four Friends, stating: "We meddle not with the affairs of government; but we desire to do all we can to preserve and promote peace." This defined their status as nonparticipating observers (Savery 1837, entry for August 1794).

Joseph Brant politely declined to attend. He observed that the president, however attentive he had been in other matters, had ignored the main issue, the boundary line. An obligation to attend a meeting with the "Lake Indians" made it impossible for him to be in Canandaigua. But if the president changed his mind about the line, Brant would sanction a meeting at Buffalo Creek, provided the basis of the treaty was to confirm the old Ohio boundary line (O'Reilly Collection, 10: 69).

One could not go safely into the woods outside of Fort Le Boeuf or Fort Franklin during the first week of September. Brant's deputies and Cornplanter's hunters treated whomever they met with insolence, exchanging ordinary arms for good rifles, taking horses, and threatening to take scalps any day (PP 62: 87).

Figure 43. Henry Abeel, son of Cornplanter. Portrait by John Bird King, 1827. Courtesy National Museum of Denmark, Copenhagen, Department of Ethnography. Photo by Lennart Larsen.

Things were not much better in Canandaigua. General Chapin, having lost his wife, was ill himself, exhausted by the Presque Isle journey. On top of grief and illness weighed the burden of the treaty (O'Reilly Collection, 10: 70). By the time Pickering set out on the tenth, the Six Nations had yet to respond to the invitation. The chiefs could not give Captain Chapin a direct answer, nor had they fulfilled their promise to send a deputation instructed to make arrangements. Having waited patiently, General Chapin now wanted to know why. He sent interpreter Horatio Jones to ask, would they please give him their decision? Everything was ready for the treaty at Canandaigua, the place to which the president had seen fit to remove the council fire, which he hoped would not prevent them from attending. The president "wishes you to hear his voice," wrote Chapin, and "I [ask you] to pay attention" (O'Reilly Collection, 10: 71).

Pickering must have felt relieved to get away from his desk. Besides the duties of postmaster general, for the past month he had paid invoices covering Indian goods: silver arm bands, wrist bands, ear bobs, nose jewels, brooches, kettles, clothing, calico, blankets, rolls of gartering, handkerchiefs, looking glasses, linen and fine black cloth for the chiefs, vermilion and lead for the warriors, transportation on the same, besides cutlery, foodstuffs, cheese, and Madiera for his own table, and rum, the essential treaty commodity. There was the keep of a public horse, Henry Abeel's mount. At the last minute, two public saddles had to be repaired for the use of Henry and the servant, Pitcher. Pickering drew $2,000 from the bank for expenses and contingencies. His journal of expenses covers the itinerary, daily expenses, and distances covered as his party traveled to Canandaigua (PP 62: 175-84). He provided himself with a conversion table for currencies, a table of distances, maps, and copies of laws and treaties, and as a literate man, he took along a copy of Walker's *Critical and Pronouncing Dictionary* (1791). Indeed, here was a model civil servant of the federalist period.

Two days before Pickering arrived, and while the Quakers were still on the road, an edge of uncertainty about the treaty lingered in Canandaigua. From the west a letter from William Ewing, employed as a spy, brought the first written confirmation of Wayne's action, which Captain Chapin heard first from Indians and then from returned captives. There now appeared no doubt of its truth (Chapin to Knox, 17 September 1794, O'Reilly Collection, 10: 72; Pickering to Knox, 20 September, PP 60: 201).

For the month past the British had made every effort to keep the Six Nations from honoring the treaty invitation. They tried desperately to persuade them to join the hostile Indians, but on failing to get a commitment allowed that they might attend and accept the American presents.

While Cornplanter debated with the women at Buffalo Creek, Genesee Seneca leaders decided to attend the treaty and showed up in Canandaigua at the stated time, one hundred fifty strong. Chapin, however, persuaded them to go back to the Genesee crossing and await the Buffalo and Allegheny contingents, to which they consented. While they were still in town, Chapin afforded them a glimpse of the goods and stores that Pickering had forwarded for the treaty. Chapin gained confidence that the treaty would bring out the factions friendly to the United States, and possibly the remainder.

Timothy Pickering, Henry Abeel, and servant Pitcher arrived at Canandaigua on Friday, 19 September, having ridden the three hundred miles from Philadelphia in nine days (PP 62: 180). Pickering immediately got to work, receiving and dispatching Indian runners. On Saturday he wrote to Knox confirming the report of Wayne's victory (PP 60: 201). To Becky, his wife, he related the first of a series of intimate accounts beyond his official reports.[1] Pickering's timing was perfect: within several hours of his arrival, two runners came from the council at Buffalo Creek carrying answers to the invitation to meet Pickering at Canandaigua. (As

1. In the 1940s, PIckering's descendants, who still occupied his house on Chestnut Street in Salem, discovered a bundle of these letters beneath a roof rafter. A member of the family transcribed them for me. I am extremely grateful.

he wrote Becky, he was not authorized to treat with them elsewhere.) Their excuse for the delay was that they had been held up waiting for Cornplanter to appear. The council, moreover, felt bound by its then-explicit declaration that "the place of council must be Buffaloe Creek." The Indians expected Pickering to come there.

Chapin, however, felt confident that in view of the news of Wayne's victory, the chiefs would come to Canandaigua. Pickering confided to his wife that the chiefs' objection to coming to Canandaigua was "wholly grounded on British reasons," by their influence on the chiefs, "many of whom are sufficiently corrupt to play a double game." He predicted that it would take another ten days for them to get there and get down to business. From the runners he learned that Colonel Simcoe had given an assembly of Buffalo Creek chiefs at Fort Erie an interpretation of Wayne's action more favorable to the British, minimizing Indian losses and exaggerating the number of Americans killed as three hundred, more than double the number reported by Wayne.

Indeed the Indians were playing a double game. They charged the runners with two replies to the president's invitation, each position supported by wampum strings. Pickering noted that when he answered the runners by refusing to go to Buffalo, "the runners then took out another bunch of strings, *all white*, and said the Chiefs directed them to tell me, That if it was not in my power to confer with them at Buffaloe Creek, they would meet me at Kanandaigua" (PP 60: 202; 62: 180). Having reassured the runners, Pickering sped them homeward and urged their leaders to come forward promptly. It would take the runners two and one-half days to cover the nearly one hundred miles, and another week for their leaders to reach Canandaigua, since "they travel with their women and children, and are never in a hurry." Pickering still had something to learn about Indian time.

Differing conceptions of time and custom would impress the thoughtful Quaker James Emlen: "Perhaps no people are greater masters of their time, hence in their public transactions we often complain of their being tedious, not considering that they and we estimate time with very different judgements. We are very apt to condemn any natural practices which differ from our own, but it requires a greater conquest over prejudices & more penetration than I am Master of clearly to decide that we are the happier people" (Emlen journal [Fenton, ed., 1965a]: 333).

□□◇□□

Colder weather marked the fourth week of September, warning the Indians to get in their harvest and the commissioner to get on with the treaty. A hoarfrost covered the ground at Canandaigua on Monday, 22 September. Next day Pickering dispatched the interpreter Horatio Jones with a message to the Indians at Buffalo Creek, urging them on (PP 62: 180).

Just then the council was in session, according to runners who came to Canandaigua with a message from that body. The previous runners, they reported, who had left Canandaigua on the twentieth, had reached Buffalo Creek on the twenty-second. The chiefs had held councils for two days and then sent runners to Grand River to inform the Mohawks where the treaty would be held and to invite them to attend. Further, "*in five days from this time*" (2 October), the Indians at Buffalo Creek "would rise from their seats" to travel to Canandaigua. Meanwhile, "Cornplanter had returned home to collect his people and bring them to the treaty." The date fixed for leaving Buffalo Creek depended on the number of days estimated for the Mohawks to join them and for Cornplanter to return with his people. Pickering calculated that the main body would need a week coming from Buffalo to Canandaigua. Given the contingencies that beset such movements of people, he saw "little chance of opening the treaty for business until the middle of October." Rumor promised a great assembly (Pickering to Knox, 27 September 1794, PP 60: 202).

Henry Abeel became something of a trial to Timothy Pickering, who had sons of his own. Among other habits, he had acquired in Philadelphia a taste for finery. To get Henry ready to visit his mother at Kahnawagens, Pickering paid two shillings for a "waistcoat pattern" and advanced three dollars and a quarter toward traveling expenses (PP 62: 176). Henry set out on the twenty-fifth, the day the Quakers arrived and the Oneida-Tuscarora delegation came in. (Cornplanter, who now lived at Allegheny, separated from Henry's mother, had spared this son to be educated at Philadelphia. His mother remained behind at Kahnawagens on the Genesee, Cornplanter's old home, where Henry went to visit his matrilineage. Both the separation of his parents—"brittle monogamy"—and lineage loyalty are characteristic of Iroquois society.) Henry returned on the weekend not to miss any of the fun in town (PP 62: 180).

The Oneida-Tuscarora contingent numbered 135. As loyal veterans of the Revolution, they had a special claim on Pickering's attention. Three of their leaders, Nicholas Cusick (Tuscarora), Captain John, and Kohicktoton, claimed that General Schuyler had promised them all the perquisites of American officers, which had not been forthcoming. Cusick held an uncashed certificate worth three hundred pounds. Pickering would have to take this matter up with James Dean (PP 62: 180).

The Quakers, having just arrived, were invited to sit in this conference. Pickering had reason to be joyful at their coming because they brought a letter from his wife telling him that his family was well, despite the warm weather and the threat of yellow fever.[2] Timothy wrote to Becky that night, hoping that the cold front that brought frost to Canandaigua would soon be felt in Philadelphia and check the prevailing diseases.

As Emlen noted, upper New York had been unusually sickly that summer, with "bilious fever . . . the general complaint." Whether influenza or malaria, it afflicted both Indians and whites. Thirty Indians died that season at Oneida. At Onondaga, most of the Indians were reported sick; and thirteen white people engaged in salt making died. Public health fared better along the Genesee.

Like most busy people leaving home, Pickering forgot something. He instructed his wife just where on his desk to find an invoice from Tench Francis covering fine cloth purchased for the chiefs, which he needed for inventory and accounting before the treaty.

The Oneida-Tuscarora delegation gained fifteen members for a second conference next day. Few had come from Onondaga, where Death, the Faceless, had taken some of their great men (Emlen journal; also David Bacon's diary, 26 September 1794, Haverford College Library). Pickering condoled with them, for he, too, had

2. September in Philadelphia can be hot, and that year (1794), yellow fever and other diseases had taken many persons.

lost a son. (Such an appeal to a loss in one's family affects the Iroquois profoundly and evokes elaborate expressions of sympathy.) This delegation, its ears unstopped and its throat cleared, was ready to do business.

Horatio Jones had a busy week at Buffalo Creek. It was the fifth of October before he returned to Canandaigua to report. Charged with hastening the departure of the local Indians for the treaty and with removing any obstacles the British might continue to throw in their way, Jones went directly to the principal village, assembled the chiefs, and delivered Pickering's message. Farmer's Brother immediately gave orders to prepare for the journey, which entailed getting in the harvest, and he set the date for departure as on or about 1 October. The assembly appeared pleased (Pickering to Knox, 8 October, PP 60: 203).

At Winney's tavern, Jones encountered Johnson, the British interpreter, and Colonel Powell of Fort Erie, who manifested surprise and disgust that the Indians were actually preparing to attend the treaty at Canandaigua. The most remarkable evidence of their intention, Jones reported, which marked the breakdown of the usual sex division of labor, was that the men and boys were pitching in to help the women harvest the corn in time to meet the deadline for departure.

Next day, Jones and Captain Chapin returned to the Genesee "to hang a kettle for Indians" who were expected to arrive that evening or the following day (Pickering to Knox, 8 October, PP 60: 203). It being inconvenient for Colonel Pickering to go there himself, he had sent along a speech of condolence to be delivered by Jones at the woods' edge to comfort the relatives of the Delaware Indian killed at Venango (O'Reilly Collection, 10: 74). To his son John, Pickering described Indian travel to treaties in great numbers so that all might witness the great event and share in the distribution of presents and the feast. They sent their wisest men. "The women attend, because they carry the baggage of the family, their young children at their backs, cut and bring wood to the fire places, and cook."

Knowing they had at least two weeks to get ready, Chapin and Pickering concentrated on the problems of the Oneidas. The Quakers held meetings of neighboring Friends and visited the Indians in camp (Emlen and Savery journals). They noted that fertile areas were fast filling up, although Indians were still all around. David Bacon's concerns did not prevent his trying the local fishing with small success.

The Oneidas had a complaint against the state of New York about the boundary of their reservation. It was over a misunderstanding in the survey as to just where the line ran from the Deep Spring, situated just north of the path leading from Chittenanago to present-day Manlius, which spring had always marked the boundary with Onondaga. The line was supposed to run due north to Canasaraga Creek, which surveyor Simeon DeWitt had mislabeled "Chittenanga," and the new line cut off a large piece of their land. The confusion of two Iroquois place names had deteriorated into a fraud. Pickering wisely deferred judgment until he could examine the facts on the ground.

Over the first October weekend, General Chapin estimated 450 Indians in town for the treaty. But the main body of the Six Nations was slow in coming from Buffalo Creek. Being free on Tuesday, the Quakers called on Jemima Wilkinson, the frontier prophet and self-styled "Universal Friend," of whom both Savery and

Emlen give compelling descriptions. This "artful and designing woman," as Savery called her, would inflict her presence and advice on the Indians during the treaty a fortnight later, and the Indian women would use this pretext to air their views.

Governments have a way of deferring and cutting expense accounts. Hendrick Aupaumut and his Stockbridge-Mahican companions who had run errands to the Miami rapids wanted reimbursement and the guns promised them. Hendrick was tired of putting things down on a piece of paper for forgetful white officials (PP 62: 89).

Mindful that the Six Nations would want something more than a piece of parchment attesting to the treaty articles, Pickering commissioned an Indian to make a large wampum belt, fifteen rows deep, which cost him two dollars (PP 62: 177).

On the morning of October ninth, Emlen and Parrish rode out to meet the Indians who were reported at the Genesee crossing. By nightfall the main body of Indians had not arrived. "Patience . . . will always be needed by those who attend Indian treaties," wrote Savery. The two Friends paused in the Indian camp to watch a Brag Dance before lodging at Gilbert Berry's tavern. They got little sleep, what with Indian drunks. By this time, meetings of Seneca medicine and war societies had degenerated into drinking bouts. As Emlen observed, any spectator might, after presenting a bottle of rum, boast of feats performed during his lifetime. Bystanders, both Indian and white, participated in rotation, recounting war records. There was a sensible doctor present who, after presenting a bottle, made his brag. He had been a man of peace, he claimed; in his profession he had striven to save men's lives and had succeeded in many cases. A child could take the life of a fellow, but "it required a Man of Judgement and Skill to save it." This novel brag gained universal approval.

As if to compensate for the annoyance suffered by the Friends during the drunken brawl at night, tavernkeeper Berry took them on a tour of lands he occupied within the preemption of Robert Morris. West of the Genesee River they saw corn on the ground estimated to yield eighty bushels to the acre, bark longhouses, evidently in use, and the ruin of a former Indian castle. Berry's contact with the Indians predated Morris's purchase of the preemption right from the state. He might need the support of the Friends later on.

In the evening the two Friends met and congratulated their "Indian Brethren," many of whom Parrish knew. The Indians returned thanks that the Quakers had survived the arduous journey to attend the treaty. That same evening, Cornplanter's party, which was encamped at Geneseo, sent word by two runners that it would take a shortcut to Canandaigua, saving ten miles, and not come by way of Kahnawagens. Emlen marveled at the physique of Sharp Shins, the noted distance runner who had once covered the ninety miles to Niagara in twelve hours and some minutes from sunrise to sunset (Emlen journal: 296). The Seneca delegates could not be expected to arrive in Canandaigua before the twelfth; they actually made it two days later.

□□◇□□

Back in Canandaigua, Pickering, Savery, and Bacon learned about Oneida factionalism during an all-day council held on 11 October. Captain John undertook to expound the role of sachem and contrast it with the office of war chief during peacetime. This issue would rise again among the Senecas. It was a pity that Samuel Kirkland did not attend the treaty, as invited, for no one understood Oneida politics better. He could have explained how the long factional struggle at Oneida had evolved into political parties of traditionalists versus Christians. Pickering was left to seek consensus as best he could during the treaty. Five strings of wampum symbolized his concern for friendship and unanimity, stressed the importance of the Oneidas among the Six Nations, and recognized their attachment to the United States. He hoped they might live in harmony on their own land (PP 60: 218–23).

Indeed, land had become the issue, and the traditional rules no longer applied. How the Oneida leaders handled this gesture of mediation indicates the importance they attached to the issue and reveals how custom treated such cases. Captain John addressed a few words to his colleagues, asked Pickering to keep his seat, and directed the sachems to withdraw "to converse among themselves." Presently, on their return, Captain John spoke their mind: "Now, Brother, listen to what we have to say."

After reviewing the substance of Pickering's speech, as was always done, he again admonished him to listen as he spoke the mind of the council in the sachems' presence. Following the usual invocation to the Great Spirit, and after disclaiming that they were a poor and ignorant people to be pitied, in contrast with the white people, he said, "Still we have rules of conduct—those of our forefathers, which they handed down, that they might be preserved and practiced by their children."

Despite repeated appeals for them to unite over policy, these rules were now inoperable in the new situation. "Our minds are divided on account of our lands." He then recited instances of repeated requests to sell and reviewed the controversy attending each case. "Brother, this was the cause of our minds being broken apart." The most eloquent of those opposed to selling had been "Our Head-Chief (Good Peter) who died at Buffalo Creek" in July 1792. It was over the lease by the sachems that the head warrior had risen in protest. And this had divided the nation into factions. The land controversy had shaken the Tree of Peace to its roots, so that the chiefs could no longer sit comfortably in its shade smoking their pipes (PP 60: 219).

At this, Captain John handed five strings representing Pickering's speech to the then head warrior, also named Peter, who, after a few remarks, handed them to Pickering. It was now up to Pickering to put the two factions back on the same path.

Pickering had learned the protocol of forest diplomacy. Accordingly, he would retire to consider and reply two days later. Both parties had fairly stated the case. Nevertheless, it was a matter of such importance that he needed time to consider and prepare a reply (PP 60: 218–23).

That evening, returning Quakers reported that the five hundred Senecas now at the Genesee crossing appeared somewhat apologetic at the delay they had occasioned. Until they came in, everyone was glad it was Sunday. In the afternoon the Friends went at four o'clock to the Indian camp, where some fifty white people who had somehow got word of it joined them. The Oneidas had camped in a cutover woodlot, the felled logs affording seats for council and guests. Here was enacted a scene quite novel to any Quaker meeting. One of the chiefs went round the camp shouting the "signal for them to assemble, which they did in large numbers" (Savery journal). After a moment of silence, the interpreter announced that they desired to sing a hymn (Bacon journal). Hymn singing before and after preaching the gospel struck the Quakers as quite unorthodox, but they did not object. Missionary Kirkland had taught the Oneidas to sing hymns in their native language. Disturbing as psalm singing might strike Quaker ears, the rendering by the choir of twelve moved Emlen to write:

> The Indian language being one of the softest in the World, their singing exceeded anything of the kind that I remember to have heard, the voices of the squaws were truly melodious; to a mind which could drop its exercise & listen with satisfaction to the harmony of sound it would have been truly delightful. . . . I must acknowledge that part of our Meeting . . . was to me the most exercising. (Emlen journal: 299–300)

Savery ruminated on the state of Oneida acculturation and found it slight. Though they were better instructed in religion than the others, it had affected their manners and morals little.

Pickering, having spent the weekend at his desk drafting a memorandum on the Oneida land question, delivered his advice on Monday. The Quakers joined him at the Oneida camp. In effect, he ruled that the governor of New York had disregarded the general government's 1790 law; therefore, the lease in question was out of order.[3] "No sale of Indian land should be valid, unless made at a public treaty held under the authority of the United States." In delivering to the council a copy of the United States statute, he acknowledged that others might tell them that the United States had no right to meddle with their lands. (Indeed, the state of New York has never acknowledged the right to treat with the Indians within its borders as belonging to the federal government.) This was the context that had prompted President Washington to appoint Colonel Pickering sole commissioner to treat with the Six Nations.

As a guide to future transactions, he laid out a program under eight heads for the Iroquois to follow (PP 60: 223–30). Among other things, he recommended substitution of a vote by two-thirds of the warriors and all of the sachems instead of unanimity. This time Pickering and the Quakers withdrew while the Oneida council considered the advice.

Captain John reported on their deliberations. The council had asked the chief warrior, Peter, to speak his mind on the subject. He said that he approved of it but had nothing further to say on the subject. Then he and the other warriors walked out, as if they disapproved, leaving only sachems and councilors to face Pickering. (One way to attain unanimity was for dissenters to withdraw.) The warrior faction evidently went home. Sorry as the sachems might be for the continued dissatisfaction of the warrior faction, the sachems would have welcomed more pointed fault-finding and professed that more pointed criticism would not have offended them. Captain John, as head chief, accepted the blame personally for the disputed

---

3. The full text of Pickering's speech is preserved in his papers at the Massachusetts Historical Society.

land cession. He underscored the nature of Iroquois polity by adding: "Brother, All nations have a head, or officers to manage their business. The Indians have theirs. *Among us, the affairs of peace are conducted by Sachems and Councilors.* But to speak the plain truth, our Head Warrior wants to interfere & control them" (PP 60: 229).

Indeed, the Seneca nation would air the same internal struggle between sachems and warriors within the fortnight.

The rest of Captain John's speech gave a somewhat humorous account of how white men of half their ability had mulcted Oneidas of their land by plying them with drink. Like the best of Indian humor it was self-directed. Meanwhile, he would speak to the head warrior with a view to reconciliation. Evidently, Peter had designs on becoming head sachem.

The Indians were slow coming in, but those in town were big eaters. In the month since he had arrived, Pickering observed that pressure on his larder was enormous, bills were mounting, and but a third of the Indians had reached town. On 13 October, the eve before the Buffalo Creek Senecas came in, he estimated fifteen hundred Indians in the neighborhood. They already had consumed 800 pounds' worth of provisions and supplies, and the daily consumption rate was rising. He appealed to Secretary Knox for an additional $5,000. It looked as if the treaty would cost some $10,000 (O'Reilly Collection, 10: 76, 77).

Underbudgeting is a common failure. There were such unforeseen items as stringing twenty-five thousand wampum beads, and Mr. Berry's tavern bills covering whiskey for Red Jacket and Farmer's Brother.

Having duly announced their presence in the neighborhood, the Buffalo Creek contingent of Senecas and Onondagas filed into Canandaigua on 14 October to be properly received with all the formalities of the ancient welcoming ceremony by the Oneidas, representing the junior moiety of the confederacy, and General Chapin for the United States. Friends Parrish and Emlen rode out to meet them, and Bacon noted that "they came in great order." The chiefs sent a rider to announce their coming and to ride back and meet them. "He appeared to think himself as Important as a General at the head of a great Army."

The woods'-edge camp was four miles out. Farmer's Brother, Little Billy, Red Jacket, and their followers of the Seneca nation had encamped the previous evening. The next morning, while the villagers of Canandaigua waited or rode out, the Senecas deliberately painted and ornamented themselves as etiquette required. It was midafternoon when they filed into town, 472 strong, entering at the upper end of town, where the previous arrivals lined up. Both sides fired a salute. Savery (1837) described the scene:

> The Oneidas, Cayugas, and Onondagoes were drawn up, dressed and painted, with their arms prepared for a salute before Chapin's door. The men able to bear arms marched in, assuming a good deal of importance, and drew up in a line facing the Oneidas, &c. colonel Pickering, general Chapin, and many white people being present. The Indians fired three rounds, which the other Indians answered by a like number, making a long and loud echo through the woods. Their commanders then ordered them to form a circle around the Commissioner and general Chapin; then sitting down on the ground they delivered a speech through the Farmer's Brother

(Honayewas),[4] and returned the strings of wampum which were sent them when they were requested to come to the treaty.

Emlen added that Farmer's Brother apologized for their late arrival but returned thanks to the Great Spirit for "favouring them to arrive in health," which they believed was his ordering, "whom they acknowledge to be the great disposer of events, that they were thus long delayed."

Pickering sought to make their minds easy. When they were ready, they would proceed to business. He assured them that everything necessary would be provided for their accommodation, and he ordered several kettles of rum to be brought in, after which they dispersed and went to set up camp. Each chief delivered a bundle of sticks accounting for the number of men, women, and children in his party, which together totaled 472 persons. "They made a truly terrific and warlike appearance" (Bacon and Savery journals).

Ethnographic niceties abound in these Quaker observations: face-painting, salutes, belief in predestination, return of wampum invitations, and stick tallies.

□□◇□□

It would be several days before the Indians were ready for business. Cornplanter and the Allegheny contingent would not come in before Thursday afternoon, the sixteenth, at the same hour. Meanwhile, Pickering spent Wednesday the fifteenth writing to his wife and reporting to General Knox. He rounded off the Buffalo Creek count at 500, estimated Cornplanter's people at 400, and added the Oneidas and Onondagas in residence to reach 1,200 certain and 1,500 probable total attendance (PP 60: 204). He used these figures to support Chapin's plea for funds. Fish Carrier, the head Cayuga chief, had not yet started from Buffalo Creek but was reported waiting for a delegation of Mohawks from Grand River. If they failed to show he would come along without them. Fish Carrier was held in such esteem by the other Iroquois chiefs that it remained doubtful whether any important business could be done until he arrived (Pickering to Knox, PP 60: 204).

The Indians appeared as friendly as Pickering ever knew them. He discounted press reports that the Six Nations would go to war right after the treaty. Observed behavior disputed such a view. Although they might resent being deprived of their lands, and British propaganda to the contrary—that they would become like other tribes, "mere makers of baskets and brooms"—Pickering still did not think that war would follow. He had a higher opinion of the Six Nations.

Both the Six Nations and Chapin now had the truth about Fallen Timbers. Independent confirmation came from a trustworthy Buffalo Creek chief and a letter written by Brant from Detroit, mentioning numbers killed in particular tribes; of the fifty wounded, half had died. This was the letter that Jones, the interpreter, told Pickering about on his return from Buffalo Creek. Brant had asked the chiefs for their advice, but they concluded to give none.[5] Such shared intelligence had a profound effect on the conduct and outcome of the treaty.

The Indians got bored waiting, and when bored or frustrated, they got drunk. Deadly brawls ensued. Two Tuscaroras, while drinking, fell to quarreling and got in a fight. A kinsman who attempted to separate them was stabbed under the ribs.

4. Honanyawus (Hodge 1912, 1: 453).
5. On Brant's 1794 visit to Detroit, see Kelsay 1984: 513–15.

The one who drew a knife in the dark mistook his uncle for his opponent. The victim soon died. The required condolence would cause a further delay.

On 16 October it looked as if the treaty might soon commence. Fish Carrier's Cayugas were reported nearby. Cornplanter's party, together with Senecas from the upper Genesee, filed into town at mid-afternoon.[6] The Oneidas, Tuscaroras, Onondagas, and other predecessors lined up on three sides of the square facing the newcomers. Each side fired three rounds "and performed some maneuvers; all in full Indian dress and painted in an extraordinary manner." They then encircled the commissioners and Friends and exchanged short speeches of congratulation, and because it rained, "the rum was soon brought and the company dispersed" (Savery 1837).

The little drama of the woods' edge had its third run next day to greet Fish Carrier's Cayugas. No one bothered to write a notice (PP 62: 180). There were now about sixteen hundred Indians present to attend the treaty.[7] That many Indians, Savery complained, were "very noisy night and day, dancing, yelling, and constantly intruding . . . to beg for rum." Attendance at Indian treaties could be painful for Euro-Americans and required resignation.

But the Indians were not entirely idle. They hunted deer and sold venison for three half-pence or less per pound. Nor were they without charm. Savery wrote: "I sat in company with an Indian Queen, who had a small child in one of their kind of cradles, hung with about one hundred small brass bells, intended to soothe the child to rest" (1837: 354). Pickering would describe a similar scene in a letter home.

A concern on which the Quakers sought advice of the Six Nations related to ownership of the Hopewell lands in Virginia that members of the Society of Friends had settled and for which they desired to compensate the heirs of the previous native owners. Two years previously, when Seneca leaders had visited Philadelphia, concerned Friends asked them on departing to inquire of any living descendants. After devoting several councils to the subject, it appeared clear to the Senecas that the lands in question were part of the hunting grounds of the Conestoga Indians. Cornplanter pointed out two elderly men present as descendants of these former Iroquoians of the Susquehanna Valley who professed to remember well the question of this title and who no doubt would satisfy the Quakers as to the details at a later time. Meanwhile, they would withdraw (Emlen and Savery journals).

That afternoon, townspeople and Friends witnessed the formalities of the Condolence Council. No business could start without it. Unfortunately, no one bothered to interpret the ritual addresses, and only the Quakers, to whom Henry Abeel brought a message from the Indians inviting them to attend, described its external features.

Different tribes met and condoled each other, according to custom, on account of having lost some of their chiefs, men of distinction on both sides, notably

6. Cornplanter's party of four hundred consisted largely of other-than-Allegheny Senecas, of whom few were in attendance (M. H. Deardorff, personal communication).

7. Savery (journal: 358) estimated the maximum Six Nations population at 4,000 and listed 3,900, omitting the Oneidas: Seneca 1,900, Tuscarora 300, Cayuga 400, Onondaga 500, Mohawk 800. The Tuscarora figure may include the Oneidas.

Senecas and Oneidas, who lived widely separated (Bacon journal). Besides these chiefs of opposite confederate moieties who had died since their last meeting, the Delaware nephews of the Senecas had had a man killed near Fort Franklin. The Quaker journals describe a scene that none of them understood because the speeches, which were not treaty business but merely fulfilled custom law, were not interpreted. "Captain John and another of the Oneidas spoke, addressing themselves to [village bands] who lived westward, holding in their hands as they spoke one after the other, several strings of wampum and belts; which they handed to the Seneca chiefs one by one at certain periods of their address, till they had delivered all they had." Clearly what Savery recorded is the action of the clearminded during recitation of the Requickening Address. Savery alludes to three bare words of requickening: wiping tears, brightening countenances, and unstopping throats. He noted that Fish Carrier (Cayuga), Clear Sky (Onondaga), and Red Jacket (Seneca)—from Buffalo Creek—returned the condolences, handing belts and strings back to the eastern Indians. This reciprocal act united them as one heart and one mind. Emlen commented: "There is something pleasing in their natural & unaffected eloquence as it proceeded from their Lips unadorned by art."

The council might now open, as they informed Colonel Pickering. The Six Nations would proceed to wipe the tears from the eyes of the Delawares and take the hatchet out of the head of the deceased on Monday afternoon. The council fire now kindled was covered for the weekend.

An opening address lit the council fire for a second session on Monday afternoon, 20 October. Commissioner Pickering performed the symbolic ceremony of burying the Delaware killed by an American. With fifteen strings of requickening he proceeded to gather the bones and bury them out of sight, to wipe away the tears of the aggrieved, and to cover the grave with leaves beyond the sight of passersby. He took the hatchet out of the deceased's head, uprooted a large pine, flung the hatchet into the hole, and replanted the pine tree that it might never be taken up again. He cleansed the blood from the bed, wiped tears from their eyes, opened the path of peace, and requested the Indians to keep it open at their end; the United States would keep open the other end for "*as long as the sun shone.*" The Senecas to this day remember and treasure Pickering's phrase, which appears in Pickering's and Savery's journals but not in the treaty. All of this was in the symbolic language of the Condolence Council, which Pickering had learned. He valued the wampum given at near one hundred dollars (Savery and Emlen journals).

Having completed the condolences, Pickering announced that he had something further to communicate but inquired whether the chiefs had any comment on what he had said. After consulting apart at length, the Indians appointed Farmer's Brother to speak their mind. He spoke briefly but with great energy, telling the commissioner that they were not ready to answer but would reply tomorrow. Emlen described him: "The Farmer's Brother is a man of Large stature, the Dignity and Majesty of his appearance, his sonorous voice and expanded arm, with the forcible Manner of his Utterance delivered in a Language to us unintelligible reminded me of the ancient orators of Greece and Rome."

After this speech, according to Savery, "the council fire was covered and the rum brought in as usual." Pickering would have to save his further remarks until after the Indians replied.

Two noteworthy events marked the third session, on Tuesday, 21 October. It snowed; and Jemima Wilkinson, "the Universal Friend," appeared before the council. Fish Carrier returned the commissioner's condolences of the previous day. The tone was conciliatory: although the death of their nephew caused sorrow among them, yet the commissioner's sympathy afforded them relief. Indeed, accidents happened among all nations. They would bury his death in oblivion (Emlen). He touched all the topics of requickening until all the strings that had been given them had passed through his hands. (The return of the fifteen strings of condolence is normally expected of the bereaved moiety as evidence that their minds are lifted up.) The Six Nations would hold the chain of friendship with the fifteen fires (there were by now fifteen states in the union).

Colonel Pickering now announced himself as the sole commissioner on behalf of the United States. He said he hoped the Indians knew from previous dealings with him that they could regard him with confidence. He was ready to hear their grievances and any other business they had to communicate. He assured them that he desired "the happiness and peace of their nations" and "he would never deceive them."

Pickering introduced the Quakers, their old friends, who had come forward at the request of the Six Nations and with the president's sanction. Jasper Parrish, who knew their idiom as well as that of the Senecas, read the Friends' address, which the Indians heard with frequent expressions of approval (Savery 1837).[8]

The Onondaga chief Clear Sky briefly acknowledged their speech while reserving a full reply until next day, as dignity demanded. That should have ended business, but Jemima Wilkinson, who sat with her retinue in the center of the council, asked to be heard.

As an act of ill grace, nothing in the annals of white and Indian affairs quite approaches Wilkinson's performance before the Indian council during the Canandaigua treaty. She and her three adherents fell upon their knees, and she prayed and then preached through an interpreter until daylight faded and cut her short, to everyone's immense relief. One cannot tell from the journals who was most displeased.

The Indians had some business of their own to attend to before covering the fire for the night. They had prepared memorial belts for several deceased chiefs as records of their service to the nation. Each belt required a short speech to the deceased's kindred, and their "words" were given into the custody of an ancient chief to become part of the cultural heritage, whereupon they covered the council fire (Savery 1837).

□□◇□□

No public treaty council met during the next two days. Rather, the chiefs and Colonel Pickering held private conferences. The Friends, clearly disturbed by the intrusion of the prophet Wilkinson, tried to adjust doctrinal differences with her and despaired. On the twenty-third, the commissioner held a private council at his residence to which he invited the Quakers and forty chiefs. Captain John of Oneida opened the council by informing the commissioner in a humorous way of

---

8. Savery heard *entaw* (*nen:tah*, "this" [Chafe 1963: 10]), although *nyoh*, or *yohe:*, is more common usage.

a council to which they had all been called, but on arriving, the chiefs were first invited upstairs to partake of a dram. "Perceiving that Berry was to be the commissioner, they concluded that it was [a] no good council fire, so he came off and drew the rest of the Indians with him" (Savery 1837). Obviously the design was to get the chiefs drunk and then convey some land to Berry. Pickering commended their conduct and promised to have Berry removed from the lands in question (Savery and Bacon journals).

Two instances of custom usage followed. No sooner had the previous exchange occurred when word came of the death of an Oneida ancient named Beech Tree. Ordinarily, on hearing the death cry, the chiefs would have suspended all business, had they adhered to custom law. Obviously concerned over further delay in the treaty proceedings, the commissioner informed them that his people did not let such occasions suspend transaction of important business; only the relatives of the deceased retired. But it was up to them. Apparently the Oneida chiefs were as eager as Pickering to get on with the business, and it is noteworthy how they rationalized setting aside a precedent. Because the deceased had long been ill, his passing was not unexpected, "although the loss would be much felt, particularly by his own Nation, yet it was the will of the Great Spirit." Contrary to usual practice—deferring business—the work of peace came also from the Great Spirit, and they thought they should proceed (Emlen).

Having decided that the Great Spirit would countenance this breach of custom, they went on with the council. Just then three elderly matrons entered with Red Jacket as their speaker to demand equal time to present their views in council in reply to "That White woman" who had been permitted to speak. Red Jacket addressed the sachems and warriors, and also the commissioner, asking their indulgence of the women. He explained his role as speaker for the women, who had charged him to deliver their views. He expatiated on the importance of women in Iroquois society—it was they who made men, and although they did not sit in council, yet "they were acquainted from time to time with the transactions at the Treaties." They had an abiding interest in the affairs of their nations. They had heard the opinions of their sachems and concurred that the white people were at the root of Indian distress, that they had pressed and squeezed them together until it pained their hearts, and that the white people should restore the lands they had taken. Yesterday that white woman had told the Indians to repent; "they now called upon the white people to repent, for they had as much need as the Indians" (Savery 1837: 355-56). They asserted that their right to speak derived from having "made the Men, both Sachems and Warriors" (Bacon journal).

The commissioner, in thanking the women for their speech, said he would always be willing to hear them whenever they had anything of importance to say. He did not regard Wilkinson's intrusion as a precedent. But he was willing to grant the women's request to speak through Red Jacket. After taking a glass of wine, the women withdrew (Emlen, Bacon, and Savery journals).

The commissioner then opened the council for business by recapitulating the speeches of Cornplanter and Red Jacket the previous day, 22 October. Cornplanter had spoken as chief warrior, and Red Jacket for the sachems. Pickering outlined his remarks in his notes under six major points with subheads, with frequent references to the "Indian Book" from the War Department (PP 62: 95-96). He dwelt on two themes in Cornplanter's and Red Jacket's speeches: the chain of friendship (Savery 1837: 356; Emlen journal: 306-7) and the haughty demeanor of the U.S. commissioners at Fort Stanwix. Cornplanter would never dissociate himself from the terms he had accepted ten years earlier at Fort Stanwix; any credit for terms reached at Canandaigua would redound to Farmer's Brother and to Red Jacket, as speaker.

The chain theme retained a remarkable consistency during the eighteenth century. By the end of the American Revolution, the chain of friendship had rusted away. The Seneca speakers had alleged that it was the fault of the white people. The attitude of the U.S. commissioners at Fort Stanwix had hardly contributed to renewing the chain, they said. The Indians were much aggrieved at the commissioners' conduct, which had scarcely improved at the treaties of Fort Harmar and Fort McIntosh.[9] At Fort Stanwix the commissioners had asserted that the country was now all theirs and had used such haughty and threatening language that the Indians present became so intimidated that they signed agreements contrary to their better judgment. It was now time to brighten the rusty chain. From the Seneca viewpoint, the United States should confirm to them a strip of land twenty to thirty miles deep from Lake Erie and extending from the Seneca country in southwestern New York State to "the Western territory." This strip represented the Allegheny corridor.

Having recapitulated the Seneca argument, the commissioner during two hours based his legal argument on Indian records and previous treaties. To the question, What nations are owners of the disputed lands? the answer required determining "the ancient boundaries of the Six Nations" and their extent.

First, Pickering said, Cornplanter's declaration at Fort Stanwix, backed up by the Delaware, Wyandot, Ottawa, and Chippewa declaration at Fort McIntosh, defined the division between the western tribes and the Six Nations. The Delawares seemed content with that treaty.

Second, as to the speeches of Cornplanter and Red Jacket, Pickering made two points: indeed the language of the U.S. commissioners at Fort Stanwix was harsh, but conquerors become haughty. He reminded the Six Nations of their own boast of having made women of the Delawares only a generation ago—to have put them in petticoats, armed them with corn pounders, told them to let their hair grow, and forbidden them to go on the warpath. And the Stanwix commissioners' haughtiness arose partly from a mistaken idea of the meaning of the peace treaty between the United States and Britain. Pickering was prepared to explain its true meaning as declared to the western Indians the previous year. This same interpretation had been sent to Lord Dorchester.

Pickering queried how far westward the land heretofore claimed by the Six Nations extended (Emlen journal: 307). Tribal territory being the province of war chiefs in American Indian societies, Cornplanter replied: "At the conclusion of the

9. Of the two Fort Harmar treaties, both executed on the same day, 9 June 1789—one with the Six Nations, the other with the western tribes, lest the two come to an accommodation—the treaty with the Six Nations (less the Mohawks) reaffirmed the 1784 treaty at Fort Stanwix and defined the western limits of Six Nations territory. The treaty with the western tribes confirmed the treaty of Fort McIntosh (1785), wherein the western tribes ceded lands to Pennsylvania, now part of Ohio.

war . . . with the Lake Indians it was mutually agreed that their hunting ground should be bounded to the Westward by a line drawn from Cuyahoga Creek on Lake Erie to the mouth of the Muskingum River on the Ohio." This area included a large tract in Pennsylvania, west of the Allegheny River, which the commissioner informed them had been purchased from the Delawares and Wyandots at the treaty of Fort McIntosh. This was also land that the western Indians fought for. A frequent difficulty in purchasing lands from Indians arose from different tribes' claiming the same territory.

Third, anticipating the Six Nations' concern about the western country, which the western "Hostiles" also claimed, Pickering had prepared seven points: (1) Chief Billy had stated the Six Nations' pretensions at Philadelphia. (2) The United States could not give up these lands for two reasons: previous sales, and gifts paid to warriors. (3) The previous year the commissioners to the Miami rapids were ready to relinquish particular lands to get a settlement, but failed. (4) Despite the regret of the hostile Indians, British agents McKay and Bunbury defeated the treaty. (5) These men made a fortune as traders. Pickering planned to withhold mentioning these data and the crown appropriation for Indians and present them last if needed. (6) The hostile Indians would have made peace the previous winter had not the British prevented it. (7) He left unstated "reasons why the same terms will not now be offered."

I find no record that Pickering spoke to three additional major heads for which he had prepared documentation. We may assume that he touched on these subjects during the two hours he was on his feet. For reasons cited under his first three heads, he contended that "the Six Nations at this treaty need now attend only to their own concerns." In a systematic way he sought to delimit the problem by repeating the boundaries set by the treaties of Forts Stanwix and Harmar; he could cite Cornplanter's speeches acknowledging that the Six Nations were bound by them. Ever since the fur trade began, logistics had demanded a path from Lake Ontario to Lake Erie, and a former treaty had granted four miles around Niagara to the king. A speech of Cornplanter's attested to his having sold to Pennsylvania the land between Tioga and Lake Erie. To this bombshell Pickering might add the fact that at Fort Harmar, Cornplanter and other chiefs had deeded to Pennsylvania the "Triangle" that comprised Presque Isle. Further, there was a release signed by Cornplanter and Half Town for these transactions in the amount of $800. Finally, Pennsylvania had granted 1,500 acres to Cornplanter and 200 acres to Big Tree, including an island in the Allegheny River.[10]

Regardless of how other Six Nations chiefs viewed these transactions between their war chief and the governor of Pennsylvania, Pickering meant to assure them that "rights of individual states [were] not to be taken away by the General Government." Pennsylvania was in fact proprietor of the land in question. It was not unlike separate property rights of the Six Nations. Plainly, the rights of the general government and Pennsylvania to the land were complete, and all rights of the "fifteen fires" had been conveyed to Pennsylvania.

---

10. This is, of course, the famous Cornplanter grant, since virtually inundated by the Kinzua reservoir during the 1960s.

As for the question in Indian minds—how had the chain in U.S. hands grown rusty?—it was sheer rhetoric. Pickering realized that they thought these transactions had rusted the chain, and he was prepared to admit and show why the Americans had then been angry. He could cite Cornplanter's remarks. But despite non sequiturs on his and their parts, he would proceed to brighten the chain anyway, first by the payment of goods and second by the payment of annual rent forever. The motive for these gifts was the Indians' gradual civilization; they were not given to prepare them to war against enemies of the United States. As a third measure, Pickering considered releasing to the Indians land bounded by the Buffalo meridian south to the Pennsylvania line, but he marked this proposal "Perhaps." The concession, were it to be made, would be questioned by Secretary Knox and would surely raise questions in Congress.

Pickering contrasted his generosity with the conduct of the British, whose obvious motives were to prepare the Indians for war. Lord Dorchester's speeches to the contrary and Simcoe's fort only illustrated British perfidy. Their Indian appropriations totaled 40,000 pounds sterling, then some 175,000 dollars.

The final head on Pickering's agenda would explain the law protecting Indian lands, presumably the Non-Intercourse Act of 1790. Among numerous supporting references to the "Indian Book," Pickering noted disclaimers by Wyandot and Delaware chiefs at Fort McIntosh to the lands lying between the Muskingum, the Allegheny, French Creek, and the Cuyahoga, which the Six Nations now claimed, and the willingness of the former to adjust the line to accommodate the original thirteen fires, or states. There were also references to a Cornplanter speech promising to hold fast to the position of the United States, saying that "the Six Nations and the U, States are one people" and mentioning a blacksmith and clothing. The Oneida Good Peter, now deceased two years, had said of the 1784 Stanwix treaty: "Let the peace be firm and unchangeable; We heartily rejoice at the present peace." At the time Cornplanter had been in accord, but he had shifted to new ground (Pickering notes, 23 October 1794, PP 62: 95–96).

Savery summed up the day: "This council held five hours, and much was said on both sides." Pickering had applied some oil and rubbed off rusty spots on the chain of friendship in an effort to assure the Indians that it was not in such bad shape as they apprehended. But the debate would heat up in the following days.

CHAPTER 42

THE COUNCIL FIRE GROWS WARM

It snowed nearly all day at Canandaigua on 24 October, sufficient to enable the Indians to track deer, which was a good thing. It gave some relief to the townspeople, who were losing their stock. The previous day, Richard Crosby had filed an affidavit in Ontario County Court for stock stolen by Indians: one cow, two large hogs, valued at forty dollars. They must have made good eating. Next to bear, the Senecas were partial to pork. To the deer hunter, snow is a blessing, and an hour in the open sobers one quickly. The Indians took no less than one hundred deer within a few miles of Canandaigua, some in sight of town. One man killed three in short order (Savery 1837). Plenty of venison would hang in the Indian camps, with some for sale at one or two shillings per pound, or in exchange for ʔoːneːkaʔ, "firewater" (whiskey). Things could have been a lot worse (Savery 1837; NYHS, O'Reilly Collection, 10: 80).

Commissioner Timothy Pickering condescended to cover the council fire until the morrow while two Oneidas were buried in a single grave. The funeral of old Beech Tree and friend was a unique event. Dressed in clean shirts, leggings, and moccasins, the two were enclosed in one square box; observers could not see whether grave goods accompanied the deceased. A man walked before the coffin to the grave carrying a three-gallon keg of rum under each arm, while holding a bottle in his hands. "The chiefs spoke at the grave, and then the warriors fired three salutes over it, whereupon the mourners fell upon the rum and got completely drunk before night" (Savery in Taylor 1925: 153–54).

With the treaty suspended, the Indians drunk, snow falling, and the days shortening, Emlen lapsed into the Indian metaphor of impending doom. "A dark cloud seems now gathering around us," he wrote in his journal (Fenton, ed., 1965a: 308). The British Indian interpreter, Johnson, had arrived in town, which greatly disturbed Pickering, who resolved not to let him attend and obstruct the treaty proceedings.

Pickering had every reason to be annoyed. He had at last begun the treaty; he had broached the question of boundaries, the issue at the bottom of all Indian wars with the whites. The Indians manifested a good disposition, although they spoke strongly. He saw the way to get through the business in a week. He thought the outcome would be satisfactory. But he still lacked confirmation of Wayne's victory from Knox, who was characteristically delinquent in informing his people in the field. Demanding as Knox was to receive regular reports from subordinates, he sometimes left them in the dark to discern their own direction. Not until 25 October did he sit down to acknowledge Pickering's letters of 20 September and 16 October. By the time a courier reached Canandaigua ten days later, the treaty would be all but over.

Knox's letter, when received, would tell of John Jay's successful negotiations with the British ministry the previous summer, during the hostilities, which would result in the British withdrawing their garrisons from the Miami rapids and ultimately from Detroit and Niagara. The letter mentioned the Whiskey Rebellion, the French Revolution, and frontier incursions in Kentucky. Chapin would get the $6,000 requested for treaty expenses, and he was expected to account for it promptly (MHS, PP 62: 93; O'Reilly Collection, 10: 82).

Had Pickering known all this, he might have been a little more generous to Johnson as an intruder and a little less irascible. His loss of temper in what Savery termed "a tense little drama" is particularly interesting because it highlights differences in character structure between whites and Indians.

The commissioner had requested the Friends to attend council that day in order to witness his reprimand of the British agent. Johnson had arrived in the neighborhood from Fort Erie two days earlier, bearing a message from Joseph Brant to the assembled Indians. The preceding day he had met with some of the chiefs and delivered the message, which urged them to stand fast on the Muskingum boundary (Kelsay 1984: 515).

He appeared at the Saturday council "in the character of a British interpreter" and appeared quite intimate with the Buffalo Creek contingent (Savery 1837). Cornplanter, aware of the anxiety that Johnson's appearance caused Pickering, rose to vindicate Johnson's presence in council. He expressed surprise that the British and Americans could not sit together in council, inasmuch as he understood from what had passed at Fort Stanwix ten years earlier "that no objection could be made to some of that nation being present at any future treaty" (Emlen journal).

Pickering kept detailed notes of the proceedings on 25 October, including attendance of both citizens and Six Nations chiefs, Cornplanter's speech, and his own reply (PP 60: 233–41). According to those notes, Cornplanter made the following points: (1) Why, since the peace, could the British and Americans, people of one color, not sit side by side at a treaty with Indians? (2) We sachems and warriors requested the British interpreter to attend the treaty and witness it. We all are pleased he is here. (3) He repeated Brant's message, brought by Johnson, regarding the council with hostile Indians at the Miami rapids, where Brant alone represented the Six Nations. Brant held that the British had frustrated the peace effort in 1793. The western Indians acknowledged the superiority of the Six Nations and would hear them in the matter of the boundary.

It would appear that Brant, in sending his compliments to the chiefs assembled at Canandaigua, still hoped to make a settlement based on the old line for which he had long contended, namely, the Ohio River, and which he now held out as the price of peace, requesting that it be mentioned at Canandaigua. Further, by Brant's messenger the Six Nations chiefs were invited immediately, when the present treaty council concluded, to come to Buffalo, where Brant would await their return, and to bring with them General Chapin, their superintendent.

Cornplanter, repeating Brant's message as he had heard it from Johnson, must have sensed that he was making a losing plea—he had already lost his audience. As he spoke, the ears of his Iroquois listeners were attuned to his words, but their eyes shifted alternately between the countenance of Colonel Pickering and that of the British interpreter. Pickering's face revealed the rising emotions of anger and righteous indignation, while Johnson appeared embarrassed. The Iroquois beheld this revelation with fascination and horror. Eighteenth-century civilization provided a New England Yankee or a Loyalist frontiersman no mechanism to mask his feelings, whereas generations of informal education in Longhouse society had schooled native diplomats to clothe themselves in a facade of imperturbability. Iroquois culture internalized what English civilization openly exploited.

The commissioner rose from his writing table in the center of the room to face Cornplanter and accuse Johnson of coming to spy for the British. He spoke from notes (PP 60: 233–41; Quaker journals). He inferred from remarks that the councilors sensed his displeasure at the appearance of the British interpreter at a council fire kindled by the United States. He admitted that his countenance revealed his feelings, that he could not conceal them. His indignation would have been even greater had not the recess occasioned by the funeral of old Beech Tree afforded him time to cool off.

If indeed the Indians had invited Johnson, Pickering asked, why had he not come with them? He had waited until Simcoe returned from the west and ordered him here to observe. Pickering felt warranted in calling him a British spy.

He reminded the Six Nations that they had requested that he be appointed to kindle the council fire and that the Society of Friends send observers. Where was their former confidence? How should he regard the intrusion of a British agent? Pickering confessed to pride at not sitting down with British agents. His pride stemmed from integrity and seeking truth: "I will never do you wrong." American agents, he declared, were never invited to sit in British councils with the Six Nations.

"Brothers, we are a free and independent nation, treating with the Six Nations, who also profess to be free and independent." (This was a partial recognition of Iroquois sovereignty.) "We have never asked the mediation of the British."

The United States, Pickering told the chiefs, "requested your assistance as friends to achieve peace with people of your color, the hostile western Indians." He thanked them for their efforts during the previous two years, though they had been unsuccessful. Contrary to Brant's letter, just read, the Six Nations had not led the hostiles astray; it was the British. It was also the British who prevented a treaty with the western Indians at Buffalo Creek in 1793, when the U.S. commissioners returned from Detroit. Brant himself had admitted it to General Chapin.

Pickering then enumerated four instances of British injustice: (1) failure to give up the forts on the American side of the peace treaty boundary, (2) armed interference with the settlement of Sodus Bay, (3) Lord Dorchester's speech that war between the British and Americans was inevitable ("We threw the King upon his back, and established our independence"), and (4) the policies that caused the American Revolution. Even when the king and councilors dropped warlike designs, the governors of Canada persisted in the old policy.

Next, Pickering felt obliged to mention several instances of British pride. (1) Brant and a delegation of western Indians at Niagara a year ago had appeared amenable to running a new line to replace the Ohio, when the British had agreed the difficulty was removed. (2) A second delegation frustrated the commissioners by raising fresh difficulties at Detroit, saying the first delegation was mistaken. The commissioners were never called to council at the Miami rapids; they could go only as far as Sandusky. (3) The western Indians determined not to go to Sandusky but would have met the commissioners on the Miami River, which Farmer's Brother confirmed. But Governor Simcoe, behind the scenes, pulled other strings. (4) When the western Indians sent runners to General Wayne the preceding winter to arrange peace, British agents heard and interfered. "Whenever there was a prospect of making peace with the Western Indians, the British have not failed to interfere and prevent it."

Pickering, obviously fed up both officially and personally with British interference, had stated his reasons for not tolerating a British agent's sitting at a council fire kindled by the United States. He summed up his position by quoting the president's instructions "not to suffer a British agent to attend this council Fire."

Having given his reasons and repeated his orders, he put the onus on the Six Nations to determine whether the business for which they were met should go on or whether the council fire should be extinguished. "You are a free and independent people: and as such you will determine this question."

The threat to cover the council fire shocked the Indians, and Pickering's speech impressed the Quakers. Captain Hendrick Aupaumut had confirmed the charge of British interference when the Quakers first arrived in Canandaigua. He had an ear in the council of the western Indians and had witnessed British dictation of Indian answers to the commissioners. James Emlen observed that the commissioner's challenge "seemed from the countenances of the Indians, to strike them with awe and surprise: as the breaking off of the treaty might be attended with dangerous consequences." Savery noted that the Indians appeared amazed at the warmth of the commissioner's delivery. When he sat down, one said: "the council fire grows warm, the sparks . . . fly about very thick. Johnson appeared like one condemned to die, and now rose and left us."

To recover their composure and frame an answer, the Indians requested that the commissioner, the Quakers, and the public withdraw. They counseled among themselves for half an hour and, when ready, sent a messenger to call in the other side. This is the age-old Iroquois council procedure.

It was now Cornplanter's turn to lecture the white people. His colleagues had stood him on his feet because it was his idea to bring Johnson to the treaty, and it was now up to him to explain away their embarrassment. He informed the commissioner that the sachems, after deliberating on the subject, realized there was no other way but to proceed with the treaty. As for himself, he could observe only that the reason why the council fire had not been uncovered that day was because a British man was present. But if he had the ordering of the council fire, he would be inclined to let Johnson stay, "because if the worst or most suspected man in the world should be disposed to sit in the council he would have no objection, in hope that it would tend to his reformation" (Emlen journal). He admitted that his people had caused the delay in the proceedings, but the real fault lay with the white people who had deceived them ten years ago at Fort Stanwix.

Now our sachems and warriors say, "What shall we do?" We will shove Johnson off: yet this is not agreeable to my mind, for if I had kindled the council fire, I would suffer a very bad man to sit in it that he might be made better; but if the peace you made had been a good peace, all animosities would have been done away, and you could have then sat side by side in council. I have one request to make, which is, that you would furnish him with provisions to carry him home. (Savery 1837: 357)

The council had sat for five hours. Pickering, satisfied with the conclusion, covered the fire for the night. Indeed, a certain logic governed Cornplanter's argument, but the pressure of politics did not favor it. Having won his point, Pickering invited the principals to dinner. The commissioner and his fifteen guests, including Red Jacket, Little Beard, Big Sky, Farmer's Brother, Little Billy, and Fish Carrier, dined by candlelight. Savery did not list Cornplanter! Horatio Jones interpreted the native repartee, which manifested a high turn for wit and humor. Red Jacket had the most conspicuous talent. Savery (1837: 357) described him as "a man of pleasing countenance, and one of the greatest orators among the Six Nations." The speaker for the women at Buffalo Creek emerged as the principal native voice at Canandaigua, just as Fort Stanwix in 1784 had been Cornplanter's treaty.

□□◇□□

The good humor of Saturday night dissipated in the tension of Sunday until Johnson was safely out of town. He was actually in some danger. The town was full of Revolutionary veterans who prepared to take action if Colonel Pickering did not. The *Albany Gazette* of 17 November ran an account of the affair, captioned "And Satan came among them," implying that the townspeople were prepared to inflict "the Yankee Punishment, or Tar and Feathers."

The council met despite the snow and drizzle. Little was accomplished. Cornplanter produced a letter that the Indians had drafted for Johnson to take to Brant, which stated that they intended to adhere to the original line between them and the lake Indians as acceptable for a settlement. The letter displeased Pickering, who wrote a letter of his own, as did General Chapin. However Brant might interpret the three letters, Pickering remained determined to reach a solution that the Six Nations would accept. Although "the Indians appeared pretty high" that day (Savery 1837), insisting that the settlement should be at Buffalo, and although "the Senecas appeared rather more uncompromising than heretofore," they were actually bluffing, hoping desperately that Pickering did not possess the intelligence that Johnson had brought from Brant—news of Wayne's victory at Fallen Timbers, when the British had shut the gates to the fort. In effect, the western Indians were telling the Six Nations that the British had stood by and let them be defeated the previous summer; but if the United States would agree to the line made last year between them and the Six Nations (and the United States), there would be peace. Details could be arranged next spring at Buffalo Creek. The Seneca sachems acted as if they were unaware that Pickering and Chapin had heard the news of Wayne's victory and British perfidy within days of its reaching Buffalo Creek. All that remained was official confirmation from Secretary Knox (O'Reilly Collection, 10: 83; PP 60: 211).

A sure sign that tension was mounting that Sunday evening: the chiefs got drunk. Seeing that they were hung over on Monday morning, Pickering postponed proceeding with the treaty until Tuesday. Instead, he devoted the morning to private conferences with individual chiefs—principally with Cornplanter, "on whom seems to rest the principal weight of the Business" (Emlen journal). Cornplanter was being troublesome, and Pickering wanted to prepare his mind for proposals next day in council to redress the Indians' grievances. This gesture followed the time-worn custom of "talk in the bushes" before bringing an issue formally before a council. Having lost several days to Beech Tree's funeral, the Johnson incident, and hangovers, Pickering nevertheless assured Becky, his wife, that he could wind up the treaty in a week (T. Pickering to B. Pickering, 28 October 1794).

A crisis of leadership between warriors and sachems threatened. On Tuesday morning, the twenty-eighth, Red Jacket brought his wife and five children to call on the Quakers formally. Savery remarked that "they were exceedingly well clad in their manner, and the best behaved Indian children I have ever met with." Jones came along to interpret. Red Jacket related the views of his people that had led to the Friends' being invited as observers at the treaty. They believed that the Quakers were honest people and their friends; they wanted them present that they might not be deceived or imposed upon. Red Jacket confided that the chiefs and warriors were very uneasy at Cornplanter's frequent private sessions with the commissioner, particularly the session on Monday.

Over the weekend in the Indian camp, Little Billy spoke roughly to Cornplanter, admonishing him to consider who he was: he was a war chief, and it did not become him to give the appearance of being so forward; "it was the business of sachems, more than his [as a war chief], to conduct the treaty" (Savery 1837). In defense of his conduct, Cornplanter protested that "he had exerted himself for several years and taken great pains for the good of the nation, but if they had no further occasion for him he would return home" (Savery 1837). The Seneca sachems might be thoroughly disgusted with Cornplanter for usurping the role of sachem, but Pickering and Chapin interested themselves in detaining him. They felt he should not be allowed to withdraw.

Pickering was in a spot. Chapin, who had been his main support in the conduct of affairs, was deathly ill. The loss to the country threatened a void that could not be filled. There was no one to replace him in the Indian department. Pickering faced the task of holding the factions together until they signed the treaty (T. Pickering to B. Pickering, Pickering to Knox, 28 October 1794). October was expiring. They were just getting into the substantive part of the business.

Pickering had been up the past two nights writing until after midnight, presumably the terms of the treaty. Among his papers (PP 62: 97), a long memorandum dated simply "October, 1794" identifies issues as hypothetical questions with answers. It lists points used in his speech under twelve heads (without argument), as follows:

1. Encroachments and unfair purchases. Reference to Stanwix 1768.
2. Path along the Lake. None on British side.
3. Injuries done U.S. in late war. Never compensated, but by cessions.
4. Indian protocol with wampum.
5. Question of British indemnity for war losses?

6. President's speech of 29 December 1790: Indian access to Federal courts.

7. Cornplanter's second speech to the President: too little land left; why did they sell to New York and Phelps?

8. The important question: restoring land between Buffalo meridian and eastern line of Erie Triangle [modern Chautauqua, part of Cattaraugus, and Erie counties]. Stipulation: Seneca settlements never to be disturbed. Possible satisfaction. Best way to treat issue of Indian title: ignore it [Yankee pragmatism].

9. Lands designated for Revolutionary War veterans. Indian war has prevented settlement.

10. Peace has opened a path through all the states. Lands surrounding forts ceded by Britain 1783.

11. The law regulating intercourse with the Indians. Explain.

12. There ought to be a law prohibiting re-sale of treaty goods to traders—particularly guns.

The course of debate would determine just how Pickering used this agenda of topics on which he briefed himself. He left no formal speech; rather, we depend on Quaker sources for the council proceedings on 28 October.

□□◇□□

Dissatisfaction among the Senecas reached such a pitch that it seemed improbable that the Tuesday council would convene. It finally met at three o'clock to hear Pickering. Cornplanter was conspicuously absent.

The commissioner reported on the conferences he had held with the chiefs since the last public council, summarizing the business discussed. He expressed sorrow that the chief warrior's conduct had excited their jealousy, and he tried to exculpate him by saying that he himself had invited Cornplanter to meet with him in his quarters inasmuch as Cornplanter had engaged in former transactions between the United States and the Six Nations and knew best what had transpired (Emlen journal: 314). This explanation somewhat pacified the chiefs. The business of the treaty had already been delayed too long; "he was now determined to open for them fully and candidly the terms upon which the chain of friendship would be brightened" (Savery 1837: 358).

Pickering then produced his commission, signed by the secretary of state, by which President Washington had granted him "full power to propose and adjust the accommodation of all differences between them and the United States," which he handed to Friend Savery to read. Because they had already spent many days without getting much done, Pickering told the council, he had resorted to the device of private councils with particular chiefs that they might digest the issues prior to their being opened in public treaty. Realizing now that this plan had caused dissatisfaction, he had decided to change plans and openly address the terms in public council.

The chiefs, he said, had indicated to him the two rusty places on the chain. He had disposed of one of them by taking the hatchet out of the head of the Indian killed at Venango. The other spot of corrosion ran much deeper, in the estimation of their chief warrior, although the sachems thought it less important; Cornplanter had proposed a new line between the Six Nations and the United States to begin where the Allegheny crossed the border between New York and Pennsylvania, to run thence to French Creek below the forks of Cussawago Creek, and to continue thence to the forks of the Muskingum and down that river to the Ohio. This new line would remove the rusty spot, reminiscent of Brant's insistence. But, as Pickering reminded the council, it involved land preempted by the western Indians, and it restored parts of Pennsylvania ceded at the 1784 Stanwix treaty, as well as that of 1768. Moreover, Pennsylvania had paid the Six Nations ten thousand dollars at the earlier treaty for an agreement not to sell lands within the boundaries of Pennsylvania except to the proprietors of that province, and they had reaffirmed this agreement at Muskingum in 1786.

He then referred to the Erie Triangle, which Pennsylvania had purchased of Congress, and showed them on the map that it was within lands ceded by them to the United States at the 1784 Fort Stanwix treaty. Pennsylvania had paid them two thousand dollars at the Muskingum treaty two years later to confirm the title. The commissioners then mistakenly assumed that the east line of the triangle would extend to Buffalo Creek. To correct this error, the commissioner offered to cede back to them all the land lying between the triangle and a meridian drawn from the mouth of Buffalo Creek due south to the Pennsylvania line. This area comprised four times the area of the Erie Triangle. The one exception reserved "the four-mile path"—a strip always four miles wide—beginning at Johnson's landing, some four miles east of Fort Niagara, and running thence along the inlet until it came within four miles of Buffalo Creek. From there it ran to the creek at a mile distant from its mouth, and thence along Lake Erie to the triangle (Bacon, Emlen, and Savery journals; see Pickering's agenda item 8 in the foregoing list). Pickering ignored any boundary west of the triangle, perhaps because Wayne's victory had made it irrelevant.

The commissioner reminded the council that the four-mile path beside the inlet between Lakes Ontario and Erie had been ceded to the British during Sir William Johnson's day. It now belonged to the United States, yet the Indians retained the right to hunt on those lands, as well as on all lands that they had ceded at the Fort Stanwix treaty. Their existing settlements thereon should remain undisturbed.

To sweeten the deal, in addition to the previous annuity of $1,500, the president had authorized him to offer the Indians an additional $3,000, increasing the annuity to $4,500, to be paid to them and their posterity forever. It was intended to advance their gradual civilization. Besides, he was prepared to distribute among them goods valued at $10,000, should the treaty attain mutual satisfaction. He hoped they would join him in digging a deep pit in which to bury former differences and in taking firm hold of the chain of friendship. They should take his proposals under consideration and answer when ready (Savery 1837: 350).

The council huddled briefly, and its speaker announced that the chiefs would take what had been said under consideration and reply when they were of one mind.

For the next two days (29–30 October), the Indians either consulted among themselves or else were too drunk to hold a public council with the commissioner. But their young men, free of responsibility, enjoyed the fine weather by racing horses with the local blades and engaging in social drinking. Their activity amused Revolutionary veterans but vexed more concerned men who yearned to get home. It is a pity that we are dependent solely on Quaker accounts of the sporting events—horse racing and the Brag Dance—which they deplored; they were more sympathetic observers of Indian camp life.

Bacon admired how quickly the natives could build a town of three hundred houses in two days so as to live comfortably in their way. The women were busily engaged in making moccasins, fashioning belts (or sashes), plaiting baskets, or cooking venison. Skins of some one hundred deer were stretched to dry. From a council being held in the open, the voice of an orator reached them.

The sachems and headmen debated until nightfall just how to answer the commissioner's propositions. The revelation of Cornplanter's role at Fort Stanwix and his subsequent activities put him in a difficult situation with other segments of the Seneca nation. The councilors could not conceive what he had done with the eight hundred dollars the Pennsylvania government had paid him in Philadelphia, or what had induced Pennsylvania to grant him fifteen hundred acres for a personal farm. These gratuities made other headmen jealous (Savery 1837: 360).

They were not ready to answer the commissioner by the last day of October. Maybe the Quakers knew something the council didn't? The general council deputized Red Jacket (Seneca), Clear Sky (Onondaga), Sword Carrier (Tuscarora), and an unnamed Cayuga, with Jones as interpreter, to call on the Quakers for advice. After apologizing for not having paid more attention to the Quakers earlier, their speaker, Red Jacket, requested that the room be cleared of others, for what they were about to say should be kept secret. He then invoked the presence of the Great Spirit among honest men and friends (Bacon journal). The council understood from a preliminary visit by Sword Carrier that the Quakers were willing to help if requested.

"Brothers," said Red Jacket, "we hope that you will make our minds easy. We who are now here are but children" (in contrast with the deceased ancients).[1] He acknowledged that their respective fathers (Iroquois and proprietors) had transacted business together. The council needed to know the will of Congress and the extent of the commissioner's powers. The council was willing to give up the four-mile path from Johnson's landing to Cayuga Creek, consistent with their compact with Sir William Johnson. But they wished to reserve the part from Cayuga to Buffalo Creek for the fisheries. Could the Quakers tell the council why the Erie Triangle could not be given up (Savery 1837: 360)?

Cornplanter and Brant, only war chiefs, as delegates to the 1784 treaty at Fort Stanwix, were supposed to have referred proposals to the general council for wider consideration. At the time, Old Smoke—then the acknowledged head of the Senecas, a man of great understanding and a war chief, though not a league chief—was yet alive, but Red Jacket did not say that Old Smoke had attended the treaty. He held that the delegation was threatened into compliance and that Brant had gone off to Canada leaving Cornplanter to make the best possible deal.

Seven strings of wampum attested to the seriousness the council attached to this request for advice. The delegation returned at mid-afternoon as directed, but finding the Friends not fully prepared, told them not to hurry. They would come tomorrow (Savery 1837: 361).

1. An appeal to the wisdom of the ancients should always be made by their grandchildren, the living who, by contrast, are impoverished. This deprecatory note precedes recitation of the Great Law to this day in the Condolence Council.

The Quakers wrote out their reply, which Savery delivered next day. The Indians had put them squarely in the middle. The Quakers could not advise the Indians to hold out, which would directly oppose the policy of their own government. Savery called on General Chapin and Colonel Pickering, but just what he revealed of the Indians' intentions is not clear, although he learned that both men seemed confident that the Indians would come to their terms.

Saturday morning, 1 November, dawned in a cold rain. At two o'clock, the same four Indians from the council came with their interpreter to hear the advice of the Friends. The Quakers had done their best to digest the request, but knowing, in the Indian idiom, that they were treading where the earth was narrow, they were as brief as possible. Holding seven strings of wampum in his hand, Savery spoke through an interpreter, returning the strings at the end of his speech in the Indian manner.

The Quakers expressed sympathy and concern, and they disclaimed a knowledge of civil affairs. They explained that they did not dispute the commissioner's position and they regarded the land sale to Pennsylvania as a fait accompli. Their only original suggestion, a forlorn hope at that, reminded the Six Nations that they might appeal to the president and to Congress.

Red Jacket reiterated the three points of the Quaker advice to make certain that he understood them, so that he might deliver their views to the general council. He thanked the Friends for their advice and remarked that although they might deem it of small value, the chiefs did not consider it so, but thought it would strengthen their position.

□□◇□□

During the closing days of October, while the chiefs were weighing these matters, Pickering occupied himself with accounts for goods and services, checking an enumeration of tribal delegations against estimates of village populations, and making lists of probable signers of the treaty. Estimates of expenses by December approached $3,000 (PP 62: 189, 147–54).

How many Indians were present, their tribal affiliations, how many stayed home, and the quantity of land held by them concerned both Pickering and the Friends. Emlen reduced to a table the estimates available to the Friends in Canandaigua (Table 7).

A considerable part of the Cayuga and Onondaga populations had moved off their reservations to reside with the Senecas and Tuscaroras, and a few had joined the Mohawk migrants in Canada. The sixth nation, Tuscarora, was chiefly settled in the Seneca country. The Stockbridge Indians, remnants of New England tribes, had removed to Oneida; they possessed 23,040 acres. About 150 lived at Brotherton on 3,840 acres. The Quaker journals put treaty attendance at 1,600.

Commissioner Pickering, burdened with the treaty distribution, sought more precise statistics. Instead of relying on previous estimates of overall tribal populations, he compiled a table of settlements and bands, individually enumerated by tribe, listing warriors, children, and women and separating those present and at home, to reach a total for the settlement and a total for the nation. Then he prepared a roster of delegations attending the treaty (PP 62: 147).

The figures in Table 8, compiled from his list, contrast populations and attendance. The table warrants several comments: I have reduced in square brackets

TABLE 7
EMLEN'S SUMMARY OF POPULATION AND
TERRITORY ESTIMATES FOR THE SIX NATIONS, 1794

TRIBE	NUMBER	TERRITORY HELD
Seneca	1,900	4,000,000 acres
Oneida	600	256,000 acres
Tuscarora	300	No land of their own
Cayuga	400	64,000 acres
Onondaga	500	70,400 acres
Mohawk	800	Grand River and Bay of Quinte
Total	4,500	

TABLE 8
PICKERING'S ESTIMATES OF
TRIBAL POPULATIONS AND TREATY ATTENDANCE, CANANDAIGUA, 1794

TRIBE	BAND		POP.	ATTENDANCE
Seneca on Genesee	1.	Big Tree	96	[91]
	2.	Kaneaudeo	148	148
	3.	Jenesheo	91	[89]
	4.	Squaukee Hill	190	[185]
	5.	Canawaugus	22	22
	6.	Tonawanda	104	104?
	7.	Cornplanter's		
		Allegheny Senecas	331	41
	8.	Cattaragaras	225	225?
	9–10.	Buffalo Creek	379	302
Onondaga	11.	Buffalo Creek	215	90
	12.	Old Onondaga	166	17
Oneida	13–14.	Oneida & Genesee	600	264
Tuscarora	15.	Niagara 262?	at Oneida	63?
Cayuga	16.	Including Delaware		
		and Saponi	324	125
	17.	Munsee Delaware	143	143?
	18.	Stockbridge	315	42
	19.	Mohawk at Grand		
		River	200	2
Total			3,874	1,890

Note: Spellings of band names are Pickering's.

several of Pickering's attendance figures where he indicated a family or two stayed home. And I question attendance figures represented by a check in his "present" column, where he simply repeated the total population as attending. Both Deardorff, who vetted these figures, and I question, for example, how 143 Munsees could be both present and at home; and a portion of the 225 Cattaraugus Senecas listed as present may be subsumed under the Buffalo Creek figure of 302. Unless Indians kept coming in as late as 31 October, an attendance figure of 1,890 seems too high, particularly since total attendance is stated elsewhere at 1,600.

Pickering may not have seen Kirkland's 1890 census,[2] but he obtained comparable results from General Chapin and the interpreters, Horatio Jones and Jasper Parrish. For the same set of settlements or bands represented at the treaty, the three men listed local populations, compiled a roster of attendance, and estimated the absentees, exclusive of the Grand River Mohawks. Their total came to 3,537, contrasted with Pickering's corrected total of 3,874 who were "to share the annuity of 4,500 Indians." They counted 2,176 present. The figure 4,500, as given in the Quaker estimates (Table 7), is close to Kirkland's 1790 total; it was attained by rounding off estimates. Its purpose was to ascertain the Iroquois population within the United States to share the annuity. Three out of four eligible Indians were present or counted as such.

Pickering labored over rounded estimates in order to make an equitable distribution of treaty goods between the Senecas and all the rest of the Six Nations. He decided to "let the Senekas be as 8 to 16 of all the others." An adjusted total of 3,400 was easier to work with. He then listed the goods by item and tabulated the shares in seven columns labeled "Senekas, Cayugas, Onondagas, Oneidas, Tuscaroras, Munsees, Stockbridges." No Mohawks! He apportioned each item according to his formula. Thus, of 210 kettles, 110 went to the Senecas and 100 to the rest. For the latter 100, he established percentage shares for the smaller tribes: Cayuga, 10 percent; Onondaga, 20; Oneida, 35; Tuscarora, 20; Munsee, 10; and Stockbridge, 5. Quantities of all items available and listed did not equal the number of Indians present. Items in short supply did not go around. Vermilion, powder, and lead, all bulk items, were most easily apportioned among the men. Items of clothing and adornment for women proved difficult. The items listed suggest Indian desires and reveal something of their way of life just then. The distribution of treaty goods at Canandaigua would affect Iroquois expectations for the next two hundred years.

These figures illuminate the political history of the Iroquois Confederacy. The Iroquois League of tradition had its roots in village government; the village chiefs of its time accepted a message of peace and power and formed a confederacy, their names descending as titles in matrilineages. The league tradition persisted as an ideal charter, but active governing roles were usurped by local chiefs who achieved status as sachems. Together they governed the Five (and later Six) Nations, which operated as a magnificent fiction, for power and control never left the village.

2. In October 1790, Samuel Kirkland left Oneida to take a census of the Six Nations, going from village to village as far as Buffalo Creek. He listed the names of heads of families, grouped the families by "tribes" (clans), and noted distribution of ages and sexes in each house. In December, he tabulated the data by nation, tribe (clan), village, village chiefs, wigwams per village, and individuals by sex and age per household. He omitted the Oneidas from the tabulation, which totaled 2,465, to which he added an estimate of 1,200 persons at Grand River, bringing the figure to 3,665. The following year he revised the census to include five villages of 588 Oneidas and some neighboring settlements of Tuscaroras and Stockbridges, which were omitted from the previous count. He arrived at a figure of 4,685, exclusive of a more conservative estimate of 1,100 at Grand River. The supporting data for the 1790 census are not among Kirkland's papers at Hamilton College but would be most valuable for ethnohistorical research if they could be found, for in 1792 he transmitted the census to the American Academy of Arts and Sciences in Boston in fulfillment of his election to that learned body, retaining only a summary. All attempts to locate the original document so far have failed.

Nominally the Canandaigua treaty convoked the Six Nations, but the invitations went out to village bands that decided individually whether to attend or stay home. Of these, the ten Seneca village bands together made up the Seneca nation and consistently throughout history equaled or outnumbered the other nations combined. The Canandaigua treaty was primarily a Seneca affair. The total Iroquois population represented at the treaty had declined during the late eighteenth century. Indeed, as they said, "we have grown poor."

The Great Law of the Hodinonhsioni, or People of the Longhouse, got but slight recognition at the treaty. The Mohawk nation, its first adherents, did not participate; only the Onondagas and Senecas of the senior moiety, and the Oneidas and Cayugas of the junior moiety, sent delegations. Onondaga participation was slight; Thadada:ho⁹ was nowhere in evidence. Such of their leaders who held league titles and were present signed at the heads of tribal rosters, but in most cases the designated head sachem had achieved his status.

CHAPTER 43

THE TREATY CONCLUDES

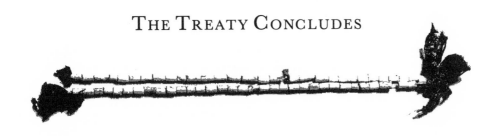

The full council convened on Sunday, 2 November, to hear the reply of the Six Nations. The Onondaga Clear Sky, in opening the council, remarked that he hoped the delay of a few days while they considered Commissioner Pickering's proposals and formulated their answer had occasioned no hard thoughts. The subject to them was of such importance that achieving unanimity, which was vital to attain and preserve because their whole system rested on it, took time. Red Jacket would now speak the mind of the Six Nations (Savery 1837). In this speech, Red Jacket performed one of his better oratorical efforts.

Having invoked the presence of the Great Spirit, Red Jacket addressed the commissioner as the president's emissary and voice of the fifteen fires. As charged, he said, the Six Nations had taken the matter under deliberate consideration, consulted each other, and identified the rusty spots in the chain of friendship, which they were assured would be brightened.

Instead of complying with their request regarding the spots where the chain was rusty, Pickering had offered to relinquish land along Lake Erie, eastward of the Erie Triangle, but proposed to retain the four-mile strip between Cayuga and Buffalo Creeks, thinking that that would brighten the chain. "Brothers, We thought you had a sharp file to take off the rust, but we believe it must have been dull. Or else you let it slip out of your hands."

The Senecas wanted the four-mile path for their fisheries. Although they were but children, Red Jacket said, the Senecas were sharp-sighted. They could see that the government wanted the strip for an access road to harbors and vessels on the lakes.

A second rusty spot covered land. "We wish . . . the treaty at fort Stanwix may be broken. You white people have increased very fast on this island, which was given to us Indians by the Great Spirit; we are now become a small people, and you are cutting off our lands piece after piece—you are a very hard-hearted people, seeking your own advantages."

Red Jacket praised the Quakers as promoters of peace whom both parties were using to bolster their respective positions. But he admonished Pickering for not using the file effectively: "We have told you of the rusty part, which the file passed over without brightening it. We wish you to take up the file again and rub it very hard. You told us . . . you would apply oil."

It is clear that the chiefs regarded the portage from Niagara to Buffalo harbor as threatening the fisheries and ultimately their settlement on Buffalo Creek. Steel files appeared on late-seventeenth-century Seneca sites, and Red Jacket's generation thoroughly understood their use.

Pickering made the mistake of replying then and there, and hedging. He said he understood that their minds were easy except over the strip of land between the two lakes. He then recapitulated Red Jacket's points, as custom demanded. He reminded the Indians why they had decreased while white people increased, and he suggested how the trend might be reversed and they become a great people.

Impatient at this gratuitous advice, Red Jacket interjected in Seneca: "Keep straight!"

Calling on his experience in improving agricultural arts in his native Massachusetts, Pickering hinted at a plan for transforming the Indian way of life. But Red Jacket did not deem a lecture on the acculturation process, or on "civilization of the native Indians," as Pickering might have termed it, quite appropriate just then, in the context of the treaty, and he had no intention of listening to such a discourse in lieu of the issues before the council.

Pickering then suggested that the title to the four-mile strip remain in the Seneca nation and that the United States offer compensation for cutting the road and the right of passage. It would be most inconvenient not to have taverns to accommodate travelers. And in the native metaphor, if the Senecas should travel it themselves, a house where one could get a "walking staff" (a drink) would be a welcome amenity. A harbor would be of no advantage without the privilege of building houses and stores.

Pickering's commission did not call for giving up any land. He took the risk of ceding back the strip in order to conclude the treaty. But since the Indians did not appear ready to accept his offer, and land was a tender point with them, he proposed that they consider the matter and reply tomorrow. Meanwhile, he would confer with some of the chiefs at his lodgings.

If the Six Nations were not ready to answer Pickering, there remained another matter they could discharge that day. Adhering to their custom following the death of a kinsman, they returned to the donor any present received by the deceased as a mark of respect. Red Jacket returned to the commissioner a silver gorget that had belonged to a chief deceased in the previous year, which the United States had presented to that chief.[1] Farmer's Brother made a condolence address suitable to the occasion and presented strings of black wampum to the deceased's family (Savery 1837).

Clear Sky, who had uncovered the fire (opened the council), exercised his privilege and performed the duty of covering the fire in a few words.

□□◇□□

Monday, 3 November, dawned cold and rainy and no business was done because the chiefs avoided the issue and got drunk. Red Jacket and Captain John, among others, called on the Quakers early begging for rum, with no luck. Some sober Oneidas wanted to discuss their lands (Bacon journal). Meanwhile, Fish Carrier

---

1. The deceased may have been one of the Seneca chiefs who visited Philadelphia with Cornplanter in 1791.

and five other Cayuga chiefs went to see Colonel Pickering at his lodgings hoping to discuss a matter "which lays very heavy on our minds and has . . . for some time." They appealed for his help in selling their reservation to New York state in exchange for an annuity. Pickering went on writing as Fish Carrier spoke and opened their minds.

Although the "York People" had gotten most of their country for a trifle, Fish Carrier said, they were not coming forward for the rest. The Cayugas wanted Pickering to sign a paper conveying their intent to the New York people. The Cayugas would accept an annuity of five hundred dollars, payable to General Chapin, their superintendent. So far they had received nothing. They left it to the commissioner's discretion to mend their speech as he saw fit and have it interpreted to them.

An agreement between New York and the Cayuga nation had been sealed on 22 June 1790 (Hough 1861, 2: 428–29). With the pressure of the treaty, the lateness of the season, and a council to hold at Oneida, it seemed unlikely that Colonel Pickering would manage to stop at Albany long enough to take up this matter with Governor Clinton.

The Oneidas and the Quakers made no progress in solving the problem of the residual heirs to the Hopewell lands, the descendants of the original owners being scattered among the Six Nations.

The Friends were learning fast that they could not simply be observers without participating as witnesses to the treaty. On Tuesday, 4 November, as the day of signing the treaty articles approached, they found themselves courted by the Indians, who would not open the council without their presence, and solicited by Colonel Pickering, who needed their moral support if not their imprimatur on the document.

Two Tuscarora chiefs came to talk about the Hopewell lands. Hard on their heels came Colonel Pickering bearing the proposed treaty articles, which, in his certainty that the Indians would accede to his terms, including the road over the Niagara portage, he had reduced to writing and now wished to read to the Friends. They knew this request was coming and for several days had been considering among themselves how to respond in the event they were called upon to witness the document. Signing such a treaty was not an act that a Quaker could do in conscience. Pickering was no more pleased than were the chiefs at the Friends' withholding support. They had just begun to learn to suffer at Indian treaties, as Savery put it.

At two o'clock the chiefs assembled in council to resume the business that they had broken off two days earlier. But not seeing the Quakers present, they refused to start without them. Accordingly, they dispatched a messenger to go lead them by the arm and seat them in the principal place, as custom prescribed.

The council now declared in session, Red Jacket addressed the commissioner. The treaty had convened to brighten the chain of friendship between the Six Nations and the "fifteen fires." But a small piece of land occasioned the remaining rust. "Now we are conversing together in order to make the chain bright." Here he characterized Pickering's proposal regarding the strip of land between Cayuga and Buffalo Creeks, where the white people planned to build houses: "But we apprehended, you would not only build houses, but towns." He said, "We have taken these matters into consideration."

Clearly the chiefs perceived cultural differences. "We conclude that we do not understand this as the white people do; if we consent to your proposal, we know it will injure us. If these houses should be built they will tend to scatter us and make us fall in the streets [by drinking to excess], instead of benefiting us. You want land to raise provisions, hay [and other crops]; but as soon as the white people settle there, they would think the land theirs, for this is the way of the white people" (Bacon and Savery journals).

Indeed, Red Jacket's prediction about the attitude of white people toward the land at Buffalo Creek would come true, and it is equally true today of non-Indians living on leased lands of the present Seneca reservations.

A very small thing kept the chain from being brightened, Red Jacket said. If Pickering would consent to release this small piece of land and build no houses on it, the chain would be made bright. As for the harbors, he would have to adjust that with the British.[2]

"I see there are many of your people now here, watching with their mouths open to take up this land: if you are a friend to us, then disappoint them; our patience is spent; comply with our request; dismiss us and we will go home."

In the debate that followed, the commissioner agreed to a road, somewhat wider than the existing portage path, from Johnson's landing to Buffalo Creek, the Senecas to retain the title. He proposed adjusting differences over minor injuries in an executive session with some of the chiefs at his lodging. Early agreement seemed imminent.

In replying to Red Jacket's speech, the commissioner appealed to an earlier treaty between the Six Nations and Sir William Johnson, by which Johnson had obtained the right of free passage through their country. What had been granted to the king was transferred to the United States in the 1783 peace treaty. As a concession, if they would grant freedom to pass and repass, he would give up the rest. He requested only the liberty to improve an already existing path—to clear it of stumps and logs. He was confident that they would make no difficulty over such a small matter.

In Iroquois councils there is always a period of quiet, as if to let the words settle in their minds before a reply is in order. After such a pause, Pickering himself broke the spell to observe that he had forgotten to inform them that the road would be opened under the supervision of "Canadesago" (General Chapin), who would take care to have the work done in a manner that would do as little injury to the Indians as possible.

A measure of Indian interest in settling the issue, a minor point, may be judged from the sachems' taking but a half-hour to consult together and charge Red Jacket with a rejoinder. They had made up their minds. He expected and demanded the commissioner's undivided attention. He was tired of seeing words being written down. Addressing General Washington on such a serious matter as brightening the chain of friendship demanded eye and ear contact. Pickering was absorbed with writing down what was said. Red Jacket paused and would not proceed until Pickering looked him in the face.

The Senecas, he said, did not want the Americans to go to the great expense of clearing a road. "We have agreed to grant you a road from fort Schlosser to

2. The might of Britannia weighed heavily on the minds of Seneca headmen, who wanted the path to Erie Triangle along the lakeshore kept for their exclusive use.

Buffalo-creek, but not from Buffalo-creek down this way at all. We have given you an answer; if, on considering it you have any reply to make, we will hear you" (Savery 1837). It would appear that the commissioner had requested an access road paralleling Lake Ontario in addition to the Niagara portage. The sources are not clear on the exact route.

One thing is clear, however: Red Jacket was a greater prophet than he thought. If he could see from where he lies in Forest Lawn cemetery the high rises, the rusting steel mills, the maze of railways, and the avenues of concrete that today cover south Buffalo, he would be certain that he was right.

Pickering had fully expected the Six Nations to agree to his proposal. This not being the case, he would give it up, he said, reserving only the road from Fort Schlosser to Buffalo. Each party had given a little, which he regarded as the best way of settling business. He thought he could clear up in executive sessions several other matters preliminary to signing the articles. One matter that he had been working on concerned the distribution of the goods and the annuity. Fixing some mode for settling disputes required consultation. He recognized that there were bad people on both sides, and whatever plan they devised could be introduced in council to the public. He invited two Seneca sachems and two warriors, and a sachem and warrior of each of the other nations, to breakfast with him the next morning. Upon this, he covered the council fire.

□□◇□□

Again there is evidence of tension in attaining unanimity as the decision to sign the treaty faced the sachems and warriors of the Six Nations. Once more the syndrome of frustration—bickering, compulsive drinking, and not holding council—postponed the settlement for nearly a week. The sachems, drunk themselves, manifested disgust for one another, with the warriors, and with the commissioner. Nothing was accomplished on the fifth, sixth, and seventh of November; they sobered up on the eighth only because the commissioner ordered no more booze sold until they signed. Cornplanter revolted on the ninth. On the tenth, when the warriors were ready to sign, the sachems managed to get drunk.

At this juncture, Brant and his British friends at Niagara and Fort Erie must have been consumed with curiosity for news of Canandaigua. Brant, who had had no news since Johnson returned, wrote to General Chapin expressing sorrow at his illness and looking forward to a meeting at Buffalo to hear a report on the treaty. The two were trusted friends. Brant was beginning to realize that the time for rigid insistence on the boundary line had passed. He would welcome Chapin's opinion. He sent his regards to Captain Chapin, who had escorted him to Philadelphia, and in a postscript asked the general to procure him a "Bolting Cloth," which was not to be had at Fort Erie. He also wrote to Pickering, mainly about the Johnson affair but also to denigrate some of his own people—certain "unprincipaled Indians who will say anything or go any Place for the Sake of Pecuniary Gratification."

On the fifth, in the afternoon, the Quakers rode out to Cornplanter's camp, where they saw an old woman called "Graney Wagus" who was said to be over a hundred years old. She had walked the hundred miles from her home to attend the treaty (Bacon and Savery journals).

No public council sat on Thursday, 6 November, because the commissioner and the national representatives passed the day disputing "some little matters which we thought had been settled" (Bacon journal). Presque Isle and annuities paid to particular chiefs comprised the small matters that hindered the drafting committee. The latter rankled the sachems. Several principal chiefs started new objections to relinquishing Presque Isle. That Cornplanter, Little Billy, and others had gotten two thousand dollars' worth of goods from Pennsylvania at Muskingum, and two thousand dollars at Philadelphia, surprised them. Hearing the news disturbed the minds of the sachems so much that they broke up the conference. For people who were anxious to get home while the weather held, this incident came as a sad disappointment (Savery 1837).

During this fuss General Chapin remained hopeful: the Indians needed time to cool. There was no use protesting. The Indians would say only, "Brother, you have your way of doing business, and we have ours. Sit easy on your seats."

Although the Indians would not settle, they were not too proud to beg. Pickering loaned Skenandoa $24. He paid Horatio Jones, the interpreter, $40 to cover a rifle for Farmer's Brother and a horse for Red Jacket. Presents never hurt Indian and white relations, if paid to the right Indians.

The sachems were still drunk and disgusted on Friday, 7 November. Nothing was accomplished. Pickering, at tea with the Friends, related that he had inferred from a conversation with a bright Tuscarora, and for the price of a forty-dollar horse, that fear of offending the British blocked the minds of the sachems. They were unwilling to confirm previous sales of lands lying west of the area just ceded back to them. Having gotten a strip of present-day Chautauqua County, they now wanted the Erie Triangle. Pickering's legal justification for the lands ceded at Fort Stanwix failed to convince the Friends. He reasoned that those parts of the Six Nations who allied themselves to the British in the late war had inflicted great injury to persons and property, and he, therefore, regarded the terms as just. They should make compensation in the form of the lands they relinquished at the time. "Such is the reasoning of conquerors," concluded Savery.

Timothy Pickering confided to his wife that day that he was weary of the treaty and as impatient to get home as the Quakers. "Yesterday, I expected to fix the terms of the treaty with the Indians, but they were perverse and shifting, thro' fear of offending the British and the Western Indians, and today the principal chiefs are drunk."

His only consolation was good news from home. Earlier in the week, a courier from Philadelphia had brought Knox's letter of 25 October, containing the now redundant news of Wayne's victory but also Philadelphia gossip and news of the steps taken to suppress the Whiskey Rebellion. In his reply, Pickering explained the hangups in the proceedings. "The chiefs wanted fresh confirmation of their lands; but they were unwilling to *relinquish* or *give up*, or use any words of that import, respecting the lands ceded by former treaties to the United States." When pressed, "they would answer, that those lands having been ceded by former treaties, there was no need of saying anything about them." When asked explicitly "did they acknowledge themselves bound by those cessions, including those made by the Delawares and Wyandots, which they mentioned, as far the Muskingum and Cayahoga [*sic*], they gave no answer." They would not say they would give them up; but would they claim them later? "No," the commissioner answered his own question (Pickering to Knox, 7 November 1794, PP 60: 206a, MHS).

A Tuscarora war chief from Niagara found a solution: he tipped Pickering that British influence blocked the minds of the sachems—"They are afraid of offending the British." Cornpranter and Little Billy, both Seneca war chiefs, and several others present that evening failed to deny the assertion. Later on, Captain Billy put the onus on the sachems and said he had reproached them for pretending they were a free people. The following evening Farmer's Brother acknowledged to General Chapin that these fears made all the difficulty in the present negotiations. This had been a meeting of war chiefs who, as expanders of frontiers, had the say on delimiting boundaries. Generally in Native American polity, the warriors took charge of external relations.

The same war chiefs finally stated that they perceived "no objection to pledge that they would never claim any land outside their acknowledged boundaries; and of course no part of Pennsylvania, or the Triangle including Presque Isle: if the Sachems also say *yes*, we shall soon close the treaty." Here apparently was the source of Pickering's language, "and they shall never claim the same" (Pickering to Knox, 7 November 1794, PP 60: 206a).

At that writing the head sachems of the Seneca nation in particular were too drunk to say yes or no to any proposition, and until they sobered up, business stalled. "But if I do not finally obtain an explicit cession," Pickering concluded, "or confirmation of former cessions, I think I shall get an absolute renunciation that will be as effectual." (This was to be article 4 of the Canandaigua treaty.)

Today one might say, Pickering had had it. Summing up the situation, he wrote: "I was never more weary of Indian negotiations: more than the patience of Job is requisite, to endure their delays, their trifling, and their drunkenness."

On Saturday, 8 November, the Indians were sober, but not of their own choice. Chapin and Pickering ordered that no more liquor be sold to Indians until the treaty was over. No signatures—no booze. What is more, it rained. The sachems and warriors were engaged with the commissioner until three o'clock. They agreed on all the articles so that they could be written up and signed the next day (Savery 1837).

The Indians, too, were showing signs of wanting to go home. Friend Bacon heard that over one hundred head of cattle had been killed for the Indians, weighing an average of seven hundred pounds each.

On Sunday afternoon, 9 November, everything was set for the signing when Cornplanter intervened, refused to sign, and threatened a walkout by the warriors.[3] According to Savery, a messenger came to inform the Friends that the Indian council was gathered and waiting.

Two large parchments with the articles of the treaty engrossed, being ready for signing, we were in hopes the business would now close. . . . [W]e soon discovered some dissatisfaction among the Indians, by their putting their heads down and whispering. After waiting impatiently for bout an hour, not knowing what it meant, Cornplanter rose and spoke as follows:

"Brothers,—I respect your attention, whilst I inform you of my mind as an individual. I consider the conduct of the United States, since the war, to have been very

3. Bacon and Savery are the only sources for this incident. Pickering was so preoccupied that he did not summarize the events of the last three days until he reported to _nox several days later.

bad. I conceive they do not do justice. I will mention what took place at New York at one particular time. After the treaty at fort Stanwix, I went to New York under an apprehension that the commissioners had not done right; and I laid before Congress our grievances on account of the loss of our lands at that treaty; but the thirteen fires approved of what the commissioners had done, and in confirmation of it; they held up the paper [the treaty with the British] with a piece of silver hanging to it.

"Now, colonel Pickering, you have told us at this treaty, that what was given up by the British, was only the land around the forts. I am very much dissatisfied that this was not told to us before. There has already been too much blood spilt; if this had been known at the close of the war, it would have prevented any blood from being shed. I have, therefore, told our warriors not to sign this treaty. The fifteen fires have deceived us; we are under the sachems and will listen to what they do. Though we will not sign it, yet we shall abide by what they do, as long as they do right. The United States and the Six Nations are now making a firm peace, and we wish the fifteen fires may never deceive them, as they have done us warriors; if they once deceive the sachems, it will be too bad." (Bacon and Savery journals)

Savery did not comment on Cornplanter's behavior but left that to Pickering. He continued: "Eel, the herald, then made a warm speech to the Indians, exhorting them to abide by the decision of the sachems, which was received with loud shouts of applause: *Entaw! Entaw! Entaw!*"[4]

It was now Pickering's turn to rebuke Cornplanter for raising old issues. Savery took down his remarks:

Brothers of the Six Nations and your associates, I confess I am greatly surprised at the speech of your head warrior, after all the pains I have taken to make the articles of the treaty easy. I endeavored to please both sachems and warriors, they were both present when the articles were agreed on, and there was not a word of objection.

Brothers,—The design of this treaty is, to bury all differences; you know that I candidly and explicitly disapproved of the conduct of the commissioners at fort Stanwix, but as this treaty was to establish a firm friendship between the Six Nations and the United States, I did not wish to bring former transactions into view, which was also the desire of your chief warrior; now he brings up the old matters to make a division in your councils.

Brothers,—I wish for calmness and deliberation, as the subject is of importance to us, and of utmost importance to you. He expresses dissatisfaction that our treaty with the British was not explained before; but this was done last year to the Western Indians, when many of the Six Nations were present; . . . many of the chiefs must remember it. . . . A certain line was drawn between the British and us; what the British had obtained of the Indians on our side of that line before the peace, was transferred by that treaty to the United States; it was agreed that the British should not interfere with the land on this side of that line, nor were we to interfere with the land on their side of the line.

Brothers—I am very sorry that these objections are made now when we are about to sign the treaty. The chief warrior has called it the treaty of the sachems . . . that

---

4. The usual shout of approbation sounded *yohe:! yohe:! yohe:!*, although *netho* may be what Savery heard.

they only were to sign it; but the warriors as well as the sachems were present when it was agreed on, and made no objection to it. He says, they will abide by what the sachems do so long as they do right. Does he mean that they will abide by them no longer than the warriors think them right? If this be the case, we may as well let things remain as they are.

Pickering would not consider a treaty made between the United States and the sachems alone. Unless the sachems and warriors united, it would only produce divisions among them and lead to dangerous consequences. As for the United States deceiving the sachems, "I represent the United States, I have told you I will not deceive you; I can add nothing on that head to what I have told you already."

Pickering remained adamant that he would not accept any such arrangement. He had taken too many pains to be fair and make things easy for the Indians. He suggested they take a day to reconsider and answer tomorrow. "If the warriors expect to live in peace with the United States as well as the sachems; if they desire to brighten the chain of friendship; if they wish to act to the advantage of themselves and the children, I am sure they will sign this treaty."

Cornplanter briefly urged the warriors to hold firm and steady to their agreement.

□□◇□□

Several factors not in the sources motivated Cornplanter's behavior. As a war chief, he had attended the Fort Stanwix treaty, and unlike Brant, he had stayed for the proceedings. He was bluffed into signing articles that relinquished land out of all proportion to what the sachems expected, while they waited at Buffalo Creek for him to report. The sachems lived in the shadow of the British garrison, but they were also asserting the prerogatives of their status as "Lords of the League," which by then was a convenient memory. Now, a decade later, the roles were reversed: the sachems were in charge.

Cornplanter had reached a point where the earth was narrow. The sachems had repudiated his actions at Fort Stanwix, and having made the first overtures to the Americans in New York and Philadelphia afterward to get some relief from its harsh terms, he had received special consideration for his friendship in land and presents. But having incurred the enmity of his brother chiefs at Buffalo, who regarded him with suspicion—particularly Red Jacket, who rose to prominence as speaker for the sachems during the present treaty—Cornplanter had reasserted his war role as defender of the Allegheny corridor. The Seneca matrons had denied him support for his war policy in the corridor, and the old men at Buffalo sustained them on appeal.

Red Jacket, who had reached an accommodation with Pickering at Tioga, had the support of Farmer's Brother and Little Billy, the Cayuga Fish Carrier, the Onondaga Clear Sky, and Captain John of Oneida, none of whom held a league title but several of whom acted as sachems. This being a sachem's treaty, Cornplanter felt their authority and prestige. Little Billy rebuked him at a council fire for having exceeded his role as a war chief. A proud man with a solid war record found this censure hard to accept, and he threatened to lead the Allegheny Senecas home. No wonder Cornplanter and Pickering did not hit it off. Pickering represented everything that had gotten Cornplanter into trouble with his own people. He could withdraw; that was the Indian way. But since he did not lead his people back to Burnt House, he would at least try to withhold the sanction of the warriors by not signing the treaty. This would fix his enemies at Buffalo Creek. It would also please the British, and this might be good insurance.

In this predicament, the only course was to renegotiate the issue among the warriors. Some sachems, while waiting for the warriors to make up their minds, would get drunk, prolonging the climax till another day. Friend Bacon found it trying being detained, as he put it, by their slothful and slow way of doing business. They were so often drunk. "But they are not to be hurried."

Consequently, no business was accomplished on Monday, 10 November. The warriors of the Six Nations met in council in the forenoon to consult over signing the articles and came to a judgment (Savery 1837). They met again in the afternoon to include the commissioner and the sachems, but several of the sachems were too drunk to attend, so nothing was done.

Just what role the Quakers played in mediating the crisis is not disclosed by their journals. Red Jacket and Farmer's Brother called on them that afternoon, and later on Savery and Bacon went to see Pickering, who does not say either what transpired.

□□◇□□

Fifty-nine sachems, war chiefs, and warriors finally met with Timothy Pickering on 11 November 1794 to sign the Canandaigua treaty. Negotiations filled the morning as chiefs came and went on visits to the commissioner's and the Quakers' lodgings. There had been enough talk; it was time to sign. The great council gathered after noon, when the sun stops to rest; at two o'clock heralds went about the camps to summon the principals. A great number assembled to witness the proceedings.

An Onondaga chief named Eel opened the council in what Savery termed "a pathetic manner," exhorting the chiefs and warriors to attain unanimity ("one mind") in closing the business. One must understand that unanimity is crucial for the preservation of Iroquois polity and for the continuity of society. The customary way of attaining it depended on an able speaker from among the chiefs persuading the parties to one mind. An Onondaga firekeeper usually performed the role of presiding officer on such occasions.

Savery described the closing scene:

> Colonel Pickering . . . held up the two parchments containing the articles of the treaty, and asked if we should proceed, which they assented to. He told them he would give one of the parchments to one of their friends to examine, while he read the other. I accordingly examined one, and informed them they were word for word alike. They then agreed to sign and pointed out the two head warriors, who though they were young men, were by some custom in their nation, the persons who were to stand foremost in ratifying tracts; they signed, and then the chiefs and warriors, some of the most eminent in each nation, being in all upwards of fifty.[5]

5. There is a deputy chief, or warrior, for each moiety of the Seneca council, one from the Wolf clan, the other a Snipe. They are Then:won:ya?s ("Awl" or "Chain Breaker") and Sonehsow:wa:? ("Big Burden Strap"), respectively. The latter is sometimes rendered Shosheowa:?. They run errands and perform other duties for the sachems, or civil chiefs, and perform special roles in the Condolence Council.

The duplicate copies of the parchment treaty have survived. The copy that went to the Senecas is now on view in the Ontario County Historical Society Library in Canandaigua, within an arrow shot of where it was executed, as tradition says, on Jasper Parrish's kitchen table. The government's copy may be seen in the National Archives in Washington (fig. 44). The "Indian copy" shows some wear.

Pickering drew up two preliminary lists of eligible signers (PP 62: 152–59). The two Seneca hereditary warriors appear as numbers ten and eleven on Pickering's systematic tribal list of signers, and their names appear together as nine and ten among the Seneca signers on the treaty document. Their two titles, Sonehso:wa:? (or Shosheowa:?) and Then:won:ya?s, survived into modern times. The pair are of opposite moieties, and they act as messengers for the two keepers of the western door of the Longhouse, transmitting messages to the other nations, especially on the death of a sachem. A third hereditary Seneca war chief, Kanon?jowa:neh, "Big Kettle," is ascribed no ceremonial duties.

Pickering was one of those conscientious administrators who leaves little to chance. In advance of the signing, and while drafting the articles in varying ways to accommodate the Indians, he drew up lists of who should sign for each of the Six Nations and their dependents. He ranked the several rosters and inscribed the names by nation at the feet of the two parchments, leaving room for a mark and a seal at the right of each name.

Starting at the righthand column and reading to the left, he put down 26 Senecas, whose names filled the adjacent second column. Six Onondagas headed the third column, followed by seven Cayugas. Six Oneidas headed column four, followed by two Munsees, two Tuscaroras, a Seneca, and a lone Mohawk. Column five is a miscellany: two Onondagas, two Cayugas, two Mahicans (Stockbridge), and two Tuscaroras. At the extreme left appear witnesses and interpreters. He thought there were going to be 26 Seneca signers, but Sonehso:wa:? came around and signed at the foot of column four. Local considerations may account for the displacement of a sachem and a war chief of each nation to the miscellany column, unless they formed an executive committee.

Each of the national rosters is rank ordered. First, "Hoonayawus," or Farmer's Brother, of the "Crane tribe" (Heron clan), is designated "Head Sachem of the nation to do business." (Here I reproduce the spellings on the treaty document, except where league titles occur.) Next, Sagoyewhatha,[6] "He Keeps Them Awake," or Red Jacket, of the Wolf clan, enjoys the same rank. Then come two genuine sachems with league titles: Kanyotai:yo?, Handsome Lake, of the large Turtle clan, "Head Sachem of the Nation by birth" (S-1, RC 43);[7] and Sha?takeonye:s, Skies of Equal Height (S-2, RC 44), who is similarly ranked. The next five on the Seneca roster are denominated "Chief councillor by birth." They are Burning Day, Sky Carrier, Parot Nose (sic), Heap of Dogs, and Thagenshota?, "Carry Me" (number 19). Next come the paired "Hereditary Head Warriors," already discussed, and a third of this rank, Big Kettle. Cornplanter—Kayenthwahkenh, "At the Field"—is designated "Active Head Warrior," an achieved status. He

6. *Shakoye:wa:tha?*, "he makes them look for it in vain" (Chafe 1963: 56).
7. A variant of the name Handsome Lake appears three times on the list: as a Seneca sachem, as an Onondaga war chief, and as the fifth signer on the Oneida roster.

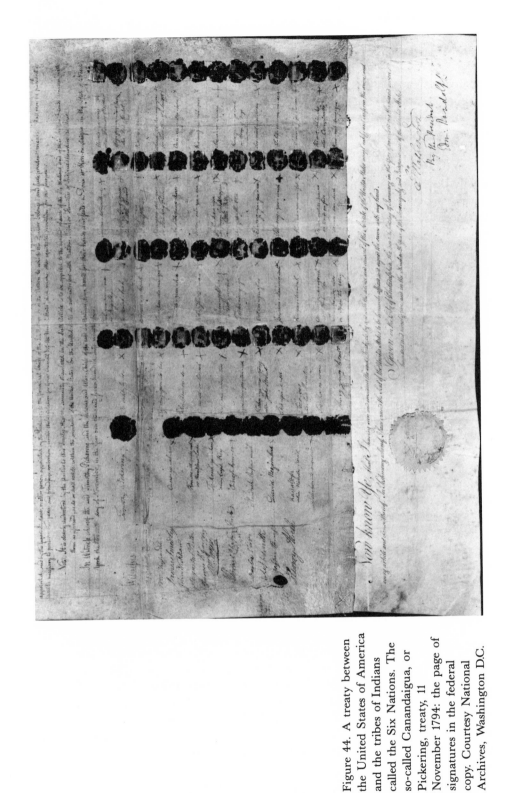

Figure 44. A treaty between the United States of America and the tribes of Indians called the Six Nations. The so-called Canandaigua, or Pickering, treaty, 11 November 1794: the page of signatures in the federal copy. Courtesy National Archives, Washington D.C.

is paired with Green Grasshopper, alias Little Billy. The remainder of the Seneca roster are "War chiefs by merit." Such distinctions are subtle and not entirely clear.

Sonh-yoo-wau-na, or Big Sky, heads the Onondaga roster. By birth a Cherokee, he had earned the status of head sachem by merit. A resident of Buffalo Creek, he was deemed "a sensible old man, not to be tempted over the fire by the British." He is marked not present. Pickering also listed in the number-one spot Big Earth (Yoenjowa:nenh), who was lame and did not attend the treaty. Pickering marked him "Head sachem by birth." A variant interpretation of the name of one person may explain the coincidence, although two statuses conflict. Next come two sachems: one by merit and the other a league chief, Hotoshahenh (One?sa:hen, Oa-2, RC 20). Next follow three warriors: one bears the picturesque title "Divides the Soup," and another "Sturgeon on a Stick," reflecting subsistence activities. The preceding were Onondagas from Buffalo Creek.

A sachem from old Onondaga, O-yo-ne-ah-nee, heads a column of honorables to the left; the name resembles Hoyonnyenni (Oa-10, RC-28). Below him appears Kon-ni-at-or-lee-oo, clearly a variant of Handsome Lake, but this one was a war chief at Onondaga.

Fish Carrier, Oo-jau-geht-a (O:kenjonkehte?), head chief by merit, headed the Cayuga signers, coming before three of the ten Cayuga holders of league titles: Teyoenhyongo: (C-6, RC 38), Kadagwarasonh ("Bruised," C-3, RC 35), and Tsinondawerhon, or Kaji?nontaweheh (C-2, RC 34), all sachems by birth. There follow three war chiefs, of whom one, Broken Axe, is designated "Head Warrior of the nation by birth." These were from Buffalo Creek.

The names of two other Cayugas appear in the column of the distinguished and are designated "Cayugas from the East"—from old Cayuga, the mucky land at the crossing, their traditional homeland. They are Te-kenh-yoo-hau (Haga?en: yonk, C-1, RC 33), alias Captain Key, followed by a war chief named Oneshausee. With four league titles, this was a strong delegation.

Three Oneida sachems signed before three war chiefs. The leading league title, Otatshehte, Quiver Bearer (Oe-1, RC 10), properly heads the roster, followed by Kanonkwenyodon, "Standing Ears of Corn" (Oe-2, RC 11). The third sachem, Tos-song-gau-lo-lus, defies recognition. Of the three war chiefs, one is named O-ne-at-or-lee-oo, a variant of Handsome Lake. A league title in the Seneca nation may appear in another nation as the name of a war chief.

The same rank order by birth and merit for sachems, followed by war chiefs of several grades, was adhered to for the smaller ethnic entities. Rank and locality were the important distinctions. I have inferred this from the documents; Pickering does not tell us how he arrived at the system. He simply followed the way the Iroquois leaders and interpreters instructed him (PP 62: 152–54).

The structure and arrangement of signatures to the treaty mirror the nature of Iroquois polity just then. Although invitations to the treaty were addressed to the Six Nations, they went out to local bands and villages. The attendance by settlements added up to a predominantly Seneca treaty, and the Seneca nation was segmented into Genesee, Allegheny, Cattaraugus, and Buffalo Creek contingents, each with its own leaders. The greater part of the Onondaga nation was at Buffalo Creek; less than half remained at old Onondaga. The Cayugas were likewise segmented between Buffalo Creek and Cayuga proper. Save a few east of the Genesee, the Oneida delegation represented a population still in place, who would sign a separate treaty afterward. The Mohawk nation sent no delegates, although Pickering managed to find a lone Mohawk to sign the treaty. Buffalo Creek and Allegheny were at the cutting edge of issues affecting the peace. Although the peace treaty aimed to comprehend all the Six Nations and their dependents, as such the Six Nations were a convenient fiction. Canandaigua was primarily a Seneca treaty, and Red Jacket emerged as its dominant figure.

The priority in ranking the signatures to the treaty, which accorded to sachems by birth the privilege of signing near the heads of the national rosters, marks the persistence of the Iroquois League tradition, even though "sachems by merit" signed ahead of the Seneca and Cayuga hereditary chiefs. Of the nine Oneida league titles that were intact a few years later, the first two and a third of that roster signed. Four of the ten Cayuga titles appear, including the leading pair, who are as "father and son."

The fourteen traditional Onondaga titles, which included Thadoda:ho?, presiding officer of the league, and his six firekeepers, produced but a single signer, number ten on that roster, whose name heads the far left column. Big Sky, whose name heads the Onondaga list, was not the title of an Onondaga founder.

Handsome Lake and Skies of Equal Height were the first two of eight Seneca founders. Both names follow the signatures of Farmer's Brother and Red Jacket. But the name of the Seneca prophet who held the leading hereditary Seneca sachemship, Handsome Lake, appears again among the honorees at the left and as the name of an Oneida war chief. In all, the holders of ten league titles who signed the treaty represented 20 percent of the original fifty founders.

Clearly, chiefs of achieved status had usurped the statuses and roles of sachems whose titles were ascribed in matrilineages. This erosion of the traditional system had been ongoing since early in the century. In the process, the Iroquois League, which had arisen as a compact of village chiefs, became a confederacy of local war leaders and speakers who came up through the age grades to the status of sachems. The so-called sachems included a smattering of "chiefs by birth" with prestigious titles. The league became a cherished memory of a symbolic system preserved by ritual but no longer a functioning government. It began at the local level and returned to the local level.

□□◇□□

Once the treaty was signed, Pickering had a breather in which to communicate some of the behind-the-scenes negotiations. The following day he wrote to Becky, his wife, the bare fact of his accomplishment. To Secretary Knox he transmitted the treaty with a detailed report of what had been accomplished. In this important letter he explained to Knox the concept of the quitclaim and why it was not a cession, to which Knox took exception, a dispute that would continue while Knox was in office (Pickering to Knox, 12 November 1794, PP 60: 207–9). Knox presently resigned, and Pickering succeeded him as secretary of war, which relieved Pickering of having to write a full report of the treaty negotiations.

In the Knox letter, Pickering summarized his view of the treaty's achievement immediately afterward: "Yesterday Peace and Friendship with the Six Nations were established; I hope for perpetuity; and on terms that may prove acceptable to the President and the Senate. A copy is enclosed" (ASPIA, 1: 545). He continued:

> The fear of offending the British on the one hand, and the Western Indians on the other, induced the Chiefs to persist in their opposition to an *explicit* cession of land; tho' finally they said they were willing to declare that they would never claim any of the land which we were solicitous to have relinquished. On this ground the treaty has assumed its present form. I had previously molded it into various shapes: but not one gave them satisfaction.
>
> You will see the great object is obtained; an express renunciation, which takes in all of the lands in Pennsylvania, including the Triangle which comprehends Presqu'Isle; and a pointed declaration that they will never disturb the people of the U. States in the free use and enjoyment of them, or any other lands not contained within the present described boundaries of the lands of the Six Nations. These boundaries, as they respect the Senekas' country, differ from those agreed on at Ft. Stanwix: Yet not a foot of land has been relinquished falling within the preemption right of Massachusetts, and lying within the state of New York. The tract extending from the eastern end of the Triangle to a line running due south from the mouth of Buffalo Creek to the Pennsylvania line [Chautauqua, parts of Cattaraugus and Erie counties], is as important to the Senekas as any part of their country. They have settlements upon it, which contain nearly as many people as the whole Oneida nation [some 600].
>
> The strip four miles wide along the strait of Niagara, I strove to secure in such manner, that although the United States could not take possession, by virtue of former treaties, they might transfer the Indian title to those who have the preemption right; but it was in vain. They were extremely tenacious of this tract. When they desired me to add 500 dollars to the proposed annuity (to make it 5,000), I asked them, as a consideration to cede only four small pieces of a mile square each, between fort Schlosser and Lake Erie, for a landing place on the Lake, and convenient stages between that and fort Schlosser: but they chose rather to relinquish the annuity of 500 dollars. In this they were influenced by their fears of offending the British; and not by the particular value of the land, even the whole strip. I therefore gave it up; knowing that as soon as we should possess Magara, it would be ceded of course. This has since been declared to me by a very sensible and influential war-chief: "As soon (said he) as you get Niagara, that strip will be yours."
>
> But tho' I have relinquished what title the U. States acquired to this strip, by the treaty of Fort Stanwix, I have secured the important part of it which extends from the fort of Niagara to fort Schlosser, comprehending the Carrying Place: and this is in full right: if by the treaty of peace with Britain the United States became entitled to the land which belonged to the Crown. As soon as I mentioned this old cession to the King, the Seneka Chiefs acknowledged it; and immediately produced an old man who was present at running the line as I have described it. The original treaty being in the possession of the British, and not attainable, I thought it of some consequence to get an explicit acknowledgement of it from the Six Nations.

Pickering was still annoyed at Cornplanter for delaying the treaty. Cornplanter's reputation as a friend of the United States would never quite recover after the lecture that Pickering intended to deliver to Knox on reaching Philadelphia. By way of preparing Knox, Pickering wrote: "Cornplanter continued his opposition to the last: but finding himself unsupported, has joined with the other chiefs and signed the treaty. When I return, I shall give you the true character of that Chief" (PP 60: 207-9).

Pickering told Knox that he was entrusting his report and the treaty to one John Connor, "late a soldier in our Army, who was taken between forts St. Clair and Jefferson . . . a year ago, and . . . just returned from captivity." Pickering furnished Private Connor with ten dollars as an advance to be taken from his wages when he reached Philadelphia and collected back pay, and before he proceeded to rejoin the western army. Not often did a treaty commissioner entrust a diplomatic pouch to an army private and commend him to the secretary of war (PP 60: 207-9).

Pickering estimated that it would take at least two days to divide and distribute the goods among the Indians. Concluding accounts, correspondence, and other business would keep him until the eighteenth before he went on to Oneida to settle the Revolutionary claims of loyal Indians. He wrote Becky that he would be three or four days on the road to Oneida, "for the roads are intolerably bad, as we have had rain almost daily these three weeks." It should be December before he could reach Philadelphia. Both letters end on a note of quiet satisfaction. To Becky he confided: "If the treaty I have made should be approved by the President and the Senate (which I expect), it will afford me very great pleasure to have accomplished it." He had come through in good health, and now he wanted to get home in safety and see his family.

Private Connor reached Philadelphia safely to deliver both copies of the treaty to Secretary Knox, who read and transmitted the treaty to the president at year's end. On 2 January 1795, President Washington communicated to the Senate both the Canandaigua and Oneida treaties (ASPIA, 1: 544-46).

The Senate ratified both treaties promptly. On 22 January 1795, Pickering, now in Philadelphia, sent a ratified copy of the Canandaigua treaty to General Chapin by Captain Chapin for delivery to the chiefs at Buffalo Creek. With it Pickering forwarded a message to the chiefs that he asked be interpreted to them together with the ratification of the treaty. It pleased Pickering to know that General Chapin had survived, on whose behalf Pickering had consulted Dr. Benjamin Rush, "the first physician in America," whose advice he hoped might relieve the general (NYHS, O'Reilly Collection, 11: 3).

George Washington firmly believed that treating for peace was less expensive than fighting an Indian war. He was undoubtedly right, but the combined Canandaigua and Oneida treaties put a lien on a slim treasury. Before he even left Philadelphia, Pickering had ordered and shipped Indian goods valued at $10,000. While at Canandaigua he had requested an advance of $6,000 for treaty expenses. The annuity guaranteed to the Six Nations came to $4,500, and this did not include gratuities to certain chiefs at $50 each. Returning to Philadelphia, he reported traveling expenses of $2,739.02 (PP 60: 193-96), $55.35 for advances and incidentals for Henry Abeel, besides subsistence at Canandaigua of $364.76, which brought the Canandaigua account to $3,160. The "treaty for peace and friendship" at Canandaigua alone cost the government not less than $18,000. Expenses of the following Oneida treaty amounted to $3,433. Twenty thousand dollars was no paltry sum in 1794.

CONCLUSION

THE LATER EVOLUTION OF THE LEAGUE AND CONFEDERACY

> The Five Nations . . . have nominal Sachems or Chiefs, hereditary in the female line, yet if these show no talent, they enjoy no other distinction than that of a seat in the Council, and the honour of sanctioning, by their signature, some . . . surrender of the territory of the Nation: the warriors, who surpass them in abilities and eloquence, universally take the lead. —John Norton, Journal, 1816

The reader may wonder why the Canandaigua treaty marks the end of my narrative. Indeed, much happened between Canandaigua and the onset of the reservation period. To bring the story of land sales from the Treaty of Big Tree in 1797 down to the sale of Buffalo Creek Reservation in 1842, to cover Iroquois relations with the United States and Canada down to 1924, when I first met the Senecas, and to describe my fieldwork in the 1930s and 1940s would fill another book. Sources for such a book crowd my files, and they expand exponentially with time. Although I had originally planned to cover the period, this book was already too long, so I decided to cut the chain at 1794, which marks the final act of the Six Nations confederacy and of the Iroquois League, which passed into tradition.

The Canandaigua treaty marked the high tide of the federal treaty period. It established peace and friendship between the United States and the Six Nations, defining a charter for those Iroquois who remained within U.S. boundaries. The league tradition reasserted itself among the émigrés to the Grand River in Upper Canada, where they recalled the model of the league, reinvented the traditional government, and perpetuated the Condolence Council for mourning and installing life chiefs. This model of local government continued until 1924, when the Canadian Indian Act replaced the life chiefs with elected councilors and sent the adherents of the Great Law underground to maintain the tradition to the present day.

Following the breakup at Buffalo Creek, the Seneca Nation of Indians emerged as a republic with a written constitution out of an 1848 revolution that supplanted the life chiefs with elected councilors. Traditional elements withdrew to Tonawanda, Onondaga, and Tuscarora, where councils of life chiefs still govern. Together they comprise the present grand council at Onondaga, which claims lineal descent from the ancient league. They exchange condolences among their members and with the Six Nations of Canada. Duplications of title on both sides of the Niagara frontier are inevitable.

The league tradition had faded to a dim memory by the time of the Canandaigua treaty. But ten sachems by birth, 20 percent of the famous fifty founders of the league, showed up to claim their honor and assume precedence in signing the treaty. The principals who represented the Six Nations and headed their national delegations had achieved their rank on the warpath or in council. They had not been invested with antlers and did not carry names of the fifty founders.

A common complaint following previous negotiations, notably those at Fort Stanwix in 1784, maintained that the "signers," particularly Cornplanter, lacked authority to sign for the Six Nations. His role there, as we have seen, and the subsequent dispute at Buffalo Creek, put his status in limbo at Canandaigua. Pickering soon learned the basis of the complaint and undertook to ensure that the signers of the treaty for peace and friendship indeed represented the Six Nations. In drawing up lists of possible signers, he arrived at Sir William Johnson's distinction between "hereditary chiefs" and "chiefs to do business."

To my question years ago—Why was it that sachems so seldom signed treaties? —both John Norton, in the passage quoted at the beginning of this chapter (Klinck and Talman 1970: 133), and Merle Deardorff provide answers. Deardorff wrote: "Few appear on Pickering's list because by this time such authority had in these premises been eroded away. The 'Hereditary League' was now but a shadow . . . [that] had no meaning for anyone except 'old Indians' " ("Memorandum on the League," Fenton Papers, APSL).

Deardorff recognized three leagues: the original Iroquois League, Sir William Johnson's league at mid-eighteenth century, and "League III," the one the émigré Six Nations reinvented on the Grand River in Canada. One might add a League IV—that which emerged after the treaty at Buffalo Creek in 1842, when the conservative Senecas at Tonawanda, the Tuscaroras at Niagara, and the returned Onondagas rehabilitated the grand council in New York state.

Early on in this book I made a distinction, following Daniel Richter's lead, between the Iroquois League and the Iroquois Confederacy. Certainly the league tradition, continually renewed by repeated ritual for condoling and installing new chiefs, persisted into modern times as a symbolic entity of sacrosanct faith in the Great Law, while the operating basis of Iroquois government and politics passed into other hands. The league tradition has traceable roots that extend back into the eighteenth century. Parts of its ceremonial components go back to the beginnings of Iroquois history and were shared by other woodland and prairie peoples. But already by the end of the seventeenth century, according to French sources, and certainly quite early in the eighteenth century, Iroquois political leaders, with rare exceptions, carried names other than titles of the founders. Evidently, men raised up in the titles of league founders, who occupied prestigious statuses ascribed by birth but who were seldom complete as a political body, had relinquished operations to men of achieved status who went on embassies, conducted negotiations in the name of the league, and signed the treaties. The league was a ceremonial entity, the confederacy its operating agency. The grand council at Onondaga preserved elements of both, and it is never clear which is which.

What was, early in the nineteenth century, the "New Religion" of the so-called Pagan Iroquois became the vehicle of conservatism a century later. Today, the followers of the Great Law consist of the Longhouse congregations of Handsome

Lake's followers. The two exceptions are the Newtown and Coldspring longhouses of the Seneca Nation of Indians, where the league tradition has vanished. Even at Six Nations Reserve a substantial portion of the population, largely members of Christian sects, support a government of elected councilors (Weaver 1994).

Between 1784 and 1800, a considerable part of the Six Nations population had removed from New York to the Grand River in Upper Canada. They included Loyalist Mohawks, Cayugas, a band of Onondagas, a few Seneca families, some Tuscaroras, and odd Tutelos. (They did not include descendants of the nearly half of the Iroquois who emigrated to Christian settlements on the St. Lawrence at the end of the seventeenth century.) There were virtually no Mohawks left in New York. Others followed at the breakup of Buffalo Creek Reservation in 1842.

Toward the end of the Revolutionary War, the council fire symbolic of the league was removed from its ancient site at Onondaga to Buffalo Creek. There, most of the Onondaga population lived among the Senecas. Issues only remotely related to the old league—or to the confederacy, for that matter—divided the New York Iroquois into factions. Land cessions generated the greatest controversy, and the question of who had the right to represent the Six Nations in the negotiations leading up to the Buffalo Creek treaty fanned the smoldering spark of the league fire. Since the interests of more than one nation were at stake, people naturally turned to the old model, which might enable them to present a facade of unity in advancing their claims. But the plan self-destructed. At issue was the time-worn question: just who are the chiefs? Each faction presented a list of "authentic chiefs," and no two lists were alike. To fill the seats in the traditional council and to maintain the tribal rosters, advocates resorted to some unorthodox procedures. Land office politics intruded; men were bribed. Chiefs were installed only to be deposed, depending on their views.

The memory of the old league was fading. The published records of three councils held in 1839, 1846, and 1862 demonstrate the decline of the ancient system (Parker 1916b: Appendixes C, B, and D, 125–51). In removing to Buffalo Creek, the Onondaga wampum keeper (traditionally, Oa-7, RC 25) shouldered the hemp bag of wampums and carried a spark from the ancient fire of the league, which the Six Nations rekindled at the new Onondaga Longhouse. His load was lightened by half when the wampums were divided, half going in the outmigration to Grand River.

A few old men at Buffalo Creek recalled the ceremony for naming and installing candidates in the seats of the founders. Their ancient government had long since metamorphosed, and few understood how it really worked. The odd ritualist recalled the ceremony for renewing the league, which the Buffalo residents hastened to reconstitute in a single performance. The Reverend Asher Wright made a list of chiefs installed at an 1839 council at Buffalo Creek, among whom he identified two Senecas (S-3, RC 45, and S-8, RC 50) as "Sachems of the Long House of the Six Nations." The remainder of the names listed are predominantly of warriors of achieved status who were indeed active councilors.

Asher Wright left a partial record of the 1839 Condolence Council for raising chiefs, which he witnessed at the Onondaga Longhouse.[1] I recognize in his account

---

1. Asher Wright understood and probably spoke the Seneca language. I have read into his account things that he failed to understand, and I have interpreted other items that he did not explain fully.

the essential elements of the ceremony. Clans of the two moieties nominated candidates; they rehearsed ancient customs beforehand. An Onondaga sachem (Oa-4, RC 22) and one Elijah Williams exchanged the Three Bare Words. Blacksnake, a Seneca war chief (who must have been borrowed by the clearminded), led the Oneida condoling moiety in procession. The second man carried the bag of wampum, chanting the names of the founding chiefs and the offices of the Six Nations. "What must be the feeling of these men!" Wright commented. "These were the principals, the Founders." The recitation was not without error, however, which prompted guarded smiles. The Six Songs followed behind a drawn curtain. (The lead singer and choir moved Wright.) Then came Over the Forest, the appeal to the grandfathers, and the council names of the confederated nations. A description (with black wampum) of the war chief's duties preceded the Requickening Address by the clearminded, which was followed by the reply of the mourners.

Two sets of requickening wampum were exchanged and kept until the next condolence ceremony. Wright wondered whether the tribal moieties represented a merging of two confederacies in ancient times.

The Charge to the New Chiefs, who were largely replacements for those recently deposed (because they had voted the wrong way), climaxed the ceremony. The cooks then brought in the kettles. As the food was ladled out and passed, Hayahdajiwak (Skanya?dadji:wak, Oa-4, RC 22) delivered the valedictory, urging the new sachems to renew their strength before going forth on their duties. He then promised visitors who might anticipate enjoying "our young women that we shall not withhold them." This is the standard remark that still precedes the social dance called Rubbing Antlers that reunites the confederate moieties.

The grand council held at Tonawanda in 1845 was said to be unique, the lone one held in a number of years. It combined an installation ceremony with preaching of the Handsome Lake code, and because of the limitations of the observers, the report contains few illuminating details (Parker 1916b: 126–32). During the 1840s, Tonawanda counted but one league chief, S-8, RC 50, a title held by John Blacksmith and passed on to Ely S. Parker. It is unclear just when the other seven Seneca league titles reached Tonawanda—possibly after the 1857 treaty when the Tonawanda band of Senecas repurchased their reservation (E. Tooker, personal communication).

By the mid-nineteenth century, the components of the old confederacy were widely dispersed. Mohawks resided in Upper Canada, at the Bay of Quinte, and were long established on the St. Lawrence. The main body of Oneidas had removed to Green Bay, Wisconsin, a small group resided on the Thames in Upper Canada, and few families remained at home in New York. The Onondagas had resettled the valley south of Syracuse, although related family bands emigrated to Grand River and settled between the upper and lower Cayugas. The main body of Senecas withdrew to the Cattaraugus and Allegany reservations, while the Tonawanda band of Senecas retained and adapted the system of Seneca life chiefs, as did the resettled Onondagas and the Tuscaroras near Niagara.

Nicholson Parker, who was the brother of Ely S. Parker and who also collaborated with L. H. Morgan, was a native Seneca speaker who for years served as United States interpreter, residing at Cattaraugus among the Seneca nation. He was uniquely prepared to record a council of the Six Nations held at Cattaraugus in

1862. In twenty years, knowledge of the ancient ways had dimmed considerably (Parker 1916b: 144–51). A decade later, when writing *Ancient Society* (1877), Morgan asked Parker to inquire among Seneca sources about the league tradition. After encountering different versions from everyone he asked, Parker concluded: "The difficulty seems to be that there is now no one who actually understands the laws of the 'Confederacy' as it was" (Morgan Papers, University of Rochester Library, quoted in Armstrong 1978: 174). The generation of Senecas who threw out the hereditary chiefs during the 1848 revolution following the sale of Buffalo Creek Reservation had functioned for twenty-five years under a written constitution that sanctioned elected councilors to govern the Allegany and Cattaraugus reservations, which comprise the Seneca Nation of Indians.

Traditionalists still hankered for the old system and tried to revive it. Meanwhile, the league had been requickened in Canada, and Six Nations on Grand River became the source of the league tradition, both for the Iroquois people and for anthropologists.

According to Nic Parker's minutes of the 1862 council, ritualists from Canada came to conduct the ceremony. The minutes mention an Onondaga wampum keeper (Oa-7, RC 25) and a Seneca holder of a doorkeeper title (S-8, RC 50) as opening the bag of wampum. The former, as speaker, deplored the poverty of knowledge at that time, a customary caveat, and called on the other side of the fire to support him. In response, a Seneca speaker referred to a recitation on a previous day of the traditional origin of the league, and stated that the Tuscaroras had joined the confederacy later. "Our forefathers foretold . . . the destiny of the Indians . . . We have now come to that." Those who really knew were in their graves. Such words still precede recitations of the Eulogy to the Founders and Over the Forest.

The grand council that meets today at Onondaga bears small resemblance to the legendary league, whose functions have largely disappeared. Its replica at Six Nations on Grand River lacks an Oneida component, but it proclaims the great tradition, it produces virtuoso ritualists, and it has survived by assuming responsibilities unrelated to its original purpose. The Condolence Council still raises up chiefs in the titles of the founders, not unlike *honoris causa*. The recipients still enjoy prestige without much power.

The ultimate fiction, Deardorff thought, was the unwitting creation of anthropologists following in the footsteps of Lewis Henry Morgan (1851). Beauchamp, Hewitt, Parker, Goldenweiser, Speck, Shimony, and I have all, in our concerted effort to recover the nature of the original league by salvaging its surviving legends, rituals, and political structure, contributed to the invention of a tradition. What Parker (1916b) labeled a "constitution" and Goldenweiser proclaimed a "fiction" now enjoys the sanction of law among Iroquois nationalists. Both the Newhouse versions of the league tradition and the work of the committee of chiefs represent attempts to legitimize a traditionary system of government and head off reform. Hanni Woodbury (1992) has recovered the Gibson-Goldenweiser version of the founding of the Iroquois League in its complete Onondaga text, with linguistic and literary translations, which has now become the standard work on the league tradition, both for native Iroquois and for Iroquoianists. Chief Jacob Thomas currently recites the tradition from the English text and assigns his students my account of the Cayuga condolence ceremony of 1945 (Fenton 1946). In the present book I have endeavored to search the historical record for evidence of the original league, its structure, and rituals and to interpret that evidence in the light of the great tradition.

Mastering the Roll Call of the Founders represents the ultimate participation in the great tradition. At least eight lists of the founders of the league exist for the nineteenth and twentieth centuries.[2] When I tabulated these on a spreadsheet to facilitate comparison, the several lists showed a remarkable consistency of sequence and titles. Here was solid footing for investigating the titles historically. Were these indeed the names of the founders? How did they appear and at what dates in the historical sources? Why did these names occur infrequently on treaties?

The emergence of the titles in the historical sources appears in Table 6. The distribution of league titles at various times yielded some striking occurrences. The leading chiefs of four nations appeared in the seventeenth century, but not those of Onondaga. Thadoda:ho? (Oa-1, RC 19) did not appear for certain until the middle of the next century, when he showed up in 1745. Virtually the entire Onondaga roster, including Thadoda:ho?, presented itself to Sir William Johnson for confirmation in 1765. The Oneida roster was complete in 1803. I attribute the scarcity of titles during the first four decades of the eighteenth century to English ignorance.

One cannot be certain what these data mean. The titles may or may not go back beyond the recorded dates. The record of twelve Onondaga titles in 1765 approaches the same number that signed the Canandaigua treaty. Tribal rosters were seldom complete. The sachems were frequently older men who did not travel to public events, and titles were not recorded because the scribes who wrote the minutes were ill prepared, if even interested, to hear Iroquoian names pronounced by interpreters who had learned an Iroquoian language as captives and were themselves illiterate. This does not mean that complete rosters as we know them go back to the seventeenth century. But the rigor with which they were recalled at the mid-nineteenth century and my data argue for their existence at mid-eighteenth century.

Horatio Hale thought he could connect the Iroquois "Book of Rites" through a series of copy books, the original of which had burned, to one David of Schoharie who flourished around 1745 and was most probably informant to Pyrlaeus. The ethnohistorical sources support Hale's assumption. Four of the five component rituals of mourning and installation specifically comprised a ceremony at Onondaga in 1750 to condole the death of Canasatego of Lancaster treaty fame and raise Red Head in his place. Neither Canasatego nor Red Head held a league title, yet they were titular heads of the Onondaga council.

Records of the condolence ceremony go back to the seventeenth century, when it was already no new thing. Kiotsaeton, "the Hook," staged a magnificent display for the French at Three Rivers in 1645. The Jesuit fathers had already experienced the ceremony among the Hurons, and Father Le Moyne adapted the Eulogy to the Founders for his approach to Onondaga in 1654. Thirty-one years later, the

2. The eight lists are those of John Skanawati Buck (Hale 1883); Peter Wilson, Cayuga of New York State, 1845 (Morgan 1851); Seth Newhouse, 1885; Josiah Hill; Abraham Charles, 1889; William Beauchamp (1907); John Arthur Gibson 1899, 1912; and J.N.B. Hewitt (Fenton 1950).

burghers of Albany heard condolence law extolled, songs of peace sung, and the chain legend recited. Within a decade, a Mohawk singer led a eulogy procession down State Street hill toward the old Dutch church, for years the site of Indian treaties, where he sang three songs of peace. By now, one end of the chain was attached at Onondaga, the traditional seat of the league, and the other at Albany, the seat of treaties.

There are at least ten records of the eulogy chant dating between 1667 and 1794. And a version of the opening chant of the eulogy, or roll call, flourished at Oswegatchie among the émigré Onondagas in 1754 (Piquet 1754), for which we have both score and text.

The league as such was in disarray at the mid-eighteenth century. Headmen of ascribed status holding league titles no longer controlled affairs; headmen of achieved status such as Canasatego and Red Head had usurped their roles. Yet the new leaders observed the ceremonial forms and appealed to the league tradition, to the "whole house" motif, and to related symbolism to sanction their acts. The Five Nations, now Six, had become the Iroquois Confederacy.

Required condolences took so many short and long forms that colonials wondered what the essentials were. The five essentials were the three bare words, wiping the bloody seat, and covering the grave. The order seems not to have been set. The number grew with the years.

Indeed, the league had grown old, but its tradition lingered. We have no descriptions apart from the tradition of what it was like in the beginning.

To be certain, the league was a confederacy of village chiefs who accepted Deganawi:dah's message of peace and agreed to cooperate and meet annually to settle differences but to preserve their local autonomy. It derived its structural models from the tribal and local level. The village council was ever the heart of the system. It was composed of the ancients and included others than its leading chiefs; its members met in tribal or national councils and were persuaded to join in the grand council that met at Onondaga. Local patterns for gaining consensus were projected to higher levels of integration. For mourning dead chiefs and raising their successors, the nations adapted the moiety model of the upper Iroquois nations, ranging Mohawk-Onondaga-Seneca father's kinsmen on one side of the fire opposite Oneida-Cayuga "offspring" on the other. But in sessions of the grand council, the nations adapted the tripartite model of the Mohawks and Oneidas, seating the Mohawks and Senecas across the fire from the Oneidas and Cayugas, with the Onondaga firekeepers at the head, between the two pairs, in position to moderate (see fig. 22). This model carried over into modern times.

The several rules governing the conduct of matron, warrior, chief, succession, malfeasance, and the council in raising and deposing chiefs and installing their successors in office assume the character of bylaws codified and written in the nineteenth century to assist in maintaining the league tradition in action.

Wampum came into prominence during the seventeenth century for attesting to political agreements between Indian nations and Europeans. Its manufacture became a colonial cottage industry for use in the fur trade, as a medium of exchange. Its symbolism shifted from utilitarian to sacred with the passage of time. As the volume available for circulation increased during the eighteenth century, belts of greater length and depth, featuring elaborate designs, passed from the hands of Sir William Johnson and others into Iroquois hands, to be racked up at Onondaga and stored in a great hemp bag. None of these large belts dates from the founding of the league. As mnemonics, they reminded learned men who had memorized the oral texts and could read them so long as both the spatial arrangement and the verbal stream remained together in the same mind.

The military campaigns of the old regime from Champlain to Frontenac contributed little to understanding the nature of the *rotinonhsioni*, the "extended house" or "whole house" of Mohawk speakers. There is scant evidence that the league as such operated as a military force or that the several nations of the confederacy rallied to support one another. French *police* concentrated on the fur trade; only Jesuit scholars such as Bruyas and, later, Lafitau concerned themselves with linguistics and ethnology.

The transformation of the league into the confederacy began in the late seventeenth century, and the metamorphosis completed itself when the Five Nations became the Six Nations with the adoption of the Tuscaroras early in the eighteenth century. Semblances of league behavior, nevertheless, persisted. Holders of league titles dominated the odd delegation that signed a peace agreement with the French following Denonville's invasion of the Seneca country.

The Dutch traders on the Hudson were all business. They showed remarkably little intellectual interest in the natives. Van den Bogaert's trade mission up the Mohawk River in 1635 did measure houses, estimate village populations, and record some noteworthy observations. At Oneida he heard the Five Nations denominated for the first time (Gehring and Starna 1988: 15–17).

Dominie Megapolensis, alone of the Hollanders, sketched native ethnography and made a stab at the native language. But Mohawk polity escaped him. Friendships grew between Dutch and Mohawk trading partners, and liaisons between Dutch men and native women spawned generations of interpreters who grew up bilingual in Dutch and Mohawk or the Algonquian language of the River Indians. Several notable Mohawk headmen shared both genetic pools.

The gun trade on the Connecticut River first armed Mohawk warriors and transformed Mohawk military power among the Five Nations. Guns enabled them to hijack northern fur fleets. Firepower engendered a kind of arrogance and the taking of tribute from neighboring natives.

None of these factors contributed to league solidarity. Iroquois speakers had a genius for making their loose-knit confederacy sound like a solid structure when no such cohesion existed. A part could represent the whole, as in "Five Nations speak through my mouth." The speaker might not even hold a league title. Iroquois genius ran to diplomacy.

Toward the end of the Dutch regime, affairs in Iroquoia deteriorated. Even the palisades of the three Mohawk "castles" had rotted, and the sachems could not summon sufficient manpower to restore them. Instead, they appealed to Dutch friends for horses to haul the logs out of the woods. Plague followed military defeats. Old enemies beset the Five Nations. The supply of furs diminished.

Although the Dutch forged an iron chain alliance with the Mohawks in 1643 and renewed it periodically, the great era of treaties and the covenant chain began with the English takeover in 1664. The English, Albany, and the Iroquois emerged together. Established trade relations with Dutch partners continued, since Albany and the Dutch were one. Mohawk war parties earned a fierce reputation in New England and became a concern whenever New Englanders came to Albany.

Relations with New France were even worse. Mohawk-Oneida raids on the Laurentian settlements inspired Governor de Tracy to restore His Majesty's glory by sacking the Mohawk towns, which the Mohawks failed to rebuild. Instead they came to Albany begging for powder and lead, which was in short supply.

The Indian Records for 1677 began with the Albany magistrates attempting to persuade the Mohawks to make peace with the River Indians, something that would take another decade. The Mohawks made their first land cession at Schenectady. The schism between upriver and downriver interests began, which continues today in New York as upstate versus downstate.

The chain motif and its legend came into prominence in the 1690s, and thereafter the league and the chain evolved together. Actually, the first of the "silver chain" treaties occurred in 1677 at Albany, linking three New England colonies with the Five Nations. There is virtually no firm evidence of league solidarity at this time. One looks in vain for names of founders. The sachems present at the treaty protested that they could not control the warriors—a theme that runs throughout Iroquois history. Local autonomy prevailed, each nation replied separately to propositions (there was no league response as such), and sachems admitted they could not return captives, whom the warriors owed to maternal families. In short, the Iroquois Confederacy had inherent weaknesses.

New York governor Thomas Dongan, who inherited the silver chain in 1683, perceived that keeping the goodwill of the Iroquois in trade and politics held the key to British success in North America. He insisted that Lord Howard of Virginia come the four hundred miles to Albany to treat with the Five Nations. He undertook to strengthen the confederacy by suggesting it form an executive committee of sachems and warriors from each nation to meet in emergencies. Dongan believed it was unnecessary and expensive to feed huge crowds attending treaties, but the native polity required both observation and participation at every level of society. Moreover, treaties were fun. The idea went nowhere.

English officials began to comprehend Iroquois political symbolism, to observe order of precedence in speaking, and to experience the priority that native peoples placed on reciprocity, song, and ritual. Planting a tree and burying the ax were symbolic acts—rarely, if ever, actual behavior. The path and the fire acquired a reality of their own. Laying down wampum belts became a colonial obsession.

Reassurances that the league was intact through professions of unity denied the considerable evidence of disunity. Council rules and condolence law, however, governed the protocol of treaty making.

Rival governors, Dongan and Denonville, reaped a harvest of disaster to Indian victims. Despite Dongan's facility in French and his urging the Mohawk and Seneca doorkeepers (often enemies) to bring the interior nations to harmony, the Denonville expedition wasted the Seneca country. The crisis drove Dongan to seek aid from Massachusetts and Connecticut. Uniting the colonies over the Indian problem became a concern for the next century. Dongan's efforts to expand Iroquois territory in the name of the crown met with mild tolerance but no real concession of title. When Dongan departed, the Albany magistrates resumed control.

The La Barre fiasco illustrates how the grand council worked. The Five Nations united to confront a common threat. This incident illustrates temporary suspension of the autonomous action previously cited.

The "voices of the Five Nations" represent Iroquois role models in action: bright men and scoundrels who manifested aspects of Iroquois independence and who afford rare insights into political behavior. None of the holders of league titles cited in the late-seventeenth-century sources approached the distinction of these men.

The two cultures, Iroquois and European, employed kinship terms for each other that had different meanings for each. To Europeans the term "father" implied subordination to authority, whereas in Iroquois society "father" took second place to "mother's brother." The Five Nations never really acknowledged themselves "subjects" of either France or Britain. They preferred the term "brothers" in political discourse. Nor did they submit to the conquest theory of the state.

Peace with Canada could be a left-handed affair. The grand council might dignify a mission by sending a delegation of sachems with league titles, which suggests that on occasion they could revive the league, if only to buy time before sacking Lachine.

Smashing the Longhouse at its center and raiding Schenectady, accomplishments of the French and their Indian allies, grabbed the attention of the English colonists, who gave some thought to a common cause in supporting the Five Nations and reducing Canada. Even the crown manifested concern. Governor Fletcher hastened upriver, earning the name "Great Swift Arrow"—a pun on his surname. He put Peter Schuyler in charge of Iroquois affairs, replacing Secretary Livingston, and created a three-man board of commissioners. Promises failed to impress the old men at Onondaga, who kept the paths open to both European powers. The English were big on talk but short on action.

The grand council continued to assert its independence. It sent Teganissorens on a mission to Canada, but it also sent a delegation to Albany, where it had planted a Tree of Peace and kept a perpetual fire burning. At a full-scale treaty to assert British dominance, the Five Nations approached in procession chanting the eulogy. Their speaker reviewed the evolution of the covenant chain and recommended renewing and extending it. The Five Nations, now diminished, needed support. Efforts to return the "praying" Indians from the St. Lawrence had come to naught.

The Grand Settlement at Montreal in 1701 stabilized a de facto situation at a time when all parties were exhausted.[3] Though greatly weakened militarily and beset on all sides, the Five Nations triumphed diplomatically to follow a policy of neutrality for the next half-century. All parties needed to keep their adversaries alive lest the extinction of one disturb the balance of power. Not to be outdone, the English held a separate treaty at Albany, featured some of the same actors, and relied on the covenant chain to secure their end.

Just then, pro-French and pro-English loyalties divided the Five Nations into factions that prevented the grand council from attaining one mind. Advantage

3. La Potherie left the best account of the proceedings, which I have analyzed for ethnographic content.

resided with the French Jesuit missionaries such as Bruyas and Lafitau, who perceived the nature of Iroquois polity, which remained obscure to most Englishmen.

Young blades on the town were forever after known as "Mohawks" following the visit of four "sachems," dubbed "kings," who took London by storm in the greatest publicity stunt of Queen Anne's reign. The mission arose from common needs, and its success involved melding native and British protocols. The hoopla aside, it had some substantive results, notably Anglican missions to the Mohawk Valley, crown attention to funding the reduction of Canada, and the importance of the Iroquois for the success of the enterprise. It required cooperation between colonies as well as the restoration of the Iroquois Confederacy. No matter that the kings were not proper sachems; they maintained the fiction of an ideal pattern and performed the roles.

The adoption of the Tuscaroras as the sixth nation increased the manpower of the Iroquois Confederacy and enhanced Iroquois political posture considerably. The Tuscaroras came in under the wing of the Oneidas and settled among them, becoming siblings in the junior moiety, but without a vote in the grand council. The original Five Nations enjoyed a privileged position in the minds of both natives and newcomers for a time, until the idea of the Six Nations caught on. An internal schism rent the body politic of the confederacy during the first quarter of the eighteenth century as the sachems failed to control the warriors in the war against the Catawbas. Concern mounted in adjacent colonies and in New England for some joint action.

The council brand next passed to Pennsylvania, as the council fire was lit in a series of treaties at Philadelphia, Lancaster, Carlisle, and the forks of the Delaware. Conrad Weiser enlisted the confederacy in settling Delaware land cessions.

During the first quarter of the century, Iroquois politics gained clarity through the writings of Lafitau (1724) and Cadwallader Colden (1727). The Great Law as system is nowhere explicit. Its external features were quite apparent, and these were shared with neighboring peoples. The grand council asserted its independence. Succession of chiefships is mentioned, but not the rules. Participation by nations remained irregular. Pennsylvanians perceived the weakness of the confederation and urged consolidation. Benjamin Franklin found in the treaties a species of native literature—a new genre—and began a sustained fascination with the Iroquois Confederacy.

The confederate council, meeting at Onondaga in 1743 to hear Weiser's petition, fulfilled the major rituals of the league tradition, although the participants apparently did not hold titles of the founders. The speaker, Canasatego, employed the council names of the nations. The council observed proper protocol and agreed to treat at Lancaster. The policy of neutrality was wearing thin.

The Lancaster treaty proved a pivotal event for the colonies. The Iroquois controlled the agenda, and native protocol prevailed. Canasatego offered his famous valedictory on confederation, which advice awakened some inquiring minds in the colonies and elicited amusement among English readers. The Lancaster treaty made a considerable impact at home and abroad. Weiser's answers to Thomas Lee's queries on Iroquois government emphasized procedure over structure.

Factionalism beset the confederacy at mid-century. Canasatego returned home to Onondaga at the height of his power to face bitter opposition from the pro-

French party. The struggle threatened neutrality, which only the interior nations upheld, while Seneca inclined to the French and Mohawk to the English.

The 1745 Albany treaty proved a fiasco. Governor Clinton was inept, the Indian commissioners were reluctant, the Mohawk leaders—concerned over land scams—were unready to abandon neutrality, and the New England delegates went home unhappy. Colden did his best to smooth over affairs the following year. Smallpox beset the town, carried off Far Indian visitors, and prevented the Six Nations from fulfilling military quotas. Johnson mobilized Mohawk warriors, but the upper nations remained aloof. Clinton fired the Indian commissioners and handed Johnson the management of Six Nations affairs.

In the seven years preceding the Albany Congress, the chain was both broken and mended. French influence rent the confederacy. The westward drift of Iroquois and dependent peoples created new loyalties beyond the reach of the old men at Onondaga. The persistent Catawba war resisted colonial efforts to settle the dispute. Sentiment for union among the colonies would emerge from Indian affairs.

Franklin generated a model for union while preparing for the Albany Congress, but I found no evidence that he received additional instruction on the league while mending the chain. Mohawks held Albany in contempt, pressed for cancelling fraudulent land claims, and pinned their hopes on Johnson to manage their affairs.

At first Johnson's influence did not extend much beyond the Mohawks. He had to rely on minor ethnic entities dependent on Oneida, while the upper nations remained aloof. How to restore control of the Delaware émigrés in Ohio perplexed everyone. In making over the confederacy to do business, Johnson began by journeying to Onondaga to settle the Delaware question and to retrieve the émigrés from Oswegatchie.

Just then, Teedyuscung emerged as the voice of the eastern Delawares during the Easton treaties, which were more celebrated in rhetoric and symbolism than in accomplishment. The Onondagas displaced the Mohawks as the leading force in the confederacy. Protocol became more important than substance. The practical necessity of doing business with Europeans favored the confederacy.

The want of a consistent policy kept the confederacy fragmented during the Seven Years War. The French ear for language, sense of ceremony, and concept of grandeur appealed to the upper nations. The Mississauga threat from the west immobilized the upper nations and exploded any myth of an invincible confederacy.

With scant Mohawk support, Johnson, as crown superintendent, turned his attention to settling the troubles between Pennsylvania and the Delawares. An Iroquois presence, notably Cayuga, put Teedyuscung in his place. Communication difficulties contributed to inefficient operations. The 1758 Easton treaty ended Pennsylvania's ascendancy in treaty negotiations and highlighted the need for defining a boundary line between colonists and Indians.

The Iroquois reasserted their dominance by reintroducing the chain, which in their view meant something different from an alliance between them and the British. Throughout the treaties, the Iroquois managed to adapt tradition and symbol to the particular situation. They survived by being flexible.

Lord Jeffrey Amherst was a soldier of the king, and he disliked Indians. At Johnson's invitation, he did look in on Oneida. He mollified Iroquois participants in the Montreal campaign by naming his flagship HMS *Onondaga* and flying an "Onondaga flag," although the Indians' later behavior horrified him. Johnson never convinced him that subsidizing whole tribes was the way to keep them peaceable. The summer of 1760 witnessed a high watermark in Indian affairs. Canada became English; the Six Nations fell from the balance of power. Amherst stopped presents. From now on the British would call the shots.

At Detroit the following summer Johnson promoted the confederacy idea among Wyandot and Central Algonquian tribes but failed to find takers. The Seven Nations of Canada applied for admission to the chain. Although crown superintendent of Indian affairs, Johnson could not prevent the Pennsylvania governor from holding a further Easton treaty. The leading Cayuga league chief (C-1, RC 33) spoke for the Six Nations, after which Johnson assembled the confederacy, except for the Senecas, and reasserted his position. As Pontiac's Rebellion loomed in the west, Seneca involvement appeared inevitable. Land claims persisted as the burning issue of the century. The first definition of Indian rights came in the British North America Act of 1763, which prohibited settlement west of a line defined as bounding crown lands reserved for Indians.

Johnson sought to strengthen the confederacy. Having mastered the ritual forms, he could instruct others how to approach Indians. He understood the confederate moiety system. He had researched the Indian Records and kept a book of rules. Observing Indian customs paid off. In 1765, the Onondagas asked him to ratify candidates for chiefships whom they had raised up in the place of deceased councilors, specifying their names, clans, and sponsors. The list of eight, possibly nine, league titles comprised a substantial part of the Onondaga roster. It is the largest assemblage known for a single nation, and it is the earliest record of the titles in the literature. The league tradition persisted at Onondaga.

Negotiating the Cherokee peace and establishing the boundary line of colonial settlement occupied Johnson and the Six Nations during the decade preceding the 1768 Fort Stanwix treaty. On the opening day of that treaty, Johnson had the Mohawk speaker reiterate the rules governing council procedure. Johnson himself renewed the chain. Circumstances moved Johnson to exceed his instructions. The Iroquois were in no position to enforce their claims to western lands in what proved the greatest "giveaway" in history, but they tried to reserve hunting rights. The confederacy still projected a powerful image. But they could no longer back up words with deeds or prevent the alienation of the Delawares and Shawnees in Ohio. Johnson's policy advocated keeping the several confederacies from uniting. He had learned that adhering to Iroquois ways guaranteed getting what he wanted from a council. It was against the background of these transactions that he wrote his famous letters on Iroquois politics to Dr. Arthur Lee of Virginia that reached the Royal Society of London.

To the missionary Samuel Kirkland we owe a vivid account of the death syndrome, trial by village council, the alienation of the Oneidas to the patriot cause, a census of the Six Nations after the American Revolution, and a plan for the education of Indians. He explored the nature of Iroquois polity and kept an ear attuned to the grand council at Onondaga. He understood the role of women in matters of war and peace. Inevitably he broke with the royalist Johnsons, but he maintained a lifetime correspondence with Joseph Brant.

The climax of British relations with the Six Nations came in 1774 with the passing of Sir William Johnson and the raising up of Guy Johnson in his place, with Iroquois support and ceremony. That year the "she sachems" recalled Cayuga warriors from participating in Lord Dunmore's War. The grand council of the confederacy raked up its fire three years later. Confederacies tend to segment into their original autonomous units when unanimity fails.

The 1775 treaty at Albany between commissioners of Congress and the Six Nations, the last treaty held on the Hudson, followed the established mode. Iroquois presence was sparse, the upper nations absent; it was an Oneida affair. An Oneida sachem appealed to a confederate rule: one or more nations might act for the confederacy and inform the others, and if there was no objection, the matter was binding.

Other confederacy rules that are evident in the ethnohistorical sources include the following: Ancient custom required that whenever a fire was kindled and a tree of peace planted, some person should be appointed to watch it. Those who kindled a council fire should provide the wherewithal to wash the mouths of those they invited to sit around it. A council fire kindled for a stated purpose (peace) could not admit of another purpose (war). Whoever kindled a fire (as host) spoke first. A first fire must be extinguished before a second fire could be kindled. The host might rake up (cover) a fire for the night to uncover it next day, but once a fire was extinguished (logs scattered), it must be rekindled.

Even a condolence held at Oneida in 1776 could not save a fragile neutrality. The amenities over, the symbolically mourning Cayugas and the mourning Oneidas of the junior moiety engaged in the fiercest debate since the founding of the union before the Oneidas prevailed in their attachment to the colonies. Attaining "one mind" became impossible as outside pressures tore the Six Nations apart.

Even less mindful were the commissioners at the 1783 Treaty of Paris, who, in ceding territory east of the Mississippi to the United States, ignored the Six Nations entirely. The Iroquois naturally resented it. Confusion reigned among American officials as to who was responsible for making peace with the confederacy's hostile members and sustaining their welfare. The distinction lay between the authority of Congress to make peace with Indians and the territorial rights of states over Indians who were considered members of a state. Were the Six Nations members of New York state, or did jurisdiction over them reside in the general government?

Congress seized the initiative, appointed an Indian Committee, defined its responsibilities, and designated commissioners to treat with the Six Nations. Ignoring President Washington's more humane view, the committee took a hard line and visited conquest theory on the Six Nations.

The 1784 Stanwix treaty yielded a decade of disaster. From the wreckage on the Indian side emerged the breakup of the Six Nations, factionalism among the Senecas, revival of the league tradition at Grand River, extension of the idea of confederation to the western tribes, and a decade of Indian warfare in Ohio. On the American side, failure to resolve the constitutional issue of where Indians belonged in the scheme of things produced two centuries of ambiguity. The question of federal versus state jurisdiction was never settled. Before the decade was out, the United States lost two armies to Indian victories, and a coalition of Indians met defeat at Fallen Timbers. Not until 1794 was Timothy Pickering able to negotiate peace and tranquillity at Canandaigua.

In the words of the old people, this is as far as I can carry the story; I lay down my bundles for the night. We who come in later times are impoverished for information. The league tradition has grown old; it persists in new forms and finds new purposes. Its history is not seamless.

Da ne?ho nengen nigaiwanongeh, Dane?ho. "This is the sum of my words."

Summary of Elements
of the Condolence Council

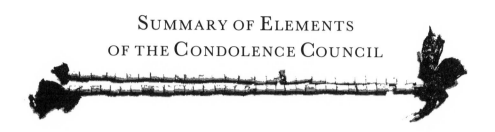

The text of the Condolence Council that Chief John Arthur Gibson dictated to Alexander Goldenweiser in 1912 described a ceremony in which the Four Brothers moiety of chiefs (Oneidas, Cayugas, and dependents) had suffered a death and were condoled by the Three Brothers (Mohawks, Onondagas, and Senecas). This was also the situation I witnessed in 1945 at lower Cayuga (Fenton 1946). My 1945 observations and my field notes on a reverse ceremony at Onondaga in 1951, coupled with an analysis of Gibson's 1912 text that I presented at the Iroquois Conference in 1986, enabled me to isolate reciprocal and spatial patterns between mourners and clearminded. The analysis isolated some forty-five incidents of spatial and reciprocal behaviors. The following is my attempt to reduce the ritual of the condolence council to a schematic outline, with the mourning moiety on the left and the clearminded moiety on the right. The arrows indicate which side approaches the other in performing a specific role. Numbers in parentheses indicate sections of Gibson's 1912 text. This outline might be considered a rough set of stage directions for performing the Condolence Council, so that people can revive the ceremony if it ever fails.

MOURNERS		CLEARMINDED
1	Notify by death cry and dark string ⟶	(Firekeepers), or M-1, or S-1.
2		Dispatch runner: death cry (*gwa:?...heh*) rallies phratry.
3	Death site ⟵	Phratry
	Perform condolences (Hale 1895:49)	
	a) family	
	b) chiefs	
	c) public	
	Grave-side words	
	Matron picks up title string (183)	
4	Three days after burial, hold death feast if ready; otherwise, on tenth day ⟵	(Enter at door) Requickening: 13 words, lift up minds

5   When ready, matron notifies own
    phratry chiefs, who consider, reach
    one voice   ⟶   (Fire)

6   Appoint day for ceremony:
    (word of date)   ⟵   when will enter the door

    Owner of title (matron) gets ready:
        enlists hunters
        cooks
        speaks at installation

7   White string to notify   ⟶   Handed among chiefs in token of
                                                     acceptance (of candidate) (187; here
                                                     Gibson anticipates the climax of
                                                     the ceremony)

8   Empty bench filled   ⟵   Notice of speaker to charge
                                                     candidate (187)

9   Life sustainers to be served   ⟶
        chiefs   chiefs
        public   public
        young people   young people

10 Should a chief die suddenly
    wearing antlers:
        Lift horns at graveside (189)
        Proper way: chiefs summon
            matron—antlers—matron
            (She picks it up) (190)

11 In case of threat to the chiefs, hang
    a pouch on a horizontal pole, drop
    in a short, dark mourning string for
    either side to retrieve (1 of 13 con-
    dolence strings owned in severalty).
    Then follow the path to the death
    site and console the matron. There,
    at edge of the dirt (hearth):

    Mutual condolences   ⟷   Mutual condolences

                          Proper Way (191)

12 Mourners prepare to respond to   At time of Dead Feast:
    clearminded during ceremony   Rehearse all the words of the Great
                                                     Law

                                                     Lay down 13 strings
                                                         Cries, in turn
                                                         Words, in turn.

13		← Appointed warrior notifies those in darkness: ready to take up the path (on the way) (192).
	Everything ready	→ Runner returns: all set.

At the Woods' Edge (193, 196)

14	Kindle fire by road	← Procession (Hale 1895: 51)
	Hear chanting	
	People assemble (chiefs, warriors, young)	
15		Each chief picks up a string to carry on the path; singer picks up the cane; crier appointed.
.1		← Eulogy to Founders (194)
16	Moiety separation: Oneida, Cayuga	Mohawk, Onondaga, Seneca (Three Brothers)
17	Welcome	→ Strangers (Hale 1895: 51)
	Chanter paces to and fro, his side fire.	
18	Three Bare Words of Requickening → eyes, ears, throat "It affects both sides equally" (197)	
19		← Reply and return by Three Brothers (201–4)
20	Leading visitors by the arm to the → main bench (206), a warrior role	
21		Eulogy resumed to door
22		Visitors seated (207)
23		Entire eulogy repeated in house, with cries for 1–50 chiefs recalled (Hale 1895:53–54) (208).
24	← Stretch curtain →	
25		Requickening strings arranged for use later (210).
26		Six Songs (Hymn to Dead Chief) less one: 1. League 2. Kindred

3. Warriors
4. Womenkind
5. Grandsires (Founders)

27   ← Withdraw curtain →

28   Over the Forest, part 1: 1–4
                      (Singer traverses house) (212)
                          1. Hail Grandfathers,
                             Your children weep,
                             The League has grown old.
                          2. (Caveat for error)
                          3. Words taken into grave
                          4. You said, it shall endure

29   ← Stretch curtain →

30   The interpolated Sixth Song (213):
                      "Grandsires, continue to hear us."

31   ← Withdraw curtain →

32   Over the Forest, part 2: 5–11
                          5. Antlers
                          6. Lift title dying chief
                          7. Child discovers corpse
                          8. Uproot a tree, cast down
                             trouble, replant
                          9. Imminent loss of chief
                         10. Hand pouch and deposit
                             short string mourning
                         11. Principal founders;
                             extending rafters

33   ← Requickening, part 2: words 4–15
                          4. Water of pity
                          5. Wipe bloody mat
                          6. Darkness of grief
                          7. Loss of sky
                          8. Loss of sun
                          9. Her mind rolls atop the grave
                         10. Death: the great enigma
                         11. Council fire logs stomped
                             and scattered
                         12. Woman and warrior rolls
                         13. Path of the chief
                         14. Suicide: mind
                         15. Loss of the torch (215–25)

34   Condolence Law: "Show his
                      Face"

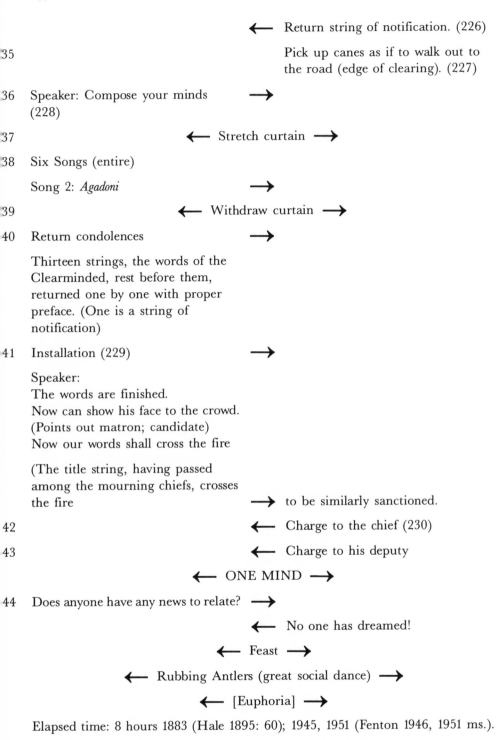

⟵ Return string of notification. (226)

35   Pick up canes as if to walk out to
                                                the road (edge of clearing). (227)

36   Speaker: Compose your minds   ⟶
     (228)

37   ⟵ Stretch curtain ⟶

38   Six Songs (entire)

     Song 2: *Agadoni*   ⟶

39   ⟵ Withdraw curtain ⟶

40   Return condolences   ⟶

     Thirteen strings, the words of the
     Clearminded, rest before them,
     returned one by one with proper
     preface. (One is a string of
     notification)

41   Installation (229)   ⟶

     Speaker:
     The words are finished.
     Now can show his face to the crowd.
     (Points out matron; candidate)
     Now our words shall cross the fire

     (The title string, having passed
     among the mourning chiefs, crosses
     the fire   ⟶ to be similarly sanctioned.

42   ⟵ Charge to the chief (230)

43   ⟵ Charge to his deputy

                       ⟵ ONE MIND ⟶

44   Does anyone have any news to relate? ⟶

                              ⟵ No one has dreamed!

                       ⟵ Feast ⟶

            ⟵ Rubbing Antlers (great social dance) ⟶

                  ⟵ [Euphoria] ⟶

Elapsed time: 8 hours 1883 (Hale 1895: 60); 1945, 1951 (Fenton 1946, 1951 ms.).

    Some explanations by a native Iroquois may assist the reader in understanding the foregoing schematic. Simeon Gibson interpreted his father's text to me during October 1943. Selections from my transcriptions of his comments on the

Onondaga text follow. He asserted that by rights, Mohawk was the official language of the Condolence Council, especially for chants and the Requickening Address as given in Hale (1883). In recent years, Cayuga and Onondaga have supplanted Mohawk for prose speeches. In what follows, numbers in parentheses indicate sections and paragraphs of Gibson's 1912 text. Simeon Gibson's comments are keyed by number to the numbered items in the foregoing list. My own comments are in square brackets.

1. When a chief dies, the mourning side appoints a runner to carry the message to the chiefs of the opposite side and to cry out the death cry, *gwa:...a?!*, three times repeatedly on the path. People may stop him to inquire his message. In later years he rode a horse or a bicycle or drove a car (sec. 77, par. 180, 181).

3. Convened by a runner of their own, the clearminded chiefs assemble at the home of the dead chief for the burial and requickening (78, 184).

5. The family shall elect a chief and notify the council. It is first up to the phratry. When the maternal family (within the clan) selects a candidate, they first notify the chiefs of their own phratry, and then they pass their decision over to the chiefs on the other side, the clearminded (C). The mourning phratry chiefs (M) must first judge the candidate's character before approving. They hit a drunkard on the head right away as unfit. The order of approval is (1) within the clan by the maternal family; (2) when the clan chiefs pass, the head of the clan notifies the chiefs of the confederacy on their side of the fire (phratry or moiety). The mourning chiefs have the right only to reject the candidate.

When approved (M), they notify the chiefs of the opposite moiety across the fire (C) (79, 185).

6. The clearminded have the right to set the date for the Condolence Council (80, 186).

The candidate is in effect installed by his own mourning chiefs who send back the short white string, notifying the condolers that the new chief has been horned. [The great ceremony will sanction this fact.]

9. Whenever there is a feast involving chiefs, the food, particularly meat, is served first to the chiefs, and whatever is left over goes around to the crowd (81, 187). [It is an honor for a guest to receive meat in the first round.]

11. Wampum strings were kept in a pouch made from the skin of a small squirrel-like rodent, which was hung on a pole set up horizontally (84, 190).

The clearminded, having removed the pouch, proceed to the place where the matron is mourning, and there, "at the edge of the dirt," or the bare earth where the dirt of the clearing surrounding the house meets the grass, shall stand and condole the bereaved. Around every house is a worn patch of earth. The speaker shall stand at the edge of the grass (85, 190).

12. At the rehearsal for the ceremony, the clearminded shall return thanks; the mourners are silent (86, 191).

13. Both moieties of a single nation are represented on the mourning side (87, 192). [This is within the system of which the moieties of the confederacy are a projection.]

15. Procession to the woods' edge (88, 193, 196). Simeon explained: "At the rehearsal they (C) lay out the thirteen strings of requickening in order of use in the ceremony, and then they are hung over a horizontal cane. Just before going

out [of the longhouse] on the road, they pick them up and put them in a bag." This practice is contrary to what the text says about chiefs in the procession each carrying a string. The cane refers to that described in Fenton 1950, which bears mnemonic pegs and pictographs. The singer is preceded by scouts and an appointed crier (88, 194). The order of procession is (1) chiefs, (2) warriors, and (3) the public, including children, and this is how they line up on both sides of the fire at the woods' edge behind their chiefs (98–99, 196).

17. The mourners greet the clearminded as strangers. The chanter reminds the visitors that the founders decreed that here at the woods' edge they should kindle a fire and say a few preliminary words but refer the main business of mutually rubbing down each other's bodies (the name of the ceremony) to the principal place (the council house), where the visitors would momentarily be led by the hand (Hale 1883: 119, 1895: 51; Gibson, sec. 103, par. 472).

18–19. In the preliminary exchange of mutual condolences at the fire, when the clearminded send the first string back across the fire, then the mourners get back in their grasp their own message. For each side of the confederacy has its own set of requickening strings, and the speaker means that the wampum goes back to the owners who first sent it across the fire (114, 202).

The string goes over the fire at the end of each speech. An appointed man carries that wampum string across the fire and, when it is delivered, returns and sits by the speaker again. At the end of the article, the speaker hands him another string. His job lasts only for the duration of the rite (115, 203).

23. On reaching the door of the longhouse, a new singer takes over the eulogy, or roll call chant, recommencing from the beginning so that persons within the house who have assembled to witness the new chief raised and crowned will hear the chant in its entirety (119, 206). The singer proceeds to put their house in order from the formation of the league to the present (121, 208).

In enumerating the roll of the founders, each of the tribal chiefs, as they hear their own titles sung out, cry "Yohen:::!" The chiefs of their own phratry (Three Brothers or Four Brothers) respond in support, "Hi:::yah!" (122, 208). These cries continue until the end of the roll (Hale 1895: 53–54).

24. A line or wire is stretched across the longhouse at the middle dividing it equally, and a quilt is hung on the side where the two sets of chiefs are seated at opposite ends of the room. It does not obscure what transpires at the other end of the room (123, 209).

25. A cane or staff is put across between the laps of chiefs seated opposite on benches near the speaker, and on this stick all the fourteen requickening strings are arranged in order (124, 210).

26. Song four of the Six Songs relates to women. The key word is *age⁹sen:ni⁹*, "the cook," according to Jemima Gibson. Each chief has a female cook (*godihont*), an official ordinarily for longhouse feasts, who is appointed from within the maternal family at the same time that the chief is raised. She serves for life and is replaced at death by another. She is not the same official as the *goyanego:nah*, clan matron (141, 229). Her duties are to cook the corn soup for the ceremony of making a chief, corn bread if she is smart enough, and boiling the meat. At a special council, should special meals be needed, the chief may call on his special cook and ask her to cook the corn soup (see also 145, 229).

41. Installation. The new chief stands before the seated mourning chiefs with the speaker beside him. The clearminded listen to the presentation of the candidate. At the moment they stand him up and show his face to the crowd they crown him with symbolic antlers (142–43, 520–21).

Each chief has his own string, which is called "the guardian," and this goes over the fire. Each chief handles it as it passes among them, an act of confirmation, and then it is returned across the fire with a speech (146, 522).

42. The charge by the clearminded. Told that his skin is now seven thumbs thick, seven spans of the measuring worm, the chief is now impervious to criticism, to satirical or diffuse sanctions such as gossip. He simply will not feel it (147, 230–31).

The Songs

The chants and songs of the Condolence Council were recorded at Six Nations Reserve for the Library of Congress in 1945 by David Thomas (Onondaga) and Cayuga chief Alex General (Desgahe?). "Dawit" Thomas performed solo both Athahinon?keh—the chant "Going on the Road," which recites the eulogy, or Roll Call of the Founders—and the Six Songs. Chief General chanted the welcome address performed at the woods'-edge fire, and also "Over the Forest," which proclaims the bylaws of the Great Law. Tradition holds that this repertoire should be performed in Mohawk, the language of the first nation to grasp the Great Law, but inevitably the first language of the performer colors the singer's rendering. The *Iroquois Book of Rites* (Hale 1883) carries the Mohawk texts, which Chief General's versions followed, but David Thomas derived his renderings from the oral tradition. Spoken text and song text are not quite the same; the singer inevitably accommodates the text to the melodic line. This is apparent in the scores of the Six Songs, where words are divided to fit the meter.

My colleague, the late Gertrude Kurath, musicologist and student of the dance, transcribed the recordings, which appear here as musical scores with song texts (fig. 45). The chants and songs contain archaic terms as in the formal speeches made during the ceremony. Small wonder that few contemporary ritualists know these terms and most listeners fail to comprehend them. Such ignorance is no new thing.

Indeed, two eighteenth-century observers, in replying to queries from the great Scottish historian William Robertson, confirmed how little then-contemporary Iroquois understood the song texts. George Croghan, William Johnson's deputy among the Ohio contingents, wrote in his semiliterate style: "They have Some Songs in their Condoling for the Dead, which is little understood by themselves, & makes it almost imposible [*sic*] to gain a litreal Translation" (Wainwright 1947: 158). And Guy Johnson, nephew and successor to Sir William, remarked that songs contained remains of ancient rites then little understood, although retained in nonsense vocables (Hamilton 1953: 317–18). Guy Johnson, in answering another query, held that although their songs were too short to convey traditions, the chiefs "frequently repeat their History and Mythology to the young Men, to be transmitted to Posterity" (Hamilton 1953: 323).

What Croghan and Guy Johnson were at a loss to describe, Abbé Francois Piquet (1708–89), a Sulpician priest, heard at Oswegatchie and scored with texts as sung by renegade Onondagas who joined his mission at La Presentation,

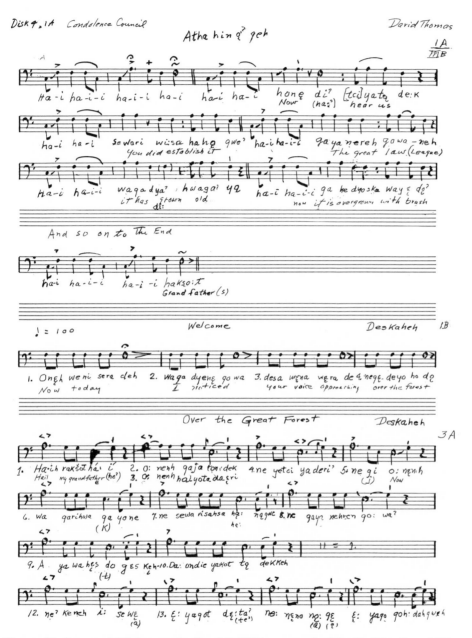

Figure 45. Scores of "Going on the Road," "Welcome at the Wood's Edge," and "Over the Forest," transcribed by Gertrude Kurath from recordings by David Thomas and Alex General in the Library of Congress.

situated at the mouth of the Oswegatchie River on the St. Lawrence (now Ogdensburg, New York).[1] Piquet contributed the scores and texts of three Iroquois songs to the *Journal Etranger* for May 1754. The third score and text is clearly a version of the introduction to the roll call chant of the Condolence Council sung by the clearminded before starting on the path to the house of the mourning confederate moiety. It is marked "Air Funebre, tres Lent" (fig. 46).[2]

Figure 46. Scores of condolence songs transcribed by Father Piquet, 1754. Courtesy Newberry Library, Chicago.

Tsia-ton-te-ni-on   (Swariwissa-anno kwe, ahi!ahi!::/
                Ka, ahi ahi i:/
Sewannon h[w]arrata-nion,ahi ahi!
                (Onnen Saga-ri-waton ahi!ahi!://

Hear us, alas alas!

You who founded it, alas!
You who established the Great Law! Alas!

Which should be observed as always, Alas!

The recorded songs and texts represent an arbitrary selection from the repertoire, although the score for each is complete musically. From tapes of copies of the field recordings in the Library of Congress, which Kurath transcribed, now in the library of the American Philosophical Society, I vetted Kurath's rendering of the native texts as they appear beneath the musical scores. Naturally, the texts are incomplete, but they are sufficient to document the musical scores, which repeat to the end of each text. The English translation follows for each recording.

GOING ON THE ROAD

Ha-i [6 times]: Now then Hear us
Ha-i [twice]: You who established it
Ha-i [twice]: The Great Law [league]
Ha-i [twice]: It has grown old
Ha-i [twice]: It is overgrown with brush
Ha-i [thrice]: Hail Grandfather(s)
[And so on to the end]

1. The mission at La Presentation was founded in 1749 and lasted until 1806. Piquet returned to France to live in retirement, publish, and die. See Hough 1880: 33–35; see also DCB, 4: 636–38.
2. Roy Wright, that reincarnation of the wandering medieval scholar, found this gem in the Newberry Library and sent me a photocopy of his notes "sur Trois Airs Iroquois, *Journal Etranger, Mai 1754*, pp. 229–35 (Paris: Saugrain le fils)." John Aubrey of the Newberry Library supplied copies of the text and musical scores. Dr. Hanni Woodbury compared the texts and I compared the musical scores with Gertrude Kurath's transcription of David Thomas's rendering.

WELCOME AT THE WOODS' EDGE

Now today . . .
I noticed your voice . . .
Coming this way . . .
Over the forest . . .
[And so on to the end]

OVER THE FOREST

Hail Grandfathers
Now hear us
While your grandchildren
Cry mournfully to you
For now it has grown old
What you established
Namely, the Great Law [League]
We hope that they may hear us.
Hail Grandfathers
You said that
It would be tough on those
Who came in later times . . .
[And so on to the end]

THE SIX SONGS

These are the three recorded songs that Kurath transcribed.

1. Ha-i [ten times]
I come to greet my kindred
Ha-i [ten times and repeat]
I come to greet my kindred

2. Ha-i [ten times]
I come to greet the Great Law [league]

3. Hear us, hear us, hear us
My grandfathers, hear us
[The Sixth Song]

CONDOLENCE CEREMONIES
INVOLVING SIR WILLIAM JOHNSON

In April 1756, Sir William Johnson received an invitation belt from the Onondaga council to attend a congress there with representatives of the Shawnee and Delaware tribes (NYCD, 7: 97). His embassy departed during the first week of June. During this grand council, Johnson would take part in a ritual to condole the death of the leading Onondaga sachem, Red Head, or Kakhswenthioni, "Hanging Wampum Belt" (NYCD, 7: 133). Peter Wraxall, then secretary of Indian affairs, was taken ill soon after the embassy departed and did not accompany the expedition or witness the treaty proceedings; nevertheless, he wrote them up afterward in the form of the journal that Johnson transmitted to the Lords of Trade in September. The document offers one of the finest examples of condolence and council protocol on record. Johnson must have kept notes.

Reaching Oneida on 13 June, en route to Onondaga, Johnson and the Mohawk warriors who escorted him, as members of the mourning moiety, were condoled next day by the speaker for their hosts—the Oneidas, Tuscaroras, Cayugas, and Nanticokes—these being the moiety of the clearminded. The speaker uttered the Three Bare Words, which he stated was their custom whenever they met with the English, their siblings, "or they enter our Fireplace to condole the losses of their people" (NYCD, 7: 131). Tears, throat, and heart were the words employed for clearing Johnson's throat and cleaning the council place of blood spilt by a common enemy. But the Oneida speaker gave only one string of wampum when at least three were required, which suggests a shortage of wampum at Oneida. Johnson gave three strings in reply, one for each word, as was proper. Johnson obviously had more wampum to pass (NYCD, 7: 131).

Concerned though the Oneida council might be about English intentions, their speaker discounted worrisome reports as rumors not accompanied by a wampum belt. Before Johnson replied to the Three Bare Words, the Oneida speaker buried the bad rumor with a belt "under the roots of the largest tree in the woods," a metaphor reminiscent of Deganawi:dah's prophecy of the end of the Iroquois League. Johnson, having acknowledged the condolences, silenced the rumor and quieted factionalism at Oneida with a belt of his own. The council then opened for business, which consisted largely of news related to dealings with the French (NYCD, 7: 131–32).

In getting ready for the grand council at Onondaga, Johnson followed customary protol. This required an embassy to prepare its speeches, select or commission the requisite belts proper to the occasion, and appoint speakers before reaching the principal place of council. While at Oneida, Johnson and the sachems of the clearminded nations, his hosts, prepared their speeches and chose the belts for condoling the death of Red Head.

Johnson and his party, now accompanied by representatives of the clearminded moiety, resumed their march to Onondaga. Anticipating their arrival, the Cayugas sent two runners from Onondaga to meet them some five miles outside the town. The runners asked them to send word about when they would enter town so that the Cayuga representatives might arrange to meet them and join the procession to condole the Onondagas. Presumably the Cayuga delegation had come forward, as was proper, to align themselves with the Oneidas and their dependents on the clearminded side, in the moiety now called the "Four Brothers."

Johnson replied, "Today," and marched within an English mile of Onondaga, where three Cayugas met him. There the party halted for two hours to settle condolence formalities. We are told that this was the ancient custom of the Six Nations. This meeting was one step removed from the ceremony at the woods' edge.

The act of the clearminded in taking the ceremony over the path or road to the house of the mourners, calling out the names of the founders on the way, and crying out the kinship terms of the opposite moiety of chiefs still constitutes the opening performance of the modern Condolence Council—the eulogy on the path to the woods' edge (Fenton 1957: 23). Johnson led the procession of "Sachems singing the condoling song which contains the names laws and Customs of their renowned ancestors." Abraham, the leading Mohawk, and the two chief sachems of Oneida carried the ceremony (NYCD, 7: 133-34). By rights, Abraham, as a Mohawk, was of the moiety of the Three Brothers, which included the mourning Onondagas and Senecas. Johnson had co-opted him for the occasion.

Welcome at the woods' edge proper occurred when Johnson's column of eulogy singers came within sight of Onondaga castle and was met by the mourning chiefs and warriors, who placed themselves in a semicircle across the path, "sitting in profound silence." This rite took an hour. It is not clear from the text which side performed which role. Ordinarily the eulogy sung on the path stops at the moment of confrontation, whereupon one of the mourning side recites the welcome chant, and then the two sides exchange the Three Bare Words. According to the text, "the aforesaid sachems [I take this to be the Onondagas] sung the condoling song," which could refer to the welcome chant. At the end of the rite, Rozinoghyata and several other Onondaga headmen stood, took Johnson by the hand, and welcomed him to their settlement. This is called today "taking one by the arm" and ushering him to the principal place.

As is the case today, the singer heading the procession resumed the eulogy where he had left off and continued to the place of council. A fusillade of gunfire greeted the visitors on entering town, and they reciprocated it. They were conducted to a "green bower" erected for the purpose of the council adjoining the house of the deceased sachem. The text does not specify seating arrangements, but it is customary for moieties to sit on opposite sides of the "fire." We are told that when the sachems were seated they sent for Johnson, and when he came, the mourners addressed him with the customary Three Bare Words—tears, throat, and heart.

Today this is done at the woods'-edge fire, and the bare words are tears, ears, and throat, the heart having become a following burden when metaphorical medicine restores internal organs. This rite ended Johnson's introduction to Onondaga on 18 June (NYCD, 7: 134).

Next day the full council of nations present met to perform the complete condolence ceremony for the death of Kakhswenthioni, who had been the chief sachem of Onondaga. (Contrary to league tradition, this was not Thadoda:ho?, as in recent times.) The published minutes represent Johnson as head of mission, but Mohawk chief Abraham was speaker. The journal enumerates a program of five parts for that first day's council at Onondaga. (1) The speaker covered the grave with a large belt. (2) He comforted the mourning relatives with a belt. (3) A third belt admonished the surviving councilors to adhere to the covenant chain. (4) A fourth belt dispelled clouds and restored the sun so that the participants might continue deliberation. (5) Since the warriors of the Six Nations met in night councils, a fifth belt dispelled dark clouds, restored the moon and stars, and removed obstructions to their deliberations.

This is but part of the requickening paradigm of the Condolence Council as we now know it, but, significantly, the journal adds that the condolence messages were reinforced by eleven belts and three strings, fourteen in all, plus a scalp to replace the deceased, the total of which equals fifteen, the number of "words" in the present Requickening Address (Hewitt 1944). A glass of rum went around to wash down sorrow and grief. The journal does not mention a terminal feast.

On the second day of the council meeting, 20 June, the mourning Onondagas, having waited overnight, returned thanks for the condolences with the same number of belts. Johnson then condoled the death of the son of Teyohaqueande, the third Oneida league sachem (Deyohagwendeh, Oe-3, RC 12), who the previous day was "bit by a Raddle Snake," a rare occurrence. He covered the grave with a Strouds blanket and a shirt.

This courtesy ended the condolence business. Johnson's party, the clearminded, then withdrew to camp at the landing on Onondaga Lake, five miles away, near bateaux and supplies, an act reminiscent of a gesture in the modern ritual.

Conferences at Johnson's camp in the following days illustrate various uses of wampum, the moiety divisions of the league (which Johnson apparently understood), and symbolic kinship usage between negotiating parties. Condolence elements also appear.

When Waadory, an Oneida warrior who had defected to the French but then returned, petitioned for a conference with a black string, and then in conference tendered a black belt in repentance, Johnson gave a black belt in return and sent him back to Oswegatchie to spy.

A meeting of the sachems of the Six Nations on the twenty-fourth included some Nanticokes, some Siouan-speaking Tutelos, and an Algonquian Mahican, namely Abraham, the deceased Hendrick's brother, then head sachem of the upper Mohawk castle, who also spoke Mohawk. Abraham spoke for the Three Brothers' side, or Mohawk-Onondaga-Seneca. An Oneida speaker, Conoghquieson, responded, repeating several speeches for the Four Brothers' side (NYCD, 7: 136–37).

Kinship terminology between nations evidently varied according to context. Formally, the Delawares and Shawnees were termed "nephews" (sister's sons) by the Six Nations, their "uncles" (mother's brothers). But in council address the respondents addressed each other as "brethren" (NYCD, 7: 149, 157). This whole matter needs sorting out elsewhere.

At the 24 June session of the council, the Onondaga chief Tyaworondo produced a parcel of belts and strings received from the governor of Canada. These included a string to condole Five Nations' losses, a large black belt inviting them to treat at Montreal, a similar belt inviting two chief warriors to guard the sachems en route but limiting the size of the delegation, and a white belt to condole sachems lately deceased. One wonders whether the recorder reversed the colors of invitation and condolence belts, the latter being usually purple or "black." Also, it is unlikely that the French governor included the Mohawks in his message.

The subsequent proceedings contained few condolence items, although they are relevant as political behavior. As now, a speaker might cross the fire to speak for the opposite moiety. We read that the Onondaga speaker moved his seat to a place among the Oneida chiefs to speak for one of them. He produced a white covenant-chain belt with the figure of a man at each end, symbolizing the governor of Canada and the Five Nations, hand in hand in friendship. It was given hoping the Oneidas would forgive the recent destruction by the French of Fort Bull at the Great Carrying Place. The rest of the message is unimportant in this context.

Of a Sunday evening, 27 June, the death shout (*kwaʔaːh* or *koːweh*) announced the arrival of two messengers from the Susquehanna bearing news that the Nanticoke "king" had died at Otseningo. Next day Johnson, in conjunction with the Six Nations, performed the usual condolence ceremony with strings of wampum and then covered the graves of the dead with two black strouds. The mourners expressed satisfaction and reciprocated. The usual expected glass of rum ended the ceremony (NYCD, 7: 141-42).

By the end of the council at Onondaga, Johnson had mastered requickening protocol. He was even prepared to raise up chiefs. As in the modern Condolence Council, which reaches a climax when the face of the new chief is held up to the assembly, Johnson turned to the Onondaga speaker, who had just thanked him for his generosity with presents, and proceeded to make the speaker a sachem by hanging a medal around his neck. Such acts are recalled today in referring to a name or title borrowed from another clan as "a name hung about the neck." The name is not passed down in the matrilineage.

Journeying home, Johnson observed two sorts of protocol. A customary alternative to the woods'-edge approach was to enter a village with scalps. In the first instance his entourage gained support by calling at the Tuscarora village and presenting two French scalps, which a Tuscarora warrior grabbed and carried around the castle singing the war song (NYCD, 7: 150).

That same evening, the Oneida sachems came out to meet Johnson in camp, expressing concern for his safety on the road. A death had occurred—the head sachem had lost his nephew that very morning—and this required the woods'-edge protocol. Courtesy demanded a condolence ceremony, and Johnson still had a belt for the purpose. In the evening he entered the castle, called a council of the people, and performed the ceremony. It is clear that observing such ceremonial amenities enhanced rapport. In thanking him, the Oneida speaker commented that his act was convincing proof of his regard for them and that he did not neglect the necessary ceremonies even when busy (NYCD, 7: 151).

The next winter, smallpox swept the Mohawk Valley, two leading sachems died, and Johnson was deeply engaged in condoling them. In early January 1757, a delegation of Oneida and Tuscarora chiefs headed by Conoghquieson, the second Oneida league chief, their speaker, was on its way down to condole the losses in two Mohawk castles (SWJP, 2: 665). Johnson met with two Mohawk chiefs of the Bear and Turtle clans, proposed condoling the death of his friend Abraham, the late Hendrick's brother, and sent, with their approval, a large black belt to show the people and cover the grave. It was to go to the nearest kin, never to be returned or exchanged (SWJP, 9: 589). The same day, Chief David of Schoharie, to whom Hale (1883: 42) attributed the Mohawk version of the "Book of Rites," arrived to notify Johnson of the death of Seth, their head; they were now "in darkness." On 25 January, all the Mohawk chiefs came to Fort Johnson to settle details of Abraham's condolence. Johnson sent a second black belt to "drape up the grave" and a third to achieve unanimity between sachems and warriors. Altogether, the ceremony would require ten belts and two strings, but the sachems did not specify the burdens. To requicken the deceased, Johnson sent a scalp in lieu of prisoners (SWJP, 9: 593, 595), which greatly pleased the mourners. No further business could be transacted until after the ceremony (SWJP, 9: 600, 603).

Six years later, at a critical time in affairs, the Six Nations came to Johnson's hearth to condole the death of Sir William's father. The Onondaga speaker, with three strings, wiped Johnson's tears, removed obstructions from his breast, wiped the blood from the bed, collected the bones of his relatives, covered the grave, dispersed the clouds and restored the sun, and cleared his mind. Having "gone through the Ceremony . . . necessary on those Melancholly occasions . . . have now only to add that with these Strings of Wampum wipe all dust from your feet to your Head (3 strings)." He was then ready for business. Johnson condoled the nations in turn for their war losses (SWJP, 10: 674–76).

When Sir William Johnson himself died suddenly during a conference at Johnson Hall in the summer of 1774, runners with belts were sent through the Five Nations, and the death cry was heard the length of the Longhouse. The nations individually and together arrived at Johnson's hearth to condole his death and lift up the mind of his mourning nephew, Guy Johnson. Some seventeen condolence messages were received, including covering the grave, the three bare words, water of pity to cleanse his body and restore his heart, disperse clouds and restore the sun, and rekindle the fire. Particular chiefs returned medals and other important presents that Johnson had bestowed. And finally, they sought to requicken Guy Johnson in the great man's status and roles (NYCD, 8: 471; Gage Papers, Clements Library, Ann Arbor, Michigan).

BIBLIOGRAPHY

Abler, Thomas S. 1967. "Seneca Nation Factionalism: The First Twenty Years." In *Iroquois Culture, History, and Prehistory: Proceedings of the 1965 Conference on Iroquois Research*, ed. Elisabeth Tooker, 25–26. Albany: New York State Museum and Science Service.

———. 1980. "Iroquois Cannibalism: Fact Not Fiction." *Ethnohistory* 27(4): 309–16.

———. 1984. "The Kansas Connection: The Seneca Nation and the Iroquois Confederacy Council." In *Extending the Rafters: Interdisciplinary Approaches to Iroquoian Studies*, eds. Michael K. Foster, Jack Campisi, and Marianne Mithun, 81–93. Albany: State University of New York Press.

Abler, Thomas S., ed. 1989. *Chainbreaker: The Revolutionary War Memoirs of Governor Blacksnake as told to Benjamin Williams.* Lincoln: University of Nebraska Press.

American State Papers—Indian Affairs, 1832–34. Class 2, 25 May 1789–1 March 1827. Eds. Walter Lowrie et al. Washington, D.C.

Amherst, Jeffrey. *Journals, 1758–60, 1762.* Public Record Office, London.

———. 1931. *The Journal of Jeffrey Amherst.* Chicago: University of Chicago Press.

Aquila, Richard. 1983. *The Iroquois Restoration: Iroquois Diplomacy on the Colonial Frontier, 1701–1754.* Detroit: Wayne State University Press.

Armstrong, William Howard. 1978. *Warrior in Two Camps: Ely S. Parker, Union General and Seneca Chief.* Syracuse, N.Y.: Syracuse University Press.

Axtell, James. 1981. *The European and the Indian: Essays in the Ethnohistory of Colonial North America.* New York: Oxford University Press.

———. 1985. *The Invasion Within: The Contest of Cultures in Colonial North America.* New York: Oxford University Press.

Bacqueville de La Potherie, Claude C. Le Roy. 1722. *Histoire de l'Amérique septentrionale.* 4 vols. Paris: Nion et F. Didot.

Bailey, Alfred G. 1933. *The Conflict of European and Eastern Algonkian Cultures, 1504–1700: A Study in Canadian Civilization.* Publication of the New Brunswick Museum, Monograph Series 2. Saint John, New Brunswick. Reprint, Toronto: University of Toronto Press, 1969.

Barbeau, C. Marius. 1915. *Huron and Wyandot Mythology.* Anthropological Series 11, Memoirs of the Canadian Geological Survey 80. Ottawa.

———. 1960. *Huron-Wyandot Traditional Narratives in Translations and Native Texts.* Anthropological Series 47, National Museum of Canada Bulletin 165. Ottawa.

Barreiro, Jose. 1990. "The Return of the Wampum." *Northeast Indian Quarterly* 7(1): 8–20.

Beauchamp, William M. 1880. "Wampum Belts of the Six Nations." *American Antiquarian* 2: 28–230.

———. 1885. "Permanence of Early Iroquois Clans and Sachemships." *American Antiquarian and Oriental Journal* 8: 82–91.

————. 1886. "Permanence of Early Iroquois Clans and Sachemships." *Proceedings of the American Association for the Advancement of Science* 34: 381–92.

————. 1891. "Hi-a-wat-ha." *Journal of American Folk-Lore* 4(15): 295–306.

————. 1892. *The Iroquois Trail; or, Foot-prints of the Six Nations, in Customs, Traditions, and History, in which are included David Cusick's "Sketches of the Ancient History of the Six Nations."* Fayetteville, N.Y.: H. C. Beauchamp.

————. 1895. "An Iroquois Condolence." *Journal of American Folk-Lore* 8(31): 313–16.

————. 1898. "Wampum Used in Council and as Currency." *American Antiquarian* 20(1): 1–13.

————. 1901. "Wampum and Shell Articles Used by the New York Indians." *New York State Museum Bulletin* 41: 319–480.

————. 1905. "A History of the New York Iroquois, Now Commonly Called the Six Nations." *New York State Museum Bulletin* 78: 125–461.

————. 1907. "Civil, Religious and Mourning Councils of the New York Indians." *New York State Museum Bulletin* 113: 341–451.

————. 1921. *The Founders of the New York Iroquois League and Its Probable Date.* Researches and Transactions of the New York State Archaeological Association 3(1).

————. 1922. *Iroquois Folk Lore Gathered from the Iroquois of New York.* Syracuse, N.Y.: Onondaga Historical Association.

Beauchamp, William M., ed. 1916. *Moravian Journals Relating to Central New York, 1745–66.* Syracuse, N.Y.: Onondaga Historical Association.

Bell, Whitfield J., Jr., ed. 1973. *A Journey from Pennsylvania to Onondaga in 1743.* (Reprints the journals of John Bartram and Lewis Evans and the report of Conrad Weiser.) Barre, Mass.: Imprint Society.

Berkhofer, Robert F., Jr. 1965a. "Faith and Factionalism among the Senecas: Theory and Ethnohistory." *Ethnohistory* 12(2): 99–112.

————. 1965b. *Salvation and the Savage: An Analysis of Protestant Missions and American Indian Response, 1782–1862.* Lexington: University of Kentucky Press.

————. 1978. *The White Man's Indian: Images of the American Indian from Columbus to the Present.* New York: Alfred A. Knopf.

Biggar, H. P., ed. 1922–36. *The Works of Samuel de Champlain.* 6 vols. Toronto: Champlain Society.

————, ed. 1924. *The Voyages of Jacques Cartier.* Publications of the Public Archives of Canada, 11. Ottawa.

Billington, Ray A. 1944. "The Fort Stanwix Treaty of 1768." *New York History* 25(2): 182–94.

Birket-Smith, Kaj. 1920. "Some Ancient Artifacts from the Eastern United States." *Journal de la Société des Américanistes de Paris* 12: 141–69.

Black, William. 1877. "Journal of the 1774 Lancaster Treaty." *Pennsylvania Magazine of History and Biography* 1: 117–32, 232–49, 404–19.

Blair, Emma H., ed. 1911–12. *The Indian Tribes of the Upper Mississippi Valley and Region of the Great Lakes, as Described by Nicolas Perrot, French Commandant in the Northwest; Bacqueville de La Potherie, French Royal Commissioner to Canada; Morrel Marston, American Army Officer; and Thomas Forsyth, United States Agent at Fort Armstrong.* 2 vols. Cleveland: Arthur H. Clark.

Blau, Harold, Jack Campisi, and Elisabeth Tooker. 1978. "Onondaga." In *Handbook of North American Indians, vol. 15: Northeast,* ed. Bruce G. Trigger, 491–99. Washington, D.C.: Smithsonian Institution.

Bloch, Marc L. B. 1953. *The Historian's Craft.* Trans. Peter Putnam. New York: Alfred A. Knopf.

Boas, Franz. 1897. "Horatio Hale." *The Month in Literature, Art, and Life* 1(3): 262–63.

————. 1907. "Ethnological Problems in Canada." *Proceedings of the Fifteenth International Congress of Americanists,* 1: 151–60.

Bond, Richmond P. 1952. *Queen Anne's American Kings*. Oxford: Clarendon Press.

Boucher, Pierre. 1664. *Histoire véritable et naturelle des moeurs et productions du pays de la Nouvelle France, vulgairement dite le Canada*. Paris: F. Lambert.

———. 1881 [1664]. *Canada in the Seventeenth Century*. Trans. E. L. Montizambert. Montreal: George E. Desbarats.

Bougainville, Louis Antoine de. 1964. *Adventure in the Wilderness: The American Journal of Louis Antoine de Bougainville, 1756-1760*. Ed. and trans. Edward P. Hamilton. Norman: University of Oklahoma Press.

Boyce, Douglas W. 1973. "A Glimpse of Iroquois Culture History through the Eyes of Joseph Brant and John Norton." *Proceedings of the American Philosophical Society* 117(4): 286-94.

———. 1987. "'As the Wind Scatters the Smoke': The Tuscaroras in the Eighteenth Century." In *Beyond the Covenant Chain: The Iroquois and Their Neighbors in Indian North America, 1600-1800*, eds. Daniel K. Richter and James H. Merrell, 151-63. Syracuse, N.Y.: Syracuse University Press.

Boyd, Julian P., ed. 1938. *Indian Treaties Printed by Benjamin Franklin, 1736-1762*. Philadelphia: Historical Society of Pennsylvania.

Boyle, David. 1898. "The Pagan Iroquois." In *Annual Archaeological Report for 1898, Being Part of the Appendix to the Report of the Minister of Education, Ontario*, 54-211. Toronto.

———. 1906. "The Making of a Cayuga Chief." In *Annual Archaeological Report for 1905 . . .*, 56-59. Toronto.

Bradford, William. 1694. "An Account of the Treaty between his Excellency Benjamin Fletcher, Captain General and Governor in Chief of the Province of New-York &c. And the Indians of the Five Nations, viz. The Mohaques, Oneydes, Onnondages, Cajouges and Sennekes at Albany, beginning the 15th of August, 1694." New York: William Bradford.

Bradford, William. 1952. *Of Plymouth Plantation, 1620-1647*. Ed. Samuel Eliot Morison. New York: Knopf.

Bradley, James W. 1980. "Ironwork in Onondaga, 1550-1650." In *Studies in Iroquoian Culture*, ed. Nancy Bonvillain, 109-18. Ridge, N.H: Occasional Publications in Anthropology.

———. 1987. *Evolution of the Onondaga Iroquois: Accommodating Change, 1500-1665*. Syracuse, N.Y.: Syracuse University Press.

Brandão, J. A., and William A. Starna. 1996. "The Treaties of 1701: A Triumph of Iroquois Diplomacy." *Ethnohistory* 43(2): 209-44.

Brant, Joseph. 1801. "Answers to Queries Respecting the Six Nations." Manuscript, Miller Papers I. New York Historical Society, New York.

Brasser, Ted J. C. 1971. "The Coastal Algonkians: People of the First Frontiers." In *North American Indians in Historical Perspective*, eds. Eleanor B. Leacock and Nancy O. Lurie, 64-91. New York: Random House.

Braunholtz, H. J. 1953. "The Sloane Collection: Ethnography." *British Museum Quarterly*, 18: 23-26.

Bruyas, Jacques. 1863. *Radices verborum iroquaeorum* (Radical words of the Mohawk language, with their derivatives). Ed. John Gilmary Shea. Shea's Library of American Linguistics 10. New York: Cramoisy Press.

Buffington, Arthur H. 1922. "The Policy of Albany and English Expansion." *Mississippi Valley Historical Review* 8(4): 327-66.

Bushnell, David I., Jr. 1906. "The Sloane Collection in the British Museum." *American Anthropologist* n.s. 8: 671-85.

Campisi, Jack. 1978. "Oneida." In *Handbook of North American Indians, vol. 15: Northeast*, ed. Bruce G. Trigger, 481-90. Washington, D.C.: Smithsonian Institution.

———. 1984. "Six Nations Policy, States' Rights, and Indian Sovereignty." In *Extending the Rafters: Interdisciplinary Approaches to Iroquoian Studies*, eds. Michael K. Foster, Jack Campisi, and Marianne Mithun, 95-108. Albany: State University of New York Press.

Campisi, Jack, and William A. Starna. 1995. "On the Road to Canandaigua: The Treaty of 1794." *American Indian Quarterly* 19(4): 467–90.

Canfield, William Walker. 1902. *The Legends of the Iroquois, Told by "The Cornplanter."* New York: A. Wessels.

Ceci, Lynn. 1977. "The Effects of European Contact and Trade on the Settlement Pattern of Indians in Coastal New York, 1524–1664." Ph.D. diss., City University of New York.

———. 1980. "The First Fiscal Crisis in New York." *Economic Development and Culture Change* 28: 839–47.

———. 1987. "Native Wampum as a Peripheral Resource in the Seventeenth-Century World System." Unpublished manuscript.

Chadwick, E. M. 1897. *The People of the Longhouse.* Toronto: Church of England Publishing Co.

Chafe, Wallace L. 1961. *Seneca Thanksgiving Rituals.* Bureau of American Ethnology Bulletin 183. Washington, D.C.

———. 1963. *Handbook of the Seneca Language.* New York State Museum and Science Service Bulletin 388. Albany.

———. 1967. *Seneca Morphology and Dictionary.* Smithsonian Contributions to Anthropology 4. Washington, D.C.

Charlevoix, Pierre F. X. de. 1761. *Journal of a Voyage to North America.* 2 vols. London. Readex Microprint, 1966.

———. 1866–72. *History and General Description of New France.* 6 vols. Ed. John G. Shea. Reprint, Chicago: Loyola University Press, 1962.

Chase, E. P. ed. 1929. *Our Revolutionary Forefathers: The Letters of Francois, Marquis de Barbe-Marbois.* New York.

Chazonoff, William. 1970. *Joseph Ellicott and the Holland Land Company: The Opening of Western New York.* Syracuse, N.Y.: Syracuse University Press.

Churchill, Winston S. 1957. *A History of the English-Speaking Peoples, vol. 3: The Age of Revolution.* New York: Dodd, Mead.

Clark, Joshua V. H. 1849. *Onondaga; or, Reminiscences of Earlie and Later Times; Being a Series of Historical Sketches Relative to Onondaga; with Notes on the Several Towns in the Country, and Oswego.* 2 vols. Syracuse, N.Y.: Stoddard and Babcock.

Clarke, Noah T. 1931. "The Wampum Belt Collection of the New York State Museum." *New York State Museum Bulletin* 288: 85–121.

Claus, Daniel. 1755. "Letter to the Secretary, Canajoharie, July 10." In *Pennsylvania Provincial Council Minutes* 6: 468–75.

Clinton, DeWitt. 1812. *Discourse Delivered before the New-York Historical Society, at Their Anniversary Meeting, 6 December, 1811.* New York: James Eastburn.

Colden, Cadwallader. 1724. "A Memorial Concerning the Furr Trade of the Province of New York." In *Documents Relative to the Colonial History of the State of New York*, ed. Edmund B. O'Callaghan, 5: 726–33. Albany: Weed, Parsons.

———. 1727. *The History of the Five Indian Nations Depending on the Province of New-York.* Reprint with introduction and notes by John Gilmary Shea, New York: T. H. Morrell, 1866.

———. 1750. *The History of the Five Indian Nations of Canada, Which Are a Barrier between the English and the French. . . .* 2d ed. London: John Whiston.

———. 1937. *History of the Five Nations: Continuation, 1707–1720.* Colden Papers 9. New York Historical Society Collections 68.

Converse, Harriet (Maxwell). 1908. "Myths and Legends of the New York State Iroquois." Ed. Arthur C. Parker. *New York State Museum Bulletin* 125: 5–195.

Cornplanter, Jesse. 1938. *Legends of the Longhouse.* New York: Lippincott.

Count, Earl W. 1952. "The Earth Diver and the Rival Twins: A Clue to the Time Corre-
lation in North-Eurasiatic and North American Mythology." In *Selected Papers of the
Twenty-ninth International Congress of Americanists: Indian Tribes of Aboriginal America*, ed. Sol Tax,
55–62. Chicago: University of Chicago Press.

Craig, Neville B. 1876. *Olden Time*. 2 vols. Cincinnati. (Pittsburgh 1846–48 in pamphlet form.)

Curtin, Jeremiah, and J.N.B. Hewitt. 1918. "Seneca Fiction, Legends, and Myths." Ed.
J.N.B. Hewitt. *Thirty-second Annual Report of the Bureau of American Ethnology for the Years
1910–11*, 37–813.

Cusick, David. 1825. *Ancient History of the Six Nations*. Tuscarora, N.Y. Reprint, Lockport,
N.Y., 1828, 1848. (Included in Beauchamp 1892.)

Day, Gordon M. 1968. "Iroquois: An Etymology." *Ethnohistory* 15(4): 389–402.

———. 1971. "The Eastern Boundary of Iroquoia: Abenaki Evidence." *Man in the Northeast*
1(1): 7–13.

———. 1978. "Western Abenaki." In *Handbook of North American Indians, vol. 15: Northeast*,
148–59. Washington, D.C.: Smithsonian Institution.

Deardorff, Merle H. 1951. "The Religion of Handsome Lake: Its Origin and Development." In *Symposium on Local Diversity in Iroquois Culture*, ed. William N. Fenton, 77–107.
Bureau of American Ethnology Bulletin 149. Washington, D.C.

DeMille, George E. 1946. *A History of the Diocese of Albany*. Church Historical Society
Publication no. 16. Philadelphia.

DePuy, Henry F., comp. 1917. *A Bibliography of the English Colonial Treaties with the American
Indians, Including a Synopsis of Each Treaty*. New York: Lennox Club.

Desrosiers, Léo-Paul. 1947. *Iroquoisie*. Montreal: Études de l'Institute d'Histoire de
l'Amérique Française.

———. 1954. "Preliminaires du massacre de Lachine." *Cahiers de Dix* 19: 47–66.

———. 1955. "Iroquoisie, terre française." *Cahiers de Dix* 20: 34–59.

———. 1956. "Negotiations de paix (1693–1696)." *Cahiers de Dix* 21: 55–87.

———. 1957. "L'expedition de M. de La Barre." *Cahiers de Dix* 22: 105–35.

———. 1958. "Denonville." *Cahiers de Dix* 23: 107–38.

———. 1959. "La paix-miracle (1653–1660)." *Cahiers de Dix* 24: 85–112.

———. 1960. "Il y a trois cents ans." *Cahiers de Dix* 25: 85–101.

———. 1961. "Les années terribles." *Cahiers de Dix* 26: 55–90.

———. 1962. "Revers et succès (1662–1663)." *Cahiers de Dix* 27: 77–95.

———. 1963. "Frontenac, l'artisan de la victoire." *Cahiers de Dix* 28: 93–145.

———. 1964. "La paix de 1667." *Cahiers de Dix* 29: 24–45.

———. 1965. "Fort Orange (Albany) a l'époque des guerres indiennes." *Cahiers de Dix* 30:
19–33.

———. 1966. "Guérillas dans l'île de Montréal." *Cahiers de Dix* 31: 79–85.

Dictionary of Canadian Biography. 1967–. Toronto: University of Toronto Press.

Dobyns, Henry F. 1966. "Estimating Aboriginal American Population: An Appraisal of
Techniques with a New Hemisphere Estimate." *Current Anthropology* 7(4): 395–416.

———. 1983. *Their Number Become Thinned: Native American Population Dynamics in Eastern North
America*. Knoxville: University of Tennessee Press.

Donck, Adrian van der. 1841. "A Description of New Netherlands, Together with Remarks
on the Character and Peculiar Customs of the Savages or Natives of the Land." *Collections
of the New-York Historical Society*, 2d. ser., 1(5): 125–242.

Downes, Randolph C. 1940. *Council Fires on the Upper Ohio: A Narrative of Indian Affairs in the
Upper Ohio Valley until 1795*. Pittsburgh: University of Pittsburgh Press.

Drake, Samuel G. 1851. *Indian Captivities; or, Life in the Wigwam: Being the True Narratives of
Captives Who Have Been Carried Away by the Indians, from the Frontier Settlements of the U.S., from
the Earliest Period to the Present Time*. Auburn, N.Y.: Derby and Miller.

Driver, Harold E. 1961. *Indians of North America.* Chicago: University of Chicago Press.

Druke, Mary A. 1983. "The Structure and Meanings of Mohawk-Oneida Leadership." Ph.D. diss., University of Chicago.

———. 1985. "Iroquois Treaties: Common Forms, Varying Interpretations." In *The History and Culture of Iroquois Diplomacy: An Interdisciplinary Guide to the Treaties of the Six Nations and Their League*, eds. Francis Jennings et al., 85–98. Syracuse, N.Y.: Syracuse University Press.

———. 1987. "Linking Arms: The Structure of Iroquois Intertribal Diplomacy." In *Beyond the Covenant Chain: The Iroquois and Their Neighbors in Indian North America, 1600–1800*, eds. Daniel K. Richter and James H. Merrell, 29–40. Syracuse, N.Y.: Syracuse University Press.

Duane, James. 1869. "Opinion on New York Indian Treaties for Gov. George Clinton." New York Historical Society Collections 130: 409–15.

Du Creux, François. 1951–52. *History of Canada, or New France.* 2 vols. Ed. James B. Conacher, trans. Percy J. Robinson. Toronto: Champlain Society.

Eccles, William J. 1959. *Frontenac: The Courtier Governor.* Toronto: McClelland and Stewart. Reprint, Toronto: Carleton Library, 1965.

———. 1964. *Canada under Louis XIV, 1663–1701.* Toronto: McClelland and Stewart; New York: Oxford University Press.

———. 1969. *The Canadian Frontier, 1534–1760.* New York: Holt, Rinehart, and Winston.

———. 1972. *France in America.* New York: Harper and Row.

Eid, Leroy V. 1979. "The Ojibwa-Iroquois War: The War the Five Nations Did Not Win." *Ethnohistory* 26(4): 279–324.

———. 1985. "National" War among Indians of Northeastern North America. *Canadian Review of American Studies* 16(2): 125–54.

Evans, Griffith. 1784–85. "Journal of a Trip from Philadelphia to Fort Stanwix to Attend 'Northern Treaty' with the Indians." Manuscript HM 608, Henry E. Huntington Library, San Marino, Calif.

———. 1941. "Journal of Griffith Evans, 1784–1785." Ed. Hallock F. Raup. *Pennsylvania Magazine of History and Biography* 65: 202–33.

Feest, Christian F. 1978. "Virginia Algonquians." In *Handbook of North American Indians, vol. 15: Northeast*, ed. Bruce G. Trigger, 253–70. Washington, D.C.: Smithsonian Institution.

Feister, Lois M. 1973. "Communication between the Dutch and the Indians in New Netherland, 1609–1664." *Ethnohistory* 20: 25–38.

———. 1982. "Indian-Dutch Relations in the Upper Hudson Valley: A Study of Baptism Records in the Dutch Reform Church." *Man in the Northeast* 24: 89–113.

Fenton, William N. 1933–38. Field notebooks. Fenton Papers, American Philosophical Library, Philadelphia.

———. 1936. *An Outline of Seneca Ceremonies at Coldspring Longhouse.* Yale University Publications in Anthropology 9. New Haven, Conn.

———. 1940. "Problems Arising from the Historic Northeastern Position of the Iroquois." In *Essays in Historical Anthropology of North America*, 159–252. Smithsonian Miscellaneous Collections 100. Washington, D.C.

———. 1941. "Iroquois Suicide: A Study in the Stability of a Culture Pattern." *Bureau of American Ethnology Bulletin* 128(14): 80–137.

———. 1942. "Contacts between Iroquois Herbalism and Colonial Medicine." *Annual Report of the Smithsonian Institution for 1941*, 503–26. Washington, D.C.

———. 1944. "Simeon Gibson: Iroquois Informant, 1889–1943." *American Anthropologist* 44(2): 231–34.

———. 1946. "An Iroquois Condolence Council for Installing Cayuga Chiefs in 1945." *Journal of the Washington Academy of Sciences* 36(4): 110–27.

———. 1949a. "Collecting Materials for a Political History of the Six Nations." *Proceedings of the American Philosophical Society* 93(3): 233–38.

———. 1949b. "Seth Newhouse's Traditional History and Constitution of the Iroquois Confederacy." *Proceedings of the American Philosophical Society* 93(2): 141–58.

———. 1950. "The Roll Call of the Iroquois Chiefs: A Study of a Mnemonic Cane from the Six Nations Reserve." *Smithsonian Miscellaneous Collections* 111(15): 1–73.

———. 1951a. "Locality as a Basic Factor in the Development of Iroquois Social Structure." *Bureau of American Ethnology Bulletin* 149(3): 35–54. Washington, D.C.

———. 1951b. "Iroquois Studies at the Mid-Century." *Proceedings of the American Philosophical Society* 95(3): 296–310.

———. 1953a. *The Iroquois Eagle Dance: An Offshoot of the Calumet Dance; with an Analysis of the Iroquois Eagle Dance and Songs by Gertrude P. Kurath.* Bureau of American Ethnology Bulletin 156. Washington, D.C.

———. 1953b. "A Calendar of Manuscript Materials Relating to the History of the Six Nations in Depositories Outside of Philadelphia, 1750–1850." *Proceedings of the American Philosophical Society* 97(5): 578–95.

———. 1955. "Factionalism in American Indian Society." *Acts of the Fourth International Congress of Anthropological and Ethnological Sciences* 2: 330–40. Vienna.

———. 1956. "Toward the Gradual Civilization of the Indian Natives: The Missionary and Linguistic Work of Asher Wright (1803–1875) among the Senecas of Western New York." *Proceedings of the American Philosophical Society* 100(6): 567–81.

———. 1957. *American Indian and White Relations to 1830: Needs and Opportunities for Study.* Chapel Hill: University of North Carolina Press.

———. 1960. "The Hiawatha Wampum Belt of the Iroquois League for Peace: A Symbol for the International Congress of Anthropology." In *Selected Papers of the Fifth International Congress of Anthropological and Ethnological Sciences*, ed. Anthony F. C. Wallace, 1–7. Philadelphia: University of Pennsylvania Press.

———. 1961. "Iroquoian Culture History: A General Evaluation." In *Symposium on Cherokee and Iroquois Culture*, eds. William N. Fenton and John Gulick, 257–77. Bureau of American Ethnology Bulletin 180. Washington, D.C.

———. 1962. "This Island, the World on the Turtle's Back." *Journal of American Folklore* 75(298): 283–300.

———. 1963. Review of *Conservatism among the Iroquois at the Six Nations Reserve*, by Annemarie Anrod Shimony. *American Anthropologist* 65(2): 444–47.

———. 1965. "The Iroquois Confederacy in the Twentieth Century: A Case Study in the Theory of Lewis H. Morgan in *Ancient Society*." *Ethnology* 43(3): 71–85.

———. 1967. "From Longhouse to Ranch-Type House: The Second Housing Revolution of the Seneca Nation." In *Iroquois Culture, History, and Prehistory: Proceedings of the 1965 Conference on Iroquois Research*, ed. Elisabeth Tooker, 7–22. Albany: New York State Museum and Science Service.

———. 1968. "Introduction." In *Parker on the Iroquois*, ed. W. N. Fenton, 1–47. Syracuse, N.Y.: Syracuse University Press.

———. 1971a. "The Iroquois in History." In *North American Indians in Historical Perspective*, eds. Eleanor B. Leacock and Nancy O. Lurie, 129–68. New York: Random House.

———. 1971b. "The New York State Wampum Collection: The Case for the Integrity of Cultural Treasures." *Proceedings of the American Philosophical Society* 115(6): 437–61.

———. 1972. "Statement of Chief Henan Scrogg on the Six Nations' Meeting of the Handsome Lake Religion at Tonawanda in 1935." Fenton field notes, 6 September 1935. Fenton Papers, American Philosophical Society Library, Philadelphia.

———. 1975. "The Lore of the Longhouse: Myth, Ritual, and Red Power." *Anthropological Quarterly* 48(3): 131–47.

————. 1978a. "Northern Iroquoian Culture Patterns." In *Handbook of North American Indians, vol. 15: Northeast*, ed. Bruce G. Trigger, 295–321. Washington, D.C.: Smithsonian Institution.

————. 1978b. Review essay. *American Anthropologist* 80: 929–35.

————. 1979. "The Great Good Medicine." *New York State Journal of Medicine* 79(10): 1603–9.

————. 1985. "Structure, Continuity, and Change in the Process of Iroquois Treaty Making." In *The History and Culture of Iroquois Diplomacy: An Interdisciplinary Guide to the Treaties of the Six Nations and Their League*, eds. Francis Jennings, William N. Fenton, Mary A. Druke, and David R. Miller, 3–36. Syracuse, N.Y.: Syracuse University Press.

————. 1986a. "A Further Note on Iroquois Suicide." *Ethnohistory* 33(4): 448–57.

————. 1986b. "Leadership in the Northeastern Woodlands of North America." *American Indian Quarterly* 10(1): 21–45.

————. 1987. *The False Faces of the Iroquois*. Norman: University of Oklahoma Press.

————. 1989. "Return of Eleven Wampum Belts to the Six Nations Iroquois Confederacy on Grand River, Canada." *Ethnohistory* 36: 392–410.

Fenton, William N., ed. 1941. *Symposium on Local Diversity in Iroquois Culture*. Bureau of American Ethnology Bulletin 149. Washington, D.C.

————, ed. 1957. "Seneca Indians, by Asher Wright (1859)." *Ethnohistory* 4(3): 302–21.

————, ed. 1965a. "The Journal of James Emlen Kept on a Trip to Canandaigua, N.Y., September 15 to October 30, 1794, to Attend the Treaty between the United States and the Six Nations." *Ethnohistory* 12(4): 279–342.

————, ed. 1965b. "Captain Hyde's Observations on the Five Nations of Indians at New Yorke, 1698." *American Scene Magazine* (Thomas Gilcrease Institute of American History and Art, Tulsa, Oklahoma).

Fenton, William N., and Ernest S. Dodge. 1949. "An Elmbark Canoe in the Peabody Museum of Salem." *American Neptune* 9(3): 185–206.

Fenton, William N., and Simeon Gibson, trans. and eds. 1941. "The Deganawi:dah Legend: A Tradition of the Founding of the League of the Five Iroquois tribes." English translation of text given by John Arthur Gibson to J. N. B. Hewitt, 1899. Bureau of American Ethnology, mss. 1517b and 1517c, National Anthropological Archives, Smithsonian Institution, Washington, D.C. Copy in American Philosophical Society Library.

Fenton, William N., and John Gulick, eds. 1961. *Symposium on Cherokee and Iroquois Culture*. Bureau of American Ethnology Bulletin 180. Washington, D.C.

Fenton, William N., and Gertrude P. Kurath. 1951. "The Feast of the Dead, or Ghost Dance, at Six Nations Reserve, Canada." *Bureau of American Ethnology Bulletin* 149(7): 139–65. Washington, D.C.

Fenton, William N., and Elizabeth L. Moore, eds. and trans. 1974. *Customs of the American Indians Compared with the Customs of Primitive Times*, by Father Joseph-François Lafitau, vol. 1. Toronto: Champlain Society.

————, eds. and trans. 1977. *Customs of the American Indians Compared with the Customs of Primitive Times*, by Father Joseph-François Lafitau, vol. 2. Toronto: Champlain Society.

Fitting, James E. 1978. "Prehistory." In *Handbook of North American Indians, vol. 15: Northeast*, 14–15, 44–57. Washington, D.C.: Smithsonian Institution.

Flannery, Regina. 1939. *An Analysis of Coastal Algonquian Culture*. Catholic University of America Anthropological Series, 7. Washington, D.C.

Flexner, James T. 1959. *Mohawk Baronet: Sir William Johnson of New York*. New York: Harper.

Foley, Denis. 1973. "The Iroquois Condolence Business." *Man in the Northeast* 5: 47–53.

Force, Peter, ed. 1837–53. *American Archives . . . A Documentary History of . . . the North American Colonies*. 5 ser., 3 vols. (1776). Washington, D.C.: Peter Force.

Foster, Michael K. 1974. *From the Earth to beyond the Sky: An Ethnographic Approach to Four Longhouse Iroquois Speech Events*. National Museum of Man, Ethnology Division, Mercury Series Paper 20. Ottawa.

———. 1984. "On Who Spoke First at Iroquois-White Councils: An Exercise in the Method of Upstreaming." In *Extending the Rafters: Interdisciplinary Approaches to Iroquoian Studies*, eds. Michael K. Foster, Jack Campisi, and Marianne Mithun, 183–207. Albany: State University of New York Press.

———. 1985. "Another Look at the Function of Wampum in Iroquois-White Councils." In *The History and Culture of Iroquois Diplomacy: An Interdisciplinary Guide to the Treaties of the Six Nations and Their League*, eds. Francis Jennings, William N. Fenton, Mary A. Druke, and David R. Miller, 99–114. Syracuse, N.Y.: Syracuse University Press.

Francis, Turbot. 1836. "Journals." Massachusetts Historical Society Collections, ser. 3, vol. 5: 75–100. Boston.

Franklin, Benjamin. 1962. *The Papers of Benjamin Franklin*, vol. 5. Ed. Leonard W. Labaree. New Haven, Conn.: Yale University Press.

———. 1987. *Writings*. Ed. J. A. Leo LeMay. New York: Library of America.

Freeman, Douglas Southall. 1948. *George Washington: A Biography*, vol. 1. New York: Charles Scribner's Sons.

Freilich, Morris. 1958. "Cultural Persistence among the Modern Iroquois." *Anthropos* 53(3–4): 473–83.

Fried, Morton H. 1967. *The Evolution of Political Society*. New York: Random House.

Friends, Society of. 1840. *The Case of the Seneca Indians in the State of New York*. Philadelphia: Merrihew and Thompson.

Galinée, René de Bréhant de. 1903. *Exploration of the Great Lakes, 1669–1670*, pt. 1. Ed. James H. Coyne. Papers and Records of the Ontario Historical Society 4. Toronto.

Garrad, Charles, and Conrad E. Heidenreich. 1978. "Khionontateronon (Petun)." In *Handbook of North American Indians, vol. 15: Northeast*, ed. Bruce G. Trigger, 394–97. Washington, D.C.: Smithsonian Institution.

Gehring, Charles T., and J. A. Schiltcamp, trans. and eds. 1987. *New Netherland Documents, vol. 17: Curaçao Papers (1640–1665)*. Interlaken, N.Y.: Heart of the Lakes Publishing.

Gehring, Charles T., and William A. Starna. 1988. "Preface." In *A Journey into Mohawk and Oneida Country, 1634–1635: The Journal of Harmen Meyndertsz van den Bogaert*, trans. and eds. C. T. Gehring and W. A. Starna. Syracuse, N.Y.: Syracuse University Press.

Gehring, Charles T., William A. Starna, and William N. Fenton. 1987. "The Tawagonshi Treaty of 1613: The Final Chapter." *New York History*, October: 373–93.

Gillette, Charles E. 1970. "Wampum Beads and Belts." Typescript, New York State Museum.

Gipson, Lawrence Henry. 1936–70. *The British Empire before the American Revolution*. 15 vols. Caldwell, Idaho: Caxton Printers; New York: Alfred Knopf.

———. 1939. *The British Empire before the American Revolution, vol. 4: Zones of International Friction: North America, South of the Great Lakes Region, 1748–1754*. New York: Knopf.

———. 1942. *The British Empire before the American Revolution, vol. 5: Zones of International Friction: The Great Lakes Frontier, Canada, the West Indies, India, 1748–1754*. New York: Knopf.

Goddard, Ives. 1978. "Delaware." In *Handbook of North American Indians, vol. 15: Northeast*, ed. Bruce G. Trigger, 213–39. Washington, D.C.: Smithsonian Institution.

———. 1984. "Agreskwe: A Northern Iroquian Deity." In *Extending the Rafters: Interdisciplinary Approaches to Iroquoian Studies*, eds. Michael K. Foster, Jack Campisi, and Marianne Mithun, 229–35. Albany: State University of New York Press.

Goldenweiser, Alexander A. 1912a. "On Iroquois Work, 1911." In *Summary Report of the Geological Survey Branch of the Canadian Department of Mines for the Calendar Year 1911*, 386–87. Ottawa.

———. 1912b. "The Death of Chief John A. Gibson." *American Anthropologist* 14(4): 692–94.

———. 1912–14. Field notebooks on Iroquois research, Six Nations Reserve, Canada, and Tuscarora, New York. National Museum of Man, Ottawa. Photocopies in American Philosophical Society Library, Philadelphia.

———. 1914a. "On Iroquois Work, 1912." In *Summary Report of the Geological Survey Branch of the Canadian Department of Mines for the Calendar Year 1912*, 464–75. Ottawa.

———. 1914b. "On Iroquois Work, 1913–1914." In *Summary Report of the Geological Survey Branch of the Canadian Department of Mines for the Calendar Year 1913*, 365–72. Ottawa.

———. 1916. Review of "The Constitution of the Five Nations" by Arthur C. Parker. *American Anthropologist* 17(2): 431–36.

———. 1922. *Early Civilization*. New York: Alfred A. Knopf.

Gookin, Daniel. 1792. "Historical Collections of the Indians in New England; of Their Several Nations, Numbers, Customs, Manners, Religion, and Government. . . ." Massachusetts Historical Society Collections, 1st ser., 1: 141–232.

Gottschalk, Louis R. 1950. *Lafayette between the American and the French Revolutions (1783–1789)*. Chicago: University of Chicago Press.

Grassman, Thomas, ed. 1969. *The Mohawk Indians and Their Valley; Being a Chronological Documentary Record to the End of 1693*. Schenectady, N.Y.: Eric Hugo Photography and Printing Co.

Graymont, Barbara. 1972. *The Iroquois in the American Revolution*. Syracuse, N.Y.: Syracuse University Press.

Green, Michael. 1982. *The Politics of Indian Removal: Creek Government and Society in Crisis*. University of Nebraska Press.

Griffin, James B. 1944. "The Iroquois in American Prehistory." *Papers of the Michigan Academy of Science, Arts, and Letters* 29: 357–74.

———. 1967. "Eastern North American Archaeology: A Summary." *Science* 156(3772): 175–91.

Grumet, Robert S. 1995. *Historic Contact: Indian People and Colonists in Today's Northeastern United States in the Sixteenth through Eighteenth Centuries*. Norman: University of Oklahoma Press.

Guldenzopf, David. 1986. "The Colonial Transformation of Mohawk Iroquois Society." Ph.D. diss., State University of New York at Albany.

Hagedorn, Nancy L. 1988. "'A Friend to Go between Them': The Interpreter as Cultural Broker during Anglo-Iroquois Councils, 1740–70." *Ethnohistory* 35: 60–80.

Hale, Horatio E. 1882. "A Lawgiver of the Stone Age." *Proceedings of the American Association for the Advancement of Science*. 30: 324–41.

———. 1883. *The Iroquois Book of Rites*. Philadelphia: D. G. Brinton. Reprint, Toronto: University of Toronto Press, 1963.

———. 1888. "Huron Folk-lore." *Journal of American Folk-lore* 1(3): 177–83.

———. 1891. "An Iroquois Condoling Council." *Proceedings and Transactions of the Royal Society of Canada*, 1st ser., 9(2): 77–112.

———. 1895. "An Iroquois Condoling Council." *Proceedings and Transactions of the Royal Society of Canada*, 2d. ser., 1(2): 45–65.

———. 1896. "Four Huron Wampum Records: A Study of Aboriginal American History and Mnemonic Symbols." *Journal of the Royal Anthropological Institute* (London) 26: 221–47.

Hallowell, A. Irving. 1946. "Some Psychological Characteristics of the Northeastern Indians." In *Man in Northeastern North America*, ed. Frederick Johnson, 195–225. Papers of the Robert S. Peabody Foundation for Archaeology, 3. Andover, Mass.

———. 1955. *Culture and Experience*. Philadelphia: University of Pennsylvania Press.

———. 1957. "The Backwash of the Frontier: The Impact of the Indian on American Culture." In *The Frontier in Perspective*, eds. Walker D. Wyman and Clifton B. Kroeber, 229–58. Madison: University of Wisconsin Press.

———. 1960. "The Beginnings of Anthropology in America." In *Selected Papers from the American Anthropologist, 1888–1920*, ed. Frederica de Laguna, 1–90. New York: Row, Peterson.

———. 1976. *Contributions to Anthropology: Selected Papers of A. Irving Hallowell*, eds. Raymond D. Fogelson et al. Chicago: University of Chicago Press.

Hamilton, Milton W., ed. 1953. "Guy Johnson's Opinions on the American Indian." *Pennsylvania Magazine of History and Biography* 77: 311–27.

Harris, George H. 1903. "Life of Horatio Jones." *Buffalo Historical Publications* 6: 383–526.

Heckewelder, John G. E. 1881. *An Account of the History, Manners, and Customs of the Indian Nations, Who Once Inhabited Pennsylvania and the Neighbouring States*. Rev. ed. Memoirs of the Pennsylvania Historical Society, 12. Philadelphia.

Heidenreich, Conrad E. 1971. *Huronia: A History and Geography of the Huron Indians, 1600–1650*. Toronto: McClelland and Stewart.

Hertzberg, Hazel W. 1966. *The Great Tree and the Longhouse: The Culture of the Iroquois*. New York: Macmillan.

Hewitt, J. N. B. 1892. "Legend of the Founding of the Iroquois League." *American Anthropologist* 5(2): 131–48.

———. 1894. "Era of the Formation of the Historic League of the Iroquois." *American Anthropologist* 7(1): 61–67.

———. 1902. "Orenda and a Definition of Religion." *American Anthropologist* 44(1): 33–46.

———. 1903. "Iroquoian Cosmology, Part 1." *Annual Report of the Bureau of American Ethnology for the Years 1899–1900*, 21: 127–339. Washington, D.C.

———. 1912. "White Dog Sacrifice." In *Handbook of American Indians North of Mexico*, ed. Frederick W. Hodge, 2: 939–44. Bureau of American Ethnology Bulletin 30. Washington, D.C.

———. 1916. "The Requickening Address of the League of the Iroquois." In *Holmes Anniversary Volume: Anthropological Essays Presented to William H. Holmes in Honor of His Seventieth Birthday*, 163–79. Washington, D.C.: J. W. Bryan Press.

———. 1917. "Some Esoteric Aspects of the League of the Iroquois." *Proceedings of the Nineteenth International Congress of Americanists*, 322–26. Washington, D.C.

———. 1919. "Explorations and Field-Work of the Smithsonian Institution." *Smithsonian Institution Publication* 2851, 69–71.

———. 1920. "A Constitutional League for Peace in the Stone Age of America: The League of the Iroquois and Its Constitution." *Annual Report of the Smithsonian Institution for 1918*, 527–45. Washington, D.C.

———. 1928. "Iroquoian Cosmology, Part 2." *Annual Report of the Bureau of American Ethnology for the Years 1925–1926*, 43: 449–819. Washington, D.C.

———. 1936. "Field Studies of the Iroquois in New York and Ontario, Canada." *Explorations and Field-Work of the Smithsonian Institution in 1936*, 83–86. Washington, D.C.

———. 1944. "The Requickening Address of the Iroquois Condolence Council." Ed. William N. Fenton. *Journal of the Washington Academy of Sciences* 34(3): 65–85.

———. Papers. National Anthropological Archives, Smithsonian Institution, Washington, D.C.

Hewitt, J.N.B., and William N. Fenton. 1945. "Some Mnemonic Pictographs Relating to the Iroquois Condolence Council." *Journal of the Washington Academy of Sciences* 35(10): 301–15.

Hodge, Frederick W., ed. 1912. *Handbook of American Indians North of Mexico*. 2 vols. Bureau of American Ethnology Bulletin 30. Washington, D.C.

Homans, George Caspar. 1962. *Sentiments and Activities: Essays in Social Science*. New York: Free Press.

Hough, Franklin B. 1880. *The Thousand Islands of the River St. Lawrence*. Syracuse, N.Y.: Davis, Bardeen.

Hough, Franklin B., ed. 1861. *Proceedings of the Commissioners of Indian Affairs, Appointed by Law for the Extinguishment of Indian Titles in the State of New York.* 2 vols. Albany: Joel Munsell. (Original manuscript in the Albany Institute.)

Hubbard, J. Niles. 1886. *An Account of Sa-go-ye-wat-ha, or Red Jacket and His People, 1750–1830.* Albany: Joel Munsell's Sons.

Hudson, Charles. 1976. *The Southeastern Indians.* University of Tennessee Press.

Hunt, George T. 1940. *The Wars of the Iroquois: A Study of Intertribal Trade Relations.* Madison: University of Wisconsin Press.

Innis, Harold A. 1956. *The Fur Trade in Canada: An Introduction to Canadian Economic History.* 2d. ed. Toronto: University of Toronto Press.

Jackson, Halliday. 1830a. *Civilization of the Indian Natives.* . . . Philadelphia.

———. 1830b. "Sketch of the Manners, Customs, Religion and Government of the Seneca Indians in 1800." 34-page addendum found in some copies of *Civilization of the Indian Natives.* . . .

Jacobs, Wilbur R. 1950. *Diplomacy and Indian Gifts: Anglo-French Rivalry along the Ohio and Northwest Frontiers, 1748–1763.* Stanford, Calif.: Stanford University Press.

Jenness, Diamond. 1933. "Three Iroquois Wampum Records." *Annual Report of the National Museum of Canada for 1931,* 25–28. Ottawa.

Jennings, Francis. 1975. *The Invasion of America: Indians, Colonialism and the Cant of Conquest.* Chapel Hill: University of North Carolina Press.

———. 1978. Susquehannock. In *Handbook of North American Indians, vol. 15: Northeast,* ed. Bruce G. Trigger, 362–67. Washington, D.C.: Smithsonian Institution.

———. 1984. *The Ambiguous Iroquois Empire: The Covenant Chain Confederation of Indian Tribes with the English Colonies from Its Beginnings to the Lancaster Treaty of 1744.* New York: W. W. Norton.

———. 1988. *Empire of Fortune: Crowns, Colonies, and Tribes in the Seven Years War in America.* New York: W. W. Norton.

Jennings, Francis, William N. Fenton, Mary A. Druke, and David R. Miller, eds. 1985a. *The History and Culture of Iroquois Diplomacy: An Interdisciplinary Guide to the Treaties of the Six Nations and Their League.* Syracuse, N.Y.: Syracuse University Press.

———, eds. 1985b. *Iroquois Indians, a Documentary History of the Diplomacy of the Six Nations and Their League: Guide to the Microfilm Collection.* Woodbridge, Conn.: Research Publications.

Jesuit Relations and Allied Documents: Travels and Explorations of the Jesuit Missionaries in New France, 1610–1791. 1896–1901. 73 vols. Reuben Gold Thwaites, ed. Cleveland: Burrows Brothers. Reprint, New York: Pageant Press, 1959.

Johannsen, Christina B., and John B. Ferguson, eds. 1983. *Iroquois Arts: A Directory of People and Their Work.* Waterville, N.Y.: Association for the Advancement of Native North American Arts and Crafts.

Johansen, Bruce E. 1990. "Native American Societies and the Evolution of Democracy in America, 1600–1800." *Ethnohistory* 37(3): 279–90.

Johnson, Elias. 1881. *Legends, Traditions and Laws of the Iroquois, or Six Nations, and History of the Tuscarora Indians.* Lockport, N.Y.: Union Printing and Publishing.

Johnson, Frederick, ed. 1946. *Man in Northeastern North America.* Papers of the Robert S. Peabody Foundation for Archaeology, 3. Andover, Mass.

Johnson, Sir William. 1756. "An Account of Conferences Held." London.

———. 1921–65. *The Papers of Sir William Johnson.* 14 vols. Eds. James Sullivan et al. Albany: University of the State of New York.

Johnston, Charles M., ed. 1964. *The Valley of the Six Nations: A Collection of Documents on the Indian Lands of the Grand River.* Toronto: University of Toronto Press.

Jones, Dorothy V. 1982. *License for Empire: Colonialism by Treaty in Early America.* Chicago: University of Chicago Press.

Journals of the Continental Congress, 1774–1789. 1904–37. Washington, D.C.: Government Printing Office.

Kalm, Peter. 1964. *The America of 1750: Peter Kalm's Travels in North America. The English Version of 1770.* 2 vols. Ed. Adolph B. Benson. New York: Dover.

Kelsay, Isabel Thompson. 1984. *Joseph Brant, 1743–1807: Man of Two Worlds.* Syracuse, N.Y.: Syracuse University Press.

Kennedy, Archibald. 1751. *The Importance of Gaining and Preserving the Friendship of the Indians to the British Interest, Considered.* New York: James Parker. London: E. Care, Jr., at the St. John's Gate, 1752. (Includes Benjamin Franklin's letter of 1750, pp. 38–46. Copy seen at the American Philosophical Society Library.)

Kent, Donald H., ed. 1979. *Early American Indian Documents, Treaties and Laws. Pennsylvania and Delaware Treaties, 1629–1737,* vol 1. Washington, D.C.: University Publications of America.

Kent, Donald H., and Merle H. Deardorff, eds. 1960. John Adlum on the Allegheny: Memoirs for the Year 1794. *Pennsylvania Magazine of History and Biography* 84(3, 4): 265–324, 435–80.

Kirkland, Samuel. 1764–1804. Kirkland Papers. Hamilton College Library, Clinton, N.Y.

Klinck, Carl F., and James J. Talman, eds. 1970. *The Journal of Major John Norton, 1809–1816.* Toronto: Champlain Society.

Knopf, Richard C., transcriber and ed. 1960. *Anthony Wayne, a Name in Arms . . . . : The Wayne-Knox-Pickering Correspondence.* Pittsburgh: University of Pittsburgh Press.

Lafitau, Joseph-François. 1724. *Moeurs des sauvages amériquains, comparées aux moeurs des premiers temps.* 2 vols. Paris: Saugrain l'aîné.

Lahontan, Louis A., Baron de. 1905. *New Voyages to North America.* 2 vols. Ed. Rueben G. Thwaites. Chicago.

Landy, David. 1978. Tuscarora among the Iroquois. In *Handbook of North American Indians, vol. 15: Northeast,* ed. Bruce G. Trigger, 512–24. Washington, D.C.: Smithsonian Institution.

Leder, Lawrence H. 1961. *Robert Livingston, 1654–1728, and the Politics of Colonial New York.* Chapel Hill: University of North Carolina Press.

Lee, Arthur, M.D. 1772. "Extracts of Some Letters, from Sir William Johnson, Bart. to Arthur Lee, M.D. F.R.S. on the Customs, Manners, and Language of the Northern Indians of America." *Philosophical Transactions of the Royal Society of London,* 63(1): 142–48.

Lenig, Donald. 1965. "The Oak Hill Horizon and Its Relation to the Development of Five Nations Iroquois Culture." *Researches and Transactions of the New York State Archaeological Association* 15(1): 1–114.

Lévi-Strauss, Claude. 1963. *Social Anthropology.* New York: Basic Books.

l'Incarnation, Marie de (Marie Guyart). 1681. *Lettres à son fils.* Paris.

Lincoln, Benjamin. 1836. "Journal of a Treaty, 1793." Massachusetts Historical Society Collections, 3d ser., 5: 109–76.

Linton, Ralph. 1936. *The Study of Man.* New York: Appleton-Century.

Livingston, Robert. 1956. *The Livingston Indian Records, 1666–1723.* Ed. Lawrence H. Leder. Gettysburg: Pennsylvania Historical Association.

Llewellyn, K. N., and E. Adamson Hoebel. 1941. *The Cheyenne Way: Conflict and Case Law in Primitive Jurisprudence.* Norman: University of Oklahoma Press.

Long, J. C. 1933. *Lord Jeffery Amherst, a Soldier of the King.* New York: Macmillan.

Lothrop, S. K. 1848. "Life of Samuel Kirkland, Missionary to the Indians." *Library of American Biography,* ed. Jared Sparks, 2d ser., 15: 137–368. Boston.

Lounsbury, Floyd G. 1960. "Iroquois Place-Names in the Champlain Valley. Report of the New York–Vermont Interstate Commission on the Lake Champlain Basin, 1960." *Legislative Document* 9: 23–66. Reprint, New York State Education Department, Albany.

———. 1961. "Iroquois-Cherokee Linguistic Relations." In *Symposium on Cherokee and Iroquois Culture,* eds. William N. Fenton and John Gulick, 9–17. Bureau of American Ethnology Bulletin 180. Washington, D.C.

———. 1964a. "The Structural Analysis of Kinship Semantics." In *Proceedings of the Ninth International Congress of Linguists*, ed. Horace G. Lunt, 1073–93. The Hague: Mouton.

———. 1964b. "A Formal Account of the Crow- and Omaha-type Kinship Terminologies." In *Explorations in Cultural Anthropology: Essays in Honor of George Peter Murdock*, ed. Ward H. Goodenough, 351–93. New York: McGraw-Hill.

———. 1978. "Iroquoian Languages." In *Handbook of North American Indians, vol. 15: Northeast*, ed. Bruce G. Trigger, 334–43. Washington, D.C.: Smithsonian Institution.

Lydekker, John W. 1938. *The Faithful Mohawks*. New York: Macmillan.

McCausland, Richard. 1786. "Particulars Relative to the Nature and Customs of the Indians of North-America." Royal Society of London, *Transactions*, 76, part 1: 229–35.

McIlwain, Charles H. 1915. "Introduction." In *An Abridgement of the Indian Affairs Contained in Four Folio Volumes, Transacted in the Colony of New York from the Year 1678 to the Year 1751*, by Peter Wraxall. Harvard Historical Studies 21. Cambridge, Mass.: Harvard University Press.

MacNeish, Richard S. 1952. *Iroquois Pottery Types: A Technique for the Study of Iroquois Prehistory*. Anthropological Series 31, National Museum of Canada Bulletin 124. Ottawa.

Madison, James. 1900–1910. *Writings*. 9 vols. Ed. Gaillard Hunt. New York: G. P. Putnam's Sons.

Manley, Henry S. 1932. *The Treaty of Fort Stanwix, 1784*. Rome, N.Y.: Rome Sentinel Co.

Margry, Pierre, ed. 1876–86. *Découvertes et établissements des Français dans l'ouest et dans le sud de l'Amérique septentrionale, 1614–1754: Mémoires et documents originaux*. 6 vols. Paris: D. Jouaust.

Marshe, Witham. 1800. "Witham Marshe's Journal of the Treaty Held with the Six Nations by the Commissioners of Maryland, and Other Provinces, at Lancaster, in Pennsylvania, June, 1744." Massachusetts Historical Society Collections, 1st ser., 7: 171–201.

Megapolensis, Johannes, Jr. 1857. "Short Sketch of the Mohawk Indians in New Netherland, etc." Translated, revised, and introduced by John Romeyn Brodhead. *New-York Historical Society Collections*, 2d. ser., 3(1): 137–60. New York: D. Appleton.

———. 1909 [1644]. "A Short Account of the Mohawk Indians . . . 1664." In *Narratives of New Netherland, 1609–1664*, ed. J. Franklin Jameson, 163–80. New York: Charles Scribner's Sons.

Michelson, Gunther. 1973. *A Thousand Words of Mohawk*. National Museum of Man, Mercury Series no. 5. Ottawa.

———. 1974. "Upstreaming Bruyas." In *Papers in Linguistics from the 1972 Conference on Iroquois Research*. ed. Michael K. Foster, 36–46. National Museum of Man, Ethnology Divison, Mercury Series Paper 10. Ottawa.

———. 1977. "Iroquois Population Statistics." *Man in the Northeast* 14: 3–17.

———. 1988. "An Account of an Iroquois Condolence Council." *Man in the Northeast* 36: 61–75.

———. 1991. "Iroquoian Terms for Wampum." *International Journal of American Linguistics* 57(1): 108–16.

Mithun, Marianne. 1984. "The Proto-Iroquoians: Cultural Reconstruction from Lexical Materials." In *Extending the Rafters: Interdisciplinary Approaches to Iroquoian Studies*, eds. Michael K. Foster, Jack Campisi, and Marianne Mithun, 259–81. Albany: State University of New York Press.

Monroe, James. 1898–1903. *Writings*. 7 vols. Ed. S. M. Hamilton. New York: G. P. Putnam's Sons.

Montbas, Vicomte de. 1929. *Avec Lafayette chez les Iroquois*. Libraire de Paris: Firmin-Didot.

Mooney, James. 1894. *The Siouan Tribes of the East*. Bureau of American Ethnology Bulletin 22. Washington, D.C.

————. 1900. "Myths of the Cherokee." *Nineteenth Annual Report of the Bureau of American Ethnology for the Years 1897–1898*. Pt. 1, 3–548. Washington, D.C.

————. 1928. *The Aboriginal Population of America North of Mexico*. Ed. John R. Swanton. Smithsonian Miscellaneous Collections 80(7). Washington, D.C.

Moorehead, Warren King. 1922. *The Hopewell Group of Ohio*. Anthropological Series 6(5). Chicago: Field Museum of Natural History.

Morgan, Lewis H. 1850. "Report to the Regents of the University upon the Articles Furnished to the Indian Collection." *New York State Cabinet of Antiquities' Annual Report* 3: 65–97. Albany.

————. 1851. *League of the Ho-de-no-sau-nee, or Iroquois*. Rochester, N.Y.: Sage. Reprinted as *League of the Iroquois*, New York: Corinth Books, 1962.

————. 1852. "Report on the Fabrics, Inventions, Implements, and Utensils of the Iroquois." *New York State Cabinet of Antiquities' Annual Report* 5, 66–117. Albany.

————. 1871. *Systems of Consanguinity and Affinity in the Human Family*. Smithsonian Contributions to Knowledge, 17. Washington, D.C.

————. 1877. *Ancient Society; or, Researches in the Lines of Human Progress from Savagery through Barbarism to Civilization*. New York: Henry Holt.

————. 1901. *League of the Ho-de-no-sau-nee, or Iroquois*. 2 vols. Ed. Herbert M. Lloyd. New York: Dodd, Mead.

————. 1964. *Ancient Society*. Ed. Leslie A. White. Cambridge, Mass.: Harvard University Press.

————. Papers. Department of Rare Books and Special Collections, University of Rochester Library, Rochester, N.Y.

Morison, Samuel Eliot. 1952. *The Oxford History of the American People*. New York: Oxford University Press.

Nammack, Georgiana C. 1969. *Fraud, Politics, and the Dispossession of the Indians: The Iroquois Land Frontier in the Colonial Period*. Norman: University of Oklahoma Press.

Narratives of New Netherland, 1609–1664. 1909. J. Franklin Jameson, ed. New York: Charles Scribner's Sons.

Newhouse, Seth. 1885. "Cosmogony of De-ka-na-wi-da's Government of the Iroquois Confederacy: The Original Literal Historical Narratives of the Iroquois Confederacy." Manuscript. Public Archives of Canada, folder MG 19 F. 26, Ottawa. Photocopies in the American Philosophical Society Library, Philadelphia.

New York Assembly. 1889. *Report on the Indian Problem*. Assembly Document 51. Albany.

New York Secretary of State. 1887. *Journals of the Military Expedition of Major General John Sullivan against the Six Nations of Indians in 1779*. Ed. Frederick Cook. Auburn, N.Y.: Knapp, Peck and Thomson.

New York State Historical Association. 1933–37. "The Sullivan-Clinton Campaign of 1779." In *History of the State of New York*, ed. Alexander C. Flick, 4: 185–216. New York: Columbia University Press.

Niemczycki, Mary Ann Palmer. 1984. *The Origin and Development of the Seneca and Cayuga Tribes of New York State*. Rochester Museum and Science Center Research Records 17. Rochester, N.Y.

Noon, John A. 1949. *Law and Government of the Grand River Iroquois*. Viking Fund Publications in Anthropology, 12. New York.

Norton, John (Teyoninhokarawen). Ca. 1809–16. "Letter Book." Ayer Collection, ms. no. 654. Newberry Library, Chicago.

Norton, Thomas Elliot. 1974. *The Fur Trade in Colonial New York, 1686–1776*. Madison: University of Wisconsin Press.

O'Callaghan, Edmund B., ed. 1849–51. *Documentary History of the State of New York*. 4 vols. Albany: Weed, Parsons.

————, ed. 1853–87. *Documents Relative to the Colonial History of the State of New York, Procured in Holland, England and France, by John R. Brodhead.* 15 vols. Albany: Weed, Parsons.

Orchard, William C. 1929. *Beads and Beadwork of the American Indians: A Study Based on Specimens in the Museum of the American Indian, Heye Foundation.* Contributions from the Museum of the American Indian, Heye Foundation, 11. New York.

O'Reilly Collection (Indians of Western New York). 15 vols. New York Historical Society, New York.

Palstits, Victor H., ed. 1910. *Minutes of the Executive Council of the Province of New York; Administration of Francis Lovelace, 1668–1673.* 2 vols. Albany.

Pargellis, Stanley M. 1933. *Lord Loudoun in North America.* New Haven, Conn.: Yale University Press.

Parker, Arthur C. 1909. "Secret Medicine Societies of the Seneca." *American Anthropologist* n.s. 11(2): 161–85. (Reprinted in Parker 1913, 113–30.)

————. 1910. "Iroquois Uses of Maize and Other Food Plants." *New York State Museum Bulletin* 144(482): 5–113. Albany.

————. 1912. "Certain Iroquois Tree Myths and Symbols." *American Anthropologist* 14(4): 608–12.

————. 1913. "The Code of Handsome Lake, the Seneca Prophet." *New York State Museum Bulletin* 163. Albany.

————. 1916a. "The Origin of the Iroquois as Suggested by Their Archaeology." *American Anthropologist* 18(4): 479–507.

————. 1916b. "The Constitution of the Five Nations." *New York State Museum Bulletin* 184: 7–158.

————. 1919. "The Life of General Ely S. Parker, Last Grand Sachem of the Iroquois and General Grant's Military Secretary." *Publications of the Buffalo Historical Society* 23. Buffalo.

————. 1923. "Seneca Myths and Folk Tales." *Buffalo Historical Society Publications* 27: 59–73. Buffalo, N.Y.

————. 1968. *Parker on the Iroquois.* Ed. William N. Fenton. Syracuse, N.Y.: Syracuse University Press.

Parkman, Francis. 1865–92. *France and England in North America: A Series of Historical Narratives.* 9 vols. Boston: Little, Brown. (1899 New Library ed., 12 vols.)

————. 1884. *Montcalm and Wolfe.* 2 vols. Boston: Little, Brown.

————. 1889. *Count Frontenac and New France under Louis XIV.* Boston: Little Brown.

Peckham, Howard H. 1947. *Pontiac and the Indian Uprising.* Princeton, N.J.: Princeton University Press.

Pendergast, James F. 1994. "The Kakouagoga or Kahkwas, an Iroquoian Nation Destroyed in the Niagara Region." *Proceedings of the American Philosophical Society* 138(1): 96–144.

Pennsylvania Archives, 1852–1949. 138 vols. Eds. Samuel Hazard et al. Philadelphia: Joseph Severns; Harrisburg: Commonwealth of Pennsylvania.

Pennsylvania Provincial Council. 1838–53. *Minutes of the Provincial Council of Pennsylvania from the Organization to the Termination of the Proprietary Government, March 10, 1683, to September 27, 1775.* 16 vols. Ed. Samuel Hazard. Harrisburg: Commonwealth of Pennsylvania.

Pickering, Timothy. 1896. "Calendar of Pickering Papers." Massachusetts Historical Society Collections, 6th ser., 8. Boston.

Pilkington, Walter, ed. 1980. *The Journals of Samuel Kirkland: Eighteenth-Century Missionary to the Iroquois, Government Agent, Father of Hamilton College.* Clinton, N.Y.: Hamilton College.

Pilling, James Constantine. 1888. *Bibliography of the Iroquoian Languages.* Bureau of American Ethnology Bulletin 6. Washington, D.C.

Piquet, Abbé François. 1754. "Sur trois airs Iroquois." *Journal Etranger*, May 1754, 229–35. Paris: Saugrain le fils.

Proctor, Thomas. 1791. "Narrative." In *American State Papers—Indian Affairs*, 149–65.

———. 1864–65. "Narrative of Col. Thomas Proctor." In *An Authentic and Comprehensive History of Buffalo*, by William Ketchum, 2 vols., 1: 413–26, 2: 305–18. Buffalo: Rockwell, Baker and Hill.

Quain, Buell H. 1937. "The Iroquois." In *Cooperation and Competition among Primitive Peoples*, ed. Margaret Mead, 240–81. New York: McGraw-Hill. Reprint, Boston: Beacon Press, 1961.

Radcliffe-Brown, A. R. 1958. *Method in Social Anthropology, Selected Essays*. Ed. B. Srinivas. Chicago: University of Chicago Press.

Radisson, Pierre E. 1865. *Voyages of Peter Esprit Radisson, Being an Account of His Travels and Experiences among the North American Indians, from 1652–1684*. Boston: Prince Society.

———. 1967. *The Explorations of Pierre Esprit Radisson*. Ed. Arthur T. Adams. Minneapolis: Ross and Haines.

Randle, Martha C. 1951. "Iroquois Women, Then and Now." In *Symposium on Local Diversity in Iroquois Culture*, ed. William N. Fenton, 167–80. Bureau of American Ethnology Bulletin 149. Washington, D.C.

———. 1953. "The Waugh Collection of Iroquois Folktales." *Proceedings of the American Philosophical Society* 97: 629.

Richter, Daniel K. 1982. "Rediscovered Links in the Covenant Chain: Previously Unpublished Transcripts of New York Indian Treaty Minutes, 1677–1691." American Antiquarian Society, *Proceedings* 92: 63–66.

———. 1983. "War and Culture: The Iroquois Experience." *William and Mary Quarterly*, 3d ser., 11: 528–59.

———. 1985a. "Iroquois versus Iroquois: Jesuit Missions and Christianity in Village Politics, 1642–1686." *Ethnohistory* 32(1): 1–16.

———. 1985b. "Up the Cultural Stream: Three Recent Works in Iroquois Studies." *Ethnohistory* 32(4): 363–69.

———. 1987. "Ordeals of the Longhouse: The Five Nations in Early American History." In *Beyond the Covenant Chain: The Iroquois and Their Neighbors in Indian North America, 1600–1800*, eds. Daniel K. Richter and James H. Merrell, 11–28. Syracuse, N.Y.: Syracuse University Press.

———. 1992. *The Ordeal of the Longhouse: The Peoples of the Iroquois League in the Era of European Colonization*. Chapel Hill: University of North Carolina Press.

Ritchie, William A. 1944. *The Pre-Iroquoian Occupations of New York State*. Rochester Museum of Arts and Sciences Memoir 1. Rochester, N.Y.

———. 1955–56. "The Indian in His Environment." *New York State Conservationist*, Dec.–Jan.: 23–27.

———. 1965. *The Archaeology of New York State*. Garden City, N.Y.: Natural History Press. Rev. ed. 1969.

Ritchie, William A., and Robert E. Funk. 1973. *Aboriginal Settlement Patterns in the Northeast*. New York State Museum and Science Service Memoir 20. Albany.

Robertson, William. 1777. *The History of America*. London: W. Strahan.

Rogers, E. S. 1978. "Southeastern Ojibwa." In *Handbook of North American Indians, vol. 15: Northeast*, 760–771. Washington, D.C.: Smithsonian Institution.

Rothenberg, Diane. 1976. "Friends Like These: An Ethnohistorical Analysis of the Interaction between Allegany Senecas and Quakers, 1798–1823." *Dissertation Abstracts International* 36(12): 8156–57A.

Rotstein, Abraham. 1967. "Fur Trade and Empire: An Institutional Analysis." Ph.D. diss., Department of Economics, University of Toronto.

Ruttenber, Edward M. 1872. *History of the Indian Tribes of Hudson's River: Their Origin, Manners and Customs, Tribal and Sub-tribal Organizations, Wars, Treaties, etc.* Albany: J. Munsell.

Sagard, Gabriel. 1939. *The Long Journey to the Country of the Hurons*. Ed. George M. Wrong. Toronto: Champlain Society.

Sanson d'Abbéville, Nicholas. 1657. *L'Amérique en plusiers cartes*. Paris: Chez L'Auteur. (Copy in Beinecke Library, Yale University.)

Sapir, Edward. 1916. *Time Perspective in Aboriginal American Culture: A Study in Method*. Anthropological Series 13, Memoirs of the Canadian Geological Survey 90. Ottawa.

Savery, William. 1837. "A Journal of the Life, Travels and Religious Labours of William Savery." Comp. Jonathan Evans. *The Friends Library* 1: 325–68ff. Philadelphia.

Schoolcraft, Henry R. 1839. *Algic Researches, Comprising Inquiries Respecting the Mental Characteristics of the North American Indians*. 2 vols. New York: Harper and Brothers.

———. 1846. *Notes on the Iroquois; or, Contributions to the Statistics, Aboriginal History, Antiquities and General Ethnology of Western New York*. New York: Bartlett and Welford.

Schuyler, Peter. Papers. New York Public Library.

Scott, Duncan C. 1912. "Traditional History of the Confederacy of the Six Nations, Prepared by a Committee of the Chiefs." *Transactions of the Royal Society of Canada*, 3d. ser., 5(2): 195–246.

Seaver, James E. 1925. *A Narrative of the Life of Mary Jemison, the White Woman of the Genesee*. New York: New York Historical and Preservation Society.

Service, Elman R. 1971. *Primitive Social Organization: An Evolutionary Perspective*. 2d. ed. New York: Random House.

Sewall, Samuel. 1973. *Journal, 1674–1729*. 2 vols. Ed. M. Halsey Thomas. New York: Farrar, Straus, and Giroux.

Shetrone, Henry Clyde. 1930. *The Mound Builders*. New York: Appleton.

Shimony, Annemarie A. 1961. *Conservatism among the Iroquois at the Six Nations Reserve*. Yale University Publications in Anthropology 65. New Haven, Conn.

Smith, Donald B. 1987. *Sacred Feathers: The Reverend Peter Jones (Kahkewaqonaby) and the Mississauga Indians*. Lincoln: University of Nebraska Press.

Smith, Erminnie A. 1883. "Myths of the Iroquois." *Second Annual Report of the Bureau of American Ethnology for the Years 1880–1881*, 47–116. Washington, D.C.: Smithsonian Institution.

Smith, William. 1757. *The History of the Province of New-York*. London: Thomas Wilcox.

Snow, Dean R. 1984. "Iroquois Prehistory." In *Extending the Rafters: Interdisciplinary Approaches to Iroquoian Studies*, eds. Michael K. Foster, Jack Campisi, and Marianne Mithun, 241–57. Albany: State University of New York Press.

Snow, Dean R., and Kim M. Lamphear. 1988. "European Contact and Indian Depopulation in the Northeast: The Timing of the First Epidemics." *Ethnohistory* 35(1): 15–33.

Snow, Dean R., and W. A. Starna. 1989. "Sixteenth-Century Depopulation: A View from the Mohawk Valley." *American Anthropologist* 91: 142–49.

Snyder, Charles M. 1978. *Red and White on the New York Frontier . . . from the Papers of Erastus Granger, Indian Agent 1807–1819*. Harrison, N.Y.: Harbor Hill Books.

Snyderman, George S. 1948. "Behind the Tree of Peace: A Sociological Analysis of Iroquois Warfare." *Pennsylvania Archaeologist* 18(3–4): 3–93.

———. 1953. "A Preliminary Survey of American Indian Manuscripts in Repositories of the Philadelphia Area." *Proceedings of the American Philosophical Society* 97: 596–610.

Speck, Frank G. 1920. "Decorative Art and Basketry of the Cherokee." Public Museum of the City of Milwaukee, Bulletin 2, 158–86.

———. 1945. *The Iroquois: A Study in Cultural Evolution*. Cranbrook Institute of Science, Bulletin 23. Bloomfield Hills, Mich.

———. 1949. *Midwinter Rites of the Cayuga Longhouse*. Philadelphia: University of Pennsylvania Press.

Speck, Frank G., and W. C. Orchard. 1925. "The Penn Wampum Belts." Museum of the American Indian, Heye Foundation, *Leaflets* 4: 1–20. New York.

Stone, William L. 1838. *Life of Joseph Brant—Thayendanegea, Including the Border Wars of the American Revolution, and Sketches of the Indian Campaigns of Generals Harmer, St. Clair, and Wayne, and Other*

Matters Connected with the Indian Relations of the United States and Great Britain, from the Peace of 1783 to the Indian Peace of 1795. 2 vols. New York: George Dearborn.

———. 1841. *The Life and Times of Red Jacket, or Sa-go-ye-wat-ha; Being the Sequel to the History of the Six Nations.* New York: Wiley and Putnam.

Swanton, John R. 1938. "John Napoleon Brinton Hewitt." *American Anthropologist* 40: 286–90.

Swanton, John R., and Roland B. Dixon. 1914. "Primitive American History." *American Anthropologist* n.s. 16: 376–412.

Tanner, Helen Hornbeck. 1987. *Atlas of Great Lakes Indian History.* Norman: University of Oklahoma Press.

Taylor, Francis R. 1925. *Life of William Savery of Philadelphia (1750–1804).* New York: Macmillan.

Thomas, Robert. 1964. "Powerless Politics." Paper read at the annual meeting of the American Anthropological Association, Detroit.

Thompson, Stith. 1929. *Tales of the North American Indians.* Cambridge, Mass.: Harvard University Press.

———. 1932–36. *Motif-Index of Folk-Literature: A Classification of Narrative Elements in Folk-tales, Ballads, Myths, Fables, Mediaeval Romances, Exempla, Fabliaux, Jest-Books, and Local Legends.* 6 vols. Indiana University Studies 96–97, 100–101, 105–6, 108–12. Rev. and enl. ed., Bloomington: Indiana University Press, 1955–58.

Thomson, Charles. 1759. *An Enquiry into the Causes of the Alienation of the Delaware and Shawanese Indians from the British Interest, and into the Measures Taken for Recovering Their Friendship.* London.

Tooker, Elisabeth. 1964. *An Ethnography of the Huron Indians, 1615–1649.* Bureau of American Ethnology Bulletin 190. Washington, D.C.

———. 1968. "On the New Religion of Handsome Lake." *Anthropological Quarterly* 41: 187–200.

———. 1978. "The League of the Iroquois: Its History, Politics, and Ritual." In *Handbook of North American Indians, vol. 15: Northeast,* ed. Bruce G. Trigger, 418–41. Washington, D.C.: Smithsonian Institution.

———. 1980. "Isaac N. Hurd's Ethnographic Studies of the Iroquois: Their Significance and Ethnographic Value." *Ethnohistory* 27(4): 363–69.

———. 1984. "The Demise of the Susquehannocks: A Seventeenth-Century Mystery." *Pennsylvania Archaeologist* 54(3–4): 1–10.

———. 1988. "The United States Constitution and the Iroquois League." *Ethnohistory* 35(4): 305–36.

———. 1989. "On the Development of the Handsome Lake Religion." *Proceedings of the American Philosophical Society* 133: 35–50.

———. 1990. "Rejoinder to Johansen." *Ethnohistory* 37(3): 291–97.

Tooker, Elisabeth, ed. 1967. *Iroquois Culture, History, and Prehistory: Proceedings of the 1965 Conference on Iroquois Research.* Albany: New York State Museum and Science Service.

———, ed. 1985. *An Iroquois Source Book, vol. 1: Political and Social Organization.* New York: Garland.

Trelease, Allen W. 1960. *Indian Affairs in Colonial New York: The Seventeenth Century.* Ithaca, N.Y.: Cornell University Press.

Trigger, Bruce G. 1971. "The Mohawk-Mahican War (1624–1628): The Establishment of a Pattern." *Canadian Historical Review* 52(3): 276–86.

———. 1976. *The Children of Aataentsic: A History of the Huron People to 1660.* 2 vols. Montreal: McGill-Queen's University Press.

———. 1978. "The Strategy of Iroquoian Prehistory." In *Archaeological Essays in Honor of Irving B. Rouse,* ed. R. C. Dunnell and E. S. Hall, Jr., 275–310. The Hague: Mouton.

———. 1982. "Ethnohistory: Problems and Prospects." *Ethnohistory* 29: 1–19.

———. 1985. *Natives and Newcomers: Canada's "Heroic Age" Reconsidered*. Montreal: McGill-Queen's University Press.

———. 1986. "Ethnohistory: The Unfinished Edifice." *Ethnohistory* 33(3): 253–67.

Trigger, Bruce G., ed. 1978. *Handbook of North American Indians, vol. 15: Northeast*. Washington, D.C.: Smithsonian Institution.

Tuck, James A. 1971. *Onondaga Iroquois Prehistory: A Study in Settlement Archaeology*. Syracuse, N.Y.: Syracuse University Press.

Tylor, E. B. 1896. "The Hale Series of Huron Wampum Belts." *Journal of the Royal Anthropological Institute* (London) 26: 248–54.

van den Bogaert, Harmen M. 1988. *A Journey into Mohawk and Oneida Country, 1634–1635: The Journal of Harmen Meyndertsz van den Bogaert*. Trans. and eds. Charles T. Gehring and William A. Starna. Syracuse, N.Y.: Syracuse University Press.

Van Doren, Carl. 1938a. *Benjamin Franklin*. New York: Viking Press.

———. 1938b. "Introduction." In *Indian Treaties Printed by Benjamin Franklin, 1736–1762*, ed. Julian P. Boyd. Philadelphia: Historical Society of Pennsylvania.

Van Laer, Arnold J. F. 1923. *Minutes of the Court of Fort Orange and Beverwyck, 1657–1660*. 2 vols. Albany.

———. 1924. *Documents Relating to New Netherland, 1624–1626, in the Henry E. Huntington Library*. San Marino, Calif.: Henry E. Huntington Library.

Van Laer, Arnold J. F., ed. 1908. *Van Rensselaer Bouvier Manuscripts, Being the Letters of Kiliaen Van Rensselaer, 1630–1643, and Other Documents Relating to the Colony of Rensselaerwyck*. Albany: University of the State of New York.

Vaughan, Alden T. 1965. *New England Frontier: Puritans and Indians, 1620–1675*. Boston: Little, Brown.

Wade, Mason. 1988. "French and Indian Policies." In *Handbook of North American Indians, vol. 4: History of Indian-White Relations*, ed. Wilcomb E. Washburn, 21–24. Washington, D.C.: Smithsonian Institution.

Wadsworth, Benjamin. 1852. "Journal." Massachusetts Historical Society Collections, ser. 4, 1: 102–10.

Wainwright, Nicholas B. 1947. "The Opinions of George Croghan on the American Indian." *Pennsylvania Magazine of History and Biography* 71: 152–59.

———. 1959. *George Croghan, Wilderness Diplomat*. Chapel Hill: University of North Carolina Press.

Wallace, Anthony F. C. 1949. *King of the Delawares: Teedyuscung, 1700–1763*. Philadelphia: University of Pennsylvania Press.

———. 1952. "Halliday Jackson's Journal to the Seneca Indians." *Pennsylvania History* 19: 117–47, 325–49.

———. 1956. "Revitalization Movements: Some Theoretical Considerations for Their Comparative Study." *American Anthropologist* 58(2): 264–81.

———. 1957a. "Origins of Iroquois Neutrality: The Grand Settlement of 1701." *Pennsylvania History* 24(3): 223–35.

———. 1957b. "Political Organization and Land Tenure among the Northeastern Indians, 1600–1830." *Southwestern Journal of Anthropology* 13(4): 301–21.

———. 1958a. "The Dekanawideh Myth Analyzed as the Record of a Revitalization Movement." *Ethnohistory* 5(2): 118–30.

———. 1958b. "Dreams as Wishes of the Soul: A Type of Psychoanalytic Theory among the Seventeenth-Century Iroquois." *American Anthropologist* 60(2): 234–48.

———. 1970. *The Death and Rebirth of the Seneca*. New York: Alfred A. Knopf.

———. 1978. "Origins of the Longhouse Religion." In *Handbook of North American Indians, vol. 15: Northeast*, ed. Bruce G. Trigger, 442–48. Washington, D.C.: Smithsonian Institution.

Wallace, Paul A. W. 1945. *Conrad Weiser, 1696–1760, Friend of Colonist and Mohawk*. Philadelphia: University of Pennsylvania Press.

———. 1946. *The White Roots of Peace*. Philadelphia: University of Pennsylvania Press.

———. 1948. "The Return of Hiawatha." *New York History* 29(4): 385–403.

Waller, G. M. 1960. *Samuel Vetch, Colonial Enterpriser*. Chapel Hill: University of North Carolina Press.

Washington, George. 1891. *The Writings of George Washington, vol. 10: 1782–1785*. Ed. Worthington Chauncey Ford. New York: G. P. Putnam's Sons.

Waugh, Frederick W. 1916. *Iroquois Foods and Food Preparation*. Anthropological Series 12, Memoirs of the Canadian Geological Survey 86. Ottawa.

Weaver, Sally M. 1973. "Politics of the Iroquois: An Analysis of Political Change." Manuscript. Fenton Papers, ser. 4. American Philosophical Society Library, Philadelphia.

———. 1978. "Six Nations on the Grand River, Ontario." In *Handbook of North American Indians, vol. 15: Northeast*, ed. Bruce G. Trigger, 525–36. Washington, D.C.: Smithsonian Institution.

———. 1984. "Seth Newhouse and the Grand River Confederacy at Mid-Nineteenth Century." In *Extending the Rafters: Interdisciplinary Approaches to Iroquoian Studies*, eds. Michael K. Foster, Jack Campisi, and Marianne Mithun, 165–82. Albany: State University of New York Press.

———. 1994. "The Iroquois: The Consolidation of the Grand River Reserve in the Mid-Nineteenth Century, 1847–1875." In *Aboriginal Ontario*, eds. Ed Rogers and Donald Smith, 182–212. Toronto: Dundern Books.

Webb, Stephen Saunders. 1984. *1676: The End of American Independence*. New York: Alfred A. Knopf.

Weld, Isaac. 1807. *Travels through the States of North America and the Provinces of Upper and Lower Canada during 1795, 1796, 1797*. 2 vols. London.

Weslager, Clinton A. 1972. *The Delaware Indians: A History*. New Brunswick, N.J.: Rutgers University Press.

White, Marian. 1978a. "Erie." In *Handbook of North American Indians, vol. 15: Northeast*, ed. Bruce G. Trigger, 412–17. Washington, D.C.: Smithsonian Institution.

———. 1978b. "Neutral and Wenro." In *Handbook of North American Indians, vol. 15: Northeast*, ed. Bruce G. Trigger, 407–11. Washington, D.C.: Smithsonian Institution.

Williams, Lorraine E., and Karen A. Flinn. 1990. *Trade Wampum, New Jersey to the Plains*. Trenton: New Jersey State Museum.

Williams, Roger. 1643. *A Key into the Language of America*. London: Gregory Dexter. Reprint, Detroit: Wayne State University Press, 1973.

Winsor, Justin, ed. 1884–99. *Narrative and Critical History of America*. 8 vols. Boston: Houghton, Mifflin.

———. 1895. *The Mississippi Basin: The Struggle in America between England and France (1697–1763)*. Boston: Houghton, Mifflin.

Winthrop, John, Jr. 1929–47. *Winthrop Papers*. 5 vols. Ed. Allyn B. Forbes. Boston: Massachusetts Historical Society.

Woodbury, Hanni. 1992. *Concerning the League: The Iroquois League Tradition as Dictated in Onondaga by John Arthur Gibson*. Algonquian and Iroquoian Linguistics Memoir 9. Winnipeg.

Wraxall, Peter. 1915. *An Abridgement of the Indian Affairs Contained in Four Folio Volumes, Transacted in the Colony of New York from the Year 1678 to the Year 1751*. Ed. Charles H. McIlwain. Harvard Historical Studies 21. Cambridge, Mass.: Harvard University Press.

Wray, Charles. 1973. *Manual for Seneca Iroquois Archeology*. Rochester, N.Y.: Cultures Primitive; Cambridge, Mass.: Harvard University Press.

Wray, Charles, and Harry L. Schoff. 1953. "A Preliminary Report on the Seneca Sequence in Western New York, 1550–1687." *Pennsylvania Archaeologist* 23(2): 53–63.

Wright, James V. 1966. *The Ontario Iroquois Tradition*. Anthropological Series 75, National Museum of Canada Bulletin 210. Ottawa.

———. 1984. "The Cultural Continuity of the Northern Iroquoian-Speaking Peoples." In *Extending the Rafters: Interdisciplinary Approaches to Iroquoian Studies*, eds. Michael K. Foster, Jack Campisi, and Marianne Mithun, 259–82. Albany: State University of New York Press.

Wroth, Lawrence C. 1928. "The Indian Treaty as Literature." *Yale Review* 17: 749–66.

Zeisberger, David. 1887. *Zeisberger's Indian Dictionary*. Cambridge, Mass.: John Wilson.

Zoltvany, Yves F. 1974. *Phillippe de Rigaud de Vaudreuil, Governor of New France, 1703–1725*. Toronto: McClelland and Stewart.

INDEX

DATE DUE